OXFORD

HANDBOOK *of* **Deaf Studies, Language, and Education**

EDITED BY

Marc Marschark and Patricia Elizabeth Spencer

OXFORD
HANDBOOK
of

Deaf Studies, Language, and Education

OXFORD
UNIVERSITY PRESS

OXFORD
UNIVERSITY PRESS

Oxford University Press, Inc., publishes works that further
Oxford University's objective of excellence
in research, scholarship, and education.

Oxford   New York
Auckland   Cape Town   Dar es Salaam   Hong Kong   Karachi
Kuala Lumpur   Madrid   Melbourne   Mexico City   Nairobi
New Delhi   Shanghai   Taipei   Toronto

With offices in
Argentina   Austria   Brazil   Chile   Czech Republic   France   Greece
Guatemala   Hungary   Italy   Japan   Poland   Portugal   Singapore
South Korea   Switzerland   Thailand   Turkey   Ukraine   Vietnam

Published by Oxford University Press, Inc.
198 Madison Avenue, New York, New York 10016

First issued as an Oxford University Press paperback, 2005

www.oup.com

Oxford is a registered trademark of Oxford University Press

Library of Congress Cataloging-in-Publication Data
Oxford handbook of deaf studies, language, and education /
    edited by Marc Marschark and Patricia Elizabeth Spencer.
        p. cm.
Includes bibliographical references and index.
ISBN-13 978-0-19-514997-5; 978-0-19-518913-1 (pbk.)
ISBN 0-19-514997-1; 0-19-518913-2 (pbk.)
1. Deaf—Social conditions.   2. Deaf—Education.   3. Deaf—
Means of communication.   4. Sign language.   I. Marschark,
Marc.   II. Spencer, Patricia Elizabeth.
HV2380.O88 2003
362.4'2—dc21

2002010496

9 8 7 6 5 4 3 2 1

Printed in the United States of America
on acid-free paper

Preface

A handbook is a tricky undertaking. It is supposed to be an authoritative source book for investigators and service providers in a field, but it also should be able to serve as a reference for students and lay readers interested in the topic. It should offer both breadth and depth in the subject matter, but it also has to be written in accessible language, as free of jargon as possible. Finally, a handbook must be based on the most current research, and thus, while a handbook is large and thorough, its chapters have to be prepared within a very limited time frame and be contained in a limited number of pages. That means asking literally dozens of contributors to abide by short and inflexible deadlines to produce high-quality, comprehensive chapters.

As daunting and contradictory as the above goals may seem, there is also the possibility that a project of this sort can bring about a spirit of collaboration that motivates contributors to work under what normally would be seen as a set of patently unreasonable expectations. The result can be a kind of synergy, as authors and editors see all of the pieces of the puzzle fall into place and create something much bigger than just a collection of thematically related chapters. Indeed, such was the fate of this project. Due largely to the collective will of the contributors (with perhaps just a bit of pres-

sure, and, admittedly, maybe a little nagging), this volume was completed in a single academic year, including three rounds of editorial review and editing. Not even edited books a quarter of this length on well-circumscribed topics are assembled that quickly, especially not while contributors and editors are also involved in teaching, service provision, research, professional responsibilities, and writing projects committed to long before. But in this case, perhaps there was some other motivation for participating in this project and an alternative explanation for its success. That "higher purpose," we believe, lies in the nature of the subject matter. Let us take a few steps back and explain.

When the possibility of this handbook was raised by Oxford University Press, it appeared to offer an exciting opportunity to draw together the various threads of the "field of deafness" and create a comprehensive summary of the issues that are of interest to all the various stakeholders concerned with the lives of deaf adults and children. The field of deafness, however, has always been rather amorphous, if not fractured. Originally—and we're talking as far back as the ancient Greeks here—it consisted largely of educators and parents seeking ways to educate deaf children. In Plato's *Cratylus* (360 B.C.), for example, Socrates mentions the use of signs by deaf people. Deafness is also mentioned in the writings of Aristotle and the poet Lucretius. In Pliny the Elder's *Natural History* (completed just two years before he died during the 79 A.D. eruption of Mount Vesuvius . . . so much for royalties), he mentions Quintus Pedius, the deaf son of a Roman consul, who gained permission from the Caesar Augustus to become an artist. Pedius turned out to be extremely talented artist, but more important, the fact that he required the emperor's permission to pursue his training tells us something of the lives of deaf individuals during that period. Much later, during the Renaissance, many more deaf artists gained fame throughout Europe, and by the mid-seventeenth century, deaf people, their talents, and their communication systems were of interest to a variety of noted scientist-philosophers. But participation in those discussions by *deaf* scientists and philosophers was still almost 200 years away.

From the beginnings of this multifaceted field, there clearly were disagreements about the role of deaf people in society and whether they should or could be educated. Even then, the debate between those who favored educating deaf children via spoken language and those who supported signed language (or "visible gesture") was contentious. Both sides surely wanted what was best for deaf children, but they differed widely in their underlying perspectives and in how to go about achieving it. Unfortunately, instead of resolving over time, the issue came to divide the field and threatened (some would say succeeded) in placing internal politics over optimizing the welfare of deaf children.

At least by the sixteenth century, organized interest in deaf education had spread throughout Europe and was soon to come to the new world. By the beginning of the twentieth century, the field of deafness had expanded to include psychology and, with it, the study of intellectual functioning among deaf persons. Much of this interest was more akin to the anthropological search for strange and interesting peoples (and languages) in the prior century. But there also was a truly scientific quest to understand the mental processes of deaf people and to develop nonverbal testing instruments that would allow valid and reliable evaluation of thinking skills among deaf individuals, again largely with education in mind. At this point, signed communication had already been around for centuries, if not longer, but sign languages were not yet recognized as true languages. Therefore, much of the early research gained its anthropological flavor from the fact that deaf people were seen as a tribe that somehow thought without language—a fascinating group, indeed!

It was not until the second half of the twentieth century, with recognition that signed languages had all of the features of spoken languages (all of the important ones, anyway) that a true scientific revolution began *with* deaf people, rather than *for* or *about* deaf people. This distinction is an important one. Paolo Freire, the Brazilian educational reformer, once noted that a revolution for the people is a revolution against the people. In this particular case, until deaf people became involved in the study of Deaf[1] communities, deaf education, sign language, and social and psychological issues associated with hearing loss, they often seemed little more than an anthropological group to be studied or pitied. Surely there had been deaf champions and famous deaf people before: Laurent Clerc, Helen Keller, Thomas Edison, and Frederick Barnard (for whom Columbia University's Barnard College is named) are the first names that come to mind. There also have been hearing individuals who championed the cause, socially and scientifically, of equality of opportunity for deaf individuals, including Charles Michel Abbé de l'Epée, Thomas Hopkins Gallaudet, and William Stokoe, just to name a few. Still, the fact that the struggle was necessary has put some onus on investigators and educators to give something back to this multifaceted field and work with some urgency to enhance the opportunities for future deaf children.

Since the late 1970s or so, this effort has truly blossomed. From the early work on the linguistics of sign language to current imaging studies of brain function in deaf individuals, an interdisciplinary variety of researchers, both deaf and hearing, have collaborated with teachers, parents, service providers, and policy makers to understand and improve the development and education of deaf children and level the playing field for deaf adults in higher education and employment. Far from being motivated by paternalism—something that deaf individuals have long had to tolerate—work being done today in Deaf studies, language, and education reflects a new appreciation and respect for the Deaf community, signed languages, the contributions of deaf individuals, and the benefits of social diversity.

Consistent with this *zeitgeist*, the guiding principle of this project, from the outset, has been the need to bring together experts from diverse areas of the field who are both sensitive to its history and able to weave together a stronger fabric of understanding than has been available previously. The necessity for such an approach lies in the fact that, for all of the advances that have been made in the field, everyone involved in research, education, or provision of services for deaf children and adults will admit that in some areas progress has fallen well short of our goals. Among the more obvious of these shortcomings are the literacy skills of deaf students; the provision of mental health services for deaf individuals; access to communication by people who are deaf and hard of hearing; understanding the challenges of deaf children with multiple handicaps; and the universal provision of hearing screening, early intervention, and appropriate educational options for deaf children. Clearly the problem is not due to lack of effort. Rather, it is the way of science and pedagogy (and, yes, bureaucracy) that understanding complex challenges and methods to surmount them tend to evolve over time, rather than being resolved by sudden insights or findings.

For all of the shortcomings and complaints that could be leveled at research and practice in this field, the chapters that follow make it clear that we are now in a better position than ever before to make progress in these areas. And progress is being made! Basic and applied research over the last 25 years have clarified many of the psychological and contextual factors influencing the language, social, and cognitive development of deaf children, while technology and educational innovation have provided new opportunities for change. As the field has grown, however, so has the diversity of investigators, the specialization of service providers, and the number of publication outlets for their work. Meanwhile, the expectations of those seeking answers to practical questions—especially deaf individuals and the parents of deaf children—have also increased. It thus seemed incumbent on those of us in the field to gather up some of the strands of research and practice and present them in one place, within a single format, with an eye toward offering a resource for all those interested in Deaf studies, language issues, and the education of individuals who are deaf or hard of hearing.

With this agenda in mind, what was to become the *Oxford Handbook of Deaf Studies, Language, and Education* began with a discussion of the intended scope the work, seeking to ensure that it would cover as much information as possible without too much overlap across chapters, but also without too many gaps. With the help of several anonymous reviewers and Catharine Carlin, our esteemed editor at Oxford University Press, we were able to include essentially all important aspects of deaf studies: language, social/psychological issues, neuropsychology, culture, technology, and education. Then we began seeking contributors who were experts in each content area and were willing and able to take on the selected areas, providing state-of-the-art reviews that were both objective and comprehensive. This meant that contributors would need to consider alternative perspectives on their subject matter, not just those they found most comfortable or familiar. There was thus a lot of sharing, as contributors contacted each other and read drafts of chapters in contiguous areas to ensure that the fit and the tone were right.

As editors, we have watched the development and progress of this work from the day it was first suggested. Now that it is finished, we can admit to the contributors and others that the project met all of the original goals far better than we ever imagined possible. We owe great debt to all those who wrote the chapters and whose ideas enabled them to do so. With regard to ideas, an anecdote is in order.

About a quarter of the way into the project, a group of several contributors and other colleagues in the field attended a conference in Europe. In discussing the various topics and authors included in the volume (all of which had been posted on a contributors' website), one of the contributors remarked that it was surprising that professors X and Y had not been included, because surely they were two of the most prominent people in the field. That was the first time that we articulated the fact that contributors for this project were selected very differently from how they would be selected for a typical edited volume. As we have noted, the topics were decided first. Then, the challenge was to find people who are conducting cutting-edge research in each of those areas and who could describe them in a way that would mesh with the other topics. With this opposite-of-usual approach to editing the volume, we were led to particular individuals who could craft contributions to fit particular niches, yet could live with all of the limitations described above. In some cases, that meant that contributions were to be somewhat outside the areas in which the authors write most often; in other cases, contributors could include only a sampling of what they would have liked to write about. In all cases, however, this group of professionals somehow managed to set aside all distractions and produce a volume that is authoritative but accessible, current yet complete, and research-based while still being useful for essentially anyone interested in this broad and diverse field. And they actually did it on time!

At this writing, as the *Handbook* is about to go to press, we are still amazed at how well it turned out, how smoothly it all went, and just how much larger this volume is than the sum of its chapters. Although we had described in advance the general contents and scope of the volume, we never would have predicted the comprehensiveness of its coverage nor the extent of the synergy and the excitement that would emerge. To all those who contributed to its preparation and production, we owe great thanks. To all those who will make use of this work, we urge you to take advantage of the pages that follow, not just the words, but the paths they lay out for theoretical and practical progress in a field that is only beginning to appreciate its responsibilities and potential.

Note

1. Throughout this volume, "deaf" is used to refer to an audiological status while "Deaf" is used in reference to the linguistic minority that makes up the Deaf community, shares Deaf culture, and is composed of individuals who identify themselves as Deaf people.

Contents

Contributors

C. Tane Akamatsu
Toronto Board of Education
Student Support Services
155 College Street
Toronto, Ontario M5T 1P6, Canada

John A. Albertini
Department of Research
National Technical Institute for the Deaf
Rochester Institute of Technology
96 Lomb Memorial Drive
Rochester NY 14623, USA

Jésus Alegria
Laboratoire de Psychologie Expérimentale
Université Libre de Bruxelles, C.P. 191
B-1050 Brussels, Belgium

Shirin D. Antia
Department of Special Education, Rehabilitation,
and School Psychology
University of Arizona
PO Box 210069
Tucson, AZ 85721-0069, USA

David F. Armstrong
Budget Office

Gallaudet University
800 Florida Avenue, NE
Washington, DC 20002-3695, USA

Kathleen S. Arnos
Department of Biology
Gallaudet University
800 Florida Avenue, NE
Washington, DC 2002-3695, USA

Edward T. Auer, Jr.
Department of Communication Neuroscience
House Ear Institute
2100 West Third Street
Los Angeles, CA 90057, USA

Matthew Bakke
Department of Audiology and Speech–Language
Pathology
Gallaudet University
Washington, DC 20002-3695, USA

Lynne E. Bernstein
Department of Communication Neuroscience
House Ear Institute
2100 West Third Street
Los Angeles, CA 90057, USA

Peter Blamey
Department of Otolaryngology
University of Melbourne
384-388 Albert Street
East Melbourne, Victoria 3002, Australia

Barbara Bodner-Johnson
Department of Education
Gallaudet University
800 Florida Avenue, NE
Washington, DC 20002, USA

Rosemary Calderon
Psychiatry and Behavioral Sciences
University of Washington
PO Box 359300, CH-13
Seattle, WA 98105, USA

Barbara Cone-Wesson
Speech and Hearing Sciences
University of Arizona
P.O. Box 210071
Tucson AZ 85721-0069, USA

Karen Emmorey
Laboratory for Cognitive Neuroscience
The Salk Institute for Biological Studies
10010 North Torrey Pines Road
La Jolla, CA 92037, USA

Susan Fischer
Department of Research
National Technical Institute for the Deaf
Rochester Institute of Technology
96 Lomb Memorial Drive
Rochester, New York 14623, USA

Mark T. Greenberg
Pennsylvania State University
Prevention Research Center
HDFS—Henderson Building South
University Park, PA 16802, USA

Judith E. Harkins
Gallaudet University
Technology Assessment Program
800 Florida Avenue, N.E.
Washington, DC 20002, USA

Harry van der Hulst
Department of Linguistics
University of Connecticut
337 Mansfield Road, Unit 1145
Storrs, CT 06269, USA

Janet R. Jamieson
The University of British Columbia
Department of Educational and Counselling
Psychology and Special Education
Faculty of Education
2125 Main Mall
Vancouver, BC V6T 1Z4, Canada

Michael A. Karchmer
Gallaudet Research Institute
Gallaudet University
800 Florida Avenue, NE
Washington, DC 20002, USA

Thomas N. Kluwin
Department of Educational Foundations and
Research
Gallaudet University
800 Florida Avenue, NE
Washington, DC 20002-3695, USA

Harry Knoors
University of Nijmegen and
Instituut voor Doven
Theerestraat 42
5271 GD Sint-Michielsgestel, The Netherlands

Lynne Sanford Koester
Department of Psychology
The University of Montana
Skaggs Building 369
Missoula, MT 59812-1041, USA

Kathryn H. Kreimeyer
Arizona State Schools for the Deaf and Blind
PO Box 87010
Tucson, AZ 85754, USA

Paddy Ladd
Centre for Deaf Studies
University of Bristol
8 Woodland Road
Bristol BS8 1TN, UK

Harry G. Lang
Department of Research
National Technical Institute for the Deaf
Rochester Institute of Technology

96 Lomb Memorial Drive
Rochester, New York 14623, USA

Amy R. Lederberg
Department of Educational Psychology and
Special Education
Georgia State University
University Plaza
Atlanta, GA 30303, USA

Gregory R. Leigh
Royal Institute for Deaf and Blind Children
361-365 North Rocks Road
North Rocks, NSW 2151, Australia

Irene W. Leigh
Department of Psychology
Gallaudet University
800 Florida Avenue, NE
Washington, DC 20002-3695, USA

Jacqueline Leybaert
Laboratoire de Psychologie Expérimentale
Université Libre de Bruxelles, C.P. 191
B-1050 Brussels, Belgium

Susan J. Maller
Department of Educational Studies
School of Education, Purdue University
Liberal Arts and Education Building
West Lafayette, IN 47907, USA

Marc Marschark
Department of Research
National Technical Institute for the Deaf
Rochester Institute of Technology
96 Lomb Memorial Drive
Rochester, NY 14623, USA
and Department of Psychology
University of Aberdeen
Aberdeen, Scotland

Connie Mayer
95 Ferrier Avenue
Toronto, Ontario M4K 3H6, Canada

Ross E. Mitchell
Gallaudet Research Institute
Gallaudet University
800 Florida Avenue, NE
Washington, DC 20002, USA

Christine Monikowski
Department of American Sign Language and
Interpreter Education
National Technical Institute for the Deaf
52 Lomb Memorial Drive
Rochester, NY 14623, USA

Arti Pandya
Department of Human Genetics
Virginia Commonwealth University
PO Box 980033
Richmond, VA 23298, USA

Peter V. Paul
The School of Teaching & Learning
The Ohio State University
333 Arps Hall
1945 N. High Street
Columbus, OH 43210-1172, USA

Robert Q. Pollard, Jr.
University of Rochester Medical Center
300 Crittenden Boulevard
Rochester, NY 14642, USA

Des Power
Centre for Deafness Studies and Research
School of Education and Professional Studies
Griffith University
PMB50, Gold Coast Mail Centre
QLD 9726, Australia

Jerker Rönnberg
Department of Behavioral Sciences and The
Swedish Institute for Disability Research
Linköping University
S-581 83 Linköping, Sweden

Marilyn Sass-Lehrer
Department of Education
Gallaudet University
800 Florida Avenue, NE
Washington, DC 20002, USA

Brenda Schick
SLHS, Campus Box 409
University of Colorado
Boulder, CO 80309-0409, USA

Barbara R. Schirmer
Office of the Vice President for Academic Affairs
The University of Detroit Mercy

4001 W. McNichols Road
P.O. Box 19900
Detroit, MI 48219-0900

Sara Schley
Department of Research
National Technical Institute for the Deaf
Rochester Institute of Technology
96 Lomb Memorial Drive
Rochester, NY 14623, USA

Jenny L. Singleton
University of Illinois at Urbana-Champaign
Department of Educational Psychology
1310 South Sixth Street, 226 ED
Champaign, IL 61820-6990, USA

Patricia Elizabeth Spencer
Department of Social Work, HMB S334
Gallaudet University
Washington, DC 20002-3695, USA

Michael S. Stinson
Department of Research
National Technical Institute for the Deaf
Rochester Institute of Technology
96 Lomb Memorial Drive
Rochester, NY 14623, USA

Samuel J. Supalla
Department of Special Education and Rehabilita-
tion and School Psychology
College of Education
University of Arizona
Tucson, AZ 85721, USA

Meg Ann Traci
52 Corbin Hall
RTC: Rural

The University of Montana Rural Institute
Missoula, MT 59812, USA

Mathijs Vervloed
Department of Special Education
University of Nijmegen
Montessorilaan 3
6525 HR Nijmegen, The Netherlands

Ronnie B. Wilbur
ASL Linguistics Laboratory
Purdue University
Heavilon Hall
W. Lafayette, IN 47907-1353, USA

Sherman Wilcox
Department of Linguistics
University of New Mexico
Albuquerque, NM 87131, USA

Cheri Williams
Literacy Education
PO Box 210002
University of Cincinnati
Cincinnati, OH 45221-0002, USA

Elizabeth A. Winston
Educational Linguistics Research Center
1613 Leila Drive
Loveland, CO 80538, USA

Bencie Woll
Department of Language and Communication
Science
City University—London
Northampton Square
London EC1V 0HB, UK

OXFORD
HANDBOOK *of* **Deaf Studies, Language, and Education**

Patricia Elizabeth Spencer & Marc Marschark

Introduction

Covering all of the major topics addressed in research and practice related to Deaf studies, education, and language resulted in a large number of chapters in this handbook. Indeed, there are so many chapters and topics presented that we thought readers might benefit from a map or summary of its contents. That summary is presented here.

Each chapter in this volume has been written to stand alone, but also to work in concert with all of the other chapters to provide an overview of the state-of-the-art in research about hearing loss, its implications, and about people who are deaf or hard of hearing. The chapters present information from varied perspectives, reflecting the diversity of perspectives and characteristics of the population on which they focus. Authors of the chapters represent many different countries and cultures, reflecting the international nature of research efforts related to deafness. They also are from diverse academic and professional backgrounds, reflecting the interdisciplinary nature of the field. Although we might prefer a world in which it was not necessary to say so, deaf and hard-of-hearing authors, as well as hearing authors, contributed chapters. The contributors therefore reflect the increasingly important role of persons who are deaf

and hard of hearing in the study of their own population.

We have made an effort to group the book's chapters by topic, but this turned out to be an exceedingly difficult and intellectually challenging task, in large part because of the variety of types of information included and the important cross-disciplinary connections made by the contributors. Researchers in this field tend to be sensitive to and knowledgeable about information across a variety of areas, and their writings often provide the kind of synthesis across topics that should be the goal of all intellectual endeavors, but which makes it difficult to put the resulting works into a series of clearly defined categories. Chapter topics discussed in the following pages range from child development to brain–cognition relationships, from educational interventions to technological advances, and from the origins of language to considerations of characteristics of Deaf communities and sign languages. The fact that many of these topics are considered in more than one chapter further complicated our efforts at categorization.

The result is that the chapters are organized into four major topics, with some topic areas further divided. The volume begins with work focused on education, representing the importance of this topic and providing information about the changing circumstances of educational experiences for deaf and hard-of-hearing children. A first part includes chapters about general curriculum, service provision, and achievement. In the first chapter, Harry Lang provides a historical context for interpreting current educational practices and outcomes. Michael Karchmer and Ross Mitchell then give an update on demographic characteristics, academic achievement, and factors influencing achievement of deaf and hard-of-hearing students in the United States. Des Power and Greg Leigh address the general area of curriculum for deaf and hard-of-hearing students, specifically discussing ways in which this curriculum is consistent with or deviates from that generally used with hearing students.

The next three chapters in part I focus on specific types of educational placements and needs. Michael Stinson and Tom Kluwin summarize what is known about progress and experiences of deaf and hard-of-hearing students in various school placements, ranging from mainstream to special schools. Marilyn Sass-Lehrer and Barbara Bodner-Johnson then provide a description of the basis for and conduct of early intervention services for families and their young children with hearing loss. Special curriculum and service needs for children who have hearing loss plus cognitive, motor, or other developmental disabilities are then addressed by Harry Knoors and Mathijs Vervloed. This group of chapters gives a picture of the range of educational options, individual needs, and general outcomes for deaf and hard-of-hearing students.

An issue of prime importance with regard to deaf education and deaf individuals has been patterns of literacy achievement and difficulties in this area that are faced by most students who are deaf or hard of hearing. This topic is addressed in another educationally relevant section, part II, beginning with a chapter by Peter Paul that provides a theoretical perspective on the difficulties deaf and hard-of-hearing students face in acquiring literacy skills, and another by Barbara Schirmer and Cheri Williams surveying methods and practices of teaching reading. These are followed by John Albertini and Sara Schley's chapter that describes the acquisition of skills in writing, a topic addressed less often than reading. Finally, Connie Mayer and Tane Akamatsu analyze and critique the theoretical basis and practical outcomes of bilingual approaches to

building deaf and hard-of-hearing students' literacy skills.

Part III includes chapters on cultural, social, and psychological issues. These issues are addressed at several levels, considering individuals and their relationships with peers, family, and the larger community. Bencie Woll and Paddy Ladd provide a model for characterizing Deaf communities and their interactions with the hearing communities in which they are situated. Shirin Antia and Kathryn Kreimeyer consider characteristics of deaf children's interactions with deaf and with hearing peers, primarily in school environments. Aspects of deaf children's social development is further addressed by Rosemary Calderon and Mark Greenberg, who consider both family and school contexts, and by Meg Traci and Lynne Koester, who provide a detailed view of the socialization and development of deaf and hard-of-hearing infants in the context of the family. Finally, Irene Leigh and Robert Pollard give an analysis of the psychological characteristics and needs of deaf and hard-of-hearing adults in a variety of contexts related to daily living.

A fourth major topic area addresses issues related to language. It is in the area of language that barriers and challenges most often arise for persons who are deaf or hard of hearing, and, accordingly, it is an area in which much research has been conducted. This topic area is discussed in three parts. Part IV focuses on children's language, covering patterns of development and achievement, as well as methods for assessment. The chapters in Part IV well reflect the importance and diversity of alternative language approaches, illustrating the variety of methods used to promote language development of deaf and hard of hearing children.

Brenda Schick begins part IV with an overview of research focusing specifically on children acquiring a natural sign language such as American Sign Language, along with comparative information about the progress of children who are exposed to English-based signing systems such as those used in total communication programs. Peter Blamey then addresses oral language skills of deaf and hard-of-hearing children whose language experiences are primarily in spoken language environments. Amy Lederberg follows with a developmental look at young deaf children's expression of meaning, both prelinguistically and through the acquisition of formal vocabulary—signed or spoken. Jacqueline Leybaert and Jésus Alegria then discuss the effects of using cued speech to promote children's language skills. The final two chapters in part IV focus on assessment issues. These chapters include reviews of literature together with practical suggestions for assessment, with Janet Jamieson focusing on assessment of general English language skills, regardless of modality, and Jenny Singleton and Sam Supalla focusing specifically on assessing children's skills in American Sign Language.

Part V focuses on signed languages. David Armstrong and Sherman Wilcox discuss the origins of sign language, suggesting that not only did they emerge early in human evolution but that they may, in fact, have characterized the earliest human languages. Susan Fischer and Harry van der Hulst follow with a detailed description of some of the grammatical characteristics of current sign languages, emphasizing how they maximize visual and spatial potentials for the expression of meaning and connected discourse. Ronnie Wilbur's chapter continues this focus, illustrating modality influences on language structure and arguing that such influences place inherent limits on the adaptability of artificially created sign systems such as Signed English. Christine Monikowski and Elizabeth Winston provide information about an emerging research focus, that of interpreting and interpreter education, including discussion of the conceptually complex processes involved in translating information from language based on one modality to representation of the same meaning in a language based on another modality. Finally, Karen Emmorey describes the neural and neuropsychological underpinnings of sign languages, looking into an area of basic research that holds great promise for better understanding of development and education of deaf children and language functioning among deaf adults.

Part VI comprises a diverse group of chapters, but all of which, in one way or another, address aspects of hearing. Lynne Bernstein and Edward Auer provide a summary of information about speech perception by deaf persons, emphasizing the multimodal nature of that task. Kathleen Arnos and Arti Pandya describe the anatomy and physiology of the auditory system and follow with what is almost a tutorial summarizing advances in the study of genetics and their implications for children and adults with hearing loss. Barbara Cone-Wesson then gives an overview of audiological procedures for early identification of hearing loss, the process that provides the necessary foundation for movement toward early intervention during children's critical developmental period. Judith Harkins and Matthew Bakke provide information about an array of technologies and assistive devices that provide increased access and ease of communication for deaf persons in the workplace and in their daily lives. Patricia Spencer and Marc Marschark summarize information about language, education, and social-psychological outcomes of cochlear implantation, emphasizing data about children, many of whom use the information provided by implants to develop spoken language skills.

The final part of the *Handbook* covers a topic of both theoretical and practical importance. Cognitive correlates and consequences of deafness (or in some cases, the surprising lack of consequences) are addressed in three chapters. Susan Maller discusses assessment of cognitive abilities, focusing primarily on assessment of children. She discusses methodological weaknesses in some earlier studies and psychometric weaknesses in some of the instruments that have been used with this population. Based on research from around the world, Marschark proposes that some but not all cognitively related processing is affected by differences in modalities available for processing information. He suggests that a closer, objective look at some of those differences will provide basic theoretical information about human cognition as well as more effective directions for methods for teaching deaf students. Jerker Rönnberg focuses primarily on a specific cognitive process, that of working memory, and gives a detailed, theoretically cogent description of the interactive effects of memory, hearing loss, and language experience.

The amazing array of theoretical and applied topics covered in the *Handbook* display the multiple values of research and practice related to deaf persons, their language, and their lives. The results of such research can not only lead to improved services to that population but also provide basic and comparative information relevant to theory building related to human development in general. Despite the depth and breadth of topics covered in this volume, many of these areas of research are either still in an emerging stage or are undergoing radical changes in perspective that represent new avenues of study or new ways of conceptualizing topics. These changes are due at least in part to advances in technology that increase information sharing among researchers and across national boundaries as long-distance communications become faster and easier for both hearing and deaf persons. They also reflect the increasing involvement and leadership of deaf persons from diverse backgrounds and cultures in the setting of research agendas and designs for educational and related practice.

As we describe in the Epilogue, the work described in these chapters results in a sense of re-newed or strengthened energy for many topics and an openness to new ideas among those who conduct research or provide services for deaf and hard-of-hearing people. We believe that the chapters in this book, representing the cooperation of researchers and authors from so many different perspectives and specialties, will increase not only readers' knowledge but also their appreciation of the excitement that characterizes research efforts in deaf studies, education, and language in the twenty-first century.

Educational Issues

Harry G. Lang

Perspectives on the History of Deaf Education

A history of the education of deaf persons is by its very nature a study of societal and cultural change. This notion is epitomized in tracing prevailing attitudes about deaf people and how they learn. Certain fallacious attitudes, for instance, have lingered, taking on new forms over time, even with the more recent efforts of scholars to examine the issues systematically. This is especially true with regard to the issue of language and its relationship to academic achievement. That deaf students are visual learners and may benefit from a visual language, rather than an auditory one, has never been universally accepted as an established tenet guiding formal instruction. Whether speaking of the seventeenth century's metaphysical association of the human voice with the soul or divine spirit, or twenty-first-century decisions in some schools to forbid the use of signs by children with cochlear implants, misconceptions, as well as insufficient bridging of research and practice, have thwarted efforts to effectively teach language and academic content to deaf children. The well-documented cognitive and linguistic developmental delays in deaf children continue to be viewed by many as the result of deafness per se. But as Marschark, Lang, and Albertini (2002) summarize, "if there is a problem, it is much more likely to be found in the way

we teach and what we expect from deaf students than in the students themselves" (p. 7). Such an understanding of deafness as an educational condition shapes the historical highlights discussed in this chapter.

The Deaf Experience in Early Times

Throughout history, deaf people have faced a gamut of perceptions and attitudes that have influenced the quality of educational opportunities. The earliest records from classical and ancient civilizations provide scant information about the roles of signs, gestures, and spoken language in the daily lives of deaf people, leading to consideration of the extent to which deaf people were seen to be able to reason and communicate thousands of years ago. In the fifth century B.C., Herodotus authored a history of the Greco-Persian wars, a work for which he earned the title "Father of History." In that work, he mentions seeking guidance with regard to his deaf son. In Plato's *Cratylus* (360 B.C.), Socrates poses a rhetorical question related to the use of signs, implying that such a form of communication was used by deaf people in this period of history. There is also brief mention of deafness in the writings of Aristotle. In the first century A.D., we find in Pliny the Elder's *Natural History* the report of an influential father seeking an educational opportunity for his deaf child. This first recorded account of the education of a deaf child, Quintus Pedius, is unusual. The Greeks and Romans encouraged infanticide to remove children who were mentally or physically unable to contribute to a strong citizen state. During this period, the focus on disability largely precluded educational attempts. In *Politics*, for example, Aristotle wrote, "As to the exposure and reading of children, let there be a law that no deformed child shall live" (quoted in Winzer, 1993, p. 13).

Theological literature has also contributed to our understanding of attitudes toward deaf persons and the barriers to education in pre-Renaissance times. The Hebrews may have been an exception to the generally negative attitudes toward persons who were deaf or had disabilities. The *Talmud*, the rabbinical teachings and Jewish oral law begun in the fifth century A.D., raised the possibility of instructing deaf children. In the Mishnah of the *Talmud*, the writers described people with disabilities as children of God who might be capable of reasoning despite their handicaps. Christianity also brought new views on the injustice of neglecting deaf people. Saint Jerome's translation of the *Vulgate*, in the fourth century A.D., discussed deafness and the possibility of salvation through signed as well as written communication. He viewed "the speaking gesture of the whole body" as serving to communicate the word of God as well as speech and hearing. Saint Jerome's contemporary, Saint Augustine, wrote *De Quantitate Animae* and *De Magistro*, in which he specifically discussed gestures/signs as an alternative to spoken language in the communication of ideas and in learning the Gospel (King, 1996).

Over the next 10 centuries we find little biographical information that might help us understand how deaf people lived. It seems likely, however, that the Dark Ages were especially dark for deaf persons. Beliefs in mystical and magical cures for deafness were prevalent, illustrating the range of beliefs people held about hearing loss. Some stories of cures for deafness were documented with enough detail that we might surmise something about the times. Among such reports was one by the Saxon monk Bæda, known as "the Venerable Bede," the first historian of the English people. In

The Ecclesiastical History of the English Nation, written around 700 A.D., and still an important source for knowledge of the very early Anglo-Saxon period, Bede tells of Saint John of Beverley's cure of a young deaf boy (King, 1996). The story reveals a sustained view of spoken language as an inspired and theological, rather than as a physiological, function.

The Renaissance

The Renaissance is generally credited with major changes in creative thinking. Accordingly, more complex views of deaf people and deaf education can be found during this period in the writings of the Dutch humanist Rudolphus Agricola and the Italian mathematician and physician Girolamo Cardano. In the late 1400s, Agricola described a deaf person who had been taught to read and write. With signs, he explained, or some other visual or pedagogical means, deaf persons could sufficiently express themselves and understand the world (Radutzky, 1993). When Agricola's work was published 43 years after his death, it came into the hands of Cardano, who elaborated on the uniqueness of deaf people being able to communicate through reading and writing, rather than through hearing and speaking. Cardano's son had a hearing loss, but we know little about how this father's experience shaped his thinking about the connection between written characters and ideas. He took note, for example, of how a deaf person may conceive such a word as "bread" and associate the written word directly with the concept it represented.

With widespread illiteracy among hearing people, it was unusual during this period to find deaf persons who were able to read and write, but records indicate that some notable deaf artists, in particular, were leading productive lives. Before Cardano's book came out in 1575, for example, Bernardino di Betto Biagi, born in 1454, had painted Frescoes of Moses' life in the Sistine Chapel. Also in Italy, Cristoforo de Predis was a successful illuminist. In Madrid, the deaf artist Jaime Lopez decorated the sixteenth-century Hermitage of Notre Dame. Juan Fernándes de Navarette, a painter for Philip II of Spain, was best known for his exquisite coloring and experimentation with light. Deafened in 1529 at the age of three, he went on to earn the honor of being called the "Spanish

Titian," after the Italian master. He communicated in signs with the curate of the parish of Santo Vincente, who found them "as intelligible as speech" (Lang & Meath-Lang, 1995). Navarrete died in 1579, three years after Cardano's book was published. On his death bed, with pen and paper, he wrote out his own will and appointed an executor.

Navarrete had studied history and the Scriptures in a monastery of La Estrella of the Order of St. Jerome in Logroño more than a decade before the work of the great Spanish Benedictine monk Pedro Ponce de Leon. In 1578 Ponce described how he had taught the congenitally deaf sons of great lords and other notables to read and write, attain a knowledge of Latin and Greek, study natural philosophy (science) and history, and to pray. Ponce's students included the deaf brothers Pedro and Francisco de Velasco, and the congenitally deaf Fray Gaspar, who later became a priest.

Abandoned in historical anonymity are the teachers before Ponce. The success of these and other deaf individuals in Cardano's time attests to the fact that deaf people had found ways to communicate in Renaissance Europe. These appear to be the first indications of the empowerment of deaf people through education. The fruits of these labors were immediately observable in lasting works of art and other contributions to the world. In these isolated reports we find the earliest references to the importance of visual forms of communication and some promise in their relationship to academic learning.

The Age of Reason

As word of Ponce's methods of instructing deaf students spread through the writings of Juan Pablo Bonet and, later, the work of Sir Kenelm Digby, the education of deaf children in Europe slowly took root. Bonet's book, *The Reduction of Letters and the Art of Teaching the Mute to Speak*, was published in 1620. In this early treatise on the education of deaf people, a critical assumption made by Bonet was that thought precedes language (Moores, 1996). Bonet also stressed the importance of activity and what some would now call multisensory learning. In comparing and contrasting objects, for example, he wrote that "some of them are so similar as to demand feeling rather than sight to distinguish them, and these [the deaf child] must weigh in his head, so as to reorganize differences in things that need some consideration" (quoted in De Land, 1931, p. 33). In this book, we also find the roots of a theory of learning as an active construction of meaning. Bonet taught reading and writing as a precursor to speech but also added fingerspelling as part of his instructional methods.

In 1670, William Holder, a priest, and John Wallis, a mathematician, publicly argued in the *Philosophical Transactions of the Royal Society* their respective claims of being the first to teach deaf students to speak and speechread in Great Britain. Other writers influenced by Ponce's work included England's George Sibscota (*Deaf and Dumb Man's Discourse*, 1670); his countryman John Bulwer, who published a study of manual language (*Philocophus; or, the Deaf and Dumbe Man's Friend*, 1648); the Scot George Dalgarno (*Didascalocophus; or, the Deaf and Dumb Man's Tutor*, 1680); and the Dutch physician Johan Konrad Amman (*The Speaking Deaf*, 1692; *A Dissertation on Speech*, 1700). Bulwer's work with natural language and gestures brought greater acknowledgment to this form of communication, while Amman's work with speech would soon have its own followers. Amman and the Flemish naturalist Francis Mercurius van Helmont saw voice as the primary means of communicating human language and as "the expressive secret of the soul" (Ree, 1999, p. 64). As this base of literature was being established, the groundwork was also being laid for one of the most disheartening philosophical conflicts in the history of the education of deaf learners: the controversy over the use of signed and spoken communication methods.

One myth, perpetuated even into modern times, was the belief that abstractions could not be conveyed through sign language. Yet, the anecdotes of this early period reveal that the signs used by deaf people contradicted this view. Public schools were not yet established, and we have little information about how deaf children were taught individually, but we do know there were communicative exchanges between hearing persons and intelligent, if not fully educated, deaf people. There is a growing body of literature revealing that in the sixteenth and seventeenth centuries, prior to formal public schooling, the self-determination of deaf people to learn may have been bolstered by their use of sign language (see Marschark et al., 2002).

The establishment of scientific societies in the seventeenth century helped to bring legitimacy to the instruction of deaf students. The lineage of these societies has been traced back to Plato, and, as described earlier, the literary records associated with Plato's famous Academy offer a Socratic discussion of deaf persons and their ability to communicate with gestures and signs. As scientific societies spread through Europe in the sixteenth and seventeenth centuries, particularly in Naples, Rome, Leipzig, and Florence, they became centers of experimentation. In the early reports of these academies, we find studies on the anatomy of the ear and the use of tubes and trumpets for improving hearing. As the years passed, reports on the relationship between language and learning increased in number. As a result of these efforts, deaf education in the seventeenth century, even though in its infancy, has provided insights that would well influence practices today. The mathematician John Wallis (1857), for example, recognized that deaf children are perfectly capable of developing the ability to use language, questioning why it should not be possible for the eye to receive letters or other characters in representing concepts as well as the ear with sounds. Dalgarno (1680) expressed similar optimism, writing that deaf people are equal "in the faculties of apprehension, and memory . . . to those that have all their senses" and equally capable of instruction (p. 8). Dalgarno also made a provocative comment about the use of signs with deaf infants. There might be "successful addresses made to a [deaf] child, even in his cradle," he wrote, if parents had "but as nimble a hand, as commonly they have a Tongue" (p. 9). This observation of the critical nature of visual communication with deaf children during infancy shows Dalgarno was far ahead of his time.

As the scientific societies grew in Europe, the scientists and philosophers expanded their interests. Jean-Jacques Rousseau, instigator of the French Revolution; his compatriot Denis Diderot; and the naturalist Georges Louis Leclerc, Comte de Buffon, keeper of the Jardin du Roi and author of the 44-volume *Natural History*, were among those who examined the potential of deaf youth to learn. Rousseau was an early influential proponent of "learning by doing." In his book *Émile*, he expressed views which became the basis for reform in France after the Revolution. He redirected attention to learning through the senses and the importance of the child's interaction with the environment, rather than through rote memorization of the classics. As

a member of the French Academy of Sciences, Rousseau took a special interest in examining deaf children instructed by a teacher named Jacobo Pereire, who was using pronunciation, signs, fingerspelling, and speechreading. As a result of the work of Rousseau and others, the instruction of deaf pupils gained increasing respect as a profession.

John Locke's writings on empiricism and education through the senses inspired the French philosophers to examine communication of deaf people. Their work, however, was focused primarily on the origin of speech and language as means of communicating and understanding thought. They were less interested in speech and language in terms of functional communication (Winzer, 1993). Many and varied views on the abilities of deaf learners were shared during this period. In 1751, for example, Buffon expressed his opinion that deaf children "can have no knowledge of abstract and general ideas" (quoted in Presneau, 1993, p. 414). Among those who had more interaction with deaf people, such as Diderot, Rousseau, and Condillac, and whose scholarly pursuits included frequent observations of Pereire's teaching, there was a better grasp of the relation between language and learning, as well as the role of sign language and gestures in the educational process. But, as in modern times, it is difficult to examine the efficacy of specific methods used by Pereire and his contemporaries when little is known about the degree of hearing loss of the pupils who were demonstrated to the members of the academy.

Presneau (1993) points out that deaf people played a significant role in the intellectual history of the eighteenth-century. Such deaf individuals as Saboureux de Fontenay, Abelaïde Bernard, and Jean Massieu contributed meaningfully to the development of methods of communication and teaching. Their emergence as thinkers with firsthand experience with deafness bears further exploration in historical analyses.

By the 1760s, under the guidance of Charles Michel Abbé de l'Epée, France had established the world's first government-sponsored school for deaf children. L'Epée saw sign language as a natural way for deaf people to communicate. Viewing language as artificial and arbitrary, he applied what he had learned of the theories of language espoused by Locke, Diderot, Condillac, Rousseau, and others to the classroom (Winzer, 1993). In particular, he saw language as more than a verbal system of sounds and orthography. Through a combination of signs and written characters, he believed it was possible to teach deaf students to think logically.

Meanwhile, the Royal Society members were examining hearing and deafness and the abilities of deaf pupils to communicate and to learn. But it was a concerned parent whose efforts led to the first school for deaf children in Great Britain. Nearly a century after John Wallis provided an account of his work with deaf pupils, his writings fell into the hands of a merchant in Leith, Scotland. Charles Shirreff was the father of a deaf boy and encouraged Thomas Braidwood to open an academy in Edinburgh in 1760. The basal education provided at the Braidwood Academy empowered the congenitally deaf John Goodricke, for example, to become a significant contributor to the field of astronomy (Lang & Meath-Lang, 1995).

The methods used by Epée and his successor, Abbé Roch Ambroise Sicard, were particularly assailed by Samuel Heinicke, who established a school in Leipzig in 1778 based on the practice of teaching deaf pupils to speak. Influenced by the writings of Amman, Heinicke was one of the first to try to link speech to higher mental processes, arguing that articulation and vocal language were necessary for abstract thought (Lane, 1984).

The European founders of manualism (l'Epée) and oralism (Heinicke) exchanged letters expressing their irreconcilable differences on educating deaf students. Thus began the "war of methods" between the proponents of the systematic use of sign language in educating deaf children and those who stressed the use of speech, speechreading, and residual hearing without signs as an all-encompassing solution. Throughout the centuries to follow, equally bold and emotionally laden judgments regarding methods of communicating with deaf pupils have done little to bring the opposing camps together.

Epée combined the signs of deaf people with his own invented system of grammatical features and departed significantly from the "natural language." Heinecke's emphasis on speech, too, was unnatural for many deaf people. With the added demands placed on deaf learners to adjust to either of these unfamiliar communication approaches, we can only surmise the impact such approaches placed on the development of logical thought and concepts in the classroom. In addition, the seventeenth and eighteenth-century literature on educat-

ing deaf students includes little reference to the heterogeneity of deaf learners. Both then, and in modern times, many young deaf people have suffered poor education as influential figures have made sweeping generalizations about communication, language, and learning.

Deaf Education Begins in America

Despite the progressive thinking of some Europeans, colonists in the New World were still struggling to come to terms with views about deaf children and learning. Attempts to teach deaf children were seen by some in the colonies as sorcery or witchcraft. In the Massachusetts town of Scituate, the second oldest in Plymouth Colony, settlers had come from Kent and appear to have had both a higher proportion of deaf people among them and a wider acceptance of the use of signs (Groce, 1985). Families from Scituate moved to Martha's Vineyard, along with families from other towns in Massachusetts. Intermarriage on the island led to a very high rate of deafness. Through time, both hearing and deaf people used signs on such a common basis that it seemed natural to everyone. At least as far back as the 1690s, there were literate deaf people at Martha's Vineyard, but little is known about how they were taught at least a century before the first formal school was established in America.

Meanwhile, a few deaf children were sent by the colonists to Europe to receive their education, including a nephew of President James Monroe, who went to Paris, several children of Major Thomas Bolling, and the son of Francis Green, who went to Braidwood Academy. In 1783, Green published *Vox Oculis Subjecta* ("Voice Made Subject to the Eyes"). The title of this report was the motto of the Braidwood Academy and reflected Green's appreciation for the school that had succeeded so well in instructing his son.

The American Philosophical Society (founded by Benjamin Franklin) holds the distinction of having been the first scientific society in the colonies to publish a report on teaching deaf children. William Thornton, head of the U. S. Patent Office, published a treatise on elements of teaching speech and language. Thornton had probably observed the work of the followers of the Braidwoods and L'Epée during his own studies in Edinburgh and Paris, respectively. He was one of the first scholars in America to provide salient perceptions on deaf education, examining the phonological basis for reading, the importance of vocabulary building, and the varied ways available to communicate with deaf people, including speech, fingerspelling, and signs. Nearly a quarter of a century before the first school for deaf children was established in the United States, Thornton wrote, "A deaf person not perfectly skilled in reading words from the lips, or who should ask anything in the dark would be able to procure common information by putting various questions, and by telling the person that, as he is deaf, he requests answers by signs, which he will direct him to change according to circumstances" (Thornton, 1793/1903, p. 414).

Despite the controversies that raged in this period of deaf education history, much progress was made in understanding that deaf children could indeed learn to read and write and be educated through visual means, especially through the use of signs and fingerspelling.

The Nineteenth Century

After the turn of the nineteenth century, momentum in educating deaf children in America increased dramatically. Efforts by Francis Green to investigate the establishment of a special school and by the Reverend John Stanford to educate several deaf children in an almshouse in New York City did not bear much fruit. In 1812, Thomas Hopkins Gallaudet began teaching Alice Cogswell, the deaf daughter of his neighbor, Mason Fitch Cogswell, a New England physician. Cogswell eventually gathered enough financial support to send Gallaudet to Europe to study the methods used in the well-known schools begun by Braidwood and l'Epée. The efforts of Bolling, Green, and Cogswell firmly established parental leadership in the early movement toward quality education for deaf children in the United States. Unable to reach an agreement with the Braidwood Academy with regard to learning their methods of instruction, Gallaudet spent several months at the National Institution for Deaf-Mutes in Paris. There, he was able to convince Laurent Clerc, a 30-year-old deaf assistant teacher, to accompany him to Hartford, Connecticut, where they obtained funds to establish the Connecticut Asylum for the Deaf and Dumb (now named the American School for the Deaf) in 1817. Gallaudet was its director, and Clerc became the first deaf teacher in America.

The parallel movements of improved educational opportunity and empowerment can be seen during the early nineteenth century in how deaf people pioneered in establishing schools. After Clerc, about 25 other deaf people played instrumental roles in founding educational institutions in the United States. Some became superintendents. Many were among the schools' first instructors. By 1850 there were more than 15 residential schools serving deaf pupils, with nearly 4 out of every 10 teachers in these schools deaf themselves. With the attendance of students at these residential schools and the increased use of sign language to teach them, the Deaf community in the United States also began to grow.

Deaf persons also took leading roles in the early schooling of deaf children in other countries. They included, for example, Roberto Francisco Prádez in Spain (Plann, 1993) and Ivan Karlovich Arnold in Russia (Abramov, 1993). In Italy, the deaf author Giacomo Carbonieri wrote in 1858 that sign language was essential for the intellectual performance of deaf people (Corazza, 1993). The work of these and other individuals has been largely neglected.

It was not long before proposals for high schools and "high classes" for deaf pupils were presented at national conventions and published in journals for educators. In the United States, support for providing deaf individuals with greater educational opportunities was bolstered by the increasing visibility of deaf scientists, artists, and writers. Some were born deaf and others were adventitiously deafened; some were immigrants and many were Americans by birth. These talented individuals had begun to command authority in their respective fields. H. Humphrey Moore became a distinguished artist, as did Augustus Fuller and John Carlin. James Nack excelled in poetry. Leo Lesquereux, a paleobiologist, became the first member of the National Academy of Sciences (Lang, 1994). Frederick Barnard, perhaps the most prominent deaf American of his time, was a clear thinker who published in detail his perspectives on the education of deaf children only two decades after the first school for deaf students was established in Hartford, Connecticut, writing of the need for bilingualism and studying sign language scientifically (Lang & Stokoe, 2000). He saw the child's mental construction of the world as a series of inductions from which understanding grows.

It is through research on the biographical and autobiographical writings about successful deaf men and women in the nineteenth and twentieth centuries that we begin to see an evolution of the role of parents—from advocates for new schooling opportunities to a direct involvement in the cognitive and linguistic development of their children during infancy and childhood.

Higher education for deaf people received a great impetus in 1857 when Amos Kendall, the business manager for Samuel F. B. Morse and his telegraph business, met with Edward Miner Gallaudet, the son of Thomas Hopkins Gallaudet, and encouraged him to accept the responsibility as the superintendent of a school for deaf and blind children which Kendall had established the previous year in the District of Columbia. The Columbia Institution for the Deaf, Dumb and Blind, incorporated by Congress that year, was authorized to grant college degrees in the liberal arts and sciences. Years later, the college would become Gallaudet College and later Gallaudet University.

The German oralist movement was taken up in the nineteenth century by John Baptist Graser and Frederick Moritz Hill. Its influence soon spread throughout Europe. After Heinicke's death in 1874, Epée's influence there was short-lived. An increasing movement toward nationalism led the Germans to renew and intensify the emphasis on articulation. In the United States, Horace Mann and Samuel Gridley Howe incited support for the German approach after touring European schools and vigorously pronouncing judgment of the educational benefits of oralism.

The bitter debate among oralists, manualists, and combinists (those who mixed the methods in various degrees) raged in the second half of the century between Alexander Graham Bell and Edward Miner Gallaudet. Bell was also prominent in the eugenics movement, intended to keep the human race healthy by reducing hereditary deficiencies, and this added fuel to the fire generated by the oral–manual controversy. Gallaudet, the champion of deaf people, fought to have the combined system of spoken and sign language communication in instruction continued in the schools and to preserve sign language. Bell disagreed and broke away from the Convention of American Instructors of the Deaf (CAID) to form his own group to advocate for

teaching speech to deaf children and against the use of sign language. He viewed sign not as a language but as a vernacular that made it difficult for deaf people to acculturate in the larger society. That organization, later renamed the Alexander Graham Bell Association for the Deaf, is also still active today, as is CAID. Winzer (1993) writes that "deaf people themselves largely rejected the faddism and dreamy idealisms of the oralists . . . and viewed oralism as an implausible ideology, surrounded by failures" (p. 202). By 1880, however, there were nearly a dozen oral schools in the United States.

At the 1880 Congress of Milan, there was an explicit denial of the emerging Deaf empowerment. Congress participants, overwhelmingly hearing educators, voted to proclaim that the German oral method should be the official method used in schools of many nations: "The congress, considering the incontestable superiority of speech over signs, for restoring deaf-mutes to social life and for giving them greater facility in language, declares that the method of articulation should have preference over that of signs in the instruction and education of the deaf and dumb" (quoted in Lane, 1984, p. 394). Many of the proponents of sign language communication were unable to attend, and deaf people were excluded from the vote. Deaf communities around the world were infuriated by what they saw as the oppressive strategies of the hearing authorities in the schools. Partly as a result of the Milan vote, the National Association of the Deaf (NAD) was established in the United States to strengthen the political clout of deaf persons, who wanted to have control over their own destiny. The choice of communication methods was a human rights issue, in reality, and one that remains volatile today.

The Twentieth and Twenty-First Centuries

Despite the controversy, educators of the late nineteenth and early twentieth centuries established a rich knowledge base, publishing their perspectives on teaching in the *American Annals of the Deaf and Dumb*, which began in 1847. The issues of the *Annals*, as well as other nineteenth-century literature, provide numerous insightful discussions about early educational efforts. In 1888, for example, J. Scott Hutton, the principal of an educational institution for deaf children in Nova Scotia, presented a paper at the Sixth National Conference of Superintendents and Principals of Institutions for Deaf Mutes in Jackson, Mississippi, describing "action-writing" as an essential part of the curriculum. Similarly, astute educators touched on such relevant topics as reading, time on task, use of illustrations with instructional materials, motivation, memory, and the importance of hands-on activities and drawing connections to cognitive development. Adolphe Ferrière, an influential Swiss "father of the activity school" who experienced deafness himself, laid the foundation for new kind of public education in the early twentieth century. Ferrière argued that the school which offers nothing but information (i.e., lectures and reading) must disappear: "In its place must come the school which teaches the child how to use the lever which has ever raised the world above itself—purposeful activity" (quoted in Halbertstam, 1938, p. 758). The theory developed by Ferrière and his colleagues valued the child's initiative and used concrete objects to foster powers of observation and reasoning. These views still have considerable power today, particularly with regard to deaf children. They clearly point to the need to avoid "chalk and talk" teaching and the need to link new information to what students already know. Such methods also led to an increased focus on educating students in more practical matters relating to employment. Ironically, his work had less influence on deaf education, where it was much needed.

Through the first half of the twentieth century, the special education movement expanded considerably, marked by a growing tendency to place deaf children in special classes in schools attended by hearing children. Teacher training and the establishment of professional organizations helped to validate this movement, but its momentum, as well as that of the growth of associated curriculum reform efforts such as activity learning, waxed and waned with the Great Depression and with the influence of early investigations of how deaf children learn language and subject matter.

During the decades following World War II, the oral—manual controversy persisted. New issues intensified the debate, particularly the cultural versus clinical perspectives on educating deaf children. The cultural perspective was bolstered particularly by the scientific recognition of American Sign Language (ASL) as a true language. William Sto-

koe's (1960) work in that regard led to ASL receiving more respect and attention in school environments. Greater public awareness and acceptance of ASL was accompanied by a growing political voice among people who were deaf and hard of hearing. The social and political transformations that took place led to wholly new lifestyles for many deaf people in America as well as improved attitudes about deafness in general.

The clinical perspective on deaf education has also received impetus, most notably from medical and technological advances. With regard to medicine, there was the near elimination of some formerly common etiologies of hearing loss in children (e.g., maternal rubella), although there has been a relatively greater occurrence of others (e.g., premature birth). Of growing significance, however, is the rapidly increasing number of deaf children who are receiving cochlear implants. Research concerning effects of implants on aspects of development other than hearing is just beginning, and so the long-term implications for education and for language, social, and cognitive growth remain unclear. There is no sign that these seemingly disparate cultural and clinical perspectives will be easily resolved in the educational arena.

In general, the curriculum emphases in deaf education, as a field, have not been closely tied to those in public education for hearing students. In science, mathematics, and social studies, for example, the relevance of the curriculum movements of the 1960s and 1970s, especially those focused on active learning and articulation across grades, were not adequately explored for school programs serving deaf students (Lang, 1987). Although deaf education may need particular emphases in the curriculum (and instruction) to address the special needs and characteristics of deaf learners, the benefits of approaches and materials used for hearing peers have not been systematically examined.

In addition, this period was characterized by increased systematic inquiry (educational and psychological research) addressing the complex issues associated with the development and education of deaf children. In particular, much was learned about the importance of communication between parents and their deaf children during the early years, providing children with a diversity of experiences and opportunities for social interactions and the relationships of these to language ability, cognitive development, and academic achievement (see Marschark et al., 2002, for a summary of research with implications for teachers, parents, and educational leaders).

Despite this progress in research, however, educators have not been very successful in improving the general reading skills of deaf students. In the United States, deaf students, on average, graduate from high school well below grade-level in reading (Traxler, 2000). Bilingual (ASL-English) instructional programs have been proposed and experimented with through the 1980s and 1990s. In reviewing a variety of communication intervention systems and language learning-teaching approaches, McAnally, Rose, and Quigley (1994) concluded that a "combination of natural and more structured language development practices relative to the involvement and skill of the teacher and the reactions and responses of the students seems to be the most productive approach" (p. 271).

Approaching this problem of teaching language effectively has also been complicated by the inclusion movement. In most public schools, teachers lack adequate training in such areas as reading and cognition and even in the general pedagogical practices that may be more effective with deaf learners. National organizations that might have once effectively provided guidance and resources in deaf education have lost their potency. Marschark et al. (2002) point out that the appealing but dubious assumption that cognitive development is precisely the same for deaf and hearing children may be leading to ineffective or less than optimal educational practices.

The years since 1970 have been revolutionary in deaf education, and in general for the Deaf community in America. Deaf education has been characterized by significant changes in its content, orientation, and the number of children it reaches. Enrollment in special schools or classes for deaf children in the United States has fallen sharply over the past 25 years. By 1986, only 3 out of 10 deaf children in the U.S. still attended state-run residential schools; the majority attended public schools either in special classes for deaf students or in regular classes with an interpreter or special resource teacher. For the most part, those children who remained in residential schools tended to be those with congenital or early onset, severe to profound deafness.

The inroads in education and access for deaf students, and the related decline in enrollment in separate school programs, were accelerated by legislative acts that led to a much more encompassing and politically sophisticated social movement that has significantly affected the lives of deaf people in the United States. Federal legislation in education, included, in particular, Public Law 94–142, the Education of All Handicapped Children Act (1975), a landmark that guaranteed free, appropriate public education for all children with disabilities. Public Law 94–142 was further amended by Public Law 99–457 (Education of the Handicapped Amendments of 1986). Finally, the 1990 Individuals with Disabilities Education Act (IDEA) was enacted. The IDEA now refers to the entire package of laws that assures a fair and equitable public education for all children with disabilities. Although a full consideration of the virtues and criticisms of PL 94–142 is beyond the scope of the present discussion, there is no doubt that it has affected the philosophical underpinnings of deaf education in the United States. It is also clear that, while the U.S. Congress placed the obligation of deaf education squarely on parents and local school systems, it has never appropriated sufficient funds to implement the law fully. The result has been that most hearing parents of deaf children have taken on more responsibility for their children's education, but without added external support. In many cases, this situation has forced parents into greater dependence on relatives, inconsistent child-rearing practices, and the cumbersome shuffling of work schedules and residences.

In the absence of full implementation, it is difficult to determine the potential impact of PL 94-142 on deaf education and the Deaf community. Meanwhile, many schools for deaf children are finding it difficult to maintain minimum enrollments, and it remains to be determined whether regular public schools really represent less restrictive environments for deaf children than do residential schools.

Dramatic increases in enrollments of deaf students have also occurred in large postsecondary programs such as Gallaudet University and the National Technical Institute for the Deaf at Rochester Institute of Technology and in thousands of other two-and four-year programs. The enrollment of deaf students in postsecondary education has increased by a factor of 50 since 1965, numbering more than 26,000. On average, however, only one out of four of these students complete a degree. Although those students are supported by services such as interpreting, notetaking, tutoring, and real-time captioning, we know little about the impact of such support on their learning and academic achievement (Lang, 2002).

Summary and Conclusions

A study of the educational history of deaf persons reveals some positive themes that have implications for parents and educators today. One is the importance of parental involvement in the education of deaf children. Factual accounts and anecdotes have enriched our understanding of the advocacy roles parents have played, especially with regard to the establishment of school programs around the world. Over the past 30 years, more significant efforts have been made to educate parents about the critical role they must assume in the social, language, and cognitive development of their deaf children. Today, research clearly supports parental involvement in both formal and informal education, evidenced in studies demonstrating the long-term influence of mother–child relationships and early communication and the need for providing deaf children with a variety of experiences during the early years.

Another theme emerging from an examination of the educational history relates to how deaf people have taken an increasingly greater role in influencing their own education. Many histories have been published that describe how deafness was perceived in ancient times, how various societies changed with regard to their attitudes toward deaf people, and how we might understand the turning points in the education and acceptance of people who are deaf. Often, however, writers have neglected to examine how deaf people have overcome barriers in many periods of history under a wide variety of conditions to make important contributions in education and other fields. Given the rich biographical resources available today, familiarization with the wide range of accomplishments of deaf people should be an expectation in teacher preparation programs in order to challenge facile generalizations about what deaf people can or cannot do. By finding ways to circumvent the numerous barriers they have faced and by triumphing successfully as learned individuals, deaf people lay claim to being more than pupils or victims of oppression, but

contributors to the advancement of the field of deaf education as a science. Thus, a study of the history of the education of deaf individuals can also increase our understanding of the need for self-empowerment by deaf people and the shaping of Deaf communities around the world.

Third, the study of history shows that many of the emphases we find important in deaf education today are not new and that good practices have been lost or neglected over time. In history we find valuable techniques for instruction, such as providing metacognitive skills to enhance reading, or using writing as a process to assist learning the curriculum—emphases promoted by teachers of deaf children a century ago, but not applied extensively in today's classrooms. More extensive analyses are needed of the evolution of perspectives on such issues as standardized testing, the relationships between memory and reading, the construction of learning experiences through enculturation, and the impact of stigmatizing deaf people by viewing deafness as a disability.

Fourth, in the modern era, normalization efforts in various countries have particularly emphasized the integration of deaf students with hearing peers in schools. In most instances, deaf students have been placed in inclusive environments without adequate teacher education. History has repeated itself in the sense that we have often searched for best practices, whether they be technological innovations, a form of communication, or an educational environment, but we do not provide adequate resources to study the benefits and disadvantages of these approaches to instruction.

Probably the most poignant lesson we have learned from history is that controversy can grow from ignorance. This lesson emerges most obviously with regard to our failure to recognize individuality in the students we teach, particularly in terms of language skills and academic achievement.

A study of the history of deaf education provides us with many perspectives with which we may build a foundation for the instruction of deaf students in the new millennium. The twentieth century, especially its latter half, will be particularly remembered as a period when educators took significant steps to replace the view of deaf children as concrete, literal thinkers with a more thorough understanding of the interactions of language and intellectual development. We know that early access to meaningful language is essential for normal cognitive development and academic success in both deaf and hearing children. We also know that early use of sign language is a good predictor of academic success of deaf children. Delays in areas of cognitive development important to learning subject matter, however, such as classification and concept learning, have been demonstrated both in deaf children who have been educated in spoken language environments and those exposed primarily to sign language. In their summary of what we know from research, Marschark et al. (2002) point out that the lack of any simple causal link between language delays and cognitive abilities in deaf children indicates that there are undiscovered factors that influence evaluations of cognitive development in deaf children. The complexity and sometimes contradictory nature of the findings emphasize the need for care in evaluating language development, cognitive growth, and academic achievement, and they reinforce the importance of recognizing that these factors are rarely independent. In view of the advances in knowledge about deaf learners over the past few decades, the twenty-first century should be marked by comprehensive research and meaningful instruction, curriculum, and programming.

Author Note

Portions of this chapter have been drawn from Marschark, Lang, and Albertini (2002, chapter 3).

References

Abramov, I.A. (1993). History of the Deaf in Russia. In R. Fischer & H. Lane (Eds.), *Looking back: A reader on the history of Deaf communities and their sign languages* (pp. 199–205). Hamburg: Signum.

Corazza, S. (1993). The history of sign language in Italian education of the deaf. In R. Fischer & H. Lane (Eds.) *Looking back: A reader on the history of Deaf communities and their sign languages.* Hamburg: Signum, pp. 219–229.

Dalgarno, G. (1680). *Didascalocophus.* Oxford. Reprinted in the *American Annals of the Deaf, 1857, 9,* 14–64.

De Land, F. (1931). *The story of lipreading.* Washington, DC: The Volta Bureau.

Groce, N.E. (1985). *Everyone here spoke sign language: Hereditary deafness at Martha's Vineyard.* Cambridge, MA: Harvard University Press.

Halbertstam, L. (1938). The father of the activity school. *Volta Review, 40,* 757–759.

King, L.A. (1996). *Surditas: The understandings of the deaf and deafness in the writings of Augustine, Jerome, and Bede.* Unpublished doctoral dissertation, Boston University, Boston, MA.

Lane, H. (1984). *When the mind hears: A history of the deaf.* New York: Random House.

Lang, H.G. (1987). Academic development and preparation for work. In M.C. Wang, H.J. Walberg & M.C. Reynolds (Eds.), *The handbook of special education: Research and Practice* (pp. 71–93). Oxford: Pergamon Press.

Lang, H.G., & Meath-Lang, B. (1995). *Deaf persons in the arts and sciences: A biographical dictionary.* Westport, CT: Greenwood Press.

Lang, H.G., & Stokoe, W. (2000). A Treatise on signed and spoken language in early 19th century deaf education in America. *Journal of Deaf Studies and Deaf Education, 5,* 196–216.

Lang, H.G. (2002). Higher education for deaf students: Research priorities in the new millennium. *Journal of Deaf Studies and Deaf Education, 7,* 267–280.

Marschark, M., Lang, H.G., & Albertini, J.A. (2002). *Educating deaf students: Research into practice.* New York: Oxford University Press.

McAnally, P.L., Rose, S., & Quigley, S.P. (1994). *Language learning practices with deaf children.* Austin, TX: Pro-Ed.

Moores, D.F. (1996). *Educating the deaf: Psychology, principles, and practices* (4th ed.). Boston: Houghton Mifflin.

Plann, S. (1993). Roberto Francisco Prádez: Spain's first Deaf teacher of the Deaf. In R. Fischer & H. Lane (Eds.), *Looking back: A reader on the history of Deaf communities and their sign languages* (pp. 53–74). Hamburg: Signum.

Presneau, J. (1993). The scholars, the deaf, and the language of signs in France in the 18th century. In R. Fischer & H. Lane (Eds.), *Looking back: A reader on the history of Deaf communities and their sign languages* (pp. 413–421). Hamburg: Signum.

Radutzky, E. (1993). The education of deaf people in Italy and the use of Italian Sign Language. In J. Van Cleve (Ed.), *Deaf history unveiled: Interpretations from the new scholarship* (pp. 237–251). Washington, DC: Gallaudet University Press.

Ree, J. (1999). I see a voice: *Deafness, language and the senses—A philosophical history.* New York: Metropolitan Books.

Stokoe, W.C. (1960). Sign language structure: An outline of the visual communication systems of the American deaf (Occasional Papers 8). Buffalo University of Buffalo Department of Anthropology and Linguistics. (reprinted Burtonsville, MD: Linstock Press, 1993).

Stokoe, W.C. (2001). *Language in hand: Why sign came before speech*. Washington, DC: Gallaudet University Press.

Thornton, W. (1793/1903). Cadmus, or a treatise on the elements of written language. *Association Review*, 5, 406–414.

Traxler, C.B. (2000). The Stanford Achievement Test, 9th edition: National norming and performance standards for deaf and hard-of-hearing students. *Journal of Deaf Studies and Deaf Education*, 5, 337–348.

Winzer, M.A. (1993). *The history of special education: From isolation to integration*. Washington, DC: Gallaudet University Press.

2

Michael A. Karchmer & Ross E. Mitchell

Demographic and Achievement Characteristics of Deaf and Hard-of-Hearing Students

In this chapter, we focus on two essential concerns for the practice of primary and secondary education (1) Who are the children for whom school programs are responsible, and (2) How well are the aims of education being accomplished by these young people? One might begin by asking, for example, are the students from wealthy or poor families, native or immigrant, speakers of English or users of a different language, or more specific to this volume, hearing, hard of hearing, or deaf? The nature of the school program—its facilities, personnel, curriculum, and instruction—is strongly influenced by the composition of the students it is intended to serve. We present an analysis of the demographics of deaf and hard-of-hearing children in the various K-12 educational settings in the United States, with a brief review of how this profile has changed over the last three decades.

Once the demographics of students in the various educational programs are understood, it is important to consider how the students are progressing in the development of basic skills, habits, and dispositions. For deaf and hard-of-hearing students, the only widely available and nationally representative data routinely collected and analyzed have been standardized academic achievement test

scores. As such, the focus is on the following question: How well are deaf and hard-of-hearing children in the various school programs acquiring essential academic skills, especially English language literacy, the most widely studied academic competency? Though with the development of the first hearing-impaired version of the Stanford Achievement Test (SAT-HI) in 1974 (see Trybus & Karchmer, 1977), local, regional, and national studies of the mathematical competencies of deaf and hard-of-hearing students have become more common, the issue of standardized reading assessment performance remains the primary focus (obsession?) of deaf education. To begin, we place the academic achievement patterns among deaf and hard-of-hearing students in the context of variations in outcomes among hearing students. Next, we compare hearing students and deaf and hard-of-hearing students by reviewing the results from the 1996 Stanford Achievement Test, ninth edition (Stanford-9), national standardization project for deaf and hard-of-hearing students in the United States (see Holt, Traxler, & Allen, 1997). Finally, we present a synthesis of what is known about the link between student characteristics and achievement outcomes among program settings.

Demographics

When it comes to the education of deaf and hard-of-hearing students in the United States, school composition has undergone a major transformation. The Education for All Handicapped Children Act of 1975 (EAHCA; Public Law 94–142) and the laws that have succeeded it have dramatically influenced the pattern and delivery of educational services for deaf and hard-of-hearing students (see, e.g., Schildroth & Karchmer, 1986; U.S. Department of Education, 2000). By defining the right to a free, appropriate public education in the least restrictive environment for children who are hard of hearing or deaf, among other identified disabilities, a radical shift in educational ideology has occurred (see Lang, this volume). No longer are deaf and hard-of-hearing children predominantly receiving their schooling in isolated settings primarily with specially trained personnel. To the extent possible, children with educationally relevant disabilities are to be integrated into instructional settings with non-disabled children. As of spring 2001, two-thirds of all deaf and hard-of-hearing students reported to the Annual Survey of Deaf and Hard of Hearing Children and Youth (hereafter, Annual Survey) receive at least some of their academic instruction in a regular classroom with hearing students. Over the last quarter of a century, the demographic profile of schooling for deaf and hard-of-hearing students has changed substantially as well (e.g., Holden-Pitt & Diaz, 1998; Schildroth & Hotto, 1995; Schildroth & Karchmer, 1986; U.S. Department of Education, 2001).

Who Are Deaf and Hard-of-Hearing Students?

Before discussing current national demographics for deaf and hard-of-hearing students in the K-12 school system, clarity about which students are being counted is needed. This is an important question because, unlike blindness, there is no legal standard for defining who is deaf. Defining the relevant population is not a simple task—the boundaries are amorphous and contested. Though there are a variety of standards that have been developed for assessing hearing ability, there is no threshold beyond which a student is defined as "legally" deaf. The federal government applies the generic and heterogeneous label of "hearing impairment" (e.g.,

U.S. Department of Education, 2000) to identify those children who receive special services in response to an educationally relevant degree of deafness. Though some students will not be enumerated because their hearing loss is not deemed educationally relevant or because it has not been identified, the pragmatic solution to the problem of population definition is through counting those identified for special education services. The distribution of deaf and hard-of-hearing students receiving special education services may not necessarily be representative of the distribution of deaf and hard-of-hearing students in the schools. Nonetheless, these are the students for whom the schools are making some effort to accommodate their deafness in order to provide an appropriate education, and these are the students of interest in this chapter.

The best representation of this population of deaf and hard-of-hearing students is the Annual Survey. For more than 30 years now, the Gallaudet Research Institute has collected demographic, program, and service data on roughly 60% of the nation's deaf and hard-of-hearing children and youth served in pre-K through grade-12 programs in the United States (e.g., Allen, 1992; Holden-Pitt & Diaz, 1998; Mitchell & Karchmer, in press). Because the Annual Survey has been described in detail elsewhere (see Ries; 1986; Schildroth & Hotto, 1993), only a brief overview is provided here. The data were obtained by distributing machine-readable forms to all public and private schools and programs that had been identified as providing services for deaf or hard-of-hearing children and youth, with the request that one form be completed for each child. Compliance was voluntary and confidentiality strictly maintained. Though not all schools and programs were sure to have been identified, and not all that had been identified responded, the Annual Survey provides a fairly representative cross-section of the students in America's deaf education programs (see Ries, 1986, for a thorough discussion of representativeness).

Student Characteristics and Instructional Settings

The findings from the Annual Survey for the 2000–2001 school year, with particular attention to program placement, are available. This sample includes information on 37,278 deaf and hard-of-hearing students from 6 to 21 years of age. These are the students presumed to be in elementary through secondary school programs. Figure 2-1 shows the distribution of students by instructional setting. Four patterns account for 96.5% of the student placements ($n = 35,955$): (1) regular school settings that do not involve the use of resource rooms (31.7% of the total); (2) regular education settings that also include a resource room assignment (12.6%); (3) self-contained classrooms in regular schools (28.5%); and special schools or centers, such as residential or day schools for deaf students (24.7%). All except the special school placements represent situations in which educational services are delivered in facilities serving hearing students. That is, 75.3% of the students in the 2000–2001 Annual Survey can be said to be educated in a mainstream facility. This pattern of educational placement represents a great change from 1975, just after the passage of P.L. 94-142. Whereas 49% of deaf and hard-of-hearing students reported to the 1975–1976 Annual Survey were enrolled in residential or day schools for deaf students (Karchmer & Trybus, 1977), only half that percentage were reported in 2000–2001 to attend a special or center school.

For the remainder of this section, we focus on the 35,955 six- to twenty-one-year-old deaf and hard-of-hearing students receiving academic instruction in the four settings listed above according to the 2000–2001 Annual Survey.[1] For brevity, the four instructional settings described above are referred to as: (1) regular education settings, (2) resource rooms, (3) self-contained classrooms, and (4) special schools. The first two settings represent services delivered in a regular education environ-ment. Self-contained classroom settings provide separate education within facilities for hearing students. As shown below, many of the students in self-contained classrooms, although located physically in a mainstream school, participate little in regular education (see Stinson & Kluwin, this volume).

Extent of Integration

Across the four settings, two-thirds of all students are integrated academically with non-disabled hearing students, at least to some degree. The pattern of integration across the settings is not the same, however (table 2-1). Virtually all students in the regular education and resource room settings have some integration, with the majority receiving instruction with hearing students half the time or more (>16 hr per week). A large majority of the students in self-contained classrooms also are integrated; but the actual amount of integration for these students is fairly modest. Just more than one-sixth are integrated 16 hours per week or more. Finally, few of the students in special schools are academically integrated with hearing students at all. Looking at these data from another perspective, one can ask where the nonintegrated students are educated. The answer is clear: Almost three-quarters of the nonintegrated students reported to the Annual Survey are in special schools; nearly all of the rest are in self-contained classrooms.

Basic Demographic Differences

Four demographic factors included in the 2000–2001 Annual Survey are considered: gender, age, racial/ethnic background, and the written/spoken

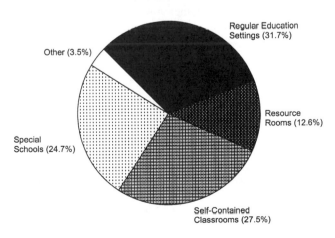

Figure 2-1. Instructional settings of deaf and hard-of-hearing students ($n = 37,278$) (Data source: Gallaudet Research Institute, 2000–2001.)

Table 2-1. Academic integration for deaf and hard-of-hearing students in four instructional settings: percent distributions

| Setting | Hours per week integrated with non-disabled hearing students for academic classroom instruction | | | | | |
	None	1–5	6–15	16–25	≥ 26	Total
Regular school setting (n = 10,679)	3.3	3.6	3.8	10.1	79.2	100.0
Resource room (n = 4,644)	0.9	4.4	14.1	33.5	47.2	100.0
Self-contained classroom (n = 10,006)	28.3	28.7	25.9	9.9	7.3	100.0
Special school (n = 8,970)	90.4	3.6	2.7	1.2	2.2	100.0
Total (n = 34,299)	33.0	11.0	11.3	10.9	33.7	100.0

Source: Gallaudet Research Institute (2000–2001).

languages used regularly in the student's home. Of these four factors, only the gender distribution is similar across settings, with about 54.0% males in each setting. Table 2-2 shows that special schools enroll older students as compared to the other settings. Of the students 6–21 years old, almost half the students in special schools are 14 or older and one sixth are older than 18. The other three instructional settings tend to serve younger students, with relatively few students 18 or older.

The four instructional settings also differ significantly by racial/ethnic composition (figure 2-2). White students make up more than 60% of the enrollments of regular school settings and resource rooms. Hispanics/Latinos are next most numerous in these programs (>16%), followed by black/African-American students (>10%). The percentage of white students in special schools is almost 50, with most of the rest of the students divided equally between Hispanic and black students. Self-contained classrooms have the lowest percentage of white students (about 41%) and the highest percentage of Hispanic students (nearly 31%). Finally,

Asian/Pacific Islanders make up about 4% of the students in each setting. Students from other racial or ethnic backgrounds, including students reported to be from more than one ethnic background, account for almost 5% of the students in each setting.

Just more than 90% of deaf and hard-of-hearing students come from homes where only one spoken/written language is used regularly. English and Spanish are the languages most commonly reported (figure 2-3). Here again there is noticeable variation among the settings. What is most salient is that the self-contained settings have a far larger percentage of students from homes where Spanish is used than is true in the other settings. Almost a quarter of the students in self-contained classrooms come from homes where Spanish is regularly used, almost twice the percentage found in the three other settings taken in aggregate.

Other Student Characteristics

Perhaps the variable that most distinguishes the instructional settings is students' degree of hearing

Table 2-2. Percentage distributions of deaf and hard-of-hearing students, by age, in four instructional settings

| Setting | Age group (years) | | | | |
	6–9	10–13	14–17	18–21	Total
Regular school setting (n = 11,823)	27.3	35.4	30.0	7.4	100.0
Resource room (n = 4,685)	22.1	38.0	31.8	16.6	100.0
Self-contained classroom (n = 10,252)	31.9	33.9	25.9	8.2	100.0
Special school (n = 9,195)	22.4	28.0	32.9	16.6	100.0
Total (n = 35,955)	26.7	33.4	29.8	10.1	100.0

Source: Gallaudet Research Institute (2000–2001).

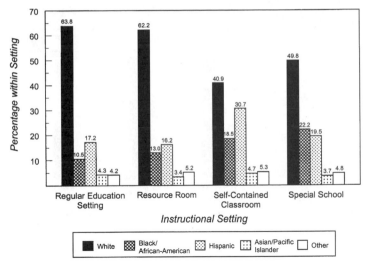

Figure 2-2. Ethnic distribution of deaf and hard-of-hearing students in four instructional settings ($n = 35,634$) (Data source: Gallaudet Research Institute, 2000–2001.)

loss (as indicated by unaided, average pure-tone thresholds across the speech range in the better ear, the "better ear average"). Figure 2-4 shows hearing profiles of students in the four settings. Special schools tend to enroll students with greater hearing impairments. Sixty percent are in the profound range (≥ 91 dB), while less than one fifth have hearing impairments in the less-than-severe (<71 dB) range. Self-contained classrooms serve students across the entire hearing spectrum (figure 2-4).

Regular school settings, including resource rooms, predominately serve students with substantial residual hearing. More than three-quarters are in the less-than-severe range, and another 9% have thresholds between 71 and 90 dB.

The primary communication mode used to teach deaf and hard-of-hearing students is strongly related to students' degree of hearing loss (e.g., Jordan & Karchmer, 1986). Specifically, profoundly deaf students typically are in programs where sign-

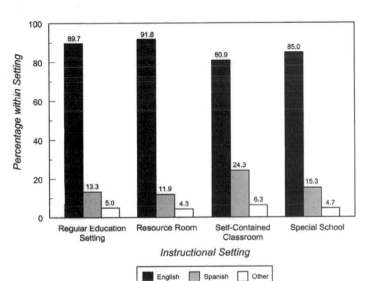

Figure 2-3. Languages in the homes of deaf and hard-of-hearing students in four instructional setting ($n = 33,979$) (Data source: Gallaudet Research Institute, 2000–2001.) *Note:* Percentages do not total 100 within settings because more than one language is indicated for some students.

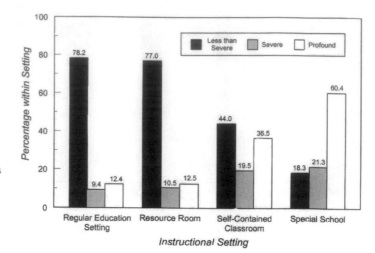

Figure 2-4. Degree of hearing loss of deaf and hard-of-hearing students in four instructional settings (*n* = 32,145). (Data source: Gallaudet Research Institute, 2000–2001.)

ing or signing together with speech is used. Students with milder losses tend to be in programs where speech is the primary medium of instruction. Because of this, the four settings not only sort students by hearing level, they also sort them by primary mode of communication used in teaching. Table 2-3 shows that 9 out of 10 students in special schools receive instruction primarily through signs or signs and speech. Just more than two-thirds of the students in self-contained classrooms also are in signing programs. In contrast, more than three-quarters of the students in the regular school settings, including those in resource rooms, receive instruction through speech only.

Many of the students have other educationally relevant disabilities or conditions. The presence of an additional disability is also related to educational placement. Overall, of the students for whom this information is reported, 43.4% have one or more additional conditions (see Knoors & Vervloed, this volume). The breakdown by type of instructional setting is shown in table 2-4 and indicates that students in the regular education setting are much less likely than students in any of the other three settings to have additional conditions. Note that certain specific conditions are more prevalent in some settings than others. For example, resource rooms are far more likely to have learning disabled students than the other settings. Self-contained classrooms and special schools are more likely than the other two settings to have students described as mentally retarded.

Finally, almost two-thirds of students in the four settings wear personal hearing aids, and 5% have a cochlear implant. Although the extent of hearing aid and cochlear implant use does not differ greatly across the settings, specific patterns of use are complicated to describe and are beyond the

Table 2-3. Primary communication modes used to teach students in four instructional settings: percent distributions

Setting	Primary communication mode of instruction					
	Speech only	Speech and sign	Sign only	Cued speech	Other	Total
Regular school setting (*n* = 11,442)	79.7	18.4	1.3	0.2	0.3	100.0
Resource room (*n* = 4,653)	75.1	22.2	1.7	0.7	0.3	100.0
Self-contained classroom (*n* = 10,190)	29.9	63.3	5.0	0.6	1.2	100.0
Special school (*n* = 9,029)	8.9	74.3	15.4	0.0	1.4	100.0
Total (*n* = 35,314)	46.6	46.1	6.0	0.4	0.8	100.0

Source: Gallaudet Research Institute (2000–2001).

Table 2-4. Percentages of students in four instructional settings reported to have one or more conditions other than deafness

Setting	Without additional conditions	With additional conditions	Total
Regular school setting ($n = 8,949$)	70.7	29.3	100.0
Resource room ($n = 3,957$)	47.3	52.7	100.0
Self-contained classroom ($n = 8,644$)	49.9	50.1	100.0
Special school ($n = 7,384$)	52.3	47.7	100.0
Total ($n = 28,934$)	56.6	43.4	100.0

Source: Gallaudet Research Institute (2000–2001).

scope of this chapter (see Karchmer & Kirwin, 1977, about patterns of hearing aid use).

Achievement

Questions about the academic achievements of deaf and hard-of-hearing students have been asked in a number of ways for nearly a century now. Chamberlain and Mayberry (2000) examined the assessment of reading performance among North American deaf and hard-of-hearing children to better understand the nature of the relationship between American Sign Language (ASL) and reading. Turner (2000) considered research discussing English literacy development from both sides of the Atlantic, as did a team of British researchers (Powers, Gregory, & Thoutenhoofd, 1998) who provided an overview of American, British, and Canadian findings on a host of educational outcomes for deaf and hard-of-hearing children published between 1980 and 1998, from which were identified factors affecting educational achievement applicable to deaf learners in the United Kingdom.

Moores (2001) reviewed academic achievement quite broadly, with an interest in the relationship between the instructional setting and the level of student performance across the content areas, with particular attention to high school mathematics achievement. Paul and Quigley (1990), in addition to providing a broad summary of achievement outcomes, specifically noted the strengths and limitations of various assessment strategies and instruments employed in the literature (also see Baker, 1991). Mertens (1990) reported on outcomes for deaf and hard-of-hearing students to

provide a conceptual model of academic achievement that would inform and direct continuing research in this area. Regardless of emphasis or purpose, however, these reviews note the same overwhelming concern: the average performance on tests of reading comprehension for deaf and hard-of-hearing students is roughly six grade equivalents lower than their hearing peers at age 15 (e.g., Allen, 1986; Traxler, 2000).

Academic achievement may be defined in various ways. The most common strategies for evaluating a student's scholastic accomplishments include testing in one or more content areas at a specified level of difficulty, grading by teachers responsible for particular classes or subjects, and granting of credentials (certificates or diplomas) by schools. Additional indicators of academic achievement include grade-to-grade advancement and the successful completion or mastery of curricular units for which grades and credentials are not awarded. The research literature discussing the academic achievement of deaf and hard-of-hearing students is substantially limited to the analysis of commercially available, norm-referenced, standardized tests, and only infrequently have any of the other indicators been examined.

Standardized test scores turn out to be the best, if not the only, indicators of academic achievement of deaf and hard-of-hearing students in the United States. Test developers have endeavored to select those curriculum content elements that are most nearly universal from the wider range of possibilities. It must be acknowledged, therefore, that this form of assessment may suffer from misalignment with local curriculum variations. To their credit, standardized tests have well-defined psychometric properties. In contrast, subject grades have too much measurement error and are too contextually bound; credentials exclude those students still in the K-12 system and those who have left early. Standardized scholastic assessment offers a glimpse of some of the important academic achievements that students have made across multiple contexts and does so in a way that permits a fair measure of comparison among groups of students.

Analysis of standardized test scores, particularly norm-referenced scores, have led to insights and concerns (see Baker, 1991; Paul & Quigley, 1990, for reviews of tests used with deaf and hard-of-hearing students). A number of small-scale studies have used individually administered tests, such as the Peabody Picture Vocabulary Test (e.g., Davis, Elfenbein, Schum, & Bentler, 1986), as well as group-administered tests such as the Comprehensive Test of Basic Skills (e.g., Bess, Dodd-Murphy, & Parker, 1998), Metropolitan Achievement Test (MAT; e.g., Stuckless & Birch, 1966), and Stanford Achievement Test (or Stanford; e.g., Bodner-Johnson, 1986; Brill, 1962; Vernon & Koh, 1970). Overwhelmingly, however, the most widely generalizable findings have come from the use of group-administered tests, namely the MAT (e.g., Furth, 1966; Wrightstone, Aronow, & Moskowitz, 1963) and the Stanford (e.g., Allen, 1986; Holt, 1993; Traxler, 2000; Trybus & Karchmer, 1977).

Student Characteristics and Academic Achievement

Rooted in the American cultural value of equity (see Stout, Tallerico, & Scribner, 1995), school professionals and policymakers have paid close attention to differences in academic achievement test scores among politically and educationally relevant student groups in the United States since the 1960s (e.g., Coleman et al., 1966). For hearing, hard-of-hearing, and deaf students, educators have consistently been concerned with differences in achievement for children grouped by family socioeconomic status, race and ethnicity, gender, home language, English language proficiency, age or grade, and special education services received. Each of these child and family demographic factors has been researched in isolation or in combination with other factors, but not all of them carry the same meaning, nor are they identified by the same indicators for hearing, hard-of-hearing, and deaf stu-

dents. Demographics that make sense across all three groups include family socioeconomic status (SES or class), race and ethnicity, and gender. But for deaf and hard-of-hearing students, home language, English language proficiency, age or grade, and special education services received have not referenced the same set of constructs and indicators as they have for hearing students. That is, within the conceptually similar categories of language use, age-related progress through school, and special services for educationally relevant needs, there are important qualitative differences.

Race, Class, and Gender

Racial and ethnic group membership is strongly associated with group mean academic achievement levels. In the United States, the reference group with which to compare all others has been white students, a designation representing the mix of numerous European ethnic groups. Though the identification of other ethnic groups is even more complicated, the socioeconomic distinction between underrepresented and overrepresented minorities is the most parsimonious for present purposes (see, e.g., National Task Force on Minority High Achievement, 1999).

Underrepresented minorities are those persons identified as belonging to a racial/ethnic group whose proportional representation in the various high-income professions and among recipients of higher-education credentials is less than would be expected based on their prevalence in the general population; the opposite pattern is true for the overrepresented minorities. Whites currently remain the majority and thus continue to serve as the reference group. Blacks/African Americans, Hispanics/Latinos, and Native Americans (American Indians/Native Alaskans) are the three underrepresented minorities that receive the greatest attention. Asian Americans are the one overrepresented minority that is given regular notice (this designation often excludes Pacific Islanders). For hearing students, underrepresented minorities have lower aggregate academic achievement scores than white students, but overrepresented minorities achieve more highly, as a group, than white students (e.g., Campbell, Hombo, & Mazzeo, 2000; Entwisle, Alexander, & Olson, 1997; Hedges & Nowell, 1999; Portes & MacLeod, 1999).

The same relative performance differences across groups are observed for deaf and hard-of-hearing students as well, except that Asian American students are less likely to outperform white students (e.g., Allen, 1986; Holt, 1993; Holt et al., 1997; Mitchell, 2002). However, handling race and ethnic–group membership as a simple divide between the underrepresented and the overrepresented misses an important confound with English language proficiency. Ethnic groups with high proportions of recent immigrants (non-English speakers)—namely, Latinos and Asian Americans—tend to perform lower on tests of reading than on the relatively less English-loaded tests of mathematics, whether these students are hearing or not (for hearing students, see Abedi, 2001; for deaf and hard-of-hearing students, see Allen, 1986; Jensema, 1975; Kluwin, 1994; Mitchell, 2002).

Student socioeconomic status is typically assigned by indicators such as parental education, parental occupational status, and family income levels. Though there is some variability in the strength of the association between SES and academic achievement due to the indicators used, a positive relationship is consistently observed. However, compared to hearing students (e.g., Alexander, Entwisle, & Olson, 2001; Campbell et al., 2000; Biddle, 2001; Portes & MacLeod, 1999), there has been much less extensive examination of the relationship between SES and achievement for deaf and hard-of-hearing students. Further, the confounding of race and ethnicity with lower socioeconomic status in the United States, particularly for recent immigrants, has made it more difficult to identify the impact of SES for deaf and hard-of-hearing students.

Studies of deaf and hard-of-hearing students and their families have not included the collection of family SES data with samples either large enough or representative enough to make reliable estimates of the independent effect of parental income, education, or occupation on student achievement. Nonetheless, deaf and hard-of-hearing students from higher SES families score higher on standardized tests of academic achievement, on average, than students from lower SES families (Jensema, 1977, Kluwin, 1994; Kluwin & Gaustad, 1992; Kluwin & Moores, 1989.

The relationship between gender and academic achievement has been the object of study for quite some time. Unlike ethnicity or family SES, gender is fairly straightforward, requiring little explanation and having little ambiguity in measurement. Female students have, in the aggregate, performed better than male students on standardized tests of language arts, but not in mathematics (see, e.g., Campbell et al., 2000). In recent years, however, the gender gap for hearing students is no longer statistically reliable for mathematics achievement—girls have essentially caught up with boys (e.g., Hall, Davis, Bolen, & Chia, 1999; Leahy & Guo, 2001; Nowell & Hedges, 1998). For deaf and hard-of-hearing students, the only difference is that there is mixed evidence on whether there is reliably higher mathematics achievement for older boys for the last three decades (e.g., Allen, 1986; Mitchell, 2002; Trybus & Karchmer, 1977).

Language, Age, and Special Education

When it comes to more strongly school-relevant characteristics, there are important differences as well as similarities between hearing students and deaf and hard-of-hearing students. That is, the achievement impact of home language, language of instruction and assessment, age–grade correlation of curriculum, and the need for special educational services is similarly understood, but the student characteristics to which educators attend are qualitatively different for deaf and hard-of-hearing students. Consider first the problem of the relationship between language and academic achievement. In the United States, there are a large number of languages used by children and youth in their homes, communities, and schools, with English and Spanish being the most common. English is far and away the preferred, if not the only, language used in large-scale assessments in schools, but not all children are equally proficient in the use of English. As such, schools have complied with bilingual education program requirements by recording the dominant spoken language of each student's home, if it is not English, and determining the English language proficiency of each student whose home language is not English (see August & Hakuta, 1997). However, this practice does not facilitate the identification of limited English proficiency (LEP) that is relevant to performance on standardized assessments for those students who use nonstandard English dialects (see, e.g., Baron, 2000; Ogbu, 1999) or who use signed languages (see, e.g., Commission on the Education of the Deaf, 1988; Woodward, 1978).

Whether students can hear or not, LEP has devastating impact on standardized test performance when the test is written in English. Large differences in academic achievement are observed among hearing students when comparing the aggregate performance of LEP students with fluent English-proficient students, students who are native English speakers, and other hearing students for whom the designation of LEP does not apply (e.g., Hao & Bonstead-Bruns, 1998; Portes & MacLeod, 1999; Schmid, 2001). Additionally, older LEP students are further behind their peers, as a group, than younger LEP students (Rumberger, 2000).

There are two issues that are commonly considered when discussing the relationship between deafness and English language fluency. First, there is the matter of first-language fluency development (see reviews by Marschark, 2001; Quigley & Paul, 1989). Children who learn English before they are no longer able to hear, often referred to as postlingual deafness, generally achieve higher scores on standardized tests, particularly in reading, than children who were unable to hear in their first years of life, called prelingual deafness (e.g., Allen, 1986; Jensema, 1975; Reamer, 1921). Among those who begin life deaf, however, those who grow up with deaf parents or parents who competently facilitate visual language interaction have higher English language reading achievement than those deaf children who did not grow up with competent visual language support (see reviews by Chamberlain & Mayberry, 2000; Kampfe & Turecheck, 1987).

Second, deafness and English language fluency are related through access to linguistic interaction both inside and outside of the family, home, or classroom setting (Marschark, 2001). For interaction in English, the focus has been on the student's speech intelligibility, ease with which the student can speechread, and ease of speech perception (except for speechreading, these concerns pertain to hearing students as well). There is little research on the association of either speech intelligibility and the ability to speechread with academic achievement. One study found that students with superior speech intelligibility and better speechreading skills were more likely to have higher standardized test scores (Pflaster, 1980, 1981). Though there are few studies that directly estimate the impact of ease of speech perception on academic achievement, the better ear average has been frequently used as a proxy indicator. Consistently, students who are profoundly deaf perform lower than or near the same level on tests of reading as students who are severely deaf, and these students generally have lower aggregate achievement than students who are less-than-severely deaf, the latter often referred to as hard of hearing (e.g., Holt, 1993; Holt et al., 1997; Jensema, 1975; Karchmer, Milone, & Wolk, 1979). Additionally, the lesser the degree of deafness, the greater the gain in reading comprehension achievement, on average, over a 3- to 5-year period (Trybus & Karchmer, 1977; Wolk & Allen, 1984).

All of these deaf and hard-of-hearing students, possibly including those with minimal sensorineural hearing loss (Bess et al., 1998), have lower aggregate reading achievement than hearing children. Further, the central tendency in reading achievement as a function of age has been observed to diverge: deaf and hard-of-hearing students are relatively further behind their same-age hearing peers in the high school years (e.g., Allen, 1986; Holt, 1993; Traxler, 2000). Mathematics performance is much higher, on average, for deaf and hard-of-hearing students, but the difference from hearing students remains noteworthy.

For interaction in sign language (e.g., ASL), the development of fluency and sophistication appears to depend on the deaf student having access to a sign language discourse community (see Marschark, 2001). With the exception of the important, but small, fraction of deaf students who grow up in ASL-fluent homes (see Mitchell & Karchmer, in press), many deaf students do not have daily access to a natural, sophisticated, and diverse sign language discourse community. Unfortunately, there is only one large-scale study that has attempted to link a student's ASL fluency with academic achievement (Moores et al., 1987; Moores & Sweet, 1990). This study, limited to high school students, had a relatively insensitive measure of ASL fluency and was unable to adequately examine this linkage (but see Chamberlain & Mayberry, 2000, for a review of small-scale studies). So instead of student fluency and the ability to express knowledge and understanding in sign language as a bridge to English language fluency development, the proxy for access to linguistic interaction has been whether the deaf child has one or more deaf parents.

As with hearing students (e.g., McDonnell, McLaughlin, & Morison, 1997; Mitchell, 2001; Reynolds & Wolfe, 1999), deaf and hard-of-hearing students who have an additional condition do not achieve as highly on standardized tests, on average, as those with no additional conditions (e.g., Allen, 1986; Holt, 1993; Holt et al., 1997). Further, as with hearing students, the kind of additional disability is important. Cognitive and behavioral disabilities have more negative impacts on achievement than physical disabilities. For hearing students and deaf and hard-of-hearing students alike, an additional disability is associated with lower aggregate achievement.

The final consideration in reviewing the relationship between student characteristics and academic achievement is a comparison between the distribution of outcomes for hearing students and deaf and hard-of-hearing students. This contrast provides an estimate of the impact of deafness across the range of student achievement. However, the problem of age–grade correlation, or lack thereof, introduces an important caveat to the hearing versus deaf and hard of hearing comparison. The normative standard for group-administered educational testing is to test all students of the same age-grade with tests of the same level of difficulty. Though there may be some students who have been retained or accelerated, so that their age may not be the same as their classmates, students are generally close in age for a given grade in school. This age–grade correlation also tends to assure that test items sample a curriculum that has been learned recently rather than materials and objectives learned earlier or that have yet to be encountered. The age–grade connection tends to remain fairly true for deaf and hard-of-hearing students as well, but the level at which they are tested does not follow the normative pattern. Because the reading/English language proficiency levels attained by many deaf students are much lower than most of their hearing age–grade peers, these students are accommodated by being tested "out of level" (see Pitoniak & Royer, 2001, pp. 53–58, for a review of issues related to testing accommodation; also Abedi, 2001). This out-of-level testing results in many deaf and hard-of-hearing students being much older than the age–grade range for which their test is typically administered. (The appropriate level, in the case of the Stanford, is determined by a screening test that indicates at which level students may be reliably assessed [e.g., Allen, White, & Karchmer, 1983; Gallaudet Research Institute, 1996a].)

Out-of-level testing means that caution needs to be exercised when interpreting academic achievement test scores. Despite the fact that test developers provide vertical equating scales, the difficulty level of the items is not perfectly comparable when the performance estimate is more than two grade levels from the intended level for testing. Additionally, the age appropriateness of the test items may be compromised. For these reasons, comparing the scores of deaf or hard-of-hearing 15-year-old students taking a 4th grade level reading test with 15-year-old hearing students taking a 10th grade level reading test, the modal comparison (Holt et al., 1997), is not entirely satisfactory.

With the foregoing cautions in mind, comparisons between hearing students and deaf and hard-of-hearing students are made. The grade equivalent metric that has been so popular in past literature is not used; the grade equivalent is an ordinal scale, rather than an equal interval scale. Instead, item response theory scaled scores are used because they provide a linear interval scale and allow for comparisons across test levels.

Figure 2.5 offers an age–grade comparison of reading comprehension scores between the Stanford-9 national norming studies for hearing students (Harcourt Brace Educational Measurement, 1997) and deaf and hard of hearing students (Gallaudet Research Institute, 1996b). The comparison matches cohorts of deaf and hard-of-hearing students of a particular age (8–15 years), whether tested out of level or not, with hearing students for the grade that is predominantly the same age (grades 2–9, respectively). This results in eight pairs of vertical lines representing the dispersion of scores from the first to the ninth decile (i.e., 10th–90th percentile), where each line has a shaded square (deaf & hard of hearing) or diamond (hearing) marking the median (5th decile or 50th percentile).

There are three patterns to note. First, the median value increases for each successively older cohort year for both the hearing and the deaf and hard-of-hearing groups. Second, the median score is consistently higher for hearing students than for deaf and hard-of-hearing students, and the difference is fairly constant across cohorts. Third, the dispersion (distance between the 1st and 9th deciles) for hearing students decreases for successive cohorts, up to age 12/grade 6, while the dispersion for deaf and hard-of-hearing students increases. The observed range of performance is much larger for a greater share of the deaf and hard-of-hearing

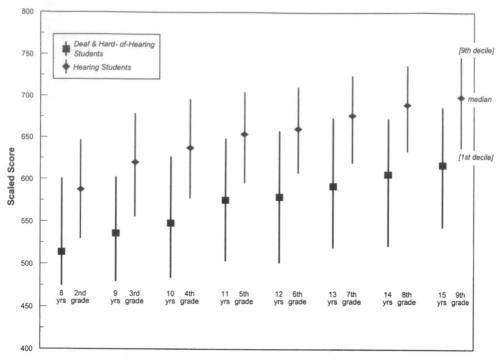

Figure 2-5. Spring 1996 Stanford Achievement Test (9th edition) 1st to 9th decile ranges in reading comprehension scaled scores for deaf and hard-of hearing/hearing students age 8, 2nd grade, through age 15, 9th grade. (Data sources: Harcourt Brace Educational Measurement, 1997; Gallaudet Research Institute, 1996b.)

students compared to hearing students. Altogether, this implies that the higher performing deaf and hard-of-hearing students are likely to be making the same amount of annual achievement growth as hearing students, though the level of performance of the top deaf and hard-of-hearing students is only on par with the middle-of-the-pack hearing students, while the lower performing deaf and hard-of-hearing students are further and further behind. These results emphasize an important point: to understand the diversity of academic accomplishments of deaf and hard-of-hearing students, analysts must attend to both the central tendency and the dispersion of achievement.

Summary and Conclusions

The first part of this chapter described how deaf and hard-of-hearing students differed in four instructional settings, suggesting that students are not randomly distributed among school programs. The deliberate process of student assignment, however

accomplished, results in distinctly different student profiles for each program type. And as reviewed in the latter part of this chapter, these differences in student characteristics across settings are associated with academic achievement differences as well. Thus, the crucial step is to determine if there is any evidence that program placement is associated with group achievement differences (see Stinson & Kluwin, this volume).

Figure 2.6 depicts the Stanford-9 reading comprehension achievement profiles for deaf and hard-of-hearing students at ages 8 and 15 (Holt et al., 1997). Three settings (not identical to the four identified earlier) are distinguished: students in special schools, students in local schools with minimal integration in the mainstream program (i.e., predominantly self-contained classrooms), and students in local schools who are substantially integrated (i.e., mostly students in resource rooms and other regular education settings). The full dispersion of student achievement (i.e., from the 1st to the 9th decile, with each decile marked on the vertical line) for each of the three settings is shown.

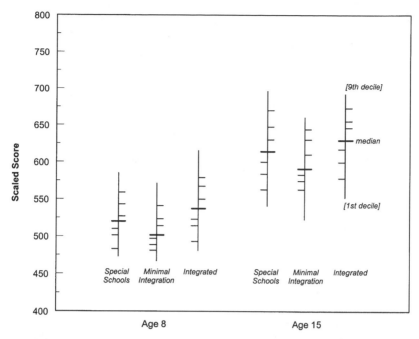

Figure 2-6. Spring 1996 Stanford Achievement Test (9th edition) reading comprehension scaled score distributions for two cohorts (ages 8 and 15) of deaf and hard-of-hearing/hearing students in three instructional settings *Note:* The 2nd through 4th deciles are indicated by horizontal lines to the left, and the 6th through 8th deciles by horizontal lines to the right. (Data source: Gallaudet Research Institute, 1996b.)

There are three important points to note, in addition to the increased dispersion for older cohorts previously described. First, the range of achievement observed is greatest among integrated students at age 8; at age 15, it is among special school students. Second, though the median performance of special school students is lower than integrated students for both cohorts, the highest 20% of the special school students at age 15 are achieving as well or better than the highest 20% of the integrated students at age 15. Third, the low-end performance in the local school programs is found among those who are minimally integrated, lower than that of students in the special schools. These patterns suggest that there is greater heterogeneity of academic achievement in special schools than in the mainstream, but not necessarily in regular schools generally. That is, there is cause to suspect that the distribution of achievement in regular schools and in special schools is similar, but the purposeful sorting of students into differentiated programs is readily apparent for the various regular education settings.

It is difficult to attribute any differences in academic achievement to the programs themselves. A handful of studies have tried to establish if there is any link between the type of program and academic achievement, but the results of these investigations suggest that there is little independent explanation of achievement differences attributable to student placement (Allen & Osborn, 1984; Kluwin & Moores, 1985, 1989). In fact, there is some reason to believe that student placement dynamics are sensitive to student performance differences, where options exist, thereby increasing the likelihood that program settings reflect sorting and selecting decisions more strongly than instructional efficacy (see Oakes, Gamoran, & Page, 1992, on ability grouping and tracking). However, because there have been few longitudinal analyses of student academic performance related to program placement changes, it is difficult to determine whether programs are responsive to student differences or whether they serve to consolidate student differences, thereby restricting opportunities (Kluwin, 1993; Mitchell & Mitchell, 1999).

Notes

We gratefully acknowledge that inclusion of data from the 2000–2001 Annual Survey of Deaf and Hard of Hearing Children and Youth was made possible by the following members of the Gallaudet Research Institute: Sue Hotto (coordinator), Kay Lam, John Woo, Anna Lex, Linda Stamper, and Russ Perkins.

1. Due to missing or unreported data, the total number of cases for each variable may be less than 35,955.

References

Abedi, J. (2001, Summer). Assessment and accommodations for English language learners: Issues and recommendations. In *CRESST Policy Brief 4*. Los Angeles: University of California, National Center for Research on Evaluation, Standards, and Student Testing.

Alexander, K. L., Entwisle, D. R., & Olson, L. S. (2001). Schools, achievement, and inequality: A seasonal perspective. *Educational Evaluation and Policy Analysis, 23*(2), 171–191.

Allen, T. E. (1986). Patterns of academic achievement among hearing impaired students: 1974 and 1983. In A. N. Schildroth & M. A. Karchmer (Eds.), *Deaf children in America* (pp. 161–206). San Diego, CA: College-Hill Press.

Allen, T. E. (1992). Subgroup differences in educational placement for deaf and hard of hearing students. *American Annals of the Deaf, 137*(5), 381–388.

Allen, T. E., & Osborn, T. I. (1984). Academic integration of hearing-impaired students: Demographic, handicapping, and achievement factors. *American Annals of the Deaf, 129*(2), 100–113.

Allen, T. E., & White, C. S., & Karchmer, M. A. (1983). Issues in the development of a special edition for hearing-impaired students of the seventh edition of the Stanford Achievement Test. *American Annals of the Deaf, 128*(1), 34–39.

August, D., & Hakuta, K. (Eds.). (1997). *Improving schooling for language-minority children: A research agenda*. Washington, DC: National Academy Press.

Baker, R. M. (1991). Evaluation of hearing-impaired children. In K. E. Green (Ed.), *Educational testing: Issues and applications* (pp. 77–107). New York: Garland Publishing.

Baron, D. (2000). Ebonics and the politics of English. *World Englishes, 19*(1), 5–19.

Bess, F. H., Dodd-Murphy, J., & Parker, R. A. (1998). Children with minimal sensorineural hearing loss: Prevalence, educational performance, and functional status. *Ear & Hearing, 19*(5), 339–354.

Biddle, B. J. (Ed.). (2001). *Social class, poverty, and education: Policy and practice*. New York: Routledge-Falmer.

Bodner-Johnson, B. (1986). The family environment and achievement of deaf students: A discriminant analysis. *Exceptional Children, 52*(5), 443–449.

Brill, R. G. (1962). The relationship of Wechsler's IQ to academic achievement among deaf students. *Exceptional Children, 28*(6), 315–321.

Campbell, J. R., Hombo, C. M., & Mazzeo, J. (2000, August). *NAEP 1999 trends in academic progress: Three decades of student performance* (NCES 2000-469). Washington, DC: U.S. Department of Education, Office of Educational Research and Improvement, National Center for Education Statistics.

Chamberlain, C., & Mayberry, R. I. (2000). Theorizing about the relation between American Sign Language and reading. In C. Chamberlain, J. P. Morford, & R. I. Mayberry (Eds.), *Language acquisition by eye* (pp. 221–259). Mahwah, NJ: Lawrence Erlbaum Associates.

Coleman, J. S., Campbell, E. Q., Hobson, C. J., McPartland, J., Mood, A. M., Weinfeld, F. D., & York, R. L. (1966). *Equality of educational opportunity*. Washington, DC: U.S. Government Printing Office.

Commission on Education of the Deaf. (1988, February). *Toward equality: Education of the deaf*. Washington, DC: U.S. Government Printing Office.

Davis, J. M., Elfenbein, J., Schum, R., & Bentler, R. A. (1986). Effects of mild and moderate hearing impairments on language, educational, and psychosocial behavior of children. *Journal of Speech and Hearing Disorders, 51*(2), 53–62.

Education for All Handicapped Children Act of 1975. Pub. L. No. 94–142, 20 USCS §§ 1400 *et seq.*

Entwisle, D. R., Alexander, K. L., & Olson, L. S. (1997). *Children, schools, and inequality*. Boulder, CO: Westview Press.

Furth, H. H. (1966). A comparison of reading test norms of deaf and hearing children. *American Annals of the Deaf, 111*(2), 461–462.

Gallaudet Research Institute. (1996a). *Stanford Achievement Test, 9th Edition: Screening procedures for deaf and hard-of-hearing students*. Washington, DC: Gallaudet University, Gallaudet Research Institute.

Gallaudet Research Institute. (1996b, November). *Stanford Achievement Test, 9th Edition, Form S: Norms booklet for deaf and hard-of-hearing students*. Washington, DC: Gallaudet University, Gallaudet Research Institute.

Gallaudet Research Institute. (2000–2001). Annual

Survey of Deaf and Hard of Hearing Children and Youth. Washington, DC: Gallaudet University, Gallaudet Research Institute.

Hall, C. W., Davis, N. B., Bolen, L. M., & Chia, R. (1999). Gender and racial differences in mathematical performance. *Journal of Social Psychology, 139*(6), 677–689.

Hao, L., & Bonstead-Bruns, M. (1998). Parent-child differences in educational expectations and the academic achievement of immigrant and native students. *Sociology of Education, 71*(3), 175–198.

Harcourt Brace Educational Measurement. (1997). *Stanford Achievement Test Series, Ninth Edition: Spring multilevel norms book.* San Antonio, TX: Author.

Hedges, L. V., & Nowell, A. (1999). Changes in the black-white gap in achievement test scores. *Sociology of Education, 72*(2), 111–135.

Holden-Pitt, L., & Diaz, J. A. (1998). Thirty years of the Annual Survey of Deaf and Hard-of-Hearing Children and Youth: A glance over the decades. *American Annals of the Deaf, 143*(2), 72–76.

Holt, J. A. (1993). Stanford Achievement Test—8th Edition: Reading comprehension subgroup results. *American Annals of the Deaf, 138*(2), 172–175.

Holt, J. A., Traxler, C. B., & Allen, T. E. (1997). *Interpreting the scores: A user's guide to the 9th Edition Stanford Achievement Test for educators of deaf and hard-of-hearing students* (Technical Report 97-1). Washington, DC: Gallaudet University, Gallaudet Research Institute.

Jensema, C. J. (1975, September). *The relationship between academic achievement and the demographic characteristics of hearing impaired children and youth* (Series R, No. 2). Washington, DC: Gallaudet College, Office of Demographic Studies.

Jensema, C. J. (1977, August). Parental income: Its relation to other characteristics of hearing impaired students. In B. W. Rawlings & C. J. Jensema, *Two studies of the families of hearing impaired children* (Series R, No. 5; pp. 9–15). Washington, DC: Gallaudet College, Office of Demographic Studies.

Jordan, I. K., & Karchmer, M. A. (1986). Patterns of sign use among hearing impaired students. In A. N. Schildroth & M. A. Karchmer (Eds.), *Deaf children in America* (pp. 125–138). San Diego, CA: College-Hill Press.

Karchmer, M. A., & Kirwin, L. (1977, December). *Usage of hearing aids by hearing impaired children in the United States* (Series S, No. 2). Washington, DC: Gallaudet College, Office of Demographic Studies.

Karchmer, M. A., Milone, M. N., & Wolk, S. (1979). Educational significance of hearing loss at three levels of severity. *American Annals of the Deaf, 124*(2), 97–109.

Karchmer, M. A., Trybus, R. J. (1977, October). *Who are the deaf children in "mainstream" programs?* (Series R, No. 4). Washington, DC: Gallaudet College, Office of Demographic Studies.

Kampfe, C. M., & Turecheck, A. G. (1987). Reading achievement of prelingually deaf students and its relationship to parental method of communication. A review of the literature. *American Annals of the Deaf, 132*(1), 11–15.

Kluwin, T. N. (1993). Cumulative effects of mainstreaming on the achievement of deaf adolescents. *Exceptional Children, 60*(1), 73–81.

Kluwin, T. N. (1994). The interaction of race, gender, and social class effects in the education of deaf students. *American Annals of the Deaf, 139*(5), 465–471.

Kluwin, T. N., Gaustad, M. G. (1992). How family factors influence school achievement. In T. N. Kluwin, D. F. Moores, & M. G. Gaustad (Eds.), *Toward effective public school programs for deaf students: Context, process, and outcomes* (pp. 66–82). New York: Teachers College Press.

Kluwin, T. N., & Moores, D. F. (1985). The effects of integration on the mathematics achievement of hearing impaired adolescents. *Exceptional Children, 52*(2), 153–160.

Kluwin, T. N., & Movres, D. F. (1989). Mathematics achievement of hearing impaired adolescents in different placements. *Exceptional Children, 55*(4), 327–355.

Leahey, E., & Guo, G. (2001). Gender differences in mathematical trajectories. *Social Forces, 80*(2), 713–732.

Marschark, M. (2001). *Language development in children who are deaf: A research synthesis.* Alexandria, VA: National Association of State Directors of Special Education. (ERIC Document Reproduction Service No. ED455620.)

McDonnell, L. M., McLaughlin, M. J., & Morison, P. (Eds.). (1997). *Educating one & all: Students with disabilities and standards-based reform.* Washington, DC: National Academy Press.

Mertens, D. M. (1990). A conceptual model for academic achievement: deaf student outcomes. In D. F. Moores & K. P. Meadow-Orlans (Eds.), *Educational and developmental aspects of deafness* (pp. 25–72). Washington, DC: Gallaudet University Press.

Mitchell, R. E. (2001). *Class size reduction policy: Evaluating the impact on student achievement in California* Unpublished doctoral dissertation, University of California, Riverside. *Dissertation Abstracts International, 62*(07), 2305A.

Mitchell, R. E. (2002). [Stanford-9 mathematics and reading achievement of deaf and hard-of-hearing students: 1996 national norms project]. Unpublished data analyses.

Mitchell, R. E., & Karchmer, M. A. (2004). Chasing the mythical ten percent: Parental hearing status of deaf and hard of hearing students in the United States. *Sign Language Studies*, 4(2), 138–163.

Mitchell, R. E., & Mitchell, D. E. (1999, August). *Student segregation and achievement tracking in year-round schools*. Paper presented at the annual meeting of the American Sociological Association, Chicago, Illinois.

Moores, D. F. (2001). *Educating the deaf: Psychology, principles, and practices* (5th ed.). Boston: Houghton Mifflin Company.

Moores, D. F., Kluwin, T. N., Johnson, R., Cox, P., Blennerhasset, L., Kelly, L., Ewoldt, C., Sweet, C., & Fields, L. (1987). *Factors predictive of literacy in deaf adolescents* (Final Report to National Institute on Neurological and Communicative Disorders and Stroke Project, No. NIH-NINCDS-83-19). Washington, DC: National Institutes of Health.

Moores, D. F., & Sweet, C. (1990). Factors predictive of school achievement. In D. F. Moores & K. P. Meadow-Orlans (Eds.), *Educational and developmental aspects of deafness* (pp. 154–201). Washington, DC: Gallaudet University Press.

National Task Force on Minority High Achievement. (1999). *Reaching the top: A report of the National Task Force on Minority High Achievement*. New York: College Board.

Nowell, A., & Hedges, L. V. (1998). Trends in gender differences in academic achievement from 1960 to 1994: An analysis of differences in mean, variance, and extreme scores. *Sex Roles: A Journal of Research*, 39(1–2), 21–43.

Oakes, J., Gamoran, A., & Page, R. N. (1992). Curriculum differentiation: Opportunities, outcomes, and meanings. In P. W. Jackson (Ed.), *Handbook of research on curriculum* (pp. 570–608). New York: Macmillan.

Ogbu, J. U. (1999). Beyond language: Ebonics, proper English, and identity in a Black-American speech community. *American Educational Research Journal*, 36(2), 147–189.

Paul, P. V., & Quigley, S. P. (1990). *Education and deafness*. New York: Longman.

Pflaster, G. (1980). A factor analysis of variables related to academic performance of hearing-impaired children in regular classes. *Volta Review*, 82(2), 71–84.

Pflaster, G. (1981). A second analysis of factors related to academic performance of hearing-impaired

children in the mainstream. *Volta Review*, 83(2), 71–80.

Pitoniak, M. J., & Royer, J. M. (2001). Testing accommodations for examinees with disabilities: A review of psychometric, legal, and social policy issues. *Review of Educational Research*, 71(1), 53–104.

Portes, A., MacLeod, D. (1999). Educating the second generation: Determinants of academic achievement among children of immigrants in the United States. *Journal of Ethnic and Migration Studies*, 25(3), 373–396.

Powers, S., Gregory, S., & Thoutenhoofd, E. D. (1998). *The educational achievements of deaf children—a literature review* (Research Report No. 65). Norwich, England: Department for Education and Employment.

Quigley, S. P., & Paul, P. V. (1989). English language development. In M. C. Wang, M. C. Reynolds, & H. J. Walberg (Eds.), *Handbook of special education: Research and practice*: Vol. 3. Low incidence conditions (pp. 3–21). Oxford: Pergamon Press.

Reamer, J. C. (1921). Mental and educational measurements of the deaf. *Psychological Monographs*, 132.

Reynolds, A. J., & Wolfe, B. (1999). Special education and school achievement: An exploratory with a central-city sample. *Educational Evaluation and Policy Analysis*, 21(3), 249–270.

Ries, P. (1986). Characteristics of hearing impaired youth in the general population and of students in special educational programs for the hearing impaired. In A. N. Schildroth & M. A. Karchmer (Eds.), *Deaf children in America* (pp. 1–31). San Diego, CA: College-Hill Press.

Rumberger, R. W. (2000, September). *Educational outcomes and opportunities for English language learners*. Santa Barbara, CA: University of California Language Minority Research Institute.

Schildroth, A. N., & Hotto, S. A. (1993). Annual Survey of Hearing-Impaired Children and Youth: 1991–92 school year. *American Annals of the Deaf*, 138(2), 163–171.

———. (1995). Race and ethnic background in the Annual Survey of Deaf and Hard of Hearing Children and Youth. *American Annals of the Deaf*, 140(2), 96–99.

Schildroth, A. N., & Karchmer, M. A. (1986). *Deaf children in America*. San Diego, CA: College-Hill Press.

Schmid, C. L. (2001). Educational achievement, language-minority students, and the new second generation. *Sociology of Education*, 74 (Extra Issue), 71–87.

Stuckless, E. R., & Birch, J. W. (1966). The influence of early manual communication on the linguistic development of deaf children. *American Annals of the Deaf, 111*(2), 452–460 (Part I); *111*(3), 499–504 (Part II).

Stout, R. T., Tallerico, M., & Scribner, K. P. (1995). Values: The 'what?' of the politics of education. In J. D. Scribner & D. H. Layton (Eds.), *The study of educational politics* (pp. 5–20). Washington, DC: The Falmer Press.

Traxler, C. B. (2000). The Stanford Achievement Test, 9th Edition: National norming and performance standards for deaf and hard-of-hearing students. *Journal of Deaf Studies & Deaf Education, 5*(4), 337–348.

Trybus, R. J., & Karchmer, M. A. (1977). School achievement scores of hearing impaired children: National data on achievement status and growth patterns. *American Annals of the Deaf, 122*(2), 62–69.

Turner, V. (2000). Deaf children and literacy: Identifying appropriate tools and learning environment. *Deaf Worlds, 16*(1), 17–25.

U.S. Department of Education. (2000). *Twenty-second annual report to Congress on the implementation of the Individuals with Disabilities Education Act.* Washington, DC: Author.

U.S. Department of Education, National Center for Education Statistics. (2001). *The condition of education 2001* (NCES 2001-072). Washington, DC: U.S. Government Printing Office.

Vernon, M., & Koh, S. D. (1970). Early manual communication and deaf children's achievement. *American Annals of the Deaf, 115*(5), 527–536.

Wolk, S., & Allen, T. E. (1984). A 5-year follow-up of reading-comprehension achievement of hearing-impaired students in special education programs. *The Journal of Special Education, 18*(2), 161–176.

Woodward, J. (1978). Some sociolinguistic problems in the implementation of bilingual education for deaf students. In F. Caccamise & D. Hicks (Eds.), *American Sign Language in a bilingual, bicultural context: Proceedings of the Second National Symposium on Sign Language Research and Teaching* (pp. 183–209). Silver Spring, MD: National Association of the Deaf.

Wrightstone, J. W., Aronow, M. S. & Moskowitz, S. (1963). A comparison of reading test norms of deaf and hearing children. *American Annals of the Deaf, 108*(3), 311–316.

Des Power & Gregory R. Leigh

Curriculum
Cultural and Communicative Contexts

The term "curriculum" is used frequently by almost everyone with an interest in education but often with little agreement on its meaning. Often curriculum is narrowly considered as being only the syllabus or other documents that shape teaching processes and content. Alternatively, curriculum can be seen broadly as being everything that happens in schools. By briefly exploring the concept of curriculum, the issues in curriculum development for deaf and hard-of-hearing students can be more clearly identified.

Defining Curriculum

The curriculum is more than a mere document or syllabus; it is much more than a collection of predetermined learning objectives and experiences. Curriculum refers not only to those elements but also to the actual effects on student learning of a variety of planned and unplanned arrangements and the interactions between participants in the educational process. These arrangements include variables as diverse as government and school policies, objectives, school administration and organization, and student assessment and reporting procedures. Broadly, then, curriculum refers to all of the arrangements that are made for students' learning, both planned and ad hoc.

This definition highlights the fact that curriculum is not merely about intended actions or outcomes (as reflected in policy documents, syllabuses, and the like) but also about actual activities (i.e., what actually happens in schools and other educational programs) (Cohen & Harrison, 1982; Lovat & Smith, 1998). Cohen and Harrison (1982) described curriculum as both intention and reality. They suggested that curriculum as intention refers to the plans that are made for the learning and development of an individual or group of learners. As such, curriculum is about objectives, predetermined learning experiences, the organization of those experiences, and methods for evaluating outcomes. In this regard, curriculum development can be seen as a process of decision-making. Indeed, Tyler (1949) argued that curriculum development was about providing the best and most justifiable decisions in response to four fundamental questions:

- What educational purposes should the school seek to attain?
- What educational experiences can be provided that are likely to attain these purposes?

- How can these educational experiences be effectively organized?
- How can we determine whether these purposes are being attained?

Answers to such questions, however they may be cast, give rise to curriculum as intention. Curriculum as reality refers to what actually happens in learning environments. Both the intended and the real curricula are products of a dynamic and complex network of relationships between people and a wide diversity of influences—explicit and implicit, human, and physical (Cohen & Harrison, 1982). This complex web of interactions and influences is central to the notion of curriculum. The nature of the curriculum, both intended and real, will depend on the context or situation in which it was developed and in which it operates. Fundamentally, the curriculum will be an expression of the values and aspirations of the community or communities in which it operates and will differ according to the nature of that social context.

The more diverse the social context is, the more difficult it will be to reach consensus on issues and priorities that affect a group collectively. Regarding curriculum, the communities served by schools and other educational programs and facilities may not easily reach agreement about what is valued in terms of objectives or educational strategies. There is considerable potential for some of the values that underpin the curriculum to be unstated and taken for granted, giving rise to what has often been called the "hidden curriculum." The hidden curriculum refers to the unplanned and usually unrecognized learning outcomes that are a consequence of curriculum activities. Common among these unplanned learning outcomes are learners' development of the beliefs, norms, perceptions, and understandings that reflect the views of the dominant culture or ideology—that is, those who are responsible for planning and implementing the curriculum (Seddon, 1983).

Lovat and Smith (1998) suggested that "many of the messages of the hidden curriculum are concerned with power, authority, access and participation: these are messages that continually shape learners' developing views of the world . . . their creating of reality" (pp. 35–36). Schools and other educational programs for deaf and hard-of-hearing students are no exception, with the messages inherent in particular statements and actions of teachers and other professionals being effortlessly learned by children (and their families). This raises obvious questions about what the dominant perspective or ideology of those professionals may be and whether they reflect all or only some constructions of reality for deaf and hard-of-hearing people.

In this chapter we address several aspects of curriculum for deaf and hard-of-hearing learners. In the first section we examine the curriculum context for deaf and hard-of-hearing learners. The second section identifies how, given this complex context of competing perspectives, there can often be significant differences between the intended and actual curriculum for those learners. In the last section we consider some of the specific issues and curriculum arrangements that are made for deaf and hard-of-hearing learners (hereafter referred to collectively, and more simply, as "deaf" learners).

Curriculum Context: Perspectives on Deafness

Demographically and socially, deafness is a complex phenomenon. The earlier use of the collective phrase "deaf and hard-of-hearing students" suggests that some agreed definitional criteria could be used for at least two subgroups of this population. In reality, such agreement is rare. Indeed, it is evident that there is considerable variety among the ways deaf people are described and regarded both by themselves and others. From different perspectives, those involved in curriculum development for such students may well describe the same circumstances very differently.

From an audiological perspective, deafness may be defined in terms of degree and when and how it occurred. At a minimum, there may be a distinction made between people who are born deaf or became deaf in early childhood and those whose deafness occurred later in life. From a developmental perspective there will be a focus on the impact that different degrees of hearing loss may have upon development (especially language and speech development), mode of communication (sign, speech, or some combination thereof), and whether there are any co-existing developmental disabilities. Equally, there could be a legal or policy perspective, a medical perspective, or a sociocultural perspective on deafness. Notably, from that last perspective, deafness is not considered in terms of degree or developmental effects but by the social and linguistic corollaries of being "Deaf" or "hard of hearing" (Padden & Humphries, 1988; Power, 1997a; Taylor & Bishop, 1991; Woll & Ladd, this volume). Each perspective has its own associated parameters for definition and description.

How deafness is defined, what is valued, and perceptions of what a "deaf life" may mean, all will be differently constructed according to the perspectives that are dominant among those who control the processes of curriculum development and implementation. Therefore, there may be quite different interpretations of the curriculum context for the same group of learners. Different constructions of the context will inevitably lead to different curriculum decisions on a range of issues. Not least among these issues will be the important and contentious questions of language and communication type and location of program delivery (i.e., separate special school or some form of mainstream environment).

To take one issue as an example, the range of potential objectives and learning experiences relating to language and communication development for young deaf children is very broad and has been subject to debate for centuries (see Lang, this volume). In early intervention programs, for example, the dominant perspectives are sometimes medical and audiological. If these perspectives are exclusive, the curriculum context that is constructed will be one where the child is seen only as a member of the broader community with a communication disability to be ameliorated rather than a potential member of a subcommunity with a need to develop the language of that community—sign language. Alternatively, if the dominant perspective is a sociocultural one, the curriculum context will be interpreted as one where the primary cultural affiliation is with the Deaf community and where the development of a sign language is seen as a preeminent curriculum objective—possibly without any corresponding emphasis on spoken language development. Baynton (1996) saw such narrow constructions of the curriculum context as being the product of people perceiving deafness as exclusively a childhood issue and failing to consider a broader context for deaf children—a whole-of-life context that may dictate wider curriculum goals.

Power (1981) argued that curricula should be "ecologically valid" for life beyond school. This ecological validity should be assured by the broadest possible conception of the context for the curriculum. To this end, all possible perspectives on the situation of the deaf individual should be taken into account. This is frequently not the case. Failure to acknowledge the potential diversity of life outcomes leads to a narrow construction of the curriculum context and the inclusion of objectives and content that may be inconsistent with either the current or future needs of the child and his or her environment. As Leigh (2001) pointed out:

> To fail to acknowledge that a particular perspective on deafness may lead to the adoption of a set of objectives for a deaf student that are not consonant with that student's current or future social circumstance may result in a situation where both educational means and ends are subsequently questioned or rejected by that student and his or her cultural community. There are, for example, unfortunate examples of young deaf students and deaf adults who have come to question, often bitterly, the lack of inclusion of sign language and deaf culture in their educational experience (Jacobs, 1989). Similarly, some deaf people educated in more socioculturally defined programs have come to question their lack of access to assistive technologies for hearing and their lack of programmed opportunity to develop expressive spoken language skills (Bertling, 1994). Clearly, there are issues relating to current and future cultural affiliation, among many other issues, that must be considered in curriculum design. (pp. 158–159)

There are many aspects of the context for curriculum design and implementation that warrant careful consideration and should be made patent for all concerned. Such consideration makes the dominant perspectives and ideologies more readily apparent. According to Leigh (2001), there are a number of issues that should be actively and openly considered by those responsible for curriculum development before important decisions on objectives and content are taken. Among others, these issues are:

- The particular perspective on deafness held by early intervention specialists, teachers, therapists, doctors, family members, and ultimately, by the children concerned.

- The value placed on certain educational, therapeutic, and/or medical interventions (e.g., cochlear implants) by each of those same individuals.
- Individual teacher's ideologies and beliefs about the special learning needs of deaf learners and their beliefs about what constitutes sound educational practice for deaf students.
- The literature (especially the research literature) on educational, linguistic, and technological interventions associated with deaf people, and the awareness, understanding, and perception of that literature by teachers and associated professionals.

Clearly, the potential for widely varying individual positions on these issues creates the opportunity for significantly different constructions of the curriculum context for the same learners. Different constructions of the curriculum context will result in different objectives and curriculum content for students, even when they may otherwise have similar physical and situational characteristics (Lovat & Smith, 1998).

It will not be possible to represent all alternative social perspectives on deafness in all aspects of the curriculum for every student. Indeed, there should, and will, be differentiation and individualization (this issue is considered later). The point of this discussion is to demonstrate that all curriculum decisions have a context that must be actively examined and understood, particularly if the development of a hidden curriculum for deaf students is to be avoided.

Curriculum: Intention and Reality

Hidden Curriculum

The hidden curriculum refers to the unplanned learning outcomes associated with learners' exposure to particular attitudes, actions, and ideas. The potential for such unplanned outcomes highlights the need for a process of analysis to ensure that perspectives and values are made clear.

Careful consideration of the context for curriculum development is often not part of the curriculum development process for deaf learners. At the level of early intervention and preschool programs, for example, the learners may be the parents and the families as much as the deaf children themselves. Many parents come to the experience of education for their young children with no relevant background or experience relating to deafness.

Professionals in early intervention programs provide families with a range of information and learning experiences related to a variety of options and possibilities, particularly about language and communication. In this context, the attitudes or messages inherent in particular statements and actions of professionals (teachers, therapists, etc.) will be highly salient for families that are making a choice about communication options and will become a potent set of learning experiences for parents. If an influential and respected professional is enthusiastic about a particular form of communication (spoken or signed), is incapable of using an alternative mode of communication comfortably, or is uncomfortable in the presence of people from a different linguistic or cultural perspective on deafness, an effective hidden curriculum will have been constructed (Leigh, 2001). The real learning experiences are not found in the intended curriculum but in the attitudes and actions of professionals that are consistent with their particular perspective on deafness.

To guard against such hidden curricula, the dominant ideologies of both programs and individuals within those programs need to be considered as part of a formal process of analysis (often called situational analysis) and should be made patent to all concerned before curriculum objectives and content are decided. This is not to suggest that a program should necessarily present every alternative perspective equally. However, open consideration of all perspectives and issues may lead to a different conceptualization of the curriculum context and the identification of objectives, learning experiences, and approaches to assessment that may not have otherwise been considered.

Official and Real Curricula

A gap between curriculum as intention and reality may also be determined by other factors. In the case of special schools for deaf students, historically, there was considerable latitude concerning compliance with standard curriculum expectations. As a consequence, the potential for a gap between official curriculum standards and the real curriculum has always been apparent. Indeed, the development of alternative curriculum priorities or teaching strategies for deaf students to achieve the same learning outcomes as their hearing peers is seen as entirely appropriate in both special and mainstream learning environments for deaf students (Bunch, 1987; Luetke-Stahlman & Luckner, 1991; Moores, 2001). However, there is a question of relative emphasis in curriculum differentiation that deserves some comment.

A mismatch between official and real curriculum for deaf students may be a consequence of the disproportionate emphasis on certain specialized objectives that relate only to deaf learners, particularly objectives that relate to spoken language and communication skills (Moores, 2001). Because of this emphasis, some commentators have expressed concern that attention to other curriculum areas such as mathematics, social studies, and science may be diminished (Lytle & Rovins, 1997). This may result in a significant gap between the curriculum planned for deaf students and that officially prescribed for their peers by the official curriculum guidelines for the broader community. This gap between the official and the real curriculum for deaf students tends to be exacerbated as deaf children move through the grade levels (Moores, 2001).

Moores (2001) noted the importance of academic achievement as a basis for entrance to higher levels of learning and highlighted the need to ensure that the gap between official and real curriculum does not become too great for deaf learners because of attention to specialized learning objectives. "Educators of the deaf must continually rethink their priorities with respect to the mix between teaching academic content and traditional training that concentrates primarily on communication skills" for deaf students (p. 7).

Central to the relationship between curriculum intention and reality are the questions identified by Tyler (1949) and outlined at the beginning of this chapter. The answers to these questions give form to the particular curriculum arrangements for any group of learners. In the next section we consider some of the specialized curriculum arrangements made for deaf learners by revisiting the questions raised by Tyler concerning purposes, organization, and assessment.

Specialized Curriculum Arrangements for Deaf Students

Curriculum Purpose: The Question of Objectives

The first two curriculum questions raised by Tyler (1949) relate to the establishment of objectives and the consequent determination of learning experiences for students. In this regard, Bunch (1987) suggested that, according to the particular perspective that is adopted, the curriculum objectives and learning experiences identified for deaf students may be the same as those applicable to hearing children, an adaptation of those applicable to hearing children, or alternative (or additional) objectives and strategies to those applicable to hearing children in regular education programs. The kind of program in which students are placed tends to influence these alternatives. Students in mainstream programs are more likely to experience a version of the curriculum closer to that of the curriculum for hearing children, whereas those in separate classrooms or schools are more likely to experience adapted and/or alternative curriculum arrangements.

Since the advent of specialized educational provisions for deaf students, alternative curriculum objectives and content have commonly been considered both appropriate and necessary. Historically, specialized curricula, particularly at the upper school levels, focused on vocational (typically industrial) rather than on academic objectives. This was particularly true in residential schools for the deaf up until the last quarter of the twentieth century (Baynton, 1996). However, the most common additional or alternative curriculum objectives for deaf students have always been in the areas of language and communication, particularly speech production and reception, audition, and the mastery of the structural (grammatical) aspects of the language of the wider community (Lang, this volume; Moores, 2001).

Currently, more than four out of every five students with impaired hearing are educated in regular mainstream schools, either in regular classrooms or special classes within regular schools (Stewart & Kluwin, 2001). Hence, the influence of and need to conform to general curriculum standards is increasing (Moores, 2001). In most western countries, standards provide the basis for curriculum design for all students. Nevertheless, there is ample evidence that deaf students have specific needs as learners that require some adaptation of both objectives and the learning experiences designed to achieve standardized outcomes (Luetke-Stahlman & Luckner, 1991; Marschark, 1997; Marschark, Lang, & Albertini, 2002; Stewart & Kluwin, 2001).

For deaf students, effective curriculum design involves determining additional or alternative educational objectives and experiences required to achieve the same overall outcomes as for other students. Determining the requirement for, and nature of, such specialized objectives and learning experiences involves considering the specific characteristics of deaf children as learners. In addition to the many issues related to the development of a first language, these characteristics include:

- The frequently large discrepancy between the levels of reading and writing ability of deaf students and their hearing peers, with the gap widening as they progress through school (Traxler, 2000).
- The possibility that deaf learners' primary or preferred language of communication will be a signed language; the associated necessity to use interpreters for some purposes (Messenheimer-Young & Whitesell, 1995); and the known limitations of interpreting as a basis for full and equitable access to classroom communication (Innes, 1994; Lang, 2002; Seal, 1998; Watson & Parsons, 1998).
- Deaf learners' dependency on visual information and their greater propensity to be visually distracted than hearing learners (Marschark, 1993; Matthews & Reich, 1993).
- The likelihood that deaf learners will have limited vocabularies and a restricted range of meanings for words with multiple meanings (Geers & Schick, 1988; McEvoy, Marschark, & Nelson, 1999).
- The difficulties that deaf students experience with simultaneous attention to communication and other visual information (viz., computer screens, overhead projection, etc.). Such attention requires constant switching of attention in a manner that is not the case for hearing learners (Matthews & Reich, 1993; Wood, Wood, Griffiths, & Howarth, 1986).
- The potential for significant differences between deaf and hearing learners in regard to their organization of knowledge and their long and short-term memory processes (Marschark, 1993).
- The often significant mismatch between the language and communication skills of deaf children and others in their day-to-day environments (particularly parents and close family). This is likely to account for reduced opportunities for linguistic mediation of their experiences and hence their active construction of knowledge (Gallaway, 1998; Marschark et al., 2002).
- The likelihood that children from certain ethnic, linguistic, or racial minorities will be overrepresented in the deaf school-age population (Lynas & Turner, 1995; Schildroth & Hotto, 1996;) and less likely to be educated in mainstream educational environments (Allen, 1992; Kluwin & Stinson, 1993).

As a consequence of these potentially differentiating characteristics, some educational objectives and methods that are appropriate for hearing students may not be appropriate for deaf students (see Marschark et al., 2002, for a review of many of these issues). Consideration of these characteristics gives rise to a range of possible alternative objectives and strategies for deaf students relative to those for their hearing peers. The nature and range of these possible differences also highlights the potential for diversity among deaf learners and the imperative to consider their learning needs on an individual basis (Stewart & Kluwin, 2001).

The concept of individualized program objectives is now well accepted in educational theory and practice. In the United States, this principle is enshrined in law through the Individuals with Disabilities Act (IDEA). The act mandates that any child with special educational needs should receive services (both educational and ancillary) that are designed to meet their particular needs through the development of an Individualized Education Program (IEP). Whether dictated by law or simply by good educational practice, individualized programming will dictate a wide range of different objectives and possible outcomes for individual deaf students across all curriculum areas.

Having acknowledged the importance of individualization of objectives and teaching strategies, it is also possible to identify a number of areas in which there are specific curriculum arrangements that are common to significant numbers of deaf learners. The following sections examine some of the curriculum areas in which specialized arrangements are, or may need to be, made for deaf learners.

Language

As a curriculum area in the education of deaf students, "language" or "language development" has no real analogue in regular education where, for the most part, children come to the educational process with first-language skills in place. For deaf students, no such assumptions can be made. Language development can include a broad range of objectives, from the acquisition of language fundamentals to the development of literacy and the language arts that are expected outcomes of education for all children. For deaf learners, language development has been expanded from a term that typically refers to monolingual language acquisition to one that may include the acquisition of language bimodally (i.e., in speech and sign) or bilingually (i.e., a spoken/written language and a sign language) (Luetke-Stahlman, 1998).

Objectives in this curriculum area may relate to the development of a spoken language and/or a signed language in one or more modes of communication (spoken, signed, cued, and written). The corresponding diversity of specific objectives for language and language skill acquisition is reflected in several chapters in this volume (see Blamey; Schick; Schirmer & Williams). This diversity exists not only in regard to choice of target language but also in regard to the specific objectives and learning experiences chosen to guide the development of that language and communication system (see Leybaert & Algeria, this volume; Mayer & Akamatsu, this volume).

For the purpose of this discussion, it is sufficient to note that a wide range of factors will influence the nature of the objectives and learning experiences identified for deaf students learning either a first or second language. These factors include:

- The motivations and linguistic abilities of both the students and their families.
- The particular theoretical and pedagogical approach to developing language skills that is adopted (i.e., naturalistic or structured interventionist).
- The availability of resources to support the chosen pedagogy.
- The availability of frameworks and strategies for the accurate assessment of the students' abilities in the target languages.

The importance of the last factor cannot be overstated. The establishment of effective language development objectives and subsequent programming strategies depends on effective assessment of linguistic abilities (Luetke-Stahlman, 1998). In bilingual programs, however, the options for assessing sign language acquisition by children are limited by both the lack of research into sign language acquisition by young children and the associated lack of specific instruments for assessing that development (Schembri et al., 2002, but see Singleton & Supalla, this volume). This lack of appropriate instruments for assessing sign language abilities is a serious limitation in establishing appropriate pedagogical objectives for children (Drasgow, 1993; Schembri et al., 2002).

It should be noted here that, as language learners, deaf students who use sign language and those who communicate orally—in regular or special schools—share a range of communication difficulties in classrooms. Among these are problems in switching attention to and from speakers to see signs or lip patterns, switching attention from speakers to visual displays such as overhead projection or interpreters (Matthews & Reich, 1993), and, in regular classrooms, monitoring multiple auditory and visual sources of communication and information. All deaf students, regardless of program location, require optimal visual and acoustic conditions to obtain maximum benefit from the language teaching/learning situation in class (Erber, 1974). None of signing, cued speech, oral communication, or simultaneous communication will be a panacea for the communication difficulties faced by deaf language learners.

The Use of Signed Language

There is insufficient space here to consider the debate about what kind of signing should be used in educating deaf children who sign. It is sufficient to acknowledge that two different kinds of signing are currently being used in programs for deaf students. Some programs use a form of signed representation of the local spoken language, typically in simultaneous communication with speech. These simultaneous communication programs use what Fischer (1998) called "artificial sign systems" (ASS, signed English, Signing Exact English, etc.). Others use what Fischer called "natural sign systems" (NSS, forms of English-like signing that occur naturally in the signing community and include those forms variously referred to a Pidgin Sign English or "contact signing"). The second form of program, now commonly referred to as "bilingual-bicultural," is based on the use of a natural sign language (NSL, e.g., ASL, LSF, BSL, Auslan). These are languages with the same linguistic, cognitive, and epistemological status as spoken languages (Klima & Bellugi, 1979; Power, 1997a, b).

Bilingual-bicultural programs are responsive to the view that life for a deaf person will involve the negotiation of two languages (signed and spoken/written) and two cultures (those of the Deaf community and the hearing world). Preparation for life in two cultural and language communities is a primary objective of such programs. The development of sign language skills is fundamental to life objectives but is also fundamental to the objectives of providing uninhibited access to curriculum content via a fully accessible language and a basis for acquisition of English as a second language via reading and writing (and possibly speaking) (Wilbur, 2000).

In simultaneous communication programs, however, the use of signed communication is typically limited to some form of English-like signing (ASS or NSS), particularly in the early years. In these programs, the use of signing is linked to specific pedagogical objectives for the development of the majority spoken language, in both oral and written forms. In such programs, the use of English-like signing is premised on the belief that aspects of spoken language content and form can be more effectively developed when they are made visually accessible by the use of a manual representation of the language (see Mayer & Akamatsu, this volume). The validity of this aim and the potential for such language learning outcomes to be realized by such an approach are hotly debated (see Schick, this volume; Schick & Moeller, 1992; Supalla, 1991).

Regardless of the debate over specific linguistic objectives, bilingual-bicultural (and to a lesser extent some simultaneous communication programs) operate on the assumption that students will access the Deaf community. Increasingly, therefore, these programs have curriculum objectives associated with students' acquisition of a bicultural status. Specific objectives and content aim to assist students in their developing awareness of, and involvement in, the two cultural milieus—Deaf and hearing. In regard to Deaf culture, there is a developing curriculum resource base to support such objectives and many programs employ deaf staff members to teach content and provide role models for their students (Stone, 2001). In regard to hearing culture, specialized objectives relate to the development of the skills necessary to be personally and vocationally successful in the culture of the wider community. All these objectives and learning experiences are typically covered under the general curriculum area of "Deaf studies" (Corson, 1992).

Deaf studies

In recent years, Deaf studies has become a separate curriculum area in its own right, with a flourishing literature and teaching resource base (Carty, Neale, & Power, 1997; Gaustad, 1997). Such curricula increase deaf students' knowledge and understanding of the Deaf community as well as improving their understanding of themselves as Deaf people and their self-esteem and confidence in working with the hearing world (Corson, 1992; de Klerk, 1998; Stewart & Kluwin, 2001.

There is evidence that children being educated in either special schools or mainstream classes may have difficulty coming to terms with their deafness and their place in a hearing world (Leigh & Stinson, 1991; Stoefan-Fisher & Balk, 1992). This situation has given rise to what Stewart and Kluwin (2001) called "the integrated approach to Deaf studies" (p. 116), which can be used with deaf and hearing students alike in separate or integrated settings. The approach allows Deaf studies objectives to be integrated into learning experiences in science, social studies, health, and language arts (Gaustad, 1997, 1999). Such programs have also proved beneficial for providing hearing students with a better understanding of deafness and deaf people.

Deaf students in separate schools and/or classes where spoken communication is used have also been shown to benefit from what Stewart and Kluwin (2001) called the Global-Interactive Approach to Deaf Studies—"*global* in the sense that students study the different ways that people with all degrees of hearing loss live . . . *interactive* because the way in which Deaf studies is taught will reflect . . . the characteristics and interests of the students" (p. 116).

The Traditional Content Areas: Mathematics, Science, and Social Studies

Lytle and Rovins (1997) argued that specific objectives and pedagogy in the content areas have tended to be ignored because the focus has been too heavy on language and communication objectives (see also Moores, 2001). For deaf students' achievements to equate with hearing students in these areas, there is a need for specific focus on objectives and learning experiences in the core content areas.

Consistent with Lytle and Rovins' (1997) concerns, critics of the teaching of mathematics to deaf students have noted the potential for teachers to be overly reliant on rote learning of the "four processes" (addition, subtraction, multiplication, and division) at the expense of the more "real world/ real problems/real materials" constructivist approaches (Daniele, 1993; Gregory, 1998; Pagliaro, 1998; Stewart & Kluwin, 2001). In recent times in the United States, there has also been criticism of the way in which teachers of the deaf are prepared for teaching mathematics and calls for more sophisticated understanding of modern curriculum and methods in mathematics by those teachers (Dietz, 1995; Pagliaro, 1998).

Most authors on this topic have identified the specialist language of mathematics and the linguistic sequencing and manipulation of events in written mathematics problems as creating the most difficulty for deaf students (Gregory, 1998; Pau, 1995). Accordingly, many commentators have noted the need for specific teaching of the language (particularly the vocabulary) of mathematics. As for all vocabulary learning, the most successful processes are deemed to be those that aim to make connections to existing knowledge and provide maximum opportunity for students to experience and manipulate the concepts in context (Stewart & Kluwin, 2001).

Beyond this emphasis on vocabulary, there are several additional principles that have been frequently identified as productive for deaf students. Commonly advocated are constructivist approaches that seek to facilitate students' personal construction of their own knowledge structures. To these ends, teachers are encouraged to identify the limits of each student's current knowledge and experience and to provide activities that permit them to add new information and extract new understandings from their experiences through both exploration and classroom discourse (Luetke-Stahlman & Luckner, 1991; Marschark et al., 2002; Stewart & Kluwin, 2001). A critical objective in such a process is that students develop an understanding of how mathematics can be practically applied to the world they live in and to problems in everyday life (Dietz, 1995). To aid this process, objectives for mathematics should be integrated into all curriculum objectives, thus highlighting relationships and maximizing language and concept development opportunities.

The latter principle is important in all content areas of the curriculum for deaf students. Teachers should be encouraged to go well beyond the social studies, science, or mathematics of their lessons and to seek ways to use all of these lessons as means of expanding cognitive and language abilities—particularly vocabulary skills (Stewart & Kluwin, 2001).

Commentators also have drawn attention to recent national curriculum developments in science and the potential mismatch between official and real curriculum initiatives for deaf students in this content area (especially in the United States; Marschark et al., 2002). The principles are essentially the same as for mathematics. There is a need to expose students to authentic problems, with the language of science being learned in concrete and meaningful contexts. Perhaps more than other content areas, however, science lends itself to visual learning and hands-on activities that meet the need for meaningful experiences and exploit the tendency for deaf learners to be highly dependent on visual information. As in mathematics, deaf children need opportunities for extended discourse about science issues—opportunities for adult-mediated and peer-mediated experiences that build concepts and understanding. As already noted, such mediation occurs frequently and incidentally for hearing students but for deaf students may need to be consciously provided. Such deliberate provision aims to account for the fact that deaf students will often need to divert their attention from an experiment or activity to engage in such discourse and vice versa. Such opportunities cannot be left to chance.

In all countries, social studies curricula strive to give students an understanding of their role as citizens and individuals. These objectives relate just as much to deaf as to hearing students. However, deaf students also stand to gain additional understanding about their role as deaf individuals in both Deaf and hearing communities through specialized Deaf studies curricula.

A priority objective in the area of social studies is to assure that students have the necessary experiential background knowledge to understand social concepts (Stewart & Kluwin, 2001). As already noted, lack of exposure to adult-mediated social experiences may place deaf learners at a disadvantage in this regard (Marschark et al., 2002). As for the other content areas, cooperative and highly interactive activities in authentic contexts (e.g., field trips and integrated, theme-based activities) are highly effective (Luetke-Stahlman & Luckner, 1991; Stewart & Kluwin, 2001). Social studies presents a particularly good opportunity for integrating objectives across the curriculum, using themes to integrate language, mathematics, science, art, and other curricular objectives and content as appropriate.

Curriculum Organization: The Question of Program Location

The third curriculum question raised by Tyler (1949) related to the organization of learning experiences to ensure the achievement of objectives. Such organization has too many possible dimensions to cover in detail here. An important aspect of this issue for deaf students is the decision about program location—whether curriculum objectives will be pursued in a separate educational setting (i.e., a special school) or in a mainstream classroom.

The majority of deaf students are educated in regular schools. Most of these students, particularly those in fully inclusive environments, communicate orally. However, the number of individuals and small cohorts of students using sign language interpreters in such environments is increasing, particularly at the upper grade levels. Such placements present the need for some highly specific curriculum arrangements (see Messenheimer-Young & Whitesell, 1995, for more detailed commentary on these issues). Regardless of their preferred language or mode of communication, most deaf students educated in regular schools access the regular curriculum, often with collabo-

ration between their class teacher and a specialist teacher of the deaf (Luckner & Miller, 1994; Lynas, Lewis, & Hopwood, 1997; Schildroth & Hotto, 1996).

Undoubtedly, some students are not well suited to mainstream placement and will experience difficulties personally, socially, and academically (Kluwin & Stinson, 1993; Marschark, 1993; Stinson & Kluwin, this volume; Stinson & Lang, 1994). For other students, mainstream educational placement is the most efficient means of providing access to the developmental and learning opportunities of the regular curriculum standards (Kluwin & Stinson, 1993; Lynas, 1986; Marschark, 1997; Powers, 1996; Stinson & Antia, 1999; Watson & Parsons, 1998). In such cases, deaf students' experiences in regular classrooms can be optimized by particular curriculum arrangements. Such arrangements include accommodations to account for the relevant learning characteristics of deaf students. This requires that mainstream teachers understand these learning characteristics and the particular communication and social needs of deaf students. This may be facilitated by a collaborative approach in which teachers of the deaf and regular teachers cooperate to develop resources and curriculum strategies for the entire class, but taking account of the deaf student's needs (Gaustad, 1999). Alternatively, it may involve less direct interventions such as the provision of multimedia instructional materials for teacher professional development relating to these issues (Bartlett & Power, 1997; Luckner & Denzin, 1998).

The question of program location is difficult and controversial. From a curriculum perspective, it is perhaps most controversial because mainstream educational placement (particularly full inclusion) is often (mis)interpreted as an objective in its own right, rather than one of a range of alternative curriculum arrangements for pursuing educational objectives (Moores, 2001). This whole issue warrants additional research, as there is little empirical evidence to support many of the claims that may be made for the relative benefits of alternative educational placements and organizational strategies. Indeed, Meadow-Orlans (2001) argued that the organization of deaf education is a major area in need of research. She noted that little research has been reported on the relationships between program location, teaching, and outcomes for student academic achievement in ordinary classes versus special classes or special schools (see Stinson & Kluwin, this volume).

Curriculum Assessment: The Question of Outcomes

The final curriculum question raised by Tyler (1949) related to determining the outcomes of learning experiences for students. Two sets of issues are of interest in regard to assessment for deaf students: issues surrounding the use and appropriateness of various strategies for assessing deaf students' achievement of curriculum objectives, and issues relating to their participation in state or national assessment programs.

In regard to state and national testing, the participation of deaf students is often questioned. Concerns are based on the potential negative effects of deaf students' language and communication differences and whether such mass assessments are capable of providing an accurate picture of their abilities. Sometimes deaf students are excused from these assessments, and in other cases accommodations have been made for them (Elliott, Kratochwill, & Schulte, 1998). Such accommodations include provision of sign interpreting and/or written instructions, provision of individual oral instructions, additional time for the test, or allowed use of a dictionary. The reasons for such accommodations, and the accommodations themselves, each complicate the process of interpreting the outcomes of such assessments for deaf students.

The other area of interest in assessment is that which is undertaken to determine curriculum-based outcomes for deaf students. In this case, assessment is largely teacher directed and comprises both formal and informal measures to determine how effectively objectives have been achieved, as a basis for subsequent planning. To these ends, Luetke-Stahlman (1999) argued that a variety of assessment approaches should be used. These approaches include criterion-referenced tools, norm-referenced instruments (i.e., measures that permit teachers to address discrepancies between a student's abilities and those of the peer group), analysis of samples of actual performance (e.g., samples of signed or spoken language, portfolios of writing, etc.), questionnaires, interviews, and observation schedules (checklists).

The issue of language differences and difficulties arises in regard to these forms of assessment also. Luetke-Stahlman (1998, 1999) argued that the question of whether assessment strategies should be modified or conducted in an alternative language depends on the purpose of the assessment. If, for example, the purpose is to determine students' understanding of information or their ability to draw inferences and conclusions based on that information, then the assessment should be conducted in the students' dominant or preferred language (e.g., sign language or spoken English). However, some cognitive and academic abilities may not be amenable to investigation through any means other than written language (Luetke-Stahlman, 1998; Paul, 1998), particularly if performance is to be compared to that of hearing peers, as in national and state testing programs and benchmarking exercises. These types of assessment may require students to demonstrate their cognitive and academic linguistic proficiency with English (or the language spoken by hearing persons in their environment) as an integral component of the assessment task. These are potentially contentious matters but are critically related to the issue of ensuring that there is no gap between the curriculum for deaf and hearing students in either intention or reality.

Summary and Conclusions

Curriculum refers to the effects on student learning of a variety of arrangements. How deafness is defined, what is valued, and perceptions of what a deaf life may mean will all differ according to the perspectives and ideologies of the people involved in making those arrangements. It is imperative, therefore, that curriculum development processes ensure that biases and ideologies are recognized and that the full range of possible social, cultural, and communicative contexts for deaf learners is considered in the process of establishing objectives and learning experiences for them.

Regardless of the increasing requirement for all students to conform to national or state curriculum standards, alternative curriculum objectives and content continue to be considered as necessary for deaf students, particularly in the areas of language and communication. Effective curriculum design for this group requires consideration of a wide range of learning characteristics that, in turn, determine specialized and individualized curriculum objectives. The goal of such differentiated objectives is not to achieve different outcomes but to ensure achievement of the same overall learning outcomes as all other students (i.e., with the notable exception of specialized additional curriculum areas such as Deaf studies).

Related to the issue of alternative curriculum objectives is the question of where those objectives should be pursued—in a separate school or program or in a mainstream setting? The overwhelming majority of deaf students are now educated in regular schools. However, this aspect of curriculum organization remains contentious. This issue warrants considerable additional research, as there is little empirical evidence to support the claims that are made for the relative benefits of alternative curriculum organizational strategies (see Stinson & Kluwin, this volume). There is, however, much in the research literature (educational, linguistic, and cognitive) that we have surveyed above that contributes to understanding how teaching-learning outcomes for deaf students can be optimized in any situation (Marschark et al., 2002). Such information warrants close attention for the optimization of educational opportunities for deaf students.

Ultimately, real improvements in curriculum outcomes are beyond the determination of state or national curriculum policies and go directly to what actually happens in classrooms—to how effectively the curriculum is designed and implemented. Optimal outcomes require commitment by all those involved to openness and accountability in considering the curriculum context for deaf students and in subsequently determining objectives for their learning. Also required is a commitment to constant experimentation with, and modification of, the strategies and teaching approaches used to meet those objectives.

References

Allen, T. (1992). Subgroup differences in educational placement for deaf and hard of hearing students. *American Annals of the Deaf, 135*, 381–388.

Bartlett, B., & Power, D. (Eds.). (1997). *Teaching students with disabilities: Hearing impairment.* Brisbane: Queensland Department of Education.

Baynton, D. C. (1996). *Forbidden signs: American culture and the campaign against sign language.* Chicago: The University of Chicago Press.

Bertling, T. (1994). *A child sacrificed to the deaf culture.* Wilsonville, OR: Kodiak Media Group.

Bunch, G. O. (1987). *The curriculum and the hearing-impaired student.* Boston: Little Brown and Company.

Carty, B., Neale, J., & Power, D. (1997). *Deaf studies program: P-7.* Brisbane: Language Australia Centre for Deafness and Communication Studies.

Cohen, D., & Harrison, M. (1982). *The curriculum action project: A report of curriculum decision making in Australian schools.* Sydney: Macquarie University.

Corson, H. J. (1992). Deaf studies: A framework for learning and teaching. In J. Cebe (Ed.), *Deaf Studies for Educators* (pp. 7–14). Washington, DC: College for Continuing Education, Gallaudet University.

Daniele, V. (1993). Quantitative literacy. *American Annals of the Deaf, 138,* 76–81.

Dietz, C. H. (1995). *Moving toward the standards: A national action plan for mathematics education reform for the deaf.* Washington, DC: Gallaudet University Pre-College Outreach Programs.

de Klerk, A. (1998). Deaf identity in adolescence. In A. Weisel (Ed.), *Issues unresolved: New perspectives on language and deaf education* (pp. 206–214). Washington, DC: Gallaudet University Press.

Drasgow, E. (1993). Bilingual/bicultural deaf education: An overview. *Sign Language Studies, 80,* 243–261.

Elliott, S. N., Kratochwill, T. R., & Schulte, A. G. (1998). The assessment accommodation checklist: Who, what, where, when, why, and how? *Teaching Exceptional Children, 31*(2), 10–14.

Erber, N. (1974). Effects of angle, distance, and illumination on visual reception of speech by profoundly deaf children. *Journal of Speech and Hearing Research, 17,* 99–112.

Fischer, S. (1998). Critical periods for language acquisition: Consequences for deaf education. In A. Weisel (Ed.). *Issues unresolved: New perspectives on language and deaf education* (pp. 9–26). Washington, DC: Gallaudet University Press.

Gallaway, C. (1998). Early Interaction. In S. Gregory, P. Knight, W. McCracken, S. Powers, & L. Watson. (Eds.), *Issues in deaf education* (pp. 49–57). London: Fulton.

Gaustad, M. G. (1997, April). *Inclusive education for deaf and hard of hearing students: Intervention with mainstream students and teachers.* Paper presented at the Annual Meeting of the Council for Exceptional Children, Salt Lake City, UT.

Gaustad, M. G. (1999). Including the kids across the hall: Collaborative instruction of hearing, deaf and hard of hearing students. *Journal of Deaf Studies and Deaf Education, 4,* 176–190.

Geers, A., & Schick, B. (1988). Acquisition of spoken and signed English by hearing-impaired children of hearing-impaired or hearing parents. *Journal of Speech and Hearing Research, 53,* 136–143.

Gregory, S. (1998). Mathematics and deaf children. In S. Gregory, P. Knight, W. McCracken, S. Powers, & L. Watson (Eds.), *Issues in deaf education* (pp. 119–126). London: Fulton.

Innes, J. J. (1994). Full inclusion and the deaf student: A deaf consumer's review of the issue. *American Annals of the Deaf, 139,* 152–156.

Jacobs, L. M. (1989). *A deaf adult speaks out* (3rd ed.). Washington, DC: Gallaudet University Press.

Klima, E., & Bellugi, U. (1979). *Signs of language.* Cambridge, MA: Harvard University Press.

Kluwin, T. N., & Stinson, M. S. (1993). *Deaf students in local public high schools: Background, experiences and outcomes.* Springfield, IL: Charles C. Thomas.

Lang, H. (2002). Higher education for deaf students: Research priorities in the new millennium. *Journal of Deaf Studies and Deaf Education, 7,* 267–280.

Leigh, G. R. (2001). Curriculum considerations. In R. G. Beattie (Ed.), *Ethics in deaf education: The first six years* (pp. 143–166). San Diego, CA: Academic Press.

Leigh, I. W., & Stinson, M. (1991). Social environments, self-perceptions, and identity of hearing-impaired adolescents. *Volta Review, 93,* 7–22.

Lovat, T. J., & Smith, D. L. (1998). *Curriculum: Action on reflection revisited* (3rd ed.). Katoomba, Australia: Social Science Press.

Luckner, J., & Denzin, P. (1988). In the mainstream: Adaptations for students who are deaf or hard of hearing. *Perspectives in Education and Deafness, 17,* 8–11.

Luckner, J. L., & Miller, K. J. (1994). Itinerant teachers: Responsibilities, perceptions, preparation, and students served. *American Annals of the Deaf, 139,* 111–118.

Luetke-Stahlman, B. (1998). *Language issues in deaf education.* Hillsboro, OR: Butte Publications.

Luetke-Stahlman, B. (1999). *Language across the curriculum when students are deaf or hard of hearing.* Hillsboro, OR: Butte Publications.

Luetke-Stahlman, B., & Luckner, J. (1991). *Effectively educating students with hearing impairments.* New York: Longman.

Lynas, W. (1986). *Integrating the handicapped into ordinary schools: A study of hearing-impaired pupils.* London: Croom Helm.

Lynas, W., Lewis, S., & Hopwood, V. (1997). Supporting the education of deaf children in mainstream schools. *Deafness and Education, 21,* 41–45.

Lynas, W., & Turner, S. (1995). *Young children with sensori-neural hearing loss from ethnic minority families.* Manchester, England: Centre for Audiology, Education of the Deaf and Speech Pathology, University of Manchester.

Lytle, R., & Rovins, M. (1997). Reforming deaf education: A paradigm shift from how to teach to what to teach. *American Annals of the Deaf, 142,* 7–15.

McEvoy, C., Marschark, M., & Nelson, D. L. (1999). Comparing the mental lexicons of deaf and hearing individuals. *Journal of Educational Psychology, 91,* 1–9.

Marschark, M. (1993). *Psychological development of deaf children.* New York: Oxford University Press.

Marschark, M. (1997). *Raising and educating a deaf child.* New York: Oxford University Press.

Marschark, M., Lang, H. G., & Albertini, J. A. (2002). *Educating deaf students: From research to practice.* New York: Oxford University Press.

Matthews, T. J., & Reich, C. F. (1993). Constraints on communication in classrooms for the deaf. *American Annals of the Deaf, 138,* 14–18.

Meadow-Orlans, K. P. (2001). Research and deaf education: Moving ahead while glancing back. *Journal of Deaf Studies and Deaf Education, 6,* 143–148.

Messenheimer-Young, T., & Whitesell, K. (1995). Communication-based learning communities: Coming to know by co-creating curriculum. *Volta Review, 97*(5). iii–viii.

Moores, D. (2001). *Educating the deaf: Psychology, principles and practice* (5th ed.). Boston, MA: Houghton Mifflin.

Padden, C., & Humphries, T. (1988). *Deaf in America: Voices from a culture.* Cambridge, MA: Harvard University Press.

Pagliaro, C. M. (1998). Mathematics preparation and professional development of deaf education teachers. *American Annals of the Deaf, 143,* 373–379.

Pau, C. S. (1995). The deaf child and solving the problems of arithmetic. *American Annals of the Deaf, 149,* 287–290.

Paul, P. (1998). *Literacy and deafness: The development of reading, writing, and literate thought.* Needham Heights, MA: Allyn and Bacon.

Power, D. (1981). Principles of curriculum and methods development in special education. In W. Swann (Ed.), *The practice of special education.* Oxford: Blackwell.

Power, D. (1997a). *Constructing lives: The Deaf experience.* Brisbane: Griffith University, Faculty of Education, Centre for Deafness Studies and Research.

Power, D. (1997b). Myths about sign languages. *Australian Language Matters, 5*(2), 8–9. [http://sunsite.anu.edu.au/language-australia/interp-trans/issues.html#myths]

Powers, S. (1996). Deaf pupils' achievements in ordinary schools. *Journal of the British Association of Teachers of the Deaf, 20,* 111–123.

Schembri, A., Wigglesworth, G, Johnston, T., Leigh, G., Adam, R., & Barker, R. (2002). Issues in development of the test battery for Australian Sign Language morphology and syntax. *Journal of Deaf Studies and Deaf Education, 7,* 18–40.

Schick, B., & Moeller, M. P. (1992). What is learnable in manually coded English sign systems? *Applied Psycholinguistics, 13,* 313–340.

Schildroth, A. N., & Hotto, S.A. (1996). Changes in student and program characteristics, 1984–85 and 1994–95. *American Annals of the Deaf, 141,* 68–71.

Seal, B.C. (1998). *Best practices in educational interpreting.* Boston: Allyn & Bacon.

Seddon, T. (1983). The hidden curriculum: An overview. *Curriculum Perspectives, 3,* 1–6.

Stewart, D., & Kluwin, T. N. (2001). *Teaching deaf and hard of hearing students: Content, strategies and curriculum.* Boston: Allyn & Bacon.

Stinson, M. S., & Antia, S. D. (1999). Considerations in educating deaf and hard-of-hearing students in inclusive settings. *Journal of Deaf Studies and Deaf Education, 4,* 163–175.

Stinson, M. S., & Lang, H. G. (1994). Full inclusion: A path for integration or isolation? *American Annals of the Deaf, 139,* 156–158.

Stoefan-Fisher, J., & Balk, J. (1992). Educational programs for children with hearing loss: Least restrictive environment. *Volta Review, 94,* 19–28.

Stone, R. (2001). A bold step: changing the curriculum for culturally deaf and hard of hearing students. In P. E. Spencer, C. J. Erting, & M. Marschark (Eds.), *The deaf child in the family and at school: Essays in honour of Kathryn P. Meadow-Orlans.* Mahwah, NJ: Lawrence Erlbaum Associates.

Supalla, S. J. (1991). Manually coded English: The modality question in signed language development. In P. Siple & S. D. Fischer (Eds.), *Theoretical issues in sign language research: Vol. 2. Psychology* (pp. 85–109). Chicago: The University of Chicago Press.

Taylor, G., & Bishop, J. (Eds.). (1991). *Being deaf: The experience of deafness.* London: Pinter & The Open University.

Traxler, C. B. (2000). Measuring up to performance standards in reading and mathematics: Achievement of selected deaf and hard of hearing students in the national norming of the 9th Edition Stanford Achievement Test. *Journal of Deaf Studies and Deaf Education, 5,* 337–348.

Tyler, R. W. (1949). *Basic principles of curriculum and instruction.* Chicago: University of Chicago Press.

Watson, L., & Parsons, J. (1998). Supporting deaf pupils in mainstream settings. In S. Gregory, P Knight, W. McCracken, S. Powers, & L. Watson (Eds.), *Issues in deaf education* (pp. 135–142). London: Fulton.

Wilbur, R. (2000). The use of ASL to support the development of English and literacy. *Journal of Deaf Studies and Deaf Education, 5,* 81–104.

Wood, D., Wood, H., Griffiths, A., & Howarth, I. (1986). *Teaching and talking with deaf children.* Chichester, UK: Wiley.

4

Michael S. Stinson & Thomas N. Kluwin

Educational Consequences of Alternative School Placements

The education of the deaf in the United States is every bit as diverse as is American education as a whole (Moores, 1996; Stewart & Kluwin, 2001). Today, a deaf or hard-of-hearing child could be in a public, private, or parochial school, in a residential program, or in a day program. A teacher of the deaf could spend his or her entire career in one school in a small town or ride the subway in a big city from one school to another. This diversity in part reflects the continuum of types of educational placement available in the United States today. This continuum is important because individual deaf students have different levels of need for support (Schirmer, 2001). (The term "deaf" will be used here to refer to the full range of deaf and hard-of-hearing students who receive special educational services.)

In this chapter we discuss four categories of alternative placements: (1) separate schools, (2) resource rooms and separate classes, (3) general education classes, and (4) co-enrollment classes. Two questions that immediately arise regarding these options are, What are the differences in the experiences of students in these alternative placement types? What are the differences in the characteristics and attainments of students in these placement types? A more complex question is, Is it possible to relate these different educational experiences to characteristics and attainments of the students? That is, do different experiences produce different educational consequences? The second and third sections of this chapter consider the research that best answers these questions. The first section provides background, description, and conceptualization that aids understanding of the research that this chapter reviews and of thinking in the field in regard to alternative types of placement.

Brief History

A common view of the education of deaf children is the residential school teacher with the self-contained class; however, this is not now and has not always been the most common situation (see Lang, this volume). Before the establishment of what is now the American School for the Deaf in Hartford, education of the deaf was a sporadic affair marked by isolated tutorial situations such as the plantation school that was the predecessor to the Virginia School for the Deaf and Blind in Staunton, Virginia. But even as the education of the deaf moved state by state toward the establishment of residential schools, there were early experiments with other approaches. In 1848, there was a "mainstream" program for deaf children in Baltimore (Moores, 1996).

During the second half of the nineteenth century and up until about World War I, the education of the deaf was divided between rural residential schools and day schools in cities. Wisconsin was a leader in the day school movement with a string of day programs dotting the shores of Lake Michigan. The golden years of the residential schools were from about 1910 to around 1950. One factor that capped their growth was the considerable cost of establishing a new school.

After World War II, America changed, and, as a result, the landscape of deaf education changed also. Families became more able and more likely to support a deaf child at home, while facilities for the education of deaf children started appearing within local school systems. The first change was a small increase in the number of deaf children in local public schools. As these numbers increased, residential school populations stayed about the same as before; however, the populations in the day schools declined. Local public school programs started to take up the excess population, and mainstreaming was on its way (Moores, 1996).

Types of Placement

Separate Schools

Separate schools, or schools for the deaf, provide intact classes with only deaf students. Although there is diversity among separate schools, the typical school has 150–200 students. High school students tend to reside at the school. Among these students, there may be a number who transferred from local public schools (Moores, 1996; Schirmer, 2001). In most separate schools there is an emphasis on sign communication, which occurs in forms with and without simultaneous speech. There is generally an excellent range of special services, such as audiologists, counselors, and psychologists. There is an extensive array of academic and vocational courses and a wide range of athletic and social programs. Separate schools are becoming increasingly varied in the extent that they provide experiences in general education classes for some of their students. According to the National Center for Education Statistics (1999), 16.8% of deaf students receive their education in separate schools.

Resource Rooms and Separate Classes

Both resource rooms and separate classes are located in public schools in which most students are hearing. The principal difference between resource rooms and separate classes is the amount of time that deaf students spend in regular classrooms. Students in separate classes receive all, or almost all, of their instruction from a teacher of the deaf with other deaf students. In contrast, students attend resource rooms only for selected subjects for part of the day. These students typically are away from the resource room and in general education classes for most of the day. The National Center for Education Statistics (1999) report indicates that 19.1% of deaf students are in resource rooms and 28.5% are in separate classes. We do not treat resource rooms and separate classes as distinct categories here.

The work of the resource room teacher falls into three general categories: consultation/collaboration, direct teaching, and regular classroom support (Glomb & Morgan, 1991). Consultation and collaboration includes responding to a general education teacher's requests for assistance with a student, developing academic, social, or behavioral goals for students in conjunction with the general education teacher, coordinating instructional plans, suggesting effective materials or strategies, and so on. To a large extent, direct teaching in the resource room involves remedial instruction, preteaching or post-teaching the content from the general education lessons, as well as tutoring deaf children when necessary. Kluwin, Stewart, and Sammons (1994) described five types of resource room teachers based on the social, administrative, or physical integration or isolation of the resource room teacher. Their typology ranges from socially, administratively, or physically isolated ("Fort Apache") teachers to completely integrated ("Happy Campers").

General Education Classes

General education classes are those with primarily hearing students and a regular teacher. Typically, only one deaf student (or only a few) is placed into any particular general education class. Deaf students in these classes commonly receive some special services. There is considerable diversity in this support, depending on the needs of the student. Often, a teacher of the deaf, called an itinerant teacher, provides consultation or supplementary instruction. A speech/language specialist may provide the only or additional consultation. Students may also receive services to support communication access and learning (Schirmer, 2001). These services include notetakers, interpreters, and real-time speech-to-text services (Stinson, Eisenberg, Horn, Larson, Levitt, & Stuckless, 1999: Stinson & Foster, 2000). The National Center for Education Statistics (1999) reported that 35.4% of deaf students received services in general education classes in 1995–1996.

More than 75% of the students taught by itinerant teachers are served on a pull-out basis; about 15% of the time, teachers work with students while they are in the general education class, and only about 5% routinely team teach with the regular education teacher. The (statistically) typical student served by an itinerant teacher is an orally educated white male without any additional handicaps who has a moderate hearing loss. The student likely wears a hearing aid, has intelligible speech, and gets along well with others (Allen, 1992; Kluwin & Stinson, 1993). The primary Individual Education Program (IEP) goals for this student tend to be language related, particularly focusing on written language. Common classroom adjustments for the student are preferential seating and the use of visual materials. These students may need materials rewritten or the use of notetakers or interpreters (Luckner & Miller, 1994).

Itinerant teachers spend much of their time traveling. The itinerant teacher sees many students in one day, whose ages can range from 2 though 21, who have a wide range of abilities, and who have varying degrees of hearing impairment (Affolter, 1985; Luckner and Miller, 1994; Swenson, 1995) Like the resource room teachers, the most important parts of the job for the itinerant teacher are providing direct service to students and consulting with other professionals and parents. The greatest barriers to providing services are the time constraints on the general education teachers and their lack of understanding of deafness (Affolter, 1985; Swenson, 1995). Additional barriers can be failure of the classroom teacher to follow through on recommendations, a lack of administrative support, and large numbers of students in the caseload (Ellis & Mathews, 1982; Olmstead, 1995).

Co-enrollment Classes

"Co-enrollment" refers to classrooms that include both deaf and hearing students, ideally in equal numbers, and a curriculum taught in both sign language and the vernacular. With the exception of the TRIPOD program in Burbank, California (Kirchner, 1994) and the program at the Kinzie Elementary School in Chicago (Banks, 1994), there have only been sporadic documented attempts in Florida (Kluwin, Gonsher, Silver, Samuels, 1996), Colorado (Luckner, 1999), and Arizona (Kreimeyer, Crooke, Drye, Egbert, & Klein, 2000) to establish co-enrollment programs. Anecdotal reports of other undocumented one-time experiments with the approach have been noted in other locations, but the practice has been quite limited. This may reflect both the strengths and the limitations of the approach. Co-enrollment appears to work well with dedicated and motivated staff when there are sufficient numbers of deaf students to create a viable free-standing program. Without the base of a moderately large deaf student population to continue year after year, as well as a dynamic and dedicated administrative structure, as in the Kinzie situation, these programs seem to flourish and disappear within a year or two. To our knowledge, there are no statistics on the number of students in co-enrollment classes.

In working in a team teaching or co-teaching situation, curriculum pace is set by the overall progress of the class (Kluwin et al., 1996). Additional communication access to the material is provided by the teacher of the deaf signing during her presentations, by an aide or interpreter, if needed, and by the general education teacher, who often begins to learn signs (Kirchner, 1994; Kluwin, 1999). Signs are taught to the hearing students both formally and informally (Kluwin et al., 1996; Kreimeyer et al., 2000). Team teaching, co-teaching, or co-enrollment means more work for the people involved because more collaborative time for planning is required (Kluwin et al., 1996). Successful team teaching depends on one person taking responsibility for getting things done (i.e., a clear team leader), commonly defined goals, and adequate time together (Kluwin et al., 1996; Kreimeyer et al., 2000).

Mainstreaming, Inclusion, and Placement

Co-enrollment classes are sometimes described as inclusion programs (Antia, Stinson & Gaustad, 2002). Descriptions of programs or placements in public schools may use the terms "mainstream" or "mainstreaming." The terms of inclusion and mainstreaming are widely used in discussions of alternative placements (e.g., Stinson & Antia, 1999; Stuckless & Corson, 1994). The following discussion considers inclusion and mainstreaming from placement, philosophical, and pragmatic perspectives.

Placement Perspective

In considering mainstreaming and inclusion from a placement perspective, the key issue is the physical setting in which children receive their education. From this perspective, inclusion implies that children who are deaf receive most or all of their education in the general education classroom. Mainstreaming implies that the deaf students receive their education in public schools that are also attended by hearing students, but not necessarily within the general education classroom (Stinson & Antia, 1999).

Philosophical Perspective

From a philosophical perspective, inclusion is more complex than mere physical placement in the general education classroom. The key philosophical concept of inclusion is that all students, including those with disabilities, are full members of the classroom and school communities (Antia, et al., 2002; Bunch, 1994). This concept implies that the general education classroom will change to accommodate all different learners and that it is desirable to offer special services to all children within the general education classroom. One major assumption is that, in an inclusive setting, the classroom teacher, rather than the special educator, has the primary responsibility for educating all children in the classroom (Jenkins, Pious, & Jewell, 1990). Another assumption is that special services that have been traditionally offered outside of the classroom setting will be offered within the classroom.

Philosophically, the central concept of mainstreaming is that it is desirable to place in the general education classroom those students with disabilities who are able to meet the expectations of that classroom. These expectations should be met with minimal assistance, or the level of the assistance should be irrelevant (Friend & Bursuck, 1996). Mainstreaming places greater emphasis on the child being able to adapt to the general education classroom, whereas inclusion places greater emphasis on the adaptation of the general education classroom to the child. To successfully mainstream a child, it is therefore first necessary to evaluate the child's readiness to function within the classroom.

Pragmatic Perspective

From a pragmatic perspective, the major question to be answered regarding inclusion is whether accommodations can be made, or are being made, in the general education classroom to appropriately educate deaf students. A pragmatic issue that needs to be resolved is whether special educators and general education classroom teachers can work in equal partnership to provide an adequate education to deaf students within the general education classroom. The primary question to be answered for mainstreaming is whether students can be appropriately identified and prepared for the general education classroom so that they can function there effectively.

Perspectives and Alternative Placements

For any educational program, its placement practices, philosophy, and pragmatic actions may be independent of each other. For example, full-time placement is not synonymous with inclusion, nor is full-time placement in the regular classroom a sufficient condition for membership. A school culture that strongly promotes inclusion and that has a shared vision of inclusion for all students among staff members can promote perceptions of membership despite part-time placement in general education classes (Antia et al., 2002). In general, resource rooms seem more closely linked with mainstreaming, and co-enrollment classes are more closely linked with inclusion. Placement in general education classes may be linked with either mainstreaming or inclusion, depending on factors such as level of support.

Achievement and Placement

Between-Group A Priori Differences

The comparison of the effectiveness of different types of placements on the basis of achievement outcomes is difficult, if not impossible, because of the differences between the children who enter these programs. Starting with the work of Jensema (1975), others such as Allen (1986), Holt (1994), and their associates at the Center for Demographic Studies at Gallaudet University have produced numerous reports about the variation in student characteristics among different placement situations. These differences fall into two large categories: student characteristics and family characteristics. Student characteristics include gender, degree of hearing loss, age of onset of hearing loss, additional handicaps, the student's current age or cohort group membership, previous achievement, ability, use of sign communication, and speech skills. Family variables include the parent's hearing status, family's home language, family's socioeconomic status, size of the family, and family's ethnic group membership.

Looking first at student characteristics that may impact placement, gender is one predictor, with males being more likely to be placed in general education classes than females (Holt, 1994; Kluwin, 1993; Kluwin & Stinson, 1993). Degree of hearing loss also consistently predicts placement, with a general trend for students with less severe hearing losses to attend general education classes (Allen, 1992; Allen & Osborn, 1984; Holt, 1994; Reich, Hambelon, & Houldin, 1977). Age of onset does not appear to be related to placement. Although several studies used age of onset as a variable in evaluating at placement decisions, it was not a statistically significant factor. The presence of additional handicaps tends to reduce the extent of placement of deaf or hard-of-hearing students in general education classes (Allen, 1992; Allen & Osborn, 1984). In addition, the older the deaf or hard-of-hearing student becomes, the more likely it is that he or she will be placed in general education classes (Allen, 1992; Holt, 1994; Reich et al., 1977). Previous achievement levels have been used as covariates in some studies of achievement differences across placement types, but generally achievement has not been considered in investigations of placement (Allen & Osborn, 1984; Kluwin,

1993; Walker, Munro, & Rickards, 1999). Finally, practitioners have stated that greater proficiency in communicating in spoken English is a factor in placing students in general education classes, but only two studies appear to have investigated the relationship between these skills and placement (Kluwin & Stinson, 1993; Reich et al., 1977). Both found that better English skills were associated with placement in general education classes.

Turning to family functions, Powers (1999) did not find parents' hearing status to be a factor in school placement for children in England. Reich et al. (1977), however, reported that the use of English as a home language was predictive of school placement for Canadian students. Although socioeconomic status and family size do not appear to be related to placement, ethnicity has been consistently shown to be a predictor of placement decisions in the United States, as children from ethnic minorities are more likely to attend separate school programs (Allen, 1992; Allen & Osborn, 1984; Holt, 1994; Kluwin, 1993).

Several studies suggest strongly that a priori differences that result in placement differences are the largest factor in the achievement of deaf students and that placement per se is not the critical factor. The original suggestion that placement was not a factor in the academic achievement of deaf students came from Carlberg and Kavalle's (1980) meta-analysis of earlier studies of mainstreaming. Carlberg and Kavalle reported effect sizes, a summary statistic in meta-analysis, for mainstreaming mentally retarded and emotionally disturbed students greater than 1.0 (plus and minus, respectively). This result meant that there was a strong relationship between these students' academic achievement and whether they were placed in special or general education classes. In contrast, for deaf students, they found an effect size that indicated that less than 5% of the variance in achievement score differences was attributable to placement. For these students the relationship between achievement and placement was weak. Subsequently, Allen and Osborn (1984) reported that about 1% of score difference was due to placement, while about 25% of the score difference was due to student characteristics. Kluwin and Moores (1985) essentially replicated this finding, but in a later study Kluwin and Moores (1989) reported that more of the unexplained variance in score differences, as well as some of the student characteristic variance, could be accounted for if a measure of teaching quality was included. More recently, Powers (1999), in England, reported nearly identical results to the original Allen and Osborn (1984) study in the United States. Consistently, the student's gender, degree of hearing loss, presence of additional handicaps, and age group have been shown to be greater factors in predicting achievement outcomes than placement itself.

Differences in Academic Experience Between Alternative Placements

Kluwin (1992) made the point that the process of education in a separate class or in a special school or a resource room is fundamentally different from the process of education in a general education class. In the Kluwin study, general education highschool math teachers were found to use more oral presentations to the group, use less individual "seat work," pose fewer questions to students, and provide more positive verbal feedback. They also were less individualized in their approach to instruction, used more whole instruction, and were more focused on moving through the content of the course than teachers of the deaf in separate classes. Some of the differences, such as less individualization and more whole group instruction, reflect differences related to small group versus large group instruction. One of the fundamental problems in sorting out placement differences is that considerations such as class size can be a confounding variable.

Cawthon (2001) looked at general education classrooms with deaf and hearing students. She reported that although teachers directed fewer and shorter utterances and fewer questions to deaf students, a higher percentage of the questions were open-ended. However, there was greater variation between the classes that Cawthon observed than between deaf and hearing students' experiences within either class. Thus, it is not clear whether teachers in general education classes treat deaf and hearing students differently.

Differences in Achievement Between Alternative Placements

In answering the question of the effectiveness of alternative placements (separate schools, resource rooms, etc.), there are three issues to be addressed. First, how can achievement be defined operation-

ally? Second, what is the size of the effect of placement on achievement? Third, what predicts achievement differences other than placement? In regard to operational definitions, several measures of achievement have been used, including reading (Allen & Osborn, 1984; Kluwin & Stinson, 1993; Reich et al., 1977), writing (Kluwin & Stinson, 1993; Reich et al., 1977), mathematics (Allen & Osborn, 1984; Kluwin & Moores, 1985, 1989; Kluwin & Stinson, 1993; Reich et al., 1977), highstakes testing (Powers, 1999), and grade point average (Kluwin & Stinson, 1999).

With regard to how much of an effect placement has on achievement, the reader is referred to the previous discussion of effect size. In those few studies where effect size is reported or it is possible to compute it from the data available, placement per se accounts for less than 5% of the difference in achievement, whereas student characteristics account for 25% of the difference, and most of the variance is unaccounted for (Allen & Osborn, 1984; Kluwin & Moores, 1985, 1989; Powers, 1999).

In regard to factors that predict achievement differences other than placement, several studies have expected a relationship between gender and achievement or between degree of hearing loss and achievement, but have not found one (Kluwin & Moores, 1985, 1989; Powers, 1999). Powers (1999) also hypothesized that age of onset would predict achievement differences, but failed to find a difference. To date, research provides no indication that gender, degree of hearing loss, or age of onset have significant impact on achievement differences within placements. One relatively consistent, positive predictor of outcome differences within placements, however, has been the absence of additional handicaps (Allen & Osborn, 1984; Kluwin & Moores, 1989; Powers, 1999).

To summarize, it is difficult to determine the efficacy of placements for deaf students for four reasons. First, unexplained variance in studies has ranged from 65% to 80%, with approximately 75% unexplained variance probably being the norm based on the size and complexity of the study sample (Allen & Osborn, 1984; Kluwin & Moores, 1989; Powers, 1999). In other words, research in this area has consistently failed to adequately describe the entire phenomenon. Second, estimates of the impact of placement per se on achievement have remained constant since the meta-analysis of

Carlberg and Kavalle (1980), at around 1% of the total variance. This finding represents, like the percentage of unexplained variance, one of the most consistent replications of findings in educational research. Third, a priori student differences exist which consistently account for between one-fifth and one-quarter of the total variance and usually more than 95% of the explained variance. Thus, the focus should be on the students first, and with the setting a distant second. Fourth, although it is easy on a theoretical and experiential basis to describe significant process differences among the placement types, seldom have instructional factors (much less quality of instruction) entered into the analysis of between-placement differences. One could easily speculate that much of the 75% of unexplained variance lies there.

Personal and Social Characteristics and Placement

Differences in Social Experiences Between Alternative Placements

Social environments for separate schools, resource rooms, general education classes, and co-enrollment programs vary between and among each other. They vary in the nature of teacher–student interaction, relationships with peers, and outside-of-class activities (Garretson, 1977; Stinson & Foster, 2000).

Separate Schools

In addition to having teachers who are skilled in communicating with deaf students through sign language, separate schools provide good opportunities for interaction with other deaf peers. In these schools, there is a critical mass of peers and adults with whom students can interact easily and where they benefit from a variety of positive social experiences (Foster & Emerton, 1991; Moores, 1996). There is usually a strong program of extracurricular activities for deaf students, including numerous opportunities for leadership. Because of the opportunities for informal communication, extracurricular activities such as junior branches of deaf organizations, and regular interaction with deaf adults, separate schools are the setting where deaf children have been socialized to acquire the values of and to identify with the Deaf community. Allen

and Karchmer (1990) reported that whereas 20% of the teachers in separate schools were deaf, only 1% of teachers in mainstream programs were deaf, and the proportion of deaf teachers in separate schools may have increased since that report.

Resource Rooms and Separate Classes

Because resource rooms and separate classes typically have several deaf peers, there are regular opportunities for deaf students to interact with each other. Stinson, Whitmire, and Kluwin (1996) examined the frequency of interaction with deaf and with hearing peers who varied in the extent they were placed in regular classes. Students who were always or almost always in separate classes reported that they interacted primarily with deaf peers in class, in school, and in out-of-school activities. Students in separate classes, however, may at times engage in lessons jointly with a general education class (Gaustad, 1999). Some large public school programs with numerous resource rooms include extensive opportunities for extracurricular activities specifically for deaf students, as well as opportunities to participate in activities with hearing schoolmates (Kluwin & Stinson, 1993). Extracurricular activities with hearing peers often include interpreter support for communication access.

General Education Classes

When deaf students are in classes with hearing students, the quality of communication access has implications for their social experiences. In formal instruction and in extracurricular activities, communication access may be relatively good because the teacher uses an FM system, speechreading is relatively easy, and/or a support service such as an interpreter is provided. In other situations, however, such as in hallways, lunchrooms, or school buses, students are on their own and may not have good access to communication with peers (Foster, 1989; Ramsey, 1997; Stinson & Foster, 2000).

Another relevant issue is the degree of social support that is provided to the deaf student in the general education classroom by the regular teacher and the teacher of the deaf. Luckner and Miller (1994) found that itinerant teachers reported that 75% of the general education teachers understood the needs of their deaf students. Afzali-Nomani (1995) found that 77% of the general education teachers and teachers of the deaf rated the classroom settings as being positive for the students' social adjustment, and 69% rated the settings as being positive for the students' self-esteem. However, Stinson and Liu (1999) noted that support personnel who worked in general education classrooms commented that the teachers were sometimes unsupportive. Furthermore, hearing students often do not know how to get deaf students' attention, how to establish eye contact, or how to speak in a manner that facilitates speechreading. Also, hearing students may misinterpret deaf students' responses, or may simply be afraid because the students seem different (Stinson & Liu, 1999).

When hearing peers have greater patience in communication, interactions are more likely to be positive. They are also more likely to be positive when deaf students have relatively more hearing, or when hearing peers develop knowledge of sign language (Afzali-Nomani, 1995; Antia & Kreimeyer, 1995; Bat-Chava & Deignan, 2001; Shaw & Jamieson, 1997). Stinson and Liu (1999) reported that five groups of individuals contribute to the active participation of deaf or hard-of-hearing students: regular classroom teachers, interpreters, teachers of the deaf, and deaf and hearing peers.

Observational studies of interactions between deaf and hearing students and studies of perceptions of social relations provide further description of deaf students' social experiences. These studies have yielded results that are consistent with a description that includes limitations in communication access, in support from classroom teachers, and in understanding by hearing peers. Findings indicate that, in general, deaf children interact more with deaf peers than with hearing ones, and hearing children interact more with hearing peers than with deaf ones (see Antia & Kreimeyer, this volume).

Associated with the limited interaction between deaf and hearing children may be feelings of apprehension that inhibit communication and make it less satisfactory (Hurt & Gonzalez, 1988; Schirmer, 2001). However, these concerns may ameliorate after time. For example, Ladd, Munson, and Miller (1984) found that the interactions between deaf and hearing peers increased over a two-year period.

Stinson and colleagues (Stinson et al., 1996; Stinson & Whitmire, 1991) found that participation with hearing peers was relatively greater for deaf students who were primarily in general education classes than for deaf students who were primarily in separate classes. Thus, self-rated partici-

pation appears to reflect opportunities for interaction.

These observational and self-report studies suggest that when deaf students are in general education classrooms, they do interact with hearing peers (Kluwin, Stinson, & Cicerini, 2002). However, when it is possible, they will interact more frequently with deaf peers. In general, social experiences in general education classes are less positive than those in separate classes or separate schools.

Co-enrollment Classes

The few studies and descriptions of co-enrollment programs (Kirchner, 1994; Kreimeyer et. al., 2000; Luckner, 1999) suggest that deaf students in this setting have more positive interaction experiences than in general education classes. Because there are several deaf students in the classroom, regular interaction with deaf peers occurs (Kreimeyer et al., 2000). These classes also encourage interaction between deaf and hearing peers by providing instruction in sign language and other strategies for deaf–hearing communication. In this environment, deaf students are involved in all class activities. Kreimeyer et al. found that there was increased interaction between deaf and hearing classmates in class and in the lunchroom in a co-enrollment program as compared to a traditional itinerant model.

Personal/Social Characteristics of Students and Consequences of Experiences in Alternative Placements

Because of the difficulty in separating personal/social characteristics that students bring with them to a placement and consequences of being in the placement for personal/social development, these are addressed simultaneously. Studies of social characteristics and consequences are grouped into three categories: social skills, sociometric status/acceptance, and affective functioning. Measures of social skills include measures of social maturity, such as the Meadow-Kendall Socio-Emotional Inventory teacher rating scales developed by Meadow (1983). Social acceptance includes sociometric ratings by peers of the extent to which deaf students are seen as desirable as friends/playmates and also self-ratings by deaf students on the extent of their acceptance by deaf and hearing peers. Affective characteristics refer to general personal dispositions, including self-esteem and loneliness.

One group of studies focused on separate schools or compared students in separate schools with those primarily in either separate classes or primarily in general education classes. A second group focused on students in special classes or compared students in special classes with those in general education classes. A third group of studies examined students in general education classes, and a fourth group examined students in co-enrollment programs. We consider studies of these characteristics separately for each of the school placements discussed thus far.

Separate Schools

Studies of students in separate schools have examined teacher and self-ratings of social skills, peer ratings of acceptance, and self-ratings of the affective dimension of self-esteem. Hagboard (1987) found that deaf students in separate (i.e., residential) schools who were rated highest in social acceptance had been at the schools the longest, and female students received higher acceptance ratings than males. Cartledge, Paul, Jackson, and Cochran (1991) found no differences between mean teacher's ratings of social skill for students in separate schools and those primarily in resource rooms. Cartledge, Cochran, and Paul (1996) reported that students in resource room programs assigned higher self-ratings of social skills than students in a residential program. Van Gurp (2001) found that students in a resource room program reported higher self-esteem on the dimensions of reading and general school than did those in a program in which they had transferred from a separate school to a new facility with deaf and hearing students. In sum, there appear to be no clear differences in social skills and affective characteristics of students in separate schools compared to those in separate classes or general education classes. In addition, studies have found differences in social acceptance among students in separate schools that are related to individual characteristics.

Resource Rooms and Separate Classes

This group of studies has either examined deaf students within resource rooms or separate classes or compared students primarily in these classes with those in primarily in general education classes. These studies have used teacher- and self-ratings of social skills, self-ratings of acceptance, and self-ratings of the affective characteristic of self-esteem.

Farrugia and Austin (1980) reported that teachers rated deaf students in general education classes as less socially mature on the Meadow-Kendall Socio-Emotional Inventory than hearing students. Kluwin and Stinson (1993) compared deaf students in general education classes with deaf students in separate classes on the Meadow-Kendall measure and reported that the separate-class students were less socially mature than the general education students. Shaffer-Meyer (1991) reported no statistically significant differences on the Meadow-Kendall between students in separate classes and those in general education classes.

Stinson et al. (1996) found that deaf students who were primarily in general education classes assigned higher ratings of comfort in relationships with deaf peers than did deaf students who were primarily in separate classes. In contrast, there was no difference between ratings of comfort in relationships with hearing students for those in separate classes and those in general education classrooms. Stinson and Whitmire (1991) also found that deaf students reported more comfort in relationships with deaf students than with hearing students, regardless of type of placement. Likewise, Musselman, Mootilal, and MacKay (1996) found that students who were primarily in separate classes were more comfortable with relationships with deaf peers. However, for students who were primarily in general education classes, there was not a significant difference between the mean rating of comfort with deaf peers and that of comfort with hearing peers. Finally, studies by Larsen (1984) and by Cohen (1989) found no differences between deaf students primarily in general education classes and those in separate classes on self-reports of self-esteem.

Research that has focused on separate classes and on comparisons of students who are primarily in that setting with students in general education indicate that students in separate classes may be less socially mature. It is not clear whether the difference is a consequence of differences in experiences or of differences in characteristics of students, such as social skills, at initial placement. Studies have also indicated that deaf students in separate and in general education classes are more comfortable in relationships with deaf peers than in those with hearing peers. Students in the two settings do not appear to be different from each other in self-esteem.

General Education Classes

Studies of students in general education classes have addressed social skills, acceptance, and affective characteristics. Three of these studies investigated degree of acceptance of the deaf students as indicated by peer ratings from hearing students. In an investigation of social functioning, Maxon, Brackett, and van den Berg (1991) found that deaf students' self-ratings on 10 scales of social functioning were not significantly different from those of hearing students, except on one scale in which the deaf students indicated that they were more likely to be emotionally expressive than did the hearing students. With respect to acceptance, Cappelli, Daniels, Durieux-Smith, McGarth, and Neuss (1995) found that deaf students in grades 1–6 received lower ratings of likeability than did their hearing classmates. Antia and Kreimeyer (1997) found that deaf children in preschool, kindergarten, and first grade general education classes received lower peer ratings of acceptance than did hearing peers. Ladd et al. (1984) reported that, over time, hearing peers rated deaf peers as being more considerate.

In regard to affective characteristics, Murphy and Newlon (1987) found that postsecondary deaf students reported they were significantly lonelier than were hearing students. Two studies that have used measures of self-esteem found interactions between the level of self-esteem and characteristics of the students. In a study with the Piers-Harris self-esteem scale, Shaffer-Meyer (1991) found that for students in general education classrooms, students with less severe hearing losses had higher self-esteem than did those with more severe hearing losses; however, for students in separate classes, there was not a significant difference between the self-esteem of students with different hearing levels. Gans (1995) did not find a significance difference between adult ratings of self-esteem of students primarily in separate classes or primarily in general education classes. She did find, however, that for students in general education classes, those with better English language skills had more positive self-esteem, but for those in separate classes there was not a significant difference.

The studies of students in general education classes indicate that the lack of acceptance by hearing peers, and deaf students' perceptions of this lack, do not adversely affect self-esteem. In addition, the findings of interactions between hearing level and self-esteem, and between language proficiency and self-esteem suggest that students must have good communication and English skills to handle the demands of the general education classroom. The lack of acceptance and the reports of loneliness and lack of comfort with hearing peers point to the importance of finding better ways of providing social support to students in general education classrooms.

Co-enrollment Classes

Two studies have investigated acceptance and affective characteristics of deaf children in co-enrollment settings (Kluwin, 1999; Kluwin & Gonsher, 1994). Kluwin and Gonsher (1994) used a peer nomination procedure in a study of a kindergarten class with team teaching. The class of 25 included several deaf children. Each child was asked to select up to three children with whom he or she would prefer to interact. Kluwin and Gonsher found that the number of times that deaf and hearing children were selected as a desirable companion were not distinguishable from each other. Kluwin (1999) found no differences in self-reported loneliness or in self-esteem between 13 deaf and 9 hearing peers enrolled in a co-enrollment program for 1–5 years. These studies indicate that, at least from a social perspective, co-enrollment classes may be a promising way of educating deaf students with hearing ones.

In summary, the social environments of separate schools, resource rooms and separate classes, and co-enrollment classes appear to be more positive than that of the general education classroom. Findings regarding loneliness at the postsecondary level and lack of acceptance by hearing peers in general education classrooms at the elementary level are consistent with the above statement. This conclusion needs to be qualified by findings that suggest that personal characteristics interact with the type of placement in influencing the social integration of the individual student.

Summary and Conclusions

Determination of the consequences of alternative placements is probably even more difficult for personal characteristics than for academic achievement. It is impossible to distinguish between personal characteristics that may have been a basis for placement and those characteristics that are due to the placement experience itself. In addition, personal characteristics are more difficult to measure than academic achievement, and there are not common, widely used measures of personal characteristics. Partly because common measures of academic achievement are available, several studies have partitioned the achievement variance accounted for by placement type and by individual differences (e.g., Kluwin & Moores, 1985, 1989). These studies have shown that individual differences in students account for 95 % of the explained variance in achievement and that placement only accounts for a small portion of the explained variance. Furthermore, the explained variance has usually been only a quarter or less of the total variance. Research currently has limited ability to describe and measure the factors that account for variation in achievement.

In contrast to the work on achievement, there are no known studies that have produced this type of partitioning for social characteristics. In these circumstances the most fruitful approach to understanding the consequences of placement on personal characteristics may be to conduct studies that provide detailed descriptions of the students in particular placements and of interventions that may improve the educational experience. This work should expand our limited understanding of how educational practices in alternative placements affect achievement and personal development, as well as help to improve the quality of education for deaf students.

References

Affolter, M. (1985). *Working with deaf students in rural areas* (Technical Report). Bellingham: WA: Western Washington University, National Rural Development Institute.

Afzali-Nomani (1995). Educational conditions related to successful full inclusion programs involving deaf/hard of hearing children. *American Annals of the Deaf, 140,* 396–401.

Allen, T.E. (1986). Patterns of academic achievement among hearing impaired students: 1974 and 1983. In A.N. Schildroth & M.A. Karchmer (Eds.), *Deaf children in America* (pp. 161–206). San Diego, CA: College Hill Press.

Allen, T.E., & Karchmer, M. (1990). Communication in classrooms for deaf students: Student, teacher, and program characteristics. In H. Bornstein (Ed.), *Manual communication: Implications for education* (pp. 45–66). Washington, DC: Gallaudet University Press.

Allen, T.E., & Osborn, T. (1984). Academic integration of hearing-impaired students: Demographic, handicapping, and achievement factors. *American Annals of the Deaf, 129*(3), 100–113.

Antia, S.D., & Kreimeyer, K.H. (1997). The generalization and maintenance of the peer and social behaviors of young children who are deaf or hard of hearing. *Language, Speech and Hearing Services in Schools, 28,* 59–69.

Antia, S., Stinson, M.S., & Gaustad, M. (2002). Developing membership in the education of deaf and hard of hearing students in inclusive settings. *Journal of Deaf Studies and Deaf Education, 1,* 214–229.

Banks, J. (1994) *All of us together: The story of inclusion at the Kinzie School.* Washington, DC: Gallaudet University Press.

Bat-Chava and Deignan, E. (2001). Peer relationships of children with cochlear implants. *Journal of Deaf Studies and Deaf Education, 6,* 186–199.

Bunch, G. (1994). An interpretation of full inclusion. *American Annals of the Deaf, 139,* 150–152.

Capelli, M., Daniels, D., Duriex-Smith, A., McGrath, P., & Neuss, D. (1995). Social development of children with hearing impairments. *Volta Review, 97,* 197–208.

Carlberg, C., & Kavale, K. (1980). The efficacy of special versus regular class placement for exceptional children. *Journal of Special Education, 14*(3), 295–309.

Cartledge, G., Cochran, L., & Paul, P. (1996). Social skill self-assessments by adolescents with hearing impairment in residential and public schools. *Remedial and Special Education, 17,* 30–36.

Cartledge, G., Paul, P.V., Jackson, D., & Cochran, L. L. (1991). Teachers' perceptions of the social skills of adolescents with hearing impairment in residential and public school settings. *Remedial and Special Education, 12*(2), 34–39.

Cawthon, S. (2001). Teaching strategies in inclusive classroom with deaf students. *Journal of Deaf Studies and Deaf Education, 6*(3), 212–225.

Ellis, J. & Mathews, G. (1982). *Professional role performance difficulties of first year itinerant specialists.* Unpublished report, Northern Illinois University, De Kalb.

Farrugia, D., & Austin, G. F. (1980). A study of social emotional adjustment patterns of hearing-impaired students in different educational settings. *American Annals of the Deaf, 25,* 535–541.

Foster, S. (1989). Educational programmes for deaf students: An insider perspective on policy and practice. In L. Barton (Ed.), *Integration: Myth or reality?* (pp. 57–82). London: The Falmer Press.

Foster, S., & Emerton, G. (1991). Mainstreaming the deaf student: A blessing or a curse? *The Journal of Disability Policy Studies, 2,* 61–76.

Friend, M., & Bursuck, W.D. (1996). *Including students with special needs: A practical guide for classroom teachers.* Boston: Allyn & Bacon.

Gans, J. (1995, July). *The relation of self-image to academic placement and achievement in hearing-impaired students.* Paper presented at the Eighteenth International Congress on Education of the Deaf, Tel Aviv, Israel.

Gaustad, M. G. (1999). Including the kids across the hall: Collaborative instruction of hearing, deaf, and hard of hearing students. *Journal of Deaf Studies and Deaf Education, 4*(3), 176–190.

Glomb, N. & Morgan, D. (1991). Resource room teachers' use of strategies that promote the success of handicapped students in regular classrooms. *The Journal of Special Education, 25*(2), 221–235.

Hagborg, W. (1987). Hearing impaired students and sociometric ratings: An exploratory study. *Volta Review, 89*(4), 221–228.

Holt, J. (1994). Classroom attributes and achievement test scores for deaf and hard of hearing students. *American Annals of the Deaf, 139*(4), 430–437.

Hurt, H. T., & Gonzalez, T. (1988). On apprehension and distorted self disclosure: The hidden disabilities of hearing-impaired students. *Communication Education, 37,* 106–117.

Jenkins J. R., Pious, C. G., & Jewell, M. (1990). Special education and the regular education initiative: Basic assumptions. *Exceptional Children, 56,* 479–491.

Jensema C. (1975). *The relationship between academic achievement and the demographic characteristics of hearing impaired children and youth* (Series R, No. 2). Washington, DC: Gallaudet College Office of Demographic Studies.

Kirchner, C. (1994). Co-enrollment as an inclusion model. *American Annals of the Deaf, 139*(2), 163–164.

Kluwin, T. (1992). Considering the efficacy of mainstreaming from the classroom perspective. In T.N. Kluwin, D.F. Moores, & M.M. Gaustad (Eds.), *Defining the effective public school program for deaf students* (pp. 175–193). New York: Teachers College Press.

Kluwin, T. (1993). Cumulative effects of mainstreaming on the achievement of deaf adolescents. *Exceptional Children, 60*(1), 73–81.

Kluwin, T. (1999). Co-teaching deaf and hearing students: Research on social integration. *American Annals of the Deaf, 144,* 339–344.

Kluwin, T., & Gonsher, W. (1994). A single school study of social integration of children with and without hearing losses in a team taught kindergarten. *The ACEHI Journal, 20*(3), 74–87.

Kluwin, T., & Gonsher, W., Silver, K., Samuels, J. (1996). Team teaching students with hearing impairments and students with normal hearing together. *Teaching Exceptional Children, 29*(1), 11–15.

Kluwin, T., & Moores, D. F. (1985). The effect of integration on the achievement of hearing-impaired adolescents. *Exceptional Children, 52*(2), 153–160.

Kluwin, T., & Moores, D. F. (1989). Mathematics achievement of hearing impaired adolescents in different placements. *Exceptional Children 55*(4), 327–335.

Kluwin, T., Stewart, D. S., & Sammons, A. (1994). The isolation of teachers of the deaf and hard of hearing in local public school programs. *The ACEHI Journal/La Revue ACEDA, 20*(2), 16–30.

Kluwin, T.N., & Stinson, M.S.(1993). *Deaf students in local public high schools: Backgrounds, experiences, and outcomes.* Springfield, IL: Charles C. Thomas.

Kluwin, T. N., Stinson, M.S., & Cicerini, G. M. (2002). Social processes and outcomes of in-school contact between deaf and hearing peers. *Journal of Deaf Studies and Deaf Education, 7,* 200–213.

Kreimeyer, K., Crooke, P., Drye, C., Egbert, V., & Klein, B. (2000). Academic benefits of a co-enrollment model of inclusive education for deaf and hard-of-hearing children. *Journal of Deaf Studies and Deaf Education, 5*(2), 174–185.

Ladd, G., Munson, H., & Miller, J. (1984). Social integration of deaf adolescents in secondary-level mainstreamed programs. *Exceptional Children, 50*(5), 420–428.

Larsen, D. S. (1984). *An investigation of the relationship between self-concept of hearing impaired students and other selected variables.* Unpublished doctoral dissertation, Brigham Young University, Provo, UT.

Luckner, J. (1999). An examination of two co-teaching classrooms. *American Annals of the Deaf, 144*(1), 24–34.

Luckner, J., & Miller, K. (1993). Itinerant teachers: Responsibilities, perceptions, preparation, and students served. *American Annals of the Deaf, 139*(2), 111–118.

Maxon, A., Brackett, D., & van den Berg, S. (1991). Self-perception of socialization: The effects of hearing status, age, and gender. *Volta Review, 93,* 7–18.

Meadow, K.P. (1983). An instrument for assessment of

social-emotional adjustment in hearing-impaired preschoolers. *American Annals of the Deaf, 128,* 826–834.

Moores, D. F. (1996). *Educating the deaf* (4th ed.). Boston: Houghton Mifflin.

Murphy, J., & Newlon, B. (1987). Loneliness and the mainstreamed hearing-impaired college student. *American Annals of the Deaf, 132,* 21–25.

Musselman, C., Mootilal, A., & MacKay, S. (1996). The social adjustment of deaf adolescents in segregated, partially integrated, and mainstreamed settings. *Journal of Deaf Studies and Deaf Education, 1,* 52–63.

National Center for Education Statistics. (1999). Retrieved December 2001 from www.nces.ed.gov.

Olmstead, J. (1995). Itinerant personnel: A survey of caseloads and working conditions. *Journal of Visual Impairment & Blindness, 89,* 546–548.

Powers, S. (1999). The educational attainments of deaf student in mainstream programs in England: Examination of results and influencing factors. *American Annals of the Deaf, 144,* (3), 261–269.

Ramsey, C. L. (1997). *Deaf children in public schools: Placement, context, and consequences.* Washington, DC: Gallaudet University Press.

Reich, C., Hambelon, D., & Houldin, B. K. (1977). The integration of hearing impaired children in regular classrooms. *American Annals of the Deaf, 122,* 534–543.

Schirmer, B.R. (2001). *Psychological, social, and educational dimensions of deafness.* Boston: Allyn and Bacon.

Shaffer-Meyer, D. (1991). *The self-concept of mainstreamed hearing impaired students.* Unpublished doctoral dissertation, University of Northern Colorado, Greeley.

Shaw, J., & Jamieson, J. (1997). Patterns of classroom discourse in an integrated, interpreted elementary school setting. *American Annals of the Deaf, 142,* 40–47.

Stewart, D. A., & Kluwin, T.N. (2001). *Teaching deaf and hard of hearing students: content, strategies, and curriculum.* Boston: Allyn and Bacon.

Stinson, M., & Antia, S. (1999). Considerations in educating deaf and hard-of-hearing students in inclusive settings. *Journal of Deaf Studies and Deaf Education, 4,* 163–175.

Stinson, M., Eisenberg, S., Horn, C., Larson, H. Levitt, H., & Stuckless, R. (1999). Real-time speech-to-text services. In R. Stuckless (Ed.), *Reports of the National Task Force on Quality Services in Postsecondary Education of Deaf and Hard of Hearing Students* (pp. 1–23). Rochester, NY: Northeast Technical Assistance Center, Rochester Institute of Technology.

Stinson, M., & Foster, S. (2000). Socialization of deaf children and youths in school. In P. Spencer, C. Erting, & M. Marschark (Eds.), *The deaf child in the family and at school* (pp. 151–174). Mahwah, NJ: Lawrence Erlbaum Associates.

Stinson, M., & Liu, Y. (1999). Participation of deaf and hard-of-hearing students in classes with hearing students. *Journal of Deaf Studies and Deaf Education, 4,* 191–202.

Stinson, M., & Whitmire, K. (1991). Self-perceptions of social relationships among hearing-impaired adolescents in England. *Journal of the British Association of Teachers of the Deaf, 15,* 104–114.

Stinson, M. Whitmire, K., & Kluwin, T. (1996). Self-perceptions of social relationships in hearing-impaired adolescents. *Journal of Educational Psychology, 88,* 132–143.

Stuckless, E.R., & Corson, H. (Eds.). (1994). Special programs, full inclusions, and choices for students who are deaf. Reference issue. *American Annals of the Deaf, 139*(20), 148–170.

Swenson, A. (1995). Itinerant teaching: An insider's view. *RE:view, 27*(3), 113–116.

Van Gurp, S. (2001). Self-concept of deaf secondary school students in different educational settings. *Journal of Deaf Studies and Deaf Education, 6,* 54–69.

Walker, L., Munro, J., & Rickards, F. (1999). Literal and inferential reading comprehension of students who are deaf or hard of hearing: *Volta Review, 100*(2), 87–103.

5

Marilyn Sass-Lehrer & Barbara Bodner-Johnson

Early Intervention
Current Approaches to Family-Centered Programming

The first 3 years of life are known as the "magic years." During this time, the developing infant is nourished and nurtured as character and capabilities unfold. The power of early life experiences on later development and the implications of a sensitive period for the acquisition of language and for cognitive and emotional development continue to amaze both researchers and educators.

For many deaf children, the early years are marked as much by confusion as by the magic of early development. Hearing loss is sometimes not apparent until the second year of life, and by that time parent–child relationships may be strained and meaningful interactions limited. Hearing caregivers struggle to identify the source of their child's developmental differences and grapple with the implications of hearing loss. Early intervention provides families with information and skills to communicate with their child. These services typically end, however, when the child becomes 3 years old and transitions to preschool. Many families experience less than a year of early intervention benefits (Meadow-Orlans, Mertens, & Sass-Lehrer, in press).

Newborn hearing-screening technology presents the opportunity for a different paradigm in the early experiences of young deaf children and their families. The expansion of newborn hearing-screening programs throughout the country means fewer children will miss the advantages of an early start. Parents and caregivers who learn about their child's hearing abilities within the first few months of their child's life may, with the support of knowledgeable and sensitive professionals, begin acquiring the understanding and skills they need to adapt their interactions to provide access to the same quality of early-life experiences as their child's hearing peers.

Educational, social, and political forces provide a context for understanding early intervention programming for deaf children and their families. Early education for deaf children has evolved from multiple sources including early childhood education, child development, special education, deaf education, and, more recently, the field of early childhood special education. The influences of European and American philosophical and theoretical views of early development from the seventeenth century to the present are reflected in the recommended guidelines for practice endorsed by the National Association for the Education of Young Children (NAEYC) (Bredekamp & Copple, 1997) and the Division for Exceptional Children (DEC) (Sandall, McLean, & Smith, 2000).

Early education for deaf children and families has struggled with its place among the disciplines of early childhood education and special education. The question, "is deafness a disability?" is fundamental to understanding the impact of deafness on the child and family and the subsequent nature of early intervention services provided. Although early childhood education is rooted in a developmental and constructivist view of learning, early childhood special education tends toward a functional/behavioral perspective. These paradigms for learning (developmental and behavioral) and their respective related practices (responsive, child-directed and directive, teacher-centered) represent the continuum of teaching and learning contexts evident in early education programs (Bailey, 1997; Bruder, 1997; Fox, Hanline, Vail, & Galant, 1994).

The importance of the early years for deaf children was recognized as early as the mid-seventeenth century when parents were urged to fingerspell to their infants (Dalgarno, 1680, cited in Moores, 2001; see also Lang, this volume). The first early intervention program for deaf children in the United States was known as a "family" school established by Bartlett in 1852 in New York City. Tensions between schools and families, however, were common in the mid-1800s, when residential schools were the norm and they assumed many of the family's child-rearing responsibilities. Barriers rather than bridges described the relationship between parents of deaf children and schools at this time (Bodner-Johnson, 1986b).

In 1942, the program known today as the John Tracy Clinic established a private, parent-initiated educational program for parents with young deaf children and continues as a model of parent involvement in early intervention (John Tracy Clinic, nd). Two decades later, Head Start became the nation's first public commitment to young children with special needs. Federal funds from the Bureau of Education for the Handicapped of the U.S. Department of Education established the Handicapped Children's Early Education Program (HCEEP) in 1968 to develop and evaluate models for early education (Bowe, 2000). SKI*HI, a parent-centered program for young deaf children, was one of the first programs to receive federal support. Research focusing on the development of the deaf child (Meadow, 1968; Schlesinger and Meadow, 1972), parent–child interactions (Meadow, Greenberg, Erting, & Carmichael, 1981), and later, family environments (Bodner-Johnson, 1986a) served to reinforce the importance of families in the education of young deaf children.

Families and children with disabilities were beneficiaries of a social and political commitment to equal opportunity and access to education in the late 1960s and early 1970s. Legislation passed in 1975, Public Law 94–142 of the Education of the Handicapped Act, provided funding to increase access to free and appropriate public education for all school-aged children with disabilities. A decade later, an amendment to this legislation (PL 99–457, Amendment to the Education of the Handicapped Act of 1986) extended this right to preschool children, and states received financial incentives to expand and establish services to infants, toddlers and their families. This legislation, amended again as Public Law 105-17, Individuals with Disabilities Education Act 1997, provides guidelines for the development and provision of early intervention and preschool programs for children with developmental delays or disabilities and their families.

Characteristics of Early Childhood Education for Deaf Children and Their Families

Over the last several decades, the field of early education for children with disabilities has reconceptualized its approach to service delivery to children and their families. Family-centered service delivery, a concept adopted from the health care profession that included families in the treatment of children with special health care needs in the 1960s (Shelton, Jeppson, & Johnson, 1987), has become a foundational characteristic of the philosophy and practice of early intervention. Other important characteristics of early intervention service delivery, such as culturally responsive and developmentally appropriate programming, define and support a family-centered approach and result in comprehensive and cohesive services for families and children. This reformulation of the field aligned with the service delivery philosophy espoused in federal legislation and came about as the result of new knowledge that emerged from data-based research as well as practice, new theoretical conceptualizations, and changes in basic social forces.

A paradigm shift in early childhood education occurred when it adopted the perspective that the family and individual behavior should be understood within an ecological (Bronfenbrenner, 1979) and family social system (Menuchin, 1974) theoretical framework. The focus of service delivery moved beyond the child to include addressing the family's goals and concerns, emphasizing the parents' role as collaborator and decision-maker with the early interventionist, and promoting the self-efficacy of the family, their individual strengths and resources, and those of their various communities. Collaborative, family-centered early education has corrected the teacher-as-expert model and utilizes family–professional partnerships to support and strengthen the parents' abilities to nurture and enhance their child's learning, development, and well-being. Further, services made available to families derive from an interdisciplinary, team-based approach so that audiologists, social workers, and deaf consultants, for example, coordinate with the early interventionist to develop individualized programs that support families and both directly and indirectly enhance the child's development.

A number of principles (Dunst, 1990; Shelton & Stepanek, 1994) and guidelines (Hallau, 2002; Bodner-Johnson & Sass-Lehrer, 1999; Bodner-Johnson, Sass-Lehrer, Hafer, & Howell, 1992) have been developed that offer a framework for developing and implementing early education programs for deaf children and their families. They are summarized below and presented as foundational characteristics of these programs.

Family Centered

The development of the young child can only be fully understood within a broad ecological context beginning with the family and extending outward to include the immediate environments with which the child interacts. The contextual framework sets the stage for developing programs and practices that establish the well-being of the family as a priority goal considered integral to planning for the child. A family-centered approach is sensitive to family complexity, responds to family priorities, and supports caregiving behavior that promotes the learning and development of the child (Shonkoff & Meisels, 2000).

Collaborative

Early intervention professionals who establish effective relationships with families, joining with them by demonstrating trust and understanding, can significantly enhance the family's ability to boost their child's development (Kelly & Barnard, 1999). The family–professional relationship is key to developing partnerships with families that facilitate shared decision-making and family participation at all levels of the program. Families should have full access to complete and unbiased information to make choices and have control over desired resources and outcomes that support self-efficacy and competency building. The relationship should develop in ways that are culturally appropriate and consistent with the family's desires.

Developmentally Appropriate Practice

Developmentally appropriate practice "is a framework, a philosophy, or an approach to working with young children" (Bredekamp & Rosegrant, 1992, p. 4). Program decisions are made on the basis of what we know about child development and also on the basis of family, community, and cultural values and priorities. Within developmentally appropriate practice, the child's unique learning and development patterns and the complexity of the family's circumstances are considered. Developmentally appropriate practice relies on the parents' knowledge about the child and family and on their decision-making role to determine what is appropriate for their individual child (Gestwicki, 1999). Professionals working with parents also need to consider what is known about working with adults (Klein & Gilkerson, 2000). Early intervention professionals benefit from an understanding of the principles of adult learning and an adult learner perspective in their work with parents and with other professionals (Bodner-Johnson, 2001).

Interdisciplinary

A comprehensive and cohesive early intervention program includes interdisciplinary child assessments, appropriate consultative services, and full implementation of an Individualized Family Service Plan (IFSP). The IFSP is a process through which families and professionals identify a child's strengths and needs, as well as the family's priorities, resources, and concerns, to develop a plan for services. The IFSP requires a commitment, for example, from professionals in the fields of medicine, social work, speech and audiology, mental health, and occupational and physical therapy, to work collaboratively toward common goals for the child and family. Any of these services can be made directly available to families, or families can benefit indirectly by professional consultation with the early interventionist (Stredler-Brown & Arehart, 2000). In addition, service providers should establish connections with community resources so that practitioners from a range of disciplines and deaf adults can share their knowledge and experience and be members of the team. The priorities of the individual family dictate the composition of each family's interdisciplinary team.

Assessment Based

The goal of early childhood assessment is to acquire information and understanding that will facilitate the child's development and learning within the family and community (Meisels & Atkins-Burnett, 2000). A number of principles of assessment in infancy and early childhood have been developed (Greenspan & Meisels, 1996). Primary among these principles when considering a family-centered, interdisciplinary model are the following:

- Assessment must be based on an integrated developmental model.
- Assessment involves multiple sources of information and multiple components.
- The child's relationship and interactions with his or her most trusted caregiver should form the cornerstone of an assessment.
- Assessment is a collaborative process.

Parents with deaf children have a vital role in collaborating with professionals by providing information regarding their child's development and learning about how family and cultural contexts influence their child's competencies. Parents and professionals can then work together to identify individual outcomes for the child and family based on the results of the assessment (Sass-Lehrer, in press).

Culturally Responsive

Families reflect a rich social, cultural, ethnic, and linguistic diversity in our society. An individual family's values and beliefs influence their perspectives regarding their child's abilities, their child-rearing practices, their relationships with profes-

sionals, and their involvement in the program; thus, it is important to understand and be responsive to cultural diversity (Christensen, 2000; Sass-Lehrer, in press; Steinberg, Davila, Collaza, Loew, & Fischgrund, 1997). Other differences in families, such as the hearing status of parents, their resources, and the parents' educational backgrounds, require that programs offer choices and flexibility in services so that parents can more fully participate (Meadow-Orlans & Sass-Lehrer, 1995).

Community Based

Within an ecological framework for developing family-centered early intervention, an important resource to the family's support system is the community in which they live. A family's community offers a personal social network as well as general community organizations and programs that can be used by families with young children as sources of support. For example, relatives and friends, church and civic groups, cultural/ethnic associations, childcare programs, colleges, and libraries are all potential resources to the family. Early intervention professionals can work with families with deaf children to identify and locate these and more specialized services, such as mental health agencies or respite care programs, that exist in their locale and that families indicate could provide support to them (Wolery, 2000).

Early Intervention Program Models

Programs for young children who are deaf or hard of hearing and their families incorporate the above characteristics and reflect legislative guidelines and professional recommendations (ASHA-CED, 1994; Commission on Education of the Deaf, 1988; Easterbrooks & Baker-Hawkins, 1994; Joint Committee on Infant Hearing, 2000; Sandall et al., 2000). Model programs have clearly defined philosophies that describe the theoretical perspectives on which they are based; also in these programs anticipated outcomes are articulated and the roles of children, families, and professionals are defined. Model programs may be replicated because the theoretical foundation is clear, and intervention approaches and guidelines for evaluating program effectiveness are provided. Linking the child's assessed abilities and needs and family's priorities and concerns with the intervention strategies and evaluations increases the likelihood that expected outcomes for both children and families are achieved. A systems approach to early education programming provides a framework for designing programs that links the program's philosophy, assessment protocols, goal setting, intervention, and evaluation (Bagnato, Neisworth, & Munson, 1997; Bricker, Pretti-Fronczak, & McComas, 1998).

The term "curriculum" is often used interchangeably with "program." Curriculum in its broadest sense encompasses all the experiences provided for a child and family (see Power & Leigh, this volume). The NAEYC and the National Association of Early Childhood Specialists in State Departments of Education (NAECS/SDE) describe curriculum as: "an organized framework that delineates the content that children are to learn, the processes through which children achieve curricular goals, what teachers do to help children achieve these goals, and the context in which teaching and learning occur" (NAEYC, 1991, p. 10).

Central curricular questions are, "What should the child learn?" "How should learning be facilitated?" (Spodek & Brown, 1993, cited in Bailey, 1997, p. 228). A family-centered perspective adds, What are the family's priorities and concerns for enhancing their child's development? The early intervention curriculum must address the uniqueness of each child and family and design programs and services that reflect developmental processes of learning within the context of the family and community.

Programs for deaf and hard-of-hearing children and families are similar to programs for children with and without special needs, but are unique in their emphasis on language and communication, the nature of the support and information for families, and the competencies of the professionals.

Language and Communication

For the majority of children with hearing loss, the acquisition of language and communication skills is the central focus of early intervention programming. Establishing effective communication between families and their young children has long been recognized as the key to early language acquisition, family functioning, and the overall development of the child with a hearing loss (Calde-

ron & Greenberg, 1997; Rosenbaum, 2000; Vaccari & Marschark, 1997).

The selection of the mode of communication that will provide the best access to early linguistic development and effective communication is an important decision. The most effective programs acknowledge the necessity of collaboration between parents and professionals and the importance of families making the ultimate decision (Moeller & Condon, 1994; Stredler-Brown, 1998). The communication modality chosen is influenced by child factors (e.g., hearing abilities), family variables (e.g., parent hearing status, previous experience with deafness), as well as information and guidance from professionals (Eleweke & Rodda, 2000; Kluwin & Gaustad, 1991; Spencer, 2000; Steinberg & Bain, 2001). Parents indicate that choice of communication approach is one of the most stressful decisions they make, and they value comprehensive, unbiased information and respect for their views (Meadow-Orlans et al., 2003).

Holistic and Comprehensive Programs

Young children with hearing loss may be short changed by programs that focus solely on the development of language and communication skills. At least one in three children in early education programs has one or more developmental concerns in addition to hearing loss (Gallaudet Research Institute, 2001; Holden-Pitt & Diaz, 1998; Meadow-Orlans, Mertens, Sass-Lehrer, & Scott-Olson, 1997). These children are not well-served by a narrow curriculum focus (Jones & Jones, in press). Curricula developed for young children with hearing loss and their families as well as curriculum resources designed for young children with and without special needs provide a comprehensive and holistic approach. Interdisciplinary models of service provision that include families and professionals with expertise in related disciplines recognize the complex developmental needs of young children with hearing loss. Early childhood best practice guidelines realize the impact of learning in one domain on development in all areas and support an integrated approach that emphasizes multiple domains (i.e., communication and language, cognitive, social-emotional, motor, and adaptive or functional skills) (Bredekamp & Copple, 1997; Sandall et al., 2000). An integrated approach strengthens development in all domains and encourages children to make meaningful connections among all areas of development.

Family Programming

With the expansion of newborn hearing screening, families are entering programs earlier than ever before. Their opportunity to learn about the implications of hearing loss and other developmental issues, how to communicate with their babies, meet other families, and find social and emotional support happens while their children are still very young. Sign language instruction is offered by the majority of early education programs (Meadow-Orlans et al., 1997); however, most programs do not provide information about Deaf culture (Stredler-Brown & Arehart, 2000). Although the majority of programs provide information on a variety of topics (e.g., deafness, amplification, and development), fewer offer counseling services or provide opportunities for families to participate in support groups (Meadow-Orlans et al., 1997; Stredler-Brown & Arehart, 2000). The goal of services is to reflect family priorities and concerns, but services are often influenced by the professionals' skills and the resources available (Meadow-Orlans et al., in press).

Qualifications of Providers

The quality of early education services hinges on the educational background and experience of the professionals providing services. One survey of programs for deaf and hard-of-hearing children reported that providers have a variety of educational backgrounds (Stredler-Brown & Arehart, 2000) with the majority employing providers with backgrounds in speech-language pathology and early childhood special education. Less than half of these providers have academic backgrounds in deaf education. Backgrounds in the above areas are likely to provide some but not all of the expertise essential for working with this population (Stredler-Brown, 1998). Professionals should have knowledge in early childhood education, deaf education, and special education. The ability to provide family-centered services and family support is essential, as are skills to work collaboratively with other professionals and community agencies. Professionals should have an understanding of Deaf culture, the ability to tap resources in various communities, and

skills to collaborate with deaf adults. Professionals need specialized preparation in language acquisition and communication and must be able to explain and use the communication approaches used by deaf and hard-of-hearing people. Also important are knowledge of amplification and other assistive technologies and the ability to monitor their effectiveness on the child's language development (Bodner-Johnson, 1994; ASHA-CED, 1994; JCIH, 2000; Easterbrooks & Baker-Hawkins, 1994; Sass-Lehrer, in press).

Models of Service Delivery

A national survey in 1990 of services for deaf children and families indicated a shift in services from individual child sessions in school to parent–child sessions in the home (Craig, 1992). Still, service delivery models vary according to the target of intervention (parent, child, others), the setting (home, school, community, other), the process of intervention (identification of children eligible for services, assessment, IFSP), the services provided (speech language, physical therapy, other), the frequency of intervention, and philosophical orientation (behaviorist, developmental, ecological) (Calderon & Greenberg, 1997; Harbin, McWilliam, & Gallagher, 2000).

Direct services that support families and build competence and confidence to facilitate children's development are believed to be more effective than child-directed instruction that does not include families (Carney & Moeller, 1998; Yoshinaga-Itano, 2000b). Family-focused services may be offered in the home, school/agency, community center, hospital, and clinic. Professionals seek to develop collaborative relationships with parents/caregivers and, as partners, develop a plan for providing support, information, and skill development to support their child's development. By working directly with parents/caregivers, professionals can better understand the broader community and cultural context of the child and can, together with families, determine how individual family routines and familiar settings can promote the child's development (Bricker et al., 1998).

Child-focused services are an important component of early education for toddlers and preschoolers and provide support for learning and development in the child's environment. Professionals, parents, and other caregivers purposely design stimulating and developmentally appropriate environments and activities in the home, the center, or other settings that encourage young children to play, interact with others, and explore. Playgroups with deaf, hard-of-hearing, and hearing siblings and peers provide a context for the young child to develop communication and social skills. Deaf and hard-of-hearing adults are effective language and cultural models for children and families; also they enhance communication as well as social development (Hintermair, 2000; Mohay, 2000; Watkins, Pittman, & Walden, 1998). Adaptation of the environment (e.g., acoustic and visual) and child-directed strategies to encourage interaction are essential to maximize the child's engagement.

Interdisciplinary and Interagency Collaboration

Harbin et al. (2000) suggest that program models also may be described by organizational structure to the extent that they coordinate and integrate their services with other programs and community resources. Early intervention is provided by special schools and programs for deaf children, programs for hearing children, community-based programs for children with and without disabilities, and public or private agencies and clinics. Referral to early intervention for deaf children is frequently managed by state service coordinators who are responsible for the implementation of services and coordination with other agencies (Stredler-Brown & Arehart, 2000). Service coordination, including assessment, IFSP development, and program monitoring, is often a collaborative endeavor including specialists from the early intervention program and professionals in other programs or agencies. Collaboration with community-based agencies may provide more comprehensive services and enhance the family's connections with their community and facilitate access to community-based resources (e.g., financial, respite, child care, mental health (Harbin et al., 2000).

Ensuring access to community-based services and programs is one of several goals of IDEA. The legislation encourages families and professionals to consider the child's "natural environment" when identifying the services to be provided. According to IDEA "to the maximum extent appropriate, [early intervention services] are provided in natural environments, including the home, and community settings in which children without disabilities participate" (section 632[4][G]). This provision of the law has been erroneously interpreted as a prohibition against center-based services for young deaf and hard-of-hearing children only and their families. In fact, services may be provided in schools for deaf children or other settings for deaf children only, however, a justification must be provided in the IFSP (section 636[d][5]). Consideration of special language and communication needs and opportunities for direct communication with peers and adults in the child's language and communication modality are typically provided as justification for center-based services.

Comprehensive Program Models

Four comprehensive early intervention programs that incorporate the curricular practices discussed above are described in tables 5-1–5-4. These programs embrace a family-centered philosophy and provide support to children and families through interdisciplinary and community-based collaborations. One program is affiliated with a school for deaf children, one with a statewide Department of Public Health, one with a college of education in a state university, and another with a national research hospital. Each program works directly with families whose children are deaf, hard of hearing, or have co-occurring disabilities. All programs are considered model in that they have clearly articulated philosophies and developmental perspectives; they use a collaborative process for identifying child and family outcomes, and services to families and children reflect the program philosophical and theoretical orientation.

Colorado Home Intervention Program

The Colorado Home Intervention Program (CHIP) is a statewide early intervention program for deaf and hard-of-hearing children and their families (table 5-1). In collaboration with the research staff at the University of Colorado, child and family assessment data have been collected and analyzed for more than 12 years. Assessments include inventories of child development, assessment of play, phonological development, and an assessment of communicative intention. The assessment protocol,

Table 5-1. Colorado Home Intervention Program

Description	Communication/language philosophy	Services to families/children	Interdisciplinary interagency collaboration	Service providers
• State-wide • Birth to 3 years • Deaf/hard-of-hearing children and families • One third ethnic minority • 40% disabilities • Family-centered • Interdisciplinary	• Focus on parent–child communication and language development • Communication mode based on input from parents, professionals, and assessment data • Individual communication plan developed	• Weekly home-based services (information to families, emotional support, parent–child communication) • Family centered multidisciplinary naturalistic assessment • In-home sign language instruction from deaf/hard-of-hearing adults	• Community-based coordination of services • Consultative services to providers and families from psychology, social work, occupational therapy, physical therapy, speech, vision	• Early intervention providers/facilitators, deaf/hard-of-hearing role models, sign language instructors, parent consultants, consumer advisors, regional care coordinators, program administrator • M.A. audiology, deaf education, speech-language pathologists, early childhood educators • Minimum standards and competencies set • On-going professional development and technical assistance • Part-time, contracted

F.A.M.I.L.Y. (Stredler-Brown & Yoshinaga-Itano, 1994), uses a transdisciplinary play-based approach (Linder, 1993) and requires observations of children at play in a variety of contexts. Statewide norms for the population of deaf and hard-of-hearing children have been generated from these data and are used to monitor each child's progress. The data are also used to generate goals and support communication decisions.

Colorado was one of the original states to establish universal newborn hearing screening and boasts a 2 to 3-month average age of identification, with 84% of those identified beginning early intervention within 2 months (Mehl & Thompson, 2002). Children and families who received services from CHIP by the time the child was 6 months of age demonstrated better outcomes than those who entered later (Yoshinaga-Itano, Sedey, Coulter, & Mehl, 1998). The CHIP children were more likely to demonstrate (1) language development within the normal range in the first 5 years of life; (2) significantly better vocabulary development; (3) sig-

nificantly better speech intelligibility; (4) significantly better social and emotional development; and (5) their families were more likely to experience faster resolution of grief (Apuzzo & Yoshinaga-Itano, 1995; Yoshinaga-Itano & Apuzzo, 1998; Yoshinaga-Itano et al., 1998).

Boys Town National Medical Research Hospital

The Parent–Infant Program at Boys Town National Medical Research Hospital in Omaha, Nebraska, provides early intervention for deaf and hard-of-hearing children from birth to 3 years (table 5-2). A cornerstone of the program is the Diagnostic Early Intervention Program (DEIP), a multidisciplinary, family-centered program that provides support for families with children with recently identified hearing losses and supports them by identifying their child's needs and family priorities and exploring options for services (Moeller & Condon, 1994). As in Colorado, child assessment and

Table 5-2. Boys Town National Research Hospital (BTNRH)

Description	Communication/language philosophy	Services to families/children	Interdisciplinary interagency collaboration	Service providers
• Birth to 3 years • Deaf/hard of hearing with/ without disabilities • Hearing children with deaf parents may be involved • Family-centered • Transdisciplinary • Center based for preschool ages, 3–5 years	• Emphasizes supporting families' exploration of communication options to determine best fit • Supports decision-making authority of families and collaborative problem solving and discovery (Moeller & Condon, 1994)	• Home visits (weekly or dependent on IFSP) • Play groups for babies and moms (weekly, 2 hours) • Parent support group (weekly) • Shared reading with deaf tutors (available) • Toddler group (twice weekly) • Preschool class (5 days/week)	• Interagency collaboration with BTNRH, 8 local education agencies and Omaha Hearing School • Service coordinators and school district special education professionals • BTNRH departments of audiology, counseling, genetics, medicine, psychology, speech pathology, cochlear implant team	• Deaf educator, speech-language pathologist, audiologist, licensed counselor • Graduate degrees and postgraduate training in related areas • All specialists housed at BTNRH and provide services on contract from local school districts • Preschool housed in local public school and staffed by deaf, hard-of-hearing, and hearing staff of BTNRH and public schools

family participation data have been collected for many years to examine child developmental outcomes including language. Moeller (2000) reported on a retrospective study of children with bilateral sensorineural hearing loss who had completed the DEIP program. Moeller examined the relationship between age of enrollment in the program and child language outcomes. Children in the study were from English-speaking homes with a hearing parent(s), and had no evidence of a co-occurring disability. Children's hearing losses were identified between the second day of life and 54 months of age with a mean of 18 months.

Assessment data included age of identification and program entry, measures of hearing, infant developmental performance or measures of nonverbal intelligence, and measures of vocabulary and verbal reasoning skills at 5 years of age. In addition to child outcomes, ratings of family involvement were obtained using a family rating scale completed by early interventionists who had worked with the family between 2 and 4 years. The family involvement ratings considered family adjustment to child's hearing loss, participation in parent–infant sessions, attendance at sessions, initiative in pursuing information, advocacy efforts on behalf of their child and family, communication skills and

effectiveness of communication with child, application of techniques to expand language, and supportive extended family members.

The findings of this study confirmed that age of enrollment in the Boys Town Parent–Infant program was significantly related to language outcomes at 5 years of age. Vocabulary and verbal reasoning skills of children enrolled by 11 months of age were significantly better than those enrolled after this time. Earlier enrolled children achieved language scores comparable (however, in the low average range) with their hearing peers by age 5 regardless of degree of hearing loss. Of equal importance was the finding that high levels of family involvement positively affected child outcomes. Limited family involvement, in contrast, was associated with language delays that were exacerbated by later enrollment in early intervention. Moeller (2001) proposed that early intervention makes a positive difference in the lives of the majority of children and should focus on enhancing communicative interactions.

Yoshinaga-Itano (2000b) and Moeller (2001) attribute the findings of these studies about child outcome, in part, to the quality of the early intervention programs. Both programs emphasize a family-centered approach that establishes partnerships with parents. Both focus on parents and caregivers and provide limited or no direct intervention or demonstration therapy with infants and toddlers. CHIP and Boys Town include strong counseling and family support components, individualize approaches to working with children and families, and describe professional interactions with families as nonjudgmental (Yoshinaga-Itano, 2000b).

SKI*HI Institute

SKI*HI provides training and technical assistance throughout the United States and around the world for early intervention programming for children who are deaf or hard of hearing, have sensory impairments, or are deaf-blind, and their families (table 5-3). The goals of the SKI*HI model are to identify children with hearing loss as early as possible, provide family-centered, home-based programming, and ensure families obtain additional services as needed. SKI*HI has collected outcome data since 1979 with findings indicating children enrolled in SKI*HI programs outperform those not enrolled in early intervention (Strong, Clark, Johnson, Watkins, Barringer, & Walden, 1994). A later study examining data from 1970 to 1991 demonstrated significantly greater rates of language development for those children enrolled than would be expected from maturation alone during the same time period (Strong et al., 1994).

More recently, SKI*HI has established deaf-mentor services to young children and their families (Watkins et al., 1998). Deaf mentors have regular visits with families and focus on American Sign Language (ASL) instruction for the family, interactions using ASL with the child, and understanding and appreciation of Deaf culture and introduction to the Deaf community. An investigation of the efficacy of the Deaf Mentor Experimental Project involved 18 children in each of 2 groups; 1 group received services from a specially trained deaf mentor; the other group did not (Watkins et al., 1998). Every family in the study participated in the SKI*HI program with weekly home visits from a SKI*HI trained parent advisor. The investigators were interested in the impact of the deaf mentor on child communication and language, on communication between children and family members, and on parent perceptions and attitudes concerning deafness. Results indicated that children whose families par-

ticipated in the Deaf Mentor Project demonstrated higher rates of language growth, had vocabularies twice as large, and scored higher on measures of communication, language, and English syntax than those who did not participate. Parents in the Deaf Mentor Project reported more comfort using both ASL and signed English than parents who did not participate in the project and were reported to have accurate perceptions about Deaf culture. The researchers concluded that early intervention programs should consider including deaf mentors in their program services.

Laurent Clerc National Deaf Education Center, Kendall Demonstration Elementary School Parent–Infant Program

The Parent–Infant Program (PIP) at Kendall Demonstration Elementary School is located on the campus of Gallaudet University in Washington, DC. PIP is a family-centered, research-based program that reflects the individual needs of families and children (table 5-4). Parent–professional relationships and partnerships are paramount to the success of this program; together parents and professionals assess child and family needs, make choices regarding program services, set goals for the child and family, facilitate achievement of goals, and document progress (Nussbaum & Cushner, 2000). PIP offers center- and home-based services as well as collaboration and consultation with programs and service providers in the community. The center-based program offers family–child playgroups for children who are deaf or hard of hearing, siblings, and extended family members two mornings each week and parent information and support sessions twice each month. In addition to the parent–infant specialist, other professionals include a teacher assistant, audiologist, communication specialist, sign and other language interpreters, physical and occupational therapists, nurse, counselor, and psychologist. The support staff provides consultation to families within the playgroup sessions as well as individually as appropriate. Deaf professionals are prominent members of the professional team, serving a variety of roles.

PIP has four primary goals: (1) to provide a nurturing environment for children and families, (2) to provide an interactive learning environment, (3) to provide access to professionals and other parents/caregivers; and (4) to develop families' com-

Table 5-3. SKI*HI Institute

Description	Communication/language philosophy	Services to families/children	Interdisciplinary interagency collaboration	Service providers
• Birth to 5 years • Deaf/hard of hearing • With/without additional disabilities • Family-centered	• Emphasis on early communication, visual and auditory • Information shared on all communication methods (ASL, auditory/oral, cued speech, signing English)	• Weekly home-based services • Child assessment • Family interviews • Individualized family service plan/Individualized Education Plan • Sign language instruction from deaf mentors • Transition services	• Consultation to families for audiology, child development, counseling, medical, psychology, physical therapy, etc. • Community based	• Parent advisors • Deaf mentors • Part-time contracted • Training for new providers and mentors • Community-based providers

Table 5-4. Parent Infant Program Laurent Clerc National Deaf Education Center

Description	Communication/language philosophy	Services to families/children	Interdisciplinary interagency collaboration	Service providers
• Birth to 2.5 years • Deaf/hard of hearing • Ethnically and linguistically diverse • Family-centered • Interdisciplinary	• Emphasis on parent–child communication and child language development • Bilingual ASL–English focus • Information provided on communication methods and assistive technology choices	• Twice weekly center-based parent-child play groups • Bimonthly center-based parent groups • Home visits as needed • Evening and weekend sign language classes for families and friends • Individual family service plan development • In-home early literacy program with deaf adults	• Center-based integrated interdisciplinary consultation (ASL, audiology, counseling, occupational therapy, physical therapy, psychology, social work, speech) • Community-based collaboration (child care, health care, social support services) • Center-based child-care integrated hearing/deaf	• Parent infant specialist (early childhood/deaf educator) • Deaf ASL specialists • Audiologists, counselors, family therapists, occupational therapists, physical therapists, psychologists, social workers, spoken language specialists, • M.A. plus minimum standards set by profession

petence and confidence. Although research outcomes are limited for this program model, annual parent evaluations provide information about the program's efficacy. Families describe the one-on-one time with experienced professionals as a strength of the program. According to parents, the professionals are good listeners who understand their family and challenge them to think from different perspectives. Families feel a sense of community through their participation in PIP, receive information on a variety of topics, feel supported, and have access to extensive resources.

Reported comments from families from the end-of-year evaluations were overwhelmingly positive. "My hearing children and my family love it . . . it's good for us to know that there are other children like [our child]" "[Our child] gets to see the other children and that helps . . . It creates a nice bond for all of the kids." "I really like it . . . I really like the coming together of all the specialists. I feel like we are part of a family." (Cushner, 2000).

Research in Early Intervention

Research in early intervention has provided the field with an important knowledge base that contributes both to the establishment of foundational principles that guide programming and to the development of practices that daily influence the work of professionals with children and families. Despite methodological challenges (Guralnick, 1997) and complications related to the low incidence of hearing loss and heterogeneity in the population of deaf children, as well as other factors (Calderon & Greenberg, 1997), evidence is accumulating that is leading to more effective early intervention outcomes.

Much of this recent research has been described above and is detailed in Sass-Lehrer (in press). Evidence suggests that the child's best chances for achieving proficiency in communication, language, and literacy are related to early identification of hearing loss and enrollment in a comprehensive early education program by 6 months of age (Apuzzo & Yoshinaga-Itano, 1995; Arehart & Yoshinaga-Itano, 1999; Moeller, 2000; Yoshinaga-Itano et al., 1998). Family involvement, described, for example, as participation in parent–infant sessions and the effectiveness of parental communication, is essential to the child's early development and is associated with language gains (Calderon, 2000; Moeller, 2000). Early interventionists, other parents, and deaf adults are important sources of social support that can strengthen the family's sense of well-being (Hintermair, 2000; Meadow-Orlans et al., 1997; Meadow-Orlans, Smith-Gray, & Dyssegaard, 1995). The availability of increased social support has beneficial effects on the stress parents feel in their parental role (Meadow-Orlans, 1994; Pipp-Siegel, Sedey, & Yoshinaga-Itano, 2002) and on mother–child interactions (Meadow-Orlans & Steinberg, 1993). Children benefit developmentally when families feel competent and confident in their abilities to nurture and support their child's development (Carney & Moeller, 1998; Kelly & Barnard, 1999; MacTurk, Meadow-Orlans, Koester, & Spencer, 1993). Research indicates that maternal communication skills are an important predictor of child language acquisition, early reading, social-emotional development (Calderon, 2000; Moeller, 2000), and enhanced parent–child relationships (Greenberg, Calderon & Kusche, 1984; Jamieson, 1995; Spencer, Bodner-Johnson, & Gutfreund, 1992). Despite years of debate, research has not found evidence to support the superiority of one modality of communication (manual versus oral) over another with very young children (Calderon & Greenberg, 1997; Calderon & Naidu, 2000; Carney & Moeller, 1998; Yoshinaga-Itano, 2000a; Yoshinaga-Itano & Sedey, 2000). Programs that support strong professional–family partnerships and active family involvement witness effective parent–child communication and child developmental achievements comparable to hearing children with similar developmental profiles (Moeller, 2000; Yoshinaga-Itano, 2000a).

Research in early intervention has moved beyond the question of whether early intervention is effective and feasible (e.g., Meadow-Orlans, 1987) and is now aiming to understand better what works best, for whom, under what conditions, and to what outcome (Guralnick, 1997). Calderon and Greenberg (1997) recommend that future research with deaf children and their families should address the complex individual, family, program, and societal factors that will yield a greater understanding of effective early intervention. Only then will we understand how individual child and family characteristics, environmental conditions, professional interactions, and program components interact to achieve successful outcomes for children with hearing loss. Also, the importance of addressing research questions within the context of contemporary social and cultural conditions (e.g., single-parent homes, increasing diversity of the population in the United States) is raised by Meadow-Orlans (2001) and seems especially pertinent for research in the field of early intervention.

Summary and Conclusions

This is an encouraging time for the field of early childhood education for deaf children and families. Since the 1970s, social, political, and legislative commitments, along with current theoretical formulations and research on development and learning, have come together to support program development and study in early intervention for children with disabilities and those at risk. For children who are deaf or hard of hearing, newborn hearing-screening programs have led to identification at earlier ages. Families who are referred to comprehensive early education programs with knowledgeable professionals and who develop accessible communication with their deaf children can expect their children to achieve linguistic and social skills commensurate with their hearing peers.

A number of research-based principles and policies for early intervention program development have emerged that reflect legislative guidelines and professional recommendations. These serve as program characteristics, variously define programs today, and are considered optimal program features that programs work toward. For example, comprehensive early intervention programs embrace a family-centered and developmental perspective and provide support to children and families through interdisciplinary and community-based collaboration. Further, professionals develop partnerships with parents, implement culturally responsive practices that reflect the family's values and strengths, and recognize parents as primary decision-makers. Programs that incorporate these characteristics are considered model in that they take the initiative to build on the most current knowledge in early intervention.

Earlier enrollment and longer stays in early intervention provide increased opportunities for families to gain greater understanding about their child's needs and future. The challenge to the education system is to provide services to younger and younger children that will support the realization of their potential and sustain the benefits of early intervention. The education system is further challenged to ensure that professionals are highly qualified, skilled communicators who are knowledgeable and sensitive to the importance of enhancing families' strengths and supporting their priorities.

References

Apuzzo, M.L., & Yoshinaga-Itano, C. (1995). Early identification of infants with significant hearing loss and the Minnesota Child Development Inventory. *Seminars in Hearing*, 16, 124–139.

Arehart, K., & Yoshinaga-Itano, C. (1999). The role of educators of the deaf in the early identification of hearing loss. *American Annals of the Deaf*, 144, 19–23.

ASHA-CED Joint Committee (1994). Service provision under the individuals with disabilities education act-Part H, as amended (IDEA-Part H) to children who are deaf and hard of hearing ages birth through 36 months. *ASHA*, 36, 117–121.

Bagnato, S., Neisworth, J., & Munson, S. (1997). *LINKing assessment and early intervention: An authentic curriculum-based approach*. Baltimore, MD: Paul H. Brookes.

Bailey, D. (1997). Evaluating the effectiveness of curriculum alternatives for infants and preschoolers at high risk. In M.J. Guralnick (Ed.), *The effectiveness of early intervention* (pp. 227–247). Baltimore, MD: Paul H. Brookes.

Bodner-Johnson, B. (2001). Parents as adult learners in family-centered early education. *American Annals of the Deaf*, 146, 263–269.

Bodner-Johnson, B. (1986a). The family environment and achievement of deaf students: A discriminant analysis. *Exceptional Children*, 52, 443–449.

Bodner-Johnson, B. (1986b). The family in perspective. In D. M. Luterman (Ed.), *Deafness in perspective* (pp. 225–239). San Diego, CA: College-Hill Press.

Bodner-Johnson, B. (1994). Preparation of early intervention personnel. In J. Roush & N. Matkin (Eds.), *Infants and toddlers with hearing loss: Family centered assessment and intervention*. Baltimore, MD: York Press.

Bodner-Johnson, B., & Sass-Lehrer, M.(1999). Concepts and premises in family-school relationships. In *Sharing Ideas*. Washington, DC: Pre-College National Mission Programs, Gallaudet University.

Bodner-Johnson, B., Sass-Lehrer, M., Hater, J., &

Howell, R. (1992). *Family centered early intervention for deaf children: Guidelines for best practice.* Unpublished manuscript.

Bowe, F. (2000). *Birth to five: Early childhood special education* (2nd ed.). Albany, NY: Delmar Publishers.

Bredekamp, S., & Copple, C. (Eds.). (1997). *Developmentally appropriate practice in early childhood programs* (revised ed.) Washington, DC: National Association for the Education of Young Children.

Bredekamp, S., & Rosegrant, T. (Eds.). (1992). *Reaching potentials: Appropriate curriculum and assessment for young children* (vol. 1). Washington, DC: National Association for the Education of Young Children.

Bricker, D., Pretti-Fronczak, K., & McComas, N. (1998). *An activity-based approach to early intervention.* Baltimore, MD: Paul H. Brookes.

Bronfenbrenner, U. (1979). *The ecology of human development: Experiments by nature and design.* Cambridge, MA: Harvard University Press.

Bruder, M.B. (1997). The effectiveness of specific educational/developmental curricula for children with established disabilities. In M.J. Guralnick (Ed.), *The effectiveness of early intervention* (pp. 523–548). Baltimore, MD: Paul H., Brookes.

Calderon, R. (2000). Parent involvement in deaf children's education programs as a predictor of child's language, early reading, and social-emotional development. *Journal of Deaf Studies and Deaf Education, 5,* 140–155.

Calderon, R., & Greenberg, M. (1997). The effectiveness of early intervention for deaf children and children with hearing loss. In M.J. Guralnick (Ed.), *The effectiveness of early intervention* (pp. 455–482). Baltimore, MD: Paul H. Brookes.

Calderon, R., & Naidu, S. (2000). Further support for the benefits of early identification and intervention for children with hearing loss. In C. Yoshinanga-Itano & A. Sedey (Eds.), *Language, speech, and social-emotional development of children who are deaf or hard of hearing: The early years. Volta Review, 100*(5), 53–84.

Carney, E.A., & Moeller, M.P. (1998). Treatment efficacy: Hearing loss in children *Journal of Speech, Language and Hearing Research, 41,* 561–584.

Christensen, K. (2000). *Deaf plus: A multicultural perspective.* San Diego, CA: Dawn Sign Press.

Commission on Education of the Deaf (1988). *Toward equality: Education of the deaf.* Washington, DC: U.S. Government Printing Office.

Craig, H. (1992). Parent-infant education in schools for deaf children: Before and after PL 99-457. *American Annals of the Deaf, 137,* 69–78.

Dunst, C. (1990). *Family support principles: Checklists for program builders and practitioners (Family Systems Intervention Monograph,* Vol. 2, no. 5). Morganton, NC: Family, Infant and Preschool Program, Western Carolina Center.

Easterbrooks, S., & Baker-Hawkins, S. (Eds.) (1994). *Deaf and hard of hearing students: Educational service guidelines.* Alexandria, VA: National Association of State Directors of Special Education.

Eleweke, C. J., & Rodda, M. (2000). Factors contributing to parents' selection of a communication mode to use with their deaf children. *American Annals of the Deaf, 145,* 375–383.

Fox, L, Hanline, M.F., Vail, C.O., & Galant, K.R. (1994). Developmentally appropriate practice: Applications for young children with disabilities. *Journal of Early Intervention, 18*(3), 243–253.

Gallaudet Research Institute. (2001). Regional and National Summary Report of Data from 1999–2000 Annual Survey of Deaf and Hard of Hearing Children and Youth. Washington, DC: GRI, Gallaudet University.

Gestwicki, C. (1999). *Developmentally appropriate practice: Curriculum and development in early education* (2nd ed.) Albany, NY: Delmar Publishers.

Greenberg, M.T., Calderon, R., & Kusche, C. (1984). Early intervention using simultaneous communication with deaf infants: The effect on communication development. *Child Development, 55,* 607–616.

Greenspan, S.I., & Meisels, S. J. (1996). Toward a new vision for the developmental assessment of infants and young children. In S.J. Meisels & E. Fenichel (Eds.), *New visions for the developmental assessment of infants and young children* (pp. 11–26). Washington, DC: ZERO TO THREE.

Guralnick, M.J. (1997). Second-generation research in the field of early intervention. In M.J. Guralnick (Ed.), *The effectiveness of early intervention* (pp. 3–20). Baltimore, MD: Paul H. Brookes.

Hallau, M. (2002). Creating partnerships with families. *Odyssey: New Directions in Education, 3*(1), 5–12.

Harbin, G., McWilliam, R.A., & Gallagher, J.J. (2000). Services for young children with disabilities and their families. In J.P. Shonkoff & S. J. Meisels (Eds.), *Handbook of early childhood intervention,* (pp. 387–415). Cambridge: Cambridge University Press.

Holden-Pitt, L. & Diaz, J.A. (1998). Thirty years of the Annual Survey of Deaf and Hard of Hearing Children and Youth: A glance over the decades. *American Annals of the Deaf, 143,* 72–76.

Individuals with Disabilities Education Act of 1997. Pub. Law 105-17.

Jamieson, J. (1995). Interactions between mothers and

children who are deaf. *Journal of Early Intervention, 19*, 108–117.

Hintermair, M. (2000). Hearing impairment, social networks, and coping: The need for families with hearing-impaired children to relate to other parents and to hearing-impaired adults. *American Annals of the Deaf, 145*, 41–51.

John Tracy Clinic. (nd). Accessed April, 2002 at http://www.jtc.org.

Joint Committee on Infant Hearing. Year 2000 Position Statement: Principles and Guidelines for Early Hearing Detection and Intervention Programs. *American Journal of Audiology, 9*, 9–29.

Jones, T., & Jones, J.K. (in press). Challenges in educating young deaf children with multiple disabilities. In B. Bodner-Johnson & M. Sass-Lehrer (Eds.), *Early education for deaf and hard of hearing Infants, Toddlers and Their Families: Integrating Best Practices and Future Perspectives*. Baltimore, MD: Paul H. Brookes.

Kelly, J., & Barnard, K. (1999). Parent education within a relationship-focused model. *Topics in early childhood special education, 19*(9), 151–157.

Klein, N.K., & Gilkerson, L. (2000). Personnel preparation for early childhood intervention programs. In J. P. Shonkoff & S.J. Meisels (Eds.), *Handbook of early childhood intervention* (pp. 454–483). New York: Cambridge University Press.

Kluwin, T. N., & Gaustad, M. G. (1991). Predicting family communication choices. *American Annals of the Deaf, 136*, 28–34.

Linder, T. (1993). *Transdisciplinary Play-Based Assessment: A functional approach to working with young children* (revised ed.). Baltimore, MD: Paul H. Brookes.

MacTurk, R.H., Meadow-Orlans, K. P., Koester, L.S., & Spencer, P. E. (1993). Social support, motivation, language, and interaction: A longitudinal study of mothers and deaf infants. *American Annals of the Deaf, 138*, 19–25.

Meadow, K. (1968). Early manual communication in relation to the deaf child's intellectual, social, and communicative functioning. *American Annals of the Deaf 113*, 29–41.

Meadow, K., Greenberg, M., Erting, C. & Carmichael, H. (1981). Interactions of deaf mothers and deaf preschool children: Comparisons with three other groups of deaf and hearing dyads. *American Annals of the Deaf, 126*, 454–468.

Meadow-Orlans, K. (1987). An analysis of the effectiveness of early intervention programs for hearing-impaired children. In M.J. Guralnick & F.C. Bennett (Eds.), *The effectiveness of early intervention for at-risk and handicapped children* (pp. 325–362). New York: Academic Press.

Meadow-Orlans, K. (1994). Stress, support and deafness: Perceptions of infants' mothers and fathers. *Journal of Early Intervention, 18*, 91–102.

Meadow-Orlans, K. (2001). Research and deaf education: Moving ahead while glancing back. *Journal of Deaf Studies and Deaf Education, 6*, 143–148.

Meadow-Orlans, K. P., Mertens, D. M., & Sass-Lehrer, M. A. (2003). *Parents and their deaf children: The early years*. Washington, DC: Gallaudet University Press.

Meadow-Orlans, K. Mertens, D., & Sass-Lehrer, M., & Scott-Olson, K. (1997). Support services for parents and their children who are deaf and hard of hearing: A national survey. *American Annals of the Deaf, 142*(4), 278–293.

Meadow-Orlans, K., Smith-Gray, S., & Dyssegaard, B. (1995). Infants who are deaf or hard of hearing, with and without physical/cognitive disabilities. *American Annals of the Deaf, 140*, 279–286.

Mehl, A.L. & Thomson, V. (2002). The Colorado newborn hearing screening project: 1992–1999: On the threshold of effective population-based universal newborn hearing screening. *Pediatrics, 109*(1), e7.

Meisels, S. J., & Atkins-Burnett, S. (2000). The elements of early childhood assessment. In J. P. Shonkoff & S. J. Meisels (Eds.), *Handbook of early childhood intervention* (pp. 231–257). New York: Cambridge University Press.

Menuchin, S. (1974). *Families and family therapy*. Cambridge, MA: Harvard University Press.

Moeller, M.P. (2000). Early intervention and language development in children who are deaf and hard of hearing. *Pediatrics, 106*(3): E43.

Moeller, M.P. (2001). Intervention and outcomes for young children who are deaf and hard of hearing and their families. In E. Kutzer-White & D. Luterman (Eds.), *Early childhood deafness* (pp. 109–138). Baltimore, MD: York Press.

Moeller, M.P. & Condon, M. (1994). D.E.I.P. A collaborative problem-solving approach to early intervention. In J. Roush & N. Matkin (Eds.), *Infants and toddlers with hearing loss: Family-centered assessment and intervention* (pp. 163–192). Baltimore, MD: York Press.

Mohay, H. (2000). Language in sight: Mothers' strategies for making language visually accessible to deaf children. In P. Spencer, C. Erting, & M. Marschark (Eds.), *The deaf child in the family and at school* (pp. 151–161). Mahwah, NJ: Lawrence Erlbaum Associates.

Moores, D.F. (2001). *Educating the deaf: Psychology, principles, and practices* (5th ed.). Boston: Houghton Mifflin.

National Association for the Education of Young Children and National Association of Early Childhood Specialists in State Departments of Education (1991). Guidelines for appropriate curriculum content and assessment in programs serving children ages 3 through 8. *Young Children, 46*(3), 135–146.

Nussbaum, D, & Cushner, D. (2000, July). *Teaming for early intervention programming.* Paper presented at the American Society for Deaf Children, Washington, DC.

Pipp-Siegel, S., Sedey, A., & Yoshinaga-Itano, C. (2002). Predictors of parental stress in mothers of young children with hearing loss. *Journal of Deaf Studies and Deaf Education, 7*, 1–17.

Rosenbaum, J. (2000). Family functioning and child behavior: Impacts of communication in hearing families with a deaf child. Washington, DC: Gallaudet University.

Sandall, S., McLean, M., & Smith, B., (2000). *DEC Recommended Practices in Early Intervention/Early Childhood Special Education.* Longmont, CO: Sopris West.

Sass-Lehrer, M. (2003). Programs and services for deaf and hard of hearing children and their families. In B. Bodner-Johnson & M. Sass-Lehrer (Eds.), *The Young Deaf or Hard of Hearing Child: A Family-Centered Approach to Early Education* (pp. 153–185). Baltimore, MD: Paul H. Brookes.

Schlesinger, H.S., & Meadow, K.P. (1972). *Sound and sign: Childhood deafness and mental health.* Berkeley: University of California Press.

Shelton, T. L., Jeppson, E. S., & Johnson, B. (1987). *Family-centered care for children with special health care needs.* Washington, DC: Association for the Care of Children's Health.

Shelton, T. L., & Stepanek, J. S. (1994). *Family-centered care for children needing specialized health and developmental services* (2nd ed.). Bethesda, MD: Association for the Care of Children's Health.

Shonkoff, J. P., & Meisels, S. J. (2000). Preface. In J. P. Shonkoff & S. J. Meisels (Eds.), *Handbook of Early Childhood Intervention* (pp. xvii–xviii). New York: Cambridge University Press.

Spencer, P. E. (2000). Every opportunity: A case study of hearing parents and their deaf child. In P. Spencer, C. Erting, & M. Marschark (Eds.), *The deaf child at home and at school* (pp. 111–132). Mahwah, NJ: Lawrence Erlbaum Associates.

Spencer, P., Bodner-Johnson, B., & Gutfreund, M. (1992). Interacting with infants with a hearing loss: What can we learn from mothers who are deaf? *Journal of Early Intervention, 16*, 64–78.

Steinberg, A., & Bain, L. (2001). Parental decision making for infants with hearing impairment. *International Pediatrics, 6*, 1–6.

Steinberg, A., Davila, J., Collazo, J., Loew, R., Fischgrund, J. (1997). A little sign and a lot of love . . . Attitudes, perceptions, and beliefs of Hispanic families with deaf children. *Qualitative Health Research 7*, (2), 202–222.

Stredler-Brown, A. (1998). Early intervention for infants and toddlers who are deaf and hard of hearing: New perspectives. *Journal of Educational Audiology, 6*, 45–49.

Stredler-Brown, A., & Arehart, K. (2000). Universal newborn hearing screening: Impact on early intervention services. In C. Yoshinaga & A. Sedey (Eds.), *Language, speech, and social-emotional development of children who are deaf or hard of hearing: The early years* [Monograph]. *Volta Review, 100*(5), 85–117.

Stredler-Brown, A., & Yoshinaga-Itano, C. (1994). F.A.M.I.L.Y. assessment: A multidisciplinary evaluation tool. In J. Roush & N. Matkin (Eds.), *Infants and toddlers with hearing loss: Family Centered Assessment and Intervention* (pp. 133–161). Baltimore, MD: York Press.

Strong, C., Clark, T., Johnson, D., Watkins, S., Barringer, D., Walden, B. (1994). SKI*HI Home-based programming for children who are deaf or hard of hearing: Recent research findings. *Infant-Toddler Intervention, 4*(1), 25–36.

Vacarri, C. & Marschark, M. (1997). Communication between parents and deaf children: Implications for social-emotional development. *Journal of Child Psychiatry, 18*(7), 793–801.

Watkins, S., Pittman, P., & Walden, B. (1998). The deaf mentor experimental project for young children who are deaf and their families. *American Annals of the Deaf, 143*(1), 29–34.

Wolery, M. (2000). Behavioral and educational approaches to early intervention. In J. P. Shonkoff & S. J. Meisels (Eds.), *Handbook of early childhood intervention* (pp. 179–203). New York: Cambridge University Press.

Yoshinaga-Itano, C. (2000a, July). *Optimal outcomes: Facts, myths, mysteries.* Paper presented at National Symposium of Hearing in Infants, Denver, CO.

Yoshinaga-Itano, C. (2000b). Successful outcomes for deaf and hard of hearing children. *Seminars in Hearing, 21*, 309–325.

Yoshinaga-Itano, C., & Apuzzo, M. (1998). Identification of hearing loss after age 18 months is not early enough. *American Annals of the Deaf*, 143(5), 380–387.

Yoshinaga-Itano, C., & Sedey, A. (Eds.), (2000). Language, speech, and social-emotional development of children who are deaf or hard of hearing: The early years [Monograph]. *Volta Review*, 100(5).

Yoshinaga-Itano, C., Sedey, A.L., Coulter, D.K., & Mehl, A.L. (1998). The language of early-and later-identified children with hearing loss. *Pediatrics*, 102, 1161–1171.

6

Harry Knoors & Mathijs P. J. Vervloed

Educational Programming for Deaf Children with Multiple Disabilities

Accommodating Special Needs

Among deaf children, there are many who have special needs.[1] Of particular interest in this chapter are children with a severe to profound hearing loss in combination with another disability. Such children generally need services beyond those provided for a child that is only deaf. Additional disabilities may include mental retardation, autism, visual impairment, specific learning disorders (e.g., dyslexia), attention deficit disorders, emotional or behavioral problems, or physical disabilities (see, e.g., Holden-Pitt & Diaz, 1998; Karchmer, 1985; McCracken, 1998). A major problem in describing the group of deaf children with special needs is the frequent use of generic definitions. These definitions "fail to explore the complex relationships that may exist between different conditions" (McCracken, 1998, p. 29). It is these complex relations that make these children special.

Definition and Etiology

One may wonder whether deaf children with special needs are inevitably multiply disabled. "Multiply disabled" does not mean the simple existence of multiple disabilities, but instead denotes a combination of two or more disabilities with an onset early in life for which, given help, education or intervention developed and suitable for children with one disability is not applicable. That is, in multiply disabled persons, the separate disabilities and the possible compensations for each disability influence one another (Gunther & de Jong, 1988; Nakken, 1993). It is the reduction in possibilities for compensation, whether spontaneously or after intervention, that makes a child multiply disabled. In this respect, deafblind, deaf, mentally retarded children, and deaf children with autism or physical disabilities are truly multiply-disabled children. For these children, a unique situation evolves from the combined presence of two or more disabilities with great repercussions for communication, education, mobility, living skills, and learning.

A completely different situation is the case for teaching deaf children with learning disabilities or attention deficit disorders (Samar, Parasnis, & Berent, 1998). Although teaching these children most certainly will require adaptations, the intervention strategy is basically the same as is the case with a deaf child. In this chapter we focus specifically on multiply disabled deaf children. We only briefly touch on the educational accommodations for deaf children with learning problems or attention deficits.

Multiple disabilities, including hearing disorders, are often consequences of the same conditions that may cause deafness (Das, 1996). These conditions may be divided into four categories, depending on the onset of the disability. Under the heading of "prenatal onset" we may categorize genetic syndromes, intrauterine infections (e.g., rubella and cytomegalovirus), and maternal illness. In 1985 these causes accounted for 40% of all cases of deafness in the United States. "Perinatal onset" includes birth trauma, anoxia/asphyxia, kernicterus, and prematurity and accounted in 1985 for 20% of all cases of deafness in the United States. Trauma, infections, and tumors may be categorized as causes with a "postnatal onset" resulting in acquired deafness or deafblindness, accounting for 10% of all cases. Finally, "idiopathic or unknown causes" accounted for 30% of all cases of deafness. In each case, these etiologies may result in either hearing loss alone or in hearing loss combined with a variety of disabilities.

Even when deafness is hereditary, it may have syndromic (e.g., the syndromes of Usher's, Pendred, and Waardenburg) or nonsyndromic causes. It is estimated that 70% of hereditary deafness is nonsyndromic. In the 1995 publication of Gorlin and colleagues, more than 450 syndromes are described with hearing impairment as one of the main features (see also Arnos & Pandya, this volume). Some, but not all, of these hereditary causes of deafness associate with multiple disabilities. Examples are hereditary syndromes that lead to deafblindness such as Usher's syndrome and Zellweger syndrome.

Deafblindness

By far the best documented group of multiply disabled deaf children is the group of deafblind children. The term deafblind came into use after 1990 instead of "deaf/blind" or "deaf-blind." The reason for using a single word is that it suggests a unique impairment, in which deafblindness is more than just deafness plus blindness (Aitken, 2000; McInnes, 1999; Van Dijk & Janssen, 1993). However, the label deaf-blind is still quite common, as well as the labels multi- or dual-sensory disabled.

McInnes (1999) gives several definitions of deafblindness, all essentially the same with respect to the following points. First, all definitions state that deafblind people have impaired vision and hearing, but are not necessary totally blind or completely deaf. Any degree and combination of hearing and vision impairment is called deafblindness. Theoretically speaking, there is no absolute threshold level for hearing or vision under which a person is labeled deafblind, in contrast to the thresholds in use for people who are solely visually or auditorally impaired (see also Aitken, 2000; McInnes & Treffry, 1982; Munroe, 2001). (For legislative purposes, definitional thresholds sometimes are established.) It is the deprivation of their distance senses that is the common feature of the group labeled as deafblind (McInnes & Treffry, 1982). Second, the two sensory impairments multiply and intensify the impact of each other, creating a severe disability, which is unique. Finally, because deafblindness is defined as not having sufficient vision to compensate for the loss of hearing and not having sufficient hearing to compensate for the loss of vision, deafblind people typically require services that are different from those designed exclusively for either blind or deaf people (McInnes, 1999).

In clinical practice, the definition of deafblindness occasionally is extended to all those who might benefit from being taught as a deafblind child. Thus, sometimes children with an impairment to only one distance sense as well as additional (often multiple) impairments may be classified as deafblind (Aitken, 2000). This includes, for instance, children with congenital visual impairment plus additional disabilities and congenital hearing impairment plus additional disabilities.

Hearing and vision are the two major distance senses; these senses provide most of the information that is beyond what we can reach out and touch (Aitken, 2000). The combined absence of these two distance senses causes almost all deafblind people to experience problems with access to communication and information and with mobility (Aitken, 2000; McInnes, 1999; Van Dijk & Janssen, 1993). However, their specific needs vary enormously according to age, onset, and type of deafblindness. Onset of deafness and blindness may differ, which is of major importance for teaching, education, and individual support needs.

Munroe (2001) and Aitken (2001) classify deafblind people in four broad categories. The first comprises persons with congenital or early-onset deafblindness. They have minimal or no vision or hearing at birth or lost their hearing or vision before the age of 2. This condition is mostly caused by prenatal insults (e.g., maternal virus), prematurity, chromosomal abnormalities, or postnatal influences up to the age of 2. Studies (Admiraal, 2000; Munroe, 2001) indicate that the number of children in this group has increased since about 1980, due to higher survival rates of children born prematurely. According to Admiraal (2000), in reality the frequency of severe prematurity, leading to multiple disorders, including deafness, may be even higher, because of the under-diagnosis or the late diagnosis of deafness in this group, at least in the Netherlands. These premature children mostly receive medical care from pediatricians, and many of these children are not enrolled in hearing screening programs. If a lack of response to sound is discovered, this is often attributed to mental retardation instead of to a possible hearing impairment.

The second category of deafblindness includes people with congenital or early onset hearing impairment and acquired vision loss. These children become deaf or hard of hearing before the age of 3 and lose their vision at a later time. Causes of this type include Usher's syndrome type 1 and infections such as meningitis. (See Arnos and Pandya, this volume, for more information about Usher's syndrome.)

The third category includes people with late-onset hearing and visual impairment. Children with this type of deafblindness acquire both vision and hearing loss, often separately, after the age of 3. Causes include several genetically inherited conditions (e.g., Usher's syndrome types 2 and 3), head trauma, metabolic conditions (e.g., diabetes), and in adults, stroke and aging.

Finally, the fourth category of deafblindness entails congenital or early-onset blindness with acquired hearing loss. This is a less common form of deafblindness than the other three categories. Causes include genetically inherited disorders (e.g., Alstrom syndrome and Norrie disease), birth trauma, and early postnatal infections.

Deafness, Mental Retardation, and Learning Disabilities

According to the American Association on Mental Retardation, mental retardation is a disability characterized by significant limitations in both intellectual functioning and conceptual, social, and practical adaptive skills. The onset of this disability is before adulthood (Luckasson, 1992). One of the key elements in this definition is the concept of intellectual functioning, usually measured by a test of intelligence. The application of these tests with deaf children is an issue with pitfalls.

The assessment of the learning potential of deaf children may lead to misdiagnoses or over-identification of learning disabilities or mental retardation (Marschark, 1993; Morgan & Vernon, 1994) because delays in spoken language and reading proficiency are often interpreted as resulting from mental retardation instead of from a profound hearing loss, especially if the assessment is carried out by clinicians without experience in deafness. Deaf children's inability to obtain sufficient non-distorted information from the environment is often confused with the inability to process it (McInnes, 1999). It therefore is important not to use regular norms for the general population with deaf and hard-of-hearing children and to use adequate test instructions (Braden, 1994; Morgan & Vernon, 1994; see also Maller, this volume). Deaf children should only be diagnosed as cognitively disabled when there is a significant retardation based on the norms for children with a severe to profound hearing loss. Unlike hearing children, deaf children's receptive and expressive spoken language competence often does not exceed their reading level very much. Therefore, written test instructions must be presented at the reading proficiency level of the child being tested. Alternatively, testing by means of sign language or, if appropriate, augmentative communication should be considered (Morgan & Vernon, 1994; Roth, 1991).

It is not always easy to differentiate between mental retardation and learning disability in deaf children. A major problem is the fact that the concept of learning disability is not straightforward (Bunch & Melnyk, 1989; Mauk & Mauk, 1998; Samar et al., 1998). Often it is described in exclusionary language. As a consequence, learning disability is often defined as a condition that does not arise from mental retardation, hearing disorders, emotional problems, or cultural or socioeconomic disadvantage. However, Laughton (1989) has redefined the concept of learning disability in a way that includes the possibility of children with hearing disorders having concomitant learning disabilities. Laughton states that these children have significant difficulty with the acquisition, integration, and use of language or nonlinguistic abilities.

As far as etiology is concerned, Admiraal and Huygen (1999), conducting a study of longitudinal patterns in the etiology of mental retardation in deaf people, found that in 30% of all cases of combined deafness and mental retardation the cause was unknown. This percentage is similar to the one for unknown etiologies of hearing loss in the general, not the multiply handicapped, deaf population. However, the proportion of hereditary deafness for children with mental retardation was half of that reported for the general deaf population, with acquired causes much more prevalent in the population of deaf, mentally retarded people. The most frequent etiologies among deaf and mentally retarded persons older than 20 years of age were congenital infections (rubella, cytomegalovirus), severe prematurity, kernicterus, and meningitis. In younger people, rubella and kernicterus were less prevalent because of the start of rubella vaccination programs and the fact that kernicterus has almost disappeared in the Western world. Severe prematurity was the main cause of deafness and associated handicaps in deaf mentally retarded children and youngsters.

As for possible causes of learning disorders in deaf children, Laughton assumed as the main causal condition a dysfunctioning of the central nervous system. Samar et al. (1998) state that "prenatal development misorganization can interact with abnormal experience or environmental trauma after birth to set up a recursive cascade of brain-environment interactions that leads to abnormal cognitive system development" (p. 207). In their view, learning disability and attention deficit disorders may result from different developmental disorganizations or environmental trauma, thus differing in presentation. This makes diagnosis difficult.

The claims of Laughton (1998) and Samar et al. (1998) receive some support from a study by Zwiercki, Stansberry, Porter, and Hayes (1976). They evaluated 88 deaf and hard-of-hearing students from one school for the deaf in the United States (total population 286 students), who were referred for neurological examination. Referrals took place over a 5-year period. Thirty-five out of the 88 students had obvious organic signs of neurological dysfunction, primarily manifested in sensory or motor problems. Another 21 students were diagnosed as having minimal brain dysfunction. EEG data of 83 students showed abnormal sharp wave activity in 44 cases. These students generally did not exhibit any classical signs of epilepsy, but the authors felt that the learning and behavior characteristics of these students resembled those of epileptic children so much that in many cases preferred treatment was use of antiepileptic medication. Diffuse and focal slow-wave disorders were seen in 35 cases. These patterns support, according to the authors, a diagnosis of cerebral injury or dysfunction.

Deafness and Autism

Autism is a behaviorally defined syndrome with core characteristics such as inadequacies in the development and maintenance of social relationships, problems with the development of communication and language, stereotyped behavior, and problems with adaptation to environmental changes (Rutter, 1978). The pathogenesis of heterogeneous etiologies, however, may result in single outcomes such as autisticlike behaviors. In the case of autism and hearing impairment with or without additional disabilities, the autisticlike features might only be a single outcome superficially. That is, quantitatively, autism and deafness show overlapping characteristics such as delays in language acquisition, peculiarities in word use and (sometimes, or under certain conditions) social difficulties in peer relations.

Qualitatively, there are sometimes large but mostly subtle differences in cause, pathogenesis, manifestation, and persistence of these behaviors. Therefore, a classification of autism in deaf and hard-of-hearing children, especially in those with additional visual impairments and/or mental retardation, should only be made by professionals familiar with deaf and hard-of-hearing, visually impaired, mentally retarded, and autistic children, or misdiagnosis is likely. Jure, Rapin, and Tuchman (1991) suggested that because of overlapping characteristics, there may be an underdiagnosis of autism in deaf and hard-of-hearing children and of hearing impairment in autistic children.

Prevalence of Multiple Disabilities

In discussing the prevalence of multiple disabilities among deaf individuals, one can take two approaches. The first approach is to establish how many people with hearing disorders, more specifically deaf people, also show characteristics of other disabilities, such as vision disorders, mental disa-bilities, motor disabilities, learning disabilities, or autism. In the second approach, one establishes what the prevalence of hearing disorders is among types of disabilities like mental retardation or au-tism. In this section, we consider both perspectives, not only to highlight the incidence of multiple dis-abilities among those typically classified as deaf, but also to show the frequency of underdiagnoses of severe hearing disorders one often sees among many disabled people.

Data of Holden-Pitt and Diaz (1998) show that an estimated 20–40% of all deaf and hard-of-hearing children have accompanying disabilities. For the 1996–1997 school year, the Center for As-sessment and Demographic Studies of the Gallau-det Research Institute reported 50,629 deaf and hard-of-hearing children in special educational programs across the United States. This number represents approximately 60% of all deaf and hard-of-hearing children receiving special education in the country. Valid responses about additional dis-abilities were obtained for 47,760 children. Of these children, 34% were reported having one or more educationally significant disabilities in addi-tion to deafness. The main problems mentioned were blindness or an uncorrected visual problem (4%); mental retardation (8%); emotional/behav-ioral problems (4%); and learning problems (9%) (Holden-Pitt & Diaz, 1998).

The prevalence of deafblindness can only be estimated because official Census data were not available. Most prevalence rates are based on counts of deafblind people who receive help from service providers or schools. Based on a national volunteer registry of persons with deafblindness in Canada, Munroe (2001) estimates the deafblind-ness ratio in Canada to be 10–15/100,000, or a population of 3,100–4,650 persons. Munroe (2001) also cites widely differing figures from Nor-wegian and English registries. In Norway the most recent numbers indicate there are 302 persons with deafblindness, 203 with acquired deafblindness and 71 with congenital deafblindness. Prevalence for Norway is estimated to be 6.9/100,000 persons. In the United Kingdom the national deafblind or-ganization SENSE has estimated there are 23,000 deafblind or dual-sensory impaired people, yield-ing an incidence rate of 40/100,000. For the United States there is the National Census for Deaf-Blind Children and Youth, ages 0–21. The Teaching Re-search Division, Western Oregon University (Mon-mouth) maintains this census for the Federal Office of Special Education Programs. The census is pro-duced annually, and information for December 1, 1999 indicated 10,198 persons aged 0–21 were on this registry (NTAC, 2001). Given the major prob-lem of identifying deaf children with additional dis-abilities and handicapped children with hearing impairment, due to the fact that conventional as-sessment techniques often fail with these popula-tions, and the fact that registration is mostly vol-untary, the reported prevalence rates can only be a conservative estimate of the true prevalence rates.

Jure et al. (1991) studied the prevalence of au-tism among deaf and hard-of-hearing children. In a sample of 1150 children, 46 (4%) met the criteria for autism. Further analysis of the charts of these 46 deaf or hard-of-hearing and autistic children re-vealed that 37 of them had a severe or profound hearing loss as opposed to a milder loss. With re-spect to cognitive functioning, data were available for 45 children who were both deaf and had autism: only 8 of the children had normal or near-normal intelligence. Seventeen children also showed signs of hyperactivity.

Mauk and Mauk (1998) reported tremendously differing estimates of the prevalence of learning dis-abilities among deaf and hard-of-hearing children of 3–60%. These estimates are based on both clin-ical judgments and surveys among educators. As stated before, overdiagnosis clearly is a problem, among other factors due to a lack of clearness in the conceptualization and problems in identifica-tion. Misdiagnosis of learning disability as a mani-festation of mental retardation is another serious error. On the basis of an analysis of four population studies in the United States regarding the incidence of learning difficulties in deaf children, Bunch and Melnyk (1989) concluded that since the early 1970s, approximately 6–7% of all hearing-impaired students had been reported as having concomitant learning problems that might be con-strued as learning disabilities. We now turn to the prevalence of hearing loss in two groups of handi-capped children: children with autism and children with mental retardation.

One of the features associated with autism is an inadequate modulation of sensory (including au-ditory) input. This raises the question of whether inadequate modulation of sensory input is caused by dysfunction of central auditory transmission or by peripheral hearing loss. Klin (1993) reviewed 11 studies of autistic children and youngsters, involving auditory brainstem measurements. Klin found no clear evidence for brainstem dysfunction in autism; however, the studies reviewed by Klin did provide indications for the manifestation of peripheral hearing loss in autistic people. Research into the prevalence of this hearing loss showed that the incidence in this group varies widely, depending on the inclusion criteria, the number of children taken into account, and the type and amount of hearing loss measured. Percentages of prevalence ranged from 13–44% (Klin, 1993). Rosenhall, Nordin, Sandström, Ahlsén, and Gillberg (1999) established a percentage of mild and moderate hearing loss (definitions by the authors) of 7.9% among a group of 199 autistic children and adolescents in Sweden. Pronounced (40–70 dB loss) or profound hearing loss (>70 dB) was found among 3.5% of the population studied. This is substantially higher than among children in the general population, where one finds profound hearing loss in no more than 0.1 or 0.2% of all children (Marschark, 1993).

Virtually all studies on hearing loss among mentally retarded children and adults have focused on people with Down syndrome. One of the major causes of this hearing loss is otitis media, which occurs relatively frequently in this group. Conditions that can cause hearing loss, such as otologic abnormalities (e.g., relatively small external ear canal and shortened cochlear spirals), have been reported (Widen, Folsom, Thompson, & Wilson, 1987), as has sensorineural hearing loss due to premature aging (McCracken, 1998). Evenhuis, Van Zanten, Brocaar, and Roerdinkholder (1992) studied the prevalence of hearing loss among a group of 44 institutionalized subjects with Down Syndrome, aged 35 years or older, in the Netherlands. Twenty subjects had what the authors call a handicapping hearing loss—that is, a bilateral hearing loss of 40 dB or more. Evenhuis (1995) found that 4.3% of a group of aging mentally retarded people had congenital or early and severe bilateral hearing loss.

Educational Accommodations

In general, specific approaches with respect to accommodations for educational programming tend to focus on deafblind children. Much less information, let alone empirical research into effects, is available with respect to deaf, mentally retarded children, deaf, autistic children, or deaf children with learning disabilities. Professionals agree that for all groups of multiply-handicapped deaf children, educational programming cannot start without proper assessment (Chen & Haney, 1995; Roth, 1991; Van Dijk & Nelson, 2001).

Assessment

Proper assessment is a precondition for treatment and educational programming because multiply disabled deaf children vary enormously with respect to individual limitations, competencies, and potentials. Assessment should be carried out by people fluent in the ways of communication preferred by the children such as sign language or forms of augmentative communication (Roth, 1991).

Because communication is the basis for education, the primary aim of assessment should be to study ways to access communication for a multiply disabled deaf child. Further, assessment should provide information about the likelihood of the child acquiring language, learning daily living skills, and possibly acquiring academic skills as a consequence of improved communication.

Unfortunately, formal psychoeducational testing of deaf and multiply disabled deaf children often presents considerable challenges. Reliable and valid assessments with respect to vision, hearing, cognition, and overall development are problematic (see, e.g., Chen, 1999; Jones, 1988; McCracken, 1998; Mauk & Mauk, 1998; Rönnberg & Borg, 2001; Roth, 1991; Van Dijk & Janssen, 1993), and there is a tremendous lack of adequate tests and normative data in these areas. Systematic observational assessment of the strength and weaknesses of children in the domains of perception, behavior, language, and motor skills is thus very important to educational planning. At present, however, it appears that the only observational instruments especially designed to assess the development of deafblind children are the Callier Azusa scales (Geenens, 1999; Stillman & Battle, 1986). Even with the help of assessment instruments, much still depends on the expertise of assessors, especially with their ability to integrate the results of the different assessments. Nevertheless, this should not be seen as an excuse to refrain from assessment. Given the numerous difficulties se-verely multiply handicapped children face, a mul-tidisciplinary holistic assessment and intervention approach is required (Chen, 1999; Eyre, 2000; Van Dijk & Janssen, 1993).

Providing Access to Communication

Speech is often beyond the grasp of multiply dis-abled deaf children. Even if their hearing loss is mild, perception and comprehension of speech can be difficult. Especially when children have addi-tional problems in the cognitive domain, their po-tential to compensate for the loss of information by speechreading or residual hearing through the use of context information is often limited. In most cases, establishing access to communication first means selection of a proper communication device based on assessment data about perception, cog-nitive processes (e.g., memory, attention), and mo-tor skills. One may then select a means of com-munication that ultimately proves to be useful to the child. Sign language may be appropriate as a communication tool if visual perception and motor production are relatively intact and if the child or adult functions cognitively near normal. If deaf children or adults are mentally retarded, commu-nication through sign language may be too difficult (Kahn, 1996). It is therefore essential to determine whether the grammatical structure of a sign lan-guage will be transparent enough for a child to comprehend and acquire it, even if at a slower pace. If sign language grammar proves to be too difficult, a set of selected signs (i.e., high-relevance vocabu-lary) may be more appropriate.

Apparently, the only available research con-cerning training deaf people with mental retarda-tion in understanding and producing sign lan-guage is a study by Walker (1977). That study involved 14 hard-of-hearing and deaf, mentally re-tarded adults, in a systematic training of a set of 110 signs for 9 months; a large gain in compre-hension ability was observed. Although it is not clear from that report whether British Sign Lan-guage or Sign Supported English was used, expres-sion through signs increased, and comprehension increased even more. More than half of the group members learned 90% of all the signs taught. It is important to note, however, that no signs were learned spontaneously.

Research by Jure et al. (1991) showed that learning sign language is promising for deaf chil-dren with autism, but is, according to the authors, certainly not a solution for all deaf children with autism. None of the children studied was judged to be a fluent signer, and a considerable proportion of the children did not sign at all. Unfortunately, Jure et al. gave no information about the intensity of the training, the language input during the day, and whether a created sign system or a natural sign lan-guage was used. Therefore, it might be that more intensive input of sign language during daily com-munication and in training sessions could lead to better results. The authors pointed out that not all children with autism may be able to produce signs adequately because of the interference of pragmatic deficits with the communicative use of signs. Some-times, the behavior of deaf, autistic children may be so disruptive that access to communication can only be established after the implementation of a behavior modification program (Brimer & Murphy, 1988).

Research on congenitally deafblind or severely mentally retarded children shows that the use of signs might be too demanding in the early stages of communication. Children may need the use of more permanent symbols such as objects (real size or miniaturized) or graphic symbols or natural ges-tures representing actions with objects (Stillman & Battle, 1986; Van Dijk, 1986). Even if ultimately some signs may be used by deafblind children, the fact that dual sensory impairments may involve profound visual impairments means that access to communication should be established by tactile means. Tactile Sign Language may be necessary (Miles, 1999, Reed, Delhorne, Durlach & Fisher, 1995).

If a multiply disabled deaf child has severe dif-ficulties with motor skills, sign language still may be good as input for communication and language acquisition, but augmentative devices, such as those based on pointing to pictographs or sign drawings, might be more useful (Aiken-Forderer, 1988). In all cases, if communication is adapted and the specific means of communication are se-lected, it is important to make sure that the people in the environment are able to use the selected means of communication. Training people in the environment and coaching them in the use of sign language or augmentative communication during important communicative activities during the day is as essential as training the children.

Providing Access to Language

Providing children access to communication does not necessarily lead to the acquisition of language. First, acquisition of language is dependent on the structure of the input. If the input consists of a set of signs without grammar, of course no acquisition of language would be expected, unless the child goes beyond the input given. In some cases, even deaf, mentally retarded persons restructure the input according to processing demands, as shown by Van Dijk, Van Helvoort, Aan den Toorn, and Bos (1998). Second, the communicative patterns in the environment should allow for language acquisition. This means that the child should gain insight into the reciprocal nature of communication. Turn-taking behaviors, for example, have to be developed, so the child should be allowed time to perceive and comprehend utterances by adults. This means that adults in the environment have to remain patient when a child tries, often with great effort, to produce a communicative message. In other words, the pace of communication should be slowed down so that the child can properly perceive, comprehend, and produce the sign. This is not easy, especially when deaf children are severely cognitively impaired or if they show a large asymmetry between their perception and production capabilities (e.g., if they have severe physical disability).

In general, even if multiply disabled deaf children have the potential to acquire language, the ultimate proficiency levels are often low compared to the ones attained by deaf children (Grove, Dockrell, & Woll, 1996). Sometimes, it is necessary to fulfill certain preconditions before children gain access to communication and language at all. This is especially the case with multiply disabled deaf children who have behavior disorders. In extreme cases, it is necessary to regulate behavior before communication can take place. Sometimes communication itself can lead to a decrease of disruptive behavior patterns, because these patterns (e.g., self-mutilation, acting-out behavior) are thought to serve as communicative signals when others are not available (Durand, 1990). However, reduction of disruptive behavior patterns sometimes can only be achieved by means of medication or by intensive psychotherapy or intensive behavior modification programming (Brimer & Murphy, 1988; Glenn, 1988).

Curricula for Congenitally Deafblind Children

A unique feature in educational programming for congenitally deafblind children is that teaching and learning has, above all, to take place by touch. It is because of the combined impairments in hearing and vision that deafblind children face problems in profiting from modeling, imitation, and incidental learning. They often experience difficulties in anticipating coming events, lack curiosity, have difficulty in setting up an emotional bond, and run a serious risk for learned helplessness whenever an individualized development/education plan is not developed (McInnes, 1999). Without proper intervention, congenitally deafblind individuals may spend much of their time in self-stimulation (Nafstad & Rødbroe, 1999). Moreover, they may be passive and rarely take the initiative to make contact with other people, to show exploratory play, or to share their feelings, thoughts, and experiences with others. Because of these serious risks, careful and deliberate educational programming is essential for deafblind children.

Professionals working with deafblind children first attempted to copy the teaching strategies so successfully used with adventitiously deafblind children such as Helen Keller (Enerstvedt, 1996). These strategies, however, did not always work with congenitally deafblind children. Although deafblind children did learn signs, they were rarely used communicatively—that is, to share feelings, thoughts, and experiences (Rødbroe & Souriau, 1999). From 1970 on, interest in the role of attachment in development gave new impetus to research on communication in congenitally deafblind children. Establishing emotional bonds with significant people, mostly the parents, was considered to be crucial for the origination of initiatives to explore the world, because access to the significant person was obtainable (Nafstad, 1989). Emotional bonding and attachment are still seen as important aspects in the education of deafblind children, as outlined in the approaches of McInnes and Treffrey (1982), Van Dijk 1986; Van Dijk & Janssen, 1993), and the early intervention strategies of Chen (Chen, 1999; Chen & Haney, 1995).

Van Dijk was among the first to design an educational approach for deafblind children. This approach is not solely directed at improving communication but takes into consideration all aspects of the development of deafblind children. Van Dijk's work, also known as the "conversational method" or "movement-based approach" is probably one of the best-known programs in the field of deafblind education. It has been described extensively by Writer (1987), Enerstvedt (1996), and by Van Dijk (Van Dijk, 1983, 1986; Van Dijk & Janssen, 1993). MacFarland (1995) and Wheeler and Griffin (1997) give concise descriptions of Van Dijk's teaching strategies. Most of his approach is based on his work with children handicapped as a result of rubella (see, e.g., Van Dijk, 1983, 1986), but it is also applicable to other congenitally deafblind children.

Van Dijk's work can best be characterized as an educational approach based on theories of sensory deprivation, psychology (i.e., attachment and social learning theory) and communication. The curriculum should not be carried out in isolation but should be used to establish the structure of the child's daily activities (Writer, 1987). In Van Dijk's approach, the need is stressed for initiating activities in natural contexts during times when they would normally take place. The approach is movement-based and distinguishes four levels of communication. The first one is the resonance level, in which the deafblind child's reactions to stimuli are seen as reflexive and preconscious. The second level, co-active movement, extends the resonance level because the child is more consciously aware of the turn-taking aspect of communication. Turn-taking is introduced by making movements together with as much physical help as needed to expand the (mostly limited) movement repertoire of the child: co-active movement. An extension of the co-active movement level is the level of imitation, the third level. The child is now able to follow the actions of the teacher without physical support and to imitate these actions. A first step toward symbolic communication is the fourth level, the one of referencing, whether it is by pointing, using objects cues (i.e., objects used in an activity or associated with a person) or objects of reference (i.e., three-dimensional objects referring to actions, objects, or people). When a child is able to understand that people can participate in each other's actions and thoughts by means of a symbolic system, a system for symbolic communication has to be chosen: speech, fingerspelling, or tactile sign language.

Setting up routines is one of the key aspects of Van Dijk's educational curriculum. Deprived of sensory input, a deafblind child has great difficulty in organizing and structuring events in daily life. By building daily routines, activities become predictable with respect to time, places, and persons. Knowing what is going to happen, with whom they are going to happen, and where they are going to happen are important prerequisites for the feeling of security to emerge, which in turn is important for the deafblind child's social-emotional development. Well-known tools introduced by Van Dijk to aide the establishment of routines include daily and weekly calendars and calendar boxes, association books to assist recognition and memory of important life events, and activity planners to simplify and decode complex tasks.

Although books on the development and educational programming for the deafblind were published before (see, e.g., Freeman, 1975; Walsh & Holzberg, 1981), McInnes and Treffrey (1982) were probably the first authors to publish a comprehensive book on the development, teaching, and education of deafblind children. Their work builds on that of Van Dijk, but extends it by including a comprehensive curriculum, based on a sound theoretical and methodological framework.

McInnes and Treffry (1982) noted that deafblind children often appeared to be either hypoactive or hyperactive as a result of sensory deprivation. For both groups of deafblind children, the goal of their program, during the first 3 years, is to make contact and to establish an emotional bond with the child. In order for that bond to be an enduring emotional one, it will need to involve frequent reciprocal interaction around activities that are challenging to the child. The second stage in their program is to create, in addition to strengthening the emotional bond, a need to use residual vision or hearing, integrate sensory input, and a need to communicate with the teacher. Further, in this stage one should provide experiences that help the child establish a positive self-image. General activities, which make up the child's day, are suited to developing these needs and to solve problems.

According to McInness and Treffry (1982), the child first has to integrate sensory input and use information to solve problems before one is able to implement a formal developmental or educational program in stage three. In this stage the teacher can begin a total program approach with regard to cognition, social, emotional, motor, and perceptual development, as well as life skills and orientation and mobility.

McInness and Treffry emphasize that the program should be activity based and implemented in a reactive environment—that is, an environment that stimulates the child to interact, to solve problems, and to communicate, and at the same time attempts to provide every effort of the child with success. According to McInness and Treffry, most deafblind children will spend considerable time in this third stage of programming. As they progress in the various program areas, elements of traditional academic and vocational programs of nonhandicapped peers can be introduced in the fourth stage. The program then becomes more formal, made up in large part by reading, writing, and mathematics.

With regard to learning, McInnes and Treffry (1982) discerned three stages in each of the four program stages described above. First the teacher and child work co-actively; that is, they work as one person together. Second, they work cooperatively, with the teacher providing the child with sufficient support to ensure success. Finally, in the reactive stage the child completes the task independently. With respect to the interaction, McInnes and Treffry anticipated that, until the child is confident enough, eight specific stages will occur in each new interaction with the environment. First, the child might resist the interaction, and then the child will tolerate the interaction in the second stage before he or she passively cooperates with the teacher in stage three. From this stage on, realistic goals for intervention can be constructed. In the fourth stage the child will enjoy the interaction because of the teacher. In the fifth stage the child will work cooperatively with the teacher. The child will follow the lead of the teacher with little direction or need for encouragement. In the sixth stage the child will lead the teacher through the activity once the initial communication has been given. In stage seven the child is able to imitate the action of the teacher upon request. Last, in stage eight the child is able to initiate the action independently.

Accommodations for Other Subgroups

There is little published information concerning educational accommodations for deaf, mentally retarded and deaf, autistic children. In general, apart from the use of touch, many of the same principles

of curricula for deafblind children seem to be used. But, the individualized programs developed for such children do not appear to have been well documented.

Compared to multiply disabled deaf children, deaf children with learning disabilities need fewer major accommodations. On the one hand, strict classroom management is advocated in order to have the attention of these children focused on educational content and to prevent undesirable behavior. Creating a sense of community and responsibility is a key element, as is discipline (Stewart & Kluwin, 2001). On the other hand, several authors stress the importance of individual, sometimes revised, instruction and support. It may be necessary to adapt the curricular content. Much emphasis should be put on experiential learning. Reduction of cognitive demands (memory) may be accomplished by means of visualization, structuring (advance organizers), and the use of specific examples. Test instructions may be modified. Also, support for the home environment is an important element (Samar et al., 1998; Stewart & Kluwin, 2001). Samar et al. (1998) point to the potential of interactive multimedia remediation, especially for deaf children with learning disability or attention deficit disorders. They claim that approaches like the ones developed by Merzenich et al. (1996) for dyslexic children who are hearing and for children with speech and language impairments could, though in adapted formats, also be used for certain multiply disabled deaf children. Currently, however, no empirical research is known into the effects of adaptations of didactic techniques or curricula content.

Summary and Conclusions

In this chapter "multiply disabled" has been used to denote a combination of two or more disabilities for which given methods of intervention and support, developed for children with only one disability, are not applicable because of the presence of another disability. A child is multiply disabled because of the reduction of the possibilities for compensation for each of the separate disabilities.

Although prevalence estimates vary, especially with respect to deaf children with learning disabilities and with autism, it is safe to state that deaf children and adults with multiple disabilities constitute a relatively large subgroup of the entire deaf community. The etiology of multiple disabilities, specifically studied for deafblind people and deaf people with mental retardation, shows a trend toward an increase of acquired causes, especially due to severe prematurity.

For the entire group of deaf children and adults with multiple disabilities, the appearance of their disabilities, their related developmental limitations, and their remaining potentials differ widely. Thorough assessment by professionals familiar with deafness and multiple disabilities is an absolute precondition for the design of an appropriate educational program. Accommodations in educational programming for deafblind children have been described and are most comprehensive for any group of deaf children with multiple disabilities. Research literature on educational programming for other groups of deaf children with multiple disabilities is largely lacking. This is typical for the research literature on deafness and multiple disabilities in general: in spite of the considerable number of children and adults concerned, there is almost no research published on proper forms of assessment, educational outcomes, or the effects of educational accommodations. The sole recommendation that needs to be made here is that a comprehensive research program focusing on deaf children and adults with multiple disabilities is very much needed.

Note

1. We use the term "deaf" in an audiological sense, indicating a mean hearing loss of at least 70 dB for the better ear.

References

Admiraal, R.J.C. (2000). *Hearing impairment and associated handicaps. An aetiological study*. Unpublished doctoral dissertation, University of Nijmegen, Netherlands.

Admiraal, R.J.C., & Huygen, P.L.M. (1999). Causes of hearing impairment in deaf pupils with a mental handicap. *International Journal of Pediatric Otorhinolaryngology, 51*, 101–108.

Aiken-Forderer, M. (1988). Home and school support for physically handicapped deaf children. In H. T. Pricket & E. Duncan (Eds.), *Coping with the multihandicapped hearing impaired* (pp. 29–36). Springfield, IL: Charles C. Thomas.

Aitken, S. (2000). Understanding deafblindness. In S. Aitken, M., Buultjens, C., Clark, J. T. Eyre, & L. Pease, (Eds.), *Teaching children who are deafblind* (pp. 1–34). London: David Fulton.

Braden, J. P. (1994). *Deafness, Deprivation, and IQ*. New York: Plenum Press.

Brimer, J., & Murphy, P. (1988). Autism and deafness: a case study of a deaf and autistic boy. In H.T. Pricket & E. Duncan (Eds.), *Coping with the multihandicapped hearing impaired* (pp. 37–44). Springfield, IL: Charles C. Thomas.

Bunch, G.O., & Melnyk, T-L (1989). A review of the evidence for a learning-disabled, hearing-impaired sub-group. *American Annals of the Deaf, 134*, 297–300.

Chen, D. (Ed.) (1999). *Essential elements in early intervention. Visual impairment and multiple disabilities*. New York: AFB Press.

Chen, D., & Haney, M. (1995). An early intervention model for infants who are deaf-blind. *Journal of Visual Impairment and Blindness, 89*, 213–221.

Das, V.K. (1996). Aetiology of bilateral sensorineural hearing impairment in children: a 10 year study. *Archives of the Diseases of Children, 74*, 8–12.

Durand V. M., (1990). Severe behavior problems: a functional communication training approach. New York: Guilford Press.

Enerstvedt, R. T. (1996). *Legacy of the past, those who are gone but have not left, some aspects of the history of blind education, deaf education, and deafblind education with emphasis on the time before 1900*. Dronninglund, Denmark: Forlaget Nord-Press.

Evenhuis, E.M. (1995). Medical aspects of ageing in a population with intellectual disability: II. Hearing impairment. *Journal of Intellectual Disability Research, 39*(1), 27–33.

Evenhuis, E.M., Van Zanten, G.A., Brocaar, M.P. & Roerdinkholder, W.H.M. (1992). Hearing loss in middle-age persons with Down Syndrome. *American Journal on Mental Retardation, 97*(1), 47–56.

Eyre, J. T. (2000). Holistic assessment. In S. Aitken, M., Buultjens, C., Clark, J. T. Eyre, & L. Pease, (Eds.), *Teaching children who are deafblind* (pp. 119–140). London: David Fulton.

Freeman, P. (1975). *Understanding the deaf/blind child*. London: Heinemann Health Books.

Geenens, D. L. (1999). Neurobiological development and cognition in the deafblind. In J. M. McInnes (Ed.), *A guide to planning and support for individuals who are deafblind* (pp. 150–174). Toronto: University of Toronto Press.

Glenn, S. L. (1988). A deaf re-education program: a model for deaf students with emotional and behavioral problems. In H. T. Pricket & E. Duncan

(Eds.), *Coping with the multi-handicapped hearing impaired* (pp. 7–18). Springfield, IL.: Charles C. Thomas.

Gorlin, R.J., Toriello, H. V., & Cohen, M. M. (1995). *Hereditary hearing loss and its syndromes.* Oxford: Oxford University Press, 1995.

Grove, N., Dockrell, J., & Woll, B. (1996). The two-word stage in manual signs: Language development in signers with intellectual impairments. In S. von Tetzchner & M. H. Jensen (Eds.), *Augmentative and alternative communication: European perspectives* (pp. 101–118). London: Whurr.

Gunther, F. A, & de Jong, C. G. A., (1988). Meervoudig gehandicapt [Multiple handicapped]. Doorn, Netherlands: Vereniging Bartiméus.

Jones, C. J. (1988). *Evaluation and educational programming of deaf-blind/severely multihandicapped students, sensorimotor stage.* Springfield, IL: Charles C. Thomas.

Jure, R., Rapin, I., & Tuchman, R. F. (1991). Hearing impaired autistic children. *Developmental Medicine and Child Neurology, 33*(12), 1062–1072.

Holden-Pitt, L. & Diaz, J. (1998). Thirty years of the Annual Survey of Deaf and Hard of Hearing Children & Youth: a glance over the decades. *American Annals of the Deaf, 143*(2), 72–76.

Kahn, J. V. (1996). Cognitive skills and sign language knowledge of children with severe and profoundly mental retardation. *Education and Training in Mental Retardation and Developmental Disabilities, 31,* 162–168.

Karchmer, M.A. (1985). A demographic perspective. In E. Cherow (Ed.), *Hearing-impaired children and youth with developmental disabilities* (pp. 36–58). Washington, DC: Gallaudet College Press.

Klin, A. (1993). Auditory brainstem responses in autism: brainstem dysfunction or peripheral hearing loss? *Journal of Autism and Developmental Disorders, 23*(1), 15–31.

Luckasson, R. (1992). *Mental retardation: definition, classification and systems of supports.* Washington, DC: American Association on Mental Retardation.

Marschark, M. (1993). *Psychological development of deaf children.* Oxford: Oxford University Press.

Mauk, G. W., & Mauk, P. P. (1998). Considerations, conceptualisations, and challenges in the study of concomitant learning disabilities among children and adolescents who are deaf or hard of hearing. *Journal of Deaf Studies and Deaf Education, 3*(1), 15–34.

McCracken, W. (1998). Deaf children with disabilities. In S. Gregory, P. Knight, W. McCracken, S. Powers, & L. Watson (Eds.), *Issues in Deaf Education* (pp. 28–37). London: David Fulton.

MacFarland, S. Z. C. (1995). Teaching strategies of the van Dijk curricular approach. *Journal of Visual Impairment and Blindness, 89,* 222–228.

Miles, B. (1999). Talking the language of the hands. *DB-Link,* 1–11.

McInnes, J. M. (1999). Deafblindness: a unique disability. In J. M. McInnes (Ed.), *A guide to planning and support for individuals who are deafblind* (pp. 3–33). Toronto: University of Toronto Press.

McInnes, J. M., & Treffry, J. A. (1982). *Deaf-blind infants and children, a developmental guide.* Toronto: University of Toronto Press.

Merzenich, M. M., Jenkins, W. M., Johnston, P., Schreiner, C., Miller, S. L., & Tallal, P. (1996). Temporal processing deficits of language-learning impaired children ameliorated by training, *Science, 271,* 77–80.

Morgan, A., & Vernon, M. (1994). A guide to the diagnosis of learning disabilities in deaf and hard or hearing children and adults. *American Annals of the Deaf, 139*(3), 358–370.

Munroe, S. (2001). *Developing a National Volunteer Registry of Persons with Deafblindness in Canada: Results from the study, 1999–2001.* Brantford, Canada. The Canadian Deafblind and Rubella Association.

Nafstad, A. (1989). *Space of interaction.* Dronninglund, Denmark: Nordic Staff Training Centre for Deaf-Blind Services.

Nafstad, A., & Rødbroe, I. (1999). *Co-creating communication.* Dronninglund, Denmark: Forlaget Nord-Press.

Nakken, H. (1993). Meervoudig gehandicapten, een kwestie van definitie [Multiple handicapped, a matter of definition]. In H. Nakken (Ed.), *Meervoudig gehandicapten* (pp. 13–33). Rotterdam: Lemniscaat.

NTAC Teaching Research Division (2001). *National deaf-blind count.* Monmouth, OR: Western Oregon University.

Reed, C.M., Delhorne, L.A., Durlach, N.I., & Fisher, S.D. (1995). A study of the tactual reception of sign language. *Journal of Speech and Hearing Research, 38,* 477–489.

Rødbroe, I., & Souriau, J. (1999). Communication. In J. M. McInnes (Ed.), *A guide to planning and support for individuals who are deafblind* (pp. 119–149). Toronto: University of Toronto Press.

Rönnberg, J., & Borg E. (2001). A review and evaluation of research on the deaf-blind from perceptual, communicative, social and rehabilitative perspectives. *Scandinavian Audiology, 30,* 67–77.

Rosenhall, U., Nordin, V., Sandström, M., Ahlsén, G., & Gillberg, C. (1999). Autism and hearing loss. *Journal of Autism and Developmental Disorders, 29*(5), 349–357.

Roth, V. (1991). Students with learning disabilities and hearing impairment: issues for the secondary and postsecondary teacher. *Journal of Learning Disabilities, 24*(7), 391–397.

Rutter, M. (1978). Diagnosis and definition of childhood autism. *Journal of Autism and Developmental Disorders, 8,* 139–161.

Samar, V.J., Paranis, I., & Berent, G.P. (1998). Learning disabilities, attention deficit disorders, and deafness. In M. Marschark & M.D. Clark (Eds.) *Psychological perspectives on deafness* (Vol. 2, pp. 199–242). Mahwah, NJ: Lawrence Erlbaum Associates.

Stewart, D.A., & Kluwin, T.N. (2001). *Teaching deaf and hard of hearing students. Content, strategies, and curriculum.* Boston: Allyn and Bacon.

Stillman, R. D., & Battle, C. W. (1986) Developmental assessment of communicative abilities in the deaf-blind. In D. Ellis (Ed.), *Sensory impairments in mentally handicapped people* (pp. 319–335).

Van Dijk, J. (1983): *Rubella handicapped children.* Lisse, Netherlands: Swets & Zeitlinger.

Van Dijk, J. (1986). An educational curriculum for deaf-blind multi-handicapped persons. In D. Ellis (Ed.), *Sensory impairments in mentally handicapped people* (pp. 374–382).

Van Dijk, J., & Janssen, M. (1993). Deafblind children. In H. Nakken (Ed.), *Meervoudig gehandicapten* (pp. 34–73). Rotterdam: Lemniscaat.

Van Dijk, J., & Nelson, C. (2001). Child guided strategies for assessing children who are deafblind or have multiple disabilities (CD ROM). Sint-Michielsgestel, the Netherlands: Instituut voor Doven & AapNootMuis Productions.

Van Dijk, R., Van Helvoort, M., Aan den Toorn, W., & Bos, H. (1998). *Niet zomaar een gebaar.* [Not just a sign]. Sint-Michielsgestel, the Netherlands: Publication Instituut voor Doven.

Walker, M. (1977). Teaching sign language to deaf mentally handicapped adults. In *Institute of Mental Subnormality Conference Proceedings* (vol. 3, pp. 3–25). Kidderminster, UK: British Institute of Mental Handicap.

Walsh, S. R., & Holzberg, R. (1981). *Understanding and educating the deaf-blind/severely and profoundly handicapped, an international perspective.* Springfield, IL: Charles C. Thomas.

Wheeler, L., & Griffin, H. C. (1997). A movement based approach to language development in children who are deaf-blind. *American Annals of the Deaf, 142*(5), 387–390.

Widen, J. E., Folsom, R. C., Thompson, G., & Wilson, W. R. (1987). Auditory brainstem responses in young adults with Down syndrome. *American Journal of Mental Deficiency, 91*(5), 472–479.

Writer, J. (1987). A movement-based approach to the education of students who are sensory impaired/multihandicapped. In L. Goetz, D. Guess, & K. Stremel-Campbell (Eds.), *Innovative program design for individuals with dual sensory impairments* (pp. 191–224). Baltimore, MD: Paul H. Brookes.

Zwiercki, R. D., Stansberry, D. A., Porter, G. G., & Hayes, P. (1976). The incidence of neurological problems in a deaf school age population. *American Annals of the Deaf, 121,* 405–408.

Literacy and Literacy Education

7

Peter V. Paul

Processes and Components of Reading

This chapter provides a perspective on the reading acquisition process of deaf and hard-of-hearing children and adolescents. The synthesis is based on a brief, overall description of reading research on hearing students, as well as a fairly comprehensive review of research on critical reading factors with deaf and hard-of-hearing students. The conflation of research on both groups is necessary to understand the reading process and to suggest areas for further study. The main focus is on reading in English as a first language with a few remarks on bilingualism and reading in English as a second language.

Reading Achievement and Deafness

Two persistent findings have been well documented in the research literature on reading achievement. First, most deaf and hard-of-hearing students do not read as well as hearing counterparts upon graduation from high school. In fact, the average 18- to 19-year-old deaf student is reading at a level commensurate with the average 8- to 9-year-old hearing student (Paul, 1998; Traxler, 2000). Two, the annual growth rate is about 0.3 grade level per year (Allen, 1986) compared to the roughly 1.0

grade level for many hearing students (Snow, Burns, & Griffin, 1998). In one sense, the growth rate portends a plateau, or leveling off, at the third or fourth-grade level. However, the growth rate for many deaf and some hard-of-hearing students might be uneven because there does not always seem to be a steady progress from year to year. This might be due to the difficulty of measuring reading achievement, artifacts of the tests, or other factors, which have not been uncovered (Ewoldt, 1987). It has also been suggested that the general achievement batteries are overestimating the reading achievement levels (Davey, LaSasso, & Macready, 1983) and that the actual levels are lowered than those reported. With few exceptions, these findings have been documented since the beginning of the formal testing movement in the early 1900s (Quigley & Paul, 1986).

The existence of reading difficulties for deaf and hard-of-hearing children is not in question; however, there is much debate on the reasons for these difficulties as on how to improve reading achievement levels (Musselman, 2000; Paul, 1998). One problem is the proliferation of reading theories at both the emergent and advanced reading stages, which offer diverse, sometimes conflicting, views. In addition, there seem to be misinterpretations of theories, particularly those that address either first-language or second-language reading in English (Mayer & Wells, 1996; Paul, 1998, 2001). These misinterpretations are related to the ongoing debates on whether the reading development of deaf and hard-of-hearing students is similar to that of hearing students, thereby validating the use of mainstream literacy models for understanding and improving reading.

Overview of the Reading Process for Students with Typical Hearing

Current reading theories can be linked to early views on reading, specifically during the eighteenth and nineteenth centuries (Bartine, 1989). Then,as now, discussions on the nature of reading were dominated by perspectives on the location of meaning—that is, on the printed page, in the reader's head, or somewhere in between or above (e.g., interactions or transactions between these two areas). Bartine (1989) remarked that a few scholars were also concerned with the influences of history, culture, or social milieus—the precursors to modern sociocultural theories. Nevertheless, some of the most acrimonious debates centered on the relationship between spoken language and the language of print. Initially, it was thought that print was speech written down. Although the use of written symbols (graphemes) is an attempt to capture speech signals (phonemes), it is clear that an understanding of the meaning of English print requires much more than understanding the phoneme–grapheme links.

Theories and research on these two issues—the location of meaning and the relationship between spoken language and the language of print—have led to a clarification of the English reading process. A thrust of ongoing research has been the study of reciprocal relations between processing print (e.g., via word identification and larger discourse processes) and comprehending or interpreting the message (e.g., making inferences, generalizing concepts or information) (Snow et al., 1998). The development of conventional reading requires processing the form (i.e., written code as in the structure of letters, words, and sentences) to construct or obtain meaning (i.e., comprehension and interpretation).

To proceed toward reading fluency (i.e., the point at which word identification becomes automatic and almost effortless and the point at which most energy can be spent on comprehending and interpreting the message), children need increased experiences with print as well as deeper and more extensive growth in language variables such as vocabulary, morphology, and syntax, and other variables such as knowledge of topics and culture. This increase in knowledge supports the word identification process and strengthens the reciprocal relations between word identification and reading comprehension.

In this chapter, it is argued that the reading difficulties of deaf and hard-of-hearing students can be categorized as difficulties with both processing and knowledge. In general, "processing" refers to the decoding (e.g., pronouncing, signing) of linguistic information in print, such as words and connected-discourse items such as syntactic structures and figurative language. The knowledge domain (e.g., knowledge of the structure of English, topic or world knowledge) is mentally represented and is necessary for comprehension and interpretation of decoded items. As an example, it is possible for a reader to pronounce or sign a word (processing), but not know its meaning (knowledge). Conversely, it is possible for readers to know a meaning of a word, but not be able to identify its written counterpart.

Research Synthesis on Text Factors

Much of the research on deaf and hard-of-hearing students has involved text factors, especially vocabulary and syntax (King & Quigley, 1985; Paul, 1998). In this section I discuss research in four text areas: word identification, vocabulary knowledge, syntax, and figurative language.

Word Identification

Word identification is sometimes referred to as word recognition, word attack, word analysis, decoding, and even single-word reading (Oakhill & Cain, 2000; Paul, 1998). Word identification means that the reader can identify (i.e., decode) the word and may or may not know its meaning. Stanovich (1991) and others (e.g., Snow et al., 1998) have argued that it is possible to possess adequate word identification skills and have poor reading comprehension ability; however, the converse has never been empirically demonstrated. In essence, poor word identification ability is a good predictor of difficulty in reading comprehension.

A few researchers have suggested the use of signs (usually American Sign Language; ASL) and/ or fingerspelling to facilitate the development of word identification skills, particularly for letter and word knowledge (Andrews & Mason, 1986; Hirsh-Pasek, 1987). In a longitudinal study of deaf preschoolers, Andrews and Mason (1986) advocated matching an internalized manual language (i.e., ASL signs) to printed words. Hirsh-Pasek (1987) argued that fingerspelling could be used to teach the task of separating words into parts. In her study, she found that young deaf students were able to identify more words when encouraged to decode into fingerspelling.

There is some evidence that cued speech/language can be used to develop decoding skills, especially with respect to the use of phonics for some deaf and hard-of-hearing children and adolescents (LaSasso & Metzger, 1998; see Leybaert & Alegria, this volume). The use of context cues, however, another type of decoding skill, appears to be problematic for identifying words or figuring out the meanings of unknown words (Andrews & Mason, 1991; deVilliers & Pomerantz, 1992). Finally, the role of morphology (as in structural analysis) in supporting word identification has yet to be explored (Gaustad, 2000).

A strong relationship between rapid word identification skills and reading comprehension has been reported for deaf and hard-of-hearing adolescents at the secondary and postsecondary levels (Brown & Brewer, 1996; Fischler, 1985; Kelly, 1993, 1995, 1996). Less skilled readers are slower and make more errors than more-skilled readers. Nevertheless, the nature of this relationship for deaf readers, in general, is being debated intensely. The controversy concerns the role of phonology in the word identification (decoding) process. In particular, the question is whether there is a need for phonological coding, that is, the use of knowledge of letter–sound correspondences to decode words, for efficiency in single-word reading as well as for connected discourse. This issue is discussed further later in this chapter.

Vocabulary Knowledge

Research on reading vocabulary knowledge can be categorized into three main areas: relations between vocabulary knowledge and reading comprehension, extent of knowledge of words and word meanings, and the ability to derive meanings of words from reading contexts either incidentally (i.e., natural reading) or deliberately (i.e., with respect to research tasks) (Paul, 1996, 1998). A number of researchers have established a strong correlation between reading vocabulary knowledge and reading achievement scores (LaSasso & Davey, 1987; Paul & Gustafson, 1991). That is, students who performed well on vocabulary assessments often performed well on reading comprehension measures.

There is a long line of empirical research and research reviews documenting the low vocabulary levels of deaf and hard-of-hearing students when compared to those of hearing peers (Paul, 1996, 1998). Not only do deaf and hard-of-hearing students generally comprehend fewer words from print, but their vocabulary knowledge seems to reflect the use of specific words in their own written language. For example, deaf students tend to use more nouns and verbs than adjectives, adverbs, and conjunctions. Given this limited range of vocabulary usage, their writings have been characterized as direct or stilted, with limited use of imaginative and idiomatic expressions (see reviews in deVilliers, 1991; Paul, 1998).

Investigations have revealed that vocabulary difficulty can be impacted by both processing and knowledge issues. For example, researchers have concluded that many deaf and some hard-of-hearing students also exhibit difficulties in understanding (i.e., have limited knowledge of) other critical English language components such as phonology, morphology, syntax, and orthography. This leads, in part, to problems in the students' ability to derive the meanings of words from natural reading situations (Davey & King, 1990; deVilliers & Pomerantz, 1992). Deaf and hard-of-hearing students can decode and learn words from context; however, they seem to be hampered by this process unless the words are couched in sentences that are relatively simple and appear a number of times (often unnaturally) in contrived passages. Kelly (1996) has argued that difficulty with major syntactic constructions in passages is a critical factor in the low vocabulary development of many students. That is, difficulty with understanding syntax curtails the development of fluent reading skills as well as the use of context cues to derive meanings of important words.

Syntax and Connected Discourse

Syntax has been one of the most researched components in reading and deafness. There are several reasons for the proliferation of investigations in this area. Individuals might have knowledge of words and still not be able to comprehend phrases and sentences. This accounts for the growth in vocabulary knowledge without a corresponding growth in reading achievement (King & Quigley, 1985; Paul, 1998). In addition, for deaf students (and perhaps for some second-language learning students), syntactic knowledge is often a good predictor of reading level because it requires the ability to integrate information across connected linguistic units such as phrases, sentences, and paragraphs.

A number of studies by Quigley and colleagues (see review in Paul, 2001) focused on deaf students' performances on nine major English syntactic structures on the sentential level: negation, conjunction, question formation, pronominalization, verbs, complementation, relativization, disjunction, and alternation. Deaf students had specific difficulties with verb inflectional processes and auxiliaries (e.g., "The window was hit"), with embedded structures such as relative clauses (e.g., "The boy who kissed the girl ran away"), and with most other sentences that did not adhere to a subject-verb-object interpretation (e.g., "The light on the blue police car turned"). With respect to processing and knowledge issues, Quigley's research indicated that syntactic difficulties were due, in part, to a lack of knowledge of the major syntactic constructions, which appear frequently in written materials. This lack of or limited understanding of syntax persisted throughout the adolescent and young adult years. These findings have been supported by later studies (Berent, 1996; Kelly, 1998).

A few researchers, including Ewoldt (1981), McGill-Franzen and Gormley (1980), and Nolen and Wilbur (1985), have argued that deaf students do not have major problems with syntax if the focus of analysis is beyond the sentence level. They have reported that students understand syntactic constructions better in context (i.e., short paragraphs) than in isolation (i.e., sentences). These investigators suggested that knowledge of syntax is not the issue; the issue is either the use of surrounding text (i.e., type of context) or that of test artifact (i.e., the manner in which knowledge of syntax is measured).

That work has been criticized, however, by King and Quigley (1985) and Paul (1998). Due to the use of highly familiar materials, they counterargued, students did not need to focus on the details of the story, particularly on the syntactic constructions. That is, understanding the syntactic structures in question was not crucial to comprehending the story. Further, the presence of a few incomprehensible syntactic constructions did not prove to be detrimental to reading comprehension because the stories were highly familiar to the students.

Similar to the research on the use of phonology in processing words, research on the importance of phonology for syntactic comprehension has been highly contentious and debated. It has been argued, for example, that the use of a phonological code (i.e., knowledge of sound–letter correspondences) exhibits its most marked influence on the comprehension of syntax and connected discourse (Lichtenstein, 1998). Processing syntactic constructions and other discourse structures seems to be most efficient if the reader uses a phonological code in short-term (working) memory. This issue is also discussed further, later in the chapter.

Figurative Language

It is problematic to conduct investigations on the understanding of figurative language constructions, especially those involving figures of speech (e.g., "It's raining cats and dogs") and verb-particle phrases (e.g., "She ran into a friend"). The major challenge is to isolate the effects of selected vocabulary and syntactic constructions that constituted many of these expressions. Regardless of type, there is some research demonstrating that many students have difficulty comprehending these expressions in printed materials (Payne & Quigley, 1987). In fact, in addition to vocabulary and syntax, figurative language is another area that presents difficulty for many students attempting to learn English as a second language (Bernhardt, 1991).

Payne and Quigley (1987) assessed the comprehension of verb-particle phrases by both deaf and hearing subjects. They developed a test using verb-particles at three levels of semantic difficulty (literal, e.g., "walks out;" semi-idiomatic, e.g., "washes up"; and idiomatic, e.g., "gives up") and in five syntactic patterns (subject, verb, adverb; subject, verb, adverb, object; subject, verb, object, adverb; subject, verb, preposition, object; and subject, verb, adverb, preposition, object). They found that the hearing subjects performed significantly better than the deaf subjects on all levels of semantic difficulty and for all syntactic constructions. In addition, Payne and Quigley reiterated two longstanding findings: there is little improvement in the performance of deaf subjects across ages, and performance is highly related to reading comprehension ability.

Deaf individuals can comprehend figurative expressions if diligent efforts have been made to control vocabulary and syntax systematically or if there is sufficient context to disambiguate the meanings of the various expressions (Iran-Nejad, Ortony, & Rittenhouse, 1981). Some researchers have argued that these expressions can be learned as a whole, despite the use of selected vocabulary and syntactic constructions (Wilbur, Fraser, & Fruchter, 1981). Nevertheless, even in these studies, an understanding of figurative expressions correlated positively with the reading comprehension scores of the students (Fruchter, Wilbur, & Fraser, 1984; Orlando & Shulman, 1989).

Whether reading difficulties are due to processing or knowledge factors, poor readers, especially those who have plateaued at the third or fourth-grade level, have problems comprehending figurative language in reading materials. Similar to the research on vocabulary and syntax, these readers also have been found to have limited skills and experiences in using context cues to derive the meanings of the expressions. Because they do not read widely, they cannot utilize information across multiple contexts to compensate for the instances where contexts do not reveal the meaning of particular figurative expressions.

Research Synthesis on Reader Factors

There has been a considerable amount of research on reader factors, especially if research on memory is included (King & Quigley, 1985; Marschark,

1993; Marschark & Harris, 1996; Paul, 1998). This section presents findings in three critical reader areas: prior knowledge, metacognition, and working memory.

Prior Knowledge

One common framework for understanding prior knowledge is to categorize it as part of one or two components: passage-specific prior knowledge or topic-specific prior knowledge. Passage-specific refers to knowledge about the language elements or information in the text. In other words, the focus is on knowledge that seems to be necessary to answer questions or perform tasks that requires an understanding of the stated information in the passage. Topic specific prior knowledge reflects information that is either not explicitly stated in the text or cannot be inferred using the existing information in the text. Examples include situations where readers are asked to apply or relate information in the current passage to other contexts such as previous stories, historical eras, or cultural events. At the very least, a reader needs topic-specific knowledge to interpret a story or to convey different levels of meaning. Research on deafness has centered on students' ability to use both passage-specific and topic-specific prior knowledge (e.g., Jackson, Paul, & Smith, 1997; Schirmer & Woolsey, 1997).

One of the earliest studies on deaf children's use of prior knowledge, particularly in the area of inferencing, is the work of Wilson (1979), who was interested in their ability to answer text explicit and inferential questions (i.e., integration of two or more segments of information in the text). Answering text-explicit questions was significantly easier than answering inferential questions in both deaf and hearing children. In addition, Wilson hypothesized that one major reason for the reading plateau (i.e., third- or fourth-grade level) for deaf and hard-of-hearing children was their inability to make inferences (see Oakhill & Cain, 2000). Beyond the third grade, reading materials require the use of prior knowledge to make inferences given the abstract and implicit nature of information in the text.

Since Wilson's seminal study, several investigators have documented individuals' ability to perform retell or recall tasks, answer questions, and understand (i.e., disambiguate) multiple interpretations of passages. Using a story retelling task, it has been shown that deaf and hard-of-hearing students have the ability to organize information for retelling a story, even when the retelling was written (Griffith & Ripich, 1988). In fact, studies on young deaf children have found that the utilization of sign language (i.e., ASL) to elicit and build prior knowledge (via summaries, organization of concepts), especially during prereading activities, resulted in an improvement of reading comprehension scores (e.g., Andrews, Winograd, & DeVille, 1996). Similar results have been obtained for "orally educated" deaf and hard-of-hearing children (e.g., Donin, Doehring, & Browns, 1991). In their study of orally educated children, Donin et al. (1991) found that age and language experiences contribute to the understanding of textual content structures. As argued by other researchers, the ability to use and organize prior knowledge can be restricted if students have difficulties with the textual demands (vocabulary, syntax, concepts, etc.) of passages and do not possess the necessary knowledge for or experience in organizing information (Jackson et al., 1997; Yoshinaga-Itano & Downey, 1986).

With respect to answering questions, Jackson et al. (1997) examined the relationship between prior knowledge and the ability to answer literal (text-explicit) and two levels of inferential (text-implicit and script-implicit) questions. Results indicated that when prior knowledge was elicited and probed extensively using a detailed form of questioning, the prior knowledge score predicted performance on both literal (no inference required) and script-implicit inferential questions (i.e., application type questions requiring knowledge from the reader's head). The use of detailed and additional probes with students before their engagement in a reading task might have assisted the students in recalling important and relevant information for understanding many of the major concepts in the texts.

At present, a comprehensive model for understanding the role of prior knowledge and deaf students' reading does not exist. A clearer perspective of the difficulties deaf students have in acquiring (i.e., representing mentally) textual features requires an in-depth study of these students' perception of information rendered through current communication systems (e.g., ASL, cued speech, signed English). Further research on prior knowledge should reveal, in part, why many deaf and hard-of-hearing students cannot take advantage of incidental learning (i.e., the learning of new information via extensive reading of printed materials).

Metacognition

Research on metacognition has been categorized as investigations into knowledge and control aspects (Pearson & Fielding, 1991). In the domain of reading, metacognitive knowledge refers to knowledge about oneself as a reader as well as knowledge about topics, language (both primary, i.e., speaking and/or signing and secondary, i.e., written language), text structures, literacy tasks, and even of teacher's expectations and literacy instructional styles. The knowledge aspects of metacognition overlap with those associated with the prior knowledge domain. Metacognitive-control refers to self-regulatory or self-monitoring strategies that individuals use during literacy and literacy-related tasks.

Research on hearing children has revealed a strong positive relationship between metacognitive skill and reading comprehension ability (Pearson & Fielding, 1991). Metacognitive skill has also been demonstrated to increase with age. In essence, older and more skilled readers know more about reading strategies, detect errors more often during reading, and have better recall of text information. A number of studies have documented improvements in reading comprehension via interventions on metacognitive control aspects. Hearing students can learn to improve their comprehension monitoring skills and their ability to answer comprehension questions (Pearson & Fielding, 1991).

With respect to deaf and hard-of-hearing individuals, one interesting line of metacognitive research has focused on text inspection tasks (e.g., looking back or rereading the text). If look-back is not permitted, then the emphasis is on the reader's ability to remember the desired information. If look-back is allowed, then, at the very least, insights into question-answering strategies can be obtained. In general, it is expected that look-back responses would be more accurate than no-look-back responses. This result has been documented for deaf adolescent readers, even though these readers did not think that they performed better on the look-back technique (Davey, 1987).

A closer inspection of deaf students' look-back performance has led to the hypothesis that this technique typically is not used as a metacognitive control-type strategy (i.e., rereading and reflecting on the information in the text). Rather, students look back to try to find an answer or to complete the task by focusing on selected words or phrases. The assumption is that these students have poorly developed inferential skills, and this influences their use of inappropriate strategies such as word association, copying, or visual-matching in responding to comprehension questions (Davey & LaSasso, 1983; LaSasso, 1985).

Another metacognitive task involves the detection of inappropriate information in passages. Similar to the research findings with good hearing readers, good deaf readers (high school age) are able to locate information, such as words or phrases, that does not belong in a particular passage or is unusual or nonsense (Gibbs, 1989). There is a relationship between this type of metacognitive awareness and reading comprehension. In fact, rarely do poor readers recognize these types of errors and contradictions.

Using what is called a "feeling-of-knowing" metacognitive task, Krinsky (1990) instructed high school-age deaf students to rank vocabulary words that they thought they missed on a vocabulary test. It was observed that deaf students were reluctant to guess at word meanings. They also used the phrase "I don't know" more often than hearing students, a response often reported among other poor readers on literacy-related tasks. As discussed previously, the guessing responses of deaf students are often reflective of a visual-matching strategy in which the focus is on specific language items (e.g., looking for words within words that match their definitions or guesses). It appears that these deaf students could not engage in making judgments about their ability (feeling-of-knowing) to select the correct meanings or definitions for vocabulary words.

A few studies have attempted to assess metacognitive knowledge in a more direct manner, using either interviews or think-aloud research paradigms (Andrews & Mason, 1991; Ewoldt, 1986; Strassman, 1992). Using an interview method with deaf and hard-of-hearing students, ages 8–14 years, Ewoldt (1986) found that they had difficulty providing appropriate responses to a question about why they thought they were good readers. The students also seemed to be reluctant to mention reading strategies to which they had been exposed that

they would use if they had difficulty with unknown items in a passage. Apparently, these students did not understand the purpose of reading and were unwilling to mention previously learned or used strategies (see also Strassman, 1992).

Using a think-aloud technique (i.e., commenting out loud or in sign during reading), Andrews and Mason (1991) examined the responses of deaf students using ASL who were between 17 and 20 years old. Although the students reported using strategies such as rereading and look-back, as well as their prior knowledge of the topic, they rarely reported the use of context clues. Overall, the deaf students reported the use of fewer strategies when compared to the hearing groups in the study. The researchers recommended that these students be assisted in the development of more effective strategies during reading.

Metacognitive skills are extremely important for effective reading. Although such skills are dependent on prior knowledge and other reading variables discussed in this chapter, there seems to be a need for more instructional efforts in this area. Strassman (1997) remarked that deaf students might not have a sufficient number of opportunities to engage in high-level metacognitive activities. If reading materials are too difficult, the students will not only be unmotivated but also will be unable to develop and apply a range of metacognitive strategies, except asking the teacher for help, which is a passive, often-used strategy of poor readers. The use of effective instructional techniques might assist in improving metacognitive skills; however, this will be limited if it is not accompanied by an improvement in the students' overall reading ability.

Working Memory, Phonological Coding, and Reading

Perhaps the most controversial line of reading research in deafness is the study of interrelations among working memory, the use of a phonological code, and reading ability (see Marschark, this volume). There have been several research thrusts, including the nature of working memory processes, the effects of phonology on processing words (i.e., word identification processes) and connected discourse structures (e.g., syntax), and the ability of deaf individuals to use a phonological code in working memory (e.g., Hanson, 1989; Leybaert, 1993; Leybaert & Alegria, 1993; Marschark & Harris, 1996; Musselman, 2000; Paul, 1998; Perfetti & Sendak, 2000).

The emerging view is that the use of a phonological code in working memory is most efficient for processing and understanding a language based on the alphabet system. The alphabet system requires an awareness that spoken language can be analyzed into separable words and that words can be segmented into syllables and phonemes (vowels and consonants). Successful reading seems to be driven by phonological knowledge (Perfetti & Sendak, 2000), but there is more to reading than knowledge of phonology. Readers need to possess phonological and phonemic awareness to make the phoneme–grapheme links (letter–sound connections). These findings are applicable to both first-language and second-language readers of English (e.g., Bernhardt, 1991).

Is knowledge of English phonology critical for deaf and hard-of-hearing readers? It has been suggested that it is possible to bypass word-level (i.e., phonological coding) processing (and even syntactic processing) and use semantic or orthographic processing during reading (e.g., Yurkowski & Ewoldt, 1986). In engaging in nonphonological processing, it is surmised that readers can effectively use or mediate via signs and/or fingerspelling.

In discussing the overall findings of this area, a few caveats should be considered, especially with respect to implications for further research efforts. First, there have been few studies on deaf and hard-of-hearing individuals that assess the use of phonological knowledge in word identification or connected discourse, thereby demonstrating whether phonological coding is used during reading. Studies that show the use of phonology to solve problems or perform reading-related tasks are not direct investigations of phonological coding during actual reading (Stanovich, 1991). Second, even when the use of phonology during reading has been demonstrated, it is still not clear whether readers possess phonological awareness before the reading task or if they acquire awareness after the reading task (e.g., before or after word identification; Leybaert & Alegria, 1993). Most of the related studies have been conducted on deaf adolescents of high school or college age, some of whom had already become good readers. Thus, there is a need to conduct additional investigations on beginning readers. Finally, even if deaf readers are sensitive to phonology at the word level, it might be that they are not using or cannot use this type of coding as efficiently as do hearing readers.

The bulk of the evidence reveals that deaf students who use predominantly a phonological code in working memory tend to be better readers than deaf students who use predominantly a nonphonological code (e.g., Hanson, 1989; Leybaert, 1993; Musselman, 2000; Paul, 1998). Although the merits of phonological coding are evident at the word level, the greatest advantage emerges during the processing of connected structures, as in complex English syntax (Kelly, 1996; Lichtenstein, 1998). Deaf adolescent readers who do not use a phonological code have difficulty simultaneously using syntactic and semantic information at the sentence level.

The work of Lichtenstein (1998) is representative of the research and findings on deaf adolescent and young-adult readers. Lichtenstein investigated deaf college students whose reading achievement levels were higher than those reported for typical prelingually deaf students. He reported that his subjects typically used two or more codes rather than just one exclusively. The most commonly used codes were sign and speech (i.e., phonological code); however, better readers relied pervasively on speech coding. The advantage of using a phonological code was most evident with respect to syntactic processing. That is, phonological coding better represented the grammatical structure of English than sign-based or visual coding. This permitted the short-term retention (in working memory) of a sufficient amount of information to decode grammatical structures that were not linear (e.g., relative clauses, passive voice).

Given the relative difficulty of many deaf individuals in accessing English phonology or in using a phonological code in reading, the use of alternative methods of coding has been suggested and investigated. In general, there has been considerable difficulty in documenting other types of coding such as orthography, fingerspelling, and sign. For example, it is problematic to distinguish the effects of phonological and orthographic similarity. Even if the use of orthographic coding (e.g., awareness of the order of letters in words) can be documented, it has not been shown to be as effective as phonological coding (Hanson, 1989; Lichtenstein, 1998). In fact, none of the nonphonological coding or alternative strategies appear to be as effective as phonological coding for reading connected discourse or for processing printed materials in English (Hanson, 1989; Kelly, 1996; Musselman, 2000).

Task and Context Factors

There have been only a few investigations of the effects of task and context factors (especially in conjunction with text and reader factors) on reading comprehension. Several of these studies were reviewed above—for example, the work of LaSasso (Davey & LaSasso, 1983; LaSasso, 1985) on text inspection (metacognition) and Jackson et al. (1997) on answering different types of questions (prior knowledge).

Early research on task and context factors entailed the study of parent–child reading sessions, observations of classroom reading instruction (including amount of time children spent on actual reading), the qualification of teachers who teach reading, and types of reading materials (King & Quigley, 1985; Paul, 1998). Although these lines of research are important, none of them has presented a comprehensive, coherent view, nor has any contributed substantially to understanding basic reading processes of deaf and hard-of-hearing children.

One promising and coherent line of research has been influenced by reader-response theory, specifically children's response to literature (Lemley, 1993; Williams, 1994; Williams & McLean, 1997). The most common research paradigm requires children to "transact" with a text (typically, reading silently or aloud or listening to others' reading) and sharing their responses (using speech/sign and/or written language) with the teacher or the entire classroom. Younger children might engage in the manipulation of objects and characters using cut-out posters or other manipulatives. This sharing of responses leads these children to notice similarities and differences among a range of responses to issues or events in the passages. Thus, improvement in reading ability is dependent on the richness of the social milieus, involving parents, teachers, and others, as well as access to literacy materials.

In the few studies with young deaf and hard-of-hearing children, it has been reported that the range and type of children's responses to beginning reading books or picture books were similar to those reported for younger hearing children (Lemley, 1993) or for hearing counterparts in kinder-

garten and first grade (Williams, 1994; Williams & McLean, 1997). This supports the view that the reading development of deaf and hard-of-hearing children is similar to that of hearing children (Paul, 1998, 2001). Despite severe language delays, these children were motivated to learn from beginning reading books and picture books, especially in socially constructed ways.

More research is needed within a reader-response purview; however, researchers should proceed with caution. Reading is primarily a solitary activity and, at some point, individuals have to be able to read alone and independently. Investigators should determine the amount of information in the text that is actually used to construct meaning. In the Jackson et al. (1997) study mentioned previously, it was observed that many deaf students provided information about the story topic (bats), which was not in the required reading passage. When asked to indicate where the information could be located in the text, the students were not willing or could not perform the task. Jackson et al. (1997) speculated that the students might have utilized their prior knowledge about bats but were having difficulty addressing passage-specific questions, particularly of the inferential type, mainly because they could not access or understand some of the textual information.

Summary and Conclusions

Considering the reading difficulties of many deaf and hard-of-hearing students, is a mature level of English reading a realistic goal for them? Perhaps it is more beneficial to ask what is necessary to become a proficient reader. It appears, based on the assertion discussed throughout this chapter, that reading acquisition difficulties are due to both processing and knowledge issues. Processing letters, words, and larger linguistic units needs to be rapid and automatic so that readers can use their knowledge to comprehend and interpret the text at the micro level (sentences and paragraphs) and the macro level (themes, motifs, layers of interpretations). For deaf and hard-of-hearing students to become proficient readers, there needs to be a beneficial, reciprocal relation between processing print and the use of knowledge to construct meaning.

Research on text and reader factors has illustrated a breakdown in the reciprocal relation between processing and knowledge for deaf and hard-of-hearing individuals who are poor readers. With respect to theories concerning English reading among hearing children, one interpretation is that there is a weak match between the spoken language level of the readers and the linguistic and cognitive demands of English print. The reciprocal relation between spoken and written language is activated by the association between phonology and orthography. In other words, readers need to be aware that English speech can be segmented into phonemes and that these are represented by an alphabetic orthography. For proficient hearing readers, phonology clearly drives the reading process.

The same seems to be true for good deaf readers, based on research on the use of a phonological code. Those deaf adolescent readers who do use a phonological code for processing print read better than deaf students who use nonphonological codes. Further research efforts should explore the use of phonological coding by younger and beginning readers. It is important to design studies to assess the actual use of phonology during reading, rather than general problem-solving skills. Given the relative difficulty of developing and accessing phonology for many deaf students, it is also critical to continue research on alternative means of processing print. Nevertheless, these research endeavors still need to address the issue of phonology because of the nature of the alphabet system.

Many deaf and hard-of-hearing students' struggles with reading are compounded because of attempts to both learn a language and to read in that language simultaneously. One of the major challenges for these students is to learn a bona fide language at as early an age as possible. Clearly, there are advantages to learning any language, especially for communication and thought. With respect to reading, a well-developed language is necessary for the enrichment and use of prior knowledge and metacognitive skills. With an adequately developed symbol system, it is possible to receive and represent information in memory about school topics as well as topics associated with the larger culture—present and past.

The exclusive use of a language that does not match the language of printed text is limiting. Deaf and hard-of-hearing readers also need to improve their working knowledge of the language of print (English). Much of the reviewed research has been conducted on factors such as vocabulary, syntax,

and figurative language. There is little research on components of reading such as morphology, orthography, or other important text factors. Morphology might be a fruitful area because of its contributions to the development of rapid word identification processes. It might be difficult to investigate orthography because of overlapping effects with phonology. In addition, some reading scholars believe that orthography cannot be taught; the reader's orthographic knowledge increases via extensive experiences with print.

One of the most neglected areas relating to reading is the affective domain (i.e., motivation, interest), which, in deafness, has been limited to surveys on reading interests and habits. Researchers should examine the relationships between motivation and interest and comprehension of texts. Similar to the research on hearing individuals, there should be additional studies of author's voice, the visibility of the author (i.e., impersonal versus personal writing styles), and the effects of literary genres such as expository and narrative passages on readers' motivation and comprehension.

Future research on deaf and hard-of-hearing students is likely to be influenced by the emerging sociocultural paradigms with a strong emphasis on task and context factors. It would be instructive to explore how children and adolescents interact with printed texts, particularly literature, within social and cultural milieus. However, investigations should not just seek to reveal deficiencies; there needs to be an attempt to use the information to improve both processing and knowledge of printed texts. Ultimately, reading means accessing and using information in texts to construct meaning.

References

Allen, T. (1986). Patterns of academic achievement among hearing impaired students: 1974 and 1983. In A. Schildroth & M. Karchmer (Eds.), *Deaf children in America* (pp. 161–206). San Diego, CA: Little, Brown.

Andrews, J., & Mason, J. (1986). How do deaf children learn about prereading? *American Annals of the Deaf, 131,* 210–217.

Andrews, J., & Mason, J. (1991). Strategy usage among deaf and hearing readers. *Exceptional Children, 57,* 536–545.

Andrews, J., Winograd, P., & DeVille, G. (1996). Using sign language summaries during prereading lessons. *Teaching Exceptional Children, 28,* 30–34.

Bartine, D. (1989). *Early English reading theory: Origins of current debates.* Columbia: University of South Carolina Press.

Berent, G. (1996). Learnability constraints on deaf learners' acquisition of English *wh*-questions. *Journal of Speech and Hearing Research, 39,* 625–642.

Bernhardt, E. (1991). *Reading development in a second language.* Norwood, NJ: Ablex.

Brown, P., & Brewer, L. (1996). Cognitive processes of deaf and hearing skilled and less skilled readers. *Journal of Deaf Studies and Deaf Education, 1,* 263–270.

Davey, B. (1987). Postpassage questions: Task and reader effects on comprehension and meta-comprehension processes. *Journal of Reading Behavior, 19,* 261–283.

Davey, B., & King, S. (1990). Acquisition of word meanings from context by deaf readers. *American Annals of the Deaf, 135,* 227–234.

Davey, B., & LaSasso, C. (1983). An examination of hearing-impaired readers' test-taking abilities on reinspection tasks. *Volta Review, 85,* 279–284.

Davey, B., LaSasso, C., & Macready, G. (1983). Comparison of reading comprehension task performance for deaf and hearing readers. *Journal of Speech and Hearing Research, 26,* 622–628.

deVilliers, P. (1991). English literacy development in deaf children. Directions for research and intervention. In J. Miller (Ed.), *Research on child language disorders: A decade of progress* (pp. 349–378). Austin, TX: Pro-Ed.

deVilliers, P., & Pomerantz, S. (1992). Hearing-impaired students learning new words from written context. *Applied Psycholinguistics, 13,* 409–431.

Donin, J., Doehring, D., & Browns, F. (1991). Text comprehension and reading achievement in orally educated hearing-impaired children. *Discourse Processes, 14,* 307–337.

Ewoldt, C. (1981). A psycholinguistic description of selected deaf children reading in sign language. *Reading Research Quarterly, 17,* 58–89.

Ewoldt, C. (1986). What does "reading" mean? *Perspectives for Teachers of the Hearing Impaired, 4,* 10–13.

Ewoldt, C. (1987). Reading tests and the deaf reader *Perspectives for Teachers of the Hearing Impaired, 5,* 21–24.

Fischler, I. (1985). Word recognition, use of context, and reading skill among deaf college students. *Reading Research Quarterly, 20,* 203–218.

Fruchter, A., Wilbur, R., & Fraser, B. (1984). Comprehension of idioms by hearing-impaired students. *Volta Review, 86,* 7–18.

Gaustad, M. (2000). Morphographic analysis as a word identification strategy for deaf readers. *Journal of Deaf Studies and Deaf Education, 5,* 60–80.

Gibbs, K. (1989). Individual differences in cognitive skills related to reading ability in the deaf. *American Annals of the Deaf, 134,* 214–218.

Griffith, P., & Ripich, D. (1988). Story structure recall in hearing-impaired, learning-disabled, and non-disabled children. *American Annals of the Deaf, 133,* 43–50.

Hanson, V. (1989). Phonology and reading: Evidence from profoundly deaf readers. In D. Shankweiler & I. Lieberman (Eds.), *Phonology and reading disability: Solving the reading puzzle* (pp. 69–89). Ann Arbor, MI: University of Michigan Press.

Hirsh-Pasek, K. (1987). The metalinguistics of finger-spelling: An alternative way to increase written vocabulary in congenitally deaf readers. *Reading Research Quarterly, 22,* 455–474.

Iran-Nejad, A., Ortony, A., & Rittenhouse, R. (1981). The comprehension of metaphorical uses of English by deaf children. *Journal of Speech and Hearing Research, 24,* 551–556.

Jackson, D., Paul, P., & Smith, J. (1997). Prior knowledge and reading comprehension ability of deaf and hard-of-hearing adolescents. *Journal of Deaf Studies and Deaf Education, 2,* 172–184.

Kelly, L. (1993). Recall of English function words and inflections by skilled and average deaf readers. *American Annals of the Deaf, 138,* 288–296.

Kelly, L. (1995). Processing of bottom-up and top-down information by skilled and average deaf readers and implications for whole language instruction. *Exceptional Children, 61,* 318–334.

Kelly, L. (1996). The interaction of syntactic competence and vocabulary during reading by deaf students. *Journal of Deaf Studies and Deaf Education, 1,* 75–90.

Kelly, L. (1998). Using silent motion pictures to teach complex syntax to adult deaf readers. *Journal of Deaf Studies and Deaf Education, 3,* 217–230.

King, C., & Quigley, S. (1985). *Reading and deafness.* San Diego, CA: College-Hill Press.

Krinsky, G. (1990). The feeling of knowing in deaf adolescents. *American Annals of the Deaf, 135,* 389–395.

LaSasso, C. (1985). Visual matching test-taking strategies used by deaf readers. *Journal of Speech and Hearing Research, 28,* 2–7.

LaSasso, C., & Davey, B. (1987). The relationship between lexical knowledge and reading comprehension for prelingually, profoundly hearing-impaired students. *Volta Review, 89,* 211–220.

LaSasso, C., & Metzger, M. (1998). An alternate route for preparing deaf children for bibi programs: The home language as L1 and cued speech for conveying traditionally-spoken languages. *Journal of Deaf Studies and Deaf Education, 3,* 265–289.

Lemley, P. (1993). *Deaf readers and engagement in the story world: A study of strategies and stances.* Unpublished doctoral dissertation, The Ohio State University, Columbus.

Leybaert, J. (1993). Reading in the deaf: The roles of phonological codes. In M. Marschark & M. D. Clark (Eds.), *Psychological perspectives on deafness* (pp. 269–309). Hillsdale, NJ: Lawrence Erlbaum Associates.

Leybaert, J., & Alegria, J. (1993). Is word processing involuntary in deaf children? *British Journal of Developmental Psychology, 11,* 1–29.

Lichtenstein, E. (1998). The relationships between reading processes and English skills of deaf college students. *Journal of Deaf Studies and Deaf Education, 3,* 80–134.

Marschark, M. (1993). *Psychological development of deaf children.* New York: Oxford University Press.

Marschark, M., & Harris, M. (1996). Success and failure in learning to read: The special case (?) of deaf children. In C. Cornoldi & J. Oakhill (Eds.), *Reading comprehension difficulties: Processes and intervention* (pp. 279–300). Mahwah, NJ: Lawrence Erlbaum Associates.

Mayer, C., & Wells, G. (1996). Can the linguistic interdependence theory support a bilingual-bicultural model of literacy education for deaf students? *Journal of Deaf Studies and Deaf Education, 1,* 93–107.

McGill-Franzen, A., & Gormley, K. (1980). The influence of context on deaf readers' understanding of passive sentences. *American Annals of the Deaf, 125,* 937–942.

Musselman, C. (2000). How do children who can't hear learn to read an alphabetic script? A review of the literature on reading and deafness. *Journal of Deaf Studies and Deaf Education, 5,* 9–31.

Nolen, S., & Wilbur, R. (1985). The effects of context on deaf students' comprehension of difficult sentences. *American Annals of the Deaf, 130,* 231–235.

Oakhill, J., & Cain, K. (2000). Children's difficulties in text comprehension: Assessing causal issues. *Journal of Deaf Studies and Deaf Education, 5,* 51–59.

Orlando, A., & Shulman, B. (1989). Severe-to-profound hearing-impaired children's comprehension of figurative language. *Journal of Childhood Communication Disorders, 12,* 157–165.

Paul, P. (1996). Reading vocabulary knowledge and deafness. *Journal of Deaf Studies and Deaf Education, 1,* 3–15.

Paul, P. (1998). *Literacy and deafness: The development of reading, writing, and literate thought.* Needham Heights, MA: Allyn & Bacon.

Paul, P. (2001). *Language and deafness* (3rd ed.). San Diego, CA: Singular.

Paul, P., & Gustafson, G. (1991). Hearing-impaired students' comprehension of high-frequency multi-meaning words. *Remedial and Special Education, 12,* 52–62.

Payne, J-A., & Quigley, S. (1987). Hearing-impaired children's comprehension of verb-particle combinations. *Volta Review, 89,* 133–143.

Pearson, P. D., & Fielding, L. (1991). Comprehension instruction. In R. Barr, M. Kamil, P. Mosenthal, & P. D. Pearson (Eds.), *Handbook of reading research* (2nd ed., pp. 815–860).

Perfetti, C., & Sendak, R. (2000). Reading optimally builds on spoken language: Implications for deaf readers. *Journal of Deaf Studies and Deaf Education, 5,* 32–50.

Quigley, S., & Paul, P. (1986). A perspective on academic achievement. In D. Luterman (Ed.), *Deafness in perspective* (pp. 55–86). San Diego, CA: College-Hill Press.

Schirmer, B., & Woolsey, M. L. (1997). Effect of teacher questions on the reading comprehension of deaf children. *Journal of Deaf Studies and Deaf Education, 2,* 47–56.

Snow, C., Burns, S., & Griffin, P. (Eds.). (1998). *Preventing reading difficulties in young children.* Washington, DC: National Academy Press.

Stanovich, K. (1991). Word recognition: Changing perspectives. In R. Barr, M. Kamil, P. Mosenthal, & P. D. Pearson (Eds.), *Handbook of reading research* (2nd ed., pp. 418–452). White Plains, NY: Longman.

Strassman, B. (1992). Deaf adolescents' metacognitive knowledge about school-related reading. *American Annals of the Deaf, 137,* 326–330.

Strassman, B. (1997). Metacognition and reading in children who are deaf: A review of the research. *Journal of Deaf Studies and Deaf Education, 2,* 140–149.

Traxler, C. (2000). The Stanford Achievement Test, 9th edition: National norming and performance standards for deaf and hard-of-hearing students. *Journal of Deaf Studies and Deaf Education, 5,* 337–348.

Wilbur, R., Fraser, J., & Fruchter, A. (1981, November). *Comprehension of idioms by hearing-impaired students.* Paper presented at the American Speech-Language-Hearing Association Convention, Los Angeles, CA.

Williams, C. (1994). The language and literacy worlds of three profoundly deaf preschool children. *Reading Research Quarterly, 29,* 124–155.

Williams, C., & McLean, M. (1997). Young deaf children's response to picture book reading in a preschool setting. *Research in the Teaching of English, 31*, 337–366.

Wilson, K. (1979). *Inference and language processing in hearing and deaf children*. Unpublished doctoral dissertation. Boston University, MA.

Yoshinaga-Itano, C., & Downey, D. (1986). A hearing-impaired child's acquisition of schemata: Something's missing. *Topics in Language Disorders, 7*, 45–57.

Yurkowski, P., & Ewoldt, C. (1986). A case for the semantic processing of the deaf reader. *American Annals of the Deaf, 131*, 243–247.

Barbara R. Schirmer & Cheri Williams

Approaches to Teaching Reading

The aim of this chapter is to provide an overview of the research on approaches to teaching reading to deaf students. Although the body of research literature on the reading processes of deaf students consistently generates implications for instruction, relatively few studies have investigated instructional interventions with deaf readers. Brief descriptions of the research published before 1990 are offered in this chapter, except in cases of early seminal studies and lone studies in major areas, as a foundation for understanding the current research that is described in greater detail. The chapter concludes with a discussion of implications for future research on instructional approaches that could serve to inform teacher practice.

Emergent Literacy

"Emergent literacy" is a term for, and a theoretical orientation to, young children's reading and writing development. It describes preschool and kindergarten children's knowledge and understanding about written language and the not-yet-conventional ways in which they read and write (Teale & Sulzby, 1986). It represents a paradigm shift, a reconceptualization of our understanding of

the nature and importance of children's early literacy development. Emergent literacy stands in contrast to "reading readiness," the dominant approach to beginning reading instruction since the 1920s. Traditionally, educators have viewed the preschool and kindergarten years as a period of preparation, a time for teachers to get children ready for formal reading instruction in first grade. Classroom activities typically focused on auditory and visual discrimination and memory, letter names and sounds, and word recognition. These reading-readiness skills were considered basic prerequisites for learning to read, and they became the scope and sequence of the kindergarten curriculum (Teale & Sulzby, 1986).

As early as the mid-1960s, however, researchers began to question major tenets of the reading-readiness perspective by demonstrating that many young children knew a good deal about written language (Clay, 1967). Now, a large body of literature documents young children's emergent literacy development (see Sulzby & Teale, 1991, for a thorough review). This research indicates that the ontogeny of literacy begins in the social contexts of the home and community and that children's early experiences with print have a direct influence on their initial understanding of literacy in school

(Wells, 1986). The period of emergent literacy is typically from birth to age 5, or when children enter school and begin receiving formal literacy instruction (Teale, 1986).

The majority of the research has focused on hearing children's emergent literacy, but studies in the field of deafness also demonstrate that young deaf children are learning about reading and writing in the early childhood years, before formal instruction.

Emergent Literacy Development

Investigations of emergent literacy development have involved observations of young deaf children engaged in reading and writing activities. Two investigations examined deaf children's early literacy learning in light of the children's delayed language acquisition; five investigations concentrated on emergent writing; and two investigations focused on interactive storybook reading.

Literacy Learning and Language Acquisition

Rottenberg and Searfoss (1992) conducted their study in a self-contained, public preschool program with seven children, ages 3–4, with moderate to profound hearing losses. For 9 months, the researchers observed the children's literate behaviors and collected drawing and writing samples. When children participate in activities that involve the use of reading or writing or the use of print in any form, "literate behaviors" are typically evident. For example, children will pretend to read both to themselves as well as to one another, even though they really cannot read. They will write using scribbles and letterlike shapes. They are doing what they see adults doing. Their behaviors are literate but not yet conventional. Results of the Rottenberg and Searfoss (1992) study indicated that the children chose to participate in reading, drawing, and writing above all other preschool activities and that they learned many initial concepts about print as they interacted with one another during these literacy events. When they did not have the necessary spoken or sign language to express themselves, they used drawing and writing to communicate. They also used literacy activities as a way to interact socially with classmates.

Williams (1994) followed three profoundly deaf children, ages 3–5, for a 6-month period. She observed within the children's preschool classrooms and visited their homes. In addition, she collected samples of the children's drawing and writing and tested their knowledge of literacy through accepted informal assessment approaches. Findings indicated that the children were immersed in literacy events both at home and in the preschool context. Most of these literacy activities supported the children's language acquisition. Further, all three children learned a great deal about written language as they participated in these events.

Both Rottenberg and Searfoss (1992) and Williams (1994) observed that the deaf children's participation in literacy activities and their early understanding about print were similar to those of hearing children, as documented in the research literature, despite the deaf children's delayed language acquisition. Further, results suggested that written language activities supported the children's development of spoken and signed language. Rather than focusing largely on language acquisition, as is the typical practice in many early childhood classrooms, the researchers argued for providing extensive experiences with reading and writing activities (see Albertini & Schley, this volume).

Emergent Writing

Ruiz (1995) collected drawing and writing papers by her deaf daughter, Elena, from ages 3 to 7. She found that many of Elena's hypotheses about English orthography were similar to those observed in hearing children, such as Elena's understanding that there should be correspondence between the size or age of the referent (i.e., an object or person) and the written word. For example, if the person is little or young, children assume that the word should have few letters. Elena also demonstrated hypotheses that seemed uniquely attributable to her deafness and use of sign language, such as her comment that "the shape of your hand when you sign a word tells you its first letter" (p. 213).

Conway (1985) investigated the purposes for which young deaf children write. The study was conducted in a self-contained auditory/oral kindergarten class with seven children, ages 5–6, with moderate to profound hearing losses. Conway observed and videotaped the children while at a writing table, from December to May, and collected writing samples. He found that the children used writing for the same purposes observed with hearing children: to organize information, interact with others, and consolidate their emerging understanding about the rules of writing. Conway considered the deaf children's emergent writing to be coincidental with spoken language development, though he provided no supporting data. He argued for instructional approaches that emphasize the communicative purposes of writing, rather than its mechanical aspects.

Ewoldt (1985) examined early concepts about print in 10 children, ages 4–5, with severe to profound hearing losses. She observed the children during drawing/writing time during a full school year, collected writing samples, and assessed the children on measures of early literacy. Results indicated that the children demonstrated several important concepts about print observed in the writing of young hearing children, including organization, generativeness (i.e., the ability to generate new and different words simply by rearranging the letters in a given word), and intentionality.

Andrews and Gonzales (1991) carried out a year-long investigation of six deaf kindergarten children, ages 6–8, who were engaged in what they referred to as a literacy-rich environment involving a variety of reading and writing activities. The researchers used samples of the children's written stories to evaluate their developing concepts about print. The researchers reported that all of the children showed growth in their acquisition of print knowledge and concluded that the instructional model effectively supported the children's emergent writing development. However, no data analyses were provided.

Williams (1999) observed five profoundly deaf children, ages 4–5, as they worked at the writing table of their preschool classroom for a 6-month period. She found that sign language served a variety of functions as the children wrote, including providing information, seeking assistance, instructing others, and maintaining social relationships. As they talked, the children made connections between fingerspelling, printed letters and words, and manual signs. The study corroborated previous findings with hearing children that social interaction is important to emergent writing development.

Collectively, these studies indicate that deaf children's emergent writing development may be similar to that of hearing children. Further, results provide limited support for two conclusions. First, deaf children learn about written language through acts of composing. Second, social interaction during writing sessions is supportive of early understanding about written language.

Emergent Reading

Maxwell (1984) videotaped a deaf child and her deaf parents interacting around storybooks from the time the child was 2 until she was 6 years of age. Maxwell found a sequence of emergent reading behaviors analogous to the sequence reported for hearing children: (1) labeling pictures with manual signs; (2) using illustrations to generate the storyline; (3) focusing on the sign print in Signed English books (sign print is the graphic representation of the sign, or sign language picture, above each English word); and (4) focusing on the printed text and using fingerspelling.

Rottenberg (2001) observed a profoundly deaf child, who was age 4 at the outset of the study, in his preschool classroom during a 9-month period. Similar to Maxwell's findings, Rottenberg found the following sequence of emergent reading behaviors: (1) labeling the illustrations with signs; (2) reading familiar words in context; (3) focusing on the sign print in Signed English texts; and (4) relating sign print to written English.

Both Maxwell (1984) and Rottenberg (2001) concluded that sign print was important to deaf children in learning to read because it provided a bridge between picture cues, sign language, and English orthography. Related research provides further evidence that sign print supports deaf children's word identification and comprehension skills (Robbins, 1983; Stoefen-Fisher & Lee, 1989; Wilson & Hyde, 1997).

Early Reading Instruction

Two primary approaches to supporting deaf children's early reading development have been investigated. In the 1980s, researchers examined explicit instruction in word recognition and used printed word cards to teach deaf children to read (Soderbergh, 1985; Suzuki & Notoya, 1984). More recently, researchers have examined the effectiveness of interactive storybook reading as an instructional approach.

Andrews and Mason (Andrews, 1988; Andrews & Mason, 1986a, 1986b) carried out a series of intervention studies incorporating storybook reading and word recognition. In each session, the teacher signed a storybook and then discussed it with the children, focusing on several target words from the story. Each child received a copy of the storybook to read, retell, and dramatize. Then the children practiced fingerspelling and printing the target words. The intervention was conducted for 30 min each week for 25 weeks at a residential school for the deaf. Participants included an experimental group of 23 deaf kindergarten and first-grade children, ages 5–8, with severe to profound hearing losses and a similar comparison group that received conventional reading instruction. Results indicated that the experimental group outperformed the comparison group on fingerspelling, book reading, story retelling, and word recognition tasks. The researchers concluded that explicitly teaching deaf children to match manual signs to printed words in the context of interactive storybook reading supported early reading.

Rowe and Allen (1995) examined interactive storybook reading in a public preschool program that integrated deaf, hard-of-hearing, and hearing children. The children ranged in age from 1.5 to 3.5 years, and the group ranged in size from 20 to 30 depending on attendance. At each session, two teachers presented each page of the story in three successive steps: one teacher read the text aloud and showed the illustrations; the other teacher signed the storyline in American Sign Language (ASL). Rowe and Allen observed the deaf children using voice inflections and mouth movements after the oral reading, and signing portions of the story in ASL during or after the ASL narration. The children often selected these books at other times of the day to explore and retell. Results suggested that interest in books generated by the intervention could provide a foundation for early reading.

Williams and McLean (1997) examined responses to storybook reading of five profoundly deaf children, ages 4–5 years, and the procedures used by their teachers to facilitate responses. They videotaped 16 storybook reading sessions over a 4-month period. Results indicated that the deaf children's responses to storybook reading demonstrated engagement and interest in ways that were similar to hearing children. Furthermore, as the teacher read, she modeled and explicitly taught a number of book-reading behaviors, reading strategies, and concepts about print. The researchers concluded that the instructional approach supported the children's early reading development.

Gillespie and Twardosz (1997) investigated a group storybook reading intervention at a residential school for the deaf with 18 deaf children, 9 in the experimental group and 9 in the control group. They ranged in age from 4 to 11 years and were reading at the preprimer or primer level. Group storybook reading intervention took place in the children's cottages (i.e., smallgroup residences) twice weekly, 30 min each session, over a period of 5 months. Group storybook reading did not occur in the cottages of the children in the control group, but counselors read to individual children upon request. Results indicated that the children in the experimental group were highly engaged during the group storybook reading sessions, particularly when the story readers used interactive and/or expressive reading styles. They displayed significantly more independence than the children in the control group. However, no statistically significant differences were found between the two groups on early reading behaviors.

These studies suggest that interactive storybook reading may be an effective approach for supporting deaf children's early reading development. Given the importance of emergent and early reading development, further intervention studies with young deaf readers are clearly needed.

Developmental Reading Instruction

Developmental reading instruction is traditionally viewed as the beginning of formal approaches to teaching literacy. Instructional approaches during emergent and early literacy development are designed to support the child's emergent reading behaviors and to extend initial concepts about print. Instructional approaches designed to encourage the continuing development of reading abilities, as children move from novice to proficient readers, compose the scope and intent of developmental reading instruction.

Alphabetics and Word Recognition

Readers have essentially five strategies for recognizing words in print. Phonic analysis involves using the cues that letter–sound relationships offer. Analogy involves using the cues that similar known words offer. Structural analysis involves using the cues that morphemes offer. Context involves using the semantic and syntactic cues of known words in the sentence. Sight word recognition involves the ability of the reader to identify a word automatically.

Phonological Coding

A number of researchers have been interested in the role of phonology in reading, given that English is an alphabetic language, and the capability of deaf readers to use phonology in word recognition.

The research on phonology has largely been concerned with determining how deaf readers cognitively code printed words (see Paul, this volume). Although researchers have been particularly interested in whether and how deaf readers use phonological or speech-based codes, they have also been interested in alternative codes such as fingerspelling and sign codes. Much of this research is predicated on the theory that phonological coding is most efficiently stored in working memory. To comprehend text, working memory must be able to hold several words long enough to process complete sentences. If the reader is using a coding strategy that puts so much demand on working memory that few words can be retained while processing the meaning of a sentence, then comprehension will suffer.

The study considered seminal to the research on phonological coding was conducted by Conrad (1979). Conrad was interested in determining whether deaf readers use "internal speech," which was his term for speech-based (phonological) codes, or a direct visual representation to code written words. Using words that sound alike but look different and words that look alike but sound different, he found that the deaf students in this study, between the ages of 15 and 16 years, who used internal speech were likely to be less deaf and more intelligent than those who did not use internal speech.

When Hirsh-Pasek and Treiman (1982) reviewed the research literature on phonological coding by deaf readers, they did not find evidence of phonological coding but did find evidence for sign coding in most deaf students. Hanson and colleagues (Hanson, Goodell, & Perfetti, 1991; Hanson, Liberman, & Shankweiler, 1984; Hanson & Wilkenfeld, 1985) carried out a series of studies on awareness of phonology by deaf readers. When Hanson (1989) reviewed the research literature, including her own studies, she found evidence that better deaf readers use phonological coding and

suggested that phonological sensitivity is important in becoming a skilled reader. Hanson also conjectured that deaf readers acquire phonology from a combination of experience with orthography through reading, experience in speaking, and experience in lipreading.

Leybaert and Alegria (1993) used a Stroop task (i.e., words printed in a color different from the color actually named) with 9- to 15-year-old oral deaf students. Schaper and Reitsma (1993) used sets of pseudo-words alike visually with different pronunciations and words visually different with similar pronunciations with 6- to 13-year-old oral deaf students. Kelly (1993) used function words and inflections with high school deaf students. Results of all three studies showed a tendency for participants to access phonological information during reading, particularly the more skilled readers. However, no evidence was provided to indicate the strength of phonological knowledge or application of phonology to word recognition.

Sutcliffe, Dowker, and Campbell (1999) examined the spelling of 17 deaf children using manual English. Results indicated that although the deaf children showed sensitivity to phonology in spelling, they made limited use of spelling strategies requiring phonological awareness. Transler, Leybaert, and Gombert (1999) investigated whether deaf children use phonological syllables as reading units in a study with 21 deaf children using French Sign Language, ages 7–12, and 21 hearing children, ages 7–8. The students were asked to read and copy pronounceable pseudo-words and real words. No evidence of phonological processing was found in the deaf readers. Although they had not set out to examine the use of fingerspelling as a coding strategy, the researchers observed that many of the hearing subjects made subvocalizations and many of the deaf subjects made fingerspelling movements.

If deaf readers are able code phonologically but often do not, as this body of research indicates, then instructional approaches aimed at speech-based coding might enable deaf readers to benefit from their abilities. Alternatively, if deaf readers more easily apply other codes, instruction might be more effective if these codes were taught.

Fingerspelling, Sign, and Other Coding

Several researchers have explored other codes that deaf readers use. Fischler (1985) found comparability of word recognition performance between deaf and hearing college readers and concluded that, by college age, word recognition was not a major factor in reading ability. Hirsh-Pasek (1987) found no evidence that deaf students ages 5–16 regularly decoded sight words into fingerspelling; however, the students showed increased word identification when they did decode into fingerspelling. Siedlecki, Votaw, Bonvillian, and Jordan (1990) found that signable words (i.e., words with a one-sign translation equivalent in ASL) were recalled more frequently by deaf college students than words with no readily available sign equivalent. They also found that imagery value of words that were read affected the recall only of better deaf readers. The researchers concluded that better deaf readers may use visual codes, including an internal sign-based code, in addition to a speech-based code.

Wauters, Knoors, Vervloed, and Aarnoutse (2001) investigated the effects of an instructional intervention designed to improve the word recognition of 14 deaf students, ages 6–10, in a bilingual deaf education program. One list of frequently appearing Dutch words was presented in speech only and one list in speech and sign. Results showed that accuracy was significantly higher for words learned through speech accompanied by sign than for words learned only through speech.

Fluent readers are able to read with speed and accuracy, and when reading aloud or in sign, with expression. Fluency can be viewed as freedom from word recognition problems that interfere with comprehension. We found no studies addressing fluency in deaf readers in the literature.

In summary, the body of research literature on word recognition does not provide a clear direction for instructional practice. Intervention studies are few. Theoretical studies, such as Gaustad's (2000) examination of the potential benefits of morphological sensitivity as a foundation for early decoding instruction with deaf readers, should lead to investigations of instructional interventions for word recognition.

Comprehension

The research literature on comprehension of deaf readers divides along two major categories: the readers' use of prior knowledge and their cognitive strategies.

Prior Knowledge

Reading has been described as an interaction between reader and text. The reader brings prior knowledge that shapes expectations for the text, and experience with text builds knowledge. This reciprocal relationship has been described by some theorists as a transaction (Marshall, 2000; Rosenblatt, 1978). The research on the prior knowledge of deaf readers falls into four areas: knowledge of syntax, background knowledge of text topic, knowledge of text structure, and vocabulary knowledge.

Knowledge of Syntax. Deaf readers' frequent difficulty with English syntax has led to numerous studies into the effects of syntactic difficulties on reading performance as well as investigations into ameliorating these difficulties through syntactic manipulation of text material. The *Reading Milestones* reading series, which was targeted for deaf readers, consisted of stories written with simple and then increasingly more complex sentence structures that paralleled the linguistic structures of deaf students that had been observed in research studies conducted in the 1970s (Quigley, McAnally, King, & Rose, 1991). No assessment of the effectiveness of the series with deaf readers was found in the research literature.

Early studies on syntactic knowledge showed that deaf students seek to make connections between sentences (Nolen & Wilbur, 1985), deaf readers show better comprehension with context beyond the sentence level (McKnight, 1989), semantic issues are at least as important as syntactic issues for deaf readers (Stoefen-Fisher 1987/1988), and rewriting text into simpler sentence structures does not facilitate comprehension (Israelite & Helfrich, 1988). Although Negin (1987) found that manipulating syntax improved comprehension, he only modified the visual appearance of the sentences through segmentation of meaning units and not the structure per se.

Lillo-Martin, Hanson, and Smith (1992) found that whether they were identified as good or poor readers, deaf college students were proficient in comprehending the relative clause structure. Given that difficulty with a complex syntactic structure did not appear to differentiate between deaf good and poor readers, they concluded that reading ability of deaf college students is not due to syntactic difficulties.

Kelly (1996) examined the test scores of three populations of deaf readers: 100 oral adolescents, 113 total communication adolescents, and 211 total communication postsecondary students. He examined scores on tests of syntactic and vocabulary knowledge and found that students with relatively high levels of syntactic competence were better able to apply vocabulary knowledge.

Miller (2000) sought to determine whether syntactic or semantic processing dominates the comprehension of deaf readers. He asked 32 oral and signing deaf students to read semantically leading, neutral, and misleading sentences, each followed by a multiple-choice question. He found that semantic plausibility was related to comprehension regardless of syntactic structure. However, Miller concluded that although semantic processing is predominant in deaf readers, it could not compensate for weak syntactic skills.

Determining the relative importance of semantic and syntactic knowledge is further complicated by Cavedon, Cornoldi, and DeBeni's (1984) finding that deaf 11- to 15-year-old students relied more on the structural properties of words presented in printed list format, whereas hearing peers relied more on semantic properties. Taken together, however, this body of research lends support for the importance of instructional approaches that emphasize building syntactic abilities and capitalize on deaf readers' semantic abilities.

Background Knowledge of Topic. Research with hearing readers has demonstrated that background knowledge directly influences reading comprehension (Anderson, Spiro, & Anderson, 1978; Recht & Leslie, 1988). Studies with deaf readers provide limited support for the same conclusion. However, intervention studies have shown mixed effects for approaches designed to build and activate background knowledge of deaf students.

In two investigations, a positive relationship between background knowledge and reading comprehension was found. Garrison, Long, and Dowaliby (1997) examined the relationship between background knowledge, vocabulary knowledge, and comprehension in 30 deaf college students. They found that general knowledge significantly contributed to reading comprehension of five expository passages. Jackson, Paul, and Smith (1997) investigated the contribution of

prior knowledge to the reading comprehension of 24 public school and 27 residential school deaf and hard-of-hearing students, ages 12–20 years, in oral and total communication settings. They found that reading comprehension was more positively promoted by asking the students a series of questions about an upcoming passage (e.g., "Describe bats. What do bats look like? What is on the bodies of bats? How are bats and birds different?"), rather than asking just a single question (e.g., "What do bats look like?").

In two intervention studies, the effectiveness of approaches for teaching background knowledge was assessed. Schirmer and Winter (1993) gave signing deaf students, ages 10–16 years and reading at least at the third-grade level, a thematic organizer summarizing major ideas in the upcoming story. The organizer did not improve comprehension, and the researchers concluded that reading the organizer prior to the story was either not sufficient for activating background knowledge or that activation did not ensure application of background knowledge to the reading situation. Andrews, Winograd, and DeVille (1994) used ASL summaries prior to reading for activating background knowledge with deaf students, ages 11–12 years and reading at least at the high second-grade level. Findings showed significantly better story retellings and, thus, better comprehension when the students watched an ASL summary before reading the printed text than when they read the printed text alone. Results of these studies imply that building and activating background knowledge enhances the comprehension of deaf readers, though no firm conclusions emerge regarding the most effective instructional techniques.

Knowledge of Text Structure. Research has shown that hearing children expect text to have a predictable structure and demonstrate better comprehension and recall of text that adheres to predictable structures (Fitzgerald, Spiegel, & Webb, 1985; Pappas & Brown, 1987). It has been conjectured that deaf readers develop knowledge of text structure more slowly than hearing readers (Yoshinaga-Itano & Downey, 1986). There is limited evidence indicating that deaf children can develop accurate story structure knowledge but may not use this knowledge effectively for comprehension (Griffith & Ripich, 1988).

Donin, Doehring, and Browns (1991) orally

presented a well-structured folktale at the fifth-grade readability level to 48 oral severely to profoundly deaf children, ages 7–18 years, and asked the students to retell it. The students were then asked to read and recall three structurally different passages at their reading level. Results showed that although comprehension increased with age, no structure was significantly better than any other at improving comprehension.

Schirmer (1993) asked 48 signing deaf students, ages 9–16 years and reading at least at the third-grade level, to read one well-formed and one not well-formed story at the second-grade readability. Analysis of their predictions at three stop points during silent reading indicated that they made more elaborate predictions about what would happen next in the story with the stories that were not well formed. Schirmer concluded that when deaf readers encounter material that does not completely confirm their expectations, they engage in more active cognitive processing than with predictable material. This finding thus argues against a reliance solely on well-formed stories for instruction.

Intervention studies have shown several approaches to be effective in teaching story structure to deaf students. Akamatsu's (1988) intervention involved explicitly teaching story structure components and strategies for summarizing stories. Schirmer and Bond's (1990) intervention involved asking questions reflecting major story structure components. Both interventions were effective in improving comprehension through increased knowledge of story structure.

In a study by Luetke-Stahlman, Griffiths, and Montgomery (1998), intervention involved a strategy they called "teacher mediation." The teacher read a story to a 7-year-old deaf child, using signed English, and the child retold it. The teacher mediated the child's retelling by encouraging the child to include specific story structure components during the retelling. Findings showed an increase in the targeted story structure components as well as lengthier retellings as a result of the intervention.

Vocabulary. Research on vocabulary has shown a direct relationship between vocabulary knowledge and reading comprehension (Graves, 1986; Stahl & Fairbanks, 1986). Research indicates this is also true of deaf readers (Garrison et al., 1997; LaSasso & Davey, 1987). In an investi-

gation of a vocabulary intervention, deVilliers and Pomerantz (1992) examined the extent to which deaf students could learn vocabulary through written context. The intervention involved 66 severely to profoundly deaf students, all between the ages of 12 and 18; 51 used primarily spoken language, and 15 used English-based signing. Six nouns, 6 verbs, and 6 adjectives were embedded in 2- to 3-sentence passages with context that was "lean" (i.e., provided little information about meaning other than the word's grammatical category), "rich" (i.e., provided a great deal of semantic information about the word), or "explicit" (i.e., provided a clear contrast or equivalence statement). Results showed that all of the students performed better with rich and explicit context. Findings also revealed that the better deaf readers were able to gain more from context than the poorer readers, independent of their language modes.

Cognitive Strategies

Strategic readers consciously monitor comprehension and adapt their strategies to improve understanding. Research with hearing readers has shown that good readers possess metacognitive awareness, enabling them to adjust their reading strategies, whereas poor readers do not (Paris, Lipson, & Wixson, 1983), and instruction in strategies improves comprehension (Pressley & El-Dinary, 1997). The research on cognitive strategies with deaf readers has centered on metacognition and inference.

Metacognition. When applied to the reading process, metacognition refers to readers' awareness and control over their own comprehension processes (Raphael, Myers, Tirre, Fritz, & Freebody, 1981). Research on metacognitive abilities of deaf readers points to the importance of monitoring comprehension and activating strategies to improve comprehension. In one of the earliest studies of metacognition, Davey (1987) found that deaf readers were unaware that their comprehension improved when they looked back to find the answers to questions.

Three groups of researchers have examined the kinds of strategies used by high school deaf readers to improve comprehension. Ewoldt, Israelite, and Dodds (1992) asked students to suggest strategies that would help their peers better understand three texts they had previously read and compared these to strategies suggested by their teachers. The researchers found evidence of student self-monitoring of comprehension, a match between the teachers' and students' perceptions of text difficulty, but a mismatch between the teachers' and students' recommended strategies for improving comprehension. Whereas the students recommended a greater number of independent strategies, such as rereading and using picture cues, their teachers recommended a greater number of dependent strategies, such as asking for help. Andrews and Mason (1991) asked students to think aloud while filling in words or phrases deleted from expository passages. They found that the deaf students used similar strategies as the hearing students but relied more often on rereading and background knowledge, whereas the hearing readers made greater use of context clues. Strassman (1992) videotaped deaf students responding to a questionnaire about school-related reading. Results indicated that the students focused on the (unspecified) skills they had been taught and did not use metacognitive knowledge.

When Strassman (1997) reviewed the literature on metacognition and reading in deaf students, she found that instructional practices typically emphasized skills and school-related activities, such as completing worksheets and answering teacher questions. She concluded that students would benefit from more emphasis on metacognition strategy instruction. Several other investigators have assessed approaches to improving metacognition in deaf students. Results generally indicate no direct relationship between strategy instruction and greater comprehension. Schirmer (1995) investigated mental imagery as a reading comprehension strategy and Schirmer and Woolsey (1997) studied the effects of teacher questions designed to encourage analysis, synthesis, and evaluation on reading comprehension. The participants in the 1995 study were nine deaf students, ages 7–11 years and using conceptual sign (i.e., ASL signs in English word order); in 1997, the participants were six deaf children, ages 10–12 years, using conceptual sign. In both studies, the students were engaged in weekly 30- to 45-min reading lessons for 7 weeks. In the 1995 study, the lessons included instruction in mental imagery during reading. In the 1997 study, after each story was read, the students were asked comprehension questions designed to encourage analysis, synthesis, and evaluation; no literal questions were asked. Also, the students completed a story

cloze (i.e., open-ended statements) related to the major story structure components.[1] Findings of the 1995 study showed that the children demonstrated six qualities of thinking during the mental imagery phase of the study: recollection, representation, analysis, inference, integration, and evaluation. Results of the 1997 study showed a high correlation between ability to answer the comprehension questions and inclusion of details in the story cloze, indicating that the students were able to derive story details by analyzing, synthesizing, and evaluating.

Sartawi, Al-Hilawani, and Easterbrooks (1998) taught three metacognitive strategies to 15 oral deaf students in grade three. The first, reciprocal teaching, included four parts: clarifying, predicting, questioning, and summarizing. The second, experience-based activation, involved activating the students' interests before reading. For the third, key word strategy, the students identified key words in each passage, studied the sentences before and immediately after the key word, and then prompted their classmates when misunderstandings occurred. The students read three content units and answered nine questions for each unit. Findings showed overall low increases in performance with all strategies, but the highest increase were with the key word strategy.

Inference.   Inferences are made by connecting background knowledge with information in the text being read. Good readers draw heavily on background knowledge to make inferences that are necessary for understanding the text (McKoon & Ratcliffe, 1992). Only a few studies with deaf readers have addressed inferencing as a metacognitive skill, and these have shown that deaf readers are able to make inferences during reading, and that instruction can improve deaf readers' ability to make inferences.

Brown and Brewer (1996) investigated the role of inference processes in the reading performance of 40 deaf skilled, 40 deaf less skilled, and 40 hearing college readers. The students were given 40 two-sentence paragraphs. Findings indicated that good deaf readers performed similarly to hearing readers in making predictive inferences, but less skilled deaf readers made more errors. The authors concluded that there is greater differentiation between skilled and less skilled deaf readers than between deaf and hearing readers.

Walker, Munro, and Rickards (1998a) examined scores from the Stanford Diagnostic Test of Reading for 195 deaf children, ages 9–19, to determine the relationship between literal and inferential comprehension. Results showed that literal comprehension was higher than inferential comprehension, particularly for below-average readers. Although literal and inferential scores improved with age and grade level, the gap widened between below average readers and average/above average readers.

Walker, Munro, and Rickards (1998b) evaluated an intervention designed to teach inferential reading to 60 deaf students assessed as underachieving readers, ages 9–18, using cued speech, oral, and total communication modes. The 30-lesson intervention incorporated four inferential reading strategies: locating details, simple inferential skills, complex inferential skills, and comprehension skills. Results indicated that the intervention was effective in improving inferential and overall comprehension, particularly for the younger readers.

Collectively, the body of research on comprehension points to the importance of prior knowledge and cognitive strategies but offers relatively little guidance for instructional practice. The importance of building knowledge of written syntax, topic, text structure, and vocabulary is supported by the research, but few effective techniques and strategies for deaf readers have been documented. Similarly, metacognition and the ability to make inferences are apparently as important for deaf readers as for hearing readers. However, few studies have provided evidence of effective approaches for teaching deaf readers to use metacognitive strategies and to make inferences, let alone other cognitive strategies such as predicting and summarizing.

Summary and Conclusions

The research on emergent and early reading in deaf children includes a considerably greater proportion of intervention studies than the research on developing readers. Although further study is needed to identify best instructional practices with young deaf readers, the research literature has shown that interactive storybook reading, sign print, extensive reading and writing experiences, and social interaction around literacy activities support the deaf child's emergent and early literacy development. The paucity of intervention studies with developing readers provides few answers and leaves open many questions regarding best practices. Investigations are needed of instructional interventions designed to enhance the deaf reader's capability to effectively and efficiently identify words in print through speech-based codes, sign codes, fingerspelling codes, and orthographic codes. Concomitantly, investigations need to address techniques for teaching deaf readers to comprehend syntactic structures, apply background knowledge and knowledge of text structure during reading, induce the meaning of new vocabulary through context, and activate strategies that improve comprehension.

Note

1. Cloze tasks involve measuring a person's ability to restore omitted portions of an oral or written message by reading its remaining context.

References

Akamatsu, C. T. (1988). Summarizing stories: The role of instruction in text structure in learning to write. *American Annals of the Deaf, 133*, 294–302.

Anderson, R. C., Spiro, R. J., & Anderson, M. C. (1978). Schemata as scaffolding for the representation of information in connected discourse. *American Educational Research Journal, 15*, 433–440.

Andrews, J. F. (1988). Deaf children's acquisition of prereading skills using the reciprocal teaching procedure. *Exceptional Children, 54*, 349–355.

Andrews, J. F., & Gonzales, K. (1991). Free writing of deaf children in kindergarten. *Sign Language Studies, 73*, 63–78.

Andrews, J. F., & Mason, J. (1986a). Childhood deafness and the acquisition of print concepts. In D. Yaden & S. Templeton (Eds.), *Metalinguistic awareness and beginning literacy: Conceptualizing what it means to read and write* (pp. 277–290). Portsmouth, NH: Heinemann.

Andrews, J. F., & Mason, J. (1986b). How do deaf children learn about prereading? *American Annals of the Deaf, 131*, 210–217.

Andrews, J. F., & Mason, J. M. (1991). Strategy use among deaf and hearing readers. *Exceptional Children, 57*, 536–545.

Andrews, J. F., Winograd, P., & DeVille, G. (1994). Deaf children reading fables: Using ASL summaries to improve reading comprehension. *American Annals of the Deaf, 139*, 378–386.

Brown, P. M., & Brewer, L. C. (1996). Cognitive processes of deaf and hearing skilled and less skilled readers. *Journal of Deaf Studies and Deaf Education, 1*, 263–270.

Cavedon, A., Cornoldi, C., & DeBeni, R. (1984). Structural vs. semantic coding the reading of isolated words by deaf children. *Visible Language, 18*, 372–381.

Clay, M. M. (1967). The reading behaviors of five-year-old children: A research report. *New Zealand Journal of Educational Studies, 2*, 11–31.

Conrad, R. (1979). *The deaf schoolchild: Language and cognitive function*. London: Harper & Row.

Conway, D. (1985). Children (re)creating writing: A preliminary look at the purposes of free-choice writing of hearing-impaired kindergarteners. *Volta Review, 87*, 91–107.

Davey, B. (1987). Postpassage questions: Task and reader effects on comprehension and meta-comprehension processes. *Journal of Reading Behavior, 19*, 261–283.

deVilliers, P. A., & Pomerantz, S. B. (1992). Hearing-impaired students learning new words from written context. *Applied Psycholinguistics, 13*, 409–431.

Donin, J., Doehring, D. G., & Browns, F. (1991). Text comprehension and reading achievement in orally educated hearing-impaired children. *Discourse Processes, 14*, 307–337.

Ewoldt, C. (1985). A descriptive study of the developing literacy of young hearing-impaired children. *Volta Review, 87*, 109–126.

Ewoldt, C., Israelite, N., & Dodds, R. (1992). The ability of deaf students to understand text: A comparison of the perceptions of teachers and students. *American Annals of the Deaf, 137*, 351–361.

Fischler, I. (1985). Word recognition, use of context, and reading skill among deaf college students. *Reading Research Quarterly, 20*, 203–218.

Fitzgerald, J., Spiegel, D. L., & Webb, T. B. (1985). Development of children's knowledge of story structure and content. *Journal of Educational Research, 79*, 101–108.

Garrison, W., Long, G., & Dowaliby, F. (1997). Working memory capacity and comprehension processes in deaf readers. *Journal of Deaf Studies and Deaf Education, 2*, 78–94.

Gaustad, M. G. (2000). Morphographic analysis as a word identification strategy for deaf readers. *Journal of Deaf Studies and Deaf Education, 5*, 60–80.

Gillespie, C. W., & Twardosz, S. (1997). A group storybook-reading intervention with children at a residential school for the deaf. *American Annals of the Deaf, 141*, 320–332.

Graves, M. F. (1986). Vocabulary learning and instruction. In E. Z. Rothkopf (Ed.), *Review of research in education* (pp. 49–89). Washington, DC: American Educational Research Association.

Griffith, P. L., & Ripich, D. N. (1988). Story structure recall in hearing-impaired, learning-disabled, and nondisabled children. *American Annals of the Deaf, 133*, 43–50.

Hanson, V. L. (1989). Phonology and reading: Evidence from profoundly deaf readers. In D. Shankweiler & I. Y. Liverman (Eds.), *Phonology and reading disability: Solving the reading puzzle* (pp. 69–89). Ann Arbor: University of Michigan.

Hanson, V. L., Goodell, E. W., & Perfetti, C. A. (1991). Tongue-twister effects in the silent reading of hearing and deaf college students. *Journal of Memory and Language, 30*, 319–330.

Hanson, V. L., Liberman, I. Y., & Shankweiler, D. (1984). Linguistic coding by deaf children in relation to beginning reading success. *Journal of Experimental Child Psychology, 37*, 378–393.

Hanson, V. L., & Wilkenfeld, D. (1985). Morphophonology and lexical organization in deaf readers. *Language and Speech, 18*, 269–280.

Hirsh-Pasek, K. (1987). The metalinguistics of fingerspelling: An alternate way to increase reading vocabulary in congenitally deaf readers. *Reading Research Quarterly, 22*, 455–474.

Hirsh-Pasek, K., & Treiman, R. (1982). Recoding in silent reading: Can the deaf child translate print into a more manageable form? *Volta Review, 84*, 71–82.

Israelite, N. K., & Helfrich, M. A. (1988). Improving text coherence in basal readers: Effects of revisions on the comprehension of hearing-impaired and normal-hearing readers. *Volta Review, 90*, 261–276.

Jackson, D. W., Paul, P. V., & Smith, J. C. (1997). Prior knowledge and reading comprehension ability of deaf adolescents. *Journal of Deaf Studies and Deaf Education, 2*, 172–184.

Kelly, L. P. (1993). Recall of English function words and inflections by skilled and average deaf readers. *American Annals of the Deaf, 138*, 288–296.

Kelly, L. P. (1996). The interaction of syntactic competence and vocabulary during reading by deaf students. *Journal of Deaf Studies and Deaf Education, 1*, 75–90.

LaSasso, C., & Davey, B. (1987). The relationship between lexical knowledge and reading comprehension for prelingually, profoundly hearing-impaired students. *Volta Review, 89*, 211–220.

Leybaert, J., & Alegria, J. (1993). Is word processing involuntary in deaf children? *British Journal of Developmental Psychology, 11*, 1–29.

Lillo-Martin, D. C., Hanson, V. L., & Smith, S. T. (1992). Deaf readers' comprehension of relative clause structures. *Applied Psycholinguistics, 13*, 13–30.

Luetke-Stahlman, B., Griffiths, C., & Montgomery, N. (1998). Development of text structure knowledge as assessed by spoken and signed retellings of a deaf second-grade student. *American Annals of the Deaf, 143*, 337–346.

Marshall, J. (2000). Research on response to literature. In M. L. Kamil, P. B. Mosenthal, P. D. Pearson, & R. Barr (Eds.), *Handbook of reading research* (Vol. 3, pp. 381–402). Mahwah, NJ: Lawrence Erlbaum Associates.

Maxwell, M. (1984). A deaf child's natural development of literacy. *Sign Language Studies, 44*, 191–224.

McKnight, T. K. (1989). The use of cumulative cloze to investigate contextual build-up in deaf and hearing readers. *American Annals of the Deaf, 134*, 268–272.

McKoon, G., & Ratcliffe, R. (1992). Inference during reading. *Psychological Review, 99*, 440–466.

Miller, P. F. (2000). Syntactic and semantic processing in Hebrew readers with prelingual deafness. *American Annals of the Deaf, 145*, 436–451.

Negin, G. A. (1987). The effects of syntactic segmentation on the reading comprehension of hearing impaired students. *Reading Psychology, 8*, 23–31.

Nolen, S. B., & Wilbur, R. B. (1985). The effects of context on deaf students' comprehension of difficult sentences. *American Annals of the Deaf, 130*, 231–235.

Pappas, C. C., & Brown, E. (1987). Young children learning story discourse: Three case studies. *The Elementary School Journal, 87*, 455–466.

Paris, S. G., Lipson, M. Y., & Wixson, K. K. (1983). Becoming a strategic reader. *Contemporary Educational Psychology, 8*, 293–316.

Pressley, M., & El-Dinary, P. B. (1997). What we know about translating comprehension strategies instruction research into practice. *Journal of Learning Disabilities, 30*, 486–488.

Quigley, S., McAnally, P., King, C., & Rose, S. (1991). *Reading milestones*. Austin, TX: Pro-Ed.

Raphael, T. E., Myers, A. C., Tirre, W. C., Fritz, M., & Freebody, P. (1981). The effects of some known sources of reading difficulty on meta-comprehension and comprehension. *Journal of Reading Behavior, 13*, 325–334.

Recht, D. R., & Leslie, L. (1988). Effect of prior knowledge on good and poor readers' memory of text. *Journal of Educational Psychology, 80*, 16–20.

Robbins, N. (1983). The effects of signed text on the reading comprehension of hearing-impaired children. *American Annals of the Deaf, 128*, 40–44.

Rosenblatt, L. M. (1978). *The reader, the text, the poem*. Carbondale: Southern Illinois University.

Rottenberg, C. (2001). A deaf child learns to read. *American Annals of the Deaf, 146*, 270–275.

Rottenberg, C., & Searfoss, L. (1992). Becoming literate in a preschool class: Literacy development of hearing-impaired children. *Journal of Reading Behavior, 24*, 463–479.

Rowe, L., & Allen, B. (1995). Interactive storybook reading with young deaf children in school and home settings. In P. Dreyer (Ed.), *Towards multiple perspectives on literacy: Fifty-ninth Yearbook of the Claremont Reading Conference* (pp. 170–182). Claremont, CA: The Claremont Reading Conference.

Ruiz, N. (1995). A young deaf child learns to write: Implications for literacy development. *The Reading Teacher, 49*, 206–217.

Sartawi, A., Al-Hilawani, Y. A., & Easterbrooks, S. R. (1998). A pilot study of reading comprehension strategies of students who are deaf/hard of hearing in a non-English-speaking country. *Journal of Children's Communication Development, 20*, 27–32.

Schaper, M. W., & Reitsma, P. (1993). The use of speech-based recoding in reading by prelingually deaf children. *American Annals of the Deaf, 138*, 46–54.

Schirmer, B. R. (1993). Constructing meaning from narrative text: Cognitive processes of deaf children. *American Annals of the Deaf, 138*, 397–403.

Schirmer, B. R. (1995). Mental imagery and the reading comprehension of deaf children. *Reading Research and Instruction, 34*, 177–188.

Schirmer, B. R., & Bond, W. L. (1990). Enhancing the hearing impaired child's knowledge of story structure to improve comprehension of narrative text. *Reading Improvement, 27*, 242–254.

Schirmer, B. R., & Winter, C. R. (1993). Use of cognitive schema by children who are deaf for comprehending narrative text. *Reading Improvement, 30*, 26–34.

Schirmer, B. R., & Woolsey, M. L. (1997). Effect of teacher questions on the reading comprehension of deaf children. *Journal of Deaf Studies and Deaf Education, 2*, 47–56.

Siedlecki, T., Votaw, M.C., Bonvillian, J. D., & Jordan, I. K. (1990). The effects of manual interference and reading level on deaf subjects' recall of word lists. *Applied Psycholinguistics, 11*, 185–199.

Soderbergh, R. (1985). Early reading with deaf children. *Quarterly Review of Education, 15*, 77–85.

Stahl, S. A., & Fairbanks, M. M. (1986). The effects of

vocabulary instruction: A model-based meta-analysis. *Review of Educational Research, 56,* 72–110.

Stoefen-Fisher, J. M. (1987–1988). Hearing-impaired adolescents' comprehension of anaphoric relationship within conjoined sentences. *Journal of Special Education, 21,* 85–98.

Stoefen-Fisher, J., & Lee, M. A. (1989). The effectiveness of the graphic representation of signs in developing word identification skills for hearing impaired beginning readers. *Journal of Special Education, 23,* 151–167.

Strassman, B. K. (1992). Deaf adolescents' metacognitive knowledge about school-related reading. *American Annals of the Deaf, 137,* 326–330.

Strassman, B. K. (1997). Metacognition and reading in children who are deaf: A review of the research. *Journal of Deaf Studies and Deaf Education, 2,* 140–149.

Sulzby, E., & Teale, W. (1991). Emergent literacy. In R. Barr, M. Kamil, P. Mosenthal, & P. D. Pearson (Eds.), *Handbook of reading research* (Vol. 2 pp. 727–757). White Plains, NY: Longman.

Sutcliffe, A., Dowker, A., & Campbell, R. (1999). Deaf children's spelling: Does it show sensitivity to phonology? *Journal of Deaf Studies and Deaf Education, 4,* 111–123.

Suzuki, S., & Notoya, M. (1984). Teaching written language to deaf infants and preschoolers. *Topics in Early Childhood Special Education, 3*(4), 10–16.

Teale, W. (1986). The beginnings of reading and writing: Written language development during the preschool and kindergarten years. In M. Sampson (Ed.), *The pursuit of literacy* (pp. 1–29). Dubuque, IO: Kendall Hunt.

Teale, W., & Sulzby, E. (1986). Introduction: Emergent literacy as a perspective for examining how young children become writers and readers. In W. Teale & E. Sulzby (Eds.), *Emergent literacy: Writing and reading* (pp. vii–xxv). Norwood, NJ: Ablex.

Transler, C., Leybaert, J., & Gombert, J. (1999). Do deaf children use phonological syllables as reading units? *Journal of Deaf Studies and Deaf Education, 4,* 124–143.

Walker, L., Munro, J., & Rickards, F. W. (1998a). Literal and inferential reading comprehension of students who are deaf or hard of hearing. *Volta Review, 100,* 87–103.

Walker, L., Munro, J., & Rickards, F. W. (1998b). Teaching inferential reading strategies through pictures. *Volta Review, 100,* 105–120.

Wauters, L. N., Knoors, H. E. T., Vervloed, M. P. J., & Aarnoutse, C. A. J. (2001). Sign facilitation in word recognition. *The Journal of Special Education, 35,* 31–40.

Wells, G. (1986). *The meaning makers: Children learning language and using language to learn.* Portsmouth, NH: Heinemann.

Williams, C. (1994). The language and literacy worlds of three profoundly deaf preschool children. *Reading Research Quarterly, 29,* 125–155.

Williams, C. (1999). Preschool deaf children's use of signed language during writing events. *Journal of Literacy Research, 31,* 183–212.

Williams, C., & McLean, M. (1997). Young deaf children's response to picture book reading in a preschool setting. *Research in the Teaching of English, 31,* 337–366.

Wilson, T., & Hyde, M. (1997). The use of signed English pictures to facilitate reading comprehension by deaf students. *American Annals of the Deaf, 142,* 333–341.

Yoshinaga-Itano, C., & Downey, D. M. (1986). A hearing-impaired child's acquisition of schemata: Something's missing. *Topics in Language Disorders, 7,* 45–57.

9

John A. Albertini & Sara Schley

Writing
Characteristics, Instruction, and Assessment

Analyses of deaf students' writing from the 1940s through the 1960s focused on lexical and grammatical usage within the sentence. Using the linguistic tools of the day, researchers catalogued grammatical errors, word usage, and sentence length and complexity in the writing of deaf and hearing age mates. The reports indicated that sentences (and compositions) written by deaf children tended to be shorter than those written by hearing controls of the same age and that deaf students tended to reiterate words and phrases, use more articles and nouns, and use fewer adverbs and conjunctions (Heider & Heider, 1940; Myklebust, 1964). Among the most common errors noted were errors of inflectional morphology (e.g., verbs tense and agreement), the misuse of function words (e.g., articles and prepositions), and anomalies of constituent structure (i.e., the misuse of coordinating and subordinating conjunctions) (Greenberg & Withers, 1965; Stuckless & Marks, 1966; Yoshinaga-Itano & Snyder, 1985). Studies through the mid-1980s reported on length, parts of speech, error type, and sentence type (according to transformational grammar).

By the 1970s, the limitations of teaching language and writing at the sentence level were being discussed (Kretschmer & Kretschmer, 1978; Wil-

bur, 1977). Teachers and researchers began documenting deaf writers' reflections on writing and conducting studies of discourse and process alongside product. The focus of this chapter is on research conducted since the 1970s. We consider what and how deaf students write, changes in educators' conceptions of writing, and the influence of language and modality on teaching deaf students' to write considered in light of society's expectations for literacy and the uses of writing for personal, social, and academic purposes.

Background

Expectations of the Literate Citizen

Reading and writing support an information-based society. Less than a century ago, a 60% rate of literacy was acceptable (Snow, Burns, & Griffin, 1998). Today, workers in agriculture as well as in industry rely to a great extent on technology, and from all indications, the reliance on high technology and electronic communication will only increase (Allen, 1994). For example, through the 1940s the operation of printing presses required mechanical knowledge and experience, but few literacy skills. Modern printing requires technological knowledge, experience, and sophisticated literacy skills to use software and operate computers (US Ink, 2001).

Society's changing literacy expectations are reflected in school standards. The International Reading Association and the National Council of Teachers of English Standards for the English Language Arts are broader and more demanding than at any time in our history (Standards for the English Language Arts [Standards] 1996). Their standards reflect the goals of an educational system in a democratic society. Students need to become proficient and literate users of language in order to succeed in school, participate in a democracy as informed citizens, find challenging and rewarding work, appreciate and contribute to cultural activities, and pursue their own goals and interests as independent learners throughout their lives (Standards, 1996, p. vii).

Models of Writing Processes

When readers and writers interact with texts, they generate thoughts and construct meanings. Their abilities to comprehend and construct meaning determine the development of communication abilities and achievement in school. To understand this interaction, educators have proposed several models of reading and writing processes. A well-known interactive model of reading (Stanovich, 1980) describes an interaction among psycholinguistic abilities—that is, abilities related to knowledge of the language of the text and those related to world knowledge and knowledge of texts in general. Similarly, writing involves both bottom-up and top-down processes (Paul, 2001). A reader uses alphabetic and phonological information to decode print, and a writer uses grammar, spelling, and punctuation to encode thought (bottom-up processing). A reader uses language and world knowledge to interpret and predict, and the writer manipulates content, organization, and style to accommodate (or challenge) the background and perspectives of an audience (top-down processing).

From a psychological point of view, writing requires interaction between two cognitive spaces. In the content space, the writer solves problems of belief and knowledge, and in the rhetorical space, problems of organization and style. Based on their

research with hearing middle-school students, Bereiter and Scardamalia (1987) posit these cognitive spaces and two models of composing: the knowledge-telling model and the knowledge-transforming model. In the former, the writer uses existing cognitive structures to solve novel problems. An item of content from memory must "sound right" in relation to the assignment and foregoing text. In the latter, thoughts take shape as one writes and rewrites. To the extent that changing text changes thought, writing will influence the development of knowledge. In the knowledge-transforming model, the interaction between cognitive spaces is recursive and bidirectional.

Learning to write also has been characterized as a process of socialization (Kress, 1996). For the child, writing, like speaking, signing, and drawing, is a way of making and potentially sharing meaning. From a social constructivist point of view, dialogue between a writer and a reader helps the writer select content and identify problems in the rhetorical space. The function of writing becomes the representation and communication of thought in a community of writers, and, by focusing on content and process, the writer learns to communicate more clearly and effectively. Supporters of a process writing approach do not ignore grammar and mechanics (bottom-up aspects), but relegate them to the final stages of the process (see, e.g., Calkins, 1986; Cooper, 1993; Flower & Hayes, 1980; Graves, 1991; Paul, 1998, 2001).

Functions of Writing for Deaf Students

Because form and content vary with function, research and instruction should take students' experience with the functions of writing into account. Deaf students may come to school having written phone conversations (by means of a teletypewriter TTY), kitchen notes to their parents, or notes to hearing people in face-to-face conversation. Some may have written thank you notes to their relatives, made lists, or kept journals. Others may have had little need or encouragement to do such instrumental, social, or personal writing. However, deaf children's writing experiences may be increasing over time. In the mid-1980s, deaf adults retrospectively reported more use of TTYs and handwritten notes for communication in homes with deaf parents than in homes with hearing parents (Maxwell, 1985). By the mid-1990s, however, deaf adults from homes with hearing parents reported equivalent use of TTYs and handwritten notes (Albertini and Shannon, 1996).

In school, the functions of writing are generally more narrowly conceived and the forms more intellectually demanding. In the United States and Great Britain, at least, school curricula have traditionally emphasized "transactional" writing, writing to inform or persuade (Britton, Burgess, Martin, McLeod, & Rosen, 1975; Emig, 1971). Because school essays and reports require knowledge of a new form and often new content, they are more challenging to the beginner than, say, personal letters, which may assume shared context and experience. Writing a decontextualized report for a stranger requires greater attention to background and detail. The traditional function of school writing for hearing and deaf students has been evaluation. For deaf students, in addition, writing has often been used to practice the grammar and mechanics of English (Albertini, 1993). Thus, regardless of students' exposure to writing in the home, use and function narrow considerably at school. In the case of deaf students learning English through reading and writing, lack of experience at home or a narrowing of scope at school may also affect the development of language skills.

Language Learning and Writing

The development of language and literacy is interdependent. Literacy development depends on the development of interactive language skills, and literacy in turn promotes continued language growth. Monolingual and bilingual hearing children who have a solid foundation in their native language (particularly if they have academic experiences with that language), learn literacy better than those who do not have a foundation in any language (see Malakoff 1988; Snow, Cancino, De Temple, & Schley, 1991). Deaf children who know sign language show superior gains in literacy (Strong & Prinz, 1997). Yet relatively few deaf children come to school with solid knowledge of a sign language. Experience in the home may range from oral communication only, to some home-sign/gesture, to signed English, to American Sign Language (ASL), to other spoken languages and other signed languages. Deaf children's linguistic and conversational skills also vary depending on degree of hearing loss and age at which hearing loss was

identified. Whatever their backgrounds, most deaf children share a common characteristic: they are not mapping the written form of a language onto a linguistic system that they already know and understand. Instead, they are mapping a written system onto a reduced set of understandings of the language.

A well-developed linguistic system requires knowledge of the rules of conversation and discourse as well as those of vocabulary and syntax. In one third-grade classroom at a residential school, a newcomer to sign language struggled to write his own last name, and lack of interaction skills and basic ASL fluency impeded his ability to get help (see Ramsey, 1997; Ramsey & Padden, 1998). He did not know the rudimentary rules of discourse in a signing community: when to watch conversation, how to get the conversational floor for a turn, nor how to get the teacher's attention. This case points to the overlapping development of language and literacy. To learn literacy in the classroom, a deaf child must understand basic patterns of language and discourse.

Characteristics of Deaf Students' Writing

Deaf Students Compared to Hearing Peers and Non-native English Learners

On average, 17- to 18-year-old deaf students write on a par with hearing students who are 9–10 years old (Paul, 1998, 2001). Such comparisons of writing achievement parallel summaries of reading achievement (Allen, 1994; Traxler, 2000). Studies of intersentential cohesive devices (e.g., pronouns and transition words) report a difference in lexical variety or elaboration of content. Deaf children either used fewer cohesive markers (De Villiers, 1991) or fewer different lexical devices to signal cohesion (Maxwell & Falick, 1992). Where they used the same amount of markers, they elaborated content less than hearing peers (Yoshinago-Itano, Snyder, & Mayberry, 1996). Deaf children's vocabulary tends to be restricted. That is, they tend to use one lexical item per referent rather than several ("rabbit" only, vs. "rabbit," "bunny," "hare," and "bunny rabbit" in the same text) (see Paul, 1998, 2001; Marschark, Lang, & Albertini, 2002, for more detailed discussion). In the areas of spelling

and punctuation, deaf students perform more similarly to their hearing peers. Thus, studies of continuous text, like the analyses of sentences before
the 1970s, show considerable delay in deaf students' use of vocabulary and grammatical markers
when compared to hearing peers.

The writing samples of older deaf students in
many ways resemble those of hearing students
learning English as a second language (ESL)
(Langston and Maxwell, 1988). Because of this,
some have compared the learning of English and
literacy by deaf students to that of hearing ESL
students. Berent (1983, 1996) looked at deaf college students' and hearing ESL college students'
understanding of "subject control" and relative
clauses. Subject control refers to the fact that, in
spite of appearances, the infinitive phrases ("to
leave") in the following sentences have different
subjects:

John told Bill to leave.
John promised Bill to leave.

Berent's finding of similar hierarchies of difficulty
for both groups supports the comparison of deaf
students' writing to that of ESL students and points
to the potential usefulness of ESL methods with
deaf students.

Singleton, Rivers, Morgan, and Wiles (2001),
Singleton and Supalla (1998), and Schley (1994,
1996) have found effects of ASL proficiency in
their comparisons of deaf students and hearing
ESL students. Singleton et al. (2001) and Singleton, Supalla Fraychineaud, Litchfield, and Schley
(1997) found that hearing students (both ESL and
monolingual English students) produced longer
texts than did deaf learners who were moderately
or highly proficient in ASL. However, the deaf students used the same number of t-units (a t-unit is
a proposition consisting of an independent clause
and associated dependent clauses; Hunt, 1965).
The students who were more proficient ASL learners used more unique words than did either low-
proficiency ASL learners or ESL learners. Thus, the
deaf students who had some facility in ASL had a
richer vocabulary base and were less repetitive and
formulaic in their writing. Schley (1994) found
that students who had more ASL experience and
input (either from home or from a bilingual/bicul-
tural school for a number of years) scored higher
on two measures of English literacy (SAT-HI and
written samples).

Characteristics of the Beginning Writer

Andrews and Mason (1986), Conway (1985),
Ewoldt (1985, 1990), Watson (2000), and Williams (1993, 1994, 1999) have observed early writing development in deaf children. Initially, the sequence of behaviors proceeds from uncontrolled
scribbling (sometimes captioned by parents) to
controlled scribbling where "mock letters" (forms
closer to actual letters) are used for specific referents. Soon thereafter, children trace over parents'
writing, copy letters and words in their environment, and write their own names (first with mock
letters, later with real letters). Next steps include
use of invented spelling, use of print as a substitute
for drawing, and experiments with letter and story
formats. Much of this process is similar to that of
hearing children learning to write. According to
Watkins (1999), basic conditions for learning to
write include many of those known to be important
for learning to read: access to communication, an
early language base, and exposure to written language in the environment.

Hearing and deaf children differ in their early
spelling attempts. Hearing children invent spellings
based on sound/symbol relationships. Mayer and
Moskos (1998) found that young deaf children
used print-based, speech-based, and sign-based
strategies in their early spelling. Deaf children also
may focus on morphographemic relationships
(Padden, 1993). For example, they sometimes substitute letters in a word that are visually similar (tall
letters, letters with a tail) or double letters that hearing children would never double ("grren" rather
than "green"). These are print-based morphographemic errors. Sign-based errors occur when formation of a word's sign equivalent interferes with
its spelling (e.g., writing the word "cat" with an "f"
because an "f" handshape is used in the ASL sign
for cat). While deaf children can and do invent
some spellings related to phonological/symbol miscues, they often focus on the visual aspects of words
(see Ruiz, 1995).

Characteristics of Adolescent
and Adult Writers

Sentence-level grammatical and semantic anomalies persist in the writing of many deaf adolescents
and adults, and these characteristics continue to influence the perception of their overall writing skill

(Moores & Sweet, 1990; Yoshinaga-Itano et al., 1996). Here it is important to note that some lexical, grammatical, and discourse errors may be related to a learning disability. Although certain characteristics of language learning disabilities are often indistinguishable from patterns of normal language learning, one study surveyed experienced teachers and tutors of deaf students and found strong agreement that difficulties in spelling, organizing sentences coherently, and confusion of the meanings of time/space prepositions such as "before", "after", and "between" were characteristic of the writing of deaf students with learning disabilities (Berent, Samar, & Parasnis, 2000). However, acquiring English as a deaf person is not equivalent to having a learning disability, and the challenge is to determine when particular language productions indicate such a disability.

Beginning in the late 1980s, the focus of writing research broadened to include content, discourse-level structures, and fluency (e.g., Gormley & Sarachan-Deily, 1987; Klecan-Aker & Blondeau, 1990). The new focus on discourse organization uncovered unexpected similarities between hearing and deaf writers. Analyses of written stories and personal narratives, for example, showed that texts written by adolescent and college-age deaf writers were well structured when judged according to standard rubrics of text organization and when compared to texts written by hearing peers. This was true even though sentence-level grammatical characteristics of the texts differed markedly (Albertini, 1990; Marschark, Mouradian, & Halas, 1994). Key to the production of these texts was the writers' command of topic (e.g., personal narrative and fantasy). Choice of genre may also affect the quality of writing. Comparisons of dialogue journal entries with classroom compositions and personal letters with formal essays indicate that the less formal (and perhaps more familiar) genre may elicit better discourse structure and an overall higher level of performance (Albertini & Meath-Lang, 1986; Musselman & Szanto, 1998).

Writing Instruction

A Paradigm Shift

Indications of a paradigm shift in the teaching of writing became evident in the early 1970s (Elbow, 1973; Shaughnessy, 1977). Faced with non-eurocentric students unfamiliar with classical models of writing in western civilization courses, instructors in the United States, the United Kingdom, and New Zealand turned to more constructivist, process-oriented, and dialogic approaches (Hairston, 1982). Rather than asking students to write an essay on the model of Jonathan Swift, for example, teachers asked students to write from their own experience. Personal narrative was used as a gateway to writing instruction. Free writing, journals, and other process writing techniques were used to encourage reticent and less confident writers. The focus was on the process—getting one's thoughts, feelings, and memories down on paper without censoring or editing (Murray, 1976).

Freire (1970), a reformist literacy educator from Brazil, exerted particular influence on literacy educators in the United States. His formulation of pedagogy as a dialogue between teacher and student rather than as a transmission of knowledge from teacher to student ("banking") provided philosophical underpinning to "whole language" and social-constructivist approaches to literacy. Drawing on first language acquisition research, whole-language proponents argued that children should learn to read and write "naturally" in a context of real communication. From the beginning, they should be exposed to whole texts and encouraged to produce whole texts, however brief (Goodman, 1989; Weaver, 1990). Perhaps because "naturally" was never defined precisely or because some children responded better to component skills instruction, the movement has had its detractors and lost some of its momentum in mainstream classes (e.g., Dolman, 1992; Cassidy & Cassidy, 2000). Certain emphases of the philosophy persist, however, in social constructivist approaches to literacy, where construction of the curriculum (and knowledge) proceeds from student experience. Whether the objects of study are original student texts or classical models, real purposes and audiences for writing are clearly defined. In addition, writing is viewed as a tool of learning across the whole curriculum (Connolly & Vilardi, 1989).

Teaching writing to deaf students has reflected this paradigm shift. Surveying the change in literacy teaching to deaf students in English-speaking countries, Power and Leigh (2000) cite Ewoldt (1990) and others who support a top-down, whole-language approach to teaching reading and writing.

Dialogue as a metaphor for teaching and dialogue journals as a technique for teaching writing also have been proposed (Livingston, 1997; Staton, 1985; Teller & Lindsey, 1987). As noted above, writing draws on a broad range of skills, the learning of which may or may not be affected by deafness (Musselman and Szanto, 1998). Written language per se includes orthographic conventions (punctuation and spelling), lexical and grammatical expression, and intersentential relationships. The activity of writing or composing prose, however, also includes the arrangement of sentences and paragraphs according to the writer's knowledge, purpose, audience, and imagination.

Strategies

For years, writing curricula for deaf students focused almost exclusively on lexical and grammatical expression. Systems such as the Fitzgerald Key and Wing Symbols were used to teach English word order. Later, transformational grammar-based programs like Apple Tree, the Rhode Island Curriculum, and TSA Syntax Program emphasized the function of words and constituents in a sentence (see McAnally, Rose, & Quigley, 1994, for discussion of these systems and programs). Heidinger's (1984) detailed curriculum focused on the syntactic and semantic development of deaf children's writing, but again only at the sentence level. Wilbur (1977) proposed that deaf students' traditional problem areas of pronominal reference, conjunctions, and determiners (using "a" rather than "the") can mostly be traced to curricula that stop short of the intersentential relationships in writing (and language). In 1989, Livingston examined the process of revision with college students and concluded that teachers generally provided sentence-level rather than discourse-level feedback.

Process writing approaches focus the students' attention on content and continuous discourse. Writing is used to retrieve experience from memory and to record observations. Does such writing lead to improvements in lexical and grammatical expression? In a 2-year investigation that involved 325 students and 52 teachers across the United States, a holistic scoring of a variety of genres and indices of grammatical complexity indicated an improvement in overall quality of writing and an increase in grammatical complexity (Kluwin & Kelly, 1992). The authors concluded that the improve-

ments and increases in sentence complexity could have been due to students having greater freedom to experiment. When preoccupied with grammatical correctness (in more traditional approaches), students tend to experiment less with language, using simpler constructions and more familiar words (see also Andrews & Gonzalez, 1991; Brown & Long, 1992).

Because of the persistence of grammatical errors in the writing of deaf students, educators have attended to sentence-level structure, even in process-oriented programs. One relevant study investigated the use of a writing rubric as a means of combining the strengths of product and process approaches (Schirmer, Bailey, & Fitzgerald, 1999). The rubric, a grid specifying objectives and levels of performance, was used to teach and assess the writing of 4 students in grade 5 and 6 students in grade 7 throughout an entire school year. The expectation that use of the rubric would lead to grammatical as well as organizational improvement was not met. Students improved on traits related to content and organization but not on those related to vocabulary, structure, and mechanics.

For several years now, educators have suggested that writing should be used as a tool for reading and for learning. Zamel (1992) reasoned that for English learners, the process of reading becomes transactional if reading is embedded in reflective and summative writing. Writing helps the reader connect information and, in effect, compose an understanding of the text. Botstein (1986) claimed that writing in "common ordinary language" was crucial to the effective teaching of science and mathematics (p. xiii). When students (and teachers) use ordinary language to write about these subjects, it allows them to connect unfamiliar terms, theories, insights, and facts to their own experience (see also Yore, 2000). Moderate correlations in measures of reading and writing performance by deaf students indicate an overlap in these skills (Albertini et al., 1986; Moores & Sweet, 1990), yet the tendency is to teach them separately. A study by Akamatsu (1988) points to the reciprocal relationship in teaching story structure to deaf students. Her results suggested that such reading instruction contributed to the students' ability to write story summaries. Completing the loop, improvement in writing story summaries should lead to improved story comprehension. A study of uncorrected and ungraded student science writing by deaf students indeed suggested that process writing contributed to science learning and the ability of teachers to evaluate the learning (Lang & Albertini, 2001).

The use of technologies to facilitate the composing process and to teach writing to deaf students has also been investigated. Studies of TTY communication have focused on conversational interaction and language structure characteristics (Geoffrion, 1982; Johnson & Barton, 1988; Lieberth, 1988; Nash & Nash, 1982). The use of a computer is reported to have had a significant effect on the quality of deaf students' writing in the context of a process writing program (Mander, Wilton, Townsend, & Thomson, 1995). Using a nonequivalent control group design, the research team found that students' writing in a primary school class improved significantly on measures of quality and linguistic development after introduction and use of a computer. The use of local area networks for language practice and writing instruction in deaf classrooms began with ENFI (Electronic Networks for Interaction) at Gallaudet University in 1985 (Bruce, Peyton, & Batson, 1993). In tutoring younger students, college students developed their own abilities to develop ideas and write more formal academic prose (Peyton, 1989). Other quantitative and qualitative analyses of ENFI projects indicated that gains were nearly the same for ENFI and non-ENFI groups (Fowles, 1993), but that the essays written by ENFI students were more conversational in nature than those written by the non-ENFI students (Bartholomae, 1993). Thus, results are mixed with regard to teaching students the conventions of formal academic prose. However, for students who are afraid to put one foot in front of the other for fear of tripping up grammatically, fluency and a conversational style may be appropriate goals.

Languages, Modalities, and Writing

Since the late 1980s and the beginning of bilingual education programs in schools for the deaf, several studies have examined the influence of ASL on English literacy development. Although studies with older students show a positive relationship between ASL proficiency and English literacy (Prinz & Strong, 1998; Prinz & Strong, 1997), the results of studies with younger students are not as clear (Schley, 1994; Singleton et al., 1997, 2001; Singleton & Supalla, 1998). Schley (1994) found a modest positive association between ASL proficiency and English literacy in elementary-aged deaf children at an ASL/English bilingual school; however, in another study Singleton and Supalla (1998) found no clear relationship between the two. Thus, research conducted to date indicates positive effects of ASL proficiency on English literacy by middle school and high school but not before.

Studies of writing process and modality suggest variation in the use of signing across age and situation. Williams (1999) found that deaf preschool students were beginning to use writing along with ASL, Pidgin Sign English (PSE), facial expression, gesture, and pantomime as a means of communicating experience. Her analysis indicated that children were using writing to depict experience rather than to record speech (for a detailed consideration of semiotic precursors to writing, see Kress, 1997). Mayer and Akamatsu (2000) questioned the utility of ASL and a signed form of English for older students at the point of composing. Although both provide comprehensible input, Mayer and Akamatsu concluded that the signed form of English better served as the bridge between inner speech and written text.

Mayer (1999) examined the writing processes of two 13-year-old deaf writers. Both students mouthed their words (one while writing, the other while rereading her writing). Although both were skilled users of ASL, they did not sign to themselves while writing and were surprised to be asked about it. Mayer concluded that both writers were depending on an inner version of English at the point of composing. In a related study, 7 out of 20 deaf college students, all proficient signers, wrote of perceiving an inner voice when asked to comment on the metaphor of voice in writing (Albertini, Meath-Lang, & Harris, 1994). They described the experience as either hearing their own voice as they wrote or sensing a voice telling them what to do. While some of the students extended the metaphor to signing as an expression of one's voice, none reported experiencing inner signing as they wrote.

These findings notwithstanding, some deaf students report composing in sign. Accordingly, five college students were allowed mediation to produce examination essays (Biser, Rubel, & Toscano, 1998). Interpreters voiced the students' signed responses to the essay topic into a tape recorder. Using both the first (themselves on videotape) and second (transcribed) drafts, two of the students wrote passing essays. Mediation appeared to facilitate the composing process for these students, although not for the others. Further investigation is needed to determine the effects of mediation on the overall fluency and coherence of written texts.

Assessment

In the 1960s, the best predictor of teachers' ratings of writing quality was grammatical correctness (Stuckless & Marks, 1966). Then and today, most lay readers are struck by the English language errors produced by deaf writers. Indeed, we know that for deaf language learners, the acquisition of morphology, syntax, and lexical knowledge often lag behind the acquisition of vocabulary, content knowledge, and rhetorical skills. However, as the teaching of writing to deaf students has expanded beyond a focus on sentence-level grammatical correctness, so too has the scope of what is assessed.

Although grammatical correctness is one indication of writing quality, current assessments also take into account dimensions such as content and organization. Still, a single assessment will necessarily focus on a certain set of characteristics, and selection of an appropriate assessment tool will depend on the purpose for assessing students at the classroom or program levels. Schools typically assess writing in order to (1) place students appropriately, (2) determine proficiency (for exit requirements, for example) or (3) evaluate the effectiveness of a program. Teachers assess writing (1) to chart progress, (the achievement of developmental milestones, for example), (2) to assess learning, and (3) to diagnose areas of strength and weakness.

The most widely used types of writing tests today are multiple-choice, essay, and portfolio assessments. In multiple-choice tests, an indirect way of sampling performance, students' linguistic, rhetorical, and stylistic choices are taken as an indication of writing skill. Essay tests are direct in that actual writing samples are rated for correctness and competency. In the portfolio, or longitudinal approach, a number of samples are collected over the course of a term, a year, or several years. (For more detailed discussion of these types of assessments, see Luetke-Stahlman & Luckner, 1991; Marschark et al., 2002; and Paul, 1998. For more on longi-

tudinal assessments, see French, 1999; Schirmer, 1994; and Stewart & Kluwin, 2001).

With an increase in the number of deaf students entering postsecondary institutions in the United States, indirect multiple-choice tests (e.g., the Written English Expression Placement Test, 1985) are frequently used for placement in reading and writing courses. Use of these tests raises concerns of fairness and accuracy because the recognition of writing conventions and correct usage are typical areas of difficulty for deaf writers. In addition, the tests involve significant amounts of reading, a potential confound, especially for deaf students. To judge the relative validity of using available indirect assessments with deaf and hard-of-hearing college students, Berent and colleagues (1996) conducted an analysis of the ability of two widely used indirect measures of writing (The Written English Expression Placement Test and The New Jersey High School Proficiency Test: Writing Section) to predict scores on a third, direct assessment of writing (The Test of Written English, normally administered in association with the Test of English as a Foreign Language, or TOEFL). Their analyses indicated that indirect tests were poor predictors of competency as determined by performance on the direct test.

A concern regarding the use of direct assessments is agreement among raters, or interrater reliability. To achieve reliable scoring, raters need to agree on characteristics and criteria. Thus, scoring procedures and training are used to control "the disparate impact of personal experience, variation, and expectation" (Huot, 1990, p. 257). Two types of scoring procedures are now being used widely by teachers and administrators. Holistic procedures require a rater to use a single scale (e.g., 1–6) to rate a writing sample. Here, the assigned rating represents an impression of overall writing quality. Analytic procedures require assignment of separate scores to various components of writing. Grammar, organization, and content, for example, are scored on separate scales according to predetermined criteria for each. A third, less widely used procedure is primary trait scoring, which focuses on features important for a particular audience and purpose. For example, organization and use of technical vocabulary might be singled out in the rating of a chemistry laboratory report.

In one holistic rating procedure used to place deaf college students in developmental writing courses, acceptable interrater reliability was achieved by having readers assign equal weight to organization, content, language, and vocabulary (Albertini et al., 1986). The procedure used in the National Technical Institute for the Deaf (NTID) Writing Test (based on Jacobs, Zinkgraf, Wormuth, Hatfield, & Hughey, 1981) remains holistic in that ratings of the categories overlap (Bochner, Albertini, Samar,& Metz, 1992). Since its development, several studies have demonstrated external, concurrent, and predictive validity of the NTID Writing Test (Bochner et al., 1992; Albertini, Bochner, Dowaliby, & Henderson, 1996). In 1992, the state of Kansas began using a six-trait analytical scale to assess student writing, and one study suggests that it may be reliably used with deaf students (Heefner & Shaw, 1996). Yoshinaga-Itano and colleagues (1996) have used detailed analytic rating scales to determine deaf students' control of semantic written-language variables (such as lexical repetition and lexical and pronominal reference across sentences). Although used for research in that study, Yoshinaga-Itano et al. suggested that the scales might also be used for assessment purposes.

Although the use of longitudinal methods of assessment, such as portfolios and teacher logs, are frequently recommended (e.g., Isaacson, 1996), research supporting the use of these methods with deaf students has yet to appear. The studies cited above center on assessment at the school program level, but valid and reliable assessment at any level rests on how closely the tests match writing in the real world and how objective (consistent and fair) the teacher can be in rating students' process and products. In the classroom, the teacher is involved in additional activities that function, from the students' point of view, as forms of assessment. When a teacher grades, corrects, or simply responds to a students' writing, the teacher provides an assessment of student performance.

Summary and Conclusions

Several conclusions may be drawn from recent studies in the teaching and assessment of writing with deaf students. First, aspects of form (that is, grammar) are resistant to change even when deaf students write with purpose and focus on meaning. Grammatical and lexical performance will not improve significantly without direct instruction, and

by all accounts, changes in grammatical and lexical performance will occur only over periods of years and in programs where students are encouraged to write frequently and at length. However, programs that encourage students to write from personal experience and in various genres will likely foster the development of discourse organization and fluency. Analyses of organization, content, and effect of genre revealed similarities in the writing of deaf and hearing students. For deaf students, the use of more familiar genres, those that emphasize communication, self-expression, or imagination, will be beneficial.

For students learning to communicate in more than one language and modality while learning to write, theory supports linking languages and bridging modalities. Available research indicates that both ASL and signed forms of English contribute to the development of English literacy and that this contribution becomes evident by the middle and high school years. The effects of using computers, networks, and mediated texts also have been investigated. Where the teacher wishes to foreground peer review and commentary, computer networks can facilitate the writing process. If we construe writing as the physical act of making meaning, it follows that tools and techniques will influence process (Bolter, 1991). As students learn to use nontraditional tools to find information and create text, traditional ideas of reading and writing may change, and despite mandates which compartmentalize writing into component skills, the research reviewed here suggests that the teaching and testing of writing will benefit from more comprehensive, balanced, and functional approaches.

References

Akamatsu, C.T. (1988). Summarizing stories: The role of instruction in text structure in learning to write. *American Annals of the Deaf, 133*, 294–302.

Albertini, J.A. (1993). Critical literacy, whole language, and the teaching of writing to deaf students: Who should dictate to whom? *TESOL Quarterly, 27*, 59–73.

Albertini, J.A. (1990). Coherence in deaf students' writing. In J. Kreeft Peyton (Ed.), *Students and teachers writing together: Perspectives on journal writing* (pp. 127–136). Alexandria, VA: Teachers of English to Speakers of Other Languages.

Albertini, J.A., Bochner, J.H., Cuneo, C.A., Hunt, L.S., Nielsen, R.B., Seago, L.M., & Shannon, N.B. (1986). Development of a writing test for deaf college students. *Teaching English to Deaf and Second-Language Students*, 4, 5–11.

Albertini, J.A., Bochner, J.H., Dowaliby, F., Henderson, J.B. (1996). Valid assessment of writing and access to academic discourse. *Journal of Deaf Studies and Deaf Education*, 2, 71–77.

Albertini, J.A., & Meath-Lang, B. (1986). An analysis of student-teacher exchanges in dialogue journal writing. *Journal of Curriculum Theorizing*, 7, 153–201.

Albertini, J.A., Meath-Lang, B., & Harris, D.P. (1994). Voice as muse, message, and medium: The views of deaf college students. In K. Yancey (Ed.), *Voices on voice: Perspectives, definitions, inquiry* (pp. 172–190). Urbana, IL: National Council of Teachers of English.

Albertini, J.A., & Shannon, N.B. (1996). Kitchen notes, "the grapevine," and other writing in childhood. *Journal of Deaf Studies and Deaf Education*, 1, 64–74.

Allen, T.E. (1994). *Who are the deaf and hard-of-hearing students leaving high school and entering post-secondary education?* Paper submitted to Pelavin Research Institute as part of the project, A Comprehensive Evaluation of the Postsecondary Educational Opportunities for Students who are Deaf or Hard of Hearing, funded by the U.S. Office of Special Education and Rehabilitative Services. Retrieved July, 2002, from http:www.gallaudet.edu/AnnualSurvey/whodeaf.html

Andrews, J. F., & Gonzales, K. (1991). Free writing of deaf children in kindergarten. *Sign Language Studies*, 73, 63–78.

Andrews, J.F., & Mason, J. (1986). How do deaf children learn about prereading? *American Annals of the Deaf*, 131(3), 210–217.

Bartholomae, D. (1993). "I'm talking about Alan Bloom": Writing on the network." In B. Bruce, J.K. Peyton, & T. Batson (Eds.), *Network-based classrooms* (pp. 237–262). New York: Cambridge University Press.

Bereiter, C., & Scardamalia, M. (1987). *The psychology of written composition*. Hillsdale, NJ: Lawrence Erlbaum Associates.

Berent, G. P. (1983). Control judgments by deaf adults and by second language learners. *Language Learning*, 33, 37–53.

Berent, G.P. (1996). The acquisition of English syntax by deaf learners. In W. Ritchie & T. Bhatia (Eds.), *Handbook of second language acquisition* (pp. 469–506). San Diego, CA: Academic Press.

Berent, G.P., Samar, V.J., Kelly, R.R., Berent, R., Bochner, J., Albertini, J., & Sacken, J. (1996). Validity of indirect assessment of writing competency for deaf and hard-of-hearing college students. *Journal of Deaf Studies and Deaf Education*, 1, 167–178.

Berent, G.P., Samar, V.J., & Parasnis, I. (2000). College teachers' perceptions of English language characteristics that identify English language learning disabled deaf students. *American Annals of the Deaf*, 145, 342–358.

Biser, E., Rubel, L., & Toscano, R.M. (1998). Mediated texts: A heuristic for academic writing. *Journal of Basic Writing*, 17, 56–72.

Bochner, J.H., Albertini, J.A., Samar, V.J., & Metz, D.E. (1992). External and diagnostic validity of the NTID Writing Test: An investigation using direct magnitude estimation and principal components analysis. *Research in the Teaching of English*, 26, 299–314.

Bolter, J.D. (1991). *Writing space: The computer, hypertext, and the history of writing*. Hillsdale, NJ: Lawrence Erlbaum Associates.

Botstein, L. (1986). Foreword: The ordinary experience of writing. In P. Connolly & T. Vilardi (Eds.), *Writing to learn mathematics and science* (pp. xi–xviii). New York: Teachers College Press.

Britton, J., Burgess, T., Martin N., McLeod, A., & Rosen, H. (1975). *The development of writing abilities (11–18)*. London: Macmillan.

Brown, P., & Long, G. (1992). The use of scripted interaction in a cooperative learning context to probe planning and evaluation during writing. *Volta Review*, 95, 411–424.

Bruce, B., Peyton, J.K., & Batson, T. (Eds.). (1993). *Network-based classrooms*. New York: Cambridge University Press.

Calkins, L. M. (1986). *Lessons from a child on the teaching and learning of writing*. Exeter, NH: Heinemann.

Cassidy, J., & Cassidy, D. (2000). What's hot, what's not for 1999. *Reading Today*, 17, 1–28.

Connolly, P., & Vilardi, T. (Eds.) (1989). *Writing to learn mathematics and science*. New York: Teachers College Press.

Conway, D. (1985). Children (re)creating writing: A preliminary look at the purposes of free-choice writing of hearing impaired kindergarteners. *American Annals of the Deaf*, 130, 91–107.

Cooper, J. D. (1993). *Literacy: Helping children construct meaning*. Boston, MA: Houghton Mifflin.

De Villiers, P. (1991). English literacy development in deaf children: Directions for research and intervention. In J.F. Miller (Ed.), *Research on child language disorders: A decade of progress* (pp. 349–378). Austin, TX: Pro-Ed.

Dolman, D. (1992). Some concerns about using whole

language approaches with deaf children. *American Annals of the Deaf, 137,* 278–282.

Elbow, P. (1973). *Writing without teachers.* New York: Oxford University Press.

Emig, J. (1971). *The composing process of twelfth graders* (NCTE English Research Rep.No. 13). Urbana, IL: National Council of Teachers of English.

Ewoldt, C. (1985). A descriptive study of the developing literacy of young hearing-impaired children. *Volta Review, 87*(5), 109–126.

Ewoldt, C. (1990). The early literacy development of deaf children. In D. Moores & K. Meadow-Orlans (Eds.), *Educational and developmental aspects of deafness* (pp. 85–114). Washington, DC: Gallaudet University Press.

Flower, L.S., & Hayes, J.R. (1980). The dynamics of composing: Making plans and juggling constraints. In L. W. Gregg & E.R. Steinberg (Eds.), *Cognitive processes in writing* (pp. 31–50). Hillsdale, NJ: Lawrence Erlbaum Associates.

Fowles, M. (1993). Designing a writing assessment to support the goals of the project. In B. Bruce, J.K. Peyton, & T. Batson (Eds.), *Network-based classrooms* (pp. 263–285). New York: Cambridge University Press.

Freire, P. (1970). *Pedagogy of the oppressed.* New York: Continuum.

French, M. M. (1999). *Starting with assessment.* Washington, DC: Gallaudet University.

Geoffrion, L.D. (1982). An analysis of teletype conversation. *American Annals of the Deaf, 127,* 747–752.

Goodman, K.S. (1989). Whole-language research: Foundations and development. *The Elementary School Journal, 90,* 207–221.

Gormley, K., & Sarachan-Deily, A. (1987). Evaluating hearing impaired students' writing: A practical approach. *Volta Review, 89,* 157–170.

Graves, D.H. (1991). *Build a literate classroom.* Portsmouth, NH: Heinemann.

Greenberg, B.L., & Withers, S. (1965). *Better English usage: A guide for the Deaf.* Indianapolis, IN: Bobbs-Merrill.

Hairston, M. (1982). The winds of change: Thomas Kuhn and the revolution in the teaching of writing. *College Composition and the Communication, 33,* 76–88.

Heefner, D.L., & Shaw, P.C. (1996). Assessing the written narratives of deaf students using the six-trait analytical scale. *Volta Review, 98,* 147–168.

Heider, F., & Heider, G. (1940). A comparison of sentence structure of deaf and hearing children. *Psychological Monographs 52,* 42–103.

Heidinger, V. A. (1984). *Analyzing syntax and semantics: A self-instructional approach for teachers and clini-*cians. Washington, DC: Gallaudet University Press.

Hunt, K. (1965). *Grammatical structures written at three grade levels.* Champaign, IL: National Council of Teachers of English.

Huot, B. (1990). The literature of direct writing assessment: Major concerns and prevailing trends. *Review of Educational Research, 60,* 237–263.

Isaacson, S.L. (1996). Simple ways to assess deaf or hard-of-hearing students' writing skills. *Volta Review, 98,* 183–199.

Jacobs, H., Zinkgraf, S., Wormuth, D., Hatfield, V., & Hughey, J. (1981). *Testing ESL composition: A practical approach.* Rowley, MA: Newbury House.

Johnson, H.A., & Barton, L.E. (1988). TDD conversations: A context for language sampling and analysis. *American Annals of the Deaf, 133,* 19–25.

Klecan-Aker, J., & Blondeau, R. (1990). An examination of the written stories of hearing-impaired school-age children. *The Volta Review, 92,* 275–282.

Kluwin, T.N., & Kelly, A. B. (1992). Implementing a successful writing program in public schools for students who are deaf. *Exceptional Children, 59,* 41–53.

Kress, G. (1996). Writing and learning to write. In D. Olson & N. Torrance (Eds.), *The handbook of education and human development: New models of learning, teaching, and schooling* (pp. 225–256). Oxford: Blackwell.

Kress, G. (1997). *Before writing.* New York: Routledge.

Kretschmer, R., & Kretschmer, L. (1978). *Language development and intervention with the hearing impaired.* Baltimore, MD: University Park Press.

Lang, H.G., & Albertini, J.A. (2001). The construction of meaning in the authentic science writing of deaf students. *Journal of Deaf Studies and Deaf Education, 6,* 258–284.

Langston, C.A., & Maxwell, M.M. (1988). Holistic judgement of texts by deaf and ESL students. *Sign Language Studies, 60,* 295–312.

Lieberth, A. (1988, September/October). Teaching functional writing via telephone. *Perspectives for Teachers of the Hearing Impaired, 6,* 10–13.

Livingston, S. (1989). Revision strategies of two deaf writers. *American Annals of the Deaf, 134,* 21–26.

Livingston, S. (1997). *Rethinking the education of deaf students.* Portsmouth, NH: Heinemann.

Luetke-Stahlman, B., & Luckner, J. (1991). *Effectively educating students with hearing impairments.* New York: Longman.

Malakoff, M. (1988). The effect of language of instruction on reasoning in bilingual children. *Applied Psycholinguistics, 9,* 17–38,

Mander, R., Wilton, K.M., Townsend, M.A.R., & Thomson, P. (1995). Personal computers and process writing: A written language intervention for deaf children. *British Journal of Educational Psychology, 65*, 441–453.

Marschark, M., Lang, H.G., & Albertini, J.A. (2002). *Educating deaf students: From research to practice.* New York: Oxford University Press.

Marschark, M., Mouradian, V., & Halas, M. (1994). Discourse rules in the language productions of deaf and hearing children. *Journal of Experimental Child Psychology, 57*, 89–107.

Maxwell, M.M. (1985). Some functions and uses of literacy in the deaf community. *Language in Society, 14*, 205–221.

Maxwell, M.M., & Falick, T.G. (1992). Cohesion & quality in deaf & hearing children's written English. *Sign Language Studies, 77*, 345–372.

Mayer, C. (1999). Shaping at the point of utterance: An investigation of the composing processes of the deaf student writer. *Journal of Deaf Studies an Deaf Education, 4*, 37–49.

Mayer, C., & Akamatsu, C.T. (2000). Deaf children creating written texts: Contributions of American Sign Language and signed forms of English. *American Annals of the Deaf, 145*, 394–403.

Mayer, C., & Moskos, E. (1998). Deaf children learning to spell. *Research in the Teaching of English, 33*, 158–180.

McAnally, P.I., Rose, S., & Quigley, S.P. (1994). *Language learning practices with deaf children* (2nd ed.). Austin, TX: Pro-Ed.

Moores, D.F., & Sweet, C. (1990). Factors predictive of school achievement. In D.F. Moores & K.P. Meadow-Orlans (Eds.), *Educational and Developmental Aspects of Deafness* (pp. 154–201). Washington, DC: Gallaudet University Press.

Murray, D. (1976). Teach writing as process, not product. In R. Graves (Ed.), *Rhetoric and Composition* (pp. 79–82). Rochelle Park, NY: Hayden Book Co.

Musselman, C., & Szanto, G. (1998). The written language of deaf adolescents: Patterns of performance. *Journal of Deaf Studies and Deaf Education, 3*, 245–257.

Myklebust, H.R. (1964). *The psychology of deafness.* New York: Grune & Stratton.

Nash, J.E., & Nash, A. (1982). Typing on the phone: How the deaf accomplish TTY conversations. *Sign Language Studies, 36*, 193–213.

Padden, C. (1993). Lessons to be learned from the young deaf orthographer. *Linguistics and Education, 5*, 71–86.

Paul, P.V. (1998). *Literacy and deafness.* Boston: Allyn and Bacon.

Paul, P. (2001). *Language and deafness* (3rd ed.). San Diego, CA: Singular.

Peyton, J.K. (1989). Cross-age tutoring on a local area computer network: Moving from informal interaction to formal academic writing. *The Writing Instructor, 8*, 57–67.

Power, D., & Leigh, G.R. (2000). Principles and practices of literacy development for deaf learners: A historical overview. *Journal of Deaf Studies and Deaf Education, 5*, 3–8.

Prinz, P.M., & Strong, M. (1998). ASL proficiency and English literacy within a bilingual deaf education model of instruction. *Topics in Language Disorders, 18*, 47–60.

Ramsey, C. L. (1997). Deaf children as literacy learners: Tom, Robbie, and Paul. In J. Flood, S.B. Health, & D. Lapp (Eds.), *A handbook for literacy educators: Research on teaching the communicative and visual arts* (pp. 314–322). New York: MacMillan.

Ramsey, C. L., & Padden, C. (1998). Natives and newcomers: Gaining access to literacy in a classroom for deaf children. *Anthropology & Education Quarterly, 29*, 5–24.

Ruiz, E. (1995). A young deaf child learns to write: Implications for literacy development. *The Reading Teacher, 49*, 206–214.

Schirmer, B. R. (1994). *Language and literacy development in children who are deaf.* New York: Merrill.

Schirmer, B. R., Bailey, J., & Fitzgerald, S.M. (1999). Using a writing assessment rubric for writing development of children who are deaf. *Exceptional Children, 65*, 383–397.

Schley, S. (1994). *Language proficiency and bilingual education of deaf children.* Unpublished doctoral dissertation, Harvard University, Cambridge, MA.

Schley, S. (1996). What's a clock? Suppose the alarm lights are flashing. Sociolinguistic concerns in implementing BIBI education. In C. Lucas (Ed.), *Sociolinguistics in Deaf communities.* Washington, DC: Gallaudet University Press.

Shaughnessy, M. (1977). *Errors and expectations: A guide for the teacher of basic writing.* New York: Oxford University Press.

Singleton, J, Rivers, R., Morgan, D.D., & Wiles, J. (2001, April). Deaf children's written narrative and vocabulary skills: A comparison with hearing ESL writers. Paper presented at the Society for Research in Child Development's biennial meeting, Minneapolis, MN.

Singleton, J., & Supalla, S. (1998). The effects of ASL fluency upon deaf children's cognitive, linguistic, and social development (Final report of funded grant project 1993–1996 to the U.S. Department of Education, Office of Special Education and Rehabilitation Services). Urbana-Champaign, IL: University of Illinois.

Singleton, J.L., Supalla, S., Fraychineaud, K., Litchfield, S., & Schley, S. (1997, April). From sign to word: Comparing deaf children's literacy-related competence in ASL and written English. Paper presented at the biennial meeting of the Society for Research in Child Development, Washington, DC.

Snow, C.E., Burns, M.S. & Griffin, P. (Eds.) (1998). *Report on preventing reading difficulties in young children* (National Research Council). Washington, DC: National Academy Press.

Snow, C.E., Cancino, H., De Temple, J. & Schley, S. (1991). Giving formal definitions: A linguistic or metalinguistic skill? In E. Bialystok (Ed.), *Language processing and language awareness by bilingual children* (pp. 90–112). New York: Cambridge University Press.

Standards for the English Language Arts. (1996). Urbana, IL: National Council of Teachers of English and the International Reading Association.

Stanovich, K.E. (1980). Toward and interactive-compensatory model of individual differences in the development of reading fluency. *Reading Research Quarterly, 1*, 32–71.

Staton, J. (1985). Using dialogue journals for developing thinking, reading, and writing with hearing-impaired students. *Volta Review, 87*, 127–153.

Stewart, D.A., & Kluwin, T.N. (2001). *Teaching deaf and hard of hearing students*. Boston: Allyn and Bacon.

Strong, M., & Prinz, P.M. (1997). A study of the relationship between ASL and English literacy. *Journal of Deaf Studies and Deaf Education, 2*, 37–46.

Stuckless, E.R., & Marks, C.H. (1996). Assessment of the written language of deaf students (Report of Cooperative Research Project 2544, U.S. Department of Health, Education, and Welfare). Pittsburgh, PA: University of Pittsburgh.

Teller, H.E., & Lindsey, J.D. (1987). Developing hearing-impaired students' writing skills: Martin Buber's mutuality in today's classroom. *American Annals of the Deaf, 132*, 383–385.

Traxler, C.B. (2000). Measuring up to performance standards in reading and mathematics: Achievement of selected deaf and hard-of-hearing students in the national norming of the 9th Edition Stanford Achievement Test. *Journal of Deaf Studies and Deaf Education, 5*, 337–348.

US Ink (2001, November). *The history of printing*. Retrieved September 2002, from *http://www.usink. com/history_printing.html*

Watkins, S. (1999). *The gift of early literacy: For young children who are deaf or hard of hearing and their families*. North Logan, UT: Hope, Inc.

Watson, L. M. (2000). The early writing of deaf children. *Proceedings of the 19th International Convention of Educators of the Deaf and 7th Asia-Pacific Conference*. Sydney, Australia.

Weaver, C. (1990). *Understanding whole language, from principles to practice*. Portsmouth, NH: Heinemann.

Wilbur, R.B. (1977). An explanation of deaf children's difficulty with certain syntactic structures of English. *Volta Review, 79*, 85–92.

Williams, C. L. (1993). Learning to write: Social interaction among preschool auditory/oral and total communication children. *Sign Language Studies, 80*, 267–284.

Williams, C. L. (1994). The language and literacy worlds of three profoundly deaf preschool children. *Reading Research Quarterly, 29*, 124–155.

Williams, C. L. (1999). Preschool deaf children's use of signed language during writing events. *Journal of Literacy Research, 31*, 183–212.

The Written English Expression Placement Test. (1985). Princeton, NJ: Educational Testing Service.

Yore, L. (2000). Enhancing science literacy for all students with embedded reading instruction and writing-to-learn activities. *Journal of Deaf Studies and Deaf Education, 5*, 105–122.

Yoshinaga-Itano, C., & Snyder, L. (1985). Form and meaning in the written language of hearing impaired children. *Volta Review, 87*, 75–90.

Yoshinago-Itano, C., & Snyder, L., & Mayberry, R. (1996). Can lexical/semantic skills differentiate deaf or hard-of-hearing readers and nonreaders? *Volta Review, 98*, 39–61.

Zamel, V. (1992). Writing one's way into reading. *TESOL Quarterly, 26*, 463–485.

10

Connie Mayer & C. Tane Akamatsu

Bilingualism and Literacy

Although the debate over the effectiveness of bilingual education programs can be framed in many terms—social, cultural, curricular, and linguistic (Hakuta, 1986)—in this chapter we focus on the issue of text-based literacy and achievement in reading and writing. Understanding that it is simplistic to quantify the impact of bilingualism on any single dimension as either good or bad, it is nevertheless useful and necessary to consider the circumstances and consequences of opting for this approach to educating a deaf child, especially in the domain of literacy, which has such profound and lasting repercussions for the life of the learner.

Since the introduction of bilingual programs in the education of deaf students, one of the principal claims has been that, as a consequence of using a natural sign language as the primary language of instruction, students will not only have greater and easier access to curricular content but will also develop higher levels of literacy, even without exposure to the language in its primary form through speech or alternatively through signed forms of that language (Johnson, Liddell, & Erting, 1989; Lane, Hoffmeister, & Bahan, 1996). Some proponents of this position go so far as to suggest that the goal would be to achieve levels of literacy commensurate with that of hearing peers (Grushkin, 1998;

Nelson, 1998; Wilbur, 2000). The prediction that students in bilingual programs would achieve improved literacy levels and the pedagogical route through which this goal might be realized has been interrogated on theoretical grounds (Mayer & Akamatsu, 1999; Mayer & Wells, 1996; Paul, 1996, 1998). However, as yet there is not a body of research to convincingly make the case for any position. Therefore, with respect to the literacy development of deaf students in bilingual programs, much is still open for debate, leaving many unanswered questions and unresolved issues.

In an attempt to provide a comprehensive consideration of the issue of bilingualism, literacy, and the deaf learner, this chapter will first examine the theoretical frameworks that have underpinned the move to bilingual models of literacy education for deaf students. In exploring the theory on this point, it will draw on research, not only from the context of the deaf learner, but from other bilingual situations where the research has been more extensive and exhaustive and where the claims attending the theory were first examined empirically. What has been learned from the research to date is summarized and placed within the context of the outcomes suggested by the theory and the research from other bilingual settings, and in light of the claims made when bilingual programs for deaf students were first instituted.

At the outset, it is important to acknowledge the body of work that examines the use of signed forms of spoken languages in developing literacy, but by definition, this investigation of signed communication does not address issues pertinent to bilingualism (i.e., the use of two different languages). This review, therefore, is limited to studies that explicitly look at natural signed languages (e.g., American Sign Language; ASL) in a bilingual context. We conclude by making suggestions and posing questions regarding directions for future study and research.

Theory Informing Practice

The linguistic interdependence principle has provided the principal theoretical foundation and rationale for establishing bilingual education for both deaf and hearing students. Cummins (1981, 1986) proposed that model as a framework for thinking about the ways in which proficiency in a first language could be seen as positively supporting the learning of a second language. He suggested that a common underlying proficiency across languages allows for a positive transfer to occur, if there is adequate exposure to the second language (L2) and motivation to learn it. The nature of this transfer can be represented by means of a "dual-iceberg" model in which common cross-lingual proficiencies underlie the surface features of both languages (see figure 10-1)

Appealing to the linguistic interdependence

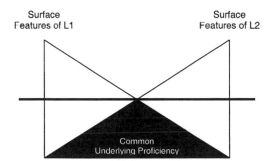

Figure 10-1. Common underlying proficiency makes the transfer of cognitive/academic *or* literacy-related skills across languages possible (Adapted from Cummins, 1989).

model, proponents of bilingual models of education for deaf students suggested that if students achieved high levels of proficiency in a native sign language as their first language (L1), then a positive transfer would occur, which would support the development of literacy in the majority language as L2. It was predicted that the model would apply despite the aspects that make the context for the deaf language learner unique; namely, that the L1 and the L2 do not share a common mode, that sign languages do not have widely accepted written forms, and that deaf learners do not have ready access to the face-to-face form of the L2.

A key feature of the model is the notion that in bilingual classrooms, the L1 and L2 can work in effective complementarity. With respect to the legend of figure 10-1, the "or" signals that there is not wholesale transfer of L1 to L2, but rather that L1 knowledge supports L2 learning in particular ways, given differences in the nature of the two languages being considered and the level of the learner's respective proficiency (oral/signed and written) in the L1 and the L2. In this regard, Cummins (1989) suggested that "there may be a threshold level of proficiency in both languages which students must attain in order to avoid any negative academic consequences and a second higher, threshold necessary to reap the linguistic and cognitive benefits of bilingualism and biliteracy" (p. 42).

This suggestion highlights the distinction between the basic interpersonal communication skills (BICS) and cognitive academic language proficiency (CALP) of any language (Cummins, 1984), as it is only when learners are able to develop CALP in their L1 that they are able to make positive links to learning the L2. From this perspective, first language conceptual and background knowledge can facilitate the acquisition of L2 literacy and subject matter content (Cummins, 1989). This position also implies the continued development of text-based literacy in the L1 because many aspects of CALP are associated with the ability to read and write.

But the continued development of CALP in the L1 is only one aspect of what goes into developing literacy in the L2. While Cummins (1988) does stress that acquiring proficiency in L2 is not simply a by-product of time spent on the target L2, he also emphasizes that "a second generalization that emerges from the data is that in order to develop conversational and academic L2 skills, learners must be exposed to sufficient L2 comprehensible input" (p. 157). This exposure is critical for developing the threshold level of L2 language proficiency that is necessary for the development of L2 literacy.

In positing the linguistic interdependence model, Cummins was assuming that the learner had the opportunity to learn both the written and spoken modes of the L1 and would then be able to use this literate proficiency to support the learning of the L2. At the same time, he assumed that there would be ample opportunities for learners to participate in a linguistic community that uses the L2 in both its spoken and written forms (Mayer & Wells, 1996). Given these assumptions, it is clear that when applying this model to the education of deaf students, there will be a singular set of concerns. This is not to question the validity of the interdependence model or its application in this context, but rather to point out that there are unique issues that must be addressed and taken into account when applying this model to the situation of the deaf learner.

Becoming Literate in a Signed or a Spoken Language

To examine how the claims for linguistic interdependence apply with respect to the literacy development of deaf learners, it is necessary to consider how anyone becomes literate in a first language, as learning to read and write in an L2 is fundamentally the same process as learning to read and write in the L1 (Fitzgerald, 1995; Paul, 1996, 1998). This process is summarized in table 10-1, which outlines four distinguishable, yet related and over-

Table 10-1. Phases in children's mastery of their first language

Phase	Hearing bridge	Deaf bridge
1. Learning the L1	Spoken L1	Natural sign language
2. Social to inner speech	Egocentric spoken L1	Egocentric sign
3. Inner to written speech	Spoken L1	?
4. Learning synoptic genres	Spoken L1	?

Note: L1, first language. Adapted from Mayer and Wells (1996).

lapping phases in children's mastery of their first language (for a detailed discussion, see Mayer & Wells, 1996). In each phase, the child uses a language and modality-specific bridge between the already mastered linguistic activity and those yet to be mastered.

In the normal course of development in phase 1, children spontaneously master the face-to-face form of their L1 provided that they have sufficient opportunities to interact with more mature members of their linguistic community as they engage in various joint activities (Bruner, 1983; Wells, 1986). This applies to both signed and spoken languages, although it is too often the case that deaf children grow up in environments with significantly less interaction to support their language development (Marschark, 1993).

In phase 2, the developmental step is from language used only in interactions with others to what Vygotsky (1987) called "inner speech," the mode of language that mediates internal verbal (i.e., language-based) thinking. Although the nature of language for interaction with others and language for inner thought are different in nature, they are similar in kind, and according to Vygotsky, the existence of the latter depends on the prior existence of the former. In this developmental process, it is egocentric speech or egocentric sign that provides the bridge between social and inner speech. It could be said that one begins to think in their L1.

The challenge of phase 3 is to realize the meanings, generated in inner speech, in a written form. Here, again, the face-to-face form of the L1 plays a critical, transitional role in that understanding of written language is first effected through the use of the face-to-face to language as a mediating tool (Vygotsky, 1978). In the case of hearing children, they typically use a strategy of first composing the text piecemeal in spoken language and then attempting to write down what they say and hear. Thus the oral, face-to-face form of the language serves as a bridge to the written form. In the case of developing linguistic competence in a natural sign language as an L1, this phase is inapplicable because there are no written forms to be mastered. However, there does remain the question of how the deaf child will bridge from inner speech in sign to written speech in L2, given that there is no one-to-one correspondence between signed and written phrase for the learner to discover and exploit as a strategy for decoding or encoding a text.

Phase 4 is concerned with learning the synoptic genres (e.g., expository texts) in which discipline-based knowledge is constructed and communicated. Again, the face-to-face form of the language plays a pivotal bridging role for the hearing child— an oral reading of a text, a discussion of the text's relationship to what the child already knows and can express in everyday speech, or the composition of texts that make use of lexicon and grammar comparable to texts that have been read (Halliday, 1975; Wells, 1999). The concerns raised with respect to phase 3 apply here as well. Although natural sign language can be used to discuss any topic, this discussion will not employ the lexical and grammatical features of written text, and therefore will not serve as a bridge to the synoptic genres in the same way that they do for the hearing learners of these forms.

Developing Literacy in a Second Language

When using this framework as a way to think about developing literacy in a second language, it is most expedient to focus on phase 3 because this is where written language first appears. The L1 learner has a fully developed face-to-face language system in place as the basis for developing reading and writing abilities in that language. L2 learners do not come to the task with the same set of L2 oral language resources. Especially for older L2 learners who are literate in L1, it is often a case of developing literacy in L2 while seeking support from an L2 language system that is still insufficiently developed to allow learners the full range of literacy practices to which they are accustomed (Eisterhold, 1990).

But learning to read and write in a second language cannot be explained simply in terms of level of oral proficiency in the L2. L2 learners will have varying levels of proficiency in using both the oral and written forms of their L1, as well as varying degrees of oral ability in the L2. L1 literacy can play a positive role in learning to read and write in the L2, but there is a need to be sensitive to, and make a distinction between, language skills and literacy skills in any discussion of how literacy in a second language develops and what aspects of the L1 can support the process.

In terms of phase 3 of the model, it can be argued that there are two bridges from inner speech in L1 to reading and writing in L2 that are potentially available for L2 learners who are fluent in both the spoken and written modes of their L1 (figure 10-2). These L2 learners can make use of their growing knowledge of the spoken form of the second language as a resource for making sense of text, in much the same way a child does in developing L1 literacy. But they can also exploit the similarities, whatever they may be, between the written modes of the L1 and L2, including the ways in which the written mode represents the spoken mode in each of the two languages (Mayer & Wells, 1996). Further, learners probably do not exclusively use one route but take advantage of all available linguistic options in their efforts to learn to read and write a second language.

This conceptualization of routes to literacy in L2 is consistent with Cummins' (1981) claims with respect to linguistic interdependence, in that he also points out that there are two routes to literacy in L2: the continued development of CALP in the L1, particularly reading and writing, and adequate exposure in quality and quantity to the L2. The implications for the literacy learning situation of the deaf signer in a bilingual environment are clear. There is no widely accepted written form of the L1

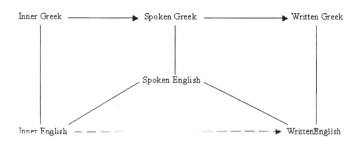

Figure 10-2. Two bridges from inner speech in first language to literacy in second language. (From Mayer & Wells, 1996; reprinted by permission of Oxford University Press.)

to be used as a scaffold to support literacy learning in the L2, and there is not access to the primary, spoken form of the L2 in order to develop the language proficiency that supports reading and writing development.

Research evidence from the context of bilingual programs for hearing learners supports the contention that higher levels of L1 proficiency are related to higher achievement in L2 literacy (for an overview, see Cummins, 1983, 1984, 1991a, 1991b, Cummins & Swain, 1986). More specifically with respect to the development of reading and writing ability in the L2, the evidence indicates a positive correlation between the ability to read and write in an L1 and the subsequent ability to master these same aspects of the L2 (Canale, Frenette, & Belanger, 1987; Cumming, 1989; Edelsky, 1982), although this relationship is less vibrant when the orthographies of the L1 and L2 are dissimilar (Cummins, 1991a). However, it is important to note that it is L1 literacy, and not L1 oral proficiency, that is associated with higher levels of L2 literacy (Cummins, 1991b; Hornberger, 1989). Furthermore, research evidence from studies of hearing learners indicates that oral proficiency in L2 is a necessary component for developing L2 literacy. Even highly developed L1 reading and writing ability cannot compensate entirely for a lack of fluency in L2 (Alderson, 1984; Reese, Garnier, Gallimore, & Goldenberg, 2000; Yau, 1991).

Thus, although supported by research evidence, the issues of linguistic interdependence and common underlying proficiencies are not as simple and straightforward as they may first appear. "If we are going to say that literacy-related skills transfer after a certain language proficiency has been reached, then we must be able to define literacy skills as opposed to language skills (a fine line) before we are able to say what exactly transfers" (Eisterhold, 1990, p. 96).

What are the language and literacy skills that are necessary for the development of high levels of L2 literacy for deaf learners? More specifically, what L1 proficiencies in a natural sign language, which has no written form, transfer to higher levels of L2 literacy? And what is the nature of the second-language proficiency that must be achieved before this transfer can occur? How can these concerns be addressed when designing bilingual models of literacy education for deaf students?

Bilingual Models of Literacy Education for Deaf Learners

Bilingual programs for deaf students have been in place since the late 1980s (Mahshie, 1995; Strong, 1995), and there is a substantial body of descriptive literature that outlines the theoretical bases for these programs, delineates their communication policies and pedagogical practices, and describes their organization and implementation (Livingston, 1997; Nover, Christenson, & Cheng, 1998; Svartholm, 1993). Most reports focus on presenting a rationale and pedagogy, derived from the linguistic interdependence theory, which suggests that proficiency in a natural sign language will be used as the basis for teaching literacy in the target L2. The pedagogical statements that attend this principle are usually some version of "teaching a natural sign language to deaf children as their primary face to face language and teaching English [or some other spoken language] as a second language through literacy" (Erting, 1992, p. 105), implying that through interactions with print, students will learn not only to read and to write, but will learn the language itself. Neither the spoken or signed forms of the L2 nor contact signing (i.e., the sign language that is the natural outcome of contact between the spoken majority language and the local signed language) are seen to play an integral role in this process. Although they are sometimes construed as possible outcomes of the bilingual learning process, they are not seen as the means to achieving the goal of L2 literacy (Livingston, 1997; Lucas & Valli, 1992).

The tenet that a natural sign language can be used to develop L2 literacy is realized in practice in two ways. In many bilingual models of literacy education, there is a heavy emphasis on using the sign language to discuss the features of the written text, a position that is influenced by the notion of metacognition as a tool for students to use in analyzing the linguistic elements of both the sign language and the print (Paul, 1998). The teaching approaches in line with this thinking are generally variations on the theme of using comparative/contrastive analyses and grammar translation techniques. Neuroth-Gimbrone and Logiodice (1992), for example, outlined strategies for using ASL to develop English literacy with a group of adolescent learners, and Akamatsu and Armour (1987) examined the use of progressive revisions of multiple drafts of text, changing from sign glosses to standard English. Andrews, Winograd, and DeVille (1996), in contrast, used ASL summaries as a pre-reading activity, whereas Christie, Wilkins, McDonald, and Neuroth-Gimbrone (1999) described ASL strategies for developing English narratives with deaf college students. In all cases, these strategies aided students in organizing the content and meaning of written texts, but there is no evidence that specific and long-term improvements in English literacy resulted.

In contrast to this vision of practice, some proponents of bilingual education make the case for a whole language, meaning focused approach to developing L2 literacy. The primary language of instruction and communication is still the natural sign language, but it is used with the recognition that "the focus of instruction is not on language but on achieving subject-area understandings, and that learning a second language in school is not exclusively for the sake of learning the language but rather as the means to achieve academic success" (Livingston, 1997, p. 17). The L1 is used to construct the meaning, leaving the learner free to convert this meaning into print.

It is useful to note that both models emphasize that the use of a natural sign language will develop L2 literacy, but opt for pedagogical approaches that take fundamentally different views as to how this L2 proficiency will be achieved. In the meta-linguistic/metacognitive bilingual model, there is an underlying assumption that deaf readers and writers are fundamentally different from their hearing counterparts because they do not have easy access to, and thus knowledge of, the spoken form of the L2. This difference necessitates the direct teaching of the linguistic aspects of both languages in order for the students to make useful comparisons and develop the ability to see one language in terms of the other (Svartholm, 1993, 1994). Taking this point of view may mean delaying the introduction of reading and writing, which, for the deaf learner, only occurs in the L2, because L1 proficiency must be developed to a high level before linguistic comparisons with L2 can be made. There is also an inherent cognitive advantage if the learner is somewhat older before reading and writing are introduced.

The underlying assumption in a whole-language model is that deaf children, as language learners, are not vastly different from their hearing peers. This is predicated on the notion that all learners learn language best when it is relevant and used in meaningful interaction (Mahshie, 1995; Livingston, 1997). Since signing in L1 and reading and writing in L2 are viewed as reciprocal processes to be acquired naturally, there would be no delay in introducing print because L2 literacy is not dependent on L1 metalinguistic knowledge.

Despite the comparisons often made between hearing and deaf second-language learners, there are fundamental differences that arise from the two paths to L2 literacy described earlier. Without access to the auditory–oral channel, deaf learners are deprived of the support that hearing learners of the written mode of a second language receive from their growing mastery of its spoken form. And deaf learners do not have text-based literacy skills in L1 to transfer to the written mode of the L2. Thus there are issues unique to the situation of the deaf learner that must be taken into account when adopting either a structured or a whole-language approach.

Therefore, it is useful to consider the literature that examines strategies to specifically develop literacy in a bilingual context. One strategy that has received considerable attention is the use of finger-spelling as a tool to connect ASL and print (Erting, Thumann-Prezioso, & Sonnenstrahl-Benedict, 2000; Padden, 1996; Padden & Ramsey, 2000). Padden and Ramsey (2000), for example, suggested that deaf children's language skills in ASL, finger-spelling, and print are interrelated and that students must be taught to orchestrate their use of these language resources. They specifically described the use of classroom discourse that uses associative "chaining structures," in which a target word is signed, fingerspelled, signed again, and related to print to highlight the relationships among these language elements.

Supalla, Wix, and McKee (2001) described a program for teaching reading and writing predicated on directly linking the acquisition of English with what children know about ASL. They suggested that children be taught to exploit their knowledge of ASL by recording signed narratives on videotape and subsequently transcribing them into a written code developed specifically for encoding ASL. The children then translate this written form of ASL to English glosses, and from there to standard English. This system allows for cross-linguistic comparison at the sentence level. By bypassing the phonological inaccessibility to English, this model works exclusively in the print modality of the two languages. The stated expectation is that the academic performance of deaf children should approach that of other late learners of English, but to date there is no evidence to support this claim.

Johnson (1994) suggested a role for contact sign in a bilingual model as "its early acquisition might provide for a natural and timely access to structures, features, and lexical categories of English that might directly be transferable to the processes of English language learning" (p. 11). He suggested that fingerspelling and the English-like mouth movements that often accompany contact sign could supply important phonological information to the deaf literacy learner. Using a prompted recall strategy, Mayer (1999a, 1999b) examined the composing strategies of four deaf students who used both ASL and contact sign in their face-to-face communication and were all scoring above the 80th percentile in reading based on the Stanford Achievement Test (SAT-HI, 8th ed.). She found that in the process of creating a written text, the students made use of a range of English-based strategies that included fingerspelling, recalling rules, and prior experiences with text, and mouthing alone or in conjunction with fingerspelling or signing. Although ASL was used to discuss the content of the text and to reflect on the composing process, the students were not seen to make use of ASL while directly engaged in the act of writing. In a related study, Akamatsu, Stewart, and Becker (2000) found that deaf children whose teachers made concerted efforts to use English-based signing as a bridge between ASL and English literacy made relatively large gains in reading comprehension, as measured by the Standard Achievement Test over a 3-year time span.

What these studies have in common is that they can all be thought of in terms of the previously described routes to L2 literacy. Those who advocate the use of fingerspelling (a unique cross-over strategy between the languages) seek to take advantage of the obvious relationship between a signed form and written text. Those who propose the use of mouthing in conjunction with fingerspelling, contact sign, or some other sign system are attempting to compensate for the phonological inaccessibility of a spoken L1 by representing its morphological and syntactic structure in a way that is cognitively and visually accessible. Those who design a written version of a signed L1 endeavor to create a potential bridge between the signed forms of the L1 and written L2. However, while there have been discussions of pedagogical models and the various strategies that can be exploited within these models, little empirical evidence has been provided as to their relative efficacy in developing L2 literacy.

Literacy Development in a Bilingual Deaf Context

With respect to bilingualism and a consideration of the effects of using a natural signed language on the subsequent development of literacy, numerous appeals have been made to those studies that looked at the performance of deaf children of deaf parents (DCDP), as it was widely presumed that this group invariably became better readers and writers than deaf children of hearing parents (DCHP) (Moores, 2001; for a discussion see Paul, 1998). Indeed, DCDP have been touted as the ideal bilingual deaf population because they come to school with a first language, ASL, and learn English in all its modalities (speech, sign, print) as a second language. Moreover, studies conducted before the widespread use of signing programs in school consistently showed that DCDP tended to do better on tests of cognitive ability and academic achievement that DCHP (Meadow, 1968; Vernon & Koh, 1970; Zweibel, 1987), in spite of roughly equivalent speech and speechreading skills.

The evidence in support of the notion that DCDP are generally advantaged is not unequivocal. Researchers have acknowledged competing explanations for why this is the case. DCDP might have advantages over DCHP in terms of genetic etiology (and lesser likelihood of additional handicapping conditions), access to a natural language from birth, age of detection of deafness, and parental acceptance of deafness and the ability to marshall resources to support their deaf child in school. Such conditions might confer a general learning advantage for these children, particularly in the early years.

Brasel and Quigley (1977) found that DCDP whose parents used signing that approximated English (what he called "manual English") scored higher on measures of academic achievement than DCDP whose parents used "forms other than manual English." Moores and Sweet (1990) found that proficiency in English-based signing was significantly correlated with reading achievement in both DCDP (who are presumably bilingual) and DCHP (who might or might not be bilingual). In other words, it is not the presence of ASL, but rather the presence of English in some accessible form, that appears to make the difference. It is sobering to remember that the advantage that DCDP enjoy may be, on average, only 2 or 3 years, still far behind their same-age hearing peers (Moores, 2001).

Some explorations have sought to determine whether fluency in ASL confers a more specific language advantage for children regardless of parental hearing status. Strong and Prinz (2000) studied the relationship among 155 students' performance on two expressive and four receptive ASL tasks and on one receptive and three expressive tests of written English. The students were between the ages of 8 and 15, attended a residential school, and had widespread exposure to the social use of ASL. They found that DCDP outperformed DCHP on measures of English literacy as well as on measures of ASL proficiency. However, there was no significant difference in English literacy levels between DCDP and DCHP within the groups of children who scored in the "high" or "medium" proficiency range in ASL. Strong and Prinz interpreted this last finding as evidence that ASL itself, rather than deaf parentage per se, advantages children in English literacy proficiency. They considered the possibility that some other factor, such as the quality of early parent–child communication or consistent linguistic input, might also be associated with later literacy levels of the children but did not investigate this.

Hoffmeister (2000) suggested that studies have not used measures sensitive enough to identify the relationship between ASL and its facilitative effect on English. He looked at the relationship between ASL and English literacy by measuring the ASL, manually coded English, and English knowledge of 50 deaf students from eight to eighteen years of age, who had either limited or intensive exposure to ASL. He found that students who received more intensive ASL exposure did better on measures of English reading achievement, English signing comprehension, and ASL than did students who received less intensive ASL, regardless of parental hearing status. He suggested that the positive correlation between ASL skills and knowledge and English skills might be explained by enhanced language functioning in deaf children who are skilled in ASL. Unfortunately, he did not report the actual

levels of English abilities in his sample, and there is no information as to whether the students took the level of the SAT that was age appropriate.

Padden and Ramsey (2000) compared the reading comprehension subtest scores from the SAT with various measures of ASL including verb agreement production and sentence order comprehension and found significant positive correlations among these skills in fourth- and fifth-grade children. These measures of ASL were also correlated with both the ability to reproduce a fingerspelled word in writing and the ability to write initialized signs presented in a sentence. Padden and Ramsey were careful not to confuse correlation with causality. Yet, it is cause for concern that even DCDP may not be reaching levels of English literacy equal to that of hearing peers. Actual levels of reading comprehension are not reported. Moreover, it still is unclear how knowledge of ASL benefits English literacy beyond the word level that was investigated in this study, or how lexical knowledge in ASL is different from that of English, particularly when combined with fingerspelling and initialized signs.

In one of the few studies that analyzed the nature of the written language of deaf children in a bilingual program, Singleton, Rivers, Morgan, and Wiles (2001) compared the written language performance of 60 deaf students with low, moderate, and high levels of ASL skill to two groups of hearing students, ESL learners and monolingual speakers of English. Students' written texts were measured on seven parameters that fell into two broad categories: measures of structural and narrative maturity and vocabulary. In the first category, structural and narrative maturity, there was no effect of ASL skill level. In terms of vocabulary, students with higher levels of ASL skill tended to use more low-frequency words and were less formulaic and repetitive in their writing than the low ASL group. A particularly telling finding was that, while ESL learners used a similar proportion of closed-class items (e.g., prepositions, conjunctions, articles) as their monolingual peers, both the high and moderate ASL groups struggled in this area, suggesting that ASL accrued the deaf participants limited syntactic benefit with respect to written English. In sum, these studies indicate consistent, positive correlations between higher levels of skill in a natural sign language and higher levels of L2 literacy, at least relative to other deaf students. However, the actual level of L2 literacy attained is not defined, and therefore there is no way to know if these learn-ers are working near grade level and no way to compare their performance to that of their hearing age peers. Although suggestive, these correlations leave much unanswered as to how deaf learners ac-tually mediate the literacy learning process.

Summary and Conclusions

As bilingual education for deaf learners has been justified on the grounds of linguistic interdepend-ence theory, it is most expedient to frame a sum-mary and set of conclusions in terms of this model. The claim has been made that L1 sign language skills transfer positively to L2 literacy learning, and the positive correlations that researchers have iden-tified between natural sign language and higher lev-els of L2 literacy can be viewed as providing sup-port for this contention. These findings can be interpreted as providing evidence that the use of a natural sign language does not hinder the L2 liter-acy learning process. Therefore, despite the contro-versies about the roles L1 and L2 play in a bilingual setting, there should be no controversy over the fact that primary language instruction in a natural sign language can confer cognitive and academic bene-fits and lead to primary language maintenance without blocking L2 literacy learning.

That being said, the development of CALP in an L1 (especially one with no written form) is, by itself, not sufficient for the development of L2 lit-eracy, and even "highly efficient reading and writ-ing ability in L1 does not make up altogether for lack of knowledge of L2" (Hornberger, 1989). The issue of proficiency in the primary form of the L2 underlies the issue of second-language literacy ac-quisition, and the argument made in the literature and supported by the research involving hearing learners is that L1 language and literacy skills trans-fer rapidly only when L2 oral proficiency has been established. Therefore, the development of reading and writing in the L2 must be understood in the context of the broader account of the role played by both L1 and language and literacy skills and L2 language proficiency, as is conceptualized by the two routes to L2 literacy described in figure 10-2.

Whole-language proponents suggest that meaningful exposure and interaction in L2 print can make up for the lack of proficiency in a pri-mary, oral form of the L2, while advocates of grammar-translation or contrastive approaches suggest that the L1 can be used to systematically teach L2 literacy by discussing, comparing, and contrasting the two languages. Neither of these two approaches incorporates an explicit discussion of the role that L2 language proficiency plays in the L2 literacy learning process.

In acknowledging this as a concern, researchers have posited compensatory strategies that serve to either stand in for L2 oral proficiencies (contact sign, mouthing, or mouthing in conjunction with speech, fingerspelling, or sign), or to bypass it and focus on sign-based strategies that bridge from L1 to L2 literacy (glossing and fingerspelling). These strategies have the potential to be exploited in ei-ther a whole-language or directed approach as a means to address the concern of providing access and a bridge to L2. This potential needs to be in-vestigated with respect to how, and how well, these strategies mediate the literacy learning process, par-ticularly with respect to how they might operate in concert to support the process of learning to read and write.

There are numerous descriptive accounts of bi-lingual programs, classroom practices, and teach-ing strategies, but there is a lack of longitudinal research that tracks literacy development over time. Although there are some reports of children in the early years of bilingual schooling who appear to be working at grade level, this evidence must be in-terpreted with caution. These young children are still at the initial stages of literacy development when the differences between hearing and deaf children would be less pronounced, and there would not be an expectation that any child would yet be a fluent reader or writer. It would be most worthwhile to continue to track these learners to see if they continued to function at grade level as their schooling progressed.

It would also be important to include measures of literacy as an aspect of future studies, with actual reading and writing levels being reported to be ex-plicit as to what we mean when we say that students have "higher" levels of literacy. This kind of evi-dence would most convincingly address the ques-tion of whether students in bilingual programs learn to read and write at a level commensurate with their hearing age peers, or at least at levels higher than those reported previously.

Longitudinal data will inform our understand-ing of the nature of the pedagogical practices related to improved literacy levels, particularly in "ascertaining the relationship of communication modes and coding strategies to the development of literacy skills" (Quigley & Paul, 1989, p. 17), and with respect to how well these practices can compensate for the lack of language proficiency in the L2. It would also help to determine the merits of various types and combinations of metalinguistic approaches for the teaching of reading and writing.

Currently, there is a much wider recognition and acceptance of the fact that deaf literacy learners will require pedagogical approaches beyond ESL methodologies and exposure to visually accessible, print forms of the target language. In the absence of any theoretical or research evidence to the contrary, it has become apparent that applying the principles of linguistic interdependence to the situation of the deaf literacy learner demands a rethinking of any simple application of this theory to the practice. Given the singular challenges facing the deaf literacy learner and taking into account the unique set of available modalities, it would be reasonable to expect that they would appropriate and manipulate all mediational means at their disposal. The goal of further scholarship and inquiry should be to investigate the nature and complexity of the relationships among the languages and modalities of L1 and L2 to better understand how they can support the literacy learning process (Mayer 1999a, 1999b; Musselman, 2000; Nelson, 1998; Singleton et al., 2001).

When interrogating the use of all available routes to literacy, it is useful to remember that all mediational tools have inherent affordances and constraints (Wertsch, 1998). Although natural sign languages can play a role in the L2 literacy learning process, they do not afford the learner any access to the primary form of the target language. Other strategies, such as mouthing, fingerspelling, signed forms of English, or contact sign, may offer an alternative route for this access but have their own set of constraints in terms of how fully they can convey meaning and to what degree they can stand in for oral L2 proficiency. In this sense, it could be suggested that with respect to bilingual literacy education for deaf learners, the errors may be ones of omission rather than commission. Is it the case that, for sociocultural and political reasons, some programs have limited the options for deaf learners? Have we opted for pedagogical prescriptions based on theory without paying enough attention to

the consequences of putting this theory into practice?

In planning future bilingual programs, "policy makers need to realize that conceptual and linguistic growth are dependent upon opportunities for meaningful interaction in both the target language and the L1" (Cummins, 1991a, p. 172). How do we design bilingual programs for deaf literacy learners that meet these criteria? Which aspects of cognitive academic language proficiency in a natural sign language most positively support the development of L2 literacy? How much and what sort of exposure to the target language is necessary to satisfy the requirement of adequate exposure in quality and quantity? What set of mediating strategies will best support literacy development? And ultimately, is it reasonable to expect, given the unique challenges facing deaf literacy learners, that the majority of these students can attain literacy levels that approach those of their hearing peers?

Addressing these questions is the challenge facing researchers and educators who have a commitment to improving the quality and efficacy of literacy instruction for deaf learners in bilingual settings. To this end, there is a need to open up and expand the possibilities for discussion and debate, despite the attendant political and pedagogical issues and tensions. Only in this way can we collectively develop a more adequate understanding, in theory and in practice, of how best to support deaf students as they take on the challenge of learning to read and write.

References

Akamatsu, C. T., & Armour, V. (1987). Developing written literacy in deaf children through analyzing sign language. *American Annals of the Deaf*, *132*(1), 46–51.

Akamatsu, C. T., Stewart, D., & Becker, B. J. (2000). Documenting English syntactic development in face-to-face signed communication. *American Annals of the Deaf*, *145*, 452–463.

Alderson, J. (1984). Reading in a foreign language: A reading problem or a language problem? In J. Alderson & A. Urquhart (Eds.), *Reading in a foreign language* (pp. 1–27). London: Longman.

Andrews, J., Winograd, P., & DeVille, G. (1996). Using sign language summaries during prereading lessons. *Teaching Exceptional Children*, *28*, 30–34.

Brasel, K., & Quigley, S. (1977). The influence of certain language and communication environments in early childhood on the development of language in deaf individuals. *Journal of Speech and Hearing Research, 20,* 95–107.

Bruner, J. (1983). *Child's talk.* New York: Norton.

Canale, M., Frennette, N., & Belanger, M. (1987). Evaluation of minority students writing in first and second languages. In J. Fine (Ed.), *Second language discourse: A textbook of current research* (pp. 147–165). Norwood, NJ: Ablex.

Christie, K., Wilkins, D., McDonald, B., & Neuroth-Gimbrone, C. (1999). GET-TO-THE-POINT: Academic bilingualism and discourse in American Sign Language and written English. In E. Winston (Ed.), *Storytelling and Conversation: Discourse in Deaf Communities* (pp. 162–177). Washington, DC: Gallaudet University Press.

Cumming, A. (1989). Writing expertise and second language proficiency. *Language Learning, 39,* 81–141.

Cummins, J. (1981). The role of primary language development in promoting educational success for language minority students. In California State Department of Education (Ed.), *Schooling and language minority students: A theoretical framework.* Los Angeles: Evaluation, Dissemination and Assessment Center, California State University.

Cummins, J. (1983). *Heritage language education: A literature review.* Toronto: Ministry of Education.

Cummins, J. (1984). *Bilingualism and special education: Issues in assessment and pedagogy.* Clevedon, Avon, UK: Multilingual Matters.

Cummins, J. (1986). Empowering minority students: A framework for intervention. *Harvard Education Review, 56,* 18–36.

Cummins, J. (1988). Second language acquisition within bilingual education programs. In L. Beebe (Ed.), *Issues in second language acquisition.* (pp. 145–166) Boston: Heinle & Heinle Publishers.

Cummins, J. (1989). *Empowering minority students.* Sacramento, CA: California Association for Bilingual Education.

Cummins, J. (1991a). Interdependence of first-and second-language proficiency in bilingual children. In E. Bialystok (Ed.), *Language processing in bilingual children* (pp. 70–89) Cambridge: Cambridge University Press.

Cummins, J. (1991b). Language development and academic learning. In L. Malave & G. Duquette (Eds.), *Language, culture and cognition* (pp. 266–283). Clevedon, Avon, UK: Multilingual Matters.

J., & Swain, M. (1996). *Bilingualism in education.* New York: Longman.

Edelsky, C. (1982). Writing in a bilingual program: The relation of L1 and L2 texts. *TESOL Quarterly, 16,* 211–228.

Eisterhold, J. (1990). Reading-writing connections. In B. Kroll (Ed.), *Second language writing* (pp. 88–101). New York: Cambridge University Press.

Erting, C. (1992). Deafness and literacy: Why can't Sam read? *Sign Language Studies, 7,* 97–112.

Erting, C., Thumann-Prezioso, C. & Sonnenstrahl-Benedict, B. (2000). Bilingualism in a Deaf family: Fingerspelling in early childhood. In P. Spencer, C. Erting, & M. Marschark (Eds.), *The deaf child in the family and at school* (pp. 41–54). Hillsdale, NJ: Lawrence Erlbaum Associates.

Fitzgerald, J. (1995). English-as-a-second-language learners' cognitive reading processes: A review of research in the United States. *Review of Educational Research, 65,* 145–190.

Grushkin, D. (1998). Why shouldn't Sam read? Toward a new paradigm for literacy and the deaf. *Journal of Deaf Studies and Deaf Education, 3,* 149–202.

Hakuta, K. (1986). *Mirror of language: The debate on bilingualism.* New York: Basic Books Inc.

Halliday, M. A. K. (1975). Talking one's way in. In A. Davies (Ed.), *Problems of language and learning* (pp. 8–26). London: Heinemann.

Hoffmeister, R. (2000). A piece of the puzzle: ASL and reading comprehension in deaf children. In C. Chamberlain, J. Morford, & R. Mayberry (Eds.), *Language acquisition by eye* (pp. 143–163). Hillsdale NJ: Lawrence Erlbaum Associates.

Hornberger, N. (1989). Continua of biliteracy. *Review of Educational Research, 59,* 271–296.

Johnson, R. (1994). Possible influences on bilingualism in early ASL acquisition. *Teaching English to Deaf and Second Language Students, 10,* 9–17.

Johnson, R., Liddell, S., & Erting, C. (1989). *Unlocking the curriculum: Principles for achieving access in deaf education* (Gallaudet Research Institute working paper 89–3). Washington, DC: Gallaudet University.

Lane, H., Hoffmeister, R., & Bahan, B. (1996). *Journey into the DEAF-WORLD.* San Diego, CA: Dawn Sign Press.

Livingston, S. (1997). *Rethinking the education of deaf students: Theory and practice from a teacher's perspective.* Portsmouth, NH: Heinemann.

Lucas, C., & Valli, C. (1992). *Contact language in the American deaf community.* San Diego, CA: Academic Press.

Mahshie, S. (1995). *Educating deaf children bilingually.* Washington, DC: Gallaudet University Press.

Marschark, M. (1993). *Psychological development of deaf children.* New York: Oxford University Press.

Mayer, C. (1999a). Shaping at the point of utterance: An investigation of the composing processes of the deaf student writer. *Journal of Deaf Studies and Deaf Education, 4,* 37–49.

Mayer, C. (1999b). *Using what is to hand, to eye, to ear and to mind: A theory of the deaf writer's meaning making*. Unpublished doctoral dissertation, University of Toronto, Toronto, Canada.

Mayer, C., & Akamatsu, C. (1999). Bilingual-bicultural models of literacy education for deaf students: Considering the claims. *Journal of Deaf Studies and Deaf Education, 4*, 1–8.

Mayer, C., & Wells, G. (1996). Can the linguistic interdependence theory support a bilingual-bicultural model of literacy education for deaf students? *Journal of Deaf Studies and Deaf Education, 1*, 93–107.

Meadow, K. (1968). Early manual communication in relation to the deaf child's intellectual, social, and communicative functioning. *American Annals of the Deaf, 113*, 29–41.

Moores, D. (2001). *Educating the deaf: Psychology, principles and practices*. Boston: Houghton-Mifflin.

Moores, D., & Sweet, C. (1990). Relationships of English grammar and communicative fluency to reading in deaf adolescents. *Exceptionality, 1*, 97–106.

Musselman, C. (2000). How do children who can't hear learn to read an alphabetic script? A review of the literature on reading and deafness. *Journal of Deaf Studies and Deaf Education, 5*, 9–31.

Nelson, K. (1998). Toward a differentiated account of facilitators of literacy development and ASL in deaf children. *Topics in Language Disorders, 18*, 73–88.

Neuroth-Gimbrone, C., & Logiodice, C. (1992) A co-operative bilingual language program for deaf adolescents. *Sign Language Studies, 74*, 79–91.

Nover, S., Christensen, K., & Cheng, L. (1998). Development of ASL and English competence for learners who are deaf. *Topics in Language Disorders, 18*, 61–71.

Padden, C. (1996). Early bilingual lives of deaf children. In I. Parasnis (Ed.), *Cultural and language diversity and the deaf experience* (pp. 99–116). New York: Cambridge University Press.

Padden, C., & Ramsey, C. (2000). American Sign Language and reading ability in deaf children. In C. Chamberlain, J. Morford, & R. Mayberry (Eds.), *Language acquisition by eye* (pp. 165–189). Hillsdale, NJ: Lawrence Erlbaum Associates.

Paul, P. (1996). First and second language English literacy. *The Volta Review, 98*, 5–16.

Paul, P. (1998). *Literacy and deafness: The development of reading, writing, and literate thought*. Boston: Allyn and Bacon.

Quigley, S. & Paul, P. (1989). English language development. In M. Wang, M. Reynolds, & H. Walberg (Eds.), *Handbook of special education: Research and practice* (Vol. 3, pp. 3–21). Oxford: Pergamon.

Reese, L., Garnier. H., Gallimore. R., & Goldenberg, C. (2000). Longitudinal analysis of the antecedents of emergent Spanish literacy and middle-school reading achievement of Spanish speaking students. *American Educational Research Journal, 37*, 633–662.

Singleton, J., Rivers, R. Morgan, D., & Wiles, J. (2001, April). *Deaf children's written narrative and vocabulary skills: A comparison with ESL writers*. Paper presented at the Society for Research in Child Development. Minneapolis.

Strong, M. (1995). A review of bilingual/bicultural programs for deaf children in North America. *American Annals of the Deaf, 140*, 84–94.

Strong, M., & Prinz, P. (2000). Is American Sign Language skill related to English literacy? In C. Chamberlain, J. Morford, & R. Mayberry (Eds.), *Language acquisition by eye* (pp. 131–141). Hillsdale NJ: Lawrence Erlbaum Associates.

Supalla, S., Wix, T., & McKee, C. (2001). Print as a primary source of English for deaf learners. In J. Nichol & T. Langendoen (Eds.), *One mind, two languages: Bilingual language processing*. Malden, MA: Blackwell.

Svartholm, K. (1993). Bilingual education for the deaf in Sweden. *Sign Language Studies, 81*, 291–332.

Svartholm, K. (1994). Second language learning in the deaf. In I. Ahlgren & K. Hyltenstam (Eds.), *Bilingualism in deaf education* (pp. 61–70). Hamburg: Signum.

Vernon, M., & Koh, S. (1970). Early manual communication and deaf children's achievement. *American Annals of the Deaf, 115*, 527–536.

Vygotsky, L. S. (1978). *Mind in society: The development of higher psychological processes*. Cambridge, MA: Harvard University Press.

Vygotsky, L. S. (1987). Thinking and speech (trans. N. Minick). In R. W. Reiber & A. S. Carlton, (Eds.), *The collected works of L. S. Vygotsky* (Vol. 1) (pp. 39–285). New York: Plenum.

Wells, G. (1986). *The meaning makers: Children learning to talk and talking to learn*. Portsmouth, NH: Heinemann.

Wells, G. (1999). *Dialogic inquiry: Toward a sociocultural practice and theory of education*. New York: Cambridge University Press.

Wertsch, J. (1998). *Mind as action*. New York: Oxford University Press.

Wilbur, R. (2000). The use of ASL to support the development of English and literacy. *Journal of Deaf Studies and Deaf Education, 5*, 81–104.

Yau, M. (1991). The role of language factors in second language writing. In L. Malave & G. Duquette (Eds.), *Language, culture and cognition* (pp. 266–283). Clevedon, Avon, UK: Multilingual Matters.

Zweibel, A. (1987). More on the effects of early manual communication on the cognitive development of deaf children. *American Annals of the Deaf, 132*, 16–20.

Cultural, Social, and Psychological Issues

11

Bencie Woll & Paddy Ladd

Deaf Communities

Records indicate that in the Western and Middle Eastern worlds, sign language-using Deaf people have gathered together for at least 7,000 years, and evidence for the existence of signed communication in various first nations indicates a Deaf presence which may be even older. By far the greatest amount of historical description and sociological research data, and consequently, theories about Deaf communities, has concentrated on European and North American Deaf gatherings in the past two centuries, particularly those of the last 25 years.

Gaining formal acceptance of the term "Deaf community" has not been unproblematic; however, its vernacular use has spread so widely that it has almost completely replaced the older term "Deaf world" in English discourse. In this present usage there is widespread agreement that, although it may not be possible to define the boundaries of Deaf communities, they are broadly understood to consist of those Deaf people who use a sign language.

In recent years, concern about the nature of these boundaries has grown, from both within and without those communities. In part this is due to the continual accumulation of academic knowledge regarding the concept of community itself and its problematic nature in both modern and postindustrial Western societies. In part it is due to the increasing headway made into the numbers of those formerly classified as "deaf children" as a result of technological developments twinned with the educational ideology of oralism. These developments, and Deaf children and adults' response to them, have resulted in community boundaries becoming cultural battlegrounds, where socializing patterns and contending cultural allegiances have become politicized. In such an emotional climate, it has become even more of a challenge to develop rational academic theory.

Moreover, the socializing patterns of both middle-aged and young Deaf people during the last 30 years have changed to the extent that Deaf clubs, the traditional centers of Deaf community and culture, perceive their continued existence to be threatened. These developments, which resemble similar patterns in wider Western societies, suggest that defining Deaf communities will become increasingly problematic.

This conceptual complexity is rendered more acute by the recent attempts to extend theorizing about Deaf communities to cover a wide variety of non-Western societies that have significant Deaf membership, ranging from tribes to farming communities, to towns both small and large, and examining not only present-day communities but ones that existed more than 300 years ago.

All these developments described above require these themes to be collated into an approach that is both coherent and sustained. This chapter represents an initial contribution to that goal.

A Conceptual Vehicle

Recent literature on Deaf communities (Bahan & Nash, 1996; Ladd, 2002; Lane, Pillard, & French, 2000) has begun the process of offering conceptual frameworks and models intended to include the various manifestations of Deaf existence. Bahan and Nash (1996) described the type of community found in industrialized societies where Deaf people form a small percentage of the population (usually less than 1 in 1,000) and where Deaf community life is organized separately from the hearing community, as a "suppressing" community. This is contrasted with those nonindustrialized societies with a high incidence of deafness, and in which Deaf and hearing life are not separated. Bahan and Nash (1996) refer to this as the "assimilating" community. Their taxonomy suggests that Deaf communities are formed in ways that correlate with how Deaf people have been treated and how sign languages have been viewed by majority societies/communities.

The establishment of these polar concepts is a valuable beginning to the discourse process. However, this dichotomy does not enable us to situate the full range of community types. The use of terms such as "suppressing" also implies that the attitudes of majority communities are the sole determinant of Deaf community structure and that Deaf communities are merely reactive ones. Similarly, such a model does not represent the dynamic qualities of Deaf communities and how they might change over time in response to both internal and external pressures.

As one means of making sense of the relevant literature, a multidimensional model of Deaf communities is presented in figure 11-1, based on attitudes, social choices, and the size of the Deaf population. A majority community with few Deaf people, negative attitudes to sign language, and different life opportunities for hearing and Deaf people will occupy a position in the upper right rear of the space in figure 11-1 (Bahan and Nash's suppressing community), which is termed here the "oppositional community" to reflect the bidirectional conflict). In such a community, hearing status defines access to society, with consequently lower socioeconomic status and educational achievement of Deaf people; the rate of marriage between Deaf people is high; and the hearing community has little or no awareness of the Deaf community. Most European and North American Deaf communities in the past 200 years can be described as existing toward the right side of the model.

It is also useful to situate within this matrix communities of only one or a few Deaf people, and where the same negative attitudes to sign language are found. Although there are many similarities to

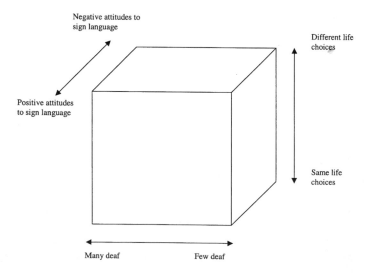

Figure 11-1. The multi-dimensional characteristics of Deaf communities.

Negative attitudes to sign language

Positive attitudes to sign language

Different life choices

Same life choices

Many deaf   Few deaf

the oppositional community, life choices for Deaf and hearing people in these nonindustrial communities are similar. Thus, these examples would be placed in the lower right rear of the model. For the time being, these will also be classed as "oppositional communities."

The front lower left of figure 11-1 is occupied by those Deaf communities that can be viewed as inseparable from the hearing community, termed here the "single community" (Bahan and Nash's "assimilating" community). In such communities, socioeconomic status and educational achievements of Deaf members are largely equivalent to those of hearing members, and there is considerable knowledge of sign language by hearing members. There is a low rate of marriage between Deaf partners, and no apparent separate community of Deaf people. Examples of such communities include those of Martha's Vineyard, Bali, and the Yucatan, discussed later. In many of these societies, some might contest the existence of a Deaf community, since there are limited cultural or social consequences of deafness and little sense of Deafhood (Ladd, 2002).

Occupying other points in this multidimensional space are Deaf communities integrated to a greater or lesser extent with the hearing community, here termed the "integrated community." In such societies, socioeconomic status and educational achievement of Deaf people is not highly differentiated from that of hearing people. However, in some cases Deaf people have gathered together consciously, and the hearing members manifest an awareness of the existence of those Deaf groupings, including various degrees of communication skills with Deaf people and some knowledge of sign language.

The Deaf Community Concept

For more than 150 years writers have discussed how Deaf people join together to create social groups and Deaf identities (Erting, 1978; Flournoy, 1856; Higgins, 1980; Ladd, 1998; Lane, 1984; Lawson, 1981; Markowicz & Woodward, 1978; Padden & Humphries, 1988). They have described how Deaf people create communities based on three factors: deafness, communication, and mutual support. Johnson (1994) reviews how these three factors lead to "communities of communica-

tion," "communities of ethnic identity," and "communities of solidarity."

The existence of Deaf communities, the identity of Deaf people, and the experience of Deafhood is here regarded equally as a consequence of Deaf people's experiences in majority societies, through exclusion, and a desire to create alternative structures to those of majority society. Through interaction with community members across generations and participation in the various activities and structures of the community, individuals are able to develop an awareness, acceptance, and celebration of both individual and collective Deaf self. This multidimensional sense of self-esteem is generally considered to be impossible for a Deaf person to develop if their lives take place solely within majority societies. Deaf community activities are felt to be sufficiently powerful to transcend the negative experiences of daily interaction with those societies. In short, by sealing off those aspects of their lives that really matter to them, Deaf people have made the existence of a positive Deaf identity possible.

All these concepts of Deaf community conceive of Deaf social and cultural lives as underpinned and driven by forms of communication that differ from those of the majority society. This differentiation primarily consists of the choice of a sign language as a preferred language. The centrality of these languages is reflected not only in the social and political organization of these communities, but in their strong cultural tradition of sign-play, jokes, storytelling, and poetry. In the most practical sense, then, the central fact of Deaf community membership is seen as linguistic membership.

Membership of these Deaf communities is also seen as determined, not by audiological measurement, but by self-identification as Deaf and reciprocal recognition of that identification—"attitudinal deafness" (Baker & Cokely, 1980). Individuals with minor hearing losses may be full members of the Deaf community, while other individuals with profound hearing losses may not identify with Deaf communities. When deaf people make the decision not to be part of the Deaf community, community members refer to them as preferring to try to live in the hearing world. On a closer consideration of the boundaries or margins of these Deaf communities, the issue is confused by different and in fact virtually opposing sets of terminology used by the two different languages in question. A good example is cited by Padden and Humphries (1988), who point out that to describe someone as acting as "hard of hearing" in the American Deaf community is to comment that a Deaf person has the behavioral and cultural characteristics of a hearing person. In English, such an expression would contrast with a hearing, rather than a Deaf norm.

Attitudinal deafness is seen by some writers as reflected in ethnic identity as it applies to membership of a Deaf community. In sociological and anthropological literature, ethnicity involves two features. "Paternity" defines members of a group in biological terms: in the case of the Deaf community, this is a hearing impairment, and additionally for some community members, Deaf family members. The other feature, "patrimony," refers to customary patterns of behavior and shared values: "ethnicity is a social force, created from within the community, that both results from and [creates] interaction and identity with the group (Johnson, 1994, p. 103).

Both the linguistic and attitudinal differences, reinforced by restricted access to society, underpin a Deaf solidarity and a sense of identification among Deaf people who share similar experiences (The Deaf Nation, 1998, Ladd, 1998). In its highest forms of expression, this community is actually referred to as a nation, as in Berthier's proposal from the 1840s that "la nation des sourds-muets" (the deaf-mute nation) should directly elect one representative to the French Parliament (Mottez, 1993).

Conceptual solidarity is also perceived to exist across national boundaries, leading to the notion of an international Deaf community. This was reported as long ago as 1815 in an account of Laurent Clerc's visit to the Braidwood School in London:

> As soon as Clerc beheld this sight [the children at dinner] his face became animated; he was as agitated as a traveller of sensibility would be on meeting all of a sudden in distant regions, a colony of his countrymen. . . . Clerc approached them. He made signs and they answered him by signs. This unexpected communication caused a most delicious sensation in them and for us was a scene of expression and sensibility that gave us the most heartfelt satisfaction. (de Ladebat, 1815)

It is generally agreed that in Western societies, Deaf residential schools and Deaf clubs form the two cornerstones of the Deaf community. In Deaf schools, Deaf children come together, learn sign languages, and begin the process of accessing the wider Deaf community. Despite continual attempts at suppression, Deaf schools ensured the continuity of sign language use and ensured the passing on of Deaf culture and Deaf historical traditions from one generation to another.

Similarly, there is widespread agreement that Deaf clubs provided a crucial central focus for Deaf adult life, not merely creating and maintaining the language and culture of childhood, but extending the Deaf experience into all the organizational forms required in adulthood. Between them, these two cornerstones are seen as encompassing what is traditionally understood as the Deaf community.

History of the Concept of Deaf Community

It is probable that deaf people who communicate by gesture or sign have existed as part of humanity from its inception; in the West, the first written evidence of their existence can be found at the rise of the Mediterranean societies in the fifth century BC. From that time onward, Greek philosophers like Herodotus, Socrates, Aristotle, and Plato, and their equivalents in Jewish and Roman society philosophized about the nature of Deaf people's existence and their place in society (see Lang, this volume).

Two characteristics of early Western approaches are particularly relevant. One is the contrast between a positive view of Deaf potential, constructed by examining groups of Deaf people; and a negative view, which only noticed Deaf individuals isolated from their peers. Van Cleve and Crouch (1989) noted the contrast between more positive Judaic/Old Testament writings about Deaf groups, and negative ones arising from Christianity's view of Deaf individuals as subjects to be healed, initially by Jesus of Nazareth, and later by followers of that religion. It is interesting in this respect to contrast the matter-of-fact attitude of the Mishnah (the first-century compendium of Jewish law) which discusses the legal status of signing and hints at the existence of a Deaf community: "A deaf-mute may communicate by signs and be communicated with by signs (Gittin 4.7); If two deaf-mute brothers were married to two deaf-mute sisters . . ." (Nashim 14:4).

The polar perspectives described above (groups

vs. individuals) have been reproduced ever since, and can be schematized as a "phobe–phile" axis. The former has considered Deaf people as less than human because of their perceived individual difficulty in communicating with "normal" people, whereas the other has marveled at their collective use of sign and gesture and seen this as enlarging the scope of what it means to be human. It is important, however, to note that variations of these opposing perspectives coexist within individuals and groups. These contrasting approaches can be traced through to the present day, assuming different patterns within varying fields and domains.

Deaf Emergence in the Middles Ages

From the fifteenth century onward, for a number of complex reasons, including the impact of the Renaissance with its revival of Greek philosophy, there was a considerable increase in both phobe and phile approaches. One recurrent theme concerns the education of Deaf people. The phobe construction (a pathological, or medical model) saw Deaf people essentially as empty vessels that could be made to resemble "normal" humanity in external appearance, by focusing on the development of their speech and discouraging contact with other Deaf people. The "phile" construction (a social model) prioritized Deaf people's ability to make sense of the world through their own visual skills, their ability to communicate in depth with each other, and the communicative power found in sign language, and perceived them as constituting a community of their own with the potential to administer their own affairs while achieving degrees of participation in the majority society. Early accounts are found in Richard Carew's (1555–1620) description of a young Deaf man, Edward Bone (cited in Jackson, 2001) and in Bulwer's dedication of a book to two Deaf brothers (1648).

Other themes concern an emerging recorded respect for Deaf people by lay society. Achievements by Deaf individuals and groups in business domains are noted by Zwiebel (1994). There is also growing evidence of the role of Deaf artists during this period (Bernard, 1993; Mirzoeff, 1995), and there appear to have been networks of Deaf artists and their Deaf friends (Plann, 1998), or even the beginnings of small Deaf communities which may be considered as proto-Deaf (existing before deaf education) communities. There is also the suggestion that monastic communities may have contained numbers of Deaf people, and had contact with Deaf people outside the community (de Saint-Loup, 1993). Finally, there are communities known to have incorporated sign language into their everyday lives (Groce, 1985).

The clearest evidence for the existence of proto-Deaf communities comes from the Ottoman court from the fifteenth century onward, where successive Sultans maintained as many as 200 deaf people charged with various responsibilities, including teaching sign language to the rest of the court (Miles, 2000). Several deaf people were among the Sultans' closest companions. One reason for this is intriguing: speech was seen as an undignified method of communication in the presence of the Sultan, and sign language was felt to be more appropriate.

It is possible to contend that the existence of such communities is contingent upon hearing people's respect for sign languages. Thus, the importance and status of secret signing societies and gesture during these periods (de Saint-Loup, 1993; Mirzoeff, 1995) can be thought of as providing a positive underpinning for the acceptance of proto-Deaf communities wherever they happened to show signs of development. Research from these periods continues to emerge, and it may be that in time it will be possible to theorize more confidently about a hidden history of Deaf communities.

Education and the Deaf Community

As Deaf educational establishments began from the 1760s onward to bring together large numbers of Deaf children and adults, sign languages also began to flourish (see de L'Epée, 1984/1776). Although it can be argued that deaf people can maintain satisfactory lifestyles while existing outside education systems (see Desloges, 1984/1779), especially where there are high enough numbers of Deaf individuals within a community, there is no doubt that the concentration of deaf children and adults within a residential school system is important in maintaining a sizeable and healthy Deaf community when the percentage of deaf people within a given population is small. Deaf education therefore was, and continues to be, the battleground on which the community's future existence and quality of life is contested (see Lang, this volume). By the early nineteenth century, the numbers of deaf graduates from these schools created a demand for Deaf meeting places; large numbers of clubs and religious societies were consequently established across Europe and the United States, many founded by Deaf people (Lysons, 1963). For the first time, Deaf school graduates attained professional positions, and Deaf magazines and newspapers were developed to facilitate regional and national communication. These developments were enhanced by the establishment in the United States in 1867 of Gallaudet College.

Documents from the era show high levels of Deaf self-confidence (Mottez, 1993), including beliefs that sign language was a "universal" language, which underpinned their conviction that hearing people could learn from their example. Attempts were also made to formalize the concept of an enfranchised or independent Deaf-Mute Nation, both in France (Mottez, 1993) and the United States (Van Cleve & Crouch, 1989).

However, the expansion of Deaf schools and clubs created something of a Trojan horse. Deaf education was often constructed to presuppose "hearing masters" of "Deaf subjects" (e.g., Sicard, 1984/1800), and an ideology of the "miracle of education" was disseminated to lay people. Deaf leaders, seeking funds to establish more schools, had little choice but to go along with this; a similar pattern occurred in the development of Deaf clubs. Deaf communities were thus vulnerable when the ideologies of the education system changed.

As the nineteenth century continued, the growth of industrialization saw the development of beliefs in the intrinsic goodness of science and progress, which constructed Deaf people as beings who could be "changed for the better." Social Darwinism applied the laws of science to human societies, and discourses of survival of the fittest were used both to reinforce colonialism and initiate repressive practices with other stigmatized groups (Foucault, 1979). Developments were reinforced by the concerns of those parents of deaf children who controlled the funding of the charitable and private school system, the upper class, now augmented by the new mercantile class. Many wanted their children to remain within their own social groups and not to join communities of the Deaf multitudes.

All these themes coalesced in the doctrine of oralism, which sought to remove sign languages and deaf teachers from the schools, to replace them by advocating the sole use of spoken communica-tion, and to prevent deaf children from signing with each other. These culminated in the famous Milan Conference of 1880. The growth of Social Darwinist eugenics also resulted in attempts to close Deaf clubs and prevent deaf marriages; laws to sterilize or castrate deaf people were placed on the statute book of 30 U.S. states (Mirzoeff, 1995); thus, even the adult Deaf community was under attack.

Deaf communities and their allies responded by founding national organizations to combat oralism; the National Association of the Deaf was established in the United States in 1880, and the British Deaf and Dumb Association (later the British Deaf Association) in Britain in 1890, both of which still exist today. International congresses were held, culminating in Paris in 1900, where deaf teachers and headmasters attempted to join the conference intended to ratify Milan. Despite outnumbering the oralists, they were refused admittance (Lane, 1984). Although the communities never gave up demanding change, their prime focus turned inward, toward preserving their language and their community and developing and refining their own social structures. Oralism was to remain essentially unchallenged for the next 70 years. Meanwhile, Deaf people's positive image with the lay public was diminished; earlier perceptions of an organic community with philosophical significance were supplanted by the medical model perception of a collection of isolated and handicapped individuals who constituted a medical and social problem.

Social Welfare Colonization

Deemed to be incapable and in need of charity and welfare support services, the adult Deaf community was rendered vulnerable to another colonialist development. In Britain, Anglican and Catholic missioners to the Deaf stepped into the vacuum left by the decline of Deaf lay preachers and the disappearance of the literate Deaf leaders of the nineteenth century to develop an absolute hold over Deaf clubs and organizations (Lysons, 1963; National Union of the Deaf, 1982).

Despite the negativity of the times, there was some evidence that lay people wanted to learn sign language (Corfmat, 1990). Deuchar (1984), however, indicates a general reluctance by the missioners to teach sign language; this enabled the missioners to retain their power as the gatekeepers of Deaf society.

Deaf Community Resurgence

During the twentieth century, despite oralism, Western Deaf communities continued to exist and grow. However, deprived of a meaningful role with deaf children, and with low rates of literacy, these communities had to curtail their political expression and focus on sustaining their social lives. It is easy to imagine that, had oralism not developed, Deaf communities would have developed an overt class system, with potential divisions between professionals and working-class Deaf people. Thus, the lowering of the achievement ceiling may have served to bond those communities more tightly.

In the mid-1970s, growing awareness of the failure of oralism, combined with the decolonization processes engendered by the liberal 1960s, enabled the beginnings of a Deaf resurgence. A number of factors contributed to this process: the development of the welfare state, which weakened the hold of the charitable sector over Deaf community life; Deaf activist organizations such as the National Union of the Deaf in Britain, and movements such as the "Deaf President Now" revolt at Gallaudet University in the 1980s; linguistic recognition of sign languages and their restoration to a place in deaf education; Deaf visibility in the media; the rediscovery of Deaf history; and the development of Deaf studies as an academic discipline.

This resurgence has resulted in an increase in the quality of Deaf community life. However, other factors suggest that these communities are not only becoming more complex, but may even be fragmenting in different ways. Indeed, the unique status of Deaf communities may itself be a problem. To define deaf people simply as disabled is to overlook the linguistic foundation of their collective life. To define them as a linguistic group is to overlook the very real sensory characteristics of their existence, both positive (a unique visual apprehension of the world out of which sign languages have been constructed), and negative (communication barriers are not simply linguistic, but auditory, too).

Case Studies of Non-Western Deaf Communities

In recent years there have been a growing number of studies of Deaf communities which differ from the Western model. These have often been per-ceived by both Deaf and non-Deaf people as representing an idyllic opposite to the Deaf communities of Europe and North America, with language, ethnic identity, and solidarity thought to be common to hearing and Deaf people. These communities include Grand Cayman Island (Washabaugh, 1981), Providence Island, off the coast of Colombia (Washabaugh, Woodward, & DeSantis, 1978), the Urubu of Amazonia (Ferreira-Brito, 1984), the Yucatan Maya (Johnson, 1994), the Enga of New Guinea (Kendon, 1980), and Martha's Vineyard (Groce, 1985). Discussion of all of these is beyond the scope of this chapter, but specific cases will be presented below.

There is also another set of circumstances where long-standing use of sign language has been a cultural norm. These are the aboriginal communities of central and northern Australia and the Native American communities. It does not seem that these languages originated with Deaf members; rather it would appear that they were developed as a means of expression in situations where spoken languages could not be used. McKay-Cody (1998) confirms that the Plains Indians used signs as a lingua franca, for ceremonies, oratory, and performance. Kendon (1988) reports similar uses of aboriginal community sign languages, as well as situations in which women were not permitted to speak—for example, after being widowed. Although both studies conclude that Deaf members of these communities must have been included to a much greater degree than found elsewhere, there is not yet sufficient evidence to assess the quality of Deaf–hearing relationships within them.

Martha's Vineyard

The best known account of a community where signing played a part in the lives of most people, hearing and deaf, is Groce's (1985) study of Martha's Vineyard, an island off the coast of Massachusetts. Martha's Vineyard is the prototypical model of Bahan and Nash's (1996) assimilating community.

Some areas of this island had a high incidence of genetic deafness through the nineteenth century. Groce (1985) and Bahan and Nash (1996) reported that deafness was regarded as just a normal variation among people, comparable to handedness. Most Deaf people married hearing people and were well-respected and economically active. A sign language specific to the island formed an integral part of interaction, including prayer meetings, and in settings where distances were too great for spoken language conversation. However, town business was conducted using hearing family members as interpreters. Over time, as intermarriage with people from outside the community increased, the percentage of deaf people decreased, and the multi-generational nature of the community changed. The last deaf members of the community died in the middle of the twentieth century, and the sign language and community are now extinct.

Yucatan

Johnson (1994) described a Yucatan Mayan Deaf community. Just over 3% of the village population is deaf, and both deaf and hearing people are farmers. Hearing people appear to have a high degree of competence in the village's sign language. However, the deaf members are not fully integrated socially. Only three of the seven deaf men are married (all to hearing women), and none has deaf children. None of the deaf women is married, and they report that it is impossible for them to marry. Despite this limited integration with hearing villagers, they do not identify with deaf people from outside the village.

Compared to Martha's Vineyard, this community represents an intermediate position on the matrix, near to the front on the left of figure 11-1, representing a high percentage of deaf people, moderate degree of social integration, and high degree of economic integration.

Bali

In the community of Desa Kolok on the island of Bali (Branson, Miller, Marsaja, and Negara, 1996), 2% of the 2000 village residents are deaf, and marriage between hearing and deaf villagers is the norm. Deaf members of the community have equal status in decision-making at local community level, although few are reported to participate. Those who do, use family members to interpret because not all village members are fluent in sign language. In earlier times, village deaf children received no formal education, although there has been a school for hearing children for more than 50 years. Recent moves to offer specialist deaf education has resulted in placing deaf children in a school located outside

the village, and this has begun to alter the linguistic and social dynamics of the community.

Desa Kolok also appears to have exemplified the "single community," occupying a similar place on the matrix to the Yucatan. However, there is the suggestion that, under pressures of political, social, and demographic change, it has moved toward the central position of an integrated community. If movement continues, it may be that this community will progressively resemble the oppositional type.

In two of the examples above, the emergence of Deaf schools, which did so much for Deaf communities in general, appear to be destroying what are now seen as idyllic communities. It may be pertinent to ask what sort of community deaf people actually prefer, since it would appear that community changes have in the end taken place as a result of their own choices.

Israeli Bedouin

Kisch (2001) described a Bedouin tribe of around 2,000 people with a deaf population of more than 10%. There are no deaf–deaf marriages in the community, and indeed, no deaf women are first wives (the community are Muslim and men have up to four wives). Thus there appear to be some limits on social integration. Deaf children are better educated than hearing children because they attend a deaf school where Hebrew is taught, and hearing children often do not attend school at all. The deaf children therefore develop a degree of literacy in the majority language, which is a key to employability, and they are fully economically integrated. Although all hearing members of the community have some knowledge of the tribe's sign language, only hearing people in families with a high percentage of deaf members are fully fluent. This community, therefore, also represents an intermediate space within the matrix of community type shown in figure 11-1.

Nigeria

Schmaling (2000) provides a thorough and grounded description of a well-established Deaf community within the Hausa tribe in northern Nigeria. There is an oral tradition that deaf people have always had meeting points in towns and villages for sharing information and experiences.

Their sign language is the main subject of Schmaling's study. The Deaf community has its own leader, the Sarkin Bebaye ("Chief of the deaf"), whose office is regarded as that of representative of the deaf, paralleling the system of chiefs which is one of the basic organizational principles of Hausa society.

Deaf people are well integrated into hearing Hausa society, and interaction and communication between deaf and hearing people is high. Many hearing people are able to converse with the deaf freely and effectively through signing, at least on a basic level. Hearing people do not feel ashamed of talking with their hands; they generally try to use their hands as much as possible when communicating with deaf people and accept signing as an appropriate medium of communication. Schmaling discusses a number of features that may account for the high level of integration of deaf people in Hausa society, including life in extended families and a generally high incidence of deafness (and disability) in Hausa society.

It would appear that this is a prime example of an integrating community. Moreover, unlike the other communities described above, there is clear evidence of a level of what might be called "Deaf consciousness" among the deaf members. Schmaling does report that there is a danger that this state of integration may weaken, as individualization within Hausa society increases, with a concomitant loss of traditional societal values. If this is confirmed, it might be predicted that the community would move toward becoming an oppositional community.

Nicaragua

The apparently recent emergence of sign language in Nicaragua has been well documented (see Kegl, Senghas, & Coppola, 1999), but the development of the community itself is less well known. Senghas and Kegl (1994) reported on the social factors involved in the development of this community from an anthropological perspective. Unusually for reports of this kind, their focus is on the internal dynamics of the Deaf community as well as on relations with the hearing community.

It is claimed that until the mid-1990s, there were no deaf children of deaf parents, interaction between deaf people was limited, and there was a near total absence of a multigenerational Deaf

community structure. The modern Deaf community began to form as schools were established, consisting primarily of teenagers and young adults, and is described as having an egalitarian, grass-roots quality. This community incorporated Deaf, hard-of-hearing, and dyslexic people (all educated together). As time has passed, the two latter groups have gradually separated from the Deaf community, and the Deaf community has become more hierarchical and stratified.

Because this is a community so clearly in a period of rapid change, Senghas and Kegl's observations highlight the importance of viewing all communities as dynamic entities. The community still remains in the oppositional category, but can be said to have moved upward on the matrix, as the Deaf individuals' life choices diverge further from those of their originating villages.

Modern Deaf Communities and Subcommunities

Current changes in the Deaf communities of some Western countries may be perceived as reflecting a similarly dynamic and intermediate quality, and even in some respects indicating a move from an oppositional community to an integrated one.

It has been estimated that for every deaf person who uses British Sign Language (BSL), there are nine hearing people who have some knowledge of the language. There has been national broadcasting of television programs using BSL for more than 20 years, and around 20,000 hearing people take basic-level examinations (equivalent to 120 hours of study) in BSL every year (Woll, 2001). Furthermore, many more parents, siblings, and friends of young deaf children have begun to sign, and many more professionals working with deaf people have done likewise. The creation of the profession of interpreting, Deaf studies, and interpreting programs at universities, and the numbers of deaf young people attending those universities has resulted in hearing and deaf students beginning to form friendships.

This has had the effect of creating small subcommunities of deaf and hearing signers in certain locations, ranging from Fremont in California and Rochester in New York to Wolverhampton and Preston in Britain. Bienvenu and Colonomos (1989) refer to these types of development as constituting "the third culture," and Ladd (2002) attempts to formalize this development within a wider schematization of Deaf communities in general. Ladd's model, which identifies earlier and smaller versions of this contact in the pubs around Britain in the early and mid-twentieth century, suggests that the deaf people who socialized in this manner still retained strong links with the wider multigenerational Deaf community, but it is possible that this latter characteristic is now changing. There is also a general shift in the siting of Deaf community activity, especially among young Deaf people, from Deaf clubs to more public settings; this has served to make Deaf communities and languages more visible and contributed to the developments above.

Diversity Within Deaf Communities

In recent years researchers have begun to look at the existence of what are termed here as "subcommunities" existing within the wider Deaf communities, and there have been a number of studies of gay, black, Jewish, Hispanic, Asian and Native American subcultures within those communities. Although it is beyond the scope of this chapter to discuss these in detail, it is possible to see that the same factors that influence the nature of Deaf communities generally can also be applied to a consideration of these subcommunities. In fact, it would not be too difficult to create a matrix similar to that in figure 11-1 to situate these within the Deaf community.

In some of the above examples, subcommunities have only recently developed. Gay and lesbian Deaf people have only recently emerged from centuries of prejudice to declare themselves and develop their own groups (Lane, Hoffmeister, & Bahan, 1996). There is some evidence to show that a distinctive sign dialect exists in ASL, known as GSV (Gay Sign Variation) (Kleinfeld and Warner 1996).

An intermediate example would be the Jewish Deaf community, which had its own school in Britain for decades and still has its own Deaf club. In this example, the autonomy of the group works harmoniously as a section of the national Deaf community, rather like any other Deaf club. The extent to which this subcommunity possessed its own sign dialect is not yet clear.

In other examples, however, the majority Deaf community can be viewed as acting as an opposi-

tional community, and in its turn creating an oppositional minority Deaf community. The earliest example in Britain is the Roman Catholic Deaf community, who were educated in their own Deaf schools (with their own very different sign languages, not dialects, which originated from Irish Sign Language) and their own clubs. In some cities, such as Liverpool and Manchester, the degree of integration was greater than in others, such as Glasgow. In the last 20 years, most of the overt barriers of prejudice have come down.

The clearest example of an oppositional subcommunity can be found in the United States and in South Africa, where black and white Deaf schools were strictly segregated and where there was little interaction between the two races for the better part of two centuries (Anderson & Bowe, 2001). In this example it would seem fair to suggest that there actually were two separate communities, with their own distinct paths of origin and development (Hairston & Smith, 1983). In the case of the United States, the fact that both use American Sign Language, albeit distinctive dialects (Aramburo, 1989), would appear to contradict the analysis of separation, but it is possible to construe such use of American Sign Language as, in effect, a colonizing language brought from white Deaf people to black schools. However, the existence of a common language (as contrasted, say, with the situation in hearing South Africa), has enabled an acceleration of black and white Deaf contact. Research is needed to ascertain the degree to which this acceleration has resulted in a unified community. In South Africa, where change has been more recent, where there are more languages to integrate, and where there is a relative absence of a Deaf professional class to form a bridge, there is clearly some way to go (Aarons & Akach, 1998). It is interesting, however, to note the extent to which new Deaf television programs in South Africa are being used as a medium to unify both the sign languages and the communities.

The British black Deaf community differs from those above in that it is a very new community which began with the deaf children whose parents migrated to Britain from the Caribbean and Africa from the 1950s onward, and which is only just beginning to develop a distinctive social network and dialect of BSL (James, 2000; James & Woll, 2002). A similar pattern can be found with Asian Deaf people.[1] In some areas the small number of black/Asian

Deaf people has resulted in apparent integration with the white Deaf community. In others, however, the extent of racism experienced by Black/Asian Deaf people has caused them to withdraw from the white community altogether (Taylor & Meherali, 1991), and this may have served as the impetus for creating their own subcommunities.

Comparable American subcommunities formed by immigration, such as the Hispanic and Asian Deaf communities, have not yet been substantially researched, and although Lane, Hoffmeister, and Bahan (1996) provide a thorough discussion of issues of diversity within the American Deaf community, there appears to be little material (at least in English) available on diversity issues or Deaf subcommunities outside the United States and the United Kingdom.

A pressing issue for these subcommunities is the extent to which they have access to their hearing equivalents. Gay and lesbian Deaf groups report significant contact, and it has even been suggested that this contact is more extensive than for the rest of the Deaf community. In contrast, however, other groups have found it difficult to access the languages and cultures of their originating communities. For example, Dively (2001) described the experiences of Native American Deaf people and identified two important themes characteristic of other Deaf subcommunities: limited participation within Native American culture and difficulty in maintaining their Native American identity in the wider Deaf community. This is parallelled by research in Britain on the experiences of Deaf people of Asian backgrounds (Chambra, Ahmad, & Jones, 1998).

Summary and Conclusions

A surge in Deaf confidence and pride has taken place since the 1980s, partly due to the revelation of the linguistic complexities of sign languages. However, there has been limited consideration of social and cultural issues and of the internal and external factors responsible for creating, maintaining, and changing Deaf communities compared to the amount of linguistic research which has been carried out. Until resources are available to study Deaf communities in a consistent manner, progress will be slow.

It is hoped that these tentative beginnings to-ward the development of less static models of Deaf communities will be useful in assisting with social change and study. While static models continue, the implication that oppositional communities are incapable of significant change also continues, with the concomitant suggestion that there is no work for those majority societies to do. This static view will also retard attempts to think through what might be happening within Deaf communities; in view of the pace of increase in the number of deaf people who are professionals and the number of hearing people learning to sign, failure to consider these changes would be unwise. If we are to assist in mitigating any negative developments which the future might bring and in encouraging positive ones, we need to be able to take up positions and models which enable us to perceive Deaf communities in ways as flexible as the ones they are themselves developing.

Note

1. In Britain, this term refers to people originating from the Indian subcontinent: India, Pakistan, Bangladesh, and so on. In the United States, the term is used more widely to refer to people from countries such as Japan, Malaysia, China, and the Philippines.

References

Aarons, D., & Akach, P. (1998). South African Sign Language-one language or many? *Stellenbosch Papers in Linguistics, 31*, 1–28.

Anderson, G.B., & Bowe, F.G. (2001). Racism within the Deaf community. In L. Bragg (Ed.), *Deaf world: a historical reader and primary sourcebook* (pp. 305–308). New York: New York University Press.

Aramburo, A. (1989). Sociolinguistic aspects of the black Deaf community. In C. Lucas (Ed.), *The sociolinguistics of the Deaf community* (pp. 103–119). New York: Academic Press.

Bahan, B., & Nash, J. (1996). The formation of signing communities. In *Deaf studies IV: visions of the past, visions of the future* (pp. 1–26). Washington, DC: Gallaudet University Press.

Baker, C., & Cokely, D. (1980). *American Sign Language.* Silver Spring, MD: TJ Publishers.

Bernard Y (1993). Silent artists. In R. Fischer & H. Lane (Eds.), *Looking back: a reader on the history of Deaf communities and their sign languages* (pp. 75–88). Hamburg: Signum Press.

Bienvenu, M.J., & Colonomos, B. (1989). *Language, community and culture* [video recording]. Durham; UK: University of Durham Deaf Studies Research Unit.

Branson, J. Miller, D. Marsaja, I.G., & Negara, I.W. (1996). Everyone here speaks sign language, too: A deaf village in Bali, Indonesia. In C. Lucas, Ed.), *Multicultural aspects of sociolinguistics in deaf communities* (pp. 39–57). Washington, DC: Gallaudet University Press.

Bulwer, J. (1648). *Philocophus or the deafe and dumbe man's friend.* London: Humphrey Moseley.

Chamba, R. Ahmad, W., & Jones, L. (1998). *Improving services for Asian deaf children: parents' and professionals' perspectives.* Bristol. The Policy Press.

Corfmat, P. (1990). *Please sign here.* Worthing, UK: Churchman Publishing.

The Deaf Nation. (1998). *Sign On* [video recording]. Newcastle: Tyne Tees TV.

de Ladebat, L. (1815). *A collection of the most remarkable definitions and answers of Massieu and Clerc.* London: Cox & Bayliss.

de L'Epée, C. (1984/1776). The true method of educating the deaf confirmed by much experience. In H. Lane & F. Philip (Eds.), *The deaf experience* (pp. 49–72). Cambridge, MA: Harvard University Press.

de Saint-Loup, A. (1993). Images of the Deaf in medieval western Europe. In R. Fischer & H. Lane (Eds.), *Looking back: A reader on the history of Deaf communities and their sign languages* (pp. 379–402). Hamburg: Signum Press.

Desloges, P. (1984/1779). A deaf person's observations about an elementary course of education for the deaf. In H. Lane & F. Philip (Eds.), *The deaf experience* (pp. 28–48). Cambridge, MA: Harvard University Press.

Deuchar, M. (1984). *British Sign Language.* London: Routledge & Kegan Paul.

Dively, V.L. (2001). Contemporary native deaf experience: overdue smoke rising. In L. Bragg (Ed.), *Deaf world: a historical reader and primary sourcebook* (pp. 390–405). New York: New York University Press.

Erting, C. (1978). Language policy and deaf ethnicity in the United States. *Sign Language Studies, 19,* 139–152.

Ferreira-Brito, L. (1984). Similarities and differences in two Brazilian sign languages. *Sign Language Studies, 13,* 45–56.

Flournoy, J.J. (1856). Mr. Flournoy to Mr. Turner. *American Annals of the Deaf and Dumb, 8,* 120–125.

Foucault, M. (1979). *Discipline and punishment.* New York: Vintage Books.

Groce, N. (1985). *Everyone here spoke sign language.* Cambridge, MA: Harvard University Press.

Hairston, E., & Smith, L. (1983). *Black and deaf in America.* Silver Spring, MD: TJ Publishers.

Higgins, P. (1980). *Outsiders in a hearing world.* Newbury Park, CA: Sage.

Jackson, P. (2001). *A pictorial history of deaf Britain.* Winsford, UK: Deafprint.

James, M. (2000). *Black deaf or deaf black?* Unpublished doctoral dissertation, City University, London.

James, M., & Woll, B. (2002). Black deaf or deaf black? In A. Blackledge & A. Pavlenko (Eds.), *Negotiation of identities in multilingual contexts* (pp. 125–160). Clevedon, UK: Multilingual Matters.

Johnson, R.E. (1994). Sign language and the concept of deafness in a traditional Yucatec Mayan village. In C.J. Erting, R.E. Johnson, D.L. Smith, & B.D. Snider (Eds.), *The deaf way—Perspectives from the International Conference on Deaf Culture, 1989* (pp. 102–109). Washington, DC: Gallaudet University Press.

Kegl, J.A. Senghas, A., & Coppola, M. (1999). Creation through contact: sign language emergence and sign language change in Nicaragua. In M. DeGraff (Ed.), *Comparative grammatical change: The intersection of language acquisition, creole genesis, and diachronic syntax* (pp. 179–238). Cambridge, MA: MIT Press.

Kendon, A. (1980). A description of a deaf-mute sign language from the Engaprovince of Papua New Guinea with some comparative discussion: Parts I, II, III. *Semiotica, 32,* 1–34, 81–117, 245–313.

Kendon, A. (1988). *The sign languages of aboriginal Australia.* Cambridge: Cambridge University Press.

Kisch, S. (2001). *Deafness among a Bedouin tribe in southern Israel.* Unpublished master's thesis, Tel-Aviv University.

Kleinfeld, M.S., & Warner, N. (1996). Variation in the Deaf community: Gay, lesbian and bisexual signs. In C. Lucas (Ed.), *Multicultural aspects of sociolinguistics in Deaf communities* (pp. 3–38). Washington, DC: Gallaudet University Press.

Ladd, P. (1998). *In search of Deafhood—Understanding Deaf culture.* Unpublished doctoral dissertation, University of Bristol, UK.

Ladd, P. (2002). *Understanding Deaf culture: in search of Deafhood.* Clevedon, UK: Multilingual Matters.

Lane, H. (1984). *When the mind hears.* New York: Random House.

Lane, H., Pillard, R.C., & French, M. (2002) Origins of the American Deaf-world: assimilating and differentiating societies and their relation to genetic patterning. In K. Emmorey & H. Lane (Eds.) *The signs of language revisited* (pp. 77–100). Mahwah, NJ: Lawrence Erlbaum Associates.

Lane, H. Hoffmeister, R. & Bahan, B. (1996). *A journey into the Deaf-world.* San Diego, CA: Dawn Sign Press.

Lawson, L. (1981). The role of sign in the structure of the deaf community. In B. Woll, J.G. Kyle & M. Deuchar (Eds.), *Perspectives on British Sign Language and deafness* (pp. 166–177). London: Croom Helm.

Lysons, K. (1963). *Some aspects of the historical development and present organization of voluntary welfare societies for adult deaf persons in England 1840–1963.* Unpublished master's thesis, University of Liverpool, Liverpool, UK.

Markowicz, H., & Woodward, J. (1978). Language and the maintenance of ethnic boundaries in the Deaf community. *Communication and Cognition, 11,* 29–37.

McKay-Cody, M. (1998). Plains Indian Sign Language: a comparative study of alternative and primary signers. In C. Carroll (Ed.). *Deaf Studies IV: Toward 2000: Unity and diversity* (pp. 17–77). Washington, DC: College for Continuing Education, Gallaudet University.

Miles, M. (2000). Signing at the Seraglio—mutes, dwarves and gestures at the Ottoman Court 1500–1700. *Disability Handicap and Society, 15,* 115–134.

Mirzoeff, N. (1995). *Silent poetry: Deafness, sign and visual culture in modern France.* Princeton, NJ: Princeton University Press.

Mottez, B. (1993). The deaf mute banquets and the birth of the Deaf movement. In R. Fischer & H. Lane (Eds.), *Looking back: A reader on the history of Deaf communities and their sign languages* (pp. 143–156). Hamburg: Signum Verlag.

National Union of the Deaf. (1982). *Charter of rights of the deaf.* London: No author.

Padden, C.A., & Humphries, T. (1988). *Deaf in America.* Cambridge, MA: Harvard University Press.

Plann, S. (1998). Francisco Goya y Lucientes und Roberto Prádez y Gautier: Die Rolle der Gehörlosigkeit im Leben zweier spanischer Künstler. *Das Zeichen, 12,* 502–519.

Schmaling, C. (2000). *Maganar hannu: "Language of hands." A descriptive analysis of Hausa Sign Language.* Hamburg: Signum Verlag.

Senghas, R.J., & Kegl, J.A. (1994). Social considerations in the emergence of Idioma de Signos Nicaraguense (Nicaraguan Sign Language). *Signpost, 7,* 40–46.

Sicard, R.-A. (1984/1800) Course of instruction for a congenitally deaf person. In H. Lane & F. Philip (Eds.), *The deaf experience* (pp. 81–126). Cambridge, MA: Harvard University Press.

Taylor, G., & Meherali, T. (1991) *The other deaf community? Issues in Deafness* (block 1, unit 4). Milton Keynes: The Open University.

Van Cleve, J.V., & Crouch, B.A. (1989). *A place of their own.* Washington, DC: Gallaudet University Press.

Washabaugh, W. (1981). The deaf of Grand Cayman, British West Indies. *Sign Language Studies, 10,* 117–134.

Washabaugh, W., Woodward, J., & DeSantis, S. (1978). Providence Island sign: A context-dependent language. *Anthropological Linguistics, 20,* 95–109.

Wilcox, S. (1989). *American Deaf culture: An anthology.* Silver Spring, MD: Linstok Press.

Woll, B. (2001). Language, culture, identity and the deaf community. *The Linguist, 40,* 98–103.

Zwiebel, A. (1994). Judaism and deafness: a humanistic heritage. In C.J. Erting, R.E. Johnson, D.L. Smith, & B.D. Snider (Eds.), *The deaf way: perspectives from the International Conference on Deaf Culture* (pp. 231–238). Washington, DC: Gallaudet University Press.

Shirin D. Antia & Kathryn H. Kreimeyer

Peer Interaction of Deaf and Hard-of-Hearing Children

For all children, socialization with peers serves several crucial functions. Peer interaction allows children to develop friendships that are important for the growth of the child's social self (Fine, 1981). Some authors (Garvey, 1984; Rubin, 1980) suggest that interaction with peers leads to the development of the social skills necessary to initiate and maintain friendships. It is through interaction with peers that children learn to take multiple perspectives in social situations. They also learn negotiation, conflict management, tact, and other social communication skills important for socialization in the adult world. Positive peer interaction is, therefore, a necessary component of overall social development (Odom, McConnell, & McEvoy, 1992). Peer social interaction includes communication (nonliguistic and linguistic, positive and negative) and social play with peers. Because hearing loss in children can result in communication barriers, researchers have been interested in the quantity and quality of peer interaction of children with hearing loss, the factors that influence their peer interaction, and interventions that enhance peer interaction.

Quantity and Quality of Peer Interaction

Frequency and Duration of Peer Interaction

Frequency of peer interaction is of interest because of its inferred relationship with social competence. Most of the research with deaf and hard-of-hearing (D/HH) children is based on observations of peer interaction and social play of preschool and elementary children. This may reflect the importance of peer interaction for young children and the ease of observing them during play. Observation studies that focus on frequency of interaction typically count the number of times or number of intervals during which a child interacts with a peer. Some studies have measured the duration of time that children interact with peers. Studies that include older elementary children and adolescents typically use self-reports or teacher reports of interaction.

Several observation studies of kindergarten and elementary children show that D/HH children interact less frequently, or for less time, with peers than do hearing children. However, other studies have found no differences between D/HH and hearing children. One of the problems in drawing conclusions from such research is the difficulty in controlling factors that affect interaction, such as the D/HH children's language ability, mode of communication and age, and the partner's language ability and familiarity. No research has accounted for all of these variables within a single study. Frequency of interaction may also be affected by whether the setting is segregated or integrated (i.e., with hearing children present). Some research has been conducted in segregated settings with only D/HH children present. Presumably, the communication barriers among D/HH children are less than those between D/HH and hearing children. Thus, it is assumed that peer interactions with D/HH peers will be more frequent, of longer duration, and of higher quality than those with hearing peers. However, because many D/HH children are educated in integrated settings such as public schools, especially in the United States (Holden-Pitt & Diaz, 1998), the ability of D/HH and hearing children to interact with each other is of particular interest to researchers. Data from different integrated settings are not comparable, however, because in some settings D/HH children have access to both D/HH and hearing peers, while in others they have access only to hearing peers.

Early studies of peer interaction in integrated settings concluded that D/HH children interacted less frequently than hearing peers. McCauley, Bruininks, and Kennedy (1976) compared the interaction frequency of D/HH and hearing children in first through fourth grade in integrated classrooms. They observed 14 hearing and 14 D/HH children who had moderate to profound hearing losses. Results indicated that the hearing children had significantly more interaction and interacted with a significantly greater number of peers than the D/HH children. Similarly, Levy-Shiff and Hoffman (1985) compared the interaction of 12 children with profound hearing loss, 12 children with severe hearing loss, and 12 hearing children enrolled in five integrated kindergartens. They found that the children with profound hearing loss interacted significantly less frequently with peers than those in the other groups. Because the children were in an oral program, the authors assumed that degree of hearing loss was related to language and communication skills. Thus, they concluded that children's communication skills impacted interaction frequency.

Vandell and George (1981) examined the interaction of 16 D/HH and 16 hearing children between 3 and 5 years of age who attended a partially integrated preschool program. The children were each paired with a play partner to compare the interaction of hearing dyads, D/HH dyads, and mixed dyads (one D/HH and one hearing partner). Results indicated that although the frequency of interaction among the three kinds of dyads was similar, the hearing dyads spent more time in interaction than the D/HH dyads. The mixed dyads spent the least time interacting with one another.

Antia (1982) compared the interaction of D/HH children in special-education resource rooms, where children had the opportunity to interact only with other D/HH peers, and in general education classrooms, where they had the opportunity to interact with both D/HH and hearing peers. Her study included 32 D/HH children with mild to profound hearing losses and 84 hearing children in grades 1–6. She found that the D/HH children interacted significantly less frequently with peers (D/HH or hearing) than the hearing children. Moreover, the D/HH children had the same frequency of interaction within the general education classroom and the resource room, indicating that the presence of only D/HH peers did not increase peer interaction.

Studies examining social play have also found differences between D/HH and hearing children, even when D/HH children have been observed in segregated settings. Higginbotham and Baker (1981) compared the social play of seven D/HH and seven hearing kindergarten children aged 4–6 years. The D/HH children had severe to profound hearing loss and communicated orally. All children were in segregated settings and had access only to peers of the same hearing status. The D/HH children spent significantly more time in solitary play and less time in cooperative play than did hearing children. Furthermore, they spent most of their time in solitary play and successively less time in play that required engagement with other children (parallel, associative, cooperative). The hearing children, in contrast, spent the least time in solitary play and the most time in play that required engagement with other children.

In another study of social play, Antia and Dittillo (1998) observed 38 D/HH children with hearing losses ranging from moderate to profound and

44 hearing children. The children were observed during inside play in small groups of six to eight, of whom at least two children were D/HH. Thus the D/HH children had access to both D/HH and hearing peers. The authors found that the hearing children engaged in significantly more associative/cooperative play than the D/HH children and that the hearing children engaged primarily in social play, while the D/HH children engaged equally in nonplay and social play.

These studies indicate that D/HH children interact less with peers than do hearing children. However, they did not systematically identify variables that contributed to reduced interaction frequency. A major variable hypothesized to affect interaction frequency in D/HH children is their language and communication ability. Three studies have examined the effects of D/HH children's language ability on their peer interaction or social play. Lederberg (1991) examined the effect of D/HH children's language ability on their play-partner preferences and on the characteristics of their play and social interaction with peers. She observed 29 D/HH children between 3 and 5 years of age. The children were enrolled in self-contained classrooms in public schools and were observed during outdoor free play with D/HH peers. They were divided into high, medium, and low language ability levels, based on their scores on two language tests. Lederberg found that children who had high language ability initiated significantly more interaction and spent significantly more time playing with high language ability partners than with partners of medium or low language ability. High language ability children also used significantly more linguistic communication with high language ability partners than with other partners.

Spencer, Koester, and Meadow-Orlans (1994) examined the peer interaction of four 3-year-old D/HH children with moderate to profound hearing losses and four hearing children in an integrated day care program where all adults used sign. Two of the D/HH and two hearing children had deaf parents and were native signers. The eight children were divided into three language levels based on the length of their signed or spoken utterances. The authors reported that hearing status was not associated with frequency of peer interaction, but that children with high language ability (D/HH or hearing) engaged in peer communication at a significantly higher rate than children with medium or low language ability. Antia and Dittillo (1998) found that, while D/HH children's communication ability (measured by a standardized questionnaire) was not related to frequency of positive peer interaction, it was positively related to frequency of associative/cooperative play. Clearly, language and communication ability seem related to peer interaction.

Mode of communication is another variable that can affect peer communication, especially between D/HH children and hearing peers. Minnett, Clark, and Wilson (1994) compared the play and peer communication of 15 children with moderate hearing loss using oral communication, 15 children with profound hearing loss using simultaneous (speech and sign) communication, and 30 hearing children. The children were between the ages of 3 and 5 years and enrolled in an integrated preschool program. Minnett et al. found no differences between the D/HH and hearing children in the total amount of social play and communication directed toward peers, although all children preferred to interact with partners of similar hearing status. The mode of communication did not affect the social play, peer communication, or partner preference of the D/HH children.

Hulsing, Luetke-Stahlman, Frome-Loeb, Nelson, and Wegner (1995) observed the peer interaction of three D/HH kindergarten children: one who used oral communication, and two who used simultaneous communication. Each child was in a different general education classroom with no other D/HH children present. The researchers compared the children's interaction to three matched hearing classmates and found that the children who used simultaneous communication had less frequent interactions than their hearing peers, while the child who used oral communication had a similar number of interactions.

Researchers examining the interaction of D/HH adolescents also report that those who use oral communication are more likely to have interactions with hearing peers than those who use sign. Stinson and Kluwin (1996) collected self-reported data on the social activity, speech, and signing skills of 451 D/HH adolescents in 15 public high schools. Those adolescents who rated themselves low in signing ability reported interacting with, and having a positive regard for, hearing schoolmates. Adolescents who rated themselves high in signing skills reported interacting mostly with other D/HH schoolmates. Similarly, Stinson and Whitmire (1992) obtained self-ratings of preferred mode of communication and social participation from 64 D/HH adolescents attending a summer camp. Again, adolescents who preferred oral communication reported more frequent interaction with hearing than with D/HH peers, while those who preferred sign communication reported the opposite. Bat-Chava and Deignan (2001) examined the oral language and social relationships of 25 D/HH children with cochlear implants in general education classrooms. Parents of 81% of the children reported that oral communication improved after implantation and that, as a result, their children became more willing and able to interact with hearing peers. Conversely, children whose oral communication did not improve after implantation were reported to have difficulties in social relationships with hearing peers.

Although several researchers (Minnett et al., 1994; Spencer et al., 1994) have reported that D/HH children prefer to interact with D/HH peers, they also report that some interaction occurs with hearing partners. Interaction with hearing partners may be mediated by familiarity. Lederberg, Ryan, and Robbins (1986), who observed 14 D/HH children between 4 and 6 years of age in dyadic play with peers, reported that D/HH children had more successful initiations with familiar than with unfamiliar hearing partners. The D/HH children engaged in more physical communication and pretend play with a familiar than with an unfamiliar hearing partner. They were more likely to communicate in sign and to communicate about absent objects with a D/HH than with a hearing partner. Apparently, D/HH and hearing children who are familiar with one another may find nonlinguistic means of communication to partially overcome language and mode-of-communication barriers.

The presence of hearing partners can positively affect D/HH children's social play. Esposito and Koorland (1989) systematically compared the effects of the presence of D/HH and hearing peers on two D/HH children aged 3 and 5 years. When observed in their self-contained classroom with only D/HH peers available, both children engaged in non-interactive parallel play for 33–56% of observed intervals and in associative play for 11–32% of intervals. When observed in their day-care setting, where only hearing peers were available, the children engaged in parallel play for 7–25% of in-tervals and in associative play for 35–60% of intervals. Thus, with D/HH peers, they engaged primarily in non-interactive play, but with hearing peers they engaged primarily in interactive play.

Levine and Antia (1997) also found that the presence of hearing peers had a positive effect on social play. They examined the play of 46 D/HH children aged 3–6 years enrolled in 13 partially integrated programs. They observed the children during free play in groups of four to six children, of whom two to three children were D/HH and the remainder hearing. Similar to results reported by Minnett et al. (1994) and Spencer et al. (1994), they found that the D/HH children engaged more frequently in social play with D/HH than with hearing peers. Older children (ages 5–6 years) engaged in more group play with hearing peers than younger children (3–4 years). The most interesting finding was that group dramatic play (the most advanced form of social play) occurred most frequently in mixed groups that included at least two D/HH children and one or more hearing children. They suggested that the reason for this finding was that the hearing children in the group were able to model and organize the dramatic play. Another reason could be that the D/HH children were better able to communicate in the presence of a familiar D/HH peer.

Quality of Peer Interactions

Besides frequency of interaction, several aspects of the quality of peer interactions have been examined. One area of interest is D/HH children's ability to initiate and maintain interactions with peers. Another is the kind of communication, linguistic or nonlinguistic, used during peer interaction. Linguistic interaction includes both oral and signed communication. A final area of research is the themes of interaction. Each of these can reveal children's skills and potential sources of difficulty.

Initiating and Maintaining Interaction

To interact with peers, children must initiate interaction in a manner that will result in a peer response. Several studies indicate that D/HH children initiate peer interaction at rates similar to, or higher than, hearing children. Arnold and Tremblay (1979) examined interaction initiations of six D/HH and six hearing children between 4 and 5 years of age enrolled in an integrated preschool.

Free-play observations indicated that the D/HH children initiated interaction as frequently as the hearing children. They also received as many initiations from peers as did the hearing children. However, both groups showed a preference for initiating interaction with peers of similar hearing status. Antia and Ditillo (1998) examined initiations and responses to initiations and found no differences between D/HH and hearing children. Vandell and George (1981) found that D/HH preschool children initiated significantly more interactions to their peers, both deaf and hearing, than hearing children.

D/HH and hearing children use similar initiation strategies. Vandell and George (1981) reported that both D/HH and hearing children frequently used vocalizations, smiles, and object-related acts. However, the D/HH children's initiations were more likely to be rejected by partners than initiations of the hearing children. Messenheimer-Young and Kretschmer (1994) completed a detailed case study of the initiation strategies used by a 5-year-old hard-of-hearing child in an integrated preschool. The child used strategies similar to those of hearing classmates. Successful initiation strategies for all children included nonverbal entry, extending an invitation, offering an object, or producing a behavior similar to that in which other children were engaged. Seventeen percent of the child's initiations were successful in eliciting a positive response from other children. The hearing children had success rates of 15–74%. Thus, although the child had comparatively few successful initiations, his success rate was within the range demonstrated by classmates.

Hulsing et al. (1995) examined the interactions of three D/HH kindergarten children. The average length of each interaction was between two and three turns for all children, D/HH and hearing, and D/HH and hearing children had similar rates of successful initiation. Roberts, Brown, and Rickards (1995) examined pretend play interactions of 12 oral D/HH children (3 with age-appropriate language, 9 with language delays) and 18 hearing children between 3 and 5 years of age in integrated preschool classrooms. They also found that D/HH and hearing children had similar rates of initiation. Both groups initiated interaction with a single behavior rather than a string of behaviors and appeared equally successful with these behaviors. The most frequently used and successful initiation behavior for both groups was a play-related utterance or action. The D/HH children were more likely to use actions, while the hearing children were more likely to use utterances. This difference could reflect the language delay of the D/HH children or the expectation that their oral language would not be understood. Another difference between the groups was that the D/HH children used a wait-and-hover initiation strategy more frequently than the hearing children; this strategy was unsuccessful for both groups.

Levy-Shiff and Hoffman (1985) and Vandell and George (1981) found that D/HH children were less likely to have successful initiations than hearing children, although their initiation behaviors were similar to those of hearing children. McKirdy and Blank (1982) examined the rate and success of initiations between 12 D/HH and 12 hearing dyads, 4–6 years of age. The children were paired to play with a preferred playmate of the same hearing status. Results indicated that D/HH dyads initiated approximately half the number of initiations as hearing dyads. Besides frequency and form, McKirdy and Blank examined the "summoning power" of the children's communication initiations. They found that the majority of the initiations used by the deaf dyads were "obliges," behaviors that contained an explicit demand for a response, while the majority of the initiations of the hearing children were "comments," behaviors that contained no such demand. For the D/HH children, the obliges were more effective in eliciting responses than comments, while the opposite was true for the hearing children.

Duncan (1999) studied 11 D/HH and 11 hearing preschool and kindergarten children enrolled in the same integrated program. Each child was videotaped during free play and during dyadic interaction with a partner of the opposite hearing status. Duncan found few differences in initiation frequency or strategies between D/HH and hearing children in the dyadic setting. However, in the free-play setting D/HH children initiated fewer interactions than hearing children and were more likely to use nonlinguistic communication. When maintaining interaction, the D/HH children used more minimally contingent responses and made fewer significant contributions than the hearing children. Minimally contingent responses were those that maintained the interaction but added no new information, whereas significant contributions both maintained the interaction and added new information.

Communication During Interaction

One of the issues of interest to researchers is the kind of communication used by D/HH children when interacting with peers. One line of research examines the kinds and relative proportions of linguistic (oral or signed) and nonlinguistic (physical activity, mime, gesture) communication used by D/HH and hearing children with D/HH and hearing peers. A second line of research examines the themes and topics during interaction.

Linguistic and Nonlinguistic Communication

Antia (1982) examined the linguistic and nonlinguistic communication used by D/HH and hearing children. In the integrated classroom, D/HH children used linguistic communication for 52% of interactions, while hearing children used linguistic communication for 84%. D/HH children also used significantly more nonlinguistic communication than hearing children. In the segregated resource room, D/HH children increased linguistic communication to 77%. McCauley et al. (1976) found that D/HH children in their study used linguistic communication for 61% of interactions, while hearing children used linguistic communication for 75% of interactions. Both studies show that, although elementary-age D/HH children used more nonlinguistic communication than hearing children, they preferred linguistic over nonlinguistic communication.

Themes of Communication During Social Play

Two studies have examined the themes of D/HH children's communication during social play. Both studies used small numbers of children, therefore limiting conclusions. Brown, Prescott, Rickards, and Paterson (1997) compared the social play utterances of four oral, profoundly deaf and four hearing children between the ages of 4 and 5 years enrolled in an integrated kindergarten program. They coded pretend play episodes for object-related, role-related, and activity-related utterances. Literal object-related utterances occurred when a child requested or named an object. Non-literal object-related utterances occurred when a child symbolically transformed the object (e.g., pretending that a block was a car). They found that

D/HH children used significantly more literal references than hearing children. Role utterances in which children defined or talked about a role to be assumed by themselves or others were not analyzed but were used frequently by three hearing and one deaf child, and rarely or not at all by one hearing and three deaf children. Action-related utterances were either about current actions, where children described what they were doing, or scripted actions, where children recounted or projected the development of the pretend play. The D/HH children used significantly more current action utterances than the hearing children. It appeared that, during pretend play, the D/HH children tended to communicate more about literal and current topics and less about absent or symbolic topics than the hearing children.

Further evidence suggesting that the communication of young D/HH children during play appears to be based on literal rather than on symbolic themes was provided by Selmi and Rueda (1998). They examined the collaborative pretend play of nine oral D/HH children with severe to profound hearing losses in a segregated preschool. The authors reported that, of the 48 collaborative play episodes identified, 46 were based on themes of everyday activities. Only two episodes were based on fantasy themes.

Although the data are limited, it appears that D/HH preschool children engage in social pretend play with peers. However, their communication focuses on literal and familiar events. Because the research was conducted only with oral children, the effect of mode of communication may be an issue. Since pretend play becomes increasingly more fantasy-based and abstract with age (Brown et al., 1997), D/HH children with delayed language may be at a disadvantage when playing with hearing children.

Summary: Quantity and Quality of Peer Interactions

Available research indicates that, in many instances, D/HH children interact less frequently with peers, may spend less time in interaction, and engage in briefer interactions than hearing children. The reasons for the differences are varied. Hearing loss itself does not influence peer interaction, as several studies report that D/HH and hearing children interact equally frequently with peers. However, D/HH children's language ability may have a major influence on their communication with peers and, consequently, on the frequency and duration of peer interaction. With hearing peers, the lack of a shared communication mode can affect interaction, although familiarity may allow D/HH and hearing children to overcome mutual communication barriers. Generally, D/HH children and hearing children prefer to interact with peers of similar hearing status. However, the presence of hearing peers who can model and organize cooperative play can influence the quality of D/HH children's play. Thus, D/HH children may engage in higher levels of social play when interacting in groups where hearing peers are present.

When examining interaction initiations, the research indicates that D/HH children generally are as interested as hearing children in interacting with peers. Some researchers report that D/HH and hearing children use similar initiation strategies, but others report that D/HH children use more direct and more nonlinguistic strategies to initiate interaction. Several researchers report that D/HH and hearing children have similar initiation success rates, but others report lower success rates. One reason for the lack of initiation success may be that, despite some similarities in surface form, D/HH children's frequent nonlinguistic initiations have different "summoning power" than the linguistic initiations used by hearing children. Because the studies on interaction differ in the numbers and kinds of children who participated, the situations in which data were collected, and the kinds of peers available, it is difficult to identify the factors that influenced the quantity or quality of peer interaction in a single study. Instruments used to collect observational data also can influence the results. For example, Antia (1982) used an observation instrument that recorded data at 10-s intervals, whereas Antia and Ditillo (1998) used an instrument that recorded data at 1-min intervals. Longer observation intervals tend to overestimate behavior and thus might result in a finding of no differences.

Intervention Programs to Increase Peer Interaction

Because peer interaction is important to the development of social competence, several researchers have attempted to increase peer interaction of D/HH children through a variety of programs conducted in segregated and integrated settings. In segregated settings, the goal has been to increase the occurrence of interactions through instruction in specific peer interaction skills. In integrated settings, the goal is to increase interaction between D/HH children and hearing peers to promote social integration. The interventions typically involve teaching D/HH and/or hearing children specific interaction skills, teaching hearing children sign language and/or providing them with information about deafness, and designing educational environments that naturally promote interaction.

Increasing Social Interaction Within Segregated Educational Settings

Several interventions have been developed to teach children specific social skills as a strategy to increase peer interaction. These interventions focus on teacher-mediated instruction to develop skills such as greeting other children, cooperating, sharing materials, assisting others, initiating and maintaining conversation, complimenting, and praising. Relatively small numbers of children were involved in these studies, and most have used single-subject research designs. In such studies, interventions are introduced in a sequenced, staggered manner across targeted behaviors or participants (multiple baseline designs) or are periodically withdrawn (withdrawal designs) (Richards, Taylor, Rangasamy, & Richards, 1999). Data are collected frequently and continuously during baseline (nonintervention) and intervention phases.

Barton and Osborne (1978) designed an intervention to increase physical and verbal sharing among a class of five kindergarten children enrolled in a school for the deaf. Observational data on physical and verbal sharing were obtained during free play before, during, and after intervention. During the intervention, the teacher implemented positive practice techniques by prompting any child who was not sharing to initiate or accept a peer's verbal request for sharing. The teacher modeled the necessary language and prompted children to use it. Results indicated that physical sharing increased approximately 350% for the class when intervention procedures were implemented and remained above baseline levels after intervention ceased. In contrast, verbal sharing occurred rarely throughout the study and appeared unaffected by the intervention, despite modeling and prompting by teachers. At the beginning of the next school year, with a new teacher and several new classmates, physical sharing remained 294% above baseline levels. The increase in physical sharing suggests that this skill can be taught and maintained. Unfortunately, the design of this study did not control for maturation effects that might have influenced the long-term follow-up data, nor did it examine the effect of sharing on overall peer interaction.

Lemanek, Williamson, Gresham, and Jensen (1986) used a multiple baseline design to evaluate a social skills training program with four 11- to 18-year-old D/HH children who had difficulties with interpersonal relationships. Baseline data on smiling, body posture, eye contact, communication, appropriateness of response content, response latency, and overall social skills were obtained during role-play scenarios. A social skills training package then was sequentially implemented. During intervention, the instructor presented each child with role-play scenarios in which he instructed and modeled appropriate responses for the children to practice. Social skills performance during these role-plays increased for all children by an average of 23%. Generalization data collected in role-play situations with two high school students serving as confederates demonstrated similar levels of gain. Follow-up data obtained during role play, 2 months after the intervention ceased, indicated that social behavior increases were maintained. Thus, this study demonstrated the effectiveness of social skills training with older children, but only in role plays and not in naturally occurring interaction situations.

Rasing and Duker (1992, 1993) used multifaceted procedures to increase appropriate turn waiting, initiations, and interactions with nine 8- to 9-year-old children and nine 12- to 13-year-old children attending a school for deaf children. The intervention procedures included posting a list of appropriate and inappropriate behaviors in the classroom and living area, conducting problem-solving lessons during which examples of appropriate and inappropriate social behaviors were modeled and prompted, reinforcing appropriate behavior, and correcting inappropriate behaviors. Multiple baseline designs across the three targeted behaviors indicated the effectiveness of the intervention procedures for turn-waiting and initiations

with the youngest children (Rasing & Duker, 1992) and for turn-waiting, initiations, and interaction with others for the older children (Rasing & Duker, 1993) during school periods. Follow-up data obtained under substantially reduced intervention conditions indicated that the target behaviors remained above baseline levels.

Antia and Kreimeyer (1987, 1988) and Kreimeyer and Antia (1988) implemented a series of studies to examine the effectiveness of a social skills intervention with small groups of D/HH children (ages 3–5 years) enrolled in a self-contained preschool program. Antia and Kreimeyer (1987) used a combined multiple baseline/withdrawal design to examine the effectiveness of a social skills intervention on the occurrence of positive interaction with two groups of preschool children. Data were collected during intervention sessions on six of the nine children who participated in the intervention. Teachers planned arts and craft activities and cooperative games during which they modeled and prompted greeting, sharing, assisting, cooperating, inviting, complimenting, and praising. Positive peer interaction increased after sequential introduction of the intervention across each group and decreased when the intervention was withdrawn. This pattern indicates that the interaction increases were due to the intervention rather than other intervening variables. Additionally, the data indicated that sharing (a nonlinguistic interaction) accounted for most of the increase in interaction. Conversation (primarily a linguistic interaction) increased slightly and at a much slower rate and remained substantially below the level of sharing. Data obtained in a free-play generalization setting in which no intervention was conducted also showed an increased in peer interaction after the implementation of the intervention. To determine whether these increases were comparable to interaction of typically developing children, social validation data were collected on three hearing preschool children during free play. During the intervention, D/HH children had interacted with peers for 53–65% of observed intervals, while hearing children interacted with peers for 58–64% of observed intervals. Although total peer interaction of the D/HH and hearing children was similar, conversation rather than sharing was the primary means of interaction for the hearing children.

In an effort to increase the occurrence of conversational interaction, the intervention procedures were modified by Kreimeyer and Antia (1988) to incorporate role-play activities that necessitated linguistic interaction. Teachers modeled and prompted specific language for children to use during peer interaction. The researchers found that these intervention procedures increased the frequency of conversation over that observed in the initial study, but it remained below that observed for typically developing hearing children. Most important, generalization of results to a free-play setting was demonstrated with specific toys incorporated into the intervention activities. No generalization occurred with toys that were not incorporated into the intervention.

Because Antia and Kreimeyer (1987) had observed that interaction returned to baseline levels when intervention procedures were abruptly withdrawn, Antia and Kreimeyer (1988) also contrasted the results of abrupt and gradual withdrawal of intervention procedures. After a baseline period, intervention procedures were introduced in which teachers used the modeling and prompting procedures with particular emphasis on linguistic interaction. When the intervention was abruptly withdrawn, peer interaction returned to baseline levels. However, levels of positive peer interaction were maintained after a gradual and sequential reduction of each component of the intervention. Additionally, by the end of the study, linguistic interaction exceeded that of nonlinguistic interaction for three of the four children.

Research on social skills intervention in segregated settings thus indicates that it is possible to increase the occurrence of specific social skills, that a social skills intervention can successfully increase interaction with D/HH peers, and that the skills and resulting peer interaction can be generalized to new settings. Gains can be maintained when specific programming is incorporated into the intervention. Intervention is most successful in increasing nonlinguistic interaction.

Increasing Social Interaction Within Integrated Educational Settings

Social Skills Intervention

A second series of studies conducted by Antia and colleagues (Antia & Kreimeyer, 1996, 1997; Antia, Kreimeyer, & Eldredge, 1994) evaluated the effectiveness of social skills intervention within integrated settings where the primary goal was to in-

crease interaction between D/HH and hearing children. The first study (Antia et al., 1994) included 51 D/HH and 54 hearing children; the second study included 45 D/HH and 91 hearing children (Antia & Kreimeyer, 1996). The children (ages 3–7 years) were enrolled in preschool, kindergarten, and first-grade programs in several states. Approximately one third of the D/HH children used oral communication, while the rest used simultaneous communication. In all situations, the D/HH children spent some portion of their school day with hearing peers, at least during the intervention period.

Both the D/HH and hearing children participated in either the social skills intervention or an integrated activities intervention designed to control for the effects of peer familiarity. The social skills intervention was implemented as described previously. Sign, when used, was taught to the hearing children within the context of the social skills activities. Once an activity was initiated, teachers prompted both D/HH and hearing children to interact with one another. Teacher prompting was gradually withdrawn during the last 2 weeks of the intervention. The integrated activities intervention provided opportunities for D/HH and hearing children to become familiar with one another in a small, stable group of peers. During integrated activities children were seated together and participated in regular classroom activities that let them interact with one another. However, teachers did not specifically model or prompt social skills or interaction between children.

During the intervention children were divided into groups of four to eight, approximately half D/HH and half hearing. Teachers conducted the interventions for approximately 20 minutes a day two or three times a week. The mean number of total intervention sessions for each study was approximately 37. Peer interaction data were obtained during 20-minute free-play sessions.

Antia et al. (1994) found that interaction between D/HH and hearing children increased over the duration of the study, with no difference between treatments. Throughout the study, all children continued to interact more frequently with peers of the same hearing status than with peers of different hearing status. When children interacted with a peer of different hearing status, they used primarily nonlinguistic interaction. These results suggested that familiarity, rather than specific social skills instruction, increased peer interaction between children of different hearing status.

Antia and Kreimeyer (1996) used intervention procedures parallel to those in the first study, but free-play data collection sessions were modified. In addition to the D/HH and hearing children who participated in the intervention sessions, one or two hearing children who did not participate in the intervention sessions joined the free-play sessions. The inclusion of these "untrained hearing peers" allowed evaluation of the role of peer familiarity in interactions. A successful social skills intervention should result in increased interaction with peers participating in the intervention as well as with unfamiliar peers, as social skills acquired with one group of peers should generalize to interaction with other children. However, an intervention that increases familiarity, but does not teach social skills, should result in increased interaction only with familiar peers.

The social skills intervention resulted in increased interaction among D/HH children, but not between D/HH and hearing children. The interaction increase among D/IIII children was primarily nonlinguistic and was maintained for 3–4 weeks after the intervention ceased. The integrated activities intervention did not result in increases either among D/HH children or between D/HH and hearing children. It was not possible to analyze the impact of familiarity on peer interaction with untrained hearing peers because there was no significant change in interaction between D/HH and hearing children.

Antia and Kreimeyer (1997) evaluated the impact of the social skills and integrated activities interventions on the long-term maintenance of peer interaction and social play by conducting follow-up observation of 43 of the D/HH children who had participated in the 1996 study. They reanalyzed the original data using an instrument that provided information on peer interaction, social play, peer initiations, and responses to peer initiations. Follow-up data were obtained during free play 1 year after the intervention ceased. Results indicated that, although total peer interaction did not change as a result of either intervention, the children who participated in the social skills intervention decreased their frequency of solitary and parallel play. By the end of the intervention, associative/cooperative play became the most frequent type of play for the children in the social skills group. Data obtained 1 year later indicated a significant decrease in nonplay for the social skills group, while the increased level of associative/cooperative play was maintained.

The social skills intervention in both the integrated and segregated setting was successful in increasing interaction and social play among D/HH children. However, it was not successful in increasing interaction between D/HH children and hearing peers. There are some indications (Antia et al., 1994) that opportunities to interact with a stable group of peers without a specific teacher-directed intervention might be promising.

Sign Language and Deafness Awareness Instruction

One of the most significant deterrents to interaction between D/HH and hearing children is the lack of a common means of communication when D/HH children use sign language. Teaching sign language to hearing children is one intervention strategy that has been used to increase interaction. Kurkjian and Evans (1988) implemented a sign language curriculum with 16 fourth- and fifth-grade children who had expressed an interest in learning sign language and attended a school that included 6 D/HH children. Sixteen grade-matched students, who also had expressed interest in learning sign language, did not participate in the classes and served as a control group. The intervention addressed signing skills as well as general information about D/HH individuals and Deaf culture. Children completed a self-report about who they knew, who they recently had talked to or played with, and who they were friends with pre-, mid- and postintervention. Results indicated that both the experimental and control group showed significant increases in knowing and playing with D/HH children. Thus, time or familiarity, rather than instruction in sign language or knowledge about deafness, appeared to be the critical variable.

Vandell, Anderson, Erhardt, and Wilson (1982) taught preschool children about hearing loss and provided sign language instruction as part of an intervention designed to increase peer interaction between young D/HH and hearing children. Additionally, each hearing child was paired with a different deaf "buddy" on five occasions to engage in a structured activity or free play. Data on the frequency and duration of interaction, before and after this intervention, showed that hearing children who had participated in the intervention interacted less frequently and for shorter durations with D/HH children than those who had not. Several explanations can be provided for this unexpected result. Teaching hearing children about hearing loss may emphasize the differences between children and thus inhibit interaction. Although the children were provided opportunities to interact with one another, these opportunities were limited and, therefore, did not allow for development of familiarity.

Co-enrollment or Co-teaching Programs

One intervention that can provide intensive contact (and therefore familiarity) between D/HH and hearing children is the co-enrollment model of instruction (see Stinson & Kluwin, this volume). In co-enrollment programs, D/HH and hearing children learn together in a classroom that is taught jointly by a general education teacher and a teacher of D/HH children. The number of D/HH students typically ranges from one fourth to one third of the total classroom membership. Sign language instruction is integrated into the classroom curriculum. An interpreter may be present to facilitate communication while class members, including the general education teacher, are developing sign skills. Teachers have reported in interviews the belief that their co-enrollment programs promoted opportunities for interaction and friendship between D/HH and hearing children (Luckner, 1999). Kluwin and Gonsher (1994) also reported increased sign language use among hearing children in such a program.

Kreimeyer, Crooke, Drye, Egbert, & Klein (2000) recorded the frequency of interaction between five D/HH elementary-age children and their hearing peers at the initiation of a co-enrollment program. Observational data collected within the classroom, where teachers facilitated interaction as necessary, indicated that positive peer interaction increased between D/HH and hearing children. Increases in interaction after implementation of the program were generalized to the school lunchroom, a setting in which no teacher facilitation occurred. Although these data are encouraging, the absence of a control group or a strong single-subject design, and the few students on whom data are available, necessitate further study.

Summary and Conclusions: Intervention Programs to Increase Peer Interaction

The studies on intervention indicate that social skills intervention can successfully increase interaction among D/HH children, although greater increases are typically seen in nonlinguistic than linguistic interaction. These increases can be maintained over time and generalized to new settings. However, neither social skills nor other teacher-directed interventions appear successful at increasing interaction between D/HH and hearing children. One reason for the low success rate might be that the interventions are not sufficiently intense to overcome the communication barriers that exist between these two groups. However, long-term, intensive interventions (such as co-enrollment programs) that provide opportunities to become familiar with a group of hearing peers seem to have more success than short-term, less intensive interventions. Long-term interventions also may be successful because they promote familiarity between children. Although familiar D/HH and hearing children can overcome communication barriers by using nonlinguistic communication, linguistic communication between the groups is desirable. In some cases, hearing children will need to receive sign language instruction, but to successfully promote interaction, such instruction needs to be provided in the context of meaningful interaction between hearing and D/HH children rather than in isolation. Any intervention must include specific strategies to promote maintenance and generalization of skills if increases in peer interaction are to be sustained.

Single-subject research designs are promising tools to examine the effectiveness of interventions with low-incidence populations such as D/HH children, as these designs allow good control of intervention and subject variables. Concerns about generalization of intervention effectiveness to other children can be addressed by replications across children and contexts. Researchers also need to examine systematically the effect of child variables, such as language ability and mode of communication, and contextual variables, such as peer familiarity, on the effectiveness of specific interventions. Finally, most research has focused on interaction of young children. More attention needs to be paid to peer interaction in older elementary-school children. Interventions that succeed with preschool and elementary children may not be effective at older ages.

References

Antia, S. D. (1982). Social interaction of partially mainstreamed hearing-impaired children. *American Annals of the Deaf*, 127, 18–25.

Antia, S. D., & Dittillo, D. A. (1998). A comparison of the peer social behavior of children who are Deaf/Hard of Hearing and Hearing. *Journal of Children's Communication Development*, 19, 1–10.

Antia, S. D., & Kreimeyer, K. H. (1987). The effect of social skill training on the peer interaction of pre-school hearing-impaired children. *Journal of the Division for Early Childhood*, 11, 206–213.

Antia, S. D., & Kreimeyer, K. H. (1988). Maintenance of positive peer interaction in preschool hearing-impaired children. *Volta Review*, 90, 325–338.

Antia, S. D., & Kreimeyer, K. H. (1996). Social interaction and acceptance of D/HH children and their peers. *Volta Review*, 98, 157–180.

Antia, S. D., & Kreimeyer, K. H. (1997). The generalization and maintenance of the peer social behaviors of young children who are deaf or hard of hearing. *Language, Speech and Hearing Services in the Schools*, 28, 59–69.

Antia, S. D., Kreimeyer, K. H., & Eldredge, N. (1994). Promoting social interaction between young children with hearing impairments and their peers. *Exceptional Children*, 60, 262–275.

Arnold, D., & Tremblay, A. (1979). Interaction of deaf and hearing preschool children. *Journal of Communication Disorders*, 12, 245–251.

Barton, E. J., & Osborne, J. G. (1978). The development of classroom sharing by a teacher using positive practice. *Behavior Modification*, 2, 231–250.

Bat-Chava, Y., & Deignan, E. (2001). Peer relationships of children with cochlear implants. *Journal of Deaf Studies and Deaf Education*, 6, 186–199.

Brown, P. M., Prescot, S. J., Rickards, F. W., & Paterson, M. M. (1997). Communicating about pretend play: A comparison of the utterances of 4-year-old normally hearing and deaf or hard of hearing children in an integrated kindergarten. *Volta Review*, 99, 5–17.

Duncan, J. (1999). Conversational skills of children with hearing loss and children with normal hearing in an integrated setting. *Volta Review*, 101, 193–212.

Esposito, B. G., & Koorland, M. A. (1989). Play behavior of hearing impaired children: integrated and segregated settings. *Exceptional Children*, 55, 412–419.

Fine, G. A. (1981). Friends, impression management, and preadolescent behavior. In S. R. Asher & J. M. Gottman (Eds.), *The development of children's friendships* (pp. 29–52). London:Cambridge University Press.

Garvey, C. (1984). *Children's talk*. Cambridge, MA: Harvard University Press.

Higginbotham, D. J., & Baker, B. A. (1981). Social participation and cognitive play differences in hearing-impaired and normally hearing preschoolers. *Volta Review*, 83, 135–149.

Holden-Pitt, L., & Diaz, J. A. (1998). Thirty years of the annual survey of deaf and hard-of-hearing children & youth: A glance over the decades. *American Annals of the Deaf*, 142, 72–76.

Hulsing, M. M., Luetke-Stahlman, B., Frome-Loeb, D., Nelson, P., & Wegner, J. (1995). Analysis of successful initiations of three children with hearing loss mainstreamed in kindergarten classrooms. *Language, Speech and Hearing Services in the Schools*, 26, 45–52.

Kluwin, T., & Gonsher, W. (1994). A single school study of social integration of children with and without hearing losses in a team taught kindergarten. *ACEHI/ACEDA*, 20, 71–86.

Kreimeyer, K. H., & Antia, S. D. (1988). The development and generalization of social interaction skills in preschool hearing-impaired children. *Volta Review*, 90(4), 219–232.

Kreimeyer, K. H., Crooke, P., Drye, C., Egbert, V., & Klein, B. (2000). Academic and social benefits of a coenrollment model of inclusive education for deaf and hard-of-hearing children. *Journal of Deaf Studies and Deaf Education*, 5, 174–185.

Kurkjian, J. A., & Evans, I. M. (1988). Effects of sign language instruction on social interaction between hearing-impaired and normal-hearing children. *Child and Family Behavior Therapy*, 10, 121–134.

Lederberg, A. R. (1991). Social interaction among deaf preschoolers: The effects of language ability and age. *American Annals of the Deaf*, 136, 53–59.

Lederberg, A. R., Ryan, H. B., & Robbins, B. L. (1986). Peer interaction in young deaf children: The effect of partner hearing status and familiarity. *Developmental Psychology*, 22, 691–700.

Lemanek, K. L., Williamson, D. A., Gresham, F. M., & Jensen, B. J. (1986). Social skills training with hearing-impaired children and adolescents. *Behavior Modification*, 10, 55–71.

Levine, L. M., & Antia, S. D. (1997). The effect of partner hearing status on social and cognitive play. *Journal of Early Intervention*, 21, 21–35.

Levy-Shiff, R., & Hoffman, M. A. (1985). Social behaviour of hearing-impaired and normally-hearing preschoolers. *British Journal of Education Psychology, 55*, 111–118.

Luckner, J. L. (1999). An examination of two coteaching classrooms. *American Annals of the Deaf, 144*(1), 24–34.

McCauley, R. W., Bruininks, R. H., & Kennedy, P. (1976). Behavioral interactions of hearing impaired children in regular classrooms. *Journal of Special Education, 10*, 277–284.

McKirdy, L. S., & Blank, M. (1982). Dialogue in deaf and hearing preschoolers. *Journal of Speech and Hearing Research, 25*, 487–499.

Messenheimer-Young, T., & Kretschmer, R. R. (1994). "Can I play?" A hearing impaired preschooler's requests to access maintained social interaction. *Volta Review, 96*, 5–18.

Minnett, A., Clark, K., & Wilson, G. (1994). Play behavior and communication between deaf and hard of hearing children and their hearing peers in an integrated preschool. *American Annals of the Deaf, 139*, 420–429.

Odom, S. L., McConnell, S. R., & McEvoy, M. A. (1992). Peer related social competence and its significance for young children with disabilities. In S. L. Odom, S. R. McConnell, & M. A. McEvoy (Eds.), *Social competence of young children with disabilities* (pp. 3–35). Baltimore, MD: Paul H. Brookes.

Rasing, E. J., & Duker, P. C. (1992). Effects of a multifaceted training procedure on the acquisition and generalization of social behaviors in language-disabled deaf children. *Journal of Applied Behavior Analysis, 25*, 723–734.

Rasing, E. J., & Duker, P. C. (1993). Acquisition and generalization of social behaviors in language-disabled deaf children. *American Annals of the Deaf, 138*, 362–368.

Richards, S. B., Taylor, R. L., Rangasamy, R., & Richards, R. Y. (1999). *Single subject research: Applications in educational and clinical settings.* San Diego, CA: Singular.

Roberts, S. B., Brown, P. M., & Rickards, F. W. (1995). Social pretend play entry behaviors of preschoolers with and without impaired hearing. *Journal of Early Intervention, 20*, 52–83.

Rubin, Z. (1980). *Children's friendships.* Cambridge, MA: Harvard University Press.

Selmi, A. M., & Rueda, R. S. (1998). A naturalistic study of collaborative play transformations of preschoolers with hearing impairments. *Journal of Early Intervention, 21*, 299–307.

Spencer, P., Koester, L. S., & Meadow-Orlans, K. (1994). Communicative interaction of deaf and hearing children in a day care center. *American Annals of the Deaf, 139*, 512–518.

Stinson, M. S., & Kluwin, T. (1996). Social orientations toward deaf and hearing peers among deaf adolescents in local public high schools. In P. C. Higgins & J. E. Nash (Eds.), *Understanding deafness socially* (pp. 113–134). Springfield, IL: Charles C. Thomas.

Stinson, M. S., & Whitmire, K. (1992). Students' views of their social relationships. In T. N. Kluwin, D. F. Moores & M. G. Gaustad (Eds.), *Towards effective public school programs for deaf students: Context process and outcomes* (pp. 149–174). New York: Teachers College Press.

Vandell, D. L., Anderson, L. D., Erhardt, G., & Wilson, K. S. (1982). Integrating hearing and deaf preschoolers: An attempt to enhance hearing children's interaction with deaf peers. *Child Development, 53*, 1354–1363.

Vandell, D. L., & George, L. (1981). Social interaction in hearing and deaf preschoolers: Successes and failures in initiations. *Child Development, 52*, 627–635.

13

Rosemary Calderon & Mark Greenberg

Social and Emotional Development of Deaf Children

Family, School, and Program Effects

Establishing healthy social-emotional development is a critical foundation for life success. Competencies that are generally accepted as defining healthy social-emotional development are also applicable to helping individuals realize their academic and vocational potential (Feuerstein, 1980; Goleman, 1995). Although there have been numerous conceptualizations of competence in childhood, there is considerable agreement that competence has broad features that cross developmental periods. Specific skills arise or recede in importance in different developmental epochs. Competencies cannot only be posited for children, but the different adults or groups who are most important to supporting these developments similarly can be identified. Following from Waters and Sroufe (1983), competence is defined here as "an integrative concept that refers to the ability to generate and coordinate flexible, adaptive responses to demands and to generate and capitalize on opportunities in the environment" (p. 80). Further, across all developmental periods, competent functioning is associated with the ability to coordinate affect, cognition, communication, and behavior (Greenberg, Kusché, & Speltz, 1991; Waters & Sroufe, 1983)

Greenberg and Kusché (1993) include the following processes and outcomes when defining social and emotional competence:

- Good communication skills;
- The capacity to think independently;
- The capacity for self-direction and self-control;
- Understanding the feelings, motivations, needs, and so forth, of oneself and others;
- Flexibility in appropriately adapting to the needs of each particular situation (which includes the ability to take multiple perspectives in any situation);
- The ability to rely on and be relied upon by others;
- Understanding and appreciating both one's own culture and its values as well as those of the cultures of others; and
- Utilizing skilled behaviors to maintain healthy relationships with others and to obtain socially approved goals.

Although this is not an exhaustive list of skills to delineate social-emotional competence, it does profile several necessary characteristics for successful development. These skills are achieved over time, and each has its own developmental trajectory dependent on an individual's growth from infancy to adulthood (Weissberg & Greenberg, 1998). Each person develops these skills to a greater or lesser degree depending on their own temperament and personality, family values, educational background, peer relationships, societal and cultural norms, and so on. Social competence also includes at least one other critical characteristic, "tolerance for ambiguity" (Loevinger, 1976). This includes the ability and willingness to consider multiple perspectives of reality, not just one's own point of view, and the capacity to be flexible rather than rigid in adapting to varying circumstances. Finally, all of the above aspects of social competence are directly or indirectly related to the ability to show adaptive coping under varying levels of stress (Greenberg, Lengua, & Calderon, 1997).

Unfortunately, as a group, deaf children and adolescents demonstrate reduced mastery in many of these areas of competence and thus are at risk for a number of adverse outcomes (Greenberg & Kusché, 1989; Marschark, 1997; Meadow, Greenberg, Erting, & Carmichael, 1981). These outcomes include low academic achievement, underemployment, and higher rates of social maladaptions (violence, drug and alcohol problems) and psychological distress and disorder (Greenberg & Kusché, 1989; Marschark, 1993). However, not all deaf children develop adjustment problems, and the impact of deafness on the child's overall development is influenced by several factors, including the quality of the family environment, parental adaptation to deafness, family coping, the nature of school and community resources, and the child's characteristics and transactions with his or her ecology (Calderon, 2000; Calderon & Greenberg, 1999; Montanini-Manfredi, 1993; Stinson & Foster, 2000).

Cross-cultural studies conducted by Meadow and Dyssegaard (1983a, 1983b) support the importance of ecological analysis in understanding deaf children's social competence. They investigated teacher ratings on the Meadow/Kendall Social-Emotional Assessment Inventory (MKSEAI; Meadow, 1983) by comparing more than 700 American deaf students with 289 Danish deaf students. Results indicated that although the MKSEAI scores did not differ significantly between the two samples, the deaf children, as a group, showed a general lack of motivation and initiative. Meadow and Dyssegaard hypothesized that the deficits in motivation and initiative, important factors for so-

cial maturity, may be due to hearing parents and teachers being highly directive and not providing deaf children with rich opportunities for taking independent action and responsibility.

Challenges Specific to Deaf Children

As noted in previous reviews of social-cognition in childhood (Greenberg and Kusché, 1989), deaf children are often delayed in language development, tend to show greater impulsivity and poorer emotional regulation, and often have an impoverished vocabulary of emotion language. Thus, for some deaf children, as well as for other individuals who have experienced delays in language or who have been deprived of sufficient language-mediated experience (Feuerstein, 1980), the inability to spontaneously mediate experience with linguistic symbols and label aspects of inner emotional states may be one important factor leading to serious gaps in social-emotional development. For example, young children will generally act on their own curiosity with impulsive behavior such as touching or exploring an object that may not be safe or experience a feeling but have no linguistic label for it. After numerous warnings or feeling identification from caregivers, children can develop their own internal linguistic dialogue to temper the impulsive desire to touch and explore or understand their own feeling states by telling themselves "it's not safe," "it doesn't belong to me," "no, don't touch," or "I am sad" or "I feel angry." However, this process is interrupted (or never begun) when children do not or cannot perceive their caregivers' language. Furthermore, there are other important factors to be considered in understanding obstacles faced by deaf children in developing social and emotional competence that have direct implications for educational interventions. Several of these areas are discussed below.

Incidental Learning

Understanding ourselves, our culture, rules for how people and families communicate, and so forth, are strongly influenced by incidental learning. Incidental learning is the process by which information is learned by virtue of passive exposure to events witnessed or overheard. The meaning of such information is not directly taught nor necessarily intended for instruction; yet important information and nuances for behavior or beliefs are transmitted and absorbed either consciously or unconsciously. Because the constant use of sign language by hearing people is rare and deaf children cannot overhear spoken conversations, there are many types of messages that are not readily available to deaf children (e.g., parent or teacher discussions, problem-solving, arguments when children are out of sight but not out of hearing range, television and radio in the background environment, phone calls with relatives or friends, praise or disciplinary procedures directed toward another child). In the case of deaf children, all communications must be directed specifically to them, and they in turn must also pay close visual attention. This can be a tiring process for these children, as well as for others communicating with them, and at times may also interfere with their ongoing activities. Thus, deafness, itself, may limit some avenues of incidental learning commonly experienced by hearing children. As a result, programs to promote parent–child communication and social and emotional competence should be used with all deaf children, not only those that are manifesting problems, to help remediate understanding that may be missed or distorted through gaps in incidental learning.

Parenting Styles and Their Consequences

When parents find out that their child is deaf, they often experience an emotional crisis and loss of confidence in their ability to know what is best for their child. Parents turn to professionals for support and guidance with respect to intervention approaches. This can be a confusing time for parents given the disparate approaches advised by some professionals. Despite this initial stress, the implementation of universal screening for hearing loss in newborns, early identification, and early intervention have demonstrated significant gains in the language and communication skills for deaf children. These gains have shown lasting effects into early childhood for better success in language, academic, and social-emotional outcomes for deaf children (Calderon & Naidu, 2000; Yoshinaga-Itano, Sedey, Coulter, & Mehl, 1998). Traci and Koester (this volume) and Sass-Lehrer and Bodner-Johnson (this volume) provide an in-depth review of the importance of this initial phase in deaf children's lives to

their overall development and their families' adjustment.

After the initial impact of diagnosis and early intervention, a variety of obstacles in parenting can accompany the significant communication problems that are often found between deaf children and their hearing parents (Schlesinger & Acree, 1984; Schlesinger & Meadow, 1972; Vaccari & Marschark, 1997). Parents frequently report that because their deaf children do not understand them, they have limited options available for socializing their children. As a result, some deaf children have fewer opportunities to learn what they did wrong and why it was wrong, how their behavior affected others, and what alternatives they could have chosen instead. Moreover, their parents are more likely to model avoidance and physical action as methods for solving problems. Similarly, parental frustration due to communication barriers often leads parents to "take on" their children's problems. When this happens, deaf children are then afforded little opportunity to learn from and resolve their own difficulties. The impact of limited explanations and restricted experiences denies to many deaf children their rightful opportunity to learn to understand others.

Linguistic Overprotection

In addition to the other factors already discussed, more subtle factors are also involved in the constellation of immature behaviors that are frequently noted with deaf children. For example, for many (if not most) adults living and working with deaf children, manual/sign communication is a second language that has been acquired later in life and is never as natural as their native spoken language. Nor is it natural for hearing people to remain acutely attuned to the needs of a deaf person who relies on lip reading or on residual hearing. Therefore, in addition to the deaf child's communication difficulties, there is also an issue of lack of communication skill and insecurity on the part of many adults. This combination of fear of misunderstanding/being misunderstood and communication deficiencies in adult role models result in an insidious form of "linguistic overprotection." This often unconscious fear often leads adults to "talk down" to or reduce the linguistic and cognitive complexity of communications to deaf children (Schlesinger, 1987). This phenomenon, in turn, limits the children's opportunities to learn about social and emotional states and characteristics as well as limiting their opportunities to learn more advanced language.

Culture and Identity

Deaf children's acculturation is unusual in that they are minorities within their own families. More than 90% of deaf children are born to hearing parents (Moores, 2001). This intergenerational discontinuity in deafness leads to a significant dilemma faced by most deaf children; they are likely to become part of a clearly defined minority culture in which there are no other members in their family to show them that culture and language. To be a successful member of society and gain the full access to its richness and opportunities, they will need to learn to live at least to some extent in both worlds, that of the hearing and the deaf. Thus, family and community ecologies both play important roles in promoting healthy social and emotional development with deaf children (e.g., educational settings, day care, church, neighborhoods, and other professional and community resources).

This view is supported by Bat-Chava's (1994, 2000) investigations on theories of identity formation and self-esteem in deaf populations. She found that those deaf people who embraced values of both the hearing world and deaf culture appeared to have the highest level of self-esteem. They were able to reap professional and academic success while also being able to advocate for social change in the majority's view of their minority culture. They did not accept the differential (lower) expectations by the majority culture, which can result in deaf individuals limiting their own personal goals, developing negative self-concepts, or internalizing cognitive attributions of helplessness, failure, and inferiority.

Other relevant research in the area of identity development for deaf children has focused on the educational placements and social-interaction partners that deaf children are involved with, their level of hearing loss, primary communication mode used by the child, and the communication mode used by those who interact most with the child (e.g., parents, teachers, hearing and/or deaf peers) (Sheridan, 2000; Steinberg, 2000; Stinson & Foster, 2000). Stinson and Foster (2000) wrote about the impact on the identity and social adjustment of deaf

children as a result of the availability of hearing and/or deaf peers to socialize with in their respective educational placements. The most common placements are inclusion in the child's neighborhood school, self-contained classrooms in regular hearing schools, or deaf residential programs. Each of these placements and respective peer groups promote different aspects of social competencies and sense of identity in deaf or hard-of-hearing children. When combined with the family environment and parent–child communication strategies investigated by Sheridan (2000) and Steinberg (2000), the complex set of influences that affect the achievement of positive self-acceptance and secure identity for deaf individuals is evident. These factors related to social-emotional development are elaborated below and by Antia and Kreimeyer (this volume). Added to this is the use of and benefit from sophisticated assistive listening devices— namely, the use of cochlear implants that may or may not contribute to identity confusion (Bat-Chava & Deignan, 2001; Wald & Knutson, 2000; see Spencer & Marschark, this volume).

A Developmental Framework for Attaining Social-Emotional Competency Skills

Although there are undoubtedly many levels and perspectives by which to understand the development of social competence in deaf children, a viewpoint that considers the whole child combines developmental theory, social-cognitive models, and an understanding of dynamic educational, familial, and cultural system processes is most useful. A developmental framework for understanding both the development of social competence and maladjustment as it impacts the growing deaf child is presented below (Greenberg, 2000). We discuss development at three different developmental phases of childhood. Central to outcomes for social-emotional development is not only the prevention of social or personal ills but also the promotion of healthy growth and development (having healthy relationships, managing stress effectively, self-efficacy).

The Early Years

During early childhood, a number of developmental outcomes signal competency. They include being (1) self-confident and trusting, (2) intellectually inquisitive, (3) able to effectively use language to communicate, (4) physically and mentally healthy, (5) able to relate well to others, and (6) empathic toward others (Carnegie Task Force on Meeting the Needs of Young Children, 1994). Further, these competencies are seen as the result of loving, caring interactions with the child's parents that leads to healthy attachments and early experiences with adult caregivers that provide the building blocks for intellectual and communicative competence (Greenberg and Marvin, 1979; Lederberg & Mobley, 1990; Meadow-Orlans & Steinberg, 1993). As parents (the primary socializing agents) model healthy ways to relate to the child as well as to others, teach acceptable behavior, guide healthy habits and routines, and help the young child to manage their impulses, these competencies will unfold (Schlesinger & Meadow, 1972). Involvement in comprehensive, early intervention programs can greatly assist hearing parents with deaf children to facilitate the development of these skills.

Middle Childhood

In the early and middle years of schooling, there are vast changes in the child's cognitive and social-cognitive growth as well as the powerful influence of the peer group and the school. An excellent exemplar of a model for promoting competency is that developed by the W.T. Grant Consortium on the School-based Promotion of Social Competence (1992). Although this model encompasses all school grades, it places particular emphasis on the middle childhood years. It proposes that skills be developed in the competencies of emotions, cognitions, behaviors, and their interrelations as applied to the following six domains of functioning: personal development, family life, peer relations, school-related skills, community/citizenship, and event-triggered stressors. From middle childhood onward, being socially competent requires good communication skills (Hamilton, 1982) and the use of complex cognitive strategies, including foresight, anticipation, reflection, and imagination. These abilities help the individual to more adequately understand oneself and others, to more effectively plan and execute behavioral plans, and to receive and interpret the continual feedback from both intrapsychic and environmental sources. Below we

review research on promising practices that appear likely to lead to social competence in the middle childhood period for deaf children.

Adolescence, Competence, and Identity

The teen years provide new developmental challenges for all children. Connell, Aber, and Walker (1995) have provided a comprehensive framework for understanding the competencies needed during the teen years. The desired outcomes are grouped into three gross domains: economic self-sufficiency, healthy family and social relationships, and good citizenship practices. Although economic capacity and opportunity, community demography, and the existence of social institutions (e.g., youth organizations) are seen as important factors, Connell et al. place crucial emphasis on the density of bonds and networks among community participants (parents, neighbors, teachers, etc.) in taking responsibility for healthy youth development. Because adolescence is believed to be a time of significant risk, as well as a critical time for the formation of identity, such information is essential for the development of effective programs to strengthen identity and adaptation. In this regard, there is a need to pay special attention to the potential role of deaf adults in affecting these developmental processes, especially in the implementation of prevention programs.

Elaborating on points made earlier, both one's intimate attachment to parents and peers as well as a feeling of belonging to a social network are important in healthy identity development in adolescence. One's social network might include a variety of individuals including relatively close friends, members of one's extended family, coworkers or classmates, neighbors, casual acquaintances, and members of organizations or groups in which the adolescent actively participates. Both intimate attachments and/or one's social group can be invaluable resources for coping with stress by providing a variety of functions including emotional support, validation, information, advice, feelings of solidarity, and actual physical or financial assistance. For these reasons, it is important for deaf adolescents to feel connected with other deaf peers or adults through school programs, recreational programs, deaf clubs, or other organized activities.

Programs to Address Social and Emotional Development: Review of Efficacy Outcomes

A number of investigators have applied behaviorally oriented social skills training to deaf children with behavioral and interpersonal difficulties. In two studies, Schloss and colleagues (Schloss and Smith, 1990; Schloss, Smith, & Schloss, 1984; Smith, Schloss & Schloss, 1984) demonstrated the effectiveness of time-limited social skills training for increasing the social responsiveness and appropriateness of emotionally disturbed, hearing impaired, orally educated adolescents. Similarly, Lemanek, Williamson, Gresham, and Jensen (1986) reported positive effects of behavioral social skills training with four case studies of adolescents. Finally, Rasing and colleagues (Rasing & Duker, 1992, 1993: Rasing, Connix, Duker, van de Hurk Ardine, 1994) in The Netherlands have shown significant short-term effects of behavioral training programs for individual social skills in language-disabled deaf children. There were no control groups or long-term follow-up in any of these projects, and no assessments were made of the children's general social competence.

Although curricular-based interventions appear promising for improving the social competence of deaf children (Luetke-Stahlman, 1995), it appears that short-term interventions are not very effective in producing noticeable or lasting changes. This is indicated by results of short-term, experimental demonstrations. For example, Regan (1981) used a shortened nine-session version of a well-known, self-control training (Meichenbaum & Goodman, 1971). This intervention model focused on the development of improved self-monitoring by teaching verbal mediation as a vehicle for improved self-control. Results using a small sample of children found no effects on behavioral impulsivity. Similarly, Lytle (1987) evaluated an intervention curriculum that combined a behavioral social skills approach with social problem-solving in a residential setting over an 8-week period. Although the residential staff rated the 16 intervention adolescents improved in social skills and problem solving, there were no differences on a normed measure of behavior problems and social competence (MKSEAI; Meadow, 1983). At post-test there were no group differences in problem-solving skills, social self-efficacy ratings, or perceived competence

by the students. In a pre–post design study, Suarez (2000) used a two-part training program with 18 deaf middle school students focusing on interpersonal cognitive problem solving (provided only to the deaf students) and social skills training (provided to both deaf and hearing students). Children received 21 hours of instruction (15 and 6 hours, respectively). Results indicated that the intervention succeeded in improving deaf students' social problem-solving skills and assertive behavior as rated by their teachers and by themselves. Sociometric ratings by hearing peers did not show any pre–post differences.

It is unlikely that short-term interventions will have long-term impacts, but such studies can demonstrate the potential of social-cognitive approaches. For example, Barrett (1986) effectively used role play with a small sample of deaf adolescents and found significant short-term effects on social adjustment; there was no long-term follow-up. Lou and colleagues (Gage, Lou, & Charlson, 1993; Lou and Charlson, 1991) reported the effects of a short-term pilot program to enhance the social-cognitive skills of deaf adolescents. Although they found no effects on the students' developmental understanding of personal attributes or characteristics, there were significant increases in role-taking ability between pre- and post-test. There was no assessment of behavior or social competence and no control group or follow-up assessment reported.

Promoting Integrated Social-Emotional Competence

Recognizing the systemic problems in current approaches to educating deaf children, Greenberg and colleagues developed and evaluated the implementation of a school-based curriculum, PATHS (Promoting Alternative Thinking Strategies; Kusché & Greenberg, 1993). The curriculum is grounded in a theory of development and change: the ABCD (affective-behavioral-cognitive-dynamic) model (Greenberg & Kusché, 1993). The PATHS curriculum is a comprehensive approach for teaching self- and interpersonal understanding. The goals of the PATHS curriculum are to teach children how to develop and maintain self-control, increase their awareness of and ability to communicate about feelings, and assist them in conflict resolution through improving their problem-solving skills. Another focus of the curriculum is teaching concepts and words useful in logical reasoning and problem solving (e.g., if-then, why-because, and-or, accident-on purpose, before-after, etc). Because deaf school-aged children make up a heterogeneous population, PATHS was designed for use with a variety of developmental levels (late preschool to grade 6).

Using a design that included the random assignment of classrooms to intervention and wait-list control status, the PATHS curriculum was evaluated for effectiveness with a sample of 70 severely and profoundly deaf children who were involved in 3 consecutive years of longitudinal data collection. The children ranged in age from 6 to 13 years. All of the children had hearing parents and attended self-contained classrooms in local schools that used total communication (simultaneous use of signs and speech). All of the children had an unaided hearing loss of at least a 70 dB (better ear); the average loss was 92 dB.

The version of the PATHS curriculum that was evaluated consisted of a 60-lesson manual that was used daily in the classroom for 20–30 minutes over 6 months. The teachers and their assistants received 3 days of training before the school year and then received weekly observations, group supervision, and individual consultations. During the second year, the children in the wait-list control group (and new children who entered the classrooms) received a revised version of the curriculum that had been expanded to include approximately 15 more lessons. At each assessment time (pretest, post-test, follow-up), a variety of measures were used to assess social problem solving, emotional understanding, academic achievement, and teacher and parent ratings of behavioral adaptation.

The results generally indicated significant improvements (see Greenberg & Kusché, 1993, for an extended discussion of measures and results). Results of social problem-solving interviews indicated significant improvements in role taking, expectancy of outcome, and means–end problem-solving skills. Similar improvements were found on both emotional recognition and the reading of emotion labels. Teacher ratings indicated significant improvements in emotional adjustment and frustration tolerance. These improvements in both behavior and social-cognition were maintained up to 2 years post-intervention. Similar findings were found for an independent replication sample, as well as in a smaller sample of oral-only educated

children. Thus, teaching self-control, emotional understanding, and problem-solving skills led to changes in these skills as well as to improved behavior. In addition, a change-score analysis indicated that increases in affective-cognitive understanding were related to behavioral improvements.

As a result of these early, brief field trials, the scope and duration of the curriculum was expanded through later field testing in day and residential schools. The present form of PATHS (Kusché and Greenberg, 1993) is planned as a multiyear model adaptable to the first years of schooling (approximately ages 6–12). It is currently being used with deaf as well as hearing students in the United States, The Netherlands, Belgium, Canada, Australia, and Great Britain. An independent study assessing the effects of the PATHS curriculum with deaf children in England also showed significant impact. The intervention group showed immediate improvements on indices of emotional competence and adjustment. At 1-year follow-up these gains were maintained on measures of adjustment (Hindley & Reed, 1999).

PATHS was conceptualized as both a specific set of lesson procedures and a global model for structured education. There are extensive methods of generalization to help build and solidify these skills outside the classroom. The processes of social understanding in PATHS can also be applied to the problems of early and middle adolescence. After initial mastery of the basic PATHS concepts, there are various areas of instruction that can be incorporated into the PATHS paradigm, such as alcohol and drug abuse prevention, sex education, and AIDS awareness. Continued use of a PATHS-like curriculum in middle school and high school takes on new meaning at these ages as teenagers can use more abstract thinking and engage in more sophisticated problem solving and emotion regulation (Greenberg & Kusché, 1993; Kusché, Greenberg, Calderon, & Gustafson, 1987).

Given the importance of positive social-emotional adjustment and its relevance to academic and vocational outcomes, it is surprising and dismaying that over the last decade others have not undertaken research endeavors at this comprehensive level to either deepen our understanding or facilitate the development of social-emotional development with deaf and hard-of-hearing children. There is a great need for the development of similar curriculum models for deaf adolescents and young adults who are going through the transition to college, vocational training, or work. In addition, it is crucial to involve the child's family and community in such efforts along with the use of such school-based curriculums for promoting social-emotional competence.

Family and Ecological Influences in Promoting Healthy Social and Emotional Development

Current U. S. federal legislation and regulations explicitly state the importance of family involvement in the child's education and early intervention (Individuals with Disabilities Education Act Public Law 94-142, 1975; see Sass-Lehrer and Bodner-Johnson, this volume) and recognize the value of parents and professionals working together to address children's educational needs. The importance of a central role for families is demonstrated by a number of studies that indicate that parent attitudes, parent involvement, social support, expectations, and problem-solving skills are related to the academic and social development of deaf children in early and middle childhood (Bodner-Johnson, 1986; Calderon, 2000; Calderon & Greenberg, 1993; Calderon, Greenberg & Kusché, 1991; Watson, Henggeler, & Whelan, 1990). Similar to hearing children, deaf children with parents who are involved in the child's early formal education program show higher levels of academic success and social-emotional functioning as measured by early reading assessments and teacher and parent ratings of externalizing (acting out) symptomotology (Calderon, 2000).

Unfortunately, starting from the point of diagnosis, professionals and parents may have different priorities and approaches in understanding and working with the deaf child. These differing priorities between parents and professionals, lack of professional consensus, and advanced but unproven technology underscore the challenge in bringing parents and professionals together to work as a team and in staying focused on the overall development of the child. If parents are to feel competent in raising their deaf child and helping their child develop social and emotional competence, professionals must facilitate and support the parents' ability to step back, reflect on their feelings, and make a strategic plan with specific short- and long-term goals and objectives for their child and themselves as a family (Calderon & Greenberg, 1997; Moeller & Condon, 1994).

Parents routinely seek out resources on their own to increase their communication skills and arrange for appropriate supplementary services for their child (e.g., speech and language therapy, audiology services, recreational activities, etc.), but they are often faced with few options for such resources within their own community. This is especially true for families living in rural communities, but it is not uncommon for urban families. Support services or education programs often require a 2- to 4-hr commute, making the parent and child's engagement difficult. Furthermore, by parents' report, more often than not, school and community personnel are not very encouraging or inviting to parents regarding involvement in their children's educational process (Calderon, 2000). During the school years, mothers and fathers should be invited and encouraged to be assertive and persistent in advocating for services from the various systems with which their child is involved. Mothers and fathers should continue to play crucial roles in their children's lives in addition to teachers and other adult role models.

Services for Families

Based on our current knowledge of promoting positive social-emotional outcomes for deaf children and their families, the next generation of family services should consider the following components.

1. Services that will teach, encourage, and expand parents' knowledge and use of good problem-solving skills. An increase in parental success at solving problems is likely to increase their feelings of mastery and control. This in turn provides deaf children with influential, competent, and resourceful parental role models.

2. Program services that facilitate the development of strong support networks for parents, particularly for mothers, because they appear to use and benefit from these networks (Greenberg et al., 1997; Meadow-Orlans, 1990, 1994; Meadow-Orlans & Steinberg, 1993). These supports might come from other parents of children with hearing loss,

friends, neighbors, extended family, professionals, community (e.g., church or other organizations), school personnel, and deaf persons.

3. The development of specialized intervention programs for fathers of deaf children, who are usually not targeted by early intervention programs.

4. Parental support and guidance that continues throughout childhood and should include a developmental approach. Support services should include advanced sign language classes, family weekend retreats, exposure to deaf adults, and problem-solving groups to address deaf adolescent issues. Recognition of parents' and children's different needs at different emotional and life stages is important if families are to participate and feel that the services are meeting their needs.

School Personnel and Settings in Promoting Healthy Social and Emotional Development

Teachers provide children with alternative role models and demonstrate ways of using cognitive and affective processes for handling frustration, emotional turmoil, and interpersonal conflict. Teachers can have a major influence on children's emotional development and social competence. As children make their way from family-based to school-based services, they gain new opportunities for communication and language development, peer interactions, and structured support to help them develop more effective communication and social networks.

Either by law or policy shifts, local schools, regardless of their size or number of deaf children, have been given greater responsibility in the education of deaf children. Thus, deaf children tend to remain in the hearing community and are residing with their hearing families much longer; fewer deaf children are being introduced into the Deaf community through the cross-generational process of attending a residential educational institution. These shifts in schooling have led to new and more important roles for parents and teachers in the educational development and social-emotional adjustment of deaf children.

As might be expected, most instructional time

in the classroom (as well as preparatory teacher-training experiences) is spent on academic subjects, speech, and communication skills. Teacher-training programs in deaf education often do not require sufficient coursework in cognitive and personality and social development; as a result, most graduates do not have state-of-the-art information or knowledge of specific instructional techniques to teach social-emotional competency skills. The implementation of P.L. 94-142 resulted in the development of many smaller, geographically dispersed programs. These programs have few teachers and often no administrator, curriculum specialist, or even psychologist who work solely with students with hearing loss and who have the necessary skill and knowledge to provide appropriate training (Committee on the Education of the Deaf, 1988).

As Bronfenbrenner (1979) and others (Weissberg, Caplan, & Sivo, 1989) have suggested, person-centered models of development must be integrated with ecological models that examine how development is affected by systems-level factors. These variables include the nature of each ecological setting in which the child interacts (e.g., family, school, neighborhood, church, peer group), the linkages among those systems (e.g., school-family communication), the indirect influences of others on the family and school, and cultural values.

In summary, teachers and schools need more support and training to prevent or remediate social-emotional difficulties and their consequences for children with hearing loss. There is a clear need to develop preventive and remedial school-based interventions to ensure the healthy development of deaf children. At the present time, there is a wide gap between basic knowledge regarding deaf children and curricular practices and models of schooling. The next generation of school-based innovations might include the following:

1. The development and evaluation of preventive intervention programs in teaching social-cognitive abilities such as role-taking, understanding of emotions, and social problem-solving in the early school years; prevention programs for adolescents on problem solving as it relates to interpersonal difficulties, peer pressure, drug and alcohol use, and sexuality; and attributional training/

problem-solving programs to attempt to effect motivation, locus of control, and self-confidence of deaf adolescent and young adults.

2. The development of curricular materials on deaf culture, deaf history, and American sign Language for use in school programs for deaf children across educational settings.

3. The development of program coordination between vocational rehabilitation counselors and school personnel to facilitate the transition between school and work.

The Importance of the Deaf Community in Facilitating Healthy Adaptation in Deaf Children

Since the Deaf President Now movement at Gallaudet University when deaf students insisted that a deaf university president be selected, there has been much discussion of the importance of deaf adults in the education of deaf children. In dealing with the topic of a healthy Deaf identity, understanding of deaf persons is essential to the development of healthy school and community programming. Deaf persons need to be involved in early intervention and education as teachers, psychologists, directors of schools, support staff, volunteers, and all other related positions. Not only should they be employed at all levels in early intervention and education, but it is essential that deaf persons become members of the school advisory board and other decision-making bodies that set policy. In addition, there are other roles for deaf persons that may not be considered standard teaching positions—for example, hiring deaf persons as professionals to offer American Sign Language and Deaf culture/history classes to deaf children, parents, and teachers, including the art of storytelling. It is important that members of the Deaf community continue to develop more tolerance for the intervention choices available to deaf children. Despite continuing efforts by the medical field and hearing parents' conscious or unconscious desire to have their deaf child be hearing, to date there is no "cure" for deafness. All deaf children must be made to feel included in the Deaf community regardless of their parents' choices or interventions they choose for themselves.

New Influences on the Social-Emotional Development of Deaf Children

There are several advancements in the field of deafness that likely will have profound effects on the development of deaf and hard-of-hearing children. These include universal newborn screening and intervention beginning in infancy, cochlear implants, communication technology (e.g., increased access to computers and the internet, real-time captioning, video-relay interpreting) and innovative educational programming (bicultural, bilingual curriculums and classrooms). The collective wisdom is that these new options for deaf children and their families will promote a deeper and better understanding of deafness and bridge the communication barriers that contribute to the risk of poor social-emotional adjustment for these children. Given the recency of these advancements, long-term outcomes are not yet available to determine what benefit or detriment deaf and hard-of-hearing children and their families may experience over time. Long-term follow-up studies are imperative to understand how these changes are shaping the lives of deaf and hard-of-hearing children.

Summary and Conclusions

Deaf children can become socially and emotionally competent if given the same opportunities as hearing children to develop self-awareness, independent thinking, and good problem-solving skills over the course of their development. Such opportunities include the direct and explicit focus on teaching social-emotional skills to deaf children; emphasizing, beginning in early intervention, the powerful role parents and professionals can play in promoting social competence; and continuing to evaluate and revise what is best for the child and make the child a partner in the process. As families, schools, and the Deaf community become more connected, a sense of togetherness and recognition can develop as to the important and unique contributions that all bring to the optimal development of deaf children (Hill, 1993).

Parents and professionals need to directly address the needs of the child and consciously interweave the systems of the school, family, and community to work together to meet the child's needs. Children's developmental integration occurs from a relational standpoint—in relation to the ecology of school (teacher–student, teacher–principal, teacher–parent, and peer–peer interactions) and home (family interactions). No single main effect (ecology, personal characteristics of the participants, or the nature of the intervention) will determine the outcomes. Instead, there is a need to conceptualize the multiple, reciprocal interactions among persons and environment that determine healthy, competent behavior (Bronfenbrenner, 1979; Weissberg et al., 1989).

References

Barrett, M. (1986). Self-image and social adjustment change in deaf adolescents participating in a social living class. *Journal of Group Psychotherapy, Psychodrama, and Sociometry, 39*, 3–11.

Bat-Chava, Y. (1994). Group identification and self-esteem of deaf adults. *Personality and Social Psychology Bulletin, 20*, 494–502.

Bat-Chava, Y. (2000). Diversity of deaf identities. *American Annals of the Deaf, 145*, 420–428.

Bat-Chava, Y., & Deignan, E. (2001). Peer relationships of children with cochlear implants. *Journal of Deaf Studies and Deaf Education, 6*, 186–199.

Bodner-Johnson, B. (1986). The family environment and achievement of deaf students: A discriminant analysis. *Exceptional Children, 52*, 443–449.

Bronfenbrenner, U. (1979). *The ecology of human development*. Cambridge, MA: Harvard University Press.

Calderon, R. (2000). Parent involvement in deaf children's education programs as a predictor of child's language, reading, and social-emotional development. *Journal of Deaf Studies and Deaf Education, 5*, 140–155.

Calderon, R., & Greenberg, M. T. (1993). Considerations in the adaptation of families with school-aged deaf children. In M. Marschark & M.D. Clark (Eds.), *Psychological perspectives on deafness* (pp. 27–48). Hillsdale, NJ: Lawrence Erlbaum Associates.

Calderon, R., & Greenberg, M.T. (1997). The effectiveness of early intervention for deaf children and children with hearing loss. In MJ Guralnick (Ed.), *The effectiveness of early intervention* (pp. 455–482). Baltimore, MD: Paul H. Brookes.

Calderon, R., & Greenberg, M.T. (1999). Stress and coping in hearing mothers with children with hearing loss: Factors affecting mother and child adjustment. *American Annals of the Deaf, 144*, 7–18.

Calderon, R., Greenberg, M.T., & Kusché, C. (1991). The influence of family coping on the cognitive and social skills of deaf children. In D. Martin (Ed.), *Advances in cognition, education, and deafness* (pp. 195–200). Washington, DC: Gallaudet University Press.

Calderon, R. & Naidu, S. (2000). Further support of the benefits of early identification and intervention with children with hearing loss. In C. Yoshinaga-Itano (Ed.), *Language, speech and social-emotional development of deaf and hard of hearing children: The early years* [Mongraph]. *Volta Review, 100*(5), 53–84.

Carnegie Task Force on Meeting the Needs of Young Children. (1994). *Starting points: Meeting the needs of our youngest children*. New York: Carnegie Corporation.

Committee on the Education of the Deaf (1988). *Toward equality: Education of the deaf*. Washington, DC: U.S. Government Printing Office.

Connell, J. P., Aber, J. L., & Walker, G. (1995). How do urban communities affect youth? Using social science research to inform the design and evaluation of comprehensive community initiatives. In J. P. Connell, A. C. Kubisch, L. B. Schorr, & C. H. Weiss (Eds.), *New approaches to evaluating community initiatives* (pp. 93–125). Washington, DC: Aspen Institute.

Feuerstein, R. (1980). *Instrumental enrichment*. Baltimore, MD: University Park Press.

Gage, S., Lou, M. W., & Charlson, E. (1993). A social learning program for deaf adolescents. *Perspectives in Education and Deafness, 13*, 2–5.

Goleman, D. (1995). Emotional intelligence. New York: Bantam Books.

Greenberg, M.T. (2000). Educational interventions. In P. Hindley & N. Kitson (Eds.), *Mental health and deafness* (pp. 311–336). London: Whurr Publishers.

Greenberg, M., & Kusché, C. (1989). Cognitive, personal and social development of deaf children and adolescents. In M.C. Wang, M.C. Reynolds, & H.J. Walberg (Eds.), *Handbook of special education: Research and practice* (Vol. 1, pp. 95–129). Oxford: Pergamon Press.

Greenberg, M. T., & Kusché, C. A. (1993). *Promoting social and emotional development in deaf children: The PATHS project*. Seattle: University of Washington Press.

Greenberg, M. T., Kusché, C. A., & Speltz, M. (1991). Emotional regulation, self-control, and psychopathology: The role of relationships in early childhood. In D. Cicchetti & S. L. Toth (Eds.), *Rochester symposium on developmental psychopathology: Vol. 2. Internalizing and externalizing expressions of dysfunction* (pp. 21–56). Hillsdale, NJ: Lawrence Erlbaum Associates.

Greenberg, M. T., Lengua, L. J., & Calderon, R. (1997). The nexus of culture and sensory loss: Coping with deafness. In I.N. Sandler & S.A. Wolchik (Eds.), *Handbook of children's coping with common stressors: Linking theory, research and interventions* (pp. 301–331). New York: Plenum.

Greenberg, M. T., & Marvin, R. S. (1979). Attachment patterns in profoundly deaf preschool children. *Merrill-Palmer Quarterly, 25*, 265–279.

Hamilton, V. (1982). Cognition and stress: An information processing model. In L. Goldberger & S. Brenitz (Eds.), *Handbook of stress: Theoretical and clinical aspects* (pp. 41–71). New York: The Free Press.

Hill, P. (1993). The need for deaf adult role models in early intervention programs for deaf children. *ACEHI Journal, 19*, 14–20.

Hindley, P., & Reed, R. (1999). Promoting alternative thinking strategies (PATHS) mental health promotion with deaf children in school. In S. Decker, S Kirby, A. Greenwood, & D. Moores (Eds.), *Taking children seriously*. London: Cassell Publications.

Kusché, C.A., & Greenberg, M.T. (1993). *The PATHS curriculum*. Seattle, WA: Developmental Research and Programs.

Kusché, C.A., Greenberg, M.T., Calderon, R., & Gustafson, R.N. (1987). Generalization strategies from the PATHS Project for the prevention of substance use disorders. In G. Anderson & D. Watson (Eds.), *Innovations in the habilitation and rehabilitation of deaf adolescents* (pp. 243–263). Little Rock, AR: Rehabilitation Research Center on Deafness and Hearing Impairment.

Lederberg, A. R., & Mobley, C. E. (1990). The effect of hearing impairment on the quality of attachment and mother-toddler interaction. *Child Development, 61*, 1596–1604.

Lemanek, K.L., Williamson, D.A., Gresham, F. M., & Jensen, B. F. (1986). Social skills training with hearing-impaired children and adolescents. *Behavior Modification, 10*, 55–71.

Loevinger, J. (1976). *Ego development*. San Francisco, CA: Jossey Bass.

Lou, M. W., & Charlson, E. S. (1991). A program to enhance the social cognition of deaf adolescents. In D. Martin (Ed.), *Advances in cognition, education, and deafness* (pp. 329–334). Washington, DC: Gallaudet University Press.

Luetke-Stahlman, B. (1995). Classrooms, communication, and social competence. *Perspectives in Education and Deafness, 13*, 12–16.

Lytle, R. R. (1987). Effects of a cognitive social skills training procedure with deaf adolescents. (Doc-toral dissertation, University of Maryland, 1987). *Dissertation Abstracts International, 47* (11-B), 4675.

Marschark, M. (1993). *Psychological development of deaf children*. New York: Oxford University Press.

Marschark, M. (1997). *Raising and educating a deaf child: A comprehensive guide to the choices, controversies, and decisions faced by parents and educators*. New York: Oxford University Press.

Meadow, K.P. (1983). *Revised manual. Meadow/Kendall social-emotional assessment inventory for deaf and hearing-impaired children*. Washington, DC: Pre-College Programs, Gallaudet Research Institute.

Meadow, K.P., & Dyssegaard, B. (1983a). Social-emotional adjustment of deaf students: Teachers' ratings of deaf children: An American-Danish comparison. *International Journal of Rehabilitation Research, 6*(3), 345–348.

Meadow, K.P., & Dyssegaard, B. (1983b). Teachers' ratings of deaf children: An American-Danish comparison. *American Annals of the Deaf, 128*, 900–908.

Meadow, K.P., Greenberg, M.T., Erting, C., & Carmichael, H. S. (1981). Interactions of deaf mothers and deaf preschool children: Comparisons with three other groups of deaf and hearing dyads. *American Annals of the Deaf, 126*, 454–468.

Meadow-Orlans, K. P. (1990). The impact of child hearing loss on the family. In D. F. Moores & K. P. Meadow-Orlans (Eds.), *Educational and developmental aspects of deafness* (pp. 321–338). Washington, DC: Gallaudet University Press.

Meadow-Orlans, K. P. (1994). Stress, support, and deafness: Perceptions of infants' mothers and fathers. *Journal of Early Intervention, 18*, 91–102.

Meadow-Orlans, K.P., & Steinberg, A.G. (1993). Effects of infant hearing loss and maternal support on mother-infant interactions at 18 months. *Journal of Applied Developmental Psychology, 14*, 407–426.

Meichenbaum, D. H., & Goodman, J. (1971). Training impulsive children to talk to themselves: A means of developing self-control. *Journal of Abnormal Psychology, 77*, 115–116.

Moeller, M.P., & Condon, M.C. (1994). D.E.I.P.: A collaborative problem-solving approach to early intervention. In J. Roush & N.D. Matkin (Eds.), *Infants and toddlers with hearing loss: Family centered assessment and intervention* (pp. 163–192). Baltimore, MD: York Press.

Montanini-Manfredi, M. (1993). The emotional development of deaf children. In M. Marschark & M.D. Clark (Eds.), *Psychological perspectives on deafness* (pp. 49–63). Hillsdale, NJ: Lawrence Erlbaum Associates.

Moores, D. (2001). *Educating the deaf: Psychology, principles, and practices* (5th ed.). Boston: Houghton Mifflin.

Rasing, E. J., Connix, F., Duker, P. C., & van de Hurk Ardine, J. (1994). Acquisition and generalization of social behaviors in language-disabled deaf children. *Behavior Modification, 18*, 411–442.

Rasing, E. F., & Duker, P. C. (1992). Effects of a multifaceted training procedure on the acquisition and generalization of social behaviors in language-disabled deaf children. *Journal of Applied Behavior Analysis, 25*, 723–734.

Rasing, E. F., & Duker, P. C. (1993). Acquisition and generalization of social behaviors in language-disabled deaf children. *American Annals of the Deaf, 138*, 362–369.

Regan, J. J. (1981). *An attempt to modify cognitive impulsivity in deaf children: Self-instruction versus problem-solving strategies.* Unpublished doctoral dissertation, University of Toronto, Toronto, Canada.

Schlesinger, H.S. (1987). Effects of powerlessness on dialogue and development: Disability, poverty and the human condition. In B. Heller, L. Flohr, & L. Zegans (Eds.), *Expanding horizons: Psychosocial interventions with sensorily-disabled persons* (pp. 1–27). New York: Grune and Stratton.

Schlesinger, H. S., & Acree, M. C. (1984). The antecedents of achievement and adjustment: A longitudinal study of deaf children. In G. Anderson and D. Watson (Eds.), *The habilitation and rehabilitation of deaf adolescents* (pp. 48–61). Washington, DC: The National Academy of Gallaudet College.

Schlesinger, H.S., & Meadow, K.P. (1972). *Sound and sign: Childhood deafness and mental health.* Berkeley: University of California Press.

Schloss, P. J., & Smith, M. A. (1990). *Teaching social-skills to hearing-impaired students.* Washington, DC: Alexander Graham Bell Association.

Schloss, P. J., Smith, M. A., & Schloss, C. N. (1984). Empirical analysis of a card game designed to promote consumer-related social competence among hearing-impaired youth. *American Annals of the Deaf, 129*, 417–423.

Sheridan, M. A. (2000). Images of self and others: Stories from the children. In P. E. Spencer, C. J. Erting, & M. Marschark (Eds.), *The deaf child in the family and at school: Essays in honor of Kathryn P. Meadow-Orlans* (pp. 5–19). Hillsdale, NJ: Lawrence Erlbaum Associates.

Smith, M. A., Schloss, P. J., & Schloss, C. N. (1984). An empirical analysis of a social skills training program used with hearing impaired youths. *Journal of Rehabilitation of the Deaf, 18*(2), 7–14.

Steinberg, A. (2000). Autobiographical narrative on growing up deaf. In P. E. Spencer, C. J. Erting, & M. Marschark (Eds.), *The deaf child in the family and at school: Essays in honor of Kathryn P. Meadow-Orlans* (pp. 93–108). Hillsdale, NJ: Lawrence Erlbaum Associates.

Stinson, M. S., & Foster, S. (2000). Socialization of deaf children and youths in school. In P. E. Spencer, C. J., Erting, & M. Marschark (Eds.), *The deaf child in the family and at school: Essays in honor of Kathryn P. Meadow-Orlans* (pp. 191–209). Hillsdale, NJ: Lawrence Erlbaum Associates.

Suarez, M. (2000). Promoting social competence in deaf students: The effect of an intervention program. *Journal of Deaf Studies and Deaf Education, 5*, 323–336.

Vaccari, C., & Marschark, M. (1997). Communication between parents and deaf children: Implications for social-emotional development. *Journal of Child Psychology and Psychiatry, 38*, 793–802.

Wald, R. L., & Knutson, J. F. (2000). Deaf cultural identity of adolescents with and without cochlear implants. In B. J. Gantz, R. S. Tyler, & J. T. Rubinstein (Eds.), *Seventh symposium on cochlear implants in children Annals of Otology, Rhinology, and Laryngology,* (supplement 185, pp. 109–111).

Waters, E., & Sroufe, L. A. (1983). Social competence as a developmental construct. *Developmental Review, 3*, 79–97.

Watson, S. M., Henggeler, S. W., & Whelan, J. P. (1990). Family functioning and the social adaptation of hearing-impaired youths. *Journal of Abnormal Child Psychology, 18*, 143–163.

Weissberg, R. P., Caplan, M. Z., & Sivo, P. J. (1989). A new conceptual framework for establishing school-based social competence promotion programs. In L. A. Bond, B. E. Compas, & C. Swift (Eds.), *Prevention in the schools* (pp. 255–296). Menlo Park, CA: Sage.

Weissberg, R. P., & Greenberg, M. T. (1998). Community and school prevention. In I. Siegel and A. Renniner (Eds.), *Handbook of child psychology* (5th ed.): Vol. 4. *Child psychology in practice* (pp. 877–954). New York: John Wiley.

W. T. Grant Consortium on the School-based Promotion of Social Competence. (1992). Drug and alcohol prevention curricula. In J. D. Hawkins and R. F. Catalano (Eds.), *Communities that care* (pp. 129–148). San Francisco, CA: Jossey-Bass.

Yoshinaga-Itano, C., Sedey, A. L., Coulter, D. K., & Mehl, A.L. (1998). The language of early-and later-identified children with hearing loss. *Pediatrics, 102*, 1161–1171.

14

Meg Traci & Lynne Sanford Koester

Parent–Infant Interactions

A Transactional Approach to Understanding the Development of Deaf Infants

Families today are looking more and more to the growing body of research on human development for answers to the age-old question of how best to support the needs of their children (Horowitz, 2000). For the 5,000 American families experiencing the birth of a deaf infant each year (Thompson et al., 2001), this question comes into focus as the answers become more complex and uncertain. Research on the protective factors surrounding children who demonstrate successful adaptation to deafness represents an important effort to support these families in their search for answers (e.g., Erting, Prezioso, & Hynes, 1990; Yoshinaga-Itano, Sedey, Coulter, & Mehl, 1998; see also Sass-Lehrer & Bodner-Johnson, this volume). Such studies can provide families with deaf infants important information on the heterogeneity of individual and environmental differences within deaf populations and on the range of supports developed for deaf children and their families (e.g., Meadow-Orlans, Mertens, & Sass-Lehrer, in press; Spencer, in press). The relevance of this information is likely to vary between families with hearing parents (approximately 90% of those with deaf children) and those with at least one deaf parent (less than 10%; Marschark, 1993b). Still, paucity of rigorous studies with deaf populations, in conjunction with fre-

quent inaccessibility of the supports they recommend, weakens the utility of this research as an effective coping resource for these families (Meadow-Orlans, 2000). Therefore, concerns still exist regarding how deafness will affect the child, how the child will affect the family, and how the family's decisions and actions can support the child, both in the short-term and across the life span.

Researchers of disability (Fougeyrollas & Beauregard, 2001), child development, developmental psychopathology, and life span development (Dixon & Lerner, 1992) conceptualize these complex questions within a framework of "person–environment interaction" or "transactional adaptation" (Sameroff & Chandler, 1975). Sameroff and Chandler were among the first to emphasize the interplay between child characteristics and environmental context in efforts to understand developmental outcomes. Their transactional model has since been elaborated in ways that are particularly applicable to the study of deaf infants:

> To predict outcome, a singular focus on the characteristics of the individual, in this case the child, frequently will be misleading. An analysis and assessment of the experiences available to

the child needs to be added. Within this trans-actional model the development of the child is seen as a product of the continuous dynamic interactions of the child and the experience provided by his or her family and social context. (Sameroff & Fiese, 1990, p. 122)

The current chapter presents an integrative analysis of the dynamic interactions between deaf infants and their parents, with particular emphasis on early socio-emotional development, including communication, self-regulation, emotional expressiveness, and self-recognition. Admittedly, the diagnosis of deafness is so salient that for many families, it can become a singular focus (Sameroff & Fiese, 1990) that can distract them from considering other influences affecting developmental trajectories. Because descriptions of early development are typically drawn from research conducted with hearing dyads, a brief preface about the importance of deafness as a contextual factor influencing social development seems warranted.

Deafness as a Contextual Factor

There are qualitative differences in various aspects of the development of deaf and hearing children, and their varying experiences of the world will influence their psychological development in ways that may not yet be fully known or understood. Nevertheless, it is important not to view developmental differences as deficiencies (Marschark, 1993a). Certainly, deaf children bring different personal attributes to environmental challenges or developmental demands than do hearing children. Throughout development, personal attributes of deaf children will mandate different social supports than those required by hearing children. During the first years of life, the presence and absence of varying environmental supports affects increased individuality among deaf children, particularly through social interactions. This individuality is reflected in the different experiences of deaf toddlers (e.g., cultural contexts, parenting styles, exposure to sign language, use of hearing aids) and their different personal resources (e.g., dialogue skills, communication styles, attachment relationships, emotional regulatory skills, sense of self). Furthermore, transactional adaptation (Sameroff & Chandler, 1975) includes consideration of the impacts deaf infants

have on their social partners. Consequently, families with deaf children, though similar in one respect, may proceed along similar and distinct developmental trajectories throughout the child's lifetime.

Other Contextual Factors

To fully understand these descriptions of between-group and within-group differences, one must look beyond deafness to other factors that further define the early social contexts of deaf infants. As Papoušek and Papoušek (1997) stated, "The interplay of infantile and parental predispositions is astonishingly harmonious and mutually rewarding for both partners as long as all prerequisites function smoothly and no unfavorable contextual factors intervene" (p. 44). From clinical evidence of integrative and communicative disorders, Papoušek and Papoušek outlined four types of unfavorable contextual factors or risk factors that may negatively affect the harmonious interplay: (1) missed opportunities for initial communication as a result of perinatal complications (for results of a national survey, in which 7.6% of the 331 parent participants reported that their deaf or hard-of-hearing infants had experienced prematurity and perinatal trauma, see Harrison & Roush, 1996); (2) infant disability leading to discouragement of intuitive parental responses (hearing impairment has been reported to co-occur with other disabilities in approximately one third of deaf infants, Batshaw & Perret, 1992); (3) mismatched style between infant and parent (e.g., infant cues for more intense stimulation are misinterpreted as frailty or sickness; thus parents decrease the intensity and salience of their own behavior and exacerbate the infant's noninteractive appearance); and (4) prolonged need for infantile preverbal communication (e.g., child does not acquire language at expected age, but in the meantime loses "babyish" features that normally elicit intuitive parental communicative support, such as infant-directed speech). The first two contextual factors are discussed in this chapter generally as stressors within a family systems approach. The third factor is addressed in subsections on temperament, "goodness-of-fit," and interactional reciprocity, and the fourth is expanded upon within a subsection on communication styles. Each of these factors will be discussed as they relate to the interactive experiences of young deaf children and their families. Finally, the developmental or personal resources of deaf children that arise from these experiences are discussed.

Stress Within a Family System

Studies of the stress associated with developmental disabilities have focused on measuring the effect of stress on the family system as a context for child development (e.g., McCubbin & Patterson, 1983). Theoretically, stress of the child's hearing loss negatively affects family functioning and, consequently, the development of the child. Protective factors thought to ameliorate negative relationships between familial stress and healthy child development include parental attitudes (Hadadian, 1995), beliefs (Erting, Thumann-Prezioso, & Benedict, 2000), attributions (Miller, 1988), internal and external family resources (Pelchat et al., 1999), and the quality of social support (Meadow-Orlans & Steinberg, 1993). These factors can support parents' abilities to adapt successfully to stressors (e.g., Minnes & Nachsen, 1997), facilitating their parenting effectiveness and hence child outcomes. In one notable study, increasing parental sense of coherence was found to lessen the impact of stress on caregivers and influence the health and behavior of the child with a disability (Gottlieb, 1998).

For families with deaf infants, a unique source of stress stems from conflicting professional opinions regarding different intervention and communication options (Meadow-Orlans & Sass-Lehrer, 1995). Pipp-Siegel, Sedey, and Yoshinaga-Itano (2002) found that perceptions of greater intensity of daily hassles and ratings of fewer social and financial resources predicted parental stress in a sample of mothers of young deaf children. Social networks of families with deaf children also correspond to positive mother–child interactions (Meadow-Orlans et al., in press), perhaps effectively buffering negative effects of familial stress on children's development. Understanding how to support these families must be an ongoing, investigative process.

The Role of Temperament

The unique characteristics of each infant, such as typical levels of irritability, adaptability, and responses to unfamiliarity, are thought to influence the interactive patterns of parent–infant dyads from birth onward (Kagan, 1997). Often referred to as "temperament," the child's normal pattern of reacting to environmental cues and coping with distress represents one of many factors that is significant for a child with disabilities (Chess & Thomas, 1996; Kagan, 1983).

As Chess and Thomas (1996) have argued, temperamental characteristics consisting of constitutionally derived behavioral tendencies are evident early in ontogeny and play an important role in subsequent social relationships. Thus, an important theme in much infancy research is how parents and infants reciprocally respond to and influence each other's behaviors or what behaviors each member of the dyad contributes to their patterns of interaction. This bidirectional influence has been documented in studies of typical mother–infant interaction (Brazelton, Koslowski, & Main, 1974), as well as in studies of infants with depressed mothers (Cohn, Matias, Campbell, & Hopkins, 1990), but has only recently become the focus of attention in the literature regarding deaf babies and their families (Koester & Meadow-Orlans, 1999, in press). This concept is important to understanding healthy development among deaf children and in moving us beyond a unidirectional explanation that focuses on parenting alone.

The related concept of "goodness-of fit" between the individual and environmental context also has been convincingly applied to the development of deaf children and their families by Clark (1993):

> The individuals' unique set of characteristics may match (fit) the demands of the setting, leading to adaptive outcomes: If so, these individuals will receive supportive or positive feedback from the environment. On the other hand, the individuals' characteristics may not match the demands of the setting—showing a poor fit: Now, these individuals receive nonsupportive or negative feedback from the environment, often leading to maladaptive outcomes in development. (p. 354)

It is important to emphasize that poor or good fit is not necessarily a stable feature. Rather, as a growing body of evidence demonstrates, an initial fit of temperaments between a parent and infant, good or not, may be affected over time by parents who adapt sensitively to their infant's needs, respond with more directiveness, or decrease their level of interaction (Lamb, Ketterlinus, & Fracasso, 1992; see also Pelchat et al., 1999).

Plasticity is another related concept of particular interest to the present topic. According to this approach, certain skills or attributes may still be developed at some later point even if the typical time of emergence has been missed, and this approach is applicable to both deaf and hearing infants. Although there may be sensitive periods during which a given skill, such as language, will develop most readily and perhaps most fully (Newman, Bavelier, Corina, Jezzard, & Neville, 2002; Newport, 1990), the possibility remains for personal and contextual modifications to facilitate this development later. "Because the context and the organism actively modify or transform each other, plasticity is an inevitable feature of development" (Clark, 1993, p. 354). In primarily auditory linguistic contexts provided by most hearing families, the mode of language input may not be the best fit for the communication needs of a deaf child. It seems plausible, then, that the language delays with which most deaf children of hearing parents enter formal educational settings may be partially explained by the concept of goodness-of-fit during the preschool years (Clark, 1993).

Interactional Reciprocity

Tronick and Weinberg (1997) have developed the mutual regulation model (MRM) to describe the process of early parent–infant emotional functioning. This provides a useful tool for explaining the potentially negative effects of various factors such as maternal depression on the psychological development of the child. The MRM assumes that an infant is motivated to communicate with others and to establish intersubjectivity but also to act on the physical world. In the early months, however, the latter orientation toward physical exploration clearly is secondary to the goal of establishing mutually satisfying social relationships. According to this model, successful dyadic functioning depends on the following primary considerations: (1) the ability of the child's physiological system to organize and control states of arousal and behavioral responses; (2) the integrity of the communicative system, or an infant's capacity to generate messages

and meanings; and (3) caregivers' sensitivity to the child's communicative efforts and ability to respond appropriately.

Thus, the mutual regulation process involves "the capacity of each of the interactants, child and adult, to express their motivated intentions, to appreciate the intentions of the partner, and to scaffold their partner's actions so that their partner can achieve their goals" (Tronick & Weinberg, 1997, p. 56). In infant–adult dyads, there is a wide disparity between partners' communication capacities, mandating that adults modify their dyadic behaviors to accommodate the child's needs (Papoušek & Papoušek, 1987; Rogoff, 1990; von Salisch, 2001). In the case of a deaf child of hearing parents where sensory capacities are also disparate, compensation may be more challenging, yet necessary:

> Infants who are congenitally and profoundly deaf begin their lives lacking what is perhaps the most universal of parent-child communication devices, not only in humans, but across a variety of mammalian and other species: the oral-aural channel. Surely, there is compensation and accommodation in that situation that serves to provide a reciprocal relationship between parent and child and "bootstraps" development in an effective, if somewhat different manner than that of hearing children. It is only by understanding those differences, however, that we can hope to understand the psychological functioning of deaf individuals. (Marschark, 1993a, p. 22)

Indeed, there are a variety of ways in which parents compensate and accommodate to their children's sensory needs and social maturity to facilitate reciprocal interactions and to support development. What follows is a review of parental responses and modifications documented in studies of deaf and hearing infants.

How Do Caregivers Respond to Communicative Attempts of Infants?

Some research suggests that early dyadic communication can easily be disturbed by difficult-to-read infant signals (Handler & Oster, 2001) or by lack of infant responsiveness to caregivers' bids (Papoušek & von Hofacker, 1998). These patterns may be important predictors of later interactional and emotional difficulties between parent and child (Mundy & Willoughby, 1996). In either case, having a child diagnosed with a hearing loss can easily alter the typical flow of reciprocal interactions and thus change parent–infant dynamics, at least temporarily, until mutuality is reestablished and each partners' signals become more easily interpreted by the other. As in the case of temperament, however, the initial fit between parental expressive communication styles and the infant's receptive abilities and preferences will play an important role in determining the outcome for the deaf infant's early social, emotional, and linguistic development.

Intuitive parenting (Papoušek & Bornstein, 1992; Papoušek & Papoušek, 1987) predicts that a parent will automatically, but not necessarily intentionally, make many behavioral adjustments to facilitate a social context between the parent and the infant in which language lessons occur. Papoušek and Papoušek (1997), however, caution that these intuitive adjustments may not be made when unfavorable contextual factors are present, like those outlined above. Parents of children with developmental and physical disabilities have been described as more active and directive than parents of children without these disabilities (Pelchat et al., 1999). Parents of children with disabilities may believe that their children need more intense stimulation to elicit a response; in addition, the child's own signals may be more difficult for parents to read, as discussed earlier (for a review, see Hauser-Cram, Warfield, Shonkoff, & Krauss, 2001). The literature related to hearing parents with deaf children is replete with similar conclusions regarding parental directiveness (Meadow-Orlans & Steinberg, 1993; Pipp-Siegel & Biringen, 1998; Spencer & Gutfreund, 1990). Swisher (2000) noted that attention getting strategies observed in caregivers with deaf infants, such as tapping the child before signing or gesturing, are often prerequisite to providing language input about the child's focus of interest. These behaviors should not be interpreted as unresponsive to the child's attention focus, even when the tapping is directing the child's attention somewhere. Still, if the parent is not receiving reciprocal responses from the infant, then the parent may develop a pattern of exerting more control during interactions. When a deaf child does not orient or calm to a parent's voice, parents may gradually perceive this as a rejection or cause for concern about their caregiving abilities (Marschark, 1993a).

How Do Dialogue Skills Typically Emerge?

Infants learn to engage with social partners through repeated early interactions, usually face-to-face in most North American families. Through these frequent and usually pleasurable experiences, the infant learns how to initiate topics, how to maintain them, how to take turns, and how to elicit the partner's response to a focus of mutual interest. Because all of these subtle skills may be more complicated in the case of an infant with a hearing loss, enhancing these interactional patterns has become the focus of many early intervention efforts (Spencer, in press). Parents often need help tuning into and interpreting their deaf baby's signals, as well as trying creative and alternative means of capturing and maintaining the deaf child's attention. However, if the infant is not highly responsive, parents may tend to take over and dominate the exchange, further inhibiting the infant's efforts to initiate a turn and to develop the necessary skills as a social partner. It is sometimes useful in these cases to look to deaf parents for examples of effective, natural strategies, involving visual and physical means to promote communication with a deaf child.

Chen (1996) describes attention-getting strategies such as animated facial expressions; tactile and kinesthetic contact with the infant's hands and feet; placement of social partners' faces, hands, conversational topics and signs within infants' visual field; placing signs on the infant or on the object; and repeating signs. As Swisher (2000) asserts, deaf mothers are well prepared to respond sensitively to a deaf child by already being competent in using visual communication; in other words, they are able to provide accessible language to a deaf child from the outset. However, the visual channel must serve to take in the object world as well as the social world, so that there is still a challenge for deaf parents to help the child learn conversational and attentional rules, especially at the age (around 5–6 months) when the infant's interest shifts to objects. A recent study (Spencer, 2000) demonstrated that deaf parents meet this challenge by supporting a systematic pattern for alternating visual foci. Spencer (2000) observed that hearing and deaf infants of deaf, signing mothers learn to look longer at their mothers than infants of hearing mothers. And for deaf infants of deaf mothers, this increase was observed in conjunction with longer time spent in coordinated joint attention than that observed for deaf infants with hearing mothers.

Several additional studies (e.g., Prendergast & McCollum, 1996) have examined patterns of interaction between mothers and their deaf babies; results showed, for example, that deaf mothers responded more to their child's eye contact than did hearing mothers. Overt attentional strategies such as tapping on an infant's body and waving within their visual field have also been reported; Waxman and Spencer (1997) found that deaf mothers of deaf infants used tapping significantly more than other groups of mothers. As Swisher (2000) cautions, however, the child's ability to respond appropriately to tapping involves a cognitive process and is therefore not automatic. That is, the connection between the location of tapping (on the infant) and the intended focus of attention may not be immediately obvious to the infant: "a tap on the body is not meant to direct the child's attention to his or her own body, but to the person doing the tapping and usually to their communication. . . . In short, the child must learn that such a signal means 'look at me' or 'pay attention to what is going to come next' " (Swisher, 2000, p. 25).

Longitudinal research has demonstrated that hearing mothers with early diagnosed deaf infants can make important communicative adaptations to the needs of their infants within the first year. Specifically, this research has shown that although deaf mothers incorporate more forms of stimulation in different modalities than do hearing mothers (e.g., more smiling and highly animated facial expressions, more visual-gestural games and sign communication, and more frequent, energetic tactile stimulation), during later interactions hearing mothers with deaf infants also become accustomed to using more frequent visual-gestural activities in their face-to-face interactions (Koester, Traci, Brooks, Karkowski, & Smith-Gray, in press). Additionally, this research has shown that in free-play situations, hearing mothers of deaf 9-month-old infants differed from hearing mothers of hearing infants in their more frequent use of gestures and tactile contact. When these infants were older, the mothers of deaf infants incorporated objects into free-play interactions more frequently than did the mothers of hearing infants (Spencer, 1993).

Of course, little is known about the process of compensation that occurs before parents receive diagnostic information regarding their infant's deafness. Before newborn hearing screening, suspicion and diagnosis of infant hearing impairment occurred after most infants were 6 months of age (Harrison & Roush, 1996). Many factors may explain these delays, including the intuitive accommodations that hearing parents make for a deaf child, learning in those early months how to positively interact with their infants. As Marschark notes (1997), deaf babies may be quite adept at "training" their caregivers, or shaping parental behaviors in the direction of more physical contact and more visually accessible communication.

Spencer (in press) notes that the challenges faced by all parents change and in some cases increase in complexity as the infant matures, but that the adaptation required of parents whose child is deaf may create additional challenges. The 5-month-old infant's shift from fascination with people and faces to a keen interest in the physical and object world is a positive indication of cognitive growth. Nevertheless, it further complicates the process of maintaining joint attention and of providing linguistic input to a deaf child who is now suddenly transfixed by toys and objects to be explored, rather than by the social world which previously held so much allure (Adamson & Chance, 1998; Waxman & Spencer, 1997). Being responsive to the infant's topic of interest, learning to wait for visual attention before communicating, and developing subtle strategies for eliciting infant attention are all new skills required of the caregiver if effective interactions with a deaf child are to be achieved (Swisher, 1992, 2000).

Learning how to communicate may well be the most important and impressive accomplishment of infancy, and it requires much more than simply the acquisition of names, labels, and grammatical structures. In addition to some basic and innate predispositions, a supportive social and cultural context is needed; the infant must learn to coordinate certain motor functions, physiological systems, and cognitive capacities, and favorable conditions such as an attentive, receptive state must be met. Caregivers, by using "motherese" or infant-directed speech patterns, unknowingly provide the necessary repetitions of learning opportunities, as well as careful pacing in response to the infant's signals (Erting et al., 2000; Papoušek & Papoušek, 1997). Deaf parents have been shown to modify their signing to an infant just as hearing adults alter their speech when it is directed toward an infant (Erting et al., 1990; Masataka, 1992, 1996, 1998; Reilly & Bellugi, 1996).

Reilly and Bellugi (1996) noted that the facial expressions used in American Sign Language (ASL) to denote where, what, and why questions involve furrowed eyebrows and the head tilted slightly forward. The investigators concluded that these facial signals, if used by a parent, might communicate anger, puzzlement, or even a general termination cue to the infant, thus undermining the goal of eliciting and maintaining infant attention. Their findings demonstrated that before the child was 2 years old, deaf parents subordinated the morphological function of facial expressions and reserved these expressions almost exclusively to convey affective messages. It was not until after their infants were 2 that the parents used grammatical facial expressions with their signing to communicate linguistic information to the child. Apparently for the infant's first 2 years, facial expressions in infant-directed ASL are used primarily to communicate affect; thereafter, these expressions serve a multifunctional role by conveying both grammatical and affective information. This progression from the simple structure of manual sign to the more complex incorporation of signed morphemes such as facial expressions may facilitate language acquisition in the deaf infant.

Masataka (1992) observed eight deaf mothers using their first language, Japanese Sign Language (JSL) in interactions with their profoundly deaf infants and with other signing adults. Masataka characterized deaf mothers' infant-directed JSL as having features such as slower tempo, more repetition, and larger exaggerated movements than adult-directed JSL. He suggested that the features of signed motherese seem to "evoke more robust responses (visual) from the infant" (Masataka, 1992, p. 459), similar to infant-directed vocalizations and has demonstrated how attractive they are for deaf infants (Masataka, 1996). Masataka postulated that features of infant-directed signing facilitate language acquisition and communicate affect to infants (for further review, see Chamberlain, Morford, & Mayberry, 2000).

Supporting the Deaf Infant's Social-Emotional Needs

Forming Attachments

Developing social attachments, developing an awareness of self, being able to interpret cues from others through social referencing, and learning to regulate one's own emotional responses are important accomplishments during the first few years. The implications of these developments for deaf infants may be somewhat different than for the hearing babies typically described in the literature.

The formation of early social bonds is perhaps one of the most well-researched aspects of infant socio-emotional development, as evidenced by the abundance of literature on this topic. The infant who forms a healthy emotional attachment to a caregiver can use this as a base for further exploration and mastery of the environment, with implications extending beyond early socio-emotional development (Ainsworth & Bell, 1970; Bowlby, 1969). The secure infant uses the attachment figure for reassurance in risky or ambiguous situations, returning to this secure base during times of distress or uncertainty, whereas infants who are insecurely attached show quite different patterns both before and after reunion with the caregiver.

Researchers have found that sensitive, reciprocal, and contingent interactions with a caregiver during the first year of life foster the emergence of a secure attachment (Isabella & Belsky, 1991). Maternal intrusiveness, on the other hand, may be predictive of later avoidant attachment (Isabella, Belsky, & von Eye, 1989). Langhorst and Fogel (1982) reported that mothers who skillfully modified their behaviors in response to hearing infants' visual attention were less likely to have insecure (avoidant) babies at 12 months. In other words, sensitive caregivers appeared to be those who decreased their activity when the infant looked away, and increased it when the infant resumed visual contact—a point with particular significance in the case of interactions with a deaf infant whose use of vision is multifunctional.

The degree to which attachment is affected by deafness may also be influenced by factors discussed earlier, such as communication proficiency. It has been shown, for example, that deaf preschoolers with poor communication skills were often insecurely attached, whereas those able to communicate more easily developed secure attachments (Greenberg & Marvin, 1979). Other researchers have found that deaf children with deaf parents (presumably dyads with high communicative competence) develop attachment patterns similar to those observed in hearing children with hearing parents (Meadow, Greenberg, & Erting, 1983).

Research on attachment between hearing mothers with deaf toddlers (as well as some with deaf mothers; Lederberg & Mobley, 1990; Lederberg & Prezbindowski, 2000), emphasizes the strengths and factors contributing to positive adaptation in these families. These studies conclude that there is currently little evidence that deafness itself contributes directly to insecure attachment; it is more likely the case that other contextual influences discussed above have far greater impact on the attachment process.

Self-Recognition

An infant's ability to recognize him- or herself typically emerges during the second year and is firmly established by the end of toddlerhood. Emde (1983) notes that this accomplishment coincides with the onset of hearing children's ability to use personal pronouns when looking at pictures of themselves. Thus, even an ability such as recognizing oneself in a mirror may be grounded in certain aspects of linguistic competence. In a poignant biographical account by hearing parents, Spradley and Spradley (1985) describe the breakthrough they witnessed when their deaf preschool daughter first began to sign and learn her own name: "Of all the injuries that oralism had inflicted on Lynn, the most insidious had been to rob her of a name. We had unwittingly told her, 'You are not a person until you can see 'Lynn' on our lips, until you can say 'Lynn' with your voice. . . . Without an acceptable symbol for herself, her capacity for self-awareness and self-control had failed to take root and grow" (p. 248).

It is also assumed that this emerging skill results in part from a growing sense of self-efficacy, or an awareness of the self as an agent causing things and people in the environment to respond in predictable ways. A caregiving relationship that is both contingent upon and sensitive to the infant's particular signals and communicative style would logically contribute to these developments. For example, the phenomenon of parental mirroring of a

baby's actions, as well as parental echoing of the baby's vocalizations (or manual babbling in the case of deaf infants), may serve important functions in assisting the child's developing awareness of his or her own behaviors and effects on others.

As Lewis and Brooks-Gunn (1979) assert, social knowledge in the early years involves knowledge about self, knowledge about others, and knowledge about the self in relation to others. In other words, "I cannot know another unless I have knowledge of myself, just as I cannot know myself without knowing others" (Lewis & Brooks-Gunn, 1979, p. 2). The same authors found a significant relationship between earlier mirror recognition and greater attentional capacities on the part of the infant, a point with particular relevance for the present topic. That is, parents who share their infant's hearing status (e.g., both are deaf or both are hearing) are likely to be more effective in eliciting and maintaining the infant's attention by using visual, tactile, or auditory modes of communication. They may also be more adept at reading their infant's behavioral cues in these various modalities.

There are various ways in which early parent–child communication may be more difficult in a dyad in which one partner is deaf and the other is hearing. While vocalizations (and particularly imitations in response to the infant's vocal behaviors) typically play an important role in helping the infant develop a sense of self, similar patterns of visual-gestural communication used within deaf–deaf pairs may also be highly effective in facilitating this process. In fact, data reported by Koester and Forest (1998) show that infants in matched dyads (deaf parents with deaf children and hearing parents with hearing children) are able to develop an image of themselves as separate from others somewhat earlier than those in unmatched dyads.

Perhaps the key here is in the parent's ability to establish joint attention when the infant explores the environment visually, using opportunities to label objects and persons of interest to the child and thus leading more readily to self–other discriminations. When a deaf infant looks away from the social partner, communication is often disrupted despite the parent's efforts, often in the form of continued vocalization (in the case of hearing parents). Thus, many opportunities to provide language input and to foster the infant's awareness of the self as a causal agent in social interactions may be missed in these dyads.

Self-Regulation and Emotional Expressiveness

As Osofsky and Thompson (2000) point out, emotions are especially important to the emerging parent–infant relationship, because most early communication (and, indeed, the establishment of reciprocity) takes place through emotional expression. Concepts such as "affect attunement" (Stern, 1985) and "emotional availability" (Biringen & Robinson, 1991) are also relevant to understanding the complex interplay between parents and a prelinguistic child whose body language and nonverbal signals must provide most of the cues as to affective state, needs, and desires.

As von Salisch (2001) notes, "parents talk to their children about verbal labels for their inner experiences, about antecedents of other people's emotional expressions, and about the consequences of their own expressive displays" (p. 311). Most hearing infants in North American cultures are frequently exposed to conversations about feelings, internal states, and subjective experiences. The result is an accumulation of practice labeling and articulating their own emotions and developing strategies for modulating their emotional responses to affectively laden experiences. But how does this process occur when the infant is deaf and the primary caregiver is hearing, before establishing a shared and effective system of communication? What is the long-term effect of having missed so many of these early opportunities for learning to express one's feeling through language, making one's needs known to others through spoken communication, and of receiving the linguistic feedback that validates one's emotional responses?

Calkins (1994) describes "emotion regulation" as strategies that manage affective experiences, with one outcome being enhanced and more successful social interactions. Parents play a crucial role as the external guides to this process before the child has internalized some of these regulatory mechanisms and can call upon them when needed. In Calkins' terms, the infant initially relies on parental guidance for regulation of arousal, but then gradually becomes capable of self-regulation (see also Kochanska, Coy, & Murray, 2001). As this process unfolds, "more complex communications and interactions with the caregiver teach the child to manage distress, control impulses, and delay gratification" (Calkins, 1994, p. 53). Again, it is important to remember that the research and theorizing in this area have focused almost exclusively on hearing children and their hearing parents and therefore presume a shared communication system that makes this all possible.

> For the child who is deaf and whose parent is hearing, creating a shared meaning and relatedness through language is a greater challenge. The absence of an available symbolic system in which to share personal knowledge or create a linguistic construct for an affective or emotional inner experience makes more likely the possibility of developmental arrest or delay. Without words, without signs, without gesture or communicative silence, there is no ability to express inner experiences, thoughts, or feelings. (Steinberg, 2000, p. 95)

The concept of goodness-of-fit is perhaps applicable once again when considering the emergence of emotional regulation in a deaf child, who in the majority of cases will have hearing parents. On one side of the equation, we have the individual child's capacity for perceiving, processing, and utilizing the regulatory strategies being modeled by others in the social context. On the other side, we have the adult's perceptiveness and sensitivity in first reading the infant's emotional signals and then responding to them appropriately in ways that assist the infant in modulating intense affective experiences. The importance of shared meanings cannot be overemphasized and would appear to be critical in facilitating the emergence of flexible and adaptive self-regulatory behaviors on the part of the deaf child. Clearly, this is an important topic in need of research with this population of infants and parents.

Summary

"Children's characteristics (e.g., age, functional skills, behavioral regulation) also are associated with how parents accommodate to the process of caring for a child with disabilities. Thus, children and parents constitute an integrated, relational system, in which subsystems interact, and each subsystem, through its fusion with the whole, also influences its own well-being" (Hauser-Cram et al., 2001, p. 21). As Fabes and Martin (2000) point out, transactions between the individual and the caregiving environment change as the child matures, develops new skills, becomes more mobile or independent, or perhaps learns to communicate better. In a recent review of factors contributing to adaptive and maladaptive parenting, Osofsky and Thompson (2000) posed two important questions regarding ways in which less-than-optimal situations might be improved for families and thus lead to better outcomes: (1) how can adaptive parenting be supported and fostered? and (2) what are the conditions most likely to enhance resilience in families at risk for parent–child difficulties? Finding the most appropriate and supportive context for a deaf child (facilitating this particularly within the family during the early years) may be one of the most pressing tasks for early interventionists, deaf education specialists, parents, and researchers. A vast amount of research has been carried out with hearing infants in recent decades, providing impressive documentation of normative social, emotional, cognitive, and linguistic accomplishments within this group. Although the number of studies investigating similar developmental domains in the population of deaf infants continues to increase steadily, many gaps remain in our knowledge and understanding of these children. Both they and their parents have much to teach us, but as researchers we have only just begun to scratch the surface in our quest for insights about the world of deaf infants.

References

Adamson, L., & Chance, S. E. (1998). Coordinating attention to people, objects, and language. In A. M. Wetherby, S. F. Warren, & J. Reichle (Eds.), *Transitions in prelinguistic communication* (pp. 15–37). Baltimore, MD: Paul H. Brookes.

Ainsworth, M. D. S., & Bell, S. M. (1970). Attachment, exploration and separation: Illustrated by the behavior of one-year-olds in a strange situation. *Child Development, 41*, 49–67.

Batshaw, M. L., & Perret, Y. M. (1992). Hearing. In M.L. Batshaw and Y. M. Perret (Eds.), *Children with disabilities: A medical primer* (pp. 321–349). Baltimore, MD: Paul H. Brookes.

Biringen, Z., & Robinson, J. (1991). Emotional availability in mother-child interactions: A reconceptualization for research. *American Journal of Orthopsychiatry, 61*, 258–271.

Bowlby, J. (1969). *Attachment and loss: Vol. I. Attachment*. New York: Basic Books.

Brazelton, T. B., Koslowski, B., & Main, M. (1974). The origins of reciprocity: The early mother-infant interaction. In M. Lewis & L. Rosenblum (Eds.), *The effect of the infant on its caregiver* (pp. 49–77). New York: John Wiley & Sons.

Calkins, S. D. (1994). Origins and outcomes of individual difference in emotion regulation. *Monographs of the Society for Research in Child Development, 59* (2–3), 53–72.

Chamberlain, C., Morford, J. P., & Mayberry, R. I. (2000). *Language acquisition by eye*. Mahwah, NJ: Lawrence Erlbaum Associates.

Chen, D. (1996). Parent-infant communication: Early intervention for very young children with visual impairment or hearing loss. *Infants and Young Children, 9*(2), 1–12.

Chess, S., & Thomas, A. (1996). *Temperament: Theory and practice*. New York: Brunner/Mazel.

Clark, M. D. (1993). A contextual/interactionist model and its relationship to deafness research. In M. Marschark & M. D. Clark (Eds.), *Psychological perspectives on deafness* (pp. 353–362). Mahwah, NJ: Lawrence Erlbaum Associates.

Cohn, J. F., Matias, R., Campbell, S. B., & Hopkins, J. (1990). Face-to-face interactions of post-partum depressed mother-infant pairs at 2 months. *Developmental Psychology, 26*, 15–23

Dixon, R. A., & Lerner, R. M. (1992). A history of systems in developmental psychology. In M. H. Bornstein & M. E. Lamb (Eds.), *Developmental psychology: An advanced textbook* (pp. 3–58). Hillsdale, NJ: Lawrence Erlbaum Associates.

Emde, R. (1983). The prerepresentational self and its affective core. *Psychoanalytic Study of the Child, 38*, 165–192.

Erting, C. J., Prezioso, C., & Hynes, M. (1990). The interactional context of deaf mother-infant communication. In V. Volterra & C. J. Erting (Eds.), *From gesture to language in hearing and deaf children* (pp. 97–106). Heidelberg, Germany: Springer-Verlag.

Erting, C. J., Thumann-Prezioso, C., & Benedict, B. S. (2000). Bilingualism in a deaf family: Fingerspelling in early childhood. In P. Spencer, C. J. Erting, & M. Marschark (Eds.), *The deaf child in the family and at school* (pp. 41–54). Mahwah, NJ: Lawrence Erlbaum Associates.

Fabes, R., & Martin, C. L. (2000). *Exploring child development: Transactions and transformations*. Boston. Allyn and Bacon.

Fougeyrollas, P., & Beauregard, L. (2001). Disability: An interactive person-environment social creation. In G. L. Albrecht, K. D. Seelman, & M. Bury (Eds.), *Handbook of disability studies* (pp. 171–194). Thousand Oaks, CA.: Sage.

Gottlieb, A. (1998). Single mothers of children with disabilities: The role of sense of coherence in managing multiple challenges. In H. I. McCubbin et al. (Eds.), *Resiliency in Family Series: Vol. 1. Stress, coping, and health in families: Sense of coherence and resiliency* (pp. 189–204). Thousand Oaks, CA: Sage.

Greenberg, M. T., & Marvin, R. S. (1979). Attachment patterns in profoundly deaf preschool children. *Merrill-Palmer Quarterly, 25*, 265–279.

Hadadian, A. (1995). Attitudes toward deafness and security of attachment relationships among young deaf children and their parents. *Early Education and Development, 6*, 181–191.

Handler, M. K., & Oster, H. (2001, April). *Mothers' spontaneous attributions of emotion to infant's expressions: Effects of craniofacial anomalies and maternal depression.* Paper presented at the Biennial Meetings of the Society for Research in Child Development, Minneapolis, MN.

Harrison, M., & Roush, J. (1996). Age of suspicion, identification, and intervention for infants and young children with hearing loss: A national study. *Early Hearing, 17*, 55–62.

Hauser-Cram, P., Warfield, M.E., Shonkoff, J. P., & Krauss, M. W. (2001). Children with disabilities: A longitudinal study of child development and parent well-being. *Monographs of the Society for Research in Child Development, 66*(3).

Horowitz, F. D. (2000). Child development and the PITS: Simple questions, complex answers, and developmental theory. *Child Development, 71*, 1–10.

Isabella, R. A., & Belsky, J. (1991). Interactional synchrony and the origins of mother-infant attachment: A replication study. *Child Development, 62*, 373–384.

Isabella, R. A., Belsky, J., & von Eye, A. (1989). The origins of infant-mother attachment: An examination of interactional synchrony during the infant's first year. *Developmental Psychology, 25*, 12–21.

Kagan, J. (1983). *Stress, coping and development in children.* New York: McGraw Hill.

Kagan, J. (1997). Temperament and the reactions to unfamiliariy. *Child Development, 68*, 139–143.

Kochanska, G., Coy, K. C., & Murray, K. T. (2001). The development of self-regulation in the first four years of life. *Child Development, 72*, 1091–1111.

Koester, L. S., & Forest, D. S. (1998, April). *Self-recognition responses among deaf and hearing 18-month-old infants.* Poster presented at the International Conference on Infant Studies, Atlanta, GA.

Koester, L. S., & Meadow-Orlans, K. P. (1999). Responses to interactive stress: Infants who are deaf or hearing. *American Annals of the Deaf, 144*, 395–403.

Koester, L. S., & Meadow-Orlans, K. P. (2004). Interactions of hearing mothers and 9-month-old infants: temperament and infant stress. In K. P. Meadow-Orlans, P. E. Spencer, & L. S. Koester (Eds.), *The world of deaf infants: A longitudinal study* (pp. 57–65). New York: Oxford University Press.

Koester, L. S., Traci, M. A., Brooks, L. R., Karkowski, A. M., & Smith-Gray, S. (2004). Mother-infant behaviors at 6 and 9 months: A microanalystic view. In K. P. Meadow-Orlans, P. E. Spencer, & L. S. Koester (Eds.), *The world of deaf infants: A longitudinal study* (pp. 40–56). New York: Oxford University Press.

Lamb, M. E., Ketterlinus, R. D., & Fracasso, M. P. (1992). Parent-child relationships. In M. H. Bornstein & M. E. Lamb (Eds.), *Developmental psychology: An advanced textbook* (pp. 465–518). Hillsdale, NJ: Lawrence Erlbaum Associates.

Langhorst, B., & Fogel, A. (1982, March). *Cross validation of microanalytic approaches to face-to-face play.* Paper presented at International Conference on Infant Studies, Austin, TX.

Lederberg, A. R., & Mobley, C. E. (1990). The effect of hearing impairment on the quality of attachment and mother-toddler interaction. *Child Development, 61*, 1596–1604.

Lederberg, A. R., & Prezbindowski, A. K. (2000). Impact of child deafness on mother-toddler interaction: Strengths and weaknesses. In P. E. Spencer, C. J. Erting, & M. Marschark (Eds.), *The deaf child in the family and at school. Essays in honor of Kathryn P. Meadow-Orlans* (pp. 73–92). Mahwah, NJ: Lawrence Erlbaum Associates.

Lewis, M., & Brooks-Gunn, J. (1979). Toward a theory of social cognition: The development of self. In I. C. Užgiris (Ed.), *Social interaction and communication during infancy: New directions for child development* (pp. 1–19). San Francisco, CA: Jossey-Bass.

Marschark, M. (1993a). Origins and interactions in social, cognitive, and language development of deaf children. In M. Marschark & M. D. Clark (Eds.), *Psychological perspectives on deafness* (pp. 7–26). Mahwah, NJ: Lawrence Erlbaum Associates.

Marschark, M. (1993b). *Psychological development of deaf children.* New York: Oxford University Press.

Marschark, M. (1997). *Raising and educating a deaf child: A comprehensive guide to the choices, controversies, and decisions faced by parents and educators.* New York: Oxford University Press.

Masataka, N. (1992). Motherese in a signed language. *Infant Behavior and Development, 15*, 453–460.

Masataka, N. (1996). Perception of motherese in

signed language by 6-month-old deaf infants. *Developmental Psychology, 32,* 874–879.

Masataka, N. (1998). Perception of motherese in Japanese sign language by 6-month-old hearing infants. *Developmental Psychology, 34,* 241–246.

McCubbin, H. I., & Patterson, J. (1983). Family stress and adaptation to crises: A double ABCX model of family behavior. In H. I. McCubbin, M. Sussman, & J. Patterson (Eds.), *Social stresses and the family: Advances and developments in family stress theory and research* (pp. 7–37). New York: The Hawthorn Press.

Meadow, K. P., Greenberg, M. T., & Erting, C. J. (1983). Attachment behavior of deaf children with deaf parents. *Journal of the American Academy of Child Psychiatry, 22,* 23–28.

Meadow-Orlans, K. P. (2000). Deafness and social change: Ruminations of a retiring researcher. In P. E. Spencer, C. J. Erting, & M. Marschark (Eds.), *The deaf child in the family and at school. Essays in honor of Kathryn P. Meadow-Orlans* (pp. 293–301). Mahwah, NJ: Lawrence Erlbaum Associates.

Meadow-Orlans, K. P., Mertens, D. M., & Sass-Lehrer, M. A. (Eds.) (2003). *Parents and their deaf children: The early years.* Washington, DC: Gallaudet University Press.

Meadow-Orlans, K. P., & Sass-Lehrer, M. (1995). Support services for families with children who are deaf: Challenges for professionals. *Topics in Early Childhood Special Education, 15,* 314–334.

Meadow-Orlans, K. P., & Steinberg, A. (1993). Effects of infant hearing loss and maternal support on mother-infant interactions at 18 months. *Journal of Applied Developmental Psychology, 14,* 407–426.

Miller, C. L. (1988). Parent's perceptions and attributions of infant-vocal behaviour and development. *First Language, 8,* 125–142.

Minnes, P., & Nachsen, J. S. (1997). The Family Stress and Support Questionnaire: Focusing on the needs of parents. *Journal on Developmental Disabilities, 5,* 67–76.

Mundy, P., & Willoughby, J. (1996). Nonverbal communication, joint attention, and early socioemotional development. In M. Lewis & M. W. Sullivan (Eds.), *Emotional development in atypical children* (pp. 65–87). Mahwah, NJ: Lawrence Erlbaum Associates.

Newman, A. J., Bavelier, D., Corina, D., Jezzard, P., & Neville, H. J. (2002). A critical period for right hemisphere recruitment in American Sign Language processing. *Nature Neuroscience, 5,* 76–80.

Newport, E. L. (1990). Maturational constraints on language learning. *Cognitive Science, 14,* 11–28.

Osofsky, J. D., & Thompson, M. D. (2000). Adaptive and maladaptive parenting: Perspectives on risk and protective factors. In J. P. Shonkoff & S. J. Meisels (Eds.), *Handbook of early childhood intervention* (2nd ed., pp. 54–75). New York: Cambridge University Press.

Papoušek, H., & Bornstein, M. H. (1992). Didactic interactions: Intuitive parental support of vocal and verbal development in human infants. In H. Papoušek, U. Jurgens, & M. Papoušek (Eds.), *Nonverbal vocal communication: Comparative and developmental approaches* (pp. 209–229). New York: Cambridge University Press.

Papoušek, H., & Papoušek, M. (1987). Intuitive parenting: A dialectic counterpart to the infant's integrative competence. In J. Osofsky (Ed.), *Handbook of infant development* (2nd ed., pp. 669–720). New York: John Wiley & Sons.

Papoušek, H., & Papoušek, M. (1997). Fragile aspects of early social integration. In L. Murray & P. J. Cooper (Eds.), *Postpartum depression and child development* (pp. 35–52). New York: The Guilford Press.

Papoušek, M., & von Hofacker, N. (1998). Persistent crying in early infancy: A nontrivial condition of risk for the developing mother-infant relationship. *Child: Care, Health, & Development, 24,* 395–424.

Pelchat, D., Ricard, N., Bouchard, J-M., Perreault, M., Saucier, J-F., Berthiaume, M., & Bisson, J. (1999). Adaptation of parents in relation to their 6-month-old infant's type of disability. *Child: Care, Health and Development, 25,* 377–397.

Pipp-Siegel, S., & Biringen, Z. (1998). Assessing the quality of relationships between parents and children: The emotional availability scales. *Volta Review, 100,* (5), 237–249.

Pipp-Siegel, S., Sedey, A. L., & Yoshinaga-Itano, C. (2002). Predictors of parental stress in mothers of young children with hearing loss. *Journal of Deaf Studies and Deaf Education, 7,* 1–17.

Prendergast, S. G., & McCollum, J. A. (1996). Let's talk: The effect of maternal hearing status on interactions with toddlers who are deaf. *American Annals of the Deaf, 141,* 11–18.

Reilly, J. S., & Bellugi, U. (1996). Competition on the face: Affect and language in ASL motherese. *Journal of Child Language, 23,* 219–239.

Rogoff, B. (1990). *Apprenticeship in thinking: Cognitive development in social context.* New York: Oxford University Press.

Sameroff, A. J., & Chandler, M. J. (1975). Reproductive risk and the continuum of caretaking casualty. In F.D. Horowitz, M. Hetherington, S. Scarr-Salapatek, & G. Siegel (Eds.), *Review of child development research* (Vol. 4, pp. 187–244). Chicago: University of Chicago Press.

Sameroff, A. J., & Fiese, B. H. (1990). Transactional regulation and early intervention. In S. J. Meisels & J. P. Shonkoff (Eds.), *Handbook of early childhood intervention* (pp. 119–149). Cambridge: Cambridge University Press.

Spencer, P. E. (1993). Communication behaviors of infants with hearing loss and their hearing mothers. *Journal of Speech and Hearing Research, 36,* 311–321.

Spencer, P. E. (2000). Looking without listening: Is audition a prerequisite for normal development of visual attention during infancy? *Journal of Deaf Studies and Deaf Education, 5,* 291–302.

Spencer, P. E. (2003). Parent-child interaction: Implications for intervention and development. In B. Bodner-Johnson & M. Sass-Lehrer (Eds.), *The young deaf or hard of hearing child: A family-centered approach to early education* (pp. 333–372). Baltimore: Paul Brookes.

Spencer, P. E., & Gutfreund, M. (1990). Directiveness in mother-infant interactions. In D. F. Moores & K. P. Meadow-Orlans (Eds.), *Educational and developmental aspects of deafness* (pp. 350–365). Washington, DC: Gallaudet University Press.

Spradley, T. S., & Spradley, J. P. (1985). *Deaf like me.* Washington, DC: Gallaudet University Press.

Steinberg, A. (2000). Autobiographical narrative on growing up deaf. In P. E. Spencer, C. J. Erting, & M. Marschark, *The deaf child in the family and at school. Essays in honor of Kathryn P. Meadow-Orlans* (pp. 93–108). Mahwah, NJ: Lawrence Erlbaum Associates.

Stern, D. N. (1985). *The interpersonal world of the infant: A view from psychoanalysis and developmental psychology.* New York: Basic Books.

Swisher, M. V. (1992). The role of parents in developing visual turn-taking in their young deaf children. *American Annals of the Deaf, 137,* 92–100.

Swisher, M. V. (2000). Learning to converse: How deaf mothers support the development of attention and conversational skills in their young deaf children. In P. E. Spencer, C. J. Erting, & M. Marschark (Eds.), *The deaf child in the family and at school. Essays in honor of Kathryn P. Meadow-Orlans* (pp. 21–39). Mahwah, NJ: Lawrence Erlbaum Associates.

Thompson, D. C., McPhillips, H., Davis, R. L., Lieu, T. A., Homer, C. J., & Helfand, M. (2001). Universal newborn hearing screening: Summary of evidence. *Journal of the American Medical Association, 286,* 2000–2010.

Tronick, E. Z., & Weinberg, M. K., (1997). Depressed mothers and infants: Failure to form dyadic states of consciousness. In L. Murray & P. J. Cooper (Eds.), *Postpartum depression and child development* (pp. 54–81). New York: Guilford Press.

von Salisch, M. (2001). Children's emotional development: Challenges in their relationships to parents, peers, and friends. *International Journal of Behavioural Development, 25,* 310–319.

Waxman, R. P., & Spencer, P. E. (1997). What mothers do to support infant visual attention: Sensitivities to age and hearing status. *Journal of Deaf Studies and Deaf Education, 2,* 104–114.

Yoshinaga-Itano, C., Sedey, A. L., Coulter, D. K., & Mehl, A. L. (1998). Language of early- and later-identified children with hearing loss. *Pediatrics, 102,* 1161–1171.

15

Irene W. Leigh & Robert Q. Pollard, Jr.

Mental Health and Deaf Adults

Never before has it been so widely recognized that the majority of deaf people are mentally healthy and able to pursue self-actualizing lives. This contrasts with historical perceptions of deaf adults as maladjusted and psychologically unhealthy. Portrayals of the psychological limitations of deaf people permeate earlier deafness literature (Lane, 1999; Pollard, 1993). Given the inaccuracy of previous conceptualizations of a "psychology of the deaf" and the limited familiarity of most psychologists with well-functioning deaf adults, a clear understanding of what constitutes mental health in the deaf population remains elusive.

Part of this difficulty has to do with conceptualizing what mental health is. Although most people would agree that self-esteem and emotional and behavioral functionality are key aspects of mental health, more exact specifications are complicated by variations that arise from differing cultural norms and values as well as social factors such as education, religion, occupation, and socioeconomic status (Aponte & Crouch, 2000; Sue & Sue, 1999).

The concept of mental illness is also rooted in societal norms and perceptions and complicated by diversity. Willson (1999) defines mental illness as "specific behavioral, cognitive, emotional, or bio-logical dysfunction *in the context of* socially constructed norms and values which identify this dysfunction as harmful to the individual in terms of personal distress, individual or interpersonal disability, or increased risk of greater harm or death" (p. 185). For many deaf adults, the term "mental health" tends to be associated not with a desirable aspect of well-being, but with psychological problems, insanity, or mental health services (Steinberg, Loew, & Sullivan, 1999). The importance of fostering mental health does not receive much press in the Deaf community, in part because of the stigma associated with mental health care. Promoting culturally affirmative treatment approaches for deaf persons who have mental illness may help counteract this stigma (Glickman & Harvey, 1996; Leigh, 1999b).

Toward the end of the nineteenth century, as Western society's interest in mental health was taking shape, psychologists became interested in the unique cognitive and social experiences of deaf people. Some viewed deafness as an "experiment of nature" and, absent knowledge of the sophistication of American Sign Language (ASL), they wondered what implications the absence of oral language in deaf adults had for thought, reasoning, and even religious salvation (Pollard, 1993). Others took interest in the education of deaf children, including the development of standardized testing methods that would gauge their intellectual abilities more appropriately.

Foremost among the psychological pioneers in the deafness field in the early 1900s was Rudolf Pintner of Columbia University (Pollard, 1993). Beyond his work with deaf children, Pintner was an early advocate for mental health services for deaf adults, although he, like most psychologists of the time, presumed that hearing loss itself predisposed deaf individuals to psychopathology and intellectual inferiority. Nevertheless, he recommended that educators focus on the assets rather than on the liabilities of deaf people (Pintner, n.d.) and advocated employing deaf individuals in research and service programs that dealt with deaf people.

An undesirable consequence of Pintner's success was the entry of many unqualified psychologists into the deafness field. At the time, the oral education movement was sweeping the United States and Europe (see Lang, this volume), and few psychologists viewed sign language knowledge as requisite for conducting research. Educators of the deaf soon became disillusioned with psychologists and their research because of their conflicting and, at times, incompetent findings (Pollard, 1993). In the mental health field, similar problems emerged from the torrent of mid-twentieth-century research involving psychological testing of deaf adults that painted a skewed and disturbing picture of "the deaf personality" based on invalid instrumentation and inappropriate perceptions of deaf adults as a homogenous group.

This trend began to change with the emergence of five specialized mental health programs for deaf people between 1955 and 1966. The first was Franz Kallman's Mental Health Project for the Deaf at the New York State Psychiatric Institute, initiated at the urging of Boyce Williams, then the highest-ranking deaf individual in the U.S. Department of Education, and Edna Levine, a pioneering psychologist in the deafness field. In rapid succession, similar mental health treatment programs were founded in Washington, DC, Chicago, San Francisco, and England. The advent of these programs was coincident with the publication of the landmark *A Dictionary of American Sign Language on Linguistic Principles* (Stokoe, Casterline, & Croneberg, 1965). Pollard (1993, 1996) speculates that these mental health professionals were familiar with the emerging legitimacy of ASL, which influenced their views and writings about deaf people. In contrast to earlier scholarship, their writings began to stress psychological heterogeneity in the deaf population and examined factors other than hearing loss itself (e.g., the use of sign language or early parent–child interactions) in attempting to understand mental health and mental illness in the deaf population.

As the twentieth century drew to a close, automatically equating deafness with psychopathology became less tenable due to a confluence of factors that helped inform and normalize the deaf experience in the minds of hearing people. These factors included the rapidly expanding body of ASL research, related scholarship on sociology and deaf people, the recognition and acceptance of Deaf culture, the watershed 1988 "Deaf President Now" protest at Gallaudet University, and the passage of the 1990 Americans with Disabilities Act (ADA). Also influential were publications by deaf authors, articulately describing how they functioned normally in society but also were part of a linguistic and sociocultural minority (e.g., Jacobs, 1989; Padden & Humphries, 1988).

This changing view paralleled a trend in the United States toward increased acceptance of cultural and linguistic diversity in the population. Yet, critics such as Davis (1995) and Lane (1999) have argued that the entrenched societal presumption of able-bodied normalcy still casts deafness as a problem, which serves to marginalize and oppress deaf people. The disability rights movement (Shapiro, 1993) is a reaction against such bias and additionally helps to frame deafness as a social difference more than a medical one. Whether from a disability rights perspective or a sociocultural minority perspective, mental health scholarship and treatment programs are increasingly reflecting this perspective of deaf normalcy and diversity (Glickman & Harvey, 1996) and framing communication as a service access issue instead of a psychological problem.

Given that most deaf children are born to hearing parents (Moores, 2001), the process of Deaf enculturation (acquiring ASL fluency and socially identifying with the Deaf community) is quite different from the vertical enculturation (i.e., the passing of language and culture from parent to child) that hearing people experience. Further, one's community identity (e.g., Deaf or Latino) may be distinct from and interactive with individual, contextual identity roles such as father or teacher (Corker, 1995, 1996). Another contribution to heterogeneity is that identification as audiologically deaf may not extend to identification as culturally Deaf, especially for those who have limited exposure to ASL and deaf people (Leigh, 1999a, 1999b). Culturally Deaf individuals "behave as Deaf people do, using the language of Deaf people, and share the beliefs of Deaf people toward themselves" (Padden, 1980, p. 93).

To better understand the relationships between deaf identity development and mental health, researchers have examined the utility of disability identity models (Weinberg & Sterritt, 1986), cultural and racial identity development theories (Glickman, 1996), and acculturation theories based on the immigrant experience (Maxwell-McCaw, 2001). The emerging data suggest that culturally Deaf and bicultural (simultaneously Deaf and "hearing") identity affiliations are associated with higher self-esteem and satisfaction with life (Bat-Chava, 2000; Maxwell-McCaw, 2001) in comparison to the "hearing" identity category (reflecting hearing ways of being). "Marginal" identity (feeling unaffiliated with deaf or hearing people) appears to be the least adaptive. Although this research demonstrates some relationship between deaf identity development and mental health, the heterogeneity of the deaf population must not be overlooked. Whether one is deaf or hearing, psychological and behavioral characteristics emerge from a multiplicity of factors, including biology, ethnicity, religion, education, occupation, social experience, and more. All these factors should impact our conceptualizations of mental health and mental illness in deaf adults and, most importantly, guide continuous improvement in the prevention and treatment of mental illness.

Psychopathology: Incidence and Assessment

Despite nearly a century of investigation, our understanding of the mental health needs and characteristics of the deaf population is limited. Epidemiological studies in deafness and mental health have been narrow in scope. Most estimates of mental illness base-rates and service needs have been based on extrapolation from incidence rates of mental illness and incidence rates of deafness. The

utility of such projections is further limited by the lack of data regarding communication preferences and abilities and how these interact with service accessibility, provider competence, and other important matters.

Using population projections, Dew (1999) suggests that approximately 18,000 deaf and 670,000 hard-of-hearing Americans have psychiatric disabilities. Pollard (1996) cites larger estimates—40,000 deaf and more than 2 million hard-of-hearing Americans with severe mental illness, not counting those with less severe forms of mental illness. The prevalence of mental illness in deaf people appears to be greater than in the general population, based on the relative number of inpatients from each group (Vernon & Daigle-King, 1999). Service access limitations underlie reports that less than 2% of deaf individuals who need mental health treatment receive them, a problem that is particularly acute for deaf individuals from ethnic minority populations (Pollard, 1994, 1996; Trybus, 1983).

Pollard's (1994) study of mental illness diagnostic patterns and service trends in a sample of 544 deaf and hard-of-hearing patients in Rochester, New York, remains among the larger epidemiological studies to date. Similar prevalence rates in deaf and hearing patient samples of schizophrenia and other psychotic disorders, mood disorders, adjustment disorders, anxiety disorders, and personality disorders supported earlier studies (Grinker, 1969; Rainer, Altshuler, Kallman, & Deming, 1963; Robinson, 1978). Data regarding the prevalence of mental retardation and organic mental disorders such as dementia in the deaf population have varied, with some studies finding greater prevalence and some not (Pollard, 1994; Vernon & Andrews, 1990). The comorbidity of many hearing-loss etiologies (e.g., prematurity, rubella, meningitis) with neurological impairment suggests an increased risk for developmental and organic mental disorders in the deaf population. There are reports of an association between hearing loss and dementia in elderly deaf people, perhaps due to a common central nervous system mechanism (Pollard, 1998b).

Pollard (1994) reported a lower incidence of substance use disorders in the Rochester deaf sample but suspects this was an artifact of underreporting due to inadequate diagnostic interviews (i.e., "shock withdrawal paralysis"; Schlesinger & Meadow, 1972), service inaccessibility, or the sociocultural desire to preserve a positive image (Guthman & Blozis, 2001, Guthman, Sandberg, & Dickinson, 1999).

Because linguistically and culturally appropriate services are rarely available, deaf patients who do access mental health care often represent the most severe end of the patient continuum. The frequency of comorbid psychiatric and substance-use disorders is comparatively high in the deaf patient population, as are unemployment, abuse victimization histories, language dysfluency, and legal and other problems, leading to considerable challenges in diagnosis, treatment, and aftercare planning (Burke, Gutman, & Dobosh, 1999; Duffy, 1999; Guthman, Lybarger, & Sandberg, 1993; Merkin & Smith, 1995).

Complicating these challenges is the recognition that most deaf people do not communicate or, at times, do not behave and think in the same ways that hearing people do. The unique visual-gestural modality of manual communication systems, their varied forms (e.g., ASL vs. the many Signed English systems), the structural and production differences between ASL and English, and the behavioral norms of Deaf culture combine to yield different thought worlds between Deaf and hearing people (Dean & Pollard, 2001; Lucas, Bayley, & Valli, 2001). Moreover, limitations in literacy and knowledge base, common in the deaf population, and the greater incidence of nonpsychiatric language dysfluency (i.e., never gaining proficiency in a signed or spoken language) are additional complications that fall outside the experience of the average mental health clinician. Such factors can lead these clinicians to over- or underdiagnose psychopathology when interviewing deaf adults (Kitson & Thacker, 2000; Pollard, 1998b).

The emotive, behavioral nature of sign communication may mask depression to the untrained eye or improperly suggest agitation or mania. Language dysfluency, through writing or interpreted interviews, may improperly suggest psychosis or mental retardation. Subtle signs of psychotic language production may be overlooked because nonsigning clinicians and most interpreters will not have the dual knowledge base in sign language and psychosis to recognize such symptoms. Experiences of discrimination that deaf people may report or demands for legally mandated interpreter services may be misconstrued as paranoia or personality disorder. Clinicians may dismiss depression as a normal consequence of being deaf. In these and other ways, the risk of nonspecialist clinicians improperly assessing deaf adults, even with a competent interpreter present, is high. Pollard (1998b) details conceptual and procedural modifications recommended for clinical interviews with deaf people.

Ultimately, there is no substitute for adequate training in the unique aspects of mental health diagnosis and treatment of deaf patients, which includes sign language fluency and, if the clinician is hearing, other evidence of cross-cultural legitimacy (Pollard, 1996). The reality is that few clinicians possess these qualifications, and insufficient numbers are being trained to fill these specialized roles and meet existing service needs (Pollard, 1996; Raifman & Vernon, 1996a). For the foreseeable future, most deaf patients will be served by nonspecialist clinicians, hopefully working with qualified sign language interpreters as mandated by the ADA.

Yet, too many clinicians assume the presence of an interpreter automatically resolves communication barriers between themselves and deaf patients, believing that interpreters are mirror-like language conduits who simply translate word for word what they say. Many deaf consumers believe this, too. This is a naïve view of the challenges inherent in interpreting work (Dean & Pollard, 2001) and the impact interpreters have on the resulting communication event (Metzger, 1999). The complexity of the interpreter's role is heightened in mental health service settings where the likelihood of patient language dysfluency is greater and its significance for diagnosis and treatment is paramount. The naïve view of the interpreter's role also abdicates what is ideally a shared responsibility for communication, where everyone works to facilitate the interpreter's task of building "a semantic bridge between . . . thought worlds" (Namy, 1977, p. 25).

Additionally complicating this picture is the fact that most interpreters have little experience in psychiatric settings and are unfamiliar with the implications of dysfluent language—whether from psychiatric or nonpsychiatric origins—for the diagnostic process. Other interpreter task demands, including knowledge of clinicians' communication goals, familiarity with mental health service personnel and dynamics, and how the frequently intense emotional and interpersonal dynamics of psychiatric settings, can affect their own thoughts and feelings. All these factors can influence the nature and quality of their translations (Dean & Pollard, 2001; Pollard 1998b). Specialized training for interpreters and clinicians regarding the realities of interpreting challenges in mental health settings will improve the quality of access, diagnosis, and treatment effectiveness. Relevant curricula have been developed (Pollard, 1998a; Veltri & Duffy, 1997).

The skilled (and properly certified) interpreter with training in mental health interpreting can be an invaluable partner to the nonspecialist clinician faced with diagnosing and treating deaf adults. Although it is inappropriate to rely on interpreters for consultation outside their expertise (e.g., specific diagnostic opinions), their input on language, communication, and sociocultural factors that may impact the clinician's work should be sought before and after sessions with deaf patients. In addition, expert consultation from specialists in the deaf mental health field is available from the American Psychological Association and the American Psychiatric Association; both organizations have established special interest groups on deafness (Pollard, 1996). Further information regarding mental health interpreting can be found in Harvey (1989), Pollard (1998a), Stansfield and Veltri (1987), and Turner, Klein, and Kitson (2000).

Psychological Evaluations

In addition to psychodiagnostic information gathered from well-conducted clinical interviews and records, information such as hearing acuity, health and additional disability status (especially vision), language modality and fluency, communication preferences, cultural identity, trauma history, and family, developmental, and educational history all contribute to well-rounded case formulations and effective treatment plans for deaf adults. Psychologists may use cognitive, personality, and neuropsychological tests to yield additional information, although specialized knowledge is necessary, as many are not valid for or normed with deaf adults (Brauer, Braden, Pollard, & Hardy-Braz, 1999; Lane, 1999; Pollard, 1993). Test critiques and recommendations can be found in Blennerhassett (2000) and Ziezulia (1982) (see also Maller, this volume).

Pollard (2002) delineated five factors that determine the appropriateness of psychological tests (or other data gathering tools) for deaf individuals: purpose or goodness of fit to the evaluation question, the way instructions are conveyed, the nature and content of the items or tasks, the response modality, and the scoring methods and norms. The test or data collection tool will be biased if, in any of these five areas, there is evidence that hearing loss, fund of information, limited competency in English, or sensory or sociocultural aspects of life as a deaf or hard-of-hearing individual would play an undesirable role.

Vernon pioneered in the investigation of bias in IQ testing with deaf adults (Vernon & Andrews, 1990; see also Pollard, 1996) Braden (1994) has built upon that work, demonstrating that communication methods during test administration affect IQ scores, with oral and written instructions being particularly problematic. The validity of IQ testing with deaf individuals, including nonverbal or language-free IQ measures, remains a popular topic in the psychological testing field (Braden, 1994; Brauer et al., 1999; Maller, this volume).

The Minnesota Multiphasic Personality Inventory (Butcher, Dahlstrom, Graham, Tellegen, & Kaemmer, 1989) is the most widely used test of personality and psychopathology. To address English reading and item content bias that arises with deaf adult subjects, Brauer (1993) produced an ASL videotaped version, created through a back-translation method designed to assure linguistic equivalence between the original and ASL versions. Further research must determine whether the translated tool is clinically effective (Brauer et al., 1999).

Modifications of paper-and-pencil tests can reduce bias in item content and response modality to varying degrees (Gibson-Harman & Austin, 1985; LaSasso, 1982; Leigh, Robins, Welkowitz, & Bond, 1989). Such measures, however, are appropriate only for those deaf individuals who demonstrate adequate fluency in written English. The Beck Depression Inventory-II (BDI-II) (Beck, Steer, & Brown, 1996), a popular measure for depression with explicit differences between forced-choice response items, requires no modification and appears to be reliable based on a sample of deaf college students (Leigh & Anthony-Tolbert, 2001).

The above-mentioned bias and validity challenges apply to neuropsychological testing as well. Differentiating test findings that are a normal result of hearing loss from those that arise from unrelated neurological dysfunction can be daunting given the complex interactions between deafness etiologies, residual hearing and other sensory abilities, developmental factors, educational history, language, and sociocultural experience (Samar, Parasnis, & Berent, 1998). Few neuropsychological tests are normed with deaf adults, although this may or may not be desirable depending on the specific purpose and nature of the test at hand (Pollard, 2002). The Signed Paired Associates Test (SPAT) (DeMatteo, Pollard, & Lentz, 1987) is a neuropsychological test of learning and memory that was developed and normed specifically for use with deaf adults. It is the only such verbal (i.e., sign language-based) test, supplementing the many nonverbal tests typically used with deaf individuals. The SPAT appears to effectively differentiate between normal and clinical population samples of deaf adults (Rediess, Pollard, & Veyberman, 1997).

Neuropsychological research with stroke patients who are deaf is furthering our understanding of the fundamental nature of sign language and how it is processed in the brain (Poizner, Klima, & Bellugi, 1987). Recent improvements in computerized stimulus delivery and brain imaging techniques are pushing the boundaries of such research. Studies involving deaf and hearing subjects are demonstrating that the neural processing of sensory and language information is differentially mediated as a function of hearing status and degree of familiarity with sign language (Corina, 1998; Wilson, 2001). Functional neuroimaging research will eventually influence neuropsychological test development, test norms, and interpretation.

Advances in computer technology also are yielding psychological test procedures that are beginning to supplant traditional paper-and-pencil tests in assessment batteries. Although computerized tests are advantageous in terms of administration and scoring efficiency and in reduction of variability and error in scoring, their validity has yet to be demonstrated in most cases (Groth-Marnat, 1999). Without adequately demonstrated comparability between traditional and computerized versions of the same test, the applicability of the established body of research on the reliability and validity of the test can be questioned. Digitizing ASL videotapes of instructions and test items and thereby presenting tests via CD-ROM or other high-density media holds great promise for improvement in test reliability and validity over traditional

methods hampered by literacy barriers or variability in researcher or interpreter sign skills. An interactive, computerized, ASL version of the Psychiatric Diagnostic Interview has been developed and piloted (Eckhardt, Steinberg, Lipton, Montoya, & Goldstein, 1999; Steinberg, Lipton, Eckhardt, Goldstein, & Sullivan, 1998). One drawback of videotaped or computerized translations of psychological tests appears to be the greater length of time needed for administration in comparison to written modalities. Yet, the increased accessibility of ASL versions of tests for sign-fluent deaf adults with literacy limitations will be a major boon for clinicians if it can be shown that these approaches are valid when compared to traditional testing and interview methods.

Treatment Approaches

There is a small but slowly growing body of research on psychiatric and psychological treatment approaches for deaf adults, but practically none on medication interventions. Bird and Kitson (2000) stated that psychotropic medications can place deaf patients at risk for a greater degree of side effects depending on the etiology of their hearing loss. For example, those with renal, cardiac, or thyroid dysfunctions secondary to maternal rubella are at heightened risk for side effects from lithium, commonly prescribed to treat bipolar disorder and regulate mood. Such findings underscore the importance of a thorough medical history when evaluating and treating deaf patients.

Proper medication management depends greatly on the patient's ability to provide an accurate medical history, describe current symptoms and health status, and understand the purpose, dosage, side effects, and expected effectiveness of prescribed drugs. The effective exchange of information is commonly impeded by inadequate communication and cross-cultural interaction barriers based on educational, fund of information, literacy, and language-fluency limitations in the deaf psychiatric population (Pollard, 1998a; Steinberg et al., 1999). Harmer (1999) provided a comprehensive review of the problems and complications involved in healthcare delivery with deaf people. To achieve proper informed consent for medication treatment as well as optimal patient compliance, adequate time and communication arrangements should be assured. The addition of psychotherapy and/or case management services to psychopharmacological treatment can facilitate these goals.

It has been repeatedly emphasized that deaf persons can benefit from the full range of individual psychotherapy approaches, including psychoanalysis, humanistic, cognitive-behavioral, and family therapies, behavior modification, and other approaches with the caveat that the therapist must be sensitive to client dynamics, sociocultural aspects of deafness, and communication issues as relevant to each approach (Pollard, 1998b; Sussman & Brauer, 1999). Understanding the nature and dynamics of the ecological system affecting deaf individuals is essential for effective intervention (Harvey, 1989). Unfortunately, the literature on psychotherapy approaches with deaf persons consists primarily of case reports; empirical studies of treatment outcomes or best practices with deaf adults are rare (Pollard, 1998a).

The number of books addressing psychotherapy with deaf and hard-of-hearing persons is increasing (e.g., Corker, 1995; Glickman & Harvey, 1996; Harvey, 1989, 1998, 2001; Leigh, 1999b). The popularity of tailoring psychotherapy approaches to culturally diverse clientele (Sue & Sue, 1999) has influenced recommendations that culturally affirmative psychotherapy be used with deaf individuals, not only in relation to the unique social and linguistic aspects of the Deaf population (Glickman & Harvey, 1996) but also in relation to the impact that ethnicity and culture in the traditional sense (e.g., ancestry, religious heritage) and other diversity characteristics (e.g., sexual orientation) have on diversity and treatment responsivity in the deaf population (Leigh, 1999b). Clinicians therefore must be alert and sensitive to a range of potentially relevant cultural paradigms when working with deaf adults and use relevant sociocultural information, assessment tools, treatment methods, and community resources whatever the psychotherapeutic approach selected.

Group psychotherapy approaches have been used effectively with deaf adults in inpatient and outpatient treatment settings. Although nonverbal group methods such as dance and psychodrama (Robinson, 1978) may be preferred for individuals with severe language limitations, the full range of verbal group therapies also can be effective with most deaf individuals. Kitson, Fernando, and Douglas (2000)observed no difference between matched hearing and deaf groups using analytic psychotherapy within group settings.

Less common psychotherapeutic techniques used with deaf adults include storytelling, culturally appropriate metaphors, pictures and other visual tools, sand and art therapies, and clinical hypnosis; the latter proving effective despite altering the typical closed-eyed procedure developed for hearing subjects (Burke et al., 1999; Higgins & Huet, 2000; Isenberg, 1988; Isenberg & Matthews, 1995; Matthews & Isenberg, 1995; Morrison, 1991; Robinson, 1978).

Although it appears that most traditional and newer forms of psychotherapy can be used with deaf adults who have adequate language skills (in ASL or English), and a variety of nonverbal therapies are effective for deaf adults with language limitations, best practices research linked to specific diagnoses is particularly lacking. A rare exception is Guthman's (1996) study of outcomes for chemically dependent deaf adults enrolled in the Minnesota Chemical Dependency Program for Deaf and Hard of Hearing Individuals. Employment, participation in 12-step programs, and a communicatively accessible support system all significantly increased the chances of maintaining sobriety following inpatient treatment.

Trends in Program Development and Administration

Recognition of the underserved treatment needs of the deaf and hard-of-hearing population continues to spawn new service programs (Morton & Christensen, 2000). The need still far outweighs the availability of linguistically and culturally appropriate care, despite ADA access mandates. Fewer than 3% of providers offer mental health services to deaf people (Raifman & Vernon, 1996a). Most services are provided through interpreters, not directly with ASL-fluent clinicians. Where communicatively accessible mental health programs exist (with interpreters or sign-fluent clinicians), deaf consumers cluster and, in turn, they are underrepresented in programs that serve the general (hearing) population, even though these programs may offer more appropriate or a wider array of services than specialized deaf service programs (Pollard, 1994). If communication accessibility takes precedence over diagnostic or other treatment-specific considerations in making referrals for deaf consumers, such decisions may be discriminatory and ultimately harmful.

Litigation is a powerful method for increasing the availability and quality of mental health services for deaf individuals (Pollard, 1998a). A variety of specific advocacy and legal strategies for increasing service access and specialized care programs have been suggested, including the consent decree which defers protracted, expensive litigation in favor of mediated settlements that result in service system changes and continuing accountability (Katz, Vernon, Penn, & Gillece, 1992; Raifman & Vernon, 1996b). The legal decision in *Tugg v. Towey* (1994) set a particularly stringent standard for mental health service care with deaf individuals. In this Florida U.S. District Court case, the mental health agency in question was ordered to hire sign-fluent, specialist clinicians because providing interpreter services alone, in the court's view, did not meet the equal accessibility to treatment standard of the ADA. This case has not yet led to similar decisions in other states.

The provision of sign language interpreter services remains the primary method through which consumer access is offered in nonspecialized mental health service programs. Although better than no access at all, there is a national shortage of sign language interpreters. Interpreter services are generally limited to urban settings. Few small or private-practice mental health service settings are willing to pay for interpreter services, despite an increasing record of ADA lawsuits favoring deaf plaintiffs. Yet the effort and stress of initiating an ADA lawsuit is prohibitive for the average deaf consumer. As a result, most will turn to the public mental health system, where the availability of interpreter services is limited and the quality of care, with or without interpreter services, is questionable for this specialized population.

Public policy advocacy also has taken the form of model regional and state plans for mental health services to deaf consumers and a standards of care document (Myers, 1995; Pollard, 1995). A few states have recognized the importance of public mental health services for deaf individuals by creating dedicated administrative positions within their offices of mental health. Individuals holding these positions recently formed the Council of State Directors of Mental Health Services for the Deaf, which has been increasingly active in promoting a variety of public mental health service initiatives relevant to deaf adults and children. At the local level, the power that managed care companies have to choose providers for insurance panels is a serious concern when these often-restrictive panels overlook the importance of sign language fluency in evaluating providers or when they unquestioningly accept provider claims of sign language skill when, in fact, the provider's signing skills are very limited.

Telehealth (employing videoconferencing and other distance technologies) is emerging as a powerful new service venue in healthcare. Telehealth offers the potential of a broad array of services to rural areas as well as specialty services to both rural and urban areas. Given the shortage of ASL-proficient clinicians and accessible mental health services for deaf adults, the efficacy of providing specialized consultation and treatment services via videoconferencing is appealing. The state of South Carolina has pioneered telepsychiatry services for deaf adults, demonstrating that these services are both clinically sound and cost-effective (Afrin & Critchfield, 1999). Videoconference technology also is being used to provide sign language interpreter services to remote hospitals and other healthcare settings (Pollard, Miraglia, & Barnett, 2001). Research investigations are needed to determine if psychiatric or interpreter services provided through telehealth technology are as effective as those provided face-to-face (Jerome & Zaylor, 2000).

Training Developments

The increased post-ADA opportunities for deaf adults to pursue degrees in mental health service practice, plus the establishment of accredited graduate programs in clinical psychology, social work, and mental health counseling at Gallaudet University, have produced a surge of specialist clinicians. Many of these new clinicians are deaf. While their classroom training is generally accessible, practicum and internship opportunities are limited, especially when experience with hearing patients is desired—the primary barrier being the cost of interpreter services (Hauser, Maxwell-McCaw, Leigh, & Gutman, 2000). The University of Rochester School of Medicine has established a training program where deaf psychology interns serve hearing patients in both inpatient and outpatient settings, in collaboration with sign language interpreters as necessary, while also serving a caseload of deaf adults (Pollard, 1996). Internationally, however, deaf clinicians are rare (Klein & Kitson, 2000), with only a few scattered throughout Europe. It is essential to increase opportunities for deaf and sign-fluent hearing individuals to enter the mental health field, as well as improve outreach to nonspecialist clinicians regarding the mental health needs of deaf people and relevant sociocultural and linguistic issues.

Summary and Conclusions

In light of the dismal history of mental health portrayals of and services for deaf adults, we are in a relatively enlightened period. The recognition that simplistic frameworks do not sufficiently incorporate the heterogeneity and complexity of the deaf population nor adequately explain how psychopathology is defined, manifested, or treated in this population has fueled a search for paradigms that are inclusive not only of Deaf culture, but of other aspects of diversity such as communication modality, ethnicity, religion, family constellation, education, and myriad other factors that will allow us to develop more appropriate mental health viewpoints and service programs. Although the quality of current mental health services is uneven, a variety of specialized programs can be found throughout the United States and in other countries.

Unfortunately, there are no large research programs in the mental health and deafness field at this time. This has more to do with federal funding changes than progress or motivation in the field. Recent explorations of manifestations of psychopathology impacting ASL linguistic production (Trumbetta, Bonvillian, Siedlecki, & Haskins, 2001) and mechanisms of brain functioning in deaf adults (e.g., Corina, 1998; Emmorey, this volume) suggest that the time is approaching when it will be feasible to institute research projects that address fundamental aspects of brain functioning and psychopathology to the benefit of both deaf and hearing populations.

As we look to the advances of the future, the unsatisfactory present state of mental health services for deaf adults cannot be ignored. Reluctance to fund mandated interpreter services or establish more specialized programs for deaf individuals remains a widespread problem. Service expansion driven by litigation will continue to dominate program enhancements that arise from public policy planning, as important and hopeful as that avenue is now. Regardless, the long-term economic benefit of keeping people mentally healthy as opposed to neglecting their mental health needs should serve as justification for services, thereby sustaining the well-being of all of our nation's inhabitants.

References

Afrin, J., & Critchfield, B. (1999). Telepsychiatry for the deaf in South Carolina: Maximizing limited resources. In B. Brauer, A. Marcus, & D. Morton (Eds.), *Proceedings of the First World Conference on Mental Health and Deafness* (p. 27). Vienna, VA: Potiron Press.

Americans with Disabilities Act of 1990, 42 U.S.C.A. & 12101 *et seq.* (West, 1993).

Aponte, J., & Crouch, R. (2000). The changing ethnic profile of the United States in the twenty-first century. In J. Aponte & J. Wohl (Eds.), *Psychological intervention and cultural diversity* (2nd ed., pp. 1–17). Needham Heights, MA: Allyn & Bacon.

Bat-Chava, Y. (2000). Diversity of deaf identities. *American Annals of the Deaf, 145,* 420–428.

Beck, A.T., Steer, R.A., & Brown, G.K. (1996). *BDI-II: Beck Depression Inventory, 2nd Edition Manual.* San Antonio, TX: The Psychological Corporation.

Bird, J., & Kitson, N. (2000). Drug treatments. In P. Hindley & N. Kitson (Eds.), *Mental health and deafness* (pp. 400–413). London: Whurr.

Blennerhassett, L. (2000). Psychological assessments. In P. Hindley & N. Kitson (Eds.), *Mental health and deafness* (pp. 185–205). London: Whurr.

Braden, J. (1994). *Deafness, deprivation, and IQ.* New York: Plenum Press.

Brauer, B. (1993). Adequacy of a translation of the MMPI into American Sign Language for use with deaf individuals: Linguistic equivalency issues. *Rehabilitation Psychology, 38* 247–260.

Brauer, B., Braden, J., Pollard, R., & Hardy-Braz, S. (1999). Deaf and hard of hearing people. In J. Sandoval, C. Frisby, K. Geisinger, J. Scheuneman, & J. Grenier (Eds.), *Test interpretation and diversity* (pp. 297–315). Washington, DC: American Psychological Association.

Burke, F., Gutman, V., & Dobosh, P. (1999). Treatment of survivors of sexual abuse: A process of healing. In I.W. Leigh (Ed.), *Psychotherapy with deaf clients from diverse groups* (pp. 279–305). Washington, DC: Gallaudet University Press.

Butcher, J., Dahlstrom, W., Graham, J., Tellegen, A.,

& Kaemmer, B. (1989). *Minnesota Multiphasic Personality Inventory-2 (MMPI-2): Manual for administration and scoring*. Minneapolis: University of Minnesota Press.

Corina, D.P. (1998). Studies of neural processing in deaf signers: Toward a neurocognitive model of language processing in the deaf. *Journal of Deaf Studies and Deaf Education, 3*, 35–48.

Corker, M. (1995). *Counselling: The deaf challenge*. London: Jessica Kingsley.

Corker, M. (1996). *Deaf transitions*. London: Jessica Kingsley.

Davis, L. (1995). *Enforcing normalcy: Disability, deafness, and the body*. London: Versace.

Dean, R. K., & Pollard, R. Q. (2001). The application of demand-control theory to sign language interpreting: Implications for stress and interpreter training. *Journal of Deaf Studies and Deaf Education, 6*(1), 1–14.

DeMatteo, A. J., Pollard, R. Q., & Lentz, E. M. (1987, May). *Assessment of linguistic functions in brain-impaired and brain-intact prelingually deaf users of American Sign Language: A preliminary report*. Paper presented at the biennial meeting of the American Deafness and Rehabilitation Association, Minneapolis, MN.

Dew, D. (Ed.). (1999). *Serving individuals who are low-functioning deaf: Report from the study group, 25th Institute on Rehabilitation Issues*. Washington, DC: The George Washington University, Regional Rehabilitation Continuing Education Program.

Duffy, K. (1999). Clinical case management with traditionally underserved deaf adults. In I.W. Leigh (Ed.), *Psychotherapy with deaf clients from diverse groups* (pp. 329–347). Washington, DC: Gallaudet University Press.

Eckhardt, E., Steinberg, A., Lipton, D., Montoya, L., & Goldstein, M. (1999). Innovative directions in mental health assessment: Use of interactive video technology in assessment: A research project. *JADARA, 33*, 20–30.

Gibson-Harman, K., & Austin, G.F. (1985). A revised form of the Tennessee Self Concept Scale for use with deaf and hard of hearing persons. *American Annals of the Deaf, 130* 218–225.

Glickman, N. (1996). The development of culturally deaf identities. In N. Glickman & M. Harvey (Eds.), *Culturally affirmative psychotherapy with Deaf persons* (pp. 115–153). Mahwah, NJ: Lawrence Erlbaum Associates.

Glickman, N., & Harvey, M. (Eds.). (1996). *Culturally affirmative psychotherapy with deaf persons*. Mahwah, NJ: Lawrence Erlbaum Associates.

Grinker, R. (1969). *Psychiatric diagnosis, therapy, and research on the psychotic deaf, Final report* (grant no. RD2407-S). Washington, DC: Department of Health, Education and Welfare.

Groth-Marnat, G. (1999). *Handbook of psychological assessment* (3rd ed.). New York: John Wiley & Sons.

Guthman, D. (1996). An analysis of variables that impact treatment outcomes of chemically dependent deaf and hard of hearing individuals. (Doctoral dissertation, University of Minnesota, 1996). *Dissertation Abstracts International, 56* (7A), 2638.

Guthman, D., & Blozis, S. (2001). Unique issues faced by deaf individuals entering substance abuse treatment and following discharge. *American Annals of the Deaf, 146* 294–304.

Guthman, D., Lybarger, R., & Sandberg, K. (1993). Providing chemical dependency treatment to the deaf or hard of hearing mentally ill client. *JADARA, 27*, 1–15.

Guthman, D., Sandberg, K., & Dickinson, J. (1999). Chemical dependency: An application of a treatment model for deaf people. In I.W. Leigh (Ed.), *Psychotherapy with deaf clients from diverse groups* (pp. 349–371). Washington, DC: Gallaudet University Press.

Harmer, L. M. (1999). Healthcare delivery and deaf people: A review of the literature and recommendations for change. *Journal of Deaf Studies and Deaf Education, 4*(2), 73–110.

Harvey, M. (1989). *Psychotherapy with deaf and hard of hearing persons: A systemic model*. Hillsdale, NJ: Lawrence Erlbaum Associates.

Harvey, M. (1998). *Odyssey of hearing loss: Tales of triumph*. San Diego, CA: DawnSign Press.

Harvey, M. (2001). *Listen with the heart: Relationships and hearing loss*. San Diego, CA: DawnSign Press.

Hauser, P., Maxwell-McCaw, D., Leigh, I.W., & Gutman, V. (2000). Internship accessibility issues for deaf and hard of hearing applicants: No cause for complacency. *Professional Psychology: Research and Practice, 31*, 569–574.

Higgens, L., & Huet, V. (2000). Psychodynamic therapies: Part 2, Arts therapies. In P. Hindley & N. Kitson (Eds.), *Mental health and deafness* (pp. 357–360). London: Whurr.

Isenberg, G. (1988). The therapeutic possibilities of Eriksonian hypnosis and guided fantasy with deaf clients. In D. Watson, G. Long, M. Taff-Watson, & M. Harvey (Eds.). *Two decades of excellence, 1967–1987: A foundation for the future* (Monograph No. 14, pp. 78–82). Little Rock, AR: American Deafness and Rehabilitation Association.

Isenberg, G. & Matthews, W. (1995). Hypnosis with signing deaf and hearing subjects. *American Journal of Clinical Hypnosis, 38*, 27–38.

Jacobs, L. M. (1989). *A deaf adult speaks out* (3rd ed.). Washington, DC: Gallaudet University Press.

Jerome, L., & Zaylor, C. (2000). Cyberspace: Creating a therapeutic environment for telehealth applications. *Professional Psychology: Research and Practice, 31*, 478–483.

Katz, D., Vernon, M., Penn, A., & Gillece, J. (1992). The consent decree: A means of obtaining mental health services for patients who are deaf. *JADARA, 26*, 22–28.

Kitson, N., Fernando, J., & Douglas, J. (2000). Psychodynamic therapies: Part 1, Psychotherapy. In P. Hindley & N. Kitson (Eds.), *Mental health and deafness* (pp. 337–356). London: Whurr.

Kitson, N., & Thacker, A. (2000). Adult psychiatry. In P. Hindley & N. Kitson (Eds.), *Mental health and deafness* (pp. 75–98). London: Whurr.

Klein, H., & Kitson, N. (2000). Mental health workers: Deaf-hearing partnerships. In P. Hindley & N. Kitson (Eds.), *Mental health and deafness* (pp. 285–296). London: Whurr.

Lane, H. (1999). *The mask of benevolence: Disabling the Deaf community.* San Diego, CA: DawnSign Press.

LaSasso, C. (1982). An examination of assumptions underlying the rewriting of materials for hearing-impaired students. *Volta Review, 84*, 163–165.

Leigh, I.W. (1999a). Inclusive education and personal development. *Journal of Deaf Studies and Deaf Education, 4*, 236–245.

Leigh, I.W. (Ed.). (1999b). *Psychotherapy with deaf clients from diverse groups.* Washington, DC: Gallaudet University Press.

Leigh, I.W., & Anthony-Tolbert, S. (2001). Reliability of the BDI-II with deaf persons. *Rehabilitation Psychology, 46*, 195–202.

Leigh, I.W., Robins, C., Welkowitz, J., & Bond, R. (1989). Toward greater understanding of depression in deaf individuals. *American Annals of the Deaf, 134*, 249–254.

Linehan, M. (1993). *Skills training manual for treating borderline personality disorder.* New York: Guilford Press.

Lucas, C., Bayley, R., & Valli, C. (2001). *Sociolinguistic variation in American Sign Language.* Washington, DC: Gallaudet University Press.

Matthews, W., & Isenberg, G. (1995). A comparison of the hypnotic experience between signing deaf and hearing participants. *International Journal of Clinical & Experimental Hypnosis, 43*, 375–385.

Maxwell-McCaw, D. (2001). Acculturation and psychological well-being in deaf and hard-of-hearing people (doctoral dissertation, George Washington University, 2001). *Dissertation Abstracts International, 61*(11-B), 6141.

Merkin, L., & Smith, M. (1995). A community-based model providing services for deaf and deaf-blind victims of sexual assault and domestic violence. Sexuality and deafness. *Sexuality and Disability, 13*, 97–106.

Metzger, M. (1999). *Sign language interpreting: Deconstructing the myth of neutrality.* Washington, DC: Gallaudet University Press.

Moores, D.F. (2001). *Educating the deaf: Psychology, principles, and practices.* Boston: Houghton Mifflin.

Morrison, F. (1991). Using Eriksonian hypnotherapy with deaf people. In D. Watson & M. Taff-Watson (Eds.), *At the crossroads: A celebration of diversity,* Monograph No. 15, pp. 313–321. Little Rock, AR: American Deafness and Rehabilitation Association.

Morton, D., & Christensen, J.N. (2000). *Mental health services for deaf people: A resource directory.* Washington, DC: Department of Counseling, Gallaudet University.

Myers, R. R. (1995). *Standards of care for the delivery of mental health services to deaf and hard of hearing persons.* Silver Spring, MD: National Association of the Deaf.

Namy, C. (1977). Reflections on the training of simultaneous interpreters: A metalinguistic approach. In D. Gerver & H.W. Sinaiko (Eds.), *Language interpreting and communication.* New York: Plenum.

Padden, C. (1980). The Deaf community and the culture of Deaf people. In C. Baker & R. Battison (Eds.), *Sign language and the Deaf community* (pp. 89–103). Silver Spring, MD: National Association of the Deaf

Padden, C., & Humphries, T. (1988). *Deaf in America: Voices from a culture.* Cambridge, MA: Harvard University Press.

Pintner, R. (n.d.). *Contributions of psychological testing to the problems of the deaf.* New York: Columbia University Teachers College.

Poizner, H., Klima, E. S., & Bellugi, U. (1987). *What the hands reveal about the brain.* Cambridge, MA: Bradford Books/MIT Press.

Pollard, R. (1993). 100 years in psychology and deafness: A centennial retrospective. *JADARA, 26*, 32–46.

Pollard, R. (1994). Public mental health service and diagnostic trends regarding individuals who are deaf or hard of hearing. *Rehabilitation Psychology, 39*, 147–160.

Pollard, R. (1995). *Mental health services and the deaf population: A regional consensus planning approach* [Special issue]. *JADARA, 28* 1–47.

Pollard, R. (1996). Professional psychology and deaf people: The emergence of a discipline. *American Psychologist, 51*, 389–396.

Pollard, R. Q. (1998a). *Mental health interpreting: A mentored curriculum.* Rochester, NY: University of Rochester

Pollard, R. (1998b). *Psychopathology.* In M. Marschark & M. D. Clark (Eds.), *Psychological perspectives on deafness* (pp. 171–197). Mahwah, NJ: Lawrence Erlbaum Associates.

Pollard, R. (2002). Ethical conduct in research involving deaf people. In V. Gutman (Ed.), *Ethics in mental health and deafness* (pp. 162–178). Washington, DC: Gallaudet University Press.

Pollard, R. Q, Miraglia, K., & Barnett, S. (2001, August). *The videoconference interpreting project* Lecture presented at the biennial meeting of the Registry of Interpreters for the Deaf, Orlando, FL.

Raifman, L., & Vernon, M. (1996a). Important implications for psychologists of the Americans with Disabilities Act: Case in point, the patient who is deaf. *Professional Psychology: Research and Practice, 27,* 372–377.

Raifman, L., & Vernon, M. (1996b). New rights for deaf patients: New responsibilities for mental hospitals. *Psychiatric Quarterly, 67,* 209–219.

Rainer, J., Altshuler, K., Kallman, F., & Deming, W.E. (Eds.). (1963). *Family and mental health problems in a deaf population.* New York: New York State Psychiatric Institute, Columbia University.

Rediess, S., Pollard, R. Q., & Veyberman, B. (1997, February). *Assessment of verbal (ASL-based) memory in deaf adults: Clinical utility of the Signed Paired Associates Test.* Paper presented at the annual meeting of the International Neuropsychological Society, Orlando, FL.

Robinson, L. (1978). *Sound minds in a soundless world.* Washington, DC: U.S. Department of Health, Education and Welfare.

Samar, V., Parasnis, I., & Berent, G. (1998). Learning disabilities, attention deficit disorders, and deafness. In M. Marschark & M. D. Clark (Eds.), *Psychological perspectives on deafness* (pp. 199–242). Mahwah, NJ: Lawrence Erlbaum Associates.

Schlesinger, H. S., & Meadow, K. P. (1972). *Sound and sign: Childhood deafness and mental health.* Berkeley, CA: University of California Press.

Shapiro, J. P. (1993). *No pity: People with disabilities forging a new civil rights movement.* New York: Times Books.

Stansfield, M., & Veltri, D. (1987). Assessment from the perspective of the sign language interpreter. In H. Elliott, L. Glass, & J. W. Evans (Eds.), *Mental health assessment of deaf clients* (pp. 153–163). Boston: Little, Brown.

Steinberg, A. G., Lipton, D. S., Eckhardt, E. A., Gold-stein, M., & Sullivan, V. J. (1998). The Diagnostic Interview Schedule for Deaf patients on interactive video: A preliminary investigation. *American Journal of Psychiatry, 155,* 1603–1604.

Steinberg, A., Loew, R., & Sullivan, V. J. (1999). The diversity of consumer knowledge, attitudes, beliefs, and experiences: Recent findings. In I.W. Leigh (Ed.), *Psychotherapy with deaf clients from diverse groups* (pp. 23–43). Washington, DC: Gallaudet University Press.

Stokoe, W. C., Casterline, D. C., & Croneberg, C. G. (1976). *A dictionary of American Sign Language on linguistic principles* (rev. ed.). Silver Spring, MD: Linstok Press.

Sue, D. W., & Sue, D. (1999). *Counseling the culturally different* (3rd ed). New York: John Wiley & Sons.

Sussman, A., & Brauer, B. (1999). On being a psychotherapist with deaf clients. In I.W. Leigh (Ed.), *Psychotherapy with deaf clients from diverse groups* (pp. 3–22). Washington, DC: Gallaudet University Press.

Trumbetta, S., Bonvillian, J., Siedlecki, T., & Haskins, B. (2001). Language-related symptoms in persons with schizophrenia and how deaf persons may manifest these symptoms. *Sign Language Studies, 1* 228–253.

Trybus, R. (1983). Hearing-impaired patients in public psychiatric hospitals throughout the United States. In D. Watson & B. Heller (Eds.), *Mental health and deafness: Strategic perspectives* (pp. 1–19). Silver Spring, MD: American Deafness and Rehabilitation Association.

Tugg v. Towey, No. 94-1063, 5 Nat'l Disability Law Rep. 999-1005 (July 19, 1994).

Turner, J., Klein, H., & Kitson, N. (2000). Interpreters in mental health settings. In P. Hindley & N. Kitson (Eds.), *Mental health and deafness* (pp. 297–310). London: Whurr.

Veltri, D., & Duffy, K. (1997). *Interpreting in mental health settings.* Portland, OR: Sign Enhancers, Inc.

Vernon, M., & Andrews, J. (1990). *The psychology of deafness.* New York: Longman.

Vernon, M., & Daigle-King, B. (1999). Historical overview of inpatient care of mental patients who are deaf. *American Annals of the Deaf, 144,* 51–61.

Weinberg, N., & Sterritt, M. (1986). Disability and identity: A study of identity patterns in adolescents with hearing impairments. *Rehabilitation Psychology, 31,* 95–102.

Willson, K. (1999). Mental illness. In J. Mio, J. Trimble, P. Arredondo, H. Cheatham, & D. Sue (Eds.), *Key words in multicultural interventions: A dictionary* (pp. 184–185). Westport, CT: Greenwood Press.

Wilson, M. (2001). The impact of sign language expertise on visual perception. In M. Clark, M. Marschark, & M. Karchmer (Eds.), *Context, cognition, and deafness* (pp. 38–48). Washington, DC: Gallaudet University Press.

Zieziula, F. R. (Ed.). (1982). *Assessment of hearing-impaired people: A guide for selecting psychological, educational, and vocational tests.* Washington, DC: Gallaudet College Press.

IV

Language and Language Development

16 Brenda Schick

The Development of American Sign Language and Manually Coded English Systems

Since the acquisition of American Sign Language (ASL) was first investigated, researchers have concluded that its development parallels that of spoken languages (Newport & Meier, 1985; Schlesinger & Meadow, 1972). The primary purpose of this chapter is to present an overview of the development of ASL, mostly in deaf children acquiring it as a first language from their deaf parents. However, such children comprise only about 5–10% of the population of deaf children. The majority of deaf children have hearing parents, and most of these parents are unfamiliar with sign language until their children's hearing loss is identified (Marschark, Lang, & Albertini, 2002). It is deaf children of deaf parents (DOD) who can provide a picture of typical development of a visual language without confounding factors, such as the quality of sign input received.

Deaf children of hearing parents (DOH) are rarely exposed to ASL as a first language. Although a small percentage participate in bilingual ASL/English programs, if exposed to sign, most are exposed to sign systems designed to represent English. These systems often borrow lexical signs from ASL, but grammatical structures and often sign meanings follow English. These invented systems include signs created to represent the inflectional and derivational morphology of English (e.g., progressive,—ing; prefix, pre-). As a group, sign systems are often referred to as manually coded English, or MCE (Bornstein, 1990). However, teachers and programs differ in how faithfully they represent English via a sign system because of philosophical reasons and less than fluent signing skills. A secondary purpose of this chapter is to provide an overview of the development of English using these sign systems.

Phonological Development

Manual Babbling

The onset of babbling marks one of the earliest stages of linguistic development. Vocal babbling consists of phonological productions that are meaningless but conform to broad rules for syllable structure (Oller, Wieman, Doyle, & Ross, 1976). Babbling is considered to be a milestone in prelinguistic spoken language development because it shows that infants are learning the sound patterns of the ambient language. Both deaf and hearing children learning ASL also appear to produce meaningless manual gestures before their first words, from ages 6 to 14 months, described as manual babbles (Meier & Willerman, 1995; Petitto & Marentette, 1991). Their structural characteristics resemble vocal babbling in some respects; they are rhythmic, syllabically organized, and share phonological properties of handshape, location, and movement with adult ASL. Petitto and Marentette (1991) report that 40–70% of deaf infants' manual activity can be categorized as manual babbling. They also observe that, between 12 and 14 months, deaf children's babbling "maintained the rhythm and duration of rudimentary ASL sentences and were similar to hearing infants' use of stress and intonation in vocal jargon babbling" (Petitto & Marentette, 1991, p. 251).

Hearing children who have not been exposed to ASL also produce manual gestures, and there is disagreement about whether this behavior resembles manual babbling in deaf infants. Petitto and colleagues (Petitto, Holowka, Sergio, & Ostry, 2001; Petitto & Marentette, 1991) reported that manual gestures produced by children not exposed to sign differ in fundamental aspects from manual babbling in sign-exposed infants, particularly in rhythmic characteristics. They concluded that manual babbling is not simply a function of general motor development. In contrast, Meier and Willerman (1995) argued that there are few differences in the manual babbling produced by sign-exposed and speech-exposed infants. They believe that babble-like gestures in infants not exposed to sign occur because of structural similarities between speech and sign. They state that "rhythmical organization of speech may trigger rhythmically organized gestures" (p. 407). With this, the visual feedback that hearing children receive from their own gesturing and their exposure to gestures from nonsigning adults encourages production of manual gestures resembling those of deaf children.

Emergent Phonological Development

Like children acquiring spoken language, children learning ASL develop manual articulation skills over time. Most developmental studies have focused on the parameters of handshape, location, and movement (Bonvillian & Siedlecki, 1996; Conlin, Mirus, Mauk, & Meier, 2000; Marentette & Mayberry, 2000; Siedlecki & Bonvillian, 1997). Results confirm that articulatory errors are common in early sign production: some handshapes, loca-

tions, and movements are acquired earlier than others.

A relatively small set of handshapes consistently appears in babble and early sign productions and accounts for a large proportion of the handshapes that children use, both correctly and incorrectly in "substitutions" (Conlin et al., 2000; Marentette & Mayberry, 2000; McIntire, 1977; Siedlecki & Bonvillian 1997). For example, eight handshapes accounted for 84% of the productions of three deaf children at 7–17 months: A, C, S, 5 (including lax), bent 5, baby O, and G (Conlin et al., 2000). Incorrectly formed handshapes were usually motorically less complex than the target handshapes. This supports a model in which motor development is the primary determinant of handshape acquisition (Boyes-Braem, 1990).

Similarly, children use a relatively small set of locations in early sign productions. Face, head, and neutral space are the most common locations in the productions of children younger than 18 months of age, constituting as much as 85% of the locations they use (Bonvillian & Siedlecki, 1996; Conlin et al., 2000). Children appear to produce the location parameter more accurately and with less variability than they do handshape and movement (Conlin et al., 2000; Marentette & Mayberry, 2000; Siedlecki & Bonvillian, 1993, 1997). For example, Conlin et al. (2000) reported that the location parameter was produced incorrectly only 12% of the time, compared with 75% for handshape and 46% for movement.

Some evidence indicates that children rely on a relatively small set of movement parameters. Regarding the errors in movement, Meier (2000) reported that children often replace a movement in the distal articulators, such as the hand or wrist, with a movement in the more proximal articulators, such as the shoulder or torso. For example, a deaf child (15 months) produced the sign KITE, which requires a twisting movement in the forearm, with a twisting movement of the torso (Marentette & Mayberry, 2000). Meier (2000) argued that the use of proximal for more distal articulators reflects general principles in human motor development rather than linguistic principles.

Although gross and fine motor abilities may partially account for the order of ASL phonological development, linguistic and perceptual factors may also play a role. Marentette and Mayberry (2000) argued that some of a hearing child's handshape errors (12–25 months) were due to the child's emerging phonological organization and that motoric factors alone could not account for the developmental patterns. Perceptual salience may also be important, especially as related to development of location parameters on the face: signs near or around the face are produced more accurately, perhaps because they are within a child's central vision (Conlin et al., 2000; Marentette & Mayberry, 2000; Meier, 2000).

Lexical Development

Emergence of First Signs

Some early reports on ASL development suggested that children's first signs occurred earlier than hearing children's spoken words (Bonvillian, Orlansky, & Novack, 1983; Folven & Bonvillian, 1991; Petitto, 1990). Analyses of 20 children (mostly hearing children of deaf parents) indicated that first recognizable signs occurred at 8 months, compared with 12–13 months when most hearing children's first spoken words appear. In a more recent study of DOD children, parents reported that they observed expressive signing at 8 and 10 months (Anderson & Reilly, 2002). A developmental advantage for signs over spoken words would indicate that children are cognitively ready for word learning before 12 months but that differential development of motor control for sign and speech articulators impacts the expression of lexical knowledge. However, there are other reports that show few differences in the timing of first words between sign and speech (Caselli & Volterra, 1990; Petitto, 1988; Volterra, 1981). As Anderson and Reilly (2002) point out, hearing children have an average of 10 communicative gestures at 8 months, and it is difficult to know from available data how the earliest ASL signs compare with those gestures. Meier and Newport (1990) conclude that while there could be an early advantage for learning sign language through the one word stage, there is no indication that such an advantage extends to later developmental milestones.

Early Lexical Development

Few differences have been found between the acquisition of vocabulary in ASL and spoken languages. For example, data from 69 DOD children on an ASL version of the MacArthur Communication Development Inventory, a parent report checklist for early language development (Fenson, Dale, Reznick, Bates, Thal, & Pethick 1994), showed that vocabulary development relates to age, as is true with children learning spoken languages (Anderson & Reilly, 2002). At 12–17 months of age, productive vocabularies of DOD children were larger than those reported for hearing children, but by 18–23 months, median scores and ranges were comparable for ASL and English.

Content of the early ASL lexicon is also similar to that of English, with both having a preponderance of nouns (Anderson & Reilly, 2002; Bonvillian et al., 1983; Folven & Bonvillian 1991). In addition, Anderson and Reilly (2002) reported that the emergence of question signs (e.g., WHERE, WHAT), emotion signs, and cognitive verbs (e.g., WANT, LIKE, THINK) is similar to that of English. However, the percentage of predicates in ASL vocabularies is higher than that for children learning English, which may reflect grammatical differences between ASL and English. In contrast with reports of children acquiring spoken English, Anderson and Reilly found no evidence for a vocabulary burst (or acceleration) in a subset of the DOD children. Their vocabulary growth was steady and strikingly linear. However, it is possible that sample size and sampling intervals affected the results.

Points, Simple Sentences, and Pronouns

Early Gestures and Pointing

Gestures are a means for children to express communicative intention prior to the onset of language (Bates, Benigni, Bretherton, Camaioni, & Volterra, 1979; Fenson et al., 1994). For both deaf and hearing children, reaching, grasping, and pointing behaviors emerge at around 6–10 months, before they produce their first words (Bates, Camaioni, & Volterra, 1975; Butterworth & Morissette, 1996; Folven & Bonvillian, 1991; Petitto, 1987). For children learning ASL, the average age of emergence of communicative pointing (11 months) is earlier than the age of first referential signs (Folven & Bonvillian, 1991).

Early Sentences in ASL

One of the first milestones in grammatical development is the emergence of word combinations in a child's language. Children learning ASL begin combining pointing gestures with signs very early. Deaf parents have reported that their hearing children who are learning ASL produce signs combined with a point by about 12 months (Folven & Bonvillian, 1991; Pizzuto, 1990). The linguistic status of these early points is unclear, and they may be best considered as deictic gestures. For example, a child might point to a cookie and speak or sign "cookie." For the child who produces spoken English, the point is considered a gesture. But for the child learning ASL, because points are considered linguistic in the adult system, it is tempting to consider the child's points as linguistic. So although children produce sign and point combinations very early, it is doubtful that they should be considered true multiword combinations.

Multiword combinations of two lexical signs appear later, at about 16–18 months of age (Bonvillian et al., 1983; Folven & Bonvillian 1991; Pizzuto, 1990), as is typical for hearing children learning spoken English (Fenson et al., 1994). For ASL, as for spoken English, the types of meaning expressed in children's earliest word combinations include existence, action, and location concepts (Newport & Ashbrook, 1977).

Although the syntax of ASL has been described as having an underlying subject-verb-object word order (SVO), similar to English, ASL has many grammatical devices for altering word order so that what is actually produced is not in SVO order. It has been suggested that children learning ASL show a preference for SVO order, perhaps because alternate orders require complex morphology that they have not yet acquired (Newport & Meier, 1985). However, children learning ASL seem to be sensitive to the varieties of word orders in the adult language in that they often produce sentences with word orders other than SVO (Pichler, 2001; Schick, 2002). This may indicate awareness that word order reflects pragmatic influences, as is true in adult ASL.

Pronouns

Although there is a similarity in form between gestural points and pronominal points, the acquisition of pronouns does not appear to occur earlier in ASL than in spoken languages. Points referring to people, thus serving as personal pronouns, do not emerge until about 17–20 months of age (Petitto, 1987; Pizzuto, 1990). Both Petitto and Pizzuto found that the first pronoun to be used by children was ME (about 20 months), followed by YOU (22–24 months); with pronouns for SHE/HE the latest to emerge (24 months). Like hearing children, young deaf children have been observed to make pronoun reversal errors, such as signing YOU when they meant ME, and to use proper names or nouns rather than a pronoun (Petitto, 1987).

Morphological Development

Verb Agreement

One of the earliest morphological systems to emerge in ASL is verb agreement or directionality, in which the beginning and/or endpoint of a sign is altered to represent an argument of the verb. The verb agreement system interacts with the pronominal system in that the verb may reference a previously established pronominal loci. Spatial loci for nominals may refer to a person or object that is present in the environment, or they may be more abstract, in which a spatial loci represents a nominal that is not actually present (Emmorey, 2002; Fischer & van der Hulst, this volume).

Children learning ASL appear to use some form of directionality in their earliest gestures. Casey (1999) found that the gestures of four children contained agreement-like references to objects as early as 12 months of age. Casey concluded that verb agreement may have its roots in children's early gestures.

Studies of a few children have shown that use of verb agreement with lexical verbs emerges relatively early, ages 2–2;6. During this time, children produce verb agreement for a limited range of verbs and do not generalize the morphology to all verbs that require it (Casey, 1999; Hoffmeister, 1977; Meier, 1982). By about 3;6 years, children consistently produce verb agreement when talking about referents that are present in the environment (Hoffmeister, 1977; Meier, 1982). Even though children appear to understand the concept of an abstract pronominal reference by around age 3 (Casey, 2000; Lillo-Martin, Bellugi, Struxness, & O'Grady,

1985), the use of verb agreement with absent referents does not develop until around age 5.

Children have more difficulty with verb agreement morphology when two arguments are marked, such as the subject and the object versus when a single argument is marked. They are also more likely to mark the dative argument rather than the object in double argument verbs, as shown with children ages 3;1 to 7;0 (Meier, 1982). For example, in the sentence "He gave the hat to her," children were more likely to omit the agent agreement marker for "he" than the dative agreement for "her."

There are differing accounts to explain the development of verb agreement morphology. Meier (1982) argues that children learn verb agreement by inducing the morphological rules and that inherent spatial iconicity does not appear to facilitate development. In contrast, Casey (1999) believes that the use of verb agreement has gestural origins that become grammaticalized during acquisition and are evident in the child's earliest productions.

Development of Classifiers

An interesting aspect of adult ASL is the pervasive use of morphologically complex forms, typically termed classifiers (Schembri, 2002). These forms can be quite complex, with numerous components combined into a single predicate, or series of predicates, and they are quite productive, often being used for word formation (Klima & Bellugi, 1979; Schick, 1990a). Accounts differ on the specific types of classifiers that exist in ASL, but most descriptions include handle, entity, and SASS forms (Schembri, 2002; Schick, 1990a; Supalla, 1986). Handle forms generally refer to classifiers in which the hand is manipulating an object (e.g., BASEBALL, GOLF, DIG) or, in some descriptions, representing an object (e.g., SCISSORS, COMB-HAIR). Entity classifiers represent a category of membership and include forms for VEHICLE and PEOPLE (Baker & Cokely, 1980). SASS forms, or size-and-shape specifiers, describe the visual-geometric properties of objects, focusing on adjectival information (e.g., BUTTON, COLUMN). Each subset of classifiers has its own set of linguistic rules.

The acquisition of classifiers is prolonged, and they may not be mastered until around age 8 or 9 (Kantor, 1980; Schick, 1990c; Supalla, 1982). To produce adultlike classifiers, children must learn how to select the handshape(s), coordinate the two hands to represent figure and ground, represent spatial relationships, use classifiers to represent viewpoint, represent complex manner and motion, and order series of classifier verbs.

Early Use of Classifiers

Children acquiring ASL begin to use classifier forms as early as age 2, particularly handle and entity forms (Lindert, 2001; Slobin et al., 2000). Lillo-Martin (1988) and Supalla (1982) have shown that 3 and 4 year olds freely produce classifier forms. They do not appear to have difficulty with the concept of combining a figure and a simple path, nor the concept of using the hand to represent the handling of objects. However, they make errors in selecting handshape, coordinating the two hands, and representing space. Slobin and colleagues (2000) also reported that deaf children of hearing parents who have been exposed to ASL produce classifier forms early in development.

Handshape Selection

Although handshape selection for classifiers is not acquired without effort, children appear to produce the handshape more or less accurately by around age 5. Supalla (1982) found that a 3 year old produced at least partially correct handshapes approximately 50% of the time. A 5 year old was correct in 82% of her handshapes. Schick (1990c) also reported that most of the developmental changes in classifier handshape occur before age 5. No developmental differences in handshape use were found in 24 children ranging in age from 4;5 to 9;0.

It appears, however, that different types of classifiers may have different developmental timetables. Schick (1990c) found that entity handshapes were the most likely to be produced accurately by young children, with SASS classifiers being more difficult, and handshapes for handle forms least likely to be produced accurately. Schick (1990c) hypothesized that entity handshapes pose the least challenge for children because selection of these handshapes requires superordinate classification, a concept acquired early in development. She argued that although the handshape in handle forms requires visual-geometric categorization of the object being handled, the focus of the classifier is locative transfer. This may cause children to focus less on the properties of the object and more on the spatial mapping required to indicate the people and locations involved in its transfer. Despite the fact that a child may be able to produce a correct classifier handshape in some contexts at a fairly young age, the handshape may be incorrect in some other contexts because of linguistic complexity (Schick, 1990b).

Representation of Location

Classifiers involve more than handshape selection; children must also learn how to represent spatial relationships. Even at 6 and 7 years of age, children have difficulty integrating spatial mapping into classifier forms (Schick, 1990c; Supalla, 1982). For example, children seem to have particular difficulty representing spatial relationships that involve two objects in a figure and ground relationship. Schick (1990c) showed that children 4 and 5 years of age scored below 40% correct responses in representation of figure and ground, whereas older children scored about 70% correct. Supalla (1982) found that children ages 3 and 4 omitted a second handshape in 56% of obligatory contexts. Older children (ages 4;3 to 5;11) omitted second handshapes only about 22% of the time. When the youngest children included a secondary object, they occasionally produced it separately from the figure as an independent verb; this occurred about 20% of the time for the youngest subject (3;6 to 3;11).

Development of the Syntax of Classifiers

Often a series of classifier forms are required to represent a complex spatial relationship, and there are linguistic rules for ordering these forms. Schick (1986) observed that children ages 6;0–10;3 produced a great number of classifier predicates in which they repeated elements of the classifier construction in different predicates, combining different parts. She speculated that the children were searching for the right components as well as the correct combination. In addition, children would establish some aspect of spatial mapping, such as "a wall is located at this location" and then ignore where they had put it in a subsequent classifier form creating new spatial loci. Thus, the children often treated individual classifier forms in a series as independent classifiers.

Facial Morphology in ASL

Facial expression in ASL can serve grammatical functions as obligatory markers for certain syntactic structures, including negation, questions, topics, and conditionals, as well as adverbial notions. Children must distinguish affective from grammatical use of facial expression, learn exactly which facial behaviors accompany a given structure (i.e., eyebrow raise vs. brow furrowing), and learn the rules for the timing of the facial behavior within a signed utterance.

Children begin to use facial expression early; around 10–12 months, they use their mother's facial expression to guide their own behavior (Reilly, McIntire, & Bellugi, 1990b). Shortly after this, around ages 1;6–2;3, children begin to use facial expression with their signing, often with emotive signs. Reilly, McIntire, and Bellugi (1990b) believe that these earliest forms are frozen or unanalyzed combinations of facial expression and sign because children's production of the facial expression is often unvarying regardless of communicative intent. The facial expression is part of their lexical specification for that sign.

Numerous ASL syntactic structures include obligatory nonmanual behaviors, and acquisition differs depending on the complexity of the grammatical structure (Anderson & Reilly, 1997, 1999; Reilly, 2000; Reilly, McIntire, & Bellugi, 1990a, 1990b). For example, nonmanual markers for negation are among the earliest to emerge; negative headshakes have been observed, in isolation, at about 12 months (Anderson & Reilly, 1997). By about 20 months, children attempt to combine a manual sign, such as DON'T, and a nonmanual component, but the timing of the manual negative sign and the nonmanual behavior is not always correct. The first correctly timed nonmanual expression plus sign occurred in Anderson and Reilly's (1997) data at 27 months of age. For the majority of the children, the lexical sign for the negative emerged earlier than the nonmanual marking for the sign. Other nonmanual markers that appear at slightly older ages include adverbial nonmanual markers (Anderson & Reilly, 1999) and nonmanual markers for WH-questions (Lillo-Martin, 2000; Reilly, McIntire, & Bellugi, 1991).

A similar developmental pattern has been observed for conditionals, a more complex grammatical structure (Reilly et al., 1990a). Three- and 4-year-old children do not comprehend conditionals if they occur only with the nonmanual marker, and without the manual sign IF. By age 5, children comprehend conditionals, even without the manual sign. But children at ages 3 and 4 do not produce any nonmanual markers. At age 5, 75% of their productions occurred with a nonmanual marker, but only 20% had the correct, adultlike timing. By age 6, most of the children's productions were adultlike. This may be because children interpret the nonmanual as a lexical property of the sign IF, rather than a syntactic property of the conditional clause. A similar pattern of development can be seen for the acquisition of direct quotation, which is not produced in an adultlike manner until age 7 (Emmorey & Reilley, 1998).

As Reilly (2000) explains, there appears to be a preference in acquisition for hands first and then faces. Across several linguistic systems (i.e., questions, conditions, direct quotation, negation) children produce the linguistic concept first using a lexical sign, sometimes with fragments of the nonmanual. Only later do they integrate linguistic information occurring on both the hands and face. This acquisition pattern is repeated at different ages for different linguistic systems. Reilly and colleagues (1991) suggest several reasons for this delay in integration of hands and faces. They believe that children prefer unifunctionality in a linguistic form. They also speculate that a child views the hands as the primary articulators and thus might be predisposed to interpret facial expression as affective, not linguistic.

The Development of Syntax and Spatial Mapping in ASL

As with English, there are syntactic structures in ASL that are not fully developed until 4–7 years of age, such as conditionals as reported earlier (Reilly et al., 1990a). However, there is little research on the development of complex syntax in ASL. The complex interactions among syntax, morphology, discourse, and pragmatics appear to be the most problematic feature for children learning ASL. For example, with children 3–5 years old, aspects of syntax appear to interact with discourse. Lillo-Martin (1991) found children ages 3–5 often produce arguments explicitly rather than using null arguments, in which an argument of the verb does not appear in a sentence. She reported that children at this age often use word order to express grammatical relations, even when the sentences appeared awkward and redundant. As children gain

control of the morphology of verb agreement, beginning with arguments present in the environment, they begin to use null arguments more often and more correctly. Later, around ages 5–6, children were able to use verb agreement even with nonpresent referents, and also used more null arguments. However, certain complex structures, such as direct quotation, may interfere with correct null subject use until age 6.

Syntax is typically thought of as the ordering of words in sentences, but in ASL, there is a complex interaction between morphology and syntax both at the sentence and discourse levels. Children must learn how to coordinate spatial morphology, such as verb agreement and classifiers, within and across sentences. In addition, they must learn to use spatial morphology to structure the discourse and maintain pronominal referencing, often termed "spatial mapping" (Emmorey, 2002; Winston, 1995).

Coordinating spatial mapping across discourse appears to be difficult for children. Lowe (1984) found that a 3-year-old's storytelling was difficult to understand because she was unclear about references, often omitting arguments even though the pragmatic and discourse environment were insufficient to identify them. In addition, the child did not use spatial mapping coherently and consistently throughout the story. When she established a spatial locus, she often would abandon it in subsequent sentences. She also would stack loci on top of each other, making it difficult to determine which character was being referred to. Even at the oldest age Lowe observed, age 4;9 the child still made numerous errors in spatial mapping, although she was beginning to identify referents more consistently.

Development of MCE

Despite the fact that MCE has been used educationally for about 3 decades, there has been little systematic study of its acquisition. For children acquiring MCE, the goal is to acquire English as a first and native language, and researchers typically focus on the extent to which children adhere to or deviate from the rules of English, rather than a description of the children's overall communication skills. In addition, children learning MCE are typically learning it from hearing people, who vary widely in their fluency. Therefore, the issue of restricted input is a confound not easily separated from the issue of how well children learn MCE as a system and whether it can function as a true language (Hoiting & Slobin, 2002; Schick & Moeller, 1992).

Lexical Development in MCE

Some studies show that deaf children learning MCE have significantly delayed lexical development compared with hearing children; others show development similar to hearing children (Bornstein & Saulnier, 1981; Bornstein, Saulnier, & Hamilton, 1980; Mayne, Yoshinaga-Itano, & Sedey, 2000; Mayne, Yoshinaga-Itano, Sedey, & Carey, 2000; Schick & Moeller, 1992; Stack, 1999). For example, an early investigation of the development of MCE showed a rate of vocabulary growth for 20 children learning MCE at about 43% of that of hearing children (Bornstein et al., 1980). At nearly 6 years of age, the MCE children had an average vocabulary of a hearing 3-year-old, and by age 7, their vocabulary level was about that of a hearing 4-year-old.

Somewhat better results were found in a more recent study of 113 deaf/hard-of-hearing children, 24–37 months of age (Mayne, Yoshinaga-Itano, & Sedey, 2000; Mayne, Yoshinaga-Itano, Sedey, & Carey, 2000). Although some of the children were being educated orally and others were using English-like signing, mode of communication was not related to expressive vocabulary levels. Therefore, data from children learning sign and speech were combined. Children demonstrating cognitive development within normal limits and with hearing loss identified before 6 months had vocabulary levels significantly greater than peers who were identified later. However, even for the early-identified group, the median vocabulary level at 32–37 months fell below the 25th percentile compared with hearing children at a younger age (30 months). Receptive and expressive vocabulary results were similar.

Age of intervention also relates to vocabulary acquisition (Moeller, 2000). Five-year-old deaf children who had been enrolled in early intervention programs by 11 months of age attained receptive vocabulary scores comparable to hearing peers, with an average standard score of 94 (SD = 3.1). Children enrolled in intervention after 11 months had an average standard score of only 75, with greater variability (SD = 18). In this study, data from children in MCE and oral programming were also combined due to a lack of any group differences.

Grammatical Development in MCE

A major developmental milestone in English acquisition is when children begin to use word order. Hearing children learning spoken English appear to acquire word order with ease, using it correctly in the majority of their earliest multiword utterances (O'Grady, 1997). However, for children learning MCE, the acquisition of English word order is highly variable, with not all children consistently using word order that follows English.

Some studies have shown relatively good mastery of English word order. In a study of 13 children, ages 7–14, exposed exclusively to MCE, students were able to produce correct English word order in 80% of their spontaneously produced sentences, considering both their speech and sign production (Schick & Moeller, 1992). Similarly, in a study of a single child, age 4;5–5;3 years, Stack (1999) reported that English word order was produced correctly about 95% of the time. Geers and Schick (1988) found that 50 deaf children learning MCE, ages 5–9, correctly expressed obligatory subject and object nouns in simple sentences about 70% the time.

However, other studies have shown different results. For example, Livingston (1983) found that six deaf children, ranging in age from 6 to 16, used inconsistent sign order in most of their spontaneous utterances. Their overall syntax did not resemble English. Similar results were found by Suty and Friel-Patti (1982) who studied two 6-year-old children learning MCE. The children produced fairly accurate English structure during testing that elicited simple syntax. However, in spontaneous language, the children would often use word orders other than SVO. Supalla (1991) investigated the development of English in eight children, ages 9–11, whose parents reported minimal signing skills. In an elicitation task, the children used English word order for a mean of about 75% of their sentences. However, children ranged from 42 to 100% correct, indicating that not all were adept with English word order. Non-English word orders were used by some children for up to 32% of their utterances.

It would seem that DOD children who already have a fluent first language when they enter school would be better able to learn MCE than DOH children, who often enter school with limited language competence. However, in a study comparing MCE acquisition in DOH and DOD children ages 5–8, Geers and Schick (1988) found no group difference at ages 5 and 6. By age 7 and 8, after 4–5 years of exposure, DOD children were significantly better at MCE than DOH children, but they were still significantly behind their hearing peers. In addition, the patterns of difficulty with English structures were virtually identical for the DOD and DOH group.

Most studies on MCE have focused on the acquisition of simple grammatical structures; however, Schick and Moeller (1992) investigated the use of complex grammatical structures. They found that deaf children produced complex English sentences as frequently as a group of hearing children, although their productions contained numerous grammatical errors. They also used embedded sentences in roughly similar proportions, but there was slightly greater variability among the deaf students. Their rate of production of relative and complement clauses did not differ from a hearing control group.

Development of Morphology and Other Functional Elements in MCE

Linguists distinguish two broad categories of elements in languages: open-class or lexical categories, which can add new items; and closed-class or functional categories, containing bound inflections, modals, auxiliaries, and determiners (de Villiers, de Villiers, & Hoban, 1993). Previous research with orally educated children and children exposed to sign language before the advent of MCE systems indicated that deaf children have particular difficulty with functional elements (Berent, 1996; Kretschmer & Kretschmer, 1978; Quigley & Paul, 1984). With the development of MCE systems, educators expected that children would acquire these elements naturally because presumably they received accessible input. However, reports on the representation of these elements in MCE input show that both parents and teachers vary in their production (Luetke-Stahlman, 1991; Marmor & Pettito, 1979; Wood, Wood, & Kingsmill, 1991).

Perhaps because of variability in their input,

deaf children exposed exclusively to some form of MCE do not learn the functional grammatical categories like hearing children do. Rather, they produce these elements inconsistently, even when they are well beyond the typical age of development. For example, Schick and Moeller (1992), investigated the production of English grammar in a group of 13 deaf children, ages 7–14, whose parents and teachers were committed to using complete MCE. The students often failed to produce functional elements, even when both speech and sign production was considered. Overall, nearly half of their sentences were missing bound morphemes, articles, complementizers, auxiliaries, and other closed-class elements. There was considerable between-subject variation in the production of functional elements, with the correct use of the five most common inflectional morphemes (e.g., -ing, -ed) ranging from 19 to 100% correct. It should be noted that this study did not investigate the use of bound morphology in writing, which may better reflect underlying competence.

The results of the Schick and Moeller (1992) study show much better use of functional elements than other studies on children using MCE (Bornstein et al., 1980, 1981; Gaustad, 1986; Livingston, 1981, 1983; Stack, 1999; Supalla, 1991; Suty & Friel-Patti, 1982). For example, Supalla (1991) investigated English acquisition in a group of deaf children with restricted exposure to MCE; their teachers signed MCE and they had been exposed to MCE for at least 5 years, but the parents did not sign. None of these children produced English morphology for tense.

ASL-like Innovations by Children Learning MCE

While classifiers are pervasive in ASL, there are no linguistically similar structures in English. Despite this, children learning MCE produce classifier-like forms, sometimes quite frequently, even with little to no exposure to them (Livingston, 1983; Stack, 1999; Suty & Friel-Patti, 1982). Similarly, linguistic structures similar to verb agreement have been observed in children learning MCE, who have little to no exposure to ASL. Supalla (1991), in a previously mentioned study, found that all of his subjects produced verbs with spatial modification even though their teachers did not. It is also the case that children who are deaf and educated orally, with no exposure to sign language in any form, have been observed to produce gestural forms that share characteristics with ASL classifiers, verb agreement, and syntax (Goldin-Meadow & Mylander, 1990).

Summary and Conclusions

Children learn ASL in a manner similar to how they learn spoken languages, through interaction with fluent users of the language. They go through many of the developmental milestones observed in children learning spoken languages. Overall, learning the complex morphology in ASL does not present a problem to the young language learner, much like we see with the development of complex morphologies in spoken languages. Even DOH children learn ASL in a natural manner, albeit often with some delay (Schick & Hoffmeister, 2001; Singleton, Supalla, Litchfield, & Schley, 1998). In some ways, it is striking how ordinary ASL acquisition is.

Despite the fact that children learning MCE are rarely exposed to ASL, researchers have found structures in their linguistic innovations that resemble ASL verb agreement, classifiers, and spatial mapping. This may indicate a core property of visual languages, in that some elements may be able to emerge via gesture, albeit in a rudimentary manner that is not equivalent to the rich, structured morphology of mature ASL.

The picture of MCE development provides an alternative perspective on learning languages visually. When English grammatical structures are converted to a visual form, as with MCE, children appear to have a great deal of difficulty acquiring certain aspects of it, despite special teaching and support. Specifically, they have difficulty acquiring the functional categories and relatively simple morphology of English and produce it in a limited, fragmented manner. This may be due to the restricted input they receive, and the issue of variations in input makes interpretation difficult. But there may be something about making a spoken language into a visual one that is inconsistent with how visual languages work (Gee & Goodhart, 1985; Supalla, 1991). With this, deaf children offer us insight into what types of grammatical elements work well within a visual system and which may be relatively unlearnable.

References

Anderson, D., & Reilly, J. S. (1997). The puzzle of negation: How children move from communicative to grammatical negation in ASL. *Journal of Child Language, 18*(4), 411–429.

Anderson, D., & Reilly, J. S. (1999). PAH! The acquisition of non-manual adverbials in ASL. *Sign Language and Linguistics, 1,* 115–142.

Anderson, D., & Reilly, J. S. (2002). The MacArthur Communicative Development Inventory: Normative data for American Sign Language. *Journal of Deaf Studies and Deaf Education, 7,* 83–106.

Baker, C., & Cokely, D. (1980). *American Sign Language: A teacher's resource text on grammar and culture.* Silver Spring, MD: T. J. Publishers.

Bates, E., Benigni, L., Bretherton, I., Camaioni, L., & Volterra, V. (1979). *The emergence of symbols: Cognition and communication in infancy.* New York: Academic Press.

Bates, E., Camaioni, L., & Volterra, V. (1975). The acquisition of performatives prior to speech. *Merrill-Palmer Quarterly, 21,* 205–226.

Berent, G. P. (1996). The acquisition of English syntax by deaf learners. In W. C. Ritchie & T. K. Bhatia (Eds.), *Handbook of second language acquisition* (pp. 469–506). San Diego, CA: Academic Press.

Bonvillian, J. D., Orlansky, M. D., & Novack, L. L. (1983). Developmental milestones: Sign language acquisition and motor development. *Child Development, 54,* 1435–1445.

Bonvillian, J. D., & Siedlecki, T. (1996). Young children's acquisition of the location aspect of American Sign Language signs: Parental report findings. *Journal of Communication Disorders, 29,* 13–35.

Bornstein, H. (1990). A manual communication overview. In H. Bornstein (Ed.), *Manual communication: Implications for education* (pp. 21–44). Washington, DC: Gallaudet University Press.

Bornstein, H., & Saulnier, K. (1981). Signed English: A brief follow-up to the first evaluation. *American Annals of the Deaf, 126,* 69–72.

Bornstein, H., Saulnier, K., & Hamilton, L. (1980). Signed English: A first evaluation. *American Annals of the Deaf, 125,* 467–481.

Boyes-Braem, P. (1990). Acquisition of the handshape in American Sign Language. In V. Volterra & C. J. Ertings (Eds.), *From gesture to language in hearing and deaf children* (pp. 107–127). New York: Springer-Verlag.

Butterworth, G., & Morissette, P. (1996). Onset of pointing and the acquisition of language in infancy. *Journal of Reproductive and Infant Psychology, 14,* 219–232.

Caselli, M. C., & Volterra, V. (1990). From communication to language in hearing and deaf children. In V. Volterra & C. J. Erting (Eds.), *From gesture to language in hearing and deaf children* (pp. 263–277). Heidelberg: Springer-Verlag.

Casey, S. (1999, March. *The continuity of "agreement": Form pre-linguistic action gestures to ASL verbs.* Paper presented at the Second Annual High Desert Student Conference in Linguistics, Albuquerque, NM.

Casey, S. (2000). *"Agreement" in gestures and signed languages: The use of directionality to indicate referents involved in action.* Unpublished Doctoral Dissertation, University of California at San Diego, San Diego, CA.

Conlin, K., Mirus, G. R., Mauk, C., & Meier, R. P. (2000). Acquisition of first signs: Place, handshape, and movement. In C. Chamberlain, J. Morford, & R. I. Mayberry (Eds.), *Language acquisition by eye* (pp. 51–70). Mahwah, NJ: Lawrence Erlbaum Associates.

de Villiers, J. G., de Villiers, P. A., & Hoban, E. (1993). The central problem of functional categories in the English syntax of oral deaf children. In H. Tager-Flusberg (Ed.), *Constraints on language acquisition: Studies of atypical children* (pp. 8–47). Hillsdale, NJ: Lawrence Erlbaum Associates.

Emmorey, K. (2002). *Language, cognition, and the brain: Insights from sign language research.* Hillsdale, NJ: Lawrence Erlbaum Associates.

Emmorey, K., & Reilley, J. (Eds.). (1998). *The development of quotation and reported action: Conveying perspective in ASL.* Stanford, CA: CSLI publications.

Fenson, L., Dale, P., Reznick, S., Bates, E., Thal, D., & Pethick, S. (1994). Variability in early communicative development. *Monographs of the Society for Research in Child Development, 59*(5).

Folven, R. J., & Bonvillian, J. D. (1991). The transition from nonreferential to referential language in children acquiring American Sign Language. *Developmental Psychology, 27,* 806–816.

Gaustad, M. G. (1986). Longitudinal effects of manual English instruction on deaf children's morphological skills. *Applied Psycholinguistics, 7,* 101–128.

Gee, J., & Goodhart, W. (1985). Nativization, linguistic theory, and deaf language acquisition. *Sign Language Studies, 49,* 291–342.

Geers, A. E., & Schick, B. (1988). Acquisition of spoken and signed English by hearing-impaired children of hearing-impaired or hearing parents. *Journal of Speech and Hearing Disorders, 53,* 136–143.

Goldin-Meadow, S., & Mylander, C. (1990). Beyond the input given: The child's role in the acquisition of language. *Language, 66,* 323–355.

Hoffmeister, R. (1977). *The acquisition of American Sign Language by deaf children of deaf parents: The development of demonstrative pronouns, locatives, and personal pronouns.* Unpublished doctoral dissertation, University of Minnesota, Minneapolis.

Hoiting, N., & Slobin, D. (2002). What does a deaf child need to see? Advantages of a natural sign language over a sign system. In R. Schulmeister & H. Reinitzer (Eds.), *Progress in sign language research. In honor of Siegmund Prillwitz* (pp. 267–278). Hamburg: Signum.

Kantor, R. (1980). The acquisition of classifiers in American Sign Language. *Sign Language Studies, 28,* 193–208.

Klima, E., & Bellugi, U. (1979). *The signs of language.* Cambridge, MA: Harvard University Press.

Kretschmer, R. R. J., & Kretschmer, L. W. (1978). *Language development and intervention with the hearing impaired.* Baltimore, MD: University Park Press.

Lillo-Martin, D. (1988). Children's new sign creations. In M. Strong (Ed.), *Language learning and deafness* (pp. 162–183). Cambridge: Cambridge University Press.

Lillo-Martin, D. C. (1991). *Universal grammar and American Sign Language.* Dordrecht, The Netherlands: Kluwer Academic Publishers.

Lillo-Martin, D. (2000). Early and late language acquisition: Aspects of the syntax and acquisition of WH questions in American Sign Language. In K. Emmorey & H. Lane (Eds.), *The signs of language revisited: An anthology to honor Ursula Bellugi and Edward Kilma* (pp. 401–414). Mahwah, NJ: Lawrence Erlbaum Associates.

Lillo-Martin, D., Bellugi, U., Struxness, L., & O'Grady, M. (1985). The acquisition of spatially organized syntax. *Papers and Reports on Child Language Development, 24,* 70–80.

Lindert, R. (2001). *Hearing families with deaf children. Linguistic and communicative aspects of American Sign language development* (doctoral dissertation, University of California, Berkeley).

Livingston, S. (1981). *The acquisition and development of sign language in deaf children of hearing parents.* Unpublished doctoral dissertation, New York University, New York.

Livingston, S. (1983). Levels of development in the language of deaf children: ASL grammatical processes, Signed English structures, and semantic features. *Sign Language Studies, 40,* 193–285.

Loew, R. (1984). *Roles and references in American Sign Language: A development perspective.* Unpublished doctoral dissertation, University of Minnesota, Minneapolis.

Luetke-Stahlman, B. (1991). Following the rules: Consistency in sign. *Journal of Speech and Hearing Research*, *34*(6), 1293–1298.

Marentette, P., & Mayberry, R. I. (2000). Principals for an emerging phonological system: A case study of early ASL acquisition. In C. Chamberlain, J. Morford, & R. I. Mayberry (Eds.), *Language acquisition by eye* (pp. 71–90). Mahwah, NJ: Lawrence Erlbaum Associates.

Marmor, G., & Pettito, L. (1979). Simultaneous communication in the classroom: How well is English grammar represented? *Sign Language Studies*, *23*, 99–136.

Marschark, M., Lang, H. G., & Albertini, J. A. (2002). *Educating deaf students: From research to practice.* New York: Oxford Press.

Mayne, A. M., Yoshinaga-Itano, C., & Sedey, A. (2000). Receptive vocabulary development of infants and toddlers who are deaf or hard of hearing. *Volta Review*, *100*, 29–52.

Mayne, A. M., Yoshinaga-Itano, C., Sedey, A., & Carey, A. (2000). Expressive vocabulary development of infants and toddlers who are deaf or hard of hearing. *Volta Review*, *100*, 1–28.

McIntire, M. (1977). The acquisition of American Sign Language hand configuration. *Sign Language Studies*, *16*, 247–266.

Meier, R. (1982). *Icons, analogues, and morphemes: The acquisition of verb agreement in American Sign Language.* Unpublished doctoral dissertation, University of California, San Diego.

Meier, R. P. (2000). Shared motoric factors in the acquisition of sign and speech. In K. E. H. Lane (Ed.), *The signs of language revisited: An anthology to honor Ursula Bellugi and Edward Klima* (pp. 333–357). Mahwah, New Jersey: Lawrence Erlbaum Associates.

Meier, R. P., & Newport, E. L. (1990). Out of the hands of babes: On a possible sign advantage in language acquisition. *Language*, *66*, 1–23.

Meier, R. P., & Willerman, R. (1995). Prelinguistic gesture in deaf and hearing infants. In K. Emmorey & J. Reilly (Eds.), *Language, gesture, and space* (pp. 391–409). Hillsdale, NJ: Lawrence Erlbaum Associates.

Moeller, M. P. (2000). Early intervention and language development in children who are deaf and hard of hearing. *Pediatrics*, *106*, 1–9.

Newport, E. L., & Ashbrook, E. F. (1977). The emergence of semantic relations in ASL. *Papers and Reports on Child Language Development*, *13*, 16–21.

Newport, E. L., & Meier, R. (1985). The acquisition of American Sign Language. In D. Slobin (Ed.), *The crosslinguistic study of language acquisition: Vol. 1. The data* (pp. 881–939). Hillside, NJ: Lawrence Erlbaum Associates.

O'Grady, W. (1997). *Syntactic development.* Chicago: University of Chicago Press.

Oller, D. K., Wieman, L. A., Doyle, W. J., & Ross, C. (1976). Infant babbling and speech. *Journal of Child Language*, *3*, 1–11.

Petitto, L. (1987). On the autonomy of language and gesture: Evidence from the acquisition of personal pronouns in American Sign Language. *Cognition*, *27*, 1–52.

Petitto, L., Holowka, S., Sergio, L., & Ostry, D. (2001). Language rhythms in babies' hand movements. *Nature*, *413*(6), 35–36.

Petitto, L. A. (1988). "Language" in the prelinguistic child. In F. S. Kessel (Ed.), *The development of language and language researchers: Essays in honor of Roger Brown* (pp. 187–221). Hillsdale, NJ: Lawrence Erlbaum Associates.

Petitto, L. A. (1990). The transition from gesture to symbol in American Sign Language. In V. Volterra & C. J. Erting (Eds.), *From gesture to language in hearing and deaf children* (pp. 153–161). Berlin: Springer-Verlag.

Petitto, L. A., & Marentette, P. F. (1991). Babbling in the manual mode: Evidence for the ontogeny of language. *Science*, *251*, 1493–1496.

Pichler, D. C. (2001). *Word order variation and acquisition in American Sign Language.* Unpublished doctoral dissertation, University of Connecticut, Storrs.

Pizzuto, E. (1990). The early development of deixis in American Sign Language: What is the point? In V. Volterra & C. J. Erting (Eds.), *From gesture to language in hearing and deaf children* (pp. 142–161). New York: Springer-Verlag.

Quigley, S. P., & Paul, P. (1984). *Language and deafness*; San Diego, CA: College-Hill Press.

Reilly, J. S. (2000). Bringing affective expression into the service of language: Acquiring perspective marking in narratives. In K. Emmorey & H. Lane (Eds.), *The signs of language revisited: An anthology to Ursula Bellugi and Edward Klima* (pp. 415–434). Mahwah, NJ: Lawrence Erlbaum Associates.

Reilly, J. S., McIntire, M., & Bellugi, U. (1990a). The acquisition of conditionals in American Sign Language: Grammaticized facial expressions. *Applied Psycholinguistics*, *11*(4), 369–392.

Reilly, J. S., McIntire, M., & Bellugi, U. (1990b). Faces: The relationship between language and affect. In V. Volterra & C. J. Erting (Eds.), *From gesture to language in hearing and deaf children* (pp. 128–141). Berlin: Springer-Verlag.

Reilly, J. S., McIntire, M., & Bellugi, U. (1991). Baby face: A new perspective on universals in language acquisition. In P. Siple & S. D. Fischer (Eds.), *Theoretical issues in sign language research: Psychol-*

ogy (pp. 9–23). Chicago: University of Chicago Press.

Schembri, A. (2002). Rethinking "classifiers" in signed languages. In K. Emmorey (Ed.), *Perspectives on classifier constructions in sign language.* (pp. 3–34). NJ: Mahwah Lawrence Erlbaum Associates.

Schick, B. (1986, November). *Groping for orientation: The representation of space and form in child ASL.* Paper presented at the Boston University Child Language Conference, Boston, MA.

Schick, B. (1990a). Classifier predicates in American Sign Language. *International Journal of Sign Linguistics, 1*(1), 15–40.

Schick, B. (1990b). The effects of morphological complexity on phonological simplification in ASL. *Sign Language Studies, 66,* 25–41.

Schick, B. (1990c). The effects of morphosyntactic structure on the acquisition of classifier predicates in ASL. In C. Lucas (Ed.),*Sign Language research: Theoretical issues* (pp. 358–374). Washington, DC: Gallaudet University Press.

Schick, B. (2002). The expression of grammatical relations in deaf toddlers learning ASL. In G. Morgan & B. Woll (Eds.), *Directions in sign language acquisition* (pp. 143–158). Amsterdam: John Benjamins.

Schick, B., & Hoffmeister, R. (2001, April). *ASL skills in deaf children of deaf parents and of hearing parents.* Paper presented at the Society for Research in Child Development International Conference, Minneapolis, MN.

Schick, B., & Moeller, M. P. (1992). What is learnable in manually coded English sign systems? *Applied Psycholinguistics, 13*(3), 313–340.

Schlesinger, H. S., & Meadow, K. (1972). *Sound and sign: Childhood deafness and mental health.* Berkley: University of California Press.

Siedlecki, T., Jr., & Bonvillian, J. D. (1993). Location, handshape & movement: Young children's acquisition of the formational aspects of American Sign Language. *Sign Language Studies, 78,* 31–52.

Siedlecki, T., & Bonvillian, J. D. (1997). Young children's acquisition of the handshape aspect of American Sign Language signs: Parental report findings. *Applied Psycholinguistics, 18,* 17–39.

Singleton, J. L., Supalla, S., Litchfield, S., & Schley, S. (1998). From sign to word: Considering modality constraints in ASL/English Bilingual Education. *Topics in Language Disorders, 18*(4), 16–29.

Slobin, D., Hoiting, N., Kuntze, M., Lindert, R., Weinberg, A., Pyers, J., Anthony, M., Biederman, Y., & Thuman, H. (2000, April). *Classifiers in child sign.* Paper presented at the Workshop on Classifier Constructions, La Jolla, CA.

Stack, K. M. (1999). *Innovation by a child acquiring Signing Exact English II.* Unpublished Doctoral dissertation, University of California at Los Angeles, Los Angeles.

Supalla, S. J. (1991). Manually Coded English: The modality question in signed language development. In P. Siple & S. D. Fischer (Eds.), *Theoretical issues in sign language research* (Vol. 2, pp. 85–109). Chicago: University of Chicago Press.

Supalla, T. (1982). *Structure and acquisition of verbs of motion and location in American Sign Language.* Unpublished doctoral dissertation, University of California, San Diego.

Supalla, T. (1986). The classifier system in American Sign Language. In C. Craig (Ed.), *Noun classes and categorization.* Philadelphia: John Benjamins.

Suty, K., & Friel-Patti, S. (1982). Looking beyond Signed English to describe the language of two deaf children. *Sign Language Studies, 35,* 153–166.

Volterra, V. (1981). Gestures, signs, and words at two years: When does communication become language? *Sign Language Studies, 33,* 351–361.

Winston, F. (1995). Spatial mapping in comparative discourse frames. In K. Emmorey & J. Reilly (Eds.), *Language, gesture, and space* (pp. 87–114). Hillsdale, NJ: Lawrence Erlbaum Associates.

Wood, H., Wood, D., & Kingsmill, M. (1991). Signed English in the classroom, II: Structural and pragmatic aspects of teachers' speech and sign. *First Language, 11*(3), 301–326.

17

Peter J. Blamey

Development of Spoken Language by Deaf Children

Over the last few decades, the potential for deaf children to develop and use spoken language has improved enormously. The two main factors responsible for this improvement are technology and teaching/learning methods. The technological advances provide frequency-specific neonatal screening capabilities via the measurement of otoacoustic emissions (Norton et al., 2000) and steady-state evoked potentials (Rickards et al., 1994) and increased auditory access to speech information through high-gain hearing aids, directional microphones, radio-frequency microphones (Dillon, 2001; Skinner, 1988), and multichannel cochlear implants (Clark et al., 1987). Advances in teaching and learning include early intervention strategies (Ling, 1976, 1989; Yoshinaga-Itano, Sedey, Coulter, & Mehl, 1998) and improved knowledge of the role of hearing in language learning (Bench & Bamford, 1979; Geers & Moog, 1994; Levitt, McGarr, & Geffner, 1987; Paul & Quigley, 1994). The potential for spoken language is of fundamental importance to children because it can facilitate their access to a wide range of educational, cultural, social, and career opportunities. Spoken language proficiency is also a primary predictive factor for literacy in

hard-of-hearing and deaf adolescents (Geers & Moog, 1989).

There is now a large body of literature relevant to this topic, and the references in this chapter should be considered examples of high-quality research rather than an exhaustive list. In most cases, this review focuses on the spoken language development of deaf and hard-of-hearing children who have access to modern methods and technology and who have not learned to sign. The use of sign as a supplement or alternative to spoken communication introduces complexities that would distract from the main questions addressed in this chapter:

- What are the differences in the spoken language of hearing children, hard-of-hearing children, and deaf children?
- What is the range of spoken language performance that may be expected at different ages?
- What is the relationship between hearing and spoken language development?
- What factors affect the rate of spoken language learning?
- How can spoken language learning be accelerated?

Descriptions and Definitions of Spoken Language

Spoken language may be described from several viewpoints in terms of receptive and expressive components; sensory, cognitive, and motor components; or phonology, morphology, syntax, semantics, and pragmatics. It is obvious that hearing has a direct influence on the receptive and sensory components of spoken language processing and on the learning of the phonology (the sounds) of the language. In fact, it is easy to overstate the importance of hearing in these processes. For example, the statement "If you can't hear it, you can't understand it" ignores the importance of speechreading and context in spoken communication. The books *Hearing by Eye II* (Campbell, Dodd, & Burnham, 1998) and *Speech Perception by Ear and Eye* (Massaro, 1987) address a variety of issues related to the roles of hearing and vision in speech perception. Similarly, there are methods of teaching phonology that do not rely on hearing alone (Ling, 1976, 1989). Conversely, it is easy to underestimate the influence of hearing on the expressive, cognitive, and motor components of spoken language. This is usually a more indirect influence derived from the role of hearing in learning a spoken language rather than a direct influence during speech production. Hearing may have less influence on spoken language learning after the child has begun to read and write.

Because of the complex relationships between hearing and the components of spoken language, there is a danger that the following discussion may become circular. For example, audiologists sometimes measure "hearing" using a speech perception test. Classifications of hearing handicap are sometimes based on the difficulties that people have in recognizing speech (Davis & Silverman, 1978). At the same time, spoken language tests such as the Clinical Evaluation of Language Fundamentals (CELF; Wiig, Secord, & Semel, 1992; Semel, Wiig, & Secord, 1995) incorporate speech perception tasks as a measure of language. The CELF subtest, Recalling Sentences in Context, is interpreted as an expressive language measure because the child is required to respond verbally.

To avoid circularity, terms such as "hearing," "speech perception," "receptive language," "speech production," and "expressive language" need to be defined carefully. In this chapter, "receptive language" is defined as the ability to recognize and understand a linguistically coded input signal. Receptive language processing involves one or more sensory components and one or more cognitive components. "Speech perception" is defined as a receptive language process in which the input signal is speech. "Hearing" is one of the sensory processes that may be used in speech perception. Thus speech perception is a particular form of receptive language processing (reading is another form), and hearing is a particular sensory modality contributing to speech perception (vision is another when speechreading is used). Similarly, "speech production" is a particular form of "expressive language" (writing and signing are others). "Expressive language" is defined as the ability to convert an idea or concept into a linguistically coded output signal that may be communicated to another person. Expressive language processing involves cognitive, motor, and sensory (kinesthetic feedback) components (Levelt, 1989).

"Spoken language" is defined here to consist of speech perception and speech production as its receptive and expressive components. Unfortunately, this definition does not always conform to common usage. Sometimes "language" is quite distinct from both speech and hearing, as in the title of the well-known *Journal of Speech, Language, and Hearing Research*. In this title, "language" seems to refer exclusively to cognitive linguistic processing, as distinct from the sensory (hearing) and motor (speech) components. At other times, "speech," "speech production," and "spoken language" are synonymous. In this chapter, "speech production" and "cognitive linguistic processing" are used for the more restricted common meanings.

Measures of Spoken Language

For each component of language, measurement techniques have been devised based on controlled tests and natural language sampling (Lund & Duchan, 1993). For example, in the assessment of receptive vocabulary, the Peabody Picture Vocabulary Test (PPVT-III; Dunn & Dunn, 1997) requires the assessor to say a word and the child to respond by pointing to one of four pictures that best corresponds to the meaning of the word. The Expressive One-Word Picture Vocabulary Test (EOWPVT; Gardner, 1979) requires the assessor to show a picture and the child to say the word that represents the picture. An alternative procedure used with very young children is the MacArthur Communicative Development Inventories (CDI; Fenson et al., 1993) in which parents report whether the child uses words on a standard list. The PPVT-III requires a minimum level of hearing to be a fair test of the child's vocabulary. The EOWPVT and CDI methods require a minimum level of speech production ability in order for the child's words to be intelligible.

When the PPVT-III is used with hearing children, it is assumed that performance is limited by lexical knowledge rather than by hearing acuity. This assumption may not be valid for deaf or hard-of-hearing children. Similarly, the expressive vocabulary measures implicitly assume that speech production skills are advanced relative to the child's lexical knowledge. Research reviewed by Stoel-Gammon (1998) confirms that phoneme production skills normally precede word acquisition in that a child's first words contain a preponderance of phonemes that the child has previously or is concurrently using in babble. However, acquisition of new words seems to drive the acquisition of the later-occurring phonemes as children become older. Deaf and hard-of-hearing children may need to be considered as special cases because their speech is often unintelligible in the early stages.

It is not just vocabulary assessment that is complicated by deafness. All spoken language assessments require speech perception or speech production or both. Thus, it is difficult to separate the effects of sensory, cognitive, and motor processes from one another, especially in deaf and hard-of-hearing children. The descriptions of spoken language below must all be interpreted in the light of the potential interactions of these processes. In particular, speech perception tests usually require all three types of process and should not be interpreted simply as tests of hearing, or receptive language, or expressive language.

The Rate of Spoken Language Development

A further complication in the assessment of spoken language in children arises from its dynamic nature. Speech production and perception are both learned skills that are expected to change over time. Thus

it is often necessary to compare the spoken language abilities of deaf and hard-of-hearing children with those of age-matched hearing children to take into account the expected age-dependence of the measures. A common way of making this comparison is to calculate the "equivalent language age" of the individual child (i.e., the age at which the average raw score for hearing children is equal to the raw score of the child being assessed). The difference between the chronological age of the child and the equivalent age is the language delay. The ratio of the equivalent age to the chronological age of the child is called the language quotient (LQ). The LQ is effectively the rate of language learning averaged over the life of the child so far. An LQ value of 1 indicates a normal average learning rate. Similarly, one may calculate a normalized language learning rate over a shorter time interval by dividing the change in equivalent age by the change in chronological age. Equivalent language age, language delay, and LQ are convenient ways of summarizing the spoken language abilities of children. In particular, equivalent age can be calculated from any language test that has reliable norms for hearing children (such as the PPVT and the CELF) and thus it provides a language metric that can be used to compare results from different tests. The next section also demonstrates that equivalent language age provides a time scale that compensates for differences in language abilities of individual children, making it easier to identify the effects of hearing levels.

The continuous line in figure 17-1 shows the

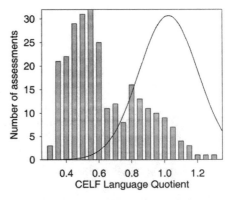

Figure 17-1. Histogram of Clinical Evaluation of Language Fundamentals (CELF) language quotients derived from a longitudinal study of children using either cochlear implants or hearing aids.

normal distribution of equivalent language age derived from the CELF for hearing children. The bars show the histogram of CELF language quotients derived from the annual evaluations of hard-of-hearing and deaf children using hearing aids and/or cochlear implants (Blamey, Sarant, et al., 2001). It is obvious that the distribution of LQ values for hearing children is quite different from the distribution found in the longitudinal study. There may be two groups of children: those whose LQ values fall within the normal range, and a larger group whose LQ values fall below the normal range. LQ is not strongly dependent on the severity of the hearing loss in this data set, consistent with the findings of Davis, Elfenbein, Schum, and Bentler (1986), Dodd, McIntosh, and Woodhouse (1998), Gilbertson and Kamhi (1995), Limbrick, McNaughton, and Clay (1992), Ramkalawan and Davis (1992), and Yoshinaga-Itano et al. (1998). Three of these studies suggest that age at first intervention is a critical factor determining rate of language acquisition; Limbrick et al. suggest that time spent reading is critical; Dodd et al. suggest that early lipreading ability is highly correlated with later language performance; and Gilbertson and Kamhi suggest that 50% of their sample of 20 children with impaired hearing also had a specific language impairment, making it difficult for them to learn new words. In considering the reasons for low LQ values, it is important to differentiate between a delay due to relatively late intervention and a continuous slow rate of learning, potentially due to environmental influences.

A Critical Level of Hearing for Speech Perception

For adults with postlinguistic hearing loss, aided speech perception scores drop rapidly once the hearing loss exceeds 90 dB (Lamore, Verweij, & Brocaar, 1990). On the basis of aided speech perception results, Davis and Silverman (1978) placed the boundary between deaf and hard-of-hearing adults at 92 dB HL. In children, the situation is more complex, with many congenitally hard-of-hearing children scoring low on speech perception tests even though their unaided hearing thresholds may be much lower than 90 dB HL. Many of these low scores are the result of language abilities that are insufficient to perform

the test rather than (or as well as) insufficient hearing levels (Blamey, Sarant, et al., 2001; Blamey, Paatsch, Bow, Sarant, & Wales, 2002). Figure 17-2 shows speech perception scores on the Bench-Kowal-Bamford Sentence Test modified for Australian use (BKB/A; Bench, Doyle, & Greenwood, 1987) as a function of equivalent language age for deaf and hard-of-hearing children using hearing aids and cochlear implants (Blamey et al., 2002). These data show that speech perception scores depend on language abilities in each group. The data for deaf children using cochlear implants and hard-of-hearing children using hearing aids fall on curves that are not statistically significantly different, but the data for profoundly deaf children using hearing aids are very different. Deaf children with hearing aids may be capable of achieving reasonably high speech perception scores on sentence materials, but they require a much greater level of linguistic competence to do so. They need to have an advanced knowledge of phonology, syntax, and semantics to compensate for their lower level of acoustic phonetic input.

These data show that a cochlear implant can move a child from the "deaf" group to the "hard-of-hearing" group (Blamey & Sarant, 2002). Boothroyd and Eran (1994) reached a similar con-

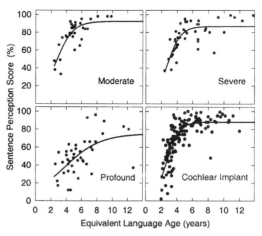

Figure 17-2. Speech (sentence) perception scores on the BKB/A Sentence Test as a function of equivalent language age from the Clinical Evaluation of Language Fundamentals for deaf and hard-of-hearing children using hearing aids and cochlear implants. (From Blamey et al., 2002, reprinted with permission of the Acoustical Society of America.)

clusion by comparing the performance of children using hearing aids and cochlear implants on the Imitated Speech Pattern Contrast Test (Boothroyd, 1991), which does not require as great a knowledge of language as the open-set BKB/A Sentence Test. In view of these demonstrations, the remainder of the chapter concentrates on the spoken language of deaf children using cochlear implants and hard-of-hearing children using hearing aids. As shown in figure 17-2, deaf children using hearing aids are likely to have poorer receptive spoken language (speech perception) and probably poorer expressive spoken language (speech production) than the other groups.

One may also ask whether there is another critical level of hearing loss that separates hearing people from hard-of-hearing people. In a classic paper, Plomp (1978) suggested that hearing loss is made up of an attenuation component and a distortion component. Hearing aids can compensate adequately for the attenuation component but not the distortion component, particularly when listening to speech in noise. The distortion component first becomes important for average threshold levels of about 24 dB, and Plomp suggested that this is the level at which auditory handicap begins. In other words, this is the boundary between hearing and hard-of-hearing people on average.

Intelligibility

Historically, one of the most obvious consequences of congenital and early-acquired deafness has been a low level of intelligibility or a lack of speech (Hudgins & Numbers, 1942), unfortunately characterized in the extreme case as "deaf and dumb." Low expectations for the development of intelligible speech by deaf children may also be found in more recent literature (e.g., Kent, 1997), despite contrary cases documented by schools such as Central Institute for the Deaf (Geers & Moog, 1994, appendix A contains excerpts from spontaneous speech samples) and proponents of auditory/oral programs (Ling, 1976, 1989; Oberkotter Foundation, 2000).

One of the difficulties in exploring this range of opinions is the subjective nature of intelligibility assessments. The fastest and most convenient method is a rating scale (Levitt et al., 1987; Shri-

berg & Kwiatkowski, 1982). Naive listeners may rate the intelligibility of a speech sample as very low, whereas experienced listeners such as parents and teachers of the deaf may have little difficulty in understanding the same sample (Shriberg & Kwiatkowski, 1982). Thus ratings depend on the listener as well as on the speaker. In an alternative procedure (McGarr, 1983), children produced known sentences that were scored by the percentage of key words recognized by naive listeners. Although this procedure is more controlled than the rating scales, the score will vary from one listener to another, and the child is required to read or to remember entire sentences to perform the task. Typical intelligibility scores for deaf children using hearing aids are about 20% for this type of assessment (McGarr, 1983; Monsen, 1978; Smith, 1975). Osberger, Robbins, Todd, and Riley (1994) reported average scores of 48% for deaf children using cochlear implants in an oral communication program. Tye-Murray, Spencer, & Woodworth (1995) found improved intelligibility for children who had been using a cochlear implant for 2 years or more and found that children implanted before age 5 showed greater benefit in speech production than children implanted at older ages.

The intelligibility of spontaneous language samples may also be assessed from the percentage of intelligible syllables (Blamey, Barry, Bow, et al., 2001). Nine deaf cochlear implant users all developed highly intelligible speech within 3 years of implantation, which was before the age of 6 years (figure 17-3). Skilled transcribers were used rather than naive listeners, and the transcribers were able to listen to the recorded conversations several times. Thus the measure should be considered as an upper bound for intelligibility and is likely to be higher than measures based on naive listeners' judgments.

Speech pathologists, teachers, and audiologists have taken a more analytic interest in speech production so that device fitting and teaching methods can be optimized. There is evidence that breath control, rate of speaking, voice quality, and voice pitch can affect intelligibility (Maassen & Povel, 1985; Markides, 1970). On the other hand, the articulation of individual phonemes (speech sounds) is considered to be the most important factor (Maassen & Povel, 1985; Shriberg, Austin, Lewis, Sweeny, & Wilson, 1997).

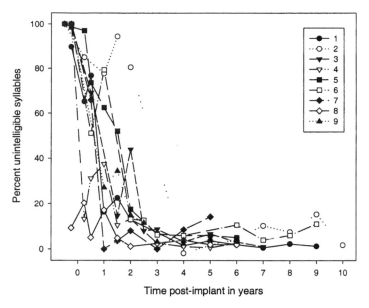

Figure 17-3. Percentage of unintelligible syllables in spontaneous language samples produced by nine children using cochlear implants as a function of time after implant. (From Blamey, Barry, Bow, et. al., 2001, reprinted with permission of Taylor & Francis.)

Phonology

The expressive phonology of children's speech has been studied extensively using formal articulation tests (e.g., Anthony, Bogle, Ingram, & McIsaac, 1971; Fisher & Logeman, 1971) and phonetic transcriptions of spoken language samples (e.g., Crystal, 1992; Lund & Duchan, 1993). The results of phonological studies are often expressed in terms of phonetic inventories (Sander, 1972), percent correct phonemes (Shriberg et al., 1997), or phonological processes (Dodd, 1976).

The expressive phonology of hearing children begins to develop at about age 1 and is not complete until about age 6 on average (for children learning English as their first language). Studies of deaf and hard-of-hearing children have generally found that phoneme acquisition occurs later than in hearing children, and reports of a full phonetic inventory are rare. Phonemes tend to be acquired in a fairly consistent order, with some variation from child to child. Table 17-1 shows the order of consonant acquisition for hearing children (Sander, 1972) and for a group of nine children using cochlear implants (Blamey, Barry, & Jacq, 2001). The order of phoneme acquisition is thought to be determined by linguistic, acoustic, and articulatory factors (Crystal, 1981). Table 17-1 shows the order of consonants ranked according to their frequency of occurrence (a linguistic factor), their intensity

(an acoustic factor), and their place of articulation from front to back (an articulatory factor). Place of articulation may also be of sensory importance for speechreading because the front-most consonants are generally the most easy to recognize visually.

Rank correlations of the columns in table 17-1 are shown in table 17-2. These correlations indicate that children using cochlear implants and hearing children acquire consonants in similar orders. Thus similar factors are likely to be involved. Frequency of occurrence has higher correlation than intensity with the order of acquisition, indicating that linguistic factors may be more important than sensory/acoustic factors in both groups of children. Stoel-Gammon (1998) suggests that early words have a tendency to contain phonemes that are acquired during the babbling stage of speech acquisition. As a child's vocabulary increases, more phonemes are required to maintain the phonetic distinctions between new and already known words. Thus the rate of vocabulary acquisition may also be related to the rate of phoneme acquisition. It has also been noted (Smith, 1975; Tobey, Geers, & Brenner, 1994) that front consonants such as /p, b, m/ occur early in the speech of deaf children. This may be because they are more visible than consonants that are produced farther back in the vocal tract; however, a similar but weaker trend is also observable in the speech of hearing children,

Table 17-1. Rankings of English consonants by order of acquisition for hearing children, order of acquisition by children using cochlear implants, order of frequency of occurrence, order of intensity, and order of articulatory place

Hearing	Implant	Occurrence	Intensity	Visibility/place
p	m	n	w	w
h	w	t	r	m
w	j	m	j	b
m	b	k	l	p
n	n	d	ʃ	v
b	d	w	ŋ	f
d	h	ð	m	ð
k	p	l	tʃ	θ
g	l	b	n	r
f	v	p	ʤ	l
j	t	h	ʒ	n
t	ʃ	j	s	s
ŋ	k	s	z	z
r	f	f	t	t
l	ŋ	g	g	d
s	r	r	k	j
ʃ	ð	ʃ	v	ʃ
tʃ	g	ŋ	ð	tʃ
z	s	z	b	ʤ
ʤ	ʤ	v	d	ʒ
v	tʃ	tʃ	h	ŋ
θ	z	θ	p	g
ð	θ	ʤ	f	k
ʒ	ʒ	ʒ	θ	h

and some front consonants such as /f, v, θ/ also occur late. Voicing, another nonvisible feature of consonants, is also often poorly controlled in the speech of deaf children (Hudgins & Numbers, 1942; Smith, 1975).

Morphology and Syntax

The phonemes of spoken language are organized into larger linguistic structures as morphemes, syllables, words, phrases, sentences, and so on. Words, phrases, and sentences increase in length and complexity as a child's language develops. Standardized measures of morphology and syntax are included in the CELF and other language measures such as the Reynell Developmental Language Scales (Reynell, 1983), and the Preschool Language Scale (Zimmerman, Steiner, & Pond, 1979). The results of these normed test instruments can be expressed as equivalent language ages. The subtests of the CELF-Preschool (Wiig et al., 1992) for children aged 2–6 years are: Linguistic Concepts, Recalling Sentences in Context, Formulating labels, Basic Concepts, Sentence Structure, and Word Structure. The CELF-3 (Semel et al., 1995) for older children has the following subtests: Sentence structure, Word Structure, Concepts and Directions, Formulated Sentences, Word Classes, Recalling Sentences, Sentence Assembly, Semantic Relationships, Word Associations, Listening to Paragraphs, and Rapid, Automatic Naming.

There are also numerous procedures for the syntactic and morphological analysis of spoken language samples, such as the mean length of utterance (Brown, 1973), the Language Assessment, Remediation and Screening Procedure (Crystal, Fletcher, & Garman, 1989) and the Index of Productive Syntax (IPSyn; Scarborough, 1990). In many cases, the language sampling procedures describe a sequence of overlapping stages of linguistic development between the ages of about 9 months and 5 years for hearing children, based on the number of elements in each utterance or another measure of complexity. For example, Brown's stages are shown in table 17-3.

Table 17-2. Rank-order correlations of English consonants ordered as in the columns of table 17-1

	Hearing		Implant		Frequency		Intensity	
	r	p	r	p	r	p	r	p
Implant	.776	<.001						
Frequency	.682	<.001	.753	<.001				
Intensity	.007	.974	.203	.340	.080	.710		
Visibility/place	.320	.127	.561	.004	.396	.056	.062	.774

Table 17-3. Early stages of morphological and syntactic development proposed by Brown (1973)

Stage	New constructs during the stage	MLU range[a]
I	Semantic roles and syntactic relations	1.0–2.0
II	Grammatical morphemes and modulation of meaning	2.0–2.5
III	Modalities of simple sentences	2.5–3.25
IV	Embedding	3.25–3.75
V	Coordination	3.75–4.25

[a]The mean length of utterance (MLU) is measured in morphemes per utterance.

In general, the spoken language development of hard-of-hearing children follows a similar sequence to that of hearing children, although at a slower rate, as illustrated by figure 17-1. Some of the data that were used to compile the histogram in figure 17-1 are shown as individual points in figure 17-4. The data for the implant users have been left out of the figure, and children with a moderate hearing loss (40–70 dB HL), severe hearing loss (70–90 dB HL), and profound hearing loss (90 + dB HL) are shown. The solid line shows the expected equivalent ages for hearing children (equivalent age = chronological age, IQ = 1). The figure shows that some children at each hearing level have age-appropriate language scores on the CELF, and some are significantly delayed. Regression analyses of these data showed that the average rate of spoken language development for hearing aid users and cochlear implant users alike was about 55% of the normal rate (Blamey, Sarant, et al., 2001).

Svirsky, Robbins, Kirk, Pisoni, and Miyamoto (2000) have reported that the rate of language development after implantation exceeded that expected for unimplanted deaf children ($p < .001$) and was similar to that of children with normal hearing. The best performers in the implanted group were reported to be developing an oral linguistic system based largely on auditory input obtained from a cochlear implant. Tomblin, Spencer, Flock, Tyler, and Gantz (1999) found that IPSyn scores improved faster for 29 children using cochlear implants than for 29 deaf children using hearing aids. Both sign and speech were used in calculating these scores. On average, the implant users' IPSyn scores improved from 30% to 65% in the first 5 years of implant use. Hearing children improved from 30% to 90% between the ages of 2 and 4 years on average (Scarborough, Rescorla, Tager-Flusberg, & Fowler, 1991). Thus, implant users were developing morphology and syntax at a slower rate than hearing children at a similar stage in their language development.

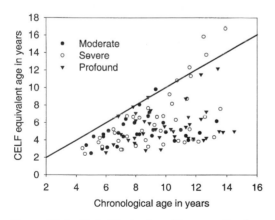

Figure 17-4. Clinical Evaluation of Language Fundamentals equivalent language age versus chronological age for children using hearing aids with different degrees of hearing loss: filled circles-moderate hearing loss (40–70 dB); open circles-severe hearing loss (70–90 dB); filled triangles-profound hearing loss (90+ dB). The solid line indicates the expected average scores for hearing children.

Vocabulary

The vocabulary of deaf and hard-of-hearing children has often been studied using the PPVT (Dunn & Dunn, 1997). The PPVT is normed for hearing children. Thus, raw scores may be converted to equivalent age, and learning rates may be expressed as a proportion of the average "normal" language learning rate of hearing children. Boothroyd, Geers, and Moog (1991) found an average learning rate of 0.43 times the normal rate for 123 hearing aid users aged 4–18 years with pure tone average (PTA) >105 dB HL. Another group of 188 children aged 4–18 years with PTA between 90 and 104 dB HL had an average vocabulary learning rate of 0.60. An average high school graduate has an estimated vocabulary of >30,000 words at age 18 (Nagy & Herman, 1987). These words are acquired at an average rate of about 5 words per day. If deaf children learn at 40% to 60% of the normal rate, they are learning 2 or 3 words per day, achieving a vocabulary of 12,000–18,000 words at age 18 years.

Some studies of deaf children using cochlear implants (Dawson, Blamey, Dettman, Barker, & Clark, 1995; Kirk & Hill-Brown, 1985) reported faster rates of vocabulary acquisition in the years immediately after implantation. For example, Dawson et al. (1995) found an average LQ of 0.43 preoperatively and an average vocabulary learning rate of 1.06 postoperatively for a group of 32 implant users aged 3–20 years at implant with an average hearing loss of 115 dB HL in the better ear preoperatively. Thus, these implant users were delayed in their vocabulary development preimplant, and some of them accelerated to a normal rate of vocabulary acquisition postimplant. Some later studies have been less optimistic. Connor, Hieber, Arts, and Zwolan (2000) found that children implanted at age 2 experienced postimplant PPVT receptive vocabulary growth of 0.63 on average, compared to 0.45 for children implanted at age 6 years and 6 months. Postimplant scores on the expressive picture vocabulary subtest of the Woodcock Johnson Tests of Cognitive Ability (Woodcock & Mather, 1989) increased at 0.7 times the normal rate. Blamey, Sarant, et al. (2001) found that hard-of-hearing implant and hearing aid users progressed on the PPVT at about 65% of the normal rate on average, as shown by the regression lines in figure 17-5.

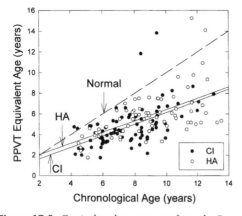

Figure 17-5. Equivalent language age from the Peabody Picture Vocabulary Test (PPVT) as a function of chronological age for children evaluated annually in a longitudinal study (Blamey, Sarant, et al., 2001, reprinted with permission from the American Speech-Language-Hearing Association.)

Relationships Among Hearing, Age, Device Use, and Spoken Language

It is clear that hearing loss can significantly affect a child's spoken language and that spoken language performance increases with age. However, it is also obvious from figure 17-4 that there are no simple relationships among spoken language, age, and hearing levels. There is wide variability in the CELF equivalent age for every category of hearing loss (moderate, severe, and profound) and every age. A similar wide scatter in PPVT equivalent ages is shown for cochlear implant users at every age in figure 17-5.

Despite the wide variability, there are consistent relationships among different spoken language measures. Spencer, Tye-Murray, and Tomblin (1998) found strong correlations among the use of bound morphemic endings, speech recognition scores, accuracy of phoneme production, and duration of implant use. Figure 17-2 shows a consistent relationship between speech perception scores and the CELF equivalent age. Blamey, Sarant, et al. (2001) found strong relationships among a variety of speech perception, speech production, and language measures. Relationships like these support the notion that hard-of-hearing children learn spoken language in a systematic and consistent fashion. Detailed studies of phonology, syntax, and vocabulary suggest that language learning in hard-of-hearing and hearing children follows a similar course. This may not be so for deaf children, as evidenced by the different relationship between auditory speech perception scores and CELF equivalent age and the greater variability for the profound hearing loss group in figure 17-2. One may speculate that some deaf children attain a high level of spoken language proficiency in spite of their limited auditory speech perception performance by learning from visual information, such as reading, lipreading, and sign. Table 17-1 is consistent with this speculation in that visibility (or place of articulation) seems to have a stronger influence on the order of phoneme acquisition for children using cochlear implants than for hearing children.

Accelerating Spoken Language Development

The main effect of hearing loss seems to be to slow down the rate of spoken language learning relative to hearing children. The rate is not affected uniformly for hard-of-hearing children or deaf children, so there must be factors additional to degree of hearing loss. Opinions differ widely as to what these factors may be, as mentioned earlier in the chapter. It is essential that research identify these factors so their effects may be overcome. It is probable that several factors interact and that several conditions have to be met simultaneously for hard-of-hearing children to fulfill their spoken language potential. Geers and Moog (1987) suggested that these conditions include nonverbal intelligence, family support, and speech communication attitude.

Audiologists emphasize the appropriate fitting of hearing aids and cochlear implants to provide an optimal auditory signal. Auditory/verbal therapists and others advocate the provision of clear and audible speech input to the child. Early interventionists advocate diagnosis, aid fitting, and commencement of therapy as early as possible in the child's life. The common feature of all these approaches is that they increase the child's auditory experience by amplifying sound, by providing an increased number of listening opportunities, and by starting the learning process as early as possible. If a hard-of-hearing child has about 40–60% of the learning opportunities of a hearing child, then it is not surprising that their learning rate is about 40–60% of normal. This model of language learning by accumulating auditory experience is consistent with the fact that phonemes occurring most often as targets in the child's language are acquired first, and less frequently occurring phonemes are learned later. This same type of sequence is likely to occur for vocabulary learning and some aspects of morphology. In contrast, the sequence of syntactic structure development in table 17-3 is determined more by length and complexity rather than by frequency of occurrence of the structures in the language.

Critical and Sensitive Periods for Language Development

Not all theories and research studies are compatible with the learning approaches described in the previous paragraph. For example, Carey and Bartlett (1978) found that hearing children can learn new words very quickly (fast mapping) and retain their knowledge with infrequent use of the words

(extended mapping). Gilbertson and Kamhi (1995) repeated this experiment with 20 hard-of-hearing children. Ten of the children learned new words quickly and retained their knowledge like hearing children. The other 10 children took longer to learn the words and did not retain them as well as hearing children (see also Lederberg, this volume). Gilbertson and Kamhi suggested that half of their sample of children had specific language impairment in addition to their hearing loss. If a large proportion of hard-of-hearing children do have language learning disability, then achieving proficient spoken language performance may not be just a question of achieving a normal amount of auditory experience.

Long-term language learning difficulties may be caused by lack of auditory input early in life. It is known that hearing children are sensitive to some aspects of their ambient language within a few days of birth (Mehler et al., 1988) and that their auditory processing adapts to language-specific features during the first year of life (Jusczyk, 1993 Werker & Tees, 1984). It is also known from biological experiments that auditory deprivation in the first few weeks or months of an animal's life can change the condition and structure of neurons in the auditory pathway (Moore et al., 1999; Shepherd & Hardie, 2001). Moore et al. (1999) have also shown that episodes of otitis media in children can temporarily disrupt binaural hearing ability and that early auditory deprivation has a similar effect in ferrets.

It is quite a leap from these experimental results to a theory predicting a permanent language learning disability as a result of early auditory deprivation, such as critical and sensitive period theories (Doupe & Kuhl, 1999). On one hand, if these theories are correct, then early intervention may be the only way to avoid permanent language learning disability. On the other hand, even if the critical period theories are incorrect, early intervention is an effective way to increase the auditory experience of deaf and hard-of-hearing children. The existence of large numbers of deaf children who have received cochlear implants at different ages provides a new opportunity to test these theories. Some studies suggest that earlier implantation produces faster learning rates, consistent with the notion of sensitive periods early in life (Connor et al., 2000; Tye-Murray et al., 1995), but it is also possible to find counter-examples where deaf children implanted later in life learn quite quickly (e.g., Dawson et al., 1995).

Summary and Conclusions

On average, the spoken language of deaf and hard-of-hearing children is delayed relative to hearing children. At least part of the delay can be attributed to late diagnosis and fitting of hearing aids or cochlear implants. Early diagnosis and intervention will directly overcome this part of the delay. There are optimistic signs that most hard-of-hearing children may then achieve spoken language performance within the normal range if universal neonatal screening and early intervention become widespread (Yoshinaga-Itano, 1999). However, hearing aids and cochlear implants do not provide normal hearing, and it is likely that special intervention will continue to be required at home and at school to maintain a normal language learning rate. Some studies of deaf children using cochlear implants claim that language learning postimplant occurs at the normal rate (Dawson et al., 1995; Svirsky et al., 2000) while others indicate a slower rate of about 60% of normal. The slower rate is consistent with studies of hard-of-hearing children using hearing aids who have similar speech perception abilities (Boothroyd et al., 1991; Blamey, Sarant, et al., 2001; Boothroyd & Eran, 1994).

Most studies show a wide range of spoken language performance at every age. This may be due in part to the inclusion of children with cognitive handicaps (including specific language impairment) that are more prevalent in the deaf population than in the hearing population (Pyman, Blamey, Lacy, Clark, & Dowell, 2000; Schildroth, 1994). Future studies of language and deafness should identify these children and treat them as a separate group so that the effects of hearing level are not confounded with other cognitive processing factors. Even after children with cognitive handicaps are excluded, a wide range of performance persists, with few deaf children attaining above-average spoken language and the majority falling significantly behind their hearing peers.

It is clear that hearing loss makes the task of learning a spoken language more difficult, but not impossible. The hard-of-hearing group of children span a wide range of audiological thresholds from about 30 to 90 dB HL. They also span a wide range

of spoken language abilities, but there is a growing body of evidence to suggest that within this group, the severity of the hearing loss is not an overwhelming factor. It seems that there is a critical level of hearing, at about 90 dB HL, which separates the deaf and hard-of-hearing groups fairly clearly in terms of their auditory speech perception performance, but not so clearly in terms of their overall spoken language performance. The multichannel cochlear implant has the potential to move a child from the "deaf" side of this critical level of hearing to the "hard-of-hearing" side.

The low correlation between severity of hearing loss on one hand and speech perception and spoken language performance on the other is possibly attributable to the success of hearing aids and cochlear implants in achieving uniformly good aided hearing thresholds for hard-of-hearing children. Although hearing aids and implants provide aided thresholds that are adequate for perception of speech at a conversational level in quiet, the speech detection thresholds are not as low as those of hearing children. Nor do hearing aids and implants compensate fully for the distorting effects that often accompany a hearing loss (Plomp, 1978). It is possible that the higher aided thresholds of children wearing hearing aids may reduce their exposure to spoken language relative to hearing children, thus accounting for their slower language learning rates. The distortion effects that accompany hearing loss may account for poorer speech perception in noise for hard-of-hearing children compared to hearing children, although the differences in quiet are not as pronounced, especially when lipreading is used.

Given that hearing aids and implants can compensate for some of the effects of hearing loss, we must seek factors other than the degree of hearing loss to account for differences in spoken language performance among hard-of-hearing children. The factors that have been most successful in explaining variation are the characteristics of the child's home and school education programs, the child's intelligence, the time spent reading, and the age at intervention (Connor et al., 2000; Geers & Moog, 1988, 1989; Limbrick et al., 1992; Sarant, Blamey, Dowell, Clark, & Gibson, 2000; Yoshinaga-Itano, 1999). These are all factors that can promote or retard learning regardless of a child's degree of hearing loss.

Some of these factors can be manipulated to accelerate the rate of spoken language learning in hard-of-hearing children. For many years, some teachers, schools, and parents have stated that direct instruction in aspects of speech production, perception, and language is beneficial to the extent that a proportion of hard-of-hearing and deaf children can achieve highly intelligible speech and good speech perception scores. Controlled research studies are supporting these statements, and early intervention, modern hearing aids, and cochlear implants are increasing the proportion of children achieving age-appropriate spoken language. However, a large proportion of hard-of-hearing children are still not receiving enough linguistic input to learn spoken language at a normal rate.

References

Anthony, A., Bogle, D., Ingram, T.T., & McIsaac, M.W. (1971). The Edinburgh Articulation Test. Edinburgh: Churchill Livingston.

Bench, R.J., & Bamford, J.M. (Eds.) (1979). *Speech hearing tests and the spoken language of hearing-impaired children*. London: Academic Press.

Bench, J., Doyle, J., & Greenwood, K.M. (1987). A standardisation of the BKB/A Sentence Test for children in comparison with the NAL-CID Sentence Test and CAL-PBM Word Test. *Australian Journal of Audiology, 9*, 39–48.

Blamey, P., Barry, J., Bow, C., Sarant, J., Paatsch, L., & Wales, R. (2001). The development of speech production following cochlear implantation. *Clinical Linguistics and Phonetics, 15*, 363–382.

Blamey, P.J., Barry, J.G., & Jacq, P. (2001). Phonetic inventory development in young cochlear implant users 6 years postoperation. *Journal of Speech, Language, and Hearing Research, 44*, 73–79.

Blamey, P.J., Paatsch, L.E., Bow, C.P., Sarant, J.Z., & Wales, R.J. (2002). A critical level of hearing for speech perception in children. *Acoustics Research Letters Online, 3*, 18–23.

Blamey, P., & Sarant, J. (2002). Speech perception and language criteria for pediatric cochlear implant candidature. *Audiology and Neuro-Otology, 7*, 114–121.

Blamey, P.J., Sarant, J.Z., Paatsch, L.E., Barry, J.G., Bow, C.P., Wales, R.J., Wright, M., Psarros, C., Rattigan, K., & Tooher, R. (2001). Relationships among speech perception, production, language, hearing loss, and age in children with impaired hearing. *Journal of Speech, Language, and Hearing Research, 44*, 264–285.

Boothroyd, A. (1991). Speech perception measures and their role in the evolution of hearing aid performance in a pediatric population. In J.A. Feigin & P.G. Stelmachowicz (Eds.), *Pediatric amplification* (pp. 77–91). Omaha, NE: Boys Town National Research Hospital.

Boothroyd, A., & Eran, O. (1994). Auditory speech perception capacity of child implant users expressed as equivalent hearing loss. *Volta Review, 96*, 151–168.

Boothroyd, A., Geers, A.E. & Moog, J.S. (1991). Practical implications of cochlear implants in children. *Ear & Hearing, 12*, 81S–89S.

Brown, R. (1973). *A first language: The early stages*. Cambridge, MA: Harvard University Press.

Campbell, R., Dodd, B., & Burnham D. (Eds.). (1998). *Hearing by eye II: Advances in the psychology of speechreading and auditory-visual speech*. Hove, East Sussex, UK: Psychology Press.

Carey, S., & Bartlett, E. (1978). Acquiring a single new word. *Papers and Reports on Child Language Development, 15*, 17–29.

Clark, G.M., Blamey, P.J., Busby, P.A., Dowell, R.C., Franz, B.K.-H., Musgrave, G.H., Nienhuys, T.G., Pyman, B.C., Roberts, S.A., Tong, Y.C., Webb, R.L., Kuzma, J.A., Money, D.K., Patrick, J.F., & Seligman, P.M. (1987). A multiple-electrode cochlear implant for children. *Archives of Otolaryngology Head and Neck Surgery, 113*, 825–828.

Connor, C.McD., Hieber, S., Arts, H.A., & Zwolan, T.A. (2000). Speech, vocabulary, and the education of children using cochlear implants: Oral or total communication? *Journal of Speech, Language, and Hearing Research, 43*, 1185–1204.

Crystal, D. (1981). *Clinical linguistics*. Wein: Springer-Verlag

Crystal, D. (1992). *Profiling linguistic disability* (2nd ed.). London: Whurr.

Crystal, D., Fletcher, P., & Garman, M. (1989). *Grammatical analysis of language disability* (2nd ed.). London: Whurr.

Davis, J.M., Elfenbein, J., Schum, R., & Bentler, R.A. (1986). Effects of mild and moderate hearing impairments on language educational and psychosocial behaviour of children. *Journal of Speech & Hearing Disorders, 51*, 53–62.

Davis, H., & Silverman, S.R. (1978). *Hearing and deafness* (4th ed.). New York: Holt, Rinehart & Winston.

Dawson, P.W., Blamey, P.J., Dettman, S.J., Barker, E.J., & Clark, G.M. (1995). A clinical report on receptive vocabulary skills in cochlear implant users. *Ear & Hearing, 16*, 287–294.

Dillon, H. (2001). *Hearing aids*. Sydney: Boomerang Press.

Dodd, B. (1976). The phonological systems of deaf

children. *Journal of Speech, and Hearing Disorders*, 41, 185–198.

Dodd, B., McIntosh, B., & Woodhouse, L. (1998). Early lipreading ability and speech and language development of hearing-impaired pre-schoolers. In R. Campbell, B. Dodd, & D. Burnham (Eds.), *Hearing by eye II* (pp. 229–242). Hove, East Sussex UK: Psychology Press.

Doupe, A. J., & Kuhl, P. K. (1999). Birdsong and human speech: common themes and mechanisms. *Annual Reviews of Neuroscience*, 22, 567–631.

Dunn, L.M., & Dunn, L.M. (1997). *Peabody Picture Vocabulary Test* (3rd ed.). Circle Pines, MN: American Guidance Service.

Fenson, L., Dale, P.S., Reznick, J.S., Thal, D., Bates, E., Hartung, J.P., Pethick, S., & Reilly, J.S. (1993). *MacArthur Communicative Development Inventories user's guide and technical manual*. San Diego, CA: Singular.

Fisher, H.B., & Logemann, J.A. (1971). *Test of articulation competence*. New York: Houghton & Mifflin.

Gardner, M. (1979). *Expressive One-Word Picture Vocabulary Test*. Novato, CA: Academic Therapy Publications.

Geers, A.E., & Moog, J.S. (1987). Predicting spoken language acquisition of profoundly hearing-impaired children. *Journal of Speech and Hearing Disorders*, 52, 84–94.

Geers, A.E., & Moog, J.S. (1988). Predicting long-term benefits from single-channel cochlear implants in profoundly hearing-impaired children. *American Journal of Otology*, 9, 169–176.

Geers, A., & Moog, J. (1989). Factors predictive of the development of literacy in profoundly hearing-impaired adolescents. *Volta Review*, 91, 69–86.

Geers, A.E., & Moog, J.S. (Eds.). (1994). Effectiveness of cochlear implants and tactile aids for deaf children: The sensory aids study at Central Institute for the Deaf. *The Volta Review*, 96, 1–231.

Gilbertson, M., & Kamhi, A.G. (1995). Novel word learning in children with hearing impairment. *Journal of Speech & Hearing Research*, 38, 630–642.

Hudgins, C., & Numbers, F. (1942). An investigation of the intelligibility of the speech of the deaf. *Genetic Psychology Monographs*, 25, 289–392.

Jusczyk, P. (1993). How word recognition may evolve from infant speech perception capacities. In G.T.M. Altmann & R. Shillcock (Eds.), *Cognitive models of speech processing: The second Sperlonga meeting* (pp. 27–56). Hillsdale, NJ: Lawrence Erlbaum Associates.

Kent, R.D. (1997). *The speech sciences*. San Diego, CA: Singular.

Kirk, K.I., & Hill-Brown, C. (1985). Speech and lan-guage results in children with a cochlear implant. *Ear and Hearing*, 6, 36S–47S.

Lamore, P.J.J., Verweij, C., & Brocaar, M.P. (1990). Residual hearing capacity of severely hearing-impaired subjects. *Acta Otolaryngologica* (Suppl.) 469, 7–15.

Levelt, W.J.M. (1989). *Speaking. From intention to articulation*. Cambridge, MA: MIT Press.

Levitt, H., McGarr, N.S., & Geffner, D. (1987). Development of language and communication skills in hearing-impaired children. *ASHA Monographs 26.*

Limbrick, E.A., McNaughton, S., & Clay, M.M. (1992). Time engaged in reading: A critical factor in reading achievement. *American Annals of the Deaf*, 137, 309–314.

Ling, D. (1976). *Speech and the hearing-impaired child: Theory and practice*. Washington, DC: Alexander Graham Bell Association.

Ling, D. (1989). *Foundations of spoken language for hearing-impaired children*. Washington DC: Alexander Graham Bell Association.

Lund, N.J., & Duchan, J.F. (1993). *Assessing children's language in naturalistic contexts* (3rd ed.). Englewood Cliffs, NJ: Prentice Hall.

Maassen, B., & Povel, D.-J., (1985). The effect of segmental and suprasegmental correction on the intelligibility of deaf speech. *Journal of the Acoustical Society of America*, 78, 877–886.

McGarr, N.S. (1983). The intelligibility of deaf speech to experienced and inexperienced listeners. *Journal of Speech and Hearing Research*, 26, 451–458.

Markides, A. (1970). The speech of deaf and partially hearing children with special reference to factors affecting intelligibility. *British Journal of Disorders of Communication*, 5, 126–140.

Massaro, D.W. (1987). *Speech perception by ear and eye: A paradigm for psychological enquiry*. Hillsdale, NJ: Lawrence Erlbaum Associates.

Mehler, J., Jusczyk, P., Lambertz, G., Halsted, N., Bertoncini, J., & Amiel-Tison, C. (1988). A precursor of language acquisition in young infants. *Cognition*, 29, 143–178.

Monsen, R.B. (1978). Toward measuring how well hearing-impaired children speak. *Journal of Speech and Hearing Research*, 21, 197–219.

Moore, D. R., Hine, J. E., Jiang, Z. D., Matsuda, H., Parsons, C. H., & King, A. J. (1999). Conductive hearing loss produces a reversible binaural hearing impairment. *Journal of Neuroscience*, 19, 8704–8711.

Nagy, W.E., & Herman, P.A. (1987). Breadth and depth of vocabulary knowledge: Implications for acquisition and instruction. In M.G. McKeown, & M.E. Curtis (Eds.), *The nature of vocabulary acqui-*

sition (pp. 19–35). Hillsdale, NJ: Lawrence Erlbaum Associates.

Norton, S. J., Gorga, M. P., Widen, J. E., Folsom, R. C., Sininger, Y., Cone-Wesson, B., Vohr, B. R., & Fletcher, K. A. (2000). Identification of neonatal hearing impairment: summary and recommendations. *Ear & Hearing, 21,* 529–535.

Oberkotter Foundation Film Project. (2000) Dreams spoken here [Videotape]. Palo Alto, CA.

Osberger, M.J., Robbins, A.McC., Todd, S.L., & Riley, A.I. (1994). Speech intelligibility of children with cochlear implants. *The Volta Review, 96,* 169–180.

Paul, P.V., & Quigley, S.P. (1994). *Language and deafness.* San Diego: Singular.

Plomp, R. (1978). Auditory handicap of hearing impairment and the limited benefit of hearing aids. *Journal of the Acoustical Society of America, 63,* 533–549.

Pyman, B., Blamey, P., Lacy, P., Clark, G., & Dowell, R. (2000). The development of speech perception in children using cochlear implants: Effects of etiologic factors and delayed milestones. *The American Journal of Otology, 21,* 57–61.

Ramkalawan, T.W., & Davis, A.C. (1992). The effects of hearing loss and age of intervention on some language metrics in young hearing impaired children.*British Journal of Audiology, 26,* 97–107.

Reynell, J.K. (1983). *Reynell Development Language Scales Manual—Revised.* Windsor: NFER-Nelson.

Rickards, F. W., Tan, L. E., Cohen, L. T., Wilson, O. J., Drew, J. H., & Clark, G. M. (1994). Auditory steady-state evoked potential in newborns. *British Journal of Audiology, 28,* 327–37.

Sander, E. (1972). When are speech sounds learned? *Journal of Speech and Hearing Research, 37,* 55–63.

Sarant, J.Z., Blamey, P.J., Dowell, R.C., Clark, G.M., & Gibson, W.P.R. (2001). Variation in speech perception scores among children with cochlear implants. *Ear & Hearing, 22,* 18–28.

Scarborough, H.S. (1990). Index of productive syntax. *Applied Psycholinguistic, 11,* 1–22.

Scarborough, H.S., Rescorla, L., Tager-Flusberg, H., & Fowler, A.E. (1991). The relation of utterance length to grammatical complexity in normal and language-disordered groups. *Applied Psycholinguistics, 12,* 23–45.

Schildroth, A.N. (1994). Congenital cytomegalovirus and deafness. *American Journal of Audiology, 3,* 27–38.

Semel, E., Wiig, E., & Secord, W.A., (1995). *Clinical Evaluation of Language Fundamentals* (3rd ed.). San Antonio, TX: The Psychological Corporation, Harcourt Brace.

Shepherd, R.K., & Hardie, N.A. (2001). Deafness-induced changes in the auditory pathway: implications for cochlear implants. *Audiology & Neurootology, 6,* 305–318.

Shriberg, L.D., Austin, D., Lewis, B.A., Sweeny, J.L., & Wilson, D.L. (1997). The percentage of consonants correct (PCC) metric: Extensions and reliability data. *Journal of Speech, Language, and Hearing Research, 40,* 708–722.

Shriberg, L.D., & Kwiatkowski, J. (1982). Phonological disorders III: A procedure for assessing severity of involvement. *Journal of Speech and Hearing Disorders, 47,* 256–270.

Skinner, M.W. (1988). *Hearing aid evaluation.* Englewood Cliffs, NJ: Prentice Hall.

Smith, C.R. (1975). Residual hearing and speech production in deaf children. *Journal of Speech and Hearing Research, 18,* 795–811.

Spencer, L.J., Tye-Murray, N., & Tomblin, J.B. (1998). The production of English inflectional morphology, speech production and listening performance in children with cochlear implants. *Ear and Hearing, 19,* 310–318.

Stoel-Gammon, C. (1998). Sounds and words in early language acquisition. The relationship between lexical and phonological development. In R. Paul (Ed.), *Explaining the speech-language connection* (pp. 25–52). Baltimore, MD: Paul H. Brookes.

Svirsky, M.A., Robbins, A.M., Kirk, K.I., Pisoni, D.B., & Miyamoto, R.T. (2000). Language development in profoundly deaf children with cochlear implants. *Psychological Science, 11,* 153–158.

Tobey, E., Geers, A., & Brenner, C. (1994). Speech production results: Speech feature acquisition. *The Volta Review, 96* (monograph), 109–129.

Tomblin, J.B., Spencer, L., Flock, S., Tyler, R., & Gantz, B. (1999). A comparison of language achievement in children with cochlear implants and children using hearing aids. *Journal of Speech, Language, and Hearing Research, 42,* 497–511.

Tye-Murray, N., Spencer, L., & Woodworth, G.G. (1995). Acquisition of speech by children who have prolonged cochlear implant experience. *Journal of Speech and Hearing Research, 38,* 327–337.

Werker, J.F., & Tees, R.C. (1984). Cross-language speech perception: Evidence for perceptual reorganization during the first year of life. *Infant Behavior and Development, 7,* 49–63.

Wiig, E., Secord, W.A., & Semel, E. (1992). *Clinical Evaluation of Language Fundamentals–Preschool.* San Antonio, TX: The Psychological Corporation, Harcourt Brace.

Woodcock, R.W., & Mather, N. (1989). *Woodcock-Johnson Tests of Cognitive Ability.* Allen, TX: DLM Teaching Resources.

Yoshinaga-Itano, C, Sedey, A.L., Coulter, D.K., & Mehl, A.L. (1998). Language of early- and later-identified children with hearing loss. *Pediatrics*, *102*, 1161–1171.

Yoshinaga-Itano, C. (1999). Benefits of early intervention for children with hearing loss. *Otolaryngological Clinics of North America*, *32*, 1089–102.

Zimmerman, I.L., Steiner, V.C., & Pond, R.E. (1979). *Preschool Language Scale*. Columbus, OH: Merrill.

18

Amy R. Lederberg

Expressing Meaning
From Communicative Intent to Building a Lexicon

This chapter addresses the development of young deaf children's communication and lexical abilities from infancy through preschool, with a focus on the development of deaf and hard-of-hearing children of hearing parents (DCHP). Comparisons with the development of typically developing hearing children with hearing parents and deaf children of deaf parents (DCDP) are made to highlight the strengths and weaknesses of the development of DCHP children. After describing communication and lexical skills, discussion focuses on aspects of children's language learning environment to elucidate ways that parents may affect their children's development.

Communication Development: 6–18 Months

Young children's first words emerge from prelinguistic communication and cognitive skills that develop from 6 to 18 months of age (Adamson, 1995; Dromi, 1992).

Babbling

Between 6 and 7 months, both deaf and hearing infants begin to produce speechlike vocalizations. These rhythmic vocalizations, or "marginal babbling," contain reduplicated sound units consisting of consonants and vowels (known as CV patterns), in which the transition between consonant and vowel is slower than is typical in speech (Masataka, 2000). The onset of marginal babbling produced by rhythmic jaw movements coincides with the onset of rhythmic hand movements and is probably controlled by motor maturation (Masataka, 2000; Wallace, Menn, & Yoshinaga-Itano, 2000). Although both deaf and hearing infants produce marginal babbles, hearing infants soon transition to more mature, speechlike syllables (referred to as canonical babble). These vocalizations consist of true syllables that are produced rhythmically and typically contain a series of CV patterns (e.g., dadada). From 7 to 12 months, the prosody and phonological attributes of hearing infants' canonical babbling begins to resemble their ambient language, thus suggesting they are analyzing and representing these linguistic features. In contrast, most deaf infants do not produce canonical babble, and the frequency of vocalizations that contain babbling does not increase developmentally (Oller & Eilers, 1988; Wallace et al., 2000).

Although deaf infants rarely produce vocalized canonical babbles, DCDP infants may babble with their hands (referred to as manual babbling) and thus be acquiring the phonological structure of their ambient language (Masataka, 2000; Petitto & Marentette, 1991). However, because research studies only included small samples (two or three infants in a group), with brief descriptions of methodology, conclusions about manual babbling await further study (see Schick, this volume).

The relation between babbling and later language development is far from clear (Masataka, 2000; Wallace et al., 2000). On the one hand, the effect of the ambient language on canonical babbling (vocalized or signed) suggests that the quality of children's canonical babbles is an indicator of phonological knowledge (Masataka, 2000). In addition, Oller and Eilers (1988) reported that only deaf infants whose canonical babbling patterns resembled those of hearing infants developed spoken words during their study. However, babbling may be neither predictive nor necessary for later language abilities. Wallace et al. (2000) found that DCHP children's speech during elementary school was related to the phonological structure (variety of consonants) of their vocalizations during preschool but not the amount of canonical babbles in infancy.

Joint Attention

During the first year of life, infants tend to attend to either people (before 6 months) or the environment (after 6 months). Typically, beginning around 12 months and increasing over their second year, toddlers' integrate attention to both. This intentional alternating of attention between the environment and the communication partner is the defining feature of "coordinated joint attention" (Adamson, 1995). Coordinated joint attention enables toddlers to communicate and share meanings with their partners about events and objects in the world and to learn the conventional words to label such events.

Deaf and hearing toddlers' engagement in coordinated joint attention with their hearing mothers typically begins to appear at 12 months and shows similar, dramatic increases throughout the second year of life (Prezbindowski, Adamson, & Lederberg, 1998; Spencer, 2000). Although DCHP and hearing toddlers are similar, DCDP toddlers spend more time than DCHP in coordinated joint

attention. Deaf mothers facilitate visual attention by directly soliciting attention to themselves (rather than to objects) and by using more attention-catching visual communication devices (gestures and signs) than hearing mothers (Waxman & Spencer, 1997). Although joint attention seems to be a robust developmental achievement for DCHP toddlers, heightened visual attention, such as that shown by DCDP infants, may be necessary for DCHP toddlers to develop language.

Intentional Communicative Behaviors

Toddlers also begin to integrate intentional communication into these joint attention episodes (Adamson, 1995). Although the early cries and movements of infants are frequently treated as communicative, infants probably do not intend to communicate with these acts. Intentional communication, expressed by gestures and vocalizations, is usually evident between 9 and 12 months and increases in frequency over the second year of life. These behaviors allow toddlers to engage in turn taking and object-focused "conversations" with their mothers before acquiring language. Hearing and DCHP toddlers intentionally communicate with equal frequency at 12, 18, and 22 months of age (Lederberg & Everhart, 1998; Yoshinaga-Itano & Stredler-Brown, 1992).

Mode of Communication and Pragmatic Function

Both hearing and DCHP toddlers communicate primarily by vocalizations (Lederberg & Everhart, 1998; Spencer, 1993a). For instance, at 22 months, Lederberg and Everhart found that 80% of DCHP and hearing toddlers' utterances contained vocalizations, while only 20% contained gestures. Although DCHP toddlers communicate as frequently and in a similar fashion as hearing toddlers, there is a clear difference in the form of their vocalizations. Hearing toddlers are more likely to use vocalizations containing canonical syllables and words than deaf toddlers (Spencer, 1993a). Hearing toddlers also frequently use conventional intonational patterns to express different meanings or pragmatic functions (e.g., demanding something vs. making a comment, Adamson, 1995). Only a small proportion of DCHP toddlers use intonation

(Obenchain, Menn, & Yoshinaga-Itano, 2000). Research on pragmatic function also suggests that these intonational markers are lacking. Although DCHP toddlers indicate a general intention to communicate with eye gaze and other markers, the pragmatic function or specific meaning of communications is unclear the majority of the time; with ambiguous utterances occurring 50% more frequently in DCHP dyads than in hearing dyads (Lederberg & Everhart, 2000; Nicholas, 2000; Nicholas & Geers, 1997). As a result, communication breakdowns occur more often in DCHP dyads than in hearing dyads (Lederberg & Mobley, 1990).

Meaning and communicative value of gestures are much clearer than nonlinguistic vocalizations, and theorists posit that gesture plays an important role in the entry into symbolic communication (Acredolo, Goodwyn, Horobin, & Emmons, 1999; Dromi, 1992). Typically, infants start using actions such as reaching (referred to as preconventional gestures) at 9 months, pointing (deictic gestures) at 12 or 13 months, and iconic, or symbolic gestures at 17 months (Adamson, 1995). Because of the ambiguity of their vocalizations, DCHP toddlers might be expected to use gestures more frequently than hearing toddlers. However, research shows DCHP and hearing toddlers use similar gestural communications at 12, 18, and 22 months (Lederberg & Everhart, 1998; Spencer, 1993a). Even more surprisingly, DCDP toddlers' nonlinguistic gestural communication during this early period is similar to that of hearing and DCHP toddlers despite the fact that DCDP children are exposed to more points and gesturelike signs in their linguistic environment (Schick, this volume). Thus, development of gestures during this early period seems unaffected by either hearing loss or large linguistic environmental variations.

In summary, many aspects of early prelinguistic communication seem impervious to the major variations in linguistic input and skills that occur for deaf and hearing children. As Adamson (1995) notes, "hearing mothers and their deaf infants . . . engage in lively, object-focused, communication-filled exchanges" (p. 198) similar to hearing toddlers. However, the meanings of these exchanges are more dependent on context for DCHP than hearing toddlers because the formers' utterances lack conventional intonational markers.

Communication Development: 18 Months–4 Years

Unfortunately, early prelinguistic communication abilities frequently do not serve as a foundation for the transition into language for DCHP children (Nicholas, 2000; Prezbindowski et al., 1998; Spencer, 1993a). After 18 months, nonlinguistic communication quickly evolves into linguistic communication among hearing and DCDP toddlers (see next section and Schick, this volume). In contrast, for many DCHP children, the use of nonlinguistic communication continues throughout the preschool years (Goldin-Meadow & Mylander, 1984; Greenberg, 1980; Lederberg & Everhart, 1998; Mohay, 1994; Nicholas, 2000; Yoshinaga-Itano & Stredler-Brown 1992). How does the reliance on nonlinguistic devices affect DCHP children's communication and interaction with others?

Joint Attention

Prezbindowski et al. (1998) found differences in the amount and nature of joint attention demonstrated by DCHP and hearing toddlers after 18 months of age. Although both DCHP and hearing toddlers increased the amount of time they spent in joint attention, the increase was greater for hearing toddlers. In addition, for hearing toddlers, but not for DCHP toddlers, the nature of joint attention changed as words became integrated in their episodes of joint attention (i.e., symbolically infused joint attention) and guided their play with objects and people approximately one third of the time. In contrast, DCHP toddlers, who used virtually no language with their mothers, spent no time in symbolically infused joint attention.

Intentional Communication and Pragmatic Function

Although DCHP children continue to increase the amount they communicate throughout the preschool years, hearing children's communication increases faster (Lederberg & Everhart, 2000; Nicholas, 2000). The pragmatic functions of DCHP children's communication continue to be more ambiguous than and different from those of hearing children (Day, 1986; Lederberg & Everhart, 2000; Nicholas, 2000; Nicholas & Geers, 1997). DCHP toddlers are more likely to use communication to direct their mothers and less likely to make statements or ask questions than hearing children. As they mature, DCHP preschoolers decrease their use of directives and increase their use of statements. However, question-asking (even through nonverbal means) remains at a low level. The pragmatic function of DCHP and hearing children's communication, especially question-asking, is related to their language abilities (Greenberg, 1980; Nicholas, 2000; Nicholas, Geers, & Kozak, 1994; Yoshinaga-Itano & Stredler-Brown, 1992). Nonverbal communication can easily be used to make requests and call attention to the environment, but information exchange (comments and question-asking) is clearly tied to producing and understanding language.

Gestures

By preschool, DCHP children gesture more and use a larger variety of gestures than hearing children (Greenberg, 1980; Lederberg & Everhart, 1998; Mohay, 1994). Research examining these gestural systems addresses two questions. To what extent do children create a complex communication system resembling language without the help of input? What is the relation between gesture and DCHP children's developing linguistic abilities?

In general, DCHP children increase use of gestures from 18 months to 3 years of age, after which gesture use stabilizes or decreases (Dromi, Fuks, & Ringwald-Frimerman, 1998; Lederberg & Everhart, 1998; Mohay, 1994). DCHP preschoolers, on average, produce 3 gestures per minute, although a few gesture as much as 6 times a minute (de Villiers, Bibeau, Ramos, & Gatty, 1993; Goldin-Meadow & Mylander, 1984; Lederberg & Everhart, 1998; Mohay, 1994). As with hearing children, the amount children gesture is related to the amount their mothers' gesture, although children occasionally gesture more than their mothers (Acredolo et al., 1999; de Villiers et al., 1993; Goldin-Meadow & Mylander, 1984). Deictic gestures (e.g., points) account for the majority of gestures, followed by conventional gestures (e.g., waving goodbye), and finally iconic or representational gestures (e.g., ball). Both DCHP and hearing children create some novel gestures that iconically resemble an action or object (Acredolo et al., 1999; Goldin-Meadow & Mylander, 1984; Mohay, 1994).

DCHP children most frequently use single-gesture utterances. Utterances that contain two or more gestures increase over time; and occur, on average, once every 4 min. Two-gesture utterances usually contain two points or a point and another gesture (de Villiers et al., 1993; Dromi et al., 1998; Goldin-Meadow & Mylander, 1984; Mohay, 1994). Thus, although DCHP children use gestures to communicate about referents and events, symbolic communication is infrequent without language. This is consistent with research that found that the amount hearing children use iconic gestures (but not points or conventional gestures) is closely related to their language development, with iconic gestures increasing as language develops (Nicoladis, Mayberry, & Genesee, 1999).

But does the gestural system show languagelike structural properties? The answer seems to depend on whether the DCHP children have access to a language model. Goldin-Meadow and colleagues (Goldin-Meadow, McNeill, & Singleton, 1996; Goldin-Meadow & Mylander, 1984) extensively analyzed the gestural system of 10 deaf preschoolers who never acquired the spoken language of their environment. The gestural system used by the children seemed to have two rule systems: one for gestures, the other for utterances. Their iconic gestures consisted of a limited number of elements that were combined to represent features of the action or referent (e.g., size, shape, movement path). The children also used a consistent order when combining points or points and iconic gestures to express an array of semantic relations. These rules did not exist in input but were created by the children. Although those gestural systems were rule governed, they differed from language in important ways. The children did not seem to create a lexicon of "words" or stable gesture–referent pairs. Instead, multiple gestures were used to refer to a given referent, and specific gestures were also used to refer to multiple referents. In addition, unlike grammatical rules, the morphological and utterance rules that the children created appear to have been based on meaning.

In contrast, DCHP children who are acquiring speech do not develop a rule-governed gestural system, even when their acquisition of speech is severely delayed. When they combine gestures into utterances, the gestures are not consistently ordered (de Villiers et al., 1993; Mohay, 1994). In addition, when DCHP children begin to acquire speech, words and gestures are almost always produced simultaneously to express equivalent meanings (e.g., the spoken word "ball" combined with a point to a ball or iconic gesture for ball), and not supplementary meanings (e.g., "ball" plus throw gesture) (de Villiers et al., 1993; Dromi et al., 1998). Thus, language-delayed DCHP preschoolers do not take advantage of the representational potential of word–gesture combinations to express semantic relations.

Vocabulary Development

Lexicon Size

Although most hearing toddlers communicate primarily with gestures and nonlinguistic vocalizations, words begin to be part of the communication repertoire beginning with their first words between 10 and 13 months (Fenson et al., 1994). New words are typically added to the lexicon slowly during the next 4–6 months, starting with only 1 per month and gradually increasing to 3 per week. This initial phase of slow word learning continues until toddlers have acquired more than 50 words, which, on average, occurs between 16 and 18 months (Dromi, 1999; Fenson et al., 1994). At this point, hearing children typically become rapid word learners, and there is a sudden acceleration in the growth rate of lexical learning. From 16 to 30 months, the median number of words learned increases from 3 to 8 new words per week. As a result, the median lexicon by 30 months contains 573 words. However, variation in the size of hearing children's lexicons is large, and this variability increases from 12 to 30 months (Fenson et al., 1994).

Research on vocabulary development of children acquiring American Sign Language (ASL) suggests that signs are acquired more rapidly than spoken words during early development, with lexicons of DCDP children from 12 to 17 months of age larger than those reported for hearing peers (Anderson & Reilly, 2002; Meier & Newport, 1990). This early "sign advantage" may occur because young toddlers are more likely to have the motor control necessary to produce words with their hands than with their mouths (Meier & Newport, 1990). This is consistent with experimental research that found that it is easier for hearing toddlers to be taught gestured words than spoken

words from 10 to 18 months (Acredolo et al., 1999). The sign advantage seems to disappear toward the end of the second year: median and ranges of lexicon size for DCDP and hearing toddlers are similar between 18 and 23 months (Anderson & Reilly, 2002).

Vocabulary development of young DCHP children is delayed, slower, and even more variable than for hearing of DCDP children (Lederberg & Spencer, 2001; Mayne, Yoshinaga-Itano, Sedey, & Carey, 2000; Moeller, 2000). Given this variability, sample size and characteristics are important to consider when generalizing research findings. Mayne et al. (2000) provided information on early lexical development for 202 DCHP children using the MacArthur Communicative Inventory (CDI), a parent-report instrument that includes an extensive word checklist. These children were enrolled in well-established, intensive, early intervention programs in Colorado. Hearing losses ranged from mild to profound and were identified for three fourths of the children by 6 months of age. One-third of parents used sign and speech with their children; the rest used only speech. One-third of the sample had cognitive impairments.

Lexical development was significantly affected by both age of identification (before vs. after 6 months old) and cognitive impairments (<80 cognitive quotient) (Mayne et al., 2000). Mode of communication, degree of hearing loss, gender, ethnicity, and education of caregiver did not relate to lexical development in this sample. Table 18-1 uses data from Mayne et al. and Fenson et al. (1993) to characterize lexical development of DCHP children in four subgroups (and hearing children for comparison) for two aspects of the lexicon: (1) the age when children transition from slow to rapid or accelerated word learning (as measured by the number of words learned per week) and (2) lexicon size at the oldest ages assessed (30 months for hearing children, 32–37 months for DCHP children).

All DCHP children who were not cognitively impaired transitioned to rapid word learning between 20 and 32 months. Early identification accelerated the transition to rapid word learning (e.g., 26 vs. 32 months at 50th percentile on the CDI) and was related to a faster rate of vocabulary growth during rapid word learning. There were some DCHP children who transitioned to rapid word learning at ages that overlapped with their hearing peers. DCHP children who were identified early

Table 18-1. Lexical development of deaf children of hearing parents and hearing children as measured by the MacArthur Communicative Inventory (CDI)

Characteristics of children	Percentile rank on CDI	Age when rapid word learning is evident (months)	Lexicon size at 30 or 32–37 months of age
Hearing children			
	50	17	568
	25	21	459
	5	26	191
DOH children			
Early identified/no cognitive disability	75	20	554
	50	26	396
	10	32	105
Later identified/no cognitive disability	75	26	413
	50	32	291
Early identified/cognitive disability	75	32	247
	50	No	37
Later identified/cognitive disability	75	32	196
	50	No	51

Note. Data are extrapolated from tables published in Fenson et al. (1993) for hearing children and (Mayne et al., 2000) for deaf/hard-of-hearing children. Early identified is ≤6 months old. Lexicon size for hearing children is at 30 months old; for deaf children it is at 32–37 months old. "No" means no rapid word learning.

and scored at or above the 50th percentile on the CDI and DCHP children who were identified late and scored at or above the 75th percentile transitioned to rapid word learning between 20 and 26 months. This was comparable to hearing children who had CDI scores between the 5th and 25th percentiles (see table 18-1). Lexicon size of these children also seemed to be comparable to their hearing peers. DCHP children in the lower percentiles transitioned to rapid word learning after 2 years of age, something not observed for hearing toddlers.

For DCHP children who were cognitively impaired, only children at or above the 75th percentile in lexicon size transitioned to rapid word learning during the study. Thus, most DCHP children with cognitive impairments were still in the slow word-learning phase at 3 years of age.

Research by Moeller (2000) indicates that age-typical vocabulary growth occurs for some DCHP children throughout preschool. She assessed receptive vocabulary by administering the Peabody Picture Vocabulary Test (PPVT) to 112 DCHP children at 5 years of age. All children had received services from one early intervention program in Nebraska for 6 months and then were placed in an auditory/oral or total communication program (approximately equal proportions), depending on which

was "determined to be most appropriate to meet the needs of the child and family" (p. 3). Age of enrollment in the early intervention program ranged from 1 to 54 months and was divided into four levels for analyses (0–11; 12–23; 24–35; and >35 months). Children with secondary (including cognitive) disabilities were excluded from the study. Half of the children scored within one standard deviation of the norms for hearing 5 years olds. Family involvement and age of intervention were the only factors affecting lexical knowledge, accounting for more than 55% of the variance of language scores. Low involvement by families was devastating and was even more important than age of intervention. Children whose parents were rated as having "ideal" or "good" involvement with their children's education (45% of the sample) had language scores comparable to hearing peers; standard scores averaged from 85 to 100, depending on age of identification. Children whose parents were less involved (average to limited) had small lexicons, with standard scores ranging from 60 to 80 depending on age of identification. Language scores were not related to mode of communication.

Other researchers have reported much smaller lexicons for samples of DCHP preschoolers than these found by Mayne et al. (2000) or Moeller

(2000), with average lexicons more than 2 standard deviations below those of hearing peers (Bornstein, Saulnier, & Hamilton, 1980; Griswold & Commings, 1974; Lederberg, Prezbindowski, & Spencer, 2000a, 2000b; Ouellet, Le Normand, & Cohen, 2001) The low achievement of these samples of DCHP children may be due to the lack of early identification and/or intensive early intervention that was available for the DCHP children studied by Mayne et al. (2000) and Moeller (2000).

Growth Rate

Thus far, rates of vocabulary growth have been inferred by comparing lexicons of children at different ages. Although such cross-sectional data are suggestive, an accurate description of changes in growth rate can only be obtained from frequent sampling of the same child over time. Such longitudinal research is especially crucial to issues of the presence of a vocabulary "burst" or suddenness in the change from slow to rapid word learning. The presence of a burst is important theoretically because it suggests a qualitative shift in word learning abilities. The majority of hearing children experience a vocabulary burst sometime between 16 and 20 months of age (Goldfield & Reznick, 1990).

It is not clear whether DCDP children show a vocabulary burst. Anderson and Reilly (2002) observed linear vocabulary growth among 13 DCDP children. However, their infrequent sampling of lexicon sizes (every 4–6 months) may have obscured sudden accelerations. In fact, two other case studies of children acquiring ASL showed a vocabulary burst (Capirci, Montanari, & Volterra, 1998; Schlesinger & Meadow, 1972). For example, one child had a vocabulary of 20 words at 16 months that expanded to 106 words in just 2 months.

There seems to be a range of growth patterns among DCHP children. There are cases of exceptional DCHP children who acquire vocabulary in a pattern similar to hearing children. In two studies (Gardner & Zorfass, 1983; Notoya, Suzuki, & Furukawa, 1994), three DCHP children who used simultaneous communication showed a rapid acceleration in word learning between 18 and 22 months. For example, one child took 8 months to learn his first 100 words and then learned 50 words in one month alone (Gardner & Zorfass, 1983).

Other longitudinal case studies (Ertmer & Mellon, 2001; Gregory & Mogford, 1981; Ouellet et al., 2001) describe a total of 14 deaf children (6 with cochlear implants) acquiring spoken language, where vocabulary growth was much slower than the very successful DCHP children described above. Three distinct patterns were observed. Two children, although delayed in their transition to rapid word learning, showed a rapid acceleration in word acquisition when their vocabulary exceeded 50 words (one at 24 months, the other at 38 months; Gregory & Mogford, 1981). Ten children showed a slow accumulation of vocabulary (learning from 2 to 4 new words per week) with no evidence of acceleration over the course of the study, even though some knew more than 100 words (Ertmer & Mellon, 2001; Gregory & Mogford, 1981; Ouellet et al., 2001). Four children (two with cochlear implants) learned almost no new words over the year(s) they were observed and finished the study with a lexicon of less than 20 words even though the children were at least 4 years old (Gregory & Mogford, 1981; Ouellet et al., 2001). As Gregory and Mogford (1981) point out, the continuation of slow word learning in DCHP children is distinctly different from what is observed in hearing children's vocabulary growth. It also suggests that vocabulary size (e.g., a lexicon of more than 100 words) may not always coincide with a transition to rapid word learning.

These longitudinal studies, although illustrative of the range of patterns possible among DCHP children, are insufficient to reach any generalizations about growth rate, especially about factors that affect vocabulary learning. For example, in these longitudinal studies, DCHP children who were in simultaneous communication environments showed age-typical vocabulary growth, but DCHP children who were acquiring speech (even with cochlear implants) did not. This effect of modality contradicts the much larger cross-sectional studies that found no effect of language mode (Mayne et al., 2000; Moeller, 2000). Clearly, more longitudinal research is needed to determine factors that lead to these very different patterns of vocabulary growth.

Content of Lexicon

In addition to the size and rate of lexical development, researchers have examined the types of words children learn. The lexicons of DCHP, DCDP, and hearing children show both similarities and differences. The specific words in most early reported lexicons (< 35 words) of DCDP, DCHP, and hearing children are remarkably similar. Among these early words are names for important people (mommy, daddy, baby), animals (dog, cat, duck, bird), objects (ball, car), food (milk, cookie), and social personal words (bye, no) (Anderson & Reilly, 2002; Gregory & Mogford, 1981; Griswold & Commings, 1974).

Nominals or names of objects and people predominate in the 50-word and 100-word lexicons of hearing, DCDP and DCHP children. However, lexicons of DCDP and DCHP children (acquiring ASL or signed or spoken English) appear to have a lower proportion of nominals than those of hearing children (Anderson & Reilly, 2002; Gregory & Mogford, 1981; Mohay, 1994; Shafer & Lynch, 1981). Their lexicons are more likely to contain action, descriptive, and personal-social words than those of hearing children at the same level of lexical development. Anderson and Reilly (2002) suggested that the increased use of predicates may occur for DCDP children because of the structure of ASL. However, differences are also found between hearing children and DCHP children acquiring signed and/or spoken English. For these latter children, other explanations have been offered (Gregory & Mogford, 1981; Mohay, 1994). Older language-delayed DCHP children may be acquiring vocabulary that is appropriate for their more advanced cognitive and social developmental level. DCHP children, in general, may be more concerned with regulating social relationships and activity and less about labeling objects than hearing children because of differences in the structure and/or content of language input. Future research should examine the impact of age and the nature of the language input (both structure and content) on the lexicon.

Word-Learning Processes or Skills That Enable Children to Learn New Words

The number and class of words that children know and the rate at which they acquire new words are all aspects of knowledge. Equally important are changes in the processes that children use when learning new words. Among hearing children, transitions from slow to rapid word learning is linked to the acquisition of new word-learning skills (Dromi, 1999; Mervis & Bertrand, 1994). These changes can be characterized in three phases of word learning.

Slow Word Learning

Diary data and experimental research with hearing infants indicate that, during the slow word learning phase, 1-year-olds only retain a new word after hearing it multiple times (Dromi, 1999; Hollich, Hirsh-Pasek, & Golinkoff, 2000). In addition, young toddlers typically only learn words for referents or events that are perceptually salient or that they find interesting (Hollich et al., 2000).

Rapid Word Learning or Fast Mapping

Sometime between 16 and 24 months, several changes typically occur in word learning that facilitate acceleration in vocabulary growth rate (Dromi, 1999; Hollich et al., 2000). First, children are able to store an initial representation of the phonological form and meaning of a word after only a few exposures Second, they quickly learn the meaning of words based on the social/pragmatic cues given by adults.

Word Learning Based on Internal Skills

Children's skill in word learning continues to grow as they develop the ability to make inferences about the meaning of new words even when the speaker gives no pragmatic cues for reference (Mervis & Bertrand, 1994). For example, hearing 2½-year-olds use the novel mapping strategy when learning new words; they know a novel word is more likely to refer to an unfamiliar rather than a familiar object. For instance, if a child is looking at a lion, elephant, and gazelle, and an adult says, "Oh, look, a gazelle," the child who already knows "elephant" and "lion" will assume "gazelle" refers to the novel animal. This allows children to learn new words in naturally occurring conversations.

Word-Learning Skills in DCHP Children

Lederberg and colleagues (Lederberg et al., 2000a, 2000b; Lederberg & Spencer, 2001) examined the development of word learning processes in 91 DCHP preschoolers. The children developed the three levels of word learning as the size of their lexicon increased. Children with small lexicons (M = 59 expressive words) could not rapidly learn new words even when they were explicitly taught (i.e., they were slow word learners). Children with moderately sized lexicons (M = 142 words) learned new words only when they were explicitly taught but not in the novel mapping context (i.e., rapid word learners). Children with the largest vo-cabularies ($M = 318$ words) learned new words rapidly when they had to infer the meaning of the word as well as when they were explicitly taught. Although word-learning abilities were related to lexicon size, they were not related to children's ages, and there were no significant differences in the pattern of results for children learning language in oral or simultaneous communication environments. Longitudinal research (Lederberg et al., 2000b) confirms that these word-learning abilities are acquired sequentially and are related to lexicon size. All DCHP children acquired the word learning skills, but some did not acquire novel word mapping until they were more than 5 years old.

Language Learning Environment

Factors Linked to Vocabulary Development

Vocabulary development is clearly linked to the way words are used in the environment. Research has identified three factors as particularly important in facilitating growth in the lexicon of both DCHP and hearing children.

Frequency

During early vocabulary development, the rate of vocabulary growth of hearing toddlers is related to the amount of language their mothers use with them (Huttenlocher, Haight, Bryk, Sletzer, & Lyons, 1991). Word frequency also plays an important role in vocabulary development for DCHP children acquiring signs. The signing ability of hearing parents varies widely, with most mothers signing only a small proportion of their communication (Lederberg & Everhart, 1998; Spencer, 1993b). The number of signs used by hearing mothers predicts the number of signs in their DCHP children's lexicon at the same age and across ages (Lederberg & Everhart, 1998; Spencer, 1993b). Thus, one reason lexical growth is slow among DCHP children acquiring sign is their impoverished sign environment.

The importance of frequency for DCHP children acquiring speech is more ambiguous. Both Harris (1992) and Gallaway and Woll (1994) point out the difficulty in describing the oral-language learning environment of DCHP children because it is impossible to determine the difference between the amount of language in the environment (input) and the amount of language the children perceive (uptake). Variables that affect perception of spoken language (e.g., degree of hearing loss, age of amplification and/or implantation) may be more important than the frequency of input.

Visual Accessibility

Accessibility of input will affect the extent of uptake, or how much is received. As numerous researchers have emphasized (Harris, 2001; Mohay, 2000; Waxman & Spencer, 1997; Wood, Wood, Griffiths, & Howarth, 1986), communicators must present words in such a way as to make them visually accessible to DCHP children. Although research on joint attention indicates DCHP toddlers can divide their attention between environment and their communicating partner, they do not appear to make their visual attention (i.e., when and where they look) contingent on their partners' visual communication (Harris, 2001; Lederberg & Everhart, 1998). Because of poor coordination between visual attention and signs, DCHP children typically miss between 20% and 30% of their parents' visual communication (Greenberg, Calderon, & Kusche, 1984; Lederberg & Everhart, 1998; Swisher, 1991, 1992). Thus, the uptake of visual language is probably considerably less than the already reduced frequency of input in the home environment.

Visual attention to the face in order to use lip movement cues for spoken words is even rarer in young children. Lederberg and Everhart (1998) found nearly two thirds of spoken utterances (that were unaccompanied by visual communication) were not seen by DCHP preschoolers. In fact, DCHP and hearing children did not differ in how much they attended to their mothers' faces while mothers were talking. In addition, this attention did not improve with age (from 22 months to 3 years of age). Thus, young DCHP children do not spontaneously look at the face to understand speech without environmental support.

Contingency

Early vocabulary development is also related to the way mothers use words and the nonverbal context in which the words are embedded. Hearing children are more likely to learn words that label objects and events that are the focus of their attention than words that require them to switch their attention (e.g., saying "truck" when child is playing or looking at truck rather than when labeling object after eliciting the child's attention) (Harris, 2000; Tomasello & Farrar, 1986). Clearly, this type of contingent naming makes the reference clear and also ensures that words refer to the child's interests. This is especially important during the slow word learning phase.

Several authors have suggested that DCHP children's language delay may be caused by their hearing mothers controlling the interaction by communicating about things that they choose, rather than following their children's interests. Although two small-sample studies (Cross, Johnson-Morris, & Nienhuys, 1980; Spencer & Gutfreund, 1990) supported this hypothesis, two other studies, with larger sample sizes (Harris, 2001; Lederberg & Everhart, 2000) did not. This research suggests that, although there may be exceptions, language delay is not due to hearing mothers' insensitivity to DCHP children's interests and attention.

Child-Directed Language

There are many aspects of motherese, or the special way language is modified when talking with young children, that, while not experimentally confirmed, appear to facilitate vocabulary development. Is it intuitive to make these modifications to older, language-delayed, DCHP children and in another modality?

Form and Structure

The answer to the preceding question seems to be yes in terms of the structure of linguistic input. Both DCHP and hearing children learning language are exposed to utterances that are simpler and more repetitive than those used with older children. In fact, there are no differences in the complexity or syntactic characteristics of speech directed to DCHP children and language-matched hearing children (see Gallaway & Woll, 1994, for a review). In addition, hearing and deaf mothers who sign to their young children use simple, one-or two-sign sentences (Harris, 2001).

Attention-Getting Features

Prosodic or paralinguistic features of child-directed language are important for eliciting and maintaining young children's attention to the linguistic input and for making words perceptually salient. Prosodic features of spoken language include a high pitch, long pauses, slow tempo, and exaggerated intonation (Masataka, 2000). Although there is no research on the prosodic characteristics of spoken input to DCHP children, Spencer and Lederberg (1997) informally observed that speech directed to young DCHP children seemed to lack these prosodic features. Perhaps even more important, it is not known what prosodic speech modifications are attention getting for DCHP children who have some access to auditory input (either because of residual hearing, amplification, or cochlear implants).

Research shows that deaf mothers who are native signers make modifications in their signing that seem analogous to the prosodic characteristics of spoken motherese. Specifically, infant-directed signing contains signs that are larger, slower, and repeated with more cycles than adult-directed signing (Erting, Prezioso, & Hynes, 1994; Holzrichter & Meier, 2000; Masataka, 2000; Spencer & Lederberg, 1997). These prosodic modifications serve an attention-getting purpose. Deaf and hearing 6-month-olds (the latter without exposure to sign) look longer at infant-directed signing than at adult-directed signing (Masataka, 2000). In addition, deaf mothers are more likely to make these modifications when their infants are not directly looking at them, as if to gain their attention (Holzrichter & Meier, 2000). It is not known if hearing mothers make similar modifications in their signing.

Other strategies used by deaf mothers to make language more visually accessible seem unique to sign language (Prendergast & McCollum, 1996; Spencer & Lederberg, 1997; Waxman & Spencer, 1997). These include moving a sign's location (on the infant or in the infant's visual field), waiting for the infant to look up before signing, and redirecting the infant's attention to mother by tapping the infant's body, moving mother's own body into the child's visual field, waving, or moving objects near mother's face. Hearing mothers of deaf infants also make these modifications but at a lower frequency than deaf mothers (Jamieson, 1994; Waxman & Spencer, 1997).

Thus, while hearing mothers may intuitively make appropriate structural modifications to their language with their deaf children, important prosodic modifications may not be intuitive (see Mohay, 2000, for a description of a program that teaches these strategies to hearing mothers). This is probably why language is not as visually accessible to DCHP children as it is to DCDP children (Harris, 2001; Lederberg & Everhart, 1998).

Summary and Conclusions

During early development, DCHP and hearing toddlers are remarkably similar in the development of joint attention, intentional communication, and the use of nonlinguistic vocalizations and gestures to communicate with others around them. However, subtle differences in linguistic knowledge are evident as early as 9 months of age. For hearing (and perhaps DCDP) infants, but not most DCHP infants, prelinguistic communication contains some phonological and prosodic features of their ambient language. This knowledge may be foundational for later language development. In addition, without these linguistic markers, the specific meaning of DCHP toddlers' nonlinguistic communication is frequently unclear to their communicative partners. For the many DCHP children who continue to be language-delayed during preschool, communication primarily consists of requests for action or attention rather than information exchange. Consequently, these DCHP children's ability to interact with the world is increasingly limited compared to developmental expectations.

Fortunately, there is evidence that in some intervention programs DCHP children are acquiring language at younger ages than ever before. In these programs (Mayne et al., 2000; Moeller, 2000), many DCHP children showed lexicons that were comparable to their hearing peers. Other research suggests that optimal lexical development consists of a period of slow word learning, followed by a period of rapid acceleration of word learning, after which new words are learned daily. Rapid word learning occurs, first, only when reference is established explicitly and, eventually, from inference. Other DCHP children experience less optimal development and remain in the slow word-learning phase for a prolonged period of time (sometimes years). These language-delayed children slowly add words to their lexicon and may never experience a rapid acceleration in word learning. Even after they have acquired rapid word learning processes, these processes do not seem to result in rapid vocabulary growth.

These different trajectories are related to age of identification and intervention, family involvement, and cognitive abilities. Early intervention and family involvement in that intervention may facilitate vocabulary development by increasing the accessibility of input through early amplification and/or cochlear implantation and through teaching families ways of modifying their input to suit their toddlers' needs. The early timing of this intervention seems critical for the ability of DCHP children to acquire language. Universal newborn hearing screening should result in more children experiencing optimal language growth. However, in addition to the timing, the type of intervention is probably important in promoting language development. Future research that relates both the timing and characteristics of different intervention programs will be critical for efforts to improve development of DCHP children.

References

Acredolo, L. P., Goodwyn, S. W., Horobin, K. D., & Emmons, Y. D. (1999). The signs and sounds of early language development. In L. Balter & C. S. Tamis-LeMonda (Eds.), *Child psychology: A handbook of contemporary issues* (pp. 116–139). New York: Psychology Press.

Adamson, L. B. (1995). *Communication development during infancy*. Madison, WI: Brown & Benchmark.

Anderson, D., & Reilly, J. S. (2002). The MacArthur Communicative Development Inventory: Normative data for American Sign Language. *Journal of Deaf Studies and Deaf Education, 7*(2), 83–106.

Bornstein, H., Saulnier, K., & Hamilton, L. (1980). Signed English: A first evaluation. *American Annals of the Deaf, 125*, 467–481.

Capirci, O., Montanari, S., & Volterra, V. (1998). Gestures, signs, and words in early language development. In J. M. Iverson & S. Goldin-Meadow (Eds.), *The nature and functions of gesture in children's communication* (Vol. 79, pp. 45–49). San Francisco, CA: Jossey-Bass.

Cross, T. G., Johnson-Morris, J. E., & Nienhuys, T. G. (1980). Linguistic feedback and maternal speech: Comparisons of mothers addressing hearing and hearing impaired children. *First Language, 1*, 163–189.

Day (Spencer), P. (1986). Deaf children's expression of communicative intentions. *Journal of Communication Disorders, 19*, 367–386.

de Villiers, J., Bibeau, L., Ramos, E., & Gatty, J. C. (1993). Gestural communication in oral deaf mother-child pairs: Language with a helping hand? *Applied Psycholinguistics, 14,* 319–347.

Dromi, E. (1992). The development of prelinguistic communication. In J. N. Anastasio, & S. Harel (Eds.), *At risk infants: Interventions, families, and research* (pp. 19–26). Baltimore, MD: Paul H. Brookes.

Dromi, E. (1999). Early lexical development. In M. Barrett (Ed.), *The development of language: studies in developmental psychology* (pp. 99–131). Philadelphia, PA: Psychology Press.

Dromi, E., Fuks, O., & Ringwald-Frimerman, D. (1998, July 1–4). *The interplay between gesture and speech in young orally trained deaf children.* Paper presented at the the XVth Biennial Meeting of ISSBD, Berne, Switzerland.

Erting, C. J., Prezioso, C., & Hynes, M. O. G. (1994). The interactional context of deaf mother-infant communication. In V. Volterra & C. J. Erting (Eds.), *From gesture to language in hearing and deaf children* (pp. 97–196). Washington, DC: Galluadet University Press.

Ertmer, D. J., & Mellon, J. A. (2001). Beginning to talk at 20 months: Early vocal development in a young cochlear implant recipient. *Journal of Speech, Language, and Hearing Research, 44,* 192–206.

Fenson, L., Dale, P. S., Reznick, J. S., Bates, E., Thal, D. J., & Pethick, S. J. (1994). Variability in early communicative development. *Monographs of the Society for Research in Child Development, 59*(5) (Serial No. 242).

Fenson, L., Dale, P. S., Reznick, J. S., Thal, D., Bates, E., Hartung, J. P. Pethick, S., & Reilly, J. S. (1993). *MacArthur Communicative Development Inventories: User's guide and technical manual.* San Diego, CA: Singular.

Gallaway, C., & Woll, B. (1994). Interaction and childhood deafness. In C. Gallaway & B. J. Richards (Eds.), *Input and interaction in language acquisition* (pp. 197–218). Cambridge: Cambridge University Press.

Gardner, J., & Zorfass, J. (1983). From sign to speech: The language development of a hearing-impaired child. *American Annals of the Deaf, 128,* 20–24.

Goldfield, B., & Reznick, J. S. (1990). Early lexical acquisition: Rate, content, and the vocabulary spurt. *Journal of Child Language, 17,* 171–183.

Goldin-Meadow, S., McNeill, D., & Singleton, J.L. (1996). Silence is liberating: Removing the handcuffs on grammatical expression in manual modality. *Psychological Review, 103*(1), 34–55.

Goldin-Meadow, S., & Mylander, C. (1984). Gestural communication in deaf children: The effects and noneffects of parental input on early language development. *Monographs for the Society for Research in Child Development, 49*(3–4).

Greenberg, M. T. (1980). Mode use in deaf children: The effects of communication method and communication competence. *Applied Psycholinguistics, 1,* 65–79.

Greenberg, M. T., Calderon, R., & Kusche, C. (1984). Early intervention using simultaneous communication with deaf infants: The effect on communication development. *Child Development, 55,* 607–616.

Gregory, S., & Mogford, K. (Eds.). (1981). *Early language development in deaf children.* London: Croom Helm.

Griswold, E., & Commings, J. (1974). The expressive vocabulary of preschool deaf children. *American Annals of the Deaf, 119,* 16–29.

Harris, M. (1992). *Language experience and early language development: From input to uptake.* Hove, UK: Lawrence Erlbaum Associates.

Harris, M. (2000). Social interaction and early language development in deaf children. *Deafness and Education International, 2*(1), 1–11.

Harris, M. (2001). It's all a matter of timing: Sign viability and sign reference in deaf and hearing mothers of 18-month-old children. *Journal of Deaf Studies and Deaf Education, 6*(3), 177–185.

Hollich, G.J., Hirsh-Pasek, K., & Golinkoff, R. M. (2000). Breaking the barrier: An emergentist coalition model for the origins of word learning. *Monographs for the Society for Research in Child Development, 65*(3).

Holzrichter, A. S., & Meier, R. P. (2000). Child directed signing in American Sign Language. In C. Chamberlain, J. P. Morford & R. I. Mayberry (Eds.), *Language acquisition by eye* (pp. 25–40). Mahwah, NJ: Lawrence Erlbaum Associates.

Huttenlocher, J., Haight, W., Bryk, A., Sletzer, M., & Lyons, T. (1991). Early vocabulary growth: Relation to input and gender. *Developmental Psychology, 27*(23), 236–248.

Jamieson, J. R. (1994). Teaching as transaction: Vygotskian perspectives on deafness and mother-child interaction. *Exceptional Children, 60*(5), 434–449.

Lederberg, A. R., & Everhart, V. S. (1998). Communication between deaf children and their hearing mothers: The role of language, gesture, and vocalizations. *Journal of Speech, Language, and Hearing Research, 41,* 887–899.

Lederberg, A. R., & Everhart, V. S. (2000). Conversations between deaf children and their hearing mothers: Pragmatic and dialogic characteristics. *Journal of Deaf Studies and Deaf Education, 5*(4), 303–322.

Lederberg, A. R., & Mobley, C. E. (1990). The effect

of hearing impairment on the quality of attachment and mother-toddler interaction. *Child Development, 61,* 1596–1604.

Lederberg, A. R., Prezbindowski, A., K., & Spencer, P. E. (2000a, July). *Deaf children's expressive vocabulary and its relation to their word learning strategies: A cross-sectional study.* Paper presented at the biennial meetings of the International Society of Infant Studies, Brighton, UK.

Lederberg, A. R., Prezbindowski, A., K., & Spencer, P. E. (2000b). Word learning skills of deaf preschoolers: The development of novel mapping and rapid word learning strategies. *Child Development, 53,* 1055–1065.

Lederberg, A. R., & Spencer, P. E. (2001). Vocabulary development of deaf and hard of hearing children. In M. D. Clark, M. Marschark, & M. Karchmer (Eds.), *Context, cognition and deafness* (pp. 88–112). Washington, DC: Gallaudet University Press.

Masataka, N. (2000). The role of modality and input in the earliest stage of language acquisition: Studies of Japanese sign language. In C. Chamberlain, J. P. Morford, & R. I. Mayberry (Eds.), *Language acquisition by eye* (pp. 3–24). Mahwah, NJ: Lawrence Erlbaum Associates.

Mayne, A. M., Yoshinaga Itano, C., Sedey, A. L., & Carey, A. (2000). Expressive vocabulary development of infants and toddlers who are deaf or hard of hearing. *Volta Review, 100*(5), 1–28.

Meier, R. P., & Newport, E. L. (1990). Out of the hands of babes: On a possible sign advantage in language acquisition. *Language, 66*(1), 1–23.

Mervis, C. B., & Bertrand, J. (1994). Acquisition of the novel name-nameless category (N3C) principle. *Child Development, 65,* 1646–1662.

Moeller, M. P. (2000). Early intervention and language development in children who are deaf and hard of hearing. *Pediatrics, 106*(3).

Mohay, H. (1994). The interaction of gesture and speech in the language development of two profoundly deaf children. In V. Volterra & C. J. Erting (Eds.), *From gesture to language in hearing and deaf children.* Washington, DC: Gallaudet University Press.

Mohay, H. (2000). Language in situ: Mothers' strategies for making language visually accessible to deaf children. In P. E. Spencer, C. J. Erting, & M. Marschark (Eds.), *The deaf child in the family and at school* (pp. 151–166). Mahwah, NJ: Lawrence Erlbaum Associates.

Nicholas, J. G. (2000). Age differences in the use of informative/heuristic communicative functions in young children with and without hearing loss who are learning spoken language. *Journal of Speech, Language, and Hearing Research, 43,* 380–394.

Nicholas, J. G., & Geers, A. E. (1997). Communication of oral deaf and normally hearing children at 36 months of age. *Journal of Speech, Language, and Hearing Research, 40,* 1314–1327.

Nicholas, J. G., Geers, A. E., & Kozak, V. (1994). Development of communicative function in young hearing-impaired and normally hearing children. *Volta Review, 96,* 113–135.

Nicoladis, E., Mayberry, R. I., & Genesee, F. (1999). Gesture and early bilingual development. *Developmental Psychology, 35*(2), 514–526.

Notoya, M., Suzuki, S., & Furukawa, M. (1994). Effect of early manual instruction on the oral-language development of two deaf children. *American Annals of the Deaf, 139*(3), 348–351.

Obenchain, P., Menn, L., & Yoshinaga-Itano, C. (2000). Can speech development at 36 months in children with hearing loss be predicted from information available in the second year of life? *Volta Review, 100*(5), 149–180.

Oller, D. K., & Eilers, R. E. (1988). The role of audition in infant babbling. *Child Development, 59*(2), 441–449.

Ouellet, C., Le Normand, M.-T., & Cohen, H. (2001). Language evolution in children with cochlear implants. *Brain and Cognition, 46*(1–2), 231–235.

Prendergast, S. G., & McCollum, J. A. (1996). Let's talk: The effect of maternal hearing status on interactions with toddlers who are deaf. *American Annals of the Deaf, 141,* 11–18.

Prezbindowski, A., K., Adamson, L. B., & Lederberg, A. R. (1998). Joint attention in deaf and hearing 22 month-old children and their hearing mothers. *Journal of Applied Developmental Psychology, 19*(3), 377–387.

Schlesinger, H. S., & Meadow, K. P. (1972). *Sound and sign: Childhood deafness and mental health.* Berkeley: University of California Press.

Shafer, D., & Lynch, J. (1981). Emergent language of six prelingually deaf children. *Journal of the British Association of Teachers of the Deaf, 5*(4), 94–111.

Spencer, P. E. (1993a). Communication behaviors of infants with hearing loss and their hearing mothers. *Journal of Speech and Hearing Research, 36,* 311–321.

Spencer, P. E. (1993b). The expressive communication of hearing mothers and deaf infants. *American Annals of the Deaf, 138*(3), 275–283.

Spencer, P. E. (2000). Looking without listening: Is audition a prerequisite for normal development of visual attention during infancy? *Journal of Deaf Studies and Deaf Education, 5*(4), 291–302.

Spencer, P. E., & Gutfreund, M. K. (1990). Directiveness in mother-infant interaction. In D. F. Moores & K. P. Meadow-Orlans (Eds.), *Educational and developmental aspects of deafness* (pp. 350–365). Washington, DC: Gallaudet University Press.

Spencer, P. E., & Lederberg, A. R. (1997). Different modes, different models: Communication and language of young deaf children and their mothers. In L. B. Adamson & M. A. Romski (Eds.), *Research on communication and language disorders: Contributions to theories of language development* (pp. 203–230). Baltimore, MD: Paul H. Brookes.

Swisher, M. V. (1991). Conversational interaction between deaf children and their hearing mothers: The role of visual attention. In P. Siple & S. D. Fisher (Eds.), *Theoretical issues in sign language research: Volume 2. Psychology* (pp. 111–134). Chicago: University of Chicago Press.

Swisher, M. V. (1992). The role of parents in developing visual turn-taking in their young deaf children. *American Annals of the Deaf, 137,* 92–100.

Tomasello, M., & Farrar, J. (1986). Joint attention and early language. *Child Development, 57,* 1454–1463.

Wallace, V., Menn, L., & Yoshinaga-Itano, C. (2000). Is babble the gateway to speech for all children? A longitudinal study of children who are deaf or hard-of hearing. *Volta Review, 100*(5), 121–148.

Waxman, R., & Spencer, P. E. (1997). What mothers do to support infant visual attention: Sensitivities to age and hearing status. *Journal of Deaf Studies and Deaf Education, 2,* 104–114.

Wood, D., Wood, H., Griffiths, A., & Howarth, I. (1986). *Teaching and talking with deaf children.* New York: John Wiley & Sons.

Yoshinaga-Itano, C., & Stredler-Brown, A. (1992). Learning to communicate: Babies with hearing impairments make their needs known. *Volta Review, 95,* 107–129.

19

Jacqueline Leybaert & Jésus Alegria

The Role of Cued Speech in Language Development of Deaf Children

Despite normal intelligence and normal potential for learning, children born profoundly deaf generally exhibit lags across all activities involving phonological representations based on speech: speech perception and speech production, oral language development, metaphonological abilities, immediate ordered memory for linguistic stimuli, reading, and spelling. In addition, their pattern of hemispheric specialization for language processing is generally atypical. The most likely explanation of these findings lies in deaf children's reduced access to oral language through lipreading.

It is now widely recognized that lip movements involved in the production of speech are automatically processed by hearing persons in normal conditions of listening. The fact that visual speech information influences the automatic processing of auditory information (McGurk & MacDonald, 1976) indicates that the visual speech information is dealt with by structures in the brain common to those involved in the processing of the auditory signal (Calvert et al., 1997). Hearing people thus develop phonological representations through access to lipreading as well as through acoustic information. The basis for the development of such amodal, perceptual representations of speech seems to occur during the first weeks of life (Burnham & Dodd,

1996; Kuhl & Meltzoff, 1988; MacKain, Studdert-Kennedy, Spieker, & Stern, 1983).

Lipreading constitutes the primary input for deaf children to gain information about the phonological structure of spoken language (Dodd, 1976). Although lipreading provides information about some phonological contrasts (e.g., place of articulation), it does not afford the perception of others, like nasality and voicing (Erber, 1974; Walden, Prosek, Montgomery, Scherr, & Jones, 1977). Through lipreading deaf children have access only to phonetically underspecified information, and they develop underspecified representations with respect to heard-and-spoken language. This hinders deaf children's acquisition of oral language and of all cognitive activities that rely upon phonological representations.

To help deaf children perceive information about the phonological structure of spoken language through the visual channel, different systems have been elaborated. One of these systems is cued speech (CS; Cornett, 1967). Reviewing previous research on the effect of CS allows one to examine whether the development of a phonological system depends on the delivery of accurate information about phonological contrasts, independently of the modality. More specifically, if phonological representations can be elaborated on the basis of a well-specified visual input, then the development of all abilities relying on such representations should be improved. Finally, a review of the research on CS also permits us to examine the question of the impact of modality: does the development of a linguistic competence from a visual input rather than from an auditory input (with the same phonological content of the input) entail differences in the cognitive processes?

Previous work has already reviewed the data on the effect of exposure to CS on language acquisition and the development of cognitive architecture (Alegria, Leybaert, Charlier, & Hage, 1992; Leybaert, 1998; Leybaert, Alegria, Hage, & Charlier, 1998). Speech production has not been noticed to improve relative to that of deaf children using other language systems (Ryalls, Auger, & Hage, 1994), but important advantages have been noted in receptive language and in the degree to which language is organized neurologically. The chapter will thus be focused on the following issues: how is the information provided by the lips and by the hands integrated, and what are the possibilities for automatic systems of cueing? How are rhyming, remembering and reading developed by deaf children using CS? Are the neural substrates involved in speech perception and in cued speech perception the same or different? Can CS provide useful information for cochlear implant users?

Cued Speech

Cued speech, developed by Orin Cornett in 1966, and adapted to more than 40 languages and major dialects (Cornett, 1994), is neither a sign language nor a manually coded system that uses signs from a sign language in a spoken-language word order. Instead, CS is a mode of communication for visually conveying traditionally spoken languages at the phonemic level (i.e., the same linguistic level conveyed via speech to hearing individuals). In CS, the speaker complements lip gestures of speech with manual cues. A cue is made up of two parameters: handshape and hand location around the mouth. The American English form of CS uses eight handshapes corresponding to groups of consonants and four hand locations to convey vowels and diphtongs (see figure 19-1). Phonemes that are distinguishable by lipreading are coded by a same

Figure 19-1. Handshape and locations of American Cued Speech © 2001, Language Matters, Inc. Reprinted by permission.

handshape (like /p/, /d/, and /zh/) or at the same location. Conversely, phonemes that have similar lipshape are coded with different handshape (like /p/, /b/, and /m/) and hand location (like /i/ and /e/). Information given by the cues and information given by lipreading is thus complementary. Each time a speaker pronounces a consonant–vowel (CV) syllable, a cue (a particular handshape at a specific position) is produced simultaneously. For example, when saying the words "bell" and "bowl," two different hand locations would be used to distinguish between the two vowels; when saying the words "bat" and "pat," two different handshapes would be used to code the initial consonant. Syllabic structures other than CV are produced with additional cues. For example, a vowel syllable is represented by the neutral handshape at the hand placement corresponding to that vowel. Syllables including consonant clusters, or codas, are coded using the handshape corresponding to the additional consonant at the neutral position.

The handshapes and hand locations used in CS, unlike those of fingerspelling, are not, by themselves, interpretable as language. Instead, the visual information provided by lipreading is also necessary. The integration of labial and manual information points to a single, unambiguous, phonological percept that deaf children could not have achieved from either source alone. Deaf children are thus in a situation in which they can interpret the oral input as a reliable visual language in which the gestures (i.e., the combination of lip movements and manual cues) are now entirely specified, both at the syllabic and at the phonemic levels. For each syllable (and for each phoneme), there corresponds one (and only one) combination of labial and manual information, and vice versa, a characteristic that makes CS entirely functional for speech perception.

Two aspects of CS design are worth commenting on. First, the arbitrary decision to code the vowels by hand locations and the consonants by hand placements seems ecologically valid. Indeed, vowels have a longer duration on the acoustic level, which corresponds to the relatively long time required to pass from one location to another (see below). In contrast, consonants are relatively short events, and it is possible to get rapidly from one handshape to another. It is noteworthy that CS appears to honor this linguistically motivated distinction. Second, the possibility to transmit information about a consonant and a vowel in one single gesture allows a rapid rate of information transmission. Actually, the production of cues seems to slow the speech rate by about 30% (i.e., from 6 syllables per second to 4 syllables per second; Duchnowski et al., 1998).

Effect of CS on Speech Perception

Deaf people's comprehension of spoken language is usually poor. Speechreaders understand only

about one fourth of what is said even in dyadic conversations (Liben, 1978). Large improvement of deaf children's speech reception skills has been demonstrated when cues are added to lipreading both for English- and French-speaking children (Alegria, Charlier, & Mattys, 1999; Nicholls & Ling, 1982; Périer, Charlier, Hage, & Alegria, 1988). Nicholls and Ling (1982) found that the speech reception scores of profoundly deaf children taught at school with CS for at least 3 years increased from about 30% for both syllables and words in the lipreading alone condition to more than 80% in the lipreading- plus-cues condition. Périer et al. (1988) showed that the advantage on sentence comprehension provided by the addition of cues was greater in children whose parents intensively used CS to communicate with them at home at an early age than in those children who benefited from CS later, and only at school, usually from the age of 6. This differential benefit displayed by the early and late CS users may be explained in two ways: early CS-users might be more familiar with words presented in CS, and/or they might have a more efficient phonological processor, which depends of the quality of the mental representations of the phonemes.

In a study by Alegria et al. (1999), early CS users displayed a larger improvement related to the addition of cues both for word perception and for pseudo-word perception. Because pseudo-words were unfamiliar for both groups of subjects, these results support the idea that experience with CS enhances the efficiency of the processing of phonological information in early users.

Automatic Generation of Cued Speech

Given the good results provided by the use of CS on the reception of speech by deaf children, various systems of automatic generation of CS have been elaborated: the Autocuer, developed in the late 1970s (Cornett, Beadles, & Wilson, 1977; Duchnowski et al., 1998), and an automatic cueing system based on automatic speech recognition (ASR) in real time (Duchnoswski et al., 1998a; 1998b). The discussion of these two systems allows one to have a clear understanding of the crucial variables to get an effective system.

The Autocuer consisted of a portable microprocessor-based device that analyzed the acoustic input, identified speech sounds, and assigned them to cues. The cues were then coded as patterns of illuminated segments projected for the receiver onto his or her eyeglasses. The cues were always delayed relative to the start times of the corresponding phonemes. It did not prove possible to develop an effective system that worked in real time.

Duchnowski et al.'s (1998) prototype automatic cueing system involves two personal computers. The talker sits facing a video camera and wears a microphone. The first computer (PC1) preprocesses the acoustic waveform and handles capture of images of the talker. The second computer (PC2) performs phonetic recognition and produces the best matched cue sequence. The digital images are stored in PC1 memory for 2 seconds before superposition of a hand image corresponding to the cue identified by PC2 and playback on a monitor for the cue receiver. The artificially cued talker, as seen by the cue receiver, is thus delayed by 2 seconds relative to the real talker's actions. The authors observed that human cuers often begin to form a cue before producing the corresponding sound; therefore, they adjusted the start times of the cues to begin 100 msec before the boundary determined from acoustic data by the cue recognizer. They also found that the timing of the conversion from one handshape to the next was nearly optimal when cues changed halfway through the transition.

The automatic cueing system has been tested by asking young hearing adults with at least 10 years of manual CS experience to identify keywords presented in low-context sentences. Word scores averaged 90% for manual CS and only 66% for automatic cueing. However, the latter scores were much larger than the average 35% for speechreading alone. The automatic cueing system thus clearly improved subjects' comprehension. Future improvement of the system will include increasing the accuracy of the phoneme recognition by the automatic recognizer (which was of only 74%), the discriminability of the handshapes by using different colors, and the refinement of the synchronization of the cues to the talker's visible facial actions.

The timing of the beginning of the cue relative to the movement of the lips had not been documented until recently. Attina, Beautemps, and Cathiard explored this issue experimentally (see Attina, 2001). They videotaped a professional cuer producing CVCVCV sequences. They discovered

that the hand gestures and the lip gestures are never really synchronized. The CS gesture starts about 200 msec. before the beginning of the lip movement corresponding to the syllable; the spatial location of the cue is reached at the beginning of the syllable and held during the production of the consonant. The next CS gesture is started during the beginning of the production of the vowel of the former syllable; the full production of the former vowel is reached before the next hand gesture reaches its location. As Duchnowski et al. (1998) anticipated, Attina et al. also found that the CS hand gesture started before the sound.

These data suggest an interesting conclusion: it could be wrong to conceive the CS hand gestures as disambiguating lip gestures that were perceived simultaneously or even before by the receiver, because the lip gestures would be dominant compared to the hand gestures. Things may be more complex. It is possible that sometimes the lip gestures disambiguate the hand gestures, while sometimes the reverse occurs. If this speculation is true, it points toward a more integrated model of CS perception than a simple "lip gestures first, cues next," at least for experienced CS receivers. (For a more detailed discussion on this point, see Alegria et al., 1992.)

Integration of Lipread and Manual Information in CS

The way information from manual cues and lipreading combine to produce a unitary percept has been explored by looking for phonological misperceptions induced by CS structural characteristics. These misperceptions might be substitutions based on the similarity between cues (i.e., perceiving /da/ for /zha/, which might result from the fact that /d/ and /zh/ share the same handshape) or intrusions of extra syllables in items requiring more CS units than they possess syllables (i.e., two CS units are required to code a single CCV or CVC syllable). Such misperceptions are potentially interesting because they might reveal the way CS is processed relative to lipread information. For example, to discriminate between /da/ and /zha/, it is necessary to pay attention to the lips posture. Using a task requiring identification of pseudowords produced in CS, it has been shown that the frequency of such misperceptions increased when CS was added to lipreading alone (Alegria et al., 1999). To further explore this issue, deaf youngsters were tested in a situation where lipread information was sometimes incongruent with CS information (i.e., the lipread syllable /va/ accompanied by the /p,d,zh/ hand-shape (Alegria & Lechat, in prep.). It was expected that the perceptual system exposed to incongruous information would adopt phonological solutions that might reveal the weights it attributes to each source. Children who learned cued speech early and late were included in the experiment. The results showed that the total number of errors was greater in the late group. The proportion of CS misperceptions, however, was larger in the early group. In addition, the processing of incongruous cues was lower when lipread information was reliable than when it was not. In short, early CS users are more efficient in exploiting CS information, which is integrated with lipreading according to the salience of this latter information.

The Development of the Three R's: Remembering, Rhyming, and Reading

Remembering

Working memory is a fundamental system for human beings, a system that allows us to retain during a brief time stimuli that have been presented, in their order of presentation. Theories of working memory have emphasized the phonological nature of this process, meaning that memory trace has an acoustic or verbal basis in hearing people (Conrad & Hull, 1964). Baddeley and Hitch (1974) elaborated one of the most influential models of working memory. Their model postulates a peripheral storage system called the "phonological loop," which is assumed to underlie performance in verbal working memory tasks. The phonological loop is divided into two components, a passive storage component ("phonological store"), into which auditory verbal material is registered, and an active rehearsal component ("articulatory loop"), which refreshes and maintains the information in the storage component. The "central executive" serves to allocate attention to these two systems. Auditory material is considered to have obligatory access to the phonological store, whereas visual material (written words, pictures) must be recoded via the articulatory loop before it is registered in the phonological store (Baddeley & Hitch, 1974). From the perspec-

tive of deaf children, the questions are. Can phonological representations be developed on the basis of visual information in the absence of reliable sound information? Would a phonological system developed on the basis of visual speech representations be totally parallel to a phonological system developed on the basis of auditory speech information?

Wandel (1989) was the first to investigate the effect of CS on the functioning of working memory. She used a procedure to evaluate hearing and deaf children's *internal speech ratio* (Conrad, 1979). The task was to memorize lists of printed words coming from two sets: rhyming words that were visually contrasted (e.g., do/few; through/zoo) and words visually similar that were not rhyming (e.g., farm, lane, have). The internal speech ratio (ISR) is the proportion of errors made on the rhyming set to the total number of errors on the two sets. An ISR greater than 52 indicates lower recall accuracy for rhyming lists than for visually similar lists. In contrast, an ISR lower than 48 results from more errors on the visually similar lists than on the rhyming lists and indicates the use of a visual code. In Wandel's study, the use of internal speech was significantly higher in deaf children exposed to CS (mean = 74.9) and in deaf children from the oral group (mean = 76.1) than in children from the total communication group (mean = 56.7). Exposure to CS thus enhances the development of the articulatory loop (Wandel, 1989).

Although the length of exposure to CS was not reported in Wandel's (1989) study, this variable seems critical in the development of the phonological loop. Indeed, children intensively exposed to CS before the age of 3 years, like age-matched hearing controls, show lower recall performance for rhyming than for nonrhyming lists of pictures (the phonological similarity effect) and lower recall performance for lists of multisyllabic words than for lists of monosyllabic words (the word length effect) (Leybaert & Charlier, 1996). In contrast, Leybaert and Charlier (1996) found that children exposed to CS only in their school environment (i.e., after the age of 6 years) did not show these effects, probably because they relied on a visual rather than on a phonological storage. The early CS users also had a larger memory span than the late CS users.

Following Baddeley's model, the phonological similarity effect and the word length effect arise from the articulatory rehearsal process, which is needed to convert pictures into phonological representations and to rehearse these representations. However, the above results leave open the question of the precise nature of this process. Indeed, rhyming words are also highly confusable in CS, because they share the same mouth shape as well as the same hand location for the vowel; similarly, multisyllabic words are also longer to produce in CS than monosyllabic words. The phonological similarity effect could be explained by the use of a rehearsal loop based on speech articulation; it is also compatible with a loop based on the use of CS articulators (i.e., mouthshapes, handshapes, and hand locations).

To address this issue, Leybaert and Lechat (2001a) examined the effects of rhyming, of mouthshape similarity, and of hand location similarity in an immediate serial recall task of stimuli presented in CS without sound. Subjects were youngsters exposed to CS with various intensity (low, medium, and high). The high group had received CS early and at home; the low group had been exposed to CS only late, at school; and the medium group had received CS at home, but inconsistently. Lists of words that sound similar and that are similar in CS provoked poorer recall than lists of phonologically dissimilar words in all three subgroups. This result confirms that hearing speech is not necessary to develop a sensitivity to the phonological rhyming effect. In addition, the deaf CS users exhibited poorer recall for lists of words similar in mouthshape (rounded lips) but which are different acoustically and are produced with different hand locations than for control lists dissimilar in mouthshapes, suggesting that the code in which information is handled in the phonological store includes the mouthshape gestures. Lists of words similar in hand location (at the corner of the lips), but not in sounding nor in mouthshape, also yielded poorer memory performance compared to control lists dissimilar in hand location, suggesting that an effect of similarity in hand location is also tied to the phonological storage buffer. The effect of hand location similarity was more important quantitatively (but not significantly) in the group with high exposure to CS, indicating that the phonological units handled by the phonological store arise in response to early linguistic experience. One may thus conceive that visual speech material has obligatory access to a visual phonological store, where it has to be re-

freshed and maintained by a CS rehearsal articulatory mechanism.

We searched for further support for this notion by investigating immediate serial recall of the same materials by hearing participants who learned CS for professional purposes or to use it with their deaf child. No effect of hand location similarity was found in these subjects, which is consistent with the idea that this effect is due to the fact that deaf subjects' phonological loop uses the same elements as those that contribute to speech perception. In contrast, the effect of mouthshape similarity was observed in these hearing adults, consistent with the notion that mouthshapes make up part of the speech perception device of hearing adults (McGurk & MacDonald, 1976).

These findings thus indicate some equivalence between the articulatory loop and the CS loop (i.e., the phonological [rhyming] similarity effects). But not all results indicate complete equivalence between these two loops: deaf subjects seemed to code hand location, whereas hearing CS users did not. Articulation is used to repeatedly feed information back into the storage buffer before it fades. In the case of lists of rhyming words, the traces left by spoken articulation and by CS articulation are highly confusable. In the case of lists of words articulated at the same hand location, the traces left by CS articulation are confusable for deaf participants only. It has been argued that the ease of imitating or rehearsing is a hallmark of the type of information that will allow for the development of the phonological loop (Reisberg & Logie, 1993; Wilson & Emmorey, 1998). The CS signal allows imitability or rehearsability to occur. These learned motor patterns thus may constitute the basis in the development of a CS-based rehearsal mechanism.

Rhyming

The abilities to judge that two words rhyme and to produce rhyming words in response to a target are among the first expressions of children's ability to appreciate the phonological structure of spoken language. In hearing children, the ability to produce and judge rhymes spontaneously is already present between 2 and 3 years of age (Read, 1978; Slobin, 1978), with some individual differences linked to the quality of their oral productions (Webster & Plante, 1995). Rhyming ability usually emerges spontaneously as a result of natural linguistic development and before any contact with literacy (Morais, Bertelson, Cary, & Alegria, 1986). Do the children who have acquired language skills via exposure to CS also have explicit metalinguistic abilities to reason about spoken language as an abstract symbolic system? Results from the reading literature suggest that metaphonological awareness, including rhyming, is a strong predictor of early reading success (Bradley & Bryant, 1978). Is the same relationship true of deaf children exposed to CS?

At present, few studies have been carried out on metaphonological abilities in deaf children exposed to CS. In one study, Charlier and Leybaert (2000) asked children to decide whether the names of pairs of pictures rhyme. Deaf children exposed early and prelingually to CS at home achieved a high level of performance, similar to that of the hearing controls, and better than the level achieved by other deaf children educated orally or with sign language. Besides the difference in general level of accuracy, the group of early CS users also differed from the other deaf children regarding the effect of two variables. First, unlike the other deaf children, the early CS users were not influenced by word spelling when they had to decide if two pictured words rhyme. This indicates that they rely on genuine phonological information rather than on orthographic information. Second, although all deaf children were misled by pairs of nonrhyming pictures with names similar in speechreading, the performance of the early CS users was less impaired by this variable than that of the other groups.

It thus seems that early exposure to CS allows the development of more precise phonological representations, which, in turn, assists in the emergence of accurate rhyming abilities. Finally, in early CS users, but not in other deaf children, the ability to judge rhymes is present before learning to read, as is the case in hearing children. How is this early metalinguistic ability related to early reading success, and is it related to the use of phonological recoding in written word recognition?

These are two topics that are being explored in an ongoing longitudinal study by Colin, Magnan, Ecalle, and Leybaert (in prep.). One aspect of their study involves rhyme judgment and rhyme generation tasks in nursery-school children and written word recognition tasks in first grade by deaf children having CS at home. The participants were deaf children educated with CS both at home and at school, deaf children who used CS at school only,

orally educated deaf children, and hearing controls. A significant correlation was found between deaf children's performance in rhyming and word recognition tasks. Children with early phonological skills, particularly early CS users, performed better in the written word recognition tasks than the other deaf children, as did hearing children. Early exposure to CS seems to allow a good integration of phonological contrasts before learning to read and consequently the development of accurate phonological representations that are essential for establishing an efficient grapho-phonemic assembling process.

Another way to evaluate rhyming abilities is to ask children to generate rhymes in response to written or pictured target words. Charlier and Leybaert (2000) reported that early CS users, like hearing children matched for reading level, achieved a high level of accuracy and produced a high percentage of correct responses that are orthographically different from the target (e.g., BLUE–few). These results contrasted with those of children exposed only late to CS who achieved only a limited level of accuracy and produced mainly words orthographically similar to the target rhyme (e.g., BLUE–glue). This indicates that early CS users relied more on phonological information, whereas late CS users used more orthographic information to generate rhymes. However, the accuracy of early CS users was slightly lower than that of their hearing controls, and the CS users were more affected than the hearing by the orthography to phonology consistency. They generated more correct responses for rhymes that have consistent pronunciations, meaning a single pronunciation (like—EEL or—OTE in English: all words ending with—EEL share the same rhyme pronunciation), than for rhymes having inconsistent (different) pronunciations (like—ERE, which has a different pronunciation in "MERE" and "WERE," or the rhyme—OOD, which is pronounced differently in "WOOD" and "BLOOD"). For some targets with inconsistent rhymes, deaf children, including early CS users, may have stored incorrect phonological representations that were derived from the spelling of the word.

The elaboration of phonological representations from spelling is not specific to deaf children: experience with the alphabetic orthography provides information that enhances the internal representations of speech segments in hearing children, too (Ehri, 1984). However, orthography might be more important for deaf children (Leybaert & Alegria, 1995), including deaf children exposed to CS.

The results of the Charlier and Leybaert (2000) rhyme generation task were replicated in English, on a sample of postgraduate deaf students (LaSasso, Crain, & Leybaert, in press). This latter study also demonstrated a relationship between deaf children's reading ability (measured by the Stanford Achievement Test score) on one hand, and the ability to generate correct responses to targets with inconsistent rhymes, as well as the ability to generate correct responses orthographically different from the target on the other hand. Taken together, these results are highly consistent with the notion that metaphonological awareness is related to reading success in deaf children as it is in hearing children.

Reading and Spelling

One of the main academic challenges encountered by deaf children is learning to read. Statistics are clear: the median reading comprehension scores of deaf and hard-of-hearing students in the Stanford 9 (SAT9) norming for ages 8–18 all fall below the median scores for hearing students at grade 4 (Traxler, 2000). This confirms previous data obtained by Conrad (1979), who found that only 5 deaf young adults out of 205 (2.4%) with hearing loss greater than 85 dB achieved a reading level corresponding to their chronological age. Apparently, a primary reason for such lags is that deaf children do not know oral language before learning to read. When they encounter a new word in their reading, they are completely lost because even if pronounced, that word does not activate anything in their mental lexicon. This is not the case for hearing children who can apply grapheme-to-phoneme correspondences to derive the pronunciation of a new sequence of letters. This pronunciation then activates the meaning of the word.

It thus seems necessary to have, before learning to read, a set of phonological representations that could be accessed from the printed words (by grapheme-to-phoneme rules) and that are linked to semantics. For hearing children, these may include how the word sounds, how it is pronounced by the vocal articulators, and how it looks on the lips. From the perspective of deaf children, the questions are: Would the phonological representations issued from visual perception allow learning to read by means of the usual grapheme-phoneme transla-

tion process? What level of reading achievement can be expected for deaf children educated with CS?

Wandel (1989) was the first researcher who compared the reading level (measured by the SAT reading comprehension scaled scores) of a deaf CS group with other deaf groups and a hearing group. She found that the CS and the oral groups attained higher reading scores than a total communication group. However, the reading level achieved by the CS group in her study was lower than that of the hearing controls. Data obtained in our studies indicate that the degree of exposure to CS is a critical variable. Children exposed early to CS attained reading levels comparable to those of hearing children of the same age, but children exposed only late to CS and children educated with sign language displayed the well-known delay in reading achievement (Leybaert, 2000; Leybaert & Lechat, 2001b).

Do early CS users learn to read and to spell using procedures similar to hearing children? Recent research has focused on the use of phonology-to-orthography correspondences in word spelling. One of the clearest indicator of the use of this procedure is the presence of phonologically accurate errors. The occurrence of errors like "brane" for "BRAIN" indicates that children have precise phonological representations, use phoneme-to-grapheme translation rules, and do not know the word-specific orthographic form. Most of the spelling errors made by hearing spellers are of this type.

In a first study Leybaert (2000) found that these types of errors were also made by early CS users. In contrast, late CS users made a lower proportion of phonologically accurate spellings and more phonologically inaccurate spellings (e.g., "drane" for "BRAIN"), which likely reflects inaccurate phonological representations, in which the identity of each phoneme is not clearly defined. The late CS group also made more transposition errors (e.g., "sorpt" for "SPORT"), which did not preserve the phonetic representation of the target word. However, in this study, intensive CS exposure was confounded with the total amount of language exposure. Early exposure to a fully accessible language may be the critical factor, rather than exposure to CS per se. Therefore, in a second study Leybaert and Lechat (2001b) compared the spelling of the early CS users to that of deaf children exposed early in life to a visual language, albeit of a different nature (i.e., sign language). The results were clear-cut:

only the hearing children and the early CS users showed evidence for predominant use of phoneme-to-grapheme correspondences when they did not know how to spell a word.

Alegria, Aurouer, and Hage (1997) also collected evidence regarding the phonological processes used by deaf children to identify written words encountered for the first time. The experiment involved leading children to elaborate phonological representations of new words during a lesson in which they were taught to associate drawings with their names via lipreading or lipreading plus CS. Before and after the lesson, each drawing was presented accompanied by four written alternatives: the correct one and three pseudowords, one of the latter being a strict lipread foil of the correct response (e.g., "prain" for "BRAIN"). Important and reliable increases in performance from the pre- to the post-test were observed in all cases, indicating that when a deaf child faces a new written word, he or she is able to identify it. The improvement in scores from pre- to post-tests were greater when CS was used during the lesson, indicating that the accuracy of the phonological representations of words was greater in this case. This improvement was larger in early than in late CS users. A post-test 7 days after the lesson revealed that the phonological information stored during the lesson remained available in the early CS group but had disappeared in the late CS group.

To conclude, the nature of the child's early linguistic experience plays a significant role in predicting reading and spelling outcomes. Early and intensive exposure to a system that makes all phonological distinctions of spoken language visually accessible seems critical to ensure adequate spelling and reading development. A late and less intensive exposure to systems such as CS does not have the same effect on the use of phoneme-to-grapheme correspondences.

Hemispheric Specialization

The differences between early and late CS users regarding linguistic, metalinguistic, and working memory developments could come from differences regarding the specialization of the left hemisphere for linguistic processing (Leybaert, 1998; Leybaert & D'Hondt, 2002). This hypothesis is grounded in several lines of evidence. First, later-

alized cerebral function for speech perception develops during the first 3 years of life of hearing children and seems more dependent on linguistic experience than on chronological age per se (Dehaene-Lambertz, Christophe, & Van Ooijen, 2000; Mills, Coffey-Corina, & Neville, 1993; Mills, Coffey-Corina, & Neville, 1997). Second, it has been argued that while the initial storage of utterances mainly depends on resources located in the right hemisphere, the analytical language processes developing around the age of 2 years would reside in the left hemisphere (Locke, 1998).

According to Locke (1998), "children who are delayed in the second phase have too little stored utterance material to activate their analytic mechanism at the optimum biological moment, and when sufficient words have been learned, this modular capability has already begun to decline" (p. 266). It might thus be the case that early CS users have stored many perceptually distinct utterances in CS in the first years of life, which would allow the analytical mechanism, housed in the left hemisphere, to work at the appropriate period. In contrast, in the late CS users who have passed the first critical years in linguistically deprived situations, the initial bias for left hemisphere specialization for language may have disappeared.

Thus far, there has been no direct evidence of the changes in left hemisphere specialization as deaf children acquire their primary language, similar to what has been found in the case of hearing children. Studies reported so far generally used the visual hemifield paradigm. This paradigm is based on the anatomy of the human visual system. The nerve fibers carrying information about stimuli presented in the right visual hemifield (RVF) project to the visual cortex of the left cerebral hemisphere, whereas the fibers carrying information about stimuli presented in the left visual hemifield (LVF) project to the visual cortex of the right cerebral hemisphere. Provided that a person is forced to fixate on the center of the presentation screen, it is thus possible to present words to the desired hemisphere. A RVF advantage for linguistic processing of stimuli would attest a superiority of the left hemisphere for that processing.

Neville (1991) has proposed that full grammatical competence in a language determines the left hemisphere specialization during processing of that language. In a hemifield study requiring the identification of written words, Neville found that while hearing subjects showed behavioral and electrophysiological left hemisphere lateralization, deaf subjects who has acquired ASL as first language did not. Most of them had not acquired full grammatical competence in English, and this may be the reason they did not display left hemisphere specialization during reading. More direct evidence for this conjecture was obtained in a study of event-related brain potentials (ERP) during sentence reading. ERPs elicited by closed-class words (function words, prepositions, adverbs) displayed a peak that was most evident over the left hemisphere, indexing grammatical processing. This specific response was absent from the ERPs of deaf subjects who scored lower on tests of English grammar than did the hearing subjects, but was present in deaf subjects who scored nearly perfectly on the tests of English grammar (Neville, 1991). These data thus support the idea that the acquisition of grammatical competence in a language is a necessary condition for the development of left hemisphere specialization for that language.

Early and intensive exposure to cued speech could provide the conditions for the development of grammatical competence in oral language (Hage, Algeria, & Périer, 1991). If this is the case, early CS users would display clear evidence for left hemisphere specialization for the processing of written and CS languages; late CS users, who do not have a fully grammatical competence in oral language, may have an atypical development of cerebral dominance for language processing.

D'Hondt and Leybaert (2002) compared the lateralization pattern of CS users for the processing of written stimuli to that of hearing subjects matched for reading level, sex, and linguistic competence. Subjects had to compare a stimulus presented at the center of the screen (hereafter "central") to a stimulus presented for 250 msec. in the left or right visual hemifield (hereafter "lateral"). Three tasks were used, including two linguistic tasks and a nonlinguistic one. The nonlinguistic task involves visual judgment: are "EeeE" (central stimulus) and "Eeee" (lateral stimulus) the same or not? No linguistic processing is required to perform this task, which could entail a similar performance of both hemispheres or even an advantage of the right hemisphere (Pugh et al., 1996). No difference between deaf and hearing subjects was observed.

One linguistic task involved semantic judgments: do "cat" (central stimulus) and "rabbit" be-

long to the same semantic category? A right visual field (left hemisphere) advantage was observed for this semantic decision task in deaf as in hearing subjects, matched for their ability to do semantic judgments in a control test (both groups reached 95% correct responses in a paper-and-pencil task). This result supports Neville's hypothesis: subjects with a full grammatical competence in French language displayed left hemisphere specialization for reading that language. The other linguistic task involved rhyming judgment of orthographically dissimilar pairs: do "feu" and "noeud" rhyme (in English, do "blue" and "few" rhyme)? In hearing subjects, a RVF advantage (left hemisphere) was observed, confirming data in the literature (Grossi, Coch, Coffey-Corina, Holcomb, & Neville, 2001; Rayman & Zaidel, 1991). Surprisingly, however, no hemifield advantage was observed in the CS users. The lack of significant laterality effect in the deaf could be related to their slightly inferior rhyming ability, indicated by their results on the paper-and-pencil test (the deaf achieved 88% correct responses, the hearing achieved 94%). Alternatively, the neural resources activated during rhyme judgment may be different in deaf CS users from those activated in hearing subjects.

Data from related research suggest that the areas activated during speechreading are not as left-lateralized in deaf people as they are in hearing people. Congenitally deaf individuals whose first language was spoken English showed significantly less left temporal activation than hearing subjects when performing a simple speechreading number task (MacSweeney et al., 2001), which suggests that "hearing speech helps to develop the coherent adult speech perception system within the lateral areas of the left temporal lobe" (p. 437). The comparison between activation displayed by CS users to that displayed by the deaf non–CS users and by the hearing may shed light on this question.

Consider next the lateralization of those aspects of processing that are directly dependent on perceptual processing. D'Hondt (2001) asked whether linguistic processing of CS stimuli might be better performed by the left hemisphere (LH), while non-linguistic processing of the same stimuli entail no hemispheric advantage, and whether the left hemisphere advantage for linguistic processing is modulated by the age at which deaf children receive formal linguistic input.

Subjects had to compare a centrally presented

video (the standard) to a video presented next, and very briefly, in the left or the right visual hemifield (the target). In the linguistic condition, they had to decide whether the same word in CS was produced in the two videos, independently of the hand that produced the stimuli. In the nonlinguistic condition, they had to decide whether the cue was produced with the same hand, independently of the word produced. A sample of subjects with early exposure to CS was compared to a sample of subjects with late exposure to CS.

The results were clear-cut: in the linguistic condition, the early CS group obtained an accuracy advantage for stimuli presented in the right visual field (LH), whereas the subjects of the late CS group did not show any hemifield advantage. In the nonlinguistic condition, no visual advantage was observed in either group (D'Hondt & Leybaert, 2002). These results confirmed the already existing evidence that the left cerebral hemisphere is specialized for language, regardless of the nature of the language medium (Emmorey, 2002). They also suggest that the neural systems that mediate the processing of linguistic information are modifiable in response to language experience. The LH superiority for language processing appears more systematically in children exposed early to a structured linguistic input than in children exposed only late to this input.

Summary and Conclusions

At the time of this review, new research questions that go beyond the issues of efficacy of CS are emerging. First, besides strong similarities between deaf CS users and hearing children, differences remain. CS users seem more dependent on word spelling than hearing subjects in rhyme generation; their phonological loop for processing CS information seems sensitive to hand location, a phonological feature in CS; and they do not display an LH advantage for rhyme judgment. Whether these differences could be explained by a common factor remains to be explored. It is also possible that functionally similar processes rely on different neural resources. The study of the cerebral regions activated by the processing of CS information, compared to audio-visual information, is on the research agenda (see Eden, Cappell, La Sasso, & Zeffiro, 2001).

A second issue that remains to be investigated is the source of individual differences. Cued speech has sometimes been supposed to be difficult in the receptive mode. This does not seem to be true for our early CS users, but it may be true for others. One obvious variable explaining the differences is intensity of exposure. Beside this, the notion of a sensitive period might be relevant here. The benefit provided by early exposure to CS may be related to the level of cortical activity in the visual cortex, which peaks around the age of 5 years (Neville & Bavelier, 2001). It might be more difficult for deaf children to process CS information effortlessly at a later age. The question of a critical or sensitive period for CS acquisition remains to be addressed.

A final topic that urgently deserves research is the benefit afforded by CS exposure to the use of cochlear implants. Collaboration rather than competition is likely here. Theoretically, it is possible that the child exposed to CS creates phonological representations that are exploitable later when the nervous system is stimulated by the electric signal delivered by a cochlear implant. It is asserted that a cochlear implant gives only degraded acoustic information, which makes it difficult to reliably discriminate fine phonetic differences in place and voicing features (Pisoni, 2000). The use of CS may help to set these fine phonetic differences. This leads one to predict that profoundly deaf children who are CS users would get better results in auditory word identification than those who are not CS users. Clinical evidence supports this hypothesis, which needs to be tested experimentally (Fraysse, Ben M'Rad, Cochard, & Van, 2002). Speech production might be another ability where the informations provided by CS and by the implant can converge. Children who receive auditory feedback through an implant may adjust their oral productions in relation to the reference points created by CS.

To conclude, CS has already afforded important benefit for language development of deaf children since its creation 30 years ago. With the new technologies available (e.g., automatic generation of CS, cochlear implants), new benefits may be foreseen.

Note

We thank our colleagues who participated to the research described in this chapter: Brigitte Charlier, Murielle D'Hondt, Catherine Hage, Carol La Sasso, and Josiane Lechat. We also thank Stéphanie Colin, Annie Magnan, Jean Ecalle, Denis Beautemps, Marie Cathiard, and Virginie Attina, who communicated their work to us and allowed us to discuss it in the chapter. The writing of this chapter was supported by a grant from the Foundation Houtman (Belgium).

References

Alegria, J., Aurouer, J., & Hage, C. (1997, December). How do deaf children identify written words encountered for the first time? Phonological representations and phonological processing. *Proceedings of the International Symposium: "Integrating Research and Practice in Literacy."* The British Council. London.

Alegria, J., Charlier, B., & Mattys, S. (1999). The role of lip-reading and cued-speech in the processing of phonological information in French-educated deaf children. *European Journal of Cognitive Psychology, 11*, 451–472.

Alegria, J., & Lechat, J. *How information from the lips and from the hands combine in CS perception.* Manuscript in preparation.

Alegria, J., Leybaert, J., Charlier, B., & Hage, C. (1992). On the origin of phonological representations in the deaf: hearing lips and hands. In J. Alegria, D. Holender, J. J. D. Morris, & M. Radeau (Eds.), *Analytic approaches to human cognition* (pp. 107–132). Bruxelles: Elsevier.

Attina, V. (2001). *Parole audiovisuelle et langage parlé complété (LPC): Etude préliminaire des coordinations main-lèvres-son.* Grenoble; France: Institut de la Communication Parlée.

Baddeley, A., & Hitch, G. S. (1974). Working memory. In G. H. Bower (Ed.), *The psychology of learning and motivation* (pp. 47–90). New York: Academic Press.

Bradley, L., & Bryant, P. E. (1978). Difficulties in auditory organization as a possible cause of reading backwardness. *Nature, 271*, 746–747.

Burnham, D., & Dodd, B. (1996). Auditory-visual speech perception as a direct process: The McGurk effect in infants and across languages. In D. Stork & M. Hennecke (Eds.), *Speechreading by humans and machines* (pp. 103–115). Berlin: Springer-Verlag.

Calvert, G. A., Bullmore, E. T. Brammer, M. J., Campbell, R., Williams, S. C. R., McGuire, P. K., Woodruff, P. W. R., Iversen, S. D., & David, A. S. (1997). Activation of auditory cortex during silent lipreading. *Science, 276*, 593–595.

Charlier, B. L., & Leybaert, J. (2000). The rhyming skills of deaf children educated with phonetically augmented speechreading. *Quarterly Journal of Experimental Psychology, 53A(2)*, 349–375.

Colin, S., Magnan, A., Ecalle, J., & Leybaert, J. A longitudinal study of deaf children's rhyming ability and written word recognition: The effect of exposure to cued speech. Manuscript in preparation.

Conrad, R. (1979). *The deaf school child.* London: Harper & Row.

Conrad, R., & Hull, A. J. (1964). Information, acoustic confusion and memory span. *British Journal of Psychology, 80*, 299–312.

Cornett, O. (1967). Cued speech. *American Annals of the Deaf, 112*, 3–13.

Cornett, O. (1994). Adapting Cued Speech to additional languages. *Cued Speech Journal, 5*, 19–36.

Cornett, O., Beadles, R., & Wilson, B. (1977, May). *Automatic cued speech.* Paper presented at the Research Conference on Speech-Processing Aids for the Deaf, Washington, DC.

D'Hondt, M. (2001). *Spécialisation hémisphérique pour le langage chez la personne à déficience auditive: Effet de l'expérience linguistique précoce.* Unpublished doctoral dissertation, Free University of Brussels, Brussels.

D'Hondt, M., & Leybaert, J. (2002). *Lateralization effects during semantic and rhyme judgment tasks in deaf and hearing subjects.* Manuscript submitted for publication.

Dehaene-Lambertz, G., Christophe, A., & Van Ooijen, V. (2000). Bases cérébrales de l'acquisition du langage. In M. Kail & M. Fayol (Eds.), *L'acquisition du langage: Le langage en émergence* (Vol. 1, pp. 61–95). Paris: PUF.

Dodd, B. (1976). The phonological system of deaf children. *Journal of Speech and Hearing Disorders, 41*, 185–198.

Duchnowski, P., Braida, L. D., Lum, D., Sexton, M., Krause, J., & Banthia, S. (1998a, December). *Automatic generation of cued speech for the deaf: Status and outlook.* In D. Burnham, J. Roberts-Ribes, & E. Vatikiotis-Bateson (Eds.), *Proceedings, International Conference on Auditory-Visual Speech Processing.* Terrigal, Australia. Sydney.

Duchnowski, P., Braida, L., Bratakos, M., Lum, D., Sexton, M., & Krause, J. (1998b, December). A speechreading aid based on phonetic ASR. In *Proceedings of 5th International Conference on Spoken Language Processing, Vol. 7* (pp. 3289–3292). Sydney, Australia.

Eden, G., Cappell, K., La Sasso, C., & Zeffiro, T. (2001, March). *Functional neuroanatomy of reading in cued and spoken English.* Paper presented at the Cognitive Neuroscience Meeting, New York.

Ehri, L. C. (1984). How orthography alters spoken

language competencies in children learning to read and spell. In J. Downing & R. Valtin (Eds.), *Language awareness and learning to read* (pp. 119–147). New York: Springer-Verlag.

Emmorey, K. (2002). *Language, cognition and the brain.* Mahwah, New Jersey: Lawrence Erlbaum Associates.

Erber, N. P. (1974). Visual perception of speech by deaf children. *Journal of Speech and Hearing Disorders, 39,* 178–185.

Fraysse, B., Ben M'Rad, B., Cochard, N., & Van, H. (2002, February). *Long term results of cochlear implants in congenital children.* Paper presented at the 6th European Symposium on paediatric cochlear implantation, Las Palmas de Gran Canaria.

Grossi, G., Coch, D., Coffey-Corina, S., Holcomb, P J., & Neville, H. J. (2001). Phonological processing in visual rhyming: A developmental ERP study. *Journal of Cognitive Neuroscience, 13*(5), 610–625.

Hage, C., Alegria, J., & Périer, O. (1991). Cued speech and language acquisition: The case of grammatical gender morpho-phonology. In D. S. Martin (Ed.), *Advances in cognition, education and deafness* (pp. 395–399). Washington, DC: Gallaudet University Press.

Kuhl, P. K & Meltzoff, A. N. (1988). The bimodal perception of speech in infancy. *Science, 218,* 1138–1141.

LaSasso, C., Crain, K., & Leybaert, J. (in press). The rhyming abilities of deaf students: Effect of exposure to cued speech. *Journal of Deaf Studies and Deaf Education.*

Leybaert, J. (1998). Phonological representations in deaf children: the importance of early linguistic experience. *Scandinavian Journal of Psychology, 39,* 169–173.

Leybaert, J. (2000). Phonology acquired through the eyes and spelling in deaf children. *Journal of Experimental Child Psychology, 75,* 291–318.

Leybaert, J., & Alegria, J. (1995). Spelling development in hearing and deaf children: Evidence for the use of morpho-phonological regularities in French. *Reading and Writing, 7,* 89–109.

Leybaert, J., Alegria, J., Hage, C., & Charlier, B. (1998). The effect of exposure to phonetically augmented lipspeech in the prelingual deaf. In R. Campbell, B. Dodd, & D. Burnham (Eds.), *Hearing by eye II: Advances in the psychology of speechreading and auditory-visual speech* (pp. 283–301). Hove, UK: Psychology Press.

Leybaert, J., & Charlier, B. L. (1996). Visual speech in the head: The effect of cued-speech on rhyming, remembering and spelling. *Journal of Deaf Studies and Deaf Education, 1,* 234–248.

Leybaert, J., & D'Hondt, M. (in press). Neurolinguistic development in deaf children: The effect of early experience. *International Journal of Audiology.*

Leybaert, J., & Lechat, J. (2001a). Phonological similarity effects in memory for serial order of cued-speech. *Journal of Speech, Language and Hearing Research, 44,* 949–963.

Leybaert, J., & Lechat, J. (2001b). Variability in deaf children's spelling: The effect of language experience. *Journal of Educational Psychology, 93,* 554–562.

Liben, L. S. (1978). The development of deaf children: An overview of issues. In L. S. Liben (Ed.), *Deaf children: Developmental perspectives* (pp. 3–40). New York: Academic Press.

Locke, J. L. (1998). A theory of neurolinguistic development. *Brain and Language, 58*(2), 265–326.

MacKain, K., Studdert-Kennedy, M., Spieker, S., & Stern, D. (1983). Infant intermodal speech perception is a left-hemisphere function. *Science, 219,* 1347–1348.

MacSweeney, M., Campbell, R., Calvert, G. A., McGuire, P. K., David, A. S., Suckling, J., Andrew, C., Woll, B., & Brammer, M. J. (2001). Dispersed activation in the left temporal cortex for speech-reading in congenitally deaf people. *Proceedings of the Royal Society of London, 268,* 451–457.

McGurk, H., & MacDonald, J. (1976). Hearing lips and seeing voices. *Nature, 264,* 746–748.

Mills, D. L., Coffey Corina, S. A., & Neville, H. J. (1993). Language acquisition and cerebral specialization in 20 months-old infants. *Journal of Cognitive Neuroscience, 5*(3), 317–334.

Mills, D. L., Coffey-Corina, S. A., & Neville, H. J. (1997). Language comprehension and cerebral specialization from 13 to 20 months. *Developmental Neuropsychology, 13,* 397–445.

Morais, J., Bertelson, P., Cary, L., & Alegria, J. (1986). Literacy training and speech segmentation. *Cognition, 24,* 45–64.

Neville, H. J. (1991). Whence the specialization of language hemisphere? In I. G. Mattingly & M. Studdert-Kennedy (Eds.), *Modularity and theory of speech perception* (pp. 269–294). Hillsdale, NJ: Lawrence Erlbaum Ass.

Neville, H., & Bavelier, D. (2001). Specificity of developmental neuroplasticity in humans: Evidence from sensory deprivation and altered language experience. In C.A. Shaw & J.C. McEachern (Eds.), *Toward a theory of neuroplasticity* (pp. 261–274). Hove, U.K.: Psychology Press.

Nicholls, G., & Ling, D. (1982). Cued speech and the reception of spoken language. *Journal of Speech and Hearing Research, 25,* 262–269.

Périer, O., Charlier, B., Hage, C., & Alegria, J. (1988).

Evaluation of the effects of prolonged Cued Speech practice upon the reception of spoken language. In I. G. Taylor (Ed.), *The education of the deaf: Current perspectives, Vol. I.* London: Croom Helm.

Pisoni, D. B. (2000). Cognitive factors and cochlear implants: some thoughts on perception, learning, and memory in speech perception. *Ear and Hearing, 21,* 70–78.

Pugh, K. R., Shaywitz, B. A., Constable, R. T., Shayxitz, S. A., Skudlaski, P., Fulbright, R. K., Brone, R. A., Shankweiler, D. P., Katz, L., Fletcher, J. M., & Gore, J. C. (1996). Cerebral organization of compenont processes on reading. *Brain, 119,* 1221–1238.

Rayman, J., & Zaidel, E. (1991). Rhyming and the right hemisphere. *Brain and Language, 40,* 89–105.

Read, C. (1978). Children's awareness of language, with an emphasis on sound systems. In A. Sinclair, R. Jarvella, & W. Levelt (Eds.), *The child's conception of language* (pp. 65–82). New York: Springer-Verlag.

Reisberg, D., & Logie, R. H. (1993). The ins and outs of working memory: Overcoming the limits on learning from imagery. In B. Roskos-Edwoldson, M. J. Intons-Peterson, & R. E. Anderson (Eds.), *Imagery, creativity, and discovery: A cognitive perspective* (pp. 39–76). Amsterdam: Elsevier.

Ryalls, J., Auger, D., & Hage, C. (1994). An acoustic study of the speech skills of profoundly hearing-impaired children who use cued speech. *Cued Speech Journal, 5,* 8–18.

Slobin, D. (1978). A case study of early language awareness. In A. Sinclair, R. Jarvella, & W. Levelt (Eds.), *The child's conception of language* (pp. 45–54). New York: Springer-Verlag.

Traxler, C. (2000). The Stanford achievement test, 9th edition: National norming and performance standards for deaf and hard-of-hearing students. *Journal of Deaf Studies and Deaf Education, 5,* 337–348.

Walden, B. E., Prosek, R. A., Montgomery, A. A., Scherr, C. K., & Jones, C. J. (1977). Effect of training on the visual recognition of consonants. *Journal of Speech and Hearing Research, 20,* 130–135.

Wandel, J. E. (1989). *Use of internal speech in reading by hearing impaired students in Oral, Total Communication and Cued Speech programs.* Unpublished master's thesis, Columbia University, New York.

Webster, P. E. & Plante, A. S. (1995). Productive phonology and phonological awareness in preschool children. *Applied Psycholinguistics, 16,* 43–57.

Wilson, M., & Emmorey, K. (1998). A "word length effect" for sign language: Further evidence for the role of language in structuring worling memory. *Memory and Cognition, 26*(3), 584–591.

20

Janet R. Jamieson

Formal and Informal Approaches to the Language Assessment of Deaf Children

From the moment deaf children are placed in school settings, language development is a primary educational goal. The accurate and authentic assessment of a deaf child's language proficiencies and language development is crucial for several practical reasons that affect initial placement and subsequent programming. School districts throughout North America require careful documentation of baseline measures of language performance of deaf students and subsequent indicators of progress on Individual Education Programs (IEPs). In addition, assessments can help identify children who are having difficulty developing language proficiency and specify the nature of the problem. Educators can then use this information prescriptively to alter curricula to more effectively meet a child's needs. On a programmatic level, the assessment of the language proficiency of a group of deaf children may be used to help determine program effectiveness.

Unfortunately, few tests can be used reliably with this population. Many standardized measures intended to assess the language knowledge and performance of hearing children are ill-suited for guiding placement decisions or for informing language goals of deaf students. Thus, educators and clinicians need to proceed cautiously when planning

for, conducting, and interpreting findings of language assessments of deaf children.

The aims of this chapter are to (1) discuss some of the important issues surrounding the language assessment of deaf children, issues that influence the selection of approaches and measures, assessment procedures, and interpretation of findings and (2) review the most commonly used formal and informal approaches to and measures for assessing deaf children's English language proficiencies. For a discussion of approaches to the specific assessment of children's sign language proficiencies or speech production, see Blamey; Schick; and Singleton and Supalla (this volume).

Assessment of Language Proficiency in Deaf Children: Unique Issues

The term "assessment" is used in this chapter to refer to a global process of obtaining and synthesizing information on an individual child's performance for the purpose of informing educational placement and instructional practice (Paul, 1998). The focus is on those children whose hearing loss gives rise to significant challenges to their language learning. The term "deaf" will be used inclusively to refer to both deaf and hard-of-hearing students.

Many deaf children are exposed to a range of language systems across home, school, and community contexts, so the assessor must determine the systems that surround the child and in which contexts they are used, as well as the child's primary or preferred modality (e.g., vision, hearing) and language system. For example, hearing parents may use spoken English at home, whereas the deaf child may be taught in a manually coded form of English, such as Signing Exact English or Signed English, and/or American Sign Language (ASL) at school (Coryell & Holcomb, 1997). In addition, the child's idiosyncratic use of a system can affect assessment. In the case of deaf children who use spoken language, the specifics of language use may be evident only to adults who are familiar with their speech. With respect to signing deaf children, there is regional variation in individual signs across North America or even from one educational program to another. Further, when language tests are used with signing deaf children, it is possible that the iconicity of the signs may artificially inflate scores. Validity of the overall assessment results thus will be enhanced by considering proficiency in all possible language systems used by the child, conducting assessment using the child's preferred language or language system whenever possible, and receiving input from informants across contexts (e.g., parents, teachers) to avoid over- and underestimating the child's language abilities.

Deaf children from non-English, spoken language backgrounds may have some language skills used only at home that could influence school decisions about the child. Thus, although assessing English proficiency is central to most placement and intervention decisions, knowledge of all possible language systems is critical for understanding a child's language skills and potential. Parents' input is critical in a comprehensive language assessment process. In the case of non–English-speaking, hearing parents, culturally sensitive interpreters and at least one parent report instrument that is valid for the home language are strongly recommended. For example, the MacArthur Communicative Development Inventories (CDI) (Fenson et al., 1993) has norms for more than 10 languages other than English, including American Sign Language (Anderson & Reilly, 2002).

Formal and Informal Approaches

The approaches to assessment and selection of tests should be based on diagnostic questions formulated on the basis of (1) preassessment observations of the child and/or input from adults familiar with the child's language use, (2) current theoretical understandings about communication, and (3) knowledge about the unique characteristics of deaf children's language use (Moeller, 1988). According to Laughton and Hasenstab (1993) the general diagnostic questions are:

1. How does the student use language to communicate in a variety of contexts? (communicative)
2. How does the student use language to learn? (metalinguistic)
3. What are regularities in the child's language performance?
4. What are the areas that need repair? (p. 153)

In practice, most formal assessment tools are selected on the basis of ease of administration and availability and are best used to specify areas of concerns. After obtaining results from initial testing, the diagnostic questions are refined to isolate those features of children's language that are priorities for intervention or foci of research. Thus, the assessor may begin with formalized tests as a means of specifying features of a child's language that appear problematic and then probe these aspects more deeply with informal strategies. Conversely, the assessor may begin with information gleaned informally through language sample analysis and then follow this up with formal testing of areas indicative of concern.

Formal Approaches

Formal, or "product-oriented," assessments are based on the premise that there is a need to isolate, identify, and describe particular individual language skills and to compare them with those of other children. Paul (1998) emphasized that formal assessment measures must be valid (i.e., measure what they purport to measure), reliable (i.e., consistent and dependable), and practical. Standardized tests are frequently used to assess students' progress objectively and to provide a comparison with some external standard. Accordingly, such tests used with deaf children are norm-referenced, that is, they compare a child's performance to that of an external reference group. Standardized tests may also be criterion-referenced, indicating a child's performance as measured against a target criterion. For example, standardized checklists tend to be criterion-referenced and are usually reported in terms of descriptions of a child's performance (e.g., "The child can determine cause/effect relations"). A list of several standardized tests commonly used in the language assessment of deaf children is presented in table 20-1. However, some cautions and limitations of formal tests normed on deaf and/or hearing populations should be kept in mind during test selection and interpretation, as discussed below.

Most standardized tests used with deaf children have been normed on hearing populations (e.g., Preschool Language Assessment Instrument; Blank, Rose, & Berlin, 1978; Test of Problem Solving; Zachman, Jorgenson, Huisingh, & Barrett, 1984). When the comparison group is hearing, caution is recommended in the interpretation of results for several reasons:

1. The language development of hearing children rests heavily on auditory input and development, so some test items unfairly penalize deaf children and make their language appear more delayed than it actually is (de Villiers, 1988).
2. The assessor often must use procedures different from those used with the normed sample. For example, the use of interpreters marks a deviation from the norming procedures and thus poses threats to both the validity and reliability of standardized tests. (Nevertheless, it is essential to work with an interpreter if the assessor is not fluent in the child's language system or the language of the home.)
3. The value of comparing the performance of younger hearing children with that of older deaf children, a common practice in assessments using tests normed for hearing children, should be done cautiously. Deaf children may show differences, as opposed to delays, in some aspects of their language development, or the linguistic skill may not be generalized to the testing context (de Villiers, 1988).
4. Because the assessments tend to occur outside of relevant communication contexts, they pro-

vide little information that is helpful prescriptively (de Villiers, 1988; Laughton & Hasenstab, 2000).

Standardized tests based on norms for deaf children may also be problematic, in that they may have an inherent sample bias (Prezbindowski & Lederberg, 2003). Samples for such norms tend to be much smaller than those of instruments for hearing children. The CDI (Fenson et al., 1993), for example, was normed on 1,789 hearing children, whereas the ASL version (Anderson & Reilly, 2002) was normed on only 69 deaf children. Additionally, the norming samples are often drawn from particular regions and/or educational programs, which limits their representativeness and can render interpretation of results difficult. The Rhode Island Test of Language Structure (Engen & Engen, 1983), for example, was normed on deaf children from the eastern part of the United States only.

How, then, can standardized tests contribute to the language assessment process? Such measures can provide a useful comparison of the progress of one group of children to another group or to deaf children nationwide. Formal test results may indicate areas of language development indicative of concern for an individual child. Alternatively, if a mainstreamed placement is being considered, it is important to know how the child compares with hearing peers on various measures of English language proficiency. However, if the goal of assessment is to obtain a comprehensive understanding of the child's language abilities, formal test results must be considered together with information collected by informal means.

Informal Approaches

Informal, or "process-oriented," assessments are based on the assumptions that language performance should be viewed in context and evaluated over time against the child's own baseline. For example, language samples are commonly used to assess deaf children's language performance informally.

Language Samples. Historically, observation of deaf children communicating with familiar conversational partners (e.g., peers, parents) has been considered a valuable means of obtaining a representative sample of the child's language. The focus of spontaneous or elicited language sampling is the child as a language user in particular con-

Table 20-1. Tests commonly used in language assessment of deaf children

Test name	Target age group	Norm/comparison group	Focus of test
Boehm Test of Basic Concepts-Revised (Boehm, 1986) (Spanish edition available)	Grades K, 1, 2	Approximately 10,000 hearing children of mixed SES, from 19 U.S. cities	To specify mastery of particular concepts required for primary school
Carolina Picture Vocabulary Test (Layton & Holmes, 1985)	4–11½ years	761 deaf children ages 2;6 to 16;0 in total communication settings in U.S.[1]	To test receptive vocabulary of signing deaf children
Expressive One-Word Picture Vocabulary Test-Revised (Gardner, 1990) (Spanish edition available)	2–12 years	1,118 hearing children from 2 to 11 years in San Francisco Bay area	To test child's expressive vocabulary by requiring child to name content of picture
Grammatical Analysis of Elicited Language Simple Sentence Level, 2nd ed. (Moog & Geers, 1985) (GAEL Pre-sentence Level and GAEL Complex Sentence Level also available)	5–9 years	323 deaf children from oral programs, 177 deaf children from total communication programs, and 200 hearing children in Missouri	To test deaf children's receptive and expressive use of English morphemes in sentences; used mostly with oral students
Kendall Communicative Proficiency Scale (Francis et al., 1980; as shown in French, 1999b)	Birth to adolescence	None	To rate the expressive communicative proficiency of deaf students in naturalistic interactions in school settings
Language Proficiency Profile 2 (Bebko & McKinnon, 1993)	3–14 years	63 deaf students ages 3;9 to 13;10 months from U.S. and Canadian programs; 104 Canadian hearing students ages 2;0 to 7;0 (28 deaf U.S. students from 3;9 to 7;4 used in one aspect of norming)	To evaluate expressive pragmatic/semantic skills, regardless of modality or language
MacArthur Communicative Development Inventories (CDI) (Fenson et al., 1993) (norms for 10 spoken languages other than English also available)	8–16 months (CDI-Words and Gestures); 16–30 months (CDI-Words and Sentences)	1813 hearing children from 8 to 30 months in 3 U.S. cities	To assess children's expressive and receptive vocabulary using norm-referenced parent checklists
MacArthur CDI-ASL (Anderson & Reilly, 2002)	8–36 months	69 deaf children of deaf parents, aged 8 to 36 months, who were learning ASL as their first language	To assess expressive vocabulary of 537 signs used by deaf children
MacArthur CDI (Norms for Deaf Children-Expressive) (Mayne et al., 2000a)	8–37 months	113 deaf children in Colorado from 24 to 37 months	To assess expressive spoken vocabulary of deaf children on the Words and Gestures and Words and Sentences subtests of the CDI
MacArthur CDI (Norms for Deaf Children-Receptive) (Mayne et al., 2000b)	8–22 months	168 deaf children in Colorado from 8 to 22 months	To assess receptive spoken vocabulary of deaf children on the Words and Gestures and Words and Sentences subtests of the CDI

Test name	Target age group	Norm/comparison group	Focus of test
Peabody Picture Vocabulary Test-III (Dunn & Dunn, 1997)	2.5 years to adulthood	2,725 hearing children and adolescents representative of 1994 U.S. census data	To assess an individual's receptive comprehension of spoken vocabulary items
Preschool Language Scale—3 (Zimmerman, Steiner, & Pond, 1992) (Spanish edition available)	Below 1 year to 6;11	1,200 hearing children between 2 weeks and 6;11 from across U.S.	To assess a broad range of expressive and receptive language skills, from precursors to language to integrative thinking skills
Preschool Language Assessment Instrument (Blank et al., 1978) (Spanish edition available)	2;9 to 5;8	288 hearing children from 36 to 71 months matched by age, SES, and sex	To assess the student's ability to respond to questions at four separate levels of cognitive abstraction
Receptive One-Word Picture Vocabulary Test (Gardner, 1985) (Spanish edition available)	2;0 to 11;11	1,128 hearing children in the San Francisco Bay area; SES and ability levels not reported	To assess children's comprehension of spoken English vocabulary
Reynell Developmental Language Scales (U.S. edition) (Reynell & Gruber, 1990) (British edition available)	1;0 to 6;11	619 hearing children ages 1;0 to 6;11 selected to approximate the 1987 U.S. census data, at nine sites	To measure verbal expressive and comprehension language skills through questions that vary in length and syntactic complexity
Rhode Island Test of Language Structure (Engen & Engen, 1983)	3–20 years (deaf), 3–6 years (hearing)	364 deaf children in Eastern U.S.; 283 hearing children in Rhode Island	An individually administered test designed to assess a student's comprehension of 20 syntactic structures
SKI*HI Language Development Scale (Tonelson & Watkins, 1979)	Birth to 60 months	None (based on 19 other norm-referenced developmental scales)	To assess deaf children's receptive and expressive use of language; children are given credit for responses, whether visual communication or spoken
Test for Auditory Comprehension of Language—3 (Carrow-Wolfolk, 1999) (Spanish edition available)	3;0 to 9;11	1,102 hearing students ages 3;0 to 9;11 in 24 U.S. states	To assess receptive skills in vocabulary and syntax
Test of Language Development—Primary 3 (Newcomer & Hammill, 1997a)	4;0 to 8;11	1,000 hearing students between 3;0 and 8;11 in 28 U.S. states	To test children's knowledge of various aspects of vocabulary and grammar
Test of Language Development—Intermediate 3 (Newcomer & Hammill, 1997b)	8;0 to 12;11	779 hearing children ages 8;6 to 12;11 from 23 states	To assess basic receptive and expressive abilities in semantics, phonology, and syntax
Test of Problem Solving (Zachman et al., 1984)	6;0 to 11;11	1578 American children ages 6;0 to 11;11 (children with special needs excluded)	To assess the student's skills in summarizing and predicting

[1]Consistent with standard practice, ages are shown as "x;x," with the first number indicating years and the second indicating months.

texts. The assessor may videotape a child in several contexts, with a variety of conversational partners, or samples of a child's written work may be obtained (see Albertini & Schley, this volume). Language samples are usually analyzed to assess deaf children's language production and comprehension skills. A first approach to analysis is often to obtain the mean length of utterance (MLU; Miller, 1981) from transcribed or student-written language samples. This provides a measure of sentence length for children who are at the stage of combining words/signs. Computer systems for managing analysis of language samples, such as Systematic Analysis of Language Transcripts (SALT; Miller & Chapman, 1983), typically provide specific information about the child's semantic, syntactic, or pragmatic performance. Written narratives may be analyzed by checklist format (e.g., Luetke-Stahlman & Luckner, 1991; Yoshinaga-Itano & Downey, 1992).

The primary contexts in which the social interactions occur, the purposes for which language is being used, and the types of information that are being conveyed or exchanged must be described (Kretschmer & Kretschmer, 1988). For a deaf child, the primary contexts are, of course, home and school. Generally speaking, the school context places more complex communication demands on the child than the home setting. Whereas home communication is generally characterized by small numbers of communicants, single, brief discourse turns, and frequent opportunities for repair, classroom discourse involves several conversational participants, demands for processing lengthy input, and far fewer opportunities for repairing conversational breakdown (Griffith, Johnson, & Dastoli, 1985; Moeller, 1988; Musselman & Hambleton, 1990). The assessment should also include information about the language of the curriculum used in the school (i.e., curriculum-based assessment, as described by Nelson, 1989).

Additional process analyses facilitate investigation of a child's language proficiency across domains within the language sampling context. Pragmatic process questions include: does the student use a variety of strategies to initiate conversation? What are the pragmatic characteristics of the conversational partner, and how do they contribute to the student's optimal language use? Questions about semantic ability include: how flexible is the child's vocabulary? What pragmatic strategies does the student use to enlarge vocabulary? The assessor may also ask, what syntactic knowledge does the student need to function in this particular environment? Language samples, thus, are a rich source of information and form a central part of the language assessment process.

A child may fail to exhibit a particular language skill during language samples obtained through naturalistic observations. The question then becomes, has the child not mastered that skill, or did the opportunity to demonstrate it in context not arise? In this case, specific elicitation tasks can be designed to increase the likelihood that certain language abilities will be shown, if a child has mastered them. Activities such as role playing, requiring the child to teach others how to play a game, or story retelling enable the assessor to obtain a language sample in a more structured but realistic situation.

Language Proficiency Assessments for Deaf Children

Most language assessment tools used with deaf children investigate language from a modular theoretical approach, which leads to the assessment of language separately in three domains: semantics, pragmatics, and syntax. Accordingly, language assessment is discussed below following these three traditional modules. However, the competition model proposed by Bates and MacWhinney (1987; MacWhinney, 1987) actually forms the theoretical underpinnings to the interpretation of assessment results in this chapter. This model is based on the notion of parallel information processing, which views language development in different domains as occurring simultaneously (and thereby affecting one another throughout the course of development), rather than sequentially. Thus, a child's abilities in a single language domain should not be interpreted in isolation, but, rather, in terms of how it facilitates or impedes language development in other domains as well.

Pragmatic Assessment

Duchan (1988) defined pragmatics broadly as "the study of how linguistic, situational, or social contexts affect language use" (p. 19). A major focus of the research on pragmatic skills in young deaf children has been the expression of communicative intents, or functions. Early findings indicated that deaf toddlers and preschoolers displayed the full range of pragmatic functions shown by hearing peers (Curtiss, Prutting, & Lowell, 1979). More recently, however, young deaf children, most of whom are delayed in use of formal language, are reported to use information-getting, or heuristic, functions less frequently than hearing peers. This has been documented for children in signing programs (Day, 1986) as well as those in oral programs (Nicholas, 2000; Nicholas, Geers, & Kozak, 1994). This finding is significant; early nonverbal requests for information in deaf children have been found to be strongly related to the later achievement of verbal communication (Yoshinaga-Itano & Stredler-Brown, 1992) and more likely to predict later language competence than the use of other pragmatic functions (Nicholas & Geers, 1997). From this perspective, then, the heuristic function in particular appears to be correlated with the acquisition of a formal language.

Research into the pragmatic development of school-age deaf students has long emphasized conversational skills, including turn-taking. For example, McKirdy and Blank (1982) and Wilbur and Petitto (1981) found that signing deaf persons, even very young children, used an elaborate set of visual regulators, such as a shift in eye gaze, as turn-taking signals in lieu of vocal intonation signals used by hearing persons. When both mother and child are deaf and use the same set of visual regulators, they demonstrate turn-taking by different, but highly effective means when compared to hearing mother–hearing child pairs (Jamieson, 1994). Thus, optimal pragmatic characteristics for hearing children may not be the same as those for deaf children, particularly those who sign.

The role of the conversational partner has been found to be highly influential in shaping both the length and the content of the response from the deaf child. This finding holds true for naturalistic interactions, both spoken and signed, observed with parents and siblings at home (Bodner-Johnson, 1991), with mothers at play (Jamieson & Pedersen, 1993), and with hearing teachers in primary classrooms (Wood & Wood, 1984). Thus, assessment of a deaf child's pragmatic skills should include a focus on the communication characteristics of the conversational partner.

Approaches to Pragmatic Assessment

Regardless of specific strategies selected to assess pragmatic skills of deaf children, the following recommendations are made: (1) use more than one strategy to assess pragmatic abilities and include a variety of conversational partners and situations (Luetke-Stahlman, 1998); (2) use caution when comparing findings from deaf children and hearing children because the specific pragmatic skills appropriate for deaf children at one point in development may not match those expected of hearing children (Jamieson, 1994); and (3) use language-matched peers, rather than age-matched peers, when comparing with hearing children (Yoshinaga-Itano, 1997). Five different tools for assessing the pragmatic skills of deaf children are described below.

Developmental Profile. Many early intervention programs assemble composite batteries to assess children's language developmental profiles. These profiles tend to include assessment of pragmatics, and that is often a major focus. One example of a comprehensive, multidisciplinary assessment battery designed for use with very young deaf children and their families is the Family Assessment of Multidisciplinary Interactional Learning for the Young Child (Stredler-Brown & Yoshinaga-Itano, 1994). The individual components evaluate nine developmental areas: communication, language, phonology, play, parent–child interaction, audition, family needs, developmental, and motor. It is completed at 6-month intervals and includes a videotape of parent–child interaction (which is later coded along several dimensions) and parent-completed checklists. The coding, in particular, is very time consuming, but the composite information is highly informative for program planning.

Other batteries have been assembled for use with older children. For example, French (1999b) designed a battery to assess deaf children's literacy development from emergent to mature. Because "conversational language [proficiency] is essential to further development in literacy" (French, 1999b, p. 25), school-based conversational language with a variety of partners and in several school-based contexts is assessed. The battery also includes checklists to determine stages of language development (including features of ASL) and reading and writing checklists, as well as surveys to obtain student and parent input. Although age-related language development information is included, the battery provides no normative data.

Program-specific Criterion-Referenced Checklists.
Judging by the proliferation of informal, unpublished pragmatic skills checklists developed over the past decade, many clinicians seem to have found checklists developed on site in response to the pragmatic skills judged to be essential for a particular group of children in their home and school context to be most useful. For example, staff of the British Columbia Family Hearing Resource Centre, an early intervention program for young deaf children and their families, developed the "Taxonomy of Pragmatic Skills: The Building Blocks to Literacy and Lifeskills" (S. Lane, personal communication, January 8, 2002). The areas of pragmatics assessed range from preverbal and communicative intent to conversational devices (such as turn-taking signals).

Communicative Proficiency Scale. A few structured instruments have been developed to assess the communicative and/or conversational proficiency of school-age deaf children and adolescents in both signed and spoken language (Akamatsu & Mussleman, 1998; Bebko & McKinnon, 1998). One instrument is the Kendall Communicative Proficiency Scale (KCPS; Francis, Garner, & Harvey, 1980), a 15-point scale for rating the communicative proficiency of deaf children in school settings. It is based on Bloom and Lahey's (1978) notion of three basic dimensions to language: content, form, and use. On the basis of naturalistic interactions with and observations of a deaf child, trained assessors assign each child a score from 0–7 in five categories (reference, content, cohesion, use, and form). The focus of the KCPS, which is part of a comprehensive language arts program (French, 1999a, 1999b), is primarily pragmatic skills, but semantic and syntactic abilities are viewed as highly interrelated, and so the overall score is a global index of language abilities.

Bebko and McKinnon have adapted the KCPS to develop the Language Proficiency Profile (LPP; Bebko & McKinnon, 1987) and the Language Proficiency Profile—2 (LPP-2; Bebko & McKinnon, 1993). The LPP-2 is a multiple-choice rating scale assessing the same five subscales of language included in the KCPS. The LPP-2 uses an informed rater approach to evaluate the child's overall developing pragmatic/semantic skills, independent of language modality or language system. The instrument has good construct validity (Bebko & McKinnon, 1998) and good concurrent validity with teacher-rated reading scores (Bebko, Calderon, & Treder, 2002), although these studies used limited sample sizes. The LPP-2 does not require extensive rater training. Both the KCPS and the LPP-2 may provide a useful initial indication of overall communicative competence before more extensive assessment.

Semantic Assessment

Meaning, or semantics, may be considered on at least three different levels of increasing complexity: word, utterance, and text (Kretschmer & Kretschmer, 1988). Historically, semantic assessment of deaf children has been conducted at the level of individual word meaning, often using hearing norms (e.g., Peabody Picture Vocabulary Tests [PPVT]—Revised; Dunn & Dunn, 1987; PPVT-III, Dunn & Dunn, 1997). Results are usually reported in terms of percentiles or age equivalencies. Delays in vocabulary and basic concept knowledge have been well documented in deaf children (e.g., Connor, Hieber, Arts, & Zwolen, 2000; Davis, 1974; see Lederberg, this volume), but, unfortunately, through the use of standardized vocabulary tests, the teacher or clinician can only verify that a significant vocabulary delay exists; the results yield no clue as to how to structure remediation (Moeller, 1988; Yoshinaga-Itano, 1997).

Contemporary researchers know there is a need to recognize semantic networks, or organizations, of particular words or groups of words (Gaustad, 2000; Scholnick, 1983). Accordingly, semantic evaluation for school-age students has become increasingly discourse oriented, focusing on narratives (spoken or written), conversations, event descriptions, and school lessons. Compared to hearing peers, deaf students' written productions tend to be marred by grammatical disfluencies and narrow vocabularies (Marschark, Mouradian, & Halas, 1994) and fewer complete propositions with increasing story complexity (Griffith, Ripich, & Dastoli, 1990). Narrative comprehension and production rests heavily on the development of semantic skills, such as the ability to make semantic associations between old and new information (Johnson, Toms-Bronowski, & Pittleman, 1982) and to apply world knowledge appropriately to language tasks (Yoshinaga-Itano & Downey, 1992). Thus, if semantic assessment is to be educationally prescriptive, it must include information not only about knowledge of individual word meanings (i.e., semantic characteristics), but also process information about the child's conceptual framework for word and concept knowledge, retrieval, and semantic operations (i.e., semantic relationships).

Formal Tests of Semantic Assessment

Parent Checklist. The CDI (Fenson et al., 1993) represents the standard parent checklist used to measure vocabulary development in hearing children, and it has been translated into several languages other than English. There are two forms of the test, Words and Gestures, for hearing infants 8–16 months of age, and Words and Sentences, for hearing infants 16–30 months of age. For the words and gestures test, parents are asked to determine which of 396 words, arranged into categories, their children understand (receptive vocabulary) and produce (expressive vocabulary). The words and sentences test consists of a 680-word expressive vocabulary checklist as well as questions about emerging grammar. When used with hearing children, the CDI has high internal reliability and is a more reliable predictor of language development than information obtained from language samples (Fenson et al., 1994).

Norms for deaf children have been developed for the original English form of the CDI (Mayne, Yoshinaga-Itano, Sedey, & Carey, 2000a, 2000b) as well as for the ASL version (Anderson & Reilly, 2002; see Singleton and Supalla, this volume). These versions of the CDI are important advances in the available tools for assessing deaf children's vocabulary development. However, they must be used with caution because of the small number of children in the deaf norming groups and, in the case of the English CDI norms, the limited geographic areas from which the children were drawn (Prezbindowski & Lederberg, 2002).

Tests Administered to the Child. The PPVT-R (Dunn & Dunn, 1987), the PPVT-III (Dunn & Dunn, 1997) and both the Receptive and Expressive One-Word Picture Vocabulary Tests (ROWPVT, Gardner, 1985; EOWPVT-R, Gardner, 1990) were designed for use with hearing children and normed on large hearing populations. The PPVT-R and the PPVT-III are individually administered tests for children from 2 years, 6 months

through adulthood that provide a measure of the receptive comprehension of spoken English. Children point to the one of four words that represents the word spoken by the assessor. Children's raw scores may be reported in standard scores, percentile ranks, stanine scores, or age equivalents. The EOWVT-R is a measure of receptive vocabulary knowledge designed for use with children 2–12 years of age. The child names the objects, actions, or concepts shown in a series of pictures. The resulting raw score may be used to generate a standard score, percentile rank, or grade equivalent score. Both the PPVT and the EOWVT-R are practical and easy to administer, although the tests may tap speechreading ability in addition to vocabulary knowledge.

The Carolina Picture Vocabulary Test (*CPVT*; Layton & Holmes, 1985), a 130-item test of receptive vocabulary, was designed specifically for signing deaf children. Children are required to point to one of four pictures that indicates the word spoken and signed by the assessor. Despite the usefulness of the CPVT as one of the few vocabulary tests for signing deaf children, there are at least two significant concerns about its use. First, it has relatively small norms: it was normed on 761 deaf children from 2½ to 16 years of age in total communication programs across the United States, or slightly more than one quarter the sample size used to establish norms for the PPVT-III (Dunn & Dunn, 1997). Second, there is often regional variation in specific signs from one program to another, so it is crucial that an assessor determine the signs that are used for test items at an individual child's home and school. It is also possible that the iconicity of some signs presented in the test may artificially inflate scores (Prezbindowski & Lederberg, 2003).

The Reynell Developmental Language Scales provide measures of receptive and expressive language development, including vocabulary. These scales have the advantage over single-word vocabulary tests of embedding language in a larger context. The scales are appropriate for use with children from 1 to 6;11 and have been widely used with deaf children. They have separate norms for British (Edwards et al., 1997) and American (Reynell & Gruber, 1990) children.

Receptive and expressive vocabulary tests, whether normed on deaf or hearing samples, can be used with children somewhat older, or at older developmental levels, than those for whom the parent report instruments are most appropriate. For example, an examiner might choose to use the CDI with an infant and a picture vocabulary test during the next stage of language learning.

Informal Strategies for Semantic Assessment

Older deaf children's semantic processing can be evaluated in written form as well as through the use of direct tests such as those described above. For example, Yoshinaga-Itano and Downey (1992) proposed a model (Colorado Process Analysis of the Written Language of Hearing-Impaired Children) for analyzing semantic characteristics in the written narratives of deaf children. A student's written story is coded for evidence of various aspects of inference and elaboration, sequence, and story. The authors used this tool with 284 severely to profoundly deaf students in Colorado between 7 and 21 years of age. Findings for the group are provided, although the authors make no claim that the scores should be considered as norms, so comparisons with study participants should made cautiously.

Syntactic Assessment

Kretschmer and Kretschmer (1988) defined syntax concisely as "the formulation and arrangement of sentences" (p. 10). There is a paucity of information about the syntactic ability of very young deaf children. Relatively more research concerning syntactic development has been conducted as deaf children approach school age, and these efforts have yielded considerable evidence that deaf children continue to develop syntactic abilities until at least the age of 12 or 13 years (e.g., Geers & Moog, 1989; Quigley & King, 1980).

Researchers investigating the language development of deaf children have increasingly recognized that various syntactic structures are not mastered outside of a discourse context or apart from a pragmatic function. Accordingly, the research focus has shifted to the process of the acquisition of syntactic skills in spoken and written discourse. For example, de Villiers (1988, 1991), using a contextually rich elicitation technique with orally educated students and a hearing comparison group, found both a difference and a delay in the acquisition of certain syntactic forms between the two groups. He reported that the deaf students were delayed in their production of relative clauses when compared with a younger hearing comparison group. Further, deaf and hearing children displayed differences in the types of errors when acquiring WH questions. Such findings suggest that not all characteristics of syntax development for typically developing hearing children apply to children who are deaf. Thus, to be educationally prescriptive, the assessment of deaf children's syntactic abilities must be sensitive to possibly idiosyncratic paths of development and the mastery (or lack of mastery) of the comprehension and production of a wide range of syntactic forms.

Formal Tests of Syntactic Development

The use of formal tests to assess deaf students' syntactic ability has been criticized on the grounds that the tests describe criterion behavior but do not provide information helpful in educational planning; that children may reduce the syntactic complexity of their utterances or code-shift from ASL into English in order to enhance tester comprehension (Kretschmer & Kretschmer, 1988); and that the tests do not test sufficient examples of a broad range of syntactic constructions to indicate mastery behavior (de Villiers, 1991). Three formal tests that are commonly used to assess deaf students' English syntactic skills are described below.

Direct Child Testing, Deaf Norms Included. The Grammatical Analysis of Elicited Language series was designed to test deaf children's expressive and receptive use of English vocabulary and grammar. It was originally developed for use with orally educated children; some limited data for children in total communication programs were also reported. The manuals also provide norms for hearing children, thereby allowing comparison to a hearing population. The GAEL Pre-Sentence Level (Moog, Kozak, & Geers, 1983), which was designed for children 3–6 years of age, has three sections: readiness, single words, and word combinations. The GAEL Simple Sentence Level, second edition (Moog & Geers, 1985) and GAEL Complex Sentence Level (Moog & Geers, 1980) were designed for students 5–9 years of age and assess expressive language and syntactic knowledge. The expressive language sections use elicited imitation (i.e., if a child's spontaneous English production is not correct, the child is asked to imitate a modeled sentence).

Findings from the GAEL should be interpreted cautiously for at least three reasons. First, elicited imitation tasks have been criticized in use with deaf children because they are lacking in communicative intent and thus may over- or underestimate a child's ability to use a particular syntactic structure in context (de Villiers, 1988). Second, in the case of children using spoken language, the test may also been seen as heavily reliant on speechreading abilities. Third, the test may overestimate functional communication because only approximations to the intended target word or sign are required for credit (Prezbindowski & Lederberg, 2003).

The Test of Syntactic Abilities (Quigley, Steinkamp, Power, & Jones, 1978) was designed for use with deaf students from 10 years to 18 years, 11 months of age. A multiple-choice format is used to determine a student's strengths or weaknesses with nine basic English structures, including negation, question formation, relativization, and nominalization. This test takes approximately 60 minutes; raw scores may be converted to age equivalents or percentiles. The test is based on Chomsky's (1965) model of transformational grammar, so the underlying assumption is that deaf children follow the same pattern of language acquisition as hearing children. In this way, when deaf children's performance is found lacking, the results suggest delay, rather than deviance or difference.

The Rhode Island Test of Language Structure (Engen & Engen, 1983) is an individually administered test designed to assess comprehension of syntax for hearing and deaf students 3–17 years of age. The student points to one of three pictures representing a stimulus sentence produced by the examiner. Comprehension of 20 grammatical structures (e.g., simple sentence patterns, imperatives, negatives, passives) is assessed. The test takes approximately 30 minutes.

Informal Strategies for Syntactic Assessment

Informal approaches to assessing a deaf child's syntactic skills have the advantage of contextual relevance. Thus, the assessor must also carefully assess the communication demands of the environment and, in the approach described next, the environment of interest is the classroom.

Classroom Assessment. French (1999a) recommended several in-classroom approaches to assessing a deaf student's comprehension of a story, and each could be used to probe a student's

knowledge of specific syntactic structures. One example, story retelling, involves students recounting a story that they have previously read. The teacher decides ahead of time which grammatical structures are of particular interest (e.g., Can the student use embedded clauses to relay aspects of the story that were described in text that way? Can the student be prompted to use embedded clauses in the retelling?). As part of a comprehensive language arts program, French (1999a) has designed developmental checklists, which include items such as breadth of vocabulary, syntactic complexity, and sequencing.

Summary and Conclusions

This chapter reviewed approaches to and measures used in the language assessment of deaf children. In spite of the crucial role of language assessment in educational placement and programming decisions for deaf children, few standardized instruments are available for use with this population. Whenever possible, the aspect of language under investigation should be assessed using a variety of formal and informal approaches, and findings should be integrated both within and across pragmatic, semantic, and syntactic domains. A case was made for the judicious use and cautious interpretation of findings from standardized tests and for the value of observations in both home and school contexts by an observer knowledgeable about the developmental impact of hearing loss and familiar with a particular child's language abilities. In sum, the assessment procedure should be tailored to respond to specific diagnostic questions and to meet the individual language and learning needs of the child.

Differences in individual child characteristics and contextual variables ensure that, at the time of school entry, deaf children will have experienced a wide range of language learning experiences. Traditional formal approaches to language assessment in deaf children have emphasized the interpretation of test results in each language domain in isolation, but this approach has yielded little educationally prescriptive information. However, the interactionist perspective (Bates & MacWhinney, 1987; MacWhinney, 1987), which emphasizes the fluid and mutually influential boundaries among language domains, appears to have potential for shedding light, both prescriptively and theoretically, on the factors that drive language growth in often idiosyncratic directions in deaf children. What are the processes by which deaf children in different educational placements and from different linguistic backgrounds sometimes ultimately achieve similar language proficiency? The investigation of this question from an interactionist perspective and by the combined use of formal and informal approaches may enable parents, practitioners, and researchers to advance toward a primary goal: to uncover unique developmental paths to optimal language learning for each deaf child.

Note

Gratitude is given to all those who responded to requests for information and data. Special thanks to Perry Leslie, Brenda Poon, and Anat Zaidman-Zait for commenting on a previous draft of this chapter.

References

Akamatsu, C.T., & Musselman, C. (1998). Development and use of a conversational proficiency interview with deaf adolescents. In M. Marschark M.D. Clark (Eds.), *Psychological perspectives on deafness* (Vol. 2, pp. 265–295). Hillsdale, NJ: Lawrence Erlbaum Associates.

Anderson, D., & Reilly, R. (2002). The MacArthur Communicative Development Inventory: Normative data for American Sign Language. *Journal of Deaf Studies and Deaf Education, 7* 83–106.

Bates, E., & MacWhinney, B. (1987). Competition, variation and language learning. In B. MacWhinney (Ed.), *Mechanisms of language acquisition* (pp. 157–194). Hillsdale, NJ: Lawrence Erlbaum Associates.

Bebko, J.M., Calderon, R., & Treder, R. (2002). *The Language Proficiency Profile-2: Assessing the global communication skills of deaf children across languages and modalities of expression.* Manuscript submitted for publication.

Bebko, J.M., & McKinnon, E.E. (1987). *The Language Proficiency Profile.* Unpublished manuscript, York University, Toronto, Canada.

Bebko, J.M., & McKinnon, E.E. (1993). *The Language Proficiency Profile-2.* Unpublished Manuscript, York University, Toronto, Canada.

Bebko, J.M., & McKinnon, E.E. (1998). Assessing pragmatic language skills in deaf children: The Language Proficiency Profile. In M. Marschark & M.D. Clark (Eds.), *Psychological perspectives on deafness* (Vol. 2, pp. 243–263). Mahwah, NJ: Lawrence Erlbaum Associates.

Blank, M., Rose, S.A., & Berlin, L.J. (1978). *Preschool language assessment instrument.* New York: Grune & Stratton.

Bloom, L., & Lahey, M. (1978). *Language development and language disorders.* New York: Wiley.

Bodner-Johnson, B. (1991). Family conversation style: Its effect on the deaf child's participation. *Exceptional Children, 57,* 502–509.

Boehm, A. (1986). *Boehm test of basic concepts—Revised.* New York: The Psychological Corporation.

Carrow-Wolfolk, E. (1999). *Test for Auditory Comprehension of Language—3.* Allen, TX: DLM Teaching Resources.

Chomsky, N. (1965). *Aspects of theory of syntax.* Cambridge, MA: MIT Press.

Connor, C.M., Hieber, S., Arts, H.A., & Zwolen, T.A. (2000). Speech, vocabulary, and the education of children using cochlear implants: Oral or total communication? *Journal of Speech, Language, and Hearing Research, 43,* 1185–1204.

Coryell, J., & Holcomb, T.K. (1997). The use of sign language and sign systems in facilitating the language acquisition and communication of deaf students. *Language, Speech, and Hearing Services in Schools, 28,* 384–394.

Curtiss, S., Prutting, C.A., & Lowell, E.L. (1979). Pragmatic and semantic development in young children with impaired hearing. *Journal of Speech and Hearing Research, 22,* 534–552.

Davis, J. (1974). Performance of young hearing-impaired children on a test of basic concepts. *Journal of Speech and Hearing Research, 17,* 342–351.

Day, P.S. (1986). Deaf children's expression of communicative intentions. *Journal of Communication Disorders, 19,* 367–385.

de Villiers, P.A. (1988). Assessing English syntax in hearing-impaired children: Eliciting productions in pragmatically-motivated situations. In R.R. Kretschmer & L.W Kretschmer (Eds.), *Communication assessment of hearing-impaired children: From conversation to classroom* (Monograph Suppl.). *Journal of the Academy of Rehabilitative Audiology, 21,* 41–71.

de Villiers, P. (1991). English literacy development in deaf children: Directions for research and intervention. In J.F. Miller (Ed.), *Research in child language disorders: A decade in progress* (pp. 349–378). Austin, TX: Pro-Ed.

Duchan, J.F. (1988). Assessing communication of hearing-impaired children: Influences from pragmatics. In R.R. Kretschmer & L.W. Kretschmer (Eds.), *Communication assessment of hearing-*

impaired children: From conversation to classroom [Monograph Suppl.]. *Journal of the Academy of Rehabilitative Audiology*, 19–40.

Dunn, L., & Dunn, L. (1987). *Peabody Picture Vocabulary Test—Revised*. Circle Pines, MN: American Guidance Service.

Dunn, L., & Dunn, L. (1997). *Peabody Picture Vocabulary Test—III*. Circle Pines, MN: American Guidance Service.

Edwards, S., Fletcher, P., Garman, M., Hughes, A., Letts, C., & Sinka, I. (1997). *Reynell Developmental Language Scales—III (British Edition)*. London: NFER-Nelson.

Engen, E., & Engen, T. (1983). *Rhode Island Test of Language Structure*. Austin, TX: Pro-Ed.

Fenson, L., Dale, P.S., Reznick, J.S., Bates, E., Thal, D.J, & Pethick, S.J. (1994). Variability in early communicative development. *Monographs of the Society for Research in Child Development*, 59(5, Serial No. 242).

Fenson, L., Dale, P.S., Reznick, J.S., Thal, D., Bates, E., Hartung, J.P., Pethick, S., & Reilly, J.S. (1993). *MacArthur Communicative Development Inventories: User's guide and technical manual*. San Diego, CA: Singular Publishing Group.

Francis, J., Garner, D., & Harvey, J. (1980). *KCPS: A pragmatic approach to language for teachers of deaf children*. Washington, DC: KDES, Gallaudet University.

French, M.M. (1999a). *Starting with assessment: A developmental approach to deaf children's literacy*. Washington, DC: Pre-College National Mission Programs, Gallaudet University.

French, M.M. (1999b). *The toolkit: Appendices for Starting with assessment: A developmental approach to deaf children's literacy*. Washington, DC: Pre-College National Mission Programs, Gallaudet University.

Gardner, M.F. (1985). *Receptive One-Word Picture Vocabulary Test*. Novato, CA: Academic Therapy Publications.

Gardner, M.F. (1990). *Expressive One-Word Picture Vocabulary Test—Revised*. Novato, CA: Academic Therapy Publications.

Gaustad, M.G. (2000). Morphographic analysis as a word identification strategy for deaf readers. *Journal of Deaf Studies and Deaf Education*, 5, 60–80.

Geers, A.E., & Moog, J. (1989). Factors predictive of the development of literacy in profoundly hearing-impaired adolescents. *Volta Review, 91*, 131–148.

Griffith, P.L., Johnson, H.A., & Dastoli, S.L. (1985). If teaching is conversation, can conversation be taught? Discourse abilities in hearing impaired children. In D.N. Ripich & F.M. Spinelli (Eds.),

School discourse problems (pp.149–177). San Diego, CA: College-Hill Press.

Griffith, P.L., Ripich, D.N., & Dastoli, S.L. (1990). Narrative abilities in hearing-impaired children: Propositions and cohesion. *American Annals of the Deaf, 135,* 14–19.

Jamieson. J.R. (1994). Instructional discourse strategies: Differences between hearing and deaf mothers of deaf children. *First Language, 14,* 153–171.

Jamieson, J.R., & Pedersen, E.D. (1993). Deafness and mother-child interaction: Scaffolded instruction and the learning of problem-solving skills. *Early Development and Parenting, 2,* 229–242.

Johnson, D., Toms-Bronowski, S., & Pittleman, S. (1982). Vocabulary development in reading and the hearing-impaired individual. *Volta Review, 84,* 11–24.

Kretschmer, R.R., & Kretschmer, L.W. (1988). Communication competence and assessment. In R.R. Kretschmer & L.W. Kretschmer (Eds.), *Communication assessment of hearing-impaired children: From conversation to classroom* [Monograph Supplement] *Journal of the Academy of Rehabilitative Audiology, 21,* 5–17.

Laughton, J., & Hasenstab, S.M. (1993). Assessment and intervention with school-age hearing-impaired children. In J. Alpiner & P.A. McCarthy (Eds.), *Rehabilitative audiology: Children and adults* (2nd ed., pp. 136–175). Baltimore, MD. Williams & Wilkins.

Laughton, J., & Hasenstab, S.M. (2000). Auditory learning, assessment, and intervention with students who are deaf or hard of hearing. In J.A. Alpiner & P.A. McCarthy (Eds.), *Rehabilitative audiology: Children and adults* (3rd ed., pp. 178–225). Baltimore, MD: Lippincott, Williams, & Wilkins.

Layton, T., & Holmes, D. (1985). *Carolina Picture Vocabulary Test for Deaf and Hard of Hearing Children*. Austin, TX: Pro-Ed.

Luetke-Stahlman, B. (1998). *Language issues in deaf education*. Hillsboro, OR: Butte.

Luetke-Stahlman, B., & Luckner, J. (1991). *Effectively educating students with hearing impairments*. New York: Longman.

MacWhinney, B. (1987). The competition model. In B. MacWhinney (Ed.), *Mechanisms of language acquisition* (pp. 249–308). Hillsdale, NJ: Lawrence Erlbaum Associates.

Marschark, M., Mouradian, V., & Halas, M. (1994). Discourse rules in the language productions of deaf and hearing children. *Journal of Experimental Child Psychology, 57,* 89–107.

Mayne, A.M., Yoshinaga-Itano, C., Sedey, A., & Carey, A. (2000a). Expressive vocabulary development of infants and toddlers who are deaf or hard of hearing. *Volta Review, 100,* 1–28.

Mayne, A.M., Yoshinaga-Itano, C., Sedey, A., & Carey, A. (2000b). Receptive vocabulary development of infants and toddlers who are deaf or hard of hearing. *Volta Review, 100,* 29–52.

McKirdy, L., & Blank, M. (1982). Dialogue in deaf and hearing preschoolers. *Journal of Speech and Hearing Disorders, 25,* 487–499.

Miller, J. (1981). *Assessing language production in children.* Baltimore, MD: University Park Press.

Miller, J., & Chapman, R. (1983). *Systematic analysis of language transcripts.* Madison: University of Wisconsin.

Moeller, M.P. (1988). Combining formal and informal strategies for language assessment of hearing-impaired children. In R.R. Kretschmer & L.W. Kretschmer (Eds.), *Communication assessment of hearing-impaired children: From conversation to classroom* [Monograph Supplement]. *Journal of the Academy of Rehabilitative Audiology, 21,* 73–99.

Moog, J.S., & Geers, A.E. (1980). *Grammatical analysis of elicited language complex sentence level.* St. Louis, MO: Central Institute for the Deaf.

Moog, J.S., & Geers, A.E. (1985). *Grammatical analysis of elicited language simple sentence level* (2nd ed.). St. Louis, MO: Central Institute for the Deaf.

Moog, J.S., Kozak, V.J., & Geers, A.E. (1983). *Grammatical analysis of elicited language pre-sentence level.* St. Louis, MO: Central Institute for the Deaf.

Musselman, C., & Hambleton, D. (1990). Creating classroom conversations with deaf children. *The ACEHI Journal, 16,* 68–90.

Nelson, N.W. (1989). Curriculum-based language assessment and intervention. *Asha, 20,* 170–184.

Newcomer, P., & Hammill, D. (1997a). *Test of Language Development-Primary 3.* Austin, TX: Pro-Ed.

Newcomer, P., & Hammill, D. (1997b). *Test of Language Development Intermediate 3.* Austin, TX: Pro-Ed.

Nicholas, J.G. (2000). Age differences in the use of informative/heuristic functions in young children with and without hearing loss who are learning spoken language. *Journal of Speech, Language, and Hearing Research, 43,* 380–394.

Nicholas, J.G., & Geers, A.E. (1997). Communication of orally deaf and normally hearing children at 36 months of age. *Journal of Speech, Language, and Hearing Research, 40,* 1314–1327.

Nicholas, J.G., Geers, A.E., & Kozak, V. (1994). Development of communicative function in young deaf and normally hearing children. *Volta Review, 96,* 113–135.

Paul, P.V. (1998). *Literacy and deafness: The development of reading, writing, and literate thought.* Needham Heights, MA: Allyn & Bacon.

Prezbindowski, A., & Lederberg, A. (2003). Vocabulary assessment of deaf and hard of hearing children: From infancy through the preschool years. *Journal of Deaf Studies and Deaf Education 8,* 383–400.

Quigley, S.P., & King, C. (1980). Syntactic performance of hearing impaired and normal hearing individuals. *Applied Psycholinguistics, 1,* 329–356.

Quigley, S.P., Steinkamp, M.W., Power, D.J., & Jones, B. (1978). *Test of Syntactic Abilities.* Beaverton, OR: Dormac.

Reynell, J.K., & Gruber, C.P. (1990). *Reynell Developmental Language Scales* (U.S. edition). Los Angeles, CA: Western Psychological Services.

Scholnick, E.K. (Ed.). (1983). *New trends in conceptual representation: Challenge to Piaget's theory?* Hillsdale, NJ: Lawrence Erlbaum Associates.

Stredler-Brown, A., & Yoshinaga-Itano, C. (1994). The F.A.M.I.L.Y. Assessment: A multidisciplinary evaluation tool. In J. Rousch & N. Matkins (Eds.), *Infants and toddlers with hearing loss* (pp. 133–161). Parkton, MD: York Press.

Tonelson, S., & Watkins, S. (1979). *The SKI-HI Language Development Scale.* Logan, UT: Project SKI-HI, Utah State University.

Wilbur, R., & Petitto, L. (1981). How to know a conversation when you see one: Discourse structure in American Sign Language conversations. *Journal of the National Speech-Language-Hearing Association, 9,* 66–81.

Wood, D.J., & Wood, H.A. (1984). An experimental evaluation of the effects of five styles of teacher conversation on the language of hearing-impaired children. *Journal of Child Psychology and Psychiatry, 25,* 45–62.

Yoshinaga-Itano, C. (1997). The challenge of assessing language in children with hearing loss. *Language, Speech, & Hearing Services in Schools, 28,* 362–373.

Yoshinaga-Itano, C., & Downey, D. (1992). When a story is not a story: A process analysis of the written language of hearing-impaired children. *Volta Review, 95,* 131–158.

Yoshinaga-Itano, C., & Stredler-Brown, A. (1992). Learning to communicate: Babies with hearing impairments make their needs known. *Volta Review, 95,* 107–129.

Zachman, L., Jorgenson, C., Huisingh, R., & Barrett, M. (1984). *Test of problem solving.* Moline, IL: LinguiSystems.

Zimmerman, I., Steiner, V., & Pond, R. (1992). *Preschool Language Scale—3.* San Antonio, TX: The Psychological Corporation.

21

Jenny L. Singleton & Samuel J. Supalla

Assessing Children's Proficiency in Natural Signed Languages

As language researchers develop a better understanding of signed language structure and acquisition processes, educators and language specialists are eager to connect that research to the practical and urgent need for reliable measures that assess deaf children's development and use of natural signed language (Haug, in press; Herman, 1998b; Maller, Singleton, Supalla, & Wix, 1999). For many deaf children born to hearing parents, the school setting is the primary context where signed language acquisition takes place. Thus, signed language proficiency is often considered a curriculum goal or learning standard and, accordingly, learning outcomes ought to be measured. Parents also need an evaluation of the initial level of their child's signed language proficiency and their subsequent acquisition progress. Assessments can help professionals identify deaf children who are having problems developing signed language proficiency. Unfortunately, few instruments are commercially available that can reliably assess a child's signed language proficiency level and identify strengths and weaknesses that can be translated into instructional or language-enrichment goals.

In practice, most educators and specialists resort to conducting informal descriptive evaluations of a deaf child's sign skills. Some school programs have developed their own checklists to document a child's signing skills. However, these informal tools rarely come with manuals describing how they were developed, how they are administered and scored, or what assessor skills or training are required. These assessment approaches are inadequate because they introduce multiple threats to the reliability and validity of the assessment results.

The aims of this chapter are to (1) provide a review of published or known assessments of children's natural signed language proficiency, (2) examine the psychometric properties of these instruments, and (3) discuss the critical issues that face the research and educational community as we continue to develop and use signed language proficiency instruments.

It is outside the scope of this chapter to discuss some of the other types of communication assessments used with the deaf population (see Jamieson, this volume). Briefly, there are some instruments designed to assess generalized communicative competence in which the focus is more on how deaf children use their signed communication. Such instruments focus on pragmatics and content rather than form or grammar (e.g., Kendall Communication Proficiency Scale; Kendall Demonstration Elementary School, 1985). Another approach has been to evaluate generalized communication abilities, independent of language or modality. With such instruments, a deaf child would be given combined credit for communication abilities demonstrated in all modalities or languages, such as simultaneous communication, speech, gesture, and natural signed language (see, e.g., Akamatsu & Musselman, 1998; Bebko & McKinnon, 1998).

Assessment of Language Proficiency

Linn and Gronlund (2000) describe assessment as "a general term that includes the full range of procedures used to gain information about an individual's learning (observations, ratings of performances or projects, paper-and-pencil test) and the formation of value judgments concerning learning progress" (p. 31). To assess language proficiency, educators and language specialists sample an individual's language performance and infer from that performance a certain competence in language knowledge or ability (Brown, 1994). The assessment can be informal (such as a teacher's overall rating of an individual's language proficiency) or highly structured (such as a comprehension test with only one correct response out of four multiple-choice items). Assessments that evaluate language *comprehension* lend themselves to structured tasks, which have the benefit of being more reliable and efficient and are easier to standardize test-taking conditions across test takers. Assessments that evaluate language *production* require performance-based approaches. A major advantage of performance-based assessments is that they measure complex language behavior that may not be adequately measured by other means. Also, emergent behaviors, or alternative rules, may be observed in a production task, whereas they could be obscured in a multiple-choice item test.

In sum, language proficiency assessments range from subjective to objective, open-ended to highly structured, and focused on small linguistic units to larger pragmatic features. The individualized needs of the assessor, the context of assessment, the goal of assessment, the needs of the child, and the language skills of the assessor are all important factors that can influence the type of instrument one designs or selects.

Designing Instruments to Assess Language Proficiency

According to Brown (1994), there are three requirements for a good language proficiency instrument. First, the instrument must be practical to administer, score, and interpret. Second, it must be reliable (consistent and dependable). Finally, the instrument must be valid (the degree to which an instrument measures what it is intending to measure). There is no absolute way to determine whether a test is valid. Convincing evidence must be gathered to support the claim that the instrument is psychometrically sound. Examples of supporting evidence include correlating results of the assessment with other related measures, involving experts to evaluate the content of the instrument, and demonstrating error-free performance on the assessment when administering it to native speakers.

Authentic and representative language samples may be obtained through an observation of the child's natural language production, elicited through a structured interview process or through structured tasks designed to elicit production and comprehension of language.

Observations/Recordings of Natural Language Production

Researchers aiming to collect spontaneous language samples often make regular visits to a family's home and videotape the child engaging in everyday routines. Videotapes may be later transcribed and all utterances are entered into a SALT (Systematic Analysis of Language Transcripts) (Miller & Chapman, 1983) or CHILDES computer database (MacWhinney, 2000). Secondary coders are used to establish coding reliability. The organized database is then used to analyze the child's utterances or extended discourse for grammatical or pragmatic structures. Parents or caregivers who know the child's linguistic abilities well can also be asked to fill out a child language inventory. This observational technique relies on parent report, not actual observations of child signing, and as a method has been shown to be highly reliable (Fenson et al., 1993).

Language Proficiency Interviews

Language proficiency interviews (LPI) are typically structured as a live interview between the assessor and interviewee. LPIs use a set of carefully constructed questions (and probes) designed to elicit particular grammatical structures, cultural knowledge, vocabulary, and fluency. With only one assessor, the LPI has come under some criticism, especially with respect to the validity of the results (Brown, 1994). One response to this criticism involves multiple assessors viewing the videotaped performance of the interviewee, and then calculating an average score across assessors. This has the effect of reducing the influence of one biased assessor. Evans and Craig (1991) argue that language samples elicited through interviews result in better samples than simple unstructured observations (e.g., language produced in a free-play session).

Language Elicitation Tasks

Researchers have used various tasks to elicit language production or comprehension from a child. For example, in barrier games, the child is asked to describe an arranged set of objects (or a picture) to the assessor, who sits across a barrier, and the assessor tries to reproduce the child's arrangement (or select the correct picture target) based solely on the child's description. Picture description and story retelling can also create a communicative context in which the child is highly likely to produce language. In some of the more structured test batteries described later, the developers have created short videotaped vignettes of particular action sequences designed to elicit particular grammatical structures (Supalla et al., in press). Structured language tests allow the researcher to control the potential variations that can emerge in a language elicitation session. A number of structured language tests have been developed by sign language researchers, especially to assess particular subsets of grammar (see also Baker, van den Bogaerde, Coerts, & Woll, 2000, for a description of methods and procedures recommended for use in sign language acquisition studies).

Evaluating an Individual's Performance

Establishing clear and specific performance criteria is critical for reliable and valid assessment of an individual's language proficiency. The two primary ways of guiding performance judgments are scoring rubrics/rating scales and checklists (Linn & Gronlund, 2000). A scoring rubric is a set of guidelines

used to evaluate the individual's responses according to the performance criteria. A scoring rubric can include very specific linguistic elements, as well as more holistic impressions of quality. A rating scale indicates the degree to which the performance characteristic is present or the frequency with which a behavior occurs. The rating scale can be numerical (e.g., 0–4), or it can be a graphic line accompanied by descriptive phrases to identify points on the scale (e.g., never, infrequently, often, always). Rating scales should have at least three but no more than seven judgment points (Linn & Gronlund, 2000). Checklists require a simple yes/no judgment as to whether the behavior is present or absent. Checklists are useful for documenting mastery of a particular skill or behavior, such as grammatical features observed in a language sample.

Interpreting the Results of an Individual's Language Proficiency Assessment

In the field of measurement and test design, there are two standard ways to interpret or contextualize the child's performance on an assessment.

A norm-referenced interpretation compares the individual's performance to a reference group's performance (i.e., "norms"). For example, if 1,000 children had been assessed with the same instrument, one could construct several reference measures (such as grade equivalent, percentile distribution, or standard scores) to determine the individual child's relative standing. While many of the instruments described in this chapter have been administered to more than 100 subjects, most of the existing signed language proficiency instruments lack the numbers (and other evidence of psychometric properties) to establish norms that would be consistent with standards used in the test development field (American Psychological Association [APA], 1985). Standardization and establishment of age norms are in progress for several instruments. Most of the remaining instruments reviewed are criterion referenced.

The goal of a criterion-referenced assessment is to determine whether the child reaches the objective, or criterion, of the test. The child's performance (a demonstration of knowledge and skills) is described against the target criterion. For example, it can be determined whether the child met certain performance standards of proficiency (as established by statewide learning standards, linguistic analyses, assessor's rating, or a scoring rubric) (Linn & Gronlund, 2000). Scores are likely to be reported in descriptive terms such as "skill is met" or "skill is emergent." Sometimes results can be reported as percent correct (e.g., percentage of task items used correctly).

Summary

Some evidence suggests that using a single performance-based tool as the only measure of an individual's competence is problematic (Linn & Gronlund, 2000). Ideally, any decision about a child's language proficiency should be supported by multiple measures or assessments (both formal and informal). The goal of language proficiency assessments is to obtain the most authentic sample one can and evaluate it in a reliable and valid way. With this information, educators and other language specialists can set language learning goals for the learner and/or measure the effects of varying instructional methods.

Signed Language Proficiency Assessments for Children

There are approximately a dozen structured instruments or test batteries designed for the purpose of assessing natural signed language proficiency in children. Several more instruments are available for the adult population, most notably proficiency interview formats and interpreter certification tests. However, when using instruments designed for adult assessment with the population of deaf children, additional validity evidence is required (APA, 1985). Although some instruments are appropriate for both children and adults, others require higher (adolescent or adult-level) cognitive skills to engage in the language elicitation task and thus may not be appropriate for a younger population.

Several instruments exist for assessing American Sign Language (ASL) and, in recent years, more instruments have been developed to assess proficiency in other natural signed languages (British Sign Language, Australian Sign Language, etc.). What follows is a brief description of the available instruments for assessing natural signed language proficiency in children.

American Sign Language

Test Battery for ASL Morphology and Syntax

The Test Battery for ASL Morphology and Syntax (Supalla et al., in press), developed in the early 1980s, includes a number of tests that are appropriate for evaluating the ASL skills of children. This test battery allows a thorough analysis of an individual's knowledge and use of specific morphological and syntactic structures in ASL. Designed for linguistic research purposes, the battery takes approximately 2 hours to administer and at least 15 hours for a trained coder to analyze and score an individual's responses. This instrument has been used with more than 100 native and non-native signers ranging in age from 3 to 75. Some test results have been published (Newport, 1990); however a description of the psychometric properties is not available. Some tasks from this test battery have been incorporated into other test batteries (Hoffmeister, Bahan, Greenwald, & Cole, 1990; Maller et al., 1999). The instrument also has been adapted for Australian Sign Language (Schembri et al., 2002).

American Sign Language Proficiency Assessment

The ASL Proficiency Assessment (ASL-PA) was developed by Singleton and Supalla, along with Wix and Maller (see Maller et al., 1999). The development of this assessment involved two stages: (1) creating a scale that identified target linguistic structures in ASL with evidence of content validity, and (2) investigating the psychometric properties of the scale. The ASL-PA checklist includes 23 morpho-syntactic linguistic structures that were culled from ASL acquisition studies (see Maller et al., 1999, for a full description of the development and psychometric properties of the ASL-PA). A trained native or near-native signer collects three 10-minute language samples from a child within three distinct discourse contexts: adult–child interview (similar to an LPI format), peer interaction (an attempt is made to select peers with similar linguistic backgrounds), and story retelling (child watches a cartoon story, then retells story to adult assessor). A trained assessor later examines the videotaped language samples and checks off a linguistic feature when it is observed in the child's production. At that point, the assessor stops searching for that target feature. The child's total ASL-PA score is the sum of checked-off target features, out of a possible total of 23.

Evidence of content validity was based on the pilot administration of the ASL-PA to four prototype native-signing children to verify that the 23 target features could be elicited within these discourse contexts. The ASL-PA was then administered to 80 deaf children between the ages of 6 and 12, with varying levels of ASL experience. Using statistical methods to determine cut-off scores (Berk, 1976), three categories of ASL proficiency were defined (low, moderate, high). Further analyses demonstrated that the linguistic background of the child strongly predicted ASL-PA proficiency category membership. This evidence was presented in support of the construct validity of the ASL-PA. The 80 deaf children in the standardization sample were also administered several ASL subtests from the Supalla et al. (in press) test battery. Analyses of these tests are currently underway to gather evidence of concurrent validity. The internal reliability of the ASL-PA was strong (KR-20 coefficient = .81). Further development of this instrument is planned, including assessor training, gathering a larger standardization sample, and verifying the cut-off scores for low, moderate, and high ASL proficiency categories. The goal for the ASL-PA is to serve as an efficient, reliable, and valid measure of ASL proficiency among children aged 6–12.

Center for ASL Literacy ASL Assessment Checklist

This instrument is used for diagnostic evaluations of ASL proficiency at the Center for ASL Literacy (CASLL) at Gallaudet University (http://gradschool.gallaudet.edu/casll/). This checklist is a revision and expansion of the Signed Language Develop ment Checklist (SLDC) developed by Mounty (1994a, 1994b). The SLDC was originally designed for assessing overall communication ability and expressive ASL competence through observation of children between the ages of 2.5 and 14 years in both structured (such as story retelling) and unstructured activities (such as free play and conversation). The focus of the SLDC was on formational, morphological, syntactic, perspective, and creative use of ASL. The revised instrument still includes multiple videotaped observations and review of language samples by a trained assessor. The assessor uses a checklist of ASL grammatical and pragmatic features to guide the diagnostic evaluation.

The revised checklist has been mostly with adults. Evidence of reliability and validity has not been published on either the SLDC or the CASLL instrument (J. Mounty, personal communication, November 30, 2001); neither is available for dissemination at this time.

Test of ASL

The Test of ASL (TASL; Prinz, Strong, & Kuntze, 1994; Strong & Prinz, 1997), developed with a sample of 155 deaf students aged 8–15 years, includes production and comprehension measures for ASL classifiers and other grammatical structures, signed narratives, and comprehension measures of time and map markers in ASL. For content validity, the authors had five nationally known deaf ASL linguists provide feedback on preliminary versions of the instrument. To date, the psychometric properties of their instrument have not been published (apart from intercoder reliabilities); however, these analyses and norming studies are planned for the future (P. Prinz, personal communication, December 6, 2001). Moreover, the TASL has been translated into Catalan Sign Language, French Sign Language, and Swedish Sign Language.

The ASL Communicative Development Inventory

The ASL Communicative Developmental Inventory (ASL-CDI Anderson & Reilly, 2002) was adapted from the MacArthur Communicative Development Inventory (Fenson et al., 1993), which also has been adapted for eight spoken languages other than English. The ASL-CDI relies on a recognition format, in which parents check off signs their child produces from an inventory of 537 sign glosses, in 20 semantic categories, to assess the early vocabularies and sentence productions of ASL-signing children ages 8–35 months. In the adaptation process, the developers consulted with deaf experts and deleted CDI words or categories that were culturally or linguistically inappropriate for an ASL version. The original MacArthur CDI has both production and comprehension forms and a grammar section. At present, the ASL-CDI has only the production form. The developers report that due to the multilayered nature of ASL grammar, with many features co-occurring in space and nonmanually, a written checklist for ASL grammar would be difficult for parents to use. Anderson and Reilly suggest that a video format with grammatical alternatives for parents to choose from may be best suited for future research.

To date, normative data have been collected from 69 deaf children of deaf parents (Anderson & Reilly, 2002), but specific age-based norms or descriptions of atypical performance have not been delineated due to the relatively small sample size, although this appears to be the planned goal for the instrument. Anderson and Reilly have conducted test–retest reliability and provided some evidence of external validity by comparing signs produced by 10 children during a videotaped home visit to the signs on the CDIs reported by parents at that time. The ASL-CDI has the advantages of requiring no specialized training to administer and targets a young age range. The assessor must have extensive knowledge of the target child's language use.

American Sign Language Assessment Instrument

The *American Sign Language Assessment Instrument* (ASLAI; Hoffmeister et al., 1990) is a collection of production and comprehension tasks designed to elicit deaf children's metalinguistic knowledge of lexical processes, morphological processes, syntactic processes, semantic processes, and narrative abilities in ASL. The instrument has been used to assess ASL knowledge in more than 200 deaf children, native and non-native signers, ages 4–16. Hoffmeister et al. field-tested the ASLAI and have conducted reliability and validity analyses on many of the subtests. Original test items that had less than 90% agreement from the field-testing participants were eliminated from the final pool of items. Tests of internal consistency within subtests facilitated further refinement of the ASLAI. Evidence of predictive validity was proposed by correlating individual's ASLAI scores with the Stanford Achievement Test for the Hearing Impaired (SAT-HI) and the Rhode Island Test of Language Structure (Hoffmeister, de Villiers, Engen, & Topol, 1997). Hoffmeister and colleagues (1990) continue to use the ASLAI with the goal of establishing age-related norms and diagnostic applications.

American Sign Language Vocabulary Test

The *American Sign Language Vocabulary Test* (ASLVT; Schick, 1997a) is a receptive vocabulary test modeled after the Peabody Picture Vocabulary Test (Dunn & Dunn, 1959). Vocabulary knowledge has been related to oral language and literacy skills among hearing children (Williams & Wang, 1997). Whether the ASLVT is a strong predictor of overall ASL proficiency is being investigated. In the ASLVT, the assessor presents an ASL sign to the child, who then selects the correct response out of four picture plates. Target signs and foils were developed for ASL with a range of difficulty (e.g., CAT [easy] to STRUGGLE [difficult] following particular criteria. A research team that included deaf and hearing native-ASL signers reviewed items. The ASLVT was pilot tested on a small group of deaf children (both native and non-native signers). Items were then revised based on pilot testing, and the final version included 61 items. The final version was administered to 97 children between ages 3 years, 11 months and 8 years as part of a larger study examining theory-of-mind issues (DeVilliers, DeVilliers, Schick, & Hoffmeister, 2000). A preliminary report of the psychometric properties of the ASLVT reveals developmental trends and differences between deaf children with hearing versus deaf parents (Schick & Hoffmeister, 2002). Further development of this instrument is planned (B. Schick, personal communication, January 28, 2002).

DeVilliers et al. (2000) have developed several production and comprehension tests to evaluate deaf children's knowledge of ASL vocabulary, morphology and syntax. This research team administered their test battery to almost 100 deaf children (ages 3 years, 11 months to 8 years) of varying ASL skill levels as part of their theory-of-mind project. Psychometric investigations of these instruments are underway.

Sign Communication Proficiency Interview

The Sign Communication Proficiency Interview (SCPI; Caccamise & Newell, 1995, 1999; Caccamise, Newell, Lang, & Metz, 1996; Newell, Caccamise, Boardman, & Holcomb, 1983) uses a conversational approach to assessing receptive and expressive sign language communication skills. The instrument is based on the LPI format in which the language-proficient interviewer and interviewee have a one-to-one conversation. Two or three trained assessors independently review the videotaped conversation and assign a skill level rating (Caccamise et al., 1996). The developers are gathering data on assessor reliability (F. Caccamise, personal communication, September 22, 2001) and have some evidence of validity from a study relating SCPI performance of signing college instructors with students' evaluations of communication ease with the instructor (Long, Stinson, Kelly, & Liu, 2000). The SCPI has been used with deaf children, in an adapted format, by some individuals in educational settings; however, psychometric analyses have not been conducted on this adaptation. Schick (1997b) adapted the SCPI format to elicit a language sample from deaf students aged 7 to 14. Schick did not score the deaf students' responses using the conventional SCPI scoring system; instead, she transcribed the students' responses and used them as a language sample for further analysis.

Gallaudet University has also developed an adaptation of the original LPI scoring process for institutional use in evaluation of sign communication proficiency among staff and students. This LPI format is now used with an adult population only. (See http://gradschool.gallaudet.edu/casll/ for more information on their version of the SCPI.) A team of assessors rates an interviewee's knowledge and use of sign production, ASL grammar, vocabulary, fluency, and comprehension.

American Sign Language Proficiency Interview

The American Sign Language Proficiency Interview (ASLPI), developed by Mel Carter at California State University Northridge in the 1980s, is another language proficiency interview assessment currently in use. Carter conducts assessor training for the ASLPI but to date has not published test development information or psychometric data. It has not been adapted for use with children (E. Laird, personal communication, February 5, 2002).

British Sign Language

Herman, Holmes, and Woll (1999) have developed a set of production and comprehension tests to assess British Sign Language development. The receptive test, now commercially available, is designed for use by professionals who work with deaf children ages 3–11 years. This published edition is based on a pilot study and standardization sample including 135 children acquiring BSL as a first language. The norming sample includes deaf and hearing native signers of BSL, deaf children attending established bilingual (BSL/English) programs, and

deaf children in total communication programs with high BSL skills, as rated by their teachers. The BSL receptive assessment is composed of a vocabulary check to determine regional dialect in BSL and vocabulary knowledge required to proceed with the remainder of the test and a 40-item receptive skills test. The instrument assesses a child's understanding of syntactic and morphological aspects of BSL. The items were developed based on the authors' review of the BSL and ASL acquisition literature.

Herman et al. (1999) have gathered solid evidence of reliability (split-half analysis of internal consistency, test–retest reliability, and intercoder reliability) and are analyzing other test data to examine concurrent and predictive validity of their instrument. An item analysis was carried out to retain the most discriminating test items for the final version used for standardization.

The BSL assessment video includes instructions for test administration in BSL and practice items. With younger children, some initial live presentation of instructions and additional exposure to the practice items allowing for tester feedback may be needed.

The BSL receptive skills test discriminates among subjects on the basis of age. This is important for developing an assessment with age-related norms. Analysis of test results also demonstrated significant differences between children according to their experience with BSL. The value of a qualitative approach to analyzing individual children's test scores is currently being explored (R. Herman, personal communication, February 19, 2002).

Other Natural Signed Language Assessments

Development efforts for tests of signed language proficiency in three natural signed languages other than ASL and BSL have begun. Jansma, Knoors, and Baker (1997) developed an assessment for Sign Language of the Netherlands (SNL) designed to assess vocabulary knowledge and deeper semantic understanding; spatial localization; and verb agreement. Knoors and colleagues have also adapted the BSL Receptive Skills test for SLN and are currently analyzing their test results. In 2002, this research group received funding for a 5-year project to develop a multimedia SLN proficiency test based on the earlier Jansma et al. SLN project developed in

1997 (H. Knoors, personal communication, March 11, 2002).

Fehrmann, Huber, Jäger, Sieprath, and Werth (1995) (as translated and reported by Haug, in press) developed the Aachen Test for Basic German Sign Language Competence (ATG). A subset of the nine tests can be used with children ages 6 and up. The test battery, based on linguistic analyses of German Sign Language (DGS; Deutsche Gebaerdensprache), ASL, and other signed languages, includes both production and comprehension measures. The criterion-referenced instrument assumes that a native DGS signer would score 90% or higher on the nine subtests. Native signing assessors evaluate the individual's performance in terms of accuracy, using a variety of scales related to each subtest. To date, more than 100 subjects have taken part or all of the ATG. The ATG requires 4 hours to administer the full test and 2 hours to administer subtests to a child. Currently, the developers are revising the instrument based on the results of the first cohort of test takers. To date, no psychometric data have been reported.

Johnston and colleagues have adapted the BSL Receptive Skills Test for use with Australian Sign Language (T. Johnston, personal communication, March 4, 2002). The instrument is intended to assist in the evaluation of an Auslan/English bilingual program attended by deaf and hearing children. Analysis of the results of pilot testing with 50 child signers and discussion of some of the psychometric properties of the instrument are to be published soon. In addition, Schembri et al. (2002) have published a Test Battery for Australian Sign Language Morphology and Syntax, adapted from the Supalla et al. test battery for ASL; however, it has not yet been used with children (A. Schembri, personal communication, March 4, 2002).

Toward Meaningful Sign Language Proficiency Assessment: Current Testing Issues and the Critical Need for Psychometric Investigations

Brown (1994) suggested that a good language proficiency instrument must be practical, reliable, and valid. Taking those recommendations in reverse order, we next consider where the field stands in terms of moving toward meaningful assessment of signed language proficiency.

Validity

The primary validity issue is whether the test or assessment procedure provides a meaningful measure of the criterion: signed language proficiency. If the measure is not valid, the end result may be an inappropriate interpretation about the proficiency of an individual child or a group of children. Evaluations of validity can take many forms.

Defining Language Proficiency

The definition of language proficiency is critically related to establishing evidence of validity. In recent years, language researchers have argued that in assessing language proficiency, it is not enough to examine an individual's mastery of particular grammatical structures. Brown (1994) reports, "along with the components of organizational (phonology, grammar, discourse) competence, language tests of the [19]90s are focusing on the pragmatic (sociolinguistic, functional) and strategic components of language abilities" (p. 265). For example, a test could assess grammatical and pragmatic language skills separately through discrete items or scales, or the assessor may need to extract grammatical and pragmatic language skills embedded in the discourse (e.g., during an interview format).

Assessors must decide the purpose or goal of language testing and the extent to which they need information about the child's mastery and use of grammatical elements and/or communicative functions of a natural signed language. At minimum, test developers need to document the theoretical assumptions they make regarding language proficiency and define the aspects of language proficiency being assessed.

For some deaf children, language specialists may decide to use a general communication assessment instead of a language proficiency measure. For example, there is a greater likelihood that deaf children born to hearing parents, rather than to deaf parents, will have a fragmented early linguistic experience and lack consistent exposure to a natural signed language. In these types of communication assessments, the child is given credit for all forms and functions of communication. However, it is important to understand that communication ability is not the same as language proficiency. For example, a deaf child with some speech, some signs, and some gestures may demonstrate poor performance on grammatical or pragmatic measures of English and ASL proficiency, yet show emergent skills on a general communication assessment. This kind of result can be interpreted in two ways. On one hand, it is positive that this child displays some communicative ability and that he or she has the cognitive and social prerequisites necessary for potential language development. On the other hand, this child has not developed native-level proficiency in any language, and with that result professionals ought to be very concerned.

Authenticity of the Language Sample

Language proficiency interviews such as SCPI, ASLPI, and a majority of the ASL-PA, approach real-life conversation and, arguably, elicit greater face validity than indirect measures such as a multiple-choice comprehension test. Moreover, with multiple samples, the assessor optimizes the chances of eliciting an authentic language sample and increases the opportunity to observe target structures. Although it is desirable to assess an individual's language proficiency based on an actual sample of language performance, the assessor must factor in the time and cost demands of these measures when deciding on an appropriate instrument.

Which language proficiency assessment approach establishes greater validity: performance-based or multiple-choice type assessment? According to Moss (1992), "performance-based assessments present a number of validity problems not easily handled with traditional approaches and criteria for validity research" (p. 230). Moss reviews various proposals for rethinking validity criteria for performance-based assessments. Moss maintains that the key concept is "an argument about consequences: the consequences of performance assessment are likely to be more beneficial to teaching and learning than are the consequences of multiple choice assessment used alone" (pp. 248–249). New validity categories such as meaningfulness, directness, or cognitive complexity support an expanded concept of validity and provide a theoretical framework for performance-based assessments.

Item Validity

There are at least three critical issues that arise in developing valid items for a signed language proficiency assessment. First when adapting an instrument from a test originally designed for spoken language, it is important to be aware of certain conflicts that can threaten the validity of the instrument. Researchers have noted that there may not be lexical equivalences between the spoken and signed language (Herman, 1998a; Kyle, 1990; Schick & Hoffmeister, 2002). For example, some sign domains such as body parts require simply pointing to the body part, which may not be as abstract as the spoken language counterpart lexical item.

Measures adapted from English are especially problematic in that the correctness of the child's responses is based on English knowledge, not on signed language knowledge. Signed translations of English-based instruments may be asking the child a question totally different from what was intended (see Schick, 1997b, for a discussion of test adaptation issues).

A second important issue is whether native signers are involved in item construction and/or review. An adapted item from a spoken language instrument may not have content and structure that is culturally and linguistically appropriate for the deaf community. For example, Anderson and Reilly (2002) eliminated "animal sound" items when adapting the MacArthur Communication Development Inventory for ASL. Novel test items that are based on linguistic or acquisition research also need to be reviewed by native signers for face validity because dialect and register variation may be considerations for item validity.

Finally, natural signed languages include morphological structures that may reveal clues about the lexical target. Test developers should verify that a less fluent signer (or even a nonsigner) could not guess the correct answer by relying on the transparency of the sign's morphological structure. Indeed, White and Tischler (1999) found that hearing children with no previous exposure to signed language were biased toward the correct picture when presented with a signed version of the Carolina Picture Vocabulary Test. In Schick's (1997a) ASL adaptation of the Peabody Picture Vocabulary Test, her distractor items (WEATHERVANE, SYRINGE, and TELESCOPE) included similar handshape or movement as the target sign (COMPASS) so that the target would not be selected purely on the basis of morphological clues.

Interpreting Results

Another important validity concern regards the appropriateness of the standard or comparison group. Herman (1998a) raises the issue of who should constitute the reference population when sign language assessments are developed and standardized. Deaf children born to hearing parents are the typical deaf child (composing 90% of the population of deaf children); however, is their sign proficiency the standard we are aiming for in a norm-referenced test? Should proficiency norms be based only on a population of native and early learners?

Another consideration rarely discussed is the fact that many deaf children have delays in their primary language acquisition. Presumably, the learning curve for signed language acquisition for an 8-year-old is different from that of a 2-year-old. Despite massive signing experience, late learners of ASL typically do not acquire complex morphology and syntax to native-signing levels (Mayberry & Eichen, 1991; Morford & Mayberry, 2000; Newport, 1990), yet the late learner can certainly function as a communicator (avoiding complex grammatical structures and demanding communication situations). Late learners may be engaging in the language acquisition process using different linguistic and nonlinguistic strategies than native or early learners of signed language. Most test developers have not presented psychometric evidence (or even a cursory discussion) about the characteristics of lower proficiency levels (i.e., what acquisition strategy or background factors may account for poorer performance) and whether these proficiency characteristics are distinct from general communicative skills.

Concurrent Validity

Since the field is in its early stages of development, no test developer has established concurrent validity by administering a different signed language proficiency instrument and correlating the new instrument results with existing instruments, although several researchers are currently working on such analyses. To date, researchers and test developers have been focused on constructing the instruments and establishing internal validity. The next stage is to establish concurrent validity as multiple instruments with psychometric evidence become available.

Predictive Validity

Many educators and researchers are interested in exploring the predictive relationship between signed language proficiency and other criterion-related measures, such as English proficiency or ac-

ademic achievement. However, there are currently no tests of English proficiency or academic achievement known to measure their constructs similarly for deaf and hearing children (Bloomquist & Allen, 1988; Maller, 1996). When deaf and hearing children of equal abilities have different probabilities of a correct response, it would appear that the test results are influenced by factors specific to deafness (Allen, 1986; Bloomquist & Allen, 1988). Some researchers have investigated the relationship between their ASL assessments and measures of English literacy normed on a deaf population (Hoffmeister et al., 1997; Singleton, Supalla, Litchfield, & Schley, 1998; Strong & Prinz, 2000).

Reliability

Test developers and consumers must be concerned with reliability of the results obtained from the chosen instrument. Reliability concerns the consistency of measurement. Are the results obtained reliable over time (e.g., test/retest), over different samples of items (e.g., split-half analysis), over different assessors (interrater reliability)? If some measure of reliability has not been obtained, it is not certain that the result obtained is generalizable. That is, if a different assessor evaluated the child's language sample, would the score be different? If the child were given a different subset of test items, would he or she perform better? If the child were assessed on Tuesday, and then again on Friday, obtaining a different proficiency score, would these test results be accepted as reliable? When an instrument is used, the assessor wants to be confident about the meaningfulness of the results.

Assessor Reliability

Two issues that come up frequently in the signed language assessment context are the signing skills and credentials of the assessor. If an assessor is not proficient in signed language, the child may perceive the task differently from the instrument's original design. The assessor should have considerable experience working with child signers. The assessor should understand the difference between child and adult proficiency standards when rating language performance. Tests that require trained examiners or assessors can improve test reliability by increasing fairness in an assessor's judgment. This can be done by improving an assessor's knowledge of scoring rubrics (which are presumably well defined and highly agreed upon), providing adequate training in assessment practices, and examining interrater consistency:

> When the evaluation of answers is not guided by clearly defined outcomes and scoring rubrics, it tends to be based on less stable, intuitive judgments. Although the judgmental scoring of . . . responses will always have some degree of unreliability, scoring reliability can be greatly increased by clearly defining the outcomes to be measured, properly framing the questions, carefully following scoring rules, and obtaining practice in scoring. (Linn & Gronlund, 2000, p. 242)

Inadequacies in assessor consistency or qualifications can put the child at a disadvantage and may open the door for complaints against the assessor, school, or district.

Procedural Reliability

Standardized instructions and test administration procedures should be used. When working with deaf children, an assessor is likely to encounter widely varying signed language skills. There is concern that an assessor may modify test administration procedures to help the low-proficiency child understand the language elicitation task. Test developers should provide clear instructions regarding the cognitive load of the task and whether alternative (e.g., assessor feedback, practice items) procedures are allowed. In this domain, especially for younger deaf children, instruments that require instructions with less language dependence are highly recommended.

Coding Reliability

Language assessments that require sign language transcription, or coding judgments, require double coding of some portion of the sample to obtain intercoder reliability. This can be accomplished by using a second coder and comparing the first and second coder's versions of the same language segment to determine the extent to which the coders agree on their judgments (Baker et al., 2000). The amount of double coding depends on the nature and amount of data; 10–25% of the data, selected at random, is not an uncommon amount. A minimum of 80% intercoder agreement is expected. Proficiency interviews that use assessors must examine interrater reliability scores to provide evidence of reliability of the assessment. Evaluation of assessor training and support (ongoing assessor reliability checks) are especially important for this format.

Practicality

Whether an assessment is performance based or is a more indirect measurement such as a comprehension language test, it still needs to be practical to administer and to score. Sign language researchers and sign language specialists know well that the scoring or coding of signed utterances is particularly challenging and time consuming. Because there is no commonly accepted written form of signed languages, scoring signed utterances generally requires training in sign language linguistics and specialized knowledge of a transcription system for signs. Due to this required assessor knowledge, it is difficult to amass large numbers of assessors to test or score language data from large numbers of deaf children. Thus, the personnel requirements for conducting large-scale studies are onerous and expensive.

Some of the available instruments are lengthy test batteries developed by sign language linguists for research purposes (e.g., Supalla et al., in press). The administration time is a problem especially for children, and the lengthy scoring time makes such test batteries impractical for educators and language specialists to use in the field. The validity of using subtests from these batteries as a proxy for assessing overall signed language proficiency needs further investigation.

Summary and Conclusions

The sign language linguistics revolution of the 1970s (Klima & Bellugi, 1979) gave rise to a number of research tools designed to assess knowledge of particular linguistic structures in natural signed languages. Acquisition studies also defined developmental milestones and natural error patterns of young deaf children raised as native signers (Lillo-Martin, 1999; Newport & Meier, 1985). Together these landmark studies created a new understanding of normal sign language acquisition, proficiency, and use. A natural extension of this research is the development of instruments to assess signed language proficiency among groups of learners who have varying linguistic experience with signed language. Research groups have developed proficiency assessments to support their own investigations, but the link from research to practice needs further strengthening.

To date, a number of test developers have examined the internal validity of their proficiency instruments, with some farther along than others. However, there is considerable work remaining to establish adequate evidence of reliability and validity. To build a sufficient database to conduct further psychometric investigations, it is necessary to administer assessments to more individuals (which is a challenge with a low incidence population). However, the current pool of available instruments includes many assessments that are complex and require a sophisticated understanding of signed language linguistics, signed language acquisition, and assessment practices. Should this challenge deter the collection of more data? This next phase of database building will likely require a commitment to highly skilled assessors until the time comes that more indirect measures of signed language proficiency can be developed that may serve as a reliable and valid proxy for the time-consuming and expensive direct assessments. Consider the amount of education and training required of speech and language clinicians to become licensed to assess the spoken language proficiency of their clients. Should the same professional standard not be expected for individuals who conduct signed language assessments with deaf children? This is a research and practice agenda that needs considerable academic and financial support.

In conclusion, to empower educators and language specialists to make informed decisions regarding selection of instruments to assess natural signed language proficiency, it is recommended that test developers create detailed manuals describing item development, test administration procedures, and the language proficiency construct underlying their instrument; provide opportunities for assessor training and support; and support continued research and validation efforts.

Note

We acknowledge the many test developers that responded to our inquiries. Also, we are grateful to Brenda Schick and members of her ASL Assessment Seminar at University of Colorado at Boulder, ASL doctoral program, for discussing a previous draft of this chapter. Our thanks to Karen Emmorey, Claire Ramsey, and Patricia Spencer for helpful discussion on assessment issues. We also acknowledge Tobias Haug in Germany, who has developed a web site dedicated to disseminating information about signed language assessment (http://www.signlang-assessment.info).

References

Akamatsu, C. T., & Musselman, C. (1998). Development and use of a conversational proficiency interview with deaf adolescents. In M. Marschark & M. D. Clark (Eds.), *Psychological perspectives on deafness* (Vol. 2, pp. 265–301). Hillsdale, NJ: Lawrence Erlbaum Associates.

Allen, T. (1986). *Understanding the scores: Hearing-impaired students on the Stanford Achievement Test, 7th ed.* Washington, DC: Gallaudet University Press.

Anderson, D., & Reilly, J. (2002). The MacArthur Communicative Development Inventory: Normative data for American Sign Language. *Journal of Deaf Studies and Deaf Education, 7,* 83–106.

American Psychological Association (1985). *Standards for educational and psychological testing.* Washington, DC: Author.

Baker, A., van den Bogaerde, B., Coerts, J., & Woll, B. (2000). *Methods and procedures in sign language acquisition studies.* Retrieved January 24, 2005, from http://www.sign-lang.uni.hamburg.de/intersign/workshop4/baker/baker.html.

Bebko, J. M., & McKinnon, E. E. (1998). Assessing pragmatic language skills in deaf children: The Language Proficiency Profile. In M. Marschark & M. D. Clark (Eds.), *Psychological perspectives on deafness* (Vol. 2, pp. 243–263). Hillsdale, NJ: Lawrence Erlbaum Associates.

Berk, R. A. (1976). Determination of optimal cutting scores in criterion-referenced measurement. *Journal of Experimental Education, 45,* 4–9.

Bloomquist, C. A., & Allen, T. (1998, April). *Comparison of mathematics test item performance by hearing and hearing impaired students.* Paper presented at the Annual Meeting of the American Educational Research Association, New Orleans, LA.

Brown, H. D. (1994). *Principles of language learning and teaching* (3rd ed.). Englewood Cliffs, NJ: Prentice Hall.

Caccamise, F., & Newell, W. (1995). Evaluating sign language communication skills: The Sign Communication Proficiency Interview (SCPI). In R. Myers (Ed.), *Standards of care for the delivery of mental* health services to deaf and hard of hearing persons (pp. 33–35). Silver Spring, MD: National Association of the Deaf.

Caccamise, F., & Newell, W. (1999). *Sign Communication Proficiency Interview (SCPI): Scheduling, interviewing, rating & sharing results* (Technical Report). Rochester, NY: National Technical Institute for the Deaf.

Caccamise, F., Newell, W., Lang, H., & Metz, D. (1996). *Sign Communication Proficiency Interview (SCPI) reliability studies* (Technical Report). Rochester, NY: National Technical Institute for the Deaf.

deVilliers, P., deVilliers, J., Schick, B., & Hoffmeister, R. (2000 July). *Theory of mind development in signing and nonsigning deaf children: The impact of sign language on social cognition.* Paper presented at the Theoretical Issues in Sign Language Research: Amsterdam, the Netherlands.

Dunn, L., & Dunn, L. (1959). *Peabody Picture Vocabulary Test.* Circle Pines, MN: American Guidance Service.

Evans, J. L., & Craig, H. K. (1991). Language sample collection and analysis: Interview compared to freeplay assessment contexts. *Journal of Speech and Hearing Research, 35,* 343–353.

Fehrmann, G., Huber, W., Jäger, L., Sieprath, H., & Werth, I. (1995). *Design of the Aachen Test of Basic Competence of German Sign Language (ATG).* Aachen, Germany: Rheinisch-Westflische Techische Hochschule (Technical University), Germanistiches Institut & Neurologische Klinik.

Fenson, L., Dale, P. S., Reznick, J. S., Thal, D., Bates, E., Hartung, J. P., Pethick, S., & Reilly, J. (1993). *The MacArthur Communicative Development Inventories: User's guide and technical manual.* San Diego, CA: Singular.

Haug, T. (1999). Review of signed language assessment instruments. Retrieved January 24, 2005, from http://www.sign-lang.uni-hamburg.de/intersign/workshop4/haug.html.

Herman, R. (1998a, October). *Issues in designing an assessment of British Sign Language development.* Paper presented at the Conference of the Royal College of Speech & Language Therapists, Liverpool, UK.

Herman, R. (1998b). The need for an assessment of deaf children's signing skills. *Deafness and Education, 22*(3), 3–8.

Herman, R., Holmes, S., & Woll, B. (1999). *Assessing British Sign Language development: Receptive skills test.* Coleford, England: Forest Book Services.

Hoffmeister, B., Bahan, B., Greenwald, J., & Cole, J. (1990). *American Sign Language Assessment Instrument (ASLAI).* Unpublished test, Center for the Study of Communication and the Deaf, Boston University, Boston, MA.

Hoffmeister, R., DeVilliers, P., Engen, E., & Topol, D. (1997). English reading achievement and ASL skills in deaf students. In E. Hughes, M. Hughes, & A. Greenhill (Eds.), *Proceedings of the 21st Annual Boston University Conference on Language Development* (pp. 307–318). Boston, MA: Cascadilla Press.

Jansma, S., Knoors, H., & Baker, A. (1997). Sign language assessment: A Dutch project. *Deafness and Education, 21*(3), 39–46.

Kendall Demonstration Elementary School. (1985). *Kendall Communicative Proficiency Scale.* Washington, DC: Author.

Klima, E., & Bellugi, U. (1979). *The signs of language.* Cambridge, MA: Harvard University Press.

Kyle, J. G. (1990). *BSL Development: Final report.* Bristol, UK: University of Bristol, Centre for Deaf Studies.

Lillo-Martin, D. (1999). Modality effects and modularity in language acquisition: The acquisition of American Sign Language. In W. Ritchie & T. Bhatia (Eds.), *Handbook of child language acquisition.* San Diego, CA: Academic Press.

Linn, R. L., & Gronlund, N. F. (2000). *Measurement and assessment in teaching* (8th ed.). Upper Saddle River, NJ: Prentice-Hall.

Long, G., Stinson, M., Kelly, R., & Liu, Y. (2000). The relationship between teacher sign skills and student evaluation of teacher capability. *American Annals of the Deaf, 144,* 354–365.

MacWhinney, B. (2000). *The CHILDES Project: Tools for analyzing talk [http://childes.psy.cmu.edu/].* Hillsdale, NJ: Lawrence Erlbaum Associates.

Maller, S. J. (1996). WISC III Verbal item invariance across samples of deaf and hearing children of similar measured ability. *Journal of Psychoeducational Assessment, 14,* 152–165.

Maller, S. J., Singleton, J. L., Supalla, S. J., & Wix, T. (1999). The development and psychometric properties of the American Sign Language Proficiency Assessment (ASL-PA). *Journal of Deaf Studies & Deaf Education, 4*(4), 249–269.

Mayberry, R., & Eichen, E. B. (1991). The long-lasting advantage of learning sign language in childhood: Another look at the critical period for language acquisition. *Journal of Memory & Language, 30,* 486–512.

Miller, J., & Chapman, R. (1983). *Systematic Analysis of Language Transcripts.* Madison: University of Wisconsin.

Morford, J. P., & Mayberry, R. (2000). A reexamination of "early exposure" and its implications for language acquisition by eye. In C. Chamberlain, J. P. Morford, & R. I. Mayberry (Eds.), *Language acquisition by eye* (pp. 111–127). Hillsdale, NJ: Lawrence Erlbaum Associates.

Moss, P. A. (1992). Shifting conceptions of validity in educational measurement: Implications for performance assessment. *Review of Educational Research*, 62(3), 229–258.

Mounty, J. (1994a). *The Signed Language Development Checklist*. Princeton, NJ: Educational Testing Service.

Mounty, J. (1994b). *A training package for assessing signed language acquisition in deaf children* (Final Report to U.S. Department of Education, Award No. H023A10035-91). Washington, DC: U.S. Department of Education.

Newell, W., Caccamise, F., Boardman, K., & Holcomb, B. (1983). Adaptation of the language proficiency interview (LPI) for assessing sign communication competence. *Sign Language Studies*, 41, 311–331.

Newport, E. (1990). Maturational constraints on language learning. *Cognitive Science*, 14, 11–28.

Newport, E., & Meier, R. (1985). The acquisition of American Sign Language. In D. I. Slobin (Ed.), *The crosslinguistic study of language acquisition. Vol. 1. The Data* (pp. 881–938). Hillsdale, NJ: Lawrence Erlbaum Associates.

Prinz, P., Strong, M., & Kuntze, M. (1994). *The Test of ASL*. Unpublished test, San Francisco State University, San Francisco, CA.

Schembri, A., Wigglesworth, G., Johnston, T., Leigh, G., Adam, R., & Barker, R. (2002). Issues in development of the Test Battery for Australian Sign Language Morphology and Syntax. *Journal of Deaf Studies & Deaf Education*, 7(1), 18–40.

Schick, B. (1997a). *American Sign Language Vocabulary Test*. Unpublished test, University of Colorado, Boulder.

Schick, B. (1997b). The effects of discourse genre on English language complexity in school-age deaf students. *Journal of Deaf Studies & Deaf Education*, 2(4), 234–251.

Schick, B., & Hoffmeister, R. (2002). *Assessing ASL skills in children: Formal tests for elementary school-aged children*. Unpublished manuscript. University of Colorado.

Singleton, J. L., Supalla, S., Litchfield, S., & Schley, S. (1998). From sign to word: Considering modality constraints in ASL/English bilingual education. *Topics in Language Disorders*, 18(4), 16–29.

Strong, M., & Prinz, P. (1997). A study of the relationship between American Sign Language and English literacy. *Journal of Deaf Studies & Deaf Education*, 2, 37–46.

Strong, M., & Prinz, P. (2000). Is American Sign Language skill related to English literacy? In C. Chamberlain, J. P. Morford, & R. Mayberry (Eds.), *Language acquisition by eye* (pp. 131–141). Hillsdale, NJ: Lawrence Erlbaum Associates.

Supalla, T., Newport, E., Singleton, J., Supalla, S., Metlay, D., & Coulter, G. (in press). *The Test Battery for American Sign Language Morphology and Syntax*. San Diego, CA: DawnSign Press.

White, A. H., & Tischler, S. (1999). Receptive sign vocabulary tests: tests of single-word vocabulary or iconicity? *American Annals of the Deaf*, 144(4), 334–338.

Williams, K. T., & Wang, J. (1997). *Technical References to the Peabody Picture Vocabulary Test-3rd Ed (PPVT-III)*. Circle Pines, MN: American Guidance Services, Inc.

V

Signed Languages

22

David F. Armstrong & Sherman Wilcox

Origins of Sign Languages

The Origins of Language

The question of how sign languages originate and evolve has had an important place in the history of ideas, and it has been intimately linked to the question of how language began in general. It can be argued that, from a phylogenetic perspective, the origin of human sign languages is coincident with the origin of human languages; sign languages, that is, are likely to have been the first true languages. This view fits within a general framework that has been called the gestural theory of the origin of language. This is not a new perspective; it is perhaps as old as nonreligious speculation about the way in which human language may have begun (in Plato's *Cratylus*, Socrates speculates about the nature of the sign language used by the deaf in relation to the origin of words). During the French Enlightenment of the eighteenth century, philosophers such as Condillac speculated that sign languages may have preceded speech (see Hewes, 1996). These writers were aware of the work of the Abbé de l'Epée and had some knowledge of the sign language of deaf people in France, at least as it was used in education (see Lang, this volume). The publication in 1859 of Darwin's *Origin of Species* heightened interest in the origin of human beings and their languages.

After publication of the *Origin of Species* a period of speculation about how languages may have arisen in the course of human evolution began. Much of the speculation was undisciplined and unsupported by evidence, such that, in 1866, the Linguistic Society of Paris banned discussion of the topic at its meetings (Hewes, 1996). However, the idea that sign languages like those used by deaf people might have something to do with the origin of language in general had become quite pervasive in the thinking even of nonscholars. This passage is from Amos Kendall's speech at the inauguration of the College for the Deaf and Dumb (later Gallaudet University) in 1864 (Gallaudet, 1983):

> If the whole human family were destitute of the sense of hearing, they would yet be able to interchange ideas by signs. Indeed, the language of signs undoubtedly accompanied if it did not precede the language of sounds . . . We read that Adam named the beasts and birds. But how could he give them names without first pointing them out by other means? How could a particular name be fixed upon a particular animal among so many species without some sign indicating to what animal it should thereafter be applied? . . . If a company of un-

educated deaf-mutes were, for the first time, brought into contact with an elephant, without knowing its name, they would soon devise a sign by which he should be represented among themselves. So, were it possible for a company of adults with their senses entire to be placed in a similar situation, they would probably point him out by a sign accompanied by some exclamation, and the exclamation might become the name of the animal. Thenceforward the perfect man would convey the idea of an elephant by sound, while the deaf-mute could only do it by a sign. (p. 211)

Except for the presence of Adam in this account and the use of politically incorrect terms to denote deaf and hearing people, some of its elements are not too different from those of contemporary gestural scenarios for the origin of language.

This might at first seem somewhat paradoxical. Most human languages, of course, are spoken. Speech is the dominant form of human communication. What could be gained theoretically by assuming a period in human history in which visual-gestural communication was predominant? The scenario presented in Kendall's speech addresses some of the key points, the most basic being how to get from an object or an event in the material world to an apparently arbitrary vocal symbol. The idea of primitive humans making mimetic gestures to refer to objects and events in their environment and coupling these with vocalizations may seem simple-minded, but it also has explanatory appeal. Nevertheless, for most of the century after the Paris society's ban on its discussion, the topic of language origins was avoided assiduously by serious scholars.

One could ask if this might not have been a good thing. After all, what can we ever know with certainty about how our ancient ancestors communicated? Behavior, famously and axiomatically, does not fossilize, and communication events are the most ephemeral of behaviors, but questions about the evolution of our ability to create languages are central to our understanding of our nature and our origins, questions about which human beings are intensely curious. In any event, in the early 1970s, a concerted movement to reopen the topic to serious scholarly study began to emerge in the United States. Important evidence was accumulating in a variety of fields that could be brought to bear on this question, most significantly, research pioneered by William C. Stokoe that suggested that full-fledged languages could exist in the visual-gestural mode.

Sign Language and Language Origins

Stokoe initiated the modern scientific study of signed languages by drawing on the insights of anthropological and structural linguists, who had come to realize that all languages have regular structures at a level below that of the individual word. According to the terminology of linguistics, languages have sublexical or phonological structure. This structure is based on systems of contrast—differences in meaning must be based on perceptible differences in language sounds, as in "bat" and "hat." It is this sublexical structure that makes phonetic writing possible, and all spoken languages have it. Stokoe's contribution was to show that American Sign Language (ASL) has such a structure and that it too can be written in a phonetic-like script (Stokoe, 1960; Stokoe, Croneberg & Casterline, 1965). By devising a workable script, he was able to convince other language scholars that ASL uses such a system of linguistic contrast, that it has a regular internal structure, and that it is, therefore, not simply ad-hoc pantomime or a corrupt visual code for English.

During the early 1970s, Stokoe began to see that his work on ASL might have a larger significance, beyond the development of increasingly complex linguistic studies and the support these were providing for the reform of deaf education. At this time, Stokoe became interested in the newly reinvigorated scientific study of the origin and evolution of the human capacity for language. Stokoe joined a small group of scholars, including Gordon Hewes, who began to synthesize new information from paleontology, primatology, neuroscience, linguistics, and sign language studies into more coherent scenarios for the evolution of language (see Harnad, Steklis, & Lancaster, 1976). Since about 1975, these scenarios have grown more sophisticated and plausible, due in large part to Stokoe's efforts.

Stokoe concerned himself especially with evolutionary problems that might be solved by postulating a signing stage in human evolution. He participated in several important symposia on this topic, one of which resulted in the book *Language Origins* (Wescott, 1974). Stokoe came to believe that iconic manual gesture must have played a key role in the transition from nonhuman primate communication to human language. In making this assertion, he was rediscovering a line of thinking that went back at least to the Abbé de Condillac, and it can be traced through the quotation from Amos Kendall. According to this line of thinking, the introduction of iconic manual gesture might solve the problem of attribution of meaning to arbitrary vocal signals. Iconic gestures which resemble the things they refer to might form a bridge to the symbolic relationship of speech sounds to their referents. But Stokoe went a step beyond this to suggest that iconic manual gestures might also have been involved in the thornier question of how syntax originated. This goes to the question at the heart of Chomskyan linguistics, which posits syntax as the defining characteristic of human languages: how do languages come to refer not only to objects and events, but to the infinite number of possible relationships among them?

Scientific Evidence for Gestural Origins

Several lines of evidence converge to support the idea that gesture-based language might have preceded speech in human phylogeny: paleontological evidence for human anatomical evolution, primatological evidence concerning the behavior of the closest living relatives of human beings, and neurological evidence concerning the organization of the substrates for linguistic behavior in the brain.

It is necessary first to review what is known about the evolutionary relationships of human beings and our closest living relatives, the apes of Africa: bonobos (sometimes referred to as pygmy chimpanzees), chimpanzees, and gorillas. Bonobos and chimpanzees are both members of the genus *Pan*, and hereafter both species will be referred to collectively as chimpanzees. Comparative studies of DNA have shown that humans are extremely closely related to the African apes, but that we are probably more closely related to chimpanzees than to gorillas (for an accessible discussion of this evidence, see Fouts & Mills, 1997). Human beings, in turn, all belong to the genus *Homo* that has only one living species, *Homo sapiens*. The traditional taxonomic term for the human lineage after its separation from the lineage that led to modern chim-

panzees is the primate family Hominidae, the hominids. There are two well-established genera of hominids, *Australopithecus*, the members of which are extinct and some of which are probably ancestral to modern humans, and *Homo*, which includes several well-established extinct species, such as *Homo erectus*, in addition to *Homo sapiens*.

There is evidence that the human lineage separated from the line leading to modern chimpanzees 5–6 million years ago, and the common ancestor may have resembled modern chimpanzees in terms of locomotor and postural adaptations and brain size (see Armstrong, 1999; Begun, 1994). During the past several decades, paleoanthropologists have established that bipedalism is the defining anatomical trait of the hominid lineage (it emerged before the enlargement of the brain, the other striking peculiarity of human anatomy; for a recent summary of the evidence, see Tattersall (1999). What bipedalism does is free the hands from their former function in locomotion for use in carrying objects, manipulating tools, and communicating by gesture. What is most significant here is that by roughly 3 million years ago, the time of the famous *australopithecine* Lucy, the human hand had begun to move toward its modern configuration (Wilson, 1998). What is equally clear is that the brain had not yet begun to enlarge, and the base of the skull, indicative of the conformation of the vocal tract, had not begun to change toward its modern, speech-enabling shape. In fact, it has been argued that hominids as recent as members of *Homo erectus*, less than 2 million years ago, would have been incapable of making the full range of modern speech sounds (Lieberman, 1991; see also Walker & Shipman, 1996). It is equally clear that, with respect to the anatomy of the hand and upper extremity, *Homo erectus* had become fully modern (Walker & Shipman, 1996; Wilson, 1998).

There is currently no fossil evidence representing the common ancestor of chimpanzees and humans, but if it resembled modern chimpanzees, it makes sense to assume that the behavior of chimpanzees might throw considerable light on the probable behavioral capacities of the common ancestor and, thus, of the early hominids. It is well known that that chimpanzees appear quite limited in the extent to which they can learn to use spoken language (see Hayes & Nissen, 1971). There appear to be at least three possible limiting factors: anatomical, neurological, and intellectual. Anatomically, it appears that the conformation of the chimpanzee vocal tract severely limits the range of sounds that can be produced (Liberman, 1991); from a neurological perspective, it has been maintained that chimpanzees lack voluntary control over their vocalizations (Myers, 1976). Although both of these claims have been challenged (Gibson, 1997; Steklis, 1985), chimpanzees do not appear capable of acquiring speech to a substantial degree. The question of the intellectual capabilities of chimpanzees with respect to the acquisition of speech (this is, of course, ultimately a neurological issue also) is much more difficult to answer, for it appears that chimpanzees are capable of comprehending speech to a much greater extent than they can produce it (see Savage-Rumbaugh, 1999). In any event, the capacity of chimpanzees, and other apes for that matter, to acquire language in a visible-gestural mode appears much greater.

Soon after the appearance of Stokoe's initial work on ASL, it occurred to researchers that sign language might provide a better test case than speech with respect to the linguistic capacities of higher primates, and, thus, those of ancestral humans. Experiments have been carried out with chimpanzees, gorillas, and the next group of Hominoidea in terms of relatedness to humans, orangutans (see Gardner, Gardner, & Van Cantfort, 1989; Fouts & Mills, 1997; Wallman, 1992). This research has been controversial with respect to what it demonstrates about the capacity of apes to acquire human language in its fullest sense, especially with respect to the acquisition of syntax. There are also important differences between apes and humans with respect to the anatomy of the hand and, therefore, the ability of apes, including chimpanzees, to form all of the handshapes of a human sign language such as ASL (see Wilson, 1998). Nevertheless, it is clear that apes, and especially chimpanzees, can acquire a substantial vocabulary of signs, and that they can use these signs to communicate productively with human beings and, at least in the case of chimpanzees, with other apes.

It is important also to look at the capacity of apes, especially chimpanzees, to produce and comprehend motivated, that is, iconic or indexic, gestures that they have not been taught by human beings, in captivity and in the wild. Burling (1999) reviews the evidence for motivated signs, generally iconic manual signs, observed among captive chimpanzees and gorillas. This includes effective gestural communication used by Viki, the chimpanzee raised by the Hayes family, who famously did not learn to speak (Hayes & Nissen, 1971); a gorilla observed using iconic gestures under naturalistic conditions at the San Francisco zoo (Tanner & Byrne, 1996); and gestures used by Kanzi and other chimpanzees studied by Savage-Rumbaugh (see Savage-Rumbaugh, 1999). In addition to the work reviewed by Burling, there is a report of spontaneous referential pointing behavior in a captive chimpanzee (Leavens, Hopkins, & Bard, 1996). As Burling (1999) points out, "almost nothing is known about the use of motivated signs in the wild" (p. 339). Although primatologists studying the behavior of chimpanzees have devoted a good deal of time to vocal behavior, it may be that until recently little attention has been given to visible gestures. Nevertheless, even cursory examination of films and photographs made by Jane Goodall at the Gombe Stream Reserve reveals that a wealth of communicative gestures, such as those for begging and dominance or submission, are used among feral chimpanzees, and many of these gestures are quite transparent to human observers (e.g., van Lawick-Goodall, 1976).

Finally, there is a tight linkage in the brain between neurological centers that control speech and signing (see e.g., Kimura, 1993; Petitto, 2000). Although this does not provide direct evidence for the primacy of signing in evolution, it does suggest at least parallel evolution for speech and sign. Moreover, there is recent evidence for the existence of "mirror neurons" in the brains of nonhuman primates, specifically in the premotor cortex of monkeys, presumed by their discoverers to be an area that is homologous with Broca's area in humans (Rizzolatti & Arbib, 1998). According to Rizzolatti and Arbib, these are neurons that fire both when a monkey observes and when it performs certain specific manual activities. This suggests the existence of a neurological system in prehuman primates that was primed to allow for the mental representation of gestural signs—the recognition that such activity can be communicative as well as instrumental.

In summary, the evidence reviewed here suggests the following scenario. The common ancestor of chimpanzees and humans probably had a limited vocal repertoire but had a substantial capacity for communication involving visible gesture, including iconic and indexic gestures. During the course of hominid evolution, the hand and upper extremity reached its modern configuration long before the upper respiratory system, including the vocal tract, did so. From this evidence, it is reasonable to conclude that the earliest languagelike behavior of the hominids involved visible, especially iconic and indexic manual, signs. There is also reason to believe that grammar, especially syntax, evolved out of iconic manual gestures.

Gesture and the Origin of Grammar

To approach the question of the origins of grammar, one must first take a position on what constitutes syntax. In the generative approach to the study of language, syntax, semantics, and lexicon are distinct. A fundamental tenet of generative grammar is that syntax is "independent of all other levels of linguistic description including semantics— and independent of all other aspects of cognition as well" (Tomasello, 1998, pp. ix–x). Under this view, grammatical ability is stipulated as part of the human genetic endowment, distinct from other perceptual and cognitive abilities.

Another approach to the study of language, cognitive grammar, takes a radically different view. A fundamental tenet of cognitive grammar is that lexicon, morphology, and syntax form a continuum of symbolic structures—symbolic because they possess both a phonological and a semantic pole. Words, of course, are symbolic structures, but according to cognitive grammar, so too is syntax. Such fundamental areas of grammar as grammatical class (e.g., nouns vs. verbs vs. prepositions), case, and basic grammatical relations (subject, direct object, indirect object) are regarded as having semantic import that derives from conceptual archetypes having a nonlinguistic origin: "pre-linguistic conceptions grounded in everyday experience" which "reflect our experience as mobile and sentient creatures and as manipulators of physical objects" (Langacker 1991, p. 285). Under the cognitive grammar view, no unique syntactic ability must be genetically specified. The human language ability is assumed to require nothing more than genetically specified perceptual, cognitive, and motoric abilities.

Naturally, these two approaches to language lead to different positions on the role of gesture and iconicity in the origin of language. For generative linguists, syntax could not have evolved out of simpler structures such as animal communication or human gestural systems. Consider Chomsky's (1972) view:

> When we ask what human language is, we find no striking similarity to animal communication systems . . . The examples of animal communication that have been examined to date do share many of the properties of human gestural systems, and it might be reasonable to explore the possibility of direct connection in this case. But human language, it appears, is based on entirely different principles. (p. 70)

The cognitive approach is compatible with a view that language (not just lexicon but also syntax) could have emerged out of animal communication and human (or proto-human) gestural systems such as those discussed above. It is here that Stokoe's notion of semantic phonology plays a critical role in linking language and gesture:

> The usual way of conceiving of the structure of language is linear: First there are the sounds (phonology), these are put together to make the words and their classes (morphology), the words in turn, are found to be of various classes, and these are used to form phrase structures (syntax), and finally, the phrase structures, after lexical replacement of their symbols, yield meaning (semantics). A semantic phonology ties the last step to the first, making a seamless circuit of this progression. The metaphor for semantic phonology that jumps to mind is the Möbius strip: the input is the output, with a twist. (Stokoe 1991, p. 112)

Semantic phonology suggests that visible gestures are primal examples of self-symbolization. Like the twist in the Möbius strip, the phonological pole of gestures and signs consists of something that acts and its action. That is, hands and their actions are iconic manifestations of the conceptual archetypes which are the prelinguistic source of grammatical structures. Hands are prototypical nouns, and their actions are prototypical verbs. A hand can act transitively on another hand, transmitting energy to the impacted object; or, a hand can act intransitively, as when we trace the path of an object that has moved. Semantic phonology links not only gesture and syntax but also signed and spoken language. It suggests that visible gestures were from the beginning critical elements in the origins of sign languages. Semantic phonology also claims that all language, regardless of modality, is essentially gestural in nature.

Thus, contrary to Chomsky's position that although human gesture may be related to animal communication, neither are directly connected to human language, semantic phonology contends that visible actions lie at the origin of all human languages. Support for this claim comes from a variety of sources. The recent evidence for mirror neurons suggests that gestural signs likely played a role in the evolution of human language. Rizzolatti and Arbib (1998) note that the "precursor of Broca's area was endowed before speech appearance with a mechanism for recognizing actions made by others" (p. 190) and suggest that this finding supports gestural theory: "language in humans . . . evolved from a basic mechanism originally not related to communication: the capacity to recognize actions" (p. 193).

Speech as Gesture

If visible gesture played a critical role in the origin of human language, a reasonable question to ask is why human language is now predominantly spoken, with signed languages being used only among certain special populations. The question is typically seen as dealing with the transition from gesture to spoken language; however, this conception of the problem is flawed in at least two ways.

First, it is important to note that all language is ultimately gestural: certain parts of the body move in a way which produces a signal. Signed languages are articulated by moving hands, face, and body to produce an optical signal that is received by the visual perceptual system. Spoken languages are articulated by moving parts of the vocal tract to produce an acoustic signal which is received by the auditory perceptual system. As the cognitive psychologist Ulric Neisser noted (1967):

> To speak is to make finely controlled movements in certain parts of your body, with the result that information about these movements is broadcast to the environment. For this reason the movements of speech are sometimes called *articulatory gestures*. A person who perceives speech, then, is picking up information

about a certain class of real, physical, tangible . . . events. (p. 156)

Whether the activity is speaking or signing, and whether the signal produced is audible or visible, the events in question are fundamentally gestural.

Second, this view of language origins does not require a transition from a period in which human ancestors used only visible gestures to one in which modern humans use only acoustic gestures. At no time in our entire evolutionary history did communication take place in a single modality. Modern primates are active vocalizers but also active gesturers. The evidence is also clear that humans gesture while they vocalize. The evolutionary link between gesture and language is so strong that even congenitally blind people who have never seen visible gesture nevertheless produce gestures when speaking with each other (Iverson, 1998). On the basis of the body of research on gesture and language, McNeill (1992) has concluded, contrary to Chomsky, that "gestures and speech should be viewed within a unified conceptual framework as aspects of a single underlying process" (p. 23).

The picture that emerges is thus one in which both visible and acoustic gestures played an early role in hominid communication and continue to be the primary means by which humans communicate. What has changed is the relative informational load carried by visible versus audible gestures. Visible gesture is clearly implicated as playing a critical role in the early evolutionary history of language. It is also evident that at some point, natural selection favored acoustic gestures as the primary means by which information is broadcast to the environment for purposes of linguistic communication, at least among hearing communities.

In spite of this shift in the balance of informational load, gesture remains a significant part of the overall human communication system, suggesting a single, unified system. Gesture also remains in other facets of signed and spoken language. Bolinger (1986), for example, posited a "gestural complex that includes intonation" (p. 197), suggesting that this gestural complex reflects an ancient mixed system of gesture and speech. Bolinger even went so far as to suggest that this mixed system survives today, though gesture and intonation have evolved along somewhat separate paths. In support of this suggestion he cites Kendon (1980, p. 211), who notes that speech and gesture are so intricately coordinated that "it is as if the speech production process is manifested in two forms of activity simultaneously: in the vocal organs and also in bodily movement." However, because vocal organ activity is also bodily movement, only one form of gestural activity need be posited. Finally, gesture remains even in signed languages. A growing body of research is now examining the gesture–language interface in signed languages (Emmorey & Reilly, 1995; Liddell, 1998; Liddell & Metzger, 1998; Morford & Kegl, 2000).

The Gesture–Sign Language Interface

A new line of research explores the process by which gesture becomes incorporated into signed languages (Shaffer, 2000; S. Wilcox, 2000, 2001; S. Wilcox et al., 2000). These studies demonstrate a variety of ways in which gesture appears with and becomes a part of signed languages. The evidence from this research suggests that nonlinguistic gestures become incorporated as lexical signs in a particular signed language.

For example, the gesture "come here" is commonly used among hearing people; it was identified as long ago as 1832 by de Jorio as functioning to call or summon someone. "Fingers extended and then brought towards the palm several times." This gesture has become incorporated into signed languages such as Catalan Sign Language with the meaning "emergency" and old ASL "necessity" (Higgins, 1923). Pragmatic inferencing, which has been shown to play a critical role in semantic change in spoken languages (Traugott, 1989), may be invoked to explain the process by which this gesture has lexicalized: one reason a person would beckon another to come is because of an urgent need.

Research on spoken languages demonstrates that lexical material may further evolve into grammatical elements of a language by the process of grammaticization (Bybee et al., 1994). One example of this is the English lexical verb "go," which has in addition to its lexical sense of movement in space a grammatical sense which is used to mark tense, typically pronounced "gonna": "I'm gonna fly to New York next week."

It now appears that gestures, in addition to lexicalizing, may undergo further development in signed languages and acquire grammatical function. One example is the evolution of the future

Figure 22-1. The Mediterranean departure-demand and departure-description gesture. Image from video.

marker in ASL. Shaffer (2000; Shaffer & Janzen, 2000) has proposed that the future marker in ASL originated as the gesture described by de Jorio (1832/2000) as "palm of the hand open and held edgewise, and moved upwards several times." (p. 260) Morris, Collett, Marsh, and O'Shaughnessy. (1979) identified this as a pan-Mediterranean departure-demand and departure-description gesture: "let's go" and "she left" (figure 22-1; note that this is not a sign, but a depiction of the gesture [Wylie & Stafford, 1977]). The gesture became incorporated into French Sign Language (LSF), appearing in a mid-nineteenth century dictionary of LSF (Broulard, 1855) as PARTIR, "depart" (figure 22-2). It also appears that this lexical sign has grammaticized in a number of signed languages as a future marker while retaining its mean-

Figure 22-2. The lexical morpheme PARTIR (depart) in French Sign Language.

ing of departure. In a passage from a 1918 National Association of the Deaf film, the form appears as DEPART (figure 22-3): "At that time, Edward Miner Gallaudet *had gone to* Philadelphia." In another 1918 film in the same series, the same form is used as a future marker (figure 22-4): "When you understand the words of our Father, you *will* do that no more."

Thus, the evidence is clear that non-linguistic gesture may become incorporated into signed languages as lexical signs. Further, these gestural elements may also become part of the grammatical repertoire of singed languages.

The process of grammaticization has been described by numerous scholars as synonymous with the evolutionary process of ritualization: "In the course of evolution, both locomotory movements and acts . . . have been selected and modified to produce signals" (Blest, 1963, p. 102). Haiman (1998) notes that this process "amounts to *the creation of a language out of other kinds of behavior*" (p. 141). Ritualization thus is implicated in the phylogenetic evolution of language from nonlinguistic behaviors, among which, visible-manual gestures played a key role. It is also implicated in the origins of sign languages with lexicalization and grammaticization of gesture playing a significant role in their ongoing development.

Figure 22-3. The lexical morpheme DEPART in American Sign Language. Image from video.

Figure 22-4. The grammatical morpheme FUTURE in American Sign Language. Image from video.

The Origin of Modern Sign Languages

There is abundant evidence that full-fledged sign languages emerge naturally among modern human populations when certain conditions are present. They appear to emerge naturally among deaf people and their hearing relatives and associates, but they also emerge among hearing people when environmental or social conditions make speech undesirable or impossible. Sign languages, or at least sign systems, are known to have arisen in hearing populations under the following conditions: (1) among Christian monks living under a code of silence (Barakat, 1975); (2) as a specialized language of women among Australian Aborigines (Kendon, 1989; Umiker-Sebeok & Sebeok, 1978); (3) as a lingua franca among North American Plains Indians (Umiker-Sebeok & Sebeok, 1978); (4) among saw mill workers in a noisy environment (Meissner & Phillpot, 1975); and (5) for use by hunters to avoid being heard by prey (Armstrong, 1999). Such systems, codes, or languages, in fact, appear to have been widespread among pre-Neolithic societies, and this may be taken as further evidence of their ancient lineage. The probability that substantial numbers of deaf people lived in these societies, especially older people who had lost their hearing, cannot be discounted.

There is evidence for the emergence of sign systems among small groups of deaf people and, especially in traditional societies in historical times, the hearing people in the communities where these deaf people live. The former systems have generally been referred to as "home signs" (see, e.g., Goldin-Meadow & Feldman, 1977), and they have been documented in a variety of areas (e.g., Torigoe & Takei, 2002). When they are restricted to use by a small number of deaf people, usually family members, and they are not transmitted across generations, they appear to remain relatively simple and syntactically impoverished. Such sign systems may not evolve into fully syntacticized languages (e.g., Washabaugh, 1986).

In some cases, however, home signs may expand beyond small groups of family members to larger social groups, including hearing people, especially in simple or traditional societies. The most famous example of this phenomenon is probably the case of the sign language that developed on the island of Martha's Vineyard (Groce, 1985). The English settlers of Martha's Vineyard, who began arriving in the mid-seventeenth century, had a high incidence of genetic deafness. Because this was a small, relatively closed, and inbred society, many families included deaf members, and an indigenous sign language developed that was apparently used by both the deaf and hearing islanders. By the time it came to the attention of scholars in the late twentieth century, the language had already died out, so not much is known about its structure. It has been inferred, however, that it may have had a significant influence on the development of American Sign Language, as many deaf island children began to attend residential schools for the deaf on the mainland, especially the American School for the Deaf in Hartford, Connecticut (Groce, 1985). Comparable sign systems have been reported in use by deaf and hearing people among the Yucatec Maya of Mexico (Johnson, 1991) and on the island of Bali (Branson, Miller, & Masaja, 1996). In his article on the Yucatec Maya, Johnson also mentions unpublished reports of similar situations in Venezuela, Africa, and on the Navaho reservation in Arizona.

The true linguistic status of sign systems such as these may be difficult to determine because they are seldom called upon to carry the full weight of social commerce in the societies in which they exist; that is, they exist in parallel with spoken languages. However, there is no doubt that when deaf people live together in sufficient numbers, full-fledged sign languages emerge. How this might happen is illustrated by the emergence of three sign languages for which historical documentation exists: French Sign Language, (*Langue des Signes Française* or LSF), American Sign Language, and Nicaraguan Sign Language.

The earliest information that comes close to providing a linguistic description of a natural sign language has to do with LSF. LSF is frequently said to have originated with the founding of the school for the deaf by the Abbé de l'Epée in Paris during the middle of the eighteenth century. It appears likely, however, that Epée drew on an existing sign language in formulating his system of "methodical" signs that were intended to support instruction in the written French language and that were grammatically modeled on that language. Little is known about natural sign languages that might have been in use by the French deaf community either before or immediately after the founding of Epée's school, but one source is what appears to be the first book ever published by a deaf author, Pierre Desloges's 1779 *Observations of a Deaf-Mute* (see Fischer, 2002). Desloges made it clear in this book that there are grammatical differences between the French language and the sign language used by deaf people, especially with respect to the use of space, including the use of directional signs (Fischer, 2002).

Desloges also proposed a taxonomy of LSF signs. According to Fischer (2002 p. 397), Desloges maintained that there are three classes of signs: "ordinary or primitive" signs, "reflected" signs, and "analytic" signs. As described, these are fairly familiar categories. The first comprises "natural signs everyone in the world, hearing or deaf, use frequently" These are the largely iconic gestures of ordinary discourse that are incorporated into the sign language. The second category of signs can be described as "natural, but that one can produce and understand only with a certain amount of reflection." Finally, analytic signs stand "for concepts that are not suited for direct, pictorial expression." Desloges, thus, categorized the signs of LSF in terms of their relative inconicity (Fischer, 2002, p. 397).

The historical route whereby LSF came to influence the development of ASL is well-known and will not be repeated in detail here. This influence began with the arrival of Laurent Clerc in the United States to begin his partnership with Thomas Hopkins Gallaudet at the American School for the

Deaf in Hartford, Connecticut, in the early nineteenth century. Gallaudet brought Clerc, a deaf teacher, from France to begin the practice of teaching deaf children in sign language in the United States. Certainly, Clerc would at first have been teaching in LSF, but eventually a new language began to emerge, almost certainly incorporating elements of existing American sign systems, probably including the sign language of Martha's Vineyard. In commenting on the belief of Jean Marc Itard that LSF was highly iconic, Lane (1976) outlines some of the processes that might have been at work, assuming as many linguists do that modern ASL is much less iconic:

> Perhaps . . . Franslan [LSF] was more iconic than Ameslan [ASL]. There are two reasons for thinking this. First, as signs are handed down from generation to generation, as the primary language of the family, from parent to child who becomes a parent in turn, they become simpler, more regular; they are shaped by the general rules for sign formation and thus become more encoded. Second, Franslan built originally on family signs brought to it by children like Massieu and his predecessors under Epée. De Gérando tells us that these children from isolated parts of France often brought similar signs for the same things. (pp. 235–236)

Now ASL is the sign language that has been most thoroughly described and analyzed in linguistic terms, and this passage from Lane reflects a theoretical position that developed during the 1960s and 1970s to explain the obvious iconicity of ASL but nevertheless preserve its linguistic status. Early theory assumed that, while elements of the language might initially be introduced iconically, most iconicity was squeezed out over time by purely linguistic processes (Frishberg, 1975; Klima & Bellugi, 1979). Wilcox (1996) refers to this as banishing the "specter" of iconicity, assumed to be necessary if the presumption is accepted that linguistic signs must be arbitrary. However, there are now linguistically sophisticated approaches to the description of ASL that assume the iconicity is not only involved at the beginnings of sign formation but that it is also basic to the ongoing grammatical processes of sign languages (Taub, 2001; P. Wilcox, 2000).

Origins of Sign Language: Emergent or Innate?

Direct evidence concerning the manner in which sign languages originally emerge has recently come to light. The appearance of what is apparently a completely new sign language among deaf students in Nicaragua has focused the attention of linguists on the factors that may be involved in the development of language in general, not just sign languages. In fact, the appearance of this language and the discussion surrounding its description has become a focal point in the ongoing debate about the modularity of language and the extent to which it represents a faculty separate in genetic determination from other human behavioral systems. The significance of this can be judged by the people who have become involved in the debate, including, according to a recent report in *Science* (Helmuth, 2001), Steven Pinker, Lila Gleitman, Ann Senghas, and Dan Slobin. Pinker (1994), citing Kegl (Kegl & Iwata, 1989), discusses the emergence of Nicaraguan Sign Language (NSL) as a key support for his "language as instinct" hypothesis:

> Until recently there were no sign languages at all in Nicaragua, because its deaf people remained isolated from one another. When the Sandanista government took over in 1979 and reformed the educational system, the first schools for the deaf were created. The schools focused on drilling the children in lip reading and speech, and as in every case where that is tried, the results were dismal. But it did not matter. On the playgrounds and schoolbuses, the children were inventing their own sign system, pooling the makeshift gestures that they used with their families at home. (p. 36)

In the popular press, the emergence of NSL into what now appears to be a full-fledged language, complete with complex syntax, has been taken as final proof of the Chomskyan hypothesis that human beings have a genetically determined "language organ" that always cranks out a language guided by principles of universal grammar, whenever social conditions are minimally adequate (see, e.g., Osborne, 1999). At least the first part of this assertion is true with respect to sign languages: they always seem to emerge when speech is not feasible. What is in question is the second part of the assertion, the degree to which the details of the grammar are genetically determined, or stipulated.

For NSL to provide a pure test case, it would be necessary for the deaf children of Nicaragua, before 1979, to have been completely cut off from human language. But how cut off were they? Certainly as suggested in Pinker's account, they, like all other deaf people, had access to at least idiosyncratic homes signs. A historical account (Polich, 2000) suggests that the situation in which the language developed may have been quite complex and may have included substantial contacts among home-signing deaf children before the early 1980s. According to Polich, there may also have been influences from foreign sign languages, including ASL and Costa Rican Sign Language. In the final analysis, however, the more fundamental question may be one that has arisen throughout this chapter, which we return to below.

Summary and Conclusions

Few would doubt that iconicity and indexicality are sources of sign language signs, but what is the source of the grammar of a new sign language like NSL? Does it arise because human brains are genetically predisposed to create certain kinds of grammatical structures, or does it come from a more plastic brain that tends to solve similar problems in similar ways? This is a question that has been at the heart of a long-running debate in the science of language generally, and sign languages may provide a key to answering it and thus answering the more general question of where all languages arise. Consider this quotation from Helmuth (2001) citing Senghas: "She focused on a form of grammar common to every known sign language but absent from spoken languages. Signers use locations in space to show how objects or ideas are related. For instance, making the sign for 'cup' in a certain spot, followed by the sign for 'tall' in that spot, makes it clear that the cup—and not necessarily the person drinking from it—is tall" (p. 1758). Does this sort of strategy for using space, common to all sign languages, and now emerging, apparently independently in NSL, represent a genetically encoded grammatical principle, or does it reflect some "natural" need to communicate and simple efficiency in using the resources at hand? Stokoe (2000) commented on a report about NSL signers that appeared in the *New York Times*:

> Their gestures naturally—not mysteriously or because of grammar rules—resemble or point at things and express actions with manual movement. For example, they sign "tell" by moving the hand from the teller to the one told. Kegl hails this as "verb agreement" and proof positive that, without any grammatical input, these children have invented grammar and language on the spot. But signing "tell" as they do is hardly a strategy requiring grammar rules, universal or otherwise. After all, these children know as we all do that telling, like a Frisbee going from thrower to catcher, is action directed from one to another. (p. 13)

A plausible case can be made for the origin of signs and the rules that allow them to refer to relationships, and, thus, of sign *languages*, in the stuff of iconic and mimetic manual gesture. Finally, and most significantly, the origin of language itself, whether signed or spoken, can be traced to the same source.

Note

A portion of this chapter appeared previously in the preface by David F. Armstrong and Michael A. Karchmer to the volume *The Study of Signed Languages: Essays in Honor of William C. Stokoe*, edited by D.F. Armstrong, M.A. Karchmer, and J.V. Van Cleve, Gallaudet University Press, 2002. It appears here by permission of the publisher.

References

Armstrong, D.F. (1999). *Original signs: Gesture, sign and the sources of language*. Washington, DC: Gallaudet University Press.

Barakat, R. (1975). On ambiguity in Cistercian Sign Language. *Sign Language Studies*, 8, 275–289.

Begun, D.R. (1994). Relations among the great apes and humans: New interpretations based on the fossil record. *Yearbook of Physical Anthropology*, 37, 11–63.

Blest, A. (1963). The concept of "ritualization." In W. Thorpe & O. Zangwill (Eds.), *Current problems in animal behavior* (pp. 102–124). Cambridge: Cambridge University Press.

Bolinger, D. (1986). *Intonation and its parts: Melody in*

spoken English. Stanford, CA: Stanford University Press.

Branson, J., Miller, D., & Masaja, I.J. (1996). Everyone here speaks sign language too: A deaf village in Bali, Indonesia. In C. Lucas (Ed.), *Multicultural aspects of sociolinguistics in deaf communities* (pp. 39–57). Washington, DC: Gallaudet University Press.

Brouland, J. (1855). *Langage Mimique: Spécimen d'un dictionaire des signes.* Gallaudet Archives.

Burling, R. (1999). Motivation, conventionalization, and arbitrariness in the origin of language. In B.J. King (Ed.), *The origins of language: What nonhuman primates can tell us* (pp. 307–335). Santa Fe, NM: School of American Research Press.

Bybee, J., Perkins, R., & Pagliuca, W. (1994). *The evolution of grammar: Tense, aspect, and modality in the languages of the world.* Chicago: University of Chicago Press.

Chomsky, N. (1972). *Language and mind.* New York: Harcourt Brace Jovanovich.

de Jorio, A. (1832/2000) *Gesture in Naples and gesture in classical antiquity.* (A. Kendon, Ed. and Trans.). Bloomington, IN: Indiana University Press.

Emmorey, K., & Reilly, J. (Eds.). (1995). *Sign, gesture, and space.* Hillsdale, NJ: Lawrence Erlbaum Associates.

Fischer, R. (2002). The study of natural sign language in 18th century France. *Sign Language Studies, 2(4),* 391–406.

Fouts R., & Mills, S.T. (1997). *Next of kin.* New York: William Morrow.

Frishberg, N. (1975). Arbitrariness and iconicity: Historical change in American Sign Language. *Language, 51,* 699–719.

Gallaudet, E.M. (1983). *History of the college for the deaf, 1857–1907.* Washington, DC: Gallaudet College Press.

Gardner, R.E., Gardner, B.T., & Van Canfort, T.E. (1989). *Teaching sign language to chimpanzees.* Albany: State University of New York Press.

Gibson, K. (1997). Review of *The wisdom of the bones* by A. Walker and P. Shipman. *Evolution of Communication, I(1),* 153–155.

Goldin-Meadow, S., & Feldman, H. (1977). The development of language-like communication without a language model. *Science, 197,* 401–403.

Groce, N.E. (1985). *Everyone here spoke sign language: Hereditary deafness on Martha's Vineyard.* Cambridge, MA: Harvard University Press.

Haiman, J. (1998). *Talk is cheap: Sarcasm, alienation, and the evolution of language.* New York: Oxford University Press.

Harnad, S.R., Steklis H.D., & Lancaster, J. (Eds.). (1976). *Origins and evolution of language and speech* [Special issue]. *Annals of the New York Academy of Sciences, 280.*

Hayes, K.J., & Nissen, C.H. (1971). Higher mental functions of a home-raised chimpanzee. In A.M. Schrier and F. Stollnitz (Eds.), *Behavior of nonhuman primates* (pp. 59–115). New York: Academic Press.

Helmuth, L. (2001). From the mouths (and hands) of babes. *Science, 293,* 1758–1759.

Hewes, G.W. (1996). A history of the study of language origins and the gestural primacy hypothesis. In A. Lock & C.R. Peters (Eds.), *Handbook of human symbolic evolution* (pp. 571–595). Oxford: Clarendon Press.

Higgins, D.D. (1923). *How to talk to the deaf.* St. Louis, MO.

Iverson, J. M. (1998). Gesture when there is no visual model. In J. Iverson and S. Goldin-Meadow (Eds.), *The nature and functions of gesture in children's communication* (pp. 89–100). San Francisco, CA: Jossey-Bass.

Johnson, R.E. (1991). Sign language, culture, and community in a traditional Yucatec Maya village. *Sign Language Studies, 73,* 461–474.

Kegl, J., & Iwata, G.A. (1989). Lenguage de Signos Necaragüense: A pidgin sheds light on the "creole?" In R. Carlson, S. DeLancey, S. Gilden, D. Payne, & A. Saxena, Eds. *Proceedings of the Fourth Annual Meeting of the Pacific Linguistics Conference* (pp. 266–294). Eugene, OR: University of Oregon.

Kendon, A. (1980). Gesticulation and speech: Two aspects of the process of utterance. In M. R. Key (Ed.), *The relationship of verbal and nonverbal communication* (pp. 207–227). The Hague: Mouton.

Kendon, A. (1989). *Sign languages of aboriginal Australia.* Cambridge: Cambridge University Press.

Kimura, D. (1993). *Neuromotor mechanisms in human communication.* Oxford: Oxford University Press.

Klima, E., & Bellugi, U. (1979). *The signs of language.* Cambridge, MA: Harvard University Press.

Lane, H. (1976). *The wild boy of Aveyron.* Cambridge, MA: Harvard University Press.

Langacker, R. W. (1991). *Foundations of cognitive grammar: Vol. II. Descriptive application.* Stanford, CA: Stanford University Press.

Leavens, D.A., Hopkins, W.D., & Bard, K.A. (1996). Indexical and referential pointing in chimpanzees (*Pan troglodytes*). *Journal of Comparative Psychology, 110,* 346–353.

Liddell, S. K. (1998). Grounded blends, gestures, and conceptual shifts. *Cognitive Linguistics, 9(3),* 283–314.

Liddell, S. K., & Metzger, M. (1998). Gesture in sign

language discourse. *Journal of Pragmatics, 30*(6), 657–697.

Lieberman, P. (1991). *Uniquely human*. Cambridge, MA: Harvard University Press.

McNeill, D. (1992). *Hand and mind: What gestures reveal about thought*. Chicago: University of Chicago Press.

Meissner, M., & Phillpott, S. (1975). The sign language of sawmill workers in British Columbia. *Sign Language Studies, 9*, 291–308.

Morford, J. P., & Kegl, J. (2000). Gestural precursors to linguistic constructs: How input shapes the form of language. In D. McNeill (Ed.), *Language and gesture* (pp. 358–387). Cambridge: Cambridge University Press.

Morris, D., Collett, P., Marsh, P. & M. O'Shaughnessy. (1979). *Gestures: Their origin and distribution*. New York: Stein and Day.

Myers, R. (1976). Comparative neurology of vocalization and speech: Proof of a dichotomy. In S. Steklis, H. Harnad, & J. Lancaster (Eds.), *Origins and evolution of language and speech* [Special issue]. *Annals of the New York Academy of Sciences, 280*, 745–757.

Neisser, U. (1967). *Cognitive psychology*. New York: Appleton-Century-Crofts.

Osborne, L. (1999, October 24). A linguistic big bang. *New York Times Magazine*, 84–89.

Pinker, S. (1994). *The language instinct*. New York: William Morrow.

Petitto, L.A., Zatorre, R.J., Gauna, K., Nikelski, E.J., Dostie, D., & Evans, A. C. (2000). Speech-like cerebral activity in profoundly deaf people while processing signed languages: Implications for the neural basis of all human language. *Proceedings of the National Academy of Sciences USA, 97*, 13961–13966.

Polich, L. (2000). The search for Proto-NSL: Looking for the roots of the Nicaraguan deaf community. In M. Metzger (Ed.), *Bilingualism and identity in deaf communities* (pp. 255–305). Washington, DC: Gallaudet University Press.

Rizzolatti, G., & Arbib, M.A. (1998). Language within our grasp. *Trends in Neuroscience, 21*, 188–94.

Savage-Rumbaugh, S. (1999). Ape language. In B. J. King (Ed.), *The origins of language: What nonhuman primates can tell us*. Santa Fe, NM: School of American Research Press.

Shaffer, B. (2000). *A syntactic, pragmatic analysis of the expression of necessity and possibility in American Sign Language*. Unpublished doctoral dissertation, University of New Mexico, Albuquerque, NM.

Shaffer, B., & Janzen, T. (2000). *Gesture, lexical words and grammar: Grammaticization processes in ASL*.

Paper presented at the 26th annual meeting of the Berkeley Linguistics Society.

Steklis, H. (1985). Primate communication, comparative neurology, and the origin of language reexamined. *Journal of Human Evolution, 14*, 157–173.

Stokoe, W.C. (1960). *Sign language structure: An outline of the visual communication systems of the American deaf*. Studies in Linguistics: Occasional Papers 8. Buffalo, NY: University of Buffalo Department of Anthropology and Linguistics.

Stokoe, W. C. (1991). Semantic phonology. *Sign Language Studies, 71*, 99–106.

Stokoe, W.C. (2000). Models, signs, and universal rules. *Sign Language Studies, 1*(1), 10–16.

Stokoe, W.C., Casterline, D.C. & Croneberg, C.G. (1965). *A dictionary of American Sign Language on linguistic principles*. Washington, DC: Gallaudet College Press.

Tanner, J.E., & Byrne, R.W. (1996). Representation of action through iconic gesture in a captive lowland gorilla. *Current Anthropology, 37*, 12–73.

Tattersall, I. (1999). *Becoming human: Evolution and human uniqueness*. New York: Harcourt, Brace and Company.

Taub, S. (2001). *Language from the body: Iconicity and metaphor in American Sign Language*. Cambridge: Cambridge University Press.

Tomasello, M. (1998). *The new psychology of language: Cognitive and functional approaches to language structure*. Mahwah, NJ: Lawrence Erlbaum Associates.

Torigoe, T., & Takei, W. (2002). A descriptive analysis of pointing and oral movements in a homesign. *Sign Language Studies, 2*(3), 281–295.

Traugott, E. C. (1989). On the rise of epistemic meanings in English: an example of subjectification in semantic change. *Language, 65*(1), 31–55.

Umiker-Sebeok D., & Sebeok, T. (1978). *Aboriginal sign languages of the Americas and Australia*. New York: Plenum Press.

van Lawick-Goodall, J. (1976). *In the shadow of man*. Boston: Houghton-Mifflin.

Walker, A., & Shipman, P. (1996). *The wisdom of the bones: In search of human origins*. New York: Random House.

Wallman, J. (1992). *Aping language*. Cambridge: Cambridge University Press.

Washabaugh, W. (1986). *Five fingers for survival*. Ann Arbor, MI: Karoma Publishers.

Wescott, R. (Ed.). (1974). *Language origins*. Silver Spring, MD: Linstok Press.

Wilcox, P.P. (2000). *Metaphor in American Sign Language*. Washington, DC: Gallaudet University Press.

Wilcox, S. (1996, October). *Hands and bodies, minds and souls: Or, how a sign linguist learned to stop worrying and love gesture*. Paper presented at the Workshop on Integrating Language and Gesture, University of Delaware, Newark, DE.

Wilcox, S. (2000, February). *Gesture, icon, and symbol: The expression of modality in signed languages*. Paper presented at the Berkeley Linguistics Society, Berkeley, CA.

Wilcox, S. (2001, July). *Conceptual spaces and bodily actions*. Paper presented at the 7th International Conference of the International Cognitive Linguistics Association, Santa Barbara, CA.

Wilcox, S., Shaffer, B., Jarque, M. J., Valenti, J. M. S. I., Pizzuto, E., & Rossini, P. (2000, July). *The emergence of grammar from word and gesture: A cross-linguistic study of modal verbs in three signed languages*. Paper presented at the 7th International Conference on Theoretical Issues in Sign Language Research, Amsterdam.

Wilson, F.R. (1998). *The hand: How its use shapes the brain, language, and human culture*. New York: Pantheon Books.

Wylie, L., & Stafford, R. (1977). *Beaux gestes: A guide to French body talk*. Cambridge: The Undergraduate Press.

23

Susan D. Fischer & Harry van der Hulst

Sign Language Structures

This chapter provides an introduction to sign language structures. The main components of sign languages are described, and some of the issues facing sign language research today are addressed. Although much of the discussion is based on American Sign Language (ASL), other sign languages are also examined for comparison.

Word Formation (Morphology)

As with most other natural languages, sign languages have a number of ways to make words out of other words or parts of words. Linguists make a distinction between *inflection*, grammatical affixes added to words for syntactic purposes, and *derivation*, lexical affixes that change the core meaning or word class. Another way to make new words is *compounding*, which takes two words and puts them together to make a new word whose meaning is often not the sum of its parts. An example of an English compound is "greenhouse," which is not a green house but rather a house in which green things are grown. It is common in compounds for not only the meaning to change but also the pronunciation; in "breakfast," the vowels in "break" and "fast" have been reduced.

Inflection

Languages differ in terms of what they express inflectionally and what they must express with independent words. English uses affixes for past tense, {-ed} and present tense (realized, e.g., as {-s} for third person singular). However, English lacks a future tense affix, using instead the independent word "will." A language like Latin has a rich inflectional system. Verbs agree with their subjects in number and gender, and can be inflected for three tenses and several moods; adjectives and nouns must agree in number and gender. Compared to Latin, English has an impoverished inflectional system, which has consequences elsewhere in the grammar; English constituent order is more fixed than Latin, and overt subjects are required in English but not in Latin, because the subject in Latin can be inferred from the verb.

Virtually all sign languages that have been studied have rich inflectional systems that free up constituent order. In ASL, although there is no grammatical expression of tense (see Neidle, Kegl, Maclaughlin, Bahan, & Lee, 2000, for an opposing, though highly controversial view), verbs can inflect for both subject and object agreement as well as a variety of aspects such as habitual, continuous, and inceptive.

Agreement

Two subclasses of verbs mark agreement with either source and goal (spatial verbs) or object and sometimes subject (agreement or inflecting verbs) (Padden, 1988). Both types of verbs do so by using referential loci (Bergman, 1980), points set up in space toward or away from which verbs move or face. In an agreement verb such as HATE, subject and object are directly encoded in the verb, both by the facing of the hands and the direction of movement (Meir, 1998). An ASL spatial verb like GO-TO can inflect for the endpoint of the action by changing its direction of movement. The ASL sign BRING (a spatial verb) moves from the real or established locus of the source (starting point) of the object to the real or established locus of the goal (endpoint). The subject of a spatial verb is not grammatically encoded and must be specified as in example 1:[1]

[1]   ME BOOK $_a$BRING$_b$
       'I bring/brought a book from point a to point b'

A third category of verbs, "plain," does not inflect at all for subject, object, source, or goal.

Liddell (1995, 1996) has argued that referential loci are outside the linguistic system of ASL, although the grammar refers to them. Many scholars disagree with this view. One argument against Liddell is that there are grammatical constructions in both ASL and, more extensively, in NihonSyuwa (NS; the sign language of Japan), that abstract away from referential loci but otherwise do not differ from other aspects of the agreement system. This involves the replacement of a referential locus with a hand in neutral space, as in example 2:

[2]   dh: CONVINCE$_a$
       nh: CL:person$_a$
       'convince him/her'

Other aspects of utterances like example 2 are discussed later. The point of this example for now is that it is the nondominant hand, which looks like the ASL number "1", rather than an established location for a previously discussed person, toward which the sign CONVINCE moves (Fischer & Osugi, 2000, call this an example of an indexical classifier).

Aspect

Sign languages also have rich inflectional means for marking aspect, which pays attention to things like beginning points or endpoints of an action or state, or the frequency of an action irrespective of time. Taking the example of GO-TO again, one can inflect it for habitual aspect by reduplicating it rapidly (Fischer, 1973). This reduplication changes the meaning (but not the core lexical meaning) of the sign in a predictable way, in this case, indicating to go to a place regularly. If the same sign is repeated with a slower, circular movement, the result is continuous aspect, and the sign means to go to a place repeated (but perhaps not regularly) for a long time (Fischer, 1973). If one begins to sign GO-TO but abruptly stops before the sign is completed, this is unrealized inceptive aspect (Liddell, 1984).

Adjectives and nouns can also undergo aspect marking; for example, the sign SICK can be inflected for habitual aspect, resulting in the meaning "sickly" (Klima & Bellugi, 1979). The sign SAME can be inflected for continuous aspect to yield the meaning "monotonous."

Plural

Many verbs can form plurals by reduplicating while sweeping the hands horizontally (Fischer, 1973). If one signs GO-TO and repeats it while moving the hands in a horizontal arc, the resulting meaning is "go to many places." For nouns, the movement need not be horizontal and the meaning may be irregular. For example, one can sign SIGNATURE repeatedly while moving the hands downward to mean a petition.

There are also other ways of forming plurals, depending partly on the sign's phonological makeup. The sign LOOK in ASL is made with two fingers extended on each hand, and can be made with only one hand. If one extends all the fingers except the thumb and uses both hands, the sign means "many people look."

Tense

As noted above, tense is an inflectional affix that indicates time. ASL indicates time but not tense. Instead, ASL uses adverbials, often at the beginning of a discourse, as time markers. For example:

[3] LONG-AGO ME SMALL ME GO-TO[ASP:HABITUAL]
FISH WITH GRANDFATHER
'When I was a child, I often went fishing with my grandfather.'

At the beginning of this discourse, a time adverbial, LONG-AGO is used to set the time frame. This time frame is assumed until and unless another time is indicated. This can occur with either another time adverbial (e.g., TOMOR-ROW, meaning the next day in a past context) or a shift of the body forward to indicate a more future time or backward to indicate a more past time.

An indirect way of expressing past time is the use of the completive aspect form FINISH in ASL. In many languages, especially Creoles (Bickerton, 1981), aspect markers tend to become tense markers, but that process has not yet occurred in ASL:

[4] YOU EAT FINISH?
'Have you eaten yet?'/'did you eat?'

With the exception of a couple of signs with which it fuses phonologically (e.g., SEE, HEAR), FINISH is still viewed as a separate word in ASL, hence by definition not a true tense marker.

Most other Western sign languages express time in the same way as ASL. However, there appear to be two true past tense markers in NS. One is a nonmanual behavior (NMB), a mouth-picture [po] as in NS:

[5] Mouth: "po" (= past)
     fe: y-nq (= question)
     dh: ₂IU₁ [you tell X]
     nh: ONNA [female_x] (= object)
     eyegaze: to addressee (= subject)
              'did you tell her?'[2]

The other is a manual sign, distinct from the NS sign OWARU ("finish"). It cannot be separated from the verb; it never occurs except after a verb, and is accompanied by the mouthing [ta], which is how the past-tense morpheme is pronounced in spoken Japanese.

Artificial sign systems (see Fischer, 1998) attempt to indicate tense with ASL forms such as PAST. However, Schick and Moeller (1992) show

that deaf children treat them as free forms, rather than as indivisible affixes on verbs.

Derivational and Other Word-Formation Processes

How do sign languages make new words with new or different content or form class? One example of a derivational process in English is the addition of the suffix -able to the verb believe to make it an adjective (believable) and then adding the prefix un- to negate it (unbelievable).

Changing of Grammatical Category

Supalla and Newport (1978) report on a subset of verbs that have corresponding nouns whose movements are different from those of the verbs. They suggest a derivational process for deriving nouns and verbs from one underlying form, adding the different types of movement when the derivation occurs. Typically, verbs have one continuous motion, while nouns have repeated, restrained movement.[3] When these derived forms enter inflectional processes such as continuous aspect, the differences in movement persist, since derivational morphological processes usually precede inflectional processes. Another example of a change of category would be the addition of the suffix AGENT to a verb like TEACH to create the noun TEACHER.

Classifiers

Classifiers are another way in which word formation in sign languages is highly productive (see Supalla, 1986). In this chapter, discussion is confined to classifiers that are represented by handshapes. When used in a verb of motion or location, a classifier functions roughly as an anaphoric pronoun; it refers back to a preceding noun (the antecedent). Here is a simple example, using what is generally known as a *handle* or *instrumental* classifier (cl.) in the dominant hand and a *semantic* classifier in the nondominant hand:

[6] dh: BOOK PUT[CL:HANDLE]
     nh: cl: long flat object
     'put the book (on a shelf)'

Classifiers are also used to coin new words. Once accepted, antecedents for these words are not required. Recent coinages involving handshapes indicating thin, flat objects include signs for laptop and handheld computers.

Classifiers as well as path movements are among the most iconic elements of sign languages; that is, there is a nonarbitrary connection between the sign and its referent. Of course, not all aspects of sign languages are iconic; sign languages contain many arbitrary elements, which is why there is no universal sign language and why users of one sign language cannot understand users of another. By the same token, the role of iconicity in spoken languages has often been minimized, pushed to the margins of sound symbolism. Spoken languages in fact differ in terms of how much iconicity they employ. In Bantu languages like Xhosa, there is a class of words called "ideophones" with a distinctive phonology for evoking sounds. Spoken Japanese also has a large repertoire of ideophones. The proportion of iconic elements in sign languages is probably higher than for spoken languages. Sign languages exploit iconicity because they can, again probably due to modality differences (Fischer, 1979; Mayberry, 1978). Most iconic elements discussed here have some characteristic form or movement that signs can imitate. However, typically there are no corresponding noises that spoken language could capture with speech sounds.

Compounding

As mentioned above, a compound is a word resulting from the combination of two other words. As described by Newport and Bellugi (1978), when two words or signs form a compound, certain deletions occur. For example, if the first member of the compound has repeated movement in isolation, the repetition of that movement is lost in a compound. This is analogous to the weakening of the vowel of the second member of a compound in English examples like "chairman." When a compound is reduplicated for plural or habitual, in ASL only the second member of the compound repeats.

Compounding is still a very productive process in the sign languages of the world. Consider the following relatively new compounds in ASL:

[7]   NAKED^ESCAPE
       'streaker'

[8]   ELECTRIC^M-A-I-L
       'e-mail' (ELECTRIC is usually signed with repeated movement; in the compound, only one movement occurs)

Phonology

In spoken language, phonology is the level of analysis at which meaningless elements are combined to form meaningful elements. The notions of features, segments, and syllables are important units of phonological analysis, regardless of modality. Words are composed of smaller, meaningless segments such as in [b][æ][t] (bat). A change in any of these three segments may result in a different word (e.g., [k][æ][t] (cat), [b][ʌ][t] (but), [b][æ][g] (bag)) but [b] has no meaning by itself. A segment that makes a difference in meaning is called a "phoneme."

Sign Parts

Stokoe (1960) was the first linguist to realize that signs are not unanalyzed wholes. He analyzed signs into meaningless parts he called "cheremes," but which most linguists now call phonemes. The difference between spoken and signed languages, Stokoe pointed out, is that the phonemes in the former are sequential, while in the latter they appear to be simultaneous. Stokoe grouped his phonemes into three types: active handshapes (what moves), location (on face, body, or another hand), and movement. Later, orientation (the way that hands point or face or interact with each other) was added as a fourth phoneme type (Battison, 1978):

[9]

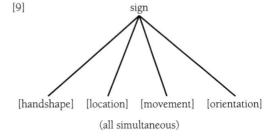

(all simultaneous)

Sign Features

Let us return to the segment [b]. Is it an unanalyzable whole, or can it be analyzed further? A comparison of [b] with [d] reveals that they are similar in several respects but different in one: they are both voiced (cf. [p], which is not voiced); they are both stops (cf. [v], which is continuous), and they are both oral (cf. [m], which is nasal). But [b] and [d] differ in point of articulation. Linguists capture these similarities and differences through the level of "features," which are units below the level of the segment. In our example, [b] and [d] would share the features [+voiced], [-continuant], and [-nasal]. Phonological processes often apply to segments that share a particular feature. For example, in some languages, a voiced stop, whether it is [b], [d], or [g], might become voiceless when in final position in a word.

Can sign phonemes also be broken down further? There have been attempts to define distinctive feature systems that analyze, for example, the handshape unit into smaller, truly atomic parts (Boyes-Braem, 1981; Friedman, 1976; Hawes & Dauenhauer, 1978; Mandel, 1981). Some of the proposed possible features for handshape refer to spread versus closed fingers and number of fingers extended. In some cases, such as for movement and location units, it has proven to be more difficult to come up with a coherent set of features. Brentari (1998) and van der Kooij (2002) offer recent discussions of proposed feature systems. A problem with previously proposed systems of features is that they are too rich (i.e., they encode too much phonetic detail that does not matter for distinguishing segments). Van der Kooij (2002) argues that the nondistinctive nature of these phonetic properties is due to two sources: phonetic predictability and iconicity. With respect to phonetic predictability at the outset of studying any new language, signed or spoken, extreme precision is necessary because investigators do not know a priori what aspects of sound or gesture are truly distinctive. Proposals for a reduced set of features require phonetic implementation rules, which van der Kooij (2002) supplies. This topic is also discussed in Crasborn (2001).

The iconicity argument is potentially controversial. It has long been noticed that many signs in sign languages are what is called "iconic" ("motivated"): aspects of the form of signs reflect aspects of the shape or action of referents. In early sign language work, it seemed crucial to deemphasize the importance of iconicity to validate the claim that sign languages have duality of patterning (independence of form and meaning, claimed to be a defining property of human language) and thus have a phonology at all. However, given the obvious relevance of iconicity, the proper question is, how can both iconicity and phonological compositionality be accounted for? The answer,

according to van der Kooij (2002), lies in allowing the lexical structure of signs to contain a specification of (iconically driven) phonetic properties alongside a phonological structure. The two routes in phonetic predictability and iconicity allow significant 'cleaning up' of the phonology which, as a result, can be shown to be quite restricted and in accordance with structural principles that appear to play a crucial role in spoken language phonology as well (van der Hulst, 2000; see Mathur, 2001, for similar discussion regarding the specification of agreement).

Sequencing

As mentioned above, Stokoe's (1960) model of the sign presented the phonemes as being simultaneous. Yet signs do have beginnings and endings, and it is possible, for example, to perform a sign backwards; the result may be an actual sign or may be nonsense. Signers would not be able to sign backward if, in their minds, signs were truly simultaneous. Furthermore, rules for agreement make reference to beginnings and endings of movements.

Phonological sequencing in sign has been a productive area of research for almost 20 years. Some proposals are discussed here in a simplified form, not necessarily in agreement with the original authors. Newkirk (1998) first drew attention to the need to recognize sequential structure. Liddell and Johnson (1989) proposed a linear sequential structure consisting of holds (H) and movements (M) to which other elements attach: [HMH]. Later researchers (e.g., Perlmutter, 1992; Sandler, 1986) incorporated essentially the same notion while using position or location instead of hold. The sequential parts of the movement (initial location [L], movement, and final location) property came to be referred to as "segments" (also called "skeletal positions"), and the internally complex location/movement property [LML] reminded researchers of the notion of syllables. Even though sequential structure had now been recognized by collapsing location and movement into a linear structure, the three remaining units, handshape, orientation, and [LML], were still taken to be simultaneous. To bring this out and also to highlight the resemblance between the [LML] skeleton and the notion of syllable, other types of diagrams (e.g., example 10) came to be used instead of the one in example 9:

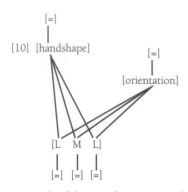

Each of the L and M units are linked to feature bundles ([=]) indicating location and properties of the movement, while handshape features and orientation features are spread over all positions in the skeleton. However, it is not the case that handshape and orientation always remain completely constant across all segments. Apart from movement of the whole hand (often called global or path movement), there can also be local movement involving either rotation of the hand (orientation change) or movement of the fingers (e.g., aperture change or wiggling). Thus the notion of movement is relevant not only in relation to the location of the whole hand, but also in relation to handshape and orientation. It would seem, then, that one needs to recognize three skeletons rather than one. In each case the units of the skeletons would have their features indicating beginning and end position and movement type (which are not indicated in example 11):

[11]

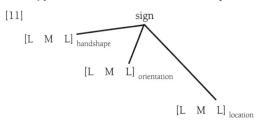

The diagram in example 11 seems to undermine the use of the term "syllable," because now there are three skeletons rather than one. There is, however, an interesting point to be made here which allows us coherently to maintain the terms "segment" and "syllable" cross-modally (van der Hulst, 2000).[4] Phonological categorization of the phonetic substance proceeds in two dimensions: vertical (sequential) and horizontal (simultaneous). Spoken language has long been considered purely in terms of an absolute precedence of vertical slicing over horizontal slicing. The vertical slicing produces a sequence of segments that can be called

syllabic structure. When the vertical slicing is completed, the horizontal slicing divides individual segments into co-temporal features, organized into units such as place, manner, and voicing. Consequently, each feature is contained within a single segment (although this idea has been relativized in Goldsmith, 1979).

Stokoe's original insight that all properties of signs are simultaneous can be said to reflect the fact that in sign language horizontal slicing of the signal takes precedence over vertical slicing, making the result of the latter (syllable structure) subordinate to segmental structure. The sequential organization thus reflects a vertical slicing that effectively produces subphonemic syllable structure. If this view is correct, single (monomorphemic) signs are monosegmental, while the smaller units of handshape, orientation, and location are subphonemic units on a par with subsegmental (simultaneous) units such as manner, place, and voicing in spoken language phonemes (van der Hulst, 1993, 1995, 2000). This difference between signed and spoken language seems due to the fact that visual information is available largely in parallel, whereas auditory information is available largely sequentially. (Apparent monomorphemic bisegmental signs are often frozen remnants of fingerspelled words, or frozen [hidden] compounds.)

Phonological Processes and Restrictions

In contrast to the static aspects of sign language phonology discussed above, what happens when signs are combined both morphologically and syntactically remains a seriously understudied area of sign phonology, although phonological effects in word formation and sentence-level phenomena have been described (Brentari, 1998; Sandler, 1989; Wilcox, 1992). Below are three examples.

First, in compound formation the handshape or orientation of one member may replace or combine with the handshape of the other member. This process can apply either regressively (the handshape of the second member of the compound is used throughout the whole sign) or progressively (the handshape of the first member of the compound continues throughout the sign). This is a genuine case of assimilation, a phonological process that conspires to ensure the preferred one handshape per word. Such processes are an extension of the single handshape or orientation that occurs as the default case within simple signs.

Second, just as in spoken language certain sequences of segments are disallowed, in sign languages certain combinations of handshapes and orientations are not permitted. Thus, a user of English knows that "brick" is a real word, and "blick" is a possible word (it could be used to name a new detergent), but "bnick" is not a possible English word. Analogously, in ASL, thumbs can touch only at the tips, which is why there is a difference in handshape between signs like SHOES (two "S" hands side by side with proximal sides touching) and WITH (two A hands facing, knuckles touching). In ASL "A" and "S" count as the same. The variants used in WITH and SHOES are determined by the fact that the knuckles of the thumbs cannot touch, so they effectively move out of the way. This constraint might not hold for other sign languages.

The third example concerns signs made with both hands. In these signs, either one hand functions as the place of articulation or both hands perform parallel actions with the same handshape. Brentari (1998) and van der Kooij (2002) have discussed one phonological process that drops one hand in two-handed symmetrical signs.

Syntax

This section discusses how sentences are put together in sign languages. A few examples beyond the level of the sentence are also discussed.

Influence of Spoken Languages and Education

In almost every country with a Deaf community, there will also be a sign language that is distinct from the spoken language of the community surrounding it. The families of sign languages do not coincide with spoken language families; for example, ASL and Langue de Signes Française (LSF) are in the same family, but British Sign Language (BSL) is in a different family and is mutually unintelligible with ASL.

Through contact and education, spoken languages can influence the grammars of sign languages. It is probably no accident that the basic structure of ASL is subject-verb-object and has other parallels to English, while the basic structure of NS is subject-object-verb and has other parallels to Japanese. Grosjean (1996) has pointed out that most signers are to some degree bilingual, and it is common in bilingual situations for a dominant language to influence the structure of a minority one. It is, however, important to note that even if a sign language exhibits the same basic word order as the spoken language, the sign language is not necessarily therefore identical to the spoken language. Conversely, the fact that an utterance does not follow the word order of the spoken language does not automatically mean that it is grammatical in the sign language of the community; it may be ungrammatical in *any* language.

Another way in which the spoken language of a region influences its sign language is the use of the writing system, especially to expand vocabulary. ASL and NS use fingerspelling (letter-for-letter visual transcription of written words) in addition to lexical signs (Padden, 1991). Further, in ASL and some other sign languages, some signs, such as I, FAMILY, and IDENTITY are initialized; that is, the sign is made with a handshape that represents the fingerspelled first letter of the corresponding English word. Although critics have condemned initialization, its use probably goes back to Old LSF. The sign DOCTOR, for example was formerly made with an M handshape; the French for "doctor" is *médecin*. Asian sign languages also borrow elements of the writing systems of the spoken languages; the sign for PERSON in both NS and Chinese Sign Language (CSL) show the shape of the character 人, NS by drawing the character in the air, and CSL by placing the index fingers of each hand in a configuration to show its shape.

Elements of the writing system can become a more integral part of the sign language. Generally, a sign can have no more than two handshapes. When a fingerspelled word is further incorporated into ASL, medial letters will be lost and replaced by a movement envelope (Akamatsu, 1985), which becomes more salient as the word is integrated into the phonological system. Examples include #JOB and #EARLY, in which only the first and last letters are visible, while the dominant hand gains movement (Battison, 1978).

When parts of the writing system become more integrated, they can participate in inflection or derivation. In ASL, for example, the fingerspelled word N-O first became a borrowed sign #NO, changing the pronunciation of the N and gaining repetition. Then it became a verb meaning 'to say no to' and gained inflection for object, subject, and number. In NS, one can substitute number handshapes for the unmarked "1" in the sign for person and correspondingly modify the meaning to "two persons," "10 persons," and so on.

If Deaf people are not exposed to the educational system, there is less chance for the spoken language to influence the sign language structure. Until recently, Thailand, for example, had no organized system for educating deaf children; Thai Sign Language makes little use of fingerspelling, and signed Thai (Thai Sign Language signs in spoken Thai order, analogous to using ASL or BSL signs in English word order) is quite rare (J. Woodward, personal communication, December 16, 2001). In contrast, some form of sign language has been used in American education for almost 200 years. In the United States, switching between signed English and ASL is quite common, especially in contexts where hearing people are present.[5]

Basic and Derived Word and Constituent Orders

As stated above, the basic constituent order of ASL is SVO, and the basic word order of NS is SOV. However, the grammar may have rules that change the basic order. Consider, for example, the use of classifiers. Because most classifiers are anaphoric, they require antecedents. Antecedents generally must precede classifiers. Assuming the classifier is in a predicate, that predicate must then occur last. Similarly, when an agreement verb requires that referential loci be set up first, the resulting sentence will have the order NP (noun phrase) NP verb. An example is:

[12] COW$_a$ INDEX HORSE$_b$ INDEX$_a$KICK$_b$
    'The cow kicked the horse.'

If the direction of the verb movement is reversed, the meaning will be "the horse kicked the cow." The presence of inflection makes the word order more flexible, and the necessity for an antecedent requires a change from the basic word order. Note that in an utterance such as that in example 12, the referential loci that attach to the verb are also anaphoric.[6]

Topicalization

In ASL, the use of classifiers and verb agreement necessitates a change from the basic word order. Most sign languages also have a process called "topicalization," where a noun phrase that the sentence or discourse is in some sense about (i.e., that represents the topic of the sentence) moves to the beginning of the utterance. The topic occurs with a special non-manual behavior (NMB) and continues until another topic is introduced (Fischer, 1973; Liddell, 1980). Notably, it does not need to be repeated in later sentences in a longer discourse, resulting in sentences with gaps that are filled in by the viewer who is cognizant of that discourse topic. An example of a topicalized structure is given below:

[13] BOOK, WHERE BUY?
    'As for the book, where did [you] buy [it]?'

Generally, topicalization occurs only in main clauses, and the topicalized constituent must indeed move to the beginning of the sentence. It can, however, move from an embedded clause:

[14] BOOK, WHO YOU THINK WANT BUY?
    'As for the book, who do you think wants to buy it?'

The Role of Nonmanuals

It has been suggested that in sign languages the face and the attitudes of the body serve the same function as intonation does in spoken languages. Signing without facial expression is certainly boring for deaf people, just as someone speaking in a monotone can put a listener to sleep. But NMBs such as facial expression and body shift are more than just intonation; in some ways they are closer to grammatical (or sometimes lexical) tone in spoken language, in that they contribute to differences in meaning. In some African languages (Goldsmith, 1979), a tone melody of high–low versus low–high can differentiate between present and past tense; in English, the noun "conduct" is stressed differently from the verb "conduct." In Chinese, depending on the tone, *ma* can mean "horse" or "mother." Recall that example 5 shows that in NS a mouth-picture like "po" can make a difference between present and past tense; this is analogous to the use of tone in Kwa (Meier, 1983) to distinguish present from future.

A second way in which NMBs are important is in showing the scope of what logicians and linguists call operators such as negation and question. The NMB for negation is either a headshake or a frown (Baker & Cokely, 1980); the NMB for a yes/no question is a raising of eyebrows and widening of the eyes, possibly with other concomitant behaviors. In ASL, the NMB for a wh-question involves eye-narrowing and furrowing of the brows. Consider these examples (hn = head nod):

```
     neg                        hn
```
[15] ME UNDERSTAND PHYSICS, MATHEMATICS
'I don't understand physics, but I do understand math.'

```
t                neg      hn
```
[16] ME UNDERSTAND PHYSICS, MATHEMATICS
'What I understand is not physics, but mathematics.'

In both examples 15 and 16, the line above the sentence indicates how far the NMB extends. Although the hands are doing the same thing, the meaning is different because what is being questioned or negated differs. Note that in these examples no inherently negative sign such as NOT is present; the negative facial expression serves as the only negator in the sentence. The same can occur in wh-questions. There are, of course, real wh signs such as WHO, WHERE, HOW, and so on. In addition, however, Lillo-Martin and Fischer (1992) have remarked the existence of what they call covert wh-constructions, words or phrases that are not normally considered to be wh-words but are made so by the addition of a wh-facial expression. For example, if someone utters either example 17 or 18, they are asking what book the addressee is reading:

```
     Wh
```
[17] YOU READ BOOK

```
     Wh
```
[18] BOOK YOU READ

In fact, as Lillo-Martin and Fischer (1992) have suggested, there are a number of signs that have been considered ordinary wh-words in ASL that can be reanalyzed as ordinary signs with the wh-facial expression added; in some cases, there is also a phonological change in the sign as well. Example

would include HOW-MANY (the sign MANY accompanied by a wh-facial expression but with added upward initial movement) and WHAT-FOR (the sign FOR with repeated and somewhat restrained motion). The examples in 19 and 20 show that even a subject or object can be inferred from a wh-facial expression:

```
     Wh
```
[19] HAPPEN
'What happened?'

```
     Wh
```
[20] EAT
'What [are you] eating?'

Both our own investigations and reports of native signers have helped confirm the existence of covert wh-facial expressions in NS, CSL, and several European sign languages.

As demonstrated in examples 17 and 18, in ASL (as in French), a wh-phrase can be fronted or can remain in its original position. How to analyze sentences like example 18 has been an object of intense discussion in recent sign language research. Petronio and Lillo-Martin (1997) have argued that such sentences are structured exactly like their English equivalent, while others (Neidle et al., 2000) have argued that the fronted wh-elements are in fact topics. (We agree with Petronio and Lillo-Martin because of sentences like example 13, which contains both a topic and a fronted wh-expression, which always must be in that order.)

Other structures in many sign languages also use NMBs for grammatical purposes. One is conditionals (if-then constructions; Baker & Padden, 1978, Fischer, 1978), which, like questions and topics, involve a brow raise; another is one type of relative clause (a clause that modifies a noun) first described by Liddell (1978); the NMB can involve a chin tuck and a tense grin.[7]

Simple and Complex Structures

Every language, signed or spoken, needs to express certain basic concepts and relationships. Some languages do so in the syntax, some with inflections, others with intonation. As discussed above, for example, a language like English expresses relations among elements almost entirely by using constituent order: "the cat chased the dog" differs from "the dog chased the cat" only in the order of elements, yet clearly the meaning is different. Latin and ASL, in contrast, can show these kinds of relations by using different inflections; in Latin, those inflections tend to be on the nouns involved, whereas in ASL they tend to be on the verb (see Nichols, 1986, for discussion of these two types of languages). As with sign languages discussed earlier, all languages have to express negation and various kinds of questions. Below are some other structures found in sign languages.

Clefts, or Rhetorical Questions

Baker and Cokely (1980) describe a structure they call a rhetorical question (rh-9). It, too, uses a specific NMB. A simplified example is

   t____
[21] P-A-T DUMB, WORK HERE GALLAUDET,
   rh-q_____
   LIVE "WHAT" O-C.
   'Pat's dumb; he works at Gallaudet, but where he lives is Ocean City.'

Wilbur (1995) argues that sentences like example 21 are not rhetorical questions at all (because rhetorical questions such as "are you kidding?" or "who do you think you are?" specifically are not answered). Rather, she suggests that these are what linguists call "pseudoclefts," as exemplified in the translation of example 21.

Sentential Complements

In addition to relative clauses and cleft structures, another common way of combining sentences in a language is to make a clause the subject or object of a sentence. English examples are given in examples 22–24, with the clauses underlined.

[22] The doctor says *that you should rest.*

[23] She regrets *having said that.*

[24] *For you to quit now* would be impossible.

Not much has been published on the equivalents of these types of sentences in signed languages. Padden (1981) discussed infinitives in ASL. From our observations, the tendency seems to be to put the clause first, possibly as a topic, followed by the predicate to which it is attached; an example is

[25] RAIN WILL, ME FEEL
   'I have a feeling it's going to rain.'

Paraphrases also occur; example 24 is really a conditional, and could therefore be signed as

  Conditional_____
[26] YOU QUIT NOW IMPOSSIBLE

The expression of complex ideas in complex sentences is an area of sign language structure that clearly warrants more research.

Summary and Conclusions

The serious linguistic study of sign languages is still in its infancy, or at best adolescence; it has been going on for only about 45 years, compared with spoken language linguistics, which goes back well over 1,000 years. Sign languages have phonological, morphological, and syntactic structures that are as complex as those structures found in spoken languages. The same levels of analysis have been found for both signed and spoken languages. Contact with education in dominant spoken languages can influence sign language grammar, but, the channel in which sign languages are communicated has countervailing effects on the grammar, especially in simultaneity and iconicity. The space allotted here is obviously inadequate to provide a complete grammatical sketch of ASL or any other sign language. It is hoped that through highlighting important issues and references to other works that readers' appetite for further reading in this important area will have been whetted.[8] Both for educational reasons and for its own intrinsic value, the linguistic study of sign languages clearly merits further study.

Notes

Research on NS reported on here was supported by a fellowship from the Japan Foundation awarded to Susan Fischer.

1. The notational conventions used here are as follows: all signs are glossed in capital letters. ASL signs are represented with capitalized words in English, and Japanese signs are represented as words in Japanese. If one sign requires more than one spoken language word, the glosses are hyphenated, as in the gloss for LONG-TIME-AGO. Aspect marking is represented by superscripts, while locus and/or agreement marking is represented by subscripts. In more complicated examples, there are separate lines for each hand (dh-dominant hand; nh-nondominant hand), as well as

separate lines to show the scope of facial expressions and other nonmanuals. Fingerspelled words are shown with hyphens separating letters, e.g., M-A-I-L. INDEX means a pointing gesture.

2. f.e. = facial expression; $_2IU_x$ shows second person subject and third person object.

3. It is important to note that not all verbs or nouns fit into this pattern. Specifically, some verbs have repeated motion already and do not have corresponding nouns.

4. van der Hulst (2000) and van der Kooij (2002) furthermore argue that the M unit in all three cases is superfluous.

5. It is not necessary for hearing persons to be present to have code-switching. Deaf–deaf dyads will code-switch as well; for a detailed discussion of influences on language choice in hearing people, see Ervin-Tripp (1972).

6. Padden (1990) argues that utterances like example 12 actually constitute a mini-discourse with each index constituting a separate predicate. If that is the case, then we would have a single-word predicate in the third sentence, $_aKICK_b$, and the question of word order would be moot.

7. Fisher and Johnson (1982) argue that the clauses Liddell described are mostly those with definite heads (e.g., English "the boy" whom I saw). Relative clauses with indefinite heads (e.g., "a boy" who can help me) often use a different structure, as exemplified below, which does not have the characteristic NMB found by Liddell.

ME SEARCH MAN SELF HELP₁ WASHING-MACHINE.
'I'm looking for a man who can help me with the laundry.'

8. Existing reference grammars include Baker & Cokely (1980) for ASL; Moody (1983) for LSF; Sutton-Spence & Woll (1999) for BSL; and Johnston (1989) for Auslan. Other useful sources include Wilbur (1987) and journals such as *Sign Language & Linguistics* and *Sign Language Studies*.

References

Akamatsu, C. T. (1985). Fingerspelling formulae: A word is more or less than the sum of its letters. In W. C. Stokoe & V. Volterra (Eds.), *Proceedings of the 3rd international symposium on sign language research* (pp. 126–132). Rome/Silver Spring, MD: CNR/Linstok Press.

Baker, C., & Cokely D. (1980). *American Sign language: A teacher's resource text on grammar and culture.* Silver Spring, MD: TJ Press.

Baker, C., & Padden, C. A. (1978). Focusing on the nonmanual components of ASL. In P. Siple (Ed.), *Understanding language through sign language research* (pp. 27–57). New York: Academic Press.

Battison, R. (1978). *Lexical borrowing in American Sign Language.* Silver Spring, MD: Linstok Press.

Bergman, B. (1980). On localization in the Swedish Sign Language. In I. Ahlgren & B. Bergman (Eds.), *Papers from the first international symposium on sign language research* (pp. 81–92). Leksand: Sveriges dövas riksförbund.

Bickerton, D. (1981). *Roots of language.* Ann Arbor, MI: Karoma Publishers.

Boyes-Braem, P. (1981). *Distinctive features of the handshape in American Sign Language.* Unpublished doctoral dissertation, University of California, Berkeley.

Brentari, D. (1998). *A prosodic model of sign language Phonology.* Cambridge, MA: MIT Press.

Crasborn, O. (2001). *Phonetic implementation of phonological categories in sign language of the Netherlands.* Unpublished doctoral dissertation, Leiden University, Leiden, the Netherlands.

Ervin-Tripp, S. (1972). An analysis of the interaction of language, topic and listener. In J. J. Gumperz & D.H. Hymes (Eds.), *Directions in sociolinguistics* (pp. 86–102). New York: Holt, Rinehart, & Winston.

Fischer, S. (1973). Two processes of reduplication in the American Sign Language. *Foundations of language, 9,* 469–480.

Fischer, S. (1978). Sign language and creoles. In P. Siple (Eds.), *Understanding language through sign language research* (pp. 309–331). New York: Academic Press.

Fischer, S. (1979). Many a slip 'twixt the hand and the lip: Applying linguistic theory to non-oral language. In R. Herbert (Eds.), *Metatheory III: Application of linguistics in the human sciences* (pp. 45–75). East Lansing, MI: Michigan State University Press.

Fischer, S. (1998). Critical periods for language acquisition: consequences for deaf education. In A. Weisel (Eds.), *Issues unresolved: new perspectives on language and deaf education* (pp. 9–26). Washington, DC: Gallaudet University Press.

Fischer, S., & Johnson, R. (1982, December). *Nominal markers in ASL.* Paper presented at the Linguistic Society of America annual meeting, San Diego.

Fischer, S., & Osugi, Y. (2000, July). *Thumbs up vs. giving the finger: indexical classifiers in ASL and NS.* Paper presented at the 7th TISLR conference, Amsterdam.

Friedman, L. (1976). *Phonology of a soundless language:*

Phonological structure of ASL. Doctoral dissertation, University of California, Berkeley.

Goldsmith, J. (1979) *Autosegmental phonology*, New York: Garland Press.

Grosjean, F. (1996). Living with two languages and two cultures. In I. Parasnis (Eds.), *Cultural and language diversity and the deaf experience* (pp. 20–37). Cambridge: Cambridge University Press.

Hawes, D. M., & Dauenhauer, J. L. (1978). Perceptual features of the manual alphabet. *American Annals of the Deaf, 123,* 464–474.

Johnston, T. (1989). *Auslan: The sign language of the Australian deaf community: Vol. 1*. Unpublished doctoral dissertation, University of Sydney, Sydney, Australia.

Klima, E., & Bellugi, U. (1979). *The signs of language*. Cambridge, MA: Harvard University Press.

Liddell, S. K. (1978). Nonmanual signals and relative clauses in American Sign Language. In P. Siple (Eds.), *Understanding language through sign language research* (pp. 59–90). New York: Academic Press.

Liddell, S. K. (1980). *American Sign Language syntax*. The Hague: Mouton.

Liddell, S. K. (1984). Unrealized-inceptive aspect in American Sign Language: Feature insertion in syllabic frames. In J. Drogo, V. Mishra, & D. Tersten (Eds.), *Proceedings of the twentieth regional meeting of the Chicago linguistic society* (pp. 257–270). Chicago IL: Chicago Linguistics Society.

Liddell, S. K. (1995). Real, surrogate, and token space: Grammatical consequences in ASL. In K. Emmorey & J. S. Reilly (Eds.), *Language, gesture, and space* (pp. 19–41). Hillsdale, NJ: Lawrence Erlbaum Associates.

Liddell, S. K. (1996). Spatial representations in discourse: Comparing spoken and signed languages. *Lingua, 98,* 145–168.

Liddell, S. K., & Johnson, R. (1989). American Sign Language: The phonological base. *Sign Language Studies, 64,* 197–277.

Lillo-Martin, D., & Fischer, S. (1992, July). *Overt and covert Wh-constructions in ASL*. Paper presented at the fifth International Symposium on Sign Language Research, Salamanca, Spain.

Mandel, M. (1981). *Phonotactics and morphophonology in American Sign language*. Unpublished doctoral dissertation, University of California, Berkeley.

Mathur, G. (2001). *Verb agreement as alignment in signed languages*. MIT Working Paper in Linguistics #MATH01. Cambridge, MA: Massachusetts Institute of Technology.

Mayberry, R. (1978). Manual communication. In H. Davis, & S. R. Silverman (Eds.), *Hearing and deafness* (pp. 400–420). New York: Holt, Rinehart & Winston.

Meier, I. (1983). Making tone markings acceptable and easy. *Notes on Linguistics, 27,* 4–10. Summer Institute of Linguistics.

Meir, I. (1998) *Verb agreement in ISL*. Unpublished doctoral dissertation, Jerusalem and Haifa Universities.

Moody, W. (1983). *La langue des signes. Tome 1. Introduction à l'histoire et à la grammaire de la langue des signes*. Pairs: Ellipses.

Neidle, C., Kegl, J., Maclaughlin, D., Bahan, B., & Lee, R.G. (2000). *The syntax of American Sign Language*. Cambridge, MA: MIT Press.

Newkirk, D. (1998). On the temporal organization of movement in American Sign Language. *Sign Language and Linguistics, 1,* 173–211.

Newport, E. L., & Bellugi, U. (1978). Linguistic expression of category levels in a visual-gestural language: A flower is a flower is a flower. In E. Rosch & B. Lloyd (Eds.), *Cognition and categorization* (pp. 49–71). Hillsdale, NJ: Lawrence Erlbaum Associates.

Nichols, J. (1986). Head-marking and dependent-marking grammar. *Language, 62,* 156–119.

Padden, C. A. (1981). Some arguments for syntactic patterning in American Sign Language. *Sign Language Studies, 10,* 239–259.

Padden, C. A. (1988). *Interaction of morphology and syntax in American Sign Language*. New York: Garland.

Padden, C. A. (1990). The relation between space and grammar in ASL verb morphology. In C. Lucas (Eds.), *Sign language research. Theoretical issues* (pp. 118–132). Washington, DC: Gallaudet University Press.

Padden, C. A. (1991). The acquisition of fingerspelling in deaf children. In P. Siple & S. D. Fischer (Eds.), *Theoretical issues in sign language research: Vol. 2. Psychology* (pp. 191–210). Chicago: University of Chicago Press.

Perlmutter, D. M. (1992). Sonority and syllable structure in American Sign Language. *Linguistic Inquiry, 23,* 407–442.

Petronio, K., & Lillo-Martin, D. (1997). WH-movement and the position of spec-CP: Evidence from American Sign Language. *Language, 73,* 18–57.

Sandler, W. (1986). The spreading hand autosegment of ASL. *Sign Language Studies, 50,* 1–28.

Sandler, W. (1989). *Phonological representation of the sign: linearity and nonlinearity in ASL phonology*. Dordrecht: Foris Publications.

Schick, B., & Moeller, M. P. (1992). What is learnable in manually-coded English sign system. *Applied Psycholinguistics, 13,* 313–340.

Stokoe, W. C. (1960). *Sign language structure.* Silver Spring, MD: Linstok Press.

Supalla, T. (1986). The classifier system in American Sign Language. In C. Craig (Ed.), *Noun classification and categorization* (pp. 181–214). Philadelphia: J. Benjamins.

Supalla, T., & Newport, E. L. (1978). How many seats in a chair? The derivation of nouns and verbs in ASL. In P. Siple (Ed.), *Understanding language through sign language research* (pp. 91–132). New York: Academic Press.

Sutton-Spence, R., & Woll, B. (1999). *The linguistics of British Sign Language: An introduction.* Cambridge: Cambridge University Press.

van der Hulst, H.G. (1993). Units in the analysis of signs. *Phonology, 10,* 209–41.

van der Hulst, H. G. (1996). On the other hand. *Lingua, 98,* 121–143.

van der Hulst, H.G. (1995). Dependency relations in the phonological representations of signs. In H.

Bos & T. Schermer (Eds.), *Proceedings of the fourth European congress on sign language research* (pp. 11–38). Hamburg: Signum Press.

van der Hulst, H.G. (2000). Modularity and modality in phonology. In: N. Burton-Roberts, P. Carr, & G. Docherty (Eds.), *Phonological knowledge. Conceptual and empirical issues* (pp. 207–244) Oxford: Oxford University Press.

van der Kooij, E. (2002). *Phonological categories in Sign Language of the Netherlands; Phonetic implementation and iconicity.* Unpublished doctoral dissertation, Leiden University, Leiden, the Netherlands.

Wilbur, R. B. (1987). *American Sign Language: linguistic and applied dimensions* (2nd ed.). Boston: Little, Brown.

Wilbur, R. B. (1995). Why so-called rhetorical questions' are neither rhetorical nor questions. In H. F. Bos & G. M. Schermer (Eds.), *Sign language research 1994: Proceedings of the fourth European congress on sign language research* (pp. 149–170). Hamburg: Signum.

Wilcox, S. (1992). *The phonetics of fingerspelling.* Philadelphia: Benjamins.

24

Ronnie B. Wilbur

Modality and the Structure of Language

Sign Languages Versus Signed Systems

The goal of this chapter is to provide an explanation for the characteristics of natural signed languages that separate them from artificially created signing systems. These characteristics are a result of the adaptations that have taken place over time as generations have learned signed languages from birth. Adaptations are the emergent result of a variety of influencing factors, such as perceptual constraints, production constraints, processes of grammaticalization, and modality influences. At the same time, the resulting linguistic system must be easy to use and learn.

To approach these issues, this chapter views fully developed signed languages from the perspective of universal grammar (UG) by discussing the design features of a model of language that is intended to be universal to all languages. From this perspective, the capacity for language is simultaneously universal to all humans, varied across languages, and individual to each person's own experience and learned grammar. To study language, linguists approach the problem by asking the following types of questions:

1. What do all languages have in common?
2. What are the constraints on how languages may vary from each other?

3. How can languages be learned by children so regularly and quickly?

Each of these questions motivates a line of research that is both independent of and yet related to the others. With respect to the first question, researchers seek to identify absolute universals (no exceptions), strong tendencies (nearly no exceptions), and other patterns that may help construct the model of natural language. This universal model, when constructed, must also address the second question, for example, that some languages use tone for lexical purposes and others do not, or that some languages have strict word order constraints while others do not; or that some are spoken and some are signed. Finally, the model must be able to contribute to the third question regarding language acquisition.

The model itself must contain the design features for natural language. Theoretical linguists engage in model building. Using data from known languages, they evaluate how well different types of models account for answering the three questions, as well as predicting what will be found is as-yet-unstudied languages. Sign language research provides an opportunity to evaluate proposed models of natural language from a different perspective—

signed instead of spoken, seen instead of heard. For example, analysis of sign languages has provided support for specific pieces of linguistic understanding originally based on spoken languages. One consequence of investigations of the design features of natural language is an explanation for why artificially created signing systems (e.g., used for signing and speaking at the same time) do not behave like natural languages and are not allowed to evolve into them. The design features of natural languages, the features that constrain linguistic adaptations to the modality of perception and production, are the focus of this discussion.

Speech Is Not a Design Feature

The study of sign languages has made it clear that natural language is not the same thing as speech. To separate language from speech, early sign language research focused on demonstrating the linguistic nature of signed languages. Stokoe and colleagues (Stokoe, 1960; Stokoe, Casterline, & Croneberg 1965) analyzed sign structure into components comparable to the linguistic units present in spoken languages, such as the phonological forms that are used to build words, word compounds, and phrases. In doing so, he presented a linguistic model of sign structure that displayed the complex hierarchical organization and duality of patterning characteristics considered to be the hallmarks of natural language. Supplemented by the structural and grammatical aspects reported by Klima et al. (1979), the evidence for considering American Sign Language (ASL) as a natural language was irrefutable. The wider linguistic community was then required to shift to a modality-free definition of natural language, although exact definitions were not always articulated. One might say that the design features of a natural language include, but may not be limited to, a hierarchically organized, constituent-based system of symbol use that serves the needs of communities of users to efficiently produce and understand infinite numbers of novel messages and that is capable of being learned by babies from birth.

The existence of created signing systems, such as signed English (SE), provides insight into the "natural" in natural language. Sentences in ASL and spoken English with equivalent information are roughly equal in duration, whereas in SE they take at least 50% longer (Bellugi & Fischer, 1972; Wilbur & Nolen, 1986). Over time ASL has adapted to minimize the number of signs while maximizing the information in a message (Frishberg, 1975), whereas SE retains the sequential word order of English despite the fact that signs take longer to make than spoken words. It is this lack of adaptation that proves the rule: the design features of natural languages require an efficient fit with the perception and production requirements of the modality in which they are used; SE is not natural and does not fit its modality efficiently. This difference in efficiency between natural languages and created systems lies in the availability and use of 'layering'. Roughly, layering is the simultaneous use of multiple articulation channels to maximize information transfer. This chapter explains layering as a largely ignored design feature of natural language, illustrates how it works in various sign languages, and then considers the implications of its absence in SE.

Surface Design Options for Languages: Sequentiality and Simultaneity

Language is a vehicle for information transfer between individuals. It entails the process by which information in one person's mind is linguistically coded and physically transmitted to another person, who physically receives and linguistically decodes it and comes to possess the information that the transmitter intended to send. Traditionally, transfer involves speech articulation and acoustic perception. With signed languages, the modality is visual/gestural, so transmission involves the hands and other articulators and perception by the eyes.

There is a strong tendency for spoken languages to use sequential information transfer: phonemes occur in sequence; word formation involves affixing before, inside of, or after the stem; and sentence formation relies on the presentation of syntactic constituents in sequence. This is not to say that simultaneous information transfer does not occur in spoken languages. Some examples are simultaneous pitch patterns for intonation; lexical tone; ablauts (e.g., German plural); vowel harmony (Turkish, Finnish); and nasalization over large domains. However, such simultaneous options are greatly outnumbered by sequentiality in spoken languages, given the nature of, for example, the speed of articulation and the transmission of sound waves for perception. In contrast, signed languages rely heavily on simultaneous information transfer, even though, ultimately, signs must be put in sequence for production and perception:

> The fact that ASL is a language with complex organizational properties implies that it will share certain principles of organization with other languages. The fact that it is a language in a different modality (visual/spatial rather than auditory/vocal) implies that there will be differences in its principles of organization. ASL exhibits formal structuring at the same two levels as spoken languages (the internal structure of the lexical units and the grammatical structure underlying sentences). However, a fundamental difference between ASL and spoken languages is its surface organization: signed languages display a marked preference for co-occurring layered (as opposed to linear) organization (Wilbur, Klima, & Bellugi, 1983, p. 314).

Simultaneity in Signed Languages: How Layering Works

Layering is the linguistic organizational mechanism by which multiple pieces of information can be sent simultaneously; it requires that the articulation of each piece cannot interfere with the others. Thus, layering is a conspiracy of form (articulation) and meaning to allow more than one linguistically meaningful unit of information (morpheme) to be efficiently transferred simultaneously. An example in spoken languages is the use of tone in tone languages, wherein consonantal and vocalic segments are sequentially articulated while tone contours are simultaneously produced with them. The articulation of the tones uses an available production channel that does not interfere with the articulation of each segmental phoneme; both are distinctly produced and perceived.

How Are Signed Languages Layered Manually?

Within the manual portion of signing, there are a variety of layering options, nearly all of which are exploited for phonological, morphological, or syntactic purposes. The availability of two hands as independent articulators is one such example (Bat-

tison, 1978). One hand can articulate a one-handed sign (e.g., a noun, name, or adjective while the other hand points to a referent of the sign, either present in the discourse situation (deixis) or established in the discourse signing space (typically a spatial location abstractly associated with the referent).

A second type of layering is the use of classifiers. Classifiers, originally reported for ASL by Frishberg (1975), are "certain handshapes in particular orientations to stand for certain semantic features of noun arguments" (p. 715) (also see Fischer & van der Hulst, this volume). Some ASL classifiers are shown in figure 24-1. These are taken from a story, *The Fox and the Stork*, narrated by Patrick Graybill in a dramatic format for a student audience. The fox invites the stork for dinner, serves the stork in a flat soup bowl which the fox can lick from (figure 24-1a) but from which the stork cannot eat (figure 24-1b). The stork then invites the fox for dinner and, distressed, goes home. Later the fox comes to dinner and the stork serves chopped fish in a tall narrow-necked container, which is fine for the stork's beak (figure 24-1c), but which the fox cannot manage (figure 24-1d). Figure 24-1e illustrates how the relationship of the two classifier handshapes conveys the main predicate of the sentence, namely, "swallowing a piece of fish." The layering of classifiers provides another source of simultaneous information transfer. In general, nouns must be introduced into the discourse first and then followed by the co-referential classifier. One-handed classifiers, or the nondominant hand from two-handed classifiers, can then be held in position while the dominant hand articulates one or more signs relevant to the referent of the first classifier.

In example 1 from Swedish Sign Language, the "hostess" and the "tray" are introduced, after which the nondominant hand used in CARRY-TRAY (figure 24-2a) is held to show where the glass is taken from (figure 24-2b) and that the hostess is still holding the tray while giving the glass to an unidentified person (figure 24-2c).[1]

[1] HOSTESS TRAY CARRY-TRAY TAKE-GLASS-FROM-TRAY GIVE$_3$-GLASS
'The hostess carried the tray, then took a glass from it and gave it to someone'

Example 1 also shows another layered classifier use; here the classifier handshape has been incorporated into the verb sign, so that the direct object of the

(a) 'fox tongue and flat bowl'   (b) 'stork beak and flat bowl'

(c) 'stork beak into
narrow container'   (d) 'fox tongue can't fit
narrow container'

(e) 'stork beak in air,
stork swallows food'

Figure 24-1. American Sign Language classifiers as contained in the story, *The Fox and the Stork*. Images from video.

verb can be articulated at the same time as the verb. This is seen in figure 24-2b, where the handshape for "glass" on the dominant hand and the handshape and position of "tray" on the nondominant hand, yields the layered verb complex "to remove something from a flat surface previously indicated to be a tray while holding something in the shape of a glass." Similarly, figure 24-2c conveys "to give something in the shape of a glass to someone while still holding the tray."

A third type of layering occurs when morphological information is "laid over" a basic lexical item. For example, if two individuals have been introduced into discourse and established in signing space, a verb may modify its starting location to reference one individual and its ending location to reference the other. Thus, there may be overt marking of verb agreement to indicate the associated referents, permitted by the ability to use each spatial location for a referent and the direction of hand movement for the verb.

This is not the only marker of agreement. Meir (1998) observed a further distinction in Israeli Sign Language (ISL): the direction of movement reflects the semantic/thematic (source, goal) structure of the agreement, whereas the *facing* of the hand, that is, which way the palm or fingertips are oriented, reflects the syntactic argument structure (subject, object). The facing is always toward the syntactic object, and the subject is marked by default. Figure 24-3a shows ISL $_1$HELP$_2$ "I help you" and figure 24-3b shows $_2$HELP$_1$ "you help me."

In so-called "backward" verbs, direction of movement and direction of facing are opposite each other: the subject is the goal and the object is the source. In the ISL sign $_2$TAKE-ADVANTAGE-OF$_1$ "I take advantage of you" (figure 24-3c) and $_1$TAKE-ADVANTAGE-OF$_2$ "you take advantage of me" (figure 24-3d), the movement starts at the source and moves to the goal, and the facing is toward the syntactic object, following the general rules, but unlike regular verbs, the source is not the subject, and the difference in thematic versus argument specifications are clearly seen as separate. Thus, there are two separate mechanisms available to be layered, the direction of movement and the facing of the hands or fingertips to the object of the verb.

A fourth type of layering is seen in verb modifications for aspectual and quantificational purposes. In their discussion of inflectional processes, Klima et al. (1979) suggested at least 8 types for

(a) CARRY-TRAY   (b) TAKE-GLASS-FROM-TRAY   (c) GIVE₃-GLASS

Figure 24-2. Classifiers in Swedish Sign Language including predicates: (a) CARRY-TRAY; (b) TAKE-GLASS-FROM-TRAY; (c) GIVE₃-GLASS. Images from video.

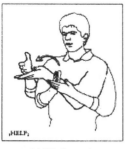
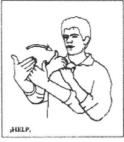

(a) 'I help you'   (b) 'You help me'

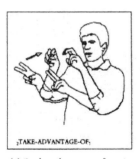

(c) 'I take advantage of you'   (d) 'You take advantage of me'

Figure 24-3. Regular and backward verbs in Israeli Sign Language (from Meir, 1998, reprinted with permission of John Benjamins Publishing.)

ASL and identified 11 phonological dimensions used to mark them. These latter fall into two groups that can be layered with respect to each other: (1) those that affect the rhythmic and dynamic temporal qualities of the movement and (2) those that affect the spatial arrangement of the movement (Wilbur et al., 1983). This phonological split is paralleled by a split in their linguistic functions. The meanings that result from the temporal modifications are interpreted with respect to the predicate

itself, whereas the spatial modifications contribute information about the arguments of the predicate.

Further layering can also occur. Klima et al. (1979) discuss combinations of "durational" and "exhaustive" on the sign GIVE. Durational alone on GIVE means "give continuously" (figure 24-4a). Exhaustive means "to each" (figure 24-4b), and, when embedded in durational, means "give to each, that action recurring over time" (figure 24-4c). In contrast, durational can be embedded in exhaustive, to yield a form meaning "give continuously to each in turn" (figure 24-4d). Embedding durational in exhaustive and then into durational yields "give continuously to each in turn, that action recurring over time" (figure 24-4e), a form that might be used to describe the distribution of food at a soup kitchen over the course of a winter. The required morphosyntactic information is layered on top of the lexical sign, conveying a bigger bundle of information in a complex sign in less time than would be required if each piece of information had to be signed separately; notice how many English words are needed to translate each complex sign. Further evidence for layering comes from the nonmanual channels, as discussed in the next section.

How Are Signed Languages Layered Nonmanually?

A unique aspect of signed languages is the systematic grammatical use of facial expressions and head or body positions. The nonmanual markers comprise a number of independent channels: the head, the shoulders, the torso, the eyebrows, the eyeballs (gaze), the eyelids, the nose, the mouth (upper lip, lower lip, mid-lip, lip corners), the tongue, the cheeks, and the chin. Each of these is capable of independent articulation and, with layering, com-

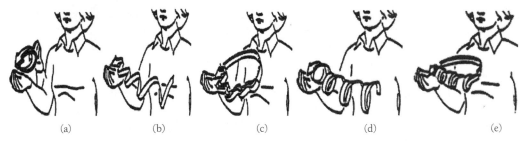

(a)   (b)   (c)   (d)   (e)

Figure 24-4. Embeddings in American Sign Language: (a) durational on GIVE; (b) exhaustive on GIVE, meaning "to each"; (c) exhaustive embedded in durational on GIVE, meaning "to give to each, recurring over time; (d) durational embedded in exhaustive on GIVE, meaning "give continuously to each in turn"; (e) durational embedded in exhaustive and then into durational, meaning "give continuously to each in turn, recurring over time." (Reprinted with permission of U. Bellugi and the Salk Institute for Biological Studies.)

plex combinations can be produced. In general, nonmanual cues may provide lexical or morphemic information on lexical items or indicate the ends of phrases or phrasal extent.

One source of layering is the use of nonmanual articulations for both grammatical and affective purposes, which are clearly separate (Baker & Padden, 1978; Coulter, 1978, 1979; Liddell, 1978). This separation is clearly seen in the acquisition of nonmanuals, with the early use of facial expressions for affective purposes and the later use for linguistic functions (Anderson & Reilly, 1997, 1998; Reilly, 2000; Reilly & Bellugi, 1996; Reilly, McIntire, & Bellugi, 1991; Reilly, McIntire, & Seago, 1992). In figure 24-5, affective facial expressions for "happy," "angry/stunned," and "bemused/sad" are seen from the story *The Fox and the Stork*. The expressions for

"happy" (figure 24-5a) and "angry/stunned" (figure 24-5b) are both produced while the sign for the narrow container is being held; that is, they are produced during holds that are at the end of a sentence (or the transition to the next one). In contrast, the affective facial expression for "bemused/sad" (figure 24-5c) is made while the sign for "go home" is articulated.

Mechanisms for Layering

There are a number of design features that permit multiple articulation of nonmanuals or affective facial expressions without mutual interference. One feature that separates affective and grammatical use is the articulation of the onset and offset—abrupt for syntactic functions, gradual otherwise (Baker-Shenk, 1983; Liddell, 1978, 1980).

(a) 'stork happy about   (b) 'fox angry about narrow   (c) 'stork goes home sad about
narrow container'   container'   the flat soup bowl'

Figure 24-5. Affective facial expressions in American Sign Language, as contained in the story, *The Fox and the Stork*. Images from video.

Another design feature is the coordination with syntactic constituents. For example, the grammatical negative headshake in ASL has an abrupt onset and offset and is coordinated with either the negative sign (if there is one) or the scope of the whole negative constituent (what is negated) (Veinberg & Wilbur, 1990). In contrast, negative headshakes used by nonsigners have gradual onsets and offsets, and occur in sentence positions seemingly unconnected with English syntax (Veinberg & Wilbur, 1990). Thus, affective use of negative headshakes in the dominant hearing culture does not have the specific constraints of articulation (abrupt start and stop) or timing with respect to the utterance that grammatical negative headshake displays in ASL. It is also clear that the linguistic use is most controlled; its onset/offset is regulated and its placement with respect to signs is specified. Presumably, there is a design feature that ensures that the linguistic uses are easily differentiated from nonlinguistic ones, as well as from each other.

The spatial distribution of nonmanuals across the face, head, and shoulders, providing clear and separate information channels, is another example of such a design feature (figure 24-6). In ASL, the nonmanual signals made on the face can be roughly divided into two groups, lower and upper. Although it is likely that other sign languages use this basic division, it is important to emphasize that the meanings associated with particular articulations are not universal, but language specific. Furthermore, nonmanual signals that appear to have the same function may in fact display very different behaviors when examined more closely.

To illustrate, consider the negative headshake, which has been examined in ASL (Veinberg & Wilbur, 1990; Wood, 1999), Swedish Sign Language (Bergman, 1995), and German Sign Language (*Deutsche Gebärdensprache* or DGS; Pfau & Glück, 2000; Pfau, in press), among many others. Pfau & Glück (2000) compare DGS and ASL negation. One difference is that ASL allows the negative sign to occur with a negative headshake (hs) on it alone as in example 2 but DGS does not (example 3; DGS glosses from Pfau, in press):

$$\overline{\text{hs}}$$
[2] JOHN NOT BUY HOUSE
     'John doesn't buy a house'

$$\overline{\phantom{\text{MUTTER BLUME KAUF}}\text{hs}}$$
[3] *MUTTER BLUME KAUF NICHT
     'Mother does not buy a flower'

In further contrast, DGS allows the negative headshake to directly negate just the verb with no manual negative sign (example 4), whereas at least one

Figure 24-6. Spatial layout of nonmanuals.

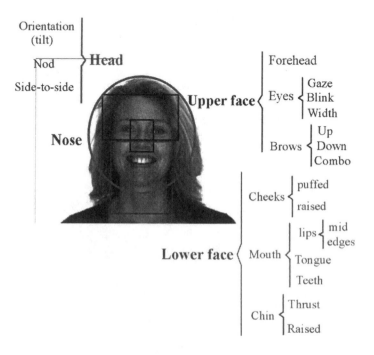

dialect of ASL does not (example 5) (Neidle et al. 2000; but see Veinberg & Wilbur, 1990 for a grammatical example from another dialect):

$$\overline{\text{hs}}$$
[4] MUTTER BLUME KAUF
'Mother does not buy a flower'

$$\overline{\text{hs}}$$
[5] *JOHN BUY HOUSE
'John doesn't buy a house"

Pfau (in press) argues that the domain of the negative headshake is syntactically determined in ASL, whereas it is determined phonologically in DGS. Thus the identification of similarities across sign languages (in this case, that they are both negative headshakes) may be misleading.

In her analysis of Danish Sign Language, Engberg-Pedersen (1990) focused on three nonmanual markers: squinted eyes, raised eyebrows, and pulled back chins. She argues that the raised eyebrows mark signs referring to thematically central information which is new or which the signer assumes the addressee is familiar with and can access without difficulty; they also mark thematic shifts. In contrast, squinted eyes are used on thematically central given information that the signer assumes may be difficult for the addressee to access (in their memory store). Pulling the chin back marks topics and may be accompanied by either raised brows (indicating thematic shift) or squinted eyes (indicating accessibility problem). Engberg-Pedersen concludes that the uses of these markers is entirely due to the signer's desire to accommodate the information to the addressee's memory and knowledge.

In contrast, the use of raised brows in ASL cannot be attributed solely to functional behavior (Coulter, 1978; Wilbur, 1996; Wilbur & Patschke, 1999). This is partly because of the fact that of the three types of topic marking ("t") with brow raise identified by Aarons (1994), one marks given/known information (Aaron's tm3) as in (example 6), one ("tm2") marks thematic shift to new topic, as in (example 7), and the third ("tm1") marks new information (example 8) ("who John really loves"). It is difficult to reconcile the use of brow raise marking on both old and new information from a pragmatic approach.

$$\overline{\text{br}}$$
[6] MARY$_a$, JOHN LOVE PT$_a$
'(You know) Mary, John loves her.'

$$\overline{\text{br}}$$
[7] VEGETABLE, JOHN LIKE CORN
'As for vegetables, John likes corn.'

$$\overline{\text{br}}$$
[8] JOHN NOT-LIKE JANE. MARY, HE LOVES *t*.
'John doesn't like Jane—it's *Mary* he loves.'

In ASL, brow raise is a feature of other constructions besides topics: conditional clauses, restrictive relative clauses, when-clauses, yes/no questions, the given clauses in wh-clefts, the new information in clefts, and generic subjects. There appears to be no such widespread use in Danish Sign Language, nor in several other sign languages. Hence, it would be both insufficient and frequently inaccurate to try to derive these linguistic usages directly from common cultural gestures without grammaticalization, which by definition means that something is brought under grammatical control and assigned a grammatical function. To be part of a natural language, nonmanual markers must have had an opportunity to evolve in this fashion, as, for example, the negative headshake that must start and stop in the right way and at the right time.

Lower Face Options

In ASL, the lower portion of the face is used to provide adverbial and adjectival information. The mouth, tongue, and cheeks provide meaningful markers that associate with specific lexical items and the phrases of which they are heads (e.g., noun/NP, verb/VP). Liddell (1978, 1980) identified three adverbial functions: (1) "mm," made with the lips pressed together, indicates "with pleasure or enjoyment of an activity"; (2) "th," made with lax jaw, slightly separated lips, and critically, a protruding tongue tip, indicates "carelessness or incorrectness"; and (3) "cs," made with a slight head tilt and shoulder raise, tight lips, and clenched teeth, indicates "recency or closeness in time or space." In Liddell's (1978) classic example (9), the nonmanual marking "mm" is adverbially associated with the predicate:

$$\overline{\text{mm}}$$
[9] MAN FISH [I:continuous]
'The man is fishing with relaxation and enjoyment.'

Similarly, puffed cheeks for "big, fat" might occur with a noun (e.g., TREE, TRUCK) and may also spread to other information in the NP (e.g., other adjectives). Numerous other configurations of lips, teeth, tongue, and cheeks have been identified for ASL (for overviews: Baker & Cokely, 1980; Reilly, 2000; Valli & Lucas, 1992; tongue positions and flaps in Davies, 1985). Again, these are linguistically controlled and must be learned.

Upper Face and Head Options

Traditional analyses of the upper face, head, and body positions were originally associated with specific syntactic structures, as though each cluster of nonmanuals were an unanalyzable whole (Baker & Padden, 1978; Baker-Shenk, 1983; Liddell, 1978, 1980). Coulter (1979) was among the first to identify the component pieces of these clusters and their individual functions. Aarons (1994), Baker-Shenk (1983), Liddell (1986), Wilbur (1994a, 1994b, 1995a, 1995b) and Bahan (1996) have subsequently identified functions for additional components. Upper face and head nonmanuals have a larger scopal domain than lower face nonmanuals. What the layering of upper face and head nonmanuals provides is information corresponding to prosody and intonation throughout the clause (Wilbur, 2000a; Brentari & Crossley, 2002). Lower face components can occur layered inside them.

It has been speculated that the source of raised eyebrows and lean forward in yes/no questions, for example, is derived from hearing person's gestures and facial expressions that accompany speech and that signal universal meanings to the viewer. Perhaps the best evidence that such speculations are off the mark is the fact that some signed languages do not use brow position to mark yes/no questions but use other markers instead (e.g., Austrian Sign Language, Hunger, Schalber, & Wilbur, 2000; Schalber, Hunger, Šarac, Alibašić, & Wilbur, 1999; Croatian Sign Language, Alibašić, Šarac, & Chen Pichler, 2002).

Scope Versus Edge Marking

Nonmanuals that are held for the duration of a signed phrase are domain markers; they show what signed information is layered under that particular nonmanual. They contrast in articulation with edge markers, which indicate the end of a phrase. Upper face and head domain markers are associated with two kinds of syntactic domains: c-command and checking domain. C(onstituent)-command domain markers are perhaps the most common. In ASL, these include negative headshake and brow-furrow

for wh-questions. Essentially, the nonmanual is articulated on all the signs following the element that triggers it, in this case negation or a wh-word or phrase. In contrast, brow raise is not articulated over all the signs that follow it and instead has a more complex explanation for when it occurs (Wilbur & Patschke, 1999). For example, if a topic is marked with a brow raise, the clause that follows does not have a brow raise unless it is itself a yes/no question (cf. example 6).

Edge markers indicate the end of particular phrases; clear cases occur *after* the last sign. One such example is the use of eyeblinks to mark the end of intonational phrases (Wilbur, 1994a). Some nonmanuals may be used for either domain or edge marking; in such cases, they are distinguished by another design feature: number of occurrences. For example, a single head nod can be used as an edge marker, whereas repeated head nodding can serve as a domain marker of assertion (Wilbur, 1994a).

Spatial Separation

Consider again the potential for layering given the spatial separation involved in these markers. Eyeblinks involve the eyes, specifically the eyelids, whereas eyegaze involves direction of eyeball looking. Many eyeblinks are accompanied by an eyegaze shift, that is, looking at a different location when the eyes reopen. Eyebrow position involves a different set of muscles than eyeblinks or eyegaze; thus all three can co-occur without interfering with each other. Head tilt involves the position of the head, whereas head nod and headshake are movements, hence separation by static versus dynamic; neck muscles are involved, but the absence or presence of movement differentiates tilt from nod and shake, while direction of movement differentiates nod (up/down) from shake (side/side). Head thrust takes advantage of the neck muscles that move the lower jaw/chin forward; nods (up/down) are differentiated by direction from thrust (forward). Body leans may be articulated in a variety of ways, including forward, backward, or sideways leaning of the head, head and shoulders, or upper body from the waist, or if the signer is standing, taking a step forward (Wilbur & Patschke, 1998) or backward (Winston, 1989). Again, the articulations required are distributed over the spatial layout of the face, head, and neck, permitting simultaneous, noninterfering production and perception.

Finally, some sign languages use mouth patterns that are integrated from the dominant spoken language. Ebbinghaus and Hessman (1996) discuss the extensive use of mouthing in German Sign Language (DGS) conversations: "the overall impression is that mouthing of German words is a natural ingredient of spontaneous interactions between German signers" (p. 24). They note no mention of such behavior in ASL, which has its own mouth patterns that do not derive from English, and report that other sign languages that do use mouthing in a manner similar to DGS are Norwegian Sign Language (Vogt-Svendsen, 1983), Swedish Sign Language (Bergman, 1984), Finnish Sign Language (Pimiä, 1990), Danish Sign Language (Engberg-Pedersen, 1993), Swiss German Sign Language (Boyes Braem, 2000, in press), and Sign Language of the Netherlands (Schermer, 1990).

Another use of mouthing is reported by Bos (1994) with respect to the auxiliary verb in Sign Language of the Netherlands (SLN). The SLN auxiliary sign glossed as ACT-ON is similar in formation to the verb GO-TO, but is differentiated by the mouthing of the Dutch word "op," meaning "on." Bos notes that the use of "op" with the sign ACT-ON means that op appears in semantic and syntactic locations in SLN that are ungrammatical in spoken Dutch. Example 10 illustrates the use of ACT-ON with op (and eyegaze, "eg," toward the established location 3a for the boyfriend); note that ACT-ON co-occurs with the main verb LOVE and that ACT-ON carries the agreement information with the arguments of the verb rather than LOVE itself:

[10] _____ br   /eg3a/
      $INDEX_1$ PARTNER $INDEX_{3a}$ LOVE $_{3a}$ACT-ON$_1$
                                      op

'My boyfriend loves me.'

Further Examples of Design Feature Distinctions

There are two types of eyeblinks distinguished on duration and tenseness: a) inhibited *periodic eyeblinks* marking the end of intonational phrases; and b) *voluntary eyeblinks* that are slower and deeper, and which co-occur with a sign, apparently for emphasis (Wilbur, 1994a). Head position may involve thrust, nod, or tilt. A head thrust typically occurs on the last sign in conditionals; its function is not understood (Liddell, 1986). Head nods may be distinguished by number of occurrences. Single head nods occur with signs to mark emphasis, assertion, or existence; they may mark syntactic locations where verbs have been omitted; and they may mark focus (i.e., the emphatic correlate of voluntary eyeblinks; Aarons, 1994; Liddell, 1978, 1980; Wilbur, 1991, 1994a). A repetitive head nod that has a higher frequency of repetition and smaller movement amplitude may signal hedging ("sort of," "kind of").

Bahan (1996) and MacLaughlin (1997) discuss the use of eyegaze and head tilt to convey agreement information. Head tilt indicates verb agreement with the subject and eyegaze, with the object, unless the object is first person. Signers cannot eyegaze at themselves and thus first-person object agreement is indicated instead by head tilt, which forces eyegaze to show the subject agreement. Thus, there is flexibility within layering, such that eyegaze and head tilt share functions.

Body leans are distinguished by direction and degree. Baker and Padden (1978) and Baker Shenk (1983) identified forward lean as part of the non-manuals associated with questions. Boyes Braem (2000) identified a rhythmic use of side-to-side body leans for prosodic purposes in Swiss German Sign Language. Leans are left and right of a center vertical line; the leans cross the center line when the signer narrates general information but are restricted to either the left or the right side for specific narrative purposes, such as indicating other signers or different locative or temporal situations. Wilbur and Patschke (1998) report that lean can indicate (1) prosodic emphasis on lexical items (forward), (2) semantic categories of inclusion, "even" (forward), and exclusion "only" (back), (3) contrastive focus, such as "selecting" (forward), "parallel" (forward/back or right/left), and (4) pragmatic affirmation (forward) or denial (backward) of a proposition or presupposition.

Movement of the body, from the waist or shoulders, serves as part of the pronoun system in ASL (Kegl, 1976a, 1976b, 1977, 1978). Body shifting also interacts with the use of space in signed conversations in ASL (Emmorey, Corina, & Bellugi, 1995; Liddell, 1995; Winston, 1991, 1995) and in Danish Sign Language (DSL) (Engberg-Pedersen, 1993). Engberg-Pedersen (1995) and Lillo-Martin (1995) report for DSL and ASL, respectively, that body shifting changes the reference system for purposes of changing the point of view (POV) to someone else such that when the signer produces the pronoun PRO. 1, "I/me," "I" refers to someone other than the signer (much as might happen in direct quotation). Lillo-Martin also notes that this perspective shift, "point of view (POV) predicate," operates at the syntactic level as though it were a verb that takes a complement clause. Unlike other nonmanuals, POV has its own timing slot with the body as the primary articulator.

This is yet another example of the resources available to be layered in the multichanneled nonmanual system of natural signed languages. In fact, only the most common options have been identified here. What is critical about these is their availability should the language have use for them in creating a layered structure uniquely its own over time. A brief comparison with signed English will make the importance of this process of selecting options and assigning linguistic functions to them more apparent.

Why Is Signed English Not a Natural Language?

From the above review, it seems that ASL and other sign languages rely on layering because the manual articulators move more slowly than the speech articulators. To compensate, signed languages have chosen extensive layering to solve the slowness-in-articulation problem.

In contrast, Wilbur and Petersen (1998), in a comparison of SE produced by fluent SE signers who do and do not also know ASL, found evidence that SE is not layered. The signers who knew ASL consistently used nonmanual markers while producing SE (with or without speech), that is, they extended layering from ASL to SE. The signers who did not know ASL used minimal and erratic nonmanual marking. Only 18% of their yes/no questions had brow raise, and another 53% were incorrectly marked with brow lowering (the wh-question marker in ASL). Thus, 71% of the yes/no questions were not correctly marked by ASL standards. Other nonmanuals (blinks, negative headshakes) also differed between the two groups, even though they were producing the same content. The signers who knew ASL were able to transfer nonmanuals to SE because SE has no linguistically specified nonmanuals of its own. The SE signers

who did not know ASL did not have accuracy or homogeneity of nonmanuals because they have not been developed for SE. Essentially, SE has not assigned functions to the available simultaneous options.

In fact, signed systems such as SE are prevented by their own construction rules from ever developing layering. Because SE is supposed to follow the English lexicon, morphology, and syntax, these domains are unavailable for modification by grammaticalization and hence cannot adapt. SE does not permit a sign to change the direction of movement to indicate subject and object. So "I give you" and "you give me" are properly produced with the same manual formation for GIVE, with the pronoun sequence indicating who is the subject and who is the recipient (it should be noted that there are many "contact sign" users whose base is SE but who freely ignore certain SE rules and vary verb starting and ending locations for agreement purposes). Compare the necessity of signing these three independent signs with the ASL production of either $_1GIVE_2$ or $_2GIVE_1$, where the starting and ending points of GIVE are spatially located at the appropriate referents. SE requires each such morpheme to be articulated separately. This requirement explains the fact that SE takes at least 50% longer to produce comparable content than either spoken English or ASL (Bellugi & Fischer, 1972; Wilbur & Nolen, 1986).

Under these constraints, SE is, in essence, recreated as it is acquired by each learner, whether child or adult. Novel innovations, such as those reported by Supalla (1991) and Gee and Mounty (1991) involving mechanisms that contribute to layering, are under adult pressure to normalize to the proper English sequence of separate signs. Hence, grammaticalization modifications cannot evolve. The absence of layering in SE provides another important insight into current understanding of the nature of natural language and the role of production/perception modality. After the extensive discussion of layering in ASL and other signed languages, one might be tempted to conclude that the presence of widespread layering is a modality effect. That is, linguistic information, forced into the manual/visual modality, must be layered because the modality demands it. Instead, the lack of layering in SE demonstrates that layering is not a modality effect, but rather is a linguistically driven adaptation to the modality. SE has not undergone the linguistically driven adaptation and is prevented from ever doing so.

Summary and Conclusions

What we see from the discussion of multiple articulation channels and distinctions within them is an architecture for language in which the production and perception modality provides options that can be used for phonological, prosodic, morphological, syntactic, and semantic purposes. This architecture is reflected in the proposed universal model known as UG. In particular, this model must contain a design feature that specifies that the linguistic form of any language must be efficiently compatible with the requirements of perception, production, and information transfer. Each language interacts with these options and assigns linguistic functions to various ones. Spoken languages have more segmental/sequential options available, and layered options are less frequently used. Sign languages are more likely to use simultaneous/layered options, but which ones will be used and what functions they are assigned differ from language to language. Universals and constraints on variation will have to be investigated to complete the model. Critically, however, the interaction between language and modality occurs over time, and the assignment of functions to available options simply emerges, it is not consciously decided by users. It is SE that demonstrates the importance of the linguistic evolution process because it lacks what natural languages have: efficiency in the modality.

At the same time, the lack of use of these available design features in SE confirms the theoretical model being developed by linguists. Fromkin (2000) summarizes: "The more we look . . . the more we realize that the asymmetry between general knowledge and linguistic knowledge shows language to be independent of general intellectual ability . . . that language itself . . . is distinct both anatomically and functionally" (p. 545). Fromkin (2000) notes that the research on sign language structure, acquisition, neuropsychological processing, and disruption after brain damage all support the notion that "the same abstract principles underlie all human languages—spoken or signed" (p. 542). These are the universal principles that theoretical linguists call Universal Grammar, the concept that accounts for the observation that the

brain is suited to the acquisition and use of any language to which a child is exposed. What the study of signed languages tells us about language in general is that natural languages share certain design features, specifically those that maximize information coding in a way that permits efficient production and perception. Further, as Fromkin notes, the brain is ready, willing, and able to do its job—namely, handling the transfer of information from one human mind to another—regardless of the modality in which that information is coded.

Notes

Thanks are due to Debbie Chen Pichler for her production assistance. This work was supported in part by National Science Foundation grant BCS-9905848.

1. These pictures are taken from videotapes of Swedish Sign Language donated to my Sign Languages Comparison Archive, in which all signed samples are elicited from the same list of target sentences. Many thanks to the Swedish data collection team and to this signer for their invaluable contribution.

References

Aarons, D. (1994). *Aspects of the syntax of American Sign Language.* Unpublished doctoral dissertation, Boston University.

Alibašić, T. Šarac, N., & Chen Pichler, D. (2002). *Question formation in Croatian Sign Language.* Unpublished manuscript, Purdue University, Lafayette, IN.

Anderson, D., & Reilly, J. S. (1997). The puzzle of negation: How children move from communicative to grammatical negation in ASL. *Applied Psycholinguistics, 18,* 411–429.

Anderson, D., & Reilly, J. S. (1998). PAH! The acquisition of adverbials in ASL. *Sign Language & Linguistics, 1,* 117–142.

Bahan, B. (1996). *Non-manual realization of agreement in American Sign Language.* Unpublished doctoral dissertation, Boston University, Boston, MA.

Baker, C. & Cokely D. (1980). *American Sign language: A teacher's resource text on grammar and culture.* Silver Spring, MD: TJ Publishers.

Baker, C., & Padden, C. (1978). Focusing on the nonmanual components of American Sign Language. In P. Siple (Ed.), *Understanding language through Sign Language Research* (pp. 27–57). New York: Academic Press.

Baker-Shenk, C. (1983). *A micro-analysis of the non-*

manual components of questions in American Sign Language. Unpublished doctoral dissertation University of California, Berkeley.

Battison, R. (1978). *Lexical borrowing in American Sign Language*. Silver Spring, MD: Linstok Press.

Bellugi, U., & Fischer, S. (1972). A comparison of sign language and spoken language: Rate and grammatical mechanisms. *Cognition, 1*, 173–200.

Bergman, B. (1984). Nonmanual components of signed language: Some sentence types in Swedish Sign Language. In F. Loncke, P. Boyes Braem, & Y. Lebrun (Eds.), *Recent research on European Sign Languages* (pp. 49–59). Lisse: Swets/Zeitlinger B.V.

Bergman, B. (1995). Manual and nonmanual expression of negation in Swedish Sign Language. In H.F. Bos & G.M. Schermer (Eds.), *Sign Language Research 1994: Proceedings of the Fourth European Congress on Sign Language Research, Munich, September 1–3, 1994* (International Studies on Sign Language and Communication of the Deaf, No. 29). Hamburg: Signum.

Bos, H. (1994). An auxiliary verb in Sign Language of the Netherlands. In I. Ahlgren, B. Bergman, & M. Brennan (Eds.), *Perspectives on sign language structure (Papers from the Fifth International Symposium on Sign Language Research, Salamanca, Spain, May 25–30, 1992)* (pp. 37–53). Durham: International Sign Linguistics Association.

Boyes Braem, P. (2000). Functions of the mouthing component in Swiss German Sign Language. In D. Brentari (Ed.), *Foreign vocabulary in sign languages*. Mahwah, NJ: Lawrence Erlbaum Associates.

Boyes Braem, P. (2001). Functions of the mouthings in the signing of deaf early and late learners of Swiss German Sign Language (DSGS). In P. Boyes Braem & R. Sutton-Spence (Eds.), *The hands are the head of the mouth: the mouth as articulator in sign languages* (pp. 87–98). Hamburg: Signum Press.

Brentari, D., & Crossley, L. (2002). Prosody on the hands and face: Evidence from American Sign Language. *Sign Language & Linguistics*.

Coulter, G. (1978). Raised eyebrows and wrinkled noses: The grammatical function of facial expression in relative clauses and related constructions. Presented at the Second National Symposium on Sign Language Research and Teaching.

Coulter, G. (1979). *American Sign Language typology*. Unpublished doctoral dissertation. University of California, San Diego.

Davies, S. N. (1985). The tongue is quicker than the eye: Nonmanual behaviors in ASL. In W. Stokoe & V. Volterra (Eds.), *SLR'83: Proceedings of the 3rd International Symposium on Sign Language Research, Rome, June 22–26, 1983* (pp. 185–193). Silver Spring, MD: CNR/Linstok Press.

Ebbinghaus, H., & Hessman, J. (1996). Signs and words: Accounting for spoken language elements in German Sign Language. In W. H. Edmondson & R. B. Wilbur (Eds.), *International review of sign linguistics* (pp. 23–56). Hillsdale, NJ: Lawrence Erlbaum Associates.

Emmorey, K., Corina, D., & Bellugi, U. (1995). Differential processing of topographic and referential functions of space. In K. Emmorey & J. Reilly (Eds.), *Language, gesture, and space* (pp. 43–62). Mahwah, NJ: Lawrence Erlbaum Associates.

Engberg-Pedersen, E. (1990). Pragmatics of nonmanual behavior in Danish Sign Language. In W. H. Edmondson & F. Karlsson, (Eds.), *SLR '87: Papers from the Fourth International Symposium on Sign Language Research, Lappeenranta, Finland July 15–19, 1987* (International Studies on Sign Language and Communication of the Deaf No. 10) (pp. 121–128). Hamburg: Signum.

Engberg-Pedersen, E. (1993). *Space in Danish Sign Language: The semantics and morphosyntax pragmatics*. Hamburg: SIGNUM-Verlag.

Engberg-Pedersen, E. (1995). Point of view expressed through shifters. In K. Emmorey & J. S. Reilly (Eds.), *Language, gesture, and space* (pp. 133–154). Hillsdale, NJ: Lawrence Erlbaum Associates.

Frishberg, N. (1975). Arbitrariness and iconicity: Historical change in American Sign Language. *Language, 51*, 696–719. New York: Academic Press.

Fromkin, V. (2000). On the uniqueness of language. In K. Emmorey & H. Lane (Eds.), *The signs of language revisited: An anthology to honor Ursula Bellugi and Ed Klima* (pp. 533–548). Mahwah, NJ: Lawrence Erlbaum Associates.

Gee, J.P., & Mounty, J. (1991). Nativization, variability, and style shifting in the sign language development of deaf children of hearing parents. In P. Siple & S. Fischer (Eds.), *Theoretical issues in sign language research: Vol. 2. Psychology* (pp. 65–83). Chicago: University of Chicago Press.

Hunger, B., Schalber, K., & Wilbur R. (2000, July). BUB WOLLEN LERNEN, WOLLEN? Investigation into the modals in the Styrian dialect of Österreichischen Gebärdensprache (OGS) with particular focus on repetition and pauses. Paper presented at the International Conference on Theoretical Issues in Sign Language Research (TISLR) Amsterdam.

Kegl, J. (1976a). *Pronominalization in American Sign Language*. Unpublished manuscript, Massachusetts Institute of Technology, Cambridge, MA.

Kegl, J. (1976b). *Relational grammar and American Sign Language*. Unpublished manuscript, Massachusetts Institute of Technology, Cambridge, MA.

Kegl, J. (1977). *ASL syntax: Research in progress and*

proposed research. Unpublished manuscript, Massachusetts Institute of Technology, Cambridge, MA.

Kegl, J. (1978). *Indexing and pronominalization in ASL.* Unpublished manuscript, Massachusetts Institute of Technology, Cambridge, MA.

Klima, E., Bellugi, U., Battison, R., Boyes-Braem, P., Fischer, S., Frishberg, N., Lane, H., Lentz, E., Newkirk, D., Newport, E., Pederson, C., & Siple, P. (1979). *The signs of language.* Cambridge, MA: Harvard University Press.

Liddell, S. K. (1978). Nonmanual signals and relative clauses in American Sign language. In P. Siple (Ed.), *Understanding sign language through sign language research* (pp. 59–90). New York: Academic Press.

Liddell, S. K. (1980). *American Sign Language syntax.* The Hague: Mouton.

Liddell, S. K. (1986). Head thrust in ASL conditional marking. *Sign Language Studies, 52,* 243–262.

Liddell, S. K. (1995). Real, surrogate, and token space: Grammatical consequences in ASL. In K. Emmorey & J. S. Reilly (Eds.), *Language, gesture, and space* (pp. 19–41). Hillsdale, NJ: Lawrence Erlbaum Associates.

Lillo-Martin, D. (1995). The point of view predicate in American Sign Language. In K. Emmorey & J. Reilly (Eds.), *Language, gesture, and space* (pp. 155–170). Hillsdale, NJ: Lawrence Erlbaum Associates.

MacLaughlin, D. (1997). *The structure of determiner phrases: Evidence from American Sign Language.* Unpublished doctoral dissertation, Boston University, Boston, MA.

Meir, I. (1998). Syntactic-semantic interaction in Israeli Sign Language verbs: The case of backwards verbs. *Sign Language & Linguistics, 1,* 3–37.

Neidle, C., Kegl, J., MacLaughlin, D., Bahan, B., & Lee, R. G. (2000). *The syntax of American Sign Language.* Cambridge, MA: MIT Press.

Pfau, R., & Glück, S. (2000, July). *Negative heads in German Sign Language and American Sign Language.* Paper Presented at 7th International Conference on Theoretical Issues in Sign Language Research (TISLR 2000), Amsterdam.

Pfau, R. (in press). Applying morphosyntactic and phonological readjustment rules in natural language negation. In R.P. Meier, K.A. Cormier, & D.G. Quinto (Eds.), *Modality and structure in signed and spoken languages.* Cambridge: Cambridge University Press.

Pimiä, P. (1990). Semantic features of some mouth patterns of Finnish Sign Language. In S. Prillwitz & T. Vollhaber (Eds.), *Current trends in European Sign Language Research: Proceedings of the third Eu-*

ropean Congress on Sign Language Research (pp. 115–118). Hamburg: Signum.

Reilly, J. (2000). Bringing affective expression into the service of language: Acquiring perspective marking in narratives. In K. Emmorey & H. Lane (Eds.), *The signs of language revisited: An anthology to Honor Ursula Bellugi and Ed Klima* (pp. 415–434). Mahwah, NJ: Lawrence Erlbaum Associates.

Reilly, J. S., & Bellugi, U. (1996). Competition on the face: affect and language in ASL motherese. *Journal of Child Language, 23,* 219–239.

Reilly, J. S., McIntire, M.L., & Bellugi, U. (1991). BABYFACE: a new perspective on universals in language acquisition. In P. Siple (Ed.), *Theroretical issues in sign language research: psycholinguistics.* Chicago: Chicago University Press.

Reilly, J. S., McIntire, M. L., & Seago, H. (1992). Differential expression of emotion in American Sign Language. *Sign Language Studies, 75,* 113–128.

Schalber, K., Hunger, B., Šarac, N., Alibašić, T., & Wilbur, R. B. (1999, October) About the Position of modals in the Styrian Dialect within the Austrian Sign Language (ÖGS): BUB FUSSBALL SPIELEN KÖNNEN? Poster presented at the Conference on Early Communication and Language Development, Dubrovnik, Croatia.

Schermer, G. M. (1990). *In search of a language: Influences form spoken Dutch on Sign Language of the Netherlands.* Delft: Eburon.

Stokoe, W. D. (1960). *Sign language structure: An outline of the visual communication system of the American deaf. Studies in Linguistics Occasional Papers 8.*

Stokoe, W., Casterline, D. & Croneberg, C. (1965). *Dictionary of American Sign Language.* Washington, DC: Gallaudet College. [Revised 1978, Silver Spring, MD: Linstok Press.]

Supalla, S. (1991). Manually coded English: The modality question in signed language development. In P. Siple & S. Fischer (Eds.), *Theoretical issues in sign language research: Vol. 2. Psychology* (pp. 85–109). Chicago: University of Chicago Press.

Valli, C., & Lucas, C. (1992). *Linguistics of American Sign Language: A resource text for ASL users.* Washington, DC: Gallaudet University Press.

Veinberg, S., & Wilbur, R. (1990). A linguistic analysis of the negative headshake in American Sign Language. *Sign Language Studies, 68,* 217–244.

Vogt-Svendsen, M. (1983). Lip movements in Norwegian Sign Language. In J. Kyle & B. Woll (Eds.), *Language in sign: An international perspective on sign language* (pp. 85–96). London: Croom Helm.

Wilbur, R. B. (1991). Intonation and focus in American Sign Language. In Y. No & M. Libucha (Eds.),

ESCOL '90: Proceedings of the Seventh Eastern States Conference on Linguistics (pp. 320–331). Columbus: Ohio State University Press.

Wilbur, R. B. (1994a). Eyeblinks and ASL phrase structure. *Sign Language Studies, 84,* 221–240.

Wilbur, R. B. (1994b). Foregrounding structures in American Sign Language. *Journal of Pragmatics, 22,* 647–672.

Wilbur, R. B. (1995a). What the morphology of operators looks like: A formal analysis of ASL brow-raise. In L. Gabriele, D. Hardison, & R. West-moreland (Eds.), *FLSM VI: Proceedings of the Sixth Annual Meeting of the Formal Linguistics Society of Mid-America: Vol. 2. Syntax II & semantics/pragmatics* (pp. 67–78). Bloomington: Indiana University Linguistics Club.

Wilbur, R. B. (1995b). Why so-called 'rhetorical questions' (RHQs) are neither rhetorical nor questions. In H. Bos & G. M. Schermer (Eds.), *Sign language research 1994: Proceedings of the Fourth European Congress on Sign Language Research* (pp. 149–169). Hamburg: Signum.

Wilbur, R. B. (1996). Evidence for the function and structure of Wh-clefts in ASL. In W. H. Edmondson & R. B. Wilbur (Eds.), *International review of sign linguistics* (pp. 209–256). Hillsdale, NJ: Lawrence Erlbaum Associates.

Wilbur, R. B. (2000a). Phonological and prosodic layering of nonmanuals in American Sign Language. In K. Emmorey & H. Lane (Eds.), *The signs of language revisited: An anthology to honor Ursula Bellugi*

and Ed Klima (pp. 215–244). Mahwah, NJ: Lawrence Erlbaum Associates.

Wilbur, R., Klima, E. S., & Bellugi, U. (1983). Roots: The search for the origins of signs in ASL. *Papers from the Parasession, Chicago Linguistic Society 19*(2), 314–333.

Wilbur, R. B., & Nolen, S. B. (1986). The duration of syllables in American Sign Language. *Language & Speech, 29,* 263–280.

Wilbur, R. B., & Patschke, C. (1998). Body leans and marking contrast in ASL. *Journal of Pragmatics, 30,* 275–303.

Wilbur, R. B., & Patschke, C. (1999). Syntactic correlates of brow raise in ASL. *Sign Language & Linguistics, 2,* 3–41.

Wilbur, R. B., & Petersen, L. (1998). Modality interactions of speech and signing in simultaneous communication. *Journal of Speech, Language & Hearing Research, 41,* 200–212.

Winston, E. A. (1989, July). *Timelines in ASL.* Paper presented at The Deaf Way, Washington, DC.

Winston, E. A. (1991). Spatial referencing and cohesion in an American Sign Language text. *Sign Language Studies, 73,* 397–410.

Winston, E. A. (1995). Spatial mapping in comparative discourse frames. In K. Emmorey & J. Reilly (Eds.), *Language, gesture, and space* (pp. 87–114). Mahwah, NJ: Lawrence Erlbaum Associates.

Wood, S. K. (1999). *Semantic and syntactic aspects of negation in ASL.* MA thesis, Purdue University, West Lafayette, IN.

25

Christine Monikowski & Elizabeth A. Winston

Interpreters and Interpreter Education

This chapter is about the profession of American Sign Language/English interpreting in the United States and the education required to succeed in that profession. It begins with a chronological summary of the most compelling research in the field, as well as issues that show the field's beginnings and reflect a vision for the future. The chapter continues with a look at relevant research and the evolution of the task of American Sign Language/English interpreting, the role of interpreters, quality control, the current status of interpreter education, and goals for the future.

Interpreting: Defining the Task

Task Analysis: The convention

The task analysis information from the 1984 convention of the Conference of Interpreter Trainers (CIT) was a seminal work in the field of interpreting and interpreter education that was the result of many circumstances that overlapped and intermingled to bridge from the past to the future. In 1983, seven people met for two and a half days at Johnson County Community College in Overland Park, Kansas, and again in 1984 at Madonna College in Livonia, Michigan.[1] The purpose of these meetings was to begin a task analysis of the interpreting process. Cokely's (1992) interpreting miscue research, the early work of Colonomos, and the expertise and experience of the entire group led to the outlining of the tasks of interpreting and transliterating (McIntire 1986).[2] Their work was reviewed by a group of 20 deaf and hearing people and resulted in the activities that were presented to and discussed by the participants at the 1984 CIT convention.[3]

One specific goal of the 1984 convention was to provide a forum for educators, leaders, and consumers to investigate, in a structured and informed way, the activities of interpreting and transliterating, and the approaches taken toward teaching these activities. In the first article in the proceedings, Cavallaro and Cook (1986) described the task analysis approach to understanding interpreting, transliterating, and interpreter education. Task analysis provides a means for (1) identifying instructional objectives that are necessary for the achievement of instructional goals; (2) sequencing the content of instruction necessary to meet the instructional goals; and (3) evaluating learner performance (attainment of instructional objectives) (Cavallaro & Cook, p. 7). This approach targets observable, overt behaviors and attempts to describe these behaviors explicitly for the practitioner.

From that introduction, participants of the convention were directed to analyze the tasks outlined for them related to interpreting, transliterating, and teaching based on the following criteria (Cavallaro & Cook, 1986):

1. All tasks should be stated in observable, measurable terms.
2. No critical steps should be omitted.
3. All of the subtasks should be relevant to the main task.
4. No trivial subtasks should be included.
5. The subtasks should be arranged in a logical order.

In a response to Cavallaro and Cook, Rust (1986) suggested a further goal for this task, the development of a theory of teaching interpreting, something that we do not yet have.

From this starting point, many new understandings, beliefs, and assumptions have become widespread in the field. One of the most basic accepted beliefs is that there are specific tasks that make up the whole of interpreting, and that these specific tasks can be taught. The exact nature of these tasks, the sequencing of these tasks, and the ways of teaching these tasks, were yet to be investigated.

Task Analysis Since the Conference

Following the work of the 1984 task analysis convention, two major models of interpreting have had a tremendous impact in the field: Colonomos's integrated model and Cokely's process model. Our current understanding of the task of interpreting has been greatly influenced by the contributions of both. Although these models were in the beginning stages of development before the convention, and both authors contributed to the task analysis work, the Cokely model seems to have had more influence on the convention, while the Colonomos model spread after the convention. Each of these models provided insight into interpreting and has had a tremendous impact on how interpreters view the task and on how educators teach it. Taylor (1993) has added to this early research with additional information on the task.

Colonomos: The Integrated Model

Colonomos (1992) has focused interpreter education on the process, on what is happening inside the interpreter's head during the actual task. She estimated the success of a product by the amount of control and responsibility the interpreter assumes in the process of interpretation. In other words, effective interpreters make informed, educated decisions about what to produce based on meaning analysis. Ineffective interpreters make no decisions; they simply move their hands or mouth without processing the speaker's underlying meaning. Colonomos proposes that interpreters process source messages for meaning by analyzing the source language for goal, for language variable, cultural variables, ideas, presenter's feelings, personality, and style, and also process contextual features.

Colonomos's (1992) pedagogical model of the interpreting process is based on her theoretical model and focuses on the three main aspects of the process: concentrating (C) on the source message (i.e., the incoming message), representing (R) the meaning, and planning (P) the target text (i.e., the produced message). An interpreter is able to analyze the process used to produce the target text and can focus practice and improvement activities on the area that appears to be interfering with that process.

As Colonomos was developing her model, the interpreting field was moving forward toward the 1984 CIT convention on task analysis. Colonomos was on the planning committee for the convention, and she was active in the implementation of the meeting as well. Colonomos had an active role in the convention and also learned much from it. As she says, "I believe I did contribute many of my perspectives that were incorporated into the final document [CIT task analysis]. It was a wonderful exchange of ideas and discussion/debate about various elements of the interpreting task. I'm sure I left there wiser and with many more questions to think about" (Colonomos, personal communication, October 26, 2001).

The Colonomos model has been integrated into basic beliefs of the interpreting field for many years. Colonomos has presented this model widely, and many educators use some form or segments from it. Unfortunately for the field, a detailed explanation of this model has never been written or substantiated by research. Interpreters and educators have not had the opportunity to study it, discuss it, and implement it. And, because there is no quotable source, no written document from which to draw, educators have different versions that may or may not include elements of their own thinking as well as those of Colonomos. The dearth of published, empirical research prevents the model from progressing to a theory, as defined by Rust (1986). One may believe that it works, and see results from applying it, but there is no documented evidence.

Cokely: The Process Model

In his work originally published in 1984, Cokely (1992) provided the field with its first research-based model of sign language interpreting, the process model. Cokely proposed a seven-stage model. It illustrated the path an interpretation takes from initial production in the source language to the final form produced in the target language. He did not claim this to be a step-by-step, linear process, but proposed that many of the processes co-occur during the overall interpreting process. The steps are: message reception; preliminary processing; short-term message retention; semantic intent realization; semantic equivalence determination; syntactic message formulation; and message production.

Cokely (1992) systematically analyzed the types and frequencies of miscues that occur in interpretations. These were additions, omissions, substitutions, intrusions, and anomalies. These categories provided a way for interpreters and consumers to judge the quality of interpretations and a way for interpreting educators to begin reanalyzing their approaches to teaching. Cokely summarized this by writing:

> Miscues are, in and of themselves, singular instances of behavior, instances in which the meaning of the interpretation differs from the meaning of the source text. After identifying miscues in a piece of work, or across several pieces of work, one then seeks possible patterns in the miscues. To form a pattern, the type of miscue must be relatively identical and the probable cause must also be identical (there could be several possible causes for a specific miscue). This then enables one to identify strategies that can address the cause of the miscue pattern. However, a miscue is merely a single instance of behavior; a piece of work containing only one miscue (virtually impossible, but for sake of argument we will assume that we have found such a piece of work) contains no pattern. . . . Certainly there are some miscues whose cause/motivation is inexplicable (i.e. anomalies), and may fall into the category of what you call "random errors." I suspect that there are very very few "random errors"; rather in the case of "random errors" I believe that we simply do not have enough material to find the pattern . . . we simply need more data. (personal communication, February 21, 2002)

Cokely's model has been published and presented at workshops as well. However, the research publication (Cokely, 1992) is not easily understood and integrated by the every day practitioner. To those without a research background, it can appear to be a string of unfamiliar terms and boxes with arrows that require much analysis before understanding and use. The Cokely model usually requires in-depth training and is not frequently available to interpreting educators. However, those who have studied it find its depth and breadth to be a valuable teaching tool.

If we compare the acceptance and spread of the Colonomos and Cokely models, the former appears to be much simpler than the latter. Cokely proposes 7 major stages and more than 20 substages. There appears to be a simpler three-stage process in the Colonomos model, usually presented to the audience in a more familiar sequence of a chronological progression. This is in comparison to Cokely's complex flow-chart approach. However, when analyzing the three-stage Colonomos model, there are between 28 and 30 factors and subfactors to consider. So, although equally complex, the Colonomos model may appear more familiar to interpreter educators. Both are in use in interpreting education programs in the United States.

Taylor: Developing a Diagnostic Tool

Taylor's (1993) research added another dimension to the field. Taylor's original goal was to investigate interpretations using the assumptions of Cokely's process and Colonomos's integrated models. But she faced the same dilemma that many interpreter educators face: these existing models assume pre-existing English and American Sign Language (ASL) skills. Her data showed that interpreters do not necessarily have those skills. She needed to categorize and work with the skills in her population of interpreters. Her research provided the field with clear evidence of this dilemma of trying to train interpreters without first establishing adequate language skills. She investigated interpretations to develop a diagnostic tool that would help interpreter educators evaluate errors. Again, the field was presented with a very valuable and essential beginning step in improving interpreter education, but most interpreter educators have not incorporated this work into their teaching.

A major difference in Taylor's approach to analyzing interpretations is that her early research categorized errors based on target features when the source language is English and the target language is ASL: fingerspelling, numbers, vocabulary, classifiers/size and shape specifiers, structuring space, grammar (all language-based features that are prerequisite skills for interpreting), and the two interpreting skills of interpreting and composure and appearance (Taylor, 1993). Her more recent research (Taylor, 2000) categorizes errors based on target features when the source language is ASL and the target is spoken English (sign to voice).

Cokely's (1992) findings gave us insight into where and why experts provide less-than-successful interpretations. Colonomos's approach provided a structure for looking at the interpreter's process. But the question that Taylor's work addressed is where, when, and under what circumstances novices can produce expertly. This information provided a valuable stepping stone to understanding the sequencing of teaching texts in interpreter education, the placement of entry-level interpreters, and the recommendation of skill enhancement activities for novices.

Taylor's (1993) conclusions were clear: while many target productions were labeled "interpretations," the greatest proportion of errors was due to weak or nonexistent language skills and not due to interpreting skills. In other words, the interpreters were not able to begin thinking about interpreting because they did not have language skills that were adequate to produce meaningful messages. Taylor's contribution has led to some changes in the field, but a frequent complaint relayed during a survey conducted in preparation of this chapter was that language skills were not adequately addressed within the imposed limits of the institution.[4] ASL requirements for entry into interpreting education programs are rare.

All three of the above models looked specifically at language use at the sentence level, with some influence from social and external context (e.g., use of vocabulary in sentences and phrases). More recently, the task has been expanded to include a broader view of interpreting as a discourse process. Discourse analysis seems to be the appropriate level of analysis for interpreters. Roy's (1989, 2000) work presented this approach with an in-depth analysis of a social interaction between interlocutors who use ASL and English. Her work influenced Wadensjo (1998), among others, and she has made a significant contribution to the field of sign language interpreting and education. Roy (2000) recognized the influence an interpreter has on an interaction: "interpreters shape events differently for all the participants. . . . the presence of an interpreter changes the event" (p. 47). This level of analysis is unprecedented in the field, but it is the level of analysis for the future.

Interpreting: Defining the Role

Research

The professionalization of sign language interpreting and interpreters is still evolving, although the actual work of the interpreter has been occurring for generations. The everyday role and responsibilities have been described for the field in three primary texts available for interpreting students: Neumann Solow's (1982) *Sign Language Interpreting: A Basic Resource Book*, Frishberg's (1986) *Interpreting: An Introduction*, and Humphrey and Alcorn's (1996) *So You Want to Be an Interpreter*. All are quite comprehensive and deal with the daily considerations of a professional interpreter. There is discussion about the history of the field, including organizations and ethical considerations for specific interpreting settings. Environmental considerations are also discussed: where is the ideal place for an interpreter to sit/stand? What kind of lighting is appropriate during a movie? and so on. This kind of information is important and can often determine success of the interpreting assignment.

Reliable research in the field of professional sign language interpretation is sparse. There is a plethora of "articles" that are actually handouts distributed at workshops and conventions. These papers are often taken as documented fact rather than as proposed approaches and methodologies. The field also has reaped the benefits of research on spoken language interpreting, and attempts are made to adjust the information to the special needs of sign language. There are also the models of the interpreting process that are grounded in scholarly research, as discussed earlier (see Cokely, 1992; Taylor, 1993). It is only in recent years, however, that research has addressed interpreting as a dynamic event and tried to analyze the actual role of the interpreter in the interpreting process. As Roy (2000) noted:

> Interpreting for people who do not speak a common language is a linguistic and social act of communication, and the interpreter's role in this process is an engaged one, directed by knowledge and understanding of the entire communicative situation, including fluency in the languages, competence in appropriate usage within each language, and in managing the cross-cultural flow of talk. (p. 3)

This discourse approach to interpreting asks as many questions as it answers and intersects all the facets of an interpreter's education, both academic and social. It would be helpful to take a step back to see how this approach evolved, beginning with the work of Seleskovitch.

Seleskovitch

The work of Seleskovitch (1978) was some of the earliest in the field of interpreting to truly investigate the role of interpreting in human communication, and specifically the role of the interpreter in the "trilogue" that occurs whenever interpretation happens. This recognition of the trilogue rather than the dialogue was an essential one for the field of sign language interpreting. This approach is slowly being incorporated into many interpreter education programs.

Seleskovitch is a spoken language interpreter. She began her research on the differences between the results of translation, which includes the luxury of time and resources, and the results of conference interpreting, with the imposition of time constraints and often limited resources and constrained working conditions. Seleskovitch (1978) defined the possibilities of interpreting under optimal conditions; she also realistically described the challenges, problems, and results when conditions for adequate interpreting were not met. She stated that

interpreting "has displayed abundant evidence of its potential, but because it has not been sufficiently studied or defined, it is not always in a position to realize that potential today" (p. 147). This conclusion about spoken language interpreting in 1978 is, sadly, a perfect description of the current state of ASL/English interpreting in the United States.

Seleskovitch (1978) presented the basic structure that most current interpreters use to discuss the interpreting process. She first discussed the need for understanding the source message and the need to analyze it deeply, thoroughly, and spontaneously. Her discussion of understanding of meaning is the basis of our understanding of interpretation today. Seleskovitch thus provided us with a wealth of information and approaches for the field of ASL/English interpreting. Her approach is reflected in the Colonomos model (see above) and the works describing interpreting from Neumann Solow (1981), Frishberg (1986), and Humphrey and Alcorn (1995), among others. The research being conducted on interpreting by Roy (2000) and Metzger (1995) also reflect the essential understanding of the task as presented by Seleskovitch. Many interpreters and interpreter educators are familiar with Seleskovitch's work; it is work that the field can still learn much from, and to which we owe a great deal of our current understanding of our tasks as interpreters.

Roy

Roy (2000, p. 53) noted that "Not much has been written about the views or perspectives" of the individuals who actually participate in an interpreted events.[5] She therefore examined the interpreter's perspective in one given interaction, and particularly on the potential influence the interpreter can have in any conversation. Her analysis, at the discourse level, focused on the turn-taking within that given interaction. "Exchanging turns is at the heart of the way people talk back-and-forth to each other" (p. 4). Roy's findings, however, gave us much more than simply the interpreter's perspective. She concluded: "the interpreter is not solely responsible for the success or the failure of an interpreting event. All three participants jointly produce this event and, as such, all three are responsible for the communicative success or failure" (p. 124). The interactional model she offers supports the work of interpreters in an unprecedented way.

Interpreting is the process by which people whose discourse systems are different communicate with each other in face-to-face interactions. Interpreting, then, coincides or happens within these processes and so is intimately bound up in discourse processes. Roy (2000) paved the way for Wadensjo (1998) and Metzger (1995) when she noted that interpreters "influence interaction via their own participation" (p. 34). Her work is also a challenge to interpreter educators to review and revise their courses to reflect the results of ongoing, quality research. Wadensjo's work is another step in this evolution.

Wadensjo

Wadensjo (1998), focusing on spoken language interpreting (specifically Swedish/Russian), also analyzed the interactive role of interpreting. Her work serves the ASL/English interpreter well. Wadensjo stated, "if interpreting is to be acknowledged as a profession . . . in the everyday life of public institutions and organizations . . . we need to have well-founded and shared ideas about what interpreting . . . is all about, what interpreters are good for, and about preferred standards to apply in various situations" (p. 4).

Wadensjo's (1998) work was tied most notably to Simmel (1964) and Goffman (1959) insofar as she emphasized that "the number of people in groups and organizations influences the social interaction that takes place in them" (p. 10). Wadensjo presented a groundbreaking analysis of "interpreter mediated encounters" (p. 93) and relied on Goffman's work on social interaction. Wadensjo, like Roy, focused on the potential influence of the interpreter in any conversation.

Wadensjo's (1998) analysis began with a thorough explanation of the *communication pas de trois* "there is reason to believe that interactions involving three or more individuals have a complexity which is not comparable to interaction in dyads" (p. 11). She stated that her goal was "to explore how the interpreter-mediated conversation is qualitatively different from encounters where the participants communicate directly" (p. 12). Her *pas de trois* clearly identified the unique conversation involving two people with an additional third person. This analysis of an actual interpreted encounter also included a comparison of ideal interpreting and actual performance, a detailed analysis of specific utterances, and an in-depth discussion of "neutrality"

and all its nuances. Finally, she described the confounded role of the professional interpreters who "are well aware of the fact that interpreting involves a complexity of activities" (p. 285).

Wadensjo's research has influenced the field of sign language interpreting in a positive way. The field has just begun to address the position of interpreter as one who has the potential to influence the interaction between two interlocutors. There are still numerous working interpreters and educators who support the "act as if I am not here" approach to interpreting. But Wadensjo's (1998) work elevated that dated approach to a more social one in that she addressed the presence of a third party and the ramifications from that third party's role.

Metzger

The next advance in thinking about interpreting was Metzger's work, which built on the research about sign language interpreting by bringing a further sociolinguistic foundation to the study of the role of interpreting. While Seleskovitch (1978), Wadensjo (1998) and Roy (1989, 2000) discussed the interpreting role as that of a triad with the interpreter in the middle, Metzger (1995) revealed a slightly different picture. She characterized the interpreted encounter as consisting "of two overlapping dyads, interpreter-Deaf participant and interpreter-hearing participant, with the interpreter as the pivotal overlap engaged in both dyads" (p. iv).

Understanding interpreted interactions from this perspective yields complexities that go beyond those raised by prior research. More than simply expanding the picture of interpreted interaction, Metzger (1995) revealed these many new complexities. She discussed each participant's frame of the interpreted encounter—what each believes is happening and expects to be happening. In addition, the concept of "footing" influences the encounter. Each participant has his or her own perceived role and perceptions about the roles of the other participants. But, more than that, Metzger revealed the "interpreter's paradox" (p. 34). While most interpreters and interpreter educators have assumed the basic neutrality of the interpreter in any interaction (indeed, deaf consumers depend on this) Metzger made it clear that the interpreter is far from a neutral participant. "The interpreters are both participants in the interaction and conveyors of the discourse" (p. 175); they have tremendous "power to influence discourse" (p. 204).

As evidence that this research is making the shift to practice, conventional wisdom now holds the view that interpreters have a definite impact on the communication event. In fact, as one respondent to the survey stated, "everybody is different when an interpreter is there." It was also noted that "[interpreting] is more difficult when they try to ignore us" (S. C. Phan, personal communication, August 29, 2001). Assuming that an interpreter's presence will ensure smooth and successful communication is an obsolete approach to the task. Each participant, including the interpreter, must put forth an effort to support the interaction, and we have come to realize that interpreter's effort is often the greatest (see Metzger, 1995; Roy, 2000; Seleskovitch, 1978; Wadensjo, 1998). There is debate over whether the interpreter is a third participant or a member of one of the dyads, but it is now generally accepted that interpreters are not invisible. The longer we hold on to that perspective, teaching it in our programs and to consumers, the more difficult our task is. Another response to the survey indicated that "not only is the style of communication influenced, but the content [in a more intimate interchange] is also influenced" by the presence of an interpreter. Another respondent noted that "misunderstandings . . . reveal a lot about what's happening" and it might be beneficial to "allow discomfort to occur." Acknowledging the differences in communication styles between the two participants would potentially support the role of the interpreter and clarify his or her footing, as discussed in Metzger.

Quality Control in Interpreting and Interpreter Education

Evaluating Interpreting Skills

In the United States, the field first began evaluating and certifying interpreters in 1972, when the national Registry of Interpreters for the Deaf (RID) began offering a performance-based certification test. This test used stimulus source tapes and required the applicant to perform live interpretations in front of a panel of evaluators. Those evaluators rated the applicant on the spot, and the applicant either passed or failed. Questions about interrater

reliability and the validity of the test led RID to review and revamp the system. After extensive research and testing, the new RID certification tests were first offered in 1989 and are still used, with some modification, today. There are three parts, a written test and two skill tests. The written test is administered separately, and applicants must receive a passing score before registering for the skill tests. One of the skills tests uses videotapes to assess interpreting skills (ASL to English monologue, English to ASL monologue, and interactive dialogue), and the other assesses transliteration (English-based signing to English monologue, English to English-based signing monologue, and interactive dialogue). RID also has developed certification tests for specialized fields such as legal interpreting, oral interpreting, and a test for certifying deaf interpreters.[6]

Many interpreters and consumers believed that the standards of this test were too high, requiring a level of skills not necessary for many jobs. In fact, most believed that beginning interpreters needed several years of experience working as interpreters before they could pass the RID certification. Due to this dilemma and due to the number of unskilled interpreters working without RID certification in areas such as public schools, some states developed their own certification tests. These are often called "quality assurance" screenings to indicate that they are not certification and that they test skills below the level of RID. These are often scored on a scale of 1–5, and interpreters need to receive a score of 3 or above to work in most states. In truth, interpreters scoring below this are rarely terminated from their jobs, and common practice has been to provide in-service training and waivers of skills requirements for as long as 5 years or more. In most states, interpreters who have already passed the RID test are not required to pass any additional quality assurance screenings at the state level.

The National Association of the Deaf (NAD) has also developed an interpreting skill test. Although there has been some friction between RID and NAD over which skills should be tested, the level of skills tested, and the approach to testing, in recent years RID and NAD have been collaborating to develop a new certification test that will be jointly administered and recognized by both organizations at a national level.

The establishment of such national tests in the United States significantly raised the level of interpreting and the recognition of interpreters in this country and gave credibility to the field. It was a giant step in the professionalization of the field. Unfortunately, many environments, most notably the public education system, have failed to move toward recognition of certified interpreters. For many years, the common practice has been to place those not yet ready to interpret for adults in the schools with deaf children. The schools, unwilling to pay for professional, skilled interpreters and often unable to find skilled interpreters, have allowed these unskilled people to work without certification or evaluation of any kind. It is encouraging that within the last 3–5 years, more and more states are addressing the need for skilled interpreters, establishing active requirements for interpreting skills for those working with children. A nationally available assessment tool, the Educational Interpreting Performance Assessment (Schick and Williams, 1993) is also being adopted in many school systems. The failure to satisfy established skills requirements has resulted in the termination of unskilled educational interpreters.

Evaluating the Teaching of Interpreting

The Issues

At the same time that RID, NAD, and various states have recognized the need for quality control of interpreting services, the CIT recognized the need to assess quality in interpreting education programs. Numerous members of CIT have, for approximately 20 years, contributed to the authorship of the current National Interpreter Education Standards (1995). This document identifies "the knowledge, skills, and perspective students need to gain in order to enter the field of professional interpreting" (p. 1). A look at these Standards can help one understand the critical parts of a successful program, as well as recognize the "benchmarks for assessing and enhancing student outcomes, evaluating and updating faculty, and improving curricula and related practices" (p. 1). This document was approved by the general membership of CIT in February 2002.

CIT members began the long process of describing and evaluating teaching in interpreting programs in 1989. At that time, CIT received a grant from the Funds for the Improvement of Post-Secondary Education program at the U.S. Department of Education and began to pilot test an approach to rating interpreter education programs. As a result, a series of issues papers and member responses were presented to the membership at the tenth biennial convention of the CIT, in October 1994 in Charlotte, North Carolina. These papers were based on many years of effort, energy, and input by the CIT membership to understand and establish standards for interpreter education. While at the convention, the members participated in meetings to discuss the appropriateness of standards that would, potentially, lead to a process for evaluating the quality of interpreter education programs. Cathy Cogen, then chairperson of the Standards Committee, instructed the membership to "remind each other about out shared vision for the field and second, to build the momentum and energy" necessary to "realize this vision" (Cogen, 1995, p. 3). Thus the wheels were set in motion. No longer were the issues and ideals the work of a committee, albeit a broad reaching and evolving one; the entire membership became involved in a dialogue of fundamental issues and standards, issues that Cogen characterized as "the heart of what we do . . . central to the direction the field will take in the coming years" (p. 3).

The papers were available to the membership before the convention, and the task was well publicized. There were four fundamental issues: faculty qualifications, diversity in interpreting education, proficiency, and entry level to the profession, as well as the overarching issue of levels of education, which hearkened back to Lane's 1985 suggestion to the profession: "If interpreting is to continue to grow and improve, if it is to be truly a profession and not a trade, then interpreters must know their foundations" (cited in Frishberg and Wilcox 1995, p. 16). The challenge to the field was, at that time (and still is today) to build a strong academic foundation so that the field will be acknowledged as a serious discipline. Frishberg and Wilcox (1995) asked the difficult questions, all associated with academic credibility:

> we must expect differences among our educational programs, acknowledge that graduates of community and technical colleges are well-prepared for some interpreting tasks, and not

for others, recognize that graduates of university programs with bachelors' and more especially masters' degrees are prepared for most interpreting tasks as well as many administrative, instructional and supervisory roles, anticipate that new roles and new educational foci will emerge. Our hope is that this paper will provoke all of us to tune the definitions of what the strata should be. (p. 18)

The vision of a qualified faculty supports the academic credibility that interpreter education so desperately needs: "an academic credential is necessary both as a basic requirement of academia and because it is valuable to the teaching of interpreting" (Winston, 1995, p. 21). For years, interpreter educators had no standards against which to measure their qualifications. While a qualified faculty member is important to a program and to the students it serves, the institutions of higher education have a responsibility to provide "support and encouragement for faculty to obtain further education" (Winston, p. 22).

One respondent to our survey said, "We have to do the work to find good Deaf teachers"; this is a problem often acknowledged by interpreting faculty. However, it appears to be much more complicated than this. Despite the opportunities for educational advancement for deaf people (as a result of the Americans with Disabilities Act), the Deaf community has yet to achieve the "critical mass" necessary to satisfy the need for ASL teachers and interpreter educators. Search committees in higher education find it difficult to develop a pool of qualified deaf applicants (R. Peterson, personal communication, September 20, 2001). Many programs include members of the local Deaf community in numerous activities: guest lecturers in Deaf Culture courses, talent for in-house videotapes, members of a program's advisory board, and so on. But the number of tenure-track, full-time deaf interpreter educators in interpreter education programs is quite small. Even when there is a qualified instructor, he or she is often responsible for the ASL courses in the curriculum (usually because there are also few ASL instructors).

The lack of commonly applied standards is also reflected in the expectations of faculty qualifications. To date, only two programs have addressed this issue. The first, the Teaching Interpreting Program at Western Maryland College, was a landmark program that offered an MA degree in teaching interpreting. The coursework focused on teaching interpreting, and graduates were able to document their skills as teachers. Unfortunately, this program closed and has not been officially reopened to students as of this writing.

The U.S. Department of Education has recently recognized the need for faculty training and education and is currently supporting one program to design, develop, and offer curriculum for teaching interpreting educators. This program, Project TIEM.Online, is a web-based university program offered through the University of Colorado at Boulder *http://www.colorado.edu/slhs/TIEM.Online/index.html*. The program is completely dependent on federal grant support, and its continuation will be in question at the end of the grant.

The National Interpreter Education Standards outline ways to define and assess faculty qualifications. However, few programs have incorporated these standards in hiring. Although most faculty need to have some type of academic degree because their institutions require it, little else is required from faculty except that they be practitioners or deaf. Knowledge of the field, of teaching interpreting, and of teaching and assessment are advantages, but are often not criteria for hiring all faculty. Thus, faculty qualifications are still an enormous issue in providing quality in interpreter education programs.

The second specific issue addressed the importance of creating "a place of prospective, qualitative production of an egalitarian, supportive environment" (Stawasz, 1995, p. 27). Interpreter education programs were encouraged to "recruit a diverse student and faculty population" (Stawasz, p. 27) and to "assure that the curriculum fosters the attitude of acceptance and respect of the diversity in the population" (p. 28). The work of an interpreter is with the general public, which implies meeting a variety of members of different populations, and it was important that CIT promote diversity in an explicit manner.

A third issue of quality assurance in interpreting education is the lack of entry and exit criteria for interpreting students. Historically, this was a nonissue because most interpreters gained their proficiency in ASL by socializing with members of the Deaf community. As our profession addressed the need to educate more interpreters, this concept of proficiency was somehow clouded. At the time of the CIT convention, there was concern that the growing need for interpreters would require more interpreting education programs. Monikowski (1995) cautioned that "knowingly accepting students into programs without requiring exemplary skills in both ASL and English fosters a linguistic façade which mars our professional standards and offends the intelligence of the Deaf community" (p. 33). To date, there has been little progress to require entry-level skills in many programs, and the challenge remains of teaching students how to interpret when they do not have adequate language skills.

It is clear that from the time of the CIT convention to today, not much progress has been made in this area. In the past, an interpreter's education was based in the Deaf community, but in recent years, the shift has been to formal education in an academic setting (Peterson & Monikowski, 2001). The price for this transition has been costly. In an effort to gain academic credibility, the field has, for the most part, lost the social interaction and relationships that apparently served the previous generations of interpreters so well; although, in retrospect, relying completely on the community for one's interpreting skills was a risky proposition. Perhaps what has been lost is the foundation in the language that one acquires when interacting with the members of the community. The gain has been the in-depth analysis of the interpreting task.

The community-based interpreter had the approval, trust, and support of deaf consumers. And the interpreter was the recipient of the in-group knowledge that made the difficult work worthwhile. Today, many students have the required academic credentials but few, if any, of the relationships with the members of the Deaf community. The issue of trust must be addressed. "It takes tremendous faith to give one's words and ideas over to another person to convey" (P. S. Kraemer, personal communication, August 3, 2001). In the past, knowledge about the interpreter's "community history . . . [was the deaf individual's] instrument to measure trustworthiness" (Kraemer, personal communication). Today, for many students, the Deaf Club is an alien place, perhaps reserved for a class observation assignment. Deaf elders are often unknown to the students and, without an experienced mentor, the work is seen as a detached activity, detached from the very community that gives life to the profession. "Students who have only [an] academic basis for learning interpreting suffer from a

lack of experience with real Deaf people; those who learn in the community lack a grounding in the linguistic and theoretical background necessary [to succeed]" (Kraemer, personal communication).

It must be stated, however, that conventional wisdom also says, in the words of one survey respondent, that a quality academic program "can outmatch the community-taught interpreter if the academic program has a strong community component." There has been an ongoing discussion in the field of second language acquisition regarding which setting is better—the natural or the educational (Ellis, 1994). Although in recent years there has been a realization that when one attempts to argue for one setting over the other, one is essentially comparing apples and oranges, there is a strong belief that "in natural settings informal learning occurs . . . from direct participation and observation" and there is "emphasis on the social significance of what is being learnt rather than on mastery of subject matter" (Ellis, p. 214). The work of an interpreter centers on social interaction with members of the Deaf community. It is essential to bring back as much community interaction as possible into current interpreting programs.

Although clarifying what "entry level" means to the profession was of extreme importance to the 1994 CIT conference, no issue paper was offered. There were, however, five papers presented that addressed this issue in an effort to continue the dialogue among the members (Frishberg, 1995; Mentkowski, 1995; Patrie, 1995; Robinson, 1995; Stauffer, 1995). To date, there has been little research on the issue of what "entry level to the profession" should be.

Currently, there are no commonly used and recognized standards for recognizing success or effectiveness for interpreting instructors, for students, or for interpreter education programs. Conventional wisdom says that students must "know" ASL, but there is neither a standardized method of assessing this knowledge nor any extensive research that addresses such skills. Educators certainly can see the benefits of teaching students who have conversational ASL skills, but when asked to be specific, comments from our survey included: "when they can hold a conversation on general topics"; "when they can [explain an academic article] in ASL." Often, honesty prevailed: "our reality is that the majority of preparation programs are at the [2 year degree] level and combine language learning with interpreting." There is the occasional 2 year program that is "fortunate to have had supportive administration and a model in the prerequisites of the nursing program which allow us [to require two years of ASL]."

The same is true for exit criteria: how does one assess whether the student, although he or she passed all required courses, is ready to interpret? Individual programs have established internships that give students the opportunity to work with a supervisor, and this is infinitely better than simply passing courses. But there is no standard for the field; one comment from a survey respondent was undeniable: "Firm statements from CIT and RID regarding . . . the separation of language learning and interpreting are long overdue."

National Interpreter Education Standards

The current National Interpreter Education Standards, approved by the CIT membership in 1984 and officially adopted in 1985, have two major sections for assessing interpreter education programs: general criteria and specific criteria. The general criteria deal with five issues: sponsorship, resources (including faculty qualifications), students, operational policies, and program evaluations. The specific criteria address the description of a program (including its mission statement and philosophical approach), curriculum design, prerequisites, and content requirements. These standards represent an enormous amount of work from many interpreter educators. The entire document has moved the field of interpreter education forward in immeasurable ways; it represents the hopes and dreams of a profession.

Implementing the Standards

The standards are rooted in a philosophy of self-study, an approach that offers the opportunity to compare a specific program with the standards of the profession. In the existing process, the CIT offers a member of the standards committee as a guide for the process, helping programs to organize documents, articulate philosophies, and explore curriculum. This requires a 2-year commitment from the program and its sponsoring institution. The self-study review is an excellent opportunity for a program to clearly see its strengths and weaknesses in specific areas and can also serve as an impetus for the sponsoring institution to make changes in an existing program. However, there is

no prestige in the field for the programs that have undertaken this self-study, and there is no tangible benefit. There is no competition among reviewed programs and non-reviewed programs. There is no outside economic benefit for any programs that have undergone review. It is hoped that the years ahead will bring change and that the self-study review will evolve into a bona fide accreditation program. This step will add to the academic credibility and professionalization the programs so desperately need. Like national recognition and certification did for the interpreting profession, national recognition and some type of certification of interpreting education programs will give credence to our work.

The self-study review process was originally a way for programs to conduct an internal review, using the standards as a gauge that reflected the conventional wisdom of the profession. It seems that, unless there is some kind of outside impetus attached to accreditation, the current approach of self-study will not move forward. For example, if the federal government required accreditation before awarding grants to those programs, there would be more interest from interpreter education programs. There is an effort underway to include more deaf professionals in the process by tapping into the expertise of the American Sign Language Teachers Association (ASLTA), although they have neither a self-study review nor an established accreditation process. And, since the standards require, as a prerequisite, that one has skills in both ASL and English, ASL teaching will not play a large part in assessing any interpreter education program. However, because it is essential that ASL courses prepare students for interpreting, the participation of ASLTA in understanding the language needs of interpreters is essential. The current self-study review process continues to move forward, with one program reviewed successfully (University of New Hampshire at Manchester), more in the process, and a commitment from CIT to continue offering the self-study review process and to investigate the accreditation of programs.

Summary and Conclusions

This chapter has presented an overview of the profession of interpreting and the educational programs that support the profession. The task analysis from the 1984 CIT convention, as well as the seminal work of Colonomos and Cokely (1992), laid the foundation for current interpreter education programs. In addition, Taylor's (1993) more recent work has become widely applied and has the potential to impact curricular improvements.

Research has given the field much needed academic credibility. The spoken language research of Seleskovitch (1978) set the bar for sign language research. To date, few have been able to match the quality of her work. However, in recent years, the number of research-based presentations at national CIT conventions appears to be increasing, and this bodes well for the profession.

The RID evaluation system and the collaboration between RID and NAD emphasize the need for qualified professionals. Because few individuals become interpreters without enrolling in an interpreter education program, the need for standards with which these interpreter education programs can be assessed is crucial. It remains to be seen whether the commitment from the field, currently being led by the CIT approach to self-study review, results in an accreditation process.

Lack of qualified faculty continues to be a problem. There is a need for formal programs that prepare the future faculty of interpreter education programs. Workshops and national conventions, although they provide useful information and are an excellent forum for collegial sharing and support, do not contribute to the academic credibility of our programs or of our faculty.

Generally, research on interpreting and interpreter education needs to be expanded. Many interpreter educators attend to the daily task of developing curricula, teaching classes, and organizing schedules, with little time for scholarly work in the field. Until the number of qualified faculty increases, the challenge of pursuing credible and reliable research will remain.

The growth of the profession has been slow but steady. There are more certified interpreters now than ever before, and there are more interpreter education programs now than ever before. As in any young professions, numerous issues need attention; too few people have too little time. However, it seems that the profession's initial stage of development has given way to an awareness of the need for academic credibility and recognition of standards to identify successful programs. As the millennium unfolds, we are hopeful that interpreters and interpreter educators will continue to advance as professionals.

Notes

1. These people were Dennis Cokely, Betty Colonomos, Janice H. Kanda, Sharon Neumann Solow, Donald G. Renzuli, Kenneth Rust, and Theresa Smith. This history was put together from information in CIT 1984 and from personal communications with Dennis Cokely.

2. Although Cokely's work was originally published in 1984, we are using the 1992 citation in our references because it is readily available to the public. Interpreting and transliterating are the mainstays of an interpreter's work. Interpreting is changing a message from one language to another language, American Sign Language (ASL) into English, and transliteration is process of changing "one form of an English message . . . into the other form, for example from spoken English into signed English" (Winston, 1989, p. 147).

3. We refer to the dates of specific events. All dates in parentheses are dates of publications. For example, the Proceedings from the 1984 convention were not published until (1986).

4. In an effort to share the conventional wisdom of those who currently teach interpreting students, we canvassed the entire CIT membership for their perspectives on a variety of issues. We are grateful for the participation of numerous interpreter educators who freely shared their thoughts and opinions. Some are quoted directly; others remain anonymous.

5. Roy's work was completed in 1989, but her 2000 publication is readily available to the public.

6. RID's approximately 3,646 certified interpreters are required to participate in a Certification Maintenance Program (CMP) and to earn Continuing Education Units (CEUs) in order to maintain certification (*Pam Jones, RID Certification Maintenance Program Coordinator, personal communication, February 1, 2002*).

References

Cavallaro, C., & Cook, L. H. (1986). Task analysis: what, why, and how. In M. McIntire (Ed.), *Proceedings of the 5th national convention, Conference of Interpreter Trainers (Asilomar 1984)* (pp. 6–20). Washington, DC: RID Publications.

Cogen, C. (1995), Castles in the air: introduction. In E. A. Winston (Ed.), *Mapping our course: a collaborative venture. Proceedings of the 10th national convention, Conference of Interpreter Trainers* (pp. 1–4). Washington, DC: Conference of Interpreter Trainers.

Cokely, D. (1992). *Interpretation: a sociolinguistic model. Sign Language Dissertation Series.* Silver Spring, MD: Linstok Press.

Colonomos, B. (1992). *Processes in interpreting and transliterating: Making them work for you.* Videotape. Westminster, CO: Front Range Community College.

Ellis, R. (1994). *The study of second language acquisition.* Oxford: Oxford University Press.

Frishberg, N. (1995) Response paper #4: internship, practicum, fieldwork, mentoring. In E. A. Winston (Ed.), *Mapping our course: a collaborative venture. Proceedings of the 10th national convention, Conference of Interpreter Trainers.* (pp. 71–74). Washington, DC: Conference of Interpreter Trainers.

Frishberg, N. (1986). *Interpreting: an introduction.* Silver Spring, MD: RID Publications. [revised 1990].

Frishberg, N., & Wilcox, S. (1995). Issue: levels of education. In E. A. Winston (Ed.), *Mapping our course: a collaborative venture. Proceedings of the 10th national convention, Conference of Interpreter Trainers* (pp. 15–19).

Goffman, E. (1990 [1959]). *The presentation of self in everyday life.* Harmondsworth, UK: Penguin.

Humphrey, J. H., & Alcorn, B. J. (1995). *So you want to be an interpreter: an introduction to sign language interpreting.* Amarillo, TX: H & H Publishers.

McIntire, M. L. (Ed.). (1986) New dimensions in interpreter education: task analysis—theory and application. *Proceedings of the 5th national convention, Conference of Interpreter Trainers.* Fremont, CA: Ohlone College.

Mentkowski, M. (1995). Issues in the analysis of change in higher education assessment. In E. A. Winston (Ed.), *Mapping our course: a collaborative venture. Proceedings of the 10th national convention, Conference of Interpreter Trainers.* (pp. 75–82). Washington, DC: Conference of Interpreter Trainers.

Metzger, M. (1995). *The paradox of neutrality: A comparison of interpreters' goals with the reality of interactive discourse.* Unpublished doctoral dissertation, Georgetown University, Washington, DC.

Monikowski, C. (1995). Issue III: proficiency. In E. A. Winston (Ed.), *Mapping our course: a collaborative venture. Proceedings of the 10th national convention, Conference of Interpreter Trainers* (pp. 31–34). Washington, DC: Conference of Interpreter Trainers.

National Interpreter Education Standards. (1995, February 24). Conference of Interpreter Trainers. Retrieved from http://www.cit-asl.org/standard.html

Neumann Solow, S. (1981). *Sign language interpreting: a basic resource book.* Silver Spring, MD: National Association of the Deaf Publications.

Patrie, C. J. (1995). Response paper #1: the "readiness-to-work" gap. In E. A. Winston (Ed.), *Mapping our course: a collaborative venture. Proceedings of the 10th national convention, Conference of Interpreter Trainers.* (pp. 53–56). Washington, DC: Conference of Interpreter Trainers.

Peterson, R., & Monikowski, C. (2001). *Introduction to the study of sign language interpreting.* Unpublished manuscript.

Robinson, R. (1995). Response paper #3: start with the end in mind. In E. A. Winston (Ed.), *Mapping our course: a collaborative venture. Proceedings of the 10th national convention, Conference of Interpreter Trainers.* (p. 61–70). Washington, DC: Conference of Interpreter Trainers.

Roy, C. (1989). *A sociolinguistic analysis of the interpreter's role in the turn exchanges of an interpreted event.* Unpublished doctoral dissertation. Georgetown University, Washington, DC.

Roy, C. (2000). *Interpreting as a discourse process.* New York: Oxford University Press.

Rust, K. (1986). Response to Cavallaro and Cook. In M. L. McIntire (Ed.), *New Dimensions in Interpreter Education: Task Analysis—Theory and Application, 5th National Convention of the Conference of Interpreter Trainers (Asilomar 1984)* (pp. 21–25). Washington, DC: RID Publications.

Schick, B., & Williams, K. (1993). The evaluation of educational interpreters. In B. Schick & M.P. Moeller (Eds.), *Sign language in the schools: current issues and controversies* (pp. 47–56). Omaha, NE: Boys Town Press.

Seleskovitch, D. (1978). *Interpreting for international conferences: problems of language and communication.* Silver Spring, MD: RID Publications.

Simmel, G. (1964). *The sociology of Georg Simmel* (transl. from German, ed. and with an introduction by K.H. Wolff). New York: Free Press.

Stauffer, L. (1995). Response paper #2: a response to the "readiness-to-work" gap. In E. A. Winston (Ed.), *Mapping our course: a collaborative venture. Proceedings of the 10th national convention, Conference of Interpreter Trainers.* (p. 57–60). Washington, DC: Conference of Interpreter Trainers.

Stawasz, P. (1995). Issue II: diversity in interpreting education. In E. A. Winston (Ed.), *Mapping our course: a collaborative venture. Proceedings of the 10th national convention, Conference of Interpreter Trainers* (pp. 27–28). Washington, DC: Conference of Interpreter Trainers.

Taylor, M. (1993). Interpretation skills: English to American Sign Language. Edmonton, Alberta: Interpreting Consolidated.

Taylor, M. (2000). Interpretation skills: American Sign Language to English. Edmonton, Alberta: Interpreting consolidated.

Wadensjo, C. (1998). *Interpreting as interaction*. New York: Longman.

Winston, E. A. (1995). Issue I: faculty qualifications. In E. A. Winston (Ed.), *Mapping our course: a collaborative venture. Proceedings of the 10th national convention, Conference of Interpreter Trainers* (pp. 21–23). Washington, DC: Conference of Interpreter Trainers.

Winston, E. A. (1989). Transliteration: What's the message? In C. Lucas (Ed.). *The sociolinguistics of the deaf community* (pp. 147–164). San Diego, CA: Academic Press.

26

Karen Emmorey

The Neural Systems Underlying Sign Language

For more than a century (since the time of Paul Broca and Carl Wernicke), it has been known that the left hemisphere of the human brain is critical for producing and comprehending speech. Damage to perisylvian areas within the left hemisphere (the language zone, see figure 26-1) produces various types of aphasia, language disorders caused by brain injury. Damage to equivalent areas within the right hemisphere does not produce aphasic symptoms, such as effortful speech, phonological and morphological errors, or difficulty understanding words or sentences. Why does the brain exhibit this asymmetry in specialization for linguistic functions? One hypothesis is that the temporal processing demands for auditory speech processing determine the lateralization pattern for language (Fitch, Miller, & Tallal, 1997). Speech perception relies on very fast temporal changes (on the order of 30–40 milliseconds [ms]), and it has been argued that the left hemisphere is specialized for processing rapidly changing sensory events. Another possibility is that the left hemisphere is specialized for general symbolic functions, including mathematics and other symbol systems (Brown, 1977). A further possibility is that the left hemisphere is specialized for the control of complex motor movements, regardless of whether they are linguistic (Kimura, 1993). Yet

another possibility is that the basis for left hemispheric specialization for language lies in the nature of linguistic systems rather than in the sensory characteristics of the linguistic signal or in the motor aspects of language production (Hickok, Klima, & Bellugi, 1996). Understanding the neural systems involved in signed language processing can help decide among these alternatives because sign languages are not based on auditory processing, are distinct from pantomime (symbolic gesture), involve complex motoric activity, and are clearly linguistic systems.

Figure 26-1 provides a road map for regions within the left hemisphere that have been linked to language function, based on data from spoken languages. Briefly (and oversimplifying), Broca's area is involved in language production, as well as in processing aspects of complex syntax. Wernicke's area is involved in language comprehension, and the supramarginal gyrus has been implicated in semantic and phonological processing. The angular gyrus is involved in reading processes. Of course, these regions are not the only brain areas involved in language functions, but they form a critical "language zone," such that if these regions are damaged, some form of aphasia generally results for hearing speakers.

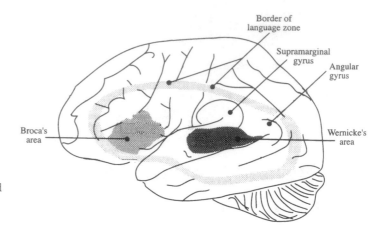

Figure 26-1. The perisylvian areas that make up the language zone within the left hemisphere. (From Goodglass, 1993, reprinted with permission of Academic Press.)

Determining the Neural Substrate For Sign Language

Evidence from brain-injured deaf signers indicates that damage to perisylvian areas of the left hemisphere (the language zone) causes sign language aphasias that are similar to spoken language aphasias (Hickok, Klima, et al., 1996; Poizner, Klima, & Bellugi, 1987). A historical review of 16 cases of signers who sustained left hemisphere damage (LHD) and 5 cases of signers with right hemisphere damage (RHD) reveals that only damage to critical left hemisphere structures led to sign language impairments (Corina, 1998b, 1998c). The poorer performance of the LHD signers cannot be attributed to group differences in onset of deafness, age of language acquisition, or age at test (Hickok, Klima, et al., 1996). Thus, data from signers with brain injury indicate that structures within the left hemisphere are critical to sign language comprehension and production, as they are for spoken language.

Evidence from studies with neurologically unimpaired deaf signers also indicates left hemispheric specialization for sign language. Using positron emission tomography (PET), McGuire et al. (1997) found left hemisphere activation when deaf signers were asked to mentally recite sentences in British Sign Language. The activated regions corresponded to the same areas that are engaged during silent articulation of English sentences by hearing subjects. Visual spatial areas within the right hemisphere did not show significant activation for "inner signing" (or for "inner speech"). Similarly, Petitto et al. (1997) observed

left hemisphere activation when deaf signers of American Sign Language (ASL) and deaf signers of Langue des Signes Québécoise (LSQ) were asked to overtly produce signs (subjects saw signed nouns and produced associated verbs). Also using PET, Emmorey et al. (2002, 2003) found activation in left inferior frontal gyrus (Broca's area) during overt picture naming in ASL, and the homologous regions within the right hemisphere were not activated. Finally, Corina, San Jose, Ackerman, Guillemin, and Braun (2000) also found activation within the left hemisphere in a verb generation task; this activation was observed whether signers produced verbs with their dominant right hand, with their left hand, or with both hands. This result suggests that the left hemisphere lateralization for sign language production is not simply due to contralateral motor control of the dominant right hand in signing.

Evidence from neuroimaging studies indicates more right hemisphere involvement during language comprehension than previously assumed, for both sign and speech. Recent studies have shown that understanding spoken language engages the right hemisphere (see Friederici, 2002, for a review); in contrast, reading appears to be strongly lateralized to the left hemisphere, with little right hemisphere involvement. Using functional magnetic resonance imaging (fMRI), Neville and colleagues (1998) investigated neural activity that occured while deaf and hearing subjects watched ASL sentences or read English sentences. For both hearing and deaf native ASL signers, fMRI revealed activation for the ASL sentences within left hemisphere structures that are classically linked to language processing (Broca's and Wernicke's areas; see figures 26-1 and 26-2). These same left hemisphere areas were also active when native speakers read English sentences. In addition, both deaf and hearing signers exhibited a comparable increase in neural activation in the equivalent areas within the right hemisphere when they saw ASL sentences, but such activation was not observed when native speakers read English sentences. Neville et al. (1998) interpreted these findings as indicating that "the specific nature and structure of ASL results in the recruitment of the right hemisphere into the language system" (p. 928).

Hickok, Bellugi, and Klima (1998b) took issue with Neville et al.'s (1998) interpretation, arguing that matching ASL processing with reading written English is not the appropriate comparison to investigate hemispheric laterality. They argued that reading is much more lateralized to the left hemisphere than auditory language processing and that both lesion studies and brain imaging studies indicate a clear role for the right hemisphere in spoken language comprehension. Supporting this hypothesis, Corina (2002) recently reported a greater

role of the right hemisphere for comprehending spoken English when subjects listened to a visible speaker (specifically, the right superior temporal gyrus, including the homologue of Wernicke's area; see figure 26-1). However, the right hemisphere activation for understanding spoken English was not as extensive as that observed for ASL (specifically, the right angular gyrus was engaged for ASL, but not for spoken English).

Furthermore, Newman, Bavelier, Corina, Jezzard, and Neville (2002) found that the right angular gyrus was engaged only for native ASL signers (hearing ASL-English bilinguals). Hearing signers who acquired ASL after puberty did not exhibit this right hemisphere activation when comprehending ASL sentences. Similarly, Neville et al. (1997) found that deaf native signers showed evidence of both left and right hemisphere activity for ASL closed-class signs (as measured by evoked response potentials or ERPs), whereas hearing late-learners of ASL did not exhibit any right hemisphere involvement. Closed-class signs convey grammatical information and include pronouns, conjunctions, and prepositions, whereas open-class signs primar-

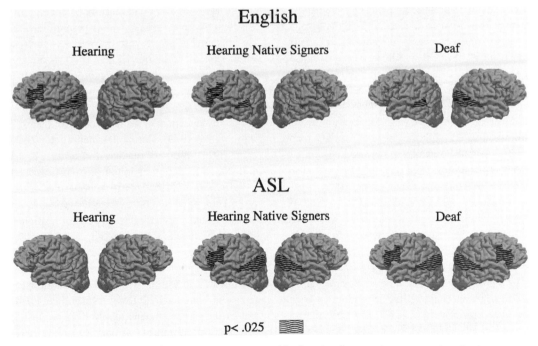

Figure 26-2. Representations of brain activation measured by functional magnetic resonance imaging in response to viewing American Sign Language (ASL) or reading English in three subject groups (hearing nonsigners, hearing native ASL signers, and deaf native signers). (From Corina, 1998b, reprinted with permission of Oxford University Press.)

ily convey semantic information and include nouns, verbs, and adjectives.

These results are intriguing and suggest a unique role for the right hemisphere in comprehending sign language (for native signers). However, not all neuroimaging studies have found evidence of a strong right hemisphere component for sign language; for example, MacSweeney et al. (2001) found little difference in right hemisphere activity for spoken language comprehension (watching and listening to a speaker) and sign language comprehension. Similarly, Söderfeldt et al. (1997) found no laterality differences for hearing signers watching and listening to a speaker compared to watching a signer tell a story (the differences between speech and sign were related to sensory modality, with greater bilateral activation in auditory cortex for speech and in visual cortex for sign). Thus, the degree of right hemisphere involvement for sign language versus spoken language comprehension remains somewhat controversial.

Dissociating Left Hemispheric Specialization for Language from Symbolic Gesture

Several studies provide convincing evidence of a dissociation between the neural systems involved in sign language versus conventionalized gesture and pantomime. Using a dual task paradigm, Corina, Vaid, and Bellugi (1992) reported left hemisphere dominance for producing ASL signs but no laterality effect when subjects had to produce symbolic gestures (e.g., waving goodbye or making thumbs-up). In addition, several studies report LHD patients who exhibited sign language impairments but well-preserved conventional gesture and pantomime (Corina, Poizner, et al., 1992; Kegl & Poizner, 1997; Poizner et al., 1987).

In a detailed case study, Corina, Poizner, et al. (1992) described patient WL, who sustained damage to perisylvian regions in the left hemisphere and was aphasic for sign language. He exhibited poor sign language comprehension, and his sign production was characterized by phonological and semantic errors with reduced grammatical structure. Nonetheless, WL was able to produce stretches of pantomime and tended to substitute pantomimes for signs, even when the pantomime required more complex movements (this tendency to pantomime was not present before his stroke).

Furthermore, WL showed a similar dissociation in his ability to comprehend ASL signs versus pantomimed gestures. When shown single ASL signs (e.g., APPLE), he was impaired in his ability to select the matching picture, but when shown pantomime (e.g., someone pretending to eat an apple), WL's comprehension was normal. Corina, Poizner, et al. (1992) concluded that such cases indicate that sign language impairments arising from left hemisphere damage cannot be attributed to general symbolic impairments.

Dissociating Neural Control for Motoric Versus Linguistic Processes

The case of WL and other LHD signers indicate that the neural systems underlying sign production and pantomime are separable (at least at some level). However, it is possible that impairments in sign language production (and spoken language production for that matter) may arise from an underlying disorder in motor movement selection and sequencing (Kimura, 1993). A motor programming deficit might affect sign language production, but not pantomime, because sign language (like speech) requires the programming of novel combinations of movements, whereas pantomime can rely on familiar, stereotypic movements (such as hammering or combing the hair). To assess the ability to produce nonsymbolic motor movements, patients with aphasia are often given a diagnostic test in which they are asked to copy meaningless movement sequences of the hand and arm (Kimura & Archibald, 1974). Corina, Poizner, et al. (1992) reported that WL performed within normal limits on this task, as did other aphasic signers described by Poizner et al. (1987). Furthermore, in a group study, Hickok et al. (1996) found that scores on this movement copy task did not correlate with linguistic impairments as measured by the Boston Diagnostic Aphasia Examination adapted for ASL (Goodglass & Kaplan, 1983).

However, it is unlikely that motor planning for signing is completely autonomous and independent of the motor systems involved in producing nonlinguistic movements. In fact, Corina (1999a) argued that the relation between linguistic processes and motor programming has not been adequately evaluated, citing the small population of aphasic signers that have been assessed and the inadequacies of measuring voluntary motor control with a test that contains only a few items.

Nonetheless, the findings to date suggest that sign language impairment arising from left hemisphere damage cannot be attributed solely to a simple disruption of motor control. For example, some types of aphasic errors are more easily explained as phonological substitutions, rather than as phonetic or motoric deficits (Corina 1999b; Corina, 2000). In addition, using the dual-task paradigm with neurologically intact signers, Corina, Vaid, et al. (1992) found no hemispheric asymmetry for producing arbitrary (nonsymbolic) gestures but a clear left hemisphere asymmetry for producing ASL signs.

Dissociating Sign Language Ability and Nonlinguistic Spatial Cognitive Ability

As already noted, single case studies and larger group studies indicate that damage to the right hemisphere does not result in sign language aphasia (Corina, 1998b, 1998c; Hickok et al., 1996; Poizner et al., 1987). These same studies have also shown that right hemisphere damage does result in various types of nonlinguistic spatial cognitive deficits. Like RHD speakers, signers with right hemisphere damage exhibit impairments of visual-spatial abilities such as perceiving spatial orientation, creating perspective within a drawing, or interpreting spatial configurations. Figure 26-3 illus-

trates the performance of LHD aphasic signers and RHD nonaphasic signers on standard spatial cognitive tasks.

The pattern of linguistic deficits observed with left hemisphere damage does not appear to simply be a function of deficits in general spatial cognitive ability. In fact, there is a double dissociation between sign language abilities and basic visual-spatial cognitive functions: sign language aphasia can occur without accompanying nonlanguage visual-spatial impairment, and severe deficits in visual spatial constructive abilities can occur without an accompanying sign language aphasia.

Left Hemisphere Organization of Language

The left hemisphere is clearly dominant for both signed and spoken language. This neural asymmetry suggests that neither perceptual mechanisms (audition or visual-spatial processing) nor motoric systems drive brain organization for language. Indeed, the evidence suggests that the brain respects distinctions in function, rather than in form. This hypothesis is now further explored by examining whether neural systems within the left hemisphere are influenced by the visual input pathways and the manual output pathways required for sign language comprehension and production.

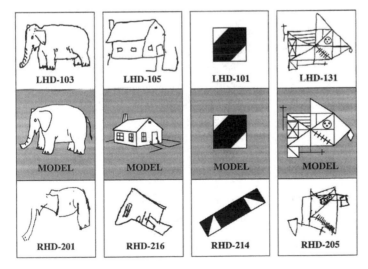

Figure 26-3. Comparison of spatial cognitive abilities in signers with left hemisphere damage (top row) or right hemisphere damage (bottom row). The first two panels show sample drawings from the drawing to copy subtest of the Boston Diagnostic Aphasia Exam (subjects are asked to draw the model pictures). The third panel illustrates the block design test from the Weschler Adult Intelligence Scale (subjects are asked to recreate the model using red and white colored blocks). The final panel provides examples of the Rey Osterreith Complex Figure (subjects are asked to copy the model figure). (Illustrations courtesy of U. Bellugi, The Salk Institute.)

Aphasic Syndromes

The left hemisphere is not homogeneous: damage to different perisylvian areas causes distinct types of language impairment for both signers and speakers, and damage outside of this region does not give rise to aphasic deficits. The patterns of impairment that have been reported for sign aphasia are similar to what has been found for spoken language aphasia, indicating that there is a common functional organization for the two forms of language. Specifically, damage to anterior language regions causes nonfluent (e.g., Broca's) aphasias, whereas fluent (e.g., Wernicke's) aphasias arise from lesions involving posterior language regions (Hickok et al. 1998a). A common feature of nonfluent aphasia is a tendency to omit grammatical morphology and to produce effortful and halting speech or sign. The following English example of nonfluent agrammatic production is from Goodglass (1993, p. 81) and the ASL example is from Poizner et al. (1987, p. 120):

ENGLISH

Examiner: What brought you to the hospital?
Patient: Yeah . . . Wednesday, . . . Paul and dad
. . . Hospital . . . yeah . . . doctors, two . . . an'
teeth

ASL

[For presentation purposes the Examiner's questions are given in English.]
Examiner: What else happened?
Patient GD: CAR . . . DRIVE . . . BROTHER . . .
DRIVE . . . I . . . S-T-A-D [Attempts to gesture "stand up"]
Examiner: You stood up?
Patient: YES . . . BROTHER. . . . DRIVE . . .
DUNNO . . . [Attempts to gesture "wave goodbye"]
Examiner: Your brother was driving?
Patient: YES . . . BACK . . . DRIVE . . . BROTHER
. . . MAN . . . MAMA . . . STAY . . . BROTHER
. . . DRIVE

In contrast to these production deficits, signers and speakers with anterior lesions often have relatively spared language comprehension (Goodglass, 1993; Hickok et al., 1998b). The reverse is true for posterior lesions, which often result in language comprehension deficits.

Posterior perisylvian lesions generally result in fluent aphasia, in which signing or speaking is fluent but often ungrammatical, and there is a tendency to select inappropriate words or to produce nonsense words. The following are examples of fluent aphasic production in English (from Goodglass, 1993, p. 86) and in ASL (from Poizner et al., 1987, p. 98:

ENGLISH [in response to "How are you today?"]
I feel very well. My hearing, writing have been doing well. Things that I couldn't hear from. In other words, I used to be able to work cigarettes I didn't know how . . . Chesterfeela, for 20 years I can write it.

ASL [asterisks indicate errors]
AND HAVE ONE* WAY-DOWN-THERE (unintelligible). MAN WALK, MAN SEE THAT *DISCONNECT E-X-T-E-N-T-I-O-N O-F *EARTH ROOM. HAVE FOR MAN CAN *LIVE ROOF, LIGHT, SHADE [seriated plural] *PULL-DOWN[[+dual]+habitual]

ENGLISH
"And there's one way down at the end [unintelligible]. The man walked over to see the disconnected, an extension of the earth room. It's there for the man can live a roof and light with shades to keep pulling down."

The ASL example is from patient PD who was somewhat unusual because although his output was similar to a Wernicke's aphasic, his ASL comprehension was relatively spared.

The findings thus far indicate that the pattern of within-hemispheric organization for sign language broadly mirrors that for spoken language. The general dichotomy between anterior-posterior lesions and nonfluent-fluent aphasia holds for sign language as well. Next, the specific neural systems involved in sign language production and comprehension are assessed to explore whether there is evidence for within-hemisphere reorganization for language in deaf signers.

The Functional Neuroanatomy of Sign Language Production

Damage to the left hemisphere can cause not only aphasia but hemiparesis (weakness) in the right hand, and thus some right-handed aphasic signers must use their left hand as the dominant hand for signing after their stroke. However, the signing errors produced by these patients do not arise from a lack of agility with their left hand. When right-handed signers without brain injury are asked to sign with the left hand, they do not produce the phonological errors observed with aphasic signers (Vaid, Bellugi, & Poizner, 1989). For speakers, the vocal tract and tongue are mid-line structures innervated bilaterally (i.e., by both hemispheres), but it is the left hemisphere that unilaterally controls speech production. One might hypothesize that because the two hands are independent articulators controlled to a large extent by opposite hemispheres, there might be less unilateral control over sign language production. However, the evidence strongly indicates left hemisphere control for the production of linguistic movements in sign language.

Broca's area has long been thought to play an important role in speech production. Broca's area is just anterior to the primary motor areas for the lips and tongue, and it is reasonable to expect that an area involved in the control of speech would be anatomically located near the speech articulators. Is this same area involved in sign language production? Or is the functional equivalent of Broca's area shifted superiorly so that it is next to the motor representation for the hand and arm? To answer these questions, Hickok, Kritchevsky, Bellugi, and Klima (1996) studied a native deaf signer (RS) who had a left hemisphere lesion principally involving Broca's area (specifically, the left frontal operculum and inferior portion of the primary motor cortex). RS exhibited good comprehension but deficits in sign production. Specifically, she tended to "shadow" one-handed signs with her nondominant (left) hand, and she had difficulty coordinating the two hands in two-handed signs. The deficits in bimanual coordination were specific to sign language production and were not present when RS produced nonlinguistic hand movements. Such deficits in coordinating the two hands may be similar to the phonetic deficits observed for speakers with nonfluent aphasia who have difficulty coordinating independent speech articulators (e.g., the larynx, tongue, and lips; see Blumstein, 1998). The case of RS suggests that Broca's area plays a similar role in language production for both speech and sign.

Further evidence for the role of Broca's area in sign language production comes from a cortical stimulation mapping study by Corina et al. (1999). Stimulation of Broca's area resulted in sign execution errors, even though this area was just anterior to the motor representation of the lips for this deaf signer. The errors produced by stimulation to Broca's area were characterized by a lax articulation of the intended sign. For example, handshapes were reduced (e.g., a loose fist, rather than the indented Y handshape of the sign COW), and movement was nonspecific (e.g., repeated tapping or rubbing, rather than the intended twisting movement). In general, stimulation of Broca's area resulted in a disruption of the global articulatory integrity of sign production. This finding is consistent with the hypothesis that Broca's area participates in the motoric execution of language output, particularly at the level of phonetic implementation.

In contrast, stimulation of the supramarginal gyrus (see figure 26-1) produced both phonological and semantic errors, rather than the reduced articulations that characterized signing under stimulation to Broca's area (Corina et al., 1999). The phonological errors involved misselections of phonological components; for example, the signer produced a clearly articulated X handshape for the open-A handshape of the intended sign PEANUT and a 3 handshape for the B handshape in PIG. The semantic errors were generally formationally similar to the intended targets. For example, when shown a picture of a horse, the signer produced COW, which differs only in handshape from the sign HORSE. Corina et al. (1999) hypothesized that the supramarginal gyrus (SMG) plays a critical role in the selection of phonological feature information and the association of this information with semantic representations during language production. Support for this hypothesis comes from a PET study by Emmorey et al. (2003). This study revealed more activation in the left SMG when deaf signers produced native ASL signs compared to fingerspelled words in a picture-naming task. Native signs engage phonological processes that are violated by fingerspelled words, suggesting that the SMG is indeed involved in the selection of phonological features of ASL signs.

Corina et al. (1999) also found sporadic semantic and phonological errors with stimulation to other areas within the left temporal lobe. Some semantic and phonological errors or paraphasias occur with almost all forms of aphasia, and this is true for sign language aphasia as well (Hickok et al., 1998a). Examples of a phonological and a semantic paraphasia from English-speaking aphasics would be saying "paker" for "paper" and "atlas" for "globe" (Goodglass, 1993). Sign aphasics also produce semantic paraphasias, for example, signing YEAR for HOUR, BED for CHAIR, GRAND-MOTHER for GRAND-DAUGHTER, or FOX for WOLF (Brentari, Poizner, & Kegl, 1995; Poizner, et al., 1987). Figure 26-4 provides examples of phonological errors made by signers with left hemisphere damage.

In sum, the data from sign language suggest that there are invariant principals for the organization of neural systems underlying language production. Neural reorganization for language production systems does not occur for deaf signers, despite the considerable differences between the vocal tract and the hands as articulators. Thus, the functional specialization of neural systems is not dependent on the nature of the motor systems involved in language production. Rather, the abstract nature of phonology as a level of linguistic representation and the interface between phonology and semantics may drive the organization of neural systems within the brain.

The Functional Neuroanatomy of Sign Language Comprehension

Impairments in auditory language comprehension occur with damage to the left temporal lobe in regions bordering primary auditory cortex (Goodglass, 1993). Given that linguistic input is visual for deaf signers, one can ask whether the temporal lobe plays the same role in sign language comprehension as it does for spoken language. Hickok, Love-Geffen, and Klima (2002) conducted a large group study with 19 LHD and RHD signers, comparing performance on sign language comprehension tasks with respect to whether the signers' lesions involved the temporal lobe. Only the signers with left temporal lobe lesions performed poorly on all sign comprehension tasks; signers with lesions outside the temporal lobe performed quite well, particularly on single sign and simple sentence comprehension tasks. Thus, language comprehension depends on intact left temporal lobe structures, regardless of whether language is perceived auditorily or visually.

What about the role of auditory cortex within the temporal lobe? Primary auditory cortex (the first cortical area to receive input from the cochlea

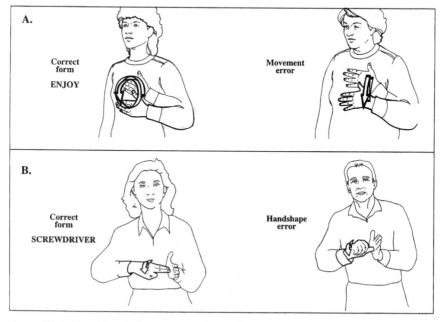

Figure 26-4. Examples of phonemic paraphasias from left-hemisphere-damaged signers. (A) Movement substitution error (from Poizner et al., 1987). (B) Handshape substitution error (from Corina, Poizner et al., 1992). (Illustrations courtesy of U. Bellugi, The Salk Institute.)

or Heschl's gyrus) is buried within the superior temporal gyrus (STG); the area posterior to Heschl's gyrus is called the planum temporale (PT) and contains secondary auditory association cortex. Several recent PET and fMRI studies have found activation in posterior STG (and the planum temporale) for deaf signers when they were watching signed language (MacSweeney et al., 2002, for British Sign Language; Nishimura et al., 1999, for Japanese Sign Language; Petitto et al., 2000, for ASL and LSQ). This neural area has long been known to respond to spoken language input (either internally or externally generated), but the language input was completely visual in the sign language studies. Petitto et al. (2000) suggested that

> the PT can be activated either by sight or sound because this tissue may be dedicated to processing specific distributions of complex, low-level units in rapid temporal alternation, rather than to sound, *per se*. Alternatively, the cortical tissue in the STG may be specialized for auditory processing, but may undergo functional reorganization in the presence of visual input when neural input from the auditory periphery is absent. (p. 8)

The rapid temporal alternations of sign do not approach the 40-ms rate found for the sound alternations of speech, arguing against Petitto et al.'s (2000) first hypothesis. Support for their alternative hypothesis can be found in the study by MacSweeney et al. (2002). MacSweeney et al. found that the activation in left STG during sign language comprehension was significantly less in hearing native signers compared to deaf native signers, suggesting that auditory association cortex is predominantly reserved for processing auditory input for hearing signers, but this neural region is engaged when processing visual signed input for deaf signers. Thus, the STG may be initially specialized for auditory processing, and this neural region retains its specialization when auditory input is received during development (as for hearing signers) but undergoes functional reorganization to process visual sign language input when no auditory input is received (see also Söderfeldt et al., 1997).

Other left hemisphere structures also appear to be involved in both spoken and signed language comprehension. Specifically, the SMG appears to be involved in phonological processing of speech (Caplan, Gow, & Makris, 1995) and of sign (Corina

et al., 1999; Love et al., 1997). Signers with lesions involving the SMG performed significantly worse on a test of phonological ability (choosing which two pictures corresponded to rhyming signs), compared to those with no damage to this area (Love et al., 1997). The PT is another structure thought to be involved in spoken language comprehension because of its proximity to primary auditory cortex. Using PET, Petitto et al. (1998) found bilateral activation in the PT for native deaf signers when they were asked to make phonological judgments (i.e., deciding whether two signs were the same or different, with the different signs varying by only a single phonological parameter). When hearing nonsigners were asked to make such same–different judgments, no activation was observed in the PT. Since the same–different task was a purely visual task for the hearing nonsigners, but a linguistic task for the deaf signers, Petitto et al. (1998) hypothesized that the PT is involved in processing sublexical aspects of sign language.

In sum, although the neural areas surrounding primary auditory cortex within the left hemisphere receive minimal auditory input for congenitally deaf signers, these areas nonetheless come to subserve language functions. In addition, several structures within the left hemisphere that have been shown to be involved in spoken language comprehension are also recruited for sign language processing. These results suggest a great deal of neuronal plasticity, and they also imply that there are biological or developmental constraints that cause specific brain areas within the left hemisphere to be well suited for processing linguistic information, independent of input modality.

The Role of the Right Hemisphere in Language Processes

Although aphasia does not result from right hemisphere damage, the right hemisphere is clearly not alinguistic. The right hemisphere has been shown to exhibit linguistic abilities at both lexical and discourse levels (Beeman & Chiarello, 1998; Joanette, Goulet, & Hannequin 1990), and, as already noted, it is becoming clear that the right hemisphere is more engaged when individuals are listening to spoken language than when they are either reading or speaking, which both appear to be more left lateralized. This section explores whether the right hemisphere is also similarly involved in sign language comprehension and whether it might also play a unique role in certain aspects of sign language processing.

Lexical Processing

The right hemisphere has been claimed to be much better at processing words with imageable, concrete referents (e.g., bed, flower) compared to words with abstract referents (e.g., truth, rule) (e.g., Day, 1979). Chiarello, Senehi, and Nuding (1987) hypothesized that this effect is postlexical, occurring after semantic information has been retrieved. They suggested that "once the lexicon has been accessed, and a semantic representation retrieved, subsequent right hemisphere semantic processing is mediated by imagery, while the left hemisphere can utilize either verbal or imaginal codes" (Chiarello et al., p. 56). Several studies have shown that signers exhibit enhanced imagery abilities that are hypothesized to be tied to certain processing requirements of ASL (Emmorey, Kosslyn, & Bellugi, 1993; McKee, 1987; Talbot & Haude, 1993). Furthermore, this enhancement seems to be linked to the right hemisphere (Emmorey & Kosslyn, 1996).

Emmorey and Corina (1993) used the visual hemifield technique to investigate the pattern of laterality for imageable and abstract signs, hypothesizing that imagery might play a greater role in processing ASL. The results supported this hypothesis. Deaf signers showed a right hemisphere advantage for recognizing imageable signs and a left hemisphere advantage for abstract signs. In contrast, hearing subjects tend to simply show improved performance for imageable words within the right hemisphere (compared to abstract words), rather than a processing advantage of the right over the left hemisphere. Emmorey and Corina speculated that the superior imagery abilities of ASL signers may enhance some linguistic processes within the right hemisphere when a high degree of imagery is involved.

Topographic Functions of Signing Space

Signing space can function iconically to represent spatial relations among objects, and signers with right hemisphere damage have been reported to exhibit impairments in the topographic function of signing space. For example, when a RHD signer

(BI) was asked to describe her room, she displaced all of the objects to the right in signing space and did not respect spatial relations, haphazardly placing the furniture in one place.[1] Emmorey, Corina, and Bellugi (1995) asked another RHD signer (DN) to immediately repeat two types of ASL stories, each 30 seconds long.[2] In one set, signing space functioned topographically (e.g., a description of the layout of a dentist's office), and in the other set, no topographic information was conveyed (e.g., a discussion of favorite foods). The stories were matched for the amount of information they contained (i.e., the number of propositions). The RHD signer DN correctly retold the stories that contained no topographic information, remembering even slightly more information than control signers. However, she was quite impaired in her ability to retell the spatial stories. The impairment was not in remembering the items in the stories, but in the correct placement of classifier signs within signing space to indicate the spatial relations among those items. Figure 26-5 provides a schematic of the nature of her errors. Neither of these RHD signers were aphasic for ASL, their descriptions of spatial layouts were fluent and grammatical, but the location and orientation of the objects were described incorrectly.

Further evidence that the right hemisphere is crucially involved in processing the topographic functions of signing space comes from a PET study by Emmorey et al. (2002). In this study, deaf native ASL signers viewed line drawings depicting a spatial relation between two objects (e.g., a cup on a table) and were asked either to produce a two-handed classifier construction depicting the spatial relation or to name the figure object that was colored red. In the classifier construction, the left hand represented the ground object and the right hand represented the figure object (the located object). The relation between the two hands schematically represented the spatial relation between the two objects. Compared to naming objects, describing spatial relationships with classifier constructions engaged the inferior parietal cortex bilaterally, with more extensive activation on the right. Parietal regions of the cortex in both hemispheres have long been known to be involved in the attention to and perception of the spatial location of physical objects in the environment (e.g., Posner & Petersen, 1990; Ungerleider & Mishkin, 1982).

When hearing English speakers were given the

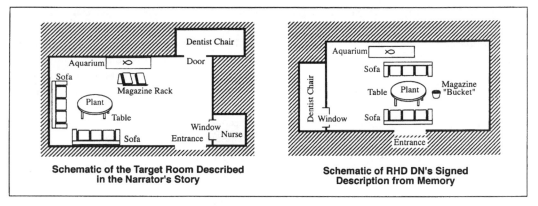

Figure 26-5. Illustration of the breakdown in the use of topographic space after right hemisphere damage (RHD). The figure is a schematic of RHD signer DN's retelling of a spatial description (adapted from Emmorey, Corina, & Bellugi, 1995).

same task, Damasio et al. (2001) found that naming spatial relations with English prepositions engaged only left parietal cortex. Thus, for sign language, additional neural areas within the right hemisphere appear to be recruited when signers describe spatial relationships using classifier constructions (see Fischer & van der Hulst, this volume). The right hemisphere may be specifically engaged when spatial locations in signing space must be related to another representation of spatial locations, either in the form of a mental image (e.g., when describing a room from memory) or in the form of physical objects (e.g., within a picture or scene). A reasonable hypothesis suggested by Corina (1998a) is that the difficulties that RHD patients exhibit in producing and comprehending classifier constructions and the topographic functions of signing space may stem from a more general problem with encoding external spatial relations into body-centered manual representations, particularly when two articulators are used. Thus, the right hemisphere may play a unique role in the interpretation of ASL spatial descriptions, a role that is not required for English spatial descriptions.

Overall, these results indicate that both the production and comprehension of classifier constructions that express spatial relationships engage neural areas within both left and right hemispheres. With respect to language, parietal regions may be uniquely engaged during the production and comprehension of spatial language in signed languages, particularly for locative classifier constructions in which the location of the signer's

hands in space specifies the spatial relation between objects.

Discourse Processes

Evidence from spoken language users indicates right hemisphere engagement in higher-level discourse processes, suggesting some degree of dissociation between sentence and discourse levels of language processing (see Joanette et al., 1990, for a review). Mildly or moderately impaired (hearing) aphasics exhibit relatively preserved narrative discourse skills; for example, narrative superstructure is preserved (there is a setting, a complicating action, and a resolution), despite grammatical deficits at the sentence level. In contrast, nonaphasic RHD subjects do not produce grammatical errors but nonetheless show impairments in discourse coherence. They exhibit an overall difficulty maintaining a topic and integrating information, and they produce uninformative details and circumlocutions within a narrative.

Although only a few case studies of discourse in RHD signers have been conducted, the results suggest the same neural organization for signed and spoken language at the discourse level. Two types of discourse-level deficits have been reported with right hemisphere damage for ASL signers. Hickok et. al (1999) found that the RHD signer AR had difficulty with topic maintenance and frequently produced tangential utterances. Similarly, Corina, Kritchevsky, and Bellugi (1996, p. 325) reported that the RHD signer JH produced occasional non-sequiturs and exhibited an abnormal attention to detail; they provide the following example from JH's description of the "cookie theft picture" (a standard picture used to elicit a language sample):

JH: ME SEE₁ KITCHEN LITTLE BOY STEP-UP #L-A-D-D-E-R AND MAYBE HIS MOTHER STAND #B-Y #S-I-N-K, WINDOW WASH #D-I-S-H-E-S. OUTSIDE, LITTLE COLD. SEE₁ WINDOW CURTAIN #D-R-A-P-E-S #C-U-R-T-A-I-N-S. MAYBE ASK HIS MOTHER PERMIS-SION?

ENGLISH TRANSLATION
"I see a kitchen, a little boy is stepping up a ladder. Perhaps, his mother, is standing by the sink under the kitchen window washing dishes. Outside it appears cold. I see the window curtains, the drapes. Maybe the boy has asked his mother permission [to get the cookies]?"

Another type of discourse deficit that can occur independently of a deficit in topic maintenance is an impairment in spatial co-reference across a discourse, which is often accompanied by errors in the use of referential shift (a discourse device used to the indicate point of view of a referent within a narrative). Two RHD signers (SJ and DN) have been reported to have difficulty maintaining consistent spatial locations for referents within a discourse (Hickok et al., 1999; Poizner & Kegl, 1992). For example, when retelling the "paint story" about a boy and girl painting on each other, the RHD signer SJ initially associated the referents (the boy and girl) with spatial locations along the midsagittal (front-back) plane, but then switched the association to the horizontal (left-right) plane, and he switched back and forth between planes without any marking to indicate a referential shift (Hickok et at., 1999). The RHD signer DN appeared to compensate for her difficulty in maintaining the association between referents and spatial locations across a discourse by frequently substituting fully specified noun phrases where pronouns would be more suitable; this rendered her narratives stylistically awkward, although they were still intelligible (Poizner & Kegl, 1992). Loew, Kegl, and Poizner (1997) also reported that DN was impaired in her ability to nonmanually signal changes in perspective with appropriate shifts in eyegaze, and she did not produce the affective facial expressions that control signers

produced to convey the perspective of a given character within a referential shift.

It is important to note that none of these RHD signers (JH, SJ, AR, or DN) made errors in pronoun use or verb agreement within a sentence or across short discourses (two or three sentences). Furthermore, the discourse deficits described above cannot be accounted for by general deficits in visual-spatial processing (Hickok et al., 1999). For example, SJ and AR both exhibited relatively severe visual-spatial deficits, but only SJ was impaired in maintaining spatial co-reference; in addition, DN suffered only mild visual-spatial impairments, but exhibited the same type of discourse impairments observed for SJ. These initial results indicate that the right hemisphere is engaged in similar discourse-encoding functions for both spoken and signed languages: topic maintenance, discourse cohesion, and interpreting character mood.

Summary and Conclusions

One overarching finding that emerges from studies of both neurologically intact and brain-injured signers is that the left cerebral hemisphere is critical for sign language processes, as it is for spoken language. The data from sign language eliminates two competing hypotheses regarding the nature of this specialization. First, sign language does not rely on the generation or perception of fast acoustic transitions, and yet the left hemisphere is dominant for processing sign language to the same degree that it is for spoken language. Second, complex gesture can be dissociated from sign language production, suggesting distinct underlying neural systems. This result also suggests that neither complex motor requirements nor symbolic functions underlie the left hemispheric specialization for language (although it is possible that there is no nonlinguistic equivalent that can match the high level of motoric complexity of either speech or sign). In addition, the data argue against the hypothesis that the co-evolution of language and the neuro-anatomical mechanisms of speech production is what led to the left hemisphere specialization for language (e.g., Liberman, 1974). Rather, it may be that neural structures within the left hemisphere are particularly well suited to interpreting and representing linguistic systems, regardless of the biology of language production and perception. The critical question, of course, is why are these neural structures well suited for language, or put another way, what is it about linguistic systems that causes them to be left lateralized? These questions remain unanswered, but the study of signed languages provides a tool by teasing apart those aspects of linguistic systems that are fundamental and inherent to the system from those aspects that can be affected by language modality.

Both neural plasticity and rigidity are observed for the neural organization within the left hemisphere for deaf signers. Neural plasticity is observed for auditory-related cortex, which has received little or no auditory input, but nonetheless is engaged in processing the visual input of sign language. More striking, perhaps, is that the same neural structures (e.g., Broca's area, Wernicke's area) are engaged for the production and comprehension of both signed and spoken language. This neural invariance across language modalities points to a biological or developmental bias for these neural structures to mediate language at a more abstract level, divorced from the sensory and motoric systems that perceive and transmit language.

There is currently some controversy regarding the role of the right hemisphere in sign language processing (e.g., Hickok, Bellugi, & Klima, 1998b; Paulesu & Mehler, 1998; Peperkamp & Mehler, 1999). As seen in figure 26-2, functional brain imaging reveals a large amount of right hemisphere activity during sign language comprehension. For both spoken and sign language comprehension, the right hemisphere appears to be involved in processing some discourse-level functions (e.g., cohesion), lexical imagery, and even some aspects of complex sentence comprehension (Caplan, Hildebrandt, & Makris, 1996; Hickok et al., 2002). Nonetheless, for sign language, the right hemisphere may play a unique role in the production and comprehension of the topographic functions of signing space, particularly as conveyed by classifier constructions.

Finally, the research reviewed here will probably be out of date relatively soon. With the accessibility of new brain imaging techniques, there is currently an explosion of studies investigating the neural systems underlying sign language production and comprehension, as well as research that explores the effects of auditory deprivation and/or sign language experience on language-related cortices and cortical regions involved in visual-spatial and motion processing. As we learn more about the brain, new questions will emerge that can be investigated by studying signed languages and deaf people. As our understanding of sign language processing and the relation between language and cognition grows, it is certain to be complemented by an increased understanding of the neural systems that give rise to linguistic and cognitive functions.

Notes

Portions of this chapter appeared in K Emmorey, *Language, Cognition, and the Brain: Insights from sign language research* (2002, Lawrence Erlbaum Associates, Mahwah, NJ). I gratefully acknowledge the support of the National Science Foundation (Linguistics Program; SBR-9809002), the National Institute of Child Health and Development (R01 HD 13249) and the National Institute on Deafness and other Communicative Disorders (R01 DC00201).

1. Lesion information was not published, but BI exhibited neurological symptoms and behavior typical of right hemisphere-damaged patients.

2. This signer was referred to by the initials AS in Poizner and Kegl (1992) and in Loew, Kegl, and Poizner (1997).

References

Beeman, M., & Chiarello, C. (1998). (Eds.). *Right hemisphere language comprehension: Perspectives from cognitive neuroscience*. Mahwah, NJ: Lawrence Erlbaum Associates.

Blumstein, S. (1998). Phonological aspects of aphasia. In M. T. Sarno (Ed.), *Acquired aphasia* (3rd ed.), pp. 157–185). San Diego, CA: Academic Press.

Brentari, D., Poizner, H., & Kegl, J. (1995). Aphasic and parkinsonian signing: Differences in phonological disruption. *Brain and Language, 48*, 69–105.

Brown, J. W. (1997). *Mind, brain, and consciousness: The neuropsychology of cognition*. New York: Academic Press.

Caplan, D., Gow, D., & Makris, N. (1995). Analysis of lesions by MRI in stroke patients with acoustic-phonetic processing deficits. *Neurology, 45*, 293–298.

Caplan, D., Hildebrandt, H., & Makris, N. (1996). Location of lesions in stroke patents with deficits in syntactic processing in sentence comprehension *Brain, 119*, 933–949.

Chiarello, C., Senehi, J., & Nuding, S. (1987). Semantic priming with abstract and concrete words: Differential asymmetry may be postlexical. *Brain and Language, 31*, 43–60.

Corina, D. P. (1998a). Aphasia in users of signed languages. In P. Coppens, Y. Lebrun, & A. Basso (Eds.), *Aphasia in atypical populations* (pp. 261–310). Mahwah, NJ: Lawrence Erlbaum Associates.

Corina, D. P. (1998b). Neuronal processing in deaf signers: Toward a neurocognitive model of language processing in the deaf. *Journal of Deaf Studies and Deaf Education, 3*(1), 35–48.

Corina, D. P. (1998c). The processing of sign language: Evidence from aphasia. In B. Stemmer & H. A. Whitaker (Eds.), *Handbook of neurolinguistics* (pp. 313–329). New York: Academic Press.

Corina, D. P. (1999a). On the nature of left hemisphere specialization for signed language. *Brain and Language, 69*, 230–240.

Corina, D. P. (1999b). Neural disorders of language and movement: Evidence from American Sign Language. In L. S. Messing & R. Campbell (Eds.), *Gesture, speech, and sign* (pp. 27–43). New York: Oxford University Press.

Corina, D. P. (2000). Some observations on paraphasia in American Sign Language. In K Emmorey & H. Lane (Eds.), *The signs of language revisited: An anthology to honor Ursula Bellugi and Edward Klima* (pp. 493–508). Mahwah, NJ: Lawrence Erlbaum Associates.

Corina, D. P. (2002, February). *The development of brain specializations for sign language systems.* Paper presented at the American Association for the Advancement of Science Annual Meeting, Boston, MA.

Corina, D., Kritchevsky, M., & Bellugi, U. (1996). Visual language processing and unilateral neglect: Evidence from American Sign Language. *Cognitive Neuropsychology, 13*(3), 321–356.

Corina, D. P., McBurney, S. L., Dodrill, C., Hinshaw, K., Brinkley, J., & Ojemann, G. (1999). Functional roles of Broca's area and supramarginal gyrus: Evidence from cortical stimulation mapping in a deaf signer. *NeuroImage, 10*, 570–581.

Corina, D. P., Poizner, H., Bellugi, U., Feinberg, T., Dowd, D., & O'Grady-Batch, L. (1992). Dissociation between linguistic and non-linguistic gestural systems: A case for compositionality. *Brain and Language, 43*, 414–447.

Corina, D., San Jose, L., Ackerman, D., Guillemin, A., & Braun, A. (2000). A comparison of neural systems underlying human action and American Sign Language processing. *Journal of Cognitive Neuroscience* (Suppl.), 43–44.

Corina, D., Vaid, J., & Bellugi, U. (1992). The linguistic basis of left hemisphere specialization. *Science, 253*, 1258–1260.

Damasio, H., Grabowski, T., Tranel, D., Ponto, L., Hichwa, R., & A. R. Damasio (2001) Neural correlates of naming actions and of naming spatial relations. *NeuroImage, 13*, 1053–1064.

Day, J. (1979). Visual half-field word recognition as a function of syntactic class and imageability. *Neuropsychologia, 17*, 515–520.

Emmorey, K., & Corina, D. P. (1993). Hemispheric specialization for ASL signs and English words: differences between imageable and abstract forms. *Neuropsychologia, 31*, 645–653.

Emmorey, K., Corina, D., & Bellugi, U. (1995). Differential processing of topographic and referential functions of space. In K. Emmorey & J. Reilly (Eds.), *Language, gesture, and space* (pp. 43–62). Hillsdale, NJ: Lawrence Erlbaum Associates.

Emmorey, K., Damasio, H., McCullough, S., Grabowski, T., Ponto, L, Hichwa, R., & Bellugi, U. (2002). Neural systems underlying spatial language in American Sign Language. *NeuroImage, 17*, 812–824.

Emmorey, K., Grabowski, T., McCullough, S., Damasio, H., Ponto, L, Hichwa, R., & Bellugi, U. (2003). Neural systems underlying lexical retrieval sign language. *Neuropsychologia, 41*(1), 85–95.

Emmorey, K., & Kosslyn, S. (1996). Enhanced image generation abilities in deaf signers: A right hemisphere effect. *Brain and Cognition, 32*, 28–44.

Emmorey, K., Kosslyn, S., & Bellugi, U. (1993). Visual imagery and visual-spatial language: Enhanced imagery abilities in deaf and hearing ASL signers. *Cognition, 46*, 139–181.

Fitch, R. H., Miller, S., & Tallal, P. (1997). Neurobiology of speech perception. *Annual review of Neuroscience, 20*, 331–353.

Friederici, A. (2002). Towards a neural basis of auditory sentence processing. *Trends in Cognitive Sciences, 6*(2), 78–84.

Goodglass, H. (1993). *Understanding aphasia.* San Diego, CA: Academic Press.

Goodglass, H., & Kaplan, E. (1983). *The assessment of aphasia and related disorders* (Reference ed.). Philadelphia, PA: Lea and Febiger.

Hickok, G., Bellugi, U., & Klima, E. (1998a). The basis of the neural organization for language: Evidence from sign language aphasia. *Reviews in the Neurosciences, 8*, 205–222.

Hickok, G., Bellugi, U., & Klima, E. (1998b). What's right about the neural organization of sign language? A perspective on recent neuroimaging results. *Trends in Cognitive Science, 2*, 465–468.

Hickok, G., Klima, E. S. & Bellugi, U. (1996). The neurobiology of signed language and its implications for the neural basis of language. *Nature, 381*, 699–702.

Hickok, G., Kritchevsky, M., Bellugi, U., & Klima, E. S. (1996). The role of the left frontal operculum in sign language aphasia. *Neurocase*, 2, 373–380.

Hickok, G., Love-Geffen, T., & Klima, E. S. (2002). Role of the left hemisphere in sign language comprehension. *Brain & Language*, 82(2), 167–178.

Hickok, G., Wilson, M., Clark, K., Klima, E. S., Kritchevsky, M., & Bellugi, U. (1999). Discourse deficits following right hemisphere damage in deaf signers. *Brain and Language*, 66, 233–248.

Joanette, Y., Goulet, P., & Hannequin. D. (1990). *Right hemisphere and verbal communication*. New York: Springer-Verlag.

Kegl, J., & Poizner, H. (1997). Crosslinguistic/crossmodal syntactic consequences of left-hemisphere damage: evidence from an aphasic signer and his identical twin. *Aphasiology*, 11, 1–37.

Kimura, D. (1993). *Neuromotor mechanisms in human communication*. Oxford: Oxford University Press.

Kimura, D., & Archibald, Y. (1974). Motor functions of the left hemisphere. *Brain*, 97, 337–350.

Liberman, A. (1974). The specialization of the language hemisphere. In F.O. Schmitt & F.G. Worden (Eds.), *The neurosciences third study program* (pp. 43–56). Cambridge, MA: MIT Press.

Loew, R. C., Kegl, J. A., & Poizner, H. (1997). Fractionation of the components of role play in a right-hemispheric lesioned signer. *Aphasiology*, 11, 263–281.

MacSweeney, M., Woll, B., Campbell, R., McGuire, P. K., David, A. S., Williams, S. C., Suckling, J., Calvert, G. A., & Brammer, M. J. (2002). Neural systems underlying British Sign Language and audio-visual English processing in native users. *Brain*, 125, 1583–1593.

McKee, D. (1987). *An analysis of specialized cognitive functions in deaf and hearing signers*. Unpublished doctoral dissertation, University of Pittsburgh, Pittsburgh, PA.

McGuire, P., Robertson, D., Thacker, A., David, A.S., Kitson, N., Frackovwiak, R.S.J., & Frith, C.D. (1997). Neural correlates of thinking in sign language. *NeuroReport*, 8(3), 695–697.

Neville, H., Bavelier, D., Corina, D., Rauschecker, J., Karni, A., Lalwani, A., Braun, A., Clark, V., Jezzard, P., & Turner, R. (1998). Cerebral organization for language in deaf and hearing subjects: Biological constraints and effects of experience. *Proceedings of the National Academy of Sciences, USA*, 95, 922–929.

Neville, H., Coffey, S., Lawson, D., Fischer, A., Emmorey, K., & Bellugi, U. (1997). Neural systems mediating American Sign Language: Effects of sensory experience and age of acquisition. *Brain and Language*, 57, 285–308.

Newman, A., Bavelier, D., Corina, D., Jezzard, P., & Neville, H. (2002). A critical period for right hemisphere recruitment in American Sign Language processing. *Nature Neuroscience*, 5(1), 76–80.

Nishimura, H., Hashikawa, K., Doi, D., Iwaki, T., Watanabe, Y., Kusuoka, H., Nishimura, T., & Kubo, T. (1999). Sign language 'heard' in the auditory cortex. *Nature*, 397, 116.

Paulesu, E., & Mehler, J. (1998). Right on in sign language. *Nature*, 392, 233–234.

Peperkamp, S., & Mehler, J. (1999). Signed and spoken language: A unique underlying system? *Language and Speech*, 42, 333–346.

Petitto, L. A., Zatorre, R. J., Nikelski, E. J., Gauna, K., Dostie, D., & Evans, A. C. (1997). Cerebral organization for language in the absence of sound: A PET study of deaf signers processing signed languages (abstr. no. 867.8). *Abstracts of the 27th Annual Meeting of the Society for Neuroscience*, 23, 2228.

Petitto, L. A., Zatorre, R. J., Nikelski, E. J., Gauna, K., Dostie, D., & Evans, A. C. (1998). By hand or by tongue: Common cerebral blood flow activation during language processing in signed and spoken languages. *NeuroImage*, 7(4), S193.

Petitto, L. A., Zatorre, R. J., Gauna, K. Nikelski, E. J., Dostie, D., & Evans, A. (2000). Speech-like cerebral activity in profoundly deaf people processing signed languages: Implications for the neural basis of human language. *Proceedings of the National Academy of Sciences, USA*, 97(25), 13961–13966.

Poizner, H., & Kegl, J. (1992). Neural basis of language and motor behaviour: perspectives from American Sign Language. *Aphasiology*, 6(3), 219–256.

Poizner, H., Klima, E. S., & Bellugi, U. (1987). *What the hands reveal about the brain*. Cambridge, MA: MIT Press.

Posner, M. I., & Petersen, S. E. (1990). The attention system of the human brain. *Annual review of Neuroscience*, 13, 25–42.

Söderfeldt, B., Ingvar, M., Rönnberg, J., Eriksson, L., Serrander, M., & Stone-Elander, S. (1997). Signed and spoken language perception studied by positron emission tomography. *Neurology*, 49, 82–87.

Talbot, K. F., & Haude, R. H. (1993). The relationship between sign language skill and spatial visualization ability: Mental rotation of three-dimensional objects. *Perceptual and Motor Skills*, 77, 1387–1391.

Tallal, P., Miller, S., & Fitch, R. H. (1993). Neurobiological basis of speech: A case for the preeminence
of temporal processing. *Annals of the New York
Academy of Sciences, 682,* 27–47.

Ungerleider, L. G., & Mishkin, M. (1982). Two cortical visual systems. In D. J. Ingle, M. A. Goodale,
& R. J. W. Mansfield (Eds.), *Analysis of visual
behavior* (pp. 549–589) Cambridge, MA: MIT
Press.

Vaid, J., Bellugi, U., & Poizner, H. (1989). Hand dominance for signing: Clues to brain lateralization of
language. *Brain and Language, 27,* 949–960.

VI

Hearing and Speech Perception

27

Lynne E. Bernstein & Edward T. Auer, Jr.

Speech Perception and Spoken Word Recognition

Speech is an important mode of communication for many people with hearing losses, even with losses at severe (60–89 dB HL) or profound (>90 dB HL bilaterally) levels. Individuals with hearing losses of these magnitudes occupy positions on a continuum between relying exclusively on spoken language and relying exclusively on manual language. Speech perception can depend totally on heard speech at one extreme and on seen speech (lip-reading/speechreading) at the other.[1] In addition, communication conditions can determine where on the continuum an individual is at any particular time. For example, students at Gallaudet University who relied on manual language in their classrooms and elsewhere on campus reported reliance on spoken language for communicating with their hearing friends, families, and the public (Bernstein, Demorest, & Tucker, 1998).

This chapter focuses on spoken communication by adults with severe or profound hearing loss, although it includes relevant discussion of results from studies involving participants with mild to moderate hearing losses or with normal hearing. The chapter describes several fundamental issues in speech perception and spoken word recognition and reviews what is known about these issues in relation to perceivers with severe-to-profound hearing losses.

Speech Perception

When talkers produce speech, their articulatory gestures typically produce acoustic and optical signals that are available to perceivers. The auditory and visual perceptual systems must categorize the linguistically relevant speech information in the speech signals. The physical forms of speech have a hierarchical structure. The segmental consonants and vowels comprise subsegmental features. Those features can be described in articulatory terms such as place of articulation (e.g., bilabial, dental, alveolar), manner of articulation (e.g., stop, liquid, vocalic, nasal), and voicing (voiced, unvoiced) (Catford, 1977).[2] The speech segments are used in language combinatorially to form morphemes (minimal units of linguistic analysis such as "un," "reason," "able" in "unreasonable"), which in turn combine to form words. Language differs from other animal communication systems in its generativity, not only to produce infinitely many different sentences out of a set of words but also to gen-

erate new words by combining the finite set of segmental consonants and vowels within a particular
language.

That consonants and vowels are structurally
key to the generation of word forms has also
suggested that they are key to the perception of
words. However, discovering how perceivers recognize the consonant and vowel segments in the
speech signals produced by talkers has not proved
straightforward and has not yet been fully accomplished (e.g., Fowler, 1986; Liberman & Whalen,
2000; Nearey, 1997). The reason for this difficulty
is that the speech segments are not produced like
beads on a string, and so do not appear as beads on
a string in the acoustic signal (Liberman, 1982).
The speech articulators—the lips, tongue, velum,
and larynx—produce speech gestures in a coordinated and overlapping manner that results in overlapping information. The speech production gestures change the overall shape of the vocal tract
tube, and those shapes are directly responsible for
the resonances (formants/concentrations of energy)
of the speech signal (Stevens, 1998). However, different vocal tract shapes can produce signals that
are perceived as the same segment, further complicating matters.

Numerous experiments have been conducted
using synthesized, filtered, and edited speech waveforms to isolate the parts of the speech signal that
are critical to the perception of speech. Although it
is not yet completely known how auditory perceptual processes analyze acoustic speech signals, it is
known that listeners are remarkably capable of perceiving the linguistically relevant information in
even highly degraded signals (e.g., Remez, 1994).
The questions of importance here are what auditory
information can be obtained by individuals with
severe or profound hearing loss and how speech
perception is affected by individual hearing loss
configurations. Work on this problem began with
examining how speech perception with normal
hearing is affected by various manipulations such
as filtering. For example, Miller and Nicely (1955)
showed that perception of place of articulation
(e.g., /b/ versus /d/ versus /g/) information depends
greatly on the frequencies above 1000 Hz, but voicing (e.g., /b/ versus /p/) is well preserved with only
frequencies below 1000 Hz. The manner feature
involves the entire range of speech frequencies and
appears to be less sensitive to losses in the higher
frequencies.

Auditory-only Speech Perception of Listeners with Impaired Hearing

As level of hearing loss increases, access to auditory
speech signals decreases. At severe or profound levels of hearing loss, hearing aids can help overcome
problems with audibility of speech sounds for some
individuals, particularly when listening conditions
are clear. Amplification systems are designed to restore audibility by boosting intensity in regions of
the spectrum affected by the loss. Unfortunately,
when hearing loss is severe or profound, simply
increasing the amplitude of the signal does not always restore the listener's access to the information
in the speech signal: At those levels of hearing loss,
the speech information that can be perceived auditorily is typically highly degraded due to limitations imposed by the listener's auditory system. For
example, high sound-pressure levels required to
amplify speech adequately to compensate for severe
or profound levels result in additional distortion,
apparently equivalent to the distortion experienced
by hearing people under equivalent signal presentation conditions (Ching, Dillon, & Byrne 1998).
However, it is difficult to generalize across individuals. Results vary, and many different factors may
be involved in how well a hearing aid ameliorates
the effects of the hearing loss. These factors include
the specific type of hearing loss (e.g., the specific
frequencies and the magnitude of the loss for those
frequencies), and, quite likely, factors involving
central brain processing of the auditory information, including word knowledge and experience listening to the talker.

Specific speech features are affected at different
levels of hearing loss. Boothroyd (1984) conducted
a study of 120 middle- and upper-school children
in the Clarke School for the Deaf in Northampton,
Massachusetts. The children's hearing losses, measured in terms of pure-tone averages in decibels of
hearing level (dB HL) ranged between 55 and 123
dB. The children were tested using a four-
alternative, forced-choice procedure for several
speech segment contrasts. The results showed that
as the hearing losses increased, specific types of
speech contrasts became inaudible, but information
continued to be available even with profound
losses. After correcting for chance, the point at
which scores fell to 50% was 75 dB HL for consonant place, 85 dB HL for initial consonant voicing,
90 dB HL for initial consonant continuance, 100

dB HL for vowel place (front-back), and 115 dB HL for vowel height. Boothroyd thought these might be conservative estimates of the children's listening abilities, given that their hearing aids might not have been optimized for their listening abilities.

Ching et al. (1998) reported on a study of listeners with normal hearing and listeners with hearing losses across the range from mild to profound. They presented sentence materials for listening under a range of filter and intensity level conditions. Listeners were asked to repeat each sentence after its presentation. Under the more favorable listening conditions for the listeners with severe or profound losses, performance scores covered the range from no words correct to highly accurate (approximately 80–90% correct). That is, having a severe or profound hearing loss was not highly predictive of the speech identification score, and some listeners were quite accurate in repeating the sentences. In general, the majority of the listeners, including listeners whose hearing losses were in the range of 90–100 dB HL (i.e., with profound losses), benefited from amplification of stimuli for the frequencies below approximately 2800 Hz. (Telephones present frequencies in a range only up to approximately 3200 Hz, suggesting that perceiving frequencies up to 2800 could be very useful.)

Turner and Brus (2001) were interested in the finding that when hearing loss is greater than 40–80 dB HL for the higher frequencies of speech, very little benefit is achieved by increasing the amplification of those higher frequencies, and, in some cases, the amplification actually results in lower performance. However, amplification of lower frequency regions does seem to provide benefit. They hypothesized that there might be an interaction between effects due to the frequency regions for which hearing loss occurred and the types of speech information the listeners were able to perceive, depending on amplification characteristics. Listeners who had hearing losses from mild to severe were asked to identify consonant-vowel and vowel-consonant nonsense syllables that were low-pass filtered at the cutoff frequencies of 560, 700, 900, 1120, 1400, 2250, and 2800 Hz. That is, only the frequencies below the cutoff were in the stimuli.

A main question for Turner and Brus (2001) was whether amplification of the lower frequencies of speech was helpful regardless of the level of hearing loss; affirmative findings were obtained across listeners and filter conditions. Turner and Brus also analyzed their data to determine how the speech features of manner, voicing, and place were independently affected by the filtering conditions and the degree of hearing loss. The manner feature refers to the distinction between consonants that are stops (e.g., /b, d, g/) versus fricatives (e.g., /f, s, z/), versus affricates (e.g., /j, č/), versus liquids (e.g., /l, r/). For this feature, performance generally improved as the filter cutoff allowed more frequencies into the stimuli. The voicing feature refers to the distinction between voiced (e.g., /b, d, g/) and voiceless (e.g., /p, t, k/) consonants. This feature was transmitted well to all the listeners, even when the low-pass filter cutoff was at its lowest levels, and even for the listeners with the more severe losses. That is, the voicing cue is robust to extreme limitations in the low frequency range of audible speech. The place feature refers to the position in the vocal tract where the consonant occlusion is formed (e.g., /b/ is formed by closure of the lips and /k/ is formed by closure of the back portion of the tongue against the velum). This feature was most sensitive to addition of higher frequencies and was most sensitive to the degree of hearing loss. Listeners with the more severe losses were unable to benefit much as additional higher frequencies were allowed into the stimulus.

In general, Turner and Brus (2001) confirmed the Ching et al. (1998) findings, suggesting that listeners with severe or profound hearing loss benefit most from amplification of the lower frequencies of speech. Nevertheless, in comparisons with hearing listeners, amplification for those with severe or profound hearing losses does not restore speech perception accuracy to normal levels.

Lipreading

As the level of hearing loss increases, and/or in environmental noise increase, people with severe or profound hearing losses typically must rely on being able to see visual speech information to augment or substitute for auditory speech information. The literature on lipreading does not necessarily encourage the view that visual information is a good substitute for auditory information. Estimates of the upper extremes for the accuracy of lipreading words in sentences have been as low as 10–30% words correct (Rönnberg, 1995; Rönnberg, Samuelsson, & Lyxell, 1998). Estimates of the ability to perceive consonants and vowels via lipreading alone have varied across studies and the particular stimuli used. Such studies typically involve presentation of a set of nonsense syllables with varied consonants or varied vowels and a forced-choice identification procedure. In general, consonant identification is reported to be less than 50% correct (e.g., Owens & Blazek, 1985), and vowel identification is reported to be somewhat greater than 50% correct (e.g., Montgomery & Jackson, 1983).

Several authors have asserted that the necessity to rely on visible speech due to hearing loss does not result in enhanced lipreading performance (e.g., Summerfield, 1991), and that lipreading in hearing people is actually better than in deaf people due to auditory experience in the former (Mogford, 1987). Furthermore, several authors assert that lipreaders can only perceive visemes (e.g., Fisher, 1968; Massaro, 1987, 1998). That is, the consonant categories of speech are so highly ambiguous to lipreaders that they can only distinguish broadly among groups of consonants, those broad groups referred to as visemes. Finally, some estimates of how words appear to lipreaders have suggested that approximately 50% of words in English appear to be ambiguous with other words (Berger, 1972; Nitchie, 1916).

To investigate some of these generalizations, Bernstein, Demorest, and Tucker (2000) conducted a study of lipreading in 96 hearing students at the University of Maryland and in 72 college students at Gallaudet University with 60 dB HL or greater bilateral hearing losses. All of the Gallaudet students reported English as their native language and the language of their family, and they had been educated in a mainstream and/or oral program for 8 or more years. Seventy-one percent of the students had profound hearing losses bilaterally. Sixty-two percent had hearing losses by age 6 months. The participants were asked to lipread nonsense syllables in a forced-choice procedure and isolated words and sentences in an open set procedure. The stimuli were spoken by two different talkers who were recorded on laser video disc.

Results of the study revealed a somewhat different picture of lipreading from that of previous studies. Across all the performance measures in this study, deaf college students were significantly more accurate than were the hearing adults. Approximately 65–75% of the deaf students outperformed 75% of the hearing students. The entire upper quartile of deaf students' scores was typically above the upper quartile of hearing students' scores. For example, one sentence set produced upper quartile scores of percent correct words ranging between 44 and 69% for the hearing students and ranging between 73 and 88% for the deaf students. When the results were investigated in terms of the perceptual errors that were made during lipreading of sentences, the deaf students were far more systematic than the hearing students: when deaf students erred perceptually, they were nevertheless closer to being correct than were the hearing students. When the nonsense syllable data were analyzed in terms of the subsegmental (subphonemic) features perceived, the results showed that the deaf students perceived more of the features than did the hearing students. Finally, among those deaf students with the highest performance were ones with profound, congenital hearing losses, suggesting that visual speech perception had been the basis for their acquisition of knowledge of spoken language, and that reliance on visible speech can result in enhanced perceptual ability.

Bernstein, Demorest, et al. (1998) investigated possible correlations between lipreading performance levels in the Bernstein et al. (2000) study and other factors that might affect or be related to visual speech perception. They examined more than 29 variables in relationship to the deaf students' identification scores on nonsense syllables, isolated words, and isolated sentences. The broad categories of factors that they investigated included audiological variables, parents' educational levels, home communication practices, public communication practices, self-assessed ability to understand via speech, self-assessed ability to be understood via speech, and scores on the Gallaudet University English Placement Test. The parents' educational levels were found not to be correlated with lipreading scores. Neither were most of the audiological variables, such as when the hearing loss occurred, when it was discovered, or level of hearing loss.

Important variables related to lipreading scores included (1) frequency of hearing aid use, which was generally positively correlated with speech scores, such that the more frequently the hearing aid was used the more accurate the student's lipreading (r ranged from .350 to .384);[3] (2) communication at home with speech, which was correlated with better lipreading scores (r ranged from .406 to .611); (3) self-assessed ability to be understood via speech in communication with the general public (r ranged from .214 to .434); and (4) the reading subtest of the English Placement Test (r ranged from .257 to .399).

Regression analyses were used to investigate the best predictors of lipreading scores among the variables that produced significant correlations. Only three factors survived the analysis as the significant predictors for scores on words and sentences: self-assessed ability to understand the general public, communication at home with speech, and the English Placement Test score. In fact, the multiple R values obtained from the analysis were quite high, ranging from .730 to .774 for scores on lipreading words and sentences. That is, more than 50% of the variance in the scores was accounted for by the three best factors. To summarize, lipreading ability was highly related to experience communicating successfully via speech and was also related to the ability to read.

Spoken Word Recognition

The focus on perception of the segmental consonants and vowels in the speech perception literature might leave the reader with the impression that perception of speech terminates in recognition of the speech segments. Indeed, some researchers theorize that perception of spoken language involves perceptual evaluation of subsegmental units to categorize the consonant and vowel segments at an abstract level (e.g., Massaro, 1998). Recognition of words would then depend on assembling the abstract segmental categories and matching them to the segmental patterns of words in long-term memory. According to this view, perception terminates at the level of recognizing segments. However, research on spoken word recognition suggests that perception extends to the level of lexical processing.

Abundant evidence has been obtained showing that the speed and ease of recognizing a spoken word is a function of both its phonetic/stimulus properties (e.g., segmental intelligibility) and its lexical properties (e.g., "neighborhood density," the number of words an individual knows that are perceptually similar to a stimulus word, and "word frequency," an estimate of the quantity of experience an individual has with a particular word) (Lahiri & Marslen-Wilson, 1991; Luce, 1986; Luce, & Pisoni, 1998; Luce, Pisoni, & Goldinger, 1990; Marslen-Wilson, 1992; McClelland & Elman, 1986; Norris, 1994).

"Segmental intelligibility" refers to how easily the segments (consonants and vowels) are identified by the perceiver. This is the factor that segmental studies of speech perception are concerned with. Word recognition tends to be more difficult when segmental intelligibility is low and more difficult for words that are perceptually similar to many other words (see below). This factor shows that perception does not terminate at the level of abstract segmental categories. If perception did terminate at that level, it would be difficult to explain stimulus-based word similarity effects. Word recognition tends to be easier for words that are or have been experienced frequently. This factor might be related to perception or it might be related to higher level decision-making processes. All of these factors have potential to be affected by a hearing loss.

General Theoretical Perspective

Theories in the field of spoken word recognition attempt to account for all the factors defined above within a framework that posits perceptual (bottom-up) activation of multiple word candidates. Activation is a theoretical construct in perception research but is thought to be directly related to activation of relevant neural structures in the brain. The level of a word's bottom-up activation is a function of the similarity between the word's perceptual representation and that of candidate word forms stored in long-term memory (e.g., Luce, 1986; Luce, Goldinger, Auer, & Vitevitch, 2000; Luce & Pisoni, 1998; Marslen-Wilson, 1987, 1990; McClelland & Elman, 1986; Norris, 1994). Once active, candidate word forms compete for recognition in memory (Luce, 1986; Luce & Pisoni, 1998; Marslen-Wilson, 1992; McClelland & Elman, 1986; Norris, 1994). In addition to bottom-up stimulus information, recognition of a word is influenced by the amount and perhaps the type of previous experience an individual has had with that word (Goldinger, 1998; Howes, 1957). It is important to emphasize here that the long-term memory representations of stimulus word forms are hypothesized to be similar to the perceptual information and therefore different from memory representations for other types of language input (e.g., fingerspelling), as well as different from abstract knowledge about words (e.g., semantics; McEvoy, Marschark, & Nelson, 1999).

An implication of the view that the perceptual word information is used to discriminate among words in the mental dictionary (lexicon) is that successful word recognition can occur even when the speech signal is degraded. This is because recognition can occur even when the speech signal contains only sufficient information to discriminate among the word forms stored in the mental lexicon. For example, an individual with hearing loss may distinguish the consonants /p/, /t/, and /k/ from the other segments in English but might not distinguish within this set. For this individual, the word "parse" could still be recognized because "tarse" and "karse" do not occur as words in English. That is, words are recognized within the context of perceptually similar words, and therefore intelligibility is a function of both segmental intelligibility as well as the distribution of word forms in the perceiver's mental lexicon.

Visually Identifying Words with Reduced Speech Information

One fundamental question is what effect reduced speech information, such as the information available to the lipreader, has on the patterns of stimulus words that are stored in the mental lexicon. Nitchie (1916) and Berger (1972) investigated the relationship between reduced segmental intelligibility and the distribution of word forms for individuals with profound hearing losses who relied primarily on visible speech for oral communication. They argued that as a result of low consonant and vowel accuracy during lipreading, approximately 50% of words in English that sound different lose their distinctiveness (become homophenous/ambiguous with other words).

Auer and Bernstein (1997) developed computational methods to study this issue for lipreading and any other degraded perceptual conditions for speech. They wondered to what extent words lost their distinctive information when lipread—that is, how loss of distinction would interact with the word patterns in the mental dictionary. For example, even though /b/, /m/, and /p/ are similar to the lipreader, English has only the word, "bought," and not the words "mought" and "pought." So "bought" remains a distinct pattern as a word in English, even for the lipreader.

Specifically, the method incorporates rules to transcribe words so that only the segmental distinctions that are estimated to be perceivable are represented in the transcriptions. The rules comprise mappings for which one symbol is used to represent all the phonemes that are indistinct to the lipreader.[4] Then the mappings are applied to a computer-readable lexicon. For example, /b/ and /p/ are difficult to distinguish for a lipreader. So, words like "bat" and "pat" would be transcribed to be identical using a new common symbol like B (e.g., "bat" is transcribed as BAT and "pat" is transcribed as BAT). Then the transcribed words are sorted so that words rendered identical (no longer notationally distinct) are grouped together. The computer-readable lexicon used in these modeling studies was the PhLex lexicon. PhLex is a computer-readable phonemically transcribed lexicon with 35,000 words. The words include the 19,052 most frequent words in the Brown corpus (a compilation of approximately 1 million words in texts; Kucera & Francis, 1967).

Auer and Bernstein (1997) showed that when all the English phonemes were grouped according to the confusions made by average hearing lipreaders (i.e., the groups /u, ʊ, ɚr/, /o, aʊ/, /ɪ, i, e, ɛ, æ/, /ɔ, ɪ/, /ɔ, aɪ, ə, ɑ, ʌ, j/, /b, p, m/, /f, v/, /l, n, k, ŋ, g, h/, /d, t, s, z/, /w, r/, /ð, θ/, and /ʃ, tʃ, ʒ, dʒ/), 54% of words were still distinct across the entire PhLex lexicon. With 19 phoneme groups, approximately 75% of words were distinct, approximating an excellent deaf lipreader. In other words, small perceptual enhancements will lead to large increases in lipreading accuracy.

In addition to computational investigations of the lexicon, lexical modeling provides a method for generating explicit predictions about word identification accuracy. For example, Mattys, Bernstein, and Auer (2002) tested whether the number of words that a particular word might be confused with affects lipreading accuracy. Deaf and hearing individuals who were screened for above-average lipreading identified visual spoken words presented in isolation. Results showed that identification accuracy across deaf versus hearing participant groups was not different. The prediction that words would be more difficult, if there were more words with which they might be confused, was born out: Word identification accuracy decreased as a negative function of increased number of words estimated to be similar to the lipreader. Also, words with higher frequency of occurrence were easier to lipread.

In another related study, Auer (2002) applied the neighborhood activation model (NAM) of auditory spoken word recognition (Luce, 1986; Luce, & Pisoni, 1998) to the prediction of visual spoken word identification. The NAM can be used to obtain a value that predicts the relative intelligibility of specific words. High values are associated with more intelligible words. Deaf and hearing participants identified visual spoken words presented in isolation. The pattern of results was similar across the two participant groups. The obtained results were significantly correlated with the predicted intelligibility scores (hearing: $r = .44$; deaf: $r = .48$). Words with many neighbors were more difficult to identify than words with few neighbors. One question that might be asked is whether confusions among words really depends on the physical stimuli as opposed to their abstract linguistic structure. Auer correlated the lipreading results with results predicted on the basis of phoneme confusion patterns from identification of acoustic speech in noise, a condition that produces different patterns of phoneme confusions from those in lipreading. When the auditory confusions replaced the visual confusions in the computational model, the correlations were no longer significant. This result would be difficult to understand if word recognition were based on abstract phoneme patterns and not on the visual speech information.

Auditorily Identifying Words Under Conditions of Hearing Loss

The NAM has also been used to investigate auditory spoken word recognition in older listeners (52–84 years of age) with mild to moderate hearing loss (Dirks, Takayanagi, Moshfegh, Noffsinger, & Fausti, 2001). Words were presented for identification from word lists that varied the factors of neighborhood density (word form similarity), mean neighborhood frequency (frequency of occurrence of words in the neighborhood), and word frequency. All of the factors were significant in the results. Overall, high-frequency words were identified more accurately than low-frequency words. Words in low-density neighborhoods (few similar neighbors) were recognized more frequently than words in high-density neighborhoods. Words in

neighborhoods of words that were generally low in frequency were recognized more accurately than words in neighborhoods of words that were generally high in frequency. The pattern of results was overall essentially similar to results with a different group of listeners with normal hearing. However, the difference between best and worst conditions for listeners with hearing losses (20 percentage points) was greater than for listeners with normal hearing (15 percentage points). This difference among listeners suggests that lexical factors may become more important as listening becomes more difficult. Although the participants in this study had mild to moderate hearing losses, the study suggests that the processes of spoken word recognition are substantially similar across listeners.

In a related study, characteristics of the listeners included hearing loss versus normal hearing and native versus non-native listeners to English (Takayanagi, Dirks, & Moshfegh, in press). Participants were 20 native listeners of English with normal hearing, 20 native listeners with hearing loss, 20 non-native listeners with normal hearing, and 20 non-native listeners with hearing loss. Hearing losses were bilateral and mild to moderate. In this study, there were two groups of words, ones with high word frequency and in low-density neighborhoods (easy words), and ones with low word frequency and in high-density neighborhoods (hard words). Familiarity ratings were obtained on each of the words from each of the participants to statistically control for differences in long-term language experience. In general, there were significant effects obtained for hearing differences and for native language differences: listeners with normal hearing were more accurate than listeners with hearing losses, and native listeners were more accurate than non-native listeners. Easy words were in fact easier than hard words for all of the listeners. However, the difference between native and non-native listeners was greater for the easy words than for the hard words. These results suggest that the neighborhood structure affects both native and non-native listeners, with and without hearing losses. Additional analyses showed that important factors in accounting for the results included the audibility of the words (how loud they had to be to be heard correctly) and also the listener's subjective rating of their familiarity with each of the words.

Estimating Lexical Knowledge

An individual's knowledge of words arises as a function of his or her linguistic experience. Several variables related to lexical experience have been demonstrated to have some impact on the word recognition process, including the age at which words are acquired, the form of the language input (e.g., spoken or printed), and the frequency of experience with specific words (as discussed earlier). Prelingually deaf individuals' linguistic experience varies along all of these dimensions. Impoverishment in the available auditory information typically leads to delayed acquisition of a spoken language, often resulting in reductions in total exposure to spoken language. Prelingually deaf individuals are also likely to use some form of manual communication as their preferred communication mode, and/or as a supplement to lipreading. Several forms of manual communication can fulfill this role, including a form of English-based signing, American Sign Language (ASL), and cued speech (see Leybaert & Alegria, this volume). As a result of variation in these experiential factors, the prelingually deaf population comprises individuals who differ dramatically in the quantity and quality of their perceptual and linguistic experience with spoken words.

In this section, some studies are discussed that focused on lexical knowledge in expert lipreaders. The participants were all individuals who reported English as their native language and as the language of the family, were educated in a mainstream and/or oral program for 8 or more years, and were skilled as lipreaders.

Estimates of the relative quantity of word experience for undergraduates with normal hearing are based on objective word frequency counts based on text corpora (e.g., Kucera & Francis, 1967). However, this approach has its detractors, especially for estimating experience with words that occur infrequently in the language (Gernsbacher, 1984). Furthermore, the approach is clearly insensitive to individual differences that may occur within or between populations of English language users with different lexical experience.

An alternative to using objective counts to estimate word experience is to collect subjective familiarity ratings by having participants rate their familiarity with words presented individually using a labeled scale. Although several sources of knowledge likely contribute to these ratings, general agreement exists that familiarity partly reflects quantity of exposure to individual words. Auer, Bernstein, and Tucker (2000) compared and contrasted familiarity ratings collected from 50 hearing and 50 deaf college students. Judgments were made on a labeled scale from 1 (never seen, heard, or read the word before) to 7 (know the word and confident of its meaning). The within-group item ratings were similar ($r = .90$) for the two participant groups. However, deaf participants consistently judged words to be less familiar than did hearing participants.

Another difference between the groups emerged upon more detailed analysis of the ratings within and across participant groups. Each participant group was split into 5 subgroups of 10 randomly selected participants. Mean item ratings for each subgroup were then correlated with those of the other nine subgroups (four within a participant group and five between). The correlation coefficients were always highest within a participant group. That is, deaf participants used the familiarity scale more like other deaf participants than like hearing participants. The results suggested that despite the global similarity between the two participant groups noted above, the two groups appear to have experienced different ambient language samples. Thus, these results point to the importance of taking into account experiential differences in studies of spoken word recognition.

Another factor in the developmental history of an individual's lexicon is the age at which words are acquired. The age of acquisition (AOA) effect—faster and more accurate recognition and production of earlier acquired words—has been demonstrated in hearing participants using several measures of lexical processing (for a review, see Morrison & Ellis, 1995). Ideally, AOA for words would be based on some objective measure of when specific words were learned. However, AOA is typically estimated by the subjective ratings of adults. These ratings have been shown to have both high reliability among raters and high validity when compared to objective measures of word acquisition (Gilhooly & Gilhooly, 1980).

Auer and Bernstein (2002) investigated the impact of prelingual hearing loss on AOA. In this study, 50 hearing and 50 deaf participants judged AOA for the 175 words in form M of the Peabody Picture Vocabulary Test-Revised (PPVT; Dunn &

Dunn, 1981) using an 11-point scale labeled both with age in years and a schooling level. In addition, the participants rated whether the words were acquired through speech, sign language, or orthography.

The average AOA ratings for stimulus items were highly correlated across participant groups ($r = .97$) and with the normative order in the PPVT ($r = .95$ for the deaf group, and $r = .95$ for the hearing group), suggesting that the groups rated the words as learned in the same order as the PPVT assumes. However, the two groups differed in when (~ 1.5 years difference on average), and how (hearing: 70% speech and 30% orthography; deaf: 38% speech, 45% orthography, 17% sign language) words were judged to have been acquired. Interestingly, a significant correlation ($r = .43$) was obtained in the deaf participant group between the percent words correct on a lipreading screening test and the percentage of words an individual reported as having been learned through spoken language, with the better lipreaders reporting more words learned through spoken language. Taken together, the results suggested that despite global similarity between the two participant groups, they appear to have learned words at different times and through different language modes.

Bimodal Speech Perception

The preceding sections reveal that individuals with severe or profound hearing losses can potentially obtain substantial speech information from auditory-only or visual-only speech stimuli. That visual speech can substantially enhance perception of auditory speech has been shown with listeners having normal hearing and hearing losses (e.g., Grant, Walden, & Seitz, 1998; Sumby & Pollack, 1954).

Estimates of how audiovisual speech stimuli can improve speech perception have been obtained from children and adults with hearing losses. Lamoré, Huiskamp, van Son, Bosman, and Smoorenburg (1998) studied 32 children with pure-tone average hearing losses in a narrow range around 90 dB HL. They presented the children with consonant-vowel-consonant stimuli and asked them to say and write down exactly what they heard, saw, or heard and saw. Extensive analyses

of the results were provided, but of particular interest here were the mean scores for totally correct responses in the auditory-only, visual-only, and audiovisual conditions. When the children were subdivided into groups according to their pure-tone averages, the group with the least hearing losses (mean 85.9 dB HL) scored 80% correct auditory-only, 58% visual-only, and 93% audiovisual. The group with the greatest hearing losses (mean 94.0 dB HL) scored 30% auditory-only, 53% visual only, and 74% audiovisual. The audiovisual combination of speech information was helpful at both levels, but especially for those with the greater hearing loss.

Grant et al. (1998) presented auditory, visual, and audiovisual sentence stimuli to adult listeners from across a range of hearing losses from mild to severe. Overall, sentence scores were audiovisual, 23–94% key words correct, audio only, 5–70% key words correct, and visual only, 0–20% key words correct. Every one of the listeners was able to improve performance when the stimuli were audiovisual. This was true even when the lipreading-only stimuli resulted in 0% correct scores. Benefit from being able to see the talker was calculated for each participant (benefit $= (AV - A)/(100 - A)$; $A =$ audio only, $AV =$ audiovisual). Across individuals, the variation was large in the ability to benefit from the audiovisual combinations of speech information: the mean benefit was 44% with a range from 8.5–83%.

That even highly degraded auditory information can provide substantial benefit in combination with lipreading has also been shown in adult listeners with normal hearing. Breeuwer and Plomp (1984) presented spoken sentences visually in combination with a range of processed auditory signals based on speech. Lipreading scores for the sentences were approximately 18% words correct. One particularly useful auditory signal combined with lipreading was a 500-Hz pure tone whose amplitude changed as a function of the amplitude in the original speech around that frequency. When this signal was combined with lipreading, the mean score for the audiovisual combination was 66% percent words correct. When the same stimulus was then combined with another pure tone at 3160 Hz, also changing in amplitude as a function of the amplitude changes in the original speech around that frequency, performance rose to a mean of 87% words correct.

For neither type of auditory signal alone would there likely have been any words correctly identified. These results demonstrate that being able to hear even extremely limited speech information can be effective, as long as it is combined with visual speech.

Vibrotactile Cues

Under certain conditions, a hearing aid could provide useful vibrotactile information that could combine with seeing speech. Frequencies in the range of the voice pitch (approximately between 70 and 300 Hz) can be perceived by vibrotactile perception (Cholewiak & Collins, 1991). When hearing loss is profound, hearing aids must operate at high output levels that result in perceptible mechanical vibration (Bernstein, Tucker, & Auer, 1998). Boothroyd and Cawkwell (1970; see also Nober, 1967) studied the problem of distinguishing vibrotactile from auditory perception in adolescents with hearing losses. They found that sensation thresholds below 100 dB HL for frequencies as high as 1000 and even 2000 Hz might be attributable to detection of mechanical rather than acoustic vibration.

Perception of information for voicing might be obtained via a hearing aid through mechanical stimulation of the skin and might account for why some individuals with profound hearing losses obtain benefit from their hearing aids when communicating via speech. That voicing information can combine effectively with lipreading has been demonstrated in a number of studies. For example, Boothroyd, Hnath-Chisolm, Hanin, and Kishon-Rabin (1988) presented an acoustic signal derived from the voice pitch in combination with sentences presented visually to hearing participants. The mean visual-only sentence score was 26% words correct, and the audiovisual sentence score was 63%. Furthermore, we and others have demonstrated, using custom vibrotactile devices, that lipreading can be enhanced when voice fundamental frequency information is presented as vibration patterns on the skin, although the vibrotactile studies have generally failed to produce the same impressive gains obtained with analogous auditory signals and hearing participants (Auer, Bernstein, & Coulter, 1998; Eberhardt, Bernstein, Demorest, & Goldstein, 1990; Boothroyd, Kishon-Rabin, & Waldstein, 1995).

Summary and Conclusions

Speech information can withstand extreme degradation and still convey the talker's intended message. This fact explains why severe or profound hearing loss does not preclude perceiving a spoken language. Studies reviewed above suggest that listeners with hearing loss can profit from even minimal auditory information, if it is combined with visual speech information. Some individuals with profound hearing loss are able to perform remarkably well in auditory-only conditions and/or in visual-only conditions. However, the performance level that is achieved by any particular individual with hearing loss likely depends on numerous factors that are not yet well understood, including when their hearing loss occurred, the severity and type of the loss, their family linguistic environment, and their exposure to language (including their relative reliance on spoken vs. manual language).

Early studies of speech perception in hearing people focused on perception of the segmental consonants and vowels. More recently, research has revealed the importance of perceptual processes at the level of recognizing words. The studies reviewed above suggest the possibility that factors at the level of the lexicon might interact in complex ways with specific hearing loss levels. A complete understanding of the effectiveness of speech perception for individuals with hearing loss will require understanding relationships among the configuration of the hearing loss, the ability to amplify selected frequency regions, and the distinctiveness of words in the mental lexicon. These complex relationships will, in addition, need to be considered in relationship to developmental factors, genetic predispositions, linguistic environment, linguistic experience, educational and training opportunities, and cultural conditions.

Notes

1. The terms "lipreading" and "speechreading" are sometimes used interchangeably and sometimes used to distinguish between, respectively, visual-only speech perception and audiovisual speech perception in people with hearing losses. We have used both terms for visual-only speech perception. In this chapter, "lipreading" refers to perception of speech information via the visual modality.

2. The place distinction concerns the position in

the vocal tract at which there is critical closure during consonant production. For example, /b/ is a bilabial due to closure of the lips, and /d/ is a dental due to the closure of the tongue against the upper teeth. Manner concerns the degree to which the vocal tract is closed. For example, /b/ is a stop because the tract reaches complete closure. But /s/ is a fricative because air passes through a small passage. Voicing concerns whether or not and when the vocal folds vibrate. For example, /b/ is produced with vocal fold vibration almost from its onset, and /p/ is produced with a delay in the onset of vibration.

3. This correlation could have arisen because, at Gallaudet University, students who used their hearing aids more frequently were also more reliant on speech communication. That is, hearing aid use was a proxy in this correlation for communication preference/skill.

4. A phoneme is a consonant or vowel of a language that serves to distinguish minimal word pairs such as /b/ versus /p/ in "bat" versus "pat."

References

Auer, E. T., Jr. (2002). The influence of the lexicon on speechread word recognition: Contrasting segmental and lexical distinctiveness. *Psychonomic Bulletin & Review, 9*, 341–347.

Auer, Jr., E. T. & Bernstein, L. E. (1997). Speechreading and the structure of the lexicon: Computationally modelling the effects of reduced phonetic distinctiveness on lexical uniqueness. *Journal of the Acoustical Society of America, 102*(6), 3704–3710.

Auer, E. T., Jr., & Bernstein, L. E. (2002). *Estimating when and how words are acquired: A natural experiment examining effects of perceptual experience on the growth the mental lexicon.* Manuscript submitted.

Auer, E. T., Jr., Bernstein, L. E. & Coulter, D. C. (1998). Temporal and spatio-temporal vibrotactile displays for voice fundamental frequency: An initial evaluation of a new vibrotactile speech perception aid with normal-hearing and hearing-impaired individuals. *Journal of the Acoustical Society of America, 104*, 2477–2489.

Auer, Jr., E. T., Bernstein, L. E., & Tucker, P. E. (2000). Is subjective word familiarity a meter of ambient language? A natural experiment on effects of perceptual experience. *Memory & Cognition, 28*(5), 789–797.

Berger, K. W. (1972). Visemes and homophenous words. *Teacher of the Deaf, 70*, 396–399.

Bernstein, L. E., Demorest, M. E., & Tucker, P. E. (1998). What makes a good speechreader? First you have to find one. In R. Campbell, B. Dodd, &

D. Burnham (Eds.), *Hearing by eye (II): The psychology of speechreading and auditory-visual speech* (pp. 211–228). East Sussex, UK: Psychology Press.

Bernstein, L. E. Demorest, M. E., & Tucker, P. E. (2000). Speech perception without hearing. *Perception & Psychophysics, 62*, 233–252.

Bernstein, L. E., Tucker, P. E., & Auer, E. T., Jr. (1998). Potential perceptual bases for successful use of a vibrotactile speech perception aid. *Scandinavian Journal of Psychology, 39*(3), 181–186.

Boothroyd, A. (1984). Auditory perception of speech contrasts by subjects with sensorineural hearing loss. *Journal of Speech and Hearing Research, 27*, 134–143.

Boothroyd, A., & Cawkwell, S. (1970). Vibrotactile thresholds in pure tone audiometry. *Acta Otolaryngologica, 69*, 381–387.

Boothroyd, A., Huath-Chisolm, T., Hanin, L., & Kishon-Rabin, L. (1988). Voice fundamental frequency as an auditory supplement to the speechreading of sentences. *Ear & Hearing, 9*, 306–312.

Boothroyd, A., Kishon-Rabin L., & Waldstein, R. (1995). Studies of tactile speechreading enhancement in deaf adults. *Seminars in Hearing, 16*, 328–342.

Breeuwer, A. & Plomp, R. (1984). Speech reading supplemented with frequency-selective sound-pressure information. *Journal of the Acoustical Society of America, 76*, 686–691.

Catford, J. C. (1977). *Fundamental problems in phonetics.* Bloomington, IN: Indiana University.

Ching, T. Y. C., Dillon, H., & Byrne, D. (1998). Speech recognition of hearing-impaired listeners: Predictions from audibility and the limited role of high-frequency amplification. *Journal of the Acoustical Society of America, 103*, 1128–1139.

Cholewiak, R., & Collins, A. (1991). Sensory and physiological bases of touch. In M. A Heller & W. Schiff (Eds.), *The psychology of touch.* Hillsdale, NJ: Lawrence Erlbaum Associates.

Dirks, D. D., Takayanagi, S., Moshfegh, A., Noffsinger, P. D., & Fausti, S. A. (2001). Examination of the neighborhood activation theory in normal and hearing-impaired listeners. *Ear & Hearing, 22*, 1–13.

Dunn, L. M & Dunn, L. M (1981). *Peabody Picture Vocabulary Test-Revised.* Circle Pines, MN: American Guidance Service.

Eberhardt, S. P., Bernstein, L. E., Demorest, M. E., Goldstein, M. H. (1990). Speechreading sentences with single-channel vibrotactile presentation of voice fundamental frequency. *Journal of the Acoustical Society of America, 88*, 1274–1285.

Fisher, C. G. (1968). confusions among visually perceived consonants. *Journal of Speech and Hearing Research, 11*, 796–804.

Fowler, C. A. (1986). An event approach to the study of speech perception from a direct-realist perspective. *Journal of Phonetics, 14*, 3–28.

Gernsbacher, M. A. (1984). Resolving 20 years of inconsistent interactions between lexical familiarity and orthography, concreteness, and polysemy. *Journal of Experimental Psychology: General, 113*, 256–281.

Gilhooly, K. J., & Gilhooly, M. L. M. (1980). The validity of age-of-acquisition ratings. *British Journal of Psychology, 71*, 105–110.

Goldinger, S. D. (1998). Echoes of echoes? An episodic theory of lexical access. *Psychological Review, 105*(2), 251–279.

Grant, K. W., Walden, B. E., & Seitz, P. F. (1998). Auditory-visual speech recognition by hearing-impaired subjects: Consonant recognition, sentence recognition, and auditory-visual integration. *Journal of the Acoustical Society of America, 103*, 2677–2690.

Howes, D. H. (1957). On the relation between the intelligibility and frequency of occurrence of English words. *Journal of the Acoustical Society of America, 29*, 296–305.

Kucera, H., & Francis, W. (1967). *Computational analysis of present-day American English*. Providence, RI: Brown University.

Lahiri, A., & Marslen-Wilson, W. (1991). The mental representation of lexical form: A phonological approach to the recognition lexicon. *Cognition, 38*, 245–294.

Lamoré, P. J. J., Huiskamp, T. M. I., van Son, N.J.D.M.M., Bosman, AJ., & Smoorenburg, G. F. (1998). Auditory, visual and audiovisual perception of segmental speech features by severely hearing-impaired children. *Audiology, 37*, 396–419.

Liberman, A. M. (1982). On finding that speech is special. *American Psychologist, 37*, 148–167.

Liberman, A. M., & Whalen, D. H. (2000). On the relation of speech to language. *Trends in Cognitive Sciences, 4*, 187–196.

Luce, P. A. (1986). *Neighborhoods of words in the mental lexicon*. (Research on Speech Perception, Technical Report No. 6). Bloomington, IN: Speech Research Laboratory, Department of Psychology, Indiana University.

Luce, P. A., Goldinger, S.D., Auer, E.T., Jr., & Vitevitch, M.S. (2000). Phonetic priming, neighborhood activation, and PARSYN. *Perception & Psychophysics, 62*(3), 615–625.

Luce, P. A., & Pisoni, D. B. (1998). Recognizing spoken words: The neighborhood activation model. *Ear & Hearing, 19*, 1–36.

Luce, P. A., Pisoni, D. B., & Goldinger, S. D. (1990). Similarity neighborhoods of spoken words. In G.T.M. Altmann (Ed.), *Cognitive models of speech processing* (pp. 122–147). Cambridge, MA: MIT Press.

Marslen-Wilson, W. D. (1987). Functional parallelism in spoken word recognition. *Cognition, 25*, 71–102.

Marslen-Wilson, W. D. (1990). Activation, competition, and frequency in lexical access. In G. T. M. Altmann (Ed.), *Cognitive models of speech processing* (pp. 148–172). Cambridge, MA: MIT Press.

Marslen-Wilson, W. D. (1992) Access and integration: Projecting sound onto meaning. In W. D. Marslen-Wilson (Ed.), *Lexical representation and process* (pp. 3–24). Cambridge, MA: MIT Press.

Massaro, D. W. (1987). *Speech perception by ear and eye: A paradigm for psychological inquiry*. Hillsdale, NJ: Lawrence Erlbaum Associates.

Massaro, D. W. (1998). *Perceiving talking faces: From speech perception to a behavioral principle*. Cambridge, MA: Bradford Books.

Mattys, S., Bernstein, L. E. & Auer, E. T., Jr., (2002). Stimulus-based lexical distinctiveness as a general word recognition mechanism. *Perception & Psychophysics, 64*, 667–679.

McClelland, J. L., & Elman, J. L. (1986). The TRACE model of speech perception. *Cognitive Psychology, 18* 1–86.

McEvoy, C., Marschark, M., & Nelson, D. L. (1999). Comparing the mental lexicons of deaf and hearing individuals. *Journal of Educational Psychology, 19*, 312–320.

Miller, G. A., & Nicely, P. E. (1955). An analysis of perceptual confusions among some English consonants. *Journal of the Acoustical Society of America, 27*, 338–352.

Mogford, K. (1987). Lip-reading in the prelingually deaf. In B. Dodd & R. Campbell (Eds.), *Hearing by eye: The psychology of lip-reading* (pp. 191–211). Hillsdale, NJ: Lawrence Erlbaum Associates.

Montgomery, A. A., & Jackson, P. L. (1983). Physical characteristics of the lips underlying vowel lipreading performance. *Journal of the Acoustical Society of America, 73*, 2134–2144.

Morrison, C. M., & Ellis, A. W. (1995). Roles of word frequency and age of acquisition in word naming and lexical decision. *Journal of Experimental Psychology: Learning, Memory, and Cognition, 21*(1), 116–133.

Nearey, T. M. (1997). Speech perception as pattern recognition. *Journal of the Acoustical Society of America, 101*, 3241–3254.

Nitchie, E. B. (1916). The use of homophenous words. *Volta Review, 18*, 83–85.

Nober, E. H. (1967). Vibrotactile sensitivity of deaf children to high intensity sound. *Larynoscope, 78*, 2128–2146.

Norris, D. (1994). Shortlist: A connectionist model of continuous word recognition. *Cognition, 52*, 189–234.

Owens, E., & Blazek, B. (1985). Visemes observed by hearing impaired and normal hearing adult viewers. *Journal of Speech and Hearing Research, 28*, 381–393.

Remez, R. E. (1994) A guide to research on the perception of speech. In: M. Ann Gernsbacher (Ed.), *Handbook of psycholinguistics* (pp. 145–172). San Diego, CA: Academic Press.

Rönnberg, J. (1995). Perceptual compensation in the deaf and blind: Myth or reality? In R. A. Dixon & L. Bäckman (Eds.), *Compensating for psychological deficits and declines* (pp. 251–274). Mahwah, NJ: Lawrence Erlbaum Associates.

Rönnberg, J., Samuelsson, S., & Lyxell, B. (1998). Conceptual constraints in sentence-based lipreading in the hearing-impaired. In R. Campbell, B.

Dodd, & D. Burnham (Eds.), *Hearing by eye: II. The psychology of speechreading and auditory-visual speech* (pp. 143–153). East Sussex, UK: Psychology Press.

Stevens, K. N. (1998). *Acoustic phonetics*. Cambridge, MA: MIT Press.

Sumby, W. H., & Pollack, I. (1954). Visual contribution to speech intelligibility in noise. *Journal of the Acoustical Society of America, 26*, 212–215.

Summerfield, Q. (1991). Visual perception of phonetic gestures. In I. G. Mattingly & M. Studert-Kennedy (Eds.), *Modularity and the motor theory of speech perception* (pp. 117–137). Hillsdale, NJ: Lawrence Erlbaum Associates.

Takayanagi, S., Dirks, D. D., & Moshfegh, A. (in press). Lexical and talker effects on word recognition among native and non-native normal and hearing-impaired listeners. *Journal of Speech, Language, Hearing Research, 45*, 585–597.

Turner, C. W., & Brus, S. L. (2001). Providing low- and mid-frequency speech information to listeners with sensorineural hearing loss. *Journal of the Acoustical Society of America, 109*, 2999–3006.

28

Kathleen S. Arnos & Arti Pandya

Advances in the Genetics of Deafness

Genetic factors are believed to account for more than half of all cases of congenital or early-onset moderate to profound deafness. The recent identification of several dozen genes for deafness, one of which accounts for a high proportion of all childhood deafness, has enabled the identification of the exact cause of deafness in many children through genetic testing. Parents, family members, deaf and hard-of-hearing adults, as well as health care and educational professionals often are unaware of the exact process and goals of genetic evaluation and may have questions about the usefulness of genetic testing. Sensitive and appropriate genetic evaluation and testing, coupled with appropriate interpretation and information through genetic counseling, can be invaluable to many families. Health professionals and those who work with deaf children in educational and service settings play an important role in helping parents and family members understand the value of a genetic evaluation and making referrals to genetics professionals.

Basic Principles of Heredity

Epidemiologic Characteristics of Deafness

The incidence of congenital severe to profound deafness is at least 1 in 1,000 births. It is estimated that genetic factors account for 50–60% of moderate to profound sensorineural hearing loss present at birth or in early childhood (Marazita et al., 1993). More than 400 different forms of hereditary deafness are known to exist (Gorlin, Torielo, & Cohen, 1995). These forms can be distinguished from one another by audiologic characteristics of the hearing loss (type, degree, or progression), vestibular characteristics (balance problems), mode of inheritance, or the presence or absence of other medical or physical characteristics. In the majority of cases (two thirds), deafness occurs as an isolated finding. This is referred to as nonsyndromic deafness. The remaining one third of types of hereditary deafness have associated medical or physical features and are called syndromes. For example, some deafness syndromes are associated with ocular (eye) findings such as two different colored eyes or changes in visual functioning, heart defects such as irregular heart rhythm, malformations of the external ears such as ear pits or

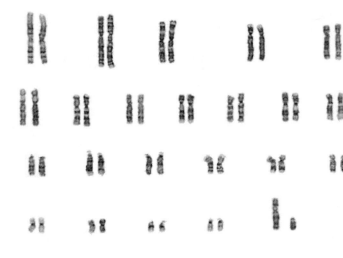

Figure 28-1. Karyotype of a normal human male. (Microphotograpy courtesy of C. Jackson Cook, Cytogenetics Laboratory, Department of Human Genetics, Virginia Commonwealth University.)

tags, and kidney malformations. Although it is not essential that professionals who work with deaf children be familiar with all of the features of syndromic forms of deafness, an appreciation of the complexity of these disorders and the effect they can have on the health of deaf individuals as well as on family members (siblings and offspring) underscores the importance of referrals for genetic evaluation and for encouraging families to follow through with the referrals. A few of the more common syndromic forms of hearing loss will be described later.

Chromosomal Inheritance

The genetic material DNA (deoxyribonucleic acid) is contained in every nucleated cell in the human body. This biochemical material is organized within the dividing nucleus into structures called chromosomes. There are 23 pairs, for a total of 46 chromosomes in each cell (figure 28-1). One of each pair of chromosomes is inherited from the mother and the other from the father. The only difference between males and females occurs in one pair of chromosomes known as the sex chromosomes; females have two X sex chromosomes and males have an X and a Y sex chromosome. Egg and sperm cells contain only one chromosome of each pair for a total of 23. A small amount of genetic material (37 genes) is included in organelles known as the mitochondria that are found in the cytoplasm of each cell. Mitochondria are responsible for energy production for the cells and contain thousands of copies of a circular

chromosome composed of genes inherited only from the mother.

Each of the nuclear chromosomes contains hundreds of genes, the biochemical instructions responsible for directing the body's growth and development. Genes code for (that is, control the production and function of) proteins, which form the structural and regulatory elements of the functioning body. Genes are composed of a specific sequence of the four chemical bases of DNA, known as adenine (A), guanine (G), thymine (T), and cytosine (C). These chemical bases combine in sequences that are hundreds or thousands of bases long to form the genes. Recent evidence gathered with the completion of the draft of the human genome by the Human Genome Project has suggested that there are somewhere between 30,000 and 40,000 genes in humans (International Human Genome Sequencing Consortium, 2001). Estimates suggest that at least 10% of all genes are involved in determining the structure and functioning of the organ of hearing. Recent progress in identification of these genes has given insight into how the ear functions and how changes (mutations) in a single gene can lead to deafness. A single gene mutation can also affect and alter the development of other tissues and organs in the body, which explains how a single gene change can lead to syndromes with a variety of physical manifestations in different organs. Genes can also express themselves at different times during prenatal development or during postnatal life, resulting in variability in the effects of specific mutations. For example, the onset of hearing loss caused by a gene mutation may occur at birth, shortly after birth, during later childhood, or at any time during adulthood. The functioning of a specific gene can also be influenced by environmental events.

Mendelian Inheritance

In the late 1800s, Gregor Mendel pioneered and studied the biological laws determining inheritance of traits in a plant species, giving rise to the term "Mendelian inheritance." It later became clear that these same laws of inheritance applied to the inheritance of many human traits. Most forms of hereditary deafness are caused by alterations (mutations) in the genes that code for structural or regulatory proteins of the ear. These alterations can be inherited in one of three common patterns known as autosomal dominant, autosomal recessive, and X-linked recessive. Autosomal refers to the 22 pairs of non-sex chromosomes (autosomes) in the nucleus of the cell. X-linked or sex-linked traits are caused by genes on the X sex chromosome.

Autosomal Dominant Inheritance

About 15–20% of hereditary deafness is inherited as an autosomal dominant trait (Marazita et al., 1993), when only a single copy of a pair of genes is altered. The dominant (altered) gene is usually inherited from only one of the parents. A person with one copy of an altered gene (Dd) is deaf and has a 50/50 chance to pass the dominant gene for deafness to a child with each pregnancy, regardless of the outcome of previous pregnancies (figure 28-2). The deafness can occur in multiple generations, and, on average, 50% of the offspring of any deaf person are also deaf. In some families the severity of the hearing loss can differ across individuals from mild to profound. This is known as variable expression. The hearing loss can also vary in age at onset and may be progressive. In rare situations, individuals with the altered gene have no hearing loss, but can have deaf offspring. This is referred to as reduced penetrance. An example of a form of dominant hearing loss with reduced penetrance is otosclerosis, characterized by progressive overgrowth of the bony ossicles with onset in the late 30s. Due to reduced penetrance, however, only 60% of individuals with the altered gene have symptoms of otosclerosis. Variable expression and reduced penetrance can occur in

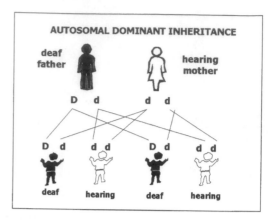

Figure 28-2. Autosomal dominant inheritance. A deaf person has one dominant gene for deafness (D) and a corresponding gene for hearing (d). Each child has a 50/50 chance of inheriting the deafness gene (D) from the parent who has this gene.

both nonsyndromic and syndromic forms of deafness. In syndromic forms, the associated medical and physical characteristics can vary from person to person in a family in which the altered gene is being passed.

Autosomal Recessive Inheritance

Autosomal recessive inheritance accounts for 75–80% of hereditary deafness (Marazita et al., 1993). For these types of genetic deafness, an individual must receive two copies of the altered gene, one from each parent, in order to be deaf. Persons with one copy of the gene for deafness and one copy of the unaltered gene are called carriers and do not express the trait. Two hearing parents who each carry a gene for deafness have a one in four or 25% chance of having a deaf child with each pregnancy (figure 28-3). An individual with recessive deafness may have another deaf sibling or may be the only deaf person in the family. In such a situation it is likely that many of the relatives are carriers of the gene for deafness. The frequency of recessive genes for deafness in the United States is estimated to be quite high, with one in eight individuals being a carrier of a recessive gene for deafness. About 1 in 31 Americans has been estimated to be a carrier of the most common autosomal recessive gene for nonsyndromic deafness, *GJB2* (Cohn et al., 1999; Rabionet, Gasparini, & Estivill, 2001). A history of consanguinity, when blood relatives have children together, is important to recognize in the diagnostic

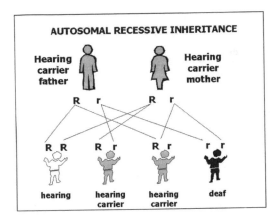

Figure 28-3. Autosomal recessive inheritance. Deaf individuals must have two genes for deafness (r), one inherited from each of the parents. The parents are hearing carriers (Rr) and have a 25% chance of having a deaf child with each pregnancy.

evaluation for a deaf child, since blood relatives are much more likely to have inherited the same recessive gene from a common ancestor.

X-linked Recessive Inheritance

X-linked recessive inheritance accounts for only a small percentage of hereditary deafness (Marazita et al., 1993). As shown in figure 28-4, a female who is a carrier for an X-linked recessive gene for deafness (Xx) has a 50/50 chance of passing the gene to each of her sons who will be deaf, and a 50/50

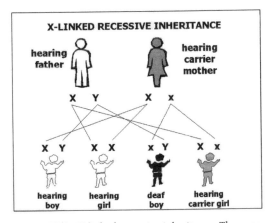

Figure 28-4. X-linked recessive inheritance. The sons of a woman who is a carrier of the X-linked gene for deafness (x) have a 50/50 chance of being deaf. The daughters have a 50/50 chance of being hearing carriers.

chance of passing the gene to each of her daughters, who will be hearing carriers. Males with X-linked hearing loss will not pass the gene for hearing loss to their sons, since a father contributes a Y chromosome (and no X chromosome) to each of his sons. However, a male with X-linked recessive hearing loss will pass the gene to all of his daughters, who will be carriers.

Mitochondrial Inheritance

As mentioned previously, mitochondria are small organelles in the cytoplasm of the cell responsible for energy production to support cellular activities. Mitochondria contain multiple copies of a small circular DNA molecule with 37 genes. Mitochondria are inherited solely from the mother through the egg cell; they are never passed from the father through the sperm cell. This results in a unique inheritance pattern for traits, which are expressed in both males and females but are only passed from mother to child. Several forms of syndromic and nonsyndromic deafness are caused by mutations in mitochondrial genes (Van Camp & Smith, 2001). The A1555G mitochondrial mutation causes deafness when individuals are exposed to aminoglycoside antibiotics (e.g., streptomycin, gentamicin) (Prezant et al., 1993). Some individuals with this mutation have been described to be deaf even without exposure to such antibiotics (Estivill, Govea et al., 1998). Although mitochondrial mutations account for only a small proportion of deafness (2–5%) overall, the incidence is much higher (10–30%) in some populations, most notably in Spanish and Asian ethnic groups (Fischel-Ghodsian, 1998; Estivill, Govea et al., 1998; Pandya et al., 1999, 2001).

Mechanisms of Hearing

To understand the effects of changes in specific genes on the anatomical and physiologic components of the ear, it is helpful to have a basic understanding of the structure and function of this organ. The three anatomical components of the organ of hearing are the external, middle, and inner ear. The external ear helps to funnel sound waves to the external auditory canal and the tympanic membrane. The sound waves are then transmitted to the middle ear, behind the tympanic membrane. Movement of the three bones (ossicles) of the middle ear, the malleus, incus, and stapes, transmit the sound waves to the oval window. The inner ear consists of the vestibular system (semicircular canals, the utricle, and the saccule), which regulates balance, and the cochlea, which mediates sound perception.

The cochlea is a snail-shaped sensory organ embedded within the dense temporal bone. It is divided longitudinally into three scalae or compartments (fluid-filled spaces separated by membranes) that spiral together along the length of the cochlea. The middle compartment, the scala media, contains a fluid called endolymph, which contains ions—small, charged molecules. The endolymph has high potassium ion and low sodium ion concentrations.

The organ of Corti (figure 28-5) sits on the basilar membrane and contains the hair cells which act as transducers to convert sound-induced mechanical waves into electrical impulses. There are one row of inner hair cells and three rows of outer hair cells. The organ of Corti is covered by the tectorial membrane, a thick and elastic flap. Each hair cell has three rows of stereocilia (hairs) of different lengths. The longest hairs of the outer hair cells are embedded in the tectorial membrane. The stereocilia are rigid and tend to move together in a bundle because they are linked to each other. A bending of the stereocilia occurs as a result of the movement of the basilar membrane and the tectorial membrane. This movement of the stereocilia allows potassium ions to enter the hair cells. The recycling of potassium ions entering the hair cells seems to be critical for the normal process of hearing to occur. Stimulation of the hair cells also activates calcium channels, allowing calcium influx into the hair cells, which triggers the release of neurotransmitters, which activate the acoustic nerve.

As genes for deafness are identified, the exact physiologic functioning of the inner ear is increasingly understood. Some of these newly discovered genes are described in the following section.

Identifying Genes for Deafness

Genetic research since the 1990s has led to the identification of several dozen genes for syndromic and nonsyndromic deafness (Van Camp & Smith, 2001). Genetic mapping refers to the localization of a region on a particular chromosome. This is achieved by identifying and studying large, three- or four-generation families with various forms of genetic deafness. Once a region is mapped, it is often possible to identify genes in the region and determine the exact sequence of the chemical bases (A, T, G, C) that make up the gene. At this point, it may then be possible to determine the protein product for which the gene codes and how the protein functions in the body. As of this writing, more than 30 genes for syndromic deafness have been mapped. Additionally, about 70 genes for nonsyndromic deafness have been mapped (Van Camp & Smith, 2001). A comprehensive review of recent progress in identifying genes for deafness can be found in Tekin, Arnos, and Pandya (2001) and in Steel and Kros (2001).

Common Syndromic Forms of Hereditary Deafness

Pendred syndrome, estimated to occur in up to 10% of deaf children, is an autosomal recessive condition characterized by sensorineural hearing loss and enlargement of the thyroid gland (goiter) (Reardon et al., 1997). Most individuals with Pendred syndrome have normal thyroid function. Pendred syndrome is also characterized by a structural change of the inner ear, an enlarged vestibular aqueduct (EVA) that can be diagnosed with magnetic resonance imaging (MRI) or computerized tomography (CT) scan. Many individuals with Pendred syndrome also have Mondini dysplasia of the cochlea, a condition in which one of the turns of the cochlea is missing. Mutations in the Pendred syndrome gene SLC26A4 result in symptoms of the syndrome (Scott, Wang, Kreman, Sheffield, & Karnishki, 1999).

Usher syndrome refers to a group of several disorders that are inherited as autosomal recessive traits and are associated with deafness and retinitis pigmentosa, a progressive degenerative disease of the retina leading to night blindness and tunnel vision (Gorlin et al., 1995; Keats & Corey, 1999). Usher syndrome is classified into three different types. Type 1 Usher syndrome is the most severe form and is characterized by congenital, severe to profound sensorineural deafness, retinitis pigmentosa with onset before 10 years of age, and severe vestibular (balance) problems. Type 2 Usher syndrome is characterized by congenital, moderate sensorineural hearing loss, and normal vestibular

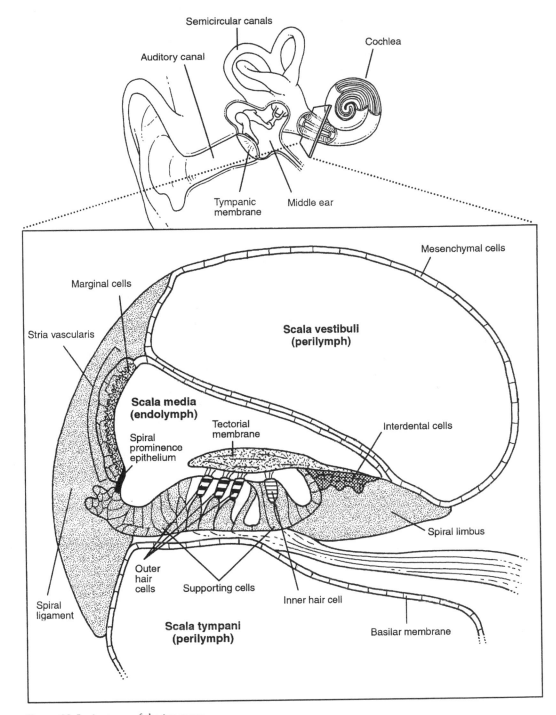

Figure 28-5. Anatomy of the inner ear.

function. The retinitis pigmentosa in this type has a later onset and is less severe. Type 3 Usher syndrome involves retinitis pigmentosa and a progressive form of hearing loss. Mutations in at least nine different genes are known to cause Usher syndrome (Van Camp & Smith, 2001).

Waardenburg syndrome (WS) occurs in about 2% of deaf children and includes pigmentary changes such as different colored eyes and white patches of skin or hair (Gorlin et al., 1995). WS can be classified into two distinct types. Type 1 WS is characterized by the appearance of wide-spaced eyes, a condition known as dystopia canthorum. Dystopia canthorum does not occur in type 2 WS, but the spectrum of other pigmentary changes is the same for the two forms. Both types of WS are inherited as autosomal dominant traits, with variable expression of the clinical features; individuals may have only one or all of the associated physical features. About 20–25% of individuals with type 1 WS are deaf, whereas deafness occurs in about 50% of individuals with type 2 WS. The deafness is sensorineural, severe to profound in degree, and can occur in one or both ears. Type 1 WS is caused by mutations in the *PAX3* gene on chromosome 2 (Tassebehji et al., 1992). At least two genes for type 2 WS have been identified, *MITF* (Pingault et al., 1998) and *SOX10* (Tassabehji, Newton, & Reed, 1994). A rare type 3 WS has also been described in which pigmentary changes are associated with limb defects (Gorlin et al., 1995; Hoth et al., 1993).

Jervell and Lange-Nielsen (JLN) syndrome is a rare form of deafness that is inherited as an autosomal recessive trait. The deafness is profound, congenital and sensorineural. This syndrome is associated with the sudden onset of fainting spells due to a defect in the conduction activity of the heart (Gorlin et al., 1995). Children with JLN can die suddenly. The heart defect can be identified through an electrocardiogram (EKG) or through a more complete monitoring of the electrical activity of the heart over a period of time (Holter monitor). In this condition, the electrical activity of the heart is characterized by an elongation of the QT interval, seen on the EKG. The risk of sudden death from this heart condition can be greatly reduced with the use of medications or pacemakers. To date, mutations in two genes are known to be responsible for this condition. These genes, known as KVLQT1 and KCNE1, are responsible for the movement of potassium ions in and out of the cells of the heart as well as the ear (Neyroud et al., 1997; Schulze-Bahr et al., 1997).

Nonsyndromic Forms of Deafness

Genes That Transport Ions Across Membranes

Gap junctions are structures embedded in cell membranes through which ions and other small molecules important to the function of those cells can pass. Gap junctions, composed of connexin proteins, are important in the process of recycling potassium ions through the structures of the organ of Corti. The potassium ions are essential to the 'electrical' activity of the hair cells. Mutations in genes coding for potassium channels or channels responsible for calcium transport between cells occur in Jervell and Lange-Nielsen and Pendred syndromes. Mutations in several genes that control the development of gap junctions cause several forms of nonsyndromic deafness (e.g. the connexin 26, 30, and 31 genes) (Van Camp & Smith, 2001).

Connexin 26 (GJB2). The *GJB2* (gap junction beta 2) gene, which codes for the protein connexin 26, was first described in 1997 (Denoyelle et al., 1997; Kelsell et al., 1997). This protein product forms gap junctions between the supporting cells underlying the hair cells in the cochlea. By the end of 2001, researchers had identified more than 80 mutations in the *GJB2* gene that can alter the connexin 26 protein (Rabionet et al., 2001). One mutation, called 30delG or 35delG (a deletion of a guanine at position 35 in the gene sequence), is the most common variant and accounts for about 70% of the connexin 26 changes that can cause deafness (Denoyelle et al., 1997). Another mutation, called 167delT (a deletion of a thymine at position 167 in the gene sequence), accounts for a large proportion of deafness in the Ashkenazi Jewish population (Morrell et al., 1998).

The majority of mutations in connexin 26 associated with deafness are inherited in an autosomal recessive pattern. Mutations in this gene are common. It has been estimated that about 1 in 31 Americans is a carrier of a mutation of the connexin 26 gene (Cohn et al., 1999). The frequency of mutations varies in different ethnic groups, being very high in deaf individuals of Western European decent. Connexin 26 mutations are the cause of deafness in 50–80% of deaf individuals who have deaf siblings and hearing parents (Denoyelle et al., 1997). In addition, it has been estimated that changes in connexin 26 account for up to 37% of people with unknown causes of deafness (Estivill, Fortina et al., 1998). Typically, this gene causes severe to profound deafness present at birth, but some individuals have mild to moderate hearing loss, which may or may not be progressive (Cohn et al., 1999). In some rare cases, a single mutation of *GJB2* has been associated with deafness and is passed through families in a dominant pattern (Rabionet et al., 2001; Tekin, Arnos, Xia, et al., 2001).

Although most children who become deaf from alterations in connexin 26 have hearing parents, this gene is also an important cause of deafness in families where deaf parents have all deaf children. It has been estimated that 70% of marriages in which deaf partners have all deaf children are in fact marriages between individuals with connexin 26 deafness (Nance, Liu, & Pandya, 2000).

Due to the small size of this gene and the existence of a common mutation, testing for connexin 26 mutations is relatively easy in comparison to other more complex genes. Many genetics programs now offer testing for connexin 26 on a research or clinical basis. A few centers have made prenatal testing available as well.

Genes That Have Regulatory Functions

Certain genes control pathways by which the DNA message is processed into the protein product. One class of these regulatory genes is called transcription factors. Transcription factors control protein production by binding to DNA and either "turning on" or "turning off" genes. The combination of these factors in a cell will also determine which genes are turned on or turned off and at what time during development this happens (Mullen & Ryan, 2001). Transcription factors are important in directing cells to develop as a specific organ (such as the cochlea or middle ear) during embryonic life. At least two groups of regulatory genes in the inner ear have been identified, the *POU* and *EYA* genes. The *POU4F3* gene codes for a transcription factor that is necessary for the development and survival of hair cells. Alterations in this gene lead to the incomplete development or early death of these cells, resulting in hearing loss.

Genes Involved in Structural Integrity of the Cochlea

Several genes have been identified that are important in coding for proteins that form structural components of the cochlea. The *TECTA* gene encodes the protein alpha-tectorin, which is an important structural component of the tectorial membrane overlying the stereocilia of the hair cells. Different mutations in this gene result in autosomal dominant, nonsyndromic deafness (Verhoeven et al., 1998) and autosomal recessive deafness (Mustapha et al., 1999). This is one example of several documented situations in which different mutations of the same gene cause hearing loss with a different mode of inheritance or clinical characteristics.

Other structural proteins that are important in the inner ear are collagens. There are more than 30 genes that code for collagen proteins. Collagen molecules combine to form the tectorial membrane. Mutations in different collagen genes are known to cause syndromic forms of hearing loss such as osteogenesis imperfecta (progressive hearing loss with fragile bones), Alport syndrome (hearing loss with cataracts and the kidney disease nephritis), and Stickler syndrome (hearing loss with cleft palate, myopia, retinal detachment, and premature degeneration of the joints) (Van Camp & Smith, 2001). One collagen gene also causes a form of autosomal dominant, nonsyndromic hearing loss (McGuirt et al., 1999).

Unconventional myosins are proteins that are located in the hair cells. Mutations in the *MYO7A* gene which codes for the myosin 7A protein result in a type of Usher syndrome (Weil et al., 1995) and also cause nonsyndromic hearing loss—both an autosomal recessive form (Liu, Walsh, Mburu, et al., 1997) and a autosomal dominant type (Liu, Walsh, Tamagawa, et al., 1997).

Clinical Implications of Genetic Testing

In the near future, genetic testing for deafness will become more common as more genes are identified and diagnostic testing moves from the research laboratory to clinical practice. At this time, most families do not have direct access to genetic testing unless they participate in a research protocol, or they are referred for genetic evaluation upon identification of deafness in a family member. There are many clinical benefits to genetic testing. In many cases, an early diagnosis of a specific genetic cause of deafness can eliminate the need for other invasive and expensive medical testing to identify syndromes, such as tests of heart function, ophthalmologic screening for Usher syndrome, thyroid testing, and tests to identify prenatal infections. The precise diagnosis of the cause at an early stage enables parents to understand what changes in the child's hearing or health may occur, so that appropriate amplification and educational intervention can be planned. Parents of deaf children may also obtain a psychological benefit from the early diagnosis of the exact cause of deafness because this information can alleviate guilt, prevent misinformation, and expedite the process of parental acceptance of the diagnosis of the deafness.

Genetic Evaluation and Counseling

Genetic evaluation and counseling should be viewed as an important part of the diagnostic process once a child is identified as deaf. Such an evaluation can allow parents of deaf and hard-of-hearing children to get accurate information about the cause of deafness, other medical implications, the chance of recurrence in future children, and implications for other family members. Genetic testing is often used as a part of the genetic evaluation in an attempt to confirm a specific diagnosis. Because many individuals with hereditary deafness are the only deaf person in the family, the genetic evaluation process is important for hearing parents who have one deaf child, as well as for families where there are multiple deaf or hard-of-hearing individuals. Deaf parents of deaf children as well as deaf and hard-of-hearing adults should also be given the option of participating in genetic evaluation and counseling services. Many such individuals do not know the exact cause of their deafness and could benefit from information to assist with health care and family planning issues.

The goal of genetic evaluation is to provide information and assist families in making choices that are appropriate for them. A genetic evaluation is performed by a clinical geneticist (an MD), who is responsible for the medical evaluation and diagnosis, as well as a genetic counselor, who is

trained to provide information to families in a sensitive and caring fashion and also to recognize the emotional state of the family and work with them on issues related to grieving, adjustment, acceptance of the diagnosis, and making choices based on the information provided. Social workers, psychologists, and audiologists are also often part of the genetic counseling team and play an important role in providing emotional and medical support and guidance for the family. Medical, educational, and other professionals who work with families with deaf or hard-of-hearing children or adults play a critical role in the referral process for genetic evaluation.

The process of genetic evaluation for a deaf individual is described in detail elsewhere (Arnos, Israel, Devlin, & Wilson, 1996) and includes the collection of detailed family and medical history, a thorough physical examination to search for evidence of syndromic forms of deafness, and comparison of audiologic test results from family members. An accurate family history is one of the most important clues to the etiology of the deafness. The genetic counselor collects details about the health and hearing status of siblings, parents, grandparents, and other close family members. The ethnicity of the family is also important to document, as well as any instances of consanguinity in the family. Even though the details of the family history are important in making a diagnosis, individuals for whom collection of family history information is not possible because of adoption or loss of contact with family members can also benefit from genetic evaluation.

Other components of the genetic evaluation can provide information that allow a precise diagnosis. For example, the geneticist also collects a detailed medical history for the deaf family member and other relatives. In some cases, medical records may be requested. This information is often helpful in making an accurate diagnosis or excluding previously reported causes of deafness. Audiograms are also an important component of the genetic evaluation process, although the audiogram alone will not provide the information necessary for an exact diagnosis of the cause of deafness.

The physical examination is used to identify features of syndromic forms of deafness or to confirm nonsyndromic deafness and identify other minor physical or medical features that may give clues about the cause of the deafness. The geneticist will determine if the medical history of the deaf individual or other family members is related to the cause of deafness, determine which types of medical or genetic testing are appropriate, and then evaluate and interpret any test results. At this point, families who might benefit from genetic testing are informed about the availability of such tests and given appropriate information about the benefits, risks, and implications of such information. Individuals who are to be tested should have a full understanding of all of these aspects and must give consent. In most situations this testing is done by obtaining a small blood sample, from which the DNA can be extracted and testing for certain genes performed.

Once a diagnosis has been made, complete information will be provided to the family by the genetics team. Information discussed may include medical information about the diagnosis and any accompanying conditions, the mode of inheritance, medical prognosis, implications for future children or other family members, treatment options, and any research efforts that may be underway. The focus of the genetics team is to provide this information in an atmosphere that is supportive of the cultural differences and psychosocial needs of the family.

The Role of Genetic Testing, Evaluation, and Counseling as an Adjunct to Newborn Hearing Screening

As countries worldwide implement newborn hearing screening (see Cone-Wesson, this volume), it is anticipated that in the coming years, the parents of babies who are identified as having a hearing loss through newborn hearing screening will also be offered genetic testing as part of the evaluation process for the hearing loss. Although there are many benefits of this type of testing, as mentioned above, parents will have the option to decline participation in genetic testing. The American College of Medical Genetics recently established genetic evaluation guidelines for the etiologic diagnosis of congenital deafness for primary care physicians and other health care providers (American College of Medical Genetics Expert Panel, 2002). The document fully addresses the medical and psychosocial benefits of genetic evaluation and the appropriate timing of such an evaluation, which may vary from family to family.

Psychosocial and Ethical Issues Related to Genetic Testing

General Issues Related to Genetic Testing

The bioethics of genetic testing for hereditary conditions has been a topic of discussion in the genetics literature for some time and continues to be a focus of concern. The Human Genome Project devotes a significant proportion of its annual budget to a program known as Ethical, Legal and Social Implications (ELSI), which supports research into the ethical implications of genetic testing and educational programs in genetics for allied health professionals, attorneys, and judges (Human Genome Project, 2001). The field of bioethics is concerned with identifying, analyzing, discussing, and proposing solutions to ethical difficulties and genetic risks as well as determining at what point the introduction of a clinical genetic test is useful and appropriate. Consumer and professional education, cost–benefit analysis, data collection to determine reliability and quality control, and public evaluation should be important steps that occur before the introduction of specific genetic tests.

Concerns regarding the ethics of genetic testing center around issues of discrimination, access to genetic information, privacy and confidentially, and informed consent (Cunningham, 2000). With appropriate informed consent, individuals who participate in genetic testing are fully informed of the benefits as well as the risks of such tests. Risks include the possible psychological burden of the information and potential negative effects on family dynamics and relationships and implications for employment and insurance coverage. Families should be informed about these risks before participating in genetic testing. There is a risk that participants in genetic testing may inadvertently learn information about their genetic make-up, perhaps unrelated to the original reason that genetic testing was undertaken, which they did not wish to know or which they find upsetting. If their reasons for wanting genetic testing are not carefully thought out, they may have to make choices they would have preferred to avoid or that they were not ready to make. If individuals are undertaking genetic testing for the purpose of prenatal diagnosis, choices regarding termination of pregnancy after receiving the results of such testing should be carefully explained by a genetic counselor. Genetic counselors are trained to provide detailed information on benefits and risks, including psychological risks that may be encountered through genetic testing.

Implications of Genetic Testing for Deafness

As of this writing, genetic testing for deafness is not widely available. Tests for common forms of hereditary deafness such as connexin 26 will become increasingly available as part of newborn hearing screening programs or potentially as part of newborn screening done at birth. These tests will also become more readily available to members of the Deaf community, which could be viewed as both empowering and threatening. Because of the existence of Deaf culture, many may view genetic testing as a threat to their way of life. Others may realize the potential of genetic testing to allow them to either avoid or ensure the birth of deaf children simply by means of selection of a marriage partner (Nance et al., 2000). It remains to be seen what the impact of genetic testing on the Deaf community may be. Some of the concerns of genetic testing and implications for the Deaf community are discussed by Jordan (1991). Initial studies of consumer attitudes have been performed, as described below, and have paved the way for further examination of this important issue.

Consumer Attitudes Toward Genetic Testing for Deafness

Several recent studies have documented the attitudes of deaf and hard-of-hearing people as well as hearing parents of deaf children toward genetic testing for deafness. Middleton, Hewison, and Mueller (1998, 2001) devised a questionnaire that included items to assess preference for having deaf or hearing children, opinions about the use of genetics technology, and whether genetic testing devalued deaf people. This survey was initially distributed to a small group of 87 deaf adults from the United Kingdom and then to a much larger group of more than 1,300 deaf, hard-of-hearing and deafened, and hearing individuals also from the United Kingdom with either a deaf parent or a deaf child. The results demonstrated that self-identified culturally Deaf participants were significantly more likely than hearing or hard-of-hearing/deafened participants to say that they would not be interested

in prenatal testing for deafness. Of those hearing, hard-of-hearing/deafened and deaf participants who would consider prenatal diagnosis, the majority of participants said they would use such information for preparing personally or preparing for the language needs of that child. Only a small number in each group said that they would have prenatal diagnosis to terminate a deaf fetus, and only 3/132 (2%) of deaf respondents said that they would have prenatal diagnosis to terminate a hearing fetus in preference for a deaf one.

Stern et al. (2002) used an adaptation of the Middleton questionnaire to examine the attitudes of deaf and hard-of-hearing individuals in the United States. The 337 respondents to the survey included members of the National Association of the Deaf and Self Help for the Hard of Hearing People, Inc., and students at Gallaudet University. This survey results were similar to those of Middleton et al. (2001); overall, the deaf/hard-of-hearing participants had a positive attitude toward genetics, had no preference about the hearing status of their children, did not express an interest in prenatal diagnosis for hearing status, and thought pregnancy termination for hearing status should be illegal. As prenatal diagnosis for deafness becomes more widely available, a better idea of the demand for this procedure for hereditary deafness can be obtained.

Summary and Conclusions

More than half of childhood deafness is caused by hereditary factors. Significant progress has been made in the identification of the more than 400 different forms of hereditary deafness. As more genes for deafness are discovered, techniques for testing for those genes will be improved and refined. This testing will become more widely available in the future.

It is possible that techniques such as preimplantation genetic diagnosis and gene therapy for deafness will also become available. Preimplantation genetic diagnosis is a technique in which a specific genetic trait or condition is identified in a fertilized embryo *in vitro*, outside the mother's body. Embryos that are found to carry the desired genetic trait can then be transplanted into the mother in the hopes of a successful pregnancy and delivery. This method is expensive and therefore will not be widely accessible, and it currently has only been used successfully for a few genetic conditions. Gene therapy is the use of genes as therapeutic agents. This technique is in the early stages of development and its usefulness is limited. Gene therapy may become available in the future for treatment of progressive forms of hearing loss or for forms of deafness having onset after birth.

It is clear that there is a need for discussions between professionals and consumers regarding research and the availability of new genetic technologies to deaf and hard-of-hearing individuals and their families. These discussions have already begun under the guidance and support of federal health agencies such as the National Institutes of Health and the Centers for Disease Control. Consumer organizations representing deaf and hard-of-hearing individuals have also begun to educate themselves by sponsoring informational workshops for their members. The implications of the developments in genetics for the diagnosis and treatment of hereditary deafness will be wide ranging and controversial. It is important for all stakeholders to have an understanding of these implications so that these important discussions can continue.

Acknowledgment

The authors thank Lydia Prentiss for preparation of figures 28-2, 28-3, and 28-4.

References

American College of Medical Genetics Expert Panel (2002). Genetics evaluation guidelines for the etiologic diagnosis of congenital hearing loss. *Genetics in Medicine 4* (3), 162–171.

Arnos, K. S., Israel, J., Devlin, L., & Wilson, M. (1996). Genetic aspects of hearing loss in children. In J. Clark & F. Martin (Eds.), *Hearing care in children* (pp. 20–44). Needham Heights, MA: Allyn & Bacon.

Cohn, E. S., Kelley, P. M., Fowler, T. W., Gorga, M. P., Lefkowitz, D. M., Kuehn, H. J., Schaefer, G. B., Gobar, L. S., Hanh, F. J., Harris, D. J., & Kimberling, W. J. (1999). Clinical studies of families with hearing loss attributable to mutations in the Connexin 26 gene (GJB2/DFNB1). *Pediatrics, 103,* 546–550.

Cunningham, G. C. (2000). The genetics revolution: ethical, legal, and insurance concerns. *Postgraduate Medicine, 108,* 193–202.

Denoyelle, F., Weil, D., Maw, M. A., Wilcox, S. A., Lench, N. J., Allen-Powell, D. R., Osborn, A. H., Dahl, H-H. M., Middleton, A., Houseman, M. J., Dode, C., Marlin, S., Boulila-ElGaied, A., Grati, M., Ayadi, H., BenArab, S., Bitoun, P., Lina-Granade, G., Godet, J., Mustapha, M., Loiselet, J., El-Zir, E., Aubois, A., Joannard, A., McKinlay Gardner, R. J., & Petit, C. (1997). Prelingual deafness: high prevalence of a 30delG mutation in the connexin 26 gene. *Human Molecular Genetics, 6,* 2173–2177.

Estivill, X., Fortina, P., Surrey, S., Rabionet, R., Melchionda, S., D'Agruma, L., Mansfield, E., Rappaport, E., Govea, N., Mila, M., Zelante, L., & Gasparini, P. (1998). Connexin-26 mutations in sporadic and inherited sensorineural deafness. *Lancet, 351,* 394–398.

Estivill, X., Govea, N., Barcelo, A., Perello, E., Badenas, C., Romero, E., Moral, L., Scozzari, R., D'Urbano, L, Zeviani, M., & Torroni, A. (1998). Familial progressive sensorineural deafness is mainly due to the mtDNA A1555G mutation and is enhanced by treatment with aminoglycides. *American Journal of Human Genetics, 62,* 27–35.

Fischel-Ghodsian, N. (1998). Mitochondrial mutations and hearing loss: Paradigm for mitochondrial genetics. *American Journal of Human Genetics, 62,* 15–19.

Gorlin, R. J., Torielo, H. V. & Cohen, M. M. (1995). *Hereditary hearing loss and its syndromes.* New York: Oxford University Press.

Hoth, C. F., Milunsky, A., Lipsky, N., Sheffer, R., Clarren, S. K. & Baldwin, C. T. (1993). Mutations in the paired domain of the human PAX3 gene cause Klein-Waardenburg syndrome (WS-III) as well as Waardenburg syndrome type I (WS-I). *American Journal of Human Genetics, 52,* 455–462.

Human Genome Project. (2001). Human Genome Project homepage. Retrieved December 2001, from http://www.nhgri.nih.gov/

International Human Genome Sequencing Consortium. (2001). Initial sequencing and analysis of the human genome. *Nature 409,* 860–921.

Jordan I. K. (1991). Ethical issues in the genetic study of deafness. *Annals of the New York Academy of Sciences, 630,* 236–239.

Keats, B. J., & Corey, D. P. (1999). The Usher syndromes. *American Journal of Medical Genetics, 89,* 158–166.

Kelsell, D. P., Dunlop, J., Stevens, H. P., Lench, N. J., Liang, J. N., Parry, G., Mueller, R. F., & Leight, I. M. (1997). Connexin 26 mutations in hereditary non-syndromic sensorineural deafness. *Nature, 387,* 80–83.

Liu, X. Z., Walsh, J., Mburu, P., Kendrick-Jones, J., Cope, M. J., Steel, K. P., & Brown, S. D. M.

(1997). Mutations in the myosin VIIA gene cause non-syndromic recessive deafness. *Nature Genetics, 16,* 188–190.

Liu, X. Z., Walsh, J., Tamagawa, Y., Kitamura, K., Nishizawa, M., Steel, K. P., & Brown, S. D. M. (1997). Autosomal dominant non-syndromic deafness caused by a mutation in the myosin VIIA gene. *Nature Genetics, 17,* 268–269.

Marazita, M. L., Ploughman, L. M., Rawlings, B., Remington, E., Arnos, K. S., & Nance, W. E. (1993). Genetic epidemiological studies of early-onset deafness in the U.S. school-age population. *American Journal of Medical Genetics, 46,* 486–491.

McGuirt, W. T., Prasad, S. D., Griffith, A. J., Kunst, H. P., Green, G. E., Shpargel, K. B., Runge, C., Huybrechts, C., Mueller, R. F., Lynch, E., King, M. C., Brunner, H. G., Cremers, C. W. R. J., Tasanosu, M., Li, S. W., Arita, M., Mayne, R., Prockop, D. J., Van Camp, G., & Smith, R. J. H. (1999). Mutations in COL11A2 cause non-syndromic hearing loss (DFNA13). *Nature Genetics, 23,* 413–419.

Middleton, A., Hewison, J., & Mueller, R. F. (1998). Attitudes of deaf adults toward genetic testing for hereditary deafness. *American Journal of Human Genetics, 63,* 1175–1180.

Middleton, A., Hewison, J., & Mueller, R. F. (2001). Prenatal diagnosis for inherited deafness—what is the potential demand? *Journal of Genetic Counseling 10,* 121–131.

Morrell, R. J., Kim, H. J., Hood, L. J., Goforth, L., Frederici, K., Risher, R., Van Camp, G., Berlin, C. I., Oddoux, C., Ostrer, H., Keats, B., & Friedman, T. B. (1998). Mutations in the connexin 26 gene (GJB2) among Ashkenazi Jews with nonsyndromic recessive deafness. *The New England Journal of Medicine, 339,* 1500–1505.

Mullen, L. M., & Ryan, A. F. (2001). Transgenic mutations affecting the inner ear. *Hearing and hearing disorders in children.* American Speech-Language-Hearing Association, Special Interest Division 9 Newsletter, 11, 7–16.

Mustapha, M., Weil, D., Chardenoux, S., Elias, S., El-Zir, E., Beckmann, J. S., Loiselet, J., & Petit, C. (1999). An alpha-tectorin gene defect causes a newly identified autosomal recessive form of sensorineural pre-lingual non-syndromic deafness, DFNB21. *Human Molecular Genetics, 8,* 409–412.

Nance, W. E., Liu, X. Z., & Pandya, A. (2000). Relation between choice of partner and high frequency of connexin-26 deafness. *Lancet, 356,* 500–501.

Neyroud, N., Tesson, F., Denjoy, I., Leibovici, M., Donger, C., Barhanin, J., Faure, S., Gary, F., Coumel, P., Petit, C., Schwartz, K., & Guicheney, P. (1997). A novel mutation in the potassium channel gene KVLQT1 causes the Jervell and Lange-Nielsen cardioauditory syndrome. *Nature Genetics, 15,* 186–189.

Pandya, A., Erdenetungalag, R., Xia, X. J., Welch, K. O., Radnaabazar, J., Dangaasuren, B., Arnos, K. S., & Nance, W. E. (2001). The role and frequency of mitochondrial mutations in two distinct populations: The USA and Mongolia [abstract 97]. *Proceedings of the Molecular Biology of Hearing and Deafness.*

Pandya, A., Xia, X. J., Erdenetungalag, R., Amendola, M., Landa, B., Radnaabazar, J., Danguaasuren, B., VanTuyle, G., & Nance, W. E. (1999). Heterogeneous point mutations in the mitochondrial tRNA Ser(UCN) precursor coexisting with the A1555G mutation in deaf students from Mongolia. *American Journal of Human Genetics, 65,* 1803–1806.

Pingault, V., Bondurand, N., Kuhlbrodt, K., Goerich, D. E., Prehu, M. O., Puliti, A., Herbarth, B., Hermans-Borgmeyer, I., Legius, E., Matthijs, G., Amiel, J., Lyonnet, S., Ceccherini, I., Romeo, G., Smith, J. C., Read, A. P., Wegner, M., & Goossens, M. (1998). SOX10 mutations in patients with Waardenburg-Hirschsprung disease. *Nature Genetics, 18,* 171–173.

Prezant, T. R., Agapian, J. V., Bohlman, M. C., Bu, X., Oztas, S., Hu, D., Arnos, K. S., Cortopassi, G. A., Jaber, L., Rotter, J. I., Shohat, M., & Fischel-Ghodsian, N. (1993). Mitochondrial ribosomal RNA mutation associated with antibiotic-induced and non-syndromic deafness. *Nature Genetics 4,* 289–294.

Rabionet, R., Gasparini, P., Estivill, X. (2001). Connexin 26. Retrieved December, 2001, from http://www.crg.es/deafness.

Reardon, W., Coffey, R., Phelps, P. D., Luxon, L. M., Stephens, D., Kendall-Taylor, P., Britton K. E., Grossman A., & Trembath, R. (1997). Pendred syndrome—100 years of underascertainment? *Quarterly Journal of Medicine, 90,* 443–447.

Schulze-Bahr, E., Wang, Q., Wedekind, H., Haverkamp, W., Chen, Q., Sun, Y., Rubie, C., Hordt, M., Towbin, J. A., Borggrefe, M., Assmann, G., Qu, X., Somberg, J. C., Breithardt, G., Oberti, C., & Funke, H. (1997). KCNE1 mutations cause Jervell and Lange-Nielsen syndrome. *Nature Genetics, 17,* 267–268.

Scott, D. A., Wang, R., Kreman, T. M., Sheffield, V. C., & Karnishki, L. P. (1999). The Pendred syndrome gene encodes a chloride-iodide transport protein. *Nature Genetics, 21,* 440–443.

Steel, K. P., & Kros, C. J. (2001). A genetic approach to understanding auditory function. *Nature Genetics, 27,* 143–149.

Stern, S. J., Arnos, K. S., Murrelle, L., Welch, K. O., Nance, W. E., & Pandya, A. (2002). Attitudes of deaf and hard of hearing subjects toward genetic testing and prenatal diagnosis of hearing loss. *Journal of Medical Genetics, 39,* 449–453.

Tassabehji, M., Newton, V. E., & Read, A. P. (1994). Waardenburg syndrome type 2 caused by mutations in the human microphthalmia (MITF) gene. *Nature Genetics, 8,* 251–255.

Tassabehji, M., Read, A. P., Newton, V. E., Harris, R., Balling, R., Gruss, P., & Strachan T. (1992). Waardenburg's syndrome patients have mutations in the human homologue of the Pax-3 paired box gene. *Nature, 355,* 635–636.

Tekin, M. Arnos, K. S., & Pandya, A. (2001). Advances in hereditary deafness. *Lancet, 358,* 1082–1090.

Tekin, M., Arnos, K. S., Xia, X. J., Oelrich, K., Liu, X. Z., Nance, W. E. & Pandya, A. (2001). W44C mutation in the connexin 26 gene associated with dominant non-syndromic deafness. *Clinical Genetics, 59,* 269–273.

Van Camp, G., & Smith, R.J.H. (2001). Hereditary hearing loss homepage. Retrieved December, 2001, from http://dnalab-www.uia.ac.be/dnalab/hhh/

Verhoeven, K., Van Laer, L., Kirschhofer, K., Legan, P. K., Hughes, D. C., Schatteman, I., Verstreken, M., Van Hauwe, P., Coucke, P., Chen, A., Smith, R. J., Somers, T., Offeciers, F. E., Van de Heyning, P., Richardson, G. P., Wachtler, F., Kimberling, W. J., Willems, P. J., Govaerts, P. J., & Van Camp, G. (1998). Mutations in the human alpha-tectorin gene cause autosomal dominant non-syndromic hearing impairment. *Nature Genetics, 19,* 60–62.

Weil, D., Blanchard, S., Kaplan, J., Guilford, P., Gibson, F., Walsh, J., Mburu, P., Varela, A., Levilliers, J., Weston, M. D., Kelley, P. M., Kimberling, W. J., Wagenaar, M., Levi-Acobas, F., Larget-Piet, D., Munnich, A., Steel, K. P., Brown, S. D. M., & Petit, C. (1995). Defective myosin VIIA gene responsible for Usher syndrome type 1B. *Nature, 374,* 60–61.

29

Judith E. Harkins & Matthew Bakke

Technologies for Communication
Status and Trends

The last twenty years of the twentieth century have seen remarkable innovation in communication technology. People who are deaf or hard of hearing have benefited enormously from new communication products and services. The great strides industry has made in data processing power, miniaturization, and digitization of analog technologies, plus the rapid growth of the Internet, have resulted in significant improvement in both visual communication technologies and those designed to restore or enhance hearing. Electronic mail, the World Wide Web, mobile telephones, and interactive pagers have altered the communication habits of hundreds of millions of people, with the result that deaf and hard-of-hearing people can communicate directly with hearing friends, family, co-workers, and businesses. Fast processing in small chips has led to improved hearing aids and cochlear implants. Concurrent with these developments, new public policies have required companies in the communications industries to improve the accessibility of their products.

This chapter describes key developments in a wide range of communication technologies used by deaf and hard-of-hearing people, concentrating on the 1990s and beyond. The first section of the chapter focuses on visual access to communication technologies, and the second section addresses developments in hearing-related technologies such as hearing aids, cochlear implants, and assistive listening devices.

Visual Communication Technologies

Visual communication technologies are those that make use of text, video, or flashing signals. In the past decade, such technologies have become much more diverse, lower in cost, and more widely available.

Text Telephones

Text telephones are devices developed for conducting live conversation in text form over telephone lines. The first text telephones were developed in the United States in the 1960s as a self-help effort by deaf people. Robert Weitbrecht, a deaf physicist, invented a modem to send and receive teletypewriter (TTY) signals over telephone lines (see Lang, 2000). The American text telephone is popularly known as the TTY, reflecting its roots in the teletypewriter. It is also sometimes called TDD (Telecommunication Device for the Deaf).

In recent years there have been two major trends in TTY technology: addition of new communication protocols that improve transmission performance, and integration of TTY with personal computers, computer networks, and paging networks.

American TTY manufacturers began to introduce new protocols in the 1990s, eliminating the drawbacks of the original TTY while conserving its strengths. This development has also introduced new problems of incompatibilities, as the leading new protocol is not standardized but is proprietary. Aside from North America, development of text telephones has occurred primarily in Europe, where there are approximately six incompatible protocols (Olesen, 1992).

To encourage the voluntary international harmonization of text telephone technology, an international standard was developed in the International Telecommunications Union's Technical Sector (ITU-T). The goal of this standard, Recommendation V.18 (ITU-T, 1993), is to enable interoperability among the many incompatible text telephone protocols in the world and to integrate these protocols smoothly with conventional modems for data communications. In developing V.18, it was expected that manufacturers of conventional modems would immediately incorporate the protocol, and TTY would be present in all conventional modems (Brandt, 1994). This has not occurred. Although text telephone capability has not been integrated into all computer modems, there has been gradual progress in using computers to communicate with TTYs. Specialized TTY modems and software transform the computer into a call-management device with directories, automatic dialing, large screen, memory for storing conversations, time and date stamps, split screen, color, and comfortable keyboards. When conventional data modems with digital signal processing were introduced in the marketplace, some companies produced software that causes such modems to produce and decode TTY tones. This "soft TTY" approach integrated TTY and Internet access into one device and opened up the possibility of traveling with a laptop that has built-in TTY functionality.

The TTY has also become integrated with computer and paging networks via network servers equipped with TTY modems. Using client software for the calling functions, anyone on the network can handle TTY calls.

A striking trend is that the TTY is being supplemented and partially supplanted by other text-based technologies that, while not performing the precise functions of a text telephone, take care of a rising proportion of the needs of deaf people for text telecommunications. Electronic mail, instant messages and text chat, and interactive paging have replaced many telephone calls. However, the TTY remains the only direct way a deaf person can call emergency services (9-1-1 in North America). The Americans with Disabilities Act requires that all 9-1-1 centers be able to converse via TTY (Department of Justice, 1992), but no other text technologies are supported or required.

Telecommunications Relay Service

Telecommunications Relay Service (TRS) is an operator service that facilitates telephone communication between people who are deaf and those who are hearing. TRS is also used by some hard-of-hearing people and hearing people with speech disabilities. Any telephone or TTY user can call a central number to be connected to an operator, sometimes called a communications assistant or relay agent. The operator places a call based on the instructions of the caller and relays the conversation between the two parties by typing the spoken words of the person who is speaking and speaking the typed words of the person who is using text. TRS is available nationwide, 24 hours per day, 7 days a week, in a number of countries, such as Australia, Canada, Czech Republic, Denmark, Finland, Holland, Iceland, Malta, the Netherlands, Norway, Spain, Switzerland, Sweden, the United Kingdom, and the United States (A. Kremp, personal communication, December 18, 2001). Some other countries offer more limited relay services.

There are a number of variants of the basic TRS service. For example, voice carry-over (VCO) permits the deaf or hard-of-hearing person to use speech for self-expression instead of typing and to read the text typed by the TRS agent. The voice of the deaf party is passed through so that the hearing party can listen. Two-line VCO is a service in which both parties can hear the other's speech, while the TTY user, who in this case is typically hard of hearing, can also read the TRS agent's text. Conceptually this service is similar to captioned television, in that the hard-of-hearing person can both listen and read.

Each country with nationwide TRS offers a different constellation of services to facilitate text communication via telephone. For example, in the United Kingdom, network services can automatically route direct telephone calls from a hearing person to a text telephone user via the relay service. In Sweden, the relay service offers a gateway for one-way messaging services such as text telephone to fax, mobile short messaging, and e-mail. In Australia, the relay service assists, routes, and handles all emergency-number TTY calls to facilitate fast and accurate communication.

Some TRS providers are experimenting with Internet relay services, also known as IP relay. The deaf user reaches a TRS website via a web browser instead of calling in via TTY and phone line. Web chat is used for the text component of the conversation. The user can set up the call on the web rather than through the slower process of interaction with the relay operator.

Video Relay Service (VRS) employs sign language interpreters in place of typists. Deaf callers use videoconferencing equipment in place of TTYs. The VRS center calls the hearing party on a telephone line and interprets the conversation in both directions. VRS telephone calls are faster and more natural than manually typed calls. VRS also allows callers to navigate voice menus, which are difficult and often impossible to handle on a text relay service.

Fax

Facsimile, or fax, is technology for transmitting a copy of a document via telephone line. Fax machines became cheap and ubiquitous in the 1990s. They are particularly useful to deaf and hard-of-hearing people for telecommunications in countries where there are no text telephones or relay services.

Internet

The Internet is an open network of computer networks, all operating on common, open protocols called Transmission Control Protocol and Internet Protocol (TCP/IP). Designed as a decentralized model for computer communications and shared computing resources, the Internet grew out of research funded by the U.S. Defense Advanced Research Projects Agency (ARPA). A source of pride to many people who are deaf or hard of hearing is that Vinton Cerf, one of the fathers of the Internet, is hard of hearing.

The Internet's most popular application has been electronic mail. The adoption of electronic mail by the general public has enabled direct communication between hundreds of millions of hearing people and those who are deaf or hard-of-hearing. Electronic mail lists and discussion boards allow deaf people to be included where they might formerly have been excluded, such as in workplace communications.

The World Wide Web was developed in 1991, and 10 years later there were an estimated 30 million web servers on the Internet (Zakon, 2001). Access to information that could previously be obtained only by telephone has been an extremely important benefit of the Web to many people, but especially to deaf and hard-of-hearing people. Intranets, internal corporate webs, give deaf and hard-of-hearing employees equal access to important information in the workplace.

The Web also provides a convenient and easy-to-use interface for new forms of communication. For example, a web page can be used to stream live captioning of a conference call or other meeting, through the services of a trained stenographer. Video communications are easily set up over the Web.

Text and short messaging are also popular communication tools that have opened up direct, live communication among deaf and hard-of-hearing people and their hearing associates. A favorite is America Online's Instant Messenger, which can be used by non–America Online subscribers and which is being incorporated into a growing number of paging services. The most popular chat media available today are proprietary, meaning that their use is controlled by a company which may or may not permit other companies to use it. One result is that most messaging protocols do not work with other protocols. Standardizing chat media would improve the current situation by opening up the possibility of communicating with anyone else on any network.

Mobile Communications

Throughout the industrialized world, there has been a strong market for mobile communications technologies. The current generation of mobile services consists of voice and text communications.

The next generations will include video communications as well.

Mobile Telephones

Like many other types of products and services, mobile telecommunications have moved from analog to digital technologies. Digital wireless telephones are currently less accessible to people who use TTYs and hearing aids than their analog counterparts were.

The digital wireless telephone's antenna communicates with the nearest base station via a radio frequency signal that has a pulsing, or on-off pattern. When a digital wireless telephone is held close to the ear for listening, many hearing aids pick up this energy, demodulate the radio frequency signal as a buzz, and amplify the buzz for presentation in the hearing aid wearer's ear. As a result, hearing aid wearers often hear annoying noise mixed with speech; some users hear only noise. Digital wireless telephones also garble TTY transmission. The digital encoding process is optimized for speech, and the TTY's coded signals although falling within the same range of frequencies, have a binary pattern that confounds voice coders.

The U.S. Federal Communications Commission (FCC) ordered the wireless telecommunications industry to make their digital services accessible by TTY in 2002 (FCC, 2001a). There is no similar requirement for compatibility with hearing aids, but the Hearing Aid Compatibility Act of 1988 required that its exemption for wireless phones be periodically reviewed by the FCC. A review of the exemption was begun in 2002 (FCC, 2001b).

Mobile Text Communications

Mobile text messaging refers to sending and receiving e-mail and short messages using a wireless terminal. Today's technology evolved from technologies for paging or "beeping" people whose occupations were mobile in nature. In the 1990s, pager technology took a leap forward with the introduction of two-way text paging, bridged to the Internet.

Mobile text messaging can be done on a variety of types of equipment and networks. Service providers offer packages of services and equipment. Depending on the service package, the consumer may buy a pager, wireless telephone, or personal digital assistant. The network carrying the service may be a dedicated paging network or part of the cellular telephone network. The provider of text messaging services may be a third-party reseller of services that run on a paging network, or it may be a wireless telephone service provider.

In the United States, the Deaf community has quickly adopted the interactive pager as the mobile device of choice. Service providers offer some combination of electronic mail and short messaging, with some offering fax, voice messaging, and even TTY calling and messaging.

In Europe and Australia, networks dedicated to mobile text have been phased out in favor of integrating short messaging services, data transfer, and web access with the digital wireless telephone services. Short messaging services in particular are very popular among deaf people, who find it convenient to have a single device that can reach other wireless telephone users.

Video Communications

Two-way live video communication is of obvious interest to both deaf and hard-of-hearing people. The ideal is a robust multimedia video network that can be used for interpersonal conversation in sign language, text, and/or speech, depending on the needs and preferences of the users. Video conferencing technology can be used for relay service, as previously described, and for remote interpretation of meetings and lectures. It can also be used to retrieve informational and entertainment video rendered in sign language.

This technology made significant strides during the 1990s. Video cameras and processing hardware became more affordable. Digital image processing and data compression techniques improved dramatically. Some of the early adopters in the Deaf community are finding current digital video transmission quality to be satisfactory, if not yet optimized, for sign communication. For them, video communications has become an important option for daily communication.

The two main communications networks used for sign language communication are integrated services digital network (ISDN) and Internet accessed by a high-speed connection. ISDN is a service in which calls are switched through the telephone network just as they are for ordinary (analog) voice calls A drawback of ISDN is the limited number of subscribers on the network. It is difficult to find someone to call.

The Internet is an attractive alternative to ISDN because the network of Internet users numbers in the hundreds of millions. It is also relatively easy to use, since the familiar web browser is the interface. The main drawback of video transmission through Internet is the shared and decentralized nature of the network. During busy periods on the Internet, the conversation can literally come to a halt. A high-speed digital connection purchased from a telephone or cable television company is desirable, but this alone does not ensure that a high-speed data exchange will persist throughout a conversation.

Captioning

In the United States, "captioning" has traditionally been used to describe the subtitling of the audio track of video productions for access by deaf and hard-of-hearing people. Captions differ from foreign language subtitles in that they include descriptions of audio events and nuances that convey information but are not part of the spoken language of the video. For example, the words "phone ringing" would not appear in subtitles, but would appear in closed captions to inform deaf and hard-of-hearing viewers.

Television

On broadcast television, captions are typically "closed," meaning that they can be viewed only with a decoder. Developed in the 1970s by the Public Broadcasting System with support from the U.S. Department of Education, closed-captioning began in 1980 with the introduction of special caption decoders and airing of the first closed-captioned television programs. Captioned programming grew steadily in the 1980s, subsidized by the U.S. Department of Education under statutory authority governing captioned media. In 1990, Congress passed the Television Decoder Circuitry Act (P.L. 101-431), which mandated that all televisions 13 inches or larger manufactured for sale in the United States have built-in decoder circuitry.

The British Broadcast System also developed a method of closed-captioning television (in the United Kingdom called "subtitling") during the 1970s. The resulting TeleText system provides not only closed captions, but also pages of information that fill the television screen with text and graphical displays of sports scores, currency exchange rates, weather reports, and news. Other countries that currently use Teletext for closed captioning include Australia, Sweden, Norway, Denmark, and Japan.

The amount of captioned programming available is, of course, critically important to media access. Canada and the United States lead in the quantity of closed-captioned television available, due to government requirements. In the United States, the Telecommunications Act of 1996 requires captioning of all broadcast and cable television programming, including news. The FCC has granted the industry a phase-in period until 2006 to comply (FCC, 2000b). In Canada, it has been mandated that 90% of television licensees' national programming must be captioned (Canadian Radio-Television and Telecommunications Commission 2001).

Digital Television

As television technology in the United States gradually migrates from analog to digital forms, the U.S. government is mandating updated and improved standards for closed caption decoders in digital televisions. New digital closed caption decoders, required for digital television sets made after July 1, 2002, provide consumers with a choice of font, font size, font color, and background color. They will also allow caption providers to send multiple versions of captions (FCC, 2000c).

Emergency Broadcasts and Alerts

The FCC requires local television broadcasters to provide access to emergency programming in visual form, either by captioning or by other methods that provide substantive information about the emergency (FCC, 2000d). The FCC also requires accessibility of televised messages of the Emergency Alert System (EAS). The EAS is a nationwide network for alerting the country in the event of national emergency, but it has never been used for that purpose. It is used frequently by local authorities to alert the public to severe weather and other emergencies. EAS messages must be available as crawl captions in cable systems served by more than 5,000 subscribers. For smaller systems, alternative methods of alerting may be used.

Stored Video Media

No law requires closed captioning of stored video media such as videotapes, CD-ROMs, digital videodiscs (DVD), or video games. Videos of theatrical releases with large markets are generally captioned voluntarily in the United States, and subtitling of foreign-language videos provides some degree of accessibility to deaf and hard-of-hearing viewers in other countries. Instructional video is far less likely to be captioned than entertainment video. Currently the legal burden of captioning educational video falls on educational institutions that wish to make their materials accessible. The U.S. Department of Education has for many years subsidized captioning of selected educational videos and sponsored the Captioned Media Program, currently operated by the National Association of the Deaf, that lends these captioned videos free of charge to schools and individuals.

Movie Theaters

Captioning in movie theaters has been the subject of advocacy efforts in the U.S., where there has been slow but notable progress. Open-captioned prints of movies are occasionally shown at selected, typically off-peak times in movie theaters. In addition, a small but growing number of movie theaters provide closed captioning. Rear Window captioning is a system that allows deaf patrons to attend any showing of a film and to sit anywhere in the theater, with the use of a small device available at the theater. The clear plexiglass device reflects captions that appear in reverse on an LCD display stationed at the rear of the theater. Once fastened to the seat, it can be angled by the viewer for positioning its reflected-caption image. The system was developed at WGBH, the Boston local affiliate of the Public Broadcast System, where much of the U.S. research and development on closed captioning has occurred since the 1970s.

Internet Video

Digital video may also be stored on the web for download or streaming, or "webcast" live. Much of this type of video is not captioned, as there are no legal requirements to do so.

However, guidelines have been developed for closed captioning web video. The Web Access Initiative of the World Wide Web Consortium (W3C) is an organization that develops guidelines for web accessibility. The W3C specifies captioning via a format known as Synchronized Multimedia Integration Language (SMIL). SMIL permits synchronization of several media streams, including video, audio, and text for closed captions. Features such as choice of font, font size, color, and caption background are supported. Captions appear below the video image. Software tools that assist in the creation of captions for web-based video material have begun to appear on the marketplace. Real-time closed captioning on the web is the next technical challenge. There are currently no W3C standards for real-time captioning. Captioning of live webcasts, where available, currently uses open captioning, meaning that all viewers see the captions.

Real-Time Captioning, CART, and CAN

Real-time captioning (RTC) refers to "the contemporaneous creation of text from speech" (Robson, 1997, p. 67). RTC is currently the only method for live captioning of television programming such as unscripted news reports, sports, weather forecasts, and live talk shows. RTC is produced by trained stenotypists, who use a specialized chord keyboard with which they can represent letters, syllables, words, or even sentences with a combination of key presses. Computer software rapidly looks up the chord combinations in a dictionary and prints out the standard text version.

CART, or Communication Access Real-Time Transcription, is an adaptation of RTC for live transcription during meetings, lectures, religious services, court proceedings, classroom instruction, and other group events. CART allows people with a wide degree of hearing loss to better understand the proceedings of an event. It can also serve as a type of record keeping for review of the content of meetings.

High-speed typing on a QWERTY keyboard can also provide a more limited degree of access to speech in group situations or in one-to-one meetings. Computer-Assisted Notetaking (CAN) requires no special equipment, but does require a skilled typist who can either attempt to attain verbatim transcription, if the speech is sufficiently slow, or to summarize the proceedings. Keyboard expansion software can be used to increase the number of words produced per keystroke; this process has been most extensively applied in the C-Print system developed for text transcription at Rochester Institute of Technology in Rochester, New York (Elliot, Stinson, McKee, Everhart, & Francis, 2001).

Automatic Speech Recognition

Automatic speech recognition (ASR) refers to technology that converts speech to text form. Among deaf and hard-of-hearing people, it has long been hoped that ASR would be capable of captioning the speech of any hearing person in any situation, seamlessly, unobtrusively, and accurately (Woodcock, 1997).

ASR technology made significant progress in the 1990s, in part due to improvements in data processing power of computers. Current systems can transcribe very large vocabularies. Users may speak continuously, as opposed to pausing between words, which was necessary in previous generations of the technology. Consumer-grade ASR products are largely speaker dependent, meaning that training of the system to a user's speech patterns is required for optimum performance. Optimum performance also requires that the user speak clearly and wear a headset microphone of good quality. When a user is practiced in ASR transcription and able to concentrate on the dictation task, a high degree of accuracy, 95% or better, is possible. However, ASR performance is highly variable depending on the conditions of use and the characteristics of the user's speech. The technology was not designed to transcribe live lectures or conversation, and there is evidence that in conversational speech, the accuracy rate falls below levels acceptable for communication (Harkins, Haravon, Tucker, Eum, & Fisher, 2000). The nature of errors can be very confusing, sometimes humorous, and invariably distracting. There are particular difficulties with single-word utterances, often used in conversation; for example, "okay" may be transcribed as "cocaine," and "deaf" as "death."

The use of a third party to repeat the spoken words of others into an ASR system has been suggested as a solution for telecommunications relay service automation (Harkins, Levitt, & Strauss, 1994). Companies are now experimenting with this mode of ASR transcription. Trained ASR specialists repeat the spoken words of the hearing party into an automatic speech recognition system, which transcribes the words into text form. The text is then transmitted via modem. Using ASR instead of keyboards increases the speed of transmission beyond normal typing speeds and may prevent worker injury due to repetitive stress caused by sustained typing. As with other communication-related applications, the accuracy of this method will determine its success.

Companies are beginning to embed ASR into mobile devices to enable hands-free command and control when hands and eyes are busy—for example, when driving. The spread of ASR in the user interface could disadvantage people with nonstandard speech, unless alternative input procedures using keyboards, keypads, and touchscreens or also provided.

Hearing Technologies

Technologies that provide amplified sound and direct stimulation of the cochlea have also improved significantly since 1990 due to advances in digital processing technologies.

Hearing Aids

Hearing aids constitute the primary and most fundamental technology for the rehabilitation of sensory hearing loss. Hearing aids are intended for use in a variety of circumstances and environments. They are designed to amplify sound, with the goal of raising the levels of important auditory signals, particularly speech, above the hearing thresholds of the user. Amplification must be done selectively, according to the hearing loss configuration, across the acoustic frequencies that are important for easy and clear speech understanding. These frequencies fall in the range from about 100 Hz to about 5000–8000 Hz. Furthermore, hearing aids must limit the level of the amplified signal to prevent the user from loudness discomfort.

Before the advent of very small, powerful, and efficient computer chips, hearing aids were essentially miniature amplifiers with electronic circuits designed to amplify, filter, and control the levels of signals. These analog circuits work very well, but have limited signal-processing capabilities. In recent years, digital hearing aids have moved to the forefront of the hearing aid industry and have become both smaller and more energy efficient, allowing the use of low-power hearing aid batteries. Digital hearing aids contain computer circuits that convert sound into a string of numerical values that can be mathematically transformed and then converted back into sound in the ear of the hearing aid wearer. Digital hearing aids are capable of implementing complex signal-processing algorithms that increase the flexibility and adaptability of the instruments, thus improving their ability to address the many problems that hearing aid wearers face, such as loudness discomfort, audibility of soft sounds, interference from background noise, and acoustic feedback. In addition, they permit more precise frequency shaping, enabling an audiologist to more accurately match the amplification of the hearing aid to the hearing loss of the user, thus resulting in better speech understanding.

A problem with digital hearing aids is their complexity. It is a challenge for an audiologist to achieve the "best fit" for hearing aids in which such a large number of variables are at play. For this reason, digital hearing aids are typically marketed with software that implements fitting strategies unique to the features of the particular hearing aid.

Noise Reduction

The most basic and ubiquitous complaint of people who use hearing aids is interference from background noise (Bakke, Levitt, Ross, & Erickson, 1999). Noise reduction in hearing aids with single omni-directional microphones has been largely unsuccessful in improving speech understanding in noise (Dillon & Lovegrove, 1993). More recent development efforts have focused on multiple-microphone, directional hearing aids. Directional hearing aids are most sensitive to sounds coming from the front of the listener and suppress sounds from other directions. Current hearing aids are often equipped with switches that permit the user to choose a directional pattern that suits the situation. In some situations, as when walking in a public area, users may prefer to have an omni-directional pattern so that they can monitor the environment in all directions. In other situations, such as in a conversation in a noisy restaurant, users may prefer to switch to a highly directional pattern in order to improve the signal-to-noise ratio of the desired speech.

Loudness Control

Another major problem for people with hearing loss is recruitment, a phenomenon in which the perceived loudness of sound grows more rapidly with increased sound intensity than it does for people with normal hearing. Thus, for a person with a hearing loss, a sound that is just detectible at 70 dB may be intolerably loud at 110 dB, resulting in a narrow dynamic range of hearing. Hearing aids are designed to address this phenomenon by compressing speech into a narrower dynamic range. They adjust the growth of loudness and limit their output by using circuits that adaptively control their gain. Such circuits are often called automatic gain control (AGC), or automatic volume control (AVC) circuits. Simple AGC circuits control the gain across all frequencies together. However, because an individual's hearing loss, and therefore recruitment, may be different at different frequency bands, multichannel hearing aids have been developed in which separate AGC characteristics are applied to two or three different frequency bands. Multichannel hearing aids also help in more closely matching the frequency characteristics of the hearing aid to the hearing loss of the user. In the more sophisticated digital hearing aids, adaptive compression circuits can modify their temporal parameters depending on the characteristics of the incoming sound. Thus, for a sudden loud sound, the hearing aid may adjust its gain very quickly, while for a sound with a more gradual onset, gain may decrease and increase more slowly.

Feedback Reduction

Another important feature of modern digital hearing aids is feedback cancellation. Acoustic feedback is a problem for hearing aids because it limits the amount of gain that the hearing aid can provide. Feedback is traditionally controlled by making sure that the ear canal is tightly sealed with a well-fit ear mold, but even under the best of circumstances, feedback can be troublesome when a great deal of gain is required to achieve audibility. Complex feedback reduction algorithms in digital aids can adaptively identify the presence of feedback and reduce gain only in the frequency region of the feedback itself. This improves the performance of the hearing aid by raising the maximum possible level of gain, particularly for the higher frequency sounds (important for speech understanding) where feedback is a particularly irksome problem.

Implantable Hearing Aids

Implantable hearing aids, or middle ear implants, are hearing aids in which the receiver is replaced by an implanted magnet that is fixed onto one of the bones of the middle ear (ossicles). A coil that is worn in the ear canal or behind the ear causes the implanted magnet to vibrate and stimulate the inner ear. There is one implantable hearing aid currently approved by the Food and Drug Administration and available for implantation (Ashburn-Reed, 2001). A major advantage of implantable hearing aids is their cosmetic appeal; they are virtually invisible. A second major advantage is that they eliminate the need for an earmold and reduce the problem of acoustic feedback by replacing amplified sound with mechanical stimulation of the small bones of the middle ear. The problem of efficiently coupling the hearing aid to the ossicles has proven somewhat troublesome, and sales of the FDA-approved implantable hearing aid have not been overwhelming. It remains to be seen whether implantable hearing aids will become a significant part of the overall hearing aid market.

Cochlear Implants

Cochlear implants have revolutionized hearing rehabilitation for many people with severe to profound hearing loss (see Spencer & Marschark, this volume). Unlike hearing aids, which amplify sound and present it to the impaired hearing mechanism, cochlear implants bypass the hearing mechanism and directly stimulate the auditory neurons of the

inner ear. The components of a cochlear implant system include a microphone, a speech processor, a transmitter, and an internal receiver/stimulator connected to an electrode array, as shown in figure 29.1

The microphone of a cochlear implant is mounted on the user's head. It may be mounted on a behind-the-ear (BTE) speech processor, or on a unit resembling a behind-the-ear hearing aid in the case of body-worn speech processors, or mounted on the head-worn transmitter. Sound is collected from the user's environment by the microphone and the signal is passed on to the speech processor.

The speech processor is essentially a specialized computer that converts the audio signal into a coded set of instructions for stimulating the electrodes in the array. The instructions vary according to the speech processing strategy that is chosen and the individual's sensitivity to electrical stimulation. When fitting the cochlear implant, an audiologist measures the user's sensitivity to electrical stimulation by conducting a behavioral evaluation of thresholds for just-detectable stimulation and most comfortable levels of stimulation for each electrode in the array. This procedure is often referred to as a "tune-up." The threshold and comfort levels are stored in the speech processor and used in the pro-

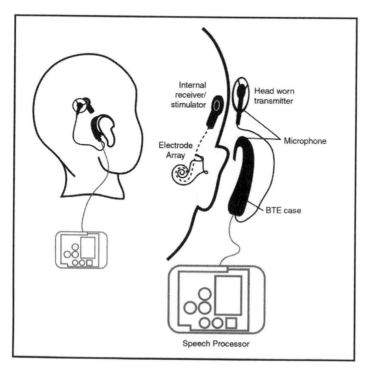

Figure 29-1. The components of a cochlear implant system. The smaller figure on the left shows the position in which the head-worn transmitter and behind the ear (BTE) unit are worn relative to the internal electrode array. The body-worn speech processor is outlined in gray to illustrate the fact that it is optional: each of the currently approved implant systems may be obtained with the speech processor entirely housed in the BTE case. The microphone is most often mounted on the BTE case; however, one implant system has a microphone mounted on the head-worn transmitter. (Figure courtesy of B. Moran, Lexington School for the Deaf, Jackson Heights, NY.)

cess of encoding sound into electrical stimulation of the intracochlear electrode array. The speech processor may be housed in a small body-worn box or it may be completely self-contained in a BTE case. All three of the currently available cochlear implant devices (Clarion, MED-EL, and Nucleus) have BTE processors available.

Because speech is a rapidly changing, wide-band signal, the speech processors need to provide both spectral and temporal information. The implant provides spectral information to the user by breaking the signal into narrow frequency bands and representing the energy detected in each band to an electrode along the array that stimulates a limited set of auditory neurons in the cochlea. Temporal information is provided through rapid sampling of the signal and updating of the stimulation at the electrodes. Rapid updating of speech information and high rates of stimulation with pulsatile strategies help users to recognize the rapidly changing resonances of the articulators during speech. The relative value to speech understanding of these two parameters in cochlear implants is not fully understood. There are limits to the technology: the more rapidly the information is updated and the greater the number of electrodes that require updating during each cycle of stimulation, the higher the cost in terms of power consumption and processing capability. For this reason, different speech-processing strategies emphasize temporal and spectral information to differing degrees. Each of the strategies now being used has been successful in helping many users understand speech, although adults who are fit with cochlear implants appear to be quite definite about which strategy they prefer (Waltzman, 2001).

Speech-processing strategies differ in their availability according to the implant manufacturer. Each implant offers two or more options from which the user, guided by the audiologist, chooses one that sounds most acceptable and yields better speech understanding. Upon initial stimulation, more than one option is made available because the speech processors contain two or more memories in which different strategies may be stored. Very young children clearly do not have the ability to make this decision, so the choice of the first strategy to try is most often made on the basis of the experience of the cochlear implant center and the audiologist. During a trial period, the child's responses to sound will be assessed by parents, teachers, and the implant team and changes made as required.

The transmitter's function is to pass the instructions generated by the speech processor across the skin via a radio frequency signal to the internal receiver/stimulator. It is worn on the head, attaching to the implanted internal receiver by means of a magnet. Depending on the model of cochlear implant, the transmitter is connected either to the BTE speech processor by a cable, to the body-worn speech processor by a cable passing through the BTE microphone, or directly to the body-worn speech processor.

The internally implanted receiver/stimulator is a single unit that consists of both the internal receiver and the electrode array. It contains circuitry that accepts radio frequency signals and electrical power across the skin from the head-worn transmitter. It carries out the instructions of the speech processor, distributing electrical stimulation to the electrodes as required. It also feeds information back across the skin to the speech processor for purposes of monitoring and control. The speed with which this information can be exchanged constitutes a limitation of the implant's flexibility. Manufacturers have tried to achieve maximum transmission flexibility so that if more advanced speech-processing strategies become available in the future, it will be possible to implement them on existing internal implant receiver/stimulators.

Although the first cochlear implant commercially available in the United States used a single implanted electrode (House 3M Single-channel Device), all implants now available in the United States use multiple electrodes. The inner ear is organized tonotopically, that is, the auditory neurons of the inner ear are arrayed according to frequency, similar to the way in which a piano keyboard is arranged. The electrode array distributes its electrodes along a distance of 25–30 mm. When a patient is selected for cochlear implantation, the surgeon places an electrode array into one of the fluid-filled chambers of the inner ear, the scala tympani (see Cone-Wesson, this volume). The electrode winds its way along the coiled inner ear, distributing electrodes along the tonotopically-organized auditory neurons. This arrangement results in a perception of pitch change as different electrodes are stimulated along the array. This representation of pitch constitutes a strong advantage of multichannel over single-channel implants.

Assistive Listening Systems

Because people who are hard of hearing have an increased need for a favorable signal-to-noise ratio (Nabelek, 1993; Plomp, 1978), assistive listening devices and systems (ALDS) were developed to overcome problems of reverberation and ambient noise found in many environments such as theaters, churches, schools, auditoriums, and arenas. A remote microphone is placed close to the desired sound source (e.g., on the speaker's lapel) and connected via wire or wireless transmission to the hearing aid (or other transducer in instances where hearing aids are not worn). Currently available ALDS use three different media to transmit and receive signals: magnetic induction (induction loops, or IL), frequency modulated radio frequencies (FM) and infrared light (IR).

FM systems use the same radio signal as commercial FM radio, but they use special bands (72–75 MHz and 216–217 MHz) that are essentially unregulated at the time of this writing. In 2001, the U.S. government considered selling these frequency bands, and their future is uncertain. Infrared systems use light as a medium. Infrared light is outside the visible spectrum. Channels are band limited to reduce interference from other light and heat sources. The light carrier is modulated by a subcarrier frequency, usually 95 kHz, although this is being changed in some systems because of interference problems. The three components include the transmitter, which encodes the audio and sends it to the emitter; an emitter (an array of specialized light bulbs that beams the light to the audience); and a receiver. The IR receiver always has some kind of "eye" that is capable of picking up the IR light signal. Direct line of sight is usually required for IR to work effectively (as in a television remote control). Bright sunlight will interfere with the signal, adding static, although there are systems that are resistant to light interference. As with FM there are compatibility issues because of individual differences in field strength, sensitivity, filter width, and preprocessing of signals before transmission.

Magnetic induction is a simple technology and was the first to be developed as an assistive hearing technology. The first application of magnetic induction was telephone listening. Early telephone handsets created magnetic fields around the earpiece as an unintended byproduct. Telecoils in hearing aids were designed to pick up the modulations of the magnetic fields and present the signal to the user. Telephones that work in this way with hearing aids are said to be hearing-aid compatible. Wireline telephones manufactured for sale in the United States are required to be hearing-aid compatible.

Magnetic induction has been widely applied in group listening systems. A loop of wire is placed around a room (floor or ceiling height). AC current carrying the signal is passed through the loop, setting up a modulated magnetic field. The speaker uses a microphone, and the speech is transduced by the IL system. Hearing aid wearers switch their hearing aids to telecoil mode or telecoil/microphone mode to hear the speech. For users who do not have hearing aids with telecoils, special IL receivers are available that can be used with headphones.

A significant advantage of magnetic induction is that no receiver is needed for a user with a hearing aid equipped with a telecoil. It solves many listening problems of hearing aid wearers and can be found on most telephones. Unfortunately, only 30% of hearing aids in the United States are dispensed with a telecoil. IL systems do not provide privacy, and the spillover of signals to adjacent rooms is notorious. A specially configured loop system, 3-D loop, has been marketed that addresses both the spillover problem and the orientation problem. The loop is configured so that the magnetic field is directed upward only.

Microphone Placement

Microphone placement is often a challenge in the use of assistive listening systems. Ideally, one wants a microphone in close proximity to every relevant sound source. This may mean using multiple microphones, requiring a microphone mixer, or it may mean passing the microphone from person to person. Directional microphones and conference microphones can sometimes avoid this inconvenience by picking up speech of many speakers. Many assistive listening systems have environmental microphones on the receivers. These are important for personal systems if the user wants to hear not only the remote signal, but also the proximate signal and his or her own voice. They are also important in educational settings where it is important for children with hearing loss learning to speak to hear their own voices.

Device Compatibility

Incompatibility among devices of different manufacturers creates a problem for people who want to use their own receivers when they attend events like plays, movies, and lectures. Many consumers have expressed the need for a universal receiver that is flexible enough to work with any available transmitter (Bakke et al., 1999).

Summary and Conclusions

The world is in the midst of a surge in innovation, spurred by the high power and small size of computer processing components, developments in display technology, the growth of the Internet as an alternative to the closed networks of the telecommunications industry, and many other trends. Deaf and hard-of-hearing people have been enjoying a golden age of communications, as text and graphical media have provided new capability at reasonable cost. There is every reason to believe that text communications will continue to be important, that progress in automatic speech recognition will continue, and that video communications will grow. As hearing aids and cochlear implants improve, they introduce another element of choice, as more people will have access to communications through the audio channel.

The first 10 years of the third millennium, will, however, also see rapid spread of digital voice technologies and multimedia communications that may create new barriers and reintroduce some old ones. Any technology that requires the user to listen and/or speak and that does not have a fully accessible visual mode has the potential to create new problems. New technologies that are incompatible with specialized technologies such as the text telephone, hearing aid, and cochlear implant may create inequitable situations where the hearing public can communicate but the deaf and hard-of-hearing public cannot. Can these challenges be prevented by industry by designing products that are accessible from the outset?

Large companies have rarely solved the access problems of deaf and hard-of-hearing people through their normal market incentives because this group is a relatively small market. Small companies have produced successful innovations, but have also faced frustrations in trying to convince large companies to accommodate their products. Government action has therefore been vitally important for making voice-based communication technologies such as telephone and television accessible.

Nonetheless, government is often reluctant to act early on emerging accessibility problems. For example, in 1988, cellular telephones were provisionally exempted from requirements for hearing-aid compatibility. Government has been reluctant to apply rules on telecommunications to Internet voice and broadcast services. After technologies have become entrenched and a negative impact on the lives of deaf and hard-of-hearing people can be demonstrated, governments sometimes are able to garner the will to regulate accessibility. Unfortunately, it is much more difficult and costly to retrofit than to build-in a feature from the beginning.

Although general trends in government policy toward business have been decidedly in the direction of deregulation, two pieces of legislation in the United States are attempting a proactive regulatory approach to accessibility. Section 255 of the Telecommunications Act requires that telecommunications equipment be accessible to and usable by people with disabilities, if this can be done without much difficulty or expense on the part of the company (FCC, 1999). Section 508 of the Rehabilitation Act (1998) requires that electronic and information technology acquired by the U.S. government be accessible to people with disabilities. As of this time, the impact of the laws is not yet clear, but the direction is promising. Some companies are beginning to consider accessibility while developing products, at the stage at which these features are least expensive.

Industry standards can also lay the groundwork for accessible design of products. During the 1990s, a number of technical standards for communication accessibility were approved in industry standards bodies, such as the International Telecommunications Union. These voluntary industry standards have not appeared in mainstream products; only those specifically required by law have been successful to date. It is hoped that the new U.S. laws on technology access will have an impact internationally and that these standards will eventually be incorporated into products.

In conclusion, it is likely that the future of technology benefiting deaf and hard-of-hearing people will come from a combination of industry and government, with industrial innovation providing new choices to the marketplace and government filling in the most important accessibility gaps. Deaf and hard-of-hearing people will need to continue to work together to safeguard their access to technology.

References

Ashburn-Reed, S. (2001). The first FDA-approved middle ear implant: The Vibrant Soundbridge. *The Hearing Journal, 54*, 47–48.

Bakke, M. H., Levitt, H., Ross, M., & Erickson, F. (1999). *Large area assistive listening systems: Review and recommendations* (Final report to United States Architectural and Transportation Barriers Compliance Board [U.S. Access Board]. Report retrieved November 30, 2001, from http://www. hearingresearch.org

Brandt, R.P. (1994). ITU-T Recommendation V.18: The first communication standard for the deaf. *Technology and Disability, 3*(3), 199–202.

Canadian Radio-Television and Telecommunications Commission (2001). Decision CRTC 2001-730. Report retrieved December 3, 2001 from http:// www.crtc.gc.ca/archive/ENG/Decisions/2001/ db2001-730.htm

Department of Justice (1992). Telephone emergency services (28CFR35.162).

Dillon, H., & Lovegrove, R. (1993). Single-microphone noise reduction systems for hearing aids: A review and an evaluation. In G. A. Studebaker & I. Hochberg (Eds.), *Acoustical factors affecting hearing aid performance* (2nd ed., pp. 353–372). Needham Heights, MA: Allyn & Bacon.

Elliot, L. B., Stinson, M. S., McKee, B. G., Everhart, V. S., & Francis, P. J. (2001). College students' perceptions of the C-Print speech-to-text transcription system. *Journal of Deaf Studies and Deaf Education, 6*, 285–298.

Federal Communications Commission. (1999). Report and Order: *Implementation of sections 255 and 251(a)(2) of the Communications Act of 1934, as enacted by the Telecommunications Act of 1996; Access to Telecommunications Service, Telecommunications Equipment and Customer Premises Equipment by Persons with Disabilities*. Washington, DC: Author.

Federal Communications Commission. (2000a). Second Report and Order: *Telecommunications relay services and speech-to-speech services' individuals with hearing and speech disabilities*. Washington, DC: Author.

Federal Communications Commission. (2000b). Second Report and Order: *Part 79—Closed captioning of video programming*. Washington, DC: Author.

Federal Communications Commission. (2000c). Report and Order: *Closed captioning requirements for digital television receivers; closed captioning and video description of video programming, implementation of section 305 of the Telecommunications Act of 1996, Video Programming Accessibility*. Washington, DC: Author.

Federal Communications Commission. (2000d). Report and Order: *Accessibility of programming providing emergency information*. Washington, DC: Author.

Federal Communications Commission. (2001a). Fourth Report and Order: *Revision of the commission's rules to ensure compatibility with enhanced 911 emergency calling systems*. Washington, DC: Author.

Federal Communications Commission. (2001b). Notice of Proposed Rulemaking: *In the matter of section 68. 4(a) of the commission's rules governing hearing aid compatible telephones*. Washington, DC: Author.

International Telecommunication Union, Technical Sector (1993). Recommendation V.18: *Operational and interworking requirements for DCE:s operating in the text telephone mode*. Geneva, Switzerland.

Harkins, J.E., Haravon, A.B., Tucker, P.E. Eum, J., & Fisher, L. (2000). Evaluating automatic speech recognition as a conversational aid for people with hearing loss. In R. Simpson (Ed.) *Proceedings of 24th Annual RESNA Conference* (pp. 106–108). Alexandria, VA: RESNA Press.

Harkins, J.E., Levitt, H., & Strauss, K. P. (1994). Technology and telephone relay service. *Technology and Disability, 3*(3), 173–194.

Lang, H. G. (2000). *A phone of our own: The deaf insurrection against Ma Bell*. Washington, DC: Gallaudet University Press.

Nabelek, AK (1993). Communication in noisy and reverberant environments. In G. A. Studebaker & I. Hochberg (Eds.), *Acoustical factors affecting hearing aid performance*, (2nd ed., pp. 15–28). Needham Heights, MA: Allyn & Bacon.

Olesen, K. G. (1992). *Survey of text telephones and relay services in Europe: Final Report* (EUR14242 EN). Luxembourg: Office of Official Publications of the European Communities.

Plomp, R. (1978). Auditory handicap of hearing impairment and the limited benefit of hearing aids. *Journal of the Acoustical Society of America, 63*, 533–549.

Robson, G. D. (1997). *Inside captioning*. Castro Valley, CA: CyberDawg.

Rehabilitation Act, S 508, as amended, 29 U.S.C. § 794(d) (1998).

Television Decoder Circuitry Act of 1990. Pub. L. No. 101–431 (1990).

Waltzman, S. (2001, May). *State of the science in assistive hearing devices for people who are hard of hearing*. Paper presented at the State of the Science Conference on Assistive Technologies for People with Hearing Loss, Graduate Center, City University of New York, New York.

Woodcock, K. (1997). Ergonomics and automatic speech recognition applications for deaf and hard of hearing users. *Technology and Disability*, 7(3), 147–164.

Zakon, R. H. (2001). WWW growth. Report retrieved November 29, 2001, from *http://www.zakon.org/robert/internet/timeline/*

30

Barbara Cone-Wesson

Screening and Assessment of Hearing Loss in Infants

During the 1990s there was a grass-roots effort by audiologists, otologists, teachers of the deaf, parents, and early interventionists to create programs for systematic detection of deafness and "educationally significant" hearing loss through universal newborn hearing screening. The result is that at the beginning of the twenty-first century, there are newborn hearing screening programs in a majority of the U.S. states, in the European Union, and in other industrialized nations. With newborn hearing screening comes the need for diagnostic methods optimized for very young infants. Along with comprehensive assessment, there is a crucial need to have early intervention programs focused on the family and social structures in which the infant will be raised. The rationale for all of these programs is the hypothesis that early detection of hearing loss or deafness is directly related to best outcomes for the child—a hypothesis supported by studies by Yoshinaga-Itano and colleagues (Yoshinaga-Itano, Coulter, & Thomson, 2000; Yoshinaga-Itano, Sedey, Coulter & Mehl, 1998). Early detection of hearing loss and early habilitation can capitalize on the considerable plasticity of the developing brain and nervous system. Therefore, programs designed to stimulate language and cognition should be most effective when applied as early as possible.

This chapter will briefly review how infant hearing develops as a background for methods used to screen or assess infant hearing. Then various methods used for audiological assessment and screening will be presented.

Development of Infant Hearing

Anatomically, the cochlea (inner ear) has developed by 24 weeks gestational age, 3 months before birth (Rubel, Popper, & Fay, 1998). Cochlear hair cells and their innervation appear to be differentiated by 22 weeks gestational age, presaging the onset of auditory function. Brain responses to sound, auditory evoked potentials (AEPs), can be recorded in premature infants at 26–28 weeks gestational age (Graziani, Weitzman, & Velasco, 1968; Starr, Amlie, Martin, & Sanders, 1977), indicating that the peripheral and brainstem auditory system are functional well before term. Studies of fetal behaviors in response to sound (movement, heart rate acceleration, or deceleration) delivered through the abdominal wall also indicate that hearing begins well before birth (Werner & Gray, 1998; Werner & Marean, 1996).

One method of studying auditory system de-

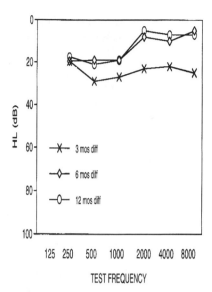

Figure 30-1. Pure-tone threshold results from 3-, 6-, and 12-month-old infants, indicating the difference (diff) in thresholds for infants compared to adults; 0 dB HL indicates pure-tone thresholds for adult listeners. (Figure created by T.E. Glattke, used with permission.)

velopment focuses on threshold. the lowest (sound pressure) level of sound to which the infant will respond behaviorally. Systematic observation of infants' responses suggest that threshold is elevated (poorer) in comparison to adults throughout early infancy and childhood (figure 30-1). However, behavioral responses of very young infants are difficult to quantify reliably, owing to their limited and labile behavioral repertoire. Even normally hearing newborns may not demonstrate a clear behavioral response to sound unless it is very loud (e.g., 90 dB HI). At 3 months of age, when more sophisticated psychophysical procedures can be used, infants still may not respond unless sound is presented at 30–40 dB above adult threshold levels. By 6 months of age, infants demonstrate reliable responses to sound at levels within 10–15 dB of adult thresholds, when tested under well-controlled conditions. But even at 10 years of age, thresholds for low frequency sounds appear to be slightly elevated compared to adult values. Some of these threshold differences are attributable to differences in external and middle ear function, which are not fully mature until puberty.

Another approach to the study of threshold development employs electrophysiologic methods.

Auditory evoked potentials measuring electrical activity in response to sound can be recorded from the auditory nervous system, including auditory nerve, brainstem, thalamus, and cortex. Thresholds for auditory brainstem responses (ABR) are elevated by 20–30 dB in the newborn compared to those of adults (Sininger, Abdala, & Cone-Wesson, 1997). Although the latency (timing) of the ABR component wave I (thought to be generated by the auditory nerve, C.N. VIII) reaches adult values by 6 months (for sounds presented above threshold), latencies of later ABR waves do not reach maturity until 18 months of age. The latency maturation is attributed to continued myelination and dendritic arborization of the brainstem auditory nervous system, which influence neural synchrony, and thus hearing thresholds (Sininger et al., 1997).[1] Thresholds for evoked potentials are, therefore, elevated with respect to adult values until brainstem development is complete. ABR thresholds have not been carefully studied as a function of age, however, despite the ubiquity of the ABR technique in both research and clinical applications. For evoked potentials generated at thalamic and cortical levels of the auditory system, adult values for component latencies and amplitudes and response detectability may not be reached until the late teenage years (Goodin, Squires, Henderson, & Starr, 1978; Kraus, Smith, Reed, Stein, & Cartee, 1985).

Methods for Assessing Hearing Sensitivity in Infants and Children

Methods for evaluating hearing sensitivity in infants and children include those based upon careful observation of an infant's behavior in response to sound with reinforcement of sound-attending behaviors, and also electrophysiologic and electroacoustic techniques.

Behavioral Methods

Behavioral Observation and Observer-based Psychophysical Procedures

Newborn infants demonstrate changes in heart and respiration rates and in motor activity in response to sound, as well as eye widening and localization toward sound. These behaviors are too labile to be used reliably in the clinical assessment of hearing threshold, although they have been exploited in research (Werner & Marean, 1996). Using the observer-based psychophysical procedure (OPP), thresholds can be reliably determined for infants as young as 3 months of age (Werner, 1995; Werner & Marean, 1991). OPP methods have greater validity and reliability compared to methods used by clinicians, specifically, behavioral observation audiometry (BOA). The difficulty with BOA, as compared to OPP, is that there is no systematic attempt to measure the observer's behavior—that is, to determine how well the observer can detect the infant's response to sound in comparison to an infant's random activity.

The OPP, in contrast, provides feedback and reinforcement to the observer on each test trial, which may be a stimulus (sound present) or a control (no sound) trial. If the infant responds to sound and the observer judges that correctly, reinforcement is provided to both the observer and the infant. Responses by the infant in the absence of sound, or the observer's failure to detect a response during a stimulus trial, are also recorded. In this way, the test performance of the observer is known. The infant also learns to emit behaviors in response to sound to gain reinforcement. BOA uses no such controls, nor is the infant reinforced for demonstrating hearing behaviors, so the procedure tends to have unrepeatable results. Although the observation of young infants' natural response to sound is an important part of the clinician's art, BOA cannot be used to validly or reliably determine hearing threshold unless the rigor of OPP is used. OPP is currently used primarily as a research technique and has not yet been applied in clinical tests for individual infants with hearing loss.

Visual Reinforcement Audiometry

By 4–6 months of age, most infants have developed sufficient head control to be able to participate in a threshold determination method known as visual reinforcement audiometry (VRA). In the traditional technique, the infant is seated on the parent's lap and test sounds (warbled tones, band-passed noise or speech) are presented through a loudspeaker. When the infant turns toward the source of the sound, a visual reinforcer is activated. The reinforcer is a mechanized toy that has been obscured in a smoked-plexiglass box. Correct responses (head turns toward sound) result in illumination and movement of the toy. The presentation of a

visual reinforcer has been shown to increase and maintain infant response rates at a high level compared to nonreinforced conditions (Primus & Thompson, 1987). Like OPP, the performance of both infant and observer can be monitored by providing control trials during which no stimulus is presented (Widen, 1993). The procedure is very robust when used for infants aged 6 to about 18 months, although motor or visual impairment diminish its effectiveness (Widen et al., 2000). Current practice of VRA employs insert earphones for individual ear tests rather than loudspeaker (sound field) presentation. The lowest level at which an infant makes a response, by convention, is referred to as the minimum response level rather than as threshold.

VRA loses its effectiveness with older infants (18–24 months). Sometimes tokens or food reinforcers are used in combination with visual and social reinforcers to maintain toddler responsiveness. When a toddler is able to learn and participate in a game, play audiometry is used. A game is structured to encourage the toddler to make a response whenever a test signal is heard. Games include dropping blocks in a bucket, putting pegs in a hole, or manipulating simple puzzle parts. A full audiogram can usually be obtained with these methods. Neurodevelopmental status and cognitive ability of the infant or toddler must be taken into account for the successful use of VRA or play audiometry techniques.

Electrophysiologic Methods for Threshold Determination

The reception of sound involves changes in electrical potentials at the level of the cochlea, auditory nerve and at higher brain levels. These AEPs can be recorded using noninvasive methods and computerized technologies. AEPs may be used to estimate threshold.

Electrocochleography: Compound Nerve Action Potential

The 1960s saw the use of electrocochleography (ECOG), recording electrical activity from the cochlea and auditory nerve in response to sound, to estimate threshold. The technique relies on placing a recording electrode close to the site of generation. A needle electrode is surgically introduced into the middle ear (through the eardrum) and placed on the bony prominence near the round window of the cochlea. Sound will evoke a compound nerve action potential (CAP) from the auditory nerve that can be recorded by the electrode, and amplified and processed by an averaging computer. Clicks and brief (< 10 ms) tone bursts can be used to evoke the response, and the lowest level at which the CAP is evident corresponds with hearing threshold (Eggermont, Spoor, & Odenthal, 1976; Schoonhoven, Lamore, de Laat, & Grote, 1999). An advantage of ECOG for testing threshold is that the CAP does not appear to adapt or habituate, even when recorded during sedated sleep and/or from young infants. A major disadvantage is that general anesthesia and surgery is required for optimal recording conditions in infants and toddlers, raising costs for assessment. Although electrodes placed (nonsurgically) in the ear canal can also be used to record the CAP, these methods are not as sensitive as the trans-tympanic technique.

Auditory Brainstem Response

A lower cost, noninvasive method for estimating hearing threshold in infants is the auditory brainstem response (ABR). The nuclei and neural pathways in the brainstem auditory nervous system (specifically, auditory nerve, cochlear nucleus, superior olive, and inferior colliculus and their connections) are activated by sound and produce brain electrical potentials that can be detected using computerized methods. ABR is unaffected by sleep state (in fact, sleep is preferred in order to reduce physiological noise) and does not adapt or habituate under normal recording conditions. Threshold and timing (latency) of the ABR correspond to different degrees and types of hearing loss (Gorga, Worthington, Reiland, Beauchaine, & Goldgar, 1985). Clicks and tone bursts can be used to evoke responses to estimate sensitivity. Although threshold and latency of ABRs show developmental effects, 25 years of clinical research have provided age-appropriate norms that are used to interpret responses. ABRs can be recorded using EEG electrodes that are placed on the scalp with water-soluble paste. This is a considerable advantage over ECOG tests, and most ABR evaluations are conducted in outpatient clinics; medical surveillance is needed only when sedation is used. A disadvantage of the ABR (in comparison to ECOG) is that several thousand responses to rapidly repeating test signals are needed for each trial. Eight

to 12 min of computerized averaging may be needed to determine threshold for one frequency, and more than an hour may be needed to develop a three- or four-frequency audiogram estimate. Test stimuli can be presented by both air and bone conduction (Cone-Wesson, 1995), so conductive versus sensorineural hearing losses can be detected. Infants older than 6 months are usually given an oral sedative for the test, and, even then, two or more test sessions may be needed to obtain air and bone conduction threshold estimates for several frequencies in both ears.

ABR tests have excellent validity, and regression formulae have been developed that relate ABR threshold to behavioral threshold (Stapells, Gravel, & Martin, 1995). These can be used to estimate behavioral audiograms (Stapells, 2000). ABRs are regularly used to estimate hearing threshold in infants and toddlers, even those who have been tested successfully using behavioral methods. Figure 30-2 shows an example of ABR tracings obtained for clicks presented well above threshold (60 dB nHL)[2] and down to threshold level (10 dB nHL). The audiologist determines the lowest stimulus level for which a response is present by visual inspection of the traces.

Limitations of ECOG and ABR

One limitation of both ECOG and ABR for estimating threshold is that neither is a test of hearing, which implies perception, but merely reflects synchrony in neural responses. Neural synchrony and perceptual threshold are correlated, but it is possible to have good neural synchrony and poor perception, particularly if there is dysfunction at neural centers higher than the brainstem. Similarly, neural synchrony can be disrupted at the nerve or brainstem level, while higher centers are able to respond to a poorly synchronized neural signal; in this case, CAP or ABR may be abnormal or absent, while perceptual thresholds may show only a mild or moderate hearing loss.

Cochlear mechanics are a major determinant of neural synchrony. In normally hearing ears, neural synchrony is greatest in response to high frequency (≥ 2.0 kHz) tone bursts and/or stimuli that have a fast or instantaneous onset, such as clicks. Thus, CAPs and ABRs are more robust in response to such stimuli and may be evident down to levels within 5–10 dB of perceptual threshold. For mid- and low-

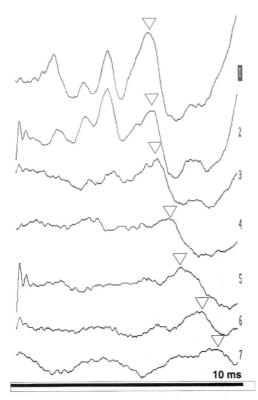

10 ms

Figure 30-2. Auditory brainstem responses obtained as a function of stimulus (click) level. 1 = 70 dB nHL, 2 = 60 dB nHL, 3 = 50 dB nHL, 4 = 40 dB nHL, 5 = 30 dB nHL, 6 = 20 dB nHL, 7 = 10 dB nHL. Arrowheads point to "wave V" or the most prominent component of this evoked response. The latency (timing) of wave V is prolonged as a function of decreasing stimulus level. A response is evident down to 10 dB nHL (i.e., 10 dB above the listener's threshold for the click stimulus).

frequency tone bursts, threshold estimates are less precise, and evoked potentials may only be evident at 20–30 dB above perceptual threshold (Stapells, 2000). When cochlear mechanics are disrupted, such as by sensorineural hearing loss, the correspondence between perceptual and CAP/ABR threshold may also be affected.

Finally, experienced observers are needed to interpret the waveforms obtained in ECOG and ABR tests, and this interpretation may be subject to observer bias. Algorithmic, statistical methods also can be used in computer software to detect responses (Hyde, Sininger, & Don, 1998) and have been used successfully in newborn hearing screening.

Auditory Steady-State Response

During the 1990s an alternative to ECOG and ABR was developed to estimate hearing threshold from AEPs, the auditory steady-state responses (ASSR) technique. The ASSR is similar to CAP and ABR in that brain potentials to sound are measured. The stimuli used to evoke ASSRs are pure tones that are amplitude and/or frequency modulated. The ASSR appears to be generated by the same neural structures as the AEPs evoked by transient sounds, but this depends on both modulation rate and subject state. In sleeping infants and young children, pure tones modulated at rates of 60–120 Hz yield reliable responses, and the characteristics of ASSRs at these rates are similar to those for the ABR.

The presence of the ASSR is critically dependent on the integrity of the cochlea for the carrier (test tone) frequency. If there is hearing loss at the carrier frequency, the ASSR threshold will be elevated, consistent with the degree of hearing loss (Rance, Dowell, Rickards, Beer, & Clark, 1998; Rance, Rickards, Cohen, DeVidi, & Clark, 1995). Thresholds for ASSR have been established in normal newborns, infants, and children (Cone-Wesson et al., 2002, Rickards et al., 1994), and the ASSR has been used to predict pure-tone threshold in infants and children with hearing loss (Aoyagi et al., 1999; Cone-Wesson et al., 2002; Lins et al., 1996; Perez-Abalo et al., 2001; Rance et al., 1995, 1998). The ASSR technique overcomes one limitation of tone-burst–evoked ABR tests by incorporating a detection algorithm, so that threshold searching and audiogram estimation can be implemented automatically.

The ASSR has the same limitation as CAP and ABR with regard to neural synchrony, and ASSR thresholds may be similarly elevated with respect to perceptual threshold. An advantage of ASSR is that it is possible to test at very high stimulus levels and reveal residual hearing in those with moderately severe to profound hearing losses, even when ABRs are absent (Rance et al., 1998). This makes ASSR an important test when amplification or cochlear implantation is being considered.

Electroacoustic Methods: Evoked Otoacoustic Emissions

The auditory nervous system, at least at the level of the inner ear, has an acoustic as well as an electrical response to sound. That is, the ear creates sound in the process of responding to sound. Although the exact mechanism for this process is unknown, it appears that the deflection of the fine cilia on top of the hair cells, which occurs during sound transduction, changes the ion concentration of the hair cell, and the hair cell elongates or contracts with these ion fluctuations (Brownell, 1990). This motility of the outer hair cells (OHCs) in synchrony with the frequency of the stimulating tone is thought to increase the amplitude of the basilar membrane motion for that tone, and thus improve sensitivity and sharpen frequency tuning of the inner ear.

A byproduct of this process is the creation of mechanical energy in the inner ear, which is transmitted from the basilar membrane, through the middle ear and the tympanic membrane outward to the external auditory canal. These cochlear emissions or "echoes" can be detected by a sensitive microphone placed in the external ear. The signal detected by the microphone undergoes further electronic amplification and computerized signal processing.

Emissions evoked by clicks or tone bursts are known as transient-evoked otoacoustic emissions (TEOAE) and those in response to two-tone combinations that create harmonic distortion within the cochlea are known as distortion product otoacoustic emissions (DPOAE). Because the TEOAE and DPOAE are generated by different types of stimuli, creating different mechanical events within the cochlea, there are some differences in their stimulus-response properties. For clinical use, the most important property is that TEOAE and DPOAE are present when the OHCs are functional and diminished or absent when OHCs are nonfunctional (Lonsbury-Martin, Whitehead, & Martin, 1991). The majority of sensory hearing losses involve damage or loss to the OHCs; thus, the evoked otoacoustic emissions (EOAEs) can be used to indicate when such abnormality exists.

The amplitude of the DPOAE may be related to the degree of hearing loss, at least for mild and moderate hearing losses (Gorga, Neeley, & Dorn, 1999). The absence of EOAEs (when the middle ear is normal) indicates hearing loss, but this loss may be mild, moderate, severe, or profound. This limits their use for threshold estimates; however, the recording of EOAEs is an important component of the audiological evaluation because their presence signifies OHC integrity. The detection and analysis of EOAEs, like ASSRs, can be completely automated. Figure 30-3 displays the waveform of a TEOAE along with its spectrum. This analysis forms the basis of TEOAE interpretation. EOAEs have gained widespread use in newborn hearing screening programs because of their sensitivity to sensory hearing loss and the efficient, automated methods available for recording and analysis.

Like the CAP, ABR, and ASSR, EOAEs do not test hearing directly. EOAEs only indicate the functional status of cochlear OHCs. There are pathological conditions that appear to affect inner hair cell (IHC) and afferent nerve function but leave OHCs and EOAEs intact. Auditory neuropathy is one form of hearing loss that appears to affect the IHC and auditory nerve function (Starr, Picton, & Kim, 2001). In these cases, EOAEs are present, but CAP and ABR are absent. Pure-tone hearing thresholds can be normal or show any degree of loss, including profound (Rance et al., 1999; Sininger & Oba, 2001). Speech perception abilities are usually very poor, even when pure-tone thresholds indicate normal hearing or show only a mild or moderate hearing loss (Cone-Wesson, Rance, & Sininger, 2001). Because EOAEs do not depend on IHC or afferent integrity, they may fail to identify a child with auditory neuropathy.

Methods for Evaluating Speech Perception

Very young hearing infants have remarkable speech perception skills (Werker & Tees, 1999). They are able to discriminate speech features, such as a voiced-voiceless contrast (/ta/ vs. /da/), or place-of-articulation (/ba/ vs. /da/) or good versus poor exemplars of vowel sounds. There is evidence that newborns can use prosody to differentiate different grammatical classes of words. But little is known about speech sound discrimination and perception abilities of infants with hearing loss. In addition, methods used for investigating infant speech perception abilities in research contexts have had little carry-over to clinical methods for evaluation. Because decisions about amplification, cochlear implantation, and language-learning methods may be based on speech perception abilities, valid clinical assessment methods are needed for infants and toddlers.

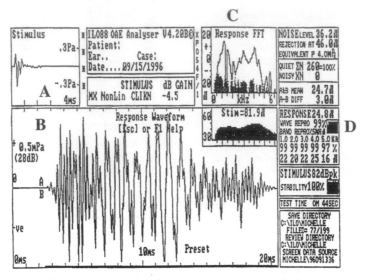

Figure 30-3. Computer screen display from a transient-evoked otoacoustic emissions (TEOAE) test, using ILO-92 hardware and software to obtain and analyze TEOAEs. (A) Stimulus waveform; in this case, a click was used to evoke the otoacoustic emission. (B) Response waveform. (C) Spectrum (Fast Fourier Transform) of the TEOAE shown in panel B. The shaded area of the spectrum indicates noise, and the unshaded area indicates the response. In this example, response energy is present across the range of frequencies analyzed, with peaks at 1.0, 2.5, and 4.0 kHz. (D) Statistical analyses of TEOAE shown in panel B. Computer software calculates the amplitude of the response (24.8 dB SPL), wave reproducibility (99%), wave reproducibility as a function of analysis bandwidth (1.0–5.0 kHz, in this example, 99% for all but 5 kHz), and signal-to-noise ration (SNR) as a function of analysis bandwidth. (Figure created by T.E. Glattke, used with permission.)

Behavioral Tests of Speech Perception

Methods for determining speech perception abilities in infants and toddlers are not well established, and, as for pure-tone threshold testing, the behavioral and cognitive repertoire of the infant must be considered.

For infants who have head control and who can localize sound (5–6 months or older), the visually reinforced infant speech discrimination (VRISD) procedure may be used to demonstrate that a speech sound or feature has been discriminated. In this procedure, the infant/toddler is reinforced for detecting a change in a train of stimuli (Eilers, Wilson, & Moore, 1977). For instance, the word "pat" can be presented repeatedly, and the change word interspersed in this pat-train may be "bat." The infant is reinforced for detecting (indicated with a head turn or other behavior) when the stimulus changes. For toddlers and older children, the Speech Feature Test (Dawson Nott, Clark, & Cowan, 1998), may be used. This is similar to the VRISD technique, except that children make a behavioral response as they play a listening game (e.g., putting a peg in a pegboard for each stimulus change detected). This method has been used to test young deaf children with cochlear implants. These techniques have not yet gained widespread clinical use but appear to be a logical extension of VRA and play audiometry procedures.

When toddlers have developed a receptive language age of at least 2.6 years and motor skills for pointing, some speech perception testing may be completed with a picture-pointing task. In these tests, such as the NU-Chips (Elliot & Kate, 1980) the child is shown drawings of four objects. There is a common phonetic element among the objects pictured, such as boat, coat, stove, comb (common element is /o/). The child is asked to "point to comb" and thus discriminate among several like-sounding possibilities. There are also similar tests using small objects that children are able to point to or manipulate, such as the Kendall Toy Test. Like the NU-CHIPs, this is a closed-set test, in which the child has a limited number of response possibilities.

Speech perception and speech discrimination are inextricably linked to language abilities. Infants who lack a receptive vocabulary for spoken language, whether because of deafness or immaturity, will not be testable with these methods. A child's ability to use sound can also be evaluated by parents' responses to an inventory of auditory behaviors. The Meaningful Auditory Integration Scale (MAIS) was developed to evaluate the benefit obtained by children initially fit with amplification or cochlear implants (Robbins, Svirsky, Osberger, & Pisoni, 1998). Probe items relate to how the child responds to sound in the environment, including speech. Results of this inventory have been shown to be sensitive to emerging hearing and speech perception abilities.

Electrophysiologic Tests of Speech Perception

Although evoked potentials from auditory cortex (also known as event related potentials, ERPs) have a prolonged time course for development, they are present in young infants and offer a means for indicating speech perception abilities. ERPs are defined as being either obligatory or cognitive. For speech sounds, obligatory potentials appear to be sensitive to differences in voice-onset time, as in /ta/ versus /da/ (Novak, Kurtzberg, Kreuzer, & Vaughan 1989). Cognitive ERPs are evoked when the listener is asked to attend or respond to some aspect of the test stimuli. A number of studies have used obligatory and cognitive ERPs to study speech perception in older children and adults (Cheor, Korpilahti, Martynova, & Lang, 2001; Kraus & Cheor, 2000), children with language disorders (Shafer et al., 2001), and to study auditory system development (Ponton, Eggermont, Kwong, & Don 2000). This research reveals significant limitations for the application of these techniques for diagnosis or prognosis of speech perception abilities in individual subjects. That is, while ERPs averaged over a group of listeners may produce a significant result, their reliability and validity for use with individuals has not yet been established (Wunderlich and Cone-Wesson, 2001).

Newborn Hearing Screening

History

Early detection of hearing loss and early habilitation can capitalize on the considerable plasticity of the developing brain and nervous system (Sininger, Doyle, & Moore, 1999). There have been efforts to detect hearing loss at birth since the latter half of the twentieth century. Downs and Sterritt (1964) evaluated the reliability of behavioral observation of newborns' responses to tones or to noise for screening. Although they reported that BOA screening tests were not effective, the notion that hearing should be screened as early as possible in life has been a mainstay of audiology since that time. The 1972 Joint Commission on Infant Screening suggested the concept of risk-register screening (Hayes & Northern, 1996), based on evidence that family history and pre- and perinatal conditions indicated risk for hearing loss (Bergstrom, Hemenway, & Downs, 1971). It was recommended that infants who had one or more of these risk factors should receive hearing assessment. The risk factors disseminated by the joint commission have undergone several revisions since the first published list in 1972 (see table 30-1).

There are several problems with risk factor screening, the most significant being that up to 50% of infants with congenital hearing loss have no risk factors and would be missed by risk factor screening alone. Risk factors, used individually or in combination, have poor sensitivity for indicating hearing loss or deafness (Cone-Wesson et al., 2000; Turner and Cone-Wesson, 1992).

A groundswell of support for universal newborn hearing screening came to a head in 1993. Following a consensus conference, the National Institutes of Health developed a position statement that encouraged screening of all graduates of neonatal intensive care units before hospital discharge, and the screening of all other infants by 3 months of age (National Institutes of Health, 1993). Two technologies, ABR and EOAES, used individually or in combination, were recognized as suitable for newborn hearing screening. By mid-2002, more than 40 of the U.S. States had passed legislation

Table 30-1. Neonatal and infant/toddler risk indicators associated
with sensorineural and/or conductive hearing loss

1972 (Hayes and Northern, 1996)
1. All infants with a family history of childhood deafness in some member of the immediate family (i.e., father, mother or sibling)
2. All infants whose mothers had rubella documented or strongly suspected during any period of pregnancy
3. All infants with a family history of, or presence of congenital malformations of the external ear, cleft lip or palate, including bifid uvula
4. All infants weighing 1500 g
5. All infants having bilirubin values of 20 mg/100 mg or more, or who had an exchange transfusion
6. All infants with abnormal otoscopic findings

2000 (Joint Committee on Infant Hearing, 2000)
1. An illness or condition requiring admission of 48 or greater to a neonatal intensive care unit
2. Stigmata or other findings associated with a syndrome known to include a sensorineural and/or conductive hearing loss or eustachian tube dysfunction, including syndromes associated with progressive hearing loss such as neurofibromatosis, osteopetrosis, and Usher's syndrome
3. Craniofacial anomalies including those with morphological abnormalities of the pinna and ear canal.
4. Family history of permanent childhood sensorineural hearing loss
5. In-utero infection such as cytomegalovirus, herpes, toxoplasmosis, or rubella
6. Postnatal infections associated with sensorineural hearing loss including bacterial meningitis
7. Neonatal indicators, specifically hyberilirubinemia as levels requiring exchange transfusion, persistent pulmonary hypertension of the newborn associated with mechanical ventilation, and conditions requiring the use of extra-corporeal membrane oxygenation
8. Neurodegenerative disorders such as Hunter syndrome, or sensorimotor neuropathies such as Friedrich's ataxia and Charcot-Marie-Tooth syndrome
9. Head trauma
10. Recurrent or persistent otitis media with effusion for at least 3 months
11. Parent or caregiver concern regarding hearing, speech, language and/or developmental delay

---

mandating universal newborn hearing screening. A number of countries belonging to the European Union have Universal newborn hearing screening programs and are leaders in this area.

Principles of Screening

Screening refers to those methods used to divide a population into two groups: a small group of individuals at risk for having the target condition and a much larger group at low risk for having the target condition. Screening methods are evaluated on the basis of the sensitivity and specificity of the test. Sensitivity refers to the percentage of those with the target condition who will fail the screening test, and specificity refers to the percentage of those without the target condition who will pass the screening test. No screening test has perfect sensitivity and specificity. Test performance will vary with the target condition (e.g., degree and/or type of hearing

loss), the prevalence of the target condition within the population, and the criterion used for the screening test.

Identification refers to those methods used to determine when hearing loss is present, after screening. Only those identified with the target condition will go on to the assessment or evaluation protocol, wherein the type and degree of hearing loss are evaluated using a variety of audiologic and medical tests.

Bilateral hearing loss is generally thought to meet criteria warranting initiation of population-based screening programs. The first criterion is that the occurrence of the target condition is frequent enough to warrant mass screening. Bilateral hearing loss of ≥ 35dB HL[3] in the better ear occurs in 1 in every 750 births. This is an exceptionally high prevalence for a potentially disabling condition. Second, the condition must be amenable to treatment or prevention that will change the expected outcome.

Medical treatment for (conductive) hearing losses and aids-to-hearing (amplification technologies and cochlear implants) can be used to provide access to sound and alleviate sensory deprivation. In addition, early intervention for language (manual or oral) can limit or prevent language delays. Third, there facilities for diagnosis and treatment must be available. This must be addressed on a local level, but, in general, both federal and state programs offer diagnostic and treatment facilities for infants with hearing loss. Fourth, the cost of screening must be commensurate with the benefits to the individual. Costs for Universal newborn hearing screening are U.S. $13.00–25.00 per infant at present but are expected to decrease with improvements in technology for testing and data management.

Fifth, screening must be accepted by the public and professional community. Most parents of newborns opt to have their infant screened when the tests are offered. Parental anxiety regarding screening test outcomes has been evaluated and has been found to be benign (Young & Andrews, 2001). The Joint Committee on Infant Hearing (2000), with representatives from major professional bodies of nursing, education, medicine, and audiology has endorsed universal newborn hearing screening.

Finally, there must be screening tools that are valid and that can differentiate those with hearing loss from those with normal hearing. ABR and EOAE have been shown to have good test performance when used for newborn hearing screening (Norton, Gorga, Widen, Vohr, Folsom, Sininger, Cone-Wesson, & Fletcher 2000).

Technologies for Screening

Universal newborn hearing screening became feasible when methods for performing ABR and EOAE became automated and efficient. Computerized methods developed for detection of the ABR, implemented in a hardware-software package specifically for newborn hearing screening purposes (Hermann, Thornton, & Joseph, 1995) made automatic ABR affordable as a screening tool. The automatic ABR has excellent test performance when compared to results from diagnostic ABR procedures (Jacobson, Jacobson, & Spahr, 1990; see Sininger et al., 2000, for an in-depth review).

EOAE technology was very rapidly adopted for newborn hearing screening because of the ease and availability of automatic (computerized) detection and analysis methods. Like the AABR methods, EOAEs have been scrutinized for newborn hearing screening, along with the factors that can influence screening outcomes (Gorga et al., 2000; Norton, Gorga, Widen, Vohr, et al., 2000).

Evaluation of Screening

There have been numerous studies in which the sensitivity of automatic ABR and EOAE tests has been determined. In most studies, infants who did not pass automatic ABR or EOAE received a diagnostic ABR as the gold standard against which the screening result was compared (Stevens et al., 1990). Only one large-scale study compared hearing screening technology performance with behavioral hearing tests (Norton, Gorga, Widen, Folsom, Sininger, Cone-Wesson, Vohr, & Fletcher, 2000). Several thousand newborns were tested with automatic ABR, TEOAE, and DPOAE tests. Regardless of the neonatal test outcomes, the infants and their families were asked to return for VRA tests, against which the neonatal tests were compared. Automatic ABR and EOAE test performance was not significantly different for detecting mild or greater hearing loss at 2.0–4.0 kHz, but automatic ABR had slightly better performance for detecting hearing loss averaged over 1.0, 2.0, and 4.0 kHz (Norton, Gorga, Widen, Vohr et al., 2000). Overall, sensitivity was greater than 80% for each measure, with a false positive rate of 20%. Both EOAE and AABR are considered good, well-researched, but not perfect technologies for newborn hearing screening applications. Neonatal screening does not identify all early childhood hearing loss. Infants can develop hearing loss due to otitis media in the first year of life, and progressive sensorineural losses also may not manifest in the newborn period (Cone-Wesson et al., 2000).

Costs for newborn hearing screening programs have been modeled (Kezirian, White, Yueh, & Sullivan, 2001) and are usually weighed against the costs of ongoing special education owing to hearing loss or deafness detected later in life (Mehl & Thompson, 1998). The actual cost of performing a hearing screening test is negligible compared to overall universal newborn hearing screening program costs, including those for personnel, methods for ensuring follow-up of those infants who are referred, and record keeping.

Problems

Universal newborn hearing screening is not without its detractors. The costs of universal newborn hearing screening are high compared to targeted screening, for example, of all infants who are neonatal intensive care unit graduates (Bess & Paradise, 1994). For a limited increase in yield, perhaps only 25–40% more infants detected with universal newborn hearing screening compared to targeted screening, it costs 10 times as much. Another issue is the effectiveness of universal newborn hearing screening programs for improving population outcomes. The desired population outcome would be intervention for hearing loss that leads to improved language and educational (and perhaps, vocational) outcomes. At the present time, there is limited evidence that newborn hearing screening results in improved language outcomes (U.S. Preventive Services Task Force, 2001). In a series of analyses, Yoshinaga-Itano, Sedey, Coulter, and Mehl (1998) showed that language outcomes were better in infants with hearing loss identified before 6 months of age compared to those who were identified after 6 months of age. Although there were more than 150 infants in this research program, outcomes cannot be generalized with confidence to the larger population. Generalization would require a large-scale, randomized control trial in which a large cohort of infants screened at birth were followed for language outcomes over a period of years and compared to a comparable group of infants who did not receive screening.

Two large-scale studies (Prieve et al., 2000; Norton, Gorga, Widen, Folsom, et al., 2000) show that follow-up of infants is a weakness of most screening programs. Screening programs in the United States have been underfunded, perhaps because of a failure to complete critically needed research on outcomes or modeling studies to estimate true costs of such a large-scale public health program.

The Future: Genetic Screening?

Much progress has been made in the identification of genes causing nonsyndromic and syndromic sensorineural hearing loss (see Arnos and Pandya, this volume), and there are suggestions that newborn screening programs could include testing for genetic indicators. Genetic screening may eventually supersede the need to test all infants with tests of function such as automatic ABR and EOAE. An alternative program might include conventional screening tests for those with a risk factor for hearing loss and genetic screening for all other infants. Currently, no universal newborn hearing screening program has included a genetic test as part of the efforts for detecting hearing loss in newborns.

In general, the same problems encountered with screening in general, such as adequate follow-up of infants referred from the genetic screen, would likely be manifest. Still, the addition of molecular analysis methods for detecting hearing loss will likely improve the overall performance of screening protocols.

Summary and Conclusions

Technologies exist to screen for hearing loss at birth and to provide accurate assessment of the degree of hearing loss in the first months of life. There is an exclusive reliance electrophysiologic and electroacoustic methods for screening and for assessment in infants under the age of 6 months. After 6 months of age, behavioral measures of hearing are used, although their application and accuracy may be limited when visual or developmental disability is present. Clinically applicable methods for assessing speech perception abilities in infants and toddlers are extremely limited, using either behavioral or electrophysiologic techniques. Because one of the desired outcomes of early identification and intervention for hearing loss is improved receptive and expressive language, more research is needed on development and application of evaluation and prognostic techniques. When screening and assessment are tied to effective intervention programs, the goal of helping children reach their full potential can be realized.

Notes

Marilyn Dille and Judith Widen provided insightful critique of earlier versions of this chapter; I am grateful for their expertise. T.E. Glattke provided figures 30-1 and 30-3, which he developed for teaching at the University of Arizona, Department of Speech and Hearing Sciences; this contribution is gratefully acknowledged.

1. The electrical activity recorded from an electrode at the surface of the nerve or from electrodes

placed at some distance from auditory neuclei is an averaged sum of neural discharges generated in a large number of nerve fibers or cells. The timing of the discharge of individual fibers contributing to a response may be described as synchronous, when many discharges occur nearly simultaneously, or nonsynchronous, when the discharges are distributed in time.

2. The notation "nHL" is used to designate normal hearing level for a transient signal, such as a click or a toneburst. 0 dB nHL is the perceptual threshold for these signals for listeners with normal hearing. "HL" is used to designate hearing level for pure tones, and 0 dB HL is the perceptual threshold for pure tones for listeners with normal hearing.

3. Whether or not mild or unilateral losses meet these criteria has not been specifically addressed. These types of losses are considered to be risk factors for the development of more significant hearing losses and so are generally included in the target condition for which screening is implemented.

References

Aoyagi, M., Suzuki, Y., Yokota, M., Furuse, H., Watanabe, T., & Ito, T. (1999). Reliability of 80-Hz amplitude modulation-following response detected by phase coherence. *Audiology and Neuro-otology, 4*, 28–37.

Bergstrom, L., Hemenway, W., & Downs, M. (1971). A high risk registry to find congenital deafness. *Otolaryngology Clinics of North America, 4*, 369.

Bess, F., & Paradise, J. (1994). Universal screening for infant hearing impairment: Not simple, not risk free, not necessarily beneficial and not presently justified. *Pediatrics, 93*, 330–334.

Brownell, W.E. (1990). Outer hair cell electromotility and otoacoustic emissions. *Ear and Hearing, 11*, 82–92.

Cheour, M., Korpilahti, P., Martynova, O., & Lang, A.H. (2001). Mismatch negativity and late discriminative negativity in investigating speech perception and learning in children and infants. *Audiology and Neuro-Otology, 6*, 2–11.

Cone-Wesson, B, (1995). Bone-conduction ABR tests. *American Journal of Audiology, 4*, 14–19.

Cone-Wesson, B., Rance, G., & Sininger, Y. (2001). Amplification and rehabilitation strategies for patients with auditory neuropathy. In Y. Sininger & A. Starr (Eds) *Auditory neuropathy: A new perspective on hearing disorders* (pp. 233–249). San Diego, CA: Singular.

Cone-Wesson, B., Rickards, F., Poulis, C., Parker, J., Tan, L., Pollard, J. 2002, *The auditory steady-state response: Clinical observations and applications in infants and children*. Submitted. *Journal of the American Academy of Audiology 13*, 270–282.

Cone-Wesson, B., Vohr, B., Sininger, Y.S., Widen, J.E., Folsom R.C., Gorga M.P., and Norton, S.J. (2000). Identification of Neonatal Hearing Impairment: Infants with hearing loss. *Ear and Hearing, 1*, (5) 488–507.

Dawson, P.W., Nott, P.E., Clark, G.M., & Cowan, R.S. (1998). A modification of play audiometry to assess speech discrimination ability in sever-profoundly deaf 2 to 4 year old children. *Ear and Hearing, 19*, 371–384.

Downs, M.P., & Sterritt, G.M. (1964). Identification audiometry for neonates. A preliminary report. *Journal of Auditory Research, 4*(1), 69–80.

Eggermont, J.J., Spoor, A., & Odenthal, D.W. (1976). Frequency specificity of tone-burst electrocochleography. In R.J. Ruben, C. Elberling, & G. Salomon (Eds.), *Electrocochleography* (pp. 215–246). Baltimore, MD: University Park Press.

Eilers, R.E., Wilson, W.R., & Moore, J.M. (1977). Developmental changes in speech discrimination in infants. *Journal of Speech & Hearing Research, 20*, 766–780.

Elliot, L. & Katz, D. (1980). Development of a new children's test of speech discrimination. St. Louis, MO: Auditec.

Goodin, D.S., Squires, K.D., Henderson, B H., & Starr, A. (1978). Age-related variations in evoked potentials to auditory stimuli in normal human subjects. *Electroencephalography and Clinical Neurophysiology, 44*, 447–458.

Gorga, M.P., Neely, S.T., & Dorn, P.A. (1999). Distortion product otoacoustic emission test performance for a priori criteria and for multifrequency audiometric standards. *Ear and Hearing, 20*, 345–62.

Gorga, M.P., Norton, S.J., Sininger, Y.S,. Cone-Wesson, B., Folsom, R,C., Vohr, B.R., Widen, J.E., & Neely, S.T. (2000). Identification of neonatal hearing impairment: Distortion product otoacoustic emissions during the perinatal period. *Ear and Hearing, 21*, 400–424.

Gorga, M.P., Worthington, D.W., Reiland, J.K., Beauchaine, K.A., & Goldgar, D.E. (1985). Some comparisons between auditory brainstem response threshold, latencies and the pure-tone audiogram. *Ear and Hearing, 6*, 105–112.

Graziani, L.J., Wietzman, E.D., & Velasco, M.S.A. (1968). Neurologic maturation and auditory evoked responses in low birh weight infants. *Pediatrics, 41*, 483–494.

Hayes, D., & Northern, J.L. (1996). *Infants and hearing*. San Diego, CA: Singular.

Hermann, B.S., Thornton, A.R., & Joseph, J.M.

(1995). Automated infant hearing screning using the ABR: Development and validation. *American Journal of Audiology*, *4*, 6–14.

Hyde, M., Sininger, Y.S., & Don, M. (1998). Objective detection and analysis of auditory brainstem responses: an historical perspective. *Seminars in Hearing 19 (1)*, 97–113.

Jacobson, J.T., Jacobson, C.A., & Spahr, R.C. (1990). Automated and conventional ABR screening techniques in high-risk infants. *Journal of the American Academy of Audiology*, *1*, 187–195.

Joint Committee on Infant Hearing (2000). Joint Committee on Infant Hearing Year 2000 *Position Statement*: Principles and Guidelines for Early Hearing Detection and Intervention Programs. *Pediatrics*, 106(4): 798–817. Rockville, MD: American Speech-Language-Hearing Association.

Kezirian, E.J., White, K.R., Yueh, B., & Sullivan, S.D. (2001). Cost and cost-effectiveness of universal screening for hearing loss in newborns. *Otolaryngology—Head & Neck Surgery*, *124*, 359–367.

Kraus, N., & Cheour, M. (2000) Speech sound representation in the brain. *Audiology and Neuro-Otology 5*, 140–150.

Kraus, N., Smith, D., Reed, N.L., Stein, L.K., & Cartee, C. (1985). Auditory middle latency responses in children: Effects of age and diagnostic category. *Electroencephalography and Clinical Neurophysiology*, *62*, 343–351.

Lins, O.G., Picton, T.W., Boucher, B.L., Durieux-Smith, A,. Champagne, S.C., Moran, L.M., Perez-Abalo, M.C., Martin, V., & Savio, G. (1996). Frequency specific audiometry using steady-state responses. *Ear and Hearing*, *17*, 81–96.

Lonsbury-Martin, B.L., Whitehead, M.L., & Martin, G.K. (1991). Clinical applications of otoacoustic emissions. *Journal of Speech and Hearing Research*, *34*, 964–981.

Mehl, A.L., & Thompson, M.A. (1998). Newborn hearing screening: The great omission. *Pediatrics*, *101*, E4.

National Institutes of Health. (1993). NIH Consensus Statement: Early identification of hearing impairment in infants and young children. *Consensus Statements, Vol. 11* (1). Bethesda, MD: NIH.

Norton, S.J., Gorga, M.P., Widen, J.E., Folsom, R.C., Sininger, Y., Cone-Wesson, B., Vohr, B.R., & Fletcher, K.A. (2000). Identification of neonatal hearing impairment: A multicenter investigation. *Ear and Hearing*, *21*, 348–356.

Norton, S.J., Gorga, M.P., Widen, J.E., Vohr, B.R., Folsom, R.C., Sininger, Y.S., Cone-Wesson B., Mascher, K, & Fletcher, K. (2000). Identification of neonatal hearing impairment: evaluation of transient evoked otoacoustic emission, distortion product otoacoustic emission and auditory brain stem response test performance. *Ear and Hearing*, *21*, 508–528.

Novak, G.P., Kurtzberg, D., Kreuzer, J.A., & Vaughan, H.G. (1989) Cortical responses to speech sounds and their formants in normal infants: maturational sequence and spatiotemporal analysis. *Electroencephalography and Clinical Neurophysiology*, *73*, 295–305.

Perez-Abalo, M.C., Savio, G., Torres, A., Martín, V., Rodríguez, E., & Galán, L. (2001). Steady-state responses to multiple amplitude-modulated tones: An optimized method to test frequency-specific thresholds in hearing-impaired children and normal-hearing subjects. *Ear and Hearing*, *21*, 200–211.

Ponton, C.W., Eggermont, J.J., Kwong, B., & Don, M. (2000). Maturation of human central auditory system activity: evidence from multi-channel evoked potentials. *Clinical Neurophysiology*, *111*, 220–36.

Prieve, B.A., Dalzell, L., Berg, A, Bradley, M., Cacace, A., Campbell, D., De Cristofaro, J., Gravel, J, Greenberg, E., Gross, S. Orlando, M., Pinheiro, J., Regan, J., Spivak, L., & Stevens, F. (2000). The New York State universal newborn hearing screening demonstration project: Outpatient outcome measures. *Ear and Hearing*, *21*, 104–117.

Primus, M.A., & Thomspson, G. (1987). Response and reinforcement in operant audiometry. *Journal of Speech and Hearing Disorders*, *52*, 294–299.

Rance, G., Beer, D.E., Cone-Wesson, B., Shepherd, R.K., Dowell, R.C., King, A.M., Rickards F.W., & Clark, G.M. (1999). Clinical findings for a group of infants and young children with auditory neuropathy. *Ear and Hearing*, *20*, 238–252.

Rance, G., Dowell, R.C., Rickards, F.W., Beer, D.E., & Clark, G.M. (1998). Steady-state evoked potential and behavioral hearing thresholds in a group of children with absent click-auditory brain stem response. *Ear and Hearing 19*, 48–61.

Rance, G., Rickards, F.W., Cohen, L.T., DeVidi, S., & Clark, G.M. (1995). The automated prediction of hearing thresholds in sleeping subjects using auditory steady-state evoked potentials. *Ear and Hearing*, *16*, 499–507.

Rickards, F.W., Tan, L.E., Cohen, L.T., Wilson, O.J., Drew, J.H., & Clark, G.M. (1994). Auditory steady-state evoked potential in newborns. *British Journal of Audiology*, *28*, 327–337.

Robbins, A.M., Svirsky, M., Osberger, M.J., & Pisoni, D.B. (1998). Beyond the audiogram: The role of functional assessments. In F. Bess (Ed.), *Children with Hearing Impairment: Contemporary Trends* (pp. 105–126). Nasville, TN: Vanderbilt Bill Wilkerson Center Press.

Rubel, E.W., Popper, A.N., & Fay, R.R. (1998). *Development of the Auditory System*. New York: Springer-Verlag.

Schoonhoven, R., Lamore, P.J., de Laat, J.A., & Grote, J.J. (1999). The prognostic value of electrocochleography in severely hearing-impaired infants. *Audiology, 38*, 141–54.

Shafer, V.L., Schwartz, R.G., Mor, M.L., Kessler, K.L., Kurtzberg, D., & Ruben, R.J. (2001). Neurophysiological indices of language impairment in children. *Acta Oto-Laryngologica, 121*, 297–300.

Sininger, Y.S., Abdala, C., & Cone-Wesson, B. (1997). Auditory threshold sensitivity of the human neonate as measured by the auditory brainstem response. *Hearing Research, 104*, 27–38.

Sininger, Y.S., Cone-Wesson, B., Folsom, R.C., Gorga, M.P., Vohr, B.R., Widen, J.E., Ekelid, M., & Norton, S.J. (2000). Identification of neonatal hearing impairment: Auditory brain stem responses in the perinatal period. *Ear and Hearing, 21*, 383–399.

Sininger, Y.S., Doyle, K.J., & Moore, J.K. (1999). The case for early identification of hearing loss in children. Auditory system development, experimental auditory deprivation, and development of speech perception and hearing. *Pediatric Clinics of North America 46* (1), 1–14.

Sininger, Y., and Oba, S. (2001). Patients with auditory neuropathy: Who are they and what can they hear? In Y. Sininger & A. Starr (Eds.), *Auditory neuropathy: A new perspective on hearing disorders* (pp. 15–35) San Diego, CA: Singular.

Stapells, D.R. (2000). Threshold estimation by the tone-evoked auditory brainstem response: a literature meta-analysis. *Journal of Speech-Language Pathology and Audiology, 224*, 74–83.

Stapells, D.R., Gravel, J.S., & Martin, B.A. (1995). Thresholds for auditory brainstem responses to tones in notched noise from infants and young children with normal hearing or sensorineural hearing loss. *Ear and Hearing, 16*, 361–371.

Starr, A., Amlie, R.N., Martin, W.H., & Sanders, S. (1977) Development of auditory function in newborn infants revealed by auditory brainstem potentials. *Pediatrics, 60*, 831–839.

Starr, A., Picton, T.W., & Kim, R. (2001). Pathophysiology of auditory neuropathy. In Y. Sininger & A. Starr, (Eds.), *Auditory neuropathy: A new perspective on hearing disorders* (pp. 67–82). San Diego, CA: Singular.

Stevens, J.C., Webb, H.D., Hutchinson, J., Connell, J., Smith, J.F., & Buffin, J.T. (1990). Click evoked otoacoustic emissions in neonatal screening. *Ear and Hearing, 11*, 128–133.

Turner, R., & Cone-Wesson, B. (1992). Prevalence rates and cost-effectiveness of risk factors. In Fr. Bess (Ed.), *Proceedings of the International Symposium on Screening Children for Auditory Function* (pp. 79–104) Nashville, TN: Bill Wilkerson Center Press.

U.S. Preventive Services Task Force (2001). Recommendations and rationale: Newborn hearing screening (D. Atkins, Ed.). Rockville, MD: Author.

Werker, J.F., & Tees, R.C. (1999) Influences on infant speech processing: toward a new synthesis. *Annual Review of Psychology 50*, 509–535.

Werner, L.A. (1995). Observer-based approaches to human infant psychoacoustics. In G.M. Klump, R.J. Dooling, R.R. Fay, & W.C. Stebbins (Eds.), *Methods in comparative psychoacoustics* (pp. 135–146). Boston: Birkhauser.

Werner, L.A., & Gray, L. (1998). Behavioral studies of hearing development. In E.W. Rubel, A.N. Popper, & R.R. Fay (Eds.), *Development of the auditory system* (pp. 12–79). New York: Springer Verlag.

Werner, L.A., & Marean, G.C. (1991). Methods for estimating infant thresholds. *Journal of the Acoustical Society of America, 90*, 1867–1875.

Werner, L.A., & Marean, G.C. (1996). *Human auditory development*. Boulder, CO: Westview Press.

Widen, J. (1993) Adding objectivity to infant behavioral audiometry. *Ear and Hearing 14*, 49–57.

Widen, J.E., Folsom, R.C., Cone-Wesson, B., Carty, L., Dunnell, J.J., Koebsell, K., Levi, A., Mancl, L., Ohlrich, B., Trouba, S., Gorga, M.P., Sininger Y.S., Vohr, B.R., & Norton, S.J. (2000) Identification of neonatal hearing impairment: hearing status at 8 to 12 months corrected age using a visual reinforcement audiometry protocol. *Ear and Hearing, 21*, 471–487.

Wunderlich, J.L., & Cone-Wesson, B. (2001). Effects of stimulus frequency and complexity on the mismatch negativity and other components of the cortical auditory-evoked potential. *Journal of the Acoustical Society of America, 109*, 1526–1536.

Yoshinago-Itano, C., Coulter, D., & Thomson, V. (2000). The Colorado Hearing Screening Program: Effects on speech and language for children with hearing loss. *Journal of Perinatology (Supplement), 20*(8), S132–142.

Yoshinaga-Itano, C., Sedey, A.L., Coulter, D.K., & Mehl, A.L. (1998). Language of early- and later-identified children with hearing loss. *Pediatrics, 102*, 1161–1171.

Young, A., & Andrews, E. (2001). Parents experience of universal newborn hearing screening: A critical review of the literature and its implications for the implementation of new UNHS programs. *Journal of Deaf Studies and Deaf Education, 6*, 149–160.

Patricia Elizabeth Spencer & Marc Marschark

Cochlear Implants
Issues and Implications

For both adults and children who have significant hearing losses, hearing aids have long provided some support for hearing language and environmental sounds. However, because they essentially are just amplifiers (but see Harkins & Bakke, this volume), their benefits generally are inversely related to the degree of hearing loss. More recently, cochlear implants have been developed to assist individuals with greater hearing losses. Cochlear implants convert sound into electrical signals that are delivered directly to peripheral portions of the auditory nerve (Harkins & Bakke, this volume; Lucker, 2002), giving many profoundly deaf persons access to information typically carried by sound. Restored hearing increases the availability of spoken language and other sounds, and thus it is expected that implants will lower many of the barriers confronting persons with greater hearing losses.

An Abbreviated History

More than 200 years ago, Alessandro Volta connected a battery to two metal rods inserted in his ears. He described the result as a "jolt" or a "boom in the head," accompanied by a "boiling-type" noise (Volta, 1800, cited in Simmons, 1966). Given this rather unpleasant description, it is not surprising that Volta's experiment was not often repeated. It established, however, that a perception of sound can result from electrical stimulation to peripheral parts of the auditory system.

Basic research on effects of electrical stimulation of the auditory system continued intermittently after Volta's experiment. It was not until 1957, however, that Djourno and Eyries reported that direct stimulation from an electrode placed near the auditory nerve allowed a patient to discriminate some sounds and words—evidence that "activation of the auditory periphery through an electrified device was practical and capable of providing . . . useful (auditory) information" (Niparko & Wilson, 2000, p. 105). In the 1970s, the 3M/House cochlear implant system, which used a single active electrode plus a "ground" electrode outside the cochlea, was developed by William House and his colleagues, and the U.S. Food and Drug Administration (FDA) officially approved its use with adults in 1984 (Estabrooks, 1998). The device gave users limited information about loudness and timing of speech and other sounds occurring in the environment. However, the benefits were eventually deemed to be insufficiently helpful, and its manufacture and use ended later in the 1980s.

During the late 1970s, scientists around the world actively experimented with more complex cochlear implant systems (Niparko & Wilson, 2000). Multichannel devices that provided stimulation at multiple locations in the cochlea, where the auditory nerve endings are located, were in wide use by the late 1980s. In addition, advances in speech processors (i.e., small computers that organize information for presentation to the cochlea) allowed more efficient reception and transmission (e.g., Estabrooks, 1998, Harkins & Bakke, this volume). These advances allowed more specificity in the information received by the auditory nerve, thus increasing users' ability to distinguish among sounds.

Clinical trials of multichannel cochlear implants with children began in 1980, and by the mid-1980s they were provided to children as well as to adults. In 1990, the FDA formally approved their use with children as young as 2 years of age. Clinical experience and results of research on the effects of cochlear implants were positive enough that the FDA lowered the minimum age for implantation to 18 months in 1998 and to 12 months in 2002. Children younger than 12 months currently are receiving them at the discretion of surgeons. By 2002, more than 70,000 adults and children around the world were using cochlear implants. Refinement of implant hardware, software, and surgical techniques continue at a rapid pace. Some pioneers in the development of cochlear implants expected that the devices would serve only to provide late-deafened people with enough information about sound to supplement and assist speechreading (Christiansen & Spencer, 2002), but expectations quickly increased. In a survey by Kluwin and Stewart (2000), for example, parents reported the primary reason for getting cochlear implants for their children was to allow them to develop understanding and production of spoken language.

As the emphasis shifted from using cochlear implants as assistive listening devices for late-deafened people to the support of spoken language development of young deaf children, controversy erupted. Provision of cochlear implants to children has been attacked on the grounds that they are insufficiently effective and also that they interfere with children developing their identity as a Deaf

person, becoming part of a Deaf community, and acquiring the sign communication skills needed to participate in that community (e.g., Lane & Bahan, 1998). Deaf people in some countries objected to public monies being spent to provide individual children with cochlear implant technology while deaf individuals' access to other technologies (such as telephone relay systems) continued to be limited (Christiansen & Spencer, 2002). On the other side, those who raise such arguments have been accused of being short-sighted and focusing on perceived group needs at the expense of the needs of individuals (e.g., Balkany, Hodges, & Goodman, 1998). Although efforts have been made to decrease the emotion and increase the objectivity of this debate (e.g., Christiansen, 1998; Niparko, 2000), and the National Association of the Deaf in the United States now supports cochlear implants as one alternative in a range of options for deaf children (National Association of the Deaf, 2001), the debate has continued into the twenty-first century.

Efficacy Studies

Extensive clinical and research efforts indicate that, although most users find them useful, cochlear implants do not change deaf people into hearing people. Information provided by implants is less specific and differentiated than that provided by a fully functional cochlea, and their output is described as "coarse" or "degraded" compared to the sounds received by hearing persons (Cleary, Pisoni, & Geers, 2001; Pisoni, 2000). Late-deafened adults and children who become deaf after having developed a spoken language must learn to associate the qualities of this new input with their stored representations of speech and distinctions among the phonological elements of that language. In this process, they are able to use some of the redundancy offered by the grammar, morphology, phonology, and semantic units of the spoken language they have already acquired. In addition, through their early experience with spoken language, late-deafened individuals will have developed memory and other cognitive processes that match the sequential processing demands of spoken language (see Marschark, this volume; Wilbur, this volume).

Children who are born deaf or become deaf before spoken language is well established have a quite different task in learning to use cochlear implant input. They must develop auditory-based language from exposure to input with fewer distinctions than input received by hearing children. Further, most deaf children have significant delays in spoken language development before obtaining the implant, and they generally lack preexisting schemas for the structure of the spoken language they will receive from this coarse input.[1] Therefore, top-down processing—or the use of linguistic context to aid in identification and discrimination of the sounds of language—will be limited. In contrast, children up to about age 8 years may have an advantage over adults in adjusting to input from a cochlear implant because younger auditory systems tend to have more plasticity or adaptability (e.g., Robinson, 1998). Given these conflicting influences, what kind of progress in spoken language has been documented for children who use cochlear implants?

Development of Speech Perception, Production, and Language

"Speech perception" includes awareness and discrimination of different sounds (phones) and recognition of different classes of sound units (phonemes) in isolation, as well as in the context of words and connected speech (see Bernstein & Auer, this volume). Speech perception is frequently tested using closed-set tasks, in which a response has to be selected from a number of options provided, or open-set tasks, which involve more open-ended responses, such as imitating a phoneme, word, or sentence, or responding to a spoken question or statement.

Tests of "speech production" include assessment of intelligibility and the accuracy of production of phonemes, words, or connected speech. "Language assessments," in contrast, typically focus on recognition and production of vocabulary and syntactic (grammatical) structures. Studies generally have confirmed that abilities in speech perception, speech production, and language are usually interrelated, as advances in one area typically are associated with advances in the other two (Connor, Hieber, Arts, & Zwolan, 2000; O'Donoghue, Nikolopoulos, Archbold, & Tait, 1999; L. Spencer, Tye-Murray, & Tomblin, 1998).

A number of studies have shown advantages in speech perception, production, and spoken language repertories for children using cochlear implants compared to children with similar hearing losses using traditional or tactile hearing aids (e.g., Geers & Moog, 1994; Meyer, Svirsky, Kirk, & Miyamoto, 1998; Osberger, Fisher, Zimmerman-Phillips, Geier, & Barker, 1998; Svirsky, Robbins, Kirk, Pisoni, & Miyamoto, 2000).[2] Nonetheless, benefits from cochlear implants are limited, and most children with implants have speech and language skills similar to those of severely hard-of-hearing children. Children with hearing losses greater than 100 decibels dB, for example, who are unlikely to benefit from hearing aids, have been found after cochlear implantation to develop speech perception skills similar to those expected for children with losses in the 88–100 dB range who use hearing aids (Boothroyd & Eran, 1994; Svirsky & Meyer, 1999; Vermeulen et al., 1997). Vermeulen et al., however, found that children deafened by meningitis (and, therefore, usually with considerable auditory experience before becoming deaf) showed more improvement, performing more like aided children with 70–80 dB hearing losses.

Blamey et al. (2001) found that speech perception, production, and language skills of 47 children, 4 years after implant, were similar to those of children with hearing losses of about 78 dB who used hearing aids. Blamey et al. speculated that their more positive findings reflected their participants' relatively extended experience with cochlear implants compared with most children in earlier studies. Children in this more recent study also could have benefited from recent technological advances in implant speech-processing strategies (i.e., software algorithms). These and other factors lead to significant interindividual differences in benefits from cochlear implants and suggest caution in the interpretation of results from any single study.

Individual Differences in Speech and Language-Related Outcomes

Reports of children's development using cochlear implants almost universally emphasize great variability in speech and language outcomes (e.g., Dowell, Blamey, & Clark, 1997; Osberger, Robbins, Todd, & Riley, 1994; Svirsky, Robbins, et al., 2000). "Average" functioning levels can disguise the important fact that a few children get little if any benefit, while some learn to function within a range typical for their hearing peers. Many researchers have addressed potential reasons for this variability in hopes of determining who is most likely to benefit from cochlear implantation and how to design interventions to maximize use of information from the devices.

Anatomical, Physiological, and Technological Influences

Anatomical and physiological factors likely contribute significantly to the variance observed in success with cochlear implants. For example, in some individuals, a proportion of nerve endings in the cochlea are compromised (Loizou, 1998) and will not transmit signals from implant electrodes. Disruptions in signal transmission also can occur more centrally, in parts of the auditory nervous system beyond the cochlea.

Proximity of electrode placement to nerve endings will also affect abilities to discriminate among stimuli. With greater distance from auditory nerve endings, the electrical signals provided by an electrode tend to spread, thus limiting discriminability. Speech perception also has been found to be better when the electrode array can be inserted more deeply into the cochlea (Vermeulen et al., 1997). In addition, children seem to need access to more functional channels than adults in order to reach a given level of speech perception or word recognition (Dorman, Loizou, Kemp, & Kirk, 2000).

Other factors, such as advances in implant system processing strategies also influence the ability to make sense of signals provided by an implant. Processing strategies currently available vary in the degree to which stimulation is presented simultaneously and/or sequentially to the electrode array (see Harkins and Bakke, this volume), and different individuals appear to function better with some than other strategies (Arndt, Staller, Arcaroli, Hines, & Ebinger, 1999; Osberger & Fisher, 1999).

Duration of Profound Deafness Before Implantation

For both adults and children, longer periods of profound hearing loss generally are associated with less benefit from implants (Blamey, 1995; Dowell et al., 1997). Short of profound hearing loss, however, even partial hearing apparently maintains auditory

processing pathways sufficiently to allow more effective use of a cochlear implant later (Miyamoto et al., 1994). Use of traditional hearing aids thus is encouraged for individuals while they await cochlear implantation.

Duration of Cochlear Implant Use

Children, as well as adults, require time and rehabilitation to gain maximum benefit from implants (Meyer et al., 1998). Mondain et al. (1997), for example, found that young children were able to discriminate between some phonemes in a closed-set listening task as early as 3 months after implant activation. Both closed-and open-set perception abilities continued to develop with time, however, and it was 3 years before average word identification scores reached 86% (see also Meyer et al., 1998; O'Donoghue, Nikolopoulos, & Archbold, 2000).

Age of Implantation

In children with congenital or very early profound hearing loss, age of implantation frequently has been negatively related to long-term speech and language outcomes, as children implanted at younger ages eventually achieve higher level skills than those implanted later (Cheng, Grant, & Niparko, 1999). A number of researchers have compared the postimplant progress of children who obtained cochlear implants before and after specific ages. Advantages have been found for speech perception by children implanted before rather than after age 6 (Papsin, Gysin, Picton, Nedgelski, & Harrison, 2000), age 5 (Barco, Franz, & Jackson, 2002), and age 3 (Miyamoto, Kirk, Svirsky, & Sehgal, 1999). Kileny, Zwolen, and Ashbaugh (2001) found that children who received implants between 2 and 4 years of age performed better on open-set speech perception tasks than children implanted between 5 and 6 years of age or children implanted between 7 and 15 years. However, the two younger groups' closed-set perception did not differ significantly. Papsin et al. reported that the children implanted before age 6 continued to close the gap between chronological age and expected perception skills as long as 4 years after implant, with no evidence of a plateau in abilities.

Barker et al. (2000) found better speech production by 10 children implanted before 2 years compared to 7 children implanted between 4 and 7 years of age. Although the groups were similar in their ability to produce sounds in isolation, the younger group was better able to integrate sounds into words and connected speech.

Age of implantation also correlated negatively with language (primarily syntax skills) in a small group of children implanted between 13 and 38 months of age and without pre-implant hearing experience (P. Spencer, 2002). Based on a larger group of children, Nikolopoulos, O'Donoghue, and Archbold (1999) also reported age effects for language skills as well as speech perception and production. They pointed out, however, that it takes time with the implant before the advantage for early implantation can be adequately measured. Older children may show faster initial gains because cognitive and other communication prerequisites are in place, ready to make use of the stimulation provided by an implant. Their actual functioning levels nevertheless typically remain below those of hearing age-peers, presumably because of the delay that had accrued before implantation. Very young children may show slower initial improvement after implantation, but improvement continues over time, and they eventually acquire skills higher than older children (Harrison, Panesar, El-Hakim, Mount, & Papsin, 2001). Despite the strength of findings related to age of implantation, no specific age has been identified as marking a critical boundary beyond which progress is not possible. Future studies may provide a better understanding of the relation between success with cochlear implants and plasticity (flexibility at the point of origin) and malleability (susceptibility to change after maturation) in the auditory system. Meanwhile, existing data suggest a gradual lessening with age of potential gains from implantation in perception, production, and language (Dowell et al., 1997; but see Osberger et al., 1998).

Communication Modalities

The impact of the type of language programming on cochlear implant outcomes has attracted much research effort and debate. The issue essentially resolves to whether children with implants will benefit differentially from being in an environment that offers spoken language only, which provides stimulation necessary for the acquisition of hearing and speech information/strategies, or an environment that includes sign language (usually with accompanying speech), which provides redundant linguistic cues and optimizes comprehension. Some investigators comparing children in oral (or auditory-verbal) versus signing (or total communication) programs have failed to indicate whether children in the two groups had equivalent hearing and spoken language skills before implantation; others have indicated initial equivalence or have statistically controlled for initial differences (e.g., Osberger et al., 1998). However, the overwhelming majority of reports indicate that, although children in both kinds of programming make gains after cochlear implantation, those in oral or auditory-verbal programming make faster progress. This pattern has been shown for speech intelligibility (Geers et al., 2000; Svirsky, Sloan, Caldwell, & Miyamoto, 2000; Miyamoto et al., 1999; Osberger et al., 1994; Tobey et al., 2000), speech perception (Dawson, McKay, Busby, Grayden, & Clark, 2000; Dowell et al., 1997; Geers et al., 2000; Miyamoto et al., 1999; Osberger et al., 1998), and for receptive and expressive language (Geers et al., 2000; Levi, Boyett-Solano, Nicholson, & Eisenberg, 2001).

In contrast with those findings, Svirsky, Robbins et al. (2000) found no difference in overall language levels between a group of children enrolled in a total communication program and a group in oral programming. However, the children in the oral program had better skills when only spoken language was considered. Connor et al. (2000) found that speech production did not differ between children in total communication and oral programs if the children began using implants by 5 years of age. Moreover, expressive vocabulary (in the child's preferred mode) and receptive vocabulary (presented orally only) scores were better for children in total communication than oral programs if implants were obtained before age 5. Children in this study, regardless of program type, received consistent and extensive speech and spoken language training. Preisler, Ahlstrom, and Tvingstedt (1997), in contrast, reported little spoken language progress for implanted children attending a program that emphasized sign language and provided relatively little speech-focused intervention. Although Tobey et al. (2000) reported better intelligibility 3 years after implant for children in auditory-verbal than total communication programming, the former group of children had experienced almost twice the hours of therapy as the latter.

Finally, Vieu et al. (1998) studied children in oral, sign language, and cued speech programs, finding that, after 3 years of implant use, those in cued speech had the best speech intelligibility and were most likely to produce grammatical elements in their language. This finding is of particular interest because the manual signals used in cued speech, unlike those in signs, have a specific, consistent relationship with speech sounds produced simultaneously (see Leybaert & Alegria, this volume). General syntactic skills related to sentence structures were better in children in oral or cued speech programs than in sign programs. However, all three groups made progress with time.

The above studies indicate that children generally increase their speech and language skills after cochlear implantation regardless of type of language programming (oral or auditory-verbal, sign, cued speech), if sufficient spoken language exposure and/or intervention is provided. Faster progress is usually made by children in oral than in sign language programs, but more information is needed about cued speech programs and interactions between program type and a variety of intervening factors. Despite advantages from cochlear implants, perception, speech, and language skills tend to trail hearing children's norms. No type of programming or language modality has yet resolved deaf children's continuing language delays after cochlear implantation.

Concerns have been raised that using signs in combination with spoken (or heard) language may overwhelm a child's processing capability. It is also feared that children with imperfect hearing will focus almost solely on signed language if it is available because it is so easily perceived. Marschark (1997), for example, noted that deaf preschoolers preferred signed over spoken communication when both were available. This appears to result because signed communication is more likely to be successful for preschoolers, regardless of the extent of exposure to spoken language. In contrast, a study by Tomblin, L Spencer, Flock, Tyler, and Gantz (1999) involving 29 children with cochlear implants in a program using total communication, suggested that this may not be an issue for children with implants. Children in their study scored much higher than the norming group of deaf children on the Rhode Island Test of Language Structure, a test

of receptive English grammar. Children with cochlear implants also performed better than a matched group of deaf children (without implants) on production of grammar (i.e., noun and verb phrases, question forms, negation, sentence structure) in a story retelling task. Perhaps most important, children with cochlear implants used spoken language without accompanying signs for more words than did deaf children using hearing aids. That is, these children increased their spoken language skills despite having the option of relying on signing.

L. Spencer et al. (1998) also reported that children with cochlear implants produced bound grammatical English morphemes (meaning units indicating tense, number, etc.) more often than children using hearing aids. Individual morphemes tended to emerge in the same order as in hearing children. In addition, the children with implants tended to express these morphemes vocally, even when they produced signs for the content words to which the morphemes were attached. Children were able to combine modalities in language production, using the vocal modality to express elements that seem to be structured in ways that specifically match processing characteristics of auditory-based language (see Schick, this volume).

Other Predictive Factors and Early Indicators of Progress

Only about 40–60% of the variance in outcomes for children with implants has been accounted for by the factors of duration of use, age at implantation, modality of language programming, and processing strategy used in the cochlear implant system (Dowell et al., 1997; Miyamoto et al., 1994; Snik, Vermeulen, Geelen, Brokx, & van den Broek, 1997). Osberger (1994) noted that degree of hearing loss before implantation was also a negative predictor of spoken language outcomes, and Osberger and Fisher (2000) concluded that greater preoperative speech perception abilities were a positive predictor. This is consistent with reports that both adults and children with some residual hearing before implantation perform very well post-implant (Eisenberg, Martinez, Sennaroghi, & Osberger, 2000; Rubenstein, Parkinson, Tyler, & Gantz, 1999 and again argues for amplification before cochlear implantation.

Cognitive skills also have been suggested as predictors of spoken language skills after implantation. For example, Pyman, Blamey, Lacy, Clar, & Dowell (2000) found that children with motor and/or cognitive delays developed speech perception skills more slowly after implantation than children without such disabilities (see Knoors & Vervloed, this volume). P. Spencer (2002) found that children with average or higher levels of nonverbal cognitive skills had better post-implant language outcomes than children with either lower overall intelligence quotients or relative deficiencies in sequencing abilities.

Other researchers have failed to find significant associations between cognitive skills and language development after cochlear implantation (e.g., Knutson, Ehlers, Wald, & Tyler, 2000). However, Pisoni (2000; Pisoni, Cleary, Geers, & Tobey, 1999) proposed that differences in the use of specific information processing skills, including memory and patterns of lexical access, contribute to post-implant progress. Pisoni and his colleagues (1999) reported that implant users who achieve higher levels of spoken language make greater use of phonologically based working memory and have a faster "global information processing rate" (p. 139) than those who do less well. However, because assessment of these abilities has not included pre-implant baseline measures, no strict causal relationship has yet been demonstrated.

Positive family involvement and support for a child's development has also been associated with post-implant outcome (Bevilacqua, Costa, Moret, & Freitas, 2001), as has a measure of parent vocabulary (Stallings, Kirk, & Chin, 2001). P. Spencer (2001) found that parents' styles of acquiring information about cochlear implantation were associated with their children's performance with implants. Parents who actively searched for information on cochlear implantation and carefully considered myriad factors tended to be most satisfied with their decision. Their children's language outcomes were also better than those in families that took a less analytical approach. This association is consistent with earlier reports that parental self-efficacy contributes to effectiveness of early interventions in general (Calderon & Greenberg, 1997, this volume). In addition, parents' reports of decision-making processes may reflect their level of support of their children's development, both before and after implantation.

Children's pre-implant behaviors and characteristics of parent–child interactions also have been reported to associate with post-implant speech and language progress. Knutson et al. (2000) found that behavioral difficulties before cochlear implantation continued afterward and predicted poorer results. Tait, Lutman, and Robinson (2000) reported that frequency of children's prelinguistic communicative contributions during pre-implant interactions, regardless of modality, related to their post-implant speech perception and production outcomes. These findings suggest that factors such as child temperament, participation in reciprocal early interactions, and perhaps parenting skills influence the development of children with implants in much the way that has been documented for other deaf children (Marschark, 1993).

Early post-implant indicators of later development also have been identified. Tait et al. (2000) reported that children who eventually made the most progress increased their production of spoken prelinguistic communication within a year of getting the implant. Bass-Ringdahl (2001) similarly reported a sharp increase in the frequency of vocalizations and canonical or variegated babbling, a precursor of spoken language in hearing children (Oller & Eilers, 1988), within 3–8 months after implantation for children implanted before 20 months of age. These early indicators are worthy of further investigation and may provide useful information for decisions for individual programming and intervention decisions.

Beyond Spoken Language: Other Outcomes

Education

Many parents and educators hope that cochlear implants will ameliorate the academic difficulties typically faced by deaf children (P. Spencer, 2000b; see Karchmer & Mitchell, this volume). While it is specifically hoped that increases in spoken language abilities will lead to increased literacy, research in this area remains scarce. L. Spencer et al. (1997) reported improved scores for reading comprehension for children with cochlear implants compared with other deaf children. In contrast with earlier reports (e.g., Yoshinaga-Itano & Downey, 1996) for a larger group of deaf children, L. Spencer et al. reported that the gap between expected and achieved reading skills did not widen with age for children with cochlear implants. Wauters, van Bon, and Tellings (2002) reported a study involving 566 deaf students (hearing losses ≥ 80 dB), 47 of whom had cochlear implants). They found no difference in either reading comprehension or in word versus nonword judgments as a function of whether children had implants, although comprehension scores (on a Dutch test similar to the Stanford Achievement Test) were uniformly low.

Other studies have indirectly addressed academic outcomes after cochlear implantation by reporting trends for movement from deaf-only to more integrated or mainstreamed school placements, with the assumption that such moves indicate language and academic skills sufficient for functioning in the more inclusive setting. Francis, Koch, Wyatt, and Niparko (1999) found that, after at least 2 years of experience using a cochlear implant, 35 children who received significant amounts of aural habilitation were more than twice as likely to be in a mainstreamed placement than children without an implant. Hours of special education services were reported to correlate −.10 with length of time using an implant.[3] The authors provided a cost–benefit analysis supporting that significant public monies were saved by the children's trend toward less intensive educational services.

A study of 121 deaf children in the United Kingdom found that those who received cochlear implants at an early age were more likely to move from segregated to mainstreamed educational placements than those who received implants later. Approximately half of the younger children were placed in mainstream environments after 2 years of implant use (Archbold, Nikolopoulos, O'Donoghue, & Lutman, 1998). A nonsignificant trend toward mainstream placements after cochlear implantation also was found in a Canadian study (Dayas, Ashley, Gysin, & Papsin, 2000). Thirty percent of school-aged children and 43% of preschool children with implants were mainstreamed; higher speech perception abilities were related to the likelihood of being mainstreamed. Parents' ratings of satisfaction with their children's educational placement were higher after implantation, and parents indicated that their children were better able to "cope with the demands of their class" (Daya et al., p. 226).

Easterbrooks and Mordica (2000) surveyed teachers of 51 children with implants to obtain their impressions of the children's implant use. Children who lived in urban or suburban areas, used spoken language at home, and were not in separate schools using signs were said to use their implants more successfully for classroom communication. Children with a known etiology of hearing loss were rated less likely to use their implants for communication than those with unknown etiologies. Easterbrooks and Mordica emphasized that teachers' attitudes, as well as their knowledge and skills about working with children with cochlear implants, have important influences on children's progress.

Attention

Visual attention is especially important to children and adults with hearing losses (P. Spencer, 2000a). Although some research has indicated that deaf adults may have enhanced visual attention skills (e.g., Neville & Lawson, 1987; see Marschark, this volume), Quittner, Smith, Osberger, Mitchell, and Katz (1994) found that deaf children performed less well than hearing children on tests of selective visual attention. Because a group of older deaf children's visual attention performance improved after they began to use cochlear implants, Quittner et al. suggested that audition influences visual attention development. However, Tharpe, Ashmead, and Rothpletz (2002), using the same task, found no difference between deaf children with and without cochlear implants. Although a group of hearing children scored significantly higher than the cochlear implant group, all three of the groups were said to perform well. Performance on the visual attention task was related to nonverbal intelligence as well as age, however, and the researchers suggested that these variables should be controlled in future studies.

Psychological Outcomes

According to Niparko, Cheng, and Francis (2000), postlingually deafened adults reported "marked improvement" in their quality of life after cochlear implantation, indicating that cochlear implants allowed them to reestablish patterns of interaction similar to those before their hearing losses. However, there have been concerns that cochlear implantation will have negative effects on children by interfering with development of self-image as deaf persons and damaging self-esteem due to lack of a peer group. This could be exacerbated if children move from schools or classrooms with other deaf children to become one of a minority of students with hearing loss in mainstreamed educational settings (Antia & Kriemeyer, this volume).

Tooher, Hogan, Reed, and Code (2001) asked Australian adolescents with cochlear implants to evaluate their quality of life. The resulting scores were so positive that the authors suspected over-reporting or lack of insight. Nonetheless, similar positive results were obtained in another study in which adolescents and their parents were asked to rate the benefits and problems associated with cochlear implantation (Chmiel, Sutton, & Jenkins, 2000). Both parents and implant recipients reported positive value in the adolescents' increased awareness of environmental sounds. The adolescents further rated having access to "a larger variety of activities" (Chmiel et al., p. 104) as an advantage. In response to the question, "What do you like best about your cochlear implant?" adolescents most often reported that they enjoyed being able to hear. However, they also indicated that some sounds were "bothersome." There were no indications of unusual psychological or social difficulties related to using cochlear implants.

In an extensive U.S. study, Christiansen and Leigh (2002) interviewed parents of children with cochlear implants about child and family experiences. The majority of parents said their children were happier, more independent, and had more self-confidence after beginning to use a cochlear implant. Some said that their children slowly acquired more hearing friends and became more comfortable socially. Christiansen and Leigh noted that parents who perceived their children as unsuccessful with their implant may have been unlikely to volunteer to participate in the interview study. Nevertheless, in an associated written survey, 60% of parents reported that their children had never refused to use their implant. Eighty-four percent of parents reported no lapse as long as a month in their children's implant use. This indicates some but not a large amount of intermittent resistance to the cochlear implants. Overall, given children's willingness to use the implants, it appears that they reacted favorably to their use.

About 90% of the parents in the Christiansen and Leigh (2002) study reported that their children socialized often with hearing children after acquiring cochlear implants. Kluwin and Stewart (2000) similarly reported that some children increased their number of friendships after implantation, but children who either had a large friendship group or a single friend before implantation did not change afterward. Thus, sociability and friendship patterns did not change drastically in either a positive or negative direction. Bat-Chava and Deignan (2001) reported that parents of children with cochlear implants and enrolled in spoken language programs generally indicated that their children became more outgoing after implantation and interacted more frequently with hearing children. Some ongoing difficulties were nonetheless noted and were attributed both to the children's continuing language delays and to attitudes of hearing peers. Perhaps as a consequence, Bat-Chava and Deignan found that about a fourth of the parents supported children's continuing relationships with deaf peers.

Given the apparent psychological importance of peer-group identification (Bat-Chava, 1994), Wald and Knutson (2000) administered the Deaf Identity Development Scale to deaf adolescents with and without cochlear implants. Adolescents with implants were more likely than those without to rate "hearing" identity items positively, although both groups tended to give highest ratings to "bicultural" identity. High ratings for hearing identity did not associate with teachers' ratings of student behavior problems nor with social status indicated by peers. In general, little difference was found between the two groups of deaf students.

In an observational study, Boyd, Knutson, and Dalstrom (2000) found that children with cochlear implants were unlikely to successfully enter into interactions with hearing children. Results did not vary with the length of time using the implant (either more or less than 24 months), although older children tended to be more successful than younger ones. These results are consistent with reports about deaf children without cochlear implants (Lederberg, 1991; Marschark, 1993).

Overall, available reports give no evidence of any strong negative effects on social or emotional status of deaf children using a cochlear implant. At the same time, they indicate that use of a cochlear implant does not resolve social interaction difficulties documented for other deaf children in a context with hearing peers (see Antia & Kriemeyer, this volume). Effects may relate not only to the degree of auditory access obtained through the implant but also to individual personality variables and social contexts.

Effects of a cochlear implant are not limited to the person with the implant but affect the entire family. Beadle, Shores, and Wood (2000) found that parents' ratings of overall quality of life related to the degree to which they perceived the outcome of their child's implant to be positive. Parents reported no increased stress related to either the child's hearing loss or the implant, but high levels of social support from education and cochlear implant teams were said to be helpful.

Another study focusing on families produced less positive results. However, a direct comparison is problematic because the studies were very different. Approximately one-fourth of 57 German parents of children with cochlear implants gave evidence of elevated stress levels in their responses to a formal questionnaire (Spahn, Richter, Zschocke, Lohle, & Wirsching, 2001). In addition, a large proportion of the parents expressed interest in counseling or other assistance. This report of high levels of stress in parents of children with cochlear implants is consistent with findings from an earlier report by Quittner, Steck, and Rouiller (1991). Therefore, it does not appear that obtaining a cochlear implant eliminates parents' stress related to their child's hearing loss.

Summary and Conclusions

Cochlear implants have given many late-deafened adults renewed access to auditory information and to their habitual social and communicative networks. For many children, cochlear implants also have provided access to the world of sounds and of auditory-based language. The process of learning to use information generated by a cochlear implant is typically lengthy, however, and focused practice and therapy are necessary. Eventual speech perception, production, and spoken language skills (including vocabulary and syntax development) are interrelated and vary widely, with some children receiving almost no benefits and others acquiring skills much like those of their hearing peers. Preliminary evidence indicates some reading and academic skill benefits from children's increased access to audition, but results are mixed, and more research is needed.

Many factors have been found to contribute to interindividual variability in outcomes after cochlear implantation. Some factors, such as intactness of auditory pathways at and beyond the auditory nerve, are beyond external control. Others, including continued development of implant technology, age of implantation, reinforcement of residual auditory sensitivity before implantation, and choice of language modality, are subject to decisions and control by families and professionals involved with individual children. In general, maintaining some auditory input before implantation, using a cochlear implant during the first years of life, and participating in educational programs emphasizing spoken language are predictive of more successful cochlear implant use. Despite apparent advantages of oral or auditory-verbal programming, most children improve their speech and language skills using cochlear implants regardless of the type of language program in which they are enrolled. Most children in oral or auditory-verbal programming remain delayed in language skills after implantation relative to hearing children. The identification of interactions between language mode and factors such as age, as well as emerging reports of the progress of children using cued speech, suggest a need for continued objective assessments of this issue.

Although recent reports indicate trends toward more mainstreamed school placements for deaf children using cochlear implants, information about children's actual academic achievements remains scarce. It is clear, however, that educational and other support systems should reconsider assumptions about individual development and needs, given the increased auditory access cochlear implants provide many deaf children. Emerging data about psychological and social-emotional functioning, however, give no strong evidence that using a cochlear implant either significantly resolves or exacerbates the kinds of social and psychological issues faced by hearing families of children who are deaf—or by the children themselves—as they interact with and participate in a largely hearing society.

Notes

1. Language delays typically are not found among deaf children of deaf parents who acquire a sign language as a first language (see Lederberg, this volume; Schick, this volume). As yet, however, there does not

appear to be any published information specific to such children who have received cochlear implants.

2. For reasons that are as yet unclear, tactile hearing aids are far more popular in Europe than in North America (see Harkins & Bakke, this volume).

3. The −.10 correlation (*n* = 35) was reported as statistically significant. Correspondence with the authors has confirmed that this is in error, but further information is not yet available.

References

Archbold, S., Nikolopoulos, T., O'Donoghue, G., & Lutman, M. (1998). Educational placement of deaf children following cochlear implantation. *British Journal of Audiology, 32,* 295–300.

Arndt, P., Staller, S., Arcaroli, J., Hines, A., & Ebinger, K. (1999). *Within-subject comparison of advanced coding strategies in the Nucleus 24 cochlear implant.* Lane Cove, NSW, Australia: Cochlear Corporation.

Balkany, T., Hodges, A., & Goodman, K. (1998). Ethics of cochlear implantation in young children. *Otolaryngology—Head and Neck Surgery, 114*(6), 748–755.

Barco, A., Franz, D., & Jackson, K. (2002, February). *Cochlear implant performance as a function of age at implantation.* Paper presented at the 6th European Symposium on Paediatric Cochlear Implantation, Las Palmas de Gran Canaria, Spain.

Barker, E., Daniels, T., Dowell, R., Dettman, S., Brown, P., Remine, M., Psarros, C., Dorman, D., & Cowan, R. (2000, June). *Long term speech production outcomes in children who received cochlear implants before and after two years of age.* Paper presented at the 5th European Symposium on Pediatric Cochlear Implantation, Antwerp, Belgium.

Bass-Ringdahl, S. (2001, February). Trends in the rate of vocalization development in young cochlear implant recipients. Paper presented at the 8th Symposium, Cochlear Implants in Children, Los Angeles, CA.

Bat-Chava, Y. (1994). Group identification and self-esteem in deaf adults. *Personality and Social Psychology Bulletin, 20,* 494–502.

Bat-Chava, Y., & Deignan, E. (2001). Peer relationships of children with a cochlear implant. *Journal of Deaf Studies and Deaf Education, 6,* 186–199.

Beadle, E., Shores, A., & Wood, E. (2000) Parental perception of the impact upon the family of cochlear implantation in children. *Annals of Otology, Rhinology & Largygology* (Suppl. 185), *109*(12), 111–114.

Bevilacqua, M., Costa, O., Moret, A., & Freitas, J. (2001, February). *Psychosocial outcomes of cochlear implant in pre-lingual children.* Paper presented at the 8th Symposium, Cochlear Implants in Children, Los Angeles, CA.

Blamey, P. (1995). Factors affecting auditory performance of postlinguistically deaf adults using cochlear implants: Etiology, age, and duration of deafness. In *Cochlear implants in adults and children* (pp. 15–20). Bethesda, MD: National Institutes of Health.

Blamey, P., Sarant, J., Paatsch, L., Barry, J., Bow, C., Wales, R., Wright, M., Psarros, C., Rattigan, K., & Tooher, R. (2001). Relationships among speech perception, production, language, hearing loss, and age in children with impaired hearing. *Journal of Speech, Language, and Hearing Research, 44*(2), 264–285.

Boothroyd, A., & Eran, O. (1994). Auditory speech perception capacity of child implant users expressed as equivalent hearing loss. *Volta Review, 96*(5), 151–167.

Boyd, R., Knutson, J., & Dalstrom, A. (2000). Social interaction of pediatric cochlear implant recipients with age-matched peers. *Annals of Otology, Rhinology & Larygology* (Suppl. 185), *109*(12), 105–109.

Calderon, R., & Greenberg, M. (1997). The effectiveness of early intervention for deaf children and children with hearing loss. In M. Guralnick (Ed.), *The effectiveness of early intervention* (pp. 445–483). Baltimore, MD: Paul H. Brookes.

Cheng, A.K., Grant, G.D., & Niparko, J.K. (1999). Meta-analysis of pediatric cochlear implant literature. *Annals of Otology, Rhinology, & Laryngology, 108,* 124–128.

Chmiel, R, Sutton, L., & Jenkins, H. (2000). Quality of life in children with cochlear implants. *Annals of Otology, Rhinology & Laryngology* (Suppl. 185), *109*(12), 103–105.

Christiansen, J. (1998). Cochlear implants. *Disability Studies Quarterly, 18*(2), 105–109.

Christiansen, J., & Leigh, I. (2002). *Cochlear implants in children: Ethics and choices.* Washington, DC: Gallaudet University Press.

Christiansen, J. (with Spencer, P.) (2002). History of cochlear implants. In J. Christiansen & I. Leigh (Eds.), *Cochlear implants in children: Ethics and choices* (pp. 15–44). Washington, DC: Gallaudet University Press.

Cleary, M., Pisoni, D., & Geers, A. (2001). Some measures of verbal and spatial working memory in eight- and nine-year-old hearing-impaired children with cochlear implants, *Ear & Hearing, 22*(5), 395–411.

Connor, C., Hieber, S., Arts, A., & Zwolan, T. (2000). Speech, vocabulary, and the education of children using cochlear implants: Oral or total communication? *Journal of Speech, Language, and Hearing Research, 43*(5), 1185–1204.

Dawson, P., McKay, C., Busby, P., Grayden, D., & Clark, G. (2000). Electrode discrimination and speech perception in young children using cochlear implants. *Ear & Hearing, 21*(6), 597–607.

Daya, H., Ashley, A., Gysin, C., & Papsin, B. (2000). Changes in educational placement and speech perception ability after cochlear implantation in children. *The Journal of Otolaryngology, 29*(4), 224–228.

Dowell, R., Blamey, P., & Clark, G. (1997, March). *Factors affecting outcomes in children with cochlear implants.* Paper presented at the XVI World Congress of Otorhinolaryngology Head and Neck Surgery, Sydney, Australia.

Dorman, M., Loizou, P., Kemp, L., & Kirk, K. (2000). Word recognition by children listening to speech processed into a small number of channels: Data from normal-hearing children and children with cochlear implants. *Ear & Hearing, 21*(6), 590–596.

Easterbrooks, S., & Mordica, J. (2000). Teachers' ratings of functional communication in students with cochlear implants. *American Annals of the Deaf, 145*(1), 54–59.

Eisenberg, L., Martinez, A., Sennaroghi, G., & Osberger, M. (2000). Establishing new criteria in selecting children for a cochlear implant: Performance of "platinum" hearing aid users. *Annals of Otology, Rhinology & Laryngology* (Suppl. 185) *109*,(12), 30–32.

Estabrooks, W. (1998). *Cochlear implants for kids.* Washington, DC: Alexander Graham Bell Association for the Deaf.

Francis, H , Kock, M., Wyatt, R., & Niparko, J. (1999). Trends in educational placement and cost-benefit considerations in children with cochlear implants. *Archives of Otolaryngology Head and Neck Surgery, 125*, 499–505.

Geers, A., Nicholas, J., Tye-Murray, N., Uchanski, R., Brenner, C., Crosson, J., Davidson, L., Spehar, B., Terteria, G., Tobey, E., Sedey, A., Scrube, M. (2000). Cochlear implants and education of the deaf child: Second-year results. Retrieved, September, 2000, from http://www.cid.wustl.edu/research

Geers, A., & Moog, J. (1994). Spoken language results: Vocabulary, syntax and communication. *Volta Review, 96*, 131–150.

Geers, A., & Tobey, E. (1992). Effects of cochlear implants and tactile aids on the development of speech perception skills in children with profound hearing impairment. *Volta Review, 94*, 135–163.

Harrison, R., Panesar, J., El-Hakim, H., Mount, R., & Papsin, B. (2001, February). *The use of recursive partitioning analysis to explore the effect of age of implantation on speech perception outcomes in prelingually deaf children.* Paper presented at the 8th Symposium, Cochlear Implants in Children, Los Angeles, CA.

Kileny, P., Zwolan, T., & Ashbaugh, C. (2001). The influence of age at implantation on performance with a cochlear implant in children. *Otology & Neurotology, 22*(1), 42–46.

Kluwin, T., & Stewart, D. (2000). Cochlear implants for younger children: A preliminary description of the parental decision and outcomes. *American Annals of the Deaf, 145*(1), 26–32.

Knutson, J., Ehlers, R., Wald R., & Tyler, R. (2000). Psychological predictors of pediatric cochlear implant use and benefit. *Annals of Otology, Rhinology & Laryngology* (Suppl. 185), *109*(12), 100–103.

Lane, H. & Bahan, B. (1998). Ethics of cochlear implantation in young children: A review and reply from a DEAF-WORLD perspective. *Otolaryngology—Head and Neck Surgery, 119*, 297–313.

Lederberg, A. (1991). Social interaction among deaf preschoolers: The effects of language ability and age. *American Annals of the Deaf, 136*, 53–59.

Levi, A., Boyett-Solano, J., Nicholson, B., Eisenberg, L. (2001, March). *Multi-lingualism and children with cochlear implants.* Paper presented at the 8th Symposium, Cochlear Implants in Children. Los Angeles, CA.

Loizou, P. (1998, September) Introduction to cochlear implants. *IEEE Signal Processing Magazine*, 101–130.

Lucker, J. (2002). Cochlear implants: A technological overview. In J. Christiansen. & I. Leigh (Eds.), *Cochlear implants in children: Ethics and choices* (pp. 45–64). Washington, DC: Gallaudet University Press.

Marschark, M. (1993). *Psychological development of deaf children.* New York: Oxford University Press.

Marschark, M. (1997). *Raising and educating a deaf child.* New York: Oxford University Press.

Meyer, T., Svirsky, M., Kirk, K., & Miyamoto, R. (1998). Improvements in speech perception by children with profound prelingual hearing loss: Effects of device, communication mode, and chronological age. *Journal of Speech, Language, and Hearing Research 41*, 846–858.

Miyamoto, R., Kirk, K., Svirsky, M., & Sehgal, S. (1999). Communication skills in pediatric cochlear implant recipients. *Acta Otolaryngologica, 119*, 219–224.

Miyamoto, R., Osberger, J., Todd, S., Robbins, A., Stroer, B., Zimmerman-Phillips, S., & Carney, A.

(1994). Variables affecting implant performance in children. *Laryngoscope, 104,* 1120–1124.

Mondain, M., Sillon, M., Vieu, A., Lanvin, M., Reuillard-Artieres, F., Tobey, E., & Uziel, A., (1997). Speech perception skills and speech production intelligibility in French children with prelingual deafness and cochlear implants. *Archives of Otolaryngology Head and Neck Surgery, 123,* 181–184.

National Association of the Deaf (2001). NAD position statement on cochlear implants. *The NAD Broadcaster, 23*(1), 14–15.

Neville, H., & Lawson, D. (1987). Attention to central and peripheral visual space in a movement detection task. III. Separate effects of auditory deprivation and acquisition of a visual language. *Brain Research, 405,* 284–294.

Nikolopoulos, T., O'Donoghue, G., & Archbold, S. (1999). Age at implantation: Its importance in pediatric cochlear implantation. *Laryngoscope, 109,* 595–599.

Niparko, J. (2000). Culture and cochlear implants. In J. Niparko, K. Kirk, N. Mellon, A. Robbins, D. Tucci, & B. Wilson (Eds.), *Cochlear implants: Principles and practices* (pp. 371–381). New York: Lippincott Williams & Wilkins.

Niparko, J., Cheng, A., & Francis, H. (2000). Outcomes of cochlear implantation: Assessment of quality of life impact and economic evaluation of the benefits of the cochlear implant in relation to costs. In J. Niparko, K. Kirk, N. Mellon, A. Robbins, D. Tucci, & B. Wilson (Eds.), *Cochlear implants: Principles and practices* (pp. 269–288). New York: Lippincott Williams & Wilkins.

Niparko, J., & Wilson, B. (2000). History of cochlear implants. In J. Niparko, K. Kirk, N. Mellon, A. Robbins, D. Tucci, & B. Wilson (Eds.), *Cochlear implants: Principles and practices* (pp. 103–107). New York: Lippincott Williams & Wilkins.

O'Donoghue, G., Nikolopoulos, T., & Archbold, S. (2000). Determinants of speech perception in children after cochlear implantation. *The Lancet, 356,* 466.

O'Donoghue, G., Nikolopoulos, T., Archbold, S., & Tait, M. (1999). Cochlear implants in young children: The relationship between speech perception and speech intelligibility. *Ear & Hearing, 20*(5), 419–425.

Oller, D.K., & Eilers, R.E. (1988). The role of audition in infant babbling. *Child Development, 59,* 441–449.

Osberger, M. (1994). Variables affecting implant performance in children. *Laryngoscope, 104,* 1120–1124.

Osberger, M., & Fisher, L. (1999). SAS-CIS preference study in postlingually deafened adults implanted with the Clarion cochlear implant. *Annals of Otology, Rhinology and Laryngology* (Suppl. 177), *108,* 74–79.

Osberger, M., & Fisher, L. (2000). Preoperative predictors of post-operative implant performance in children. *Annals of Otology, Rhinology & Laryngology* (Suppl. 185), *109*(12), 44–45.

Osberger, M., Fisher, L., Zimmerman-Phillips, L., Geier, L., & Barker, M. (1998). Speech recognition performance of older children with cochlear implants. *The American Journal of Otology, 19,* 152–175.

Osberger, M., Robbins, A., Todd, S., & Riley, A. (1994). Speech intelligibility of children with cochlear implants. *Volta Review, 96*(5), 169–180.

Papsin, B., Gysin, C., Picton, N., Nedgelski, J., & Harrison, R. (2000). Speech perception measures in prelinguistic deaf children up to 4 years after cochlear implantation. *Annals of Otology, Rhinology and Laryngology* (Suppl. 185), *109*(12), 38–42.

Pisoni, D. (2000). Cognitive factors and cochlear implants: Some thoughts on perception, learning, and memory in speech perception. *Ear & Hearing, 21,* 70–78.

Pisoni, D., Cleary, M., Geers, A., & Tobey, E. (1999). Individual differences in effectiveness of cochlear implants in children who are prelingually deaf: New process measures of performance. *Volta Review, 101,* 111–164.

Preisler, G., Ahlstrom, M., & Tvingstedt, A. (1997). The development of communication and language in deaf preschool children with cochlear implants. *International Journal of Pediatric Otorhinolaryngology, 41,* 263–272.

Pyman, B., Blamey, P., Lacy, P., Clark, G., & Dowell, R. (2000). Development of speech perception in children using cochlear implants: Effects of etiology and delayed milestones. *American Journal of Otology, 21,* 57–61.

Quittner, A., Smith, L., Osberger, M., Mitchell, T., & Katz, D. (1994). The impact of audition on the development of visual attention. *Psychological Science, 5,* 347–353.

Quittner, A., Steck, R., & Rouiller, R. (1991). Cochlear implants in children: A study of parental stress and adjustment. *American Journal of Otology* (Suppl.) *12,* 95–104.

Robinson, K. (1998). Implications of developmental plasticity for the language acquisition of deaf children with cochlear implants. *International Journal of Pediatric Otorhinolaryngology, 46* (1–2), 71–80.

Rubenstein, J., Parkinson, W., Tyler, R., & Gantz, B.

(1999). Residual speech recognition and later cochlear implant performance: Effects of implantation criteria. *American Journal of Otolaryngology-Head and Neck Surgery, 20*(4), 445–452.

Simmons, F. (1996). Electrical stimulation of the auditory nerve in man. *Archives of Otolaryngology, 84,* 2–54.

Snik, A., Vermeulen, A., Geelen, C., Brokx, J., & van den Broek, P. (1997). Speech perception performance of children with a cochlear implant compared to that of children with conventional hearing aids. II. Results of prelingually deaf children. *Acta Otolaryngologica, 117,* 755–759.

Spahn, C., Richter, B., Zschocke, I., Lohle, E., & Wirsching, M. (2001). The need for psychosocial support in parents with cochlear implant children. *International Journal of Pediatric Otorhinolaryngology, 57,* 45–53.

Spencer, L., Tomblin, J. B., & Gantz, J. (1997). Reading skills in children with multichannel cochlear implant experience. *Volta Review, 99*(4), 193–202.

Spencer, L., Tye-Murray, N., & Tomblin, J. B. (1998). The production of English inflectional morphology, speech production and listening performance in children with cochlear implants. *Ear & Hearing, 19*(4), 310–318.

Spencer, P. (2000a). Looking without listening: Is audition a prerequisite for normal development of visual attention during infancy? *Journal of Deaf Studies and Deaf Education, 5*(4), 291–302.

Spencer, P. (2000b). Every opportunity: A case study of hearing parents and their deaf child. In P. Spencer, C. Erting, & M. Marschark (Eds.), *The deaf child in the family and at school* (pp. 111–132). Mahwah, NJ: Lawrence Erlbaum Associates.

Spencer, P. (2001, March). *Language performance of children with early cochlear implantation: Child and family factors.* Paper presented at the 8th Symposium, Cochlear Implants in Children, Los Angeles, CA.

Spencer, P. (2002). Language development of children with cochlear implants. In J. Christiansen & I. Leigh (Eds.), *Cochlear implants in children: Ethics and choices* (pp. 222–249). Washington, DC: Gallaudet University Press.

Stallings, L., Kirk, K., & Chin, S. (2001, February). *The influence of linguistic environment on language development by pediatric cochlear implant users.* Paper presented at the 8th Symposium on Cochlear Implants in Children, Los Angeles, CA.

Svirsky, M., & Meyer, T. (1999). Comparison of speech perception in pediatric CLARION cochlear implant and hearing aid users. *Annals of Otology, Rhinology, & Laryngology, 177* (Suppl.), 104–109.

Svirsky, M., Robbins, A., Kirk, K., Pisoni, D., & Miyamoto, R. (2000). Language development in profoundly deaf children with cochlear implants. *Psychological Science, 11,* 153–158.

Svirsky, M., Sloan, R., Caldwell, M., & Miyamoto, R. (2000). Speech intelligibility of prelingually deaf children with multichannel cochlear implants. *Annals of Otology, Rhinology & Laryngology* (Suppl. 185), *109*(12), 123–125.

Tait, M., Lutman, M., & Robinson, K. (2000). Preimplant measures of preverbal communicative behavior as predictors of cochlear implant outcomes in children. *Ear & Hearing, 21,* 18–24.

Tharpe, A., Ashmead, D., & Rothpletz, A. (2002). Visual attention in children with normal hearing, children with hearing aids, and children with cochlear implants. *Journal of Speech, Language, and Hearing Research, 45,* 403–413.

Tobey, E., Geers, A., Douek, B., Perrin, J., Skillett, R., Brenner, C., & Toretta, G. (2000). Factors associated with speech intelligibility in children with cochlear implants. *Annals of Otology, Rhinology, & Laryngology* (Suppl. 185), *109,* 12(2), 28–30.

Tomblin, J. B., Spencer, L., Flock, S., Tyler, R., & Gantz, B. (1999). A comparison of language achievement in children with cochlear implants and children with hearing aids. *Journal of Speech, Language, and Hearing Research, 42,* 497–511.

Tooher, R., Hogan, A., Reed, V., & Code, C. (2001, February). *Adolescent cochlear implant outcomes: Quality of life and psychosocial wellbeing—Preliminary results.* Paper presented at the 8th Symposium, Cochlear Implants in Children, Los Angeles, CA.

Vermeulen, A., Snik, A., Brokx, J., van den Broek, P., Geelen, C., & Beijk, C. (1997). Comparison of speech perception performance in children using a cochlear implant with children using conventional hearing aids, based on the concept of "equivalent hearing loss." *Scandinavian Audiology, 26* (Suppl. 47), 55–57.

Vieu, A., Mondain, M., Blanchard, K., Sillon, M., Reuillard-Artieres, F., Tobey, E., Uziel, A., & Piron, J. (1998). Influence of communication mode on speech intelligibility and syntactic structure of sentences in profoundly hearing impaired French children implanted between 5 and 9 years of age. *International Journal of Pediatric Otorhinolaryngology, 44,* 15–22.

Wald, R., & Knutson, J. (2000). Deaf cultural identity of adolescents with and without cochlear implants. *Annals of Otology, Rhinology & Laryngology* (Suppl. 185), *12*(2), 87–89.

Wauters, L. N., van Bon, W. H. J., & Tellings, A. (2002, June). *Reading comprehension of deaf students in primary and secondary education*. Paper presented at the Society for Scientific Studies of Reading, Chicago.

Yoshinaga-Itano, C. & Downey, D. (1996). The psychoeducational characteristics of school-aged students in Colorado with educationally significant hearing losses. *Volta Review, 98*(1), 65–96.

VII

Cognitive Correlates and Consequences of Deafness

32

Susan J. Maller

Intellectual Assessment of Deaf People
A Critical Review of Core Concepts and Issues

This chapter addresses cognitive assessment of deaf children and adults. Emphasis is placed on the psychometric properties (e.g., reliability, validity, norms, item analysis) of published intelligence tests when administered to this population. The use of intelligence tests with deaf people has a long history that can be traced back to the early years of formal intelligence testing aimed at identifying those students in need of special education due to "mental retardation" (Kamphaus, 2001). Intelligence tests continue to serve as a primary component of the assessment process for special education (Hutton, Dubes, & Muir, 1992; Stinnett, Havey, & Oehler-Stinnett 1994) Practitioners who serve deaf children regularly are faced with the dilemma of choosing from a variety of published tests that may lack sufficient evidence of validity (the test measures what it claims to measure) for this population.

There are several potential reasons psychometric evidence is lacking for tests when administered to deaf people. First, deaf people constitute a low-incidence population, and sufficient sample sizes are difficult to obtain to conduct the necessary investigations. Second, the deaf population is composed of a diverse group in terms of a variety of variables, such as communication modalities, degree of hearing loss, parental hearing loss, age of

onset, etiology, presence of additional disabilities, race/gender, socioeconomic status (SES), and educational placement. Third, funding is often not available to support investigations by test publishers and independent researchers for low-incidence populations. Finally, many independent researchers may lack the skills both for working with deaf people and in psychometrics that are required to conduct the necessary studies. Thus, valid cognitive assessment remains a difficult dilemma for practitioners whose goals may include helping educators understand a deaf child's intellectual abilities and educational needs.

Historical Perspectives

Perceptions of the cognitive abilities of deaf people have been largely influenced by scores obtained on early intelligence tests. Moores (1982) provided a model for labeling the phases of the development of general perceptions of the cognitive abilities of deaf people. He labeled the initial stage as "the deaf as inferior," which primarily was defined by the work of Pintner, Eisenson, and Stanton (1946), who reported that deaf children were cognitively inferior to hearing children. These conclusions were based on the results of numerous studies, involving a variety of verbal, nonverbal, and performance intelligence (e.g., Draw-A-Man Test, Binet-Simon Scale) tests, and contradicted Pintner and Paterson's (1915) earlier statements recognizing the inappropriateness of similar tests. Specifically, Pintner and Paterson had recognized that (1) verbal intelligence tests could not "be applied satisfactorily to deaf children" (p. 210), (2) existing performance tests were "so inadequately standardized" (p. 210) that they were not useful, and (3) no existing instrument had been adapted for deaf children.

The next stage, defined by the work of Myklebust (1964), was labeled as the "the deaf as concrete" (Moores, 1982). Myklebust rejected the notion that deaf children were cognitively inferior to hearing children. Myklebust believed that because the other senses must serve different functions for deaf people, deaf and hearing children's thinking was structured differently, or qualitatively different. He further asserted that this difference resulted in more "concrete" thinking and a lag in academic performance.

The final stage, termed "the deaf as intellectually normal" (Moores, 1982), was defined by the work of Rosenstein (1961) and Vernon (1967), who reported deaf children scored similarly to hearing children on tests involving nonverbal tasks. Other research also has found that deaf and hearing people perform similarly on nonverbal intelligence tests (e.g., Braden, 1984, 1985; Lavos, 1962; Maller & Braden, 1993; Rosenstein, 1961) based on scores obtained on versions of the same intelligence tests that continue to dominate the modern practice.

The Practice of Assessing Deaf People

Intelligence tests play an important role in the assessment of deaf persons for a variety of purposes, such as developing individualized education plans, determining educational program placement, and monitoring progress. In addition, deaf children may be referred for evaluation when they are suspected of being gifted or cognitively impaired.

Nonverbal Tests

Nonverbal and performance intelligence tests have been recommended for use with deaf people (Sul-

livan & Burley, 1990). Several studies have reported that deaf and hearing children obtain similar Performance IQs (PIQs) on the Wechsler Intelligence Scale for Children-Revised (WISC-R; Wechsler, 1974); Hishoren, Hurley, & Kavale, 1979; Kelly & Braden, 1990; Phelps & Branyan, 1988, 1990) and the Wechsler Intelligence Scale for Children-Third Edition (WISC-III; Wechsler, 1991; Maller & Braden, 1993; Sullivan & Montoya, 1997). These tests have been the most widely used intelligence tests with deaf children (Gibbins, 1989; Maller, 1991; McQuaid & Alovisetti, 1981) in North America, and possibly in the world (Braden & Hannah, 1998).

The results from studies of deaf individuals' performance on other widely used nonverbal intelligence tests have led to somewhat inconclusive results about how their functioning compares to that of hearing persons. Specifically, deaf children have been reported to obtain IQs in the normal range (Ulissi, Brice, & Gibbins, 1989) on the Kaufman Assessment Battery for Children (K-ABC; Kaufman & Kaufman, 1983) Nonverbal Scale. Lower IQs have been reported for deaf than for hearing examinees on the Leiter International Performance Scale-Revised (LIPS-R; Roid & Miller, 1997), the Comprehensive Test of Nonverbal Intelligence (CTONI; Hammill, Pearson, & Wiederholt, 1997), and the Universal Nonverbal Intelligence Test (UNIT; Bracken & McCallum, 1998). Research is needed to sort out whether these findings can be explained by sampling or test characteristics. Specifically, the following questions might be asked regarding the sample that participated: is the sample representative of deaf individuals? Does the sample include deaf persons who have unidentified disabilities? The following questions might be asked regarding the test: do deaf examinees understand the directions? Do the items have a different meaning for deaf children, due to different opportunities to learn or different exposure to the material?

Another factor that has been reported to affect nonverbal IQs relates to the manipulation of test materials. Deaf people obtain scores in the normal range on performance tasks that require the manipulation of materials (e.g., puzzles or blocks), although they have been reported to obtain scores about one-third of a standard deviation lower than the mean for hearing people on motor-free nonverbal intelligence tests (i.e., tests that do not require manipulation of materials, such as matrices or tasks involving pictures) (Braden, 1994). Braden offered several interesting possible explanations for this finding, including the possibility that deaf examinees may understand the required task better when they see materials manipulated, have manual dexterity skills that assist in the manipulation of materials, or use verbal mediation (strategies involving linguistic thought) to attempt to solve motor-free tasks.

Verbal Intelligence Tests

Deaf examinees tend to obtain Verbal IQs (VIQs) that fall one standard deviation below the mean of hearing examinees (Braden, 1994; Maller & Braden, 1993; Moores et al., 1987). This has led to concerns regarding test validity for deaf people (Maller & Braden, 1993: Sullivan & Vernon, 1979; Vernon, 1976) and investigations of item and test bias (Maller, 1996, 1997; Maller & Ferron, 1997). Regardless of these concerns, many psychologists have continued to give nonstandardized administrations to deaf children (Gibbins, 1989; Maller, 1991), with the results frequently contained in psychological reports (Maller, 1991). Gibbins (1989) reported that some psychologists stated that they used the information "for purposes other than assessing cognitive ability" (p. 98). These psychologists probably noticed that some deaf children perform better than others (e.g., $SD = 19.91$ for the WISC-III; Maller, 1994), and variability suggests that the test is sensitive to differences between examinees. Second, VIQ is a better predictor of academic achievement than is PIQ (Maller & Braden, 1993). Furthermore, practitioners may continue to use the Verbal Scale in an attempt to identify deaf children with unusual strengths or weakness in processing verbal information so that a suspected verbally gifted deaf child will not be limited to an average academic experience, and a deaf child with suspected learning disabilities will not be overlooked. Although the Verbal Scale may seem to provide useful information regarding a deaf examinee, tests should not be used in the absence of sufficient validity evidence for a given purpose. For this reason, several legal mandates and professional recommendations concerning the development and use of tests will be discussed next.

Legal Mandates and Professional Recommendations

The Individuals with Disabilities Education Act Amendments of 1997 states that tests must "have been validated for the specific purpose for which they are used" and "be administered in the child's native language or other mode of communication." In addition, professional organizations have provided recommendations concerning test development and uses, including the widely cited Code of Fair Testing Practices in Education (Joint Committee on Testing Practices, 1988) and Standards for Educational and Psychological Testing (Joint Committee on the Standards for Educational and Psychological Testing, 1999). These documents outline important considerations when testing individuals from diverse and special populations. Scores should be interpreted with caution when they may have different meanings for subgroups of examinees because of differences related to test administration modifications, language, culture, ethnicity, gender, or disability status. Furthermore, the use of a test without sufficient validity evidence is strongly discouraged. Although test consumers depend on the development of technically sound tests, few published tests provide such evidence for deaf examinees.

Core Measurement Concepts, Issues, and Applications

Ultimately, practitioners must take responsibility for understanding the psychometric properties and potential unintended consequences, as discussed by Messick (1989), of using tests without the necessary evidence of validity. Thus measurement concepts pertaining to the assessment of deaf examinees will be explained below.

Test Adaptations

Testing "accommodations" are defined as adaptations that provide equal access for persons with disabilities. Special seating arrangements or enlarged print are two examples. Accommodations do not change the nature of the test or the construct (i.e., trait or ability) measured by the test. Conversely, "modifications" are distinguished from accommodations, because modifications may alter the intended content (Thurlow, Ysseldyke, & Silverstein, 1995) and thus may alter test constructs. An important consideration when adapting a test for deaf examinees is whether the adaptation is an appropriate accommodation or if it is a modification that changes the nature of the test construct.

Several attempts have been made to adapt intelligence tests in various ways (e.g., gestural administrations; signed instructions of nonverbal tests; translations of items on verbal tests, including the use of interpreters) for deaf examinees (e.g., Kostrubala & Braden, 1998; Maller, 1994; Miller, 1984; Porter & Kirby, 1986; Ray, 1979; Ray & Ulissi, 1982; Sullivan & Montoya, 1997). However, convincing empirical evidence regarding the measurement properties of adapted versions generally has been lacking or questionable, probably due to insufficient sample sizes. When sample sizes were available for the necessary analyses, the findings suggested that specific modifications appeared to compromise validity (Maller, 1996, 1997).

One adaptation often used by psychologists is test translation (e.g., Kostrubala & Braden, 1998; Maller, 1994; Miller, 1984). Specific guidelines have been suggested for test translation (Bracken & Barona, 1991), which include the following steps: (1) initial translation by a fluent bilingual translator, (2) a blind-back translation (i.e., translation of the translated version back to the original language by a person who is fluent bilingually), (3) careful comparison of the two versions to identify any discrepancies, (4) repetition of steps 1 and 2 to resolve discrepancies until no more improvements can be made, and (5) evaluation of the translated version by a bilingual review committee. It is important that the translated and original versions measure equivalent constructs (Sireci, Bastar, & Allalouf, 1998), as determined by the necessary empirical validity evidence (Hambleton, 1996). Methods for obtaining such evidence are discussed later.

Norm-Referenced Tests

Norm-referenced tests are used to compare an individual to a representative peer group. When choosing or interpreting the results of a test, the representativeness of the standardization sample (also known as the norm sample) should be considered. To make the sample more representative, it has been recommended that special subgroup norms be established for deaf people (Anderson & Sisco, 1977; Hiskey, 1966; Sullivan & Vernon, 1979; Vernon & Brown, 1964; Vonderhaar & Chambers, 1975). Deaf norms were developed for the WISC-R Performance Scale (Anderson & Sisco, 1977). However, Braden (1985) argued that the use of deaf norms should be reconsidered because there was no evidence to suggest that deaf norms improved the psychometric properties of the test for that population. Furthermore, Maller (1996) pointed out that when test constructs are measured differently for deaf and hearing examinees, subgroup norms may be a superficial solution to a larger problem concerning validity. If test items have different meanings for deaf examinees, then subgroup norms result in comparing deaf individuals to each other on some trait not claimed to be measured by the test. Moreover, because the deaf population is so heterogeneous in terms of hearing loss, mode of communication, parental hearing status, ethnicity, educational experiences, and so on, deaf norms still may not be representative or useful.

Reliability

Reliability refers to consistency in measurement. Test–retest reliability assesses the consistency of scores over time, requiring the administration of a test on two occasions. Test–retest reliability coefficients indicate the stability of scores, or the extent to which examinees maintain their positions in the distribution upon retesting. Test manuals rarely include test–retest reliability studies with samples representing special populations, such as samples of deaf examinees. Therefore, the extent to which educational and psychological tests scores of deaf examinees are stable over time is generally unknown. Some older studies have reported that IQs are stable for deaf examinees (Birch, Stuckless, & Birch, 1963; DuToit, 1954; Lavos, 1950), but studies are needed with currently used tests.

The other type of reliability coefficient that might be reported for deaf examinees is internal consistency reliability (e.g., split half, Kuder Richardson 20, Cronbach coefficient alpha), which requires that a test be administered only once. This type of reliability provides an index of item homogeneity (interrelatedness of the items). Internal consistency reliability coefficients rarely have been reported for the IQs of deaf examinees in independent research (e.g., Hishoren et al., 1979), and the extent to which reliability coefficients may differ for deaf and hearing examinees has remained in question.

Validity

Construct validity refers to whether the test measures what it claims to measure. According to Messick (1989), all types of validity ultimately serve as evidence of construct validity. Braden and Hannah (1998) discussed Messick's (1989) concept of construct underrepresentation, which characterizes tests that too narrowly define a construct. Maller (1996) and Braden and Hannah (1998) discussed Messick's (1989) concept of construct-irrelevant variance, which involves the use of tests that systematically reflect factors extraneous to the construct claimed to be measured by the test. For example, verbal intelligence tests may, in fact, measure degree of hearing loss or other factors specific to deafness. When tests are used with deaf children or adults, they may too narrowly measure the construct, but even worse, they may introduce construct-irrelevant variance. For these reasons, and in accordance with the mandates and professional recommendations, validity evidence is crucial when choosing tests for deaf people.

Content Validity

Content validity refers to the appearance of validity to experts in the content domain of the test. For example, a test publisher might hire high school math teachers to assist in the development of high school math achievement test. Test companies traditionally have not employed experts in the field of deafness when developing widely used standardized tests.

Criterion-related Validity

Criterion-related validity refers to the relationship between the test and some relevant criterion. The criterion is typically another well-established test of either the same construct measured at the same time (concurrent validity) or a construct that should be predicted by the test (predictive validity). To obtain evidence of concurrent or predictive criterion-related validity, correlation coefficients are used to determine the relationship between scores on the test and scores on the criterion variable.

Concurrent validity coefficients for deaf children on the Wechsler Performance Scale have included moderate to high correlations between PIQ and scores from the Hiskey-Nebraska Test of Learning Aptitude (H-NTLA; Hiskey, 1966), a nonverbal test constructed for and normed on deaf children (Hirshoren et al., 1979; Phelps & Branyan, 1988; Watson, Sullivan, Moeller, & Jensen, 1982). Moderate to high correlations also have been reported for deaf children between WISC-R PIQs and scores from the K-ABC Nonverbal Scale (Phelps & Branyan, 1988, 1990) and the Raven's Progressive Matrices (Blennerhassett, Strohmeier, & Hibbett, 1994).

Several researchers have investigated the predictive validity of deaf children's scores on nonverbal and performance intelligence tests. The findings include weak correlations between WISC-R PIQ and the Stanford Achievement Test-Hearing Impaired Edition (SAT-HI; Allen, 1986) grade equivalents and age-based percentile ranks (Braden, 1989). Kelly and Braden (1990) later reported somewhat higher (low to moderate) correlations between WISC-R PIQs and SAT-HI percentile ranks. Moderate correlations have been reported between WISC-R PIQ and Wide Range Achievement Test-Revised (WRAT-R; Jastak & Wilkinson, 1984; Phelps & Branyan, 1990) scores. WISC-III PIQs were moderately correlated with SAT-HI scores (Maller & Braden, 1993). Predictive validity coefficients for the K-ABC nonverbal scale include high correlations with the SAT-HI combined reading scale (Ulissi, Brice, & Gibbins, 1989) and moderate correlations with the WRAT-R reading and spelling tests (Phelps & Branyan, 1990).

The WISC-III Verbal Scale has been found to predict academic achievement of deaf students, with high correlations with SAT-HI scores (Maller & Braden, 1993). However, Maller and Braden (1993) emphasized that their findings should be interpreted with caution because "the Verbal Scale is not necessarily a valid measure of the deaf child's underlying cognitive abilities" (p. 110). Sullivan and Burley (1990) stated that, although the Verbal Scale predicts achievement, it is inappropriate as the "the sole measure of mental abilities in deaf children" and "should be interpreted with caution" (p. 777).

Criterion-related validity coefficients are insufficient evidence to conclude that a test is measuring what it claims to measure (Messick, 1989)—that is, that it has sufficient construct validity. Tests may be correlated for systematic reasons other than what the test claims to measure. For example, degree of hearing loss may affect performance on both intelligence and achievement tests and may explain, in part, the relationship between these two tests (e.g., correlations between WISC-III VIQ and SAT-HI scores). Thus, the correlation of a test with another measure should not be used as the sole evidence of its validity for deaf persons. Rather, direct evidence of construct validity also should be examined.

Factor Analysis as Direct Evidence of Construct Validity

The method of factor analysis is probably the most widely used method of obtaining direct evidence of the construct validity of intelligence tests for deaf people. A test's factor structure should be equal for deaf and hearing samples if the test measures the same construct across groups. Factor structure differences may be used as an indication of test bias because, if relationships between subtests and factors differ across groups, scores may have different meanings across the groups. There are two major types of factor analysis: exploratory (EFA) and confirmatory (CFA) factor analysis. EFA should be used when the researcher does not have an a priori theory regarding the underlying structure of the instrument, whereas CFA is used to test a hypothesized theoretical model. For more information regarding EFA and CFA, the reader is referred to Gorsuch (1983) and Bollen (1989), respectively.

EFA has been used to examine the factorial similarity of intelligence tests across deaf and hearing samples. For example, Braden (1984) investigated the factorial similarity of the WISC-R performance scale between a large sample of deaf children ($N = 1,228$) and the WISC-R standardization sample ($N = 2,200$), which was composed of hearing children. One factor was extracted, and the factor was highly correlated across samples, as determined by the coefficient of congruence (a type of correlation coefficient that indicates the similarity of the factor loadings across groups), indicating that the Performance Scale measured the same underlying trait for both samples. However, the sample of deaf children did obtain significantly lower than expected scores on all subtests, leading to concerns regarding the representativeness of the sample.

Whereas Braden (1984) factor-analyzed subtest scores from the Performance Scale only, EFA also has been used to factor analyze Verbal and Performance Scale subtest scores. For example, Blenner-hasset, Moores, and Anderson (1988) factor-analyzed the Wechsler Adult Intelligence Scale (WAIS-R; Wechsler, 1981). Verbal and Performance Scale subtest scores of 135 profoundly deaf adolescents were factor-analyzed. The small sample was divided into two smaller samples based on parental hearing status: deaf children of deaf parents (DCDP) and deaf children of hearing parents (DCHP). Because a two-factor solution (verbal and performance) was obtained for the DCDP sample and a three-factor solution, including verbal, performance, and freedom from distractibility (attention) factors, was obtained for the DCHP sample, these investigators concluded that the results supported the hypothesis that cognitive structures differ within the deaf population.

The WISC-R Verbal and Performance Scale scores of 368 hard-of-hearing (<60 dB hearing loss) and deaf children (>60 dB hearing loss) were factor-analyzed by Sullivan and Schulte (1992). The tests were administered using the child's preferred mode of communication by psychologists who either signed or used sign language interpreters with the signing children or who used oral language with the children from oral programs. Because hard-of-hearing and deaf samples obtained identical factor structures in separate analyses, they were combined into a total sample analysis. The mean PIQ was 117.22 ($SD = 19.13$), indicating that the sample included some very high-functioning children and greater variability than for the norm sample. A Freedom from Distractibility factor (that had been identified in the hearing norm group) was not extracted in the analysis of deaf children's performance. This led to the conclusion that the factor structure for the deaf and hard-of-hearing sample was different from that of the standardization sample. These findings were interpreted as evidence for the "differential cerebral organization indigenous to the handicap" (Sullivan & Schulte, p. 539), a neuropsychological explanation for the deaf people's higher scores on visual-spatial tests. However, this conclusion is questionable given that the coefficient of congruence was not used to compare factors, mean score differences do not affect factor loadings, and, later research reported that WISC-III Freedom from Distractibility scores were not correlated with other measures of attention for hearing children (Cohen, Becker, & Campbell, 1990), thus raising doubt about the interpretation of this factor.

Sullivan and Montoya (1997) used EFA to factor-analyze the WISC-III subtest scores of 106 deaf and hard-of-hearing children. Two factors were extracted: visual-spatial organization and language comprehension. Again, no Freedom from Distractibility factor was identified in the deaf and hard-of-hearing children's performance. Although this finding is consistent with results reported by Sullivan and Schulte (1992), it differs from the results reported by Blennerhasset et al. (1988). The samples appeared to differ in terms of age, degree of hearing loss, and parental hearing status. Regardless, replication is needed on samples representative of specific subgroups of deaf people to determine the reliability of the findings. In addition, the processing speed factors identified for the norm group was not obtained in analysis of the deaf/hard-of-hearing children's scores. Based on this same study, Sullivan and Montoya encouraged a reconsideration of the taboo of using the verbal scale with deaf examinees because most deaf children are in schools where they must compete with hearing students, VIQ is a better predictor of achievement than PIQ, and deaf persons will obtain better jobs if they are more English literate, have better mathematical skills, and can communicate with their hearing peers. However, the test does not claim to measure these skills, and empirical evidence suggests items and test constructs may have different meanings (Maller, 1996, 1997; Maller & Ferron, 1997) for deaf and hearing examinees.

The methods used in several of the EFA studies are questionable because (1) the use of varimax rotation (cf., Blennerhassett et al., 1988; Sullivan & Montoya, 1997; Sullivan & Schulte, 1992) is inappropriate when factors are correlated, or (2) the sample sizes were somewhat small because EFA requires a minimum of 10 cases per variable (Crocker & Algina, 1986) or even 20 cases per variable (Velicer & Fava, 1998) to guarantee stable estimates of factor loadings. Furthermore, EFA should be reserved for use when there is no a priori theoretical model, which is rarely the case. As stated by Crocker and Algina (1986), "very little factor-analytic research is purely exploratory" (p. 304).

Reynolds (1982) stated, "bias exists in regard to construct validity when a test is shown to measure different hypothetical traits (psychological constructs) for one group than another or to measure the same trait but with different degrees of accuracy" (p. 194). That is, test scores for one group cannot be interpreted the same way as scores for the other group. Reynolds argued that multisample CFA is a more promising and sophisticated method for detecting construct bias than the previously relied upon method of EFA. CFA requires smaller sample sizes (as few as 100 cases) (Boomsma, 1982). The idea behind multisample CFA is to test the theoretical model on which the test is constructed simultaneously across groups. If the model fits across groups, as determined by a variety of fit statistics, the factor structure is said to be invariant (not different), and it is concluded that scores do not measure intended test constructs differently across groups. An advantage of this method is that specific factor loadings, their associated error variances, and the relationship between factors can be individually tested to determine the specific differences between groups and better understand what aspect(s) of the test structure differ across groups.

Multisample CFA was used in only one published study, with a sample of 110 deaf children (Maller & Ferron, 1997). Using this procedure, adequate fit was found for the general form of the WISC-III four-factor model for deaf as well as hearing children. However, factor loadings, error variances, and factor variances and covariances differed for deaf and hearing standardization samples, suggesting that test scores may have different meanings across these groups. Similar investigations are needed for other intelligence tests recommended for use with deaf people, such as the ASL translation of the WAIS-III (Kostrubala & Braden, 1998), LIPS-R, CTONI, and UNIT.

Profile Analysis

A few previous researchers have suggested that interpretations of specific score patterns on the Wechsler Performance Scale might provide insight into a deaf child's patterns of strengths and weakness. For example, low Picture Arrangement scores were suggested to indicate poor social judgment (Vonderhaar & Chambers, 1975), whereas the Coding subtest was said to be sensitive to academic and learning problems (Braden, 1990). Although previously little had been known about the characteristic WISC-III profiles of deaf children as compared to standardization sample profiles, Maller (1999) found that, although hearing children exhibit unique profiles at a rate of 5%, 35.5% of deaf children exhibited WISC-III unique profiles that differed from those found in the standardization sample. This finding is in sharp contrast to the low rate (6.2%) of unique profiles found for hearing students receiving services for learning disabilities (Maller & McDermott, 1997), a group that was expected to display unique profiles, but did not. The majority of the deaf children exhibited profiles that were either average Performance Scale and below average Verbal Scale subtest scores or below average Performance Scale scores and well below average Verbal Scale scores. Deaf children almost always have a discrepancy between VIQ and PIQ, with VIQ significantly lower than PIQ. Furthermore, the WISC-III has been reported to measure the construct of intelligence differently at the item and factor structure levels when administered to deaf children who use sign language (Maller, 1996, 1997; Maller & Ferron, 1997). For this reason, as well the high rate of unique profiles, psychologists should question the validity of interpreting the WISC-III profiles of deaf children. Similar studies are needed for other intelligence tests.

Differential Item Functioning

To study whether specific groups may have difficulties with items due to factors specific to their language, culture, gender, or other differences, researchers or psychometricians do more than examine the language content of the items. They use highly quantitative statistical procedures that are based on probability theory to determine if a specific subgroup is less likely to answer an individual item correctly because an item may be more difficult or discriminating (separating high- and low-ability examinees) for a given group. Differential item functioning (DIF), previously known as item bias, is the statistical difference in the probability of correct response to an item between deaf and hearing groups of equal ability (e.g., intelligence, as measured by as set of nonbiased items). The presence of DIF indicates that group membership accounts for at least some of the differences in item performance and thus threatens the validity of

scores for a given subgroup. Items that do not exhibit DIF are said to be invariant. Several methods have been developed to investigate DIF. Because relatively large sample sizes are needed for DIF investigations and because state-of-the-art DIF detection procedures are quite technical and time consuming, DIF studies can be expensive for test publishers and are seldom reported for deaf samples. Although the CTONI was evaluated for item bias against deaf children, obsolete methodology was used (see Camilli & Shepard, 1994; Drossman & Maller, 2000). Another test claimed to be especially suitable for deaf children is the LIPS-R, because it is administered completely by gesture and symbols. The LIPS-R test manual, however, provides insufficient information regarding DIF and the validity of the test for deaf children. Finally, DIF investigations are needed for the WAIS-III ASL (American Sign Language) translation (Kostrubala & Braden, 1998).

Independent DIF investigations have reported that numerous WISC-III Verbal Scale and Picture Completion items exhibit DIF against a sample of deaf children when compared to a matched sample of hearing children (Maller, 1996) and the hearing standardization sample (Maller, 1997). An independent DIF investigation also was reported for the Universal Nonverbal Intelligence Test by Maller (2000). No items were found to function differently for a sample of deaf examinees and a matched sample from the UNIT hearing standardization sample data. That is, all items were invariant. Because similar evidence, based on state-of-the-art DIF detection methods, is not available for other nonverbal tests, the UNIT is recommended for use with deaf children.

Diversity Issues

Deaf people comprise a very heterogeneous group in terms of several background and demographic characteristics that can be expected to influence their test scores. Mean intelligence test score differences have been reported in the general hearing population based on a variety of demographic classifications (e.g., gender, SES, race/ethnicity; Jensen, 1980). However, these mean score differences might be explained by a number of factors, including item or test bias, differences in opportunities to learn, socialization, and exposure to content, among countless other factors (Maller, 2001). Few researchers have investigated differences between deaf people based on these classifications, probably due to the difficulty in obtaining the sufficient sample sizes. In the limited research available, inconsistent results have been reported concerning gender differences among deaf children on the Wechsler scales. These findings range from reports of no gender differences on the WISC-III (Sullivan & Montoya, 1997), differences in WISC-R coding subtest scores (females outperforming males) only (Phelps & Ensor, 1987), and statistically significantly higher WISC-R and WISC-III (up to one standard deviation) for deaf males than deaf females (Slate & Fawcett, 1996). No recent studies of IQ differences between deaf people from various race, ethnic, or SES groups have been reported. Certainly, practitioners should consider the possibility that a deaf person's intelligence test score may be influenced by additional background and diversity variables.

Variables of particular relevance to deaf people include parental hearing status, age of onset, presence of an additional disability, degree of hearing loss, and educational placement (Braden, 1994; Sullivan & Burley, 1990). Unfortunately, there is a dearth of research concerning how these variables influence IQs, again, most likely due to the difficulty in obtaining the sufficient sample sizes. Of the available research, DCDP, as well as deaf children with hearing parents and deaf siblings (DCDS) consistently have been reported to have statistically significantly higher Wechsler PIQs than DCHP and even hearing children (Conrad & Weiskrantz, 1981; Kusche, Greenberg, & Garfield, 1983; Sisco & Anderson, 1980). However, there is disagreement concerning the explanation for these findings (e.g., genetics, environment, unidentified disabilities among the deaf children with hearing parents). For example, it initially was believed that DCDP obtained higher IQs than DCHP, because they were exposed to language earlier and more naturally than DCHP. That is, their deaf parents were likely to use ASL. However, the IQs of DCDP and DCDS did not differ, but both groups' IQs were higher than DCHP IQs. The lower IQs of DCHP, were thought to be a result of potential co-existing disabilities (Conrad & Weiskrantz, 1981). The IQs of DCDP and DCDS also were subsequently reported to be higher than those of hearing children, leading other researchers to conclude

that their higher IQs might be explained by heredity (Braden, 1987; Kusche, Greenberg, & Garfield, 1983).

Such differences also were found in Braden's (1994) meta-analysis, which synthesized the results of numerous studies of IQ and deafness. The results also indicated that (1) prelingually deaf children obtain lower VIQs than children who became deaf after around age 5, and (2) degree of hearing loss is not correlated with nonverbal intelligence but is moderately to highly associated with verbal intelligence. Certainly, the presence of various disabilities (e.g., cognitive or neurological) may affect intellectual ability, whereas other disabilities may inhibit specific test performance (e.g., motor or visual), regardless of hearing status. Braden (1994) concluded that students with additional disabilities have lower IQs than those without additional disabilities; however, insufficient information was available to assign participants in the included studies to disability categories.

Braden, Maller, and Paquin (1993) reported that students in residential schools have lower PIQs than students enrolled in day (e.g., nonresidential, commuter deaf education) programs. However, after a 3- to 4-year period, residential students' PIQs tend to increase, and there are no significant differences between residential and day students' PIQs, when controlling for differences attributed to other variables (e.g., age of onset, parental hearing loss, and presence of additional disabilities). These findings contradict the arguments that residential schools have a detrimental effect on IQ (e.g., Raviv, Sharan, & Strauss, 1973).

Potential Misuses of Tests

In light of the legal mandates, professional recommendations, and available research, practitioners are encouraged to carefully consider their decisions regarding if and how an intelligence test will be used, especially in terms of the social consequences (Messick, 1989). Some potential misuses of tests with deaf persons include the following:

- Translating test directions or items without using recommended procedures for test translation,
- Oral, written, gestural administrations of tests or items without validity evidence,

- Using tests with deaf persons who have additional disabilities, such as nonverbal tests requiring vision for deafblind examinees or performance tasks with students with physical disabilities that inhibit motor skills,
- Reporting verbal intelligence scores (subtest or scale) in the body of the psychological report,
- Using verbal intelligence tests for measuring constructs other than cognitive ability (e.g., of achievement or as a predictor of academic success in an educational setting with hearing peers), even though the test does not claim to measure these constructs and lacks validity evidence for these purposes,
- Not considering diversity (e.g., gender, race/ethnicity, SES) issues that also may affect test scores, and
- Analyzing profiles of deaf students without available normative comparisons.

Summary and Conclusions

Published intelligence tests routinely are administered to deaf children to determine eligibility for special education, to plan continued services, and to predict academic achievement. Although the majority of deaf and hearing children obviously have different educational needs because of communication differences rather than because of intellectual deficits, intelligence tests continue to dominate the assessment process. Intellectual assessment may be necessary for any child, deaf or hearing, who is suspected of being gifted or cognitively impaired. Unfortunately, psychologists have lacked instruments with the necessary psychometric evidence, including reliability, validity, and item invariance evidence, for use with deaf examinees. Although deaf children tend to obtain PIQs in the normal range, they tend to obtain VIQs that are one standard deviation below the mean for hearing examinees. Many psychologists continue to modify verbal intelligence tests to predict academic achievement and to measure constructs not claimed to be measured by these tests, even though there may be evidence of item and test bias.

There is a critical need for tests with sufficient psychometric evidence for deaf people, although such evidence may be difficult to obtain for a variety of reasons, including the heterogeneous na-

ture of the deaf population, the difficulty in obtaining sufficient sample sizes, and the cost and skills required to obtain such evidence. Given this difficult situation, practitioners may ask "what instruments are currently available that are appropriate for providing information regarding a deaf child's ability?" At present, the answer may be discouraging. There currently are no available verbal intelligence tests with evidence of construct validity for deaf children. The WISC-III Verbal Scale, specifically, is known to contain numerous items that exhibit DIF against deaf children. Although the WISC-III performance scale has been the most popular intelligence for use with deaf children, there is some evidence that it lacks item and factor invariance. The UNIT is recommended for use with deaf children because there is some evidence, using state-of-the-art methods, that the UNIT contains no items that exhibit bias against deaf children. Research is needed to examine the predictive validity and factor structure invariance of the UNIT. Although the UNIT is limited to the assessment of nonverbal ability, it can provide an idea of whether the child may have a cognitive disability. After all, this originally was, and probably continues to be, the main reason for assessing intelligence—especially for members of a population who generally should qualify for special education on the basis of a hearing test alone, but like members of the hearing population, may have special needs related to cognitive ability.

Test publishers and independent researchers are strongly encouraged to promote more psychometric studies of tests used with deaf examinees. Furthermore, practitioners are urged to choose a test based on the empirical evidence of its psychometric properties, regardless of how much the test may seem to measure something meaningful, especially given the potential unintended social consequences of test use.

References

Allen, T. (1986). *Understanding the scores: Hearing-impaired students and the Stanford Achievement Test* (7th ed.). Washington, DC: Gallaudet College Press.

Anderson, R. J., & Sisco, F. H. (1977). Standardization of the WISC-R Performance Scale for deaf children (Office of Demographic Studies Publication

Series T, No. 1). Washington, DC: Gallaudet College.

Birch, A., Stuckless, E. R., & Birch, J. W. (1963). An eleven year study of predicting school achievement in young deaf children. *American Annals of the Deaf, 103*, 236–240.

Blennerhasset, L. D., Moores, D. F., & Anderson, B. (1988, April). *Factor analysis of the WAIS-R for two groups of deaf adolescents.* Paper presented at the Annual Meeting of the National Association of School Psychologists, Chicago.

Blennerhassett, L., Strohmeier, S. J., & Hibbett, C. (1994). Criterion-related validity of Raven's Progressive Matrices with deaf residential school students. *American Annals of the Deaf, 139*, 104–110.

Bollen, K. A. (1989). *Structural equations with latent variables.* New York: Wiley.

Boomsma, A. (1982). The robustness of LISREL against small sample size in factor analysis models. In K. G. Jöreskog & H. Wold (Eds.), *Systems under indirect observation: causality* (pp. 149–173). New York: Elsevier Science Publishers.

Bracken, B. A., & Barona, A. (1991). State of the art procedures for translating, validating and using psychoeducational tests in cross-cultural assessment. *School Psychology International, 12*, 119–132.

Bracken, B. A., & McCallum, S. (1998). *Universal Nonverbal Intelligence Test.* Chicago: Riverside Publishing.

Braden, J. P. (1984). The factorial similarity of the WISC-R performance scale in deaf and hearing children. *Journal of Personality and Individual Differences, 5*, 405–409.

Braden, J. P. (1985). WISC-R deaf norms reconsidered. *Journal of School Psychology, 23*, 375–382.

Braden, J. P. (1987). An explanation of the superior Performance IQs of deaf children of deaf parents. *American Annals of the Deaf, 132*, 263–266.

Braden, J. P. (1989). The criterion-related validity of the WISC-R Performance Scale and other nonverbal IQ tests for deaf children. *American Annals for the Deaf, 134*, 329–332.

Braden, J. P. (1990). Do deaf persons have a characteristic psychometric profile on the Wechsler Performance Scales? *Journal of Psychoeducational Assessment, 8*, 518–526.

Braden, J. P. (1994). *Deafness, deprivation, and IQ.* New York: Plenum Press.

Braden, J. P., & Hannah, J. M. (1998). Assessment of hearing-impaired and deaf children with the WISC-III. In A. Prifitera & D. Saklofske (Eds.), *WISC-III clinical use and interpretation* (pp. 175–201) San Diego, CA: Academic Press.

Braden, J. P., Maller, S. J., & Paquin, M. M. (1993). The effects of residential vs. day placement on hearing-impaired children's performance IQs. *Journal of Special Education, 26*, 423–433.

Camilli, G., & Shepard, L. A. (1994). *Methods for identifying biased test items.* Thousand Oaks, CA: Sage.

Cohen, M., Becker, M. G., & Campbell, R. (1990). Relationships among four methods of assessment of children with attention deficit-hyperactivity disorder. *Journal of School Psychology, 28*, 189–202.

Conrad, R., & Weiskrantz, B. C. (1981). On the cognitive ability of deaf children with deaf parents. *American Annals of the Deaf, 126*, 995–1003.

Crocker, L., & Algina, J. (1986). *Introduction to classical and modern test theory.* Fort Worth, TX: Harcourt.

Drossman, E. R., & Maller, S. J. (2000). [Review of *Comprehensive Test of Nonverbal Intelligence*]. *Journal of Psychoeducational Assessment, 18*, 293–301.

Du Toit, J. M. (1954). Measuring intelligence of deaf children. *American Annals of the Deaf, 99*, 237–251.

Gibbins, S. (1989). The provision of school psychological assessment services for the hearing impaired: A national survey. *Volta Review, 91*, 95–103.

Gorsuch, R. L. (1983). *Factor analysis.* Hillsdale, NJ: Lawrence Erlbaum Associates.

Hambleton, R. K. (1996, April). *Guidelines for adapting educational and psychological tests.* Paper presented at the annual meeting of the National Council on Measurement in Education, New York.

Hammill, D. D., Pearson, N. A., & Wiederholt, J. L. (1997). *Comprehensive Test of Nonverbal Intelligence.* Austin, TX: PRO-ED.

Hirshoren, A., Hurley, O. L., & Kavale, K. (1979). Psychometric characteristics of the WISC-R Performance Scale with deaf children. *Journal of Speech and Hearing Disorders, 44*, 73–79.

Hiskey, M. S. (1966). *The Hiskey-Nebraska Test of Learning Aptitude Manual.* Lincoln, NE: Author.

Hutton, J. B., Dubes, R., & Muir, S. (1992). Assessment practices of school psychologists: Ten years later. *School Psychology Review, 21*, 271–284.

Individuals with Disabilities Education Act of 1997, Pub. L. No. 105–17, § 1400 *et. seq.* (1997).

Jastak, S., & Wilkinson, G.S. (1984). *Wide Range Achievement Test—Revised administration manual.* Wilmington, DE: Jastak Associates.

Jenson, A. R. (1980). *Bias in mental testing.* New York: Free Press.

Joint Committee on Testing Practices (1988). *Code of fair testing practices in education.* Washington, DC: National Council on Measurement in Education.

Joint Committee on the Standards for Educational and Psychological Testing (1999). *Standards for educational and psychological testing.* Washington, DC: American Educational Research Association.

Kamphaus, R. W. (2001). *Clinical assessment of children's intelligence (2nd ed.)*. Boston: Allyn and Bacon.

Kaufman, A., & Kaufman, N. (1983). *Kaufman Assessment Battery for Children*. Circle Pines, MN: American Guidance Service.

Kelly, M., & Braden, J. P. (1990). Criterion validity of the WISC-R Performance Scale with the Stanford Achievement Test-Hearing Impaired Edition *Journal of School Psychology, 28*, 147–151.

Kostrubala, C. E., & Braden, J. P. (1998). *The American Sign Language Translation of the WAIS-III*. San Antonio, TX: The Psychological Corporation.

Kusche, C. A., Greenberg, M. T., & Garfield, T. S. (1983). Nonverbal intelligence and verbal achievement in deaf adolescents: An examination of heredity and environment. *American Annals of the Deaf, 128*, 458–466.

Lavos, G. (1950). The Chicago Non-Verbal Examination. *American Annals of the Deaf, 95*, 379–388.

Lavos, G. (1962). WISC psychometric patterns among deaf children. *Volta Review, 64*, 547–552.

Maller, S. J., (1991, August). *Cognitive assessment of deaf children: Current issues and future trends*. Paper presented at the annual meeting of the American Psychological Association, San Francisco, CA.

Maller, S. J., (1994). *Validity and item bias of the WISC-III with deaf children*. Unpublished doctoral dissertation, University of Arizona, Tucson, AZ.

Maller, S. J. (1996). WISC-III Verbal item invariance across samples of deaf and hearing children of similar measured ability. *Journal of Psychoeducational Assessment 14*, 152–165.

Maller, S. J. (1997). Deafness and WISC-III item difficulty: Invariance and fit. *Journal of School Psychology, 35*, 299–314.

Maller, S. J. (1999, April). *The validity of WISC-III subtest analysis for deaf children*. Paper presented at the annual meeting of the American Educational Research Association, Montreal.

Maller, S. J. (2000). Item invariance in four subtests of the Universal Nonverbal Intelligence Test across groups of deaf and hearing children. *Journal of Psychoeducational Assessment, 18*, 240–254.

Maller, S. J. (2001). Differential item functioning in the WISC-III: Item parameters for boys and girls in the national standardization sample. *Educational and Psychological Measurement, 61*, 793–817.

Maller, S. J., & Braden, J. P. (1993). The construct and criterion-related validity of the WISC-III with deaf adolescents. *Journal of Psychoeducational Assessment, WISC-III Monograph Series*: WISC-III, 105–113.

Maller, S. J., & Ferron, J. (1997). WISC-III factor invariance across deaf and standardization samples. *Educational and Psychological Measurement, 7*, 987–994.

Maller, S. J., & McDermott, P. A. (1997). WAIS-R profile analysis for college students with learning disabilities. *School Psychology Review, 26*, 575–585.

McQuaid, M. F., & Alovisetti, M. (1981). School psychological services for hearing-impaired children in the New York and New England area. *American Annals of the Deaf, 126*, 37–42.

Messick, S. (1989). Validity. In R. L. Linn (Ed.), *Educational measurement* (3rd ed., pp. 13–103). New York: American Council on Education/Macmillan.

Miller, M. S. (1984). Experimental use of signed presentations of the verbal scale of the WISC-R with profoundly deaf children: A preliminary report of the sign selection process and experimental test procedures. In D. S. Martin (Ed.), *International Symposium on Cognition, Education and Deafness, Working Papers, Vol. 1* (pp. 167–185). Washington, DC: Gallaudet University.

Moores, D. F. (1982). *Educating the deaf (2nd ed.)* Boston: Houghton Mifflin.

Moores, D., Kluwin, T., Johnson, R., Cox, P., Blennerhassett, L., Kelly, L., Sweet, C., & Fields, L. (1987). *Factors predictive of literacy in deaf adolescents with deaf parents: Factors predictive of literacy in deaf adolescents in total communication programs (Contract No. NO1-NS-4-2365)*. Washington, DC: National Institute of Neurological and Communicative Disorders and Stroke.

Myklebust, H. R. (1964). *The psychology of deafness: sensory deprivation, learning, and adjustment (2nd ed.)* New York: Grune & Stratton.

Phelps, L., & Branyan, B. J. (1988). Correlations among the Hiskey, K-ABC Nonverbal scale, Leiter, and WISC-R Performance scale with public-school deaf children. *Journal of Psychoeducational Assessment, 6*, 354–358.

Phelps, L., & Branyan, B. J. (1990). Academic achievement and nonverbal intelligence in public school hearing-impaired children. *Psychology in the Schools, 27*, 210–217.

Phelps, L., & Ensor, A. (1987). The comparison of performance by sex of deaf children on the WISC-R. *Psychology in the Schools, 24*, 209–214.

Pintner, R., Eisenson, J., & Stanton, M. (1946). *The psychology of the physically handicapped*. New York: Grune.

Pintner, R., & Paterson, D. G. (1915). The Binet Scale and the deaf child. *Journal of Educational Psychology, 6*, 201–210.

Porter, L. J., & Kirby, E. A. (1986). Effects of two instructional sets on the validity of the Kaufman Assessment Battery for Children Nonverbal Scale with a group of severely hearing impaired children. *Psychology in the Schools*, 23, 37–43.

Raviv, S., Sharan, S., & Strauss, S. (1973). Intellectual development of deaf children in different educational environments. *Journal of Communication Disorders*, 6, 29–36.

Ray, S. (1979). Adapting the WISC-R for deaf children. *Diagnostique*, 7, 147–157.

Ray, S., & Ulissi, S. M. (1982). *An adaptation of the WPPSI for deaf children*. Northridge, CA: Steven Ray Publications.

Reynolds, C. R. (1982). The problem of bias in psychological assessment. In C. R. Reynolds & T. B. Gutkin (Eds.), *The handbook of school psychology* (pp. 178–108). New York: John Wiley.

Roid, G. H., & Miller, L. J. (1997). *Leiter international performance scale—revised*. Wood Dale, IL: Stoelting.

Rosenstein, J. (1961). Perception, cognition and language in deaf children. *Exceptional Children*, 27, 276–284.

Sireci, S. G., Bastari, B., Allalouf, A. (1998, August). *Evaluating construct equivalence across adapted tests*. Paper presented at the annual meeting of the American Psychological Association, San Francisco, CA.

Sisco, F. H., & Anderson, R. J. (1980). Deaf children's performance on the WISC-R relative to hearing status of parents and child-rearing experiences. *American Annals of the Deaf*, 125, 923–030.

Slate, J. R., & Fawcett, J. (1996). Gender differences in Wechsler performance scores of school-age children who are deaf or hard of hearing. *American Annals of the Deaf*, 141, 19–23.

Stinnett, T. A., Havey, J. M., & Oehler-Stinnett, J. (1994). Current test usage by practicing psychologists: A national survey. *Journal of Psychoeducational Assessment*, 12, 331–350.

Sullivan, P. M., & Burley, S. K. (1990). Mental testing of the hearing impaired child. In C.R. Reynolds & R.W. Kamphaus (Eds.), *Handbook of psychological and educational assessment of children* (pp. 761–788). New York: Guilford.

Sullivan, P. M., & Montoya, L. A. (1997). Factor analysis of the WISC-III with deaf and hard-of-hearing children. *Psychological Assessment*, 9, 317–321.

Sullivan, P. M., & Schulte, L. E. (1992). Factor analysis of the WISC-R with deaf and hard-of-hearing children. *Psychological Assessment*, 4, 537–540.

Sullivan, P. M., & Vernon, M. (1979). Psychological assessment of hearing impaired children. *School Psychology Digest*, 8, 271–290.

Thurlow, M. L., Ysseldyke, J. E., & Silverstein, B. (1995). Testing accommodations for students with disabilities. *Remedial and Special Education*, 16, 260–270.

Ulissi, S. M., Brice, P. J., & Gibbins, S. (1989). Use of the Kaufman-Assessment Battery for Children with the hearing impaired. *American Annals of the Deaf*, 134, 283–287.

Velicer, W. F., & Fava, J. L. (1998). Effects of variable and subject sampling on factor pattern recovery. *Psychological Methods*, 3, 231–251.

Vernon, M. (1967). Relationship of language to the thinking process. *Archives of Genetic Psychiatry*, 16, 325–333.

Vernon, M. (1976). Psychological evaluation of hearing impaired children. In L. Lloyd (Ed.), *Communication assessment and intervention strategies*. Baltimore, MD: University Park Press.

Vernon, M., & Brown, D. W. (1964). A guide to psychological tests and testing procedures in the evaluation of deaf and hard-of-hearing children. *Journal of Speech and Hearing Disorders*, 29, 414–423.

Vonderhaar, W. F., & Chambers, J. F. (1975). An examination of deaf students' Wechsler Performance subtest scores. *American Annals of the Deaf*, 120, 540–543.

Watson, B., Sullivan, P., Moeller, M. P., & Jensen, J. (1982). The relationship of performance on non-verbal intelligence test and English language ability in prelingually deaf children. *Journal of Speech and Hearing Disorders*, 47, 199–203.

Wechsler, D. (1974). *The Wechsler Intelligence Scale for Children-Revised*. New York: The Psychological Corporation.

Wechsler, D. (1981). *Manual for the Wechsler Adult Intelligence Scale-Revised*. New York: The Psychological Corporation.

Wechsler, D. (1991). *Wechsler Intelligence Scale for Children-Third Edition*. San Antonio, TX: The Psychological Corporation.

Marc Marschark

Cognitive Functioning in Deaf Adults and Children

Research on cognitive functioning in deaf individuals, like more specific topics such as intelligence (see Maller, this volume) or social functioning (see Antia & Kreimeyer, this volume), could seem like a slippery slope within the field of deaf studies. That is, such research might be seen by some as having an outmoded or even sinister agenda (e.g., Lane, 1992). Recent studies, however, have obtained findings of significant theoretical and practical importance for parents and educators of deaf children and others who seek to discover how hearing loss and the use of a visuospatial language might influence social, language, and cognitive functioning. Not only has this work led to a more objective understanding of deaf individuals and signed languages, but they offer great hope for improving deaf education.

The interpretation of findings from such research is influenced by the orientation of the investigator (and the observer), the context in which the research is designed and carried out, and the *zeitgeist*, or the spirit of the times, in which it is conducted. Insofar as the last of these will influence the other two, it is worth considering some profound changes that have occurred in the area. Then, cognitive research involving deaf individuals can be considered in detail.

Historical Perspectives on Cognitive Research with Deaf Individuals

I. King Jordan, a psychologist and later president of Gallaudet University, once told graduating students that "deaf people can do anything except hear." As a statement of the "new attitude" among Deaf individuals and Deaf communities (see Woll & Ladd, this volume) and as an affirming and motivational message for young deaf people, Jordan's statement was an important and in some ways a revolutionary one. Yet, pointing out that deaf people can be every bit as competent as hearing people should not be taken as equivalent to the claim that deaf individuals necessarily think, learn, or behave exactly like hearing peers. Beyond the normal heterogeneity seen in the hearing population, differences in the environments and experiences of deaf children and hearing children might lead to different approaches to learning, to knowledge organized in different ways, and to different levels of skill in various domains. Ignoring this possibility not only denies the reality of growing up deaf in a largely hearing world, but jeopardizes academic and future vocational opportunities for deaf children (Marschark, Lang, & Albertini, 2002).

Four Approaches to Studying Cognition in Deaf Individuals

The Deaf as Inferior

Moores (1996) described three historical stages of investigation of cognition among deaf individuals. The first, which he termed "the deaf as inferior," was depicted as largely a consequence of the work of Rudolph Pintner and his colleagues, early in the twentieth century, showing apparent deficits in deaf children relative to hearing children. Pintner and Patterson (1917) had shown that deaf individuals, aged 7 years through adulthood, had shorter memory spans than hearing age-mates. Although Moores appears to dismiss those findings, the Pintner and Patterson results are particularly timely and important today in the context of research with deaf and hearing individuals concerning linguistic and visuospatial aspects of working memory (Rönnberg, this volume). Far from being an atypical finding, Pintner and Patterson's results are remarkably robust (e.g., Krakow & Hanson, 1985; Lichtenstein, 1998; MacSweeney, Campbell, & Donlan, 1996).

Pintner and Patterson (1917) also found that deaf individuals raised in "oral" environments had memory spans for digits longer than those raised in "manual" environments. That finding fits well with recent research, described below, showing that deaf students with better speech skills rely primarily on speech coding in memory tasks and also remember more than peers with low to moderate speech coding abilities, who tend to use both speech and sign strategies (Campbell & Wright, 1990; Lichtenstein, 1998; Marschark, 1996, cited in Marschark & Mayer, 1998). Pintner and Patterson's claim that deaf individuals are retarded cognitively relative to hearing peers grates on twenty-first-century nerves, but looking at performance in domains such as reading and mathematics (e.g., Traxler, 2000), one can still see the lags they observed decades ago. Further, while the generality of their conclusion was overstated, it fit well with the *zeitgeist*, one in which language reigned supreme and oralism had come to dominate deaf education (see Lang, this volume; Woll & Ladd, this volume). It is important to note that Pintner's studies were conducted almost half a century before it was recognized that American Sign Language (ASL) and other signed languages are true languages, and thus deaf people were seen to be cognitively functioning without the benefit of any fluent language.

The Deaf as Concrete

Moores (1996) referred to the second stage of cognitive research involving deaf individuals as "the deaf as concrete," a notion that he lays at the feet of Myklebust (1964). Myklebust argued that a lack of hearing would change the entire psychological makeup of an individual, a position supported by research in a variety of domains and well-documented by several chapters in this volume. In Myklebust's view, such changes were almost always negative, leading, for example, to older deaf children functioning in a manner similar to that observed by Piaget as characteristic of younger, pre-operational and concrete-operational children (e.g., Furth, 1964, 1966; Furth & Milgram, 1965; Oléron, 1953). Research in the 1960s and 1970s showing deaf children's lack of understanding for figurative language appeared to confirm their characterization as concrete and literal thinkers (e.g., Blackwell, Engen, Fischgrund, & Zarcadoolas, 1978; Boatner & Gates, 1969).

More recently, deaf children's difficulties with nonliteral language have been shown largely due to the fact that most relevant research involved comprehension of printed language, and we now know that they produce just as much figurative language in sign language as hearing peers do in spoken language (see Marschark, 2005). While deaf people are no longer seen as being less capable of abstract thought than hearing people, educators continue to struggle with deaf children's academic difficulties and their tendencies to behave in apparently concrete ways in various problem solving, academic, and social situations.

The Deaf as Intellectually Normal

The stage Moores (1996) refers to as "the deaf as intellectually normal" largely began with a series of studies by Vernon. In perhaps the best known article in the series, Vernon (1968) reviewed prior studies on intelligence in deaf children and found that they did "remarkably well" relative to hearing peers, given the impoverished language environments of most deaf children and their relatively high incidence of multiple disabilities (now recognized as around 40%; see Karchmer & Mitchell, this volume; Knoors & Vervloed, this volume).

The year 1967 also saw the establishment of

cognitive psychology as a field of study (Neisser, 1967). The work of Vernon and a host of investigators more interested in specific cognitive functions than deafness per se created a new understanding of cognitive functioning in deaf people. Rather than seeing them as lacking something, research turned to better understanding the influences of deaf children's early language and social experiences on development and on task-specific behaviors. It is that work, on perception, mental representation, memory, and problem solving, that is the focus of the remainder of this chapter. As a means to put the research into a contemporary perspective, however, consider one more perspective on cognition among deaf individuals.

Different Does Not Mean Deficient

Tharpe, Ashmead, and Rothpletz (2002) offered a perspective on deaf individuals similar to that of Mykelbust (1964):

> Interaction and integration of input from the various senses are normal aspects of the development process. As a result, it is expected that impairment of one sensory system influences the organization and functioning of the remaining senses. Two primary hypotheses exist regarding the effect of sensory impairment. The deficiency hypothesis states that impairment in one sensory system adversely affects the others as a consequence of the interdependence of all sensory systems. In contrast, the compensation hypothesis proposes that superior abilities may develop in one or more sensory systems as a compensatory response to impairment in one of the others. (Tharpe et al., p. 403)

Although perhaps more balanced than Myklebust in their perspective, Tharpe et al. asserted that the consequences of deafness must be either positive or negative. Amidst findings of differences in deaf and hearing individuals' performance across several cognitive domains, however, there are few results that indicate hearing loss per se as a causal factor. Rather, most results suggest that the two groups simply vary in their approaches to cognitive tasks, are influenced by the primary mode of communication (speech versus sign), and differ in their amounts of relevant knowledge (including strategic knowledge; Bebko, 1998; Bebko & Metcalfe-Haggert, 1997). This general view, that "different does not mean deficient," argues for research ex-

amining such variability within the deaf population and between deaf and hearing populations as a means of better understanding cognitive processes in deaf individuals and optimizing early experiences of deaf children. Work of this sort has expanded our understanding of language and cognition (Emmorey, this volume; Rönnberg, this volume), in general, and specifically with regard to educating deaf students (Marschark et al., 2002).

Recognizing that many of the studies cited below yielded results that could be interpreted as indicating that deaf individuals have advantages or disadvantages relative to hearing peers, the goal is to put the pieces together in a way that provides both theoretical coherence and directions for research and educational programming.

Attention and Perception

Early experience has significant impact on the development of the nervous system and organization of function within the brain. As indicated by the Tharpe et al. (2002) quotation above, the sensory compensation hypothesis thus suggests that because deaf children lack hearing, they should be particularly adept in the visual domain, and that advantage presumably would increase over time and visual experience. In general, however, there is no overall enhancement of vision, visual perception, or visuospatial processing skills in deaf individuals; indeed, they are more likely to have vision problems than hearing individuals (Parasnis, 1998).

The visual modality is certainly important for deaf individuals, and depending on the specific kind of visuospatial task used, they have been found to perform better, worse, or the same as hearing individuals. For example, deaf adults who use sign language show relatively better performance in some aspects of visual perception relative to both hearing individuals and deaf individuals who use spoken language: the ability to rapidly shift visual attention or scan visual stimuli (Parasnis & Samar, 1985, Rettenback, Diller, & Sireteanu, 1999), visual detection of both motion (Neville & Lawson, 1987a) and sign language (Swisher, 1993) in the periphery, and face recognition (Bellugi et al., 1990).

The finding that deaf adults are able to rapidly shift their visual attention supports the compensation argument of Neville and Lawson (1987a) that auditory deprivation from birth should have a major effect on the development of the visual system. They suggested that because deaf individuals have to devote more attention than hearing individuals to the peripheral visual environment in order to receive orienting signals and simultaneously process language and object information (Harris, 1992; Swisher, 1993), they also should have relatively more cortex devoted to peripheral vision. Neville and Lawson found both behavioral and ERP (reflecting electrical activity in the brain) evidence supporting that prediction.

Studies by Corina, Kritchevsky, and Bellugi (1992) and Parasnis and Samar (1985) also found that deaf college students are better at detecting motion in the visual periphery and show enhanced ability to perceive and remember complex visual signs. Quittner, Smith, Osberger, Mitchell, and Katz (1994), in contrast, found that deaf children, aged 6–13 years, had more difficulty than hearing children in a visual attention task (see also, Smith, Quittner, Osberger, & Miyamoto, 1998, Spencer, 2000. More recently, Tharpe et al. (2002) were unable to replicate that finding using the same methodology but controlling for age and nonverbal intelligence. While this issue is in need of further study, there do not appear to be any studies using other paradigms indicating deaf children or adults to have lesser visual attention skills.

Modes, Codes, and Nodes

It should not be surprising that there are interactions among experience, language, and cognitive development in deaf and hearing children; that is what learning is all about. Considerations of cognitive processes in deaf people therefore must take into account the nature of the material to be processed and its mental representation as well as individual characteristics/experience. Three differences between deaf and hearing individuals are relevant in this regard. One of them relates to the observation that some cognitive processes in deaf individuals who use sign language may differ from those in individuals (hearing or deaf) who rely on spoken language. In fact, most deaf people use both modes of communication, varying across contexts, thus raising a host of interesting challenges for research. A second well-documented difference be-

tween deaf and hearing individuals concerns their dealing with sequential information relative to more simultaneously presented material (e.g., Todman & Seedhouse, 1994), where spoken language appears to confer an advantage in retention of sequential information, even among deaf people. The third dimension to be considered in this respect is what appears to be a difference in relational versus item-specific processing in various cognitive tasks, where deaf children and adults tend more toward the latter, relative to hearing age-mates (e.g., Ottem, 1980). These three dimensions are considered below in the contexts of visual cognition, memory, and problem solving, all of which are involved in formal and informal learning.

Visual Imagery and Visual Cognition

The development of visual attention skills is enhanced by environments rich in stimulation and connections between different sense modalities. Although sound appears to contribute to some aspects of (visual) perceptual and cognitive development (Quittner et al. 1994; Smith et al., 1998; Tharpe et al., 2002), signed communication does, too.

Conlin and Paivio (1975) first showed that the concreteness of words in a list-learning task had comparable effects on memory in deaf and hearing individuals, suggesting that deaf people do not have any generalized advantage in visual imagery skills (cf. Chovan, Waldron, & Rose, 1988). Several investigators nonetheless have demonstrated a link between the use of ASL and enhanced visuospatial abilities in several domains. Emmorey, Kosslyn, and Bellugi (1993) and Emmorey and Kosslyn (1996), for example, found that both deaf and hearing signers were faster in generating mental images than were nonsigning peers. Emmorey et al. (1993) also investigated mental rotation skills in deaf and hearing signers and nonsigners using a two-dimensional, block rotation task. They found that although there was no overall advantage for deaf individuals, both deaf and hearing users of ASL showed faster response times at all orientations (i.e., faster mental rotation; see also Emmorey, Klima, & Hickok, 1998). Chamberlain and Mayberry (1994) further demonstrated that deaf individuals who relied on spoken language did not differ from hearing nonsigners in rotation speed (see also Emmorey, this volume), and Talbot and Haude (1993) showed that level of sign language expertise (but not age of acquisition) affected mental rotation of three-dimensional block figures. But such findings indicate differences between individuals with and without sign language experience, not with and without hearing.

Findings parallel to those in image generation and mental rotation have been found in face recognition. Bettger, Emmorey, McCullough, and Bellugi (1997) found that experience in discriminating facial expressions that have linguistic interpretations enhances performance for discriminating among faces in people who use ASL. They also examined face recognition in 6- to 9-year-old deaf children with deaf parents (early signers) or hearing parents (late signers) and a group of hearing agemates. Bettger et al. found that the deaf children with deaf parents generally scored higher than either of the other two groups, which did not differ. Such advantages typically are not found among deaf children who rely on spoken language (e.g., Parasnis, Samar, Bettger, & Sathe, 1996), and so the results again speak more to the effects of sign language use than deafness per se. This situation contrasts with that found in memory, where the modality of mental representation, experience, and organization of knowledge lead to differences in performance between deaf and hearing individuals.

Memory

Linguists first recognized that signed languages were true languages in the early 1960s (Stokoe, 1960). Until that message reached psychology in the mid- to late 1970s, it was unclear to many investigators and educators how deaf individuals could retain linguistic information without the use of acoustic, articulatory, or phonological memory codes.

Underlying much of the early work in this area was the erroneous assumption that use of nonverbal materials such as objects or pictures in memory tasks guaranteed nonverbal memory coding by deaf (or hearing) individuals (e.g., Blair, 1957; see Marschark, 1993, for a review). Research in the late 1960s, however, found that hearing children and adults tend to label nonlinguistic stimuli, and that those labels influence memory functioning. Campbell and Wright (1990), for example, investigated memory for pictures by deaf children exposed only to spoken language. Consistent with typical findings in immediate serial recall, they obtained word-length effects in memory, as recall was better for pictures for which the spoken names would take less time to pronounce than those with names that would take more time to pronounce. Early conclusions about verbal and nonverbal memory processes in deaf adults and children thus need to be reconsidered in the context of the ways in which memory is influenced by alternative language codes (e.g., ASL versus English), early language and educational experience, and differences in conceptual and world knowledge.

Working Memory

There is now a substantial body of evidence indicating that hearing individuals rely primarily on a temporary, phonologically based memory system for a variety of cognitive tasks, including acquisition of vocabulary, mental arithmetic, and temporary retention of verbal sequences. Patterns of performance on these tasks under various conditions have been interpreted as reflecting the operation of a phonological loop that includes a temporary, speech-based phonological store and a time-limited mental, speech-based rehearsal system (see Baddeley & Logie, 1999).

Complementary studies have pointed to a similar memory system for visual, spatial, and movement-based information variously used in mental imagery tasks, interactions with objects, and movement (Logie, Engelkamp, Dehn, & Rudkin, 2001). While concurrent spoken input and output have been shown to disrupt retention of verbal sequences held in the phonological loop (i.e., articulatory suppression), motoric output disrupts immediate memory for visuospatial material or for movement sequences. These two systems are thought to compose two components of a multiple-component working memory (Baddeley & Logie, 1999; for alternative views, see Miyake & Shah, 1999).

The modality-specific nature of the speech-based and visuospatial systems within working memory has specific implications for the coding of information for short-term retention by both deaf and hearing populations. In remembering short lists of printed stimuli, hearing people and "oral" deaf people rely heavily on speech-based coding (e.g., Conrad, 1964), while deaf people who primarily use sign language have been assumed to rely more heavily on visuospatial processing of information (e.g., Moulton & Beasley, 1975; Wilson & Emmorey, 1997b). The use of only printed materials in most relevant research (and only signed materials in most other studies), however, creates a confound, as many people with congenital or early onset hearing losses depend on sign language rather than on spoken language and tend to have relatively poor reading abilities (Traxler, 2000). Few memory studies have been conducted in which either participants' fluencies in signed and spoken language or the language of presentation has been systematically varied or controlled.

Studies involving both linguistic and nonlinguistic stimuli generally demonstrate that visual and speech-based codes are equally effective for deaf adults and children in memory tasks involving visual presentation of two to five stimuli (i.e., less than memory span limits; see Marschark & Mayer, 1998, for a review). Beyond subspan tasks, deaf adults and children have been found to evidence shorter memory spans and remember less in other short-term memory tasks compared to hearing peers, using a variety of verbal and nonverbal materials (e.g., Blair, 1957; Hanson, 1982, Krakow & Hanson, 1985; Lichtenstein, 1998; Pintner & Patterson, 1917; Waters & Doehring, 1990; Wilson & Emmorey, 1997a, 1997b). The locus of such differences has been unclear, as has the possibility of a link between reliance on alternative working memory codes and observed performance differences in educational domains (Marschark & Harris, 1996; Todman & Seedhouse, 1994).

Speech-based phonological coding appears to be more likely in deaf individuals with lesser hearing losses or those who lost their hearing after acquiring spoken language (Conrad, 1972; Lichtenstein, 1998). Individuals with greater congenital or early onset hearing losses thus would be expected to use sign-based codes in working memory. Consistent with that suggestion, several studies have demonstrated that lists of similar signs tend to disrupt memory performance in individuals who have ASL as their first language (e.g., Hanson, 1982; Krakow & Hanson, 1985; Poizner, Bellugi, & Tweney, 1981; Siple, Caccamise, & Brewer, 1982; Wilson & Emmorey, 1997b).

Krakow and Hanson (1985), for example, examined serial recall for printed, signed, and finger-spelled words by deaf college students who were either native signers (and had deaf parents) or late sign language learners (and had hearing parents) as compared to hearing students' memory for printed words. No differences were found between the two groups of deaf participants, but serial recall for printed words by the deaf participants was significantly lower than that of the hearing participants. Patterns observed in recall indicated that the deaf students used both sign-based and speech-based coding in working memory. Hanson and Lichtenstein (1990) later found that good deaf readers tend to use primarily speech-based codes.

Research of this sort suggests a strong link between phonological or speech-based skills and performance in serial memory tasks (see Musselman, 2000). Consistent with that expectation, Lichtenstein (1998) reported that deaf students with better spoken language skills tended to rely primarily on speech recoding as a strategy in both memory tasks and reading, whereas deaf students with low to moderate speech skills used both speech and sign strategies. He found a high correlation between memory span and memory errors on phonetically similar lists, suggesting that the use of signs relative to speech in working memory might be the cause of observed shorter memory spans in deaf individuals (see similar findings in Hamilton & Holtzman, 1989; Kyle, 1981).

These findings indicate that although at least some deaf individuals use both sign-based and speech-based coding in working memory, speech-based memory codes are more facilitative for serial recall in deaf individuals, just as they are in hearing individuals. Still unclear is the extent to which alternative coding modalities are under strategic control; the way in which coding may differ as a function of the information presented; or whether the use of sign-based coding in working memory is a function of sign language expertise, available to all language users, or whether it is limited to deaf individuals.

Most of the studies described above have been interpreted as indicating that speech-based and sign-based memory codes have somewhat different characteristics and depend on qualitatively different processing systems. Studies by MacSweeney et al. (1996), Marschark (1996), and Wilson and Emmorey (1997a), however, offer the possibility that these results could be explained by a phonological loop that is not as modality limited as has been assumed but is involved in retention of both spoken and signed words.

Marschark (1996), for example, conducted two memory span experiments in which hearing adults showed significantly longer digit spans (i.e., memory for sequences of digits) than deaf peers. In addition, their memories were reduced by an oral articulatory suppression task but not by a manual suppression task. The deaf participants, in contrast, were adversely affected by both interference tasks. Articulation times were longer for the signed than spoken digits (as determined in a separate task), however, and dividing individuals' digit spans by their average digit production times, revealed that there was no difference in the "lengths" of their phonological loops (Wilson & Emmorey, 1998). Thus, deaf and hearing people appear to have essentially the same working memory capacity; but because digit production is faster in speech than in sign, hearing or deaf individuals who use speech-based coding can fit more information into their time-limited articulatory loops than deaf individuals who use sign-based coding (see Ellis & Hennelley, 1980). Consistent with that conclusion, Marschark found that among deaf students, sign language skill was strongly and inversely related to memory span in the no-interference and manual interference conditions, whereas speech skill was strongly and positively related to memory in both conditions.

MacSweeney et al. (1996) similarly found that both two-handed sign production and a simple hand-tapping task reduced memory span for pictures in deaf 11- to 15-year-olds who normally used simultaneous communication. The students also showed effects of phonological coding, indicating that they had available multiple coding strategies for memory. Chincotta and Chincotta (1996), in contrast, did not find oral or tapping interference for Chinese children exposed primarily to spoken language, although oral suppression interfered with memory in hearing children. Deaf children showed lower recall than hearing children in all conditions, and it may be that they had no consistent strategies for short-term memory coding.

Wilson and Emmorey (1997a) examined serial recall for lists of similar and dissimilar signs among deaf signers. They found independent interference from sign similarity and manual suppression, suggesting disruption of an active manual rehearsal or maintenance system. They concluded that the rehearsal loop of fluent signers is like that of fluent speakers in having a buffer that retains information based on the phonological structure of the language and an active rehearsal process involving the (manual) articulators. This conclusion is consistent with findings of Wilson, Bettger, Niculae, and Klima (1997), who found that deaf children of deaf parents performed equally well on span tasks involving a sequence of words that had to be recalled either in forward or backward order. Hearing children showed the usual advantage for forward recall, suggesting that, unlike in spoken language, encoding of serial information in ASL does not entail any directional dominance. The native-signing deaf children also showed better memory than hearing children on a nonlinguistic, visuospatial task involving Corsi blocks (for comparable effects with adults, see Mayberry & Eichen, 1991). Finally, Todman and Cowdy (1993) and Todman and Seedhouse (1994) found that deaf children surpassed hearing peers in short-term memory for complex visual figures, except when the task involved serial presentation of parts of a stimulus and serial (ordered) recall.

The above results suggest that, as in visual perception, mental representation in deaf individuals who are fluent in sign language may have different characteristics from individuals who rely on spoken language. Depending on the nature of the task, the materials to be remembered, and the cognitive functions used, those differences can lead to deaf individuals having better, equal, or worse memory than hearing individuals. Although deaf individuals do not appear to use visual imagery in place of verbal codes in memory, native deaf signers are able to use spatial coding in the retention of serial information in a way that deaf and hearing nonsigners cannot (Mayberry & Eichen, 1991; Wilson et al., 1997).

Semantic Memory

Long-term or semantic memory influences learning and essentially all aspects of human behavior. Whether acquired through implicit or explicit learning, information in memory normally is retrieved spontaneously and effortlessly, as needed, even if it is conscious attempts at memory retrieval that are most intuitively obvious. In general, organization of knowledge in memory is assumed to be roughly the same for most individuals, although people who are more knowledgeable in any particular area (e.g., mathematics, wine, chess) may have qualitatively different strategies for coding and retrieval as well as more content knowledge. With regard to deaf and hearing individuals, however, there may be significant differences in both the amount and organization of knowledge in semantic memory. As noted earlier, those differences would arise from the early experiences and education of deaf and hearing children and the greater heterogeneity of deaf individuals, as a group, relative to hearing peers.

Few studies have examined the link between the memory performance of deaf individuals and the breadth and organization of their conceptual knowledge, and none has explicitly examined the way in which those differences affect academic performance. Several studies conducted through the 1970s found only small differences in semantic memory for highly familiar stimuli between deaf and hearing children. Both populations viewed familiar objects in similar ways, as reflected in the way that they would sort the objects into groups and cluster semantically similar items in recall of words or pictures in lists. Deaf students tended not to use that conceptual or taxonomic information in recall, however, and typically remembered less than hearing peers, even when they did (see Marschark & Mayer, 1998).

McEvoy, Marschark, and Nelson (1999) explicitly examined the organization of conceptual knowledge in deaf and hearing college students. Using a single-word association task, they found high overlap ($r = .77$) in responses from the two groups. At the same time, differences on several dimensions indicated that hearing students had greater coherence and consistency in conceptual organization, whereas deaf students had smaller and less well-defined sets of associations. Marschark, Convertino, McEvoy, and Masteller (2002) extended that study with three experiments. In one, they found that differences in vocabulary knowledge led to significant differences in the kinds of associative responses given. In a second, using a similar paradigm but with category names and category members (exemplars) as stimuli, high overlap was again observed as deaf students produced the same primary associates as hearing peers for 82% of the stimuli ($r = .64$ overall). More interesting for the present purposes was the finding of asymmetric patterns of responding, as hearing students were

equally likely to respond to a category exemplar with a category name as the reverse. Deaf students, in contrast, were significantly more likely to respond to an exemplar with a category name than the reverse, and they were significantly less likely than hearing peers to respond to a category name with an exemplar. These findings provided further evidence that deaf students tend to have less strongly interconnected, less readily available, and more "fuzzy" word meanings than hearing peers. Such results are consistent with research showing that deaf students are familiar with semantic categories and can produce category exemplars when asked but are less likely than hearing students to use such knowledge spontaneously (e.g., Liben, 1979).

What little evidence is available thus suggests that, despite marked similarities in the knowledge organizations of deaf and hearing individuals, there are consistent differences that can influence academic and other cognitive performance. Indeed, the finding of such differences in knowledge organization clarifies results from earlier problem-solving studies that were interpreted as indicating deficits in the cognitive abilities of deaf children and adults. At issue, then, is how such differences affect performance in various tasks beyond explicit memory tests.

Problem Solving

Research involving problem solving among deaf adults and children has followed the paradigmatic trends in developmental and cognitive psychology at large. In the 1950s and 1960s, for example, Furth, Oléron, and others conducted a variety of studies that examined the acquisition of simple single- or multidimensional nonverbal concepts. Other studies involved classic Piagetian conservation tasks or classification tasks in the North American verbal learning tradition (see Marschark, 1993, for a review). Ways in which early experience and language skills affected performance were rarely considered, if only because spoken language skills were seen to be poor; sign language skills were not recognized at all.

Sharpe (1985), for example, examined the solving of analogy problems (A is to B as C is to X?) by deaf and hearing 14- to 19-year-olds. Analogies were presented in both word and picture form;

hearing students significantly outscored their deaf peers on both tasks. Although Sharpe interpreted the results as indicating the superiority of spoken language for cognitive processing, the signed and spoken language skills of deaf participants were not evaluated. Sharpe's study also lacked a comparison of deaf students who used spoken language but still might have had less language fluency than their hearing peers. As a result, Sharpe's findings do not speak to the relative utility of signed or spoken language in such tasks. Also using an analogies task, Marschark et al. (2002) found that hearing college students successfully solved more verbal analogies than deaf students. Among hearing students, performance reflected the active application of conceptual knowledge (i.e., as indicated by patterns of associative responses). Deaf students' performance showed no such relation, although their performance was strongly related to their English reading skills.

Marschark and Everhart (1999) used a form of the 20 questions game to examine problem-solving skills of deaf and hearing students aged 7 years to college age. Each participant saw a matrix of 42 colored pictures that included items in different taxonomic categories (e.g., animals), functional categories (e.g., tools), and perceptual categories (e.g., red items). The object of the game was to discover which picture the experimenter had selected, asking 20 or fewer yes no questions. Hearing students were more likely than deaf age-mates to solve the game at all ages, although the difference was not significant among college students. Hearing participants also asked significantly more efficient questions (i.e., questions that eliminated more alternative answers). Such constraint questions (e.g., "is it round?") depend on recognizing the categories inherent in the matrix and on using taxonomic or ad hoc category knowledge to help narrow the search for the target. Analyses of transcribed protocols, however, showed that the deaf students did not apply any consistent strategies, again reflecting the heterogeneity of their conceptual knowledge and its application (McEvoy et al., 1999; Strassman, 1997).

The finding that deaf children rarely asked constraint questions in the 20 questions game led Marschark and Everhart to conclude that they were less likely than hearing peers to use category information in problem solving. The McEvoy et al. (1999) and Marschark et al. (2002) findings, however, indicated that deaf students do not have any particular difficulty in automatically activating categorical information in response to exemplars. On the basis of the latter study, it seems more likely that children in the 20 questions task recognized the categories subsuming the pictures in the matrix but did not appreciate the utility of using category members as a way to reduce the potential response set (Liben, 1979). Even then, Marschark and Everhart found that deaf students who had experience with the 20 questions game performed just as well as the hearing students, emphasizing the role of experience in both the organization and use of knowledge in semantic memory.

Relational and Individual-Item Processing

Beyond possible differences in content knowledge per se, deaf and hearing individuals appear to differ in the information processing strategies used in problem-solving tasks as well as memory tasks. Ottem (1980) reviewed over 50 earlier studies involving various kinds of problem solving and found that when tasks involved only a single dimension (e.g., number or color), deaf adults and children usually performed comparably to hearing age-mates. When a task required simultaneous attention to two or more dimensions (for example, the height of water in a container and the shape of the container), the performance of hearing individuals usually surpassed that of their deaf peers. Such findings reflect differing orientations toward relational versus individual item processing, a dimension shown to affect performance in a variety of cognitive tasks (e.g., Huffman & Marschark, 1995). Most likely a result of early educational experiences (Marschark et al., 2002), many deaf individuals appear to tend to item-specific processing, rather than to relations among items. Results from two experiments involving deaf children's reading (literally and metaphorically a problem-solving situation for them) provide additional evidence in this regard.

Banks, Gray, and Fyfe (1990) had children read passages appropriate for their reading levels and then tested them for recall of passage content. Deaf and hearing children recalled equal amounts of text, but, in contrast to the hearing children, deaf children's recall tended to be composed of disjointed parts rather than whole idea units. This finding also held when the stories were signed rather than printed, indicating that it was not solely a consequence of reading difficulties or a lag in the development of reading skills.

Marschark, DeBeni, Polazzo, and Cornoldi (1993) obtained similar findings in a reading study involving deaf adolescents and hearing students matched either for age or reading ability. Students read reading-level appropriate passages and then were asked to recall them. Recall protocols were scored for the number of relational units or individual words recalled. Overall, the deaf adolescents recalled significantly less than their hearing age-mates, but more than the younger (8–9 years of age) reading-matched children. Consistent with the Banks et al. (1990) findings, deaf students remembered proportionately fewer relations than words. Because the reverse was true for both groups of hearing students, the effect cannot be ascribed to differences in reading abilities per se. It is the relations among words, phrases, and idea units that underlie text comprehension, and the item-specific processing strategies apparently used by deaf students in other domains appear to be used (somewhat unsuccessfully) in reading as well. Richardson, McLeod-Gallinger, McKee, and Long (1999) recently obtained convergent results in an investigation of the study habits of deaf and hearing college students. Although the two groups reported remarkably similar strategies in the way they studied written materials, deaf students reported significantly more difficulty than hearing students in integrating ideas across materials.

Taken together, these results suggest that deaf individuals, at least in some contexts, are less likely than hearing peers to attend to or to recognize relational information. Such findings are consistent with earlier studies demonstrating their similar performance on problem-solving and memory tasks involving only a single relevant dimension, while hearing individuals performed better than deaf individuals when two dimensions (and a relation between them) had to be considered simultaneously. An item-specific orientation in information processing also is likely to affect performance in other academic domains, such as mathematics, science, and even history, where multiple factors must be considered in order to understand the causes and effects of events.

Summary and Conclusions

Politics and presumption aside, almost 100 years of research involving cognition and memory among deaf and hearing individuals consistently shows both similarities and differences in their performance. In working memory tasks, recent evidence has indicated that earlier claims that deaf individuals had smaller memory capacities than hearing individuals derived from lack of theoretical understanding about the nature of memory and confounds due to language use. Although the rate of information exchange in signed and spoken languages is the same, individual signs take longer to produce than individual words and thus take up more "space" in the limited-capacity, phonological working memory system. Deaf individuals who use sign language for coding in such tasks thus may show shorter memory spans than either hearing individuals or deaf individuals who use speech-based coding. Similar variation can be seen among spoken languages when words take more or less time to produce (e.g., Welsh versus English; Ellis & Hennelley, 1980). Those results therefore reflect differences in cognition, with implications for performance in various tasks, but they do not indicate any kind of memory deficit.

In both short-term and long-term retention, deaf individuals often remember less than hearing individuals, even when pretests indicate similar knowledge of the materials. Such findings could reflect less efficient retrieval strategies, less reliance on relations among concepts, or lower strength in associative connections which, in turn, influence the reliability of recall. Any of these alternatives would be consistent with previous findings in the literature, and it will require further research to determine which (if any) are the locus of the robust memory differences and in whom, under what circumstances. Meanwhile, deaf individuals show an advantage relative to hearing peers in several domains of visuospatial processing, but primarily as a function of their experience using a signed language. Hearing people show similar benefits accruing to sign language use, and there is not yet any indication that deaf individuals benefit from any form of sensory compensation other than, perhaps, increased attention to the visual periphery (see Swisher, 1993). Even in this area, however, there is some evidence that hearing individuals raised in a signing environment (i.e., with deaf parents), show similar benefits (Neville & Lawson, 1987b).

The above differences among deaf individuals and between deaf and hearing individuals are no doubt at play in a variety of learning and problem-solving situations, from categorization to social skills, and from reading to mathematics. There is considerable evidence that deaf children have specific difficulties in both of the latter areas, but it is still unclear to what extent they may be attributable to causes of a more generic, cognitive nature rather than being task specific. Certainly, differences observed between deaf and hearing students in the breadth and depth of their conceptual knowledge have implications far beyond any particular task or setting. By more fully understanding how language modality and experience influence learning and cognitive strategies, we can both clarify the theoretical nature of these processes and contribute to enhancing academic opportunities for deaf children.

References

Baddeley, A.D., & Logie, R.H. (1999). Working memory: The multiple component model. In A. Miyake & P. Shah (Eds.), *Models of working memory* (pp. 28–61). New York: Cambridge University Press.

Banks, J., Gray, C., & Fyfe, R. (1990). The written recall of printed stories by severely deaf children. *British Journal of Educational Psychology, 60,* 192–206.

Bebko, J. (1998). Learning, language, memory, and reading: The role of language automatization and its impact on complex cognitive activities. *Journal of Deaf Studies and Deaf Education, 3,* 4–14.

Bebko, J.M., & Metcalfe-Haggert, A. (1997). Deafness, language skills, and rehearsal: A model for the development of a memory strategy. *Journal of Deaf Studies and Deaf Education, 2,* 133–141.

Bellugi, U., O'Grady, L., Lillo-Martin, D., O'Grady, M., van Hoek, K., & Corina, D. (1990). Enhancement of spatial cognition in deaf children. In V. Volterra and C. J. Erting (Eds.), *From gesture to language in hearing and deaf children* (pp. 278–298). New York: Springer-Verlag.

Bettger, J.G., Emmorey, K., McCullough, S.H., & Bellugi, U. (1997). Enhanced facial discrimination: Effects of experience with American Sign Language. *Journal of Deaf Studies and Deaf Education, 2,* 223–233.

Blackwell, P., Engen, E., Fischgrund, J., & Zarcadoo-las, C. (1978). *Sentences and other systems: A language and learning curriculum for hearing-impaired children.* Washington, DC: National Association of the Deaf.

Blair, F.X. (1957). A study of the visual memory of deaf and hearing children. *American Annals of the Deaf, 102,* 254–263.

Boatner, M.T., & Gates, J.E. (1969). *A dictionary of idioms for the deaf.* Washington, DC: National Association for the Deaf.

Campbell, R., & Wright, H. (1990). Deafness and immediate memory for pictures: Dissociation between "inner speech" and "inner ear." *Journal of Experimental Child Psychology, 50,* 259–286.

Chamberlain, C., & Mayberry, R.I. (1994, May). Do the deaf "see" better? Effects of deafness on visuospatial skills. Poster presented at TENNET V meetings, Montreal.

Chincotta, M., & Chincotta, D. (1996). Digit span, articulatory suppression, and the deaf: A study of the Hong Kong Chinese. *American Annals of the Deaf, 141,* 252–257.

Chovan, J.D., Waldron, M.B., & Rose, S. (1988). Response latency measurements to visual cognitive tasks by normal hearing and deaf subjects. *Perceptual and Motor Skills, 67,* 179–184.

Conlin, D., & Paivio (1975). The associative learning of the deaf: The effects of word imagery and signability. *Memory and Cognition, 3,* 333–340.

Conrad, R. (1964). Acoustic confusions in immediate memory. *British Journal of Psychology, 55,* 75–84.

Conrad, R. (1972). Short-term memory in the deaf: A test for speech coding. *British Journal of Psychology, 63,* 173–180.

Corina, D.P., Kritchevsky, M., & Bellugi, U. (1992). Linguistic permeability of unilateral neglect: Evidence from American Sign Language. In *Proceedings of the Cognitive Science Conference* (pp. 384–389). Hillsdale, NJ: Lawrence Erlbaum Associates.

Ellis, N.C., & Hennelley, R.A. (1980). A bilingual word-length effect: Implications for intelligence testing and the relative ease of mental calculation in Welsh and English. *British Journal of Psychology, 50,* 449–458.

Emmorey, K., Klima, E.S., & Hickok, G. (1998). Mental rotation within linguistic and nonlinguistic domaines in users of American Sign Language. *Cognition, 68,* 2221–226.

Emmorey, K., & Kosslyn, S., (1996). Enhanced image generation abilities in deaf signers: A right hemisphere effect. *Brain and Cognition, 32,* 28–44.

Emmorey, K., & Kosslyn, S., & Bellugi, U. (1993). Visual imagery and visual-spatial language: Enhanced imagery abilities in deaf and hearing ASL signers. *Cognition, 46,* 139–181.

Furth, H.G. (1964). Research with the deaf: Implications for language and cognition. *Psychological Bulletin, 62*, 145–164.

Furth, H.G. (1966). *Thinking without language.* New York: Free Press.

Furth, H.G., & Milgram, N. (1965). The influence of language on classification: Normal, retarded, and deaf. *Genetic Psychology Monograph, 72*, 317–351.

Hamilton, H., & Holtzman, T.G. (1989). Linguistic encoding in short-term memory as a function of stimulus type. *Memory & Cognition, 17*, 541–550.

Hanson, V. (1982). Short-term recall by deaf signers of American sign language: Implications of encoding strategy for order recall. *Journal of Experimental Psychology: Learning, Memory, and Cognition, 8*, 572–583.

Hanson, V.L., & Lichtenstein, E.H. (1990). Short-term memory coding by deaf signers: The primary language coding hypothesis reconsidered. *Cognitive Psychology, 22*, 211–224.

Harris, M. (1992). *Language experience and early language development: From input to uptake.* Hove, UK: Lawrence Erlbaum Associates.

Huffman, C.J., & Marschark, M. (1995). Influences of relational and item-specific processing on the magnitude of concreteness effects. *European Journal of Cognitive Psychology, 7*, 169–182.

Krakow, R.A., & Hanson, V.L. (1985). Deaf signers and serial recall in the visual modality: Memory for signs, fingerspelling, and print. *Memory & Cognition, 13*, 265–272.

Kyle, J.G. (1981), Signs and memory: The search for the code. In B. Woll, J. Kyle, & M. Deuchar (Eds.), *Perspectives on British Sign Language and deafness* (pp. 71–88). London: Croom Helm.

Lane, H. (1992). *The mask of benevolence.* New York: Knopf.

Liben, L.S. (1979). Free recall by deaf and hearing children: Semantic clustering and recall in trained and untrained groups. *Journal of Experimental Child Psychology, 27*, 105–119.

Lichtenstein, E. (1998). The relationships between reading processes and English skills of deaf college students. *Journal of Deaf Studies and Deaf Education, 3*, 80–134.

Logie, R.H., Engelkamp, J., Dehn, D. & Rudkin, S. (2001). Actions, mental actions, and working memory. In M. Denis, R.H. Logie, C. Cornoldi, J. Engelkamp, & M. De Vega (Eds.), *Imagery, language and visuo-spatial thinking.* (pp. 161–183). Hove, UK: Psychology Press.

MacSweeney, M., Campbell, R., & Donlan, C. (1996). Varieties of short-term memory coding in deaf teenagers. *Journal of Deaf Studies and Deaf Education, 1*, 249–262.

Marschark, M. (1993). *Psychological development of deaf children.* New York: Oxford University Press.

Marschark, M. (1996, November). *Influences of signed and spoken language on memory span.* Paper presented at annual meetings of the Psychonomic Society, Chicago.

Marschark, M. (2005). Metaphor in sign language and sign language users: A window into relations of language and thought. In H. Colston & A.N. Katz (Eds.) *Figurative language comprehension: Social and cultural influences* (pp. 309–334). Mahwah, NJ: Lawrence Erlbaum Associates.

Marschark, M., Convertino, C., McEvoy, C., & Masteller, A. (2002). *Organization and use of the mental lexicon in deaf and hearing individuals.* Manuscript submitted for publication.

Marschark, M., DeBeni, R., Polazzo, M. G., & Cornoldi, C. (1993). Deaf and hearing-impaired adolescents' memory for concrete and abstract prose: Effects of relational and distinctive information. *American Annals of the Deaf, 138*, 31–39.

Marschark, M., & Everhart, V S. (1999). Problem solving by deaf and hearing children: Twenty questions. *Deafness and Education International, 1*, 63–79.

Marschark, M., & Harris, M. (1996). Success and failure in learning to read: The special case (?) of deaf children. In C. Cornoldi & J. Oakhill (Eds.), *Reading comprehension disabilities: Processes and intervention* (pp. 279–300). Hillsdale, NJ: Lawrence Erlbaum Associates.

Marschark, M., Lang, H.G., & Albertini, J.A. (2002). *Educating deaf students: From research to practice.* New York: Oxford University Press.

Marschark, M., & Mayer, T. (1998). Mental representation and memory in deaf adults and children. In M. Marschark & M. D. Clark, (Eds.), *Psychological perspectives on deafness, Vol. 2* (pp. 53–77). Mahwah, NJ: Lawrence Erlbaum Associates.

Mayberry, R.I., & Eichen, F. B. (1991). The long-lasting advantage of learning sign language in childhood: Another look at the critical period for language acquisition. *Journal of Memory and Language, 30*, 486–512.

McEvoy, C., Marschark, M., & Nelson, D. L. (1999). Comparing the mental lexicons of deaf and hearing individuals. *Journal of Educational Psychology, 91*, 1–9.

Miyake, A., & Shah, P. (1999). *Models of working memory: Mechanisms of active maintenance and executive control.* New York: Cambridge University Press.

Moores, D.F. (1996). *Educating the deaf: Psychology, principles, and practices.* Boston: Houghton Mifflin.

Moulton, R.D., & Beasley, D.S. (1975). Verbal coding strategies used by hearing-impaired individuals.

Journal of Speech and Hearing Research, 18, 559–570.

Musselman, C. (2000). How do children who can't hear learn to read an alphabetic script? A review of the literature on reading and deafness. *Journal of Deaf Studies and Deaf Education, 5,* 9–31.

Myklebust, H.E. (1964). *The psychology of deafness, 2nd ed.* New York: Grune & Stratton.

Neisser, U. (1967). *Cognitive psychology.* New York: Appleton-Century-Crofts.

Neville, H.J., & Lawson, D. (1987a). Attention to central and peripheral visual space in a movement detection task: an event-related potential and behavioral study. II. Congenitally deaf adults. *Brain Research, 405,* 268–283.

Neville, H. J., & Lawson, D. (1987b). Attention to central and peripheral visual space in a movement detection task: An event-related potential and behavioral study: III. Separate effects of auditory deprivation and acquisition of a visual language. *Brain Research, 405,* 284–294.

Oléron, P. (1953). Conceptual thinking of the deaf. *American Annals of the Deaf, 98,* 304–310.

Ottem, E. (1980). An analysis of cognitive studies with deaf subjects. *American Annals of the Deaf, 125,* 564–575.

Parasnis, I. (1998). Cognitive diversity in deaf people: Implications for communication and education. *Scandinavian Journal of Audiology, 27* (Suppl. 49), 109–114.

Parasnis, I., & Samar, V.J. (1985). Parafoveal attention in congenitally deaf and hearing young adults. *Brain and Cognition, 4,* 313–327.

Parasnis, I., Samar, V.J., Bettger, J.G., & Sathe, K. (1996). Does deafness lead to enhancement of visual spatial cognition in children? Negative evidence from deaf nonsigners. *Journal of Deaf Studies and Deaf Education, 1,* 145–152.

Pintner, R., & Patterson, D. (1917). A comparison of deaf and hearing children in visual memory for digits. *Journal of Experimental Psychology, 2,* 76–88.

Poizner, H., Bellugi, U., & Tweney, R. D. (1981). Processing of formational, semantic and iconic information in American Sign Language. *Journal of Experimental Psychology: Human Perception and Performance, 7,* 1146–1159.

Quittner, A.L., Smith, L.B., Osberger, M.J., Mitchell, T.V., & Katz, D.B. (1994). The impact of audition on the development of visual attention. *Psychological Science, 5,* 347–353.

Rettenback, R., Diller, G., & Sireteneau, R. (1999). Do deaf people see better? Texture segmentation and visual search compensate in adult but not in juvenile subjects. *Journal of Cognitive Neuroscience, 11,* 560–583.

Richardson, J.T.E., McLeod-Gallinger, J., McKee, B.G., & Long, G.L. (1999). Approaches to studying in deaf and hearing students in higher education. *Journal of Deaf Studies and Deaf Education, 5,* 156–173.

Sharpe, S.L. (1985). The primary mode of human communication and complex cognition. *American Annals of the Deaf, 130,* 39–46.

Siple, P., Caccamise, F., & Brewer, L. (1982). Signs as pictures and signs as words: Effect of language knowledge on memory for new vocabulary. *Journal of Experimental Psychology: Learning, Memory, and Cognition, 6,* 619–625.

Smith, L.B., Quittner, A.L., Osberger, J.J., & Miyamoto, R. (1998). Audition and visual attention: The developmental trajectory in deaf and hearing populations. *Developmental Psychology, 34,* 840–850.

Spencer, P.E. (2000). Looking without listening: Is audition a prerequisite for normal development of visual attention during infancy? *Journal of Deaf Studies and Deaf Education, 5,* 291–302.

Stokoe, W. C. (1960). *Sign language structure: An outline of the visual communication system of the American deaf.* Studies in Linguistics, Occasional Papers 8. Buffalo, NY: Department of Anthropology and Linguistics, University of Buffalo.

Strassman, B. (1997). Metacognition and reading in children who are deaf: A review of the research. *Journal of Deaf Studies and Deaf Education, 2,* 140–149.

Swisher, M. V. (1993). Perceptual and cognitive aspects of recognition of signs in peripheral vision. In M. Marschark & M.D. Clark (Eds.), *Psychological perspectives on deafness* (pp. 229–265). Hillsdale, NJ: Lawrence Erlbaum Associates.

Talbot, K.F., & Haude, R.H. (1993). The relationship between sign language skill and spatial visualizations ability: Mental rotation of three-dimensional objects. *Perceptual and Motor Skills, 77,* 1387–1391.

Tharpe, A., Ashmead, D., & Rothpletz, A (2002). Visual attention in children with normal hearing, children with hearing aids, and children with cochlear implants. *Journal of Speech, Hearing and Language Research, 45,* 403–413.

Todman, J., & Cowdy, N. (1993). Processing of visual-action codes by deaf and hearing children: Coding orientation of—capacity? *Intelligence, 17,* 237–250.

Todman, J., & Seedhouse, E. (1994). Visual-action code processing by deaf and hearing children. *Language and Cognitive Processes, 9,* 129–141.

Traxler, C.B. (2000). Measuring up to performance standards in reading and mathematics: Achievement of selected deaf and hard-of-hearing students in the national norming of the 9th Edition Stanford Achievement Test. *Journal of Deaf Studies and Deaf Education, 5*, 337–348.

Vernon, M. (1968). Fifty years of research on the intelligence of deaf and hard of hearing children: A review of literature and discussion of implications. *Journal of Rehabilitation of the Deaf, 1*, 1–12.

Waters, G.S., & Doehring, D.G. (1990). Reading acquisition in congenitally deaf children who communicate orally: Insights from an analysis of component reading, language, and memory skills. In T.H. Carr and B.A. Levy (Eds.), *Reading and its development* (pp. 323–373). San Diego, CA: Academic Press.

Wilson, M., Bettger, J.G., Niculae, I., & Klima, E.S. (1997). Modality of language shapes working memory: Evidence from digit span and spatial span in ASL signers. *Journal of Deaf Studies and Deaf Education, 2*, 152–162.

Wilson, M., & Emmorey, K. (1997a). A visuo-spatial "phonological loop" in working memory: Evidence from American Sign Language. *Memory & Cognition, 25*, 313–320.

Wilson, M., & Emmorey, K. (1997b). Working memory for sign language: A window into the architecture of the working memory system. *Journal of Deaf Studies and Deaf Education, 2*, 121–130.

Wilson, M., & Emmorey, K. (1998). A "word length effect" for sign language: Further evidence on the role of language in structuring working memory. *Memory & Cognition, 26*, 584–590.

34

Jerker Rönnberg

Working Memory, Neuroscience, and Language

Evidence from Deaf and Hard-of-Hearing Individuals

In this chapter I review behavioral and neuroscience data concerning the role of cognitive functions in visual language processing in hard-of-hearing and deaf individuals. It starts by introducing the notion of working memory as a general umbrella concept to which several other cognitive functions and visual language processing, signed or spoken, can be related. The concept of working memory allows for effective comparison of research across a variety of domains of enquiry and is productive in generating new research questions and answers. The chapter draws on behavioral and neuroscience data pertinent to the interplay among working memory, language, and communication mode.

Working Memory

Working memory refers to a limited-capacity system responsible for the temporary storage and manipulation of information necessary to deal with tasks that require comprehension, learning, and reasoning (Baddeley & Hitch, 1974). Working memory can, in the language context, be conceptualized as a "mental work-bench" serving attention, inference-making, disambiguation of anaphoric references, storage of modality-specific

information, and predictions of future actions and events (Daneman & Merikle, 1996; Rönnberg, 1995). Working memory is an active, on-line storage and processing system, not a passive, short-term memory system (Hitch, 1985).

There are several classes of working memory models in cognitive psychology, developed for different theoretical and applied purposes, and supported by different kinds of data (e.g., Richardson et al., 1996). The tradition following the Baddeley and Hitch (1974) model emphasizes that working memory resources comprise amodal as well as modality-specific components. Thus, initially, a central executive component as well as two modality-specific slave systems (i.e., the phonological loop and the visuospatial scratch-pad), serving different storage and processing demands, was assumed (Baddeley & Hitch, 1974). Later research has prompted Baddeley (2000) to add a new buffer, capable of binding long-term memory information with information from the two slave systems. Thus, this buffer serves an amodal integrative function.

An alternative type of model follows the work of Just and Carpenter (1992), where language processing resources are seen as more global, modality-free processing and storage capacities, with no assumptions about modality-specific loops. Recognizing both the modality-specific and modality-free nature of sign language, Wilson (2001) has reviewed and discussed the empirical similarities and differences that exist between working memory for signed and spoken language. It is against this background that the current chapter examines a variety of behavioral and neuroscience evidence pertinent to the issue of modality-free and modality-specific working-memory components in language processing in the deaf and hard of hearing.

Cross-Language Aspects of Working Memory

A significant breakthrough came about with the advent of neuroscience work on sign language (see, e.g., Bavelier, Corina, Jezzard, et al., 1998; Bavelier, Corina, & Neville, 1998; Rönnberg, Söderfeldt, & Risberg, 2000). When addressing working memory and its involvement in the understanding and production of sign and speech, a necessary first step is to address the modality-free aspects across languages, which may imply an abstract design of such a system.

Modality-Free Aspects of Working Memory

Behavioral Data

Behavioral data suggest that there are similarities across signed and spoken languages with respect to the function of the phonological loop system. This indicates that, despite its name, the phonological loop is not limited to auditory processing but is a more general, modality-free process. For example, Wilson and Emmorey (1997a, 1997b, 1998) have used signed language stimuli in short-term serial recall to demonstrate that sign similarity may produce a phonological similarity effect (cf. using rhyming items for speech), irrelevant hand movements may produce articulatory suppression (cf. saying "ba," repeatedly to yourself), and finally, sign length may produce the classic word length effect. With respect to the sign language capacity of the phonological loop, Marschark (1996, cited in Marschark and Mayer, 1998) has also produced such data. In addition, Marschark (1996) observed that when articulation rate is controlled with respect to sign language use, the capacity estimates of working memory for deaf participants are similar to those of persons with unimpaired hearing, and not

inferior as has been suggested elsewhere (e.g., Hanson & Lichtenstein, 1990). On the whole, then, many classic working memory effects are analogous for sign and speech.

Developmental data also suggest that there are similar developmental courses for sign and speech regarding phonology, morphology, and grammatical universals (e.g., Siple, 1997). In analogy with speech, there are also sensitive periods of acquisition for signed language (Mayberry, 1993; Mayberry & Eichen, 1991, Newman, Bavelier, Corina, Jezzard, & Neville 2002). Inasmuch as development of working memory in children depends on the developmental steps of language, similar developmental paths may be expected comparing working memory for sign and working memory for speech in children.

Neuroscience Data

An abundance of data obtained from patients who have suffered brain lesions and data from neurophysiological testing demonstrate interesting similarities in the ways in which left-hemisphere neural networks are active across languages, thus potentially enabling an amodal working memory system. The classic work by Poizner, Bellugi, and Klima (1990) has demonstrated that similar types of signed and spoken language aphasias have similar origins: fluent aphasia with comprehension problems is characteristic of patients with posterior left hemisphere lesions; anterior, left hemisphere brain damage is associated with nonfluent production, but intact comprehension.

Neuroimaging studies have also demonstrated that there are similarities between languages (see Emmorey, this volume) and that the similarities hold true across different levels of language and imaging technique (Rönnberg et al., 2000). Given that silent articulation of oral sentences engages the phonological loop in working memory, a parallel has been found in an imaging study that focused on "inner signing" of sentences. This task also engages functional networks in the brain similar to those associated with the activation of the phonological loop: specific frontal areas, rather than visuospatial areas (McGuire et al., 1997). Further, recent neurophysiological evidence seems to support the notion of an amodal site for carrying phonological, syllable-like representations, the planum temporale (PT). The PT forms part of Wernicke's area and is located in the posterior and superior parts of the temporal lobe; it is active bilaterally when either sign or speech are processed in syllable tasks (Petitto et al., 2000).

Thus, the overall inference from the behavioral and neuroscience data is that there may be a common, modality-free linguistic capacity, which can be used for working memory and phonological processes.

Modality-Specific Aspects

Behavioral Data

Although many functional, working memory–related similarities have been observed across languages, there is also a set of modality-specific findings: recall-order effects are modality specific (i.e., spatial order, not temporal order, dominates in deaf participants) and spatial rehearsal of signs and an irrelevant-sign effect are found for sign language (Wilson, 2001). The irrelevant-sign effect, which may not be as obvious as the other effects, occurs for serial recall of signs when disrupted by pseudo-signs or irrelevant moving shapes. This modality-specific and sensorimotor coding dimension is assumed to off-load some of the executive cognitive processes in working memory (Wilson, 2001).

Neuroscience Data

Lesion data and recent neuroimaging data (e.g., from functional magnetic resonance imaging [MRI] and positron emission tomography [PET] scans) have indicated that similar left hemisphere cortical structures are at work during sign and speech processing. However, other new modality-specific activation patterns are also beginning to emerge: analytical comparisons between visual speech understanding and sign-language show differences in left-hemisphere areas responsible for visual movement (Söderfeldt et al., 1997), and neuroimaging results show that specific right hemisphere effects during sign perception can be documented for the lexical level (Nishimura et al., 1999), the sentence level (Neville et al., 1997, 1998), and the discourse comprehension level of sign language (Söderfeldt, Rönnberg & Risberg, 1994, Söderfeldt et al., 1997). The exact nature of these right hemisphere effects is less well understood, but hypotheses about the level or type of processing responsible for the right hemisphere effects are (1) the discourse level (Hickok et al., 1999), (2) the prosodic functions of sign language (Bavelier, Corina,

& Neville, 1998), and (3) the role of spatial encoding of objects (Emmorey & Kosslyn, 1996; Hickok, Bellugi, & Klima, 1998). Consistent with these hypotheses is the finding that specific language-processing areas in the right hemisphere are active during American Sign Language (ASL) processing only in native signers, not in those who have acquired ASL after puberty (Newman et al., 2002). Finally, auditory cortex can be recruited by sign language in prelingually deaf individuals, a form of cross-modal plasticity that inhibits later reactivation of auditory cortices and auditory speech understanding with a cochlear implant (CI) (Soo Lee et al., 2001). This implies that neural networks laid down during early sign language acquisition engage modality-specific areas that do not permit easy recovery of language activation in speech form. However, it does not exclude the possibility that simultaneous, early use of both sign language and a CI could be beneficial (see Spencer & Marschark, this volume).

Thus, both behavioral and neuroscience data show evidence of sensory processing specific to sign language and to the right hemisphere. We know relatively little about right hemisphere effects, but early cross-modal sign-language effects may constrain further speech processing. Potential associations with sign language-specific working memory also may occur for the visuospatial level of processing (see below).

Dissociations. Neuropsychological tests of visuospatial cognition suggest that these functions are not connected to the visuospatially specific aspects driven by signed language (Hickok, Klima & Bellugi, 1996). Several adults demonstrate this type of dissociation: Corina, Kritchevsky, and Bellugi (1996), for example, described a deaf patient with left visual-field neglect, who performed very poorly in a test of memory for complex figures, whereas sign identification was unimpaired. Hickok et al. (1999) similarly found that visuospatial impairment assessed by neuropsychological tests was dissociated from the ability to process signed language grammatically and also from grammatical functions conveyed by the face (Corina, 1989; cf. Campbell, Woll, Benson, & Wallace, 1999). The reverse is also empirically true: sign aphasic patients may perform normally in pantomime and apraxia tests (Kegl & Poizner, 1997; Poizner & Kegl, 1992).

Associations. Whereas dissociations may exist

at the perceptual level, there are interesting associations between specific working memory–related functions and sign language use. These functions are presumably rooted in the specific communicative demands imposed by signed language or in a lack of auditory processing. For example, compensatory improvements have been observed for visuospatial cognition and imagery generation in deaf signers (Emmorey & Kosslyn, 1996; Emmorey, Kosslyn, & Bellugi, 1993; Parasnis, Samar, Bettger, & Sathe, 1996). The expertise of deaf (or hearing) native signers in extracting and remembering facial features with communicative importance (Bettger, Emmorey, McCullough & Bellugi, 1997; McCullough & Emmorey, 1997) further adds to the general picture of modality-specific changes in cognitive functioning as a direct result of hearing loss. In this context, it is important to note that face processing in native sign-language users is not superior when it comes to recognition memory as such, nor is the superiority tied to global features such as overall configuration of faces (i.e., shadows in black and highlights in white). Rather, enhanced performance is seen primarily in the detection and discrimination of local features, such as altered nose or eyes, that is, features that may carry grammatical functions (McCullough & Emmorey, 1997).

One particularly important finding from this research is that the ability to generate and mentally rotate images in working memory is connected to the inherent linguistic properties of signed language, such as referent visualization, perspective shifts, and reversals during sign perception (Emmorey et al., 1993; see Marschark, this volume). Experience with sign language also affects mental rotation of nonlinguistic objects within a scene (Emmorey, Klima, & Hickok, 1998). A less obvious connection may tentatively be made with perspective-rotation inherent in theory-of-mind (ToM) tasks (but see Benetto, Pennington, & Rogers, 1996). One way of connecting a physical perspective rotation in a scene with the mental perspective shifts involved in ToM tasks is to view the former rotation as a precursor of the latter ability of attributing false beliefs (Courtin, 2000). In the most common ToM task (false belief), participant X has to figure out what a right answer might be from the perspective of another person, Y. For example, Y leaves the room, knowing that a doll has been put in box #1. Before Y returns, the experi-

menter hides the doll in box#2. X's task is to say *where* Y will start looking for the doll when he or she re-enters the room. Both image and ToM "rotations" utilize a capacity to evaluate current perspectives ("rotated" and "nonrotated") in working memory, which again is associated with the capacity for comparing current perspectives during signing (Courtin, 2000). Consistent with this reasoning, the general variable of conversational opportunities in sign seems to promote the development of ToM in native signers (see Marschark, this volume; Marschark, Green, Hindmarsch & Walker, 2000; Peterson & Siegal, 1999; Rhys-Jones & Ellis, 2000).

Thus, native sign language use brings about modality-specific, especially right hemisphere, neural changes that typically serve working memory–based image generation and mental rotation. Furthermore, ToM "rotations" may share an affinity with the mental rotation capacity and these compensatory effects are dissociated from classical perceptual tests of neuropsychological function.

Summary: Cross-Language Aspects of Working Memory

Behavioral and neuroscience data strongly suggest that there are amodal links between signed and spoken language. Manipulations of working memory for sign—where the phonological loop is the most researched component—show effects qualitatively similar to those for spoken materials. The syllable may turn out to constitute an intermodality link for the phonological loop in a modality-free, working-memory system.

Although these data show impressive similarities and modality-free components of working memory, there is also an important set of data that suggests working-memory–related, modality-specific cognition (e.g., memory for face features, mental rotation, ToM "rotation," and imagery), representing compelling examples of cognitive compensation in sign language users. Particular kinds of visuospatial working memory may be lateralized to the right hemisphere in the deaf signer, but explicit testing remains to be carried out. Further specific effects are that early sign language acquisition may constrain later spoken language understanding with a cochlear implant (Soo Lee et al., 2001).

Cross-Modal Speech-Understanding Aspects of Working Memory

Speech understanding for people with hearing loss depends on perception of poorly specified or distorted speech signals, whether they are provided through sensory aids, or in conditions of speech understanding in noise, or as pure visual speech understanding (i.e., speechreading or lipreading), being complemented by different kinds of cognitive operations that facilitate inference-making (Lyxell et al., 1998). Understanding speech implies extracting the meaning of a message, and sometimes also co-constructing meaning in an ongoing dialogue (Markova & Linell, 1996). Thus, speech understanding may capitalize on a multitude of sources of information: poor or distorted sensory signals, additional visual speech cues, contextual factors, the acoustic environment in general, as well as the nonverbal gestures accompanying the dialogue (Arnold, 1997). Ease of speech understanding is correlated with the storage and processing capacities of working memory. When the linguistic input is poorly specified, top-down cognitive processes such as verbal inference making are needed (Rönnberg, Andersson, Andersson, et al., 1998), perhaps to a larger extent than for signed language.

Modality-Free Aspects

Behavioral Data

Visual Speech Understanding. The collective evidence from different speech-understanding modes suggests that we should be looking for underlying multifactor working-memory architectures (Baddeley, 2000). Examples of predictors of sentence-based visual speech understanding are skill at visual decoding of isolated spoken words (Gailey, 1987; Lyxell & Rönnberg, 1991), speed of information processing in lexical and semantic tasks (Rönnberg, 1990; cf. Pichora-Fuller, in press), and quality of phonological representations in long-term memory (Andersson, 2001). Time-restricted verbal inference-making tests, where the participant is required to write missing key words from a brief, printed sentence exposure, also represent a significant predictor (Gailey, 1987; Lyxell & Rönnberg, 1989).

Other related predictors of sentence-level visual speech understanding are (1) a short-lived visual memory-trace (Rönnberg, Arlinger, Lyxell, & Kinnefors, 1989; Samar & Sims, 1983, 1984; Shepherd, DeLavergne, Frueh, & Clobridge, 1977), (2) complex information-processing and storage tasks (Daneman & Carpenter, 1980; Lyxell & Rönnberg, 1989), and (3), verbal ability (Lyxell & Rönnberg, 1992). These are related in the sense that they contribute to decoding (i.e., the visual-neural memory trace; Rönnberg et al., 1989), or to verbal inference making (i.e., complex information processing and verbal ability). Thus, there is an emerging cognitive architecture underlying visual speech understanding. It is composed of decoding and inference-making processes that may represent components of a working-memory system, applicable across communication modes.

Visual–tactile speech understanding. Moving to visual speech supplemented by tactile speech stimulation, Bernstein, Tucker, and Auer (1998) have demonstrated that deaf speechreaders can improve their decoding skills by early, intense, and long-term visual-tactile information processing, induced by high-powered hearing aids (see Bernstein & Auer, this volume). Studies of the case GS (Plant, Gnosspelius, & Levitt, 2000; Rönnberg, 1993) demonstrate this point: relatively early and long-term use (> 50 years) of tactilely mediated visual speech understanding (i.e., picking up mainly prosodic elements of speech by placing the palm on the speaker's shoulder and the thumb on the speaker's neck/collar bone) has produced a speechreading expert, who is very efficient in establishing phonological representations based on nonsound input (Rönnberg, 1993). The primacy of decoding skills is further shown in studies of tactile benefit after practice. Type of tactile display (one-channel vs. multichannel) does not have any major effect on speech-tracking performance for the adventitiously hearing impaired. Cognitive predictor tests that assess visual word decoding or speed of phonological retrieval do, however, account for major portions of performance (Rönnberg, Andersson, Lyxell, & Spens, 1998).

Cued Speech Understanding. Early use of cued speech facilitates several cognitive functions. Supplementary visual cues augment visual speech understanding such that easily lipread phonemes share a hand shape or hand position, whereas those phonemes that are hard to discriminate use cues that belong to distinctly different groups (see Leybaert & Alegria, this volume). Research by Leybaert and colleagues has shown that early practice in phonological cued-speech distinctions in deaf children augments lipreading, spelling, rhyme judgments, reading (e.g., Leybaert, 1998; Leybaert & Lechat, 2001b), left hemisphere specialization (Leybaert & D'Hondt in press), and short-term memory (Leybaert & Charlier, 1996). There is no doubt that this system is effective in establishing phonological representations important for working memory and visual language use.

Cochlear Implants in Speech Understanding. Lyxell et al. (1996, 1998) empirically demonstrated that cognitive predictions of visual speech understanding with a CI are tapped by phonological tasks, as well as by individual capacity for simultaneous information processing and storage. There seems to be agreement that these cognitive functions are prerequisites for information processing with a CI (cf. Pisoni, 2000), and the amodal, integrative functions seem especially important (Lachs, Pisoni, & Kirk, 2001). In the same vein, the ability to flexibly take advantage of different signal–noise processing modes in digital hearing aids also seems to capitalize on the high capacity for simultaneous information processing and storage in working memory (Lunner, in press).

Thus, there is an impressive generality in the reliance on certain bottom-up (i.e., visual decoding and phonological functions) and top-down processing skills (i.e., verbal inference-making) in working memory, across different modes of speech understanding.

Neuroscience Data

Recent data are very powerful when it comes to demonstrations of cross-modal and "auditory" cortical activity by means of different sensory inputs: cochlear implants in postlingually deaf users reactivate auditory cortical areas (Zatorre, 2001); tactile stimuli in congenitally deaf tactile aid users activate secondary auditory areas (Levänen, 1998); silent speechreading also engages auditory cortex (Calvert et al., 1997; Ludman et al., 2000; MacSweeney et al., 2000), and the activation is dependent on speechreading skill (Ludman et al., 2000) and auditory deprivation (MacSweeney et al., 2001) Thus, these data give grounds for optimism when

it comes to neural flexibility and an amodal language processing potential—a pattern of data compatible with the relative invariance of cognitive processing skills across speech modes.

Modality-Specific Aspects

Behavioral Data

In memory tests based on recall of word lists, recall superiority is found for words toward the end of the list (recency effect) for heard speech but not for cued speech (Leybaert & Lechat, 2001a) or lipread speech (e.g., Campbell & Dodd, 1980). Modality specificity can also be demonstrated for the preferred free recall order of long word lists, in other words, backward order recall dominates for visual lists in print compared to spoken lists for hearing participants, whereas deaf participants display mixed strategies, and blind participants tend toward backward strategies (Rönnberg & Nilsson, 1987). Thus, there are short-term/working memory data that suggest both quantitative and qualitative modality-specific recall differences and compensations.

Neuroscience Data

We now know from several studies that for postlingually deaf individuals, rehabilitative efforts with CI overactivate auditory cortices (Fujiki et al., 1999; Naito et al. 2000). Auditory cortical overcompensations as well as visual cortical recruitment (primary visual areas) may represent new perceptual strategies, in part depending on the post-implant phase (Giraud et al., 2000; Giraud, Price, Graham, Trey, & Frackowiak, 2001). Further studies using different levels of complexity of speech material, and hence different demands on cognitive function, reveal under- and overactivation patterns, with increased phonological processing and decreased semantic processing, as well as memory compensations to keep stimuli in mind during online comprehension (Giraud et al., 2000). A preliminary appraisal of these data suggests that not only are cognitive resources taken into account to a larger extent with postlingual CI patients, but both the behavioral and neuroscience data imply an individual potential for developing a working memory system for maintaining several modality-specific sources of information while synthesizing and decoding ambiguous information.

Summary: Cross-Modal Speech-Understanding Aspects of Working Memory

Involvement of working memory in speech communication draws on bottom-up functions such as speed of lexical processing and phonological representations, as well as on complex, top-down information processing and storage capacities. These modality-free indices represent crucial predictors both within and across communication modes, sensory-aid domains, and speechreading expertise (e.g., Andersson, 2001; Rönnberg, 1995, Rönnberg, Andersson, Andersson, et al., 1998; Leybaert & Alegria, this volume; Lyxell et al., 1996). These modality-free functions are interrelated in specific ways, forming the components of a relatively general working-memory architecture, supported by neuroscience data on "auditory" activations by means of nonauditory stimuli.

The modality-specific aspect constrains generalization across speech-communication modes and is tied to the development of new strategies for understanding speech with cochlear implants, with corresponding over- and undercompensations in cortical areas, and with compensatory recall strategies in persons with deafness and blindness. Although these new perceptual strategies may be strenuous, they may still capitalize on the same components of working memory.

Bilingual and Mulitimodal Case Studies

Case studies of highly skilled speechreaders show that certain working-memory skills are relatively invariant across communicative habits: tactile-visual speech understanding (Rönnberg, 1993); bilingual mode (Rönnberg et al., 1999); pure visual speech understanding (Lyxell, 1994); and onset of impairment prelingual and postlingual (Rönnberg, 1995). It has been shown that the contribution of bottom-up processing is generally critical up to a certain threshold (Rönnberg, Samuelsson, & Lyxell, 1998) and is generalizable to children (e.g., Lyxell & Holmberg, 2000) and to nonnative language processing (Plant et al., 2000). A threshold for bottom-up processing is presumed to be constrained by the speed of visual-neural processing and lexical access and by the quality of phonological representations in long-term memory (Andersson 2001) and the speed at which they are activated

(Pichora-Fuller, in press; Pichora-Fuller, Schneider, & Daneman, 1995). Nevertheless, top-down resources are additional prerequisites for expert speech understanding (Lyxell, 1994; Plant et al., 2000; Rönnberg, 1993; Rönnberg et al., 1999).

Abstract Working Memory Processes: Generalizing Across Language and Speech-Understanding Modes

It is clear from the discussion thus far that there are several modality-free aspects of working memory for language and communication mode that can be used as a starting point for conceptualizing a general, abstract design of working memory. It is equally clear that there are modality-specific constraints. Current general models in the literature on working memory (e.g., Baddeley, 2000; Logie, 1996; Wilson, 2001) assume that the working memory system depends on perceptual input and long-term memory, as well as active working memory, with slave systems. In short, these models allow for both modality-free and modality-specific aspects of working memory.

However, following the tradition of Just and Carpenter (1992) and Daneman and colleagues (Daneman & Merikle, 1996; Daneman & Hannon, 2001), one way of summarizing the data in this chapter is first to recognize the impressive bulk of modality-free findings pertinent to working memory for sign and speech: phonological accuracy and precision at the sublexical, syllable level may represent an important multilanguage and multimodal interface between perceptual input channels and long-term memory (Andersson, 2001; Giraud et al., 2001; Petitto et al., 2000). This common base may then represent the human propensity for amodal and sublexical, combinatorial cognitive processing, which is at the root of an explanation for parallel phonological loop effects for speech and sign and similar cortical networks for "inner signing" (McGuire et al., 1997; Rönnberg, Andersson, Andersson, et al. 1998; Wilson, 2001). Equally important, and generally supportive of the amodal phonological assumption and multimodal plasticity, is the fact that "auditory" cortical activations may be generated by nonauditory stimuli (e.g., Calvert et al., 1997; Levänen, 1998).

A general speed component can also be assumed to be important: access speed of long-term memory is important for perceptual decoding and lexical and semantic retrieval for both signed and spoken languages under a variety of conditions (Kegl, Cohen, & Poizner, 1999; Pichora-Fuller et al., 1995; Rönnberg, 1990) and also for the articulatory aspects of loop functions (Marschark & Mayer, 1998).

A further mechanism put forward here is that of implicit processing. As long as language processing is automatic or implicit (i.e., for typical, expected materials and with sufficient speed of phonological lexical access in long-term memory), bottom-up functions such as phonology and speed determine performance. Current working-memory models have not fully recognized the processing economy inherent in such an assumption; for example, Logie (1996) and Baddeley (2000) seem to assume that for a given visual or auditory input, long-term memory, as well as the corresponding modality-specific processes and stores, are active most of the time. This seems appropriate for memory and cognitive tasks as such, but less so when cognition is in action in time-constrained, on-line language processing.

When a mismatch occurs (see Näätänen & Escera, 2000; Rönnberg in press, for details) between perceived input and long-term memory i.e., when materials are too atypical, or signals too distorted (due to the impairment or signal properties), or when phonological representations in long-term memory are too inaccurate, working memory is more actively invoked. Here, it is assumed that an amodal storage and processing capacity (Daneman & Merikle, 1996) of working memory is used as a function of the degree to which explicit, top-down processing, inference-making, and complex information processing is necessary to resolve the communicative task, or for expert-processing of language (Rönnberg et al., 1999).

In contrast to the amodal processing assumptions, clear evidence for modality-specific working-memory effects have also been reported for working memory for sign (Wilson, 2001; see Marschark, this volume). Brain imaging studies have revealed new cognitive processing strategies for cochlear implantees (Giraud et al., 2000, 2001), and compensatory associations between native sign language use and particular aspects of visuospatial working memory (Emmorey et al., 1998) are abundantly clear. On the basis of independent neuroimaging data, it is also known that there are domain-specific

working-memory effects that oppose the simple language or object-neutral amodal view (e.g., Smith & Jonides, 1997), showing different cortical sites for visuospatial and verbal working memory (Smith, 2000).

However, some crucial evidence is still needed in order to reconcile the modality-free with the modality-specific evidence. It is possible to think of modality-specific processing being done in the same mold of working memory in that neuroimaging data suggest that the same brain areas are more or less activated (e.g., Giraud et al., 2001). Given that different brain areas are responsible, some modification of Logie's (1996) visuospatially relevant working-memory model may be the closest candidate. Therefore, future neuroimaging studies should attempt to compare the classical working-memory effects for sign with those obtained for speech to directly assess the modality-free versus modality-specific issue in terms of neural networks.

Summary and Conclusions

This chapter has examined modality-free and modality-specific aspects of working memory for language and speech communication modes. Impressive, cross-language, classical working memory parallels have been reported and supported by neuroimaging data on phonology. There is also an impressive generality and similarity in terms of certain supporting kinds of bottom-up and top-down working-memory functions both within and across communication-modes, sensory-aid domains, and speechreading expertise. The modality-free cognitive aspects were summarized in terms of phonology, speed, explicit processing, and general storage and processing capacity in working memory.

Modality-specific compensatory enhancements are seen especially for visuospatial aspects of working memory in the native sign language user. Modality specificity is also observed in terms of new cognitive and neural working memory strategies for cochlear implantees and for modality-specific recall strategies in sign, speech, and print. It is hoped that future research will determine whether the modality-free aspects can be reconciled with the modality-specific ones, whether the differences are profoundly embedded in working memory and cognition, or whether they are superficial manifestations of the operations of some common cognitive elements.

Note

This research is supported by a grant from the Swedish Council for Social Research (30305108).

References

Andersson, U. (2001). *Cognitive deafness. The deterioration of phonological representations in adults with an acquired severe hearing loss and its implications for speech understanding.* Doctoral dissertation, Studies from the Swedish Institute for Disability Research No 3, Linköping, Sweden.

Arnold, P. (1997). The structure and optimisation of speechreading. *Journal of Deaf Studies and Deaf Education, 2,* 199–121.

Baddeley, A.D. (2000). The episodic buffer: a new component of working memory? *Trends in Cognitive Sciences, 4,* 417–423.

Baddeley, A.D. & Hitch, G. (1974). Working memory, In, G.H. Bower (Ed.), *The psychology of learning & motivation: Advances in research and theory,* Vol. 8 (pp. 47–89). New York: Academic Press.

Bavelier, D., Corina, D., Jezzard, P., Clark, V., Karni, A., Lalwani, A., Rauschecker, J.R., Braun, A., Turner, R., & Neville, H.J. (1998). Hemispheric specialization for English and ASL: left invariance—right variability. *Neuroreport, 9,* 1537–1542.

Bavelier, D., Corina, D., & Neville, H.J. (1998). Brain and language: a perspective from sign language. *Neuron, 21,* 275–278.

Bennetto, L., Pennington, B.F., & Rogers, S.J. (1996). Intact and impaired memory functions in autism. *Child Development, 67,* 1816–1835.

Bernstein L. E., Tucker P. E., & Auer E. T. (1998). Potential perceptual bases for successful use of a vibrotactile speech perception aid. *Scandinavian Journal of Psychology, 39,* 181–186.

Bettger, J.G., Emmorey, K., McCullough, S.H. & Bellugi, U. (1997). Enhanced facial discrimination: Effects of experience with American sign language. *Journal of Deaf Studies and Deaf Education, 2,* 223–233.

Calvert, G., Bullmore, E., Brammer, M., Campbell, R., Woodruff, P., McGuire, P., Williams, S., Iversen, S. D., & David, A. S. (1997). Activation of auditory cortex during silent speechreading. *Science, 276,* 593–596.

Campbell, R. & Dodd, B. (1980). Hearing by eye. *Quarterly Journal of Experimental Psychology, 32,* 85–99.

Campbell, R., Woll, B., Benson, P., & Wallace, S.B. (1999). Categorical perception of face actions: Their role in sign language and in communicative facial displays. *Quarterly Journal of Experimental Psychology. A, Human Experimental Psychology, 52A,* 67 95.

Corina, D. (1989). Recognition of affective and noncanonical linguistic facial expressions in heaaring and deaf subjects. *Brain and Cognition, 9,* 227–237.

Corina, D., Kritchevsky, M., & Bellugi, U. (1996). Visual language processing and unilateral neglect: Evidence from American sign language. *Cognitive Neuropsychology, 3,* 321–356.

Courtin, C. (2000). The impact of sign language on the cognitive development of deaf children: the case of theories of mind. *Journal of Deaf Studies and Deaf Education, 5,* 266–276.

Daneman, M., & Carpenter, P.A. (1980). Individual differences in integrating information between and within sentences. *Journal of Experimental Psychology: Learning, Memory and Cognition, 9,* 561–584.

Daneman, M., & Merikle, P M. (1996). Working memory and language comprehension: A meta-analysis. *Psychonomic Bulletin & Review, 3(4),* 422–433.

Daneman, M., & Hannon, B. (2001). Using working memory theory to investigate the construct validity of multiple-choice reading comprehension tests such as the SAT. *Journal of Experimental Psychology: General, 130,* 208–223.

Emmorey, K., & Kosslyn, S.M. (1996). Enhanced image generation abilities in deaf signers:A right hemisphere effect. *Brain & Cognition, 32,* 28–44.

Emmorey, K., Kosslyn, S. M., & Bellugi, U. (1993). Visual imagery and visual-spatial language. Enhanced imagery abilities in deaf and hearing ASL signers. *Cognition, 46,* 139–181.

Emmorey, K., Klima, E., & Hickok, G. (1998). Mental rotation within linguistic and non-linguistic domains in users of American Sign Language. *Cognition, 68,* 221–246.

Fujiki, N., Naito, Y., Hirano, S., Kojima, H., Shiomi, Y., Nishizawa, S., Konishi, J., & Honjo, I. (1999). Correlation between rCBF and speech perception in cochlear implant users. *Auris Nasus Larynx, 26,* 229–236.

Gailey, L. (1987). Psychological parameters of lipreading skill. In B. Dodd and R. Campbell (Eds.), *Hearing by eye: the psychology of lipreading* (pp. 115–141). London: Lawrence Erlbaum Associates.

Giraud, A-L., Price, C.J., Graham, J. M., Truy, E., & Frackowiak, R.S.J. (2001). Cross-modal plasticity underpins language recovery after cochlear implantation. *Neuron, 30,* 657–663.

Giraud, A.-L., Truy, E., & Frackowiak, R.S.J., Grégoire, M-C., Pujol, J-F., & Collet, L. (2000). Differential recruitment of the speech processing system in healthy subjects and rehabilitated cochlear implant patients. *Brain*, *123*, 1391–1402.

Hanson, V.L., & Lichtenstein, E.H. (1990). Short-term memory coding by deaf signers. The primary language coding hypothesis reconsidered. *Cognitive Psychology*, *22*, 211–224.

Hickok, G., Bellugi, U., & Klima, E.S. (1998). What's right about the neural organization of sign language? A perspective on recent neuroimaging results. *Trends in Cognitive Sciences*, *2*, 465–467.

Hickok, G., Klima, E.S., & Bellugi, U. (1996). The neurobiology of sign language and its implications for the neural basis of language. *Nature*, *381*, 699–702.

Hickok, G., Wilson, M., Clark, K., Klima, E.S., Kritchevsky, M., & Bellugi, U. (1999). Discourse deficits following right hemisphere damage in deaf signers. *Brain and Language*, *66*, 233–248.

Hitch, G.J. (1985). Short-term memory and information processing in humans and animals: Towards an integrative framework. In L.-G. Nilsson & T. Archer (Eds.), *Perspectives on learning and memory* (pp. 119–136). Hillsdale, NJ: Lawrence Erlbaum Associates.

Just, M. A., & Carpenter, P. A. (1992). A capacity theory of comprehension—individual differences in working memory. *Psychological Review*, *99*, 122–149.

Kegl, J., Cohen, H., & Poizner, H. (1999). Articulatory consequences of Parkinson's desease: perspectives from two modalities. *Brain and Cognition*, *40*, 355–386.

Kegl, J., & Poizner, H. (1997). Crosslinguistic/crossmodal syntactic consequences of left-hemisphere damage: evidence from an aphasic signer and his identical twin. *Aphasiology*, *11*, 1–37.

Lachs, L., Pisoni, D.B., & Kirk, K.I. (2001). Use of audiovisual information in speech perception by prelingually deaf children with cochlear implants: A first report. *Ear and Hearing*, *22*, 236–251.

Levänen, S. (1998). Neuromagnetic studies of human auditory cortex function and reorganization. *Scandinavian Audiology*, *27, suppl 49*, 1–6.

Leybaert, J. (1998). Phonological representations in deaf children: The importance of early linguistic experience. *Scandinavian Journal of Psychology*, *39*, 169–173.

Leybaert, J., & Charlier, B.L. (1996). Visual speech in the head: The effect of cued speech on rhyming, remembering and spelling. *Journal of Deaf Studies and Deaf Education*, *1*, 234–248.

Leybaert, J., & Lechat, J. (2001a). Phonological similarity effects in memory for serial order of cued speech. *Journal of Speech, Language, and Hearing Research*, *44*, 949–963.

Leybaert, J., & Lechat, J. (2001b). Variability in deaf children's spelling: The effect of language experience. *Journal of Educational Psychology*, *93*, 554–562.

Leybaert J, & D'Hondt M. (in press). Neurolinguistic development in deaf children: The effect of early language experience. *International Journal of Audiology Suppl.*

Logie, R.H. (1996). *The seven ages of working memory*. In J.T.E. Richardson et al. (Eds.), *Working memory and human cognition* (pp. 31–59). Oxford: Oxford University Press.

Ludman, C.N., Summerfield, A.Q., Hall, D., Elliott, M., Foster, J., Hykin, J.L., Bowtell, R., & Morris, P. G. (2000). Lip-reading ability and patterns of cortical activation studied using fMRI. *British Journal of Audiology*, *34*, 225–230.

Lunner, T. (in press). Cognitive functions in relation to hearing aid use. *International Journal of Audiology, Suppl.*

Lyxell, B. (1994). Skilled speechreading—a single case study. *Scandinavian Journal of Psychology*, *35*, 212–219.

Lyxell, B., Arlinger, S., Andersson, J., Bredberg, G., Harder, H., & Rönnberg, J. (1998). Phonological representation and speech understanding with cochlear implants in deafened adults. *Scandinavian Journal of Psychology*, *39*, 175–179.

Lyxell, B., Arlinger, S., Andersson, J., Harder, H., Näsström, E., Svensson, H., & Rönnberg, J. (1996). Information-processing capabilities and cochlear implants: Preoperative predictors for speech understanding. *Journal of Deaf Studies & Deaf Education*, *1*, 190–201.

Lyxell, B., & Holmberg, I. (2000). Visual speechreading and cognitive performance in hearing-impaired and normal hearing children (11–14 years). *British Journal of Educational Psychology*, *70*, 505–518.

Lyxell, B., & Rönnberg, J. (1989). Information-processing skills and speechreading. *British Journal of Audiology*, *23*, 339–347.

Lyxell, B., & Rönnberg, J. (1991). Visual speech processing: Word decoding and word discrimination related to sentence-based speechreading and hearing-impairment. *Scandinavian Journal of Psychology*, *32*, 9–17.

Lyxell, B., & Rönnberg, J. (1992). The relationship between verbal ability and sentence-based speechreading. *Scandinavian Audiology*, *21*, 67–72.

MacSweeney, M., Amaro, E., Calvert, G.A., Campbell, R., Davis, A.S., McGuire, P. Williams, S.C.R, Woll, B. & Brammer, M.J. (2000). Silent speechreading in the absence of scanner noise: an event-related fMRI study. *Neuroreport, 11,* 1729–1733.

MacSweeney, M., Campbell, R., Calvert, G.A., McGuire, P.K., David, A.S., Suckling, J., Andrew, C., Woll, B., & Brammer MJ. (2001). Dispersed activation in the left temporal cortex for speechreading in congenitally deaf people. *Proceedings of the Royal Society of London Series B-Biological Sciences, 268,* (1466), 451–457.

McCullough, S., & Emmorey, K. (1997). Face processing by deaf ASL signers: Evidence for expertise in distinguishing local features. *Journal of Deaf Studies and Deaf Education, 2,* 212–222.

McGuire, P.K., Robertson, D., Thacker, A., David, A.S., Kitson, N., Frackowiak, R.S.J., & Frith, C.D. (1997). Neural correlates of thinking in sign language. *Neuroreport, 8,* 695–698.

Marschark, M. (1996, November). Influences of signed and spoken language on memory span. Paper presented at the Annual Meeting of the Psychonomic Society, Chicago IL.

Marschark, M., Green, V., Hindmarsh, G., & Walker, S. (2000). Understanding theory of mind in children who are deaf. *Journal of Child Psychology and Psychiatry and Allied Disciplines, 41,* 1067–1073.

Marschark, M., & Mayer, T. S. (1998). Interactions of language and memory in deaf children and adults. *Scandinavian Journal of Psychology, 39,* 145–148.

Markova, I., & Linell, P. (1996). Coding elementary contributions to dialogue: Individual acts versus dialogical interactions. *Journal for the Theory of Social Behavior, 26,* 353–373.

Mayberry, R. (1993). First-language acquisition after childhood differs from second-language acquisition: The case of American Sign Language. *Journal of Speech and Hearing Research, 36,* 1258–1270.

Mayberry, R., & Eichen, E. (1991). The long-lasting advantage of learning sign language in childhood: Another look at the critical period for language acquisition. *Journal of Memory and Language, 30,* 486–512.

Näätänen, R., & Escera, C. (2000). Mismatch negativity: Clinical and other applications. *Audiology and Neuro-otology, 5,* 105–110.

Naito, Y., Tateva, I., Fujiki, N., Hirano, S., Ishizu, K., Nagahama, H., Fukuyama, H, & Kojima, H. (2000). Increased cortical activation during hearing of speech in cochlear implant users. *Hearing Research, 143,* 139–146.

Newman, A.I., Bavelier, D., Corina, D., Jezzard, P., & Neville, H.J. (2002). A critical period for right hemisphere recruitment in American Sign Language processing. *Nature Neuroscience, 5*(1), 76–80.

Neville, H.J., Bavelier, D., Corina, D., Rauschecker, J.,

Karni, A., Lawani, A., Braun, A., Clark, V., Jezzard, P., & Turner, R. (1998). Cerebral organization for language in deaf and hearing subjects: Biological constraints and effects of experience. *Proceeding of the National Academy of Sciences, USA, 95,* 922–929.

Neville, H. J., Coffey, S. A., Lawson, D. S., Fischer, A., Emmorey, K., & Bellugi, U. (1997). Neural systems mediating American Sign Language: Effects of sensory experience and age of acquisition. *Brain and Language, 57,* 285–308.

Nishimura, H., Hashikawa, K., Doi, K., Iwaki, T., Watanabe, Y., Kusuoka, H., Nishimura, T., & Kubo, T. (1999). Sign language "heard" in the auditory cortex. *Nature, 397,* 116.

Parasnis, I., Samar, V., Bettger, J., & Sathe, K. (1996). Does deafness lead to enhancement of visual spatial cognition in children? Negative evidence from deaf nonsigners. *Journal of Deaf Studies and Deaf Education, 1*(2), 145–152.

Peterson, C.C., & Siegal, M. (1999). Representing inner worlds: Theory of mind in autistic, deaf, and normal hearing children. *Psychological Science, 10,* 126–129.

Petitto, L.A., Zatorre, R.J., Gauna, K., Nikelski, E.J., Dostie, D., & Evans, A.C. (2000). Speech-like cerebral activity in profoundly deaf people processing signed languages: Implications for the neural basis of human language. *Proceedings of the National Academy of Sciences, USA, 97,* (25) 13961–13966.

Pichora-Fuller, M. K. in press. Processing speed: Psychoacoustics, speech perception, and comprehension. *International Journal of Audiology.*

Pichora-Fuller, M. K., Schneider, B. A., & Daneman, M. (1995). How young and old adults listen to and remember speech in noise. *Journal of Acoustical Society of America, 97,* 593–608.

Pisoni, D.B. (2000). Cognitive factors and cochlear implants: Some thoughts on perception, learning, and memory in speech perception. *Ear & Hearing, 21,* 70–78.

Plant, G., Gnosspelius, J., & Levitt, H. (2000). The use of tactile supplements in lipreading Swedish and English: A single-subject study. *Journal of Speech, Language and Hearing Research, 43,* 178–183.

Poizner, H., Bellugi, U., & Klima, E.S. (1990). Biological foundation of language: Clues from sign language. *Annual Review of Neuroscience, 13,* 283–307.

Poizner, H., & Kegl, J. (1992). Neural basis of language and motor behavior: perspectives from American Sign Language. *Aphasiology, 6,* 219–256.

Rhys-Jones, S.L., & Ellis, H.D. (2000). Theory of mind: Deaf and hearing childrens' comprehension of picture stories and judgments of social situations. *Journal of Deaf Studies and Deaf Education, 5*, 248–261.

Richardson, J.T.E., Engle, R.W., Hasher, L., Logie, R.H., Stoltzfus, E.R., & Zacks, R. T. (1996). *Working memory and human cognition*. New York: Oxford University Press.

Rönnberg, J. (1990). Cognitive and communicative function: The effects of chronological age and "handicap age." *European Journal of Cognitive Psychology, 2*, 253–273.

Rönnberg, J. (1993). Cognitive characteristics of skilled tactiling: The case of GS. *European Journal of Cognitive Psychology, 5*, 19–33.

Rönnberg, J. (1995). What makes a skilled speechreader? In G. Plant & K. Spens (Eds.), *Profound deafness and speech communication* (pp. 393–416). London: Whurr.

Rönnberg, J. (in press). Cognition in the hearing impaired and deaf as a bridge between signal and dialogue. *International Journal of Audiology Suppl.*

Rönnberg, J., Andersson, J., Andersson, U., Johansson, K., Lyxell, B., & Samuelsson, S. (1998). Cognition as a bridge between signal and dialogue: Communication in the hearing impaired and deaf. *Scandinavian Audiology, 27* (Suppl. 49) 101–108.

Rönnberg, J., Andersson, U., Lyxell, B., & Spens, K. (1998). Vibrotactile speechreading support: Cognitive prerequisites for training. *Journal of Deaf Studies & Deaf Education, 3*, 143–156.

Rönnberg, J., Andersson, J., Samuelsson, S., Söderfeldt, B., Lyxell, B., & Risberg, J. (1999). A speechreading expert: The case of MM. *Journal of Speech, Language and Hearing Research, 42*, 5–20.

Rönnberg, J., Arlinger, S., Lyxell, B., & Kinnefors, C. (1989). Visual evoked potentials: Relation to adult speechreading and cognitive function. *Journal of Speech and Hearing Research, 32*, 725–735.

Rönnberg, J., & Nilsson, L-G. (1987). The modality effect, sensory handicap, and compensatory functions. *Acta Psychologica, 65*, 263–283.

Rönnberg, J., Samuelsson, S., & Lyxell, B. (1998). Conceptual constraints in sentence-based lipreading in the hearing impaired. In R. Campbell, B. Dodd, & D. Burnham (Eds.), *Hearing by eye: Part II. Advances in the psychology of speechreading and audiovisual speech* (pp. 143–153). London: Lawrence Erlbaum Associates.

Rönnberg, J., Söderfeldt, B., & Risberg, J. (2000). The cognitive neuroscience of signed language. *Acta Psychologica, 105*, 237–254.

Samar, V.J., & Sims, D. G. (1983). Visual evoked-response correlates of speechreading performance in normal-hearing adults: A replication and a factor analytic extension. *Journal of Speech and Hearing Research, 26*, 2–9.

Samar, V. J., & Sims, D. G. (1984). Visual evoked-response components related to speechreading and spatial skills in hearing and hearing-impaired adults. *Journal of Speech and Hearing Research, 27*, 162–172.

Shepherd, D. C., DeLavergne, R. W., Frueh, F. X., & Clobridge, C. (1977). Visual-neural correlate of speechreading ability in normal-hearing adults. *Journal of Speech and Hearing Research, 20*, 752–765.

Smith, E. E. (2000). Neural bases of human working memory. *Current Directions in Psychological Science, 9*, 45–49.

Smith, E. E., & Jonides, J. (1997). Working memory: A view from neuroimaging. *Cognitive Psychology, 33*, 5–42.

Siple, P. (1997). Universals, generalizability, and the acquisition of sign language. In M. Marschark and V. S. Everhart (Eds.), *Relations of language and thought: The view from sign language and deaf children* (pp. 24–61). Oxford: Oxford University Press.

Söderfeldt, B., Ingvar, M., Rönnberg, J., Eriksson, L., Serrander, M., & Stone-Elander, S. (1997). Signed and spoken language perception studied by positron emission tomography. *Neurology, 49*, 82–87.

Söderfeldt, B., Rönnberg, J., & Risberg, J. (1994). Regional cerebral blood flow in sign-language users. *Brain and Language, 46*, 59–68.

Soo Lee, D., Sung Lee, J., Ha Oh, S., Kim, S.-K., Kim, J. W, Chung, J.-K., Chul Lee, M., & Kim, C.S. (2001). Crossmodal plasticity and cochlear implants. *Nature, 409*, 149–150.

Wilson, M. (2001). The case for sensorimotor coding in working memory. *Psychonomic Bulletin & Review, 8*, 44–57.

Wilson, M., & Emmorey, K. (1997a). A visuospatial "phonological" loop in working memory: Evidence from American Sign Language. *Memory & Cognition, 25*, 313–320.

Wilson, M., & Emmorey, K. (1997b). Working memory for sign language: A window into the architecture of the working memory system. *Journal of Deaf Studies and Deaf Education, 2*, 121–130.

Wilson, M., & Emmorey, K. (1998). A "word length" for sign language: Further evidence for the role of language in structuring working memory. *Memory and Cognition, 26*, 584–591.

Zatorre, R. J. (2001). Do you see what I'm saying? Interactions between auditory and visual cortices in cochlear implant users. *Neuron, 31*, 13–14.

Marc Marschark & Patricia Elizabeth Spencer

Epilogue

What We Know, What We Don't Know, and What We Should Know

Upon completing an article, chapter, or book, authors and editors are sometimes left with bits and pieces that did not quite fit, scraps of text looking for a good home, or whole topics that had to be omitted for one reason or another. More often than not, there is the feeling that there was more to say, more that could have been said, if only time, space, and publishers permitted. This is certainly one of those situations. Over the course of preparing this volume, we have learned much but also gained a better appreciation of just how much more there is to know.

Normally, authors have a fairly good idea of what they know and what they do not know in their own field or subfield of interest. In assembling a collection as diverse as this volume, however, we have discovered new studies, new ideas, and new questions of research interest that one or the other of us never knew existed (and, in some cases, perhaps did not exist before this massive collaboration). Thus, as much as the preceding chapters have provided a wealth of information about social, psychological, linguistic, and pragmatic aspects of deafness, we finish this project feeling that there are still many questions in need of answers and findings in need of good (or at least better) explanations. Indeed, the integration of previously inde-

pendent lines of research here has provided several new lines to follow, as contributors have all indicated the "hot" issues still unresolved in their areas and pointed the way to research and application that lie ahead.

Looking across the chapters of this book, one question that arises is what the future of communities of Deaf people will be, and how their culture, defined for several centuries by shared language and identity, might evolve in th face of technological and social change. As the chapter by Woll and Ladd, as well as that by Lang, emphasize, the story line has shifted from one of a population seen as being in need of care by well-meaning but often oppressive hearing powers to that of an empowered community that offers its own mechanisms for change. Despite the diversity in communication preferences and group identities within the population of people who are deaf or hard of hearing, there has been a thriving and creative Deaf community for hundreds of years. Now, as perhaps always, that community faces perceived threats both from within and without. Though the story is yet to be written, there is concern in some quarters of the Deaf community about the changes to be wrought by cochlear implants, gene therapy, and other medical advances that promise to reduce the incidence of deafness and simultaneously threaten a social structure. The chapters by Arnos and Pandya, Bernstein and Auer, Blamey, Cone-Wesson, Harkins and Bakke, and Spencer and Marschark indicated that even while accepting sign language and deaf individuals for what and who they are, society at large continues efforts to "habilitate" (in the case of prelingually deaf children) or "rehabilitate" deaf persons by developing new means of augmenting hearing and enhancing the acquisition of spoken language skills. Although these initiatives are seen as positive by some individuals who are deaf, they are perceived as negative by others, and as a direct threat to the existence of Deaf communities and Deaf culture by others.

Many other ongoing issues relate to communication, both with regard to mass media and in educational settings. Monikowski and Winston described progress in the provision and understanding of sign language interpreting (both from sign language into spoken language and vice versa), a part of the field that is still in its infancy. While we know that there are not enough qualified interpreters to meet the demand, we have little empirical evidence concerning how much information is successfully communicated in three- (or more) party communication situations (i.e., including the interpreter) or the effectiveness of interpreting in different educational contexts for students with varying sign language and spoken language skills. Similarly, Harkins and Bakke described technological advances that appear to promise greater communication access by deaf people and enhanced opportunities for interactions with hearing friends, family, and services; but the speed and consequences of adopting of technology are erratic and often mystify prognosticators and become clear only in hindsight.

Chapters by Blamey, Jamieson, Lederberg, Leybaert and Alegria, Mayer and Akamatsu, Singleton and Supalla, and Schick described communication alternatives for deaf individuals and the courses and implications of their acquisition. Those by Bernstein and Auer, Fischer and van der Hulst, and Wilbur provided additional insights into the nature of signed and spoken languages. Chapters by Stinson and Kluwin and Karchmer and Mitchell offered some indication of how alternative communication methods influence educational placement and success for deaf and hard-of-hearing children, while Emmorey, Marschark, and Rönnberg each sug-

gested ways in which different modes of communication may be relevant to brain and cognitive processes. Yet the ways in which language, learning, and social functioning interact in deaf individuals remain largely unknown, or at least are still at a point where the application of available research on the topic remain theoretical, with only a few tentative forays into the classroom and the board room.

One thing we do know is that no single method of communication is going to be appropriate for all deaf children. The goal, therefore, must be to identify hearing losses as early as possible and begin interventions that match the strengths and needs of each child and the child's family. However, we still are unable to predict which children will be able to acquire spoken language competence, with or without the assistance of speechreading and the use of specialized technologies. To date, there appears to be little emphasis on development of specialized teaching or habilitation strategies to build on the potential provided by cochlear implants and other advances in hearing amplification. Moreover, there is a glaring lack of objective information about ways in which sign systems might or might not be helpful in supporting development of spoken language in the context of new technologies. A complete picture of the full benefits of acquisition of a natural sign language (e.g., American Sign Language, British Sign Language, Auslan), the process of truly bilingual development in sign and spoken language, and the generality of literacy findings obtained with French cued speech also remain to be provided by future research and practice. In the same vein, factors that allow hearing parents of deaf children—usually unfamiliar with deafness and sign language—to learn sign language remain unclear (see Schick, Singleton & Supalla). Chapters by Antia and Kriemeyer, Marschark, Mayer and Akamatsu, Power and Leigh, and Stinson and Kluwin thus all suggest the need for taking a long, hard look at some of the assumptions that guide the field and the need to ensure that various practices have their foundations in fact rather than wishful thinking.

For centuries, deaf people who used spoken communication and those who used sign communication have coexisted, but the relationship has rarely been a comfortable one. In a world where the oppressed often become oppressors themselves, deaf individuals are often willing to admit that the tension between "oral" and "signing" deaf people is both painful and detrimental. Unfortunately, perhaps, while they are willing to discuss it in private, there appears to be little research being done on the relations within the diverse Deaf community (but see Woll & Ladd with regard to minority issues in general). How similar is the spoken language versus sign language divide to the class distinction seen among other minority communities? How is the issue seen by individuals of different generations and social standing? When we sought a chapter for this volume on "oral deaf communities," we came up empty. "Oral deaf people don't want to be seen as a community," we were told, "they are trying to be part of the hearing world." So, while there are a number of biographical and autobiographical stories available about deaf individuals' struggles between the two worlds, we know little for certain about the social dynamics involved, beyond research involving infants and children through school age, described here by Antia and Kriemeyer, Calderon and Greenberg, and Traci and Koester. We do have considerable research on the interactions of deaf and hearing children, but there is little information available on the interactions of deaf children who use spoken language with those who use sign language. If we knew more about this and about interactions involving hard-of-hearing children, perhaps we would be in a better position to know how cochlear implants might change the Deaf community and whether they will, as some fear, end it completely.

No place is the influence of cochlear implants—and the lack of information about their consequences—more obvious than in the schools, both public schools and traditional schools for the deaf. Historical and contemporary issues in educating deaf children, as seen in chapters by Antia and Kriemeyer, Lang, Power and Leigh, Sass-Lehrer and Bodner-Johnson, and Stinson and Kluwin, well describe the overt and covert challenges of parents, teachers, and students in optimizing educational opportunities for deaf children and preparing them for adulthood and the world of work. At this point, there is essentially no information available on how implants (or other technologies, for that matter; see Harkins & Bakke) are affecting social or academic functioning of younger deaf individuals. Will they help to lower some social and pragmatic barriers, or will they merely create yet another audiological class of people?

One oft-cited hope for cochlear implants is that they will facilitate the development of literacy as well as other academic skills. Results of research in this area, as reported by Spencer and Marschark, are just emerging. Leybaert and Alegria report some work indicating improvements in literacy attainment by children who are immersed in cued speech, but there is no doubt that literacy remains one of the biggest challenges for young deaf children, and one that will influence their entire educational histories and opportunities after the school years. Chapters by Albertini and Schley, Mayer and Akamatsu, Paul, and Schirmer and Williams take on various aspects of the literacy issue directly. Descriptions of the challenges in reading and writing for deaf individuals are accompanied by assessments of alternative methods for teaching literacy and supporting the literacy-related efforts of deaf learners of all ages.

But new solutions to such challenges seem to come along every few years, and even their cumulative effects thus far appear small. Many educational systems have been built on the quest for literacy in deaf children, and movements championing various forms of manually-coded English, particular educational placements, and specific teaching-learning methods (Albertini & Schley; Leybaert & Alegria; Mayer & Akamatsu; Paul; Schick; Schirmer & Williams) have lost much of their glamor, if not their adherents. Despite decades of creative efforts, however, deaf children today are still progressing at only a fraction of the rate of hearing peers in learning to read. On average, 18-year-old deaf students leaving high school have reached only a fourth to sixth grade level in reading skills, only about 3% of those 18-year-olds read at a level comparable to 18-year-old hearing readers, and more than 30% of deaf students leave school functionally illiterate (Karchmer & Mitchell; Stinson & Kluwin). We know that some deaf adults and children are excellent readers and writers, but we do not know how many there are or how achieved this level of literacy. Simply put, thus far we have been unable to match the correct teaching methods with students' strengths and weaknesses to raise the literacy bar. How can we account for those young deaf children who take to reading so readily? How much of it is their home environments, early intervention programming, or just natural talent? How can we identify them early enough to really make a difference?

Beyond literacy, there are other academic domains that remain challenging for both deaf students and their teachers, although with the possible exception of mathematics, none of them seem to present content-specific problems. Even in mathematics, recent research suggests that it is not dealing with numbers that is problematic but that there are some more basic cognitive issues to be dealt with. That is, it may be that the nature of early language and early educational experiences, as well as the lack of hearing and related perceptual-cognitive-neurological development, lead to some subtle (or not so subtle) differences in cognition and learning among deaf children (Emmorey; Maller; Marschark; Rönnberg). Only by understanding those differences can we hope to tailor experiential and educational settings to optimize learning. Such differences also may influence social-emotional development, from birth onward, suggesting the need to better understand the complex interactions among factors if the educational and social progress of deaf individuals is to move forward (Antia & Kriemeyer; Calderon & Greenberg; Traci & Koester).

At this juncture, the publication of the *Oxford Handbook of Deaf Studies, Language, and Education* seems both a trivial accomplishment and a dramatic step forward. The feeling of triviality lies in realizing the extent to which these chapters have shown us not how much we know (though they certainly have done that!), but shown us how much we do not know and, occasionally, how much we thought we knew but really do not. In a real sense, these pages indicate not just how far we have come, but how much father we have to go. At the same time, all of us involved in this project recognize that a journey of a thousand miles begins with a single step. In providing an objective and comprehensive analysis of the current state of this interdisciplinary field, the contributors have offered a detailed map for that journey, clearly marking promising routes, danger zones, and scenic overlooks. With this map in hand, the journey becomes better defined and less daunting, exciting for all its formidable complexities. But, then, after all, isn't that what handbooks (and journeys) are all about?

Author Index

Subject Index

Please remember that this is a library book,
and that it belongs only temporarily to each
person who uses it. Be considerate. Do
not write in this, or any, library book.